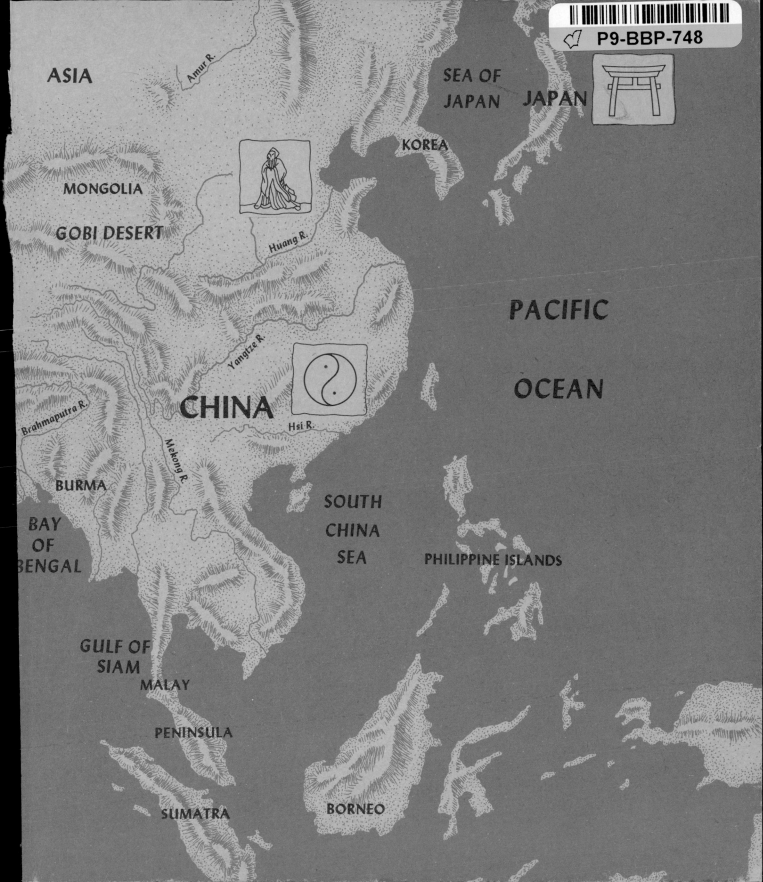

ASIA

Amur R.

SEA OF
JAPAN   JAPAN

KOREA

MONGOLIA

GOBI DESERT

Huang R.

PACIFIC

Yangtze R.

OCEAN

CHINA

Brahmaputra R.

Hsi R.

Mekong R.

BURMA

SOUTH
CHINA
SEA

BAY
OF
BENGAL

PHILIPPINE ISLANDS

GULF OF
SIAM

MALAY

PENINSULA

SUMATRA

BORNEO

Man's Religions

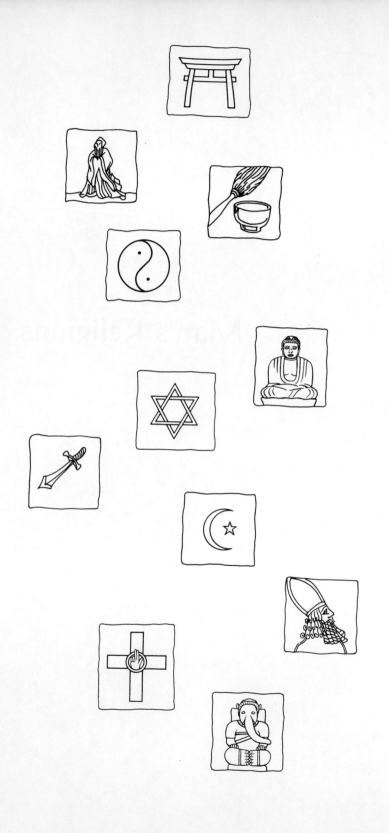

John B. Noss

Man's Religions

FOURTH EDITION

The Macmillan Company

Collier-Macmillan Limited, London

First Printing

Earlier editions copyright 1949 and © 1956 and 1963 by The Macmillan Company.

Library of Congress catalog card number: 69–11587

The Macmillan Company
Collier-Macmillan Canada, Ltd., Toronto, Ontario

Printed in the United States of America

Chuang Tzu: Mystic, Moralist and Social Reformer, edited and translated by H. A. Giles. Copyright 1889 by Kelly and Walsh, Shanghai.

China's Religious Heritage by Y. C. Yang. Copyright 1934 by Whitmore and Stone.

The Analects of Confucius, edited and translated by Arthur Waley. Copyright 1938 by George Allen and Unwin.

The Story of Confucius, edited by Brian Brown. Copyright 1927 by David McKay Company.

Men and Ideas by Lin Mousheng. Copyright 1942 by John Day Company, Inc.

Master K'ung by Carl Crow. Copyright 1937 by Carl Crow.

Philosophy—East and West, edited by Charles A. Moore. Copyright 1944 by Princeton University Press.

The Chinese Mind by Gung-hsing Wang. Copyright 1946 by Gung-hsing Wang.

The Origin and Development of the State Cult of Confucius by John K. Shryock. Copyright 1932 by The American Historical Association.

Tohoku, the Scotland of Japan by Christopher Noss. Copyright 1918 by the Board of Foreign Missions of the Reformed Church in the U.S.

Human Bullets by Tadayoshi Sakurai. Translated by M. Honda and A. M. Bacon. Copyright 1906 by T. Sakurai.

Zoroaster, the Prophet of Ancient Iran by A. V. W. Jackson. Copyright 1898 by The Macmillan Company.

The Zoroastrian Doctrine of a Future Life by Jal Dastur Cursetji Pavry. Copyright 1926, 1929 by Columbia University Press.

The Bible—An American Translation by J. M. Powis Smith and E. J. Goodspeed. Copyright 1935 by the University of Chicago.

Archaeology and the Bible by George A. Barton. 6th edition, revised. Copyright 1933 by the American Sunday School Union.

The Holy Bible—A New Translation by James Moffatt. Copyright 1922, 1924, 1926 by George H. Doran Company.

The Religion of the People of Israel by Rudolph Kittel. Translated by R. C. Micklem. Copyright 1925 by The Macmillan Company.

A History of the Jews by Abram Leon Sachar. Copyright 1930 by Alfred A. Knopf, Inc.

Stranger than Fiction—A Short History of the Jews by Lewis Browne. Copyright 1925 by Lewis Browne.

The Reform Movement in Judaism by David Philipson. Revised edition. Copyright 1907, 1931, by The Macmillan Company.

The American Jew—A Composite Portrait by O. I. Janowski. 2nd edition. Copyright 1942 by Harper and Brothers.

A Source Book for Ancient Church History, edited by Joseph C. Ayer, Jr. Copyright 1913 by Charles Scribner's Sons.

A History of the Christian Church by Williston Walker. Copyright 1918 by Charles Scribner's Sons.

Christianity; Past and Present by Charles Guignebert. Copyright by The Macmillan Company.

The Koran Interpreted by A. J. Arberry. Copyright © George Allen & Unwin, Ltd. 1955.

A History of the Arabs by Philip K. Hitti. Copyright 1937 by The Macmillan Company.

Mohammed and Islam by I. Goldziher. Translated by K. C. Seelye. Copyright 1917 by Yale University Press.

Islam: Muhammad and His Religion, edited by Arthur Jeffery. Copyright 1958 by Liberal Arts Press.

Modern Trends in Islam by H. A. R. Gibb. Copyright 1947 by University of Chicago Press.

To M. B. N.
in inexpressible
gratitude

And what place is there
in me into which my God can come,
even He who made heaven and earth?
Is there anything in me, O Lord my God,
that can contain Thee? . . .
Or should I not rather say,
that I could not exist unless I were
in Thee, from whom are all things,
by whom are all things, in whom
are all things?

—AUGUSTINE

Preface to the Fourth Edition

SINCE THE FIRST EDITION of this book went to press in 1949, significant developments have occurred in the study of man's religions. Research has widened its interests by moving from concentration on collection of objective data about gods, doctrines, and institutions to the study of how people respond in commitment of themselves to gods, doctrines, and institutions. The great amount of material published recently has elicited unusual interest. Curiosity has given place to sympathetic study. The "observer" is still reporting his finds, but the "insider" commands even more respect. For the religions are now regarded as viable options rather than as strange or unacceptable alternatives. People have stopped saying "How wrong!" or "How absurd!" and are now more apt to say "How significant!" and "How meaningful!"

The first edition sought to meet the need for an introduction to the world's faiths at a time when undergraduates were in almost total ignorance about them. At that time library shelves contained relatively little that combined the needed introduction with sufficient original source material to lend interest and a confessional quality to the outline of beliefs and practices. The last two decades have seen the outpouring of a spate of books both in hardcover and in paperback dealing with most phases of man's religions, and these books have been wondrously suited to undergraduate study.

There have been other changes. One result of the heightened interest in the subjective element in religious life is the fresh recognition of the particularity and "givenness" of each faith, the fact being that each religion is different from any other, as different and individual as persons and cultures are, with a uniqueness that cannot quite be analyzed and explained. Paradoxically, this irresolvable uniqueness is consistent with the common claim of all religions, with one doubtful exception, that within and beyond the natural and human orders there is a divine order of things that is their source and ground, and further, that there is a spiritual self within the psychophysical one. This common claim of the religions is advanced in a great variety of ways, through metaphors and symbols that faithfully reflect the variant cultures of mankind and have a uniqueness that renders them fascinating in themselves and in their suggestion of ultimate truth.

The present edition has the same underlying purpose as the first, to "make the highly human quality of each religion evident." But it is a complete revision, especially of Parts One to Three. Besides the aim of adding to the evidence of the human quality of each religion, two other aims have been sought: to bring the book into line with growing knowledge, and to go to greater depths.

While preparing his revision the author was greatly aided by the criticism and advice of specialists whom Mr. John D. Moore, then of the Macmillan editorial staff, persuaded to go over certain chapters. The author wishes to tender his thanks both to Mr. Moore and to these very helpful critics and advisers. The chapter on prehistoric and primitive religions was examined in detail by Professor Annemarie de Waal Malefijt of Hunter College of the City University of New York, those on Hinduism by Professor Hans H. Penner of Dartmouth College, those on Buddhism by Professor Alex Wayman of the University of Wisconsin, that on Shinto by Professor Joseph M. Kitagawa of the University of Chicago, and that on Islam by Professor Reuben W. Smith of the University of Chicago. The entire book was reviewed by Professor Charles J. Adams, Director of the Institute of Islamic Studies, McGill University. The author wishes also to thank Professor Richard DeMartino, a Zen Buddhist, who in his friendly way helped the author to a better understanding, he hopes, of Zen. To his great benefit also Mr. Joginder Singh, then at Indiana University, sent the author a detailed review and criticism of the chapter on Sikhism, together with books that have been helpful in detecting what his benefactor politely called "unintentional antagonism to the spirit of the Sikh tradition," something of which the author was unaware, because to the contrary he felt quite sympathetic. The chapters cited have been understandably subjected to considerable revision (as have all the chapters), although the author must bear the blame for omissions and errors still remaining.

The author also owes special thanks to Charles E. Smith, the religion editor of The Macmillan Company, who gave him his unrestricted assistance in the preparation of this edition.

The prefaces to the second and third editions, here omitted, contained a pointer to teachers that may need to be repeated. As in the first edition, the index contains an abundance of cross-references under many major entries. Such entries could prove useful in the assignment of term papers. Entries such as "Ancestor-worship," "Angels," "Asceticism," "Atheism," "Christology," "Church," "Creation," "Ethics," "Future life," "God," "Gods," "Heaven," "Hell," "Incarnation," "Magic," "Man (doctrine of)," "Monism," "Mysticism," "Prayer," "Priesthood," and "Sacrifice" contain references to many faiths of the world. A comprehensive essay based on any of these entries, or on any one of many others contained in the index but not here listed, could prove of great value to the student, especially if he is encouraged to widen his reading in the absorbing literature concerning man's religions, and thus go beyond this book.

Teachers who might want their students to read beyond this book now have a wealth of paperback books at their disposal. Comprehensive treatments of all the religions now appear in this form. In the bibliographies appended to each chapter, paperbacks are designated with the symbol *pb* and might well be used by a teacher who may wish a fuller treatment of a particular chapter (as for instance in considering the religions of Greece and Rome) or who may desire to assign term papers on a particular religion or topic. (After all, libraries seldom have enough copies to go around when term papers are assigned.) Both teacher and student will find exceedingly helpful the general bibliographies in *A Reader's Guide to the Great Religions*, edited by Charles J. Adams and published by The Free Press, a division of The Macmillan Company.

This is perhaps a large book for a one-semester

course. Should it be necessary to do so, or should concentration on specific areas be advisable, the teacher could select for study particular chapters or groups of chapters and ask the student to read further in paperback or hardcover texts. First-rate supplementary reading is now possible in general anthologies and collections of the scriptures of particular religions.

J. B. N.

Note: All letters and numbers in the text following quotations, e.g.,^{A1}, refer to References for Quotations, pp. 564 ff. See footnote on p. 10 for further explanation. For pronunciation of unfamiliar names see the index. **xiii**

THIS BOOK HAS BEEN WRITTEN to meet two specific needs: that, first, for an introduction to the world's religions containing adequate amounts of descriptive or interpretative details from the original source materials; and that, second, for a presentation of man's most noteworthy faiths in a time-setting that will do justice to their development as well as to their origins. A sufficient number of books now deal with the founders or founding of the great religions, and many others present the various religions as they are or recently have been. This book seeks, as a major aim, to bridge the interval between the founding of the religions and their present state. It is hoped, incidentally, that the frequent quotations from the original source materials—or from authoritative accounts—will make the highly human quality of each religion evident, and thus excite the reader to further reading in a vast field.

Had the author foreseen all that would be involved in his task when he began, he would have been appalled, but he now hopes he would have continued anyway, for the difficulty of the work confronting him over a long period of intensive study and composition has been more than matched by the fascination and enjoyment that have steadily accompanied it. It seems to him a certainty that any sympathetic inquiry into the faith and understanding reflected in man's religions must have such results, and he earnestly prays that readers of his book, not content with what is set down here, may go on to their own greatly rewarding research and discovery. If they find errors in his account, they may then be able to correct him.

It has been a major problem in the making of this book to present an adequate account of the great faiths within what must be called, in spite of many pages, a limited space. To tell the story of religion with as complete objectivity as one can muster, and in accordance with the findings of the latest scholarship, is difficult enough, but to be fair and yet brief, comprehensive and yet concise, interested in the riches of humanizing detail and yet true to proportion and balance of treatment are aims still more

Preface to the First Edition

difficult, perhaps impossible, to attain. Moreover, the judgment expressed in some reviews of recent books on the world's religions, that no one person can any longer write a competent book on the entire field, because the subject requires for its adequate treatment a panel of experts, is a cause for great diffidence. On the other hand, one may remark, a book by a panel of experts may run into difficulties, too. The chapters may vary widely in the amount of detail that is thought necessary; in spite of every effort to avoid it, there may be overlapping, or the opposite—hiatuses; and there usually are marked differences in pace and literary quality. Not only schematic completeness, but even unity of perspective, may be absent.

Perhaps, then, when there is so much need in our time for books that will broaden our understanding of all peoples, this one needs no further warrant to make its appearance.

It would be impossible here to make the many acknowledgments to the men and books, teachers, fellow-students, and scholars whence this book has drawn everything of value that it contains. The bibliographies at the end of each chapter, the long list of books under copyright from which so many of the quotations have come, and the still longer list of quoted references at the end of the book are inadequate gestures in this direction. To readers for The Macmillan Company, who made many helpful comments on the incomplete first draft of this book, the author owes special thanks. One of them, Professor Horace L. Friess of Columbia University, since known to him, read the manuscript when it was nearing its final form. To his discerning judgment on both general and particular points he wishes to pay special tribute; whatever errors and shortcomings this book still possesses must surely exist despite his aid and counsel, for his scholarship is as exact as it is wide.

Finally, to his wife, who encouraged, sympathized with, and endured him during the summers on Mt. Desert Island, on the coast of Maine, where most of this book was written, the author owes most of all.

J. B. N.

Contents

Illustrations

List of Illustrations and Maps

xix

Maps

One

Primitive and Bygone Religions

ALL RELIGIONS IMPLY in one way or another that man does not, and cannot, stand alone, that he is vitally related with and even dependent on powers in nature and society external to himself. Dimly or clearly, he knows that he is not an independent center of force capable of standing apart from the world.

This realization ranges from primitive conceptions of dependence on powers and forces in the immediate social and natural environment to conceptions in the high religions of a first cause of all things, a being personal or impersonal that has produced the universe and is the present basis of its existence and functioning. In either case the religions, as a general rule, relate men closely with the power or powers at work in nature and society.

Although belief in God in the higher religions has sometimes led men to think meanly of the world around them, in the faith that they are pilgrims and strangers here on earth and heaven is their home, this belief is far from typical of man's religions in general; it is in fact a special sort of belief produced under special conditions. The general attitude is that the relation between man and his world is organic and vital, not accidental and external. If the outer face of nature is sometimes mistrusted, it is usually in the name of something deeper within that is assigned a higher degree of reality.

Most men, from primitives in the jungles to members of societies far advanced in technology and intercultural relationships, do not think that men are all that matters. To think this is to run counter to a very deep feeling, namely, that man depends for life and fullness of being on forces outside himself that share in some sense his nature and with which he must be in harmony. The harmony thus sought is sometimes a harmony in action, as in primitive religions; or it is a moral and spiritual harmony, as in the great religions of the Near East; or the harmony sought is more than a harmony, it is a complete and final identity, as in most of the religions of India and the Far East.

To realize all this is to have sympathy with primitive as well as with advanced religions. The former may say what they have to say mythically, or unscientifically, or in unquestioning acceptance of sense experience or of inherited tradition, but their quest is not unlike that of religions in the larger and more inclusive cultures.

Before we enter on the story of early and bygone religions, we might consider the word *primitive* we have just used. Many careful students of the world's cultures use it with hesitancy, because it connotes lack of development and inferiority. As a matter of fact, primitive cultures are often richly developed and have much to commend them qualitatively. Even more out of favor is the word *savage*. This word suggests cruelty, amorality, and barbarism, three terms that are as far from being universally characteristic of non-literate cultures as they are of presumably "higher" literate ones. We can drop its use without loss, but the word *primitive* is hard to replace. *Non-literate* is not satisfactory because it calls attention too emphatically to only one aspect of the cultures to which it applies. With some hesitancy, then, we shall use the word *primitive* hereafter for those smaller, less informed, and more isolated societies whose technology is not as highly developed as in "civilized" societies and whose religious systems arc regarded by all in the group, without exception, as indispensable to social harmony and satisfactory adaptation to the immediate environment.

1 Religion in Prehistoric and Primitive Cultures

To ONE who is confined to it yet does not have the resources of scientific language and description to explain it, the immediate environment is full of mysteries. This is the case of primitive man. His religion has been a necessity to him, for it has provided ways of behaving with the least strain toward mysterious realities—natural forces, ancestral spirits, and the powers felt to be present in men and their social institutions. But when he has acquired the experience to locate his immediate environment in a larger natural setting, he has developed a longer reach of thought and a wider kind of relationship, in which "high gods," "national gods," and "lords of heaven" appear.

In order to understand this, it is well to begin as far back in time as we can go. We turn therefore briefly to prehistoric times.

I Stone Age Religion

> O ancient cousin,
> O Neanderthaler!
> What shapes beguiled, what shadows fled across
> Your early mind?
>
> Here are your bones,
> And hollow crumbled skull,
> And here your shapen flints—the last inert
> Mute witnesses to so long vanished strength.
>
> What loves had you,
> What words to speak,
> What worships,
> Cousin?

Could we find answers to these questions, they might help us to determine when and how religion began. But that is not certain. Because religion is a product of the earliest attempt of the human mind to achieve a sense of security in the world, the Neanderthaler may not have been the first religious man. But who was? There is no telling. It is most unlikely that such prehominids as the South African Australopithecus and the East African Zinjanthropus of (perhaps) two

4

million years ago were capable of religious feeling, for when we consider the remains they left—the sharp-edged flints they seem to have picked up as implements in their difficult struggle for existence—we can tell very little about the degree of their intelligence, much less whether they were religious or not. Even the nearer-to-our-time Peking Man (Sinanthropus), roughly the contemporary of the Javan Pithecanthropus and the Heidelberg Man, cannot be known to have behaved religiously, although he heated his caves with fire, shaped stones into tools and weapons, was a mighty hunter, and collected human heads, whose brains he seems to have extracted and eaten. (Was it because he had a respect for the magical powers of the human brain or simply because he was a delicacy-loving cannibal? We simply do not know.)

As to the Neanderthalers, who, after a long gap, flourished from one hundred thousand to twenty-five thousand years ago, definite evidence of their religion is in their graves. The burial of their dead suggests that food offerings (of which broken bones remain) and flint implements, such as hand axes, awls, and chipped scrapers, were placed in the grave during a ceremonial interment. There are signs also of other beliefs. Evidence has recently accumulated that the Neanderthalers treated the cave bear with special reverence. They hunted him at great peril to themselves and respected his spirit even after he was dead. They appear to have set aside certain cave bear skulls, without removing the brains, a great delicacy, and also certain long (or marrow) bones, and to have placed them with special care in their caves on elevated slabs of stone, on shelves, or in niches, probably in order to make them the center of some kind of ritual. Whether their bear-cult was a propitiation of the bear-spirit during a ritual feast, or whether it was a form of hunting magic to insure the success of the next hunt, or yet again whether it was a sacrifice or votive offering to some divinity having to do with the interrelations of man and bear, is a matter of controversy among authorities. Another subject of debate is the Neanderthal treatment of human skulls. Some of the skulls are found, singly or in series, with-

out the accompaniment of the other bones of the body, each decapitated and opened at the base in such a way as to suggest that the brains were extracted and eaten. The evidence is inconclusive as to whether the emptied skulls were placed in a ritual position for memorial rites or whether the Neanderthalers were head hunters who ate in some sacramental way the brains, whether of sacrificial victims, the newly dead, or enemies, to acquire the soul-force in them. In any case it would seem that the awareness of spirit-powers was rather far advanced.

When we come to the later and higher culture levels of the Old Stone Age, since twenty-five thousand years ago—to the period of the so-called Cro-Magnon men of Europe and their African peers—we are left in less doubt as to the precise nature of Old Stone Age religious conviction and practice.

The Cro-Magnons were, like the Neanderthalers, members of the genus *homo sapiens*, but they were more fully developed true men, somewhat taller and more rugged than modern man. They came into a milder climate than that which had made so hazardous the existence of the Neanderthalers whom they replaced. In the warmer months, like the Neanderthalers before them, they lived a more or less nomadic life following their game; during the colder seasons they used caves and shelters under cliffs. They lived by gathering roots and wild fruits and by hunting, their larger prey being bison, aurochs, an occasional mammoth, and especially the reindeer and the wild horse. Evidence of their hunting prowess has been found at an open-air camp of theirs discovered at Solutre, in south-central France, where archeologists have unearthed the bones of a hundred thousand horses, together with those of reindeer, mammoths, and bison—the remains of centuries of feasting. The Cro-Magnons never tamed and domesticated the horse, but they found him good eating. The horse, bearded and small, moved in large herds, was highly vulnerable to attack, and not dangerous.

In somewhat similar fashion as the Neanderthalers, the Cro-Magnons buried their dead, choosing the same kind of burial sites, not unnaturally at the

5

mouth of their grottos or near their shelters, and they surrounded the body with ornaments such as shell bracelets, and with stone tools, weapons, and food. Of great interest is the fact that they practiced the custom of painting or pouring red coloring matter (red ochre) on the body, or at a later time on the bones during a second burial.

Paint played a large part in their lives, in fact. The most remarkable cultural achievement of the Cro-Magnons was their painting and modeling. They could draw, paint murals, mold clay figures, carve in the round, or engrave on bone and antlers, with a realism unsurpassed by the art of any known primeval men. Their chief subjects were animals of the hunt, the bison, the horse, the wild boar, reindeers, cave bears, and mammoths. Human figures were comparatively rare; they usually appear in the form of statuettes and are extraordinarily fat and obviously symbolic.

Many of the engravings and paintings were executed on the walls of gloomy caves, by the light of torches or shallow soapstone lamps fed with fat. So far from the cave-mouth and in such nearly inaccessible places did the artists do their work that they could hardly have had public display of their murals chiefly in view. What then had they in mind, it may be asked.

The answer that seems the most consistent with all the facts is that the practices of the Cro-Magnons included a magical use of the painted and carved

The sorcerer of Les Trois Frères. This famous Upper Paleolithic mural from a subterranean cave in France depicts a Cro-Magnon shaman (or perhaps "spirit" controlling the hunt) wearing a costume made out of reindeer antlers, the ears of a stag, eyes of an owl, beard of a man, paws of a bear, tail of a horse, and a patchwork of animal skins. The feet are human. The "sorcerer" is perhaps engaged in a hunting dance. (Courtesy of the American Museum of Natural History.)

figures. There may have been some recognition of a kinship and interaction of animal and human spirits, with overtones of religion, but there was certainly magic, that is, an attempt to control events. That there were medicine men among them seems beyond doubt. A vivid mural in the cavern of Trois Frères shows a masked man, arrayed in reindeer antlers, bear's ears, and the tail of a horse, who probably represents a well-known figure in primitive communities, the medicine man or shaman. Whether or not the actual artist, a shaman probably led in magical use of the paintings and clay figures. Just as among primitive peoples today it is believed that an image or picture can be a magical substitute for the object of which it is the representation, so the Cro-Magnons evidently felt that whoever made an image of an animal subjected it to his influence or somehow brought it into his power. The magical use made of the realistic murals and plastic works of the Paleolithic era is suggested in several clear examples. In the cavern of Montespan there is a clay figure of a bear whose body is covered with representations of dart thrusts. Similarly, in the cavern of Niaux an engraved and painted bison is marked with rudely painted outlines of spears and darts, mutely indicating the climax of some primeval hunt; clearly, the excited Cro-Magnon hunters (gathering before the hunt?) ceremonially anticipated and insured their success by having their leaders (medicine men?) paint upon the body of their intended quarry, so vividly pictured on the cave wall, the crude representations of their hunting weapons. They went on the assumptions of magic that to foresee is to foreordain, and that like produces like.

Another sort of interest in painting and carving appears in many of the representations of human beings. Tiny sculptured figures of the human female, usually from four to six inches high, are sometimes found in Upper Paleolithic art. Most of them, like the famous Venus of Willendorf, are obviously meant to symbolize fecundity: the extremities of the figures taper away without much attempt at realistic representation, the faces are usually blank and round,

The Venus of Willendorf. The Upper Paleolithic artist who made the limestone figure (now in the Museum of Natural History, Vienna) obviously dwelt on its sexual features. The downward-turning face, crowned by curly hair, is almost blank, and the feet are absent altogether, but the breasts, abdomen, and hips are full and rounded, suggesting that the figure was used in fertility or mother-goddess rituals. The latter use may be indicated by the way in which the thin arms press down the breasts as though in breast-feeding. (Courtesy of the American Museum of Natural History.)

whereas exaggerated emphasis is placed upon fatness or largeness of hips, breasts, and abdomen. The use of such mother figures in either fertility magic or a cult of the clan mother seems indicated. In painting, one mural shows mares in foal, and another, in the rock shelter of Cogul, Spain, depicts nine women sur-

7

rounding a naked male, who seems to be either the subject of a tribal initiation at puberty or the leader in a ritual connected with fertility magic.

It thus appears that Paleolithic man used both fertility and hunting magic, with evident faith in their value as methods of control.

Of direct religious significance are the beliefs implicit in the burial customs of the Cro-Magnons and related peoples of the Upper Paleolithic period. Because the dead, or their bones, were covered with red paint (symbolizing, no doubt, the redness of the life-blood), the belief cannot have been less than that the dead survived in some real sense, although there may have been no conception of the survival of a non-physical spiritual entity; whatever survived had a ghostly corporeality and actual bodily needs and desires.

Associated with such beliefs there may have been both awe and fear of the dead.* Memories of the dead while they yet lived could have contributed to both these feelings, and so also dreams and visions in which the dead appeared. But the determinative factor in creating such a sense of something superhuman about the dead could have been a conception perhaps then already well developed—that of a highly potent realm of being or process operative in the forms and forces of nature.

There are indications from about 15,000 B.C. that some Upper Paleolithic peoples made offerings to powers of nature as well as to their dead. In Germany, at Meierdorf and later on at Stellmoor, young does with large stones placed inside their rib cages were evidently submerged in run-off lakes left by the retreating glaciers of the last ice age; perhaps the hunters sacrificed these animals to some nature power or supernatural "master of the animals" on whom their success depended. The Upper Paleolithic peoples also had a bear-cult, not unlike that of the Neanderthalers; they may have wished to propitiate

---

* This would *seem* to be established by the skeletons of Stone Age dead, which show that corpses were trussed up, bandaged, and buried under heavy stones, perhaps to keep them from coming back to torment the living.

a bear-god, or to keep him in a favorable frame of mind. If so, however, they also applied coercive measures (magic), as is shown by their murals and clay figures of bears, the clay images sometimes punctured with wounds and the painted figures spouting blood from mouth, nostrils, and body wounds, apparently in the death agony. Clearly, whatever religion they had was inextricably combined with procedures designed to ensure magical success.

This brings us to the Mesolithic Age (beginning about 10,000 B.C.), the age in which was developed the art of polishing stone implements like the axe and the arrowhead for greater smoothness and keenness. It was perhaps in this period that men learned to grow grain and tend plants. The relics of this age suggest an awe of nature. They include numerous round symbols of the sun and moon. Stones and pillars were probably venerated. There are suggestions of star- and tree-worship as well. The mingling of old fears with a certain sophistication rising from the power obtained by the use of new inventions is shown in the fact that axes, spears, and spoked wheels were seemingly venerated as fetishes. That magic had grown into a complex system in the Mesolithic Age is suggested by the many painted pebbles that have been preserved, covered with crude symbols probably having magical significance, although this may not afford a correct explanation of their use, because no one can at this distance be sure what they really mean.

The Neolithic Age (7000 to 3000 B.C.) is distinguished by several revolutionary developments: early forms of agriculture, the domestication of animals, the arts of pottery, plaiting, and weaving, the building of rude houses and boats, and the first surgery. Marked developments occurred in religion. The cult of the mother-goddess expanded and spread. Burial rites increased in importance and complexity. Funerals were conducted with elaborate ceremony, for they included sacrifices of animals and cereals, if not men. Burials were made under gigantic boulders, in stone chambers, sometimes sunk in the earth, and in cavelike tombs, often constructed with incredible labor out of

Neolithic Swiss lake dwelling. This model of prehistoric dwellings built on piles driven into the lake bottom shows considerable knowledge and skill on the part of the builders. Note also the dugout canoe, the pole for propelling it, the nets, the slain animal being carried across the bridge, and the table of the cooks and their water pots. (Courtesy of the American Museum of Natural History.)

huge stones. Another important development in some regions was cremation of the dead.

Among the mysteries of archeological research are the megalithic monuments of Neolithic times, known as *menhirs* (single stones on end), *dolmens* (two upright stones bridged by a cap-stone), *alignments* (stones in rows), and *cromlechs* (stones in circles, like Stonehenge). The only certain fact seems to be that they were in some way connected with religion, perhaps marking a sacred spot or a burial area, and serving as a center for death- and fertility-cults, as other remains suggest. As for Stonehenge, the burials associated with it and the remains of burnt offerings point to rites performed among its stones that connected the death of men and of vegetation with renewed life and fertility: so far as vegetation is concerned, it must die at the end of the year before it can revive in the spring. But this may not have been all.

The arrangement of the stones is so exact that they may have marked the procession of the lunar year or provided, to take one example, a sighting of the exact spot on the horizon where the sun would rise at midsummer. Perhaps the Stonehenge people (between 1500 and 2000 B.C.) conjoined their magic and religion with something like science.

With this we pause. What have we found? Already developed religious beliefs and practices. But how did religion *begin?* This is the still-unsolved problem. It is evident that the relics of the Stone Age form no more than a check or control upon a more fundamental, psychological inquiry—one outside the scope of this volume—that must proceed by a careful use of conjecture. Such conjecture cannot be attempted without a profound knowledge of contemporary primitive religion. Our inquiry now turns in this direction.

II Some Characteristic Features of Religion in Primitive Cultures Today

Among primitive peoples today the supernatural scene is infinitely variegated. When we measure the beliefs and practices of any one locality against those of another, almost any particular belief or practice can be matched with its opposite or contradiction. On the surface, generalization would appear to be difficult.

But similarities exist. Primitive men have certain general characteristics, and their religious practices have a number of common features.

1. *Awe before the sacred.* An outsider visiting a primitive group would find that the first sign of the religious significance of a place, person, thing, ritual, or event is that it is clearly regarded as sacred. All men regard anything sacred or holy with a distinctive attitude uniting respect and caution. Rudolph Otto, in his famous study *The Idea of the Holy,* based the experience of the holy upon an encounter with a *mysterium tremendum et fascinosum,* and found awareness of it in all religions. But the degree of awareness varies from religion to religion. For the primitive man the sacred possesses such significance that he never deals with it carelessly or casually, or in the way that he may handle his oar and his spear or converse with the members of his family. The sacred signifies supernatural potency, both enlivening and deadly, a power for quick good or bad, and one's attitude toward it may determine whether good or bad will ensue. Anything sacred carries with it the promise of a blessing; but among primitives rarely can any but qualified persons, such as chiefs, shamans, priests, and heads of families, deal with the sacred without harm. Impious handling of sacred objects may cause sudden death. The proper approach therefore is with a sense of holy mystery, awe, reverence, and devout "fear of the Lord."

2. *Expression of anxiety in ritual.* In the presence of the sacred there is a certain anxiety. Will the holy power be stirred to action? Will this action be favorable? As soon as this anxiety arises, there is a need to act and speak in ways that may promise a favorable outcome. This is one of the fundamental bases of all religious ritual. Malinowski, the famous anthropologist, has put this point well so far as primitive magical rituals are concerned:

> In a maritime community depending on the products of the sea there is never magic connected with the collecting of shellfish or with fishing by poison, weirs, and fish traps, so long as these are completely reliable. On the other hand, any dangerous, hazardous, and uncertain type of fishing is surrounded by ritual. In hunting, the simple and reliable ways of trapping or killing are controlled by knowledge and skill alone; but let there be any danger or any uncertainty connected with an important supply of game and magic immediately appears. Coastal sailing as long as it is perfectly safe and easy commands no magic. Overseas expeditions are invariably bound up with ceremonies and ritual.^A*

Many religious rituals are similarly motivated. Although it is true that praise, thanksgiving, and desire for communion with divine beings become progressively more important in the higher religions and provide much of the content of religious ritual, many anthropologists claim that among primitives in a large proportion of religious situations anxiety exists in at least two forms. First, there is a primary anxiety arising from crises or strains in the life of the individual or the community, and this calls forth rituals whose purpose is to provide restoration and reassurance. But once these rituals have been firmly established, with their mythical and institutional accompaniments, a secondary anxiety lest the rituals have *not* been promptly enough nor properly performed gives rise to further rituals of purification and expi-

---

* In this book the sources of all quotations are designated by a small capital letter, followed by a number if a book is quoted from more than once. Books quoted from are listed on p. 564 and succeeding pages, and are there designated by capital letters. This device is adopted for the convenience of readers and to save space.

ation.* The rituals of primitive peoples therefore not only comfort and reassure but also bind the individuals participating in them to their further performance, for fear that failure to do so will be followed by unhappy consequences.

3. *Ritual and expectancy.* But not all rituals are expressions of anxiety, although those that allay anxiety have a more than average intensity and urgency. Many rituals are expectant in character. They presuppose their own causal efficacy; they are performed to bring health, offspring, productivity of the soil, fertility of cattle, and other benefits desired by the community as well as the individual. Rituals also celebrate such annual events as the return of spring, sowing, and harvesting; they fit into a calendar of periodic rites. Other rituals are less regular in their recurrence because they mark spaced-out changes in the status of individuals, such as elevation to tribal leadership or kingship, which often have a pronounced sacral character, or they may mark transition of maturing individuals from one social status to another. Among the latter rites are those recognized and named by Arnold van Gennep as "rites of passage"; that is to say, they are rites in connection with birth, name-giving, initiation, betrothal, marriage, death, and the like. These events change the status not only of the individual involved but also of his parents and relatives. Typical of the rites of passage are the initiation rites we shall note among the Australian aborigines (pp. 26 f.).

But rituals also have a basis in myth, and vice versa.

4. *Myth and ritual.* The making of myths is universal among mankind.† For myths are a necessity.

* See pp. 85–118 of Lessa and Vogt, *Reader in Comparative Religion* for discussion of these points by Malinowski, Radcliffe-Brown, and George C. Homans. The last makes on especially valuable summary statement.

† Because of the vastness of this subject and the tendency of the word *myth* to lose specific meaning when it is made to stretch over so many different kinds of tales, some scholars seek to limit the meaning of the word. "True myths," it is said, have the function of corroborating or validating tribal traditions, rituals, and sacred sites. Thus, in an article in *Folklore* (December, 1957) E. O.

Primitives, like all men, find them vital for the maintenance of the patterns of group-life. Among the Australian aborigines, for example, myths have a great importance, for they are invoked to explain and give the weight of a supernatural origin and authority to the customs, ceremonials, and beliefs of the tribes (p. 28). This is a major aspect of ritual development. It frequently happens that primitives find themselves following old customs and rituals whose precise meaning now eludes them. In this situation it is natural to seek an explanation of the necessity they feel to follow what would otherwise be meaningless rites by saying, "The Fathers taught us to do these things," and then to push back the origins beyond remembered fathers to mythical Progenitors or Culture Heroes at the beginning of the world. Or some "high god" (p. 17) may be cited as the first author of "our tribe and way of life." It will be seen at once that myths here serve the very necessary function of providing binding sanctions for tribal custom and belief. Specifically, they tell in story form of the imposition, by an original authoritative father-figure, of an awesome primeval decree that is expressed in

James distinguishes true myths sharply from fantasy, poetry, romance, philosophy, theology, and psychology, because the function of myth is to "validate and justify, conserve and safeguard" established tradition and does not share therefore the interests of several types of lore that are merely speculative, playful, or in answer to the promptings of curiosity. This rules out Plato's *mythos* as true myth and excludes the folklore that is an exercise of sportive imagination. The present account follows the looser, more inclusive practice of defining myths as sacred tales of wondrous and often supernatural deeds of gods and men, especially in "beginning times," deeds that supply clues to the real nature of man and his world and are therefore memorable and significant, as deeds in tales of sheer fantasy are not. Due acknowledgment is made, it is hoped, of the fact that myths of great anthropological importance have arisen to validate and justify tribal tradition and ritual.

Incidentally, one of the issues much debated by anthropologists is whether myths arise from rituals or rituals from myths. This account follows Clyde Kluckhohn in saying that the facts do not justify an *either-or* but rather a *both-and* in this case. Myth and ritual are mutually interdependent and are both causes and effects of each other, depending on circumstances.

the institutions and traditions of the community: "Do thus-and-so without fail. It is for your good."

5. *Other functions of myth.* Myths have other roles to play. A large place must be given to cosmogonic or "creation" myths. It is of course speculative to seek reasons for their being told in such numbers and in such variety. One reason is undoubtedly the need to have an explanation of why the earth is so suited to human habitation. Someone—perhaps the High God or a Culture Hero—dove into the waters to bring up the sand with which he made the earth habitable, or he forced apart the close-lying sky-father and earth-mother to make room for the gods, men, animals, and vegetation they had engendered, or he brought these forth from an underground cave, or fought with giants for the materials with which he put the world together. Whereas questions like "Was there a First Cause?" would be greeted by primitives with incomprehension, specific questions like "Why are men, bears, and wolves as different as they are?" might stir an individual of imagination to compose and pass on to others a myth drawn from his memories and dreams and particularly from what he thought the old men of his youth might say, were they alive.

Again, many myths are expressions in fantasy-form of subconscious criticism of the injustices and maladjustments of familial and social organizations. Like dreams, they are in this respect full of meaningful symbolism, and when told and retold they afford release to hidden tensions by giving them a disguised but effective voice. This is an important aspect of mythology.

The quasi-historical myth is of another sort. It is the elaboration of an original happening, involving usually a hero or pioneer figure, into a tale of wonder, through all of whose episodes thrills the magic of the hero's name, until his character, looming transfigured through the magico-religious aura in which it is invested, glows with divinity.

6. *The bi-polarity of religion and magic.* That religion and magic are polarities within a continuous context, so that one easily shades into the other, is more and more apparent. They should be distin-

guished, however. There have been many attempts to do so, but with only moderate success. Sir James G. Frazer, for example, saw a chronological as well as a formal difference. He believed that magic was early man's attempt to coerce the powers of nature by the use of certain procedures, such as the rituals of sympathetic magic, the effect of which was to establish control over these powers. Such rituals constituted a false science, but early man trusted in them. Sometimes, however, he found that the powers of nature were beyond the control of magic, and so he resorted to coaxings and persuasions (prayer) in the hope of favorable response. Religion appeared when magic failed. Although this attempt at a distinction has some value, it has been rejected by investigators of primitive societies because (1) no chronological sequence from magic to religion can be found, and (2) religious and magical procedures, even when their distinction in definition is allowed, are often so inextricably combined that they must be seen as at most two aspects of one ritual. There is real value in saying that where rituals are coercive in intent, they have the character of magic, and where they are persuasive, they are religious. Value may also attach to Émile Durkheim's view that religious rites are obligatory and magical ones optional, but this holds true only partially. Much the same thing may be said of Malinowski's suggestion that magic is a means to a precise end in view, whereas religion has no immediate practical result in mind but is an end in itself. The difficulty with all these distinctions is that instances can be found where no one of them completely applies. For example, a primitive magician may in the course of a single ritual coax, beg, peremptorily command, and even threaten the spirits. Frazer's distinction obviously loses point here, but so do Malinowski's and Durkheim's. Perhaps we can say that each of these distinctions has some use, provided we bear in mind that magic and religion are not to be sharply separated but seen as two distinguishable aspects of the rituals used in primitive societies.°

° It could well be added that even in theologically sophisticated religious systems, religion can seldom be

7. *Types of magic.* Magic may be loosely defined as an endeavor through utterance of set words, or the performance of set acts, or both, to control or bend the powers of the world to man's will. It cannot be wholly divorced from religion, as we have heretofore noted, but it is discernibly present when emphasis is placed on forcing things to happen rather than asking that they do.

Sir James G. Frazer has made one type of magic famous. The inclusive name he gave it is "sympathetic magic." One subdivision of it, which he called "imitative magic," is based on such assumptions as that look-alikes act alike, or, more significantly, that like influences or even produces like; therefore, if one imitates the looks and actions of a man or an animal (or even of a thunder cloud), one can induce a like and desired action in the imitated being or object. The hunting magic of Cro-Magnon man, we can readily see, was a form of imitative magic. Primitive agriculture furnishes another example: it is believed that if the grower goes to his field when the grain is sprouting and, with words of encouragement or command addressed to the emerging plants, leaps again and again as high as he is able, he can induce and even compel the grain to grow at least as high. To cite still another example out of a countless number, primitives often seek an end to drought by going to a steep hill and rolling rocks down its slope while beating drums and shouting "boom!" This is done to bring on a rainstorm. (We shall come upon an instance of this before the end of this chapter, on page 30.)

Black magic has the same basis. If someone, for example, makes an image (imitation) of his enemy, perhaps in wax, and stabs it with pins, the hated one will die. It is frequently quite enough just to describe in detail the terrible things that will happen to an enemy, and then either command (usually by curse) or pray and predict that they must occur, and they may!

Frazer also found a form of sympathetic magic that he called "contagious." Things conjoined and then separated remain sympathetic with each other. Thus severed hair or fingernails retain a magical sympathy with the person to whom they once belonged, and therefore black magic performed on them causes damage to that person. This type of magic has many ramifications.

These and other practices may be grouped under various headings. It will be helpful here to consider them as exemplifying three methods of control of spirit power.

The first is fetishism. This much-abused term is used here to refer to any resort to the presumed power in inanimate things. This includes the veneration and use of certain objects into which useful powers do not have to be induced, because they are already there. These are the so-called natural fetishes —the curiously marked pebbles, aerolites, bones, odd-shaped sticks, and the like—which seem from the moment of finding to bring good fortune and to frustrate the evil designs of one's foes. But on its more actively magical side, fetishism involves inducing useful powers into a variety of inanimate objects, stuffed sometimes into an antelope's horn or other receptacle, and confining them there for the purpose of securing their assistance in a great variety of projects.

Both natural and manufactured fetishes are regarded as possessing a vague sort of personality, at least an active will. This idea accounts for the prevailing attitude taken toward them, especially in Africa. There a fetish is reverenced in the most obviously anthropomorphic way. It is first treated as an object of worship, being addressed with prayer and presented with offerings. This done, a favorable issue is awaited, with hope. But if the desired result does not follow, the attitude of the owner changes; he passes to coaxing and cajoling, then proceeds to stern commands, next to scolding, and finally to whipping

---

found in a pure state. In the Christian religion, for example, baptism and the Lord's Supper are often regarded as necessary to ensure, as if automatically and by magical compulsion or coercion, the worshiper's eventual entrance into heaven.

The references for the above distinctions are Malinowski, *Myth, Magic and Religion;* Frazer, *The Golden Bough;* and Durkheim, *The Elementary Forms of the Religious Life.*

or other chastisement. If there is still no result, the conclusion is either that the spirit has left the fetish, in which case it is useless and another must be found to take its place, or that the spirit, still in the fetish, has been rendered impotent by some more powerful fetish or spirit-power in the neighborhood. In the latter case the magician must be visited and the fetish charged with more power, or substituted with another of adequate potency.

The second method of dealing with spirit-power is shamanism. In this case spirits are conjured into or out of human beings by one who is himself spirit-possessed. The shaman of Siberia has been selected to give his name to this practice because, in this aspect of his community role, he is typical of all witch-doctors, medicine men, exorcists, and sorcerers. He is able to work himself up to a frenzy of spirit-possession; that is to say, he lifts himself up to the spirit-level, in both consciousness and power, and when in that state establishes control over certain spirits, especially those of disease and death, in order either to drive them into people (bedevilment or bewitchment), or to expel them from people (exorcism), especially in case of illness.*

The third method of control—popular magic—is not different in its nature from other types of magic. It is not confined to magicians or priests, but is diffused through the group. It is the endeavor of the common folk (with or without the aid of shamans, but always by definite procedures) either to prevent the spirit-powers from doing harm to the individual or the group or to make them serve private or group interests. One set of procedures, which goes under the name of aversive magic, is innumerable in its forms; it is perhaps best typified by the ritual by which the community rids itself of an accumulated weight of guilt by transferring it magically to a "scapegoat" or other carrier, e.g., a boat which drifts out to sea. The almost infinite number of procedures working toward social and individual well-being, specifically by promoting fertility in field and flock and in womankind, is often called productive magic. We may cite the corn dances in many parts of the world, fertility rites at sowing based on sympathetic magic, human sacrifice followed by planting of the flesh or pouring of the blood in the fields, and performances magico-religious in character, such as the offering of the first-fruits and firstlings of the fields and flocks to the gods, the worship of bulls and he-goats, ceremonial marriages of fertility gods and goddesses represented by human actors, and the offering of human victims to vegetative and corn deities in order to insure the growth of an adequate food supply.*

8. *Divination.* There is a close connection between shamanism and divination, that is, between rapport with spirit-powers and insight into what is obscure and hidden in the present and future. Such insight is thought to occur during specific divination rites. Shamans may use their own inherent power (magic) or may establish dependent prophetic relations with the supernatural (a situation that is primarily religious). The general primitive belief is that the shaman or necromancer possesses the power to make contacts in the spirit-world, including communion with the spirits of the dead, and thus gains otherwise inaccessible information about things and events on,

---

* It should be said that this description presents only one aspect of the total activities of the shaman—the magical one, where outright control of spirit-powers is sought. The shaman is also a religious specialist, skilled in persuasion. He attracts the spirits, for example, in order to talk with them or to have them talk to his audience through him in many different voices; he uses his special techniques—drum-beating, dancing, auto-hypnotic concentration, chanting, drugs, and the like, while his close-packed audience watches—in order to go into a deep trance, during which his spirit travels to far places, typically over mountains, under the sea, or under the earth, where he finds out what the spirits intend, thus divining the future, or what is happening to the dead, to whom he sometimes offers his guidance, based on other spirit-journeys, especially if they are lost and cannot find their way to their final resting place. In other words, he has priestlike functions as well as those of a magician.

* The student is referred to Sir James G. Frazer's *The Golden Bough*, the one-volume abridgment, for fascinating descriptions of these procedures. The unacceptability of the central thesis does not destroy the value of these descriptions.

above, and under the earth. Often he is believed to be the "familiar" of a single spirit or soul that puts him "in the know." In other contexts, where priests rather than shamans are the central figures, divination has an explicit religious aspect. It relies on divine inspiration, either through direct communication with the god or through oracles, such as those in which the ancient Greeks believed: words whispered by the oaks of Dodona speaking for Zeus (p. 56) or entranced utterances muttered by the priestess at Delphi (p. 57) when Apollo communicated through her. Another aspect of divination is the reading of omens in the flight of birds, the sound of thunder, dreams, visions, the appearance of comets, eclipses, "signs in the stars," accidents, sudden death, and like phenomena. Divination seems to be such a necessity to primitives that it is virtually universal.

9. *Belief in mana.* Mana is a Melanesian term, adopted by anthropologists as a convenient designation for the widespread, although not universal, belief in occult force or indwelling supernatural power as such, independent of either persons or spirits. It is not the only term of the kind in circulation among primitive peoples. The same sort of reaction is reflected in various parallel terms used by some American Indians (Sious, Iroquois, Algonquin), some tribes of Morocco, the Pygmies of middle Africa, the Bantu of South Africa, and aboriginal people in many parts of the world. Although the role of this force differs from one area to another, taken together all such terms refer to the experienced presence of a powerful but silent force in things or persons, especially any occult force which is believed to act of itself, as an addition to the forces naturally or usually present. It operates most evidently and freely through persons and in living or moving things. It is a force that is thought to be transmissible from objects in nature to man, from one person to another, or again from persons to things. It has had special importance in the South Seas. Not that Melanesians, even of today, conceive of nature as being a unified system of energies, but that the whole world is felt to be energy-pervaded. In the last analysis, the concept of mana indicates response to the vitally significant or extraordinary in quality, as distinguished from the ordinary, the usual, or the normal in quality. The extraordinary in quality—whether in events or in the character of some forceful man or powerful beast—by its very nature draws attention to itself. Though a Melanesian fears whatever is eerie or mysterious, he is practical and hard-headed enough to want to have such a mysterious efficacy as mana brought to his aid or infused into himself or his spear or the vegetables in his garden. He therefore uses what measures he can to assure himself of these effects, and his heritage in fact provides him with an abundance of magical procedures toward this end.

10. *Animism.* There is general acceptance among present-day primitives of the animistic belief that all sorts of motionless objects as well as living and moving creatures have souls or spirits in them, and that every human being has a soul or souls leaving the body temporarily during dreams and with finality at death. This notion of souls and spirits has a meaning quite distinct from that of mana, the last being in itself impersonal, although a soul or spirit may manifest it or be its outlet in action. Souls and spirits are usually conceived of in a thorough-going anthropomorphic fashion. They have shape, mind, feelings, and will or purpose; they are like living people in being amenable to reason in good moods and aggressively quarrelsome when angry or upset; they like flattery, devotion, loyalty; they are often not to be trusted out of one's remembrance; eternal vigilance is the price of being on the right side of them, and one must be ever on the alert to continue in their good graces, once obtained. A cardinal fact about the world-view of the primitive peoples is that in their conception, to use the language of E. B. Tylor, "all nature is possessed, pervaded, crowded with spiritual beings."[B]

11. *Veneration and worship of spirits.* It has been said truly that man has worshiped everything he could think of beneath the earth, everything between earth and heaven, and everything in the heavens above.[C] Sometimes it is the object itself which is worshiped as living and active, heavily charged with

mana. Again, the object is not worshiped for itself but for the spirit or soul lodged or inhering in it. Once more, the object is not worshiped at all; it becomes a symbol of the reality which *is* worshiped and which it visibly and tangibly represents. All three of these modes of worship may at times go on simultaneously, for, as in the case of the worship of images in India, some ignorant worshipers regard the image itself as alive, others suppose there is a spirit resident in it, and the cultivated or philosophically-minded devotee makes use of it as a convenient thought-center for symbolizing the reality behind all.

Short of worship, which expresses adoration and is usually accompanied by prayer and praise, are veneration and awe. These include respect and the acknowledgment of the presence of sacred power or quality. Sometimes it is difficult to know where veneration ends and worship begins.

The veneration of stones has been widespread and goes back to prehistoric times. The stones may be of any size, from pebble to boulder, and in any amount, single, in series, or even in heaps. Often they are remarkable in shape or composition. Sometimes they are shaped by human art or skill, as in the case of flint tools or weapons. Aerolites are often venerated, the classic instance being that of the Ka'ba stone at Mecca, which every Muslim pilgrim kisses to acquire its saving virtue (p. 519). Veneration of shaped stones, and of any tool or implement, not only existed in prehistoric times, but may be found today in Africa, Oceania, India, Japan, and among North American Indians. Among the primitives of the Philippine Islands the headman's weapons are held to be charged with a vital force that can act of itself. A passage from an account of these people says of one chieftain: "He was no ordinary mortal. . . . His companions insisted that his headaxe and spear killed at his bidding."[D] This sort of belief is not uncommon. The axe is still venerated in the rural districts of Germany and Scandinavia. Veneration of this kind was general in the Graeco-Roman world.

The veneration of plants and trees is also widespread, not only among primitive peoples but in more complex cultures as well. Survivals of such veneration in sophisticated societies are seen in the use of the Christmas tree and of the Maypole. It is said that in Europe, in the Upper Palatinate, woodmen still murmur a plea for forgiveness to a large, fine tree before they cut it down. Not only do trees and plants inspire reverence, but they also represent an exhaustless productivity. Deification of trees, and also of plants and grains, is a natural tribute to the mysterious growth-forces of nature. Trees help crops to grow, assist flocks and herds to multiply, and make women fertile. Barren women are sometimes married to trees in order that they may become fruitful.

Animal-veneration is another widespread element of primitive religions. It springs up naturally when men believe that if they can somehow share in the magnificent powers of certain animals, they will gain greatly in strength, vision, and cunning. Another source of animal-veneration is the feeling that members of the group and certain animals are akin. The relationship is often conceived to be so near that many peoples have had little difficulty in believing that the soul of a man at death, and even during life, readily passes into the body of an animal, and vice versa. Myths and fairy tales abound in characters such as frog-maidens, bird-women, and vampires who alternately appear in human and bat shapes; were-tigers and werewolves have contributed a thrill to many a tale of disaster and bloodshed. The lion in Africa, the tiger in Malaya, the eagle, the bear, and the beaver in North America, the bull in Greece and Egypt, the cow in India, Africa, and Scandinavia, the buffalo in South India, the kangaroo in Australia are among the fierce and strong or gentle and life-sustaining creatures that men have honored with their veneration. Similarly, reverence has been paid to the goose, the dove, and the snake. The last, whether in the form of the sinuous serpent or the winged dragon, has been reverenced under a hundred forms and symbols, of which both the water connections and the phallic associations have been among the chief fascinations for the worshiper.

We may conjecture that it was later in the history

of religions that reverence for the "elements" of the world, considered in the abstract—earth, air, fire, and water—appeared, though fire, the least abstract because least diffused, has been revered since the dawn of historic times, and probably in the Old Stone Age. The Parsees still honor it. The sky (or space) came at last to be worshiped as the home of the clouds, winds, sun, moon, and stars, themselves regarded as animate. Water, more difficult to conceive of abstractly, was venerated in its discrete forms, fountains, springs, rivers, lakes, and finally the sea, whose hold upon the imagination is such that its worship characterized all early civilizations and continued late into the Middle Ages, when the Doge of Venice was annually married to the Adriatic. In much the same way men have sometimes worshiped Earth, the universal mother and grain-bearer.

12. *Recognition of high gods.* This is the natural place to raise the disputed question whether primitive peoples have been widely given to religious relationships with a high god, a Supreme Being. It is common to find among many primitive groups a recognition of the existence of a god far up in the sky or at a great remove, who has made everything—man, earth, sea, and sky—and who at a distance sees all that goes on among men, but, though he sometimes disapproves of what he sees, does not often interfere. Among the lower primitives, like the Pygmies of Africa, the Fuegians of South America, and the Australian bushmen, the belief in such a high god has been even clearer and more definite. It has been an old belief of these most backward races that the high god formerly lived on earth, instructed men in their social and moral laws, and then retired to the skyland, where he keeps an eye on men's doings and sometimes severely punishes their lapses. Lightning is his weapon, thunder his roaring, but he himself is never seen.

A dispute has arisen among anthropologists as to whether this high god has the religious significance of the nearer spirit-powers of the earth. The prevailing opinion is rather negative. Primitive men have not had to be concerned daily about the high god. He is supreme and uncreated, existing from the beginning, but other spirits are much more active as determiners of destiny down on the earth. If there have been any exceptions to this comparative evaluation, we come across them among the Australian bushmen and the Fuegians. The former in some localities address prayers for food to the Supreme Being, and the latter thought he caused all deaths. Yet the members of one of the Fuegian tribes used to speak of him in the third person, as if he had no direct dealings with them. Moreover, they sometimes issued threats against him, which precludes their having thought him really supreme. But this matter may be left in dispute. Probably, the idea of a great Originator who has little to do with men in the ordinary course of life arose very naturally when an answer was attempted to such questions as "Where did our rituals come from?" or "Who began everything?" or "Who is the First Father?" Unable to think that any of the local powers with which they had daily dealings could have originated or fathered all things, they hit upon a theistic, or better, monotheistic, explanation. But because the being they inferred seldom entered their lives, he was in most instances in the nature of a deistic postulate rather than an ever-present religious reality (pp. 26 and 33).

13. *Taboo.* Taboos are prohibitions or "hands-off" warnings applied to many things, persons, and actions. Specifically, there are things that may not be touched or handled, persons who must be avoided or who may be approached only to a certain distance, actions that may not be performed, places that may not be entered. If we define the term broadly enough, taboos are found in every religion and any society.

Many taboos are based on fear of mana; others reflect the dread of pollution. Some set up a hedge around the god. Still others seek to avoid the loss of power, health, or luck. This by no means exhausts the range of taboo. Many different things, acts, sacred words, names, and places are on the list of the avoided. Sharp weapons, iron, blood, head and hair (they contain spirit), cut hair and nails (even when severed from the body they retain a generous portion of spirit), spittle, certain foods, knots and rings, and much more are in this category.

In many parts of the world (American Indians are an exception) the person of a chief is taboo. Partly this is to protect him from harm, but even more it is because of his mana: he is thought to be so heavily charged with power that to touch him, or his clothes, or his cooking utensils, or even the carpet or floor-space upon which he walks, is highly dangerous; immediate steps must be taken to counteract the fatal consequences to the intruder which will ensue. When entering the chief's presence the utmost precautions must be observed.

More than one instance is on record of men and women who died of fright upon learning they had unwittingly eaten the remains of a chief's meal. Their bodies apparently could not survive so powerful a dosage of mana-imbued substance.

There are taboos upon other persons. The same awe with which kings and priests are regarded is easily aroused by other persons in certain circumstances. But taboos have a greater complexity than this suggests. In many parts of the world warriors are taboo before and after battle. This is only partly because they are in an awesome state of excitement and dangerous. More particularly, they are not to be distracted. Women especially should keep their distance and even remain hidden from sight; in some cultures they are strictly forbidden to approach a warrior for some hours before battle, for sex before battle drains his power. And he is taboo after battle because he has been polluted by bloodshed. Man-slayers are in fact usually untouchable until expiation or ceremonial cleansing has taken place and removed the contagion of death and the wrath of the departed spirit. Generally, a taboo is put on all those who have had any contact with the dead, and this extends even to the hired mourners.

It is generally true among primitive folk that few pass through life without at some time or other becoming taboo. A newly born child, a boy or girl during initiation ceremonies at puberty, a woman in childbed, a husband practicing the curious custom of *couvade* (bringing to bed of the father at the birth of a child), recently widowed women, celebrants in religious ceremonies—all such, in one locality or another, are temporarily tabooed.

It must be evident that almost anything and everything at one time or other has been taboo. This holds true not only for primitive peoples but for people of more advanced cultures as well.

14. *Purification rites.* Ceremonies of purification and cleansing have been referred to more than once in the above discussion of taboo. The reference was inescapable. The existence of taboos means to the primitive not only a very real element of danger in taboo-breaking, because of the vindictive or retributive action of outraged powers, but also the guilt and uncleanness of the unfortunate taboo-breaker. This uncleanness and contamination are such that the whole community may be put in jeopardy. Until the taboo-breaker is cleansed of his defilement, he is ostracized, and may even come under the sentence of death.

But taboo-breaking is not the only source of pollution. Birth, death, bloodshed, blood itself, and contact with tabooed persons are each sources of pollution. And there may be a supernatural condition, such as the presence of an unclean spirit haunting a family or a village, a condition involving as its consequence the need of driving out the objectionable presence.

Purification of ritual pollution is effected in various ways. Common among the methods are fasting, shaving the hair and cutting the nails, crawling through cleansing smoke fumes produced during an elaborate ritual, passing between fires or jumping through fire, washing with water or blood, and cutting or gashing the body so as to let the evil out with the rushing blood. If an unclean spirit haunts a community or enters a man or woman, it may be expelled by introducing a more powerful spirit whose presence will be cleansing. The modes of purification are numberless, in fact.

But while a major motive for purification rites is getting a cleansing from pollution, there also exists the motive of purifying oneself for future ritual. The officiant may purify himself for a rite he is to perform by fasting, abstention from sex, ablutions, and the like, while those who will be present may undergo similar if less stringent purification.

Again, purification (by way of expiation) may be needed if the rituals have not been properly carried out and anxiety arises as a consequence (p. 10).

15. *Sacrifice.* This has usually entailed the giving up or destruction (e.g., burning) of something, animate or inanimate, human, animal, or vegetable, in order to cause it to pass from human possession to that of the spirit-powers or gods. The simplest form of sacrifice is always the giving of offerings, gifts of value of many sorts, in the hope of pleasing the spirits. But originally the sacrifices seem to have been more radical than this and to have involved animal and human sacrifice, because the spirits as well as men need the vitality and strength present in life and blood.

When the present-day primitive discovers that certain powers behave in an unusual or uncontrollable way, he may offer sacrifices with a view to placating or conciliating the powers he cannot coerce; such sacrifices are propitiatory. When he believes he has offended the powers by his actions, he may offer piacular sacrifices, intended to expiate or atone for his misdoing. Or he may hope to open the way for the inflow of supernatural power into himself, and then his sacrifice is of a sacramental kind. One form of such sacrifice shares something—for example, a sacred meal—with the spirit-powers. All these forms of sacrifice bear the marks of religion, but magic is also generally implicated. It is obvious, for one thing, that sacrifices may do something to or for the spirit-powers; in particular, they may impart added or needed strength and vigor.* Insofar as the powers are dependent upon

---

* Survivals of this belief may be found in Homer and among the early Romans. Homer implies that the gods not only lose prestige but power as well when men cease to sacrifice to them (p. 60). The Romans, we shall find, felt that since their sacrifices increased the *numen* or spiritual power of the gods, the gods owed them a return of favors, which was confidently expected (p. 68).

man for the vitalizing elements in the sacrifices, the sacrifices gain a magical potency to coerce them. Hence primitives sometimes regard religious rituals as having guaranteed results. They thus anticipate something that occurs explicitly above the primitive level. We shall take note in another chapter that in Vedic times in India a highly sophisticated development converted worship and sacrifice into magic: the priests promised and guaranteed that their rituals would force the gods to do as they directed (p. 98 f.). This understanding is more implicit than expressed in primitive religion.

A somewhat different development has resemblances to aversive magic. Sacrifices are offered to dreaded powers in mingled fear and confidence that they will stay away or cease to afflict the group with sickness, drought, or other calamity. Sacrifices, because of their momentousness and cost to the givers, carry great weight even with ill-disposed powers.

If we take our story a little beyond the primitive level, we see in the offering of sacrifices an important element in the origin of what are now called formal religious services. One does not bring offerings and sacrifices without words, words of compliment and conciliation. This, along with the vocal expression of awe and gratitude, is the origin of praise, and along one line of development it resulted in the hymn and psalm. After praise, it is safe to petition for favors. Here is the germ of ritual prayer. Again, differentiation in the modes of worship and sacrifice could hardly have taken place without selection of sacred places for the performance of rituals—typically the sacred grove. After the passage of centuries, shrines and temples would arise at such places. To perform the sacred ceremonies exactly and effectively there arose the consecrated class of priests, set apart to devote their lives to the care of religious property, the preservation and performance of the rituals, and the discovery and declaration of the will of the gods by divination, oracle, and prophecy.

16. *Attitudes toward the dead.* Here is an important circle of ideas. The notion of the complete extinction of the personality at death is often difficult to

19

reconcile with our daily experience. A man who has been a boon companion for days and years leaves at death a great void in our lives; our habits must be adjusted to his absence; we think of him often; his influence lingers with us; our visual and auditory memories are for some time so vivid that the mere thought of him gives him back to us in living presence; at night we dream that we see him and talk to him.

These experiences were as vivid, certainly, to our prehistoric ancestors as they are to us. It is not strange that prehistoric man and his modern representatives have felt that the dead not only survive but have the same hungers and needs as in life. But close upon this conviction that the dead have an after-life comes a real uneasiness. The dead, it is realized, have a way of hanging about. This is embarrassing, because they do not play their old part in the round of daily existence.

Very early our primitive forebears developed measures of security against troublous interference by the dead. They raised a heap of stones over the dead body, or tied it up with strong cords, or in some cases even drove a stake through the chest in order to pin the body to the earth. These practices were designed to keep the dead from "walking." At the same time, offerings were left at the burial place to keep the dead satisfied and content. Many of these customs still survive. The dead in more than one region of the world are still carried out feet foremost, in order that they may be "pointed away." This procedure is often followed by a zigzag progress on the part of the corpse-bearers, so as to bewilder the dead and make them unable to find their way back. Another custom is the taking of the body out of the house by some other than the ordinary exit, through the window or through a hole made in the wall, which is immediately closed up. Negroes along the Congo strew thorns on the grave and upon the path leading back to the village, to prick the feet of the dead and prevent return. Sometimes magical barriers are erected against the dead, such as fences around the grave, or hedges of twigs to simulate a trackless forest, or deep lines drawn across the path to represent an impassable river.

It might be concluded that such customs presuppose hostility on the part of the dead. This interpretation is, however, not accurate. It would be truer to say that until the dead have found their way to their final resting place in the hereafter and are at peace, they tend not to go far away; often they feel lost and in need of comfort. They have not yet become adjusted to their new state and want to be sustained by the assurance that the living still care for them. Only if this assurance is denied them do they become disturbed and perhaps inimical. It is hard for the living, however, to know how the dead feel, whether pleased or angry. It is well to be wary—and this precaution is always taken—but the dead often are friendly. This is especially true of ancestors. Ancient Chinese civilization was founded on the optimistic faith that ancestral spirits are eager to aid their descendants, and will do so if only the living pay them proper regard.*

Out of the double purpose of serving the dead who remain nearby and of helping those who are about to depart for the bourn of the hereafter has arisen the worldwide custom of making offerings at the grave. Food and drink are as much a need of the dead as of the living. The endeavor to placate or to assist the dead begins even before burial and is especially evident when interment takes place. Weapons, clothing, furniture, every sort of precious object (including sometimes, as in historic Egypt, miniature ovens, wooden loaves, chairs, servants, and the like) are placed in the grave or tomb (p. 44). Frequently, in times past, wives and servants were "sent along," being either slain upon the grave, burned on a pyre, buried alive, or sealed in tombs. Within living mem-

* It is useful to make a distinction between (a) the dead who depart to another world and are anxiously assisted by the living to make their way there (through a cult of the dead), and (b) the dead who remain, at least for a while, as part of the community, although now invisible, and are constantly remembered and given a role to play in family life (through ancestor-worship). See Annemarie de Waal Malefijt, *Religion and Culture* (Macmillan, 1968).

ory, kings' deaths in Africa have been the occasion of the "sending along" of hundreds of men and women.

17. *Totemism.* Our survey of the general characteristics of primitive religions concludes with brief mention of a group of practices rather hard to define. There is, however, a common characteristic present in all the diverse forms of totemism. It is that totemism recognizes the existence of a more or less intimate relationship between certain human groups and particular classes or species of animal, plant, or inanimate object in nature. The recognition of this relationship results in special social groupings (a phenomenon known as social totemism) and also in rituals binding the human groups to their totemic counterparts (cult totemism). The cult rituals are so diverse as to defy generalization. The rituals of the aborigines of Australia are noteworthy in being very closely tied to tribal survival (p. 23 f.). The tribes there are hard put to it to find enough food to enable them to survive, and totemism has provided what appears to them to be a solution to the problem. Each class of animal, plant, and inanimate object having a place in the food supply has become the totem of a clan within the tribe. The basic realizations here might be put in these terms: "Our food supply depends on there being a plentiful supply of animals, plants, and substances that go into the making of food. May all animals and plants increase and be abundant! Let therefore each of the tribe's clans having an animal or vegetable totem promote the abundance of the species especially sacred to it, by practicing magic, offering prayer, and providing constant care and solicitude. Although those not belonging to the clan may eat of the totem freely, let the totemic clan regard it as taboo, and eat of it sparingly even on the allowed occasion of the periodic sacramental meal when the clan partakes of it." Included among the totems are such things as rain (necessary to the existence of animal and plant alike and infrequent in central Australia) and substances like red ochre (necessary to the decoration of those practicing, among other things, the fertility rites). Undoubtedly the logic of these arrangements was arrived at more by gradual discovery than by reasoning. The Australians have added to these practices the social provision of exogamy, prescribing marriage outside the totemic clan. Other varieties of totemism are found in North and South America, Africa, India (where it exists weakly), and the South Seas. In these areas the particular features of totemism vary, sometimes widely. Where the food supply is ample, the Australian devices for increasing it are replaced by other interests. In North America, for example, it has been characteristic for Indian tribes to divide into a number of groups that express their individuality by taking their name from some animal, bird, or natural object. In most cases the sense of special relationship with the totem has issued in a myth of descent which derives the members of the clan and their totem from a common ancestor. Sometimes the relationship between the members of the clan and the totem has taken the form of a "mystic affinity." In other cases the rituals seek to propitiate the totem group. Occasionally a tribe's totems are chosen from birds only or exclusively from animals. In Australia and elsewhere single clans have occasionally had two or even more totems. And of course the attendant rituals vary widely both in importance and complexity.

III   Some Illustrative Case Studies

That the *feel* of primitive religion cannot well be caught from the analysis by categories which we have just pursued must be obvious. Hence it is necessary for more complete understanding to project ourselves in imagination into some particular place and situation and gain thereby a sense of primitive beliefs and practices in the milieu that produced them.

We therefore go first to Australia, to see the interplay of religion, magic, and social custom at a nearly Stone Age level, then to India, to look in upon a little-known jungle tribe, and last to Africa, for an excursion into the life and thought of a more advanced group.

1. *The Dieri of Southeast Australia.*[*] Taken as a whole, the Australian aborigines are still at a stage of culture remaining somewhere between Paleolithic and Neolithic. They belong to a very ancient stock therefore. Chocolate brown in color (the white Australians call them "black fellows"), they have broad noses, deep-set eyes, receding foreheads, and thick skull bones, but unlike the now-extinct Tasmanians, whose hair was twisted like the Negro's, their hair is wavy, and the men grow abundant beards. Except in cold weather, when they put on warm kangaroo, wallaby, and opossum skins, they wear only a hip girdle, to which the men attach their weapons. They live in scattered tribes, each occupying a definite territory and speaking a common dialect. Their culture is a food-gathering one, for they are "a people which neither tills nor sows, and which does not breed and pasture animals, but only collects and kills."[E] With them, as was the case with the Tasmanians, the spear is still the most important weapon, but it is provided with a separate hardwood or flaked-stone head, often fitted with barbs, and to hurl it through the air they use a throwing stick. Their knives and axes are of chipped stone. To their credit is the evolution of two kinds of boomerang, one of which is so shaped and twisted that it returns to the sender. Their huts are rude shelters, made of twigs and leaves woven into a half-sphere with a round door at one side. Tribal life, though geographically set apart from that of other settlements, is not completely independent, reciprocity with neighboring tribes being at least as general as hostility, and here totemism plays a powerful role in establishing lines of relatedness crossing and criss-crossing the tribal barriers.

The Dieri were observed by Howitt in the 1860's, when they were still relatively undisturbed in their group beliefs and practices. They inhabited the land to the east and southeast of Lake Eyre in South Australia, a region of minimum rainfall and very high temperatures, with low trees dotting the arid plains. They were divided into two exogamous intermarrying moieties or classes, called *murdus*. The class names were Matteri and Kararu. No Matteri could marry a Matteri, no Kararu a Kararu. The Matteri were subdivided into smaller groups, each having a totem, typical examples of such being the caterpillar, cormorant, emu, eagle hawk, and wild dog. None of these totem groups, of course, could intermarry. The Kararu had as totems such diverse entities as the carpet snake, crow, rat, frog, bat, shrewmouse, red ochre, and rain. Each individual acquired his group-totem from his mother, descent being reckoned through the female line.

Executive power in each division of the tribe resided in the oldest man of the totem group, its *pinnaru* or head. The pinnarus were collectively the headmen of the tribe, and among them one was usually superior to the others. These headmen were of chief importance in the initiation ceremonies to be described later.

From the magico-religious standpoint the outstanding individual in the group was the *kunki* or medicine man. He was credited with the power to communicate directly with supernatural beings called *kutchi*, and with the *Mura-muras*, the highly regarded spirits of the legendary heroes (a superhuman race) believed to have preceded the Australians as their prototypes and to have taught them their rituals. He was thought to have obtained his power from these supernatural beings. By them he interpreted dreams, counteracted evil spells, and drove out evil spirits. It was believed

[*] One of about 500 tribes circa 1800 A.D., many of which have now disappeared. This account of them is taken from scattered references in A. W. Howitt, *The Native Tribes of South-East Australia* (Macmillan, 1904). This and the two trail-breaking books of Spencer and Gillen—*The Native Tribes of Central Australia* (Macmillan, 1899), and *The Northern Tribes of Central Australia* (Macmillan, 1904)—stand at the beginning of modern research into present-day primitive belief and practice. Anthropologists have moved beyond the categories and theories of these books, but the data contained in them is of great value, because it was gathered before many of the tribes were affected by European settlement in Australia. Note: The data presented in this and the following two studies, although not recent, have been chosen as authentically reporting the religious ideas and practices of untouched or "unspoiled" primitives from three crucial areas—Australia, India, and Africa.

he could project in an invisible manner into his victims substances such as quartz crystals or bones. That meant death, of course. He was also thought to have the power of surreptitiously abstracting from individuals the human fat which he used as a powerful magical infusion; such fat-stealing was the *real* cause of the subsequent death of the robbed individuals. A special function of his was to act as a diviner when the relatives of the dead sought the identity of the person or persons who had planned the death. For death was not considered a natural event; it was always due either to magic or to the machinations of the kutchi. As to sickness this side of death, if a kutchi had caused anyone to fall ill, the medicine man could drive it out. But sickness was not always due to a kutchi; it might be the result of a "pointing of the bone." That is, some enemy had secured an accomplice, and they had performed a secret ceremony in which they had made magical use of a human shinbone, pointing it at the person they hoped to sicken and then uttering a magic spell. As soon as a person became ill, therefore, his friends consulted the kunki and others to find out if anyone had "given him the bone." If he died, and suspicion of having "pointed the bone" fell on any person, the latter was summarily dealt with by a *pinya*, or party of revenge,

which went out at the behest of the older men of the tribe (the tribal council) to track him down and kill or severely beat him.

Because of the oft-recurring periods of drought, the medicine man acquired great importance as a rain-maker and weather-changer. The whole tribe united in the ceremony which he and his colleagues conducted. The theory was that the clouds are bodies in which rain is produced by the Mura-muras who live on the elevated plain which is the sky. For the rain-making ceremony members of the tribe dug a hole two feet deep, twelve feet long, and from eight to ten feet wide, over which they erected a long hut of twigs and boughs. The hut was occupied by the old men, and during the ceremony their arms were cut by the principal medicine man with a sharp piece of flint and the blood made to flow on the other men sitting around. Then two medicine men, whose arms had previously been lanced, threw handfuls of down in the air. The blood symbolized rain, the down clouds. The ceremony ended when the men, young and old, butted down the hut with their heads. The piercing of the hut symbolized the piercing of the clouds, and the fall of the hut a downpour of rain. Meanwhile, the rain-making Mura-muras were besought to grant heavy rainfall, in view of the damage

Pointing the bone. An Australian aborigine points a sharpened bone at a victim some distance away while "singing" an imprecation. If the victim learns of the performance, his fright and consternation are such that it is not unusual for him to sicken and die. (Courtesy of Australian News and Information Bureau.)

caused by the drought and the famine-stricken condition of the people. The significance of the following quotation needs no pointing out:

Should no clouds appear as soon as expected, the explanation given is that the Mura-mura is angry with them; and should there be no rain for weeks or months, they suppose that some other tribe has stopped their power.[F1]

Another and even more important ceremony was designed to exert an influence upon a Mura-mura called Minkani, buried deep in a sandhill, and judged by Howitt, from the description, to be one of the fossil animals or reptiles which are found in the deltas of the rivers emptying into Lake Eyre.* Because the motive of the ceremony, a typically totemic ritual, was to increase the food supply of carpet snakes and lizards in the sandhills, the men who took part in it had these reptiles as their totems.

* This is undoubtedly an erroneous inference. It is quite common among Australian aborigines to associate totemic cult-heroes with outcropping rocks which have come to be considered as the latter's remains pushing up from below.

When the actual ceremony takes place, the women are left at the camp, and the men proceed alone to the place where the Mura-mura is to be uncovered. They dig down till damp earth is reached and also what they call the excrement of the Mura-mura. The digging is then very carefully done till, as the Dieri say, the "elbow" of the Mura-mura is uncovered. Then two men stand over him, and the vein of the arm of each being opened, the blood is allowed to fall upon the Mura-mura. The Minkani song is now sung, and the men, in a state of frenzy, strike at each other with weapons, until they reach camp, distant about a mile. The women, who have come out to meet them, rush forward with loud outcries, and hold shields over their husbands to protect them, and stop the fighting. The Tidnamadukas (members of the totem-group of the Tidnama, a small frog) collect the blood dropping from their wounds, and scatter it, mixed with "excrement" from the Minkani's cave, over the sandhills.[F2]

This was expected to make the lizards and carpet snakes more plentiful.

The Dieri had the belief that the sun sets in a hole in the earth and travels underground to the east, where it rises in the morning. They called the Milky Way the river of the sky. The sky was another country, with trees and rivers. There the spirits of the dead and the Mura-muras lived. The dead who went to the

Australian aborigines dancing a corroboree. In dancing a corroboree the Australian natives imitate birds, animals, fish, and men, and also the movements of storms and floods. They accompany their dances with cries and calls, while those standing by engage in ritual chanting. (Courtesy of Australian News and Information Bureau.)

Australian rock shelter painting. These stylized paintings are associated either with a clan hero, the increase of natural species, or favors for the dead. This depends on the rituals performed before them. (Courtesy of the American Museum of Natural History.)

sky-country found it a good place, but they could, and did, roam the earth, visiting people in sleep. If the medicine man considered a dream visit by the spirit of a dead person to be a real vision and not just a fantasy, he directed the one to whom the vision had come to leave food at the grave and to light a fire at it. This was a necessary precaution, for the dead could do harm.

When a Dieri was dying, his relatives separated into two groups. The members of one group, composed of his father, his uncles and their children, and *noas* (could-be wives, according to totem rules), sat down close to him and threw themselves wildly on his body as he expired. Those of the other group, including his mother, mother's sisters, mother's brothers, younger brothers and sisters, and elder sister, remained at a distance, anxious not to look into

his face.* This was for protection, because the deceased might draw them to himself in longing, and they might die. The men of the second group dug the grave. Those of the first group went into mourning by painting themselves with white coloring matter (gyp-

* Relationship terms here are according to classifications differing widely from those used in the West. Since individuals of the same totem-group could not intermarry, the tribal nomenclature was precise enough to determine the social status of each individual, so that it was at once apparent whether he could marry this or that person in his own or another tribe. As a consequence, though a boy might know who his father was, he had no special word *father* for him, for his father and his father's brothers shared the same name—*ngaperi*. His mother and his mother's sisters were alike called *ngandri*. Relationship terms were for a group rather than an individual. One of these group designations was the word used above, *noa*, and it meant member of a group of allowable or could-be husbands or wives, i.e., not of the same *murdu*.

sum); those of the second used red ochre mixed with gypsum. If the deceased was influential, food was placed at the grave for many days, and in winter a fire was lighted for the ghost to warm himself by. Before the corpse was lowered into the grave, it was questioned as to who had caused its death; the corpse replied by falling from the heads of the two men holding it in the direction of the guilty person! Interpreters then tried to determine the identity of the culprit's tribe, and even the name of the culprit himself.

Then the curious regard of the Australian primitives for the magical properties of human fat asserted itself. An old man who stood in the relation of *kami* (maternal grandfather or cousin) to the deceased stepped into the grave and cut off all the fat adhering to the face, thighs, arms, and stomach, and passed it around to be swallowed by relatives. These partook of the fat as follows: the mother ate of her children, and the children of their mother; a man ate of his sister's husband, and of his brother's wife. Mother's brothers, mother's sisters, sister's children, mother's parents, or daughter's children were also eaten of; but the father did not eat of his children, nor the children of their father. The deeper purpose of this modified cannibalism is quite evident—the desire to be at one with and to share the virtue and strength of the deceased.

When the grave was filled in, a large stack of wood was placed over it, the whole group to which the deceased belonged shifted camp, and for fear of offending the dead no one spoke of or referred to him again. Some Dieri groups feared the rising of the dead so much that they tied the toes of the corpse together, bound the thumbs behind its back, swept the ground clean around the grave at dusk, and looked for tracks in the morning. Should tracks appear, the body was reburied elsewhere, on the theory that the first grave was not satisfactory, and the dead person, not lying easy, rose and walked.

The adult males (but not the women and the uninitiated boys) of most tribes in southeastern Australia attributed all their customs and rituals ultimately to a high god or old man of the sky who was eternal and uncreated, having existed from the beginning of all things, and was supreme and without equal, a sort of headman of the sky-country. They believed firmly that he initiated the rites and ceremonies taught them by their ancestors and practiced so faithfully in the old days by the Australian tribes. He was called among the tribes by various secret names, known only to initiated males, such as Nurrundere, Biamban, Bunjil, Munga-ngama, Nurelli, and the like. Often he was referrd to as "Our Father." Some tribesmen felt that he was not much concerned about the doings of men; others, such as the Kurnai, thought he watched over men constantly. Howitt did not find clear evidence of belief in such a primitive high god among the Dieri and their neighbors of the Lake Eyre country, but that may have been because he was not told as much as he thought he was. It begins to appear, when all the evidence is considered, that practically all of the Australian tribes held a belief in some kind of high god, and the Dieri probably did too, but we are without knowledge as to this, and so must let the matter remain undetermined.*

We come finally to the fascinating subject of the initiation ceremonies so distinctive of the aborigines all over the Australian continent. Nowhere else among primitive societies do we see so clearly the force that religious sanctions, as brought to bear by old men, can give to the tribal mores.

Whenever a Dieri boy or girl reached puberty,

---

* Most recent findings of anthropologists have introduced some concepts unknown to Howitt. In particular, one aspect of the evidence is given special prominence—the fact that the Australian cosmogony or account of the beginning of things generally starts with chaos, formlessness, and unconsciousness. Then comes a Dawn Period, known as the Alcheringa or "dream time," when certain Dawn Beings arose (they were uncreated) and, moving like figures in a dream, shaped the earth out of its pre-existent materials into its present structure and established the various species and their habits and customs. The High God was the first of these Dawn Beings, and after giving instructions concerning the customs and rituals of men in after times, he ascended to the sky-country, while other Dawn Beings, perhaps unable or forbidden to follow him, established totemic centers on earth.

initiatory rites were planned in order to complete the transformation or rebirth of the boy into a man and the girl into a woman. The ceremonies for boys were especially thorough and were carried out in different stages over a period of months. All the available tribespeople from miles around gathered for the final ceremonies. It was the principal headman of the tribe who decided when the youths should be initiated. He informed the council of elders who the youths were and when the different ceremonies should take place.

The earliest ceremony had the clear significance that the boys were about to undergo a ritual death in order to rise or be reborn as men. The death symbol was a ceremony by which each boy's two lower middle-front teeth were knocked out by chisel-shaped pieces of wood. The teeth thus dislodged were buried a twelvemonth later eighteen inches underground. At about the same time (as early as in the ninth or tenth year), a ceremony with a similar meaning took place, that of circumcision, at which time each boy's father stooped over him and gave him a new name. Some time later there occurred, suddenly and without warning to the young men, the curious Kulpi rite, or ceremony of subincision, after which, and only then, was the youth considered to be a thorough man.

Meanwhile, there took place the rite called the Wilyaru ceremony, which definitely cut a youth off from childhood and any former dependence on the womenfolk. It is thus described:

A young man without previous warning is led out of the camp by some older men who are of the relation of *Neyi* (approximately cousin in this case) to him, and not of near, but distant relationship. On the following morning the men, old and young, except his father and elder brothers, surround him, and direct him to close his eyes. One of the old men then binds the arm of another old man tightly with string, and with a sharp piece of flint lances the vein about an inch from the elbow, causing a stream of blood to fall over the young man, until he is covered with it, and the old man is becoming exhausted. Another man takes his place, and so on until the young man becomes quite stiff from the quantity of blood adhering to him. The reason given for this practice is that it infuses courage into the young man, and also shows him that the sight of blood is nothing, so that should he re-

ceive a wound in warfare, he may account it a matter of no moment.[F3]

The deeper meaning of the rite is that the spirit and wisdom of the older men was transforming the youth into an adult by making him of one blood with them.

In the next stage of the ceremony the blood-covered youth was gashed with a sharp piece of flint on neck and back, so that when the wounds would heal he would bear raised scars as a sign that he was a Wilyaru. At the completion of the rite he was given a bull-roarer, a paddle-shaped slab of wood fastened to a string made of human hair from ten to twelve feet long. This was his first face-to-face encounter with the actual source of the vibrant roar which had formerly terrified him and the women of the camp when they heard it issuing from the distance of the bush. Even the men, he now learned, considered it to have supernatural effects and to speak with an authoritative voice to all living beings. It was the symbol and the voice of the Mura-muras who had given the tribe its sacred rituals and traditions. Presented now with one which was to be returned to a secret hiding place when not used, he was taught how to whirl it and told never to show it to women or tell them about it.

After this an important psychological experience was required of him: he was sent away alone into the bush, there to be on his own until his wounds were healed and all the blood with which he was covered had been worn off. He was to rehearse in his mind the lessons he had learned.

The young man is never seen by the women, from the time he is made *Wilyaru* till the time when he returns to the camp, after perhaps many months. . . . During the time of his absence his near female relatives become very anxious about him, often asking as to his whereabouts. There is great rejoicing in the camp when the *Wilyaru* finally returns to it, and his mother and sisters make much of him.[F4]

But he was now a man and did not belong to the women any more.

The Dieri and neighboring tribes united in the remaining ceremony, the Mindari, which was a general get-together and dancing of the initiates and the men and women and was often the occasion for the amicable settlement of any disputes since the last Mindari.

Behind all this there was the running oral commentary of the older men, carefully explaining the supernatural origin and meaning of each ceremony, beginning with a retelling of the tribal myths in regard to them. The youths were admonished in their tribal duties and responsibilities. The totemic rules and relationships were defined with exactness. Plainly the laws and customs of the community were sacrosanct and on no consideration to be departed from. The tribal morality thus came to each member of the community with the full weight of religious sanctions behind it. As well rebel against nature as against it!

2. *The Birhors of Chota Nagpur, India.* * This jungle tribe is an interesting one to study, because although its practices remain as primitive as ever, it has allowed its members to entertain ideas taken over from the Hindus around them. The tribe is therefore typical of the changes in culture beginning to overwhelm even the most backward peoples of the world today.

The Birhors are an aboriginal tribe of Dravidian stock who live on a plateau in the jungles of Chota Nagpur in east-central India. The tribe is divided into two groups, Uthlus (wanderers) and Jaghis (settlers). The latter are few in number; they have settled down near the villages of the Hindus and taken up lands for cultivation. The former, with whom we are here chiefly concerned, live in small migratory bands, always on the move through the jungles, except during the rainy season, when they encamp on the sides of hills in leaf-huts in the more inaccessible regions. Sometimes called the "monkey people," because much of their food supply consists of monkey meat, they live in a very squalid condition at a Stone Age level. Their huts, made of leaves and branches pushed together like sheaves of wheat in a field, are placed in

* The details are taken from *The Birhors: A Little-Known Jungle Tribe of Chota Nagpur,* by Rai Bahadur Sarat Roy (Ranchi, India, 1925).

a circle, facing an open space in the center that is swept clean. These primitive wanderers keep no goats, pigs, or cattle themselves, but they have learned, when they need the flesh of these animals for feasts or sacrifices, to overcome their shyness and resort to the jungle edge to barter for them. Otherwise, they live on fowls, rats, and monkeys, and certain leaves and roots of the jungle.

Their social organization presents a twofold grouping, one an organization for purposes of food-quest, another for purposes of regulating marriage and kinship. By the first grouping the tribe is broken up into bands (or *tandas*) of four to ten families each, led by a headman who is both chief and priest. By the second grouping the tribe is organized into exogamous clans, with some animal, plant, fruit, flower, or other object as the totem.

The principal occupation of the Birhor man is hunting. Because he uses no bows and arrows, a great part of his time and that of his group is consumed in making rope from chop fibers and then weaving nets to snare game. The characteristic mode of food-quest —snaring monkeys—is typical of primitive procedures elsewhere, and is described as follows:

On the morning of the appointed day, the *Naya* [the headman] goes to a neighboring stream or spring, and there bathes, fills a jug with water, and brings it home. Then after changing his loincloth, the *Naya*, in company with one or two elders of the *tanda*, proceeds with a handful of rice and the jug of water to the *Jayar* (sacred grove). The *Diguar* [also called *Kotwar*, a man appointed to make all the necessary arrangements for the hunt] has carried to the *Jayar* and placed in a heap all the nets of the intending hunters of the *tanda*. Before this heap of nets the *Naya* stands on his left leg with his right heel resting on his left knee, and with his face to the east, and, with arms extended forward, pours a little water three times on the ground and invokes all the spirits by name for success in hunting, as follows: "Here I am making a libation in your names. May blood of game flow like this." The *Naya* then sits down before the nets and puts three vermilion marks on the ground before them, and on these vermilion marks sprinkles a little rice, and addresses the spirits as follows: "Today I am offering this rice to you all. May we have speedy success. May game be caught in our nets as soon as we enter the jungle."

Then they return home, leaving the nets at the *Jayar*. After breakfast each intending hunter takes up from the *Jayar* his own net and clubs and bamboo poles for fixing the nets and proceeds to the selected jungle. . . . Arrived there, all sit down together on the ground for a short while in what is called an *awas* or rendezvous.

The *Kotwar* now touches each net with a *tiril* or ebony twig and hands it over to the *Naya*. With this twig, the *Naya* performs what is known as "*bana sana*" in order to neutralize the harmful effects of the evil eye of any of their own women in the *tanda* which may have been directed, even though involuntarily, against the party. With low murmuring voice he says: "Today, I am making *bana sana* in the names of those women who cast their eyes at us while sending us away. May we have success in the hunt as soon as we enter the jungle. May oil of the marking-nut drop in the eyes of those who cast evil eyes on us."

Now some of the party are told off and go in twos in different directions to look for monkeys. . . . When these men return with the desired information, the most suitable position in the jungle is selected where the hunters set up their nets in a line from tree to tree. Two or three men remain squatting in concealment with sticks or clubs in their hands at a distance of about twenty yards straight in front of the line of nets. These men are known as *atawahas*. Two other men are selected as *atomdas* and are stationed further off, one about twenty yards to the right and another about the same distance to the left of the *atawahas*. At about the same distance further off in front of each *atomda* stands a *bajhur*, and still further ahead of them at some distance stands a *babsor*.

Two other men styled *beberas*, one from each side, drive the monkeys toward the *atomdas*. The *atawahas* also come up, and all together drive the monkeys towards the nets and strike them dead with their clubs and sticks. The game bagged, the nets are taken down and the party leave the forest.

When they arrive at a suitable spot near some stream or other water, they light a fire, generally by friction, and scorch the monkeys in it, wash them clean, and cut them up, and taking out the brains, heart, lungs, liver, entrails, and flesh of the fore-leg joint, place them in a bag improvised with *gungu* leaves sewn up with reed-needles. These are roasted by placing burning logs of wood above and below. When roasted, the meat is taken out and distributed among the members of the party. But they must not help themselves to it until the *Naya*, who was given a bit of the *ihim* (liver), has by himself roasted it by the same method and standing a little apart from the rest and with his roasted meat in hand, and his back towards them, has offered a little to all the spirits jointly, and promised them similar offerings in future if they always brought them such game.[G1]

Among both groups of Birhors it is apparent that the begetting of future hunters (and gardeners) has increased the importance of marriage and child-bearing. Marriage and birth are consequently the occasions of prolonged ceremony, permeated throughout with magic, taboo, and worship of the spirits. The children are very well cared for. Yet, while being carried about on the mother's hip or back, they cannot fail to catch from her the impression that life is difficult and that hostile spirits are everywhere.

So long as a baby is carried in the mother's arms or slung on her back, its mother, while going to some other *tanda* or to some village or marketplace, either puts a mark of soot between its eyebrows to protect it from the evil eye or evil spirits, or, while crossing a stream, . . . takes up a little sand, and ties it up at one end of her cloth. On her return journey, when her house is in sight, she takes the sand between the tips of her two fingers and throws it behind her back.[G2]

No child can escape the knowledge that evil is ever imminent.

All the ills of life—and life is brimful of ills—are believed to be caused by supernatural agencies—either by spirits hovering about in earth, air, and water, hill and forest, river and spring, or by lesser powers and energies immanent in various animate beings as well as in certain inanimate objects and even in such immaterial things as a spoken word, an expressed wish, a passing thought or emotion, a passing glance, a magic formula or diagram, and certain names and numbers. And the problem of life which has ever presented itself to the tribal mind is how to protect the community and its members and their scanty earthly possessions from the evil attentions of spirits and the harmful influences of other mysterious powers and energies so as to make life worth living.[G3]

To the Birhor "everything above, below, and around him is animated either by a spirit or by a spiritual energy or power."[G4] The most important spirits are those of the native hills of each Birhor clan, called Buru-Bongas or Ora-Bongas. With these are associated the daily-worshiped ancestral spirits (the Haprom) and the other deities and spirits recognized by the Birhors. Among the latter are the supreme god Singabonga, the creator, symbolized by the sun, who ordinarily takes no active part or even interest in human affairs but must be periodically sacrificed to, and the mother goddesses Devi Mai and Bushi Mai, intensely interested in man and, if properly served, bringing him health, progeny, and food.

Many spirits do not ordinarily require regular sacrifices from individuals or families, but at any moment they may begin to do so, very insistently, their way of making their wants known being repeated misfortune visited on some family until they call in a *mati* or ghost-doctor (of whom there are one or two in every *tanda*) and have him divine the spirit's name and wishes. For instance:

A Birhor woman picked up from the road a brass bell which had dropped down unnoticed from the neck of a bullock employed in dragging a country cart, and soon afterwards her daughter fell ill, and a *mati* or spirit-doctor was called in to find out the cause of the illness. The mati discovered by divination that the mother of the girl had picked up something made of metal which carried a spirit called *Banjari-bhut,* and that the child could be cured only if she made a *manita* of that spirit and periodically sacrificed a goat. She did so, and the child was cured. And to this day she along with her husband periodically offers sacrifices to the Banjari-bhut with a brass bell placed before them as the emblem of the spirit. . . . When the mother dies, the spirit, thus acquired by "accident," will pass to one or more of her daughters "by inheritance," so to say.[65]

The Birhors are little given to black magic or any form of witchcraft, but they have developed to some degree the aversive phases of magic. They have procedures for stopping rain, lightning, high winds, and hail storms, driving away bugs, mosquitoes, and snakes, preventing pumpkins from rotting, and so on. The following is an example of the rain-making magic of the Jaghis, the Birhors who are settlers:

Early in the morning they go up the nearest hill and roll down stones of all sizes which produce a rumbling noise in falling to the ground; and this noise is at the same time intensified by beating a drum so as to produce a low, heavy, continued sound in imitation of the pattering rain on the roof of their huts.[66]

The taboos of the Birhors, a few of which are subjoined, afford an especially clear insight into certain of the mental processes of primitive peoples:

A woman must not step over a hunting net or hunting club. Should she do so, there will be no luck in the chase. The club in such case is thrown away.

A Birhor youth must not eat an egg which emits a sound when shaken; should he do so he will get pus in his ears.

A Birhor must not point with the finger at the rainbow; should he do so, the offending finger will get maimed or curved.

If anyone looks at a Birhor with one eye in the morning, the latter will get no game or *chop* that day. To prevent this, the former is made to look at him again with both eyes open.

A Birhor must not look back when leaving home to join a hunting expedition, as that will bring him ill luck in the chase.

A Birhor family must not leave any metal utensils outside their hut. Should they do so, a thunderbolt will strike the hut.[67]

At the beginning of this sketch it was suggested that the Birhors now exemplify the changes in culture beginning to take place in even the most backward tribes of the world. This has not been very apparent in the facts so far cited. However, the interesting thing about the Birhors is the clear distinction still evident between their primitive and largely unchanged procedures and the Hindu ideas entering their lives at one particular point—through their folktales and mythology. The imaginative life of the Birhors has been immensely stimulated by Hindu legend and story. Sita, Rama, Lakshman, Ravana, and Hanuman (the monkey god) all figure in the Birhor version of the great Hindu epic, the *Ramayana.* Brahmins, kings, queens, princesses, warriors, cities, merchants, elephants, palanquins, and palaces form elements in some of their favorite fireside tales.

Meanwhile, in their daily life, the greater proportion of the Birhors stay shyly as far away as possible from the world into which they allow their imagination thus occasionally to take them.

3. *The BaVenda of South Africa.** The BaVenda are a group of tribes belonging to the Bantu peoples of South Africa. They live in northern Transvaal, just south of the Limpopo River, in a mountainous district, and number about 150,000 souls. Still showing pastoral skills, they afford an illuminating study of religion at the beginning of the agricultural stage. Physically, the BaVenda show evidences of being a composite people, with a strong Hamitic strain. Socially, they are polite and hospitable, but secretive about personal life and ancestral customs, probably because of memories of exploitation by European settlers. They are not inclined to be warlike, as are the other Bantu peoples. They live in cylindrical huts, with conical grass-thatched roofs, the main structural elements being strong stakes bound together with withes. They keep large herds of cattle, by which they reckon their wealth, but depend for actual livelihood upon agriculture. Their crops include maize, Kaffir corn, millet, beans, pumpkins, watermelons, vegetable marrow, and sweet potatoes, the ground being worked with a hoe, mainly by women. Until the introduction of manufactured products from Europe, the native industries included such arts as weaving, skin-dressing, iron-smelting, hoe-making, and copper-refining.

The social organization shows variety. Each individual is a member of a number of independent groupings. The four mentioned below are the most important. He belongs to his own small family circle. He is a member of a larger group, his patrilineal lineage, through which his descent, succession, and inheritance are reckoned. In addition to this, he has close emotional ties with his whole matrilineal lineage. Lastly, he belongs to a *sib* of totemic character

* This account, which attempts only to present the religious conceptions and practices of the BaVenda, is drawn from the very inclusive book *The BaVenda*, by Hugh A. Stayt (Oxford University Press, 1931). Quotations are by permission of the publishers.

and is called by the name of some animal, plant, or inanimate object (lion, dove, pig, elephant, goat, water buffalo, crocodile, etc.) to which he pays special regard as his totem.

The attitude of the BaVenda toward the supernatural is displayed in beliefs and practices that run the whole gamut of religious ideas, from belief in something like mana, through animism and ancestor-worship, to belief in a supreme god, mysteriously presiding over his creation.

A fundamental concept is the belief that every object, animate or inanimate, possesses a kinetic power for good or evil. For example, when Stayt inquired about a small piece of wood worn as a charm around the neck of one of the BaVenda for protection when traveling, he discovered:

It was taken from a bough of a tree overhanging a difficult climb on a well-frequented path. This bough was grasped by every passer-by in order to assist him over the difficult place. In this way the power of that particular bough was inordinately increased . . . , and it became the obvious source from which effective charms for the timid traveller could be obtained. Conversely, the history of some powdered wood, possessing a great deal of power to do evil to the traveller, disclosed the fact that in a well-trodden path a small root caused annoyance to every passer-by, being in a spot where it almost inevitably knocked his toe. This root, unlike the friendly bough, became a source of evil power, and its wood was used for charms to bring harm to the traveller.[11]

From this sort of belief have sprung the magico-religious practices of the BaVenda. The medicine man (*nganga*) and the diviner (*mungoma*) are the most important persons in the BaVenda community.

The nganga has power to cure disease. His rigorous training in his craft has qualified him to be either a specialist in one family of diseases or a general practitioner treating all diseases. By the use of such drugs, emetics, and poisons as are found in plants, he treats a great variety of ailments, such as malaria, rheumatism, pneumonia, insanity, and toothache, often with success. The healing agents are supposed to contain different types of power, and by mixing them in certain ways the nganga directs their energy into the

31

desired channels. It is an important belief, however, that the disease itself is rarely thought to be due to natural causes. It is nearly always attributed to spiritual agencies, either to the adverse influence of offended ancestral spirits or to the much more malevolent operations of the chief obsession of the BaVenda —wizards and witches.

Wizards and witches (sing. *muloi*, pl. *vhaloi*) are universally feared. Vhaloi may be of either sex, but are usually thought to be women. They are of two kinds. Those who consciously and deliberately practice the black art, by themselves or with the aid of a conscienceless nganga won over by a large fee, compose the first group. The motive that oftenest moves them is hatred, an intense desire to destroy the person or persons disliked.

A very simple way of killing an enemy is for a muloi to obtain from the nganga a death-dealing powder. Looking in the direction of the enemy he blows the powder towards him, saying at the same time, "You must die!" The closer the powder can be brought to the victim the more rapid will be his death.[H2]

The other kind of muloi is such unwittingly! The circumstances surrounding cases like this are often tragic. The sense of conscious innocence is no protection from suspicion. It is believed that anyone, at any moment, may become, subconsciously or during sleep, a person possessed by some hideous spirit that has entered him, perhaps from a hyena, crocodile, owl, or snake. During the day such a muloi, not suspecting his tragic plight, will be an innocuous member of the village community, but during the night a destroyer of health, of property, and of life! It then becomes an urgent matter to ferret out the evil one and exact the extreme penalty. A diviner or a nganga can detect a culprit by occult means, but mere appearances may be enough to fix suspicion, as the following passage proves.

A farmer at Lwamondo shot a crocodile, and to his extreme concern the bullet ricochetted from its hide and severely wounded a boy some distance away; this boy, when he returned to his village, after recovering from the wound, was straightway dubbed a muloi, and he and all his relatives were obliged to leave that part of the country. The people had absolutely no doubt that he was a crocodile, disguised in human form, otherwise the bullet that hit the crocodile could never have hit him as well.[H3]

The pathetic fact is that the supposed muloi is usually convinced, to his or her own great horror, that he is guilty as charged.

Suspected persons are haled before the diviner or *mungoma*, whose special function it is, in distinction from the nganga, to determine the identity of evildoers. Because all deaths, save those of very old people, are due to witchcraft, he specializes in detecting those who have caused death. He ostensibly does all his divining by throwing a set of dice, which are read after they come to rest, or by floating seeds in a divining bowl. Woe to the person designated by him as guilty!

The cult of the dead plays a primary role in the religious life of the BaVenda. To them human souls are a combination of breath and shadow, two elements which depart from every living creature at death. The soul after leaving the body at death must find a new place in which to rest. It usually lingers for a while at the grave, but not for long. Soon it will search around for a better abiding place. It may reveal itself to its descendants in dreams and thus make its needs known. Or it may find another body. There are isolated instances of belief among the BaVenda in reincarnation, especially of ancient chiefs, in lions, leopards, and snakes. But the most desirable state to which the souls of the dead can attain is to be held in the memory of living descendants and to be cherished and cared for by them.

When anyone dies, every relative tries to be present at the deathbed; otherwise suspicion of complicity in the death may fall upon him. The first action after death is to cut off a portion of the garment of the deceased and preserve it for the diviner against the time when the cause of death is to be determined. The relatives keep the place of burial a secret, lest an enemy dig up the remains and practice witchcraft with them. A characteristic bit of ritual is for the eldest son to murmur over the grave of his mother, as he tosses in the first clod of earth, "You can rest in peace, my mother. So do not trouble us; I will give you all that you require."[H4] The period of mourning, marked by shaving of the heads of all the relatives, continues until the cause of death has been discovered by the diviner and the death avenged. It is highly important thereafter to keep the ancestral spirit satisfied, for all trouble to the living is caused either by witchcraft or the dissatisfaction of the dead. In order that the ancestral spirits may be focused or symbolized in something tangible, the ancestors of the father's lineage are collectively represented either by a cow and a sacred black bull, regarded as the embodiments of the patrilineal spirits, or by two large, cylindrical, highly polished stones, embedded near the hut of the headman of the lineage. The spirits of the mothers are represented by a black female goat. In addition to this, the male members of the lineage are individually represented by a spear, laid up in the hut of the head of the lineage with those earlier placed there, and the female members by an iron or copper ring, or by a miniature hoe fastened to a stick and carried by a female descendant.

In addition to the ancestral spirits there exists a host of other powers, less defined in form and character. Some are mountain-spirits, the sight of whom brings death to the traveler, and spirits in streams and pools, armed with death-dealing bows and arrows. A great many spirits live in rivers and lakes, some, or perhaps most, of whom are ancestral. But the greatest and most shadowy of all spirits is the mysterious Supreme Being, Raluvhimba. This elusive, monotheistic deity is associated with the creation of the world and is thought to live somewhere in the heavens. "The word *luvhimba*," says Stayt, "means eagle, the bird that soars aloft; the BaVenda have a very real idea of this great power travelling through the sky, using the stars and wind and rain as his instruments."[H5] Raluvhimba is remote and inscrutable, as are the similar deities of the other Bantu peoples, but the BaVenda are exceptional in the amount of respect which they pay to him, usually through their chiefs. They associate him with the rain-maker, Mwari, of the Bantus of Matebeleland, and seek his favors therefore especially in time of drought, the bringing on of which is credited to him. Any thunderous noise is his voice. In 1917 a meteor burst in the middle of the day at Khalavha, with a loud humming sound and a crash like thunder. The BaVenda rushed into the open in all their villages, with cries meant to express joy, clapping their hands and blowing horns, in order to give a warm welcome to the tremendous god. The same sort of demonstration follows an earthquake, the people shouting, "Give us rain! Give us health!" But Raluvhimba is not approached by individuals nor by families in private devotion; he is worshiped either by the whole people at once or by a representative of the whole people speaking in their names. Here is an unusually clear instance of a transitional practice by which an originally aloof high god may become in the higher religions the one true God to whom, not only the group, but also individuals, may pray.

Suggestions for Further Reading

ALIMEN, H. *The Prehistory of Africa*. Tr. by A. H. Broadrick. Hutchinson & Co., London, 1957

BENEDICT, RUTH. *Patterns of Culture*. Mentor Books, 1952

BRAIDWOOD, ROBERT. *Prehistoric Men*. Chicago Natural History Museum, 1948

BREUIL, H. *Four Hundred Centuries of Cave Art*. Montignac, 1952

CHILDE, V. G. *Social Evolution*. C. A. Watts & Co., Ltd., London, 1951

CODRINGTON, R. H. *The Melanesians*. Clarendon Press, Oxford, 1891

COON, CARLETON. *The Story of Man.* Alfred A. Knopf, Inc., 1950

DURKHEIM, ÉMILE. *The Elementary Forms of the Religious Life.* Allen & Unwin, 1915

ELIADE, MIRCEA. *Shamanism: Archaic Techniques of Ecstasy.* Tr. by Willard R. Trask. Bollingen Foundation, New York, 1964

———. *Birth and Rebirth.* Harper & Brothers, 1958. A study of primitive initiation rites

ELKIN, A. P. *The Australian Aborigines: How To Understand Them.* 3rd ed., Angus and Robertson (Sydney), 1954

EVANS-PRITCHARD, E. E. *Nuer Religion.* Clarendon Press, Oxford, 1956

FRAZER, JAMES G. *The Golden Bough.* One-vol. abridgment, Macmillan, 1923

———. *The Fear of the Dead in Primitive Religion.* Macmillan, 1933–36

GENNEP, G. VAN. *The Rites of Passage.* Tr. by Vizedom and Caffee. University of Chicago Press, 1960

GOODE, WILLIAM J. *Religion Among the Primitives.* Free Press, Glencoe, Ill., 1951

JAMES, E. O. *The Beginnings of Religion.* Hutchinson's Library, 1949

———. *Prehistoric Religion.* Harper, 1957

KOPPER, W. *Primitive Man and His World Picture.* Sheed & Ward, New York, 1952

LESSA, W. A. AND VOGT, E. Z., EDS. *Reader in Comparative Religion: An Anthropological Approach.* Row, Peterson and Co., Evanston, Ill., 1958

LOWIE, ROBERT H. *Primitive Religion.* Enl. ed., Liveright, 1948. Available as Universal Library pb

LUQUET, G. H. *The Art and Religion of Fossil Man.* Yale, 1930

MALINOWSKI, BRONISLAW. *Myth in Primitive Society.* Norton, 1926

———. *Magic, Science, and Religion.* Beacon Press, 1948. Anchor pb, 1954

MARETT, R. R. *The Threshold of Religion.* Macmillan, 1914

MARINGER, J. *The Gods of Prehistoric Man.* Knopf, 1960

MEADE, MARGARET AND CALAS, NICHOLAS, EDS. *Primitive Heritage.* Random House, 1953

MURRAY, HENRY, ED. *Myth and Mythmaking.* George Braziller, New York, 1960

NORBECK, EDWARD. *Religion in Primitive Society.* Harper & Brothers, 1961

OTTO, RUDOLF. *The Idea of the Holy.* Oxford, 1924

PETTAZONI, RAFFAELE. "The Formation of Monotheism," in *Essays on the History of Religions.* E. J. Brill, 1954

RADCLIFFE-BROWN, A. R. *The Andaman Islanders.* Cambridge, 1922

———. *Taboo.* Cambridge, 1939

RADIN, PAUL. *Primitive Religion: Its Nature and Origin.* Viking, 1937. Available as Dover pb

———. *The World of Primitive Man.* Schuman, 1953

SCHMIDT, WILHELM. *The Origin and Growth of Religion.* Dial, 1931

SEBEOK, T. A., ED. *Myth: A Symposium.* American Folklore Society, Philadelphia, 1955

SPENCER AND GILLEN. *The Arunta.* Macmillan, 1928

STEINER, FRANZ. *Taboo.* Philosophical Library, New York, 1956

THE CONCLUDING PARAGRAPH of the last chapter dealt with an important transition in thought and devotion. It provided us with an instance of the emergence of nationwide religious practices transcending tribal faith. The national religions * which appeared with the rise of states and kingdoms were full of figures like Raluvhimba.

For it is no great step to go from the religion of the BaVenda, with its mysterious, eagle-swift rain-maker and thunderer, its mountain- and river-spirits and ancestor-worship, to the more highly articulated national religions which came into being when—as happened in Egypt, Mesopotamia, Greece, and Italy—scores of tribes coalesced into nations, and a king, a city, or a confederacy bound many tribes and towns together into one. Marduk, Amon, Zeus, and Jupiter were but Raluvhimba and his associates decked out with the diverse attributes and histories which a more highly developed language, culture, and historical tradition bestowed upon them.

And the later, greater religions never wholly outgrew their origins. They never withdrew their roots from the primitive soil that had first nourished them. Although men regarded the spreading branches under which they took refuge with faces upturned in wonder, they knew, without needing to recognize the fact, that they stood on ancient, hidden roots.

Little wonder that so many treatises, monographs, and books, weighty with fact and speculation, have been written on the religions which have perished among the nations but were the vital agents of transition from primitive animism and polytheism to the higher religions carrying a world message and ministering to the spiritual needs of Everyman. There is profit therefore in doing these two things: (1) studying the original context from which the primitive elements yet retained in the high religions have been drawn, and (2) seeing at what point, and with what

* The word *national* in this phrase is not satisfactory, and is used for lack of any other suitable term. It is not meant to suggest more than "widespread within the boundaries of states or kingdoms composed of ethnically or culturally similar peoples."

2 Representative National Religions of the Past

results, the upsurge to higher levels and a world faith and message began.

This chapter is devoted to the first of these objectives; the rest of the book is chiefly concerned with the second. There is much to consider. The details, encyclopedic in scope and fullness, intrigue one's curiosity and beckon eagerly for notice, but though we shall find them crowding around our path, and must indeed look closely at many of them, we hope not to be deflected from pursuing our double aim.*

I   Egypt

Perhaps Egypt gives us the simplest case of the development from early animism and fetishism to a more or less systematized polytheism and an emerging national ethic. Upper Egypt was comparatively self-contained. It experienced very much less outside interference than Mesopotamia, and there were long periods of time when there was absolutely no interference at all. But in the Delta (lower Egypt) contacts with the outside world were constant. Not only did travelers and traders, initially from Mesopotamia, come in great numbers, bringing with them new ideas and customs from abroad (many of which the Egyptians adopted along the whole Nile), but there were also invasions that wrought forced changes. Nevertheless, taking Egypt as a whole, the internal cultural and religious changes went on in a kind of simpleness

---

* Because of this book's over-all plan, the present chapter is of necessity brief. It may therefore seem to the advanced student oversimplified. Its aim, however, is to sketch in broad lines for the less informed reader the various milieus in which Judaism, Christianity, and Islam rose and spread. The college teacher who might wish to spend more time in this area could ask the students to read one or more of such works (all obtainable in paperback) as H. Frankfort, *Ancient Egyptian Religion* (Torch) and *Birth of Civilization in the Near East* (Anchor); Gilbert Murray, *The Five Stages of Greek Religion* (Anchor); M. P. Nilsson, *Greek Folk Religion* (Torch); H. J. Rose, *Religion in Greece and Rome* (Torch); T. R. Glover, *Conflict of Religions in the Early Roman Empire* (Beacon), and others.

and singleness of logical development for longer periods than elsewhere near the Mediterranean.

The Physical and Social Background of Egyptian Religion

The physical reasons for this comparative self-sufficiency are almost too well known to rehearse. Cut off from the world by the Mediterranean on the north, and by vast expanses of barren desert rising in the east slowly toward rugged Abyssinia and stretching to the west in "lone and level sands" over more than a thousand miles of Sahara wasteland, fenced off on the south by wild equatorial mountains and the six cataracts falling northward through their gorges, Egypt lay for centuries quiet under the sun, her material needs assured by the annual overflow of the great stream that was veritably her river of life in that rainless land, and the thoughts of her people, perhaps from sheer need of something to do, devoted to their cult of the dead, with its hope of endless life.

The history of Egypt is one of the longest known to us. In the Old Stone Age scattered groups of hunters crept along the mud-strips of the Nile (narrower and thinner even than now), leaving behind them their stone implements, flimsy huts, and buried dead. These wanderers gave way some time during the Neolithic period to the first permanent residents of the Nile valley, a dark-skinned pastoral folk, who, as the centuries advanced, housed themselves in wood, brick, and then stone, organized themselves into communities, and latterly began to employ a distinctive picture-writing (the first Egyptian hieroglyphics) to keep their records and send their messages. Though the wandering tribes of the Stone Age had now vanished, and rural clusters of villages had appeared, there was no nation of Egyptians as yet. Each community lived out its independent existence as a *nome*, that is, as a group of villages spread across a fertile tract of Nile mud around a larger town that was, in effect, their county seat. The people of one nome might look across the river at those of another, learn from their neighbors how to regulate and control the overflow of the Nile, but yet have separate customs and gods and be on terms of relative hostility. Then, as cultures grew more attractive, and intercommunication increased, there came amalgamation, usually by way of conquest of one nome by another. For centuries this process went on, until there were but two kingdoms, the upper kingdom of inner Egypt and the lower kingdom of the Delta, where Mesopotamian influences were felt. These two kingdoms were finally united into one by Menes (?), the founder of the first dynasty, about 3100 B.C.* Thereafter the pharaohs established themselves as divine priest-kings along the entire Nile, and the royal household became the focal point of a far-ranging political unification that embraced all the local temples and their priests, as well as the people of the land.

The Divine Kingship

From about 3100–2600 B.C.—a period of five hundred years—the official religion of the first two dynasties stressed in its rituals, for any occasion, that the pharaoh was a god, specifically, the incarnation of

* The first and second dynasties (3100–2600 B.C.), which not only united Egypt but established an ascendancy over Palestine and the coast of Syria, were succeeded by the Old Kingdom (ca. 2600–2200 B.C.), so famous for its pyramid builders (often called the Pyramid Age). After an intermediate period of breakdown of central authority (ca. 2200–2000 B.C.), the Middle Kingdom was established (ca. 1989). The Middle Kingdom in turn gave way to the New Empire when the northern conquerors, the Hyksos, who in their formidable chariots had overrun Egypt (ca. 1800), were heroically expelled (ca. 1560), and Egypt surged on to the reconquest of Palestine and Syria—a bold assertion of an imperialism that only after long centuries and many reverses was to be abandoned, because Egypt herself was to suffer total conquest at the hands successively of Persians, Greeks, and Romans. For dates see W. F. Albright, *From the Stone Age to Christianity* (Doubleday Anchor pb, 2nd ed., 1957), pp. 156–162, 178–189. See also Steindorf and Seele, *When Egypt Ruled the East* (University of Chicago Press, 1942), pp. 274 f. Slightly variant dates are proposed by other authorities. Cf. J. A. Wilson, *The Burden of Egypt* (University of Chicago Press, 1951).

Horus, the sun, without whom there would be no light nor life. As a god among the people he could mediate between them and the gods. After 2600 B.C. (in the Old Kingdom) the name of the pharaoh received an additional title; he became "the son of Re," the latter having become the chief sun-god. Gradually thereafter the pharaohs, although retaining their godlike status, became human beings within whom dwelt the sun-god and who manifested in their persons the divine will. Although the pharaoh was now more human, the situation had not greatly changed, for whatever the degree of his humanity when he played a symbolic role in religious ritual, the ordinary Egyptian who was his witness "did not distinguish between symbolism and participation; if he said that the king was Horus, he did not mean that the king was playing the part of Horus; he meant that the king *was* Horus, that the god was effectively present in the king's body."[A]

It was by means of this doctrine of the divinity of the pharaohs that a central government was consolidated and Egypt unified.

Polytheism, Faith, and Symbolism

The pharaoh was not the sole divine being. The ancient Egyptian, when he faced the world around him, found his faith—his reverence and hopefulness—focused upon divine powers of many kinds. Living as he did on a fertile strip of soil near the Nile, he found himself in close relations not only with his fellow Egyptians, male and female, but with many birds, beasts and reptiles—frogs, for instance, and herons, gazelles, mice, hares, falcons, crocodiles, geese, lions, and other fellow creatures of many kinds. With all these he had a sense of community that tended to blur unlikenesses and incompatibilities. God, man, and beast dwelt together in a relatively confined space and shared a common lot. If the pharaoh was a god in human guise, there were many other divine powers appearing in other guises. We shall soon see that the ancient Egyptian was led to think of deities as being partly animal (theriomorphic), partly human (anthropomorphic), and partly heavenly (in some cases having the qualities of birds), and they were these all at once. Whatever the analogies and metaphors he adopted in order to picture the gods, the Egyptian was a polytheist and was surrounded by gods.

Furthermore, although his prayers and those of his priests were addressed to long-established gods that were complex in function and therefore in appearance, he and his priests were quite ready at any time to alter an image of deity when needful. There was a conscious (or better, a subconscious) recognition of the descriptive relevance of altering metaphors and symbols as a means of better understanding divine powers that could not be narrowly conceived because they had more than human or animal capabilities.*

Prehistoric Mythological Concepts

The ancient Egyptians also inherited from before the time of the first dynasty a set of prehistoric ideas

___

* It would be wise here to recognize the truth in Edward Conze's observation about polytheism in another religion (Buddhism), for the same observation can be made in this connection about the tendency toward polytheism in Egypt, even in the modern period. He says in *Buddhism, Its Essence and Development* (Bruno Cassirer, Oxford, 1951, p. 41): "The Christian teaching which has to some extent pervaded our education, has made us believe that Polytheism belongs to a past period of the human race. . . . We must first of all understand that polytheism is very much alive even among us. But where formerly Athene, Baal, Astarte, Isis, Sarasvati, Kwan Yin, etc., excited the popular imagination, it is nowadays inflamed by such words as *Democracy, Progress, Civilisation, Equality, Liberty, Reason, Science*, etc. A multitude of personal beings has given way to a multitude of abstract nouns. . . . The reason for this is not far to seek. Personal deities grow on the soil of a rural culture in which the majority of the population are illiterate, while abstract nouns find favor with the literate populations of modern towns. . . . Another factor is our separation from Nature. Every tree, every well, lake or river, almost every type of animal, could once bring forth a deity. We are now too remote from Nature to think that."

that were never abandoned down through the centuries: (1) that there was a primeval sea from which earth emerged as a projecting hill on which the first living being appeared, a being conceived, in one story or another, as a serpent, a frog, a beetle, an egg, or a lotus flower; (2) that the sky could be conveniently regarded as Hathor, a heavenly cow held up from below by Shu, the air-god, while she, touching earth with her four legs, gave birth each day to the sun, her calf, and was at the same time both a celestial stream of water (the waters above the earth) and the space-body in which the stars were lodged; (3) that, alternatively, the sky was the goddess Nut, the daughter of Shu, whom he lifted up from her husband (and brother) Geb, the earth below, so that she touched down only with her toes and fingertips, and in this position did all the things that Hathor did; and (4) that the sky might also be a vulture (later on a falcon) whose wings formed the roof of the world. Of all these apparently contradictory descriptions and metaphors it has been very sensibly said: "As no symbol can encompass the whole essence of what it stands for, an increase in the number of symbols might well have appeared enlightening rather than confusing," because "a multitude of mythological concepts may exist for any single entity."B

The same observation can be made of the prehistoric local gods, with their complex features, next to be considered.

The Animal-Headed Gods

The first local Egyptian "gods" were, or at least manifested themselves as, animals. Each community had its animal guardian—a sort of urban animal-cult. Thinis and Abydos, for example, worshiped the jackal, Fayum the crocodile. Thebes had its Amon, a ram, Memphis two guardians, Sekhmet a lioness, and Apis (or Hapi) a bull. At Dendera they paid reverence to Hathor, a cow, at Edfu to the hawk Behudet (later called Horus), and Hierakonpolis honored the vulture Nekhebt. At other places like honors were bestowed on the baboon, hippopotamus, shrew-mouse, ibis, cobra, cat, frog, eel, and other creatures.

But undoubtedly these beasts and birds were not worshiped for their animal qualities alone but also for the human (or superhuman) powers and characteristics they possessed, or represented. For, in evident recognition of the belief that divine quality as such could manifest itself in either man or beast and so showed itself in both, they acquired human bodies under their animal heads, and vice versa. For the gods, as we have anticipated, seemed pictured best as composite beings. Thus Knummu had a man's body with a ram's head, and was in human fashion skillful in shaping men and beasts on the potter's wheel. Anubis, the guardian of the cemetery and guide of the dead, possessed a jackal's head. Thoth, the god of learning, bore the head of the ibis. The lioness head of Sekhmet and the cat head of Bast surmounted lithe feminine bodies. Most curious was the greyhound form of Seth, with an upright tail suggestive of the wart hog, though his legs were human. His great adversary Horus had a hawk's head, to signify he was the sun.

Divine Amalgamations

All these were early developments and reflect political as well as religious change. As we have seen, the original nomes of Egypt—some forty-two in number—were gradually fused by conquest; but each was so closely identified with the animal-like god who was its guardian that when one nome conquered another and an over-all guardian deity was sought,

Lion-headed goddess. The goddess Sekhmet, carved in diorite, sits on a throne gazing with inscrutable eyes at her worshipers. In her left hand she holds the Egyptian symbol for life triumphing over death, the ankh, which is also emblematic of generation, the union of male and female elements in nature. (The Metropolitan Museum of Art. Gift of Henry Walters, 1915.)

39

the two gods were fused along with their territories, and often bore thereafter a hyphenated name made from their two names. At times a local deity would be identified with one of the great gods in order to elevate him to a greater and more important role. It was thus that Amon-Re and Ptah-Sokar-Osiris came into being, their separate natures blended so far as possible into one, and their secondary characteristics, if resistant to such a process, separately embodied in accessory figures or symbols. Thus, on entering the Delta and merging with Ptah and Sokar at Memphis, where Apis the bull gave the shape of the godhead, Osiris retained his human form but adopted the bull as his associate. Thereafter he was sometimes called Osiris-Apis (whence the Romans may have obtained the name Serapis, their term for the immortal bull-spirit). And when Isis was identified in the Delta with the cow-goddess Hathor, she sprouted two huge horns curving high above her head.

But in some cases blending was not feasible. In this event two incompatible deities would be set against each other in the dualism of eternal enmity, or else a triad (or even a larger group) of associates would be formed, in which the special character of each god and goddess was preserved. So, when upper and lower Egypt were united under the first dynasty, Horus, the chief god of the Delta, and Seth, dominant in upper Egypt, continued their bitter struggle, for whereas Horus was now conceived to be the life-giving sun, Seth became the power of evil (the lifeless desert?). After their enmity became a major theme in the dramatic myth of Isis and Osiris, they acquired separate aims, Horus as the son-avenger (he was now the son of Isis by Osiris) and Seth, the brother of Osiris, as the fratricidal uncle and rival for the throne, although after the issue was resolved he subsided. Triads and enneads (or groups of nine) were formed also for other and quite natural reasons. It was, for example, natural to think that the gods were grouped in families. Thus at Memphis during the Pyramid Age, Ptah, the creator, Sekhmet, the lion-headed war-goddess and sender of plagues, and Imhotep, the physician who became the god of medi-

cine, were united as father, mother and son. During the same period at Heliopolis a family of nine in four generations was worshiped, namely, Atum (the oldest, originally the hill of earth that emerged from the primordial sea, later associated with the evening sun), his children Shu (the air that holds up the sky) and Tefnut (the latter's female complement), Shu and Tefnut's children Geb (the earth) and Nut (the sky), and the children in turn of Geb and Nut: Osiris, Isis, Seth, and Nephthys. In other places Osiris and Isis formed a separate triad with Horus, their son. At Thebes during the Middle and New Kingdoms the same relationship bound together Amon-Re, father sun, Mut, mother Nile, and Khonsu, the moon, their son (p. 42).

The Isis-Osiris-Horus Complex

The Isis-Osiris family group was relatively late in appearing, but its members stimulated the popular imagination as no other Egyptian gods did.

Osiris may have had a prehistoric origin. According to one view, he was initially brought in from Libya, where he was the fructifying water which produces vegetation even in the desert. But this is by no means certain, for there is perhaps better reason to think, because he always seems to have been in human form, that he came from Syria and was originally an agricultural deity. But after he was established in Egypt and became the son of Geb and Nut, he was more or less identified with the life-giving water of the Nile. His sister Isis, who was also his wife, is perhaps less ancient a figure, but from about 1500 B.C. (during the New Empire) she grew more popular, certainly more adorable, than he. Her appeal was increased by the pathos of her story. According to the Pyramid Texts,* which are our

* The so-called Pyramid Texts have been assembled from fragments of funerary hymns and rituals found incised on the walls of royal tombs of the Old Kingdom; they were designed to secure the well-being and happiness of the pharaohs and their families in the after-world

earliest sources, Osiris, the good and beneficent king, was killed by his brother Seth. (Was Seth the demon of desert heat, and did he overpower and shrink the Nile and kill the vegetation on its banks that was Osiris too?) Taking Osiris' third eye with him, Seth fled the scene. After he was gone, Isis and Nephthys found the slain god's body and wept over it. While Isis was embracing the corpse, it revived for awhile and impregnated her. She later secretly gave birth to Horus and brought him up in a place in the Delta without discovery. When the child was old enough, she sent him forth to avenge his father. Horus found the corpse of his father still preserved. Before the court of the gods presided over by his grandfather Ceb he refuted Seth's denial that he had murdered Osiris and won the acclaim of the court as Osiris' successor and king in his place. Seth had stolen the third eye of Osiris, fixed in his forehead and betokening his kingship, so Horus now fought Seth for it and recovered it, thus becoming king in actuality as well as in name. Horus immediately took the eye to the corpse of his father, and his father awoke, stood up, and recovered the control of his limbs. (So might the eye of the kingly sun bring life and resurrection to the grain lying moist in the soil.) But Osiris did not remain above ground; he went to the underworld to become the judge and god of the dead, while Horus, retaining the eye and wearing it, became the

---

to which they alone were entitled. These texts were succeeded in the Middle Kingdom by the so-called Coffin Texts, written or inscribed on the coffins of Egyptian nobles and wealthy commoners. During the New Kingdom the tombs contained texts written on papyrus rolls that were versions of the so-called Book of the Dead, designed for all those who could afford to be buried with due ceremony. The most complete texts to come down to us are from the Greco-Roman era, the Wisdom Literature, full of stories, proverbs, and guidance for life in this world (a source, by the way, of much that is to be found in the Biblical Book of Proverbs). One brief work of a theological nature comes from as far-off a time as the Old Kingdom; a version of it is inscribed on the Shabaka Stone dating from the eighth century B.C. Other important sources of our knowledge of Egyptian religion are the pictures on walls and columns of tombs and temples, with their explanatory inscriptions.

lord of the upper world, both as the ruler of Egypt (by identification with its kings) and its glittering sun.

Sun-Worship

But Horus was not the only sun deity. There were others, one of whom (Re) came to eclipse him. From one end of their land to the other, the Egyptians knew how much their crops depended on the light and warmth that sped out of the sun into the ground where the seed lay waiting. They were aware of this from the beginning. As has been said:

The all-enveloping power and glory of the Egyptian sun is the most insistent fact in the Nile valley. . . . The Egyptian saw him in different, doubtless originally local forms.
Probably the oldest notion of him goes back to the days when the prehistoric Egyptians were still leading a hunting life in the Nile marshes, when they pictured the Sun-god as a hunter poling or paddling himself across the reed-grown marshes in a boat made by lashing together two bundles of reeds like a catamaran. Glimpses of this archaic notion are still preserved in the oldest passages of the Pyramid Texts, which often picture the Sun-god ferrying across the celestial marshes in the "double reed-boat". . . .
[Later] the "double reed-boat" was succeeded by a gorgeous royal barge like that of the earthly Pharaoh. In this luminous sun-barque, one for the morning and the other for the evening, it was believed that the Sun-god majestically crossed the celestial ocean as the Pharaoh sailed the Nile.[C1]

This was Re (or Ra), the sun conceived in human form, and especially the noontide sun. The rising sun was Kheprer, who, after a brush with Apophis, the cloud-dragon, appeared in the *mandet* boat ascending the morning sky; and the declining sun, going down in the *mesektet* boat to the horizon, was Atum. These were two sun-gods older even than Re.

But the sun was also a bird and, again, a beetle. As bird he was Horus, the high-flying falcon swiftly spanning the sky. (Indeed, the symbol most often used in all Egypt was simply the widespread wings of the mounting falcon, clearest sign of the rising sun.) More unusual was the identification of the sun-god with the scarab or sacred dung-beetle. Here the Egyptian peasant with nimble imagination transferred to the sky his observation of the diligent scarab rolling along the ground the ball of dung in which it was placing its eggs; he thought of the sun as a huge ball rolled along by a mighty sky-beetle, whose name was Kheprer (or Khopri). It was common in later days for the figure of the scarab to be incised on seals, shown in amulets, or placed on the foreheads of the statues of kings; there was life and protection in it, and by it the power of death and darkness was held at bay.

At Heliopolis in lower Egypt during the Old Empire the priests of the sun-god Atum combined him with Re. This was but the first step. Next, he was coordinated and fused with the various Horuses, from the "Horus of the horizon" (Harakhte) on through the other Horuses of the daylight hours. The winged beetle Kheprer was part of him. And not only was he the sun as a natural force; he was also the power in kings that enabled them to overspread and protect their realms, as with wings. It is for this reason that the pharaohs, after having been called Horus in the early years of the Pyramid Age, assumed by 2500 B.C. the title of "Son of Re." Their obelisks were built, most likely as massive symbols of the sun's ray, and when they were lying in their long sleep within the mighty pyramids, symbols too of the sun, they were one with the sun in death as in life. The sun, their father in life, was now their immortal life in death.

In the time of the empire a thousand years later, the queen had become the high-priestess of the sun, and through the pharaohs who impersonated him the sun was the father of her children, who were gods from birth.

Meanwhile the sun had acquired still another dimension by becoming Amon-Re. Amon was originally the local god of Thebes, in upper Egypt, and of the temple of Karnak close by, often enlarged and embellished that it might be a thing of utmost magnificence and splendor. When mighty Thebes became by conquest the ruling city of all Egypt (about 2000 B.C.), Amon grew into a god of national stature, and was combined with powerful Re as the greatest of the gods. A divine family was placed around him. Mut, the goddess of Thebes, with vulture headdress, was his wife, and the moon-god, Khonsu, was their son. The ram was his representative among the animals. Before him stood the cobra, to signify that he was king of the gods, and above him hung the sun's winged disc.

The Other Gods

There were other gods. In Memphis, for example, the citizens worshiped an abstractly conceived god called Ptah, considering him to be the creator who conceived the world in his heart and by an utterance through his lips ordered it to arise from primordial mud. He was, strangely enough, always enveloped from head to foot in bandages, exactly like a mummy, as though to suggest that he came from a far past, his special history no longer known. And there was Maat, the goddess of truth, who usually appears in the Egyptian wall-paintings of the judgment, standing at the doorway of the great hall where the heart of the dead is weighed against a feather. Safekht was the goddess of writing, Hu the god of taste, Anubis the jackal-guardian of the cemetery, Neit the goddess of hunting, holding bow and arrows. There were many others. To extend the list would serve little purpose here. Suffice it to say that the names remaining only increase the feeling that the ancient Egyptians were enthusiastic polytheists, to say the least. Not only did they honor the many deities to which Egypt gave birth, but also many foreign importations, like Anaitis, the Anahita of the Zoroastrians, and Qedesh or Ashtarth, the Ishtar or Consecrated Lover of Babylonia and Palestine.[*]

* A later reaction from this (especially in the Delta) was to identify the foreign with the native gods—a process of amalgamation tending finally toward monotheism.

Doctrines of the Future Life

However much the Egyptians enjoyed life—and they did—and however devoutly they honored the sun and the Nile that helped them to prolong it, they dwelt in thought more than any other people known to us on something which at first sight seems the opposite of life—the disposal of the dead and the after-life of kings and commoners. At first they thought it was only their kings who were happy in the hereafter. But then, during the breakdown of pharaonic authority (2200–2000 B.C.), the belief began to grow that others could hope for as much— that, either in the west or in the Field of Rushes, there was a chance of blessedness for everyone.

It was not that there had ever been scepticism about an after-life. There was plenty of evidence that the dead did not perish* The Egyptians were therefore very naturally anxious to secure their immortal satisfactions.

* Breasted suggests (in *Development of Religion and Thought in Ancient Egypt*, p. 49) what some of this evidence was. "Experience in the land of Egypt has led me," he wrote, "to believe that [the insistent faith in the hereafter] was greatly favored and influenced by the fact that the conditions of soil and climate resulted in such a remarkable preservation of the human body as may be found under natural conditions nowhere else in the world. In going up to the daily task on some neighboring temple in Nubia, I was not infrequently obliged to pass through the corner of a cemetery, where the feet of a dead man, buried in a shallow grave, were now uncovered and extended directly across my path. They were precisely like the rough and calloused feet of the workmen in our excavations. How old the grave was I do not know, but anyone familiar with the cemeteries of Egypt, ancient and modern, has found numerous bodies or portions of bodies indefinitely old which seemed about as well preserved as those of the living. This must have been a frequent experience of the ancient Egyptian, and like Hamlet with the skull of Yorick in his hands, he must often have pondered deeply as he contemplated these silent witnesses. The surprisingly perfect state of preservation in which he found his ancestors whenever the digging of a new grave disclosed them, must have greatly stimulated his belief in their continued existence, and often aroused his imagination to more detailed pictures of the realm and the life of the mysteriously departed." Reprinted by permission of the publishers.

Their beliefs are hard to arrange logically. An early notion convinced them of the existence of the *ba* or animating soul—depicted as a human-headed bird whose seat was the "heart" or "abdomen," but which flew from the body with the last breath. It loved its body, and returned to it after death with longing and hunger, its physical desire for food and drink undiminished. Hence its return was not wholly satisfactory unless the body were somehow preserved, food and drink provided, and its passage into and from the tomb made easy by an opening, such as a tiny chimney or air duct. But there was another soul. This was the *ka*, or the mental aspects of personality, the source of its motives and intuitions, symbolized by two arms outstretched or by an attendant figure formed as the double of the personality. It was this soul that after death took up its residence in the life-like statue of the deceased placed in the tomb, and saw and enjoyed the pictures and the models which portrayed its former life. Apparently the ka had its higher and lower counterparts, quite aside from the ba. It was sometimes pictured as two outstretched arms with a bird mounting between them. This bird was the *ikhu* or "spirit" (the highest intelligence), which flew off to heaven at death in the form of a bird. A lower counterpart was the "shadow" that everywhere accompanies a man walking in the sunlight, his *khaibit*. (Evidently here as elsewhere the Egyptians had some power of analysis but little of the ability to reassemble or synthesize!)

That a happy hereafter was dependent on the preservation of the body seemed obvious. The Egyptians early set about securing such preservation.* Eventually they learned the secret of mummification, entrusted to skilled professionals.†

* When the idea arose that after three thousand years in the Kingdom of Osiris (see the next section) the good soul returned to earth to re-enter its old body, this motivation became still stronger.

† Herodotus tells us how in his time (relatively late, of course) the best embalming was done. The internal organs and the brain having been removed through incisions, the embalmers, he says, would proceed thus: "They fill the belly with pure myrrh pounded up with

Egyptian boat model for a tomb. A dozen rowers guided by a pilot, who holds a weight for sounding, are rowing a master and mistress across the waters to the afterworld. After arrival there, both boat and servants are at the disposal of the one whose death has made the journey necessary. (The Metropolitan Museum of Art, Museum Excavations, 1919–1920; Rogers Fund, supplemented by contribution of Edward S. Harkness.)

Not only was the body thus preserved for the ba, and a statue besides provided as an abiding place for the ka, but the tomb was filled with all manner of furniture and provisions. The needs of the ba were met by jars of water, wine, grain, dates, cakes, and other foods, such as portions of beef and fowl that had been dehydrated or reduced to ashes. The ka was provided with chairs, beds, and even with chariots, of the usual size, and with hundreds of small models of womenfolk, servants, kitchen utensils and dishes, and many simulated foodstuffs, down to little wooden loaves and fishes. Combs, hairpins, and ointments were provided for primping, and carriages, boats, and various games for pleasure and pastime. Great treasures were in some cases included. The rich were sur-

rounded in their long sleep with gilded and silver objects of art. Nothing was forgotten.

As to the models of womenfolk and servants, a whole chapter of the Book of the Dead was devoted to spells for vivifying them into action. They were expected to go to work for the dead in the underworld, and were called *ushebtis* or "answerers." The statuette of a man bearing a bag and a hoe might have a charm written upon his chest: "O statuette, counted for X (name of deceased), . . . thou shalt count thyself for me at all times, to cultivate the fields, water the shores, transport sand of the east to the west, and say 'Here am I.' "[E1] This was a spell thought sufficient to effect the desired result.

And what of the history of the soul in the other world? There was no unanimity about that. Many different ideas were current at one time or another. It was early thought that the sky-goddess Nut admitted favored souls (those of kings) to the region of the stars revolving around the Pole, a place high above all change and decay. The worshipers of Re had other expectations. In their tombs fully outfitted boats were placed so that they might sail across the eastern sea and join the barque of the sun-god. In the mythological development of this idea, all sorts of

cassia and other spices, except frankincense, and sew it together again. Having so done they keep it for embalming covered up in natron for seventy days, but for a longer time than this it is not permitted to embalm it; and when the seventy days are past, they wash the corpse and roll its whole body up in fine linen cut into bands, smearing these beneath with gum, which the Egyptians use generally instead of glue. Then the kinsfolk receive it from them and have a wooden figure made in the shape of a man, and when they have had this made they enclose the corpse, and having shut it up within, they store it in a sepulchral chamber, setting it upright against the wall."[D]

difficulties were imagined, disagreeably hampering the soul in its initial journey to meet the sun. The eastern sea became Water Lily Lake, and the only way across it was on a ferry operated by a reluctant boatman who had to be coaxed to take a passenger. Sometimes the ferryman could not be persuaded, in which case the soul would have to get itself floated over the lake in a cloud of incense, or take to wing in the form of a bird. On its way it would find everything alive and speaking, nothing inert or dead; even the boat oars, the boat itself, the objects it would have to pass after landing, had voices. Beyond the lake there would be further perils and delays, locked gates, encounters with hostile animals and serpents, strange wildernesses. When at length the soul would win its way to the sun, it might rest at last, or perhaps it might follow on with the sun to the west and under the earth into the twelve "caverns" of the night, each enclosed by the great gates that mark the hours.

It is an interesting aspect of these conceptions that the dead were often thought to become stars or to be merged into the sun-god himself, by a kind of multiple incarnation in him.

The Kingdom of Osiris

One of the oldest, perhaps *the* oldest conception of the after-life, and one destined to come into great popularity after the Pyramid Age, was that of the kingdom of Osiris. How one got to it differed with period and place. According to one view:

The transit of the soul to the blessed west of Osiris began at Abydos, up the long valley which leads to the Oasis road. The soul is represented setting out sturdily, staff in hand, to begin its long march. The Oasis was the frontier of the unknown. Beyond that lay the end of the world, at the mountains where the sun left the visible world to enter the underworld of stars, the Duat. There the fertile isles would be reached, where the corn grew higher than any on earth.[F]

But some views were that the Osirian fields were in the north (the Delta) or beyond the sea in Syria, or, more remotely, in the Milky Way, the great white Nile of the sky.

Wherever it was, it was a pleasant region. There, upon the fertile land, lush with vegetation, and with grain twelve feet high, the fortunate soul could sit at ease under the shade trees, watching his slaves (the *ushebtis*) plough the black earth with oxen or reap the enormous ears of grain or maize, while he played a leisurely game of draughts with his smiling wife or conversed with his friends.

But because not everyone deserved so blissful a lot, judgment had to be passed before the soul could gain entrance to these enchanted fields. As pictured in the Book of the Dead, the examination of the soul is made in the presence of Osiris himself and concerns goodness or wickedness. The soul is brought—as we often see in the scenes pictured in the funeral papyri—into the Hall of Truth by the jackal-headed Anubis, guardian of the cemetery, and is made to stand before Osiris, who is enthroned under a canopy and attended on either side by Isis and their sister Nephthys. When the soul beholds the lord of the dead, it immediately begins to justify itself, and does so not by confessing and repenting any sins but by telling of the evil it has *not* done:

"Hail to thee, great god, lord of Truth. . . . Behold, I come to thee, I bring to thee righteousness. . . . I knew no wrong. I did no evil thing. . . . I did not do that which the god abominates. . . . I allowed no one to hunger. I caused no one to weep. I did not murder. I did not command to murder. I caused no man misery. I did not diminish food in the temples. . . . I did not take away the food-offerings of the dead. . . . I did not commit adultery. . . . I did not diminish the grain measure. . . . I did not load the weight of the balances. I did not deflect the index of the scales. I did not take milk from the mouth of the child. I did not drive away the cattle from their pasturage. . . . I did not dam the running water [and thus divert from others the waters of the irrigation canals at the time of the inundation]. . . . I did not interfere with the god in his payments. I am purified four times, I am pure. . . ."[E2]

After a similar "negative confession" to each of the forty-two judges sitting in a gallery as representatives

Painting of the judgment. *Found in the tomb of Queen Meryet-Amun and dating from about 1025 B.C., this painting on papyrus shows the Princess Entui-ny appearing before Osiris, god of the dead, to justify herself and be admitted to his underworld realm. In this simplified conception, Maat or Truth, crowned by an ostrich feather, stands behind the princess, prompting her. (The Metropolitan Museum of Art, Museum Excavations, Rogers Fund, 1930.)*

of the nomes of Egypt, the dead man's heart is balanced by Anubis in the judgment scales against an ostrich feather. If it is a heart made light by goodness, and does not overweight the scale, the ibis-headed Thoth, who is umpire and scribe, reports the fact to Osiris, and the soul is then allowed to enter the blessed fields of Osiris' realm. But if the scales prove the soul to be evil, retribution overtakes it.

According to some conceptions, it is destroyed by a strange creature, "The Devouress," with the head and jaws of a crocodile, the forequarters of a lion, and the hindquarters of a hippopotamus, waiting hungrily nearby, who springs forward and eats it. According to other conceptions it is thrown into a fiery hell, where it is punished severely. But there is always hope for a better issue.

Akhenaton's Venture in Monotheism

So far, all the conceptions we have examined are polytheistic, but the history of Egyptian religion provides us at one point with a determined endeavor to institute a monotheistic reform.

It sprang from the conviction enkindled in a young pharaoh, Amenhotep IV, in whose court monotheism had already found voice. Undoubtedly he must have heard the Theban sun-hymn composed by two architects employed by his father Amenhotep III, which celebrated the sun under the appellation Aton (Solar Globe), in such words as these:

O creator of what the earth brings forth, . . .
   . . . good creator who takes the greatest pains with
  his innumerable creatures. . . .
He who reaches the ends of the lands every day and
  beholds those who walk there . . .
Every land adores him at his rising every day, in order to
  praise him.[G]

By such words, and probably in sympathetic response to the urging of monotheistic enthusiasts, he was led to change the name of the national god from Amon to Aton and his own name from Amenhotep ("Amon is satisfied") to Akhenaton ("Pious to Aton"), and to order Aton to be worshiped as the one and only god, the creator of all things and the sustainer of all creatures. In the temples of Egypt now, the priests who bowed before the exalted lord of creation chanted:

Thou dawnest beautifully in the horizon of the sky,
O living Aton who wast the Beginning of life!
When thou didst rise in the eastern horizon,
Thou didst fill every land with thy beauty.
Thou art beautiful, great, glittering, high over every land,
Thy rays, they encompass the lands, even to the end of
  all that thou hast made.[C2]

In some of the noblest phrases in the literature of Egyptian religion, they proclaimed the excellencies of Aton:

How manifold are thy works!
They are hidden before men,

O sole God, beside whom there is no other.
Thou didst create the earth according to thy heart.

Thou didst make the distant sky in order to rise therein,
In order to behold all that thou hast made . . .
The world subsists in thy hand,
Even as thou hast made them.

When thou hast risen they live,
When thou settest they die;
For thou art length of life of thyself,
Men live through thee.[C3]

The determined young monarch ordered the names and figures of Amon and the other gods expunged from all monuments, temples, and public records. Even Osiris was set aside as one to be forgotten. In order to create an entirely new and helpful atmosphere for his court, Akhenaton built a splendid new capital further down the Nile from Thebes and called it Akhetaton ("Horizon of Aton"). Similar cities, meant to serve as centers of the new cult, were projected in Nubia and Syria, then still within the Egyptian empire.

But the reform of Akhenaton was not destined to outlive him. His son-in-law, who succeeded him, yielded to the priests of the old Amon party and changed his name from Tutankhaton to Tutankhamon, the name by which he has become so well known today. In the restoration of the older forms of worship it was Aton's name that was now expunged in every public place.

Amon-Re, Osiris, Isis, and Horus resumed their former reign, not to yield ground again until Christianity, a more formidable foe, overthrew them beyond hope of restoration.

II   Babylonia

Cities, governments, ideographic writing, temples, and priests appeared even earlier in Mesopotamia than in Egypt, but the spirit breathing through them was sterner, more nakedly realistic, even brutal, and yet even more given to the practice of religion as an appeal to the gods for help. The reasons are clear enough. Where Egypt was protected by thinly populated deserts on the east and west, cataracts on the south, and a northern sea, Mesopotamia, lying fertile and flat between the twin rivers that watered her, was open to invasions and attack from every quarter. The temporal and the changeful were always present. Nothing remained stable for long; the pleasures of life had to be snatched quickly.

Or let us put the facts in this way: the prehistoric hunters and fishers in the swamps at the conjunction of the Tigris and Euphrates gave place to a culture of villages, each with its temple; then villages, layer on layer,* gave place to, or came under the dominance of, cities—Erech, Eridu, Lagash, Ur, Nippur, and others. Cities fought each other until one dominated another, and the Sumerian kingdoms rose, to be followed and absorbed by Semitic empires, and these by the Persian. In the same way also the gods of the fields and streams and those of the sky overhead took to the towns, organized themselves into a superstate, with governing power lodged in a council of the gods, fought, made love, and merged into a vast pantheon with names almost beyond counting.†

---

* Houses being made of sun-dried bricks crumbled in time, and new houses were built on the smoothed-out ruins.

† Although Mesopotamian history before 4000 B.C. was relatively serene, even then the Neolithic pottery makers who were the earliest villagers were displaced along the rivers by town-building colonists, possibly Semitic, before 4500 B.C. These townsmen, who had already developed irrigating canals, were conquered in the fourth millennium B.C. by Sumerian invaders, a non-Semitic, non-Indo-European people, whose origin is unknown. (They probably came in either from the south across the sea or from the east.) Thus began a struggle between Sumerians and Semites that lasted two thousand years. Gradually the Semites, perhaps with the aid of fresh arrivals from Arabia, took over in the north, while the Sumerians (in the first part of the third millennium B.C.) continued to control the south from Nippur to the Persian Gulf. Then the great king Sargon established the Akkadian dynasty in the north, and he and his successors pillaged and ultimately undermined the Sumerian kingdoms, even though the "third dynasty of Ur" re-established a Neo-Sumerian supremacy that lasted for a century. But by 2000 B.C. the Sumerians began to go under and at last

The Sumero-Akkadian Pantheon*

We hear there were nearly two thousand deities! Many of them, however, had only the status of servants, messengers, and warriors of the greater gods. Every part of nature was represented. Six deities eventually became important over wide areas. Each was the deity of a big city. An (Anu), the sky-god, was the chief deity of Erech and nominally still the "pristine king and ruler" of the gods, but he was overshadowed by Enlil (Bel), the air-god, who became the god of the lands beneath, conferring power upon kings, and a great warrior, the chief deity at Nippur. Nanna (Sin), the moon-god, reigned at Ur. Utu, who later took the Semitic name Shamash, was the sun-god at Larsa. Enki (Ea), the water-god, who was also the wisdom-god, made his home in Eridu. Ninhursag (Aruru), also known as Nintu and Ninmah, the mother-goddess, prevailed at Kish. It was usual for the male deities, major or minor, to have a con-

---

ceased to exist as a political reality. By this time the Amoritic Semites had penetrated the south, and the great Semitic king and law-giver Hammurabi of Babylon (1728–1686 B.C.) united north and south briefly into one Sumero-Akkadian kingdom. But this kingdom was overthrown by the Kassites, invading from the northeast about 1600 B.C.; they, in their turn, could not prevent the rise of the Assyrian kingdom in the north, based at Nineveh, which rose to world power about 1100 B.C. and then began a slow decline. Assyria fell before the Babylonians in 612, and the latter succumbed to Cyrus the Persian in 539 B.C. For dates see P. van der Meer, *The Chronology of Ancient Western Asia and Egypt* (Leiden, E. J. Brill, 1955); Arnold Toynbee, *A Study of History* (Oxford, 1954); Samuel N. Kramer, *Sumerian Mythology* (Harper Torchbooks, 1961, p. 6); W. F. Albright, *From the Stone Age to Christianity* (Johns Hopkins, 1957).

* The Sumerian pantheon, the first to be formulated in Mesopotamia, was largely adopted by the Akkadians when the latter established themselves in the northern half of the area; hence the title of the present topic. In the following account, the Sumerian names will be given first, with the Akkadian equivalent in parenthesis. It will be noted in the parentheses that the Sumerian name is modified in some cases, but in other cases it is replaced by a new name, probably Semitic. Only a few Sumerian myths survive intact. The rest are in fragments; we shall therefore be considering the Akkadian versions of these myths, more fully preserved, and told in a style different from that of the Sumerians.

sort, worshiped in a separate sanctuary built on to his temple. To this rule there were some exceptions. The mother-goddess, Ninhursag, was unmarried, and An's wife had no importance, her place being taken by her daughter, the virgin love-goddess and mistress of the sky, Innana. The gods were hospitable to one another. No regnant deity excluded other cults from his or her city. Though the chief fane always belonged to the chief god, other deities might have smaller sanctuaries in other parts of the city. Apparently they deserved a place there, because, as the Semitic terminology had it, each was the *bel* or "owner" of a large tract of land nearby and should have a proper residence (temple) in the nearest city.

It was natural that these deities should be grouped into triads. In due course Anu, Enlil, and Ea were believed to divide the physical universe among them as the rulers respectively of heaven above, earth beneath, and the waters on and under the earth. Another (and later) triad had a more agricultural significance. It was composed of Shamash, the sun-god, Sin, the moon-god, and Ishtar, the Semitic goddess of fertility, who, with unequaled ability to keep her name and functions dominant, was identified with the mother-goddess Ninhursag and her aliases Ninmah, Nintu, Mami, Aruru, and others, and especially Innana of Erech, the Sumerian queen of heaven and goddess of love and fertility.

A special group of gods were the Anunnaki, the nether-world gods. Their chief was Nergal, originally a sun-god but now, as the god of pestilence, the lord of the world below, the woebegone Land of No Return. His consort was the dread goddess of death and sterility, Ereshkigal, an elder sister of Ishtar.

Of all these deities Ishtar was to come closest to being universally worshiped. She was the great mother-goddess, and yet had something almost virginal about her. By her attachment to Tammuz (Sumerian *Dumuzi*), the god of the spring sun and its awakenings in soil and beast, she established herself as a great lover in her own right. As the goddess of fertility, she gave children to women and life to vegetation. As the planet Venus, she was "the queen of the heavens and the stars." Her worship was destined to spread far to the west, to Palestine and to Egypt. Even the Zoroastrians were unable to resist her, and after changing her name to Anahita, "The Spotless One" (and thus purifying her!), they gave to her almost as great prominence as to Ormazd himself. We shall meet her again.

Marduk of Babylon

The greatest rival of Ishtar was Marduk. His prominence may be assigned, curiously enough, to sheer political good fortune. It happened that the sixth king of the first dynasty of Babylon, Hammurabi, the same who issued the world-famous law code, made this city the capital of a powerful kingdom stretching from the Persian Gulf to the central provinces embraced between the Tigris and Euphrates. It was an achievement of permanent significance, for Babylon thus became and was to remain through twenty centuries of change one of the great cities of the world. And with the rise to power of Babylon, Marduk, its god, rose to greatness too. Not prominent before, he all but absorbed the surrounding gods. Not only did he link to himself Ea of Eridu as his father (whereby he absorbed Ea's earlier son, Ninurta the war-god) and make Nabu of Barsippa, the fire-god, his son, but he absorbed from them some of their functions— the wisdom of Ea and Nabu's power over destiny. The chief attributes of Enlil of Nippur were also transferred to him,* so that he might be acknowledged the lord of the heavens. Finally, the religious literature of Babylon was extensively revised to give him the prominent role his city demanded for him.

The Babylonian Myths and Epics

The Sumerians and Akkadians had fertile imaginations. They loved to tell stories about their gods

---

* Including Enlil's victory over Tiamat, the dragon of chaos. See the next section.

and heroes.* Although it does not serve our purpose to explore the whole of this mythology, the following episodes, in part because of their intrinsic qualities but also because of the parallels to the stories of the Old Testament which they present, are of more than usual interest.

A. THE CREATION. The Sumerians, we have learned, believed that the first thing that existed was the primordial sea (associated with the goddess Nammu), from which emerged heaven (An) and earth (Ki), united as though they were a large mountain in the midst of the sea. An and Ki produced within or between them Enlil, air, and as the air began to stir in the darkness within the mountain, it separated sky and earth. Then, to see better, Enlil begot the moon-god Nanna, who in turn begot the sun-god Utu, presumably to make the light brighter. By this time the world had come into being, for the sky (An) by expansion of air (Enlil) had reached a great height, and the earth (Ki) had made a solid floor below, with sun and moon to bring light. When air moved above earth (or when Enlil united with his mother Ki) and received the aid of water (Enki), plants and animals came into being. Finally, man was created by the joint efforts of Nammu, the primeval sea, Ninmah, mother-earth, and Enki, the water-god.[H]

But according to another legend (Semitic in origin?), the present world order was formed after a primeval conflict between the dragons of darkness and chaos, led by the bird-god Zu (or in other accounts by Tiamat) and the gods of light and order, headed by Ninurta, the war-god. But the Babylonian

priests rewrote whatever materials they inherited, and they made Marduk both the hero of the struggle against chaos and also the creator of the world and of man. Their story began with Apsu, the god of fresh water, and Tiamat, the dragon of the unbounded salt water (chaos). By their intermingling, this pair over a period of years produced the gods, but the youthful gods were so lively and boisterous that Apsu could not rest and resolved to destroy them, against the wish of Tiamat.

Apsu, opening his mouth,
Said unto resplendent Tiamat:
"Their ways are verily loathsome unto me.
By day I find no relief, nor repose by night.
I will destroy, I will wreck their ways.
That quiet may be restored. Let us have rest!"
As soon as Tiamat heard this,
She was wroth and called out to her husband.
She cried out aggrieved, as she raged all alone,
Injecting woe into her mood:
"What? Should we destroy that which we have built?
Their ways indeed are most troublesome, but let us attend
   kindly!"[11]

But before Apsu could execute his plan, he was destroyed by Ea, who got wind of it, whereupon Tiamat resolved on avenging him. She created monsters to be her allies, and both Anu and Ea fled before her. Not until Marduk, assured by the gods that he would be their chief, came forth to meet her in combat was she halted.

Then advanced Tiamat and Marduk, counselor of the
   gods;
To the combat they marched, they drew nigh to battle,
The lord spread out his net and caught her,
The storm wind that was behind him, he let loose in her
   face.
When Tiamat opened her mouth to its widest,
He drove in the evil wind, that she could not close her
   lips . . .
He made her powerless, he destroyed her life;
He cast down her body and stood upon it.[J1]

After next subduing the monsters she had arrayed against him, Marduk turned back to Tiamat and split

---

* Our knowledge of these, as well as of the events of Mesopotamian history, is derived from inscriptions in the cuneiform script on rock surfaces, walls, and clay tablets. Many of these last, in more or less fragmentary condition, come from the Sumerian temple library at Nippur; more are from the library assembled many centuries later for King Assurbanipal (seventh century B.C.). For a fascinating account of the decipherment and reconstruction of the Sumerian myths, see Samuel N. Kramer, *Sumerian Mythology* (Harper Torchbooks, 1961).

Marduk battling with Tiamat.
Marduk, winged and carrying a
sword and sickle, assaults Tiamat
with double tridents. Tiamat on
her part retreats, with gaping
jaws and widespread lion claws,
on bird feet and with wings out-
stretched. From a wall panel in
the palace of Ashur-nasiripal II,
885–860 B.C.

her open like a shellfish into two halves. With one half he made the canopy which holds back the waters that are above the heavens; with the other half he formed the covering which lies above the waters under the earth. He constructed stations for the gods in the heavens. With Ea's help he made man from the blood of the god Kingsu, Tiamat's ally and second husband. Seeing what he had done, the delighted gods bestowed on him many titles as their undisputed leader and king.[12]

B. THE FLOOD. The original flood story was Sumerian and came out of grim experiences with the overflowing of the two rivers. Several of the later versions of the tale, mostly fragmentary, have come down to us. The finest of these forms part of the Gilgamesh epic, into which it was inserted as an interesting interpolation. According to this narrative, the gods decided in anger to punish man's sins by a flood. Their secret decision was revealed to one man. The good god Ea felt kindly toward Utnapishtim and told him about it. The man proceeded immediately to build an ark:

120 cubits high were its sides,
140 cubits reached the edge of its roof.[12]

As Utnapishtim later told Gilgamesh (we quote in part):

"I brought up into the ship my family and household,
The cattle of the field, the beasts of the field, craftsmen,
    all of them I brought in.
A fixed time had Shamash appointed, saying,
'When the ruler of darkness sends a heavy rain,
Then enter into the ship and close the door.'
The appointed time came near, . . .
There came up from the horizon a black cloud.
Adad thundered within it . . .
Adad's storm reached unto heaven,
All light was turned into darkness . . .
The water climbed over the mountains . . .
The gods feared the deluge,
They drew back, they climbed up to the heaven of Anu.
The gods crouched like a dog, they cowered by the wall.
Ishtar cried like a woman in travail,
The queen of the gods cried with a loud voice:
'The former race is turned to clay.'
When the seventh day drew nigh, the tempest ceased; the
    deluge,
Which had fought like an army, ended.

51

Then rested the sea, the storm fell asleep, the flood
    ceased . . .
All mankind was turned to clay . . .
I opened the window and the light fell upon my face,
I bowed, I sat down, I wept,
And over my face ran my tears,
I looked upon the world, all was sea.
After twelve days (?) the land emerged.
To the land of Nisir the ship made its way,
The mount of Nisir held it fast, that it moved not . . .
I sent forth a dove and let her go.
The dove flew to and fro,
But there was no resting place and she returned.
I sent forth a swallow and let her go,
The swallow flew to and fro,
But there was no resting place and she returned.
I sent forth a raven and let her go,
The raven flew away, she saw the abatement of the
    waters,
She drew near, she waded, she croaked, and came not
    back.
Then I sent everything forth to the four quarters of
    heaven, I offered sacrifice,
I made a libation upon the mountain's peak."[13]

The close parallels to the Old Testament are obvious.

C. Ishtar's Descent to the Land of the Dead.
If the obscure reference to Tammuz at the end of this
story * is correctly interpreted, Ishtar went down into
Hades to recover her dead lover, the personification
of the strong sun of springtime, whose vigor fades
away in the autumn. When she came to the door of
the Land of No Return, she called imperiously to the
porter:

"O gatekeeper, open thy gate,
Open thy gate that I may enter!
If thou openest not the gate so that I cannot enter,

---

* The Babylonian tale is based on a Sumerian prototype in which Innana and her husband Dumuzi (Tammuz) are the central figures. The plot differs to this
extent: in the Sumerian tale Dumuzi winds up permanently in the Land of No Return in exchange for Innana,
whereas in the Babylonian one Tammuz is already in the
Land of No Return and Ishtar seeks his release. For a
reconstruction of the Sumerian tale, see S. N. Kramer,
Sumerian Mythology (Harper Torchbooks, 1961, pp. 83–
96).

I will smash the door, I will shatter the bolt,
I will smash the doorpost, I will move the doors,
I will raise up the dead, eating the living,
So that the dead will outnumber the living."[13]

Being commanded to do so by the goddess of the
dead, the porter admits the queen of heaven, but as
she passes through each of the seven gates, he takes
an article of clothing from her, until she enters the
inner circle of the lower world stark naked. Held
there in durance, she goes through much suffering,
for the pest-god Namtar afflicts her successively with
sixty diseases. Meanwhile, men and animals in the
upper world grow listless and dull, unable to reproduce their kind. Love and fertility have left the
earth. The gods are distressed.

Forth went Papsukkal before Sin his father, weeping,
His tears flowing before Ea, the king:
"Ishtar has gone down to the nether world, she has not
    come up."[14]

Ea sends a messenger to Hades, and the goddess of
the dead reluctantly orders Namtar to sprinkle Ishtar
with "the water of life." She, restored to bloom and
health, begins her journey back to the upper world,
at each gate receiving back the clothing of which
she had been divested.

No more poetically satisfying account of the disappearance of the vegetation goddess at the approach
of winter and of her return in the spring has ever
been conceived.

D. The Journey of Gilgamesh. Related in the
most finished and literary of the Babylonian epics,
the story of Gilgamesh's journey, originally Sumerian
like the others we have cited, begins with the tale of
the friendship of Gilgamesh, the ruler of the city of
Uruk (Erech), with the wild man Enkidu, who dies
prematurely. It then tells of his journey, through
many perils, in search of immortality, to the realm of
the departed beyond the western (the Mediterranean?) "waters of death," where his ancestor Utnapishtim dwells, and concludes with his disconsolate
return to Uruk, after being robbed by a serpent of the

herb of immortality which Utnapishtim enabled him to find. The whole story is full of the pathos of human disappointment in the face of death. What can one do about death, except to make this life happy? When Gilgamesh is about to embark on the waters of death in the west, he is addressed by Siduri, a barmaid dwelling by the sea, who says:

> Gilgamesh, whither hurriest thou?
> The life that thou seekest thou wilt not find.
> When the gods created man,
> They fixed death for mankind.
> Life they took in their own hand.
> Thou, O Gilgamesh, let thy belly be filled!
> Day and night be merry,
> Daily celebrate a feast,
> Day and night dance and make merry!
> Clean be thy clothes,
> Thy head be washed, bathe in water!
> Look joyfully on the child that grasps thy hand,
> Be happy with the wife in thine arms![K1]

Here breathes indeed the spirit of the people of Babylonia. They had no hopes such as the Egyptians had of pleasantness in the world beyond. All joy was in this life.

Sacrifice, Magic, and Astrology

To insure to themselves the blessings of this life, the Babylonians resorted to their priests for sacrifices, incantations, ritual prayers, and the reading of the stars. They listened in rapt attention to the songs for the flute and the songs of prostration which were offered up before the gods. The liturgies were long, but they mellowed the gods. And if the gods would not be kind, there were incantations—powerful and compelling—to which the gods must give heed perforce, and which the evil spirits could not choose but obey. The worshipers paid the priests well to supplicate Ishtar:

I have cried to thee, suffering, wearied, and distressed, as thy servant.
See me, O my Lady; accept my prayers . . .

Forgive my sin, my iniquity, my shameful deeds, and my offense.
Overlook my shameful deeds; accept my prayer . . .
Let thy great mercy be upon me.[15]

The priests could do more than pray; they could put a spell upon the evil spirits in the body of the suppliant:

Out of my body away!
Out of my body far away!
Out of my body, for shame!
My body do not oppress!
By Shamash, the mighty, be ye exorcised!
By Ea, the lord of all, be ye exorcised!
By Marduk, the chief exorciser of the gods, be ye exorcised![K2]

The priests were busy men, well organized for their task, and offering many services to their clientele. They had learned during the centuries, from before 3200 B.C. (!), to act through what must be called in each case the temple corporation, a legal entity often possessed of large land-holdings and run according to strict business methods, with all receipts and expenditures recorded in written signs on clay tablets. The temple structures administered by the corporations were large buildings, constructed of thick courses of sun-dried brick and occupying spacious temple compounds, in the center of which often stood man-built mountains encased in brick, called *ziggurats,* each with a shrine on its top. In these compounds the priests performed their lengthy rituals. Here also they conducted schools for the teaching of reading and writing and arithmetic, and here, as well, they practiced divination, in the ambitious endeavor to read the signs of the times and foretell the future. Divination was in fact one of the main functions of the priesthood. One whole order of priests specialized in the interpretation of dreams and of aberrations in natural events. They devoted much attention especially to the reading of the omens in the sheep's liver, for they thought the will and intentions of the gods were revealed in the creases on the surface and the physical peculiarities inside the liver. But the most important of their divining methods, for us if not for

53

them, was their astrology. The origins of it go back to Sumerian times, and its repute was enormous. In the attempt to establish what might be called scientific method in reading the will of the gods in the disposition of the heavenly bodies, the diviners kept accurate and detailed records of the movements they observed in the heavens, and thus prepared the way for scientific astronomy in our own day. Though each zodiacal constellation was identified with special deities, the astronomical instruments devised for space measurement and time study of the stars were amazingly precise and accurate.

III   Greece

The last century has seen a thorough revision of earlier ideas of classical Greek religion. Homer is no longer taken at face value. His pantheon, described with his bright and winged words and in conception poetically unsurpassed, was for many centuries accepted in the West as an accurate rendering of early Greek religion. In the light of recent scholarship it is not that at all. We see now that the scholars who read off the characteristics of the Greek gods from the statues of the classic age and the lines of Homer should have paid more attention to "the crude and tangled superstitions of the peasantry of the mainland,"[L1] half-revealed and half-concealed in the poetry of Hesiod. It is clear from a study of these superstitions that much that was primitive lay at the base of Greek religion. The beauty and balance of the Homeric pantheon was in truth a triumph of unification and sublimation.

In brief, we have here another case of tribal amalgamations accompanied by a mingling and reordering of the gods.

The Gathering of the Gods in Early Hellas

The determinative fact in the formation of early Greek religion is the northern invasions beginning about the twentieth century B.C. The invaders were formidable horse-borne warriors of Aryan or Indo-European speech, who came down from the northern parts of Greece in their chariots to establish themselves as masters of the earlier, so-called Helladic peoples. Historians are not certain of the origins of all the groups involved, but they are fairly agreed that the earliest true civilizations, those of the Minoans in Crete (who flourished about 2200–1100 B.C.) and of the Bronze Age Aegeans of the Greek archipelago and mainland (2500–1100 B.C.), known to the later Greeks as "Pelasgians," were pre-Greek. The Minoan civilization began to decay about 1400 B.C., perhaps as the result of invasions (by Achaeans?) from the mainland. At all events, the Cretan palace of Cnossus fell, and never recovered its earlier glory and wealth. The Cretan culture, however, had earlier spread to the Greek mainland, and produced in the northeastern parts of the Peloponnesus and further north the Mycenaean civilization, of which the Homeric (or Achaean) Age was probably a late form.* Finally, about the twelfth century B.C. another great wave of northerners—the formidable Dorians and their allies—overthrew the Mycenaean civilization, thus causing a widespread displacement that resulted in Greek settlements along the coast of Asia Minor, composed of Ionians, Aeolians, and Dorians, too. When everyone had settled down again, the historic Greek city-states came into being, and the patterns of Greek religion, now so familiar to us, began to form.

These new patterns in religion were combinations of many different elements. The Indo-European invaders contributed to the divine *sunoikismos,* or "mingling-together," at least these deities: their chief god Zeus, the sky-father and rain-maker (called Dyaus Pitar by the Indo-Aryans and Jupiter by the Romans); Demeter, the earth-mother; and Hestia (the Vesta of the Romans), virgin goddess of the

---

* It is likely that the Achaeans—leaders among the long-haired, light-skinned invaders from the north—adopted the Mycenaean culture after mastering its creators, both in Greece and in Crete.

hearth, sister of Zeus, and a goddess from the far Indo-European past, honored with libations at the beginning and end of every sacrifice. But many of the gods had no such distant origin. Rhea seems to have been Minoan, Athena Mycenaean (at least when we first glimpse her), and Hermes and Hera Aegaean or Helladic. Apollo appears to be from Ionia, Aphrodite from Cyprus or Cythera, and Dionysus and Ares from Thrace. It was as though the gods flocked together to Olympus from all points of the compass.

And this was as true of cities as it was of Greece as a whole.

It proved difficult even in a city like Athens to have gods that would appeal to the loyalty of all Attica. On the Acropolis at Athens there seem originally to have been Athena and some Kouros [Lord] corresponding with her, some Waterer of the earth, like Erechtheus. Then as Attica was united and brought under the lead of the central city, the gods of the outlying districts began to claim places on the Acropolis. Pallas, the thunder-maid of Pallene in the south, came to form a joint personality with Athena. Oinoe, a town in the northeast, on the way from Delos to Delphi, had for its special god a "Pythian Apollo"; when Oinoe became Attic a place for the Pythian Apollo had to be found on the Acropolis. Dionysus came from Eleutherae, Demeter and Korê from Eleusis, Theseus himself perhaps from Marathon or even from Trozên. They were all given official residences on Athena's rock, and Athens in return sent out Athena to new temples built for her in Prasiae and Sunion and various colonies.[1,2]

The Classical Greek's Interaction with His Gods

It is thus quite evident that the Greek of classical times felt himself surrounded by deities and that he needed their assistance in achieving his many purposes. He was a polytheist for reasons similar to those that made polytheists of the Egyptians and Mesopotamians: the powers and forces dwelling in and under the earth (the *chthon*) and in the sky and under the sea were immediately known in daily life and were found to be diverse as well as numerous. In describing them the Greeks were anthropomorphic, for they preferred to take their analogies and symbols from

human life and personality. It is important to notice that they did not think that the deities on whom they most depended were transcendent and far-removed. Rather, they were close at hand, as close as the hearth (Hestia), the *herma* or boundary stone in the street (Hermes), the shrine before the house, which was perhaps sacred to Apollo of the Roads, the large jar in the store-room sacred to Zeus Ktesios (guardian of the family possessions), and the courtyard, watched over by Zeus Herkeios. As H. J. Rose has said: "For everyday happenings, the gods were about everyone's path and might be invoked at any moment, to confirm an oath, avert evil, heal sickness, or bless all manner of actions."[14] All formal occasions required the invocation of a god or gods—marriage, for instance, or the reception of a newborn baby into the family circle, or at the death and burial of members of the family. Farming and other occupations could not be successfully pursued nor a journey on land or sea attempted without the approval of the gods. The address to the gods on such occasions was simple and courteous but not servile, a natural, almost unreflective gesture of cooperation and community, not dominated by fear.

If a god was known to be far-removed, his existence might be recognized but no prayer or sacrifice was offered to him; there was no use in sacrificing to a deity unaware of the act. Thus Hades, the god of the underworld, and Ouranos, the god of heaven, although readily believed in, were not worshiped in Greek homes. On the other hand, Zeus was often invoked because he was nearby as well as far away, and the same was true of Apollo, who, not identified with the sun until a late date, received daily honors as patron of many human arts and skills.

This down-to-earth interaction with the gods resulted in crediting them with complex functions.

The Complex Functions of the Major Gods

Geographically, Greece is a divided land, with small valleys and plains, each hedged in by mountains or straitened between a semi-circle of hills and the "unharvested" sea. Unlike Egypt and Mesopotamia, which threw people together, Greece separated them. So that before the northern invasions, the primitive or superstitious inhabitants of Helladic Greece worshiped in their isolated territories many nature-spirits, sought the aid of a variety of fertility-powers, and engaged in diverse rites connected with magic, taboo, and the cult of the dead. The northerners who came flooding in not only imposed a new language and a certain hearty cheerfulness, but uniformity in the names of the gods, and thenceforth the

Zeus enthroned. The king of the gods sits in majesty on his throne and raises his hand aloft as if holding a scepter. He is pronouncing a judgment that he expects his hearers to accept without demur. (Courtesy, Museum of Fine Arts, Boston.)

chief gods and goddesses were identified with the local powers which could in anywise be absorbed by them, taking over their functions, rites, and histories, while also adding their own qualities.

Then, and for a long time later, the chief developments in religion occurred in cities (or city-states), each with its own public cult and its own calendar of religious ceremonies and festivals. The great gods may be said to have come to the towns as "the real thing" and were accepted there as identical with the gods and godlings that had been locally known for many generations under local names. Amalgamation therefore took place within each local tradition.

Zeus is an instructive instance of how an invader's god takes over the duties of local divinities. Because he began as the great sky-father, ruler of the upper air and the giver of rains, as he made his way through Greece he was identified with many mountain tops. Not only was he Zeus of Olympus, but Zeus Lykaios in Arcadia, Zeus Laphystios in southern Thessaly, and Zeus Kithairon in Boeotia. But he also assumed other, down-to-earth duties. He was the god of fertility in many districts, and in at least three places a deity of the underworld. As Zeus Polieus he was the guardian of several city-states. As Zeus Aphiktor he was the united cry of the suppliants, itself become deity and forcibly beating its way to heaven. At Athens he was Zeus Phratrios, and received on his altar the votes cast by the members of the phratry when a father brought his child for enrollment. At Dodona he spoke oracles through the murmuring leaves of the sanctuary oak. Generally, of course, he was the Cloud-Compeller, the Rain-Maker, carrying his bright thunderbolt, hurled amid earthshaking tremors, but the thunderbolt sometimes had the judicial use of punishing the wickedness of men. The source of genius, his offspring by goddesses and women was numerous; he fathered a large progeny of heroes, kings, and founders of cities.* Nor was Hera his first wife. When he first arrived in the north at Dodona, he brought with him out of the unknown past a consort called Dione,

* Deification of heroes and kings was widespread in the Hellenic world.

and in other places he had other wives. But Hera was destined to become his permanent spouse.

Hera is an instance from the other side—the side of the conquered. She brought to her union with Zeus a past of her own. It was at least as respectable as his. Her origins are obscure and dateless. Because the cow plays an important part in early legends about her, she may originally have been a cow-goddess. In Mycenaean times she was the Argive Korê (Maiden), and sported in more than sisterly fashion on the plains of Peloponnesian Argos with Hercules, the strong young hero of that section. But she was also connected, by myth at any rate, with Argos in Thessaly, where as a matronly friend she helped Jason, another strong young hero, to launch the ship Argo, when he set out from Pagasae in search of the Golden Fleece. She seems not to have been at that time the goddess of the earth, but a majestic maiden identified with the passage of the year. For her sake Zeus parted with Dione and became her heavy-browed consort. They had their troubles. In accounting for their early quarrels, Jane Harrison has advanced the interesting theory: "The marriage of Zeus and Hera reflects the subjugation of the indigenous people by incoming Northerners. Only thus can we account for the fact that the divine husband and wife are in constant unseemly conflict. Of course, a human motive is alleged; Hera is jealous, Zeus in constant exasperation. But the real reason is racial conflict."[N] Perhaps this explanation will do, or perhaps another: she was the queen of the hinterlands and of backward mountaineers among whom the primitive matrilinear tradition persisted, and Zeus, the lord of the patrilinear northerners, married her to win a footing. However this may be, their marriage was not long unhappy. It was later declared a great success and became in Greek eyes a "holy union," the very ideal of married existence. Hera became the patroness of married women, their counselor and example.

In the person of Apollo an even greater yoking of diverse functions is seen. He was probably not Hellenic. In the *Iliad*, at least, he is on the side not of the Greeks but of the Trojans, an implacable and feared foe of the "bronze-clad" warriors besieging Troy. Perhaps, as the myths suggest, he was originally from the island of Delos, or else from the plains of Asia Minor. His origin cannot be surely traced. Very early he stood for pastoral and agricultural interests. Certainly he was not originally a sun-god. He was a shepherd for Laomedon near Troy and for Admetos in Thessaly. He may once have been a wolf-god, but as shepherd he protected his flocks and herds from the fangs of his lupine brethren. In agricultural areas, groves and trees were under his protection; the laurel was sacred to him. Out of pastoral love of song, he drew to him with his lively playing on the lyre devoted youths and maidens. He heartily believed in youth, and was the sponsor of athletic contests, himself drawing a strong bow. He was Hekatebolos, "the shooter from afar."

> Behind his shoulders hung
> His bow, and ample quiver; at his back
> Rattled the fateful arrows as he mov'd.[P1]

His arrows not only drew blood but pierced men with deadly sicknesses. (He was also the god of healing until he was displaced by his son Aesculapius.) He slew on the slopes of Mt. Parnassus in Greece the Python, whom he then displaced at Delphi. (Like Zeus he displaced and absorbed many local spirits.) His exploit at Delphi was an important act, with far-reaching results in the development of Greek religion, for as a consequence of it he became the god of revelation. No other god was the source of such direct oracles except Zeus. In the center of his temple at Delphi was the famous vent in the earth, from which issued from time to time an intoxicating vapor, and when the priestess, called Pythia, sat on the tripod amid the fumes, she muttered words that were universally thought to be from Apollo. It was in this belief that for centuries the famous men of Greece journeyed

> to Delphi, where
> Phoebus, on earth's mid navel o'er the world
> Enthroned, weaveth in eternal song
> The sooth of all that is or is to be.[Q]

57

Model of Delphi about 160 A.D. *The temple of Apollo, Parthenon-like, dominates the scene in this suggested restoration of the famed seat of the priestesses who uttered the "Delphic oracles." Five hundred years earlier, Socrates came to Delphi when there were fewer buildings and less wealth, but perhaps more belief. (The Metropolitan Museum of Art, Dodge Fund, 1930.)*

He was often asked for an oracle before a town was founded, and afterwards became its patron. Not until very late, and then perhaps as the result of Egyptian or other foreign influence, was he identified with Helios, the sun, who drives his golden car from heaven's eastern gates to the dim regions of the night.

The story of the other deities is similar. Artemis, the virginal deity of the wild, ranging through the mountains and forests with her nymphs in maidenly reserve, but thoroughly at home with the untamed animals of her domain, was also the gentle lover of children, the protectress of men and maidens, and the solicitous friend who sought to ease the pangs of childbirth. Curiously, in Ionia, where she was a favorite, she became the Artemis of Ephesus, a motherly goddess, her front covered with breasts. Hermes, who came from deep in the pre-Hellenic period, outgrew his earliest symbol, a simple cairn of stones such as peasants in the rock-strewn land raised at the edges and corners of fields and associated with their dead.* After he became identified with a square stone pillar, called the *herma*, sometimes surmounted with his head, he was, as it were, pulled up out of the ground, where he had stood immovable, and given wingèd feet. He led the spirits of the dead down to Hades, and as the swift messenger between Zeus and the earth below, was clothed in a long belted chiton and made to wear a cap or a broad-rimmed hat and wingèd boots. Other gods showed a like complexity of function: Poseidon was god of the sea, but was originally a horse-god guarding inland lakes and streams (was he driven into the sea by invaders?); Athena, the wise and virginal warrior-maiden, was originally perhaps an owl-goddess (for the owl was sacred to her, and she herself turned on occasion into a bird disappearing upward into the sky); Demeter, goddess of the fertile soil, was, as mother of slender and beauteous Persephone (the Korê, the Maiden), also connected with the underworld. In all these deities many local gods and spirits were absorbed and sublimated. Even Aphrodite, the goddess of love,

* How this came about is thus explained by M. P. Nilsson (*Greek Popular Religion,* Columbia University Press, 1940, p. 8): "If our (Greek) peasant passed a heap of stones, he might lay another stone upon it. If a tall stone was erected on top of the heap, he might place before it a bit of provision as an offering. He performed this act as a result of custom, without knowing the real reason for it, but he knew that a god was embodied in the stone heap and in the tall stone standing on top of it. . . . Our peasant or his forefathers knew that the stone heaps sometimes covered a dead man and that the stone erected on top was a tombstone. Accordingly, the god who dwelt in the stone heap had relations with the dead. . . . Perhaps our peasant wanted to look after his stock, which grazed on the meadows and mountain slopes. The god of the stone heaps was concerned with them, too." An additional fact was that cairns served in mountain tracts and elsewhere as waymarkers, and Hermes was thus thought to guide travelers to their destination.

a latecomer, perhaps the Western form of Ishtar of Babylon, was reborn from the foam of the sea, clear-skinned and delicate and beautiful, still a little amoral, yet shorn of the accompaniments of temple-prostitution and self-mutilation that attended the worship of her Oriental counterparts. Only Dionysus seemed unassimilable and untamed. (Further on, we shall see why.)

The Homeric Pantheon

It is time for us to consider the artful, intellectualized picture of the gods which Homer gives us, and to judge of its character and its effects.

In Homer the gods no longer live in widely separated places. Their common home is the acropolis on high Olympus, more a heavenly region now than the actual mountain top in Thessaly. There Zeus, the Cloud-Compeller, is kind, and white-armed Hera is his "golden-thronèd" queen. The other gods may absent themselves on occasion from their cloud-girt palaces, but usually Zeus must know where they have gone and what they have done. The gods, not without back-talk, submit to his discipline, for he is the father of most of them. His best-beloved daughter is grey-eyed Athena, the maiden goddess of wisdom. A favored son is Apollo, the archer-god, he of the flowing golden locks, who both heals and hurts. Artemis, "delighting in wild boars and swift hinds," is the shy daughter who often absents herself in the mountain fastnesses which she prefers. Ares, "piercer of shields," is the savagely warlike son whom Zeus at times scolds sternly:

> "Come no more to me,
> Thou wav'ring turncoat, with thy whining prayers:
> Of all the Gods who on Olympus dwell
> I hate thee most; for thou delight'st in nought
> But strife and war; thou hast inherited
> Thy mother, Hera's, proud, unbending mood,
> Whom I can scarce control."[P2]

Aphrodite, the enticing goddess of love, is a daughter of Zeus by Dione and is married to her half-brother, the lame god of the forge and the fire Hephaestus, a son of Zeus by Hera, but she is unfaithful to him, and has a notorious amour with Ares. Still another son of Zeus, born of his affair with Semele, is Dionysus, but in Homer he puts in an appearance and no more. Of greater importance is Hermes, the Heavenly Guide, whose birth was the consequence of the love of Zeus and Maia. He is primarily the herald and messenger of the gods, but he is sharp and cunning and not above consorting with thieves on those occasions when he gets away by himself, as when he departs from Olympus to guide souls to and from Hades. Poseidon, the god of the sea, and Hades (Pluto), the god of the underworld, are full brothers of Zeus, born like him of Kronos and Rhea, and Demeter is his sister by the same parents, but Homer does not have her come up to Olympus.

Here then is the tight-knit family group of the gods of Homer. On the whole they form a very aristocratic company. As gods they are in charge of natural forces, but not any longer such forces *themselves,* as they had been in earlier days. Their functions have been both sublimed and simplified. They are no longer primitive. The Minoan fetishes, the deities in animal form, the mother-goddesses, are gone. The Pelasgian involvements with animal and human fertility, or with vegetation, death, and the underworld have been largely refined out of them. Their personalities are no longer portentous with vague, mysterious force; they have come into the light of day and are sharply defined, clear-cut, distinct from one another. No two are alike. Indeed they are all but earthy men and women, with thoughts, desires, moods, and passions all too human. Though immortal, they are no longer incalculable and unknown and terrible. Aesthetically, they are attractive, charming, amusing, civilized, better proportioned and more beautiful than humans—they were indeed Homer's priceless gift to the future artists of Greece. In marble and bronze, their stately, poised, and unblemished bodies were in time to rise in market-places and on acropolises, their wondrous heads gazing calmly down from the pediments and pedestals of temples, lordly and aloof, as

from another and more perfect world. Mortals could look at them only with wonder and envy.

And yet the awesome quality, which makes gods bear in their persons a *mysterium tremendum,* had left them!

Perhaps the last sentence is a little overstated. The gods in Homer do exert supernatural effects, for when Zeus nods, all Olympus shakes, and once when Poseidon hurried to Olympus in three immense strides,

> Beneath th' immortal feet of Ocean's Lord
> Quak'd the huge mountain and the shadowy wood.[P3]

Poseidon's cry—and that of every god—is thunderous

> As of nine thousand or ten thousand men,
> In deadly combat meeting, is the shout.[P4]

The gods also have great power over human lives, whether for bane or blessing. By their will cities fall, men die, and armies fail. Men know they must go through the traditional rituals of sacrifice on every important occasion, or feel the grim wrath of the waiting gods. Aeneas, inside Troy, is sure the gods are angry with the Trojans for neglecting their sacrifices. As for the Greeks, because the builders failed to make the usual sacrifices, the "firm-built" wall they raised to guard their ships before Troy scarcely lasted out their need of it. Zeus watches over men's morals, too. In one lone but significant passage in the *Iliad* he is seen pouring down

> his fiercest storms in wrath to men,
> Who in their courts unrighteous judgments pass,
> And justice yield to lawless violence,
> The wrath of Heav'n despising.[P5]

But yet, with all this, the might of the gods is gravely limited. There is something more powerful than they, to which even Zeus, the Cloud-Compeller himself, submits, though he could change it by the power of his will. This is Moira or Fate, the relentless force of destiny. It does not stand alone; with it operate vague powers—Blind Folly, Terror, Strife, Turmoil, Rumor, Death. Everything considered, powerful though they are, the gods are contained within the total frame of Nature and History, like men. Though they are superhuman beings, their powers are not boundless.

The Homeric epics had a great influence in guiding the imagination of the Greeks. Recited not only to and for the aristocracy, as was first the case, but also to the masses of the people at festivals and general assemblies, they became an essential element in the education of Greek youth. And they helped to bring about a sense of unification among the Greeks, culturally and religiously. That is to say, they created a sense among the Greeks that in religion and culture all Hellas was one. And yet Homer was more satisfying for political than for religious reasons. It may be doubted whether in actual local worship, in prayer and sacrifice, the aesthetically pleasing Homeric pantheon won the people even a little away from their ancient loyalties—and interests.

Hesiod's Theogony and Everyday Religion

Hesiod (eighth century B.C.) did no better. In a characteristic effort of Greek rationalism he tried to bring the gods into some semblance of order by raising the question of their origin (theogony).

Influenced perhaps by Near-Eastern attempts in this direction, he declared in his *Theogony* that the pristine Chaos had given room or place to Earth (Gaea or Ge), Tartarus (the Pit), and Eros (Love). Chaos itself produced Night and Darkness, and they, in turn, by the power of love, mated to bring forth Day and Air. Without a mating, Night gave issue to Sleep, Dream, Death, Old Age, Misery, Friendship, and Discord. Similarly, Discord of herself gave birth to Hunger, Toil, Murder, Battle, and other forms of human strain and struggle, while Earth brought into being unaided Heaven (Ouranos or Uranus), the Mountains, and the Ocean. Mating with Ocean, Earth

produced creatures of the sea, and taking as husband Ouranos, conceived the first great gods but was unable to give birth to them because Ouranos prevented his children from emerging from the mother. With her aid, however, Kronos came forth, stole upon his sleeping father, and castrated him with a sickle. The flowing blood impregnated Earth, and she brought forth the Furies (Erinyes), the Titans (Giants), and certain nymphs, while from the sea foam forming around the castrated members sprang Aphrodite, the goddess of love. The triumphant Kronos married his sister Rhea, who had now been born, but fearing overthrow himself, swallowed his children as they were born. Then Rhea, with the help of grandmother Earth, substituted a stone for Zeus, the last born, and Kronos swallowed it unknowing. Zeus was hidden by his grandmother in a cave in Crete and finally emerged to subdue his father and force him to disgorge the young gods and goddesses he had swallowed. Thereafter Zeus began his reign as king of the gods.

This was Hesiod's attempt to bring rational order out of mythological chaos, but although he satisfied the Greeks theologically, he did not alter much the day-to-day practice of religion, which still approached chaos.

The day-to-day observance of religion by the common folk of Greece was mainly a matter of household pieties and attendance at public ceremony. The man in the country was concerned with Pan, the pasturer (a frisky male with horns, pointed ears, a tail, and goat's feet), Demeter, the earth-mother, Hermes ("he of the stone-heap"), *daimons* (spirits full of *mana*, sometimes closer than a brother—Socrates had one), ghosts, omens, taboos, magic (by which to lay ghosts and to promote the fertility of the fields, the livestock, and womankind), "heroes" (the noble dead), and chthonian deities, deep underground, to be appeased in fear. Meanwhile, the man in the town, besides adhering to the religion and magic of the household, attended the city festivals that honored the greater gods of the pantheon. To these we turn next.

The Athenian Festivals

We know most, although not enough, about the festivals of Athens, some thirty of them. The very months of the year took their names from centrally important ones.

By and large the Athenians thought of their deities by seasons of the year. Apollo and Athena were honored principally in the summer and fall, Demeter and her daughter in late summer and fall, Dionysus and Artemis in the spring. Zeus was an exception in receiving public honors all year round, he being capable of manifold functions.

The official year began in summer with a great sacrifice to Apollo, called the Hecatombaion because a hundred head of cattle were supposed to be offered up. Just before summer (May) the Thargelia honored him with a purification rite in which two filthy men, draped with black and yellow dried figs, were chased through the streets and driven as scapegoats from the city. In late summer and early fall three other festivals celebrated his power to promote neighborliness, raise up "helpers," and give aid to agriculture.

Athena, a patroness of the city, received highest honors during the Panathenaea, held every year, but every fourth year with special pageantry, to celebrate her "birthday." Performed in mid-summer, it was one of the great festivals of the city. A long procession carried a newly embroidered mantle, mounted like a sail on a ship on wheels, to her image on the Acropolis. There were accompanying sacrifices and games. Earlier in the summer each year the Kallynteria and Plynteria purified both her temple and the city and carried an ancient image of her to the sea to be bathed.

Demeter and her daughter Persephone received honor in later summer and fall at no less than five city festivals. The first in time was the Eleusinia (not to be confused with the Eleusinian mysteries); it was held every two years and with great splendor every fourth year. In the course of its games the prize given to the winning athletes was barley from one of Demeter's holy fields, the Rarian Plain.* The other festivals (the Proerosia, Thesmophoria, Haloa, and Skirophoria) included a magic ploughing, a seeding of the earth with suckling pigs and sacred cakes (a kind of fertility magic), and a magical ritual during which worthy matrons made broad jokes to encourage the fertility-powers.

The greatest of the spring festivals, the Diasia, was in honor of Zeus. It included a *holocaust,* the Greek word for a whole-burnt offering. Hera was honored along with him in January during the Gamelia, which celebrated their "holy marriage," and there were two other festivals, one in November, another in July.

Artemis' connection with animals received notice at three fertility festivals in the spring. But the great god of the season was Dionysus. In April or May the Great Dionysia took six days to perform. It had, and still has, great literary importance, because it was the occasion for the performance, under the supervision of the priest of Dionysus, of the immortal tragedies of Aeschylus, Sophocles, and Euripides and the comedies of Aristophanes. Religion and art were here memorably combined.

Of the other festivals honoring other gods there is no room to tell. Enough has been said to indicate with what the public ceremonies were concerned.† Not only was magic literally involved; there was a finer and higher magic in the poetry and drama of the splendid rituals.

The Mystery Religions

The transitional developments are only dimly known to us, but after the heroic (or Achaean) age

---

* Games in connection with religious festivals and also at funerals were as old as Homer's Achaeans. There were Pan-Hellenic festivals whose games or "meets" are world famous: the Olympic Games held at Olympia in Elis, the Pythian Games at Delphi, the Isthmian Games at the Isthmus of Corinth, and the Nemean Games at Zeus's shrine at Nemea. The first and last were in honor of Zeus; the second honored Apollo, the third Poseidon.

† Of the ceremonies of the famous Eleusinian mysteries there is more to tell in the next section.

had receded into the past and the Homeric pantheon had been established throughout Greece as the group-standard for conceiving of the appearance and behavior of the gods, an excitingly satisfying way for the Greeks to *feel* the gods within them, and thus to share in their immortal nature, made its appearance. This was the way of the mysteries—a way that offered to individuals private and personal religious satisfactions and assurances not provided by the official public sacrifices to the gods.

So ardent indeed became the devotees of these cults that they practiced their rites even when great public crises impended and average citizens were thinking only of the common danger. Herodotus in a famous passage tells of a rapt group that pursued the Eleusinian rites even while Attica was being ravaged by the land army of Xerxes and the Greeks hovering off the coast were debating whether or not to hazard their fleet at Salamis. Witnesses on the Persian side were filled with superstitious dread, Herodotus says, when they saw the procession of the devotees going along the sacred way from Eleusis toward Athens, raising "a cloud of dust such as a host of thirty thousand men might raise," and singing the mystic hymn to Dionysus. One said to another:

"Demaretus, it is certain that some great calamity will fall upon the king's host. For, since Attica is deserted, manifestly it is something more than mortal, coming from Eleusis to avenge the Athenians and their allies. If it descends upon the Peloponnese, there will be peril for the king himself and his land army; but if it turns towards the ships at Salamis, the king will be in danger of losing his fleet. This feast is held by the Athenians every year for the Mother and the Maid, and any Athenian or other Greek who wishes is initiated. The sound you hear is the song of Iacchos * which they sing at this festival."

And Demaretus answered:

"Hold your peace and tell no man of this matter, for if these words should come to the king's ears, you will lose your head, and neither I nor any man living will be able to save you."[R1]

* A name of Dionysus.

The mysteries were so called because they were rites which were kept secret from all except the initiates. Under the guidance of a hierophant ("the revealer of holy things") the candidates underwent: (1) a preparatory purification, such as a procession to the sea and washing in it, (2) instruction in mystic knowledge, usually given behind closed doors in a mystic hall, (3) a solemn beholding of sacred objects, followed by (4) the enactment of a divine story, generally in the form of a pageant or play, in which the cult divinities were impersonated, and (5) a crowning or wreathing of each of the candidates as full-fledged initiates. Accompanying these acts, which might spread over a number of days, were processions and sacred revels, including night-long ceremonies, which afforded simultaneously a release of tension and a deepening of the sense of mystic participation in supersensible realities.

The oldest and most restrained of the mysteries was the Eleusinian. The central figures in the rites were Demeter and her daughter, the Korê. As everyone knew, the Korê had been snatched away to the underworld by Hades (Pluto), that she might be his bride, but her mother, through long days of searching and mourning, had refused to make the corn grow, and at last Zeus bade Hades allow the maiden to return to earth. But the unwary maiden had eaten a pomegranate seed, cunningly given her by Hades, and when, as the hymn that has come to us from the seventh century B.C. relates, her anxious mother asked:

"Child, hast thou eaten of any food in the world below?
Tell me; for if not,
Then mayest thou dwell beside me and Father Zeus,
Honored among all the Immortals;
But if thou hast,
Thou must go back again into the secret places of the earth
And dwell there a third part of every year,
And whensoever the earth blossoms with all sweet flowers of spring,
Then from the misty darkness thou shalt rise and come again,
A marvel to gods and men,"[R2]

alas, Persephone had to confess she had done that which required her annual return to the underworld.

The entire story of Demeter and the Maiden was elaborately re-enacted, mostly by women. At some time Dionysus, as Demeter's associate (he being the god of vegetation and the vine), was introduced into the story; it is not clear when. The mystery itself was withheld from public knowledge, but the whole of Athens could see the parade to the sea to bathe the candidates, and any citizen could also witness the procession along the sacred way from Athens to Eleusis bearing along the image of the young Dionysus (Iacchos). The participants hoped to obtain a "better lot," a more glorious immortality in the next world, this, apparently, not as a reward of virtue, but rather by assimilation of the resurrective powers of Demeter, the Korê, and Dionysus.* According to the hymn quoted above:

Blessed among men upon earth is he who has seen these
    things;
But he that is uninitiate in the rites and thus has no part
    in them
Has never an equal lot in the cold place of darkness.[R3]

The decorous Eleusinian mystery cult was far surpassed in violence and excitement by the practices of the Dionysiac cult. These had a Thraco-Phrygian origin and construed the intoxication that followed the ritual use of the wine of Dionysus as possession by the god. Added excitement was provided by sacramental communion with the god in the eating of the flesh and the drinking of the blood of a kid or a bull identified with him and actually torn asunder—a rite called omophagia. All Greece was familiar with the Dionysiac *maenads* (or Bacchae)—women, maddened by divine possession, "rushing" or "raging" in

the frenzy of tearing at the sacred animal—and knew, too, of the sad fate of Orpheus, the inventor of the mysteries of Dionysus, who, become himself the victim of the rite of omophagia, was torn to pieces by the maenads in Thrace, when in grief at his second loss of Eurydice he paid them no heed.

But if the Dionysiac cult remained incurably wild, its mild Orphic offshoot, whose conventicles spread throughout the Mediterranean world—or wherever Greeks were—including Southern Italy, Crete, and Cyprus, had this to commend it: by eating the raw flesh of the suffering and dying god (Zagreus-Dionysus), the initiate might strengthen the divine element in him; by following the Orphic rules of purity, wearing white garments, abstaining from all meat (except that of the god in the mystery), avoiding the breaking of taboos against sex indulgence and pollution, and being generally ascetic, as Orphism demanded, he might refine the evil out of him and avoid going to the place of punishment after death. More positively, by being worthy he might hope to enjoy a better lot in the next world and at the same time increase his sense of spiritual security in this. Ultimately, he might altogether escape the necessity of rebirth, in which the Orphics believed, and go to the Isles of the Blest.

That these ideas should have had a part in the development of one of the great schools of Greek philosophy may seem at first sight surprising. But it is true that in the philosophic brotherhood that Pythagoras founded the Orphic coloring was strong. The Pythagorean brothers believed that the major task of one's life is to purify the soul, and by following Orpheus (or perhaps Apollo) they hoped to bring their souls into a state of serenity, understanding, and godlike poise. Their studies in medicine, music, astronomy, mathematics, and pure philosophy were designed to nourish in their souls the divine elements, so that they would not hereafter have to suffer transmigration from earth-body to earth-body, but could regain a spiritual state of purity and insight.

This was not the only case of the search in Greek thought for higher ground.

---

* That this nonmoral hope shocked even the Greeks is evident in Plutarch's preservation of a comment attributed to Diogenes the Cynic: "Is Pataikion the thief going to have a 'better lot' after death than Epaminondas, just because he was initiated?" (Cornford, *Greek Religious Thought from Homer to the Age of Alexander*, p. 51). Reprinted by permission of J. M. Dent and Sons, publishers.

Greek Religion and the Tragic Poets

The tragedies of Aeschylus, Sophocles, and Euripides revolve upon the awful theme that man's disasters are the doom brought upon him by the gods. This is what the myths long had said, but it was not always clear whether the gods were impelled by a just purpose, by sheer willfulness, or by the decrees of an inexorable Fate to which even gods are, willy-nilly, the ministrants. The great dramatists addressed themselves to the human problems that this confusion raises, and in so doing produced passages of moral and religious reflection that have no parallel in ancient literature outside the powerful utterances of the Old Testament prophets.

In the fifth century Aeschylus and Sophocles more or less followed the poet Pindar in exalting Zeus to the moral height of being the administrator of a cosmic justice. The other deities continue to exist alongside of Zeus, but they yield at once to his will when he overrules them in the name of the justice he is imposing. No longer is Fate blind. Aeschylus, in general, places Zeus in the superior position of either commanding Fate or being served by it. It is therefore really Zeus who dispatches the avenging Furies who punish the sins of man, ever continuing and multiplying from generation to generation among the wrongdoers. Aeschylus' great trilogy, the *Oresteia*, indeed vigorously declares:

> Zeus, the high god!—whate'er be dim in doubt,
>   This can our thought track out—
> The blow that fells the sinner is of God,
>   And as he wills, the rod
> Of vengeance smiteth sore. . . .
>
> For not forgetful is the high gods' doom
>   Against the sons of carnage: all too long
> Seems the unjust to prosper and be strong,
>   Till the dark Furies come,
> And smite with stern reversal all his home,
>   Down into dim obstruction—he is gone,
> And help and hope, among the lost, is none![S]

Though in *Prometheus Bound* the tortured titan who is its central figure defies Zeus as unjust, it is evident that Aeschylus thought that Zeus had learned something from this encounter, and was in no doubt that the king of the gods should now be approached with utmost piety as the righteous moral governor of the world.

Sophocles, the wise, tender-hearted, and supremely poised, gave to the character of Zeus some of his own humanity of feeling. Following some hints supplied by Aeschylus, who, however, in general makes Zeus stern and fearsome in his moral fervor, Sophocles softens the great god's judgments with mercy. He makes Polynices, for instance, in *Oedipus at Colonos*, begin his final plea to his royal father by reminding him that Clemency sits by the side of Zeus, sharing his throne and entering into all his decisions, a fact that should influence earthly potentates and make them more merciful. Yet Sophocles, also, is sure that the favor of Zeus is not easily gained, for one must be pure in word and deed, as Zeus indeed wills from on high, if he is to experience at all the divine clemency.

Euripides, a generation later, filled with doubts that had perhaps been raised in his mind by the Sophists or by such bold minds as Anaxagoras, lifts his voice with less conviction in behalf of obedience to the gods. Although it is a difficult thing for us to decide when Euripides is putting words into the mouths of his characters and when he is speaking his own mind, it seems certain that he had come to question the justice and integrity, if not of Zeus, at least of Apollo, Aphrodite, and others among the gods. Often he pities man, stricken and hurled to earth by the unpitying gods. He makes the proud and pure-hearted Hippolytus cry:

> Ah, pain, pain, pain!
> O unrighteous curse! . . .
> Thou, Zeus, dost see me? Yea, it is I;
> The proud and pure, the server of God,
> The white and shining in sanctity!
> To a visible death, to an open sod,
>   I walk my ways;
> And all the labor of saintly days
>   Lost, lost without meaning![T1]

Meanwhile a maiden of the chorus has already uttered the amazing reproof:

> Ye gods that did snare him,
> Lo, I cast in your faces
> My hate and my scorn![T2]

And the men have chanted in discouragement overwhelming their uncertain faith:

> Surely the thought of the Gods hath balm in it alway, to
>   win me
>   Far from my griefs; and a thought, deep in the dark
>   of my mind,
> Clings to a great Understanding. Yet all the spirit within
>   me
> Faints when I watch men's deeds matched with the
>   guerdon they find.
>
>   For Good comes in Evil's traces,
>   And the Evil the Good replaces;
>   And Life, 'mid the changing faces,
>   Wandereth weak and blind.[T3]

But Euripides was by no means a total disbeliever, it would seem. He was really seeking a notion of God purged of the misconceptions of mythology and tradition. His true voice perhaps comes to us in the groping words:

> Thou deep Base of the World, and thou high Throne
> Above the World, whoe'er thou art, unknown
> And hard of surmise, Chain of Things that be,
> Or Reason of our Reason; God, to thee
> I lift my praise, seeing the silent road
> That bringeth justice ere the end be trod
> To all that breathes and dies.[T4]

In this "strange prayer," as the poet himself calls it, the questing spirit of Euripides, like that of his philosophic contemporaries, seems to seek a new theology.

The Philosophers and the Gods

That the philosophers would go far beyond the Homeric point of view was clear from the start. Greek philosophy began as monism: everything in the universe is some form or other of one thing. Thales said this substance was water, Anaximenes that it was air, Heraclitus that it was fire, and Anaximander that it was an indeterminate somewhat. Whatever it was, it was creative or divine, they all agreed. Xenophanes was sure that the creative power was "one god greatest among gods and men, not like mortals in form, nor yet in mind. He sees all over, thinks all over, and hears all over."[R4] But men insist on seeing him in their likeness, and so have fallen into the anthropomorphic fallacy:

> Homer and Hesiod have ascribed to the gods all things that among men are a shame and a reproach—theft and adultery and deceiving one another.
> Mortals think that the gods are begotten, and wear clothes like their own, and have a voice and a form.
> If oxen or horses or lions had hands and could draw with them and make works of art as men do, horses would draw the shapes of gods like horses, oxen like oxen; each kind would represent their bodies just like their own forms.
> The Ethiopians say their gods are black and flat-nosed; the Thracians, that theirs are blue-eyed and red-haired.[R5]

Plato had a different criticism. In the *Republic,* where he considers the education of youth, he fears the moral ill-effects of teaching the Homeric myths in unexpurgated form.

> The narrative of Hephaestus binding Hera his mother, or how on another occasion Zeus sent him flying for taking her part when she was being beaten, and all the battles of the gods in Homer—these tales must not be admitted into our State, whether they are supposed to have an allegorical meaning or not. For a young person can not judge what is allegorical and what is literal; anything that he receives into his mind at that age is likely to become indelible and unalterable; and therefore it is most important that the tales which the young hear first should be models of virtuous thoughts.[U1]

A similar moral criticism is leveled by Plato against the mystery religions. The trouble with the mysteries is that they do not recommend justice for the sake of justice; they practice virtue for the sake of the rewards it brings, the "shower of benefits which the heavens, as they say, rain upon the pious."

They produce a host of books written by Musaeus and Orpheus, according to which they perform their ritual, and persuade not only individuals, but whole cities, that expiations and atonements for sin may be made by sacrifices and amusements which fill a vacant hour; . . . the latter they call mysteries, and they redeem us from the pains of hell, but if we neglect them no one knows what awaits us.[U2]

Plato was far from denying the existence of the gods. But they were, he said, neither as wayward and fallible as Homer pictured them nor as easily swayed from impartial justice as the mysteries implied. They were true to, and dependent in function on, a higher power. There was above them, and behind all other beings and things, a Creator, or Artisan, who had identified himself with the highest of all values, the Good. He it was who in the beginning beheld the realm of ideal forms, which not even he created, and was inspired by them to make a world that participated in their structure and that, in mountains, plains, and seas, gods, men, and animals, bodied forth the good, the beautiful, and true in various degrees. As for man, he is a soul in a body, and his soul needs to grow toward the highest good, that it may no longer have to suffer continued rebirth but go into that state in which it may, like God, behold and enjoy forever the hierarchy of the ideal forms, in all their truth, beauty, and goodness. The gods, on their part, desire none of the superstitious worships and magical rituals that men have developed in their honor. They desire and expect only that each man shall engage in the proper tendance of his soul and seek the supreme good that the high god has set before him. Firm in these beliefs, Plato in old age contended that atheism or any assertion that God is indifferent to men or can be bought off by gifts or offerings should be treated as dangerous to society.

Much more could be said both of Plato and his fellow-philosophers. It is of great interest, for example, to see how Aristotle, at least in his earlier period, found no need in his philosophy for the traditional gods of the Greeks, but yet, in considering the highest kind of being, had to posit God the Prime Mover, that is, a being causing all the movements of celestial and terrestrial bodies by attraction toward himself, while being himself actually without motion. Aristotle, the Stoics, and the Neo-Platonists were as much emancipated as Plato from the confining bonds within which their lesser countrymen were straining toward a fuller, freer life and greater wisdom.

IV Rome

What we have found true of the religion of Greece is even more true of the religion of Rome: the literature of the classical period is not as it stands a good guide to early religious belief. The writings of the Romans we know best—those who flourished during the days of the late Republic and the early Empire—must be critically analyzed, that the references to the religion of early Rome may be isolated and given their proper value. For if we wish to form a true conception of early Roman religion, we must first lift off, as it were, the accumulated upper layers, representing the borrowings from Greek religion and thought and the more esoteric importations from Egypt and the Near East, and then proceed to look at the underlying ancient customs and rituals of the Latins.

Like its Greek counterpart, the Italian peninsula was inhabited at first by a non-Indo-European population. At some time early in the second millennium B.C. there occurred invasions from the north by Indo-European (initially Celtic) tribes. Late in this period these tribes crossed the Apennines and settled down along the Tiber and on the hills to the east. They came to be known as the Latins, and their territory as Latium. They were not, however, to be left in undisturbed possession. They were joined in the eighth century B.C. by a kindred people called the Sabines, who came down from the mountains to the east. Shortly before this, the territory to the north—historic Etruria—was settled by ship-borne * invaders from the eastern Mediterranean, the energetic Etruscans, who for so long were the chief enemies of the Romans and for a while dominated them completely. Incursions of foreigners occurred also in the far south, almost too far away at first for the Romans to pay any heed. These were the Greeks of Magna Graecia, who had come to southern Italy as a result of the Dorian invasions of southern Greece. Thus the Latins found themselves in the eighth century B.C. between the Etruscans on the north and the Greeks on the south, with what effects upon the development of their religious ideas and practices will soon appear.

At first Rome was one of the lesser Latin towns. Its rise to importance dates from the complete merging of its several communities on the famous seven hills and their enclosure in the sixth century B.C. by a long, stout encircling wall. Gradually the surrounding areas came under its control; at last Rome became the mistress of all Italy. By the close of the third century B.C. Carthaginian resistance to Roman dominance was broken, and the Roman imperium thereafter extended itself over the whole Mediterranean world. Thanks to able administration, Roman world-dominion promised to endure indefinitely.

Meanwhile, even as the treasures of the world were being poured into the lap of Rome, so also foreign cults were brought and added to the native deposit of religion. Let us trace out the history of this amalgamation or *sunoikismos*.

The Religion of Early Rome

The religion of early Rome had, like the city itself, humble beginnings. The chief holy places were at first outside its territory. Diana was worshiped in the grove of Aricia on Lake Nemi, her temple there being sacred for the whole Latin federation, and on the

* This is still hypothetical. That they were from the eastern Mediterranean seems indicated by their religion and art.

Alban hill to the east all Latium united in the festival in honor of Jupiter Latiaris.

In later times the Romans referred to the earliest strata of their religion as "the religion of Numa," as though their traditional law-giver, who could not have invented it, had prescribed it for them. It was a religion very close to magic, precise and scrupulous in its sacerdotalism, with much attention given to charms, taboos, and the reading of omens. Its most general feature was the attention it paid to supernatural forces or potencies called *numina* (sing. *numen*). This word had a meaning similar to that given in the South Seas to *mana* (see again p. 15). Numen meant a kind of potency beyond the ordinary. The gods possess it in abundance, and their power and greatness depend on how much of it they have. As the chief of the gods, Jupiter has more than the rest. But numen may be found elsewhere, too, in all sorts of things and places—boundary stones, groves of trees, running rivers, springs. Men also may possess it, particularly in groups or in families. Like the mana of the Pacific, it is transferable and may be conferred by a god upon a man, his house, his field, or his tools and weapons. Or, again, by making appropriate sacrifices men may impart increased numen to their gods—a very desirable outcome indeed if the gods are to have plenty of it to confer in return where it will do men the most good. The means by which gods and men maintain contact also have numen in them, as for instance altars, rituals, and priests.

This attention to numen as of central significance led the early Romans to assign to their gods and spirits a rather vague character. These were lacking in distinct personality, and even sometimes in distinguishable sex. To put it bluntly, "ancient Roman religion knew no mythical histories of personal gods, no genealogies, no marriages or children, no heroic legends, no worship of legendary heroes, no cosmogony, no conceptions of life in the underworld—in a word, nothing of that which Homer and Hesiod had so abundantly supplied for the Greeks."[V1] So little of distinct personality had the spirits and powers of the fields and the farmhouse that the early Romans generally regarded them simply as forms or functional expressions of numen to which descriptive or personal names were to be assigned only to distinguish them from each other. Consequently, they made no anthropomorphic images of them, had no pictures of them in their minds that they cared to draw on a wall or paint on a vase. It was only later that they learned from the Etruscans and the Greeks how to visualize and humanize their gods.

Perhaps this failure to personalize their deities was owing to their interest in the diverse functions of numen, analyzed out to their logical practical limits. The total logical scheme may well have intrigued the analytical powers of the Romans sufficiently to delay any imaginative attempts to invest the powers bearing these functions with individual characteristics and personal histories. Even when we grant that the priests may have everextended themselves in elaboration and systematization, we still have a unique situation, well worth our review.

A. The Religion of the Home and the Farm. The early Romans were mainly engaged in farming, home-making, child-raising, and war. When they desired success in farming, they turned to relevant sources of numen known to and named by them from of old: to Saturnus for sowing, to Ceres for growth of grain, to Consus for harvesting, and to Ops for safe storage of the grain. Tellus was the goddess of the tilled soil. Flora brought blossoms to field and bough, Pomona ripening to the fruit on the bough. Faunus presided over the woods, the Lares over the sown fields, the Pales over the open pasture where the livestock fed. Terminus was the numen of the boundary stone, Fons of the springs, and Volturnus of the running river. Regnant over all, Jupiter as great sky-father brought rain and sunshine.*

In home-making and child-raising there was a similar assignment of deity to locus of numen (the process seems not to have been the reverse). Janus was the numen in the door, defending the threshold, and Vesta, equally, if not more, ancient and important, was on the hearth, present, as was Hestia in faraway Greece, in the flame. It was the responsibility of the man of the house, as its priest, to be on good terms with Janus, and of the women to worship Vesta at her place on the hearth and present her with a portion of each meal before anyone ate. The Penates were the numina that presided over the cupboard, preserving its store of food from harm. At first indefinitely conceived, they were in later days identified with whoever was the patron deity of the home—Ceres, Juno, Jupiter, or someone else. More closely concerned with the history of the family, as a source of numen that exercised watch and ward over the whole household was the Lar Familiaris. Originally the Lares were guardians of the sown fields and of the crossroads, then more narrowly of the family estate, and finally of the household in particular, receiving from the family regular worship on the Calends, Nones, and Ides of every month. A potency hard to define exactly was the *genius*, the energy and vitality of each male, considered as the essence of his manhood. It was almost a separate being, a guardian and exterior power, resident both in the man and in his marriage bed. Each male revered and was expectant toward his genius, as was each female toward her corresponding *juno*, but special honor was paid to the Genius Paterfamilias, particularly on the birthday of the family's head. This genius was considered to be somehow symbolized by the house snake, a sort of double of the numen of the head of the house.

It should be emphasized, before we go on, that all

---

* As if this was not complete enough: "A much minuter subdivision of functions appears in the pontifical litanies called Indigitamenta. Thus the Flamen Cerealis [the priest of Ceres] invoked no less than twelve [minor] divinities who presided over the successive steps of the husbandman's labors, from the breaking of the ground to the storing of the grain: Vervactor, Redarator, Imporcitor, In-sitor, Obarator, Occator, Sarritor, Subruncinator, Messor, Convector, Conditor, Promitor, whose functions are connected respectively with the ploughing of the fallow, second ploughing, running the furrows, sowing, ploughing under, harrowing, hoeing, weeding, reaping, carting home, storing in the granary, and bringing out for use." George Foot Moore, *History of Religions* (Scribner's, 1913, Vol. I, p. 544). Reprinted by permission of the publishers.

these sources of numen were honored and propitiated by a great variety of ceremonies and festivals, whose essence consisted not so much in words as in acts, for in them religion was inextricably bound up with magic and taboo. Where we can recover enough of it for examination, the symbolism in these worshipful performances is usually transparently clear. The Romans wasted no time in vague sentimentality. A marked feature of all their rituals is their severely formal character. We find no suggestion of close person-to-person relationship. Although the word *religion* (from *religio*—binding fast in mutual obligation?) suggests close-knit relations, its practice was singularly free from affection. The ceremonies were matter-of-fact and markedly legal, a businesslike exchange of favors. For, since the character of the Roman was essentially practical:

His natural mental attitude was that of the lawyer. And so in his relation towards the divine beings whom he worshipped, all must be regulated by clearly understood principles and carried out with formal exactness. . . . Both sides are under obligation to fulfil their part: if the man has fulfilled "his bounden duty and service," the god must make his return: if he does not, either the cause lies in an unconscious failure on the human side to carry out the exact letter of the law, or else, if the god has really broken his contract, he has, as it were, put himself out of court and the man may seek aid elsewhere.[w]

Here lies the reason why in Roman ceremonies the omission or displacement of a single word in the ritual or any deviation in the correct behavior of the participants was believed to make the whole performance of no effect. Hence, too, the need of priests, for they alone could preserve the ceremonies intact from olden times and perform them without error, or, if they were not the performers, they alone could coach the lay officiants in the right procedure.

But all this was perhaps not so true of the religion of the farm and the home as it was of the religion of the state.

B. The Religion of the Roman State. The religion of the early Roman state was in essential respects the domestic cult nationalized. It was very well organized. The chief deities had priests (*flamines*) publicly assigned to them. But the state ceremonies were not always in their charge. In the time of the monarchy, the king was the chief priest and performed some important ceremonies. In all later periods magistrates frequently did the same, even though religious affairs were supposedly placed in the hands of the pontifices.*

On the publicly prescribed days set down on the state calendar, which came to number 104 days of each year, the priests of the various deities performed a long list of ceremonies and sacrifices. They went about their tasks meticulously and drily, whether anyone but themselves was on hand or not. There was really very much to which they must attend.†

* The pontifices formed the higher judicatory of the priesthood (the pontifical college) and were headed by the Pontifex Maximus. This last was an elected office of an executive character, and laymen might fill it. (Julius Caesar, for instance, did.)

† This is abundantly clear even in an abbreviated list of the sacred events of the calendar. Near the beginning and end of the old Roman year (which began in March), the Salii, who were the warlike priests of Mars, twice conducted the festival of Equirria, whose main event consisted in races of war-horses; and on the Ides of October they conducted another race, but this time the winning horse (assuredly full of numen) was solemnly sacrificed to Mars. The same priests on March 19 and October 19 performed a purification (lustration) of the arms of the Roman legions by a vigorous dance on the Campus Martius, in which, in an act of war magic, they brandished spears and clashed shields together fiercely, as an accompaniment to their chanting. On the 23rd of March and the 23rd of May they performed a lustration of the war-trumpets. But the greater proportion of ceremonies was not warlike; they had to do with the concerns of farmer and herdsman. On April 15th, during the Fordicidia, pregnant cows were sacrificed to Tellus, the goddess of the fields, in the hope that good crops might be assured by an increase of numen and that the ashes of the fetus, removed from the womb and buried by the vestal virgins, might prove effective in imparting fertility (numen) to the sheep in the later festival of the Parilia. The Parilia took place on April 21st, and was mainly intended to purify the sheep by making them jump through a ring of burning straw or laurel. Two days before, the Cerealia had been conducted by the priests of Ceres to promote by increase of numen the growth of the grain sown in the fields. A curious ceremony was held on April 25th in a

The question may well be raised, to what gods were all these state ceremonies dedicated? In some cases no special deities seem to have been involved. We have the list, however, of the state deities who were addressed on the other occasions. This list sounds strange indeed in the ears of those accustomed to think that Greek and Roman religion were like peas in a pod. Alphabetically listed, the deities are: "Anna Perenna, Carmenta, Carna, Ceres, Consus, Diva Angerona, Falacer, Faunus, Flora, (Fons), Furrina, Janus, Jupiter, Larenta, Lares, (? Lemures), Liber, Mars, Mater Matuta, Neptunus, Ops, Pales, (Palatua), Pomona, Portunus, Quirinus, (? Robigus), Saturnus, Tellus, (? Terminus), Vejovis, Vesta, Volcanus, Volturnus."[x]

The familiar names of Janus, Jupiter, Mars, Vesta, Neptune, and Vulcan appear, but Juno, Venus, Apollo, Minerva, and Mercury are absent. Of the names on the list, nothing is known any longer about Falacer and Furinna, although flamines were appointed to serve them. Others are hardly better known to us. Many dropped from public notice altogether in later days. Why is anybody's guess. We may note, however, a significant fact: that those that survived to enjoy later prominence were as important to the city as they had been to the country.

Jupiter (Diespiter or Diovis Pater = Father Jove) was of dateless origin. He is, of course, the Indo-European Dyaus Pitar, or Zeus Pater, and came over the mountains into Italy in the same manner as he entered Greece. As in Greece, he absorbed the functions of many local Italian gods. His most exalted title was Optimus Maximus. In consequence of being the god of lightning, thunder, and rain, he acquired the epithets Fulminator, Tonans, and Pluvius, and because he was the god of light, he was honored by having the days of the full moon made sacred to him. He predetermined the course of human affairs and gave men foregleams of coming events by signs in the heavens and the flight of birds, which the augurs were appointed to read; hence he was called Jove Prodigialis, the prodigy-sender. His lightning was often a judgment, a catastrophic punishment for evildoing, for he was the guardian of the laws of the state and of the sanctity of oaths. In Rome his temple was built on the Capitoline hill, whence he was called Jupiter Capitolinus. In later days, as the special protector of Rome, he shared in the imperial glories of that city and acquired such titles as Imperator, Invictus, Victor, and Praedator. He received the worship of the consuls of the Republic when they took up their offices. The celebrated "triumphs" of returning generals were spectacular processions winding to the shouts of the joyous populace through the city, carrying booty and captives to his temple.

Mars and Quirinus were the two war-gods. Mars, identified by the Greeks with Ares, was perhaps originally the protector of the fields and herds from inimical powers of any kind, animal, human, or superhuman. He became more and more associated with war as the Roman imperium was extended, and his original character changed. But the homely, protective nature of his early activity is seen in the description Cato has left us of the procession of a farmer and his family along his farm's boundary line, three times around, accompanied by a pig, sheep, and ox, the victims that were afterwards solemnly sacrificed.

---

grove five miles from Rome; it was the Robigalia, and during it a red dog was offered up in order to prevent red rust from endangering the grain crops. In May occurred the gloomy Lemuria to quiet the uneasy dead. In June nine days (June 7–15) were devoted to the Vestalia; in that period the women came bare-footed to the temple of Vesta with cakes that the vestal virgins then burned, and the temple and its storehouse were thoroughly cleansed against the day when the new harvest should be brought in. August had no less than six festivals devoted to the various phases of the harvest. There were six also in December, including the famous Saturnalia, when the people rejoiced together in the early winter and exchanged gifts (a pre-Christian sort of Christmas). The two festivals of January were followed by six in February. On February 15th came the Lupercalia, so well known from an incident in the life of Julius Caesar. It began with a sacrifice of goats and a dog, and was concluded when the Luperci, the priests in attendance, after cutting thongs from the skins of the sacrificial victims and thus increasing their numen, ran in two bands around the walls of the old Palatine settlement, striking the women as they went and thus curing any sterility.

During the sacrifice the farmer offered libations to Janus and Jupiter and prayed thus, like a lawyer:

Father Mars, I pray and beseech thee that thou mayest be propitious and of good will to me, our house and household, for which cause I have ordered the offering of pig, sheep, and ox to be led round my field, my land, and my farm, that thou mightest prevent, ward off and avert diseases, visible and invisible, barrenness and waste, accidents and bad weather; that thou wouldest suffer the crops and fruits of the earth, the vines and shrubs to wax great and prosper, that thou wouldest preserve the shepherds and their flocks in safety, and give prosperity and health to me and our house and household; for all these causes, for the lustration and purification of my farm, land, and field, as I have said, be thou enriched by the sacrifice of this offering of suckling pig, lamb, and calf.[Y]

In Rome, where a similar ceremony took place on the Campus Martius around an altar to the god that stood there, Mars' sacred symbols were the lance and shield, his sacred animal the wolf, and his servitors the Salii and the Flamen Martialis.

Of Quirinus we know almost nothing, except that he was the war-god of the community on the Quirinal, while Mars was from the Palatine. Quirinus was served by a flamen and had a festival dedicated to him that took place on February 17th (the Quirinalia). Perhaps he represented defense where Mars stood for offense, for he seems to have been the numen of assemblies or convocations.

Janus and Vesta were ritualistically linked together as the first and last deities invoked in any ceremony. Janus, as the keeper of the door, was invoked at the opening of almost anything. He was the god of beginnings, and thus of the first hour of the day, of the Calends of every month, and, in the calendar of later days, of the first month of the year (January). His original symbol in Rome was simply a gateway standing at the northeast corner of the Forum. It was under the king's charge, and later was assigned the services of a priest called the Rex Sacrorum, highest in dignity of all the priests. Like Vesta, Janus was not originally personalized; the door, opening and closing, was his only sign, just as the pure flame, guarded by the vestal virgins in the temple of Vesta, sufficed there to show forth the goddess.

Changes Due to Etruscan Influence

Though the facts are not entirely clear, it is certain that Rome came under Etruscan dominance during the whole of the sixth century B.C. There were some significant changes as a consequence. The Etruscans were energetic and commercial-minded. Recognizing the strategic position of Rome, they built a wall around it that enclosed enough space for a population of two hundred thousand. They sought to make residence in the city attractive to plebeians, and therefore favored them as against patricians. And they introduced some entirely new trends in Roman religion.

New deities were brought in, without seriously disturbing, at first, the old entrenched customs. Diana left her grove at Aricia for a temple erected to her on the Aventine. The triumvirate of Jupiter, Mars, and Quirinus was overshadowed by a well-housed triad composed of Jupiter, Juno, and Minerva, established on the Capitoline in a bright new temple of Etruscan workmanship.

The association of Jupiter and Juno, here begun, later led to their being regarded as husband and wife. This was the first clear instance of marriage among the Roman gods. The earlier Roman religion had furnished some instances of the yoking of male and female names, but this had signified so much less than marriage or family connection that scholars find in it only fresh evidence that the early Romans did not unambiguously know what sex their numina had: sometimes, to be safe, they gave them names signifying both sexes. But Juno became Jupiter's consort and thus took on much more of the aspects of distinct personality than before. Originally, she had simply imparted numen to women and girls (. . . as men had their genius, so women had their juno), and in the form of Juno Lucina she had been invoked at the moment of childbirth. Now she attained the characteristics that caused visiting Greeks to identify her with Hera.

Minerva may have been Etruscan. Her character paralleled that of Athena. She was the goddess of wisdom and the patroness of arts and trades. In due time her aid was sought in war; hence she was represented as wearing a helmet and a coat of mail, and she carried a spear and a shield in the manner of her Greek counterpart.

This visualizing of Minerva as an anthropomorphic deity points to an innovation of the Etruscans which was of the first importance. They set images of the gods in the temples they built. In the temple on the Capitoline, they erected two rows of columns down the center of the sanctuary, and at the northwestern end they placed three images—a statue of Jupiter flanked by one of Juno and another of Minerva. Here was the initial step that led to the imaging and personalizing of all the deities. Even Janus acquired a head—but with two faces, one looking forward and one back. But these changes were not purely Etruscan.

Borrowings from the Greeks

Just as the political power of Rome under the Etruscans was extending southward through Italy, Greek cultural influence began to penetrate northward. Especially impressive to the Romans was Greek ritual. It provided vital elements of warmth and poetry hitherto lacking in Roman religion. The Romans on their part proved ready to adopt many new conceptions offered by the Greeks, without meaning to abandon any of their old ways.

Of far-reaching moment was the introduction into Rome during the sixth century B.C. of a collection of oracles credited to the Cumaean Sibyl—the famous Sibylline Books. These books, stored in the basement of the Capitoline temple, were committed to a newly created order of patrician priests, two in number, the *duovi sacris faciundis* (later increased in number to ten, and still later to fifteen). These priests were asked on many grave occasions to consult the oracles; in each case they afterward announced, without revealing the verses consulted, the course of procedure that they said was advised. Because the oracles were of Greek origin, the Duovi usually prescribed as remedies for impending or present disaster, or for public perplexity, resort to deities and ceremonies not before known, except perhaps by report, to the Romans. As a result extensive adoptions into Roman religion took place.

It cannot be said that the Duovi suggested changes without precedent. Castor and Pollux had already been brought to Rome by way of the Latin town of Tusculum, and Hercules had also arrived by way of the town of Tiber. But the Sibylline Books gave impetus to a process which might otherwise have been slow. In 493 B.C. their verses were interpreted to advise the erection of a temple to house Ceres, Liber, and Libera (= Demeter, Dionysus, and Persephone). A temple for Apollo was next prescribed. Similarly, by identifying him with the Roman Neptune, Greek rites in honor of Poseidon were imported. Hermes came to Rome also, but under the name of Mercury, for he was to be the god of commerce (*mercatura*). Later, in much the same way, and with an accompanying Greek ritual, Aphrodite made her appearance as Venus (who had been a minor Italian deity, perhaps of the garden). About the same time, a pestilence led to the advice that Aesculapius, the god of healing, be introduced at once and provided with a temple. These fully personalized deities added an entirely new dimension to Roman religion.

Sometimes the Sibylline advisers suggested a *lectisternium*. Here the Greek ritual called for the introduction of a whole group of gods, appearing as wooden figures, elegantly attired and reclining on couches around a banquet table, on which was placed a sacramental meal! Livy reports that in 399 B.C., during a severe pestilence, Apollo, Latona, Hercules, Diana, Mercury, and Neptune were together propitiated in this manner. Nor was this the last time this rite was performed. The gods were becoming more human every day.

73

And as if stirred into original creation by these importations, the Romans added (or rather, resurrected from former times) new deities of their own: Fides to personalize the quality of loyalty celebrated in the title "Fidius" assigned to Jupiter, and Victoria to do the same for his qualities as Jupiter Victor. A goddess of luck and good fortune appeared also under the name of Fortuna. Each of these was given a separate temple within the city.

Along with all this came increased interest in the myths and epics of Greece. As a consequence, many of the Greek myths were adapted to the Italian scene and to Roman history and were reissued in new form, although most were simply taken over with slight change, to become part of the Roman heritage. The life histories of Jupiter, Juno, Minerva, and others were built up out of the Greek elements into stories ranging over an international scene but with an Italian coloring. At the same time inventive (if not supremely imaginative) minds fell to work on Roman traditions and elaborated Italian myths about Romulus and Remus, Aeneas, Tiberinus, and others. The way for Ovid and Vergil, the poets of the future, was thus prepared.

Importations from the Orient

So far, the additions to the old Roman beliefs were not out of keeping with the general cultural trends that had appeared in Roman life. But we come now to some that were more esoteric. When Rome was in the process of becoming an international power contending for supremacy in the Mediterranean world, she became conscious of cultures very different from her own. Her people, as they grew entirely away from the agricultural economy of the earlier days toward a completely urban and imperial point of view, became curious about these alien conceptions. Were they perhaps worth investigating? The old Roman religious procedures seemed more and more to fail them, or at least to be inadequate. As increasing numbers of Romans lost their rootage in the soil, and

with it the day-filling activities that had once given exercise and discipline to their emotions, they found their lives lacking in the satisfactions that prevent the sense of futility from engulfing the normal feeling that life has meaning and value. Scepticism began to run a race with the search for new and reassuring faiths.

Mystic cults, promising richer emotional satisfactions, came from the Orient. The first of these was that of the Magna Mater, Cybele, introduced from Phrygia on the advice of the Sibylline oracles. An embassy of five prominent Roman citizens went during the protracted crisis of the Second Punic War (218–201 B.C.) to fetch a sacred stone, dropped from heaven, in which Cybele was thought to be resident.

But the city fathers took a rather sober view, on closer acquaintance with Cybele, of the wildness and fanaticism of her devotees. They passed a law, which was not abrogated until the Empire, forbidding Romans to enter her priesthood, because it usually meant their castration; she had to be served by priests brought in from Asia Minor. The people, however, were allowed to, and did, go to her temple to seek her aid, for this life and the next.

Following upon Cybele's arrival came the mystery religion of Bacchus (Dionysus), with its secret rites. There was swift response to it, not only in Rome but throughout the Italian peninsula. But the upper classes hated secrecy of any kind and were highly suspicious of it; they came to believe the worst of the Bacchanalian orgies. Accordingly, the cult was suppressed by a decree of the Senate in 186 B.C. But it came to life again and was allowed to continue under the strict supervision of the state.

In the years that followed, other Eastern cults gained a footing and grew in influence. Ma of Cappadocia, Adonis of Syria, Isis and Osiris (Serapis) of Egypt, and Mithras of Persia were all brought to Rome, and each in some measure supplied the religious experience and the hope of immortality that the state religion, fallen now into the hands of agnostic politicians and of priests who also had lost faith, was powerless to call forth or sustain.

The Last Phases

The history of Roman religion during the last century of the Republic (150–49 B.C.) suggests the operation of forces moving in a direction exactly opposite to those of an earlier time. The movement was no longer centripetal, but centrifugal. The state religion had degenerated into pure formalism—the structure was there, but it was empty and void. For one thing, Rome was like a deity herself (Dea Roma) and no longer needed the help of the old gods in the old way. The educated classes, enlightened or disillusioned by Greek philosophy, pursued the atheistic way of the Epicureans, or the pantheistic way of the Stoics, or else lapsed into indifference. The attitude of Cicero was typical: he inclined toward Stoicism, but he was an eclectic and would commit himself nowhere because his scepticism prevented him. Religion was something to discuss pleasantly over the dinner table or with friends in a moment of leisure, but apart from its value as a political binding element, it was of no vital concern to a thinking man.

The attempt of Augustus Caesar to bring the world back to normal, after a generation of unnerving civil wars, by reviving the old Roman religious practices led him to repair the decaying temples of Rome, induce men to enter again the old priesthoods, and build new temples, such as that on the Palatine in honor of Apollo, the patron of his house. But this was not in itself sufficient. It affected Rome only, and even there it aroused only a mild response. He knew already how advantageous it was to him politically to be regarded outside of Italy as a god. The world needed to look to some one power, worship of which might bind it together, and perhaps none might be as useful for this purpose as the ongoing genius of the imperial house. To encourage this feeling, Augustus erected a temple in the Forum, furnished with specially appointed priests and dedicated to the honor of Divus Julius (Julius Caesar, his father by adoption), who had already been declared a god by the Roman senate in 42 B.C. As for himself, he permitted the erection of shrines in which his genius was worshiped (though not himself). This marked the beginning of emperor-worship. In the provinces it became mandatory, as a sign of loyalty to the Roman imperium, to pay reverence to the emperor's genius, and sometimes to the emperor himself. Although

The Pantheon, Rome. In the Emperor Hadrian's time this outstanding surviving example of Roman architecture was rebuilt as a rotunda to replace a probably rectangular temple constructed earlier for Agrippa. It was dedicated to the deities of the Julian house and was thus not really a shrine for all the gods of Rome, as the name of the temple might imply. (Courtesy of the Italian Government Travel Office.)

throughout life Augustus steadfastly refused honors to himself in person, it was inevitable that after his death his name should be enrolled with those of the gods and that a temple should be erected to him, with priests in attendance. Not all the emperors immediately after him were accorded this honor, but in due time consecration of the emperor as a god became part of every imperial funeral. At last the aura of divinity came to attach itself to emperors *before* death. Caligula and Domitian were two who demanded worship while living, and Nero before them is said to have enjoyed being equated with Apollo.

What is significant here is this: to have real unity, the Empire needed more than uniform laws and just government. There had to be also a unifying reverence, a common loyalty to what was central, a commitment to an all-highest. When it was apparent that the multiplicity of religions led only to centrifugal scattering, emperor-worship was conceived in an attempt to reverse the flight from the common center. But it was not enough; it just barely served. In a fundamental sense, it was not cosmic enough, not able to link together man, society, and universe under one inclusive meaning or purpose. It failed to rise above the dead level of the multiplying religious faiths of the Mediterranean world. Nor was there vital power in it to stir and change individuals.

But amalgamation of the gods, or any eclecticism on the grand scale, cannot perhaps arrive at a world-faith; the result is too complex. Dynamic qualities are, rather, engendered by simple faiths. At all events, in Rome, as in Egypt, Mesopotamia, and Greece, the national religion, the result of linkages and mergings of deities from far and near, proved to be merely provisional. After serving its purpose, it yielded to a greater, simpler, more vitally meaningful faith that came to take its place.

This was Christianity, a profound and meaningful way of linking together not only man and society, but man, his neighbor, and the universe, under one sovereign God. How it triumphed will be told later in this book.

V   Europe Beyond the Alps

In the early history of Greece and Rome we met with bands of southward-surging Indo-Europeans; in northern Europe we find them everywhere. (Later in our story we shall meet them also in India, Iran, and Armenia.) One of the great puzzles of history is where these people originated and what sent them on their far-flung journeys, radiating outward like the spokes of a wheel, south, west, north, and southeast. But whatever moved them from their prehistoric homeland (in southern Russia and the Ukraine?), they succeeded, thanks to their mastery of cavalry attack and the wielding of long two-handed swords from horseback, in subjugating not only the resident tribes in their path, outnumbered though they were, but in imposing on those they conquered their language and many elements of their magic and religion. The ancient Celts, Teutons, and Slavs developed religious practices and beliefs which, in spite of assimilation of many variant local conceptions and customs, nevertheless illustrate what the original Indo-European world-view might be expected to become when not radically altered by the infusion of foreign ways of behaving and believing.*

The Celts

We have already met the Celts in northern Italy. So far as we can determine from the uncertain records, the Celts moved originally from their first homeland to northwestern Germany, where they merged with proto-Nordic and Alpine tribes to form a new amalgam of ethnic groups marked by tall, green-eyed, red-haired men. Then they broke up by migrating westward across the Channel to the British Isles, southwestward into France (Gaul) and thence into Spain, southward into Italy and Greece, and far to the southeast into Asia Minor, where they held on

* We are now to see less amalgamation and syncretism and more heightening of central themes prior to a final disintegration.

for centuries to the province to which they gave their name (Galatia, the place of the Gauls).

The Celts, according to *The Commentaries* of Julius Caesar, worshiped most a god he identifies as Mercury, but he does not give us the Celtic name. He says they also worshiped Apollo, Mars, Jupiter, and Minerva. To this list he adds Dispater, god of the netherworld, to whom he says the Gauls traced their origin. He is joined by Tacitus, the Elder Pliny, and Lucan in the statement that the Celts were led by their priests (the Druids) in human sacrifice and animal- and tree-worship.*

* When seeking the Gallic and Irish equivalents of the Roman identifications we run into difficulties. Mars, for example, was equated in Roman inscriptions with more than fifty native gods, Mercury with some thirty others, Jupiter with some twenty-five more, Apollo with some twenty, and Minerva with a half-dozen or so. In other words, if the Celts originally had a pantheon—and we cannot say definitely that they had—history and experience had led them to substitute many names for the possible original few. What seems to have happened is that the Indo-Europeans adapted their pantheon and rituals to the older Bronze Age traditions which they found locally and which focused on fertility, death, and immortality.

The difficulties to one side, we can recover many of the names of the Gallic, Irish, and English deities. Prominent among the figures represented in the surviving remains is Cernunnos, a horned god shown sometimes with three heads or portrayed pouring out grain to a stag and a bull, evidently as a fertility deity; another god is Sucellos, always carrying a hammer, the symbol of thunder and lightning, but also bearing a cup in one hand, with a gesture of hospitality; Esus, still another, is pictured with an axe cutting branches from a tree; and fertility goddesses, such as Nantosuelta and Epona, are also mentioned. All these are from Gaul. In Ireland we hear of Dagda, "the great father"; of Lug, "inventor of all handicrafts"; of Brigit, also known in Gaul and England, goddess of wisdom and poetry; of Danu and Anu, earth-goddesses, and of others. England and Wales provide us with Andrasta, goddess of victory, Belenos, a sun god, Totatis, god of war, Lyr, god of the sea, and still others, many of them destined to be demoted with the coming of Christianity into legendary kings and queens. It is perhaps a dubious speculation which merges King Arthur, hero of the Brythons of lowland Scotland, with Artor, an English god, possibly of agriculture, or Artaios, a Gallic war god. Perhaps Gwenhwyfar (Guinevere) was first a white fairy, and Myrddin (Merlin) a divine magician, but more likely they were originally as human as Arthur was. We do not know.

The Celts found divinity in nature all around them, for they revered it in the sky, mountains, stones, trees, lakes, rivers, springs, the sea, and every kind of animal—the boar, the bear, the bull, the horse, the hare, the ram, the stag, even the crow, and many female as well as male creatures—the cow, for example. (The snake also received its share of regard, so that when St. Patrick came to Ireland, there grew the legend that he not only drove the ancient gods and goddesses into the hills and glens to serve a lower function as fairies, but also rid Ireland of snakes: in short, he could not tolerate veneration of them.) Some Celtic gods and goddesses were part animal and part human in shape. Others resembled Epona, the Gallic fertility goddess, who carried a cornucopia while on horseback or while seated among horses.

Another certain fact is that the Celts were much concerned with fertility in field, flock, and womankind. There were many fertility-powers, male and female, and a number of mother-goddesses. It was common to revere the last in groups of three and to portray them holding in their laps children or baskets of fruit in evidence of their influence on fruitfulness. Among the recurrent festivals and ceremonies of which the Celts were exceedingly fond was the May Day festival. It has survived in a token form as the Maypole dance still observed in Europe and America. The ancient Celtic festivals bore all the marks of fertility magic. It was a widespread practice to light bonfires on the hills about May 1st and then do the following things: drive cattle through or between them, have the people dance a sun dance around them, bring new fires from them to the home hearths, and then carry some of the burning brands around the fields like shining suns. It may have been a general practice to sacrifice an animal or a human being in the bonfires, as an invitation to the sun to recover its strength after the long somnolence of winter. There was also a May king and a May queen who symbolized, or were thought of as incarnations of, the vegetation spirits. It is likely that they were given in marriage to each other to stimulate fertility in soil and flock.

The human sacrifices we have incidentally mentioned shocked the Romans, who took immediate steps to suppress them. We learn that such sacrifices were made not only to promote fertility but more generally to appease, thank, or gain the help of the gods. Though innocent victims were sometimes chosen—wives or children, at times—it was more common to offer up prisoners of war or thieves and other criminals. Murderers, for example, were turned over to the Druids for sacrifice to the gods. The Roman authors tell us that the victims were sometimes slain beforehand by arrows or by stakes driven through their temples, but it was common first to build a large effigy of wicker or of wood and straw, then fill it with victims human and animal and have the Druids set it on fire. It may be assumed that such sacrifices were very special occasions and that ordinarily animal sacrifices were offered, men and dogs joining in the feast after the sacrifice, the dogs, as Arrian tells us of the Galatian Celts, being decked with garlands of flowers. In modified form some of these rites have come down to our own day. Carl Clemen offers us instances from France:

In the district round Grenoble to this day a goat is slaughtered at harvest-time. Its flesh, with the exception of one piece, which is kept for a year, is eaten by the reapers, and out of its skin the farmer has a coat made, which is believed to have healing virtue. In Pouilly an ox is killed, its skin being kept till the next seed-time. Undoubtedly these animals represent the spirit of vegetation. In former days in Brie on the 23rd of June, and down to the year 1743 in a certain street in Paris on the 3rd of July, a human effigy was burnt, the people fighting for the *debris.* . . . Finally, there are certain phrases still current in many districts of France which contain an allusion to the killing of a human being or an animal at harvest-time. When the last sheaf is being garnered or threshed the people say, "We are killing the old woman," or "the hare," "the dog," "the cat," or "the ox."ᵛ²

Frazer's *The Golden Bough* assembles hundreds of similar instances of the survival in Europe of ceremonies from a pre-Christian time.

The worship of the gods was performed with the aid of priests and priestesses both in temples and in homes, but perhaps the more important ceremonies were held in sacred groves under the direction of a special class of priests—the Druids. Caesar tells us that the Druids had political as well as religious functions. They played a role in the election of kings, served as ambassadors or legates, and took part in battles. Their teachings were preserved orally only and could not be learned without a long period of training, lasting sometimes up to twenty years. These teachings, according to Caesar, concerned not only religious and magical matters but also the movements of the stars, the size of the world, and the general constitution of the universe at large.

How true this may be cannot be known, but it does seem probable that the Druids speculated that the world would someday come to an end, that there would be a doomsday overwhelming men and gods, when fire and water would swallow up the earth, the sky would fall, and all men would perish, to make way for a new heaven and earth and a new race of men.

The Teutons

Appearing in history later than the Celts, the Teutons, who were of somewhat purer Indo-European stock, began to press westward from the southern shores of the Baltic as Anglo-Saxons and Jutes, southward as Saxons, Alamanni, Lombards, Frisians and Franks, northward as Scandinavians, and southeastward as Goths and Vandals.

Teutonic tradition comes to us chiefly by way of two Icelandic works, the *Poetic Edda,* an anthology of hymns to the gods and heroic poems, said to have been brought together by Saemundr the Wise (1056–1133), and the *Prose Edda,* the work of Snorri Sturleson, a thirteenth-century Christian, scholar, and sceptic, who tried to provide a practical manual for young poets who would wish to draw upon the traditional myths of Iceland for their material. Also important as authentic sources are the Norse sagas and scalds (poems), of which eight or ten are especially significant.

From these sources we get a rather crowded picture of a score of gods and goddesses, some ancient, some late, whom we must suppose to have come forward or receded in importance with passing time. It is possible that one of the oldest of the gods was Ziu (Tiu or Tyr), whose name has possibly the same root as Zeus, Jupiter, and the Dyaus Pitar of the Indo-Aryans. (The name appears again in the word of Anglo-Saxon descent *Tuesday*.) He was originally the shining sky but relinquished his high place, perhaps because there was more need of him on earth, to become a god of war. In contrast to him, Donar or Thor, the red-bearded god of thunder (*donner*) and rain, and therefore of agriculture, grew in importance with the years, becoming the center of a cult that spread throughout the Teutonic world. Carrying his famous hammer, Miollnir, in iron-gloved hands, he rode in a sky chariot drawn by two he-goats. He became the chief god in Norway and Iceland. (We now have his name in *Thursday*.) If Thor was popular with the common man, one-eyed Wodan or Odin (also Othin) was exalted by the ruling princes and war chiefs, for he was a god of war who protected heroes and sent his two Valkyries or war-maidens to carry warriors fallen in battle to his great hall in the sky, Valhalla. When traveling through the heavens, he galloped upon the eight-legged horse Sleipnir, accompanied by his wolves, Geri and Freki. In heaven he surveyed the world from the windows of Valaskialf, his home, supporting on either shoulder two ravens, Guggin (Thought) and Muninn (Memory), who whispered in his ear their reports of all that they had seen while in flight. His dreaded spear, Gungnir, made by dwarfs, never missed. Knowing and seeing all, he was the source of the wisdom of seers and poets. (We still honor him in our *Wednesday*.) Snorri of Iceland calls him the chief of the Aesir, the gods in heaven, who dominate the Vanir, the gods beneath. He is called All-Father, and he, as we shall see, assisted at the creation.

Three things seem to have concerned the Teutonic peoples greatly—fertility, death, and the end of the world. As to the first, they did not put all their reli-ance upon the life-quickening rain of Thor. They turned also to Freyr (Frey, Fricco), the "Lord" of fertility in man, animals, and vegetation, and therefore the god of summer, and to his sister and wife Freyja (the "Lady"). Freyr and Freyja were quite possibly son and daughter of the god of wealth, Njörd, or Njörth, and the goddess Nerthus, of whom Tacitus had so much to say[*]

Freyr and Freyja were the divine May king and May queen whose embrace brought the revival of life in spring. But the cycle of spring, summer, and autumn was symbolized by other gods and goddesses, the most notable of whom is Balder, whose tragic death (autumn?) is recorded in the well-known myth. Balder (the blessed Light) was the kindest, most noble and gentle of the gods. His mother Frigg, consort of Odin and queen of the gods (for whom *Friday* is named), took oaths from all things not to hurt him, but she neglected to pledge the mistletoe. Thinking Balder to be invulnerable, the gods had great sport throwing every kind of object at him, always without harming him, but Loki, the malicious one and trickster among the gods, learned that the mistletoe had not been sworn and persuaded the blind but powerful Hödr (Höther) to hurl a sprig of mistletoe at Balder, and he was slain. Balder perforce descended to Hel,[†] there to await liberation at the end of the world. We shall encounter him again.

Death was a disturbing thought to the Teutons, for it was too often only the beginning of troubles. Until the corpse of a man decayed, it could do harm as a specter or vampire (a belief the Norse shared

---

[*] Tacitus (*ca.* 100 A.D.) names as the highest of the Teutonic gods Mercury, Mars, and Hercules, and in this case we can identify the Teutonic originals as Wodan (or Odin), Ziu (or Tiu), and Donar (or Thor). The rites in honor of the goddess Nerthus are described by Tacitus in some detail and traced by him to their origin on the shores of the Baltic. This and other information supplied by Tacitus are a valuable confirmation of Teutonic tradition.

[†] Sometimes in the Eddas the underworld, Hel, is personified by Loki's daughter, Hel, a repulsive and dreadful creature who assigns to all who are sent to her their places in the underworld.

with the Chinese on the other side of the world), and the corpse itself was in danger of being torn to pieces by wolves out of hell, by horse-shaped demons, or by swooping eagles, such as the giant wind-demon Hraesvelg. On the other hand, the spirits of the dead, if they had been good in life and were faithfully reverenced after death, could bring good fortune to their descendants.

The convictions concerning the after-life seem confused. In later times the Teutons believed both that the dead lived on in their burial barrows and yet that they traveled nine days and nights by the Hel-way to the underworld, where they sat in the great hall of Hel on benches and drank beer (mead). But the warriors went to Valhalla—at least those whom Thor favored—and there they feasted on boar's flesh behind the 540 great doors of the shield-thatched hall, and then rose to fight each other in the courtyard for self-conditioning and for sport.

The reason why the warriors of Valhalla adopted a regimen of self-conditioning lay in their knowledge that Odin would need their services in the cosmic conflict that would take place at the time of the Doom of the Gods (the Götterdämmerung). At this point Teutonic thought reached a certain profundity —or was it no more than a dramatic view of time and history?

According to Snorri (in the *Prose Edda*), the first state of things, the Ginnunga Gap—a yawning gulf or opening suspended between a region of mist and cold, Niflheim, and a region of glowing heat, Muspelheim—generated from its rime and slush a cosmic giant, Ymir. In a similar way there also emerged a cosmic cow, Audumla, whose udders fed Ymir and made it possible for him to generate other beings. Presently from under the hands and feet of Ymir came the frost-giants; the cow Audumla also, while licking the salty ice to the north, de-iced and freed Buri, a giant who became the grandsire, through his son Bor and daughter-in-law Bestla, of Odin, Vili, and Ve. Rising against Ymir, Odin and his brothers slew and dismembered the primal giant, making the earth from his flesh, trees from his hair, mountains

from his bones, the earth-encompassing sea from his blood, clouds from his brain, and the bowl of heaven from his hollow skull. (The Hindus and the Chinese have similar stories to tell. See pp. 93 and 249.) From the sparks out of Muspelheim the sun, moon, and stars were formed. The three brothers then took the eyebrows of Ymir to make a raised plain, called Midgard, to be the abode of men, and from two trees by the sea they formed the first man and woman, Askr and Embla, the parents of the human race. The three gods also created the dwarfs to live in the ground under the earth and in stones and hills. In the region above the earth they made Askgard, the abode of the gods, with its great halls and palaces, and between heaven and earth they put a rainbow bridge, guarded against the giants by the god Heimdall. So runs the story of creation in the *Prose Edda,* although other sources, such as the poem *Voluspa* in the *Poetic Edda,* tell the story somewhat differently, but it is not to our purpose to inquire further.

An uneasy world order was now established. The frost-giants were exiled to the shores of Utgard, the earth-encompassing sea; the gods dwelt in Askgard and men in Midgard; the dead gathered in Hel, its gate in Niflheim guarded by the watchdog Garm. Off in the sea all around the flat earth lay the huge coil of the dangerous Midgard serpent, and outside the world in Muspelheim, the region of heat, were the ferocious Fenriswolf, bound by a magic chain of the gods, and the giant Sutr, the bold leader of the fire-giants. The gods of Askgard, the rulers of this uneasy world, passed down Bifrost, the rainbow bridge, to stand under the world-tree and pass judgment.

How exactly the world-tree, Yggdrasil, fits into this picture it is difficult to say, but the old tree was "the pillar" between the nine regions of the world. Under its three roots were the three regions where dwelt the dead, men, and the exiled frost-giants, and the regions of the sky were sustained by its branches. (Here is a conception that the Teutons shared with the Celts, Slavs, Mesopotamians, Hindus, and numerous groups in central Asia.)

But the Teutonic peoples knew that this world

order would not last forever. In a hall under the world-tree dwelt the three Norns or Fates, representing the past, the present, and the future, who fixed the lot of each man at birth and would someday make known the hour of doomsday. That hour would come when the old tree would groan and tremble; the Fenriswolf would break his chain and come raging to earth; the giant Sutr would lead the fire-giants in an assault upon the gods; the frost-giants would storm in from the edges of the world; the Midgard serpent, thrashing heavily in the sea, would toss great tidal waves across the earth. The watchdog of Hel would set up a howl and let Loki lead his allies past him up to earth to join in the overthrow of the world order. The invaders would storm Bifrost, only to have that frail bridge break under them. Then the final battle of the world would take place on the plains of earth, with the gods and the heroes of Valhalla going down in defeat, men would suffer apparent extinction, and the earth would be burned up by the victorious forces of fire and chaos.

After a while a new earth would emerge from the sea, and the sons of Odin and Thor, together with Balder and Hödr released from Hel, would establish a new and more promising world order. Human life would begin again from two survivors of the Götter-dämmerung and its accompanying world conflagration.

This remarkable conception of time and history links the Teutonic peoples with those of India, who also believed, and still do, in world cycles. It is obvious also that Christianity, when it came, could and did profit by the expectation of the death of the old gods and the return of gentle, cruelly slain Balder from Hel.

The Slavs

With the Slavs we return to interests such as we found among the Celts. Christianity came last to the Teutons, especially to the Scandinavians, and first to the southern Celts and southern Slavs. Consequently,

a vivid remembrance of ideas concerning death and the end of the world is not so apparent among the Celts and Slavs as among the Teutons, who remained pagan a longer time.*

The Slavs used rather revealing words for their religious realities. *Bogu* (possessor and giver of wealth) was their word for "god," and *besu* (disagreeable, nasty) their word for "demon" or "devil." It is thus apparent that their gods were the source of fertility and prosperity, and that demons interfered with and spoiled what might have turned out well. Another much used term was *duchu* (in its feminine form *dusha*), which meant "spirit" or "breath" and referred to that part of a living person that departed at death to become a spirit. Death and the after-life deeply concerned and daunted the Slavs. They seemed to think the soul of a dying person fled out of the window or door in the form of some small creature, such as a bird, a mouse, or even an insect. Thereafter, if rightly treated and periodically fed or given gifts, it might come back in ghost-form (as a mild house-spirit or *domovoj*) to crouch benevolently in the darkness back of the stove and protect the house and barn by night. Or, if not well disposed, it might enter the body of a wolf and as a werewolf bring evil and terror to all. But sooner or later the soul of the departed one would begin a long and difficult journey to a sanctuary or refuge (*raji*) at the edge of the world, for which it would need food and equipment supplied by or taken from the living.

Demonic beings in general fascinated the Slavic imagination long after the coming of Christianity.

---

* Historians distinguish between the southern Slavs (the Slavs of the Danube basin and the Balkans) and the northern Slavs (now the Czechs, Slovaks, Poles, and Russians).

Since the pre-Christian Slavs left no literature and no strong oral tradition behind them, we must in part trust to the uncertainly accurate references to them by scornful or hostile Christian writers, and rely still more on philological and cultural survivals that yield us clues to pre-Christian beliefs and practices. It is extremely difficult to determine what the southern Slavs believed; what little we have to say concerns the northern Slavs.

There were, for example, malicious female spirits (the *vilen*), beautiful and shapely, who could quickly turn into swans, other birds, or serpents and do harm to those they disliked or good to those they favored. More forbidding were the *rusalken,* perhaps originally errant souls of the dead, now capable of putting spells upon the living. These demons hid among the growing crops or swung in the treetops and delighted in scoffing at or upsetting with sudden panic the passers-by. The only thing to do was to seek to appease them with gifts of food, wreaths of flowers, or offerings of cloth hung on branches or bushes. If they were lurking in streams or ponds, offerings were thrown to them in the water. Their sadism was an ever-present menace throughout life.

There were also the Fates, to whom offerings of corn, cheese, honey, and bread were due, and who, like the Teutonic Norns and the Greek and Roman Fates, spun the thread of life and fixed its length. Also important were certain female fertility-spirits, comparable to Demeter and Ceres, and a vague male figure, Rodu, a god of fruitfulness.

Of greater religious stature were the sun-god Dazibogu (Dazhbog), and the thunderer Perun, who was the Slavic Thor and was more reverenced even than Svarog, the god of fire. Volos (Viles) was the god of cattle, Stribog the wind-god. We need mention no more. These gods, whose worship was conducted by priests with animal sacrifices, libations, and the sprinkling of blood, faded away at the coming of Christianity, apparently without a struggle, leaving only the faintest of traces after the passage of time.

Suggestions for Further Reading

Egypt

Albright, W. F. *From the Stone Age to Christianity.* 2nd ed. with new introduction, Johns Hopkins Press, 1957. Available also as Anchor pb

Anthes, Rudolph. "Mythology in Ancient Egypt," in *Mythologies of the Ancient World.* Ed. by S. N. Kramer. Anchor Books, pb, 1961

Breasted, J. H. *The Dawn of Conscience.* Scribner, 1933

———. *Development of Religion and Thought in Ancient Egypt.* Scribner, 1912. Available as Harper Torchbooks pb

Budge, E. A. W. *From Fetish to God in Ancient Egypt.* Oxford, 1934

———. *The Literature of the Ancient Egyptians.* J. M. Dent, 1914

Cerny, Jaroslav. *Ancient Egyptian Religion.* London, 1952.

Erman, Adolph. *A Handbook of Egyptian Religion.* Constable, 1907

Frankfort, Henri. *Ancient Egyptian Religion.* Columbia University Press, 1948

———. *Kingship and the Gods.* University of Chicago Press, 1948

Murray, Margaret. *The Spendour That Was Egypt.* Sidgwick & Jackson, 1949

Petri, Sir Flinders. *Religious Life in Ancient Egypt.* Houghton Mifflin, 1924

Pritchard, James B., ed. *Ancient Near East Texts.* 2nd ed., rev. and enl., Princeton, 1955

Shorter, A. H. *An Introduction to Egyptian Religion.* K. Paul, Trench, Trubner, 1932

Steindorff and Seele. *When Egypt Ruled the East.* 2nd ed., University of Chicago Press, 1957

Wilson, John A. *The Burden of Egypt.* University of Chicago Press, 1951. Issued also by the same press as a Phoenix pb under the title *The Culture of Ancient Egypt*

————. "Egypt," in *The Intellectual Adventure of Ancient Man*. University of Chicago Press, 1946. Available as Penguin Books pb under the title *Before Philosophy*

Babylonia

CHIERA, EDWARD. *They Wrote on Clay*. University of Chicago Press, 1938

CONTENAU, G. *Everyday Life in Babylon and Assyria*. Edwin Arnold, 1954

DELAPORTE, L. *Mesopotamia*. K. Paul, Trench, Trubner, 1925

FINEGAN, JACK. *Light from the Ancient Past*. Princeton, 1946

FRANKFORT, HENRI. *Kingship and the Gods*. University of Chicago Press, 1948. Deals also with Egypt

HEIDEL, A. *The Gilgamesh Epic and Old Testament Parallels*. 2nd ed., Chicago, 1949

HOCART, A. M. *Kingship*. Oxford, 1927

JACOBSON, THORKILD. "Mesopotamia," in *The Intellectual Adventure of Ancient Man*. University of Chicago Press, 1946. Available as Penguin Books pb under the title *Before Philosophy*

JASTROW, MORRIS, JR. *Aspects of Religious Belief and Practice in Babylonia and Assyria*. Putnam, 1911

KRAMER, S. N. *Sumerian Mythology*. American Philosophical Society, 1944. Available as Harper Torchbooks pb

————. "Mythology in Sumer and Akkad," in *Mythologies of the Ancient World*. Ed. by S. N. Kramer. Anchor Books pb, 1961

LANGDON, S. *Babylonian Epic of Creation*. Oxford, 1923

LEONARD, W. E., TR. *Gilgamesh*. Viking, 1934

MENDELSOHN, ISAAC, ED. *The Religions of the Ancient Near East: Sumero-Akkadian Religious Texts and Ugaritic Epics*. Liberal Arts Press pb, 1955

PRITCHARD, JAMES B., ED. *Ancient Near East Texts*. 2nd ed., rev. and enl., Princeton, 1955

Greece

ADAMS, JAMES. *The Religious Teachers of Greece*. T. & T. Clark, 1908

BEVAN, E. R. *Later Greek Religion*. J. M. Dent, 1927

CORNFORD, F. M. *Greek Religious Thought from Homer to the Age of Alexander*. J. M. Dent, 1923

GRANT, F. C., ED. *Hellenistic Religions*. Liberal Arts Press pb, 1954

GUTHRIE, W. K. C. *Orpheus and Greek Religion*. Harcourt Brace, 1925

————. *The Greeks and Their Gods*. Beacon, 1950. Available in Beacon pb

HARRISON, JANE E. *Prolegomena to the Study of Greek Religion*. Cambridge, 1903. Available as Meridian pb

JAEGER, W. *Paideia: The Ideals of Greek Culture*. 3 vols., Oxford, 1943–1945

JAMESON, MICHAEL H. "Mythology of Ancient Greece," in *Mythologies of the Ancient World*. Ed. by S. N. Kramer. Anchor Books pb, 1961

LIVINGSTONE, SIR RICHARD W., ED. *The Legacy of Greece*. Oxford, 1928.

MOORE, C. H. *The Religious Thought of the Greeks*. Harvard University Press, 1916

MURRAY, GILBERT. *The Five Stages of Greek Religion*. Clarendon Press, Oxford, 1925. Available as Anchor pb

Nilsson, Martin P. *Greek Popular Religion*. Columbia University Press, 1940
———. *Homer and Mycenae*. Methuen, 1933
Oates and O'Neill, eds. *The Complete Greek Drama*. Random House, 1938
Rhode, Erwin. *Psyche*. Harcourt Brace, 1925
Rose, H. J. *Ancient Greek Religion*. Hutchinson, 1946

Rome

Altheim, Franz. *A History of Roman Religion*. Methuen, 1938
Angus, S. *Religious Quests of the Graeco-Roman World*. Scribner, 1929
Bailey, Cyril. *Phases of the Religion of Ancient Rome*. University of California Press, 1932
Carter, J. B. *The Religion of Numa*. Macmillan, 1906
Cumont, F. *The Oriental Religions in Roman Paganism*. Open Court, 1911
Fowler, W. Warde. *The Religious Experience of the Roman People*. Macmillan, 1910
Grant, F. C., ed. *Ancient Roman Religion*. Little Library of Liberal Arts pb, 1953
———. *Roman Ideas of Deity*. Macmillan, 1914
Rose, H. J. *Ancient Roman Religion*. Hutchinson, 1948. Now available along with *Ancient Greek Religion* as Harper Torchbooks pb under the title *Religion in Greece and Rome*.
Wagenvoort, H. *Roman Dynamism*. Blackwell, 1947

Beyond the Alps

Bellows, H. A., tr. *The Poetic Edda*. Princeton, 1936
Brodem, A. G., tr. *The Prose Edda*. Oxford, 1929
Clemen, Carl, ed. *Religions of the World*. Harcourt Brace, 1931. Chapters on Celtic, Teutonic, and Slavic religions
Ellis, Hilda. *The Road to Hel*. Cambridge, 1944
Fowler, Murray. "Old Norse Religion," in *Forgotten Religions*. Ed. by Vergilius Ferm. Philosophical Library, 1950
Grönbeck, Vilhelm. *The Culture of the Teutons*. Oxford, 1931
MacCulloch, J. A. *Celtic Mythology*. In *The Mythology of All Races* series, Vol. III, Marshall Jones, 1918
———. *The Celtic and Scandinavian Religions*. Hutchinson, 1948
Machal, Jan. *Slavic Mythology*. In *The Mythology of All Races* series, Vol. III, Marshall Jones, 1918

Two

The
Religions
of
India

THE RELIGIONS of India are inexhaustively fertile in the suggestions they offer for meeting the need man feels for rational and mystical adjustment to life and the world. This suggestiveness is both a present and a past fact. The religions of India can be said to have offered almost every answer to religious need that can be thought of, and to have discarded none; all the answers made in the past are preserved, like bees in amber, along with those offered in the present. One feels, in studying the development of Indian religions, like an archeologist digging down through the layers of Near East civilizations and finding the old forever preserved beneath the new.

But, whereas it is dangerous to generalize when the solutions are so various, it is true to say that there is agreement at one point. If we are to trust the testimony of their religions, the peoples of India, including the Muslims and even the Zoroastrians, are not easily satisfied with what this world offers in material fare. The physical world is always of secondary or tertiary importance to them. Other realities—life, mind and spirit—matter far more. Many would be more explicit. To most of the leading minds of India's past (but here we should except the Zoroastrians and Muslims), the world of nature not only presents real difficulties to the fulfillment of the higher potentialities of life, mind and spirit; it must be given the value of an illusional construct or else of a deceptive "appearance." The motive of much Hindu, Jaina, and Buddhist thought in India has been deliverance—deliverance, as the Jains view it, from the degrading down-drag of gross matter, or deliverance, as the Hindus and Buddhists think, from the misleading appearances and experiences of the physical world. Only mental and spiritual realms have an unshakable reality that guarantees eternal satisfactions.

The peculiarly Indian beliefs that have led to the emergence of this point of view will appear early in the story. But let us not exaggerate the pessimism. The pessimism is real but not absolute. The present and immediate are rejected, but the eternal and the ultimate are sought in hope and expectancy. The religious consciousness of India is disillusioned concerning the near and the physical because it is hungry for the joy that is to be had when the real and the eternal may be known and apprehended. The reaction here may be rather superficially compared with that of a man glowering and unhappy because he must listen to the chattering and thumping of a cheap jazz orchestra beating out a primitive rhythm, when he is hungering and thirsting for the musicians to bring him Beethoven, Brahms, or Shostakovich. The point is that reality and truth are hidden, or at best very inadequately revealed, in the images conjured up by a purely physical experience.

Perhaps it would be useful to add a word more. We shall be concerned chiefly with three religions. They differ in interesting respects, although they may be said to be actually in basic agreement with each other. By and large, philosophical Hinduism (Brahmanism) is based on the conviction that the chief error of man lies in his *thinking*: his miseries are due to fallacies in his conception of things rather than to sin in his living. Jainism, in contrast, puts primary emphasis on *behavior*, how one acts; one must behave so as to avoid contamination by matter, defiling as pitch and destructive of all spirituality of being. Early Buddhism, finally, locates the chief missteps in the area of *feeling*; it is our desires that must be reined in and prevented from flooding us with misery.

Such generalizations should, of course, not be overworked. None of these religions places exclusive emphasis on either thinking, feeling, or action, since these cannot really be divorced from one another. (That this is the case will be evident when we look into the later development of each religion.) But the early recognition that the theory of the three religions discussed is initially concerned with thinking, behaving, and feeling will make it easier later to understand their divergences.

3 Early Hinduism: The Passage from Ritual Sacrifice to Mystical Union

A TYPICAL JUDGMENT of the commentators on Hinduism is that its diversity is unlimited. It means so many different things. It attracts so many kinds of minds. It extends a promise of ultimate treasure to so great a variety of seekers of salvation. It is not one religion, but rather a family of religions. The word *Hinduism,* in fact, should not at all imply that Hindus put their faith in a completed system of doctrines standing apart from them as a measure of their orthodoxy. Hinduism is instead fluid and changing. It comprehends the living faiths of the peoples of India who call themselves Hindus. It is to them an entire way of life. Somehow it hangs together as an indivisible whole, in spite of great range and complexity.

This range and complexity of beliefs and practices has led observers to make a distinction between the "broader" and "narrower" meanings of Hinduism. As a rule, the broader definition is preferred by most Hindus. To them Hinduism* is the whole complex of beliefs and institutions that have appeared from the time when their ancient (and most sacred) scriptures, the Vedas, were composed until now. Western scholars, however, are inclined to prefer the narrower definition, according to which the so-called Vedic and Brahmanistic periods are considered as developments preparatory to Hinduism proper, the latter being identified with the vast social and religious system that has grown up among the peoples of India since about the third century B.C.

Hinduism in the narrower sense is hardly less amazing and diverse than when it is considered in its broader meaning. Hindus have an extraordinarily wide selection of beliefs and practices to choose from: they can (to use Western terms) be pantheists, polytheists, monotheists, agnostics, or even atheists;

---

* *Hinduism* as we are using the term here is of relatively recent coinage. Modern Hindus use it as a convenience when speaking or writing in English, but among themselves they use the ancient word *dharma* ("way of life and thought") when referring to what the West calls "Hinduism" or "the religion of the Hindus." It may be added that the word *Hindu* itself is derived from Persian references (Indus-Hindus-Hindu) and indicates a geographical location, the upper branches of the Indus River.

dualists, pluralists, or monists. Morally, they may follow a strict or loose standard of conduct, or they may choose instead a supramoral mysticism. They may live an active life or a contemplative one; they may spend much time on domestic religious rituals, as most of them do, or dispense with these completely. They may worship regularly at a temple or go not at all. Their only universal obligation, whatever their divergences, is to abide by the rules and rituals of their caste and trust that by doing so their next birth will be a happier one.

It seems best in telling the story of this astonishing faith to divide the exposition into two chapters, the one entitled "Early Hinduism," the second "Later Hinduism." In an attempt to preserve some semblance of historical perspective, these two chapters are separated by three others dealing with Jainism and Buddhism, for the latter religions burst in upon and for a time interrupted the orderly growth and development of Hinduism. Therefore they will be studied before considering later Hinduism. The present chapter deals with the origins of Hinduism and the double passage (a) from polytheism to monotheism and monism and (b) from sacrifice as the most blessed activity of man to mystical union with the One, a passage that takes us from the Vedic to the Brahmanistic period.

I The Religion of the Vedic Age

Pre-Aryan India

India is an old land filled with old peoples. Before 1500 B.C. its predominant group was the curly-haired ancestors of the still-numerous black-skinned Dravidians of the southern half of India. These people were, however, not aboriginal; in their midst were primitive tribes of an older and lower culture, some of whom yet survive in the jungles of south and central India.* Disputing possession of the land were

* Vide the description of the Birhors in Chapter 1.

some Mongoloid tribes holding territories in the northeast. And on the Indus River before 2500 B.C. a people of mixed origin and diverse ethnic composition combined to produce a Bronze Age civilization with a well-developed art and architecture (brought to light by excavations at Harappa in the Punjab and Mohenjo-dara in Sind), matched, it seems, by an equally advanced religion that contained at least in germ the ideas now embodied in the Hindu doctrines of the Law of Karma and reincarnation. Archeological remains appear to show that these people worshiped mother-goddesses and, with special attention, a fertility-god who may, according to one hypothesis, have been the Hindu Shiva in an earlier form. This god is represented as being horned and three-faced (the fourth face invisible on the far side?), his legs in a yoga position, heels together, while an elephant, a tiger, a buffalo, and a rhinoceros attend him. Male and female phallic symbols accompany these figures and suggest that the religious rites invoked fertility-power. Unfortunately, no decipherable writings have come down from this civilization, which vanished in an overwhelming catastrophe, very probably in the Aryan invasion about to be described.

The Coming of the Aryans

Sometime about the middle of the second millennium B.C. there came pouring over the passes of the Hindu Kush Mountains in the northwest a people of a different strain, who were eventually to conquer, remake, and be remade by India. They were a tall, light-skinned people of Indo-European stock, and they called themselves Aryans. They formed five large divisions or peoples, each composed of organized tribes. For a long time they had been moving eastward, looking for a permanent home. At last, during a period of several centuries, they issued from the mountains upon the plains of northwest India. They were of the same complex ethnic group to which belonged the powerful tribes that moved south, west, and north in Europe and with the infusion of their blood and language brought into being the historic Greeks, Latins, Celts, Germans, and Slavs. While the original migrations were still in process, the Indo-Aryans, as we call them, seemingly went south from Europe and then east toward the rising sun. After an unknown number of years spent on the steppes of Bactria and along the Oxus River, they began to migrate again, this time into India. Another large branch of the same ethnic group broke into Iran (ancient Persia). They had been fellow-wanderers with the Indo-Aryans, but at a parting of the ways had turned southward. Time was to see great changes in language, habits, and ideas among both the Iranians and Indo-Aryans, and a difference in religious outlook as wide as that between Hinduism and Zoroastrianism, but the original similarities, both in language and religion, can still be traced without difficulty.*

The Indo-Aryans, whose horse-drawn chariots, unknown to India before, terrified the unwarlike native inhabitants, settled first on the upper branches of the Indus River. They had been a nomadic people, but now they began to live in simple village groups among their flocks and herds. As they fought their way southeastward along the base of the Himalaya Mountains and began to adjust themselves to the new climate, their life became less pastoral and more agricultural in character. The men seem to have been fully occupied with herding their cattle and waging warfare, while the women carried on the home-making and gardening. The animals they brought into India with them were those of a pastoral people —cows, horses, sheep, goats, and dogs. Of elephants, monkeys, and tigers they had as yet no knowledge. They clung to their ancient diet of milk and meat and continued the custom, probably formed centuries before (indeed, the Iranians had an identical practice), of making an intoxicating liquor they called soma (squeezed from a plant whose identity is now uncertain and drunk after it was mixed with milk). They thought their gods enjoyed this potion as much

as they, and therefore offered them libations of it whenever they sacrificed.

In the van of the Aryan advance the struggle with the black-skinned Dravidians was continuous, and as successive waves of invaders piled up from the rear, there were intertribal clashes that were to be immortalized later in the great Hindu epics, the *Ramayana* and the *Mahabharata*. By the time the whole region of the Five Rivers (the upper branches of the Indus) was occupied, the problem of mastering the new territory had been met by the rise of the first distinct social classes among what had been formerly an undifferentiated nomadic people. These classes, from which the castes of later Hindu society arose, corresponded to a new division of labor among the people.

Each tribe had over it a king or chieftain, called a *rajah* (same root as Latin *rex*), whose office was generally hereditary. The functions of the king rapidly became complex, as more and more territory came under his sway, until, toward the end of the Vedic period, he was distinguished from other citizens by a large retinue, a palace, and glittering apparel. He was expected not only to maintain a private army for the protection of his people but also to gather around him numbers of priests to aid him in securing divine blessing on his subjects and the gods' approval of his own acts. Far outnumbering the warriors who formed the rajah's private army and the priests who served both ruler and people were the farmers and herdsmen, whose home life was still much like that of their forefathers. The father or *pitar* (same root as Latin *pater*, German *vater*, English *father*, etc.) was the head of the family, the owner of its property, and, in these early days, still its family priest. Descent was reckoned through him. The wife and mother or *matar* (Latin *mater*, German *mutter*, etc.) was a comparatively free individual, much less secluded than her descendants in the Ganges valley have been. Her authority in the home over the children and black servants was not subject to restraint, except on rare occasions by her husband, who was reckoned the master of the household.

* See Section I in the chapter on Zoroastrianism.

Having been accustomed for centuries to moving toward new horizons and hazards, the Aryans settled down slowly. Only one substitute for lost adventure remained to them, and they seized upon it: they continued their wanderings in imagination, when denied them in fact, and surveyed the world about them with nimble wit. They had hardly won a place for themselves in India before they began to develop further their oral tradition. Their ritual sacrifices became more elaborate. Folk-tales and epic stories took shape rapidly. At the same time the hymns and prayers of their priests gave voice to their expanding religious conceptions. Out of these last, together with ancient magic runes and spells, have come Hinduism's earliest sacred writings, the *samhitas* ("collections"), four in number: the *Rig-Veda, Sama-Veda, Yajur-Veda,* and *Atharva-Veda.* (The word *veda* means "sacred knowledge," and it has the same root as the English *wit* and *wisdom,* the Greek οἶδα, the Latin *video,* and the German *wissen.*) Our knowledge of the gods of the Indo-Aryans is principally drawn from the four Vedas.* We turn first to the oldest of the four.

* The Vedic literature is more complex than might be inferred from this sentence. Each of these "collections" was later supplemented by one or more Brahmanas, treatises containing directions for the proper ritual use of the hymns and prayers of the Vedas. The Brahmanas in turn were supplemented by Aranyakas or Forest Books explaining how persons who retired to the forests and were unable to perform ritual sacrifices were to make magical or symbolic use of the hymns and prayers. In their turn these Forest Books terminated in or were supplemented by philosophical discussions setting forth the rationale of all thought and action—the famous Upanishads. For the sake of clarity and simplicity we shall consider the Vedas, Brahmanas, and Upanishads separately as though they constitute distinct bodies of literature. But Hindus sometimes make collections that cut across these lines. For example, they may collectively consider (1) the *Rig-Veda,* (2) one of its two Brahmanas, the *Aitareya,* (3) the *Aitareya Aranyaka* contained in the latter, and finally (4) the *Aitareya Upanishad,* which is attached to the Aranyaka. (Sometimes, however, there are not so many components extant, as is the case of the *Isha Upanishad,* which springs directly from the *White Yajur-Veda.* To show how complex the situation becomes, it should be explained that the *Yajur-Veda* comes in two versions, the Shukla or White and the Krishna or Black, and that there

The Rig-Veda

The *Rig-Veda* (literally, "the Veda of stanzas of praise") is an anthology of religious poetry in ten books, containing over a thousand hymns and reflecting the religious devotion of enduring family and other groups before and during the Vedic Age. At first these hymns (some by individuals) existed only in oral form. They are prayers addressed to a single or often to two or more deities,* whose residence is found in three regions—the earth, the heavens, and the intermediate air.

When the Aryans engaged in public worship, they approached the altar joyously and confidently, except, of course, in special cases, when trouble loomed or a god was angry. In those days they had no temples, nor even sacred precincts of a permanent kind, but worshiped under the open sky, as the ancient Iranians did. They used areas of trimmed and swept grass in the center of which they prepared a rectangular space or altar-ground, either cleared off or shallowly scooped out, and large enough to contain as many as three fires—a western one (the *garhapatya,* round in shape, the only one named in the *Rig-Veda*), an eastern one (the *ahavaniya,* square in shape), and a southern one (the *dakshina,* shaped like a half-moon).†

are differing recensions of each, as is true of other works in the Vedic literature.) One more point should be made: it is common for Hindus to include under the term *the Vedas* all the works we have mentioned, the Upanishads being more particularly referred to as the Vedanta (literally, "the end or concluding portions of the Vedas").

One further note: all of the writings mentioned above are *shruti* ("heard"); that is, they are revelations to their authors and therefore sacred writ. All later writings are *smriti* ("remembered"); that is, although they derive from revelation, they have been composed by their human authors. They include the sutras, shastras, epics (the *Mahabharata* and *Ramayana*), and the puranas and tantras to which we shall be referring later.

* Called *devas* or "shining ones," a word identical with the Latin *deus* (whence also comes, of course, the English word *deity*).

† Probably in early Vedic times only one fire, the garhapatya, was used, but this is far from certain; at least it is the only one named. In later days the altar-ground

The priests officiated inside the altar-ground. A seat on strewn grass near the fires was reserved for the invisible divine guests who might be present. The offerings consisted of one or more of the following: soma, clarified (melted) butter (*ghee*), grain, and a goat, sheep, cow, ox, or horse (the horse sacrifice being the costliest and most effectual). In time, as the sacrifices lengthened into elaborate ceremonies, priests, each with special functions, took charge. One might be the *adhvaryu* or altar-builder, who also prepared the materials for sacrifice and administered them, reciting the appropriate words as he did so. Another was the *hotar*, the libation-pourer and invoker of the gods, who would with courteous words call down the gods to enjoy the sacrificial offerings and the soma set out in vessels on the grass:

Thou hast made prayers the means of thine exalting, therefore we wait on thee with hymns, O Indra. . . .
Mark well our sacrificial cake, delighted: Indra, drink Soma and the milk commingled.
Here on the sacrificer's grass be seated. . . .[A1]

Another priest might be the *agnidh* or kindler of the sacrificial fire. But as time went on the foremost came to be the *brahmin* or presiding priest, the one who offered the central sacred petition or *brahman* (the prayer).*

During the sacrifice the oblation, whether of grain, flesh, or liquid or a combination of these, was in part poured or cast into the fire, in part placed on the ground on cushions of grass or poured there for the gods, and in part eaten or drunk by the participants in the sacrifice. The proffering of the soma libation (often a separate rite) was the final act in a long series of ritual events stretching over more than one day: the finding or purchase of the plant from which the juice was to be extracted, its reverent transportation by cart or on human heads to the location of the pressing out, the drawing of the water for the soaking of the stems, the squeezing of the stems between "pressing-stones" after they were swollen with water, the straining of the liquor through woolen strainers (an act marked by a characteristic sound interpreted with some exaggeration as "the bellowing of a bull," and by a flash of "golden" color), the mixing of the liquor with milk or honey, and finally its proffering to the gods and its distribution to the human participants, in whom the intoxicating or hallucinatory effect was almost immediate.*

These sacrificial rituals both drew upon and gave rise to an ever-growing mythology. On a previous page (p. 11), we have seen how ritual gives rise to myth as well as myth to ritual. We have here cases in point. The myths of the Indo-Aryans were already well developed when the latter entered India, but did not cease to change and grow thereafter. Because the sacrificial rituals were designed to achieve human security in both changing and settled situations, the gods were at times *reconceived* and endowed with new powers. In the process, once-potent older gods faded into the background, and other gods, regarded as more capable of meeting altered needs, took their place. The rituals themselves required the introduction of divine powers or presences, such as Agni, Soma, and Brihaspati (pp. 95 f.). It will soon be seen that quite new cosmic gods emerged when the rituals were understood to affect the cosmos (p. 93). Furthermore, the sacrifice finally became so central and significant an event in itself that the whole world

---

was raised a foot or more (instead of being hollowed out) and was often built of square bricks formed into unusual shapes, so as to resemble, for example, two triangles, or a woman, a falcon, a tortoise, or something else.

* This word *brahman* was used in different senses. It had the wider meanings of "holy word," "sacred knowledge," and "incantation," with the implication in this last case of the presence of magic power. Mystic utterance was *brahman*, too. The word applies not only to the words and stanzas (*mantras*) of the *Rig-Veda* but as well to the incantations and spells of the *Atharva-Veda* (see next topic). Another word was used in the *Rig-Veda* to convey a similar meaning, *vac* or speech, with the connotation of Holy Utterance or Word, thus making it equivalent to *brahman* or an alternative to it.

* Some commentators think the soma may have been extracted from hemp or a plant like marijuana, others that it was something less pronounced in its effects, like the juice of rhubarb stalks. No exact identification now seems possible.

was encompassed in it and became a sacramental structure throughout; indeed, the universe was held to have originated in a cosmic sacrifice. There are many passages in the Vedas and the interpretive literature that conceive of the universe as having been in its totality a cosmic cow or horse or man that was primordially sacrificed and dismembered to produce the mountains, rivers, earth, and living creatures of everyday experience. Thus, according to *Rig-Veda* X.90, the original cosmic Man, Purusha, produced gods from himself who then made a sacrifice of *him*:

When they divided Purusha how many portions did they
  make? . . .
The moon was gendered from his mind, and from his eye
  the sun had birth; . . .
Forth from his navel came mid-air; the sky was fashioned
  from his head;
Earth from his feet. . . .[A2]

And the *Satapatha-Brahmana* was to say:

Verily, the dawn is the head of the sacrificial horse, the sun its eye, the wind its breath, the fire its open mouth. The year is the body of the sacrificial horse, the sky its back, the air its belly, the earth the under part of its belly. . . .[B1]

Thus the rituals gave rise to startling myths describing the origin of all things.

These new elements of myth were, of course, based on conceptions drawn from an earlier mythology. Many of the deities invoked were obviously of very ancient date. Faith in three of them was shared with the Iranians, the Hittites, the Greeks, and the Romans. They were Dyaus Pitar or Father Sky (whom we have already met as Zeus Pater of the Greeks, Jupiter of the Romans), his mate Prithivi Matar or Mother Broad-Earth (Gaia Mater of the Greeks), and Mitra (the Mithra of the Iranians), a highly moralized god representing faith-keeping and loyalty, but perhaps originally a sun-god. In the *Rig-Veda*, however, these deities are conceived of rather vaguely and appealed to seldom, being displaced from their earlier pre-eminence by gods and goddesses who appeared more effectual in northwest India.

Prominent among the latter was blustering Indra, ruler of the gods of the mid-region of the sky and particularly the god of storms, especially of the rainstorms (monsoons) that end the dry season.* He was the god of war as well. To his worshipers he seemed a gigantic figure, with long flowing hair and a wind-tossed beard through which he shouted and roared with a loud voice. Clasping in his hand the enemy-destroying thunderbolt, the vajra, he took the field as the ally and patron of the Aryans. Small wonder that their enemies fled. In the greatest of his annual feats, he smote the drought-dragon Vritra, which was holding back the waters in the mountain fastnesses. For this dangerous exploit he fortified himself well; hard-fighting, hard-drinking Aryan hero that he was, "in the three Soma-bowls he quaffed the juices." Then with his deadly thunderbolt "he slew the Serpent that rested on the mountains; and quickly flowing, swift to the ocean down sped the waters."[C1] His worshipers would chant adoringly:

In whose command are the horses, the cattle, the villages, and all the chariots; who begot the Sun and the Dawn, who is the leader of the waters—he, O men, is Indra.
Whom the two battle ranks meeting in conflict invoke, vanguard and rearguard, both the enemies; they utter various invocations—he, O men, is Indra.
Without whom men do not conquer, whom in battle they invoke for help; who is the pattern for all, who is the shaker of the unshaken—he, O men, is Indra. . . .
May we, O Indra, at all times thy friends, with goodly offspring, praise thee in the assembly.[C2]

Such laudation must not, of course, be taken as evidence of monotheism in the strict sense. The worshipers were prone to flattery that would please, and hence, unlike the ancient Greeks, whom otherwise they resembled in significant respects, they did not elevate one deity to permanent Olympic supremacy,

---

* He was an ancient Aryan deity who picked up this special characteristic in India.

but spoke of each of their divinities as supreme—at least during the prayers.*

In sharp contrast with Indra was the dread mountain-god Rudra, not often addressed but greatly feared, the fierce author of disastrous storms sweeping down from the snows of the Himalayas, who, in his proper nature, was no ally of the Aryans at all but the destroyer of their goods and persons. Fear and awe accompanied his presence. His worshipers approached him in humility and trembling supplication, beseeching him as "an immortal one" to be "auspicious" (*shiva*) rather than malevolent, and to be merciful to their children and grandchildren. They would beseech:

> Kill not our great or our small, our growing one or our full-grown man, our father or our mother. Injure not, O Rudra, our dear selves.
>
> Injure us not in our cattle or horses. In thy wrath, O Rudra, slay not our heroes. We invoke thee ever with sacrifices.[C3]

But then again Rudra was found to be at times a gentle healer, presiding (in his mountain fastnesses?) over medicinal plants. He had his helpful as well as his destructive side. This is of some importance historically, for his greatest significance lies in the fact that he is the early form of later Hinduism's great god Shiva, the Destroyer (and Reviver).

* This is not true monotheism, but ritual or devotional henotheism (i.e., temporary flattering elevation of one of many gods to the highest rank that can be accorded, verbally or ritualistically). Franklin Edgerton says of this: "Either the particular god of the moment is made to absorb all the others, who are declared to be manifestations of him; or else, he is given attributes which in strict logic could only be given to a sole monotheistic deity. Thus various Vedic gods are each at different times declared to be creator, preserver, and animator of the universe, the sole ruler of all creatures, and so on. Such hymns, considered separately, seem clearly to imply monotheism; but all that they really imply is a ritualistic henotheism. As each god comes upon the stage in the procession of rites, he is impartially granted this increasingly extravagant praise, until everything that could be said of all the gods collectively is said of each of them in turn, individually. We see that Vedic henotheism is rooted in the hieratic ritual, without which it perhaps would hardly have developed."[D]

The *Rig-Veda* attains high flights of poetry in the description of these and other nature deities. Vayu, the wind, is the bearer of perfumes. The tempestuous little Maruts or storm spirits are "swift as wind . . . robed in rain . . . the singers of heaven."[C4] Ushas, the Dawn (the Greek Eos), is a "young maid in white robes," shining afar in her chariot drawn by red spotted horses.[C5] Her male attendants, the Asvins, twin horsemen of the dawn, speed behind her through the sky on a chariot with golden seat, reins of gold, axle and wheels of gold, and with a flight so swift that it exceeds the twinkling of an eye. There are a number of sun-gods, probably representing different phases of light; for example, Surya, mounting up with fleet yellow horses and causing the constellations, flooded with the radiance of his all-beholding eye, to "pass away, like thieves, together with their beams";[A3] and Savitar, the "golden-haired, bright with sunbeams," who traverses the "ancient dustless pathways well established in the air's mid-region";[A4] and Vishnu, the far-striding, who encompasses the extent of earth, atmosphere, and sky in three swift strides and thus redeems the world from night. Of the last it may be said that, though destined along with Rudra to surpass the rest of the Vedic deities and to become a major Hindu god, he is not prominent in the *Rig-Veda* and has there lost almost all of his solar characteristics.

One of the picturesque figures in the *Rig-Veda* is Yama, the first man to die, now the god of the dead and the judge and ruler of the departed. Remembering him, the Aryans used to address the spirit of the dead man whose body was being burned on the funeral pyre.

> Honor with thine oblations the King, Yama, who gathers men together,
>
> Who travelled to the lofty heights above us, who searches out and shows the path to many.
>
> Yama first found for us a place to dwell in: this pasture never can be taken from us. . . .
>
> Meet Yama, meet the Fathers, meet the merit of free and ordered acts, in highest heaven.
>
> Leave sin and evil, seek anew thy dwelling, and bright with glory wear another body.[A5]

Not only do these verses honor Yama and the departing spirit, but in the mention of the Fathers * they express the veneration the Aryans felt for their ancestors, a very old and important part of their religion. It was their regular practice to set down on the ground a repast of cereal cakes and milk, or milk mingled with soma, or rice cakes (*pinda*), and then invite the ancestral spirits to draw near and receive nourishment.

Morally far above the other gods stood the awe-compelling deity Varuna, originally the god of the high-arched sky, who was later assigned the inclusive function (analogous to maintaining order among the stars) of directing the forces making everywhere for natural and moral orderliness. His sphere lay in part in the domain of natural laws, for it was he who upheld the physical order of the world against the forces making for its breakdown. In another direction, it was his concern to keep men obedient to the moral law. He was the discloser of sin, the judge of truth and falsehood. His spies were busy finding men out. When men sinned, it was to Varuna that they prayed for forgiveness, so that the acts that were reckoned as sins in those pioneer times appear in the prayers they addressed to him.

If we have sinned against the man who loves us, have ever wronged a brother, friend or comrade,
The neighbor ever with us, or a stranger, O Varuna, remove from us the trespass.
If we, as gamesters, cheat at play, have cheated, done wrong unwittingly or sinned of purpose,
Cast all these sins away like loosened fetters, and, Varuna, let us be thine own beloved.[A6]

Because Varuna's interest lay in maintaining order in the universe, physically and morally, it was natural that he should be associated with Mitra, the god of loyalty and promise-keeping, already mentioned, and also with the mysterious abstract principle called Rita. Rita was conceived to be the indwelling principle in everything in the universe that shows regularity and order of action; in accordance with Rita day succeeds night, summer follows spring, the sun

* The *pitris* (cf. the Latin *patres*).

keeps his appointed course, and man goes from birth to death, invisibly guided.

There are still other gods in the *Rig-Veda*—beings who might be called the liturgical gods because they were chiefly associated with and were in part or wholly outgrowths of the act of worship itself. They are Agni, the god of fire; Soma, the divine presence in the juice of the soma plant; and, not well known to the populace but very important to the priests, Brahmanaspati (or Brihaspati), the deified power of the sacred prayer-word.

No sacrifice was effectual without the presence of Agni (Latin *ignis*), the god of fire in general, celestial or terrestrial, but especially of the altar-fire. Invoked with earnest petition before his coming, which was conceived of always as a new birth (whether on altar or hearth), he was praised and adored with utmost sincerity. (Those who care for historical comparisons will here see a connecting link with the fire-ceremonies of the Zoroastrians.) As fire purifies and cleanses, so Agni removed sin and guilt. He drove away the demons and protected the home whose hearth he occupied. He was light and wisdom, a seer into dark corners, a resolver of mysteries, from whom it was well to have guidance. He consecrated marriage, was a spiritual husband of maidens, a brother of men. He was priest, oblation-bearer, and mediator between gods and men. His worshipers knew their weal depended upon his presence.

The participation of the god Soma (the Haoma of the ancient Persians) was also necessary in the sacrifice. His introduction was, we have seen, a central feature of the ritual. Both gods and men needed him. Hence, during each ceremony soma-juice was poured into the grass where the gods invisibly sat, and as they too drank, the worshipers chanted:

We have drunk Soma and become immortal;
We have attained the light, the gods discovered.
What can hostility now do against us?
And what, immortal god, the spite of mortals?[E]

The presence of a third god represented something more subtle. Brahmanaspati (Brihaspati) does not get as much mention in the hymns as Agni and Soma, but he is highly significant of later developments. He stood for the holy power in the uttered words of the prayer, able to move the gods and to compel them to grant their favors. Hence, he was sometimes regarded as a divine suppliant-priest interceding with the gods for men, much as Agni did.

Sublime Brihaspati, easy of access, granteth his friends most bountiful refreshment. . . .
Glorify him, O friends, who merits glory: may he give prayer fair way and easy passage.[A7]

It was the doctrine of the priests that Brahmanaspati had to be present along with and in the ritual, or it would be but empty sound. If he were indeed active, prayer would have an efficacy so great that it would be compulsive upon gods and men alike; there could be no failure of fulfillment. A moment's consideration will show how much importance this fact gave to the correctly pronounced prayer-word, the brahman. It took on the force of an independently existent principle. Equal importance attached to the priest who uttered it, the holy Brahmin.

Little wonder that the priests, as we shall see in the sequel, dwelt in thought on the divine force working in the magically potent prayer.

The Other Vedas

The other Vedas are in many respects dependent upon, even appendages of, the *Rig-Veda*. The *Yajur-Veda* is mostly in prose and was meant to supply dedications, prayers, and litanies to accompany the devotional use of the *Rig-Veda*. The *Sama-Veda* is a collection of rhythmic chants mainly for the use of the singing priests at the soma sacrifices, its hymns in great part being borrowed from the *Rig-Veda*.

The *Atharva-Veda* is more independent. A treasury of charms, incantations, and spells of great antiquity, it afforded expression to aspects of experience left largely inarticulate in the *Rig-Veda*—fear, passion, anger, hate, physical distress and the human effort to

amend it. It could be argued that the expensive priestly rituals we have reviewed in the previous section were for the ruling elite ("the rich"), whereas the rites of the *Atharva-Veda* were those of the common people ("the poor") in their homes and villages. This Veda abounds in magic blessings and curses. In a manner reminiscent of European magic, it presents remedial charms that were supposed to remove all evil—or bring down the fell strokes of fate on some unlucky hated head.

Away from us may thousand-eyed, immortal evil dwell! Him whom we hate may it strike, and him whom we hate do thou surely smite![F1]

An example of the type of magic spell common in this Veda may be cited. One who wished to promote the growth of his hair might gather the sacred root that prevented baldness and have these words, at various points in the procedure, chanted:

As a goddess upon the goddess earth thou wast born, O plant! We dig thee up, O nitatni, that thou mayest strengthen the growth of the hair.
Strengthen the old hair, beget the new! That which has come forth render more luxurious.
That hair of thine which does drop off, and that which is broken root and all, upon it do I sprinkle here the all-healing herb.[F2]

The ancient instructions direct that the patient have his head anointed with the black concoction made from the plant mentioned, and have it applied by a medicine man clothed in black who has eaten black food in the early morning before the rise of the crows (black, too, of course). One cannot fail to see in the symbolism here employed an expression of the hope for the growth of new black hair.

This sort of thing may invite a smile, but it was not altogether foolish, for it was linked up with inquiries of a broader kind that were more speculative in probing the secrets of the universe than even the tenth book of the *Rig-Veda*. Still other inquiries were close to being scientific. Several of the sections of the *Atharva-Veda* (particularly II.3 and X.2) exhibit great interest in the vital organs, body secretions, and bones of the human body, which are separately distinguished and often exactly described. Apparently, an anatomically informed medical art was being developed. Indeed, one of the verses in the *Atharva-Veda* says that there were then hundreds of medical practitioners at work and thousands of herbs in use. The remedial charms were very ancient, but to some at least, the drugs used suggested a more realistic and more exciting method of attack on disease. The number of diseases known was quite long. But, as might be expected, there was much confusion of exact and inexact knowledge. As Dasgupta says:

> Some of the diseases with their troublous symptoms were (poetically) personified, and diseases which often went together were described as being related as brothers and sisters. Diseases due to worms were well-known, in the case of both men and cattle. There were also the diseases due to sorcery, which played a very important part as an offensive measure in Vedic India. Many of the diseases were also known to be hereditary.[G]

Confusion or not, we are adding to the evidence that the Indo-Aryans had brilliant minds. At least they made some good beginnings in inquiries darting in many different directions.

The Close of the Vedic Period

Vedic literature, taken as a whole, illustrates the exuberant culture which the early Indo-Aryans developed. Very clearly, this vigorous people faced life positively and, in the main, confidently on many fronts. In their literary self-expression they gave promise of great things to come.

One such promise has to be mentioned. Toward the close of the Vedic period, when the priests were growing in numbers and in power and were making religion and the search for knowledge their whole life-work, the yearning for assurance of unity in the totality of things began to express itself. So we have in the later hymns of the *Rig-Veda* the sudden emergence of such grand figures as Vishvakarman, "He Whose Work is the Universe"; Prajapati, "Lord of Creatures," the Creator; and Purusha, already mentioned, the Cosmic Man or Person, giving life to all animated beings, and indeed bringing the whole world into existence out of himself. Most arresting is the 129th hymn of the tenth book, addressed to a great unnamed cosmic reality, referred to quite simply as That One Thing, a neutral principle or activity said to have existed before there was a universe. This hymn contains an early speculation about the origin of creation, and may be rendered thus:

Then there was neither being (*Sat*) nor non-being (*Asat*):
There was no air, nor firmament beyond it.
Was there a stirring? Where? Beneath what cover?
Was there a great abyss of unplumbed water?

There was no death nor anything immortal;
Nor any sign dividing day from night.
That One Thing, given no breath, was yet self-breathing;
No second thing existed whatsoever.

Darkness was hidden in a deeper darkness;
This All was as a sea without dimensions;
The Void still held unformed what was potential,
Until the power of Warmth produced the sole One.

Then, in that One, Desire stirred into being,
Desire that was the earliest seed of Spirit.
(The sages probing in their hearts with wisdom
Discovered being's kinship to non-being.

Stretching their line across the void, they pondered;
Was aught above it, or was aught below it?)
Bestowers of the seed were there; and powers;
Free energy below; above, swift action.

Who truly knows, and who can here declare it?
Whence It was born, and how this world was fashioned?
The gods came later than the earth's creation:
Who knows then out of what the world has issued?

Whether the world was made or was self-made,
He knows with full assurance, he alone,
Who in the highest heaven guards and watches;
He knows indeed, but then, perhaps, *he* knows not!

From all points of view this is an amazing composition; the last six words are especially striking in their quizzical quality. It is clear that the priests were developing by the end of the Vedic Age considerable philosophical ability. This was their response to an urge to determine the origin of the world and of all things. Before the mountains were brought forth, before the gods came into being, before any portion of the visible universe existed, there was a nameless but all-originative being. The priests were excited at the thought. Was there any name they could give it? They wondered. Men had made many attempts heretofore, with less than complete adequacy.

They call it Indra, Mitra, Varuna, Agni, and it is heavenly noble-winged Garutman.
To what is One, sages give many a title: they call it Agni, Yama, Matariśvan. . . .[48]

The Brahmins were disposed to think further of the matter.

All this time the Aryans were still on the move. They were pressing down the Ganges valley, enslaving or driving before them, eastward and southward, the black-skinned natives. The migration did not halt until the whole of north and central India to the delta of the Ganges was in the power and under the active rule of the conquering invaders. The land had gradually changed hands.

Then the invader settled down—and change overtook *him*.

II Brahmanism

The Rise of the Caste System

By about the end of the seventh century B.C. the Aryan occupation of the Ganges valley had resulted in the organization of a number of distinct principalities or states, some ruled monarchically by hereditary rajahs, many still in the form of loose groupings of clans something on the order of republics, with the tribes governed by a central council of chieftains. The Aryans occupied the upper strata of a still-fluid social order; below were the dark-skinned non-

Aryans, in the process of being submerged. And now, though the separation between classes was not hard and fast, there were definitely coming into being four distinct social groups—the Kshatriyas or nobles, the Brahmins or priests, the Vaisyas or Aryan common people * (peasants or artisans), and last the enslaved Shudras or non-Aryan blacks. The first three classes were becoming more and more careful to hold themselves aloof from the last. There had now arisen the question of "color"—*varna*, the Hindu word for caste. Not only was marriage across the color barrier forbidden, but also even friendly social intimacies, like drinking from the same cup or sitting down to the same meal, on account of the frequency with which questions regarding purity of blood arose in consequence of such connections. There also existed a struggle for social prestige between the ruling nobles and the Brahmins; each group, in the name either of use and wont, or of religion and supernatural prerogative, claiming final and supreme authority.

The Brahmins had by now developed phenomenal power. The migration down the Ganges provided them with an opportunity that they were not slow to grasp. Religion was still in the making. The nobles were busy fighting and administering new territory and had to rely upon the priests more and more to carry on the necessary religious functions. Meanwhile, the supreme regard in which all held the brahman, or holy power in the sacrificial prayer, resulted in swiftly raising the prestige of those whose function it was to utter it. Indeed, the Brahmins finally came to claim a position of more vital importance even than the gods. As we have already seen, the sacred formula, once uttered, was deemed to have a compulsive and magical efficacy. Gods as well as men had to obey it. The priests therefore declared that they occupied the central place of power; they were the pivotal beings in a vast process reaching into all parts of the universe, hell, earth, and heaven. Through the sacrifices they performed—some

* Including the Aryo-Dravidians, for there was considerable intermixture in the Ganges plain before a check could be put to it.

of which took weeks and months to complete—they changed the very course of cosmic events. By now the names of the gods possessed little more than a ritualistic significance; the sacrifice was the thing of greater moment, and especially the utterance of the sacred prayer-formulas in connection with the sacrifices.

That these rituals of the priests veered away from religious supplication toward magical coercion is clearly evident in certain treatises, the Brahmanas, which they compiled to be appended to the Vedas.

The Brahmanas

As we have seen (p. 91), each of the four Vedas had attached to it its own Brahmana or Brahmanas that sought to direct the priests in their use of the hymns and prayers. The *Rig-Veda* has two that have survived, the *Aitareya* and the *Kaushitaki*. The White *Yajur-Veda* has the famous *Satapatha-Brahmana*, the Black the *Taittiriya-Brahmana*. The *Sama-Veda* has eight Brahmanas attached to it because it was heavily used in the soma rituals, but none of them is notable enough to name. The *Atharva-Veda* has one Brahmana, the *Gopatha*.

The Brahmanas are a curious and voluminous body of literature. Originally they were oral directions committed to memory by candidates for priestly office in the various priests' schools. Written down for the first time during the period turning on 300 B.C., or perhaps even later, and then frequently redacted, they were designed both to give practical directions in exhaustive detail for the conduct of all manner of sacrifices, and also to explain the inner meaning of these rites. The Brahmanas were thus the textbooks of the different schools or families of Brahmins, with a hint here and there of a philosophy of worship. No literature affords more detailed instruction for ritual performances.

When one reads them, the Brahmanas leave behind two striking impressions: first, that the priests were fascinated by and completely absorbed in the process of elaborating and interpreting their rituals, and second, that they regarded these rituals as having not only a compelling but even a creative power, for they caused events to occur at the demand of words and ritual acts alone.

The sacrifices described in the Brahmanas can be divided into domestic and public ones. The public rites occurred at the harvesting of rice, barley, millet, and other grains, at the full and the new moon, at the beginning of spring, during the long rainy season, in the autumn, at celebration of victories in war, at the "consecration" of kings, and when gods were called down to be propitiated and persuaded. Lengthy public rites also attended the building of altars, the soma sacrifices, and the installing of the three great fires on the altar-ground. The lengthiest of all public rites was the *Asvamedha* or Horse Sacrifice, which took over a year to complete and involved in its beginning the gathering and proffering, if not the actual sacrifice, of 609 animals! But the priests assured the rajahs who wished to assert through the sacrifice their world-power and who alone could afford the expense of it: "This is the atonement for everything. He who performs the Asvamedha redeems all sin."[B2]

Domestic rites were far simpler, usually taking place within the house and using the hearth fire fed with fresh fuel by the householder. The morning and evening offerings of rice or barley to Agni (the *Agnihotra*) are an example. More complicated was the oudoor monthly proffering of pinda (cereal cakes) to the ancestral spirits. In order to provide a sampling from the Brahmanas that might indicate what they are like, the description of this ceremony in the *Satapatha-Brahmana* is condensed below. It will be noticed that each act is carefully explained. The householder or "sacrificer" stands by with his upper garment reverently tucked up under his waistband. The officiating priest is an *adhvaryu*.

He (the adhvaryu) presents it in the afternoon. The forenoon, doubtless, belongs to the gods; the mid-day to men; and the afternoon to the fathers [i.e., ancestors]; therefore he presents it in the afternoon.

While seated behind the Garhapatya, with his face

turned toward the south, he takes that material for the offering from the cart. Thereupon he rises and threshes the rice while standing north of the Dakshina fire. Only once he cleans the rice; for it is once for all that the fathers have passed away; and therefore he cleans it only once.

He then boils it. While it stands on the Dakshina fire, he pours some clarified butter on it;—for the gods they pour the offering into the fire; for men they take the food off the fire; and for the fathers they do in this very manner: hence they pour the ghee on the rice while it stands on the fire.

After removing it from the fire, he offers to the gods two libations in the fire. He offers both to Agni and Soma. To Agni he offers because Agni is allowed a share in every offering; and to Soma he offers because Soma is sacred to the fathers.

Thereupon he draws with the wooden sword one line (furrow) south of the Dakshina fire,—that being in lieu of the altar: only one line he draws, because the fathers have passed away once for all.

He then lays down a firebrand at the farther (south) end of the line. For were he to present that food to the fathers, without having laid down a firebrand, the Asuras and Rakshas [malicious spirits] would certainly tamper with it.

He then takes the water-pitcher and makes the fathers wash their hands, merely saying, 'N.N., wash thyself!' naming the sacrificer's father; 'N.N., wash thyself!' naming his grandfather; 'N.N., wash thyself!' naming his great-grandfather. As one would pour out water for a guest when he is about to take food, so in this case.

Now those stalks of sacrificial grass are severed with one stroke, and cut off near the root;—the top belongs to the gods, the middle part to men, and the root-part to the fathers: therefore they are cut off near the root.

He spreads them along the line with their tops towards the south. Thereon he presents to the fathers three round cakes of rice. With, 'N.N., this is for thee!' he presents one cake to the sacrificer's father. [Similarly he presents a cake each to the grandfather and the great-grandfather.] He presents the food in an order directed away from the present time, because it is away from hence that the fathers have once for all departed.

He then mutters, 'Here, O fathers, regale yourselves: like bulls come hither, each to his own share!'

He then turns round so as to face the opposite (north) side. 'Let him remain standing with bated breath until his breath fail,' say some, 'for thus far extends the vital energy.' However, having remained so for a moment—

He again turns round and mutters, 'The fathers have regaled themselves: like bulls they have come each to his own share.'

Thereupon he takes the water-pitcher and makes them wash themselves, merely saying, 'N.N., wash thyself!' naming the sacrificer's father; 'N.N., wash thyself!' naming his grandfather; 'N.N., wash thyself!' naming his great-grandfather.

He then pulls down the tuck of the sacrificer's garment and performs obeisance. He mutters, 'Give us houses, O fathers!' for the fathers are the guardians of houses. After the cakes have been put back in the dish containing the remains of the boiled rice, he (the sacrificer) smells at the rice; this smelling being the sacrificer's share. The stalks of sacrificial grass cut with one stroke he puts on the fire; and he also throws away the firebrand.[83]

This rite is one of the simplest; descriptions of other rites explain the logic of their procedure at greater length and with frequent citing of myths that validate and confirm them. Mingled with the directions for the sacrifices are expressions of genuine spiritual aspiration and a growing sense of a principle of unity in the universe. Progress toward the conception of such unity is made. The theories of creation suggested in the later hymns of the *Rig-Veda* are fused here into a monotheistic compromise in which Prajapati, the Lord of Creatures, becomes Brahma Svayanibhu (Brahma Self-existing), the personal creator of the universe. It had occurred to the more speculative of the priests that if the holy power which worked through the prayer-formula could alter the course of cosmic events, then that power, capable as it was of forcing obedience from gods and men alike, must be an ultimate of some kind. Was it perhaps the true central power in the universe? Could the ultimate reality of the universe be called Brahman?

The authors of the Brahmanas here took a long stride forward, and in a direction along which Indian philosophy was destined to go far.

The Philosophy of the Upanishads

One of the greatest speculative eras in the history of religion now opened. Many alert minds in India pressed on to new and philosophically profound in-

Hermitage scene. Although this is a Rajput painting from the eighteenth century, it describes a situation almost as old as Hinduism itself, the retirement of holy men and sages from the world into the forests to discuss the meaning of life and the structure of reality. Here a white-haired ascetic seems to be teaching a younger disciple in the manner of the sages of the Upanishads. (Courtesy, Museum of Fine Arts, Boston.)

terpretations of existence. The oral compositions which, over a period of three or four centuries terminating about 300 B.C., expressed these ideas are, as we have seen, among the appendages to the Vedas; they are the famous and difficult treatises, the Upanishads. Indispensable for the study of the religions of India, this is a most important series of speculations. The Upanishads (meaning "sittings near a teacher," in the sense of "discussions on ultimate wisdom") are often in the form of dialogues, composed with memorization in view and therefore frequently too repetitious for modern ears, but they are not less profound or subtle for all that. In them Kshatriyas, men of all classes, and even women are dramatized as taking part in the discussions as readily and ably as, if not sometimes more ably than, the Brahmins themselves. As a matter of fact, the Upanishads were probably not composed entirely by Brahmins. There is good reason to think that non-Brahmins, especially Kshatriyas, composed some of them—probably many of those that reflect the dualistic rather than the monistic point of view.

How all this came about is not altogether clear. Two trends of the time may be noted. First, there was a trend toward asceticism, i.e., away from activity in the world toward inward activity, that of the mind and spirit. Ascetics and brooding thinkers were increasing in number and were rivaling the priests in commanding the highest respect. Even Brahmins were retiring to the forests and engaging in meditation and dialogue. This was not really a new kind of behavior. The *Rig-Veda* mentions ascetics, calling them *muni* and *vratyas*. The mood of the Aryans was changing. More and more of them were inclined to give up the world and seek emancipation (*moksha*) from its illusion and pain.

Second, there was a trend away from ritualism. It is true that, as appendages to the Brahmanas and their supplements, the Aranyakas, the Upanishads (the earlier ones particularly) * are far from relin-

* It is generally held that of the genuinely Vedic Upanishads those that are in prose are the earlier ones. The earliest are the *Brihadaranyaka* and the *Chandogya* Upanishads, the two longest; also early are the *Aitareya*,

quishing sacrifice as a religious practice or an ideal of life, but they in effect react against ritualism by finding equivalents, not to say substitutes, for the rites around the altar. They find these in the acts and the states of body and mind of ascetics and sages (*rishis*). The *Satapatha-Brahmana* had already suggested that each sacrifice was, on the one hand, Prajapati, the Lord of Creatures (= Purusha), being offered up anew as he was at the creation, and on the other, the Sacrificer, who offers himself up with his sacrifice; so that we have the equation, the sacrificer = the sacrifice = Prajapati. Another line of reasoning, which threads the devotional life of Hinduism from beginning to end, considers the heat (*tapas*) that fires the austere devotion of the ascetic in the forest equivalent to the fire on the altar, and his mental repetition of the Vedic chants equivalent to their recitation beside the altar.* By shifting from altar sacrifices to their equivalents, one could continue living in the spirit of the rituals of the Brahmanas, and although discarding them in practice, retain them in essence. This would be to interiorize the rituals through passage from sacrifice offered to the gods "out there" to sacrifice occurring within the self.

Accompanying this shift from outer to inner sacrifice was a new emphasis on the high worth of the spirit or self, a man's inner self (*atman*). Compared with this inner self the natural world (*prakriti*, matter), including the body and its sensory and mental states, is of an inferior order, and to choose to ignore the inner self and be content with the natural world would be an act of ignorance that could only result in illusion and suffering. Hence, although ritual sacrifices as a means of altering the natural world would have some merit in improving one's lot, salvation is best attained by breaking away from the natural world and from one's sensory and mental experience in it, through asceticism and meditation, that is, by "abandoning the body" and "freeing the soul."

To take the view just outlined and to go no farther with it was to rest, as some Upanishads (e.g., the *Shvetasvatara*) did, in the minority opinion of the Upanishads, namely, in a dualism of nature (prakriti) and soul or spirit (atman). But many Upanishadic thinkers went on beyond such a point to equate and then merge these two in a unified view (monism). In their search for inner connections between things, they found equivalences and identical samenesses everywhere. For instance, in the *Chandogya Upanishad* the fire on the altar is identified with the fire in the sun and the fire in the sun with the creative power (heat, tapas) of Being itself (Brahman). The activity of bees extracting nectar from flowers by heat is the same as the activity of priests extracting the honey of blessing from soma-juice and milk heated on the sacrificial fire, and this again is exactly what the mind does when extracting the highest good from a warm contemplation of the ritual. The light that shines above all the worlds, and on everything, is the same light that is within man and that can be experienced when we touch his body and perceive the warmth of its inner fire. This tendency to view all things as essentially equivalent was intensified when the gods and all other objects in the universe were conceived to be forms or elements derived by self-distribution from one originative source or ground of being, a cosmic Person or Cow or Horse sacrificing itself by self-dismemberment and seeking now its reconstitution or reunification by drawing its parts together again. Ultimately, all things are bound together, not only by likeness of activity but in actuality, that is to say, in *being*. Man comes to see not his separateness from the gods and his fellows but his and their identity with an eternal, all-inclusive Being or Reality, and begins to seek his deliverance (moksha) from separateness by mystical union with it.

This all-inclusive being or reality is most com-

Kena, Taittiriya, and *Kaushitaki* Upanishads, the possibility being that the last three are slightly later than the others. The Upanishads composed in verse are more recent and less obviously related to the Brahmanas. They are the *Katha, Shvetasvatara, Mundaka, Prasna, Mandukya,* and *Maitri* Upanishads. Some of these are relatively short and seem to have an independent origin.

* See the description of the third stage in the life-career of the Brahmin, p. 196 f.

monly called Brahman.* No precise definitions are attempted. Descriptions vary. Some of the treatises, for the most part the later ones, conceive of Brahman as a kind of deity endowed with personality.

> Immortal, existing as the Lord,
> Intelligent, omnipresent, the guardian of this world,
> Is He who constantly rules this world . . .[H1]

Many passages indiscriminately intermingle impersonal and personal designations for this ultimate reality. In other passages the personal designation seems to be resorted to more from habit or as a concession to the troubled imagination than anything else. The "limitless One" is described as *He* [who] awakes this world."

> Verily, in the beginning this world was Brahma[n], the limitless One—limitless to the east, limitless to the north, . . . limitless in every direction. Incomprehensible is that Soul, unlimited, unborn, not to be reasoned about, unthinkable—He whose soul is space! In the dissolution of the world He alone remains awake. From that space, He, assuredly, awakes this world, which is a mass of thought. It is thought by Him, and in Him it disappears. His is that shining form which gives heat in yonder sun and which is the brilliant light in a smokeless fire, as also the fire in the stomach which cooks the food. For thus it has been said: "He who is in the fire, and he who is here in the heart, and he who is yonder in the sun—he is one."[H2]

Some treatises regularly refer to Brahman as a neuter something, without motion or feeling, the impersonal matrix from which the universe has issued and to which it will in time return. This It, this One Thing, is the substantial substratum of everything.

> Verily, this whole world is Brahma[n]. Tranquil let one worship It as that from which he came forth, as that in which he will be dissolved, as that in which he breathes.[H3]

A few Upanishads show an awareness of the problem posed by the alternative pronouns *He* and *It*. If

---

* Neuter. More rarely, Brahma. The word has moved out of its Vedic setting. It no longer refers to the holy power of prayer only but applies directly to ultimate reality. In some of the quotations that follow the rarer word *Brahma* is used, but the liberty of appending *n* in brackets is taken.

"He" is God, then "It" is beyond, while yet inclusive of, God. (In the terminology of Meister Eckhard, the medieval mystic, "It" is the "God beyond God"). These Upanishads therefore make a distinction between Brahman made manifest as a person (He) and Brahman unmanifest (It). Thus the *Maitri Upanishad* says:

> There are, assuredly, two forms of Brahman: the formed and the formless. Now that which is formed is unreal [or not fully real]; that which is formless is real [i.e., ultimately real].[H4]

In this ascription of relative unreality to the formed Brahman we have an intimation of a later more elaborated doctrine, the doctrine of *maya,* according to which the unmanifest is the source and ground of all manifested things and beings (the world and all that is in it, including the formed or personal Brahman). But these are not wholly real. Only the hidden Brahman is utterly real and imperishable.

Some Upanishads have employed yet other terms to make this distinction explicit. Faced with the problem of how a formless, actionless being could create a world of visible and changing forms, they say that the unmanifest Brahman expressed its inherent creative power by producing Hiranyagarbha, the "Golden Egg," which at the dawn of creation emerged on "the sea of Brahman" and became the active creator God, Brahmā.* Through Brahman's inherent "magical power" (maya) Brahmā created the world. As a personal god occupying a sovereign position, his title is Ishvara, "Lord," a title that is given also to Shiva the Destroyer and Vishnu the Preserver in other contexts.

In a further effort of clarification, some Upanishads say that the personal god is Saguna Brahman ("Brahman with attributes"), while the unmanifest, unknowable, imperishable, and unconditioned Brahman is Nirguna Brahman ("Brahman without attributes"). The latter is so indescribable that references to It must be abstract and negative; one is obliged to say of It "*Neti, neti,*" ("[It is] not this, nor that"). On

---

* The word *Brahmā* is masculine, not neuter.

the other hand, Saguna Brahman may be both known and described; He is the Lord God regnant in the heavens who responds to human love and prayer.

It is evident, then, that the unmanifest and form-less Nirguna Brahman is the ultimate, and the personally manifest Saguna Brahman the immediate, source of the external world; as He and It (God and the all-inclusive One) Brahman is the constitutive element and the pervasive presence in all that is objective, all that is outside of us, the whole world of nature given to us by our senses. In the conversation in the *Brihadaranyaka Upanishad* between the renowned Brahmin, Gargya Balaki, and the king of Benares, a Kshatriya who is his superior in philosophic understanding, there is a progressive definition of Brahman as the reality within and yet beyond the sun, the moon, lightning, space, wind, fire, water, mirrors, sounds that reverberate, the different quarters of the heavens, shadows and bodies.[H5] Other Upanishads have the same general tenor. All things, all creatures, are ultimately phases of That One—"the priest by the altar, the guest in the house."[H6] "Stretched forth below and above, Brahma[n], indeed, is this whole world, this widest extent."[H7]

But this is only half the fact. Brahman is also all that is subjective, the whole inward world of reason, feeling, will, and self-consciousness, with which the innermost self is identified. All that goes on in the soul of man, and the soul itself, are phases of That One. The term for the inner self here employed is *atman,* a word used philosophically to denote the innermost and unseen self of a man as distinct from his body, his sense-organs, and his mentality; that is to say, it refers to his transcendental self, not to the empirical self whose mental and psychological characteristics are developed in the body and are knowable through sense-experience. Many of the Upanishads insist that, contrary to popular belief in the absolute individuality of the human soul, there is an actual identity between Brahman and atman, and that this is true of any and every atman, whether it is found in man, beast, insect, flower, fish, or any other living thing. "Yajnavalkya," cries an eager inquirer in the *Brihadaranyaka,* "explain to me him who is the Brahma[n] present and not beyond our ken, him who is the soul in all things." "He is your soul," comes the answer.

"He who, dwelling in the earth . . . in the waters . . . in the fire . . . the atmosphere . . . the wind . . . the sky . . . the sun . . . the quarters of heaven . . . the moon and stars . . . space . . . darkness . . . light. . . . He who, dwelling in all things, yet is other than all things, whom all things do not know, whose body all things are, who controls all things from within—He is your soul, the inner Controller, the Immortal. . . .

"He who, dwelling in breath . . . in speech . . . the eye . . . the ear . . . the mind . . . the skin . . . the understanding, yet is other than the understanding, . . . He is the unseen Seer, the unheard Hearer, the unthought Thinker, the ununderstood Understander. Other than He there is no seer. Other than He there is no hearer . . . no thinker . . . no understander. . . . He is your soul, the Inner Controller, the Immortal."[H8]

Such a passage sufficiently suggests the conclusion to which this sort of reasoning led. The true self of a man and the world-soul (*paramatman,* the universal atman) are one; they are identical. This identity is expressed in the *Chandogya Upanishad* in the formula *Tat tvam asi,* which means, "That (or It) art thou!"[H9] In other words, the All-Soul is the very stuff * of which the human soul is formed. It is all being (*sat*), consciousness (*cit*), and bliss (*ananda*), and also their opposites. Nothing takes place in the individual self that does not have its source and ground in *the* Self. We may therefore equate Brahman, the objective All, and Atman, the inner self, and call the ultimate reality henceforth Brahman-Atman, recognizing thereby that the objective and subjective are one.

It may not be said that this is the unequivocal finding of all the Upanishads. Some of them do not go so far and are monotheistic rather than monistic. None of them quite reaches the later Vedantic doctrine that because Brahman-Atman alone exists, the whole universe is either outright illusion or the

* The Upanishads vary in considering whether this stuff is mental-stuff or material-stuff.

"sport," "play," or "art" of the creative All-Soul. There is still a recognition of a relative or derivative reality of the universe; it is something that has been breathed forth by Brahman-Atman and pervaded by his or its being. And yet, perhaps "breathed forth" and "pervaded by" do not sufficiently suggest the close-knit unity of being that subsists between the Subjective and the Objectve. The *Brihadaranyaka* rather clearly insists that though things and selves may be spoken of as emanations from, creations of, or constructs pervaded by Brahman-Atman, "as a razor would be hidden in a razor-case,"[H10] all things ultimately *are* Brahman-Atman without any qualifications.* Says another treatise in phrases of breath-taking sweep:

This soul of mine within the heart is smaller than a grain of rice, or a barleycorn, or a mustard-seed, or a grain of millet, or the kernel of a grain of millet; this soul of mine within the heart is greater than the earth, greater than the atmosphere, greater than the sky, greater than the worlds. . . . This soul of mine within the heart, this is Brahma[n].[H11]

The same Upanishad, playing upon the phrase *Tat tvam asi,* tells the story:

Now there was Shvetaketu Aruneya. To him his father said: "That which is the finest essence—this whole world has that as its soul. That is Reality. That is Atman. That art thou, Shvetaketu."
"Do you, Sir, cause me to understand even more."
"So be it, my dear," said he . . . "Bring hither a fig."
"Here it is, Sir."
"Divide it."
"It is divided, Sir."
"What do you see there?"
"Those rather fine seeds, Sir."
"Of these, please divide one."
"It is divided, Sir."
"What do you see there?"
"Nothing at all, Sir."
Then he said to him: "Verily, my dear, that finest essence which you do not perceive—verily, my dear, from that finest essence this great Nyagrodha (sacred fig) tree

thus arises. Believe me, my dear," said he, "that which is the finest essence—this whole world has that as its soul. That is Reality. That is Atman. *That art thou,* Shvetaketu."[H12]

The thinkers of the Upanishads did not stop here. Knowing that their philosophy was grounded in mysticism, and not alone in a search for knowledge, they said that when the human soul *knows* its complete identity with Brahman, it celebrates this knowledge with a feeling of unity approaching ecstasy. The experience of such assured knowledge was pronounced so beatific as to be indescribable, a blissfulness

Wherefrom words turn back,
Together with the mind, not having attained.[H13]

Undoubtedly, most of the writers of the Upanishads knew of, if they did not themselves practice, the technique of such realization of identity with or complete absorption into Brahman. In this technique the prospective Brahman-knower would sit meditating in profound quiet of mind, seeking to know, verily *know*, not have an opinion or a mere belief, but be spiritually certain, that he and the world of sense about him had alike the same ground of being; that he and the tree near him were one, because they were both phases of the One, in short, *were* Brahman-Atman and not any other. The certitude of such unity came to him when he was more in a nonconscious than a conscious state.* In seeking analogies for it, the later Upanishadic thinkers declared that there are three mental states which may be usefully compared with it: the state of waking consciousness, the state of dreaming sleep, and the state of deep, dreamless sleep. All are states of consciousness, but as modes of experience of truth and reality all three are found defective, especially the first two, because in them there is a persistence of the consciousness of a duality of subject and object, self and not-self, ego and non-ego. Deep, dreamless sleep is nearest to

---

* The point is that Brahman is both razor and razor-case.

* Strictly speaking, he would be neither conscious nor nonconscious. He would be as in an ecstasy.

affording an analogy for the state of union with Brahman because it represents a sinking back into a type of nonconsciousness in which subject and object are no longer distinguished. But a fourth state of consciousness that underlies but yet transcends the first three—Pure Consciousness—comes into full being only with the experience of union with Brahman (called *turiya* or *caturtha*). This state is considered to be the highest of all states of mind because it represents the purest being of soul, when the soul is sleeplessly intent and when subject and object are indistinguishable in the purity of being. A modern interpreter from India identifies it as "pure intuitional consciousness, where there is no knowledge of objects internal or external."[11] The *Mandukya Upanishad* contains an interesting definition of it.

> The fourth state is not that which is conscious of the subjective, nor that which is conscious of the objective, nor that which is conscious of both, nor that which is simple consciousness, nor that which is an all-sentient mass, nor that which is all darkness. It is unseen, transcendent, the sole essence of the consciousness of self, the completion of the world.[12]

In the turiya state the world and the self are not obliterated as they would be in deep, dreamless sleep, but both the self and the world are held together in their pure essences, stripped of all distortion and illusion and experienced as being united with the being of Brahman-Atman, where their reality is found to subsist. To experience such a state of consciousness is to attain moksha, final liberation, release from rebirth.

One doctrine evolved during this period does, however, provide for a periodical dissolution or suspended being of all souls and of the entire world. This is the famous theory of the cyclic destruction and re-creation of the world. According to this theory, the world dissolves away at the end of every *kalpa* or period of created being, and all the souls in the universe depart from their bodies into a state of suspended being. After a period of absolute nullity and repose, called a *pralaya*, the world comes again into being, and the long-quiescent souls take up a new embodiment in vegetables, animals, men, gods, and demons. The castes are re-formed, the Vedas re-composed, and another kalpa proceeds to its inevitable end, with history generally repeating itself over again.

Such conceptions contain the germs of much future philosophizing. The six great systems of Hindu philosophy were to develop from these first-fruits of speculation. The Indian mind had indeed launched out into the deep.

First Appearance in Indian Thought of Reincarnation and Karma

It was in this same period that a new color was given to Indo-Aryan thought by the adoption of two doctrines that were to become permanent elements in the outlook of India. Both make their first definite appearance in Indian literature in the Upanishads, but they were very probably not inventions of the time. They may have been taken over from Dravidian beliefs. In any case they are not in the earlier Aryan spirit; they derive their relevance, rather, from India itself, considered as the thought-evoking background of human living.

One of these doctrines, the belief in the transmigration of souls or reincarnation (known in India as *samsara*), is not, as any student knows, peculiar to India. It has been held rather widely throughout the world, both among primitives and among peoples of highly developed nations. In its Indo-Aryan form it runs like this: the soul of a man who dies does not, except in the single case of one who at death returns into indistinguishable oneness with Brahman, pass into a permanent state of being in heaven or hell or elsewhere; the soul, rather, is reborn into another existence that will terminate in due time and necessitate yet another birth. Rebirth follows rebirth, with the one exception named, in an endless chain. The successive births are not likely to be on the same plane of being. Rebirth may occur for a finite period of time in any of the series of heavens or hells, or upon earth in any of the forms of life, vegetable, animal, or human. It may thus be either higher or lower than the present or any past existence. A man of low social status now may be reborn as a rajah or a Brahmin, or, which is more likely, an out-caste, or even as an animal, a beetle, worm, vegetable, or soul in hell.

But what determines the nature of the next birth? What causes it to enter a higher or lower state of existence? The second of the new doctrines, and the one that is peculiar to India, provides the answer. One's future existence is determined by the Law of Karma (*karma* meaning "deeds" or "works"), the law that one's thoughts, words, and deeds have an ethical consequence fixing one's lot in future existences. Looked at retrospectively, karma is the *cause* of what is happening in one's life now.

The earliest statements of this important law are among the clearest. "Those who are of pleasant conduct here—the prospect is, indeed," so runs the *Chandogya Upanishad,* "that they will enter a pleasant womb, either the womb of a Brahmin, or the womb of a Kshatriya, or the womb of a Vaisya. But those who are of stinking conduct here—the prospect is, indeed, that they will enter either the womb of a dog, or the womb of a swine, or the womb of an outcast."[H14]

Though it is here much more moderately stated than it was later, this is not quite the doctrine that character makes destiny, that a man of good character when life ends is reborn good in the next existence, or that one who is evil at the moment of death is reborn in evil case. The Law of Karma gradually assumed a more terrible aspect than this. In its more literal interpretation, it implies that everything a man does, each separate deed of his life, weighed along with every other deed, determines destiny. Single acts have each their inevitable consequence that must be worked out to the uttermost, whether for good or evil. This is the extreme view. Many Hindus, who construe the law as being less rigorous in its weighing of the consequences of each separate act, say it is sim-

ply the law that a man reaps what he sows, or to put the fact in terms of another metaphor, that his deeds shape not only his character but his soul, so that in his next incarnation his soul, as having a definite shape, "can find re-embodiment only in a form into which that shape can squeeze."[J] In any case, the law operates like a law of nature. The process is quite impersonal. "There is no judge and no judgment; no punishment, no repentance or amends, no remission of sins by divine clemency . . . just the inexorable causal nexus of the eternal universe itself."[K]

In a somewhat later time than the one we are here considering, the exact recompense of one's deeds was thus precisely estimated:

In consequence of many sinful acts committed with his body, a man becomes in the next birth something inanimate, in consequence of sins committed by speech, a bird, and in consequence of mental sins he is reborn in a low caste. . . . Those who committed mortal sins, having passed during large numbers of years through dreadful hells, obtain, after the expiration of that term of punishment, the following births. The slayer of a Brahmin enters the womb of a dog, a pig, an ass, a camel, a cow, a goat, a sheep, a deer, a bird, a Kandala, and a Pukhasa. . . . A Brahmin who steals the gold of a Brahmin shall pass a thousand times through the bodies of spiders, snakes, lizards, of aquatic animals and of destructive Pukhasas. . . . Men who delight in doing hurt become carnivorous animals; those who eat forbidden food, worms; thieves, creatures consuming their own kind. . . . For stealing grain a man becomes a rat; . . . for stealing a horse, a tiger; for stealing fruits and roots, a monkey; for stealing a woman, a bear; for stealing cattle, a he-goat.[L]

The discouragement that this kind of prospect evoked is well expressed in the *Maitri Upanishad:* "In this sort of cycle of existence (*samsara*) what is the good of enjoyment of desires, when after a man has fed on them there is seen repeatedly his return here to earth? Be pleased to deliver me. In this cycle of existence I am like a frog in a waterless well."[H15] The unhappiness that characterized the emotional revulsion from the Law of Karma is here very clearly expressed. Even the enjoyment of desires is brought into question by the man of sense and reason who

107

contemplates the effects of his acts upon his future.* The prospect did indeed suggest unpleasant possibilities. And yet into all this the newly established caste system fitted perfectly.

The Place of Caste in the Religious Dogma

During the period around 500 B.C. the caste system, so distinctive of Hindu social life, was gradually establishing itself, although its final form took centuries to evolve. The order of rank was now as follows: first, the Brahmins; then the Kshatriyas; below these, the dependent Vaisyas or "vassals"; and, last, the Shudras or servants. (There is a possibility that the Brahmins had imposed upon a more complex configuration this fourfold classification, for they wanted to establish their supremacy—and succeeded.) Outside the caste system altogether—"beyond the pale"—were the out-castes, including a group that was "untouchable." The out-castes constituted the dregs of society, unclean and without the hope of ever rising in the social scale, unless they happened to be in the small group out-casted temporarily for infraction of caste rules and awaiting reinstatement after expiation of their offences. The stratification of society proceeded further. In succeeding centuries, hard and fast lines were drawn, not only between but also within each caste. The main castes fissured into scores, even hundreds, of subcastes, each forbidding intermarriage into other subcastes and otherwise restricting freedom of association.†

But our interest here is not in the social extension of the caste system, but rather in its place within the religious dogma evolved by the Brahmins. When the caste system was linked up with the Law of Karma, the inequalities of life had at once a simple and comprehensive explanation. The existence of caste in the social structure immediately acquired a kind of moral justification. If a man was born a Shudra, it was because he had sinned in previous existences and deserved no better lot. A Brahmin, on the other hand, had every right to exalt his position and prerogatives; by good deeds in previous existences he had merited his present high station. And here, too, the ranking of the castes with the Brahmins at the top, the Kshatriyas next, the Vaisyas third, and the Shudras last seemed justified by a spiritual sliding scale, as it were: the class in society with the best record of spiritual attainment should be at the top. (So, at least, the Brahmins argued, and in spite of die-hard resistance, the Kshatriyas, with no notion of contradicting the fact of transmigration and the consequences of karma in determining destiny, and thus deprived of any weighty counterargument to offer, had to be content at length with second place—after fostering some variant views that were in opposition to Brahminism, as will be seen.*)

The social consequence of the moral justification of caste was apparent in another direction. Any attempt to level up the inequalities of society and lay a broader basis for social justice and reward now became either impious or morally wrong-headed. To question the operations of the Law of Karma, as fixing the just retribution for deeds in former lives, became the rankest of heresies.

The Need of a Way of Release

The Aryans who came into India were a robust and optimistic people, but this confident frame of mind persisted only so long as the mood expressed in the Vedas did. With the rise of the caste system, the adoption of the beliefs in reincarnation and the Law of Karma, and the development of a world-denying practice of asceticism, disaffection with the world grew in the mind of ancient India. This turning away from life here and now had other causes, too.

---

* That this was a widespread feeling of the time is evident in early Buddhism, which gave even more prominence to the Law of Karma than did the thinkers of the Upanishads and their followers. See below, Chapter 5.

† Today there are more than two thousand such castes.

* The reference here is to Jainism and Buddhism.

There were undoubtedly physical and psychological conditions making for it. Up to the time of their descent into the Ganges valley the Aryans had not finally given up their nomadic habit of life. The world still appealed to them as a sphere of action and adventure; obstacles and difficult endeavors still called out their aggressive qualities; the "native hue of resolution" was not as yet "sicklied o'er with the pale cast of thought"; they were activistic, joyous, and practical. But after they had descended the Ganges River plain and ended their wanderings, their life in that hot and enervating climate became recessive, and the energies of their bodies waned. Keen minds will not cease from thinking under such conditions. Thought may substitute for legs and provide the intellectualist, sensualist, or lover of romantic dreams with vicarious adventure—that of the mind and imagination. And yet, should this world be held to be the only realm of existence, the spirit tends to grow heavy and thought to rest more and more in negations.

In the case of ancient India, those who were aware of no world but this and felt confined and hemmed in by it came to feel that reincarnation under the Law of Karma gave them little comfort. Highly reflective minds were profoundly depressed. When these contemplated the apparently endless series of rebirths that the doctrine of transmigration conjured up to their imagination, they felt acute distress. Hindus have come to speak of the process of rebirth as "The Wheel." They have tended to look upon it with dismay. Beholding it eternally revolving, their hearts have failed them at the prospect of a possible thousand million rebirths stretching out their length before them.

The inexorable character of the operations of the Law of Karma have added to this distressing consideration feelings of dread that have daunted the stoutest heart. Few can await retribution with complacency. Even the prospect of being reborn in the next life on the human plane has offered little consolation, for it is but too likely to be on a lower level.

And yet for Hindus there is a classical antidote for this discouragement, an ultimate solution for it. It is this: "You who think this life is evil and are so distressed by the prospect of ever-recurring rebirths are forgetting something. There is a realm of being that is eternal and changeless, not at all like this world that is so full of change and decay, of becoming and passing away. You can be liberated into it, if you try." Hindus are in fact saved from pessimism when they accept the faith that this world is not the only realm of existence, that endless suffering is not their inevitable lot, that there is a realm of reality not hopelessly involved in becoming, changing, disintegrating, and perishing—namely, the realm of true being and true freedom, Nirvana.

To this point the ideas we have been examining have been steadily tending. The further history of Indian religion, orthodox or heterodox, is essentially that of a search for the solution of the problem, how may one reach a state of experience or being that transcends life's imperfections? Negatively, since rebirth is seen to supply a network of suffering extended over great stretches of time and space, how may one achieve release from the round of rebirths? More positively, how may one know and experience the truly real as against the deceptively and only partially real?

Barely four centuries passed after the Aryans invaded the Ganges plain before this problem became both clear and urgent. The mind of India has been at work on it ever since.

It now becomes our task to consider the chief solutions that have been offered, and to present their divergencies and similarities.

Suggestions for Further Reading

Bloomfield, Maurice. *The Religion of the Veda.* Putnam's Sons, 1908

———, tr. *Hymns of the Atharva Veda.* Vol. XLII, *Sacred Books of the East,* Oxford, Clarendon Press, 1897

Bragdon, Claude. *An Introduction to Yoga.* Alfred A. Knopf, 1933

Dasgupta, S. *Yoga as Philosophy and Religion.* Kegan Paul, Trench, Trubner & Co., 1924

———. *Hindu Mysticism.* Open Court, 1927

Eliade, Mircea. *Yoga: Immortality and Freedom.* Pantheon Books, 1958

Eliot, Sir Charles. *Hinduism and Buddhism.* 3 vols., Routledge and Kegan Paul, 1954. Earlier ed., Edward Arnold, London, 1921

Farquhar, J. N. *An Outline of the Religious Literature of India.* Oxford, 1920

Griffith, R. T. H., tr. *The Hymns of the Rig Veda.* 2 vols., E. J. Lazarus and Co., Benares, 1895

Griswold, H. D. *The Religion of the Rig Veda.* Oxford, 1923

Hume, R. E., tr. *The Thirteen Principal Upanishads.* Oxford, 1934

Keith, A. B. *The Religion and Philosophy of the Veda and the Upanishads.* Harvard University Press, 1920

MacDonell, A. A., ed. *Hymns from the Rigveda.* London, Association Press, 1922

Mahadevan, T. M. P. *Outlines of Hinduism.* Bombay, Chetana, 1956

Morgan, Kenneth W., ed. *The Religion of the Hindus.* Ronald Press, 1953

Piggott, S. *Prehistoric India.* Penguin pb, 1950

Prabhavananda and Manchester, trs. *The Upanishads.* Mentor pb, 1957

Radhakrishnan, S., ed. *The Principal Upanishads.* Harper & Bros., 1953

——— and Moore, Charles, eds. *Source Book in Indian Philosophy.* Princeton University Press, 1957

Renou, L. *Religions of Ancient India.* Oxford, 1953

———. *Vedic India.* Calcutta, Susil Gupta, 1957

———, ed. *Hinduism.* George Braziller, 1961. Washington Square Press, pb, 1963

Sarma, D. S. *What Is Hinduism?* 3rd rev. ed., Madras Law Journal Press, 1945

Wheeler, Sir Mortimer. *The Indus Civilization. The Cambridge History of India,* Suppl. Vol., 1953

OUT OF THE JUMBLED MATRIX of early Hindu thought, in which ideas held over from pre-Aryan religion vied for attention with ideas drawn from the Vedas and elaborated in the Upanishads—ideas certainly held at that time by only a minority of the people—two religions sprang up to vex the course of Hinduism with their answers to that central problem of Indian life, how to find release from karma and the ever-lengthening round of rebirths entailed by it. Hardly had this problem issued its challenge to the mind of India and begun to bear down upon the human spirit with weight and force before the two religions appeared. One of them, Jainism, was destined to win adherents in India only, but to survive every assault upon it, so that even though it never became a religion with a great and elemental appeal, it has continued to exist in India to this day. The other religion, Buddhism, spread rapidly over the whole of India and overflowed its boundaries to the south, east, and north, winning a permanent footing to the south and east in Ceylon, Burma, Thailand, Cambodia, Laos, and Vietnam, and to the north in China, Korea, Japan, Tibet, and Mongolia. It supplied these regions with some profoundly satisfactory answers to universal human needs. But it was destined at length to all but die out in India itself, except upon the fringes of that amazing land. For a thousand years Hinduism, all but eclipsed, grew steadfastly, reaching for assent, and its eventual return to dominance over the field of religion is something of a marvel.

When we turn to see what Jainism had to offer, our Occidental minds are apt to receive an initial shock. To anyone bred in the prevailing materialistic and hedonistic attitudes of the West, Jainism may seem at first glance an adjustment to life and world as rigorously world-denying as any the history of religions affords.

Like the greater faith Buddhism, which arose about the same time, Jainism was, when it came into being, a reaction to and in some part against the tendencies set in motion by the Brahmins. At that time (the sixth century B.C.) the caste system was

4 Jainism: A Study in Asceticism

still in the making, and when the priestly class put forward their broad claims to spiritual and social ascendancy, many, although certainly not all, in the ranks of the nobility, of whose caste Mahavira was a member, resisted these claims. The Kshatriyas were at that time active and able in philosophic discussion, as the Upanishads bear witness, and many of them found in Brahmanism a system of thought that at a number of points gave them pause. Sturdy minds among them found unacceptable the monistic idealism that resolved the substantial world of everyday into a single, unknowable entity, and there were honest souls, practical and realistic in their outlook, who declared that it was not the physical world but rather this much-spoken of Brahman that was unreal. To their commonsense eyes each living thing and all manner of other entities were as real as they appeared to be. Men and men's souls, stones, trees, and hills, footed and flying creatures, and fishes of the sea all entered experience as realities that were independently and in their own right existent. The struggle against the monistic idealism of the Brahmins frequently took the form of denying the reality of all hypothetical world-souls, however defined or named —whether supreme persons or all-inclusive neutral somethings—and maintaining a position that was ultimately atheistic. Many Western authorities therefore think that because this view was widespread and appears in the Upanishads, there must have existed a pre-Aryan dualistic world-view to which many anti-monists may have adhered—a world-view that affirmed on the one hand the reality of the physical world and on the other the existence of an infinite number of living souls. This position we have already identified as the minority view in the Upanishads (p. 102); it is now known as the Sankhya philosophy. It seems to have been systematized shortly before the founding of Jainism by a thinker named Kapila, by whom it was so well worked out that it is listed by the Hindus to this day as one of the six acceptable systems of philosophy. (See infra, p. 202 f.)

To the group that rejected Brahmanism and took a position like that of the Sankhya philosophy Ma-

havira belonged. But he had a special commitment that led him to modify whatever convictions he had that coincided with the Sankhya point of view; he adhered to the teaching and ascetic practices of Parshva, who lived some 250 years earlier than he did and may be presumed to have had doctrines that were the basis on which Mahavira developed his own views.

I Mahavira's Manner of Life

Mahavira is the accepted name for the founder of Jainism. Anyone familiar with Latin and allied tongues will see at once that it is an honorific title meaning "Great Man" or "Hero." It has quite superseded Nataputta Vardhamana, the name by which he was originally known. He is said to have been born near Vaisali (in modern Bihar) in 599 B.C. and to have died in 527.* His father, it is claimed, was a rajah. Mahavira was not the oldest son—a circumstance that made his renunciation of the princely life later on easier.

It is hard to recover the truth, of course, because of the uncertain state of the records, but the data given below, lifted out of the records, probably contain it. It is the picture of Mahavira presented by one of the two main Jaina sects, the Shvetambaras.† The story is at heart a very simple one, and, whether true *in toto* or not, it is representative of all Indian asceticism.

That Mahavira was reared in the luxury of the ancient courts of India may be gathered from the assertion that he was attended by five nurses: "a wet-nurse, a nurse to bathe him, one to dress him, one

---

* These are the traditional dates set by the Shvetambara sect. However, some modern authorities think these dates are sixty years too early.

† The canon of this sect is probably the oldest, but this is a debatable point. The writers of this canon admit themselves that they are writing 980 years after the death of Mahavira! (See *Sacred Books of the East*, Vol. XXII, p. 270.)

to play with him, and one to carry him," and that, "transferred from the lap of one nurse to that of another, he grew up," living "in the enjoyment of the allowed, noble, five-fold joys and pleasures, consisting in sound, touch, taste, color, and smell,"[A1]—the pleasures of sense he was later to renounce.* He married and had a daughter. But he was not content with a prince's life. Outside of the town, in a park he must often have visited, dwelt a body of monks who followed the rule of the ascetic Parshva, mentioned above, who had founded a monastic order that took his name. Mahavira was much attracted to their mode of life. However, out of respect for his parents he decided: "It will not behoove me, during the life of my parents, to enter the state of houselessness."[A2] As soon as his parents did die (the legend has it that they died by careful prearrangement, in accordance with the rite of *sallakhana,* or voluntary self-starvation: "On a bed of kusa-grass they rejected all food, and their bodies dried up by the last mortification of the flesh"[A3]), Mahavira prepared to give up the princely life. He was now thirty years of age, but he had to ask his brother's consent, and on condition that he would remain in the palace one more year (thinking it over?), that consent was obtained. But he used the time to give up "his gold and silver, his troops and chariots"; he "distributed, portioned out and gave away his valuable treasures."[A4]

Then in the first month of winter, he "retired from the world." He joined the body of monks in their cells outside the town. As part of his initiation into their order, he took off all his ornaments and finery and retained only one garment, a robe with "a flamingo pattern." Next, he "plucked out with his right and left hands on the right and left sides of his head his hair in five handfuls." He took the required pledge: "I shall neglect my body and abandon the care of it; I shall with equanimity bear, undergo, and suffer all calamities arising from divine powers, men, or animals."[A5]

Some months after joining the order of Parshva,

* India is tolerant of the sensuous pleasures, if they be renounced in time. See p. 191 f.

Mahavira renouncing the world. This detail from a manuscript of the Kalpa Sutra *shows Mahavira seated beneath a tree and pulling out his hair "in five handfuls." He is attended by the god Indra, whose divinity is attested by his four arms and the canopy over his head. The unknown artist probably lived in the seventeenth century. (Courtesy, Museum of Fine Arts, Boston.)*

Mahavira struck out for himself. Throwing off his robe, and thenceforth going completely naked, he began a long wandering through the villages and plains of central India in quest of release from the cycle of birth, death, and rebirth. His two convictions were (1) that saving one's soul from evil (that is, purging contaminating matter from the soul) is impossible without practicing the severest asceticism, and (2) that maintaining the purity and integrity of one's own soul involves practicing *ahimsa,* or noninjury, to any and all living beings. Neither of these convictions was new, for Mahavira took them from his predecessors in the tradition of thought with which

113

his name is now associated, but the faithfulness and sincerity with which he lived by them were remarkable.

Tradition says that for some years he wandered about with Makkhali Gosala ("Gosala of the mendicant's staff"), who was later head of the sect of Ajivakas, an ascetic group holding the strictly deterministic view that all living beings must pass without abatement or curtailment through rebirths lasting through 8,400,000 kalpas, unable in all this time to alter their fate even by virtuous conduct, being bent this way and that by an inexorable and implacable destiny, until at the end of a long, predestined ascent to a higher state, release comes automatically. But the two wanderers quarreled—perhaps (who knows?) about Gosala's view that asceticism and sexual intercourse might be alike predestined for the same person in the same interval—and Mahavira went his own solitary way in the strictest non-attachment to any other individual.

In moving about, he never stayed more than one night in a village or more than five in a town. He was determined to form no attachments to any place or people that might bind him to the world and its pleasures. Only during the four months of the rainy season did he remain in the same place, because then the roads and paths were teeming with life, and the principle of ahimsa required his remaining quiescent.

The following passages from the oldest Jaina documents are worthy of close study. Every phrase counts. They constitute a unique record of consistency to principle.

The first group of passages illustrates with great vividness the unusual precautions Mahavira took not to injure any living thing, directly or indirectly.

Thoroughly knowing the earth-bodies and water-bodies and fire-bodies and wind-bodies, the lichens, seeds, and sprouts, he comprehended that they are, if narrowly inspected, imbued with life, and avoided to injure them.

Walking, he meditated with his eyes fixed on a square space before him of the length of a man. . . . Looking a little sideward, looking a little behind, attentively looking on his path, [he walked so as not to step on any living thing].

Many sorts of living beings gathered on his body, crawled about it and caused pain there. [But he exercised self-control so as not to scratch himself.]

Without ceasing in his reflections, the Venerable One slowly wandered about, and, killing no creatures, he begged for his food.A6

Other passages condense into this picture: Mahavira apparently made it his practice, when walking, to carry a soft broom for sweeping the path wherever it might be covered with insects. Out of doors he cleared the ground before lying down to rest or sleep; within doors he examined his bed to be sure it was free from eggs and living beings. He refused all raw food of any kind and took into his begging bowl only food prepared originally for someone else and left over, for if he allowed anyone to take the life out of something expressly for him, he must hold himself accountable for being the cause of the killing of a living being. He carried a cloth for straining water before drinking it,* and always went carefully through a bowl of food to see if any of it was affected by eggs, sprouts, worms, mildew, cobwebs, or any living thing, and if it was so affected, he removed the portions containing them before "circumspectly" eating the rest.

As to the strictness with which he practiced asceticism, the next group of passages is a sufficient testimony.

This is the rule followed by the Venerable One: When the cold season has halfway advanced, the houseless one, leaving off his robe and stretching out his arms, should wander about, not leaning against a tree-trunk.

When a cold wind blows in which some feel pain, then some houseless monks in the cold rain seek a place sheltered from the wind. "We shall put on more clothes; kindling wood, or well covered, we shall be able to bear the very painful influence of the cold." But the Venerable One desired nothing of the kind; strong in control, he suffered, despising all shelter.

Sometimes in the cold season the Venerable One was meditating in the shade. In summer he [exposed] himself to the heat, he [sat] squatting in the sun.

* And for holding before his mouth when speaking, lest insects fly into it.

The Venerable One did not seek sleep for the sake of pleasure; he waked up himself, and slept only a little.

Purgatives and emetics, anointing of the body and bathing, shampooing, and cleansing of the teeth do not behoove him.[A7]

Fearful of forming agreeable personal attachments, he refrained from speaking to or greeting anyone. This procured him a good deal of ill-will from inquisitive villagers, but he bore all affronts with determined indifference.

For some it is not easy to do what he did, not to answer those who salute; he was beaten with sticks, and struck by sinful people.

Giving up the company of all householders whomsoever, he meditated. Asked, he gave no answer.

Disregarding slights difficult to bear, the Sage wandered about, not attracted by story-tellers, pantomimes, songs, fights at the quarter-staff, and boxing matches.

The dogs bit him, ran at him. Few people kept off the attacking, biting dogs. Striking the monk, they cried "Khukkhu," and made the dogs bite him.

When he once sat without moving his body, they cut his flesh, tore his hair, covered him with dust. Throwing him up, they let him fall, or disturbed him in his religious postures; abandoning the care of his body, the Venerable One humbled himself.[A8]

On another occasion, it is related (though it puts a strain on credulity to believe it) that sportive villagers, seeing him sitting naked and motionless in a field, lit a fire between his feet to see if he would move, and drove "nails" into his ears; but the Venerable One remained oblivious to them, masterly in self-control. He was determined to maintain a meditative calm unaffected by the discomforts of the body.

Keeping steadfastly to this invincible self-discipline, Mahavira wandered about for twelve years, hopeful of moksha, deliverance. The crowning experience that he sought was not withheld; it came at last. The Jaina record tells of the event with great particularity.

During the thirteenth year, in the second month of summer, in the fourth fortnight . . . when the shadow had turned toward the east, . . . outside the town Grimbhikagrama, on the northern bank of the river Rigupalika, in the field of the householder Samaga, in a northeastern direction from an old temple, not far from a sal tree, in a squatting position, with knees high and head low, in deep meditation, in the midst of abstract meditation, he reached Nirvana, the complete and full . . . called Kevala.°[A9]

He thus became the Jina (the Conqueror), and all his followers Jains, for he had achieved a complete "victory" over his body and the desires that bind one to this world of matter and sin.

Having attained the experience he had been twelve years in winning, Mahavira began to seek people out and teach them. Conversions to his way of life followed. And after thirty years of successful teaching and organizing, at the age of seventy-two, apparently by the rite of voluntary self-starvation (sallakhana), he "cut asunder the ties of birth, old age, and death" and was "finally liberated, freed from all pains."[A10] He is now, according to all the Jaina sects, enjoying supreme bliss in a place of reward called Isatpragbhara, in a state no longer subject to rebirth.

II Philosophy and Ethics of Jainism

The story of Mahavira has been told in the previous section in the simplest way, with the smallest use of Jaina technical terms, in order that the essential passion for release or escape exhibited in it might stand out clearly. But the followers of Mahavira— and he himself, though doubtless to a less degree— thought of his course of life as operating within a philosophical and ethical context requiring for its description Jaina technical terms and distinctions. Karma, soul, matter, salvation—all had meanings reflecting a world-view distinct from that either of Brahmanism or Buddhism.

° Literally "cut off," i.e., from karma.

The Jains have never questioned the belief that man is gravely conditioned in his progress toward salvation by the Law of Karma; indeed the disquieting implications of this law have loomed very large in their view. They interpret the doctrine of karma strictly, in accordance with their idea that the consequences of one's deeds are literally deposited in and on the soul. Various kinds of karmas are accumulated during this and previous births like layers or incrustations of foreign substance that may form as many as five sheaths around the soul and must be worn off by the process of living. Or, as the predecessors of Mahavira, going back to the ascetic Parshva, taught, it is as if a rarefied material, poisonous and alien, has penetrated the soul and must be thrown off by the soul's activity.

This Jaina idea is based on a very interesting view of the relation between matter and mind. Matter ranges in density from solidity to the thinnest sort of being beyond the reach of the senses; in the former case it is heavy and gross, in the latter light and volatile. Matter is eternal and consists of atoms that may cluster together into any shape or quality, such as earth, water, wind, sounds, colors, and sentient bodies of all sorts, including in the last case their senses and sensations. The subtlest mode of matter is karma-matter. It forms in the soul in the following way: whenever moved by bad desire or passion, the soul becomes, as it were, sticky, and gets itself covered with matter or permeated by it. Such adhesions and infiltrations of matter affect the course of transmigration, for the soul at the end of each period of existence carries the matter that vitiates its purity along with it. If it is full of matter, it sinks lower in the scale of existence, perhaps into hell; if it has only a little matter in it, it will be light enough to rise, perhaps into the heavens, and find its embodiment there in the body of some god, or rise higher still and become an eternally "liberated" being.

In scrutinizing the nature of Karma, the Jains have distinguished at least eight kinds of it (and 148 subdivisions), depending on the effects produced.

One form of it fixes the length of an individual's life, another his physical and mental characteristics, a third his nationality and caste, a fourth his power of resolution, a fifth his intelligence and degree of knowledge, a sixth his intuitiveness, a seventh his capacity for pleasure and pain, and an eighth his attitudes, whether of faith or doubt, purity or passion, and the like. Singly and in combination these kinds of karmas fix one's lot in each existence and affect the whole course of life.

The soul's chief problem, that of managing to throw off or expel karma-matter from itself, is in part automatically taken care of, simply by the karmas' exerting their effects and passing off. But the ethical activity of the soul annihilates the old karmas more swiftly, and at the same time (because any action creates a new karma) produces only those new karmas that have the briefest effects and are quickly dissipated or neutralized.

The major fact of life that emerges from all this is the inherent opposition (or opposite tendency) of soul and flesh, matter and mind. Mahavira and his followers were pluralists, but they roughly grouped all things into two distinct categories: (1) the *ajiva* or lifeless things in the universe, composing the realm of thick, dead matter, and (2) the *jiva* or living beings in the universe, to be defined more precisely as the infinite multitude of individual souls composing the realm of spirit (or thin, lively matter). The ajiva is eternal yet evil, but the jiva, also eternal, is of an infinite value, and contains all good, for souls are indestructible and infinitely precious. Souls are classed according to the number of senses they have. Those having five senses—gods, men, animals, and hell-beings—are in the highest group. Next are the four-sensed beings, for example, the larger insects, such as bees, flies, and butterflies. Without sight and hearing, the third group includes moths and the smaller insects. The group of two-sensed beings, possessing touch and taste, includes worms, shell-fish, leeches, and minute creatures. A final group with only the sense of touch is often referred to in Jaina writings; it includes vegetables, trees, seeds, lichens, earth-bodies, wind-bodies, water-bodies, and fire-bodies.

In their pure state, when entirely freed from matter, all souls are perfect, possessing infinite perception, infinite knowledge, infinite power, and infinite bliss. When liberated from matter, they rise straight to the top of the universe, where they join the souls in Isatpragbhara that have been liberated before them.

Incidentally, the souls that have entered Isatpragbhara are not reduced to nothingness, for though they may be described as being without qualities or relations of any sort, there is no cessation of consciousness in them. "The liberated," so runs a Jaina text, "is not long nor small . . . neither heavy nor light; he is without body, without resurrection, without contact with matter; he is not feminine, nor masculine, nor neuter; he perceives, he knows, but there is no analogy (whereby to know the nature of the liberated soul)."[A11] And there, without further ado, the text lets the matter rest, as well it might!

Being indestructible and absolutely independent, souls are not phases of nor emanations thrown out by something else. The Jains from the beginning have held that there is no Brahman-Atman such as the Brahmins describe. No unity of substance or being holds the universe together. There is no Supreme Ruler of the world, such as the devout look to. There are numerous higher beings who might be called "gods" and who exist on the various levels of the celestial regions, but they are finite beings, subject like men to rebirth. No help, Mahavira taught, could be expected from such beings, themselves in need of redemption. Therefore human souls caught in the predicament of existence in the physical world and needing to find a way of escape from karma through moksha, or release, must realize that salvation is self-attained. Praying to the gods is of no avail.

A monk or nun should not say, "The god of the sky! The god of the thunderstorm! The god of lightning! The god who begins to rain! . . . May rain fall, or may it not fall! May the crops grow! May the sun rise!" They should not use such speech. But, knowing the nature of things, he should say, "The air; a cloud has gathered, or come down; the cloud has rained."[A12]

Nor does it avail to turn to other men, nor to the words of others, as having inherent efficacy to save. The priests are of no special authority. The Vedas are not especially sacred and cannot be used as miraculous agencies of release from rebirth. Rather than trust to these external aids, let each man realize that salvation lies within himself. "Man," runs one of Mahavira's most emphatic utterances, "thou art thine own friend. Why wishest thou for a friend beyond thyself?"[A13]

The surest and swiftest way to reach liberation or moksha is the practice of asceticism or austerities (*tapas*). What Mahavira meant by asceticism may be seen from his own practice of it. His followers have added fasting according to certain rules and types of meditation leading to a trance-state marked by complete dissociation from the outer world and transcendence of one's own physical states. This trance-state is supposed to be like the one that Mahavira entered in the thirteenth year of his seeking and that assured him of his final deliverance. One cannot reach such a state, the Jains hold, without severe control of the mind and passions, for acts cannot be controlled and karmas be prevented thereby from accumulating unless the mind is so controlled as to be purified of all love of or dependence upon the world and its objects, animate and inanimate.

Mahavira's ascetic practice was (probably not by himself) summed up in the "Five Great Vows" for monks. These vows were later written out in very full form. In these fuller statements[A14] there are some interesting definitions of what Mahavira meant by ahimsa and the breaking off of every attachment to the world and its objects. Ahimsa is the subject of the first vow.

1. The first great vow, Sir, runs thus: I renounce all killing of living beings, whether movable or immovable. Nor shall I myself kill living beings nor cause others to do it, nor consent to it. As long as I live I confess, and blame,

and exempt myself of these sins, in mind, speech, and body.

There are five clauses:

A Nirgrantha [ascetic; literally, naked one] is careful in his walk, not careless.

A Nirgrantha searches into his mind. If his mind is sinful, acting on impulse, produces quarrels, pains, he should not employ such a mind.

A Nirgrantha searches into his speech. If his speech is sinful, produces quarrels, pains, he should not utter such speech.

A Nirgrantha is careful in laying down his utensils of begging.

A Nirgrantha eats and drinks after inspecting his food and drink. If a Nirgrantha would eat and drink without inspecting his food and drink, he might hurt and displace or injure or kill all sorts of living beings.

The second vow concerns truth-speaking.

2. I renounce all vices of lying speech arising from anger or greed or fear or mirth. I shall neither myself speak lies, nor cause others to speak lies, nor consent to the speaking of lies by others.

There are five clauses subjoined to this vow also, and they provide that a Nirgrantha should speak only after deliberation, so as to be sure his words are true; should never be angry, greedy, nor fearful, lest these emotions betray him into falsehood; and should not be given to mirth-making, or, as we should say, "joking" or "kidding," because these forms of diversion are based on departures from fact.

3. The third great vow runs thus: I renounce all taking of anything not given, either in a village or a town or a wood, either of little or much, of great or small, of living or lifeless things. I shall neither take myself what is not given, nor cause others to take it, nor consent to their taking it.

Again there are five clauses, enjoining severe self-restraint upon every form of greed.

4. The fourth great vow runs thus: I renounce all sexual pleasure. I shall not give way to sensuality, nor cause others to do so, nor consent to it in others.

The five clauses under this vow explain how a Nirgrantha does not allow himself, even in the remotest way, to feel the allure of sex.

5. The fifth vow runs thus: I renounce all attachments, whether to little or much, small or great, living or lifeless things; neither shall I myself form such attachments, nor cause others to do so, nor consent to their doing so.

The five clauses of this startlingly comprehensive vow may be condensed as follows:

If a creature with ears hears agreeable and disagreeable sounds, it should not be attached to, nor delighted with, nor disturbed by the sounds. If it is impossible not to hear sounds which reach the ear, the mendicant should avoid love or hate originated by them.

If a creature with eyes sees forms, if a creature with an organ of smell smells smells, if a creature with a tongue tastes tastes, if a creature with an organ of feeling feels agreeable or disagreeable touches, it should not be attached to them, (and) should avoid love or hate originated by them.

Of these vows the most radically ascetic is the last. The vows concerning ahimsa and the renunciation of all sexual pleasures are important, of course. The renunciation of sex-interests was stressed by Mahavira, who is quoted as saying: "The greatest temptation in the world are women. . . . Men forsooth say, 'These are the vessels of happiness.' But this leads them to pain, to delusion, to death, to hell, to birth as hell-beings or brute beasts."[A15] The language is sufficiently strong. Nevertheless, the fifth vow is more inclusive, and by implication contains all the rest. It does in fact make sure that, though the monk may be in the world, he is, if he practices the fifth vow, emphatically not of it.

It was obvious from the beginning that the Five Great Vows could be only for Jaina ascetics. For the lay-folk, to whom the way of life prescribed in the severer code is impossible, the Jaina leaders have laid down a much modified rule of life. The lay adherents are to make twelve vows: (1) never knowingly to take the life of a sentient creature (hence, never to till the soil, nor engage in butchering, fishing, brewing, or any occupation involving the taking of life); (2) never to lie; (3) never to steal, or take what is not given; (4) never to be unchaste (or, to put it positively, always to be faithful to husband, or wife, and be pure in thought and word); (5) to check greed, by placing a limit upon one's wealth and giving away any excess; (6) to avoid temptation to sin by, for example, refraining from unnecessary travel; (7) to limit the number of things in daily use; (8) to be on guard against evils that can be avoided; (9) to keep stated periods for meditation; (10) to observe special periods of self-denial; (11) to spend occasional days as a monk; and (12) to give alms, especially in support of ascetics. Of these vows the first is undoubtedly the most important in its social effect. It constituted a limitation that must have seemed serious to the early followers of Mahavira, but at long last it actually proved to have economic as well as religious worth, for the Jains found they could make higher profits when they turned from occupations involving direct harm to living creatures to careers in business as bankers, lawyers, merchants, and proprietors of land. The other moral restrictions of their creed, which prohibited gambling, eating meat, drinking wine, adultery, hunting, thieving, and debauchery, earned them social respect and thus contributed to their survival in the social scene.

III Mahavira's Followers

So great was the impression that Mahavira made upon his followers that legend grew rapidly about him. While his followers were dividing ("in proper protestant fashion"[B]), they were busy elaborating their stories of the divine origin and attributes of Mahavira.

His birth was regarded as supernatural. He was declared to be the last of a long series of savior beings called Tirthankaras. He descended from heaven to enter the womb of a woman. When the gods discovered that this woman was a Brahmin and therefore unworthy to bear the future "corrector" of Brahmanism, they transferred the embryo to the womb of a woman of the Kshatriya caste. He grew up sinless ("whatever is sinful, the Venerable One left that undone"[A16]) and was omniscient ("he knew and saw all conditions of all living beings in the world"[A17]).

Yet as time passed, the eminence of Mahavira was a little obscured by the veneration accorded to the twenty-three Tirthankaras who were thought to have preceded him. Parshva, his immediate predecessor, and hence the twenty-third "ford-finder" (which is what the word *Tirthankara* means), had a great temple erected in his honor on Mt. Parasnath, bearing his name, two hundred miles northwest of Calcutta. Nemi, the twenty-second, had another erected to him upon the cliff under Mt. Girnar, far in western India on the peninsula of Kathiawar. Two very holy shrines, one on Mt. Satrunjaya near Palitana, in Kathiawar, and another on the plateau of Mt. Abu in the Aravalli Hills, have been built to honor Rishabha, the first of the Tirthankaras. Although the only cultus that accords with Jainist theory is "a kind of memorial service in honor of the teacher of the way of salvation,"[C] these temples are of very elaborate and distinguished design. Jainism has come, in fact, to hold a prominent place in the architectural history of India. Other temples besides those mentioned—like the ones at Ahmedebad and Ajinere in western India and a monolithic shrine of exquisite beauty at Kaligamalai in south India—have become show-places of Indian architecture. The elaborate temple shown on page 121 has its own rich beauty.

Early in the history of the faith the Jains divided on the question of wearing clothes. The Shvetambaras or "the white-clad" were the liberals who took their stand on wearing at least one garment, whereas the stricter and more conservative Digambaras got their name from their insistence on going about, whenever religious duty demanded it, "clad in atmosphere." Mahavira did not wear clothes, they pointed out, so why, when there is a religious reason for not

Bronze image of a tirthankara.
The bronze tirthankara from ca.
700 A.D. *stares into space from his*
seat on a cushion upheld by
elephants and lions. He is so
deeply engrossed in meditation
that he is oblivious to all sights
and sounds around him. (Phila-
delphia Museum of Art. Photo-
graph by A. J. Wyatt, staff
photographer.)

wearing clothes,* should they? The Shvetambaras were in the north and yielded a bit both to the cold winds and to the social and cultural influences of the Ganges River plain. The Digambaras, not looked at askance by the Dravidian residents of their south-land, have more easily maintained the earlier, sterner attitudes down the years. Another difference exists in the fact that whereas the Shvetambaras admit women to their monastic order and assume that they have a chance to experience moksha, the Digam-baras cling to Mahavira's reputed verdict that women

are "the greatest temptation in the world" and "the cause of all sinful acts" and are therefore not to be admitted to their temples or to monastic life. Women, in this latter view, cannot win salvation until they have been reborn as men. That is their only hope.

Still another Jaina sect, the Sthanakvasis, tolerate no idols and have no temples. They worship "every-where," mainly through meditation and introspection.

In general, Jaina monks and laymen are not sharply set off from each other. It is still the custom for laymen to fast as monks at least once a year, and monks are laymen who have adopted a severer self-discipline. Laymen also participate with monks in the recurring events of the Jaina calendar. On the last day of their year (about the end of August) monks and laymen, for example, together abstain from all

* I.e., while being a monk, when on pilgrimage, or during religious fasts and rituals. The Digambaras say that any monk who owns property or wears clothes cannot reach Isatpragbhara.

Jaina temple in Calcutta. The decorative details of this sumptuous temple (opposite) in Calcutta, with its architectural elements adopted from all over the world (witness the Corinthian columns), reflects the wealth of the Jains of the great eastern city of India. Note the naked elephant-borne monks in the pavilion, who symbolize renunciation of wealth! (Courtesy of Trans World Airlines.)

food and drink and take time to review and repent of the wrong-doing and misspent hours of the past year, asking forgiveness from those wronged and paying debts. This communal act of repentance (the Parushana) is next day followed by a time of general rejoicing—the New Year's Day of the Jains. Other celebrations recur at longer intervals. At Mysore, for instance, where the Digambaras are largely located, every twelve years the fifty-seven-foot monolithic statue of Gomatesvara, one of the Tirthankaras, has his head anointed from the top of the cliff against which he stands by the contents of over a thousand pots of milk, curds, and sandal paste, amid the shouted acclaim of Jaina by-standers, who hope for an increase of their merit from this expression of gratitude.

It is generally held by Jains that the universe is eternal and that it does not periodically appear, run its course, and then disappear in a *prelaya* (p. 106). But they believe it does go through long periods of improvement and decline. They say that the golden age of man lies far in the past and that we are now in the fifth and next-to-last twenty-one-thousand-year period of steady decline; men are shorter of stature than they once were, nastier, more immoral, more than ever in need of the restraints of governmental power, and they will continue to degenerate until the sixth period of decline is past. Only then will they begin slowly to improve, period by period, until after over one hundred thousand years the golden age will return once more.

Meanwhile, Jainist philosophy has had some effect on the thought of India at large, especially in the realm of logic. The effect has been that of curbing any tendency to overstatement. Jainist logic considers all knowledge relative and transient. To every question one may answer with both yes and no. No proposition is either absolutely true or false. The Jains are fond of their ancient illustration of the logical fallacy inherent in all human thought—the story of the six blind men who put their hands on different parts of an elephant and concluded, each to his own satisfaction, that the elephant was exactly "like a fan," "like a wall," "like a snake," "like a rope," and so on. It is only the free and purified soul, gone to the Jainist heaven, that possesses perfect knowledge.

Today the Jains number approximately two million, most being in the Bombay area, where in early life Mahatma Gandhi felt their influence on his own outlook. The paradox of their present status is, as already indicated, that their essentially world-renouncing religion has, in the devious course of events, secured their economic advantage among the struggling masses of India.

Suggestions for Further Reading

BARODIA, U. D. *History and Literature of Jainism.* Bombay, 1909

HASTINGS, JAMES, ED. *Encyclopedia of Religion and Ethics.* Articles "Ajivakas" and "Jainism"

JACOBI, HERMANN, TR.. *The Gaina Sutras.* Vols. XXII and XLV in *Sacred Books of the East,* Oxford, 1884

JAINI, J. *Outlines of Jainism.* Cambridge, 1916

MEHTA, M. L. *Outlines of Jaina Philosophy.* Bangalore, 1954

STEVENSON, MRS. SINCLAIR. *The Heart of Jainism.* Oxford, 1915

TATIA, N. *Studies in Jaina Philosophy.* Benares, 1951

WARREN, H. *Jainism.* Madras, 1912

ZIMMER, HEINRICH. *Philosophies of India.* Part III, Chap. 1. Meridian Books pb, 1956

Though it arose a generation later, in the lengthening perspective of time Buddhism* seems contemporaneous with Jainism. Moreover, it shares with Jainism some of its deepest motives. Like Jainism it was a world-denying movement looking toward liberation of the true self. It was also a step toward independence of thought and action, springing from the Kshatriya caste and appealing to all classes and conditions of men. Like Mahavira, the monk Gautama found the philosophy of the Brahmins unacceptable and their claims unsubstantiated. He, too, came to deny the doctrine of the saving efficacy of the Vedas and of the ritual observances based upon them, and he challenged the claim of the Brahmin priesthood to prescriptive rights in showing the way to salvation.

But though Buddhism's similarities with Jainism are in some respects close, the differences in other respects are wide. Where one faith fixed its whole hope on an uncompromising and extreme asceticism, the other found deliverance in a moderate and commonsense "middle way." To the Buddha, extreme asceticism was not common sense, any more than sensuality was. Coolly and objectively, he tested every way of salvation offered by the teachers and spiritual leaders of his time, and refused to be swept away into any vagary of religious behavior, however logically self-consistent.

5 Buddhism in Its First Phase: Common Sense in World Denial

I Life of the Founder

Youth

There is a kind of parallel between the lives of Mahavira and the Buddha that led some early schol-

---

* Like the Hindus, the Buddhists, when referring to what the West calls "Buddhism" or the "Buddhist religion," use the term *Dharma* (Pali, *Dhamma*). Their only difference from the Hindus in this respect lies in their linking of this term with the teaching and moral injunctions of one man, Gautama Buddha. An alternative term is *Sasana*, which means the whole body of beliefs and practices of the Buddhist faith, broadly the Buddhist "dispensation" or "system."

ars to regard the two men as identical. Both were, for instance (*if* we are to accept the traditional accounts),* born to high station as members of prominent Kshatriya families; both experienced dissatisfaction with their lot, and though married and having one child, abandoned their homes and became wandering mendicant monks; both rejected the monistic idealism of the Brahmins; both founded monastic orders that ruled out caste distinctions; both were non-conformists from the Hindu point of view because they denied the special sacredness of the Vedic literature. But it is now evident that they differed more pronouncedly than they agreed, that insofar as they were alike in careers and in beliefs, it was due partly to the similarity imposed upon them by their times and environment† and partly to sheer coincidence.

* As in the case of Mahavira (and we shall find the same precaution advisable in other cases that shall come before us), the reader must be on guard not to accept the traditional biographies uncritically. The historical personages who founded the great religions have been lovingly and reverently recalled by their followers, who have had a very human need to visualize them clearly, and have therefore unconsciously added to the accounts handed down to them the details that did this for them. It will be well if the reader says to himself: "Here is the story that millions have taken for truth *and have lived by.*"

It should be emphasized that historical criticism of the Oriental religions has been only recently begun, and until there is something like completion of the critical analysis of the records of these religions, it will be necessary to remain in a state of sceptical suspense.

As to India, the probability is that this suspense will always have to continue to some degree, for since the peoples of India have been more idea-centered than history-minded, the difficulty of distilling historical truth from tradition is increased. This difficulty is, moreover, made much greater by the fact that oral transmission was the principal means of preserving literature and learning for many centuries. Even when sacred texts were put in writing (*ca.* third century B.C.?), they were considered to be somehow inferior to orally transmitted materials, it being held that the voice of an understanding person reciting sacred texts imparts meanings and nuances not apprehended through the eye only. The relative lateness of written transmission obviously magnifies the uncertainties of textual criticism also.

† This similarity lay in the fact that they both came from districts north of the Ganges where Aryan dominance was still being resisted and where Brahmanism was

Siddhartha (Pali, Siddhattha) was the given and Gautama (Pali, Gotama) the family name of the founder of Buddhism. He was born in 563 B.C. in northern India, some one hundred miles from Benares, in a fertile tract of country among the foothills of the Himalayas. His father was a petty chieftain of the Sakya clan, the various families of which held their territory in joint control, their practice being to make political decisions in "full and frequent" assemblies.

Legend has been prolifically at work on the scanty facts concerning the childhood of Gautama. Tradition insists that the father hoped his son would become "a universal monarch," the emperor of all India. But if this was in actual fact his expectation, it was doomed to disappointment. The young Gautama was possessed of a mordantly clear mind and sensitive spirit. He was destined to become more and more a stranger in the house of his father. The traditions undoubtedly exaggerate the luxury that surrounded him, but there is probably some truth in the stock phrases with which Gautama was afterwards credited: "I wore garments of silk and my attendants held a white umbrella over me."[A1] It is hardly true, as later tradition asserts, that his father was a "king." The facts are more truly suggested in the statement of Kenneth Saunders that life at the house of Gautama's father was "not unlike that at a Scottish castle in the Middle Ages."[A2] Even marriage offered no lasting balm to his inner lack of peace. At sixteen, or as some accounts say, at nineteen, he married a neighboring "princess." Legend declares she was

questioned. It is significant that in each case their followers set down their doctrines initially not in Sanskrit, the language of the Aryans, but in local dialects, Ardhamagadhin in the case of Jainism, Pali in the case of Buddhism.

However, in the following pages the names of places and persons and most terms appearing in Buddhist discourse will usually be given in Sanskrit, with Pali spelling indicated when deemed advisable. Because the Sanskrit spellings have generally been used throughout the Far East as well as in the later Buddhist literature of India, resort to them is less confusing in an introduction than the use of spellings reflecting local pronunciation. (After all, Sanskrit is the Latin of the East.)

"majestic as a queen of heaven, constant ever, cheerful night and day, full of dignity and exceeding grace,"[B] a paragon of wifely devotion. But Gautama became more and more unhappy inwardly. Sometime during his twenties he seems secretly to have made up his mind to "go out from the household life into the homeless state" of the religious mendicant, and when, in his late twenties, his wife bore him a son, he felt free to follow his secret inclination.

This determination to renounce the household life has presented an interesting problem to Buddhist believers. Why, they have asked, did the fortunate prince, with so devoted a wife and father and so young a son, resolve nevertheless to renounce life

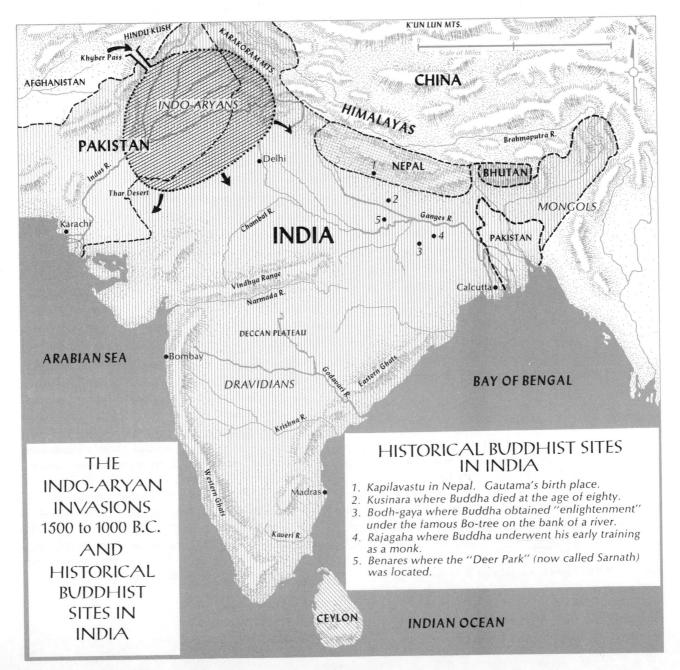

THE INDO-ARYAN INVASIONS 1500 to 1000 B.C. AND HISTORICAL BUDDHIST SITES IN INDIA

HISTORICAL BUDDHIST SITES IN INDIA

1. Kapilavastu in Nepal. Gautama's birth place.
2. Kusinara where Buddha died at the age of eighty.
3. Bodh-gaya where Buddha obtained "enlightenment" under the famous Bo-tree on the bank of a river.
4. Rajagaha where Buddha underwent his early training as a monk.
5. Benares where the "Deer Park" (now called Sarnath) was located.

under the same roof with them? With true psychological insight, they have looked for the cause not only in the spiritual reaction of the young prince to his immediate surroundings, which were of the pleasantest, but to life itself as every man must live it, whether prince or pauper. They have developed the famous legend of "The Four Passing Sights." The essence of the many variants of this story* runs something like this: Gautama's father was forewarned by soothsayers at the time of the prince's birth that his son might give up the household life and become a houseless monk, but that, on the other hand, should he be kept from taking such a step, he might become the emperor of all India ("a universal monarch"). So the father saw to it that the young prince should never experience the severities and sorrows of life, nor know the sad fact that turns so many to religion, the fact, namely, that human life is cut short by old age, disease, and death. Gautama was surrounded by young attendants. His father built him three palaces, "and in the enjoyment of great magnificence he lived, as the seasons changed, in each of these palaces."C1 So successful was the father in keeping out of sight the aged and the sick, so thoroughly did he clear from the highways all but youths and maidens when the prince went riding, that the latter grew up in ignorance of the common fate of men, the constant imminence of old age, disease, and death. The gods, therefore, looking down from the heavens and knowing that they must take a hand in the affair, sent one of their number down to earth to assume the shapes that should awaken the young prince to his true destiny. The god appeared suddenly by the wayside one day in the form of a very feeble and decrepit old man. The prince ordered the charioteer to tell him what it was they saw, and learned for the first time of the miserable close of every man's life. On another day the prince saw the second apparition, that of a loathsomely diseased man, and knew for the first time how physical illness and misery may attend man all the days of his life. The third sight was that of a dead man being carried along to a funeral pyre, and the prince knew of the dreadful fact of death. These three awful sights robbed him of all peace of mind. (It is a fact, and perhaps the legend is based upon it, that in one of the oldest passages in the Buddhist writings he is reported as saying: "I also am subject to decay and am not free from the power of old age, sickness and death. Is it right that I should feel horror, repulsion and disgust when I see another in such plight? And when I reflected thus, my disciples, all the joy of life which there is in life died within me."D1 Alarmed at the depression of spirit under which the prince labored, his father sought to cheer him with elaborate entertainment, but without success. The prince remained distraught until he beheld the fourth sight, that of a calm ascetic in a yellow robe, walking toward him as he sat under a tree by the roadside. From this person, who had gained true peace of soul, he learned how freedom from the miseries of old age, disease, and death may be won. Then, it is said, the prince made the resolve to go out from the household life into the homeless state.

The Great Renunciation

"In all the beauty of my early prime," an early passage runs, "with a wealth of coal-black hair untouched by grey—despite the wishes of my parents, who wept and lamented—I cut off my hair and beard, donned the yellow robe and went forth from home to homelessness."E1 The Buddhist legends tell in loving detail of the struggle by which the decision to renounce his high place in the world was reached: how his father ordered dancing girls to entertain the brooding prince, but all in vain, for the prince sat silently on the couch until all the dancing girls had fallen exhausted to the floor and passed into deep slumber; how the prince then rose and stepped with inward disgust over the sprawling forms of the sleepers, and made his way to his wife's apartment. There, gazing silently down on the sleeping mother with the

* The best-known account is in the *Jataka* tales.

infant Rahula at her side, he bade an unspoken farewell, then went out to leap on his great white horse and ride away, with his charioteer pacing at his side, to a far place, beyond a river. Having shaved off hair and beard and exchanged his rich garments for the coarse yellow robe, he sent back his charioteer and plunged into the forest, one of the great anonymous group of mendicants vowed to seek deliverance from the cares of mortal existence.

Thus began a six-year period of intensive struggle for realization of salvation.

The Six Years of Quest

The legends say he was anxious not to reject the Brahmin philosophy until he had tested it. He went first to Rajagaha, the royal city of the province of Magadha, and became the disciple in turn of two ascetic Brahmin philosophers living in hillside caves. He explored speculative Brahmanism with them and evidently practiced various Yoga disciplines. The first teacher, the ascetic Alara Kalama, taught him of "the realm of nothingness" to which a man might attain if he followed "the stages of meditation." But Gautama was disappointed; the temper of his mind was too objective and practical. So he went on to the second teacher, the ascetic Uddaka Ramaputta, who discoursed of "the state of neither-ideation-nor-non-ideation," with no better results.[E2] In the end, convinced that the technique and substance of Brahmanism would not conduct him to the true way of enlightenment, he withdrew and resolved, with the same objectivity, to test the extreme bodily asceticism which Jainism, among other sects, was then advocating.

After a short period of wandering, he entered a grove at Uruvela, past which flowed a clear river with, "hard by, a village for sustenance."[E3] There, sitting under the trees, he undertook for five years such rigorous self-discipline that life itself almost left him, and he became mere skin and bone. His theory, according to the earliest accounts, was that the mind becomes clearer as the body becomes more disciplined, for, thought he, "It is just as if there were a green sappy stick in the water, and a man came along with his drill-stick, set on lighting a fire and making a blaze. Do you think he could succeed by rubbing with his drill-stick that green sappy stick from the water? Toil and moil as he may, he couldn't. It is just the same with all recluses or brahmins whose life is not lived aloof from pleasures of sense in the matter of their bodies."[E4] On the other hand, he reasoned, Brahmins whose life is lived aloof from pleasures of sense in the matter of their bodies find that the dry light of understanding may flame up in them at last.

Undoubtedly, ample allowance must be made for historical exaggeration, but it is said Gautama now sat with set teeth and tongue pressed against his palate seeking "by sheer force of mind" to "restrain, coerce, and dominate" his heart, until "the sweat streamed" from his armpits.[E5] He practiced restraint of breath until he heard a roaring in his head and felt as if a sword were boring into his skull; violent pain almost drove him senseless, and still no insight came. He lived for periods on all sorts of nauseous foods, dressed in chafing and irritating garments, stood for days in one posture, or, having squatted, moved asquat. He sat on a couch of thorns, lay in a cemetery on charred bones among rotting bodies, let dirt and filth accumulate on his body till it dropped off of itself, and even ate his own excrement in the extremity of self-discipline. He reduced his diet to "only one hemp grain" or "a single grain of rice" or "one jujube fruit" a day. He became excessively thin. The *Majjhima Nikaya* credits him with these vivid words of self-description: "When I was living on a single fruit a day, my body grew emaciated in the extreme; [my limbs became] like the knotted joints of withered creepers; like a buffalo's hoof were my shrunken buttocks; like the twists in a rope were my spinal vertebrae; like the rafters of a tumble-down roof were my gaunt ribs; like the starry gleams on water deep down in the depths of a well, so shone my gleaming eyes deep down in the depths

127

of their sockets; and as the rind of a cut gourd shrinks and shrivels in the heat, so shrank and shrivelled the scalp of my head. . . . If I sought to feel my belly, it was my backbone which I found in my grasp."[E6]

Such extraordinary self-mortification should have produced results, if the psychological theory we found him adopting was sound, namely, that meditation pursued diligently in a rigorously disciplined body brought one to the goal, but to Gautama's great distress of mind he was as far from enlightenment as ever. According to the source from which we have already quoted, he thought to himself: "With all these severe austerities, I fail to transcend ordinary human limits and to rise to the heights of noblest understanding and vision. Could there be another path to Enlightenment?"[E7] Meanwhile, five other ascetics had joined him, hoping that he would share his knowledge with them. While they watched, he rose one day from his seat to go down to the stream, and fainted dead away. The five ascetics gathered round his motionless body and thought: "He will die. The ascetic Gautama will die." They wondered if he had now entered Nirvana. But he came to, and after lying in the shallow water near the bank of the stream, he was sufficiently refreshed in mind and body to begin life anew. With the objectivity of view that marked him all his life, he now concluded that the way of self-mortification had failed, that his body could not support his intellect, and that he would eat and drink and strengthen it. So he took his begging bowl in hand and resumed the life of a paribbajaka (wandering mendicant). The five ascetics were outraged. With indignant words they departed for Benares, saying that luxuriousness had reclaimed him and that, in abandoning the struggle, he had become a backslider into self-indulgence.

But though he had returned to common sense, Gautama could not rejoice. Six years of search along the two most widely recognized roads to salvation known to India, philosophic meditation and bodily asceticism, had yielded no results. But he did not give up the struggle. His thinking now became much more profound and meaningful.

The Great Enlightenment

He turned aside at a place now called Bodh-gaya, into a grove, and sat down at the foot of a fig tree (a tree that came to be known as the Knowledge- or Bodhi-tree, or more simply the Bo-tree), and there he entered upon a process of meditation that was to affect the thinking of millions of men after him. The Buddhist books insist that he set his teeth and said to himself determinedly: "Though skin, nerves, and bone shall waste away, and life-blood itself be dried up, here sit I till I attain Enlightenment."[A3] In all probability the fact was far otherwise. Psychology probably can suggest a truer version of the real course of Gautama's enlightenment: he had tried too hard altogether, so that his very determination stood between him and the state of consciousness he desired, but now, in the face of self-defeat, his will relaxed, he let his mind wander back over his previous experience. Some such questions as these must have arisen in his mind: What was he to think of his life and his search for salvation until now? Why had he failed?

And suddenly, the answer came. His inability to experience release from his suffering was due to desire (*tanha*, Sanskrit *trishna*, "thirst," "craving"), constantly and painfully thwarted. But to eliminate a misery-producing desire he must determine its causes and prevent them from issuing in the characteristic craving or thirst. A painful desire might have many causes, but they would be determinable. In fact, he could see that the whole context of life and thought in which he had lived abounded in causes of desire and pain.

The Buddhist traditions seek to illustrate this fact by setting the future Buddha symbolically in a predicament of cosmic scope. It supposes Gautama to have been approached by the Evil One in the person of Mara, the god of Desire and Death, tempting him (i.e., seeking to cause him) to give up his quest and succumb to pleasure. The tempter brought before him three voluptuous daughters accompanied by a sensuous retinue of dancers, and when they failed to beguile him, assumed his most terrible aspect and

Scenes from the life of the Buddha. In this sculptured panel from the stupa at Nagarjunikonda, dating from the third century A.D., *the Buddha (below) departs from Kapilavastu at the time of his "Great Renunciation," and (above) while seated under the Bodhi tree (broken away), is being tempted by Mara's daughters, one of whom grasps his thigh, and threatened by Mara's army of demons. But he remains immovable. (The Metropolitan Museum of Art, Fletcher Fund, 1928.)*

summoned a host of demons to assist him in terrifying the future Buddha and arousing at least his desire to cling to life. They assailed him with wind and rain and hurled at him such deadly missiles as uprooted trees, boiling mud, fiery rocks, live coals, and glowing ashes that made the pitch-black darkness livid. But the future Buddha was sitting on an "immovable" spot under the great fig tree and remained himself unmoved. The deadly missiles entered his consciousness as sprays of flowers. In the end it was the Evil One who was affrighted, for when the unmoved one touched the fingers of his right hand to the ground, a sound as of a hundred thousand roars thundered up from the sympathetic earth, and the Evil One fled.[F] Shortly thereafter full enlightenment (*bodhi*) came to him who sat so serenely under the Bo-tree, for he realized that desire arises in the context of a twelve-linked chain of causation but that he had escaped from it into a new life, a higher form of consciousness, freed of desire and its attendant pain.

Whatever the process of his thought, he was now without desire. He felt no sensual yearnings, was purged of "wrong states of mind." The Buddhist books say he then passed into a state of "awareness" or "wakefulness" suffused by an ecstasy having four phases and culminating in "the state that, knowing neither satisfaction nor dissatisfaction, is the consummate purity of poised equanimity and mindfulness."[E8] It seemed to him "ignorance was destroyed, knowledge had arisen, darkness was destroyed, light had arisen," as he sat there "earnest, strenuous, resolute."[D2] Also, he was convinced that "Rebirth is no more; I have lived the highest life; my task is done; and now for me there is no more of what I have been."[E9] He thus experienced the earthly foretaste of Nibbana (Nirvana). From now on he was the Buddha, the Enlightened One.

After the ecstasy had passed, he was immediately confronted with a problem, a temptation. This is one of the best attested facts in the Buddhist books. He had attained to a Doctrine that was "profound, recondite, hard to comprehend."[E10] Were he to preach this Doctrine or Dhamma, and were others not to understand it, that would be labor and annoyance to him. After some struggle with himself, whether he should remain a Buddha for his own sake or become a Buddha for all, a teaching Buddha, he rose and went back into the world to communicate to others his saving truth.

He sought out the five ascetics who had deserted him at Uruvela. He found them in the Deer Park at Benares, and there experienced a great personal triumph. At first, when they saw him coming toward them among the trees, they said bitterly: "Here comes the ascetic Gautama, he who eats rich food and lives in self-indulgence. Let us show him no respect, nor rise to meet him. Yet let us put out an extra seat and growl: 'If you want to sit, sit!'" But the Buddha displayed such serenity and radiance that they could not look away nor refrain from receiving him. They rose; one came forward to relieve him of his bowl and robe; another indicated his seat; another brought water to wash his feet. Then a prolonged and amiable discussion began. To their accusation that he had forfeited the possibility of enlightenment by abandoning asceticism and reverting to self-indulgence, he replied in the words of what is known as the Sermon in the Deer Park at Benares: "There are two extremes, O Almsmen, which he who has given up the world ought to avoid. What are those two extremes?—A life given to pleasures, devoted to pleasures and lusts; this is degrading, sensual, vulgar, ignoble and profitless. And a life given to mortifications; this is painful, ignoble, and profitless. By avoiding these two extremes the Truthfinder

The Buddha's first sermon in the Deer Park at Sarnath. In this panel from the stupa at Nagarjunikonda, the Buddha is seen holding up his right hand in the teaching position and addressing his five former comrades, each accompanied by a disciple. Apparently they are all converts at this point in the discourse of the Buddha. (Courtesy of the Government of India Tourist Office.)

The Buddha venerated by disciples. Three brothers, the Kasyapas, converts from Brahmanism, advance reverently toward the Buddha. At the extreme right are a Kushan noble and his wife, the latter in Greek dress. The Buddha Maitreya, flanked by devotees to right and left, appears in the top relief. The panel is intended to show the submission of Brahmanism to Buddhism. It is in the Gandhara style. (Kabul Museum, Kabul, Afghanistan.)

[the Tathagata: the Buddha's designation for himself —literally, "one who has truly arrived or has reached Truth, *Tatha*, Suchness"] has gained the knowledge of the Middle Path which leads to insight, which leads to wisdom, which conduces to calm, to knowledge, to Enlightenment, to Nirvana."[G1] He opened to them his own experience and challenged them to believe his testimony, to admit that he was an "arahat" (a monk who had experienced enlightenment), and to try the "middle way" he now advocated. The five ascetics were converted, and thus the Sangha (the Buddhist monastic order) came into being.

The Buddha then energetically entered upon his itinerant ministry in North India.

The Establishment of the Buddhist Order

As the Buddha wandered about preaching, other conversions, especially from his own caste, the Kshatriya, followed, until the number of disciples rose to sixty. Then the monks multiplied rapidly. Not only Kshatriyas and members of the lower castes, but many Brahmins joined the group of inquirers and disciples. Among these was one who became a leader among his disciples, the Brahmin Sariputta. Others came of his own class, like his cousin Ananda. Caste distinctions were then not so sharply defined in society at large as later, and in any case caste ceased to apply to individuals who joined the Buddhist order. At first all candidates for ordination into the order were brought by disciples to the Buddha, but when in course of time converts came from a distance and in increasing numbers, he authorized ordained monks to confer ordination themselves, following certain simple rules. In fact, as the converts grew in number, it became expedient to inaugurate a program and draw up rules for behavior. During the dry season the Buddha annually sent his disciples out to preach, himself setting the example. During the three months of the rainy season he and the monks gathered together, some here, some there, and lived a monastic life of self-discipline, instruction, and mutual service.

So in a very natural way rose a great order, the

131

Sangha, governed by definite rules and schedules. The essential rules, perhaps developed after the Buddha's own time, were simple: the wearing of the yellow robe, the adoption of the shaven head, the carrying of the begging bowl, the habit of daily meditation, and subscription to the initiate's confession: "I take refuge in the Buddha, I take refuge in the Dhamma (the Law or Truth), I take refuge in the Sangha (the Order)." All undertook also to obey the Ten Precepts, which may be simplified thus:

1. Refrain from destroying life (the principle of ahimsa).
2. Do not take what is not given.
3. Abstain from unchastity.
4. Do not lie or deceive.
5. Abstain from intoxicants.
6. Eat moderately and not after noon.
7. Do not look on at dancing, singing, or dramatic spectacles.
8. Do not affect the use of garlands, scents, unguents, or ornaments.
9. Do not use high or broad beds.
10. Do not accept gold or silver.[H]

The first four of these Precepts are the same as the first four vows undertaken by the Jaina monks, but instead of the extremely comprehensive fifth vow of the Jains there appears the precept against the use of intoxicants. It may be said that the Precepts illustrate the Middle Way between asceticism and self-indulgence in a specially concrete way; on the one hand self-indulgence in the pleasures of life is explicitly disavowed, and on the other the more extreme ascetic practices are not enjoined. Faithfulness in carrying out the Precepts was expected. If any monk broke any of them, he made public confession of his sin before the assembly of his chapter on the bi-monthly fast-days.

The first five of these injunctions (known as the Five Precepts) were prescribed for all lay-associates of the order. The Buddha recognized that there were those who for one reason or another could not "give up the household life" but who were so sympathetic with the ideals of the order that they should be brought into active association with it. He therefore made provision for the attachment of thousands of lay-associates to the order, on the condition that they undertook to obey the Five Precepts and evinced the spirit of helpfulness in promoting the growth and progress of the order. It was largely through the lay-membership that the order acquired its extensive property-holdings. High-born laymen of the Kshatriya caste enthusiastically donated groves, parks, and monasteries to the order.

Women clamored for admission, and the Buddha had at last, it is said, to overcome his reluctance to forming an order of nuns, but he is reported to have made the dry remark in private: "If, Ananda, women had not received permission to enter the Order, the pure religion would have lasted long, the good law would have stood fast a thousand years. But since they have received permission, it will now stand fast for only five hundred years."[D3]

It seems well attested that a fairly large group of relatives became monks and nuns. The Buddha's cousin, Ananda, stands out among all his followers as the perfect type of devoted disciple, ministering with untiring love to his teacher's personal needs and in constant attendance upon him. Another cousin, Devadatta, so personally identified himself with the order that he became guilty of an attempted schism in the interest ostensibly of greater strictness. (Buddhist tradition says he was moved by jealousy.)

Forty-five years passed in the work of preaching, teaching, and constructive planning. At last, on a journey to an obscure town by the name of Kusinara, northeast of Benares, in his eightieth year, he came to his end. He took his mid-day meal in the house of Chunda, a goldsmith. The pork he ate (or, as some would have it, the dish of truffles) brought on an attack of mortal illness. He had not gone the full distance toward Kusinara when death claimed him as he lay down between two sal trees.

These last hours were remembered afterwards in great detail. The legend says that he spoke kindly to Ananda, who had gone aside to weep: "Enough, Ananda, do not grieve, nor weep. Have I not already told you, Ananda, that it is in the very nature of all

The death of the Buddha. In this stone panel in the Gandhara style, from the third century A.D., *the Buddha enters paranirvana while reclining on a couch between two sal trees (only one of which is seen). Monks, laymen, and gods show their grief. The two smaller figures in front of the couch probably are Ananda, with his head bowed between his hands, and Subhadra, the Buddha's last convert. (Courtesy, Museum of Fine Arts, Boston.)*

things near and dear unto us that we must divide ourselves from them? How is it possible, Ananda, that whatever has been born should not perish? For a long time, Ananda, have you waited on the Tathagata with a kind, devoted, cheerful, single-hearted, unstinted service. You have acquired much merit, Ananda; exert yourself, and you will soon be free from all defect." He said he left a legacy for his followers: "The Doctrine (Dhamma) and Discipline (Vinaya) which I have taught and enjoined upon you is to be your teacher when I am gone." His last words were: "And now, O priests, I take my leave of you; all the constituents of being are transitory; work out your salvation with diligence."[1]

II The Teachings of the Buddha

Philosophical Conceptions

Paradoxically enough, one must begin study of the Buddha's philosophical conceptions with the observa-

tion that he rejected philosophical speculation as the way of salvation. Purely metaphysical issues were to him of little moment. He had an intensely practical outlook, and such issues offended his common sense. He was not interested in speculative philosophy that could not be directly related to the human situation. The Buddhist records transmit his plain-spoken repudiation of certain then-current problems in philosophy:

"Bear always in mind what it is that I have not elucidated, and what it is that I have elucidated. And what have I not elucidated? I have not elucidated that the world is eternal; I have not elucidated that the world is not eternal; I have not elucidated that the world is finite; I have not elucidated that the world is infinite; I have not elucidated that the soul and the body are identical; I have not elucidated that the monk who has attained (the arahat) exists after death; I have not elucidated that the arahat does not exist after death; I have not elucidated that the arahat both exists and does not exist after death; I have not elucidated that the arahat neither exists nor does not exist after death.° And why have I not

° The Buddha here refers to what has been called the Indian *tetralemma:* after death, does the arahat in Nir-

elucidated this? Because this profits not, nor has to do with the fundamentals of religion; therefore I have not elucidated this."

The Buddha's psychological interest is expressed in the next sentences attributed to him:

"And what have I elucidated? Misery have I elucidated; the origin of misery have I elucidated; the cessation of misery have I elucidated; and the path leading to the cessation of misery have I elucidated. And why have I elucidated this? Because this does profit, has to do with the fundamentals of religion, and tends to absence of passion, to knowledge, supreme wisdom, and Nirvana."[C2]

In other words, the basic difficulty of man is not so much in the way he philosophizes as in the way he feels. What thinking he does he ought to devote to understanding his desires and controlling them through the power of his will; in them the chief danger lurks.

The Buddha also rejected religious devotion as a way of salvation. His position was the sort of atheism we have already noted in Mahavira. He believed that the universe abounded in gods, goddesses, demons, and other non-human powers and agencies, but all without exception were finite, subject to death and rebirth. In the absence, then, of some transcendent, eternal Being, older than the Creation, the Maker of heaven and earth, who could direct men's destinies and hear and grant human wishes, prayer, to the Buddha, was of no avail; he at least did not resort to it. For similar reasons he did not put any reliance on the Vedas or on worship of their many gods through the performance of sacrificial rituals as a way of redemption, nor would he countenance going to the Brahmins as priests. (These are among the chief reasons why Buddhism is a heresy to the devout Hindu.) Like Mahavira, the Buddha showed each disciple how to rely for salvation upon himself, on his own powers, focused upon redemption by spiritual self-discipline.

Here was the strictest sort of humanism in religion.

But though the Buddha uprooted from his world-view most of what is commonly regarded as distinctive of religion as such, he held to two major Hindu doctrines that ordinarily appear in a religious context. He believed in the Law of Karma and in rebirth. He modified both of these doctrines, however.

He gave the Law of Karma more flexibility than most later philosophers were wont to do. In his view a man of any caste or class could experience so complete a change of heart or disposition as to escape the full consequence of sins committed in previous existences. The Law of Karma operated remorselessly and without remission of one jot or tittle of the full recompense upon all who went on in the old way—the way of unchecked desire—but it could not lay hold upon a man completely changed, who had achieved arahatship, "the state of him that is worthy." The arahats "who by steadfast mind have become exempt from evil desire" may feel assured that "their old karma is exhausted; no new karma is being produced; their hearts are free from the longing after a future life; the cause of their existence being destroyed, and no new longing springing up within them, they, the wise, are extinguished at death like a lamp."[J] There will be no rebirth for them.

It is those who are not emancipated from "the will-to-live-and-have" (tanha) who will be reborn.

The Buddha held firmly to the doctrine of rebirth, but the form he gave to that doctrine has puzzled men ever since. It seems he held that rebirth takes place without any actual soul-substance passing over from one existence to another. Later expositors of this doctrine declared that the Buddha, after analysis of the human person, concluded: "There is no ego [atman] here to be found."[C3] This is one of the most obscure and most profound points in the Buddha's system of thought.

Instead of the age-old faith that an imperishable and substantial soul goes over from one existence to another, its direction and status absolutely determined from stage to stage by the inexorable causal nexus of the Law of Karma, the Buddha seems to

vana exist, or not exist, or both exist and not exist, or neither exist nor not exist?

have maintained a doctrine that is surprisingly objective and modern. His reflection upon his own personality led him to deny that any of its elements had any permanence. What men have called the continuing entity of the immortal soul is really to be resolved back into an impermanent aggregation or composite of constantly changing states of being or *skandhas* (Pali *khandhas*). These skandhas are five in number: (1) the body, (2) perception, (3) feelings, (4) *sankharas* (hard to translate; literally, "configurations" or "predispositions," generated by past habits in this and previous existences; roughly, in the nearest modern equivalent, a lumping together of the "instincts" and the "subconscious"), and (5) ideation or reasoning. It is the union of these that constitutes the individual. As long as they are held together the individual functions as a single being, lives, and has a history. But each component is in perpetual flux. The body changes from day to day only a little less obviously than the other states. At death the union is dissolved, and the skandhas disperse.

What is known to us as the ego is therefore but an appearance, merely the name we give to the functional unity that subsists when the five changing skandhas set up the complex interplay that constitutes the personal life of the individual. Only the ceaseless flow of Being itself, of which these changing states are signs, has reality or permanence.

With this view of the nature of the human individual, how could the Buddha hold to the doctrine of reincarnation, as in fact he did? He could not contend that any substantial entity ("soul" or "psyche") passed over from one existence to another; that theory was precluded by his analysis. He taught, however, that there passes over to the next life a karma-laden character structure. It is as though, for example, a seal were pressed upon wax. What, in such case, passes from the former to the latter? Only the characters engraved on the seal and retained by the wax. Nothing substantial. So in respect to rebirth, at the end of one existence an individual will possess definite characteristics hardened into a kind of rigidity, but at the moment of dissolution these charac-

teristics are passed over to the soft wax of a new existence in another womb. Nothing substantial passes over, yet there is a definite connection between one complex of elements and the next.*

Buddhist lore abounds in similes for this mysterious event. Several hundred years after the Buddha the matter was regarded thus:

> Said the king [King Milinda]: "Bhante Nagasena, does rebirth take place without anything transmigrating?"
>
> "Yes, your majesty, rebirth takes place without anything transmigrating."
>
> "How, bhante Nagasena, does rebirth take place without anything transmigrating? Give an illustration."
>
> "Suppose, your majesty, a man were to light a light from another light; pray, would the one light have passed over to the other light?"
>
> "Nay, verily, bhante."
>
> "In exactly the same way, your majesty, does rebirth take place without anything transmigrating."
>
> "Give another illustration."
>
> "Do you remember, your majesty, having learnt, when you were a boy, some verse or other from your professor of poetry?"
>
> "Yes, bhante."
>
> "Pray, your majesty, did the verse pass over (transmigrate) to you from your teacher?"
>
> "Nay, verily, bhante."
>
> "In exactly the same way, your majesty, does rebirth take place without anything transmigrating."
>
> "You are an able man, bhante Nagasena."[C4]

In other words, as one process leads to another, from cause to effect, so human personality in one

---

* Because this seems to be the plain sense of the Buddha's recorded teaching, some interpreters say with good reason that he never denied that an entity of some sort goes from one life to the next. He refused to discuss what this entity might be, except to imply that it was impelled by karma. But it would seem that although he rejected the Hindu doctrine, as found in the Upanishads, that there is an imperishable soul or self (atman) residing in the perishable body apart from the mind and the other "psychic organs" of an individual person, he must have thought that a real, if only momentary, something —that is, an impermanent but death-transcending pulse of being, marked with certain causative characteristics (e.g., "clinging," karmic determinations, habits of doing, predispositions)—goes over to another life. If this be granted, it is clear that he was more ready to say what this transmigrating bit of being was *not* than what it was.

existence is the direct cause of the type of individuality which appears in the next. One text explains it thus:

This consciousness being in its series inclined toward the object by desire, and impelled toward it by karma, like a man who swings himself over a ditch by means of a rope hanging from a tree on the hither bank, quits its first resting place and continues (in the next existence) to subsist in dependence on objects of sense and other things. . . . Here the former consciousness, from its passing out of existence, is called passing away, and the latter, from its being reborn into a new existence, is called rebirth. But it is understood that this latter consciousness did not come to the present existence from the previous one, and also that it is only to causes contained in the old existence,—namely to karma called the predispositions, to inclination, an object, etc.—that its present appearance is due. . . . As illustrations of how consciousness does not come over from the last existence into the present, and how it springs up by means of causes belonging to the former existence here may serve echoes, light, the impressions of a seal, and reflections in a mirror. For as echoes, light, the impressions of a seal, and shadows have sound, etc., for their causes, and exist without having come from elsewhere, just so it is with this mind.[C5]

This does not mean, the Buddha said, that he who is born is different from the preceding person who has passed his karma on at death to him, nor does it mean that he is the same. Such an issue is as meaningless as to say that the body is different from the self or that the self and body are the same. Since there is no permanent ego-entity accompanying the skandhas, discussions as to whether the successive personalities in a continuous series of rebirths are the same or different lack point. It is better simply to know that a kind of inner necessity (karma) leads to the origination of one life as the total result of the having-been-ness of another, and that the connection is as close as that of cause and effect, or as the transfer of flame from one wick to another. It is difficult to construe, but the fundamental fact remains—that what a man does and thinks now carries over into tomorrow and tomorrow and tomorrow.

Interesting as this astute discrimination of distinctions is, the implications for the Buddha's larger conceptions of life and destiny are more important. The conclusions involved seem to be these: Wherever we observe it, the living world, whether about us or within ourselves, is constantly in flux, in a state of endless becoming. There is no central, planning world-self, no sovereign Person in the heavens holding all together in unity. There is only the ultimate impersonal unity of Being itself, whose peace enfolds the individual self when it ceases to call itself "I" and dissolves in the featureless purity of Nirvana, as a drop of spray is merged in its mother sea. The permanency of the world is an illusion, and this also holds true of the empirical ego. There remain for human experience only processes of change and decay, of becoming and passing away, of appearing and disappearing.*

The Buddha is said to have talked about all this in his Sermon at the Deer Park in Benares, when he spoke of the *turning of the Wheel*.† His followers called the symbol to which he was referring the Bhavacakra ("the Wheel of Becoming"). Taking their clues from his teaching, later followers portrayed it as having at its hub the three causes of pain, the serpent of ill-will or hatred, the pig of ignorance with its snout forever searching the ground, and the dove (or cock-bird) of lust or uncontrolled desire. The segments of the Wheel divide off the six states of rebirth: existence as a warring demi-god, as an animal, as a dweller in hell, as a human being, as a god in heaven, and as a happy soul in a Buddhist paradise. The whole is held in the of grip of the Demon of Change

---

* However, it is not true that the Buddha was a total nihilist. In *Udana* VIII.3 we find him saying: "There is, O priests, that which is unborn (*ajabam*), which has not become (*abhutam*), which is uncreate (*akatam*), which is unevolved (*asamkhatam*). Unless, O priests, there were that which is unborn, which has not become, is uncreate, and unevolved, there could not be cognized here the springing out of what is born, has become, is created and evolved."[K] It is the permanency of the world perceived in human experience that he denies, not the stream of being itself (Nirvana).

† He himself also started a wheel turning—the Wheel of the Doctrine (*Dharma*), and consequently his sermon is commonly called "The Setting in Motion of the Wheel of the Doctrine."

and Impermanence. Probably neither the Buddha nor his early disciples were this explicit, but the Wheel represents the unceasing becoming and passing away of the states of existence to which the Buddha was so sensitive.

It is likely that the Buddha spoke much more explicitly and in detail about the *human experience* of the turning of the Wheel. It is, he said, an experience of "a mass of suffering," and this suffering comes out of a twelve-linked chain of causes and effects, the first two links belonging to the previous life, the middle eight to the present, and the last two to the future existence. The Buddhist books call this Dependent Origination or the Chain of Causation. The reasoning goes like this: the first and most fundamental of the causes of the painful coming-into-being of every individual is ignorance, especially taking at face value the reality of the empirical self and the permanence of the world. This basic fault, which is carried over from the previous life, is built into the original set or bent of the personality from birth, the predispositions (sankharas). Thus predisposed, the personality becomes conscious of or cognizes the world and itself. This in turn determines the distinctive traits one has ("name and form"; the individuality one is known by). Individuality expresses itself causally in a particular exercise of the five senses and the mind. These in turn make contact with other selves and with things. Thence arises sensation. The sensations cause desire (tanha or craving). From craving comes clinging to existence. Clinging to existence entails the process of becoming. Becoming brings on a new state of being not like the one preceding it. Finally, such a new birth inevitably entails its own "old age and death, grief, lamentation, suffering, dejection and despair. Such is the origination of this whole mass of human suffering."[G2]

These convictions were not encouraging. The Buddha discerned in them his basic reasons for withdrawal from the world. As he seems to have taught, all "composite beings" able to reason suffer from three great flaws vexing their existence: impermanence (*anicca*), the ultimate unreality of the self or

soul (*anatta*), and sorrow (*dukkha*). The third aspect seemed to follow remorselessly upon the other two. The impermanence in everything that appears to exist, the ceaseless change, the endless becoming that is never quite being, filled him with weariness, a real misery; he longed for peace, the cessation of desire, for some state of consciousness with enough permanence to guarantee deliverance from "the Wheel" of perpetual and painful becoming. This, of course, is all over again the immemorial desire of India. Here, however, the thought process moves through obscure feeling states. It is *painful,* the Buddha felt, to experience continuance in a stream of consciousness made up mostly of states of incompletion.

"Now pleasant sensations, unpleasant sensations, indifferent sensations, Ananda, are transitory, are due to causes, originate by dependence, and are subject to decay, disappearance, effacement, and cessation. While this person is experiencing a pleasant sensation, he thinks, 'This is my Ego [self, atman].' And after the cessation of this same pleasant sensation, he thinks, 'My Ego has passed away.' While he is experiencing an unpleasant sensation, he thinks, 'This is my Ego.' And after the cessation of this same unpleasant sensation, he thinks, 'My Ego has passed away.' And while he is experiencing an indifferent sensation, he thinks, 'This is my Ego.' And after the cessation of this same indifferent sensation, he thinks, 'My Ego has passed away.' "[C6]

So the Buddha seems to have felt that it was human, no doubt, but it was foolish, it was stupid and ignorant, to cling with longing, as most people do, to sentient life and its pitifully few pleasures, when all through life the pain of change is so predominant. This will-to-live-and-have, this "thirst," this "clinging" to the world and its objects, was, it seemed, far and away the most striking of the characteristics that pass from one existence to the next, and if it could be made to die away, the chief cause of rebirth would be removed. If it could be made to die away, it should be made to do so!

To this conclusion the Buddha's profound psychological analysis of life and personality conducted him.

In his ethical teaching he sought to show men how to answer the questions raised by it.

Ethics*

The fundamental ethical problem to which the Buddha addressed himself was: In what way ought one to live so as to obtain surcease of pain and suffering, bring to an end the unwise will-to-live-and-have, and finally attain the fullness of the joy of liberation?

The answer to this problem he compressed into the Four Noble Truths. In the official report of his first sermon—in the Deer Park at Benares to the five ascetics—they are given thus:

"This, O Bhikkhus, is the Noble Truth of Suffering: Birth is suffering; decay is suffering; illness is suffering; death is suffering. Presence of objects we hate is suffering; separation from objects we love is suffering; not to obtain what we desire is suffering. Briefly, the fivefold clinging to existence [by means of the five *skandhas*] is suffering.

"This, O Bhikkhus, is the Noble Truth of the Cause of Suffering: Thirst, that leads to rebirth, accompanied by pleasure and lust, finding its delight here and there. (This thirst is threefold) namely, thirst for pleasure, thirst for existence, thirst for prosperity.

"This, O Bhikkhus, is the Noble Truth of the Cessation of Suffering: (it ceases with) the complete cessation of this thirst—a cessation which consists in the absence of every passion,—with the abandoning of this thirst, with the doing away with it, with the deliverance from it, with the destruction of desire.

"This, O Bhikkhus, is the Noble Truth of the Path which leads to the cessation of suffering: that holy eightfold Path, that is to say, Right Belief, Right Aspiration, Right Speech, Right Conduct, Right Means of Livelihood, Right Endeavor, Right Mindfulness, Right Meditation.' ᴸ

Analysis of these words discloses two facts: that the Buddha's ethical system balances its stress on the

---

* That is, the moral aspects of the Dhamma or Dharma. In Buddhism *Dharma* is a word with a whole complex of meanings. In various contexts it means: (a) observable objects (phenomena), facts, events; (b) the teaching or doctrine, i.e., the Truth concerning the nature and causes of observable facts and events; and (c) as here, the conduct called for in view of the Truth revealed in facts or events.

life of negation with more positive counsels, and that it is not nearly so pessimistic as Western thought has traditionally construed it to be.* It seems, in fact, that the Buddha does not condemn *all* desire, does not say that *all* existence is misery. Provisionally, and during the ordeal of human existence, there are good values in desire, if we may put it so, as well as bad values, and the wise man knows (has overcome ignorance to a sufficient degree to know) how to discriminate between them. Ultimately, of course, all desire, all attachment must be overcome if one is to realize Nirvana.

1. The first, and negative, principle in the Buddha's ethics requires strict non-indulgence of the desires known to cause suffering. But how will one know they are desires of this sort? The first three of the Four Noble Truths furnish the criteria. Reduced to the simplest form, they produce this formula: Where life becomes miserable, the misery is always found to spring from indulgence of some form of desire; hence *such* desire is to be abandoned, done away with, uprooted. Or, in one sentence, any form of desire whose indulgence entails misery is to be overcome.

So put, the ethical thought of the Buddha strikes a note of clear common sense. It is not from this *principle* that Western minds can intelligently dissent; it is from the *application* of this principle in the further reaches of Buddhist ethics. For in such application the Buddha goes far in a negative direction. Some of his ethical judgments are common enough in most ethical systems. There is widespread agreement among the ethical philosophers, for example, that pursuit of the sensuously pleasant as an end in itself is misery-producing. But though the Buddha agrees with this common enough observation, he advises far more than the abandonment of sensuous desires. Ownership of houses and lands, love of parents, wives, children, or friends—these are also ultimately woe-bringing, he taught. There is constant

---

* That the Buddha's negativism had a positive goal—the attainment of "blessedness" or spiritual happiness—is now recognized.

worry and unsatisfied desire in each case. If one loves his wife, then death, separation, the life of poverty, sickness, hundreds of situations are painful; the very intensity of love itself is painful. So it is with children, aged parents, and even with friends. "Let therefore no man love anything; loss of the beloved is evil. Those who love nothing and hate nothing have no fetters."M1

The Buddha's attitude is best presented through illustration. The legend runs that one day a grandmother appeared before him in tears. She had just lost a very dear grandchild. The Buddha looked at her gravely. "How many people are there in this city of Savatthi?" he asked, with apparent irrevelance. Upon receiving her reply, he came to the point: "Would you like to have as many children and grandchildren as there are people in Savatthi?" The old lady, still weeping, cried out yes, yes. "But," the Buddha gently remonstrated, "if you had as many children and grandchildren as there are people in Savatthi, you would have to weep every day, for people die daily there." The old lady thought a moment; he was right! As she went away comforted, she carried with her the Buddha's saying: "Those who have a hundred dear ones have a hundred woes; those who have ninety dear ones have ninety woes; . . . those who have one dear one have one woe; those who hold nothing dear have no woe."N1

If this story be true, then the Buddha would have approved, had he been alive to hear the story, of the young monk who, after being gone from home a long while, returned to his birthplace to occupy a cell built by his father for passing monks and to beg food daily at his mother's door. His mother did not recognize him in his monk's garb and emaciated condition. For three months he took food from her hands without announcing himself, and then quietly departed. When his mother heard afterwards who he was, she worshiped, saying: "Methinks, the Blessed One must have had in mind a body of priests like my son. . . . This man ate for three months in the house of the mother who bore him, and never said, 'I am thy son, and thou art my mother.' O the wonderful man!" And

the Buddhist account concludes: "For such a one, mother and father are no hindrances."C7*

The consistent Buddhist will exercise restraint even over his attachment to the Blessed One, the Buddha himself.

The venerable Sariputta said this: "As I was meditating in seclusion there arose the consideration: Is there now anything in the whole world wherein a change would give rise in me to grief, lamenting, despair? And methought, No, there is no such thing." Then the venerable Ananda said to the venerable Sariputta: "But the Master —would not the loss of him give rise in you to grief, lamenting, despair?" "Not even the loss of him, Friend Ananda. Nevertheless, I should feel thus: O may not the mighty one, O may not the Master so gifted, so wonderful, be taken from us!"N2

Also, of course, all self-regard, all emotional bias in behalf of the empirical self, must be entirely overcome. The self-defensive and self-assertive attitudes are especially ruinous to peace. The truth of the anatta doctrine must be realized in experience. Among the qualities of the true monk are those that Kassapa exhibited when, making his rounds for alms of food, he met a leper, and in order to let the leper acquire merit by alms-giving, gave him the opportunity to cast a morsel into his own outstretched bowl. Though in the process "a finger, mortifying, broke and fell," Kassapa felt no qualms but, back in the monastery, ate with undisturbed equanimity the food that lay beside the leprous finger in the bowl.P Equally the master of his emotions, Sariputta experienced complete release from ego-concern. "Serene, pure, radiant is your person, Sariputta," a monk exclaimed. "Where have you been today?" "I have been alone, in first *jhana* [Sanskrit *dhyana* or deep meditation], brother, and to me never came the thought: *I* am attaining it; *I* have emerged from it. And thus

---

* In some quarters this renunciation of family ties met with anger. "The people were annoyed, murmured, and became angry, saying: 'The ascetic Gotama causes fathers to beget no sons . . . wives to become widows . . . families to become extinct.' "G3 If his success with young men were to increase, it would threaten the existence of the human race!

individualizing and egotistical tendencies have been well ejected for a long while from Sariputta."Q

Like the Jains, the Buddhists determined to renounce all attachments disturbing to absolute peace of mind and soul. To them salvation, here and hereafter, meant just this, a state of perfectly painless peace and joy, a self-achieved freedom from misery of any kind.

This explains why Buddhist literature makes so many lists of things to be avoided, desires to be given up, bonds to be broken: "The Three Intoxications," "The Five Hindrances," "The Ten Fetters: by which beings are bound to the wheel of existence," etc. That these lists are rather exhaustive is evident in the analysis of the Ten Fetters, as follows: (1) belief in the existence of the self, (2) doubt, (3) trust in ceremonies of good works, (4) lust, (5) anger, (6) desire for rebirth in worlds of form, (7) desire for rebirth in formless worlds, (8) pride, (9) self-righteousness, and (10) ignorance.D4 This list, it will be seen, covers much ground.

2. But freedom from "fetters" obviously cannot be attained by negative means only. It is by living toward the attainment of the right or truly joy-bringing desires, those that issue in a liberating supraconsciousness, that one completely transcends and erases from everyday consciousness the kinds of desire that produce suffering.

Consider in this connection the fourth of the Four Noble Truths. The principle expressed is this: desires whose indulgence will not result in increase of misery but rather in a decrease of it (or in entire doing-away of misery) are desires that conduct steadily to salvation, the ultimate state in which *all* desires are swallowed up, even the desire for no-desire.

It was in applying this principle that the Buddha formulated the Noble Eightfold Path, "the path that leads to no-desire."

The first step in the Eightfold Path is right belief; that is, belief in the Four Noble Truths and the view of life implied in them. The next step, right aspiration or purpose, is reached by resolving to overcome sensuality, have the right love of others, harm no living being, and suppress all misery-producing desires generally. The third and fourth steps, right speech and right conduct, are defined as non-indulgence in loose or hurtful talk or in ill-will; one must love all creatures with the right sort of love in word and deed. Right means of livelihood, the fifth step, means choosing the proper occupation of one's time and energies, obtaining one's livelihood in ways consistent with Buddhist principles. The sixth step, right effort, implies untiring and unremitting intellectual alertness in discriminating between wise and unwise desires and attachments. Right mindfulness, the seventh step, is made possible by well-disciplined thought habits during long hours spent in attention to helpful topics. Lastly, right meditation or absorption refers to the climax of all the other processes, the final attainment of the trance states that are the advanced stages on the road to arahatship (sainthood) and the assurance of passage at death into Nirvana, the state of quiescence, all karma consumed, and rebirth at an end forever.

Two things ought to be noted about the steps in the Eightfold Path: first, that they fall under three headings—understanding, morals, and concentration; second, that they are so planned as to lead progressively to arahatship and thus finally to Nirvana. Of the three groups into which the steps of the Path fall, the first two groups are natural enough. Understanding of the theory and practice of the ethic of Buddhism are certainly necessary, if the Buddhist believer is to justify his faith at all. But the third group leads onto a different level. Here Buddhism is most akin to Hindu mysticism. The final goal here is the pure ecstasy, the supraconsciousness that follows on meditative exercises. By them one turns away in aversion from the unhappy world to spiritual realities beyond sense. In early Buddhism part of this mental discipline consisted in certain processes of thought the Buddha himself recommended: for example, deepening one's aversion to life by thinking concentratedly of the perishableness of the body and of the body's loathsome features, or by analyzing the disgusting changes wrought by death in the most beautiful human body, and then in grateful relief turning to the thought of the permanent and the eternal. When this kind of thinking failed, some of the early Buddhists turned to yoga methods in the hope of bringing on ecstasy psychologically. They breathed in certain ways, stared at bright objects, repeated certain formulas, and so on. The Buddha condemned giving too high a value to such technical means to ecstasy. Arahatship, he held, could be reached without resort to any special practices of the more technical sort. It was heretical, in fact, to seek entrance into Nirvana by the cultivation of ecstasy alone. The way to "bliss" was not the way of merely formalistic procedure; it was the way of meditating until one could see with a "sense-transcending eye" and gain an insight surpassing all normal awareness, something akin to an "awakening," as if all of life heretofore had been a dreaming sleep but now one had finally awakened to reality.

The steps of the Path, we have said, lead to arahatship. This is the state of him "who has awakened," of him "who has reached the end of the Eightfold Path." The arahat is the Buddhist saint. He has attained wisdom. He has conquered "the three intoxications"—sensuality, ignorance, and the "thirst" leading to rebirth—and he enjoys the "higher vision" (*sambodhi*) with its mingling of joy, pleasure, calm, benevolence, and concentration. His joy is deep, because he has already had a foretaste of Nirvana in the trance of his enlightenment, and for the balance of his days he will know the bliss of liberation from misery-bringing desires. He has reached self-fulfillment—that is, of the higher self. His energy is purely spiritual. He no longer feels suffering and takes no pleasure in earthly joys; he is able to say, "I do not wish for death, I do not wish for life." In this state he awaits with calm contentment and without apprehension the "putting out of his lamp of life"—the entrance into final Nirvana at death. Just what this final state will be he, being in this world, is in no position to say. Enough that he is now no longer unhappy. As previously noted, the Buddha refused to give any decision as to whether an arahat exists after

death or does not exist. Nirvana seems at first view a completely negative conception. It means the end, "the blowing out," of existence, so that there will be no more transmigration, and because the skandhas of the last earthly existence are dispersed and there is no ego remaining over, it would seem that Nirvana is "annihilation." But the Buddha would not say that. He did not think this was true. All he knew, or all he cared to say, was that Nirvana was the end of painful becoming; it was the final peace; it was an eternal state of neither being nor non-being, because it was the end of all finite states and dualities. Human knowledge and human speech could not compass it.*

One thing is certain: the arahat is no longer tormented by self, that is to say, by individualizing and egotistical considerations and concerns. The suggestion is made in the Pali texts—but it may be a later addition to the Buddha's teaching—that although the skandhas (i.e., "name and form," the individual known in this life) are not truly a self, when a human mind transcends its normal consciousness through dhyana (meditation at the plane of supra-consciousness), a true or spiritual self is actualized and begins to function. But even this spiritual self that then becomes manifest is annulled in Nirvana. Nirvana divests the self of self in any sense of the word.

But we have not completed our description of the arahat. One of his outstanding qualities is benevolence. He is the Buddhist ideal of what one may become and ought to be. He is magnanimous; he overflows with good will. To grasp this is very important for our understanding of the later history of Buddhism. Although fundamentally the Buddhist seeker is bent on his own self-cultivation, his own blessedness, and is often encouraged, in the words of

---

* The *Udana* quotes him as saying: "There is, monks, that plane [of realization] where there is neither extension nor . . . motion nor the plane of infinite ether . . . nor that of neither-ideation-nor-non-ideation, neither this world nor another, neither the moon nor the sun. Here, monks, I say there is no coming or going or remaining or deceasing or uprising, for this is itself without support, without continuance, without mental object."[R]

the Buddha himself, to "wander alone like a rhinoceros,"[81] forsaking houses and lands and kindred because they hinder him, nevertheless he is charged to love all mankind without exception. That the Buddha himself possessed the quality of compassion for all men is evident in a life devoted to preaching and teaching. Though he strove to sunder every personal tie to particular individuals based on emotion, on the ground, as we have seen, that any such tie is misery-producing, he charged his disciples to love all mankind with a mother's love.

"As a mother, even at the risk of her own life, protects her son, her only son, so let him cultivate love without measure toward all beings. Let him cultivate toward the whole world—above, below, around—a heart of love unstinted, unmixed with the sense of differing or opposing interests."[82]

It became a part of the Buddhist self-schooling to sit quietly in a concentrated effort to call forth from the depths of the heart a love so comprehensive that it embraced every living being in the universe and at the same time so intense that it was unlimited. It was by such loving thought that the Buddhist monk prepared himself for his evangelistic task.

But here we are brought to a pause. Is this warmth of redemptive love consistent with the cloister-seeking motive that is so primary in the life of the monk yearning for Nirvana? How can love issue from anyone engrossed in his own salvation? The question is a serious one. That there is at least a practical inconsistency here was recognized early in the history of Buddhism. In fact, it led eventually, as we shall see, to the fundamental division within Buddhism between the Mahayana and the Theravada (the Hinayana). But benevolence had a place in the full theory of the Buddha. What he evidently meant was that the love his disciples should cultivate for all mankind should be general or universal in character, the love of men as Man. This love of men (one may put it, the love of everyone, but not the love of any *one*) can be the source only of high and disinterested joy. It is not like the love of one individual for another,

which is a relation of dependence and passionate attachment and therefore fraught with the miseries attendant upon unhappy chance and change. It is the love of Man, and its benevolent ministry to individuals as representatives of mankind can be unstinted and even maternal in quality. Kept on a high, impersonal level, it can bring no pain. Rather, it may remain pure and unalloyed through every circumstance; nothing can check it, and no sorrow can enter it. Bestowed on good and evil alike without discrimination, it need not suffer a change in its warmth and saintly quality by any knowledge of good or evil. And it is not affected by the response it meets; through every rebuff, it remains inalienable.

The secret of this patience and good will is thus explained in some of the opening sentences of the *Dhammapada*:

If a man speaks or acts with a pure thought, happiness follows him, like a shadow that never leaves him. "He abused me, he beat me, he defeated me, he robbed me" —in those who harbor such thoughts hatred will never cease,—in those who do not harbor such thoughts hatred will cease. For hatred does not cease by hatred at any time; hatred ceases by love, this is an old rule.[M2]

And in the *Majjhima Nikaya* occur these words, expressive of the same lofty and inalterable good will:

If some one curses you, you must repress all resentment, and make the firm determination, "My mind shall not be disturbed, no angry word shall escape my lips, I shall remain kind and friendly, with loving thoughts and no secret spite." If then you are attacked with fists, with stones, with sticks, with swords, you must still repress all resentment and preserve a loving mind with no secret spite.[N3]

The right kind of love as the Buddha himself conceived of it is best illustrated in a story. One of his most promising disciples wished to preach, it is said, among a certain wild jungle folk. The Buddha, seeking to test him, held with him this conversation:

"But, O Punna, the men of that country are violent, cruel and savage. When they become angry at you and do you harm, what will you think then?"

"I shall think them truly good and kind folk, for whilst they speak angry and insolent words, they refrain from striking or stoning me."

"They are very violent folk, Punna. What if they strike or stone you?"

"I shall think them kind and good not to smite me with staff and sword." . . .

"And what if they kill you?"

"I shall think them kind and good indeed who free me from this vile body with so little pain."

"Well said, Punna, well said! With your great gift of patience, you may indeed essay this task. Go, Punna, yourself saved, save others."[A4]

Though one must grant a fine ethical quality to this inalienable magnanimity, the difficulty for Westerners, and for the Buddhists themselves from the first, has been this: such love is the product of an almost infinite withdrawal from everyday life. It is not a love whose chief mark is selfless self-identification with others. This was to come later. Rather, it is impartial good will on the part of one who has saved himself and wishes to teach others how to save themselves too.

That this love was so guarded and withdrawn was its historic weakness. In Buddhism's aftermath, life and the compassion it arouses were to prove too strong for the bridle of prudential control which the Buddha devised for their restraint.

But to let the matter rest here would be to do an injustice to the founder of a great faith. We should be giving less than full credit to the true humanity of the man, and that of his followers, unless we observe, as we do here, and with admiration, that his and their practice was so much more generous than their cautious, world-denying theory. How true this was of the followers we are about to see presently in this book.

SUGGESTIONS FOR FURTHER READING

ALLEN, G. F. (Y. SIRI NYANA). *The Buddha's Philosophy*. London, Macmillan & Co., 1959

ARNOLD, SIR EDWIN. *The Light of Asia*. Any ed. Famous poem on the Buddha's life based on the *Buddhacharita* of Ashvaghosa

BOAS, SIMONE BRANGIER, TR. *The Life of Buddha*. Wesleyan University Press, Middletown, Conn., 1963. An abridged translation of the now standard work of A. Foucher, *La Vie du Buddha d'après les textes et les monuments de l'Inde*, Paris, Payot, 1949

BREWSTER, E. H. *Life of Gotama the Buddha*. K. Paul, Trench, Trubner, 1926. Compiled from the Pali canon

BURTT, E. A., ED. *The Teachings of the Compassionate Buddha*. Mentor pb, 1955

CARUS, PAUL. *The Gospel of the Buddha*. Open Court, 1917. Compiled from ancient records

LORD CHALMERS, TR. *Further Dialogues of the Buddha*. Oxford, 1926

CONZE, EDWARD, TR. *Buddhist Scriptures*. Penguin pb, 1959

————, ED. AND TR. *Buddhist Meditation*. George Allen & Unwin, 1956

COOMARASWAMY, A. K. AND HORNER, I. B. *The Living Thoughts of Gotama the Buddha*. Cassell, 1949

COWELL, E. B., TR. *The Jataka*. Cambridge, 1895–1907. Reprinted in 3 vols. in Penguin Books pb, 1956

DAVIDS, T. W. RHYS, TR. *Dialogues of the Buddha*. Oxford, 1899–1921

DAVIDS, MRS. T. W. RHYS. *Buddhism, A Study of the Buddhist Norm*. Henry Holt, 1912

————. *A Manual of Buddhism*. Macmillan, 1932

————. *Psalms of the Brethren*. Oxford, 1909

————. *Psalms of the Sisters.* Oxford, 1913

DE SILVA, C. L. A. *The Four Essential Doctrines of Buddhism.* 2nd ed., Associated Newspapers of Ceylon, Colombo, 1948

HAMILTON, C. H., ED. *Buddhism, a Religion of Infinite Compassion.* Liberal Arts Press pb, 1952. Selections from Buddhist literature

JENNINGS, J. G. *The Vedantic Buddhism of the Buddha.* Oxford, 1948

LAW, BIMALA CHURN, ED. *Buddhistic Studies.* Calcutta and Simla, Thacker Spink & Co., 1931.

OLDENBURG, HERMANN. *Buddha: His Life, His Doctrine, His Order.* Tr. by William Hoey. Williams and Norgate, 1882

POUSSIN, LOUIS DE LA VALLÉE. *The Way to Nirvana.* Cambridge, 1917

PRATT, J. B. *The Pilgrimage of Buddhism,* chapters I–V. Macmillan, 1928

THOMAS, E. J. *History of Buddhist Thought.* 2nd ed., Alfred A. Knopf, 1951

————. *The Life of Buddha as Legend and History.* 3rd ed. rev., K. Paul, Trench, Trubner, 1949

WARREN, HENRY CLARKE. *Buddhism in Translation.* Harvard University Press, 1922

THE FOLLOWERS of the Buddha had what he of course could not have: they had a keen-minded, great-hearted founder to believe in and follow. It was natural that they should magnify his religious meaning for them, as indeed they did. They endowed him with a supernatural origin and intention that made him one of the world's grandest religious figures, and they surrounded him with a great company of supporting supernatural beings equally concerned as he was for human redemption from egocentricity and pain.

Whether the Buddha's own outlook was religious in the strict sense is certainly debatable. His chief concern, some commentators say, with with measures to solve the problems of the self rather than with measures to secure favorable conditions in the world below or heaven above. Religion in the sense of a hopeful appeal to the gods to alter one's circumstances was irrelevant. Heinrich Hackmann has pointed out that in original Buddhism the gods are virtually dethroned; their heavenly seats become merely transitory places of reward, no deity in the complete sense of the word exists, worship seems an absurdity, prayer has no place, to know or not to know becomes the only primary concern, and true knowledge can be found only in the narrow circle of monks or anchorites. "The great world outside is excluded. It must be left behind. The path to salvation leads not into the world and through the world, but away from it. In a life of seclusion each individual must take upon himself the heavy task of working out his own salvation by self-discipline, self-purification, study, thought, meditation, and concentration." And though the philosophical and abstract character of original Buddhism commended it to superior minds far beyond the bounds of India, "it would seem as if a special temperament were necessary to appreciate its profound appeal. Buddhism, in its original form, found no response among the masses."[A]

But the masses became interested—secondarily in the teaching, primarily in *the man*. Original Buddhism would not have had so great an effect on the history of religion in the Orient if the coolly rational

6 The Religious Development of Buddhism: Diversity in Redemptive Means

The great stupa at Sarnath. Erected in honor of the beginning of the Buddha's ministry of teaching, this stupa, 140 feet high and once covered with an outer coat of brick-work, is what remains of the monastery now being excavated at this spot near Benares. Of course, the Deer Park has long since disappeared. (Courtesy of the Government of India Tourist Office.)

philosophy of the sage of the Sakyas had not been mediated through a warm and friendly personality that could be adored. Fortunately for the future of Buddhism, its founder balanced the arahat ideal of self-salvation with the ideal of compassionate good will toward all living beings and practiced that compassion himself. Thus there grew up after him a cult that took refuge in *him,* the compassionate as well as

enlightened one, even more than it did in his teaching, so difficult to understand and practice.

When the masses became interested, they would not be denied. Original Buddhism came to them as a philosophy, but they turned it into a religion to meet their need. By a process such as we have seen in Jainism, and will see at work in other great religions, the common people laid hold of the man behind the teaching, saw divinity in him, felt a redemptive intention in his coming among men, and adoringly surrendered themselves to him. In India and beyond India, the common people who espoused Buddhism let the intellectuals, with their unusual mental gifts, go on constructing their profound and abstruse theories, and very generally admired them for their gifts, but they themselves engaged in something much more to their liking and much more satisfying to their deepest needs, the religious development of Buddhism.

This is a simplification of the matter, of course. The process was historically complex and was aided throughout, very materially, by the intellectuals who shared the feeling of the masses.

The rather odd fact is that there ultimately developed within Buddhism so many forms of religious organization, cultus, and belief, such great changes even in the fundamentals of the faith, that one must say that Buddhism as a whole is really, like Hinduism, a family of religions rather than a single religion. But families have a likeness, and if anything can be called the family likeness in these later developments, it is optimism restored, in one sense or another, to the heart of what was originally a way of liberation dominated by a sense of radical human misery.

I   The Spread of Buddhism in India and Southeast Asia

The First Two Centuries in India

During the first two centuries after the Buddha's death his doctrines found wide acceptance within the basin of the Ganges. Not only did the body of monks grow, but the lay adherents increased even more rapidly and included in their number many members of the ruling classes.

The tradition has it that immediately after the Buddha's death five hundred arahats, under the leadership of Kassapa, gathered to spend the rainy season at Rajagaha, and there recited and chanted together the precepts now found in the *Tripitaka.* Whether this be so or not, the teachings of the Buddha were early fixed in the repetitious forms of oral tradition.

When were they reduced to writing? The tradition is certainly untrue in maintaining that the monks of the so-called First Council recited the present contents of the Tripitaka. (For example, that Ananda, the Buddha's cousin and loving attendant, recited the whole of the *Sutta Pitaka,* and Upali, another prominent disciple, the *Vinaya Pitaka.*) Probably several centuries passed before the oral tradition took form as the books of the Pali canon.* When finally reduced to writing, they were divided into "three baskets" (which is what the word *Tripitaka* means), namely, the *Vinaya Pitaka,* or Monastic Rules, the *Sutta* (Sanskrit, *Sutra*) *Pitaka* or Discourses, and, last to be composed, the *Abhidhamma* (Sanskrit, *Abhidharma*) *Pitaka* or Supplement to the Doctrines. The second is the most important, because the principal voice heard in the discourses is that of the Buddha himself. It is subdivided into the *Digha Nikaya* (The Longer Discourses), the *Majjhima Nikaya* (The Shorter Discourses), the *Samyutta Nikaya* (The Connected Teachings), the *Anguttara Nikaya* (The Graduated Teachings), and the *Khuddaka Nikaya* (The Small Book Collection). The last is a sort of miscellany which includes the very important moral treatise, the *Dhammapada* (Verses on the Law), the *Buddha Vamsa,* giving the life of Gautama and his twenty-four predecessors, the *Theragatha* and the *Therigatha* (Hymns of the Elder Monks and Nuns), and the *Jataka,* a collection of some five hundred story-poems

* Let us note again that it was part of the Buddhist rejection of Brahmanism that the early books were written in the Pali dialect instead of in the Brahmins' Sanskrit.

which are said to be recollections by the Buddha of his former lives while he was still a *Bodisattva* or future Buddha.* The importance of the *Digha Nikaya* and *Majjhima Nikaya* is indicated by the number of times we have quoted them heretofore, for nowhere else do we get so clear an indication of the interests and character of the historical Buddha.

A century after the First Council, according to tradition, the Second Council met at Vesali and fought over points of doctrine and the question of moderating the severity of the early Buddhist discipline. The result was a schism, those who wanted the Doctrine and the Discipline interpreted more liberally seceding to form a new order of their own, calling itself the Mahasanghika, "Members of the Great Sangha," perhaps because they outnumbered those who were opposed to them, or because they included laymen in their number, or perhaps simply because they wanted a high-sounding title. The more orthodox monks were called the Sthaviravadins (Pali, Theravadins), "Adherents of the Teaching of the Elders." It was the latter who survived to give their name to the older Buddhism, the Theravada (or Hinayana) Buddhism.

The process of inner division, once set going, produced no less than sixteen more sects during the next three centuries and might have brought disaster to the cause had not a major accession to the Buddhist faith given it India-wide prominence.

Asoka

In 273 B.C. there came to the throne of Magadha, which then dominated the whole of India, one of the greatest emperors in Indian history. His name was

* These books were soon made the basis of commentary. In the fifth century A.D. the learned Buddhaghosa of Ceylon compiled (or is said to have compiled) them into the *Visuddhimagga* (The Way of Purification); he added a prose commentary on the poems of the *Jataka,* giving their complete setting in story form. An important independent treatise in supplementation of the Tripitaka is the *Milindapanha* (Questions of King Menander), quoted from in the last chapter.

Asoka. He was the grandson of the famous Chandragupta who, after overrunning the Macedonian garrisons left in India in 325 B.C. by Alexander the Great, went on to conquer most of the rest of India for himself. Asoka on his own part added to the great domain he inherited a fiercely resistant kingdom along the Bay of Bengal, but the bloodshed and suffering he brought on the conquered people pricked his conscience already quickened by Buddhist teachers. He publicly embraced Buddhism as his faith and became intensely interested in its propagation.

To express his "profound sorrow and regret" for the suffering he had caused by his warfare, he issued an edict, engraved upon enduring rock, for all to see, declaring that His Sacred Majesty felt remorse for the death and dislocation of so many hundreds of thousands of folk and that thenceforth "if the hundredth part or the thousandth part" of all the people who were then slain, done to death, or carried away captive "were now to suffer the same fate, it would be a matter of regret to His Sacred Majesty."[B1] His Sacred Majesty would henceforth practice gentleness and bear all wrongs done to himself with all possible meekness and patience.

Realizing that the slaughter of animals for the imperial table was inconsistent with his Buddhism, Asoka cut down the palace consumption to two peacocks and one antelope daily and then forbade even this amount. He had already abolished the royal hunt. In 259 B.C. he issued decrees regulating throughout the empire the slaughter of animals and prohibiting entirely the killing of many classes of living creatures.

Even more important were his royal exhortations to his people to live peaceably, without violence, and to practice all the Buddhist pieties. In 256 B.C. he issued a series of edicts, incised on rocks in seven widely scattered places (the "Fourteen Rock Edicts"), so that they could be read and reread by his people. These were followed by the "Seven Pillar Inscriptions," the two "Kalinga Edicts," the three "Cave Inscriptions," the four "Minor Pillar Edicts," and others. Totaling thirty-five in all, these edicts told how he wished his people to live.

Thus saith His Sacred Majesty:—"Father and mother must be hearkened to; similarly, respect for living creatures must be firmly established; truth must be spoken. These are the virtues of the Law which must be practiced. Similarly, the teacher must be reverenced by the pupil, and fitting courtesy must be shown to relations." This is the ancient nature of things—this leads to length of days, and according to this men must act.

People perform various ceremonies. In sickness, at the weddings of sons, the weddings of daughters, the birth of children, departure on journeys—on those and other similar occasions people perform many ceremonies, . . . although that kind bears little fruit. . . . On the other hand, the Ceremonial of Piety bears great fruit. In it are included proper treatment of slaves and servants, honor to teachers, gentleness toward living creatures, and liberality toward ascetics and Brahmins. . . . Even if this Ceremonial of Piety fails to attain the desired end in this world, it certainly produces endless merit in the world beyond.[B2]

This is a layman's idealistic but practical creed. There is no reference here, nor elsewhere in the edicts, to the Four Noble Truths, or to Nirvana, the goal of the arahat. What Asoka was interested in was that his people should practice the glorious ethic of the Dharma, piety, and store up merit toward rebirth in a paradise hereafter. With this prospect he was more than satisfied, for he was no monk and could not reach Nirvana without becoming one.*

In order to give effect to the moral exhortations contained in his inscriptions, Asoka required that the officials of the government, from the least to the greatest, give oral expositions of the Dharma to the people, and appointed Censors of the Law of Piety to supervise the populace in general and Censors of Women to supervise female morals in particular. These special officers were sent out to every part of

* Nirvana was for the arahats. The great mass of the people had to rest content with the prospect of accumulating enough merit to enter Swarga, heaven. In some far-off rebirth they might be monks and attain Nirvana; meanwhile the bliss of paradise awaited and invited. It was enough. Still, unsubstantiated tradition says Asoka prepared himself for monkhood by accepting ordination into the Sangha and retiring to a monastery after forty years of rule.

the empire, even to the most backward and remote districts.

Asoka was also much interested in Buddhism as an organized religion. To show his devotion to the memory of the Buddha, he made pious pilgrimages to spots sacred to the Blessed One. Realizing, too, that a divided Buddhism would be weakened in its home territory, he issued edicts discouraging schism, recommending inter-Buddhist (and also interfaith) harmony, and called together, so a doubtful and no longer verifiable tradition relates, the Third Council, which presumably reorganized and reformed the order (the Sangha).

Most important, he seems to have conceived of Buddhism as a world religion, for he sent missionaries and ambassadors of Buddhism to lands far and near. His emissaries reached Syria, Egypt, Cyrene, and Greece. His own younger brother (or son?) headed a missionary band, as we shall next see, to Ceylon. All this was the beginning of an extraordinary expansion, the full extent of which Asoka could not himself have foreseen.

Ceylon

In an exchange of gifts and compliments Asoka first broached the subject of sending teachers of the Buddhist doctrine to Ceylon. Subsequently, he sent Mahinda, said by some to be his son, by others his brother, at the head of a band of missionaries. From that time the civilization of Ceylon may be dated. Buddhist shrines and monasteries rose to perpetuate the Buddhist doctrine. For that perpetuation the rest of the Buddhist world came to be very grateful. Because Ceylon was for centuries unaffected by the sometimes catastrophic changes that went on in India itself, the Buddhist doctrine remained through the years true to the tenets of early Buddhism, with little or no change. It was, therefore, the historic destiny of the Buddhist monks of Ceylon to conserve for posterity the oldest Buddhist texts.

The story that has come down to us is this. Ma-

The Bodh-gaya temple. *The scene of the Buddha's Enlightenment under the Bodhi tree (whose lineal descendant stands nearby) was first marked by a vanished temple erected by the Emperor Asoka. The present tower, 170 feet high, was completed in the eleventh century. Part of the stone railing enclosing the original temple, and a "diamond throne" (vajrasan) marking the "immovable spot" where the Buddha sat, are still preserved. (Courtesy of the Government of India Tourist Office.)*

hinda brought no written records with him to Ceylon, but he and his associates held in memory the whole of what constitutes today the older Pali texts. The legend goes on to say that the original scriptures **149** were rendered into the Singhalese dialect, and for a time were the only complete collection of ancient texts in the whole Buddhist world. In the fifth century A.D., the great Buddhist scholar, Buddhaghosa, went to Ceylon, it is said, learned the Singhalese tongue, and began the task of retranslating the old texts back into Pali. Other scholars from India eventually brought the task to completion.

The devotional zeal of the Buddhists of Ceylon has been nourished through the years by the relics brought over from India. These include what the devout believe are the begging bowl, the left canine tooth, and a collar-bone of the Buddha. Impressive shrines—now of great age—house these treasures.

The Singhalese are to this day predominantly of the older (Theravada) Buddhist school, sometimes called the Hinayana.*

Burma and Southeast Asia

Burma and the countries of southeast Asia are also predominantly Theravadin. All at one time or another felt the influence of Hinduism, and each, at least in the northern parts and wherever the Chinese have settled, has come under Mahayana (later) Buddhist influences, but in the main the more conservative Theravadin tendencies have prevailed. What has this meant? We shall pause to see.

The General Character of the *Theravada*

In the Theravadin areas, the monk is, as he always has been, the central figure. His scriptures are the comparatively few but ancient Pali texts. He professes (sometimes because the scriptures say so, not always because the understanding assents or comprehends) that there is no atman (self), the world is transient

---

* The origin and meaning of this last term will be explained in Section II, p. 154 n. infra. Modern southern Buddhists much prefer to call their faith Theravada Buddhism.

and the scene of sorrow, and so Nirvana is the goal. The monastic discipline is that of early Buddhism. The ideal of the individual monk is the attainment of arahatship. Hence, in all the Theravadin monasteries solitary meditation is the rule. The monks go forth in the morning to beg, clad in yellow robes and with shaven heads, just as in Gautama's day, and they follow the same daily schedule as of old. The whole emphasis of life is on acquiring merit toward one's salvation.

It is typical for each monk to rise at the sound of a bell at daybreak, wash himself, sweep out his cell, fetch and filter a supply of water, light a candle before the Buddha-image in his cell, chant a salutation, and then meditate on some aspect of the Dharma and its challenge to him. After this he takes his begging bowl, and, selecting a street, goes straight down it, quietly stopping at every house, whether of high or low estate, and standing in silence for the door to be opened. If there is no response, he unobtrusively goes on to the next house. Back in the monastery, he eats his breakfast. Then, at the sound of a bell he joins the other monks in the assembly-hall for group reverences to the Buddha, chants, and instruction by the head of the monastery. From 11:00 to 11:30 he joins the other monks in eating his main (and last) meal of the day, washes and puts aside his bowl, and back in his cell devotes the afternoon to studying and copying scriptures and to meditation, choosing perhaps one of the standard themes for meditation. T. W. Rhys-Davids explained the five principal kinds of meditation thus:

There are five principal kinds of meditation, which in Buddhism takes the place of prayer. The first is called 'Metta-bhavana,' or meditation on *Love*, in which the monk thinks of all beings and longs for happiness for each. . . . The second meditation is 'Karuna-bhavana' or meditation on *Pity*, in which the mendicant is to think of all beings in distress, to realize as far as he can their unhappy state, and thus awaken the sentiment of pity, or sorrow for the sorrows of others. The third meditation is 'Mudita-bhavana,' or the meditation on *Joy*, the converse of the last, in which he is to think of the gladness and prosperity of others, and to rejoice in their joy. The fourth is 'Asubha-bhavana,' the meditation on *Impurity,* in which the mendicant thinks of the vileness of the body, and the horrors of disease and corruption; how the body passes away like the foam of the sea, and how by the continued repetition of birth and death mortals become subject to continual sorrow. The fifth is 'Upekka-bhavana,' meditation on *Serenity,* wherein the mendicant thinks of all things that worldly men hold good or bad; power and oppression, love and hate, riches and want, fame and contempt, youth and beauty, decrepitude and disease, and regards them all with fixed indifference, with utter calmness and serenity of mind.[c]

At sundown he again sweeps his cell and lights a lamp. At the sound of the evening bell he goes to another joint assembly like the morning one. After this, if he needs counsel, he goes to his superior for instruction or to confess his shortcomings and his difficulties in understanding. Finally, he retires for the night with an earnest resolve for the morrow, to work out his salvation with renewed diligence.

If one asks the Theravadin monk whether the Buddha exists or not, the correct answer is always

The great stupa at Sanchi, central India. This relic mound from the first century A.D. *is encircled by a stone railing, inside which the pilgrims move counter-clockwise. They are admitted to the enclosure by four gateways covered with carvings concerned in general with the biography and previous lives, animal and human, of the Buddha. Many of these carvings are superb examples of ancient Indian art. (Courtesy of the Government of India Tourist Office.)*

Close-up of the east gateway at Sanchi.
The top architrave or cross-piece of this richly carved gateway is devoted to the last seven Buddhas, the middle one to the Buddha's departure from Kapilavastu, and the lowest one to the visit of the Emperor Asoka to the Bodhi tree as a pious pilgrim. (Courtesy of the Information Service of India.)

that the Buddha entered Nirvana and is therefore no longer exercising an active personal influence as a living self; he is at peace, and knows nothing any more of becoming and ceasing to be.

It is still taught that everything in the universe, including gods, men, and beasts, is in a state of constant flux. To abide in flux means suffering. To experience liberation from "the scene of sorrow" requires concentration (dhyana), and this in turn demands *prajna*, the highest wisdom, that is, transcendental insight penetrating beyond phenomena to final truth; in short, enlightenment (bodhi).

But although all this is in strict conformity with Gautama's original teaching, even the Theravada doctrine has developed in the direction of religion. For one thing, Theravadin Buddhists take a reverent attitude toward the relics of the Buddha and have made images of him of every size, from the minute to the colossal. They have, we see, erected giant stupas in his name.

Even the Pali texts depart at a number of points from Gautama's own views of life and reality and contain in germ many of the ideas elaborated later in the Mahayana. For example, they declare (what Gautama himself *may* have said, though it is doubtful) that the Sage of the Sakyas was not the only Buddha to appear in the world; he had predecessors in other ages—to the number of six, say the earlier texts, or of twenty-four, says a later. They also affirm that the Buddha was a divine being, omniscient and sinless, that through countless incarnations he lived so perfectly that he became through sheer merit a divine being who lived in the Tushita heaven. From thence he came to earth, entered his mother's womb, and was born as a man. His divine nature became manifest in his enlightenment and life of pure example and teaching. His way of life is the true one for all; there is no other way out of misery into peace. He himself is at peace—perfect peace. The *next* Buddha—now a Bodhisattva (Pali, Bodhisatta), that is, a Buddha-in-the-making—is Maitreya. He is waiting for the proper time to come to earth, where he will reach enlightenment and do for men in his age what Gautama has done for this.

The religion implicit in this view of things becomes evident to any observer of the typical Theravadin religious establishment of today. In Thailand, where conditions are typical, such an establishment is called a *wat*. This is a cluster of buildings within a walled enclosure. The entrance is from the east and is guarded by large, grim-visaged animal or human figures in a protective stance, a carry-over from the animism of pre-Buddhist days when tutelary demons were thought essential to a well-guarded gateway. The main building in the enclosure is known as the *bot*. It usually has a curious threefold, red-tiled roof, one roof close upon another, with gilded finials of a horn-shape curving upward and said to represent snake heads. Inside, the building is designed as a hall for worship and preaching. Near the middle of the floor there may be a low dais for the leader of the preaching services, and on the floor around mats for the congregation—laity and monks. At the end of the hall farthest from the door is a golden Buddha-image, resplendent on a seat above the altar, with perhaps smaller standing or seated images of the same great being arranged about it, and on either side images of the two famous disciples of the Buddha, Moggalana and Sariputta, looking up worshipfully. The altar is covered with offerings of the devout, incense-burners, expensive candlesticks with their candles in place, flowers in costly vases, solid gold or plated images, dishes, and bowls. These are all precious gifts to the founder of the faith, and increase the merit of the givers.

In addition to the bot, there may be several other halls, one perhaps to house gilded Buddha-images in serried rows, and another to cover perhaps a reputed footprint of the Buddha in the solid rock. Also, distributed picturesquely through the compound there may be a number of stupas (*dagobas* or *phras* to the Thais), gilded towerlike structures of tapering designs, usually ending in a sharp-pointed pinnacle. These are built by the laity as an act of special merit. (Indeed, the highest ambition of the devout layman is to build one during his lifetime.)

Adjoining the other buildings, or outside the walls of the wat, the monasteries may be found. They are simple in structure, partitioned into cells, and very barely furnished. Here the monks live out their simple life, devoted to meditation and the duties of the wat and to lay education under government patronage. In Thailand and in Burma it is the general custom for every male at the age of twenty to live in a monastery for not less than two months—less time would not be respectable. This period is supposed to be spent in intensive study and cultivation of Theravada principles.

One question may be raised. It has to do with the services in the central hall of the wat. What is the attitude of the Theravadin toward the great Buddha-image on its throne above the flower- and gift-laden altar? The answer is that the attitude of the *average* Theravadin of Asia is undoubtedly religious. In the image he sees the representation of a living, responsive, supernatural personality who is able to hear and answer prayers, if the need be great. It is only the more learned of the monks who know better what the true doctrine is. They know that prayer increases merit, especially if it consists of the repetition of sacred words and verses, but that there is no *answer*.

II The Rise of the Mahayana in India

The Locus: Northwest India

After Asoka, Buddhism enjoyed great prestige throughout India for eight hundred years. And yet, forty years after his death, when Asoka's dynasty fell from power, influences hostile to Buddhism—like those of the empire of the Shungas—rose to ascendancy in central India.

But then Buddhism simply transferred its center of gravity westward. In northwestern India it began to flourish and take on new forms. In the second and first centuries B.C. Syrians, Greeks, and Scythians poured into the Punjab, and having made themselves its masters, became the leading spirits in a buoyant Greco-Bactrian culture. The conversion of their king, Menander (or King Milinda upon native tongues), brought the new kingdom within the reach of Buddhist influence. Then, in the first century A.D. the Kushans, a tribe of central Asian nomads akin to the Turks, overran Afghanistan and northwestern India and absorbed the arts and culture of the Greco-Bactrians. Their greatest king, Kanishka, had his capital in Peshawar and inquired into many religions, Zoroastrianism among them, before he adopted Buddhism. The Buddhist world had subsequent cause to be thankful that he gave his royal approval and patronage to the new and beautiful Greco-Buddhist sculpture and architecture, art forms that resulted when Greek artists were hired to lend their talents to the adornment of Buddhist themes. The curly-headed Buddhas, which they created, were destined to dominate the aesthetic consciousness of all later Buddhism, as far away as Japan.

It was here in northwest India that Mahayana Buddhism first came to flower.°

Sometime between the third century B.C., the age

° When the Mahayanists took their name (Mahayana means "the Great Vehicle"), the conservative, older Buddhism never accepted the name Hinayana ("the Lesser Vehicle"). *Vehicle* (*yana*) here refers to a means of transportation, such as a raft, a ferry, or a carriage. If the crossing of the river analogy is used for Buddhist salvation, then Mahayana is the Great Ferry or Raft and Hinayana the Lesser Ferry or Raft. Besides the rather derogatory juxtaposition of Great and Lesser, which the Theravadins dislike, there is an implication, sometimes pointed out, of Big and Little, the Mahayana being the Big Raft transporting whole groups of believers, with a pilot in charge, and the Hinayana the Little Raft for one-at-a-time or individual transportation.

of Asoka, whose inscriptions give us no reason to think the religious development of Buddhism had proceeded very far, and the first or second century A.D., when Kanishka ruled northwest India, the doctrines later embodied in the Mahayana, the most elaborately developed form of Buddhism, began to take shape, though they were then known only to a few. It was a momentous new development—more effective in making Buddhism a world religion than even Asoka's well-laid plans. For it turned the negativistic philosophy of early Buddhism into a religion that offered eternal rewards to the optimists.

The First Step: The Glorification of Gautama

This religious transformation of the original deposit of Buddhist tradition began to develop rapidly after Kanishka's conversion (whether with his encouragement or not is a matter of debate), and became public property. It is impossible now to determine precisely in just what order the various ideas arose, but the process expanded and developed certain intimations in the Theravada, and seems to have pursued some such course as this:

First, Gautama Buddha was adored and worshiped as a divine being who came to earth out of compassion for suffering humanity. A complete mythology, recorded in the *Jataka*, explains how through many existences the great being who became the Buddha lived according to all "the perfections" and finally reached a place in the Tushita heaven from which he came to earth. These assertions about him were a logical consequence of certain primary assumptions: (1) that the Buddha was a person of extraordinary qualities, and (2) that when we inquire about his previous incarnation, we must believe, according to the principle of the fitness of things that marks the operations of the Law of Karma, that he could not have come from hell nor from the animal and human levels, but must have come from heaven, and without doubt from the Tushita heaven, for it is a place specifically meant for highly meritorious contemplatives. The logic here runs as follows: what should or logically must have happened did, in the absence of evidence to the contrary, actually happen. Much else that the *Jataka* relates—how, as human minds apprehend, the gods went to the Tushita heaven to ask the great being to go to earth; how he assented after making five observations as to the rightness of the time and as to where and to whom he should be born; how he took the form of a white elephant and descended from heaven; how he entered the womb of his mother while she lay dreaming of this very event in a Himalayan palace of gold to which swift angels bore her for his immaculate conception; how, finally, she gave birth to him in a sacred grove with angels in attendance—all this can be understood as being logically what must have happened and therefore did happen.* To the question concerning his name before his descent to earth, the answer was, "He was a *Bodhisattva*." This word, in its Pali form Bodhisatta, occurs in rather early texts, but is there purely descriptive; it merely recites a fact that was perfectly obvious, namely, that before Gautama was enlightened he was a person destined to be enlightened. But in the growth of the Mahayana doctrine, this word was to make religious history; it became a term of great importance.

The Next Step: Discovering Other Buddhas and Bodhisattvas

Possibly the next step followed as the result of the indirect influence of Brahmanism, which insists on a reality behind all phenomena displaying itself over and over in recurring events, or perhaps the doctrine

of the avatars of Vishnu * had an influence. For whatever reason, the Mahayanists heavily emphasized a belief that the more conservative (the Theravadins) also, with less prominence, set forth, that Gautama was not the only Buddha, that there had been many Buddhas before him. Some had come to earth, and some had remained in the heavens, and some were in the making, the Buddhas of the future, the Bodhisattvas.

The myth-making process was rounded out to some sort of completion when, in a manner far surpassing the modest earlier achievements in this respect, the Mahayanists recovered the names and histories of these other Buddhas and of the Buddhas-to-be! (The reader is doubtless puzzled. How could the names and histories of these beings be recovered without the proper documents and other historical traces? In Oriental lands, those who give full credence to intuitions, revelations, and insight into past and future through trance-visions would regard such a question as barrenly sceptical.†) The literature of the Mahayana, in Sanskrit manuscript after manuscript, thus added immense stores of knowledge to the devout. Before their eyes immeasurable vistas opened up. The universe became radiant to its outer limits with compassionate beings who could and wanted to aid them. Their imaginations now had much to feed on. Furthermore, prayers were now again possible. A rich and luxuriant cultus sprang into being. The devout were furnished with wall-paintings and sculptures as aids to devotion. Salvation was no longer something to be achieved only by self-effort. Divine

---

* It may be noted that this "logic of faith" has been invoked in other religions: for example, in Jainism to tell how Mahavira was gestated in two human wombs and as a result had two mothers; in Zoroastrianism to explain how his fifteen-year-old mother came to conceive a superhuman Zoroaster; in Roman Catholicism to provide for the Virgin's immaculate conception by her parents and for her bodily assumption to heaven. Duns Scotus put the logic of the doctrinal development thus: "It could be; it ought to be; therefore it is."

* The doctrine that Vishnu has made "descents" (*avataras*) to earth by incarnating himself in men and animals will be discussed in Section V of the next chapter (p. 214 f.).

† Edward Conze, in *Buddhism, Its Essence and Development*, p. 38, has this to say: "To the Christian and agnostic historian, only the human Buddha is real, and the spiritual and magical Buddhas are to him nothing but fictions. The perspective of the believer is quite different. The Buddha-nature and the Buddha's 'glorious body' [his bodhisattva body] stand out most clearly, and the Buddha's human body and historical existence appear like a few rags thrown over his spiritual glory."

beings with vast stores of merit were eager to share with the faithful.

Much was to flow from this. Not only was the whole aspect of Buddhism changed for the believer, but its fortunes abroad improved at once. Countries that responded slowly to the appeal of the Theravada doctrines now took up the Mahayana with eagerness. And because the Mahayana was by nature expansive, it changed as it moved; the peoples among whom it made its way contributed to its development.

For this reason, it is well to see where it thus made its way before we summarize its full tenets at the height of its development.

III   The Spread of Buddhism in Northern Lands

China

The story of Chinese Buddhism is very difficult to compress into a few paragraphs. Only its broadest outlines can be touched on here.

At a very early period—perhaps as early as the third century B.C.—China and India were in contact. Military and commercial activity found both a way over the sea and a route through central Asia, but the length and difficulty of the journey tended to make the contacts few and brief. Just how much more than the name of the Buddha, in travelers' accounts of him and his teachings, was known in China before the time of the Emperor Ming Ti (58–75 A.D.), of the Later Han dynasty, is difficult to determine. Perhaps the knowledge was considerable. Chinese historians of the past have related that some half-dozen years after Ming Ti began to reign he became actively interested in Buddhism, because he had seen in a dream the golden image of the Buddha flying into his room, with head glowing like the sun. According to the ancient tale, which is very likely pure legend, he sent twelve special envoys to India to bring back more exact knowledge of the teachings of the Blessed One. The envoys brought with them on their return a library of holy books, statues of the Buddha, and what was of more importance, two Buddhist monks, full of gentle missionary zeal. The monks, it was said, unloaded their holy books from the back of their horse, entered the monastery that the emperor had erected for them, and began the work of translating their sacred literature into Chinese. Incidents *like* this occurred, but perhaps not at this time nor at an emperor's insistence. We are on sounder ground in believing that Ming Ti, in 65 A.D., permitted a statue of the Buddha to be erected and the Buddhist cult to spread, without himself being an adherent of the Blessed One.

But Buddhism made little progress in China then. It seemed in its Theravada version to be alien to the Chinese temperament and tradition. Monasticism could not easily be reconciled either with the Chinese ideal of devotion to family life or with their love of life and optimism. Moreover, the Chinese were a self-sufficient, practical, even a materialistic people, and the speculative and mystical temper of Buddhism had to prove its kinship to native Chinese mysticism (Taoism) before it held any lure for them. They had first to be shown the life-value of the doctrines of the transitory nature of the world, the unreality of worldly activity, the non-existence of the ego, and the need of salvation from the misery of existence. It is a well-founded tradition that during the two Han dynasties (206 B.C.–8 A.D. and 23–220 A.D.) family opposition to monkhood was such that a public ban lay upon the entrance of Chinese boys into monasteries.

But this attitude of coolness broke down, and for a number of reasons. During the period of the Hans, China was united and could devote itself to building upon earth an ideal feudal or Confucian society, but at last the Later Han dynasty dissolved in the turmoil that produced the Three Kingdoms (220–280 A.D.), and during the three centuries that followed the nomad tribes of central Asia, waiting beyond the Great Wall, broke into China in great numbers, pro-

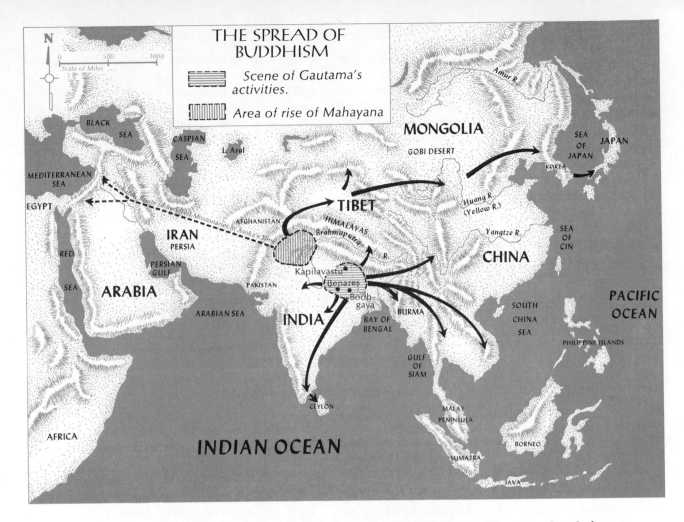

THE SPREAD OF BUDDHISM

Scene of Gautama's activities.

Area of rise of Mahayana

ducing thereby a vast disunion and misery. The scholars and intellectuals looked in vain for signs of public return to the old Chinese will to make this world a happy dwelling-place for an orderly and harmonious human family. In their great discouragement, many of them turned from the optimistic humanism of the Confucians to the mystic consolations and back-to-nature quietude of Taoism. An un-Chinese contempt for the world possessed them. They became ripe for Buddhism. Indeed, there is evidence that even in the time of the Hans the Taoists had already shown an interest in Buddhism because it seemed to them to have resemblances to their own outlook. And many others felt the same interest be-

cause the world as they knew it reduced them to hopelessness, if not actual despair.

This rather negative reason for the eventual success of Buddhism in China was more than matched by a positive one: the sheer brilliance of the advanced form of thinking discovered in the Buddhist texts, an intellectual subtlety, logical thoroughness, and profundity unparalleled in Chinese thought to that time. Intellectuals were powerfully drawn to it.

But the common people were also being readied for Buddhism. Among the nomads who broke into China through the breaches of the fabulous Great Wall were Mahayanists. They brought a gospel for the masses. From the south, too, the Mahayanist missionaries pressed in directly from India. Their flexible creed enabled them to recognize the validity of Chinese needs and modes of thought. The emphasis on filial piety that is to be found within Buddhism itself enabled them now to rank this virtue with the guarding of the sanctity of animal life, abstaining from intoxicants, and the rest of the Five Precepts of the Buddhist order. Indeed, they began to say that to fulfill the duty of filial piety, sons should add to their traditional rites Buddhist masses for the dead, as a means of making the lot of their ancestors happier. Here the vivid imagery of the Buddhist monks, who drew freely from Indian conceptions of the after-life, began to tell. There had been lacking in the life and thought of China a really satisfying conception of the future life. Chinese hopes had had little to offer in the way of comfort, except the bare faith that one would join his ancestors at death and be dependent forever thereafter on the filial piety and remembrance of one's descendants. It was in part just because Mahayana Buddhism, as it came to flower, far surpassed either Taoism or Confucianism in presenting attractive pictures of the after-life that it began by the fourth century to exercise a wider popular appeal. This is not to say that Confucianism and Taoism were entirely displaced, but only that Buddhism won a place alongside them. (One could, indeed, be at one and the same time a Confucian seeking the internal welfare and harmony of the family, a Taoist coming to terms with external natural processes, and a Buddhist aiming at security after death. The three religions seemed to complement each other.)

North China, where the racial stock was now largely intermixed with the blood of "barbarian" invaders, and where the ancient Chinese culture was most disturbed and shaken, was the first to respond generally. South China was slower to yield. Here Confucianism still had staying power, and even the Taoists were cool. Nationalistic pride was stronger in them there. But eventually, all over the land, monasteries sprang up, huge temples full of images of the various Buddhas of the Mahayana faith multiplied, and the intellectuals divided into many schools of Buddhist thought, worthy of our examination later (pp. 170 ff.).

The number of adherents to the various Buddhist groups was large, and remained large, while dynasties rose and fell. Sometimes a sternly Confucian or vigorously Taoist emperor would institute widespread persecution. One such—it was Wu Tsung of the T'ang dynasty—in 845 A.D. destroyed forty-five thousand Buddhist buildings, melted down tens of thousands of Buddha-images, and sent over four hundred thousand monks, nuns, and temple servitors back into the world. But tolerant emperors always followed the anti-Buddhist ones, and at least the physical damage was repaired.

That is the essence of the story of a thousand years.*

Korea

The introduction of Buddhism into Korea followed soon on the fourth-century spread of that religion in China. At the time, Korea was divided into three independent states, none of which had a culture much above primitive animism. When a Buddhist monk by the name of Sundo, encouraged by the Buddhist ruler of a little state in north China, crossed into Korea with Buddha-images, sacred books, and missionary ardor, in a remarkably short time the three Korean states took up the new religion and its accompanying culture. By the middle of the sixth century the king of the southwestern state was sending missionaries, images, and books to the emperor of Japan.

---

* Spiritual damage is another matter. Slow eclipse of Buddhism in the rise of Neo-Confucianism during and after the Sung dynasty led to a loss of creative influence and spiritual decline. A generation ago, although the nominal adherents of Buddhism in China (people who resorted to Buddhist shrines or priests at least occasionally) numbered perhaps 250 million souls and a Buddhist revival had had some effect in middle China, Buddhism seemed to have lost much of the force it once possessed. Today its strength is again diminishing, partly because the Communists are ideologically opposed to it.

Two monks, father and son, worshiping a Buddha. Keepers of a temple in South Korea dating from 982 A.D. and maintained by the revenues of the land it owns, father and son bow to the image that is in their care. (Courtesy of the United Nations.)

Japan

It was in the year 552 A.D. that Kimmei, the emperor of Japan, received from his Korean correspondent a gold-plated image of a Buddha, some sacred writings, some flags and umbrellas, and a letter concerning the excellent but difficult Buddhist doctrine, which should, it was claimed, produce illimitable and immeasurable good fortune—or painful retribution—and which could transform a man into a Buddha (i.e., a person possessed of bodhi). This claim probably did not impress the emperor as much as the further statement that from farthest India, through all China, even to Korea, the doctrine had found reverent acceptance. That did impress the emperor. Perhaps, he thought, there was a great deal more to the religion that a Chinese monk at Yamato had been

quietly practicing in his self-built temple these thirty years than appeared on the surface. At any rate, the emperor, the ancient story tells, took up the matter with his councilors. Some were as impressed but as cautious as himself; others were in outright opposition to the new religion, in the devout belief that the *Kami*, the native gods of Japan, would be angered. A few followed the prime minister, chief of the Soga clan, in suggesting favorable action. The emperor took the part of prudence and passed the golden Buddha-image on to the head of the Soga clan to try it out on his family, to see if the Kami would object. When a pestilence broke out among the people it was thought the Kami did object, so the golden image was thrown into a canal, and Buddhism fell irretrievably out of the emperor's favor.

In due course the emperor died, and the Korean

THE RELIGIONS OF INDIA

monarch sent another embassy, which included, besides the priests and two hundred sacred texts, a nun, an image-maker, and a temple architect. In the spirit of courtesy, the embassy was allowed to construct a temple for its own use, and once more the Soga clan supported the view that the new religion should be given a fair trial. Again, however, a pestilence broke out, and, if we are to believe the ancient tale, again the Buddha-images found a resting place at the bottom of a canal. All looked dark for Buddhism. But presently a perplexity arose. The pestilence continued! So the head of the Soga clan advanced the thought-provoking argument that it was not the Kami who were angered—else the pestilence would have ended—but it was the Buddhas, who resented the coldness of their reception. The cautious authorities decided to let matters drift.

By the time the next emperor reached the throne, Buddhism had made actual progress. In fact, the emperor, in spite of military and priestly opposition, viewed it with favor. With new Buddhist missionaries ever arriving, the tide began to turn. In 588 A.D., when the Empress Suiko ascended the throne, her nephew, Shotoku Taishi, an ardent Buddhist, became regent. He sent groups of scholars to China to bring back as complete knowledge as possible both of Buddhism and of the Chinese system of government. He built the first public Buddhist temple in Japan and organized the first monastic school. To exemplify the humanitarianism of the Mahayana, he erected a hos-

The great Buddha (Daibutsu) of Kamakura, Japan. Nearly fifty feet high over-all, this bronze image of Amida Buddha was cast in 1252 under the direction of the Japanese artist and craftsman Ono Goroyomen. The horizontal sections fit together perfectly, and earthquakes have not injured the giant figure, as the devout point out. (Courtesy of Japanese Tourist Office.)

pital, a dispensary, and a house of refuge. Other Buddhist leaders donated on their part alms-houses, irrigation canals, orchards, harbors, ferries, reservoirs, and good roads. The new religion was demonstrated to be good not only for the individual, but also for society as a whole.

Having won the adherence of the court, Buddhism began slowly to reach down to the common people. In time, as in China, various schools or sects sprang up, largely under Chinese tutelage. The whole population eventually became at least partially Buddhist. The native religion, Shinto, had offered some difficulty at first, but when the Kami, the old gods, were taken into the Buddhist pantheon as Buddhas and Bodhisattvas, the difficulties were largely removed. In fact, it was the common practice for centuries for a man to be a good Buddhist, a good Shintoist, and a good Confucianist all at the same time.*

Buddhism long was the dominant religion of Japan and reached some of its finest and noblest forms there. However, in the eighteenth and nineteenth centuries, during the time of the Tokugawa Shoguns, Shinto revived in an anti-Buddhist form (p. 324 f.) and became a rival of Buddhism in seeking the adherence of the Japanese people. Buddhism suffered a further setback during the nineteenth century with the coming of the Christian missionaries. For awhile even the government frowned on it. At present, the restrictions of World War II at an end, it is actively engaged in modernizing its methods of appeal to win back its old popular support. How far this will succeed in the face of changing Japanese needs is for the future to tell.

Tibet and Mongolia

Buddhism was late in coming to Tibet and Mongolia. It established itself in a form so different from

* Shintoism expressed gratitude for and loyalty to the national and family heritage; Confucianism provided a social ethic for the present; Buddhism took care of the future (the next life).

the Theravada and even the Mahayana, as these are usually understood, that it is called by other names. Although the Tibetans prefer that their religion be called simply Tibetan Buddhism, it is sometimes given the name of Lamaism, because of the prominence of the *lamas* in it, but this is misleading. Other names applied to it refer to its practices or doctrines. Thus it may be called the Mantrayana ("the Vehicle of Mantras," or "Holy Words," which emphasizes its magical character), or the Tantrayana (which points out its relation to Tantric Hinduism, p. 211 ff.), or, better still, the Vajrayana ("the Vehicle of the Thunderbolt," which reflects its bold theology). Because of its belated coming, strange history, and stranger doctrines, it will be described separately in the next-to-last section of this chapter (p. 180 ff.).

The Decline of Buddhism in India

Strangely enough, the up-curve of the Mahayana in China and Japan is matched by a swift down-curve in India. This is perhaps as good a place as any to note a startling fact: Buddhism steadily declined in India after the seventh century A.D. The Chinese pilgrim Fa Hien, who visited India from 405 to 411 A.D., noted with joy the flourishing condition of both the Hinayana and Mahayana monasteries, but when his countryman, Hsüan Chuang, came two centuries later (629–645 A.D.), decline had set in apace. Part of the decline may be assigned to the ferocious invasions of the White Huns in northern India during the sixth century, incursions that resulted in the raiding and destruction of the Buddhist monasteries and the disorganization of the Buddhist leadership. But this externally induced weakness was more than matched by an internal weakness of long standing: Buddhism expected the laity to feed and assist the monks but offered them in return few of the life-enveloping ceremonies the Brahmins were so ready to perform—ceremonies for birth and death and, in between, ceremonies for all the promising or threatening events that favored or deeply perturbed villages, homes, and individuals. Then, too, it had been a constant threat to Buddhism as a separate movement that the followers of Vishnu, as early perhaps as the fourth century A.D., adopted the Buddha as the ninth incarnation of Vishnu. Most serious of all was the decline of creative intellectual energy within Buddhism itself. A final blow came in the twelfth century. In 1197 the Muslims, who had entered India four centuries before, invaded the last of the Buddhist strongholds. What was left of the dispirited Buddhism in Magadha was roughly stamped out. Only a few followers of the Blessed One obscurely hung on to the faith. Except for believers in the foothills of the Himalayas, they have remained comparatively few in India to this day, although recently, through the efforts of B. R. Ambedkar, a leader among the untouchables, considerable numbers of the depressed classes of the state of Maharashtra have become converts to Buddhism.

IV   The Gospel of the Mahayana

What was the secret of the success of the Mahayana outside India? The answer is not hard to find.

The Divine Authors of Salvation

To the common people, the Mahayana offered the good news of the existence of multitudes of saviors, real and potential, whose chief desire was the cure or the amelioration of the sufferings of men. This was glad tidings. The pure benevolence of these saviors was the best of all assurances. Even the intellectuals were interested. After all, they too preferred to believe that the universe was friendly.

Of course, when the learned examined this assurance, they saw that the tenets of original Buddhism were caught up and almost lost in it, like pale-colored threads in a vivid tapestry. In the discourses of the Mahayana texts Gautama, as the golden-voiced Sakyamuni, lectured to his disciples through hun-

162

dreds of pages, yet the message he brought but faintly echoed the tenor of his discourses in the Theravada texts—it is Mahayana religion and philosophy that he is expounding. A similar recession of the themes of original Buddhism appeared in the worship and cultus of the Mahayana.*

Most Mahayanists claimed that the Buddha *privately* taught that a man does not have to save himself; he can get help.

In the Mahayana the authors of salvation are of three kinds, falling naturally into order. They are the Manushi Buddhas, the Bodhisattvas, and the Dhyani Buddhas.

Manushi Buddhas are saviors who, like Gautama, have appeared on earth in the past as human beings, attained enlightenment, instructed men in the true way of life, and then, their duty done, realized Nirvana. They are primarily teachers. Prayers cannot now reach them.

Bodhisattvas would never have become vital concepts if it had not been for the historical Buddhas, like Gautama, but in the Mahayana, if anything, they are more important and have a greater religious reality. The Theravada scriptures recognize but two beings of the kind, Gautama before his enlightenment and Maitreya. But in the full form of the Mahayana the Bodhisattvas are a great, even an innumerable, company of supernatural beings who hear prayers

* In the Chinese temples, for instance, the arahats have been indeed remembered and honored, but more because they have belonged to the pageantry of Buddhism than because they have had any vital religious function to perform. Eighteen of these early saints of Buddhism have been given a place in Chinese temples under the name of the Lohan (which is as near as the Chinese, with their tendency to pronounce r's like l's, have come to pronouncing *arahat*). They often are seated, on either hand, along the side walls of the temples, their images rendered almost grotesque by the realistic touches added to their appearance by the temple artists. Plainly, they are men and not gods; and the worshipers have not regarded them as saviors. They are there because they are a part of Sakyamuni's original company, and because many of the Chinese have believed that somewhere in the inaccessible fastnesses of the mountains they still sit in immortal, serene, and mindful meditation.

and come actively to men's aid. The prevalent popular view of Bodhisattvas, especially in China and Japan, has been that they are beings who have made a vow many existences ago to become Buddhas and have lived ever since in such a way as to acquire almost exhaustless stores of merit. This merit is so great that they could readily achieve the full status of Buddhas and pass into Nirvana, but they are compassionate beings; out of love and pity for suffering humanity, they postpone their entrance into Nirvana and transfer their merit, as need arises, to those who call upon them in prayer or give devotional thought to them. They sit enthroned in the heavens, looking down on the needy world, and sometimes, in redemptive pity, they descend in the guise of ministering angels to perform deeds of mercy.

We have space here only for brief mention of the most widely popular among them. Maitreya, the next Buddha (known in China as Milo-fo), has already been mentioned. He was honored first in India and then all over the Mahayana world. Numerous images of him show the high respect in which he has always been held, but, strange to say, the worship never has been so ardent as in the case of some other Bodhisattvas. Perhaps the faith that he is going to be the next Buddha has made for a feeling that he is, or should be, saving his merit for his earthly career and cannot give it away. The people turned to others, like Manjusri (Chinese, Wen-yu) and Avalokitesvara (Kwan-Yin). The former is one of the earliest of the Mahayana creations. He is the Bodhisattva who assists those who wish to know and follow the Buddhist Law (the Dharma). So he is represented as a princely figure, carrying in addition to his sword (logic) a book (the Buddhist Law or Truth). Near his image there often appears that of another Bodhisattva, Samantabhadra (P'u-hien), who brings happiness to his following and fosters in them his own universal kindness. But the most popular by far, in himself and in his metamorphoses, is Avalokitesvara, or Lord Avalokita. As his Indian name seems to imply (it probably means "the Lord Who Looks Down on This Age from Above"), he has a special interest in the people of the current time. The personification of divine compassion, he watches over all who inhabit the world and is said to have come to earth over three hundred times in human form, and once as a miraculous horse, in order to save those in peril who have called upon him. He averts not only moral catastrophes, such as rage, folly, and lust, but physical pains and disasters as well, such as shipwreck, robbery, or violent death. He grants to women the children they implore. His image usually represents him as in the garb of a great prince, with high headdress, carrying in his left hand a red lotus (one of his aliases is Padmapani, the Lotus-handed), and extending his right hand with a gracious gesture. Frequently he is shown seated on a large lotus, and is called, with poetic devotion, "The Jewel in the Lotus." Sometimes he is given four, or many more, arms—all laden with gifts to men. Sometimes he kneels; his postures are many.

We shall see (p. 181) that in Tibet Avalokita is accompanied by a spouse, one of the Prajnas, but in China, by a metamorphosis whose history is obscure, he changed his sex and became the enormously popular Kwan-Yin, the Goddess of Mercy, whose place in the esteem of the Chinese and Japanese is analogous to that of the Virgin Mary in Roman Catholicism. Her attitudes are exactly those of Avalokita in India, with the addition of the warmth of a madonnalike maternal feeling. Her images, upon which sculptors have lavished their highest art, show her in every variety of gracious and winsome posture. They are to be found all over China, Korea (where she is called Koan-Eum), and Japan (where her name has been further modified into Kwannon). Like her Indian alter ego, she is often shown seated on a lotus or standing on one, or she rides upon a cloud or glides on a wave of the sea. In her arms she often bears a child, for it is such she gives to her women adorers, and on her head she may wear a crown set with an image in miniature of Amitabha Buddha, the Lord of the Western Paradise, to whom she takes those faithful to her. Again, she may be shown without ornament.

Of the other Bodhisattvas one more should be mentioned. He is Kshitigarbha. In China, under the name of Ti-Tsang, and in Japan, as Jizo, he ranks high in popular regard, chiefly because, at the instance of grieving relatives and friends, he descends into the hells, delivers its sufferers, and transports them to heaven. In previous incarnations he was twice a woman, which explains his untiring kindness and tender mercy and his interest in helping women in the pangs of child-birth. As if to credit him with the endeavor to be in many places at once and thus multiply his power to aid, the Chinese declared there were six of him, one for each of the six life-levels of the universe. In Japan, in the character of a single being, Jizo was identified with the Shinto war-god, Hachiman; represented as riding on horseback, wearing a war-helmet, he became the favorite of the Japanese soldiery. But he was also the beloved friend of little children, in which relation he appeared to them in the guise of a simple, honest monk.

The third class of savior-beings is composed of Dhyani Buddhas.* These "contemplative Buddhas" differ from Bodhisattvas in having fully achieved their Buddhahood, but they stand in a different category also from the Manushi Buddhas in not having achieved their Buddhahood in human form. They dwell in the heavens, and in the indefinite interval between the present time and their compassionately postponed final entrance into Nirvana they actively minister to men's needs, as did Gautama between his enlightenment and death. Their name implies that they are Buddhas of contemplation (dhyana), and their images convey the impression of deep meditation and calm. Whereas the Bodhisattvas are usually princely in aspect and wear rich clothes, studded with gold and jewels, to symbolize their active, world-serving role, the Dhyani Buddhas sit or stand in the simple garments of the monk, their hands held in front of them or folded in their laps in the five established *mudras* or positions, their eyes turned downward, and a quiet smile lighting up their otherwise grave and composed countenances.

Taking the whole of the Mahayanist world into account, we find the three principal Dhyani Buddhas to be Vairocana, Bhaisajyaguru, and Amitabha. They are but a few among many. The first is a solar Buddha, whose functions link him with the Persian Mithra, the Vedic Savitar, and the Mediterranean Apollo. He is a Buddha of first importance in Java, and in Japan the sun-goddess Amaterasu has been called his manifestation. The second is the Buddha of Healing and has a great following in Tibet, China, and Japan. But Amitabha (known to the Chinese as O-mi-to and to the Koreans and Japanese as Amida) is one of the great gods of Asia. Once he was a monk, took the vow an incalculable number of eons ago to become a Bodhisattva, rose to his present rank, and now presides over the Western Paradise, a Buddha-field or domain he has called into existence, named Sukhavati, or the Land of Bliss, generally known as "the Pure Land." Because he is the kindly lord of this happy heaven of the western quarter and freely admits all who beseech him in faith, he has surpassed in the estimation of the masses in China and Japan even Sakyamuni, the deified Gautama.* The core of the matter is this: whereas the Bodhisattvas serve present need, Amitabha assures future bliss. The

---

* This term comes from a late Nepalese tradition and has gained currency because it is terminologically convenient. The usual name in the Sanskrit texts is Tathagatas (in the sense of "those who have traveled the same road to Suchness") or Jinas ("victorious ones").

* In answer to the question, is it really possible for a Bodhisattva to create or call into existence such a Buddha-field as Sukhavati by *thinking* it into being, Bhikshu Sangharakshita, an English convert, in his *Survey of Buddhism* says: "One who has gained the fourth [stage of] *dhyana* is able not only to produce replicas of his physical body . . . but also to 'materialize' seemingly natural objects of every kind. . . . Once [Tumo Geshe Rimpochhe, a celebrated Tibetan yogin who died in the 1930s], while traveling in Tibet with a large retinue, caused to appear in the sky a wonderful phantasmagoria of the Buddha Maitreya and His attendant Bodhisattvas. The phenomenon, which was visible for miles around, lasted for several hours. Not only was the whole countryside bathed in celestial radiance, but flowers resembling lotuses came raining down. These latter, though they could be picked up and handled, appeared to melt into the air after about half an hour. . . . Many of those who

hopeful devotee, unable to emulate Sakyamuni in helpfulness or to acquire the merit stored up by arahats and Bodhisattvas, turns to Amitabha and has merit transferred to him from the great being's store. Some sects among the Chinese and Japanese believe that the grace of O-mi-to is granted in fullness to anyone who merely repeats with devotion his sacred name. A Mahayana treatise widely read in China and Japan, *A Description of the Land of Bliss* (the *Lesser Sukhavati-vyuha*), says distinctly that faith in Amitabha, quite apart from meritorious works and deeds, is alone sufficient unto salvation. It declares:

Beings are not born in that Buddha country as a reward and result of good works performed in this present life. No, all men or women who hear and bear in mind for one, two, three, four, five, six, or seven nights the name of Amitayus,* when they come to die, Amitayus will stand before them in the hour of death, they will depart this life with quiet minds, and after death they will be born in Paradise.[E1]

In this conception original Buddhism is completely transcended.

But this is no less true of the whole of the Mahayana scheme of salvation. No one will deny that Gautama taught and practiced good will and compassion for all, but these expressions of love were to a certain degree impersonalized, as his philosophy of life demanded. So far as possible, love was made, as we have observed before (p. 142), a love for every-

one, not of any *one*, and at no time was the acquiring of merit forgotten—at least in theory. But in its conception of the character of the Bodhisattvas and Dhyani Buddhas, Mahayana Buddhism exalts pure altruism to supremacy in the moral sphere, and by insisting on its expression in supernatural beings who answer prayers, has moved directly counter to Gautama's teaching that one should not pray but should devote his energies to something really effective— saving oneself.

The Mahayanists frankly recognize this departure from early Buddhist teaching, but they have the belief that Gautama taught several kinds of doctrine, depending on the nature of the hearers: to the weak and selfish he outlined the eightfold arahat path; to those of greater understanding and strength of character he imparted the ideal of the compassionate and altruistic Bodhisattva. This version of Gautama's teaching has enabled the Mahayanists vigorously to attack the selfishness of the "Hinayanists," who are accused of abandoning the world to its fate while they seek their own salvation individually, each "wandering alone like a rhinoceros."

The Vow of the Bodhisattva

The line of thought just outlined led, in actual fact, to perhaps the most inspiring of all Buddhist teachings. It may be rather awkwardly stated thus: just as the Bodhisattvas, who are now divine but once were human, vowed in a distant past to become Buddhas and then from pure altruism postponed their entrance into Nirvana by transferring their merit to others in order to help the needy, so any human being of the present, man or woman, can, if he or she wishes, make a similar vow with regard to the future. Everyone is potentially a Buddha and should now take the vow to be a Bodhisattva. The length of time necessary to fulfil the destiny thus undertaken may be almost beyond reckoning, but true benevolence needs no urging and waits for nothing. The time to begin is now.

---

were eye-witnesses are still alive, and the substance of their united testimony is not lightly to be rejected.

"The conclusion is obvious. If it is possible to produce a phantasmagoria which lasts for a few hours and is seen by hundreds of people, it should be possible to produce one which will last for centuries and be seen by millions. If thought-power can create a flower it can, stepped up to the requisite degree of intensity, create a Buddhafield."[D1]

Because to this point of view the world and all sentient beings apparently present in it are "mind-made" or subjective phenomena, the Pure Land can be seen as of a piece with all the rest of the furniture of heaven and earth.

* The active forth-going or emanation of the unmoving Amitabha.

As the Mahayana doctrines developed into their fuller forms, this ideal was more clearly articulated and was linked up, as will shortly appear, with a vast metaphysical background. Various stages in the career of a Bodhisattva were distinguished, and a body of literature emerged to convey instructions on how to enter the initiatory stages. According to a seventh-century manual called the *Bodhicaryavatara,* the initial stages can be entered upon by anyone who feels joy in the good actions of all living beings and who wishes to spend himself in the increase of such good. A person of this temperament may then pray to the Buddhas to aid him in acquiring enlightenment—not that he may pass into Nirvana, but rather that he may secure the good of all living beings. To this end he requests the Buddhas to postpone his entrance into Nirvana until he has aided all living beings within range or until the last blade of grass shall have been set free!

In the Far East the Buddhist monks pass through successive degrees of ordination that culminate in that of a Bodhisattva. The degree that immediately precedes the last is, significantly, that of an arahat, and this order of the degrees clearly shows how the Mahayana feels it has transcended the ethical ideals of the Theravada.

V The Mahayana Philosophies of Religion

What to the people was a message of salvation was to the intellectuals and mystics a philosophy, profound and subtle. It was so all-explanatory that it intrigued the minds that believed it no less than it rejoiced them.

The Schools

Most of the Buddhist philosophizing was done in India. There the two main schools thought out their characteristic views in the second, third, and fourth centuries A.D. and were greatly influenced by, and in turn influenced, the philosophizing being done by Hindu and Jaina thinkers during what was in fact the great systematizing era in Indian thought.

In the second century A.D. Nagarjuna organized the Madhyamika (or Intermediate) school, founded on earlier speculations. It took its point of departure from the teaching of Gautama that the commonly believed-in self or ego is but a loose grouping of ever-changing skandhas. Early followers of the Buddha had reasoned that this analysis of the human personality holds good of all objects or existents whatsoever: anything at all is a loose collection of pulsating, transitory "elements." Nagarjuna now took the step of saying that these elements (dharmas), when closely examined, are no more than mental phenomena or phantasms. They are "empty" and do not really exist as experienced; they are but the fictions of ignorance-clouded minds. If one sees an object, say a man, or even the Buddha, walking down the street, one really experiences seeing such an object. The experience means something in one's mental history, but the object is nevertheless not the solid, material object one initially senses it to be. The substantiality of the external world is thus denied. "Everything is void (*sunya*)." Things are not what they seem. In reality they are empty of the characteristics assigned to them.

However, certain important qualifications must be made. What has just been argued is the transcendental truth (*paramartha-satya*). Only minds that have shed "ignorance" can apprehend it. So long as minds and consciousnesses continue to function in the ordinary or usual way, they experience everyday or relative truth (*samvriti-satya*). In the light of everyday truth things seem not to be void but to have qualities and relations that give them existence and reality for experience. This is the realm of the imperfect and impure, in which men are born and reborn (the realm of samsara).

To a mind heretofore struggling with relative truth, the thing that happens when enlightenment comes to it is a perception of the vacuity of sensed objects in the light of absolute truth (paramartha-satya).* This does not mean that nothing exists whatever. Properly interpreted, the thought runs thus: the mind liberated from the notions of everyday experience knows that things are void of the attributes assigned to them,† and indeed are not to be given any attributes at all, because they are in themselves unknowable and unknown. The reality that must be behind the appearances known to our consciousnesses as the Buddha, the world of bondage, karma, and transmigration is ineffable. (Here the thought resembles Immanuel Kant's transcendental idealism and the epistemology of other Western philosophers.) Because reality cannot be assigned any attributes, in it there is "neither production, nor destruction, nor annihilation, nor persistence, nor unity, nor plurality, nor coming in, nor going out."E2 Furthermore, entrance into Nirvana is entering a void, because it means stripping the attributes from everything and passing into what appears from "here" to be vacuity and silence.

* For instance, in any mental act of everyday experience dealing with description, the object described, the description, and the person doing the describing are all devoid of any verifiably real attributes if viewed in the light of absolute truth; they are not really existent in the way they are conceived to exist. But the phantasms have reality as phantasms. The same reasoning holds true of rest and motion, transmigration, karma, the Buddha himself, or anything whatever to which the everyday consciousness ascribes attributes.

The reason why this view is called "intermediate" is because it is a qualified realism, intermediate between the commonsense realism of early Buddhism, which grants momentary reality to dharmas in the sense given above, and the qualified idealism next to be described as characterizing the Yogacara school.

† I.e., by the everyday consciousness. Dr. Chan Wing-tsit puts the fact thus: "Reality is [presumed to be] Void in the sense of 'devoid' of any specific character." (Article, "Chinese Philosophy," in *Dictionary of Philosophy*, Philosophical Library, New York, 1942.) Another way of putting it is to distinguish, as does Bhikshu Sangharakshita, "between thoughts and things, between concepts which merely indicate realities and those realities themselves;" for "things" that are truly real subsist in "a purely spiritual world which transcends thought and speech," and human minds have therefore only uncertain and dubious concepts to go by.D2

In this void there is no form, no perception, no name, no concepts, no knowledge. There is no eye, ear, body, mind; no taste, touch, objects; no knowledge, no ignorance, no destruction of ignorance, no decay, no death, no Four Noble Truths, no obtaining of Nirvana.F

In the fifth century the Yogacara (or Idealist) school, founded in India by the brothers Asanga and Vasubandhu, began where the Madhyamika left off. In this view the mentalism or idealism at first sight seems complete. Mind or consciousness is "the imagination of unreality" (*abhutaparikalpa*), and the objects of its thought are ideas only. How then does the mind always perceive what other minds do and not just what it pleases to perceive; that is, how does it share the everyday world with other minds? How does it learn about the Buddha and seek Nirvana? The immediate answer (in terms of "the imagination of unreality") is that there is a reservoir or store of perceptions on which all minds draw, namely, "the consciousness that holds all" or "the receptacle consciousness" (*alaya-vijnana*). This "consciousness" is the store-house of all ideas. It is a cosmic all-mind. It is like an ocean; it carries on its surface the tossing and evanescent waves that are the phenomenal world apprehended by the seven illusion-making levels of consciousness—sight, hearing, smell, taste, touch, discrimination between the various phenomena of the universe, and distinguishing between subject and object. The "receptacle consciousness" is the source of the illusory phenomena "perceived" by the seven other types of consciousness. (It is itself the eighth type of consciousness.) But the alaya-vijnana is not the ultimate reality; it operates within the Void (*sunyata*), which *is* the ultimate reality, and is so named because human minds (the "imagination of unreality") cannot apprehend it. To identify with the ultimate reality is, then, to abandon all ideas (ideation), including awareness derived from the alaya-vijnana, and realize Nirvana, i.e., be lost in or rather liberated into the Void.

Earlier, in the famous treatise *The Awakening of Faith* (very uncertainly ascribed to Ashvaghosa, ca.

167

100 A.D.) the ultimate ground of consciousness had been named the Absolute Suchness (the Bhutata-thata, "that which is such as it is"), and it was said that when a mind hampered by ignorance attempts to comprehend it, the illusion that constitutes the seeming multiplicity of the phenomenal world is produced, but in itself the Absolute Suchness is pure and at rest, the "oneness of the totality of things." This way of putting the matter was destined to have great influence on later Buddhist thought.

The Wisdom That Has Gone Beyond (Prajna-paramita)

By now the language of Buddhist scholarship was no longer Pali but a variant of Sanskrit, the classical language of India. From the beginning of the Christian era and through the next five hundred years a vast literature in Sanskrit began to appear. Early examples of this literature were the *Mahavastu* and the *Lalita-Vistara,* two versions of the life of Buddha filled with miracles and wonders. Next came the *Buddha-Carita* of Ashvaghosa (ca. 100 A.D.), a famous biography of the Buddha in the noblest verse form. There followed the *Lotus of the Good Law* (the *Saddharma-Pundarika*), which is the most beloved of all Mahayanist scriptures, filled, as it is, with supposed discourses of the Buddha on Vulture Peak near Bodh-gaya; the *Sukhavati-Vyuha,* a prized description of Amitabha's Pure Land and how to get there; and a large group of sutras, a hundred or more in number, dealing with problems of philosophy of religion. Of these last the *Lankavatara* and *Surangama* sutras have been the most influential.

A special category of this literature, of which the popular *Diamond-Cutter* (the *Vajracchedika,* commonly called the *Diamond Sutra*) is typical, goes by the name of the *Prajna-paramita Sutras,* so called because they are "Discourses on the Wisdom That Has Gone Beyond" (a close translation), that is to say, teachings concerning transcendental wisdom (*prajna*).

It is in this last group of treatises that we come upon a metaphor that perfectly suggests what prajna-paramita means. It is the early Buddhist metaphor of crossing a river by raft or ferry to get to the farther shore (Nirvana). In the light of this metaphor, prajna-paramita may be translated as "the Wisdom Gone to the Other Shore."[*] The nearer bank of the river is this world, known to the senses since childhood. From it one cannot imagine at all what the Other Shore, far away, is like. But the ferry arrives, piloted by the Buddha, and when one boards it (i.e., adopts Buddhism as his faith) and begins the crossing, the receding nearer bank gradually loses reality and the far shore begins to take shape. At length only the far shore seems real, and when one arrives there and leaves behind him the river and the ferry, they too lose all reality, because one has now gained final release in the Great Beyond, which alone is utterly real. Thus, the river and both of its banks, as well as the ferry, the Buddha, and even the human goal which had been all along the ultimate bourn of Nirvana, are equally and completely void. *As concepts* they had once been the useful means of attaining prajna or transcendental wisdom, but they are empty now and useless forever.

This reasoning, we find, is based on a famous passage in the Pali *Majjhima Nikaya,* where the Buddha asks his monks:

"What would be your opinion of this man, would he be a clever man, if, out of gratitude for the raft that had carried him across the stream to safety, he, having reached the other shore, should cling to it, take it on his back, and walk about with the weight of it? . . . Would not the clever man be the one who left the raft (of no use to him any longer) to the current of the stream, and walked ahead without turning back to look at it? Is it not simply a tool to be cast away and forsaken once it has served the purpose for which it was made? . . . In the same way the vehicle of the doctrine is to be cast

---

[*] No one has written of this more graphically than Heinrich Zimmer in *Philosophies of India* (p. 475 ff. in the Meridian paperback edition). The student is recommended to read for his own enjoyment this full and fascinating description.

away and forsaken, once the other shore of Enlightenment (Nirvana) has been attained."G1

One more point needs to be added. Not only is every human concept of reality discarded in Nirvana; the empirical self, as one thinks of it in life, is discarded too. The *Astasahasrika Prajnaparamita* says this with great subtlety:

> The Enlightened One sets forth in the Great Ferryboat; but there is nothing from which he sets forth. He starts from the universe; but in truth he starts from nowhere. His boat is manned with all the perfections; and is manned by no one. It will . . . find its support on the state of all-knowing, which will serve it as a non-support. Moreover, no one has ever set forth in the Great Ferryboat; no one will ever set forth in it, and no one is setting forth in it now. And why is this? Because neither the one setting forth nor the goal for which he sets forth is to be found.G2

The Trikaya or Triple Body

In the doctrines of the Bhutatathata and the Receptacle Consciousness the reader will find no difficulty in seeing a similarity with Vedantic speculation. They point to an Absolute (the Void) that resembles in many respects the Brahman-Atman of Hindu monism. But there is a difference that must ultimately be ascribed to the influence of the career and personality of Gautama Buddha upon Mahayana speculation. Whereas in Vedantic thought Brahman-Atman remains the unpicturable, inconceivable Absolute of strictly neutral being, in Mahayana Buddhism the Absolute Essence or Suchness is identified with a sort of love-behind-things that produces Buddhas—a Buddha-essence at the heart of the universe. The importance of this conclusion for religion is surely evident. For here the Buddhas, as expressions or projections of Being-Itself, are not merely indifferent or unfeeling expressions of It, but rather a manifestation of compassionate redemptive love (*karuna*), drawing ignorance-clouded minds along the Bodhisattva way of love back to Itself.

This conclusion of the Mahayana schools reaches a great height of religious thought. Christian theology and Buddhist metaphysics can engage in dialogue at this level. This becomes still more evident in a further phase of the thought of the Mahayana metaphysical schools. In trying to relate the Absolute Suchness with the appearances of the Buddhas and other holy beings and saviors in the phenomenal world, the Mahayana systematizers evolved the doctrine of a "triple body" (Trikaya). According to it there are three "bodies" in the totality of the universe, first, "the Body of Essence and Being" (the Dharmakaya), second, "the Body of Spiritual Bliss" (the Sambhogakaya), and third, "the Body of Earthly Forms" (literally, "Transformations"), or the Nirmanakaya. The first indicates the eternal reality that is the ground and source of the phenomena (dharmas) that compose the universe known by the senses; it is identical with the Absolute Suchness, the Void, within which function or subsist the alaya-vijnana, prajna, and Nirvana. The Body of Spiritual Bliss is the heavenly manifestation of the Dharmakaya, particularly in the celestial Buddhas and Bodhisattvas, and generally in spiritual reality or force capable of redemptively entering history and taking name and form. The Body of Earthly Forms is the manifestation of the Body of Spiritual Bliss in earthly appearances, the prime example being the historical Buddha, Gautama. The first is undifferentiated and impersonal, the second differentiated and personal, and the third an earthly manifestation of the second. Applied to Gautama Buddha, this doctrine of the Triple Body led to the following formulation of the faith concerning him: the Absolute Suchness or Void is the ground of being from which emanates the Body of Spiritual Bliss manifested in such heavenly powers as Amitabha, Avalokitesvara, and the Bodhisattva who once dwelt in the Tusita heaven and who compassionately came down to earth to be the historical Gautama Buddha.* When his earthly mission

* We shall see in Section VII (p. 183) that a still later formulation, apparently Tibetan, considered Amitabha to be the celestial Buddha whose spiritual son Avalo-

was accomplished, Gautama Buddha returned to the source of all being, the Dharmakaya (= Nirvana).

Applied to the common man, these philosophical positions of the Mahayana led to the view that, because the Absolute Suchness or Buddha-essence (the Dharmakaya) is manifest in all things, there is a Buddha-nature or potentiality in every man. Anyone may take up the career of a Buddha-to-be without having to be reborn. Throughout the Far East the influence of this belief penetrated, and its optimistic implications thrilled the aspiring natures of the devout with a new zeal and a great hope.

VI Mahayana Schools of Thought in China and Japan

Our study of the religious development of Buddhism would be far from complete either in scope or interest if we did not, briefly at least, consider the leading Mahayana schools and sects in China and Japan. In general the picture is this: what the Buddhist speculative theologians of India put forward by way of suggestion and outreach, the Chinese took up and developed as the logical basis of their differentiations, and the Japanese, eager to learn, came forward to put the finishing touches on the Chinese developments, always adding something of their own in the process.

The formation of differing schools of thought was in some instances due to Indian teachers coming to China, but for the most part the Chinese were influenced toward variation in point of view chiefly by the Mahayana literature they read and discussed. This literature came to them in the form of translations from the Sanskrit originals or as literary works produced by the Chinese themselves. The first influential Mahayana text was the *Diamond-Cutter* (or *Diamond*) *Sutra*, translated in the fourth century A.D. Next came translations of the *Pure Land Sutras*, the *Lotus of the Good Law*, and the *Awakening of Faith*. Other important influences streamed from the lengthy Sanskrit works known as the *Avatamsaka Sutra* and the *Lankavatara Sutra*, which were in whole or in part translated into Chinese. The Chinese themselves seem to have composed the *Sutra of Brahma's Net*, the most widely used manual on the monastic life. Different schools of thought also justified their positions by issuing treatises like the *Practice of Dhyana for Beginners*, and the *Sutra of the Sixth Patriarch*, and others.

It would be tedious for the ordinary reader were we to attempt to trace out individually the manifold differences among the schools and sects of China and Japan. Such a study would be as detailed and difficult to follow as an inquiry, say, into the differences between Protestant sects in Europe and America. Fortunately, we may pursue another course. The main trends among the Buddhist schools are clearly distinguishable, and may be comprehensively considered under five heads.

1. *The Pure Land School*. Here the motive is one that appeals to the common man, that of getting to heaven. The chief interest and ultimate goal of the Pure Land Buddhists is the Western Paradise of Amitabha Buddha. By concentration of attention solely on this aspect of Buddhist belief an extraordinary simplification is achieved. The strenuous life of "works" is rendered unnecessary. The whole emphasis is on faith, and faith together with humility is believed to be sufficient for salvation; in fact, the practical-minded Chinese have called the Pure Land way the "short cut," and such it appears to be. An unquestioning faith in Amitabha, and the devout repetition of his name, especially by the use of the formula "Namu Omito Fo" ("Hail, Amitabha Buddha!"), are all-sufficient.

In China the Ching-t'u (Pure Land) school represents this point of view. Its founder, a converted

kitesvara brought into being the historical Gautama Buddha. However, there is a definite Tibetan tradition that Mahavairocana, the central figure among the five celestial Buddhas, gave rise to Gautama Buddha. In any case, the principle seems to be that Gautama Buddha's sambhogakaya is ultimately to be identified with one of the celestial Buddhas.

Taoist, appeared in the fourth century A.D. In Japan the chief representatives of Amidism have been the Jodo and Jodo-Shin sects. The Jodo sect was founded in the twelfth century by a Japanese scholar named Genku (later known as Honen Shonin or "Saint Honen"). As a young man he had sought vainly for peace by means of the three Buddhist disciplines ("precepts, meditation, and wisdom"), and had then found enlightenment in a library when he read in a Chinese Amidist commentary the comforting words: "Only repeat the name of Amitabha with all your heart, whether walking or standing, whether sitting or lying: never cease the practice for a moment. This is the very work which unfailingly issues in salvation."[H] He thereupon accepted salvation as coming by divine grace through faith. In old age, it is said, he claimed that after reading the Amidist commentary he began to repeat "Namu Amida Butsu!" ("Hail, Amida Buddha!") sixty thousand times a day, and increased this later on to seventy thousand times! This was the chief expression of his faith, although he also reverenced Gautama Buddha and performed good works out of gratitude and as a religious duty, knowing that he could not *earn* salvation: it was Amida's gift.

The Jodo-Shin sect, established by Genku's disciple Shinran Shonin, has introduced some radical Japanese innovations, hardly paralleled in Buddhism elsewhere, and is now the most widespread of the Japanese sects, having the greatest number of temples, monks and teachers. It has taken the confident position that humility (the sense of human powerlessness to effect redemption) and faith in Amida's love are in themselves true signs that the redeeming grace of that Buddha has already been bestowed, and that therefore the repetition of the Amidist formula (telescoped in Japan to "Nembutsu") should not be regarded as prerequisite to salvation but should be motivated by gratitude, for Amida seeks and saves without first requiring faith and good works. In fact, faith is solely his doing; it springs up spontaneously from Amida's spiritual presence in the heart.

Freed from celibacy, Shin priests are allowed to marry, eat meat, and live in the world like lay persons. As in the case of Christian churches, Shin institutions depend not on endowments but on voluntary contributions. Because the priests can marry, an innovation something like that in Tibet has occurred: the abbots are hereditary. In the past, by acquiring political and even military power, these abbots "were even more like barons than the celibate prelates"[E3] of the older, semi-militarized sects of the feudal era. The cheerful, world-accepting nature of the Shin sect has had a natural result: many persons have found it a highly attractive faith.

2. *The Intuitive School: Ch'an and Zen.* The goal here is immediate insight, enlightenment such as Gautama achieved under the Bo-tree. The method of salvation is nominally dhyana, or meditation, but salvation is actually obtained not by meditation but by insight or awakening (prajna) following on meditation. To some who are of this way of thinking scholarly research, the reading of books, listening to lectures, doing good works, the performance of rituals, and so on are not only of little merit in themselves but often a hindrance to true insight into the Buddha-reality. One must find salvation by an inward look into one's own nature.

Generally, Ch'an and Zen sects have accepted as normative four conditions:

A special oral transmission from master to disciple outside the scriptures
No dependence upon the authority of words and letters
Direct pointing to the soul of man
Seeing into one's own nature and attaining Buddhahood

In attempting to pronounce the Sanskrit word *dhyana*, the Chinese elicited their name for this way of faith, namely, the Ch'an school. The founder was said to have been an Indian scholar and teacher by the name of Bodhidharma. Now no more than a dim legendary figure, he may have come to China in the sixth century at the time when the growing influence of Buddhism had claimed an imperial convert, the Emperor Wu Ti of the Liang dynasty. The interesting old tale, which is to be viewed with historical scepti-

cism, says that when Bodhidharma came to north China and established himself there, the emperor sent for him. In the course of the interview the renowned teacher was asked how much merit flowed from making imperial donations to the Buddhist order and continuing the translations of sacred books. "No merit at all!" the gruff monk replied, and went on to say to his shocked hearer that knowledge gleaned from reading is worthless; no merit flows from good works; only meditation that admits one to direct insight into the Great Emptiness of the Buddha-reality, only truth revealed to one's thought when one turns inward to actualize the Buddha in one's heart, is of any value. To demonstrate what he meant, Bodhidharma is said next to have retired to Mt. Su and to have sat meditating with his face to a wall for nine years.

Whatever the circumstances of its origin, the Ch'an school began at first with just simple living and stern self-discipline as the preparation for meditation and the inward vision. At first it disdained all scriptures and was rigorously individualistic, iconoclastic, and averse to regarding the ultimate Buddha-principle ("Nothingness," "the Void") as in any sense definable. Gradually, however, the old aids to the religious life were reinstated and in a moderate way made use of. Nevertheless, it was realized that such aids cannot substitute for meditation, even though differences developed as to the nature of the meditation itself. There are different kinds of meditation. The question arose, should one "sit still' in meditation, carefully eliminating false views, without any specific aims or problems in mind, waiting and hoping for bodhi (by a gradual enlightenment), or should

Bodhidharma crossing the Yangtze on a reed. *The formidable reputed founder of Ch'an (Zen) Buddhism, with a characteristic scowl on his face, seems to be glaring toward the approaching shore but is actually so uninvolved in the processes of this world that, for all his bulk, he floats across the river on a fragile reed. (The Cleveland Museum of Art, John L. Severance Fund.)*

one focus upon a tough problem with intensity, hoping to wear down the intellect to the point where it gives up and "sudden enlightenment" (realization) takes place? Ultimately, of the seven Ch'an sects two survived, the Lin-Chi and the Ts'ao-tung, the first devoted to abrupt procedures and stiff problems leading to sudden enlightenment, the second to a broad development of the understanding through book-learning and instruction leading to gradual enlightenment. In either case, the ability to meditate properly was required, and one did not need to be learned in history or philosophy nor expert in the traditional rites and ceremonies to attain it. Profundity of insight into one's own "heart" was all that was required. By way of illustration, the following autobiographical passage from a Ch'an text is worth quoting, for it shows how an illiterate country boy became, on account of his intuitive qualities, the renowned Sixth Patriarch, Hui-neng:

I was selling firewood in the market (of Canton) one day when one of my customers ordered some to be sent to his shop. Upon delivery and payment for the same as I went outside I found a man reciting a Sutra. No sooner had I heard the text of this Sutra than my mind became at once enlightened. I asked the man the name of the book he was reciting and was told it was the Diamond Sutra. I asked where he came from and why he recited this particular Sutra. He replied that he came from the Tung-tsan Monastery in Wongmui; that the Abbot in charge was Hwang-yan who was the Fifth Patriarch and had about a thousand disciples under him. . . .

It must be due to my good karma accumulated from past lives that I heard about this and that later on I was given ten taels for the maintenance of my mother by a man who advised me to go to Wongmui to interview the Fifth Patriarch. After arrangements had been made for my mother's support, I left for Wongmui, which it took me about thirty days to reach.

I paid homage to the Patriarch and was asked where I came from and what I expected to get from him. I replied that I was a commoner from Sun-chow in Kwang-tung and said, "I ask for nothing but Buddhahood."

The Patriarch replied: "So you are a native of Kwang-tung, are you? You evidently belong to the aborigines; how can you expect to become a Buddha?"

I replied: "Although there are Northern men and Southern men, North or South makes no difference in their Buddha-nature. An aborigine is different from your Eminence physically but there is no difference in our Buddha-nature."[1]

This reply of the untrained country lad revealed his high capacity for understanding and insight to the Fifth Patriarch. The Patriarch subsequently expounded the *Diamond Sutra* to him, and though the younger man originally could neither read nor write, he was so thoroughly enlightened that he became the Sixth Patriarch.

Such individuals, however, are rare, and it was recognized that most beginners need careful guidance. Hence, reading of the basic sutras or texts, assigned problems for concentrated reflection, and practical suggestions as to posture and breathing during meditation have been a feature of Ch'an sects almost from the beginning.

In Japan the Ch'an school goes by the name of Zen (for thus the Chinese word was pronounced there). Three branches of Zen were established in the twelfth, thirteenth, and seventeenth centuries and have had a far-reaching, if quiet, influence on the whole of Japanese culture. The two Zen sects that are now most active are named from the two most durable Chinese sects: the Rinzai (so named from the Japanese pronunciation of Lin-Chi) and the Sōtō (from the Chinese Ts'ao-tung). In the chapter on Shinto, the native Japanese religion, we shall have occasion to mention the attraction Zen has had for the grim, taciturn army men of Japan, resolved as they have traditionally been upon self-sacrificial and single-minded devotion to emperor and country. Beyond this circle, the stress laid by both branches of Zen upon the inward search for the essential in life has had a determinative effect upon Japanese art, household furnishings, architecture, and the forms of social etiquette, especially in introducing reticence and restraint as the marks of good taste. The unexcelled Japanese art of flower-arrangement is a Zen by-product.

Let us see how this could be so.*

Zen is primarily an attempt to experience ("actualize") the unitary character of reality. "I" and "not-I" are one ("not-two"); both are aspects of Buddha-reality. This becomes clear when one "sees into one's own nature," in a moment of "awakening."

Deliberative reason will not suffice here. One cannot *think* oneself into the realization that there is no duality of oneself and the world, and that "I" and "not-I" are, in the last analysis, non-dual. Such a realization must come suddenly by an intuitive flash of insight, something that the Japanese call *satori*. There are two ways of dealing with Nature. One is to distinguish, describe, analyze, and, in pursuit of practical ends, manipulate objects from the outside; this is to deal in concepts and acts that are disjunctive (dualistic) and misleading. The other way is to contemplate Nature, much as the Taoist of China does (p. 262 f.), from the position of one who is indistinguishably at one with it; this is to pass into the True, the Void (sunyata), the Dharmakaya, concerning which "one must be silent," for to say anything about it is to apply misleading concepts to it. A favorite Zen way of saying the same thing is to assert the converse: that one does not, properly speaking, "pass into the True (Tatha), the Void, the Dharmakaya," because Nature is "nothing but one's own true mind," and therefore the Void is within, the "Beyond" is an inward "Beyond-state."

Within oneself, however, there is an illusion-making ability that is exercised to the full by all those who dwell in and cling to the world of the senses as if it were the whole of reality. But this is to submit to ignorance; truth is to be found instead "in the heart." Deep within everyone there is a Buddha-nature (a nature capable of bodhi), by actualizing which one

ceases to reason ignorantly and acquires prajna-paramita, the wisdom that has gone beyond—to the beyond that is within.

But even this language is not wholly satisfactory to Ch'an and Zen adherents. There is danger, they say, in speaking of one's Buddha-nature or the Beyond-within and the Beyond-state as if they could be viewed as objects or as having bounds and limits. They are, in truth, Buddha-reality, and as such neither external nor internal, objective nor subjective, things nor no-things; indeed such dualisms as these must be transcended by the realization (through satori) that the Buddha-reality is not outside Me but is I-Myself and that I-Myself do not stand in contrast to Not-I-Myself, because the Buddha-reality includes both in a non-dualism that is at once, at least to the finite mind, all and yet nothing, full of life and yet void, mind-itself and yet mind-like-empty-space, I-Myself and yet free from self-limitation, formless and unconditioned.

Zen masters in Japan follow their Ch'an predecessors in adopting various ways of waking novices from their illusionary slumbers, especially their clinging to objects and consequently reasoning in a dualistic strain. For the Truth cannot be known as long as they think disjunctively of myself *and* the world, the Buddha *and* I, the essence of Buddhism *for* me, the basic challenge of the Buddha *to* me, etc., because all *are* the Buddha-being (the Dharmakaya). To be able to realize their Buddha-nature, learners should stop distinguishing, separating, defining, analyzing, describing; they should stop asking questions, for these are essentially dualistic and to such questions there are no answers; they should instead await the mighty surge of "realization" that overpowers all thought. If the learner persists in trying to reason things out and keeps asking questions, the master may slap him, kick him, or throw him out into the hall. Perhaps this will break loose his hold upon objects and shock him out of his tendency to ask silly disjunctive questions; it may even suddenly fuse everything into non-duality and thus cause him to be enlightened then and there. Another tactic of the

---

* What follows is for the most part according to the point of view of Rinzai Zen, since this seems to be the more notable of the two sects, although the Sōtō sect has more members. Rinzai Zen's most vigorous advocate was the late renowned Professor D. T. Suzuki. A useful selection from his many works has been put into paperback under the title *Zen Buddhism* (edited by William Barrett; Anchor Books).

master may be to answer a question more or less nonsensically and then ask the learner to make sense of it, knowing that he will be baffled and have to "go beyond intellect to insight." (In Japanese terminology, this is to give him a *koan* to deal with.) Again, the master may recount to the learner a puzzling dialogue (which the Japanese call a *mondo*). The point is that he must realize that discursive reason misleads; that the bafflement of reason is an indication of its limited nature; that one must go beyond rational concepts to a blinding realization, an insight transcending all rational limits.

Consider the following famous koans (most of them of Ch'an derivation) as saying in effect: "Stop clinging to objects, the self included; cease asking dualistic questions; instead, know in yourself the undifferentiated Void that is at the same time the ground of all discrete being."

A monk asked Tung-shan, "Who is the Buddha?" and received the reply: "Three measures of flax."

When asked by a monk, "Is there a Buddha-nature in a dog?" Chao-chou barked, "Wu!" ("No!").

A monk asked Hui-neng to reveal the secret of Zen and was asked in turn: "What did your face look like before your parents begot you?"

The great Japanese monk Hakuin replied to an inquirer by clapping both hands and then asking, "What sound does one hand make?"

Here is a mondo:

A monk who saw Yao-shan meditating asked: "In this motionless position what are you thinking?"

"Thinking that which is beyond thinking."

"How do you go about thinking that which is beyond thinking?"

"By an act of not-thinking."

What else do the adherents of Zen stress? Several things. First, they make it a fundamental point that man and Nature are not opposed, because they are alike expressions of the Buddha-reality. To see a frog leaping into a pond is to feel at one with it in its diving, to be for the moment a frog also. The Zen monk Basho set the conditions for experiencing this

in his famous *haiku* (seventeen-syllable poem), for which it is so hard to find an English equivalent.

> An old pond, mirror-still.
> A quick frog, slanting waterward.
> A liquid *plop!**

In Zen, if one meditates on this haiku he realizes his oneness (non-duality) first with the pond, then the frog, and finally the water-sound, and with all of them together. It is one of the talents of a Zen-trained Japanese that he can contemplate beautiful things—cherry blossoms, pine trees, field-flowers, mountains—in a meditative way that allows the object and its perceiver to co-exist in a unified field, through an aesthetic trance in which object and perceiver are, as it were, relocated in a timeless continuum, where they take their place side by side, as if in a landscape, not of this world, present only to the Buddha-mind. To take an example from such a sport as archery, one does not "master" the handsome bow and shoot the arrow; the man and bow are non-dual, and the arrow shoots itself from the bow. In the tea ceremony one surrenders self to the beautiful, restrained ritual as in an aesthetic dream having the dimensions of eternity. Paradoxically, Zen imparts both a sense of cosmic non-duality and an immediate aesthetic response to sensory reality.

The way this comes about is as follows: although reality is one and all particulars are ultimately indis-

---

* This is a rather free rendition. It adds descriptive details that Japanese aesthetic perception easily supplies but that Western minds are not so skilled in interpolating. The original simply says: "Old pond—frog-plunge—water-sound."

That Japanese aesthetic perception does supply descriptive details is clearly seen in a stanza on "Basho's frog" by Sengai, a Zen monk:

> Under the cloudy cliff, near the temple door,
> Between dusky spring plants on the pond,
> A frog jumps in the water, plop!
> Startled, the poet drops his brush.

(From *Zen: Poems, Prayers, Sermons, Anecdotes, Interviews,* by Lucien Stryk and Takashi Ikemoto. Copyright © 1963, 1965 by Lucien Stryk and Takashi Ikemoto. Reprinted by permission of Doubleday & Company, Inc.)

Sand garden, Kyoto, Japan. Graceful Japanese girls contemplate the geometrically raked sand and the carefully placed rocks symbolizing the eternal Buddha-reality manifested in space and time. A Westerner seeing this abstract design might call the garden empty, but to the Zen Buddhist the very emptiness (sunyata) *is an affirmation of the nature of Being Itself. (Courtesy of Pan American Airways.)*

tinguishable, these particulars are to be welcomed and appreciated in one's immediate experience as rightful elements in the mental furniture of existence. The harmonious and the beautiful may properly delight the eye and mind of the painter or poet, while at the same time the ugly, the saddening, and the absurd have also a significant and proper place in the structure of the world. Because all things, including oneself, are transient expressions of the Buddha-reality, they are to be immediately enjoyed in all their variety and enchantment, even to the point of aesthetic intimacy and tenderness, without one's having to give up his basic non-attachment. In Zen, the Japanese say, the old Ch'an saying comes true: to begin with, everyone sees mountains as mountains and trees as trees; then when one seeks to come to terms with them (for example, as sensory aspects of an ultimate reality), mountains no longer appear as mountains, nor trees as trees; but finally when en-

lightenment is attained, mountains again are seen as mountains and trees as trees; the enlightened mind, accepting all aspects of the Buddha-reality, looks once more with open-hearted gladness at Nature, as directly and with as much childlike candor as the poets of the following haiku accepted the *is-ness* of their objects:

> As I come along the mountain path,
> What a heart-warming surprise,
> This cluster of dainty violets!
>
> > Basho
>
> Do I see a fallen flower
> Fluttering back to its branch?
> Ah! A butterfly!
>
> > Moritake
>
> Full moon, and under the trees
> Patterned shadows—how beautiful
> Alongside mine!
>
> > Baishitsu

The golden temple of Kyoto, Japan. This architecturally exquisite structure was originally a pavilion built for the fourth shogun of the Ashikaga era in the fifteenth century. It was recently rebuilt after being destroyed by fire. Painted a delicate gold color, it is more an object of Zen-like meditation than a place for Buddha-worship. (*Courtesy of Pan American Airways.*)

Finally, the Zen sects have worked out a technique of meditation that is highly disciplined and demanding. It is called *zazen* and calls for stated periods of meditation. In Rinzai Zen, in a hall designed for the purpose, the monks sit on long platforms facing each other for as long as eighteen hours day after day. Their meditations are tied in with *sanzen*, or consultation with a "master" to whom the monk regularly reports. This plan for mental and spiritual self-discipline appeals strongly to many serious-minded Japanese, not to speak of influential soul-searchers from the West, who turn to it hopefully as a means of insight.

3. *The Rationalist School.* But the intuitionist's thorough purging of the mind in the hope of enlightenment is so obviously anti-intellectualist, and moreover so fundamentally grounded in feeling-states rather than in reason, that one can easily understand the rise of the rationalist sects. In China, where they have been known as the T'ien-T'ai sects, they rose

out of, but grew away from, the Ch'an or Meditation school. The basic issue that led to their rise was the one between some hoped-for "sudden enlightenment" after the mind is emptied of all empirical content, and "gradual attainment" through study of the scriptures and a philosophically mature practice of contemplation. In the sixth century a monk in one of the Ch'an monasteries in eastern China, whose name was Chih-K'ai (or Chih-I), took a stand for an inclusive point of view. Buddhism, or the True Faith, was, he said, greater than any of its schools, and one should open his mind to insight from more than one source. Meditation (dhyana) was necessary but not all-sufficient for insight. He believed that the gathering of knowledge from teachers and scriptures, the performance of ceremonials and rituals, and the regular discipline of the monastery were all very valuable in the preparation for the ecstatic vision. Because he wished to find room for every major point of view expressed by Buddhism up to his time, Chih-K'ai evolved the doctrine that the Buddha (Gautama) taught differently at different stages of his life, according to the understanding of his hearers. At first he taught the doctrines of the Hinayana sutras, and at later periods he revealed, in progressively profounder versions, the Mahayana doctrines. The fullest revelation of the eternal truth was made near the end of the Buddha's life and embodied in the *Lotus of the Good Law,* the favorite text of the T'ien-T'ai school. The Buddha there reveals that he is a manifestation of a cosmic principle that pervades the whole universe and is present even in its smallest objects. All beings whatsoever can, T'ien-T'ai has concluded, actualize their Buddha-nature eventually and become Buddhas.

In accordance with the teaching of its founder, the T'ien-T'ai school has tried to reconcile the Hinayana and the Mahayana by subsuming both under the philosophical idealism of Nagarjuna (the Madhayamika school of India). Three levels of truth—one for the simple-minded who believe in the reality and value of the material world, another for those who seek confusedly to live a spiritual life in the material world, and a third for the seekers of intuitive insight through meditation—are discerned in Buddhist teaching. The recognition and consideration of all three levels of truth have made for tolerance and breadth of learning among T'ien-T'ai scholars.

The genetic relation between Ch'an and T'ien-T'ai in China was reversed in Japan. There, under the name of Tendai, the rationalist school of thought came first to Japan (as early as the eighth century), and Zen followed later as its intuitionist outgrowth. Tendai was founded by a Japanese noble, Saicho, later known as Dengyo Daishi ("Priest Dengyo"). Many important monasteries, with their attendant temples, have flourished under the knowledge-fostering Tendai sect. Their influence in Japan is pervasive and powerful still, though their lay membership is not so great as is that of some of the other Buddhist sects.

4. *The Mystery or True Word School.* In every religion the power of the saving name or mystic rite

has at some time been stressed. The beneficial effects are sought by a kind of holy magic, performed against a background of rational belief—a pantheon or a cosmology of impressive character. The tendency to make use of wonder-working formulas and gestures issued in China during the eighth century in the rise of the Chen Yen or Mystery school. The chief features of this school were derived from Indian Tantrism (pp. 181 and 211 ff.). The school was strongly supernaturalistic. It placed its chief reliance upon a large pantheon of Buddhist savior beings, both male and female, whose good offices were solicited through "efficacious" formulas, the use of picture charts or *mandalas,* gestures, invocations, and liturgies, which were believed to bring infallibly good results. The devotees performed their mystery rites to the accompaniment of music and bursting firecrackers, in the confident expectation of thereby obtaining the help of Buddhas in curing sickness, rescuing the dead from hell, controlling the weather, insuring health and good fortune, and the like. The school still exists in China, under the government's frown.

In Japan the Mystery school took form as the powerful Shingon sect. But the Japanese adherents widened its outlook and subdued its magical features by assimilating to it the rational and eclectic interests of the Tendai sect. The Shingon has thus turned out to be even more comprehensive and many-sided than the Tendai. Its popular appeal has been great. It was founded in the ninth century by one of Japan's great men, Kobo Daishi. This eager and forceful person went to China to study the doctrines of the Mystery school and returned to Japan to teach the "true word" that all the phenomena of the universe, including men, are manifestations of the "body, voice, and mind"—according to the Tantras the "three secrets" known only to the fully enlightened—of a single all-inclusive being, the great Dhyani Buddha (Maha-) Vairocana, the Great Sun (known in Japan as Dainichi). The other Buddhas and the Bodhisattvas are his emanations, phases of his "indestructible" energy at work in the universe. Gautama Buddha was his historical earthly manifestation. Vairocana (or

Dainichi) is thus identical with the Dharmakaya of the philosophers, but he is more personal than impersonal, for he possesses body, mind, and speech, differentiated into Buddhas, Bodhisattvas, gods, demons, men, animals, and plants, not to mention inanimate things and substances. Kobo taught that by meditation, repetition of magic formulas, and the performance of gestures with hands and fingers (the esoteric use of mind, speech, and body respectively) one can identify oneself with powerful Buddhas and Bodhisattvas. The common man can grasp something, but only something, of this, for it is but partially conveyed to him in the allegory and symbol of ritual and ceremony. Let him, however, be encouraged (as Gautama is supposed to have taught) in his love of temples and worship, for he has begun his ascent of a ladder of ten spiritual rungs or degrees: (1) absorption in "the thought of the goat": food and sex; (2) conformity to social and moral rules; (3) deliverance through the hope of heaven from the childlike fear of hell or of being either a ghost or an animal after death; (4) realization of the truth of the *anatta* doctrine that the aggregates that function as self are without a permanent soul or ego and are in flux; (5) attainment of the level of the Theravada (Hinayana) monk who subdues his desires by determining their causes and overcoming them; (6) rising to the Mahayana level of sharing the secret of liberation with all others in "the ocean of pain"; (7) meditation on the negative aspects of this world's so-called realities, their emptiness and nothingness; (8) seeing before one the true way of salvation; (9) grasping and being grasped by the ultimate truth concerning the universe, its Buddha-nature; and (10) enlightenment through realization of the mystery of the world as seen from inside, i.e., the Buddha in the heart.

In schematically presenting this synthesis of Buddhist theology, the Shingon sects have drawn up two picture-charts or mandalas, each in the form of two or more concentric circles. On one (called the Diamond Mandala), Vairocana is shown seated on a white lotus in profound meditation, while widening rings of Buddhas and Bodhisattvas wheel round him.

On the other (the Womb Mandala), the six material elements of the world appear in the form of a central ring of deities, with room for the Shinto gods on the outer rim. Kobo held that prior to the advent of Buddhism the Japanese people dimly understood the true scheme of things and embodied their insight in the gods of Shinto mythology,* who are therefore to be equated with the more precisely and truly conceived Buddhist savior beings. This was Shingon's contribution to the formation of the Ryobu or mixed Shinto described in the chapter on Shinto (p. 322 f.). Largely through the efforts of Shingon (and Tendai) the two religions, Buddhism and Shinto, were practiced as a single faith in Japan for a thousand years.

Because it presented a doctrinal and ritual synthesis, Shingon appealed strongly both to the aristocracy and to the masses. The latter had great faith in the performances of the proficient Shingon priests, whose solemn masses for the dead and elaborate temple ceremonies of a high-church character fascinated and consoled them with hopes of supernatural aid. The nobility were no less delighted, for they liked especially the teaching that just as the eternal Buddhas do not rest forever in spiritual contemplation but manifest themselves in the realm of material appearances, so a man may emerge from monastic training and show his spirituality in activities in the secular sphere. This made it possible for numbers of young nobles to retire to Shingon monasteries for their education and then re-enter the world to pursue active careers as soldiers or statesmen.

5. *The Socio-political School.* This school, the Nichiren, is an expression solely of Japanese Buddhism and reflects a social and political orientation characteristically Japanese. It was founded during the tumultuous thirteenth century, when the emperor was vainly struggling with the lords (*daimyos*) of the provinces for control of the nation and needed more religious support than he was receiving. Help came from an unexpected quarter. A monk, who thereafter took the name Nichiren ("Sun-Lotus"), experienced

---

* Especially the sun-goddess Amaterasu.

on a mountain top, while looking at the rising sun, a sense of identity between the Buddha-reality in the sun and the truth revealed in the *Lotus of the Good Law*. Previously he had studied both the Shingon and Tendai doctrines, but now he found both these systems unorthodox, along with the teachings of the Pure Land and Zen sects, so he set out to restore original Buddhism, as he thought, by launching a sect based exclusively on the doctrines of the Lotus sutra. He spoke with uncompromising forthrightness, believing that he was the incarnation of the Bodhisattva whose coming is foretold in the later sections of the Lotus sutra. In violent language he rejected as mythical and fictitious the pantheon of great Buddhas and Bodhisattvas "invented" after the time of the Lotus sutra. The Amidists and their imaginary Western Paradise were the objects of his special attack. It seemed to him a mark of a degenerate age, when men neglected the concerns of this world for the happiness of the next. He spoke with the boldness and wrath of an Old Testament prophet against the evils of his age, especially the political corruption following in the wake of the overthrow of the emperor's power by the provincial daimyos or feudal lords. Once he aroused great anger by predicting that a foreign invader would destroy Japan for its sins. He was banished to a remote region for his temerity. But the nearly successful Mongol descent upon the south coast that occurred shortly afterward seemed so clearly a verification of his prophecy that he was recalled to help avert any further danger to the nation.

To this day the welfare of Japan and the spirit of nationalism are of central importance in the Nichiren sects. Their common characteristic is that they believe that when they repeat the sacred formula "Namu Myoho Renge Kyo" ("Glory to the Lotus Sutra") their spirits become one with the eternal cosmic Buddha and experience salvation. Of the three leading contemporary Nichiren sects the most striking is the fast-growing Soka Gakkai. It maintains a temple complex and headquarters at the foot of sacred Mt. Fuji, equipped with large buildings (one being the largest temple in the world), a place to which thousands of pilgrims flock each day to chant the traditional invocation to the Lotus sutra and to gaze at the magically powerful mandala picturing the Buddhas and Bodhisattvas honored by Nichiren. It also maintains an active social and political program that includes the fostering of a political party (the Komeito or Fairness Society) that has run candidates for both houses of the Diet in the national elections, so far with spectacular success.

VII   Buddhism in Tibet*

As was said earlier, Buddhism was late in coming to Tibet. Long after the countries to the south and east of that high plateau had yielded to the gospel pleas of the Buddhist missionaries, Tibet remained unaffected. At last, about 630 A.D., a Tibetan prince, Srong Tsan Gam Po, who established a well-organized state centered in Lhasa, his capital, sent emissaries to northern India, in part with the purpose of securing the introduction of Buddhism into his realm. This sudden interest may have been due, as tradition relates, to the fact that his two wives, princesses from China and Nepal respectively, acquainted him with their own faith and desired to practice it.

Yet Srong Tsan Gam Po's introduction of Buddhism into Tibet was not very successful. The native demonolatry was too strong for it, and besides, the Tibetans found it hard to understand. A century passed before anything effective was accomplished, and then the true founder of Buddhism in Tibet came up from Bengal. He was Padma-Sambhava, a vigor-

* The Chinese occupation of Tibet since 1951 has so radically altered the situation there that the past tense is used hereafter, even up to the last paragraph in this section. It should be said also that the fact that this section is lengthier than that on, say, the Buddhism of Burma and Southeast Asia should not be construed to indicate greater comparative importance, for the fuller treatment is only a concession to general curiosity about an extraordinary land marked by equally extraordinary religious beliefs and practices.

ous teacher of the esoteric Buddhism of eighth-century northern India. Through his influence the Buddhism of Bengal, with its Tantric infusion of sex-symbolism, took root, and ultimately, after various vicissitudes and "reforms," became the religion of Tibet, and subsequently also of Mongolia, to which it spread in the thirteenth and fourteenth centuries.

It is not possible now to know just what Padma-Sambhava believed and taught, but the fact that he introduced a Tantric Buddhism gives us a clue. Tantrism is a form of devotion to natural energy (*shakti*).* It was (and is) based on manuals (*tantras*) having a distinctly magical and spell-making character and inculcating a psychological doctrine, the practice of which, its adherents admit, is "as difficult as walking on the edge of a sword or holding a tiger,"[E4] namely, the doctrine that passion can be exhausted by passion (the craving for food, drink, or sexual indulgence can best be overcome by rising above it while it is being satisfied). But this is not all. Contemplation of Nature, Tantrists say, reveals that all the great natural forces, when closely inspected, are a union of male and female elements. This is true of deity as well. Gods are in the nature of the case quiescent (i.e., profound) and aloof, but each has a complement in the form of an active spouse (a shakti), and the god's highest power is attained from union with her, for she rouses and draws it forth. Still another belief is entwined with this: in sexual union non-duality and, still more profoundly, the Void itself are momentarily experienced; there is an erasure of the distinction between male and female. The kind of Buddhism that finally took root in Tibet transformed original Buddhism by assimilating these Tantric doctrines to it.

The new and strange faith that resulted has some striking features. In the first place, the various Buddhas and Bodhisattvas were provided with spouses or consorts. But the relation between the pairs seems at first glance to be the reverse of that in Hinduism, the Buddhas and Bodhisattvas being

mentally active and creative, while their consorts are passive and contemplative (i.e., intuitive and wise), their generic name, significant of their function, being *prajna* ("higher insight"), a term that supersedes their Hindu name *shakti*. The male principle seeks to arouse each prajna to an activity likened to fire, setting the male principle aflame in turn. Moreover, a new genealogy of the gods was now made possible. It was generally said that there were five celestial Dhyani Buddhas, namely, Amitabha in the west, Akshobhya in the east, Amoghasiddhi in the north, Ratnasambhava in the south, and Vairocana at the center, all of whom were supposedly fathered by the Adi-Buddha, the originative Buddha-essence, pictured as a kind of far-off god wielding a magic thunderbolt. The five Dhyani Buddhas were paired, Amoghasiddhi with Tara, Amitabha with Pandara, Akshobhya with Mamaki, Ratnasambhava with Locana, and Vairocana with Vajradhatvisvari. They were said to give rise to the five great Bodhisattvas, who, on their part, in union with their own prajnas, produced and sent down males and females to earth. Thus Avalokita, who was an issue of Amitabha, was by some thought to be paired with a consort with whom (i.e., by embracing prajna or insight) he brought into existence Gautama Buddha in India. Others said that Vairocana was the heavenly being that caused Gautama to appear.

The human devotee meanwhile was believed able to identify himself with any of the celestial Buddhas or their consorts by a period of fasting and prayer, climaxed by the utterance of powerful mystic syllables, full of magic, and the visual evocation of the divine personage, followed by a merging of identities. This was a Tibetan version of entering Nirvana. Some further doctrines were involved: that the human being is the universe in microcosm; that just as nature is pervaded by hidden energy (shakti), so the human being has secret stores of energy coiled up in him (at the base of the spine, it was said); and that certain sounds and the display of groups of letters and images, accompanied by movements of the body and hands, aroused as if by a thunder clap the shakti of

---

* We shall hear more of it in the next chapter (p. 211 f.).

the body and put the devotee on a level with the divine power he was approaching.*

The public ceremonies that were gradually evolved appealed most strongly to the common people of Tibet. Four ritual components came to be characteristic of a complete ceremony: the *mandala* or frame, in picture form or described in the air and imagined, in which the gods were placed; the *mantras* or verses uttered; the *puja* or offering of one or more of the following: prayers, confessions of sin, sacrifices of flowers, lights, incense, perfumes, and ointments; and the *mudras* or hand positions, which were believed to establish "actual contact with the gods."ᴶ These mudras were directed to thirty-five or more Tantric deities, great and minor, and ran in sequences that often required thirty to fifty hand patterns in each sequence. They not only attracted the presence of the benevolent powers but also drove off the evil ones. By describing with the hands certain cabalistic patterns on the air and uttering at the same time the proper Sanskrit formulas, it was believed that goblins and demons (those of the mountains, desert plateaus, cemeteries, roads, air, courtyards, dwellings, hearths, wells, and fields) could be exorcised, and by the same means ferocious animals, robbers, madmen, souls of the unburied or of enemies, demons of the storm, spirits of bad dreams, or devils of disease and nervous ailments could be kept away.

The native and ineradicable demonophobia of the Tibetans † predisposed them to accept a religion so well calculated to meet their needs. The measures

taken to secure the protective presence of the Buddhas promised security at last. Their hard life on the windy plateaus of Tibet, ten thousand feet above sea level, surrounded by mountains down whose slopes whistling blasts of icy air would at any moment rush upon them, made them fear at every turn the demonic in nature. They craved supernatural protection.

The demonic in nature colored even their conception of benevolent divine beings. Not only had they pictured in imagination numerous evil powers with distorted and hideous faces; they portrayed even the mild and beneficent Buddhas and Bodhisattvas as though they were in a towering rage. The Buddha images seemed designed to frighten the wits out of the devout who approached them. But the fearsome visage had after all this good effect: it scared off the evil demons, while it merely chastened the worshiper.

The quest for protection led in more than one direction. The prayer-wheel (or mill) is an instance of the union of magic and religion. Whether the Tibetans invented it or not is a moot question, but they made a universal use of it. Not strictly wheel-like, it is to be described as a barrel revolving on an axis and containing within written prayers and pages of sacred writing. What the Communists allow now is difficult to say, but Tibetans used to carry miniature prayer-wheels about with them everywhere. (The temples had big ones, in a long line, which were whirled about one after another upon entering.) To turn the crank of the portable prayer-wheel and toss the prayers about was an act of devotion that assured the Buddhas one's heart was in the right place. Some prayer-wheels had paddles attached to them so that the blades could be dipped into a running stream and the prayers revolved automatically from one year's end to another, to the great merit of the owner.

Another protective device was the repeated utterance of the sacred Sanskrit phrase, *Om mani padme hum* ("Om! the jewel is in the lotus, hum!"). This phrase was both an expression of religious faith and a powerful spell. Repeated up the mountain and down the valley, inscribed on walls and rocks,

---

* One may now see why this system of religion has been named the Vajrayana ("The Vehicle of the Thunderbolt") to distinguish it from the Hinayana and Mahayana. Another translation of this name is "Vehicle of the Diamond." The diamond is hard and unbreakable; it cuts into everything else with the irresistibility of the thunderbolt; it flashes miniature lightning. Both are associated with bodhi or enlightenment, which comes like a lightning flash.

† Expressed in the subsurface indigenous religion called Bon, which dealt in shamanism, animal-sacrifice, devil-dancing, skull-caps, skull-drums, and thigh-bone trumpets. It was never completely suppressed. Much of it in fact crept into Buddhist ceremonies; devil-dancing, for example.

churned about endlessly in prayer-wheels, and displayed on banners and streamers, it stood for a central element in the national consciousness. Few who repeated it knew its significance; for that matter, even Western scholars are divided on whether it refers to Avalokita, as Tibetan monks have said, or to the prajnas or consorts. (In the latter case it would have a sexual meaning.) The formula was all but a Tibetan obsession.

The priests had among other things also a protective function. The people looked to them for the performance of rites and the utterance of prayers to the Buddhas that would secure long life and protection against the power of death. And when the great monasteries held their festivals, pilgrims came from all parts, supplied with quantities of butter and cloth for the monks, their priestly protectors. For days they looked on at exciting processions, masked dances, and pageants of the monks, as if their lives depended upon it. In the intervals they turned aside to honor the mythological and historical personages depicted in sculpturesque show-pieces wrought in butter and put on display; there was not only art but magic in them. Finally, they went home comforted by the blessing of the head lama and the assurance of the continued favor of the Buddhas.

The clergy of Tibet have had an absorbingly interesting history. They early acquired the name *lamas*, a term of respect meaning "one who is superior." For a thousand years they lived in thick-walled monasteries. These were originally of the unmilitary Indian model, but finally developed into fortresses of a distinctively Tibetan style, with massive walls rising firmly from the foundation-rocks to overhanging roofs far above. The climate, with its extreme cold and its long winters, made necessary the building of walled structures with plenty of room in them for winter stores. In the early days, the life that went on there was more like that of princely magicians than of monks. The Tantric Buddhism that was practiced encouraged the lamas to take spouses. Celibacy, at least among the higher clergy, became a rarity. The monasteries therefore often had hereditary heads, the

Tibetan with prayer wheel. Clothed in sheepskin, with a carrying frame on his back and his arms full of twigs, this Tibetan is twirling his prayer wheel, which revolves by a weight attached to it by a strap. He is protected not only against the weather but also against evil spirits. (Courtesy of Harrison Forman World Photos.)

abbots passing their offices on to their sons. In the ninth century the power of the monasteries was greatly increased when the king of Tibet made them grants of land and acknowledged their right to collect tithes thereon. By giving the lamas so much temporal power, the king unwittingly disintegrated his king-

Tibetan butter god. The festival of the butter gods (or Buddhas) of Tibet requires images formed from vats of colored butter. This image, shaped skillfully in an ice-cold cave, has been brought at dusk to the festival scene, but it will gradually melt down in the warmth of rows of butter lamps and the body heat of thousands of worshipful pilgrims filing by. (Courtesy of Harrison Forman World Photos.)

dom. He became a nonentity. Several centuries of civil turmoil followed. Kings disappeared from Tibet. In the thirteenth and fourteenth centuries the head lama of the Sakya monastery (apparently by appointment from Peking) ruled Tibet politically as well as religiously, though there were rival monasteries that did not submit to his authority.

With the fall of the Mongol empire in China, in the second half of the fourteenth century, the conditions were created for the attempted "reform" of Tibetan Buddhism by the great Tibetan monk Tsong-kha-pa. He organized the so-called Yellow Church, whose executive head is the Dalai Lama. Its monks are popularly known as Yellow Hats, for their hats and girdles are yellow—an evidence of Tsong-kha-pa's attempt to purify Tibetan Buddhism and take it back in theory and practice toward early Buddhism.* (Yet he reemphasized the Tantric theological doctrine of the Adi-Buddha and saw in Chenregi, which is the Tibetan name for Avalokita, that Buddha's supreme manifestation.) Tsong-kha-pa's reform was in part an imposition of a stricter monastic discipline—there was to be less alcohol and more praying—but what counted most and had the greatest future consequences was the reintroduction of celibacy. The practice of celibacy had the obvious and immediate effect of ending hereditary rule in the Yellow Hat monasteries; the abbots had no sons. But another result ultimately followed (about a century later) that gave the Yellow Church its world-famous theory of the reincarnation of the head lamas in their successors. The principle of unbroken succession has been very strong in the Orient (witness the familial organization in China and emperor-worship in Japan). But the unique thing about Yellow Hat Buddhism is that it applied this principle not to the family (as in China) nor to the state (as in Japan), but to the ecclesiastical organization (here paralleling Roman Catholicism). When celibacy broke up the old type of succession, the Yellow Hats drew out of their strong Tibetan sense of the continuity and self-perpetuating character of the ecclesiastical organization the theory that the grand lamas are the incarnations of the souls of their predecessors, who in turn were Buddhas incarnate. Thus the grand lama at Lhasa was considered to be an incarnation of Avalokita, and the abbot of Tashilunpo, the Panchen Lama, was thought to be an incarnation of Amitabha. This idea was extended to the other Yellow Hat monasteries

---

* The monasteries that resisted reform continued the use of red and constitute the "Red" sects.

and spread later to the branch establishments in Mongolia and Peking.

The search for the new living Buddha when a head lama died was often prolonged and has been known to take years. The object of the search was some child, born in the period after the head lama died, who showed familiarity with his predecessor's belongings, met the test of esoteric markings on his body, and was attended otherwise by signs such as the ghostly appearance of the symbols of the deceased lama on the walls of his home. An elaborate series of divination ceremonies was carried through. Among other things a prophetic lake was consulted for omens.

The grand lama at Lhasa acquired the name Dalai Lama in the sixteenth century, when, in response to an invitation from a powerful Mongol chieftain, the lama journeyed to Mongolia in the guise of Avalokita incarnate and revived Buddhism there by setting up a revised pantheon, a corrected system of festivals, and a new hierarchy. The grateful Mongol chieftain bestowed upon him the title "Dalai," which means "the sea" (i.e., the measureless and profound). This visit extended the operating range and power of the Yellow Church, for it resulted in the spread of Tibetan Buddhism throughout Mongolia and the establishment of a line of prelates at Urga who were believed to be incarnations of the soul of the famous Indian historian Taranatha, who traveled in Mongolia and was taken by the Mongols to be a very great man.

The success of the Yellow Church in Mongolia furnished the basis for its further spread in China, Siberia, Russia, and along the borders of India.

That Buddhism was vital in the lives of the people of the Snow Land until the Communists came is evident in the fact that one fifth of the total population resided in the lamaseries. It was a popular ambition to have at least one son out of every family enter the priesthood. The lamaseries were not only religious establishments of venerable age, but centers of political influence and seats of learning. In the Yellow Church the Dalai Lama had supreme political significance, while the Panchen Lama, of the Tashilunpo monastery, had commanding spiritual prestige.

VIII   Buddhism Today

For centuries all forms of Buddhism, except the Vajrayana, seemed to be in decline. Early Christian missionaries found the temples in decay and the priests somnolent. In some areas the revival of other faiths had dealt a blow, as when Shinto revived in Japan in the eighteenth century. Today two mighty blows have been dealt Buddhism in China and Tibet, where the Communists have put its future in doubt.

But a strong Buddhist revival has occurred in recent years in southern Asia and in Japan. This revival has had mixed causes. One cause is the arrival from the West of a religion whose purpose was to supplant the native religions, but whose missionaries in the very course of seeking more conversions provided the stimulus instead for revival. It happened in this way, in part: in seeking to find points of contact with non-Christians through a more thorough understanding of the native religions, the missionary scholars—and also Westerners who became independently interested—translated, and supplied commentaries to, hundreds of native classics, Hindu, Buddhist, Taoist, and Confucian. Thus, in the very attempt to inform themselves more fully, they opened the eyes of educated Asians to the riches of their own cultures.

Another and more widespread cause of revival has been the rise of Asian nationalisms whose early phases combined anti-colonialism with disillusionment concerning the culture and religions of the West that have proved so prone to wars. Furthermore, the social revolution that has accompanied the growing industrialization of Asia, with its inevitable adoption of many techniques and attitudes of the West, has brought new aims into view—social equality, economic justice, and political self-determination. Concrete measures toward social progress through human action have replaced resignation to fate (karma).

Humanism and secularism have appeared as rivals of the old religions. But the old religions have risen to these challenges and shown new strength.

Theravada (or Hinayana) Buddhism is self-consciously stronger and more alive today in Ceylon, Burma, and Thailand. There are about forty thousand Theravada monks in Cambodia, and it is said that 70 per cent of the population of South Vietnam is Buddhist. A great proportion of these last are Mahayanists, as are the Buddhists of Malaya and particularly of Singapore, where there are many overseas Chinese. Japanese Buddhists are also Mahayanist, with some three hundred sects existing at present as self-supporting units.

In spite of the broad historical differences between Mahayana and Theravada Buddhism, theoretical and practical efforts are being made to bring about unity. Scholars of the Buddhist world now stress the complementary nature of the two divisions of Buddhism and say that the doctrinal divergences are natural and logical and presuppose a common deposit of faith. The practical measures have taken the form of such relatively international group movements as the Maha Bodhi Society for Theravada Buddhism (founded over fifty years ago), the Young East Association for Mahayana Buddhism, and the Y.M.B.A. (the Young Men's Buddhist Association). These have had a pronounced missionary character. The first has long issued publications for world distribu-

tion. But a more recent movement has projected an even wider outreach; it is the World Fellowship of Buddhists for World Buddhism. Its aim, to bring all branches of Buddhism together, was shown when it held its first Buddhist World Congress in Ceylon and its second in Japan.

The whole Buddhist world was stirred by the Sixth Buddhist Council * held near Rangoon from May 1954 to May 1956 in the newly built World Peace Pagoda. It celebrated the 2500th anniversary of Gautama Buddha's birth. Here the delegates went carefully through the world message of early Buddhism and laid plans for the conversion of the world.

The missionary efforts of Buddhism now encircle the globe. There are active Buddhist missionaries, for example, in the United States. The Shin sect of Japanese Buddhism alone lists over a hundred missionaries at work in the United States and Canada.

It is significant, finally, that Buddhist missionaries have returned to India. In 1953 the Indian government formally handed over to Buddhist care Bodhgaya, the site of the Bo-tree under which Gautama experienced enlightenment. There is rising hope in the hearts of many Buddhists that the whole world will someday come at last to the feet of the Enlightened One.

* The first, second, and third took place, Buddhists say, in the three centuries after the Buddha's death, the fourth and fifth in Burma in the nineteenth century.

Suggestions for Further Reading

On the Buddhist World as a Whole

BAPAT, P. V., ED. *2500 Years of Buddhism*. Delhi, Government of India, 1956

CONZE, EDWARD. *Buddhism, Its Essence and Development*. Philosophical Library, 1954. Available as Harper Torchbooks pb

———, ED. AND TR. *Buddhist Scriptures*. Penguin Classics pb, 1959

———. *A Short History of Buddhism*. Bombay, Chetana, 1960

DAYAL, HAR. *The Bodhisattva Doctrine in Buddhist Sanskrit Literature*. K. Paul, Trench, Trubner, 1932

ELIOT, SIR CHARLES. *Hinduism and Buddhism*. 3 vols., Routledge and Kegan Paul, 1954. Earlier ed., Edward Arnold, 1921

GETTY, ALICE. *The Gods of Northern Buddhism*. 2nd rev. ed., Oxford, Clarendon Press, 1928

GODDARD, DWIGHT, ED. *A Buddhist Bible*. 2nd ed., rev. and enl., Dwight Goddard Estate, Thetford, Vermont, 1938. An anthology of late texts

HAMILTON, C. H. *Buddhism, a Religion of Infinite Compassion*. Liberal Arts Press pb, 1952. Selections from Buddhist literature

LAW, BIMALA CHURCH, TR. *The History of the Buddha's Religion* (The *Sasanavamsa* of Pannasami). Luzac & Co., 1952

———, TR. *A Manual of Buddhist Historical Traditions* (The *Saddhamma-Sangha* of Mahasami). University of Calcutta, 1941

———, ED. *Buddhistic Studies*. Calcutta and Simla, Thacker Spink, 1931

MORGAN, KENNETH W., ED. *The Path of the Buddha*. Ronald Press, 1956

PERCHERON, MAURICE. *Buddha and Buddhism*. Harper, Men of Wisdom pb, 1957

PRATT, J. B. *The Pilgrimage of Buddhism*. Macmillan, 1928

SANGHARAKSHITA, BHIKSHU. *A Survey of Buddhism*. Bangalore, Indian Institute of World Culture, 1957

SHARMA, CHANDRADHAR. *Dialectic in Buddhism and Vedanta*. Benares, Nand Kishore, 1952

SOOTHILL, W. E., TR. *The Lotus of the Wonderful Law*. Oxford, 1920

SUZUKI, BEATRICE (LANE). *Mahayana Buddhism*. 2nd ed., enl., Marlowe, 1948

———. *Impressions of Mahayana Buddhism*. Kyoto, Eastern Buddhist Society, 1940

SUZUKI, D. T. *The Essence of Buddhism*. 2nd ed., London, The Buddhist Society, 1947

THOMAS, EDWARD J. *The History of Buddhist Thought*. Knopf, 1933

WINTERNITZ, MORIZ. *A History of Indian Literature*. Vol. II, on Buddhist literature. University of Calcutta Press, 1933

On Indian Buddhism

AMBEDKAR, B. R. *The Buddha and His Dhamma*. Bombay, People's Education Society, 1957

BURLINGAME, E. W., ED. *Buddhist Parables*. Tr. from the Pali. Yale University Press, 1922

CONZE, EDWARD. *Buddhist Thought in India*. Allen & Unwin, 1962

DASGUPTA, S. B. *An Introduction to Tantric Buddhism*. 2nd ed., University of Calcutta, 1958

DUTT, SUKUMAR. *The Buddha and Five After-Centuries*. Luzac & Co., 1957

HORNER, I. *Women Under Primitive Buddhism*. Routledge, 1930

JONES, J. J. *The Mahavastu*. Tr. from the Sanskrit. Luzac, 1949

KEITH, A. B. *Buddhist Philosophy in India and Ceylon*. Oxford, 1923

SMITH, VINCENT A. *Asoka, the Buddhist Emperor of India*. Oxford, 1920

VASUBANDHU. *The Treatise in Twenty Stanzas on Representation—Only*. Tr. by C. H. Hamilton from Chinese version of Sanskrit original. American Oriental Society, 1938

ZIMMER, HEINRICH. *Philosophies of India*. Pantheon, 1951. Available as Meridian pb

On Buddhism in Burma, Thailand, and Southeast Asia

AUNG, MAUNG HTIN. *Folk Elements in Burmese Buddhism*. Oxford University Press, 1962

DHANINIVAT, PRINCE K. B. *A History of Buddhism in Siam*. Bangkok, The Siam Society, 1960

FINOT, L. "Outlines of the History of Buddhism in Indo-China," in B. C. Law, ed., *Buddhistic Studies*. Calcutta and Simla, Thacker Spink, 1931

RAY, NIHAR RANJAN. *An Introduction to the Study of Theravada Buddhism in Burma*. University of Calcutta, 1946

SURIYABONGS, LUANG. *Buddhism: An Introduction*. Colombo, Lanka Bauddha Mandalaya, 1957. The Thai Theravada view.

U NU. *What Is Buddhism?* Rangoon, Buddha Sasana Council Press, 1956

On Buddhism in Ceylon

BUDDHIST COUNCIL OF CEYLON, ED. *The Path of Buddhism*. Colombo, Lanka Bauddha Mandalaya, 1956

LOUNSBURY, G. CONSTANT. *Buddhist Meditation in the Southern School*. Kegan Paul, Trench, Trubner & Co., 1950

MALALASEKERA, G. P. *The Buddha and His Teachings*. Colombo, Lanka Bauddha Mandalaya, 1957

RAHULA, WALPOLA. *What the Buddha Taught*. Grove Press, 1962

On Chinese Buddhism

CHAN, WING-TSIT. *Religious Trends in Modern China*. Columbia University Press, 1953

JOHNSTON, SIR R. F. *Buddhist China*. Dutton, 1913

LEE, SHAO CHANG. *Popular Buddhism in China*. Shanghai, 1939

REICHELT, K. L. *Truth and Tradition in Chinese Buddhism*. 4th ed., rev. and enl., Shanghai, 1934

———. *Religion in Chinese Garment*. Philosophical Library, 1952

YEN-KIAT, BHIKKHU. *Mahayana Buddhism*. Bangkok, Debsriharis, 1961

On Japanese Buddhism

ANESAKI, M. A. *A History of Japanese Religion*. K. Paul, Trench, Trubner, 1930

BRIGGS, WILLIAM A., ED. *Anthology of Zen*. Grove Press Evergreen pb, 1961

ELIOT, SIR CHARLES. *Japanese Buddhism*. Edward Arnold, 1935

KITAGAWA, JOSEPH M. *Religion in Japanese History*. Columbia University Press, 1966

MASUNAGA, REIHO. *The Soto Approach to Zen*. Tokyo, Layman's Buddhist Society Press, 1958

REISCHAUER, A. K. *Studies in Japanese Buddhism*. Macmillan, 1917

STEINILBER-OBERLIN, EMILE. *The Buddhist Sects of Japan*. Allen and Unwin, 1938. Their history, philosophical doctrines, and sanctuaries

SUZUKI, D. T. *Essays in Zen Buddhism*. Luzac, 1928–1934

———. *Zen Buddhism*. Selected writings ed. by William Barrett. Anchor pb, 1956

———. *The Training of the Zen Buddhist Monk*. Kyoto, Eastern Buddhist Society, 1934

TAKAKUSU, J. *Essentials of Buddhist Philosophy*. 2d ed., University of Hawaii Press, 1949

On Tibetan Buddhism

BELL, CHARLES. *The Religion of Tibet*. Oxford, 1931

EVANS-WENTZ, W. Y. *Tibetan Yoga and Secret Doctrines*. 2nd enl. ed., H. Milford, 1958

————, ED. *The Tibetan Book of the Great Liberation, or The Method of Realizing Nirvana Through Knowing the Mind*. Oxford University Press, 1954

GUENTHER, HERBERT V. *The Origin and Spirit of Vajrayana*. San Francisco, Epicenter Press, 1959

RICHARDSON, HUGH E. *Tibet and Its History*. Oxford University Press, 1962

NEBESKY-WOJKOWITZ, RENÉ DE. *Oracles and Demons of Tibet*. 's Gravenhage, Mouton & Co., 1956

7 Later Hinduism: Religion as the Basis of Social Behavior

THE RELIGIOUS AWAKENING that occurred in India in the sixth century B.C. manifested itself in the rise of Brahmanism, Jainism, and Buddhism, which we have now considered. The urgency of the need to which the latter two were an answer had been such as to drive men to seek near-at-hand practical modes of escape from their growing sense of misery rather than to turn for remedy or solace to philosophical speculation or to priestly sacrifices that did not immediately help the individual where he hurt most. So Brahmanism had been rejected as ineffectual for souls inwardly pained. Such rejection did not require as much intellectual temerity in the sixth century B.C. as in later periods of India's history, for apart from the rituals of the Brahmanas, which were not to be deviated from by so much as a hair, Brahmanism was still open-ended and tentative, and so it was far from clear what might be settled upon as the right or true point of view. This was particularly apparent in the Upanishads. In fact, Jainism and Buddhism were not altogether novel in their philosophical and moral positions, for what they advocated in these areas was already suggested in pre-Aryan religion and in the growing oral Vedic literature, the Upanishads especially. Where their radicalism appeared was in their rejection of the sacrificial system of the Brahmanas and their refusal to give the Brahmins first place or prescriptive rights in discovering the way from misery to freedom.

Rulers and princes (the Kshatriyas) were particularly aroused to dissent. They did not like either the social or the religious implications of Brahmanism. The Kshatriyas, some of whom were of non-Aryan background, possessed among their ranks many brilliant minds, and these were not slow to detect encroachment on the ruling caste's domain. The costly sacrifices that the Brahmins prescribed might ease the anxieties of those who feared or hoped in the gods, but they did not satisfy the doubtful. Goodness had in it something more than ceremonial zeal and the offering of sacrifices. Moreover, as might be expected, the idealistic monism toward which the Upanishads and their expositors tended struck many of the realistically inclined members of the ruling class as philosophically absurd. Jainism expressed, in part, their commonsense revolt against a world-view that devaluated the individual and turned the evil of the world into illusion. On the other hand, it seemed to the ethically minded that Brahmanism's solution of the problem of human misery by sacrifices was utterly beside the point—not only a waste of goods and time but misleading. This was particularly the position taken by early Buddhism.

In the turmoil and clash of opinion that reigned, Brahmanism changed perforce its early character. That it ultimately rose victorious over its rival systems is due to its self-adaptation to changing conditions. The Brahmins never organized under a central authority, never adopted any concerted tactics either of defense or attack upon the heretical systems. They ultimately prevailed not by being intolerant and defiant toward these other creeds, but precisely by being tolerant toward them. Instead of totally outlawing the distinctive Jainist and Buddhist religions and philosophical views, they pronounced many of them good, and adopted them. The Hindus seemed endlessly hospitable to good ideas, however derived or labeled.

Meanwhile, the common people were not directly involved in these developments and were not forced into any radical change, even when so great a man as the Buddha came along. Their life-habits and religious practices altered but slowly and by a kind of internal development rather than in response to pressures built up by leaders of thought or advocates of reform. When the Brahmins underwent the revolution of thought (traced in Chapter 3) that took so many of them out of the performance of ritual and into meditation and mystical union with ultimate reality, the common people were marginally aware of it but went on with the rituals to which they were accustomed and which have largely survived to the present day. This is an important fact that needs stressing: the people of India have been and are deeply absorbed in the household rituals, community festivals, and pilgrimages that have changed so little

in form and purpose through the centuries. This is the reason that Dharma, the approved way of life, has had so central a place in Hindu private and public practice.

The inclusiveness and tolerance of the Brahmins on the one hand, and the day-to-day acceptance of custom and tradition by the people on the other, combined to bring about a quiet development of doctrines, attitudes, and laws. Here inclusion rather than exclusion was the rule. Hence, we find ourselves now facing two inclusive sets of judgments that were generally accepted, one that endorsed four permissible goals in life, and another that recognized not just one but three ways of salvation.

The Four Permissible Goals in Life

With great realism, Hinduism has recognized that men naturally and therefore legitimately seek, in the course of many rebirths, four aims in life. The first two follow the path of desire, the last two that of renunciation. (They are all included within Dharma in its most inclusive sense.)

1. *Kama*, the desire for pleasure, especially through love, is the first. So great a place does the desire for pleasure occupy in human life that some Hindus have regarded it as the presence of the god Kama, carrying a flowery bow armed with five flower-arrows that pierce the heart and fill it with desire. Not only is pleasure a permissible human goal, but pleasure-seekers need not go unguided. Those who are awkward in love or unskilled in the pleasure-bringing arts of poetry and drama may find instruction either in Vatsyayana's *Kamasutra* (if they seek knowledge of the art of love) or in the *Natyasastras* (if their interest is in the literary arts and skills). Should a man openly choose to make pleasure his aim, he is not criticized, provided he stays within the bounds set by general social rules. He may even be commended for vitality and a sense of direction. But it is thoroughly understood, nevertheless, that in this or some future existence he will come to realize that pleasure is not

enough and that he really wants something more deeply satisfying.

2. *Artha,* or power and substance—immediately, things, material possessions; ultimately, high social position or success—is the second permissible goal. A man who is able and alert may quite naturally wish for great possessions and the power and influence that may be obtained through them. This is understood to be a legitimate aspiration, but it requires ruthlessness and toughness. "The big fish eat the little ones." Machiavelli was anticipated in more than one piece of Indian literature. In the *Arthasatras* (attributed to Kautiliya, Kamandaki, and others) or in the beast fables of the *Panchatantra* one may find both sober and humorous instruction in the ruthless competition involved in this way of life. No special blame rests upon the seeker of wealth and power, for his model may well be a great and noble king, but it is recognized once again that if he is allowed to learn for himself, either in this or some future existence he will discover that he has not sought the highest goal. He will learn that a deeper satisfaction and a more authentic happiness come from following the path of renunciation.

3. *Dharma,* considered in its stricter sense as religious and moral law, sets the standards for a far worthier and more deeply satisfying life. He who follows the Dharma of doing his duty by his family, his caste, and his community, and guides himself by the *Code of Manu* and other law books (dharmasastras), renounces his egoistic desire for personal pleasure and social success and seeks instead the good of all. Profound joy attends this obedience to ethical principles, as the really good man discovers. But once more, the joy, however great, is not ultimate. There is of course only one ultimate satisfaction.

4. *Moksha,* salvation or liberation, is the highest and only truly satisfying goal. Negatively, this goal means release from the round of rebirths and all the miseries of human existence, physical and spiritual; positively, it means liberation into fullness of being in Nirvana, for description of which no human words are adequate.

The Three Ways of Salvation

The essential vigor of the older faith was demonstrated further by the fact that the three ways of release or liberation now recognized by orthodox Hinduism were clearly worked out and described.

The first of these is what has come to be known as the Karma Marga or Way of Works.[*]

I The Way of Works

The Way of Works is a very old way. It could be called the way of ritual, especially domestic ritual. Followed by the overwhelming majority of the people, it has the triple advantage of being practical, of being understandable, and of enjoying the sanctity of age-old custom (Dharma). Not markedly emotional, and still less intellectual, it is a methodical and hopeful carrying out of rites, ceremonies, and duties that add to one's merit (favorable karma). Many a Hindu has believed that by sacrificing to the gods and his ancestors, revering the rising sun, keeping the sacred hearth-fire alight, and performing meticulously the rites and ceremonies that are appropriate at a birth, a death, a marriage, or a harvest, he can acquire enough merit to pass at death into one of the heavens or be reborn as a Brahmin with a real predisposition toward achieving final union with Brahman, the Absolute.

The Way of Works is defined for the first time in the Brahmanas, where there occurs a list of "man's debts" in the way of good works. The list is simple and severe. Each man owes to the gods sacrifices, which are good works *par excellence;* in addition, he owes to his seers and teachers the study of the Vedas, to the ancestral spirits offspring, and to his fellow men hospitality. If he discharges these debts faithfully, he has done his whole duty, and by him "all is obtained, all is won."[A] But the simplicity of this con-

[*] When seen as a stage in the attainment of moksha, it is sometimes called Karma Yoga.

ception, with its heavy emphasis on sacrifices, was modified during the passage of the years, and gradually various codes sprang into existence, combining old and new customs into authoritative systems. Typical of these law books (the famous dharmasastras) is the *Code of Manu*, composed as a collection of rules of life by legalistically minded priests about 200 B.C.

All the law books, beginning with the *Code of Manu*, lay heavy stress on rites of passage, i.e., rites that mark events in the life of each individual and conduct him from birth to death and beyond. Not only must a man observe all the rules of his caste—never marrying outside of it and breaking none of the strict dietary laws and social regulations laid down for it—but he must be faithful in performing for himself and others many religious rites and ceremonies. The *Code of Manu* prescribes for each individual a long list of sacramental rites for each significant episode of life—for example, at birth, at name-giving, at the first taking out to see the sun, the first feeding with boiled rice, the first hair-cutting, initiation into manhood, marriage, and so on. But rites of passage are only part of the whole Dharma. There are honors owing to the tutelary deities of the household. The head of the house must see to it that they are properly worshiped each day and that before each meal they are presented with portions of prepared food, fresh from the hands of the lady of the house. No one may eat until this has been done.

Among the most important of all rites are those following death and directed toward ministering to the ancestral spirits. These are called the *shraddha* rites. To most Hindus it would appear true that without these ceremonies the after-life of the soul as ancestor would be cut short, and the soul would have at once to resume the course of rebirth in accordance with the Law of Karma. The shraddha rites, consisting as they do of periodical offerings of memorial prayers and food substances, are thought to be necessary to the very being of the ancestral spirits; without these attentions their strength would completely fail, and they would be swept away into the unknown. The most important elements in the food offerings are the *pinda* (food-balls, usually of cooked rice pressed into a firm cake); these are commonly supposed to provide the dead with a kind of corporeal substance, a "new body." According to one view:

On the first day the dead man gains his head; on the second his ears, eyes, and nose; on the third his hands, breast, and neck; on the fourth his middle parts; on the fifth his legs and feet; on the sixth his vital organs; on the seventh his bones, marrow, veins, and arteries; on the eighth his nails, hair, and teeth; on the ninth all the remaining limbs and organs and his manly strength. The rites of the tenth day are usually specially devoted to the task of removing the sensations of hunger and thirst which the new body then begins to experience.[B]

Pinda are offered to father and mother, to relatives on the father's and mother's side, and to those who have died away from home without rites and who are therefore especially in need of strengthening attentions. (The immature, however—girls who die unmarried and boys who have not reached the age of initiation—have no shraddha rites performed for them.) The pinda must be offered by a male descendant; hence, one must have sons or cease to exist with the same identity after death! Most spirits are considered amply provided for by the obsequy rites immediately following death, but the leading males receive further attentions, once a month for the first year, and then yearly thereafter on the anniversary of death.*

There is a Way of Works for women. It is easily stated: their duty is to serve meekly their men. The *Code of Manu* lays down the Asiatic principle:

In childhood a female must be subject to her father, in youth to her husband, when her lord is dead to her sons; a woman must never be independent.[C1]

* The domestic rites we have been considering are customarily distinguished from public ceremonies. Two groups of sutras are devoted to the two kinds of rites: the Grihya sutras, which describe the domestic ceremonies, and the Shrauta sutras, which were originally written to describe the public rites surviving from the sacrifices of Vedic days.

In line with her dependent status, she should occupy herself with household duties, yielding unquestioning obedience to the old lady at the head of the female side of the family and worshiping her men. As a faithful wife aspiring to dwell with her husband in the next existence, she should honor and obey him in this, and never displease him, even though he be destitute of virtue, unfaithful, or devoid of good qualities. "A husband must be constantly worshiped as a god by a faithful wife."[C2]* After his death she may not marry again; she may "never even mention the name of another man," but must keep watch over herself lest she entice one such to evil, and until death remain quiet, patient, and chaste, striving to fulfill "that most

---

* In certain ultraorthodox quarters, but even there with decreasing frequency, the wife is taught to show honor to her husband by prostrating herself and touching her head to his feet; or, again, she may adore the big toe of his right foot when he is about to rise in the morning, bathing it as one would an idol, and even offering incense to it and waving lights before it, as though it belonged to a great god.

In the *Padmapurana* the wife's rule of life is put in these uncompromising terms: "There is no other god on earth for a woman than her husband. The most excellent of all good works that she can do is to seek to please him by manifesting perfect obedience to him. Therein should lie her sole rule of life.

"Be her husband deformed, aged, infirm, offensive in his manner; let him be choleric, debauched, immoral, a drunkard, a gambler; let him frequent places of ill-repute, live in open sin with other women, have no affection for his home; let him rave like a lunatic; let him live without honor; let him be blind, deaf, dumb, or crippled; in a word, let his defects be what they may, a wife must always look upon him as her god, should lavish him with all her affection and care, paying no heed whatsoever to his character and giving him no cause whatsoever for disapproval.

"A wife must eat only after her husband has had his fill. If the latter fasts, she shall fast, too; if he touch not food, she also shall not touch it; if he be in affliction, she shall be so, too; if he be cheerful, she shall share his joy. She must on the death of her husband allow herself to be burnt alive on the same funeral pyre; then everybody will praise her virtue."[D]

The last part of this quotation refers, of course, to the well-known custom of *suttee*, once widely practiced in India, now forbidden by law, though isolated instances of self-immolation by widows still occur in spite of every precaution of the police.

excellent duty which is prescribed for wives who have one husband only."[C3] The widow "who, from a desire to have offspring, violates her duty to her deceased husband, brings on herself disgrace in this world," and instead of joining her husband in the next existence will "enter the womb of a jackal."[C4]

From their superior position men are required, however, to honor women. Their own welfare and happiness, as well as the blessing of offspring, depend thereon. Special gifts of ornaments, clothes, and dainty foods are enjoined on holidays and festivals. But this is the honor bestowed by superiors upon those who serve them well. The superiority of the male must not be lost sight of. A Brahmin, therefore, may not eat in the company of his wife, nor look at her while she eats, and it is prohibited for him to watch her while she dresses herself and applies collyrium to her eyes. So, at least, runs the theoretical statement of what is right and proper. It is, of course, to be borne in mind that all rules like this are never observed without exception, even in the most conservative circles, and that modern conditions have produced changes in old manners.

Many other rules might be mentioned as part of the established Hindu code down to the present day. On the whole, they prescribe a somewhat exacting way of life. But this would be an outsider's judgment. The faithful would not say so. The Way of Works is to them an action-filled way of fulfillment and a means to salvation.

By all those who studied the matter, however, the Way of Works was considered inferior to another and more philosophic road to salvation, the Jnana Marga or Way of Knowledge, also called the Jnana Yoga.

II   The Way of Knowledge

The solution of the problem of life through the Way of Knowledge is based on the reasoning in the Upanishads. Only those who shared the philosophic passion of the Upanishads could follow it.

At the threshold of the Way of Knowledge is the premise that the cause of human misery and evil is Ignorance (*Avidya*, Unwisdom or Non-seeing). Man in general is so darkly ignorant about his own nature that all his actions have the wrong orientation. Not moral transgression, then, but mental error is the root of human misery and evil.

All the Hindu philosophical systems agree in this presupposition. It is distinctive of the Hindu point of view.

And yet these same philosophical systems do not agree on the propositions to be erected on its basis. There is a good deal of difference of conception as to just what convictions constitute the mental error in the primal Ignorance. For ignorance also has its presuppositions.

It would be interesting here to go into the rival views, but space forbids. We confine ourselves therefore (for the sake of convenience and simplicity) to the best-known form of Hindu teaching about Ignorance and its cure, namely, the teaching based on the monistic philosophical position we have already found in the Upanishads.

According to the monistic view, the evil of man's situation lies in this: he persists in thinking himself a real and separate self, when such is not the fact, for since Brahman-Atman is the sole real being, in whose unity there exists no duality, man is in reality Brahman-Atman and not another. It is hard to realize such a truth, the monistic philosophers admit; too often, "in this Brahma-wheel the soul flutters about, thinking that itself and the Actuator are different."[E1] But persistence in the ignorance-fostered illusion that the individual self and the world it knows exist apart from, and are other than, the All-Soul is the cause of the world-entangled life of men and of their incessant births into one existence after another. So long as man continues ignorant and lives on in the illusion of separate selfhood, so long he is bound to the ever-turning wheel.

In seeking to clarify and illustrate this idea the monists, from the time of the Upanishads, have often resorted to analogies. They say that the relation between the individual and Brahman-Atman is similar to that between rivers and the ocean within which they disappear.

As the flowing rivers in the ocean
Disappear, quitting name and form,
So the knower, being liberated from name and form,
Goes into the heavenly Person, higher than the high.[E2]

The individual is also said to be like a wave rising from and sinking again in the sea, or like a drop of spray that momentarily flies above the sea. A brief amplification of this last analogy will further bring out the meaning. A drop of brine beheld apart from the ocean, flying, let us say, across the face of the sea, may be viewed under two aspects. Under the first, it appears to be an individual drop of a certain size and consistency, with a particular location in time and space differentiating it from any other drop or any other entity whatever. Under the second view, however, this is a misleading description of the case, for the drop is in reality only the ocean in the air, only *apparently* a thing by itself, a pure individual. This second view of the nature of the drop is that supported by Hindu monism. By analogies such as this the belief is driven home that all created things, all the "appearances" that commonsense realism accepts as being exactly as they seem, are in reality Brahman-Atman and not what they seem. They all have reality, but it is the reality of being Brahman-Atman.

For man, then, salvation comes with right understanding, and then

The knot of the heart is loosened,
All doubts are cut off,
And one's deeds (karma) cease.[E3]

There remains this point to make clear: how does one *know* "the knot of the heart is loosened"? When does faith in union become knowledge of union?

Here all the intellectual systems agree that knowledge of union is not merely a matter of accepting good doctrine. There are varieties of acceptable doctrine, and the adoption of any one variety comes short of salvation itself. Salvation itself—the saving knowledge that one has reached a state of consciousness that admits him into the realm of reality where karma ceases to exert its effects and rebirth reaches an end—comes by an ecstatic flash of certitude in the midst of deep meditation.

This flash of certitude is the ultimate goal of the Way of Knowledge. To reach it requires long preparation and self-discipline.

The classical conception of the life-preparation required to reach this last step in the Way of Knowledge is given in the *Code of Manu*. The ideal career of the pious Brahmin is there outlined for all India to admire and for Brahmins, sometimes, to emulate. There are four stages or *ashramas* in the ideal life-plan. Under one exacting program, the Way of Works and the Way of Knowledge are interfused. The stages are (1) that of student of religion, (2) that of married man and householder, (3) that of hermit, and (4) that of *sannyasin* or mendicant "holy man."

It was proposed that when the young Brahmin had passed through the sacramental rites surrounding early childhood (at birth, name-giving, the first taking out to see the sun, the first feeding with boiled rice, the first hair-cutting, and so on), he should enter upon the initial stage of his conscious journey to salvation, that of student of religion. This was to begin with ceremonial investiture with the badge of caste, the sacred cord, during which solemnity, while tending the sacred fire and going through holy rites of purification, he would experience his second or spiritual birth. His initiation into manhood thus effected, he was conducted to the home of a teacher to study the Vedas, the purificatory and sacrificial rites, and the duties of his caste. His residence at the house of his teacher was to last for an indefinite period, perhaps until his twenty-fifth year, depending on the number of Vedic treatises he wished to study. His teacher meanwhile was not expected to supply him with food; that was to be obtained by the student himself, by going from house to house, begging bowl in hand.

When he reached the end of his period of study, he was to leave his teacher and enter upon the second stage of his life. He was now to rejoin his family, marry, and take up the duties of householder. This was thought to be obligatory. No Brahmin, however deep his religious preoccupation, was considered worthy or wise unless he left a son to carry out the periodical obsequy rites for the ancestors and to leave children in his turn. The stage of householder was to be closely regulated by ancient religious rules and filled with ceremonies, all of which he was to perform with utmost diligence. He was to be well aware that every householder of necessity injures living things, especially in cooking.

A householder has five slaughter-houses as it were, viz., the hearth, the grinding-stone, the broom, the pestle and mortar, and the water-vessel, by using which he is bound with the fetters of sin. In order successively to expiate the offenses committed by means of all these five, the great sages have prescribed for householders the daily performance of the five great sacrifices. Teaching and studying is the sacrifice offered to Brahma, the offerings of water and food called Tarpana the sacrifice to the ancestors, the burnt oblation the sacrifice offered to the gods, the Bali offering that offered to the Bhutas [good and evil spirits of many sorts], and the hospitable reception of guests the offering to men.[C5]

He was to be extremely careful in his diet. He was never to break any caste rules. At length, sometimes after many years, when he saw his "skin wrinkled, and his hair white, and the sons of his sons,"[C6] he was to enter upon the third stage of his career.

As a hermit he was not expected to live an easy life. His whole thought was to be concentrated on developing a complete indifference toward everything in the world to which he had been previously attached.

Abandoning all food raised by cultivation, and all his belongings, he may depart into the forest, either committing his wife to his sons, or accompanied by her. Taking with him the sacred fire and the implements required for domestic sacrifices, he may reside there. Let him offer those five great sacrifices according to the rule. Let him wear a (deer-) skin or a tattered garment . . . be always industrious in privately reciting the Veda . . . never a receiver of gifts . . . compassionate toward all living creatures. . . . Let him not eat anything grown on ploughed land or in a village. . . . In order to obtain complete union with the supreme Soul, he must study the various sacred texts contained in the Upanishads . . . abandoning all attachments to worldly objects.[C7]

When he had become wholly and purely spiritual, he was released from any further offering of sacrifices to gods and ancestors, and free therefore to let his sacred fire die out, for it was now "reposited in his mind." He needed no longer to read the sacred texts; they, too, were reposited in his mind. If she were still with him, his wife would see he had reached liberation from all earthly ties and would depart, leaving him alone in the forest. Thus would be ushered in the fourth and last stage of his existence.

In this last stage—that of holy man—he was to seek attainment of the final goal of the Way of Knowledge: the trance of union with the Infinite. Death might overtake him before he had completely realized absorption in the eternal Brahman, but the *summum bonum* was to have the experience before death. Such an experience would come, as he knew, only in the midst of deep meditation. "All depends on meditation," says the *Code of Manu*, "for he who is not proficient in the knowledge of that which refers to the supreme Soul reaps not the full reward."[C8] The Code gives us a vivid description of the final situation:

Let him always wander alone, without any companion. . . . He shall possess neither a fire nor a dwelling. . . . Let him go to beg once a day. . . . When no smoke ascends from the kitchen, when the pestle lies motionless, when the embers have been extinguished, when the people have finished their meal, when the remnants in the dishes have been removed, let the ascetic beg. . . . The roots of trees for a dwelling, coarse worn-out garments, life in solitude and indifference towards everything, are the marks of one who has obtained liberation. Let him not desire to die, let him not desire to live, let him wait for his appointed time, as a servant waits for the payment of his wages. . . . By deep meditation let him recognize the subtle nature of the supreme Soul, and its presence in all organisms. . . . He who has in this man-

ner gradually given up all attachments reposes in Brahman alone. . . . He attains the eternal Brahman. . . .[C9]

Down to the present day this final state of absorption in the Ultimate (*samadhi*) is the goal toward which all who take the Way of Knowledge aspire. But it is not easy to attain it by purely intellectual processes. From the very first it was felt that the body had to assist the mind in suspending, in part at least, its normal functions. The Upanishads contain the first hints about a method, called Yoga, beginning with "restraint of the breath, withdrawal of the senses from objects" and ending with "contemplation" and "absorption."[E4] There is reference also to the mystic syllable *OM*, which is to be repeated over and over again, until the devotee reaches ecstasy. Of Yoga and yogis we shall hear later, for we shall appreciate their importance better in another connection. But we may note now that the followers of the Yoga disciplines gave great support to the Way of Knowledge as a primarily important method of release from the burdensomeness of life betrayed into ignorance of mind by the seductions of the senses.

III   The Way of Devotion

Perhaps the greatest single element in the successful resistance of Hinduism to absorption by Buddhism was the attitude of the common people of India. Through the long years of the crisis and slow recovery of Hinduism, the common people, not greatly affected by the intellectual excitement of the upper classes, calmly went on being religious in their own way. The Brahmins, perceiving validity in this faithfulness, worked out a justification for it. Whereas the more sophisticated minds were encouraged to seek knowledge, the people were to get help from gods and goddesses. The *Code of Manu*, in fact, contains more than one intimation of the presence of a new factor in the religious outlook, and with it the rise of a third way of salvation or release, rivaling

197

the Way of Works and the Way of Knowledge. It mentions temples and temple priests for the first time in Hindu literature. Bhakti Marga (the Way of Devotion)* had come into being.

Bhakti may be defined as ardent and hopeful devotion to a particular deity in grateful recognition of aid received or promised. It often assumes the form of a passionate love of the deity, whether god or goddess. Its marks are surrender of self to the divine being and acts of devotion in temple worship and in private life and thought.

Bhakti emerged at a comparatively late period, but it brought with it the savor of ancient faith. That it did emerge prompts the reflection that the needs of the common man can never for long be gainsaid. From primitive times he has sought the favor of gods and goddesses, and he cannot be made to believe that devotion to deities does not bring salvation. His experience has been that the world is filled with powers greater than himself from whom saving help may come. The common man never could follow the philosophers and meditative intellects down the Way of Knowledge; he was not capable of long and close introspection into the obscure movements of his own soul. Not that he held the findings of the intellectual classes to be untrue. On the contrary, he regarded with respect the opinions of the intelligentsia, much as the man of the masses today applauds, without understanding, the incomprehensible theories of an Einstein. But such acknowledgement of the rightfulness in their own sphere of the reasoning of pundits does not now, and never did in India, affect the daily course of life. The common man thinks: "The Brahmin's way may be all right for him; but I must follow my prescribed way as best I can." †

In popular Hinduism the far-reaching effect of bhakti on the external forms of religion has been incalculable. Many different sects seek salvation through devotion. No denial of the efficacy of the Way of Knowledge and of the Way of Works is implied. It is even admitted that these may have a superior efficacy. But the positive claim is made that devotion to deity is a true way of salvation in itself, whether or not one interweaves with it, as one may, certain aspects of the other two ways.

The first important literary recognition of Bhakti Marga as a true way of salvation was made in the famed *Bhagavad Gita* or *Song of the Blessed Lord,* one of the great classics of religious literature. To it we must devote special attention, for it has very greatly influenced Hinduism for over a thousand years.

This poem occurs in its present form as an episode in the enormous epic, the *Mahabharata,* which was composed over a period of eight hundred years (400 B.C. to 400 A.D.), contains one hundred thousand couplets, and deals in the main with the exploits of Aryan clans, specifically with the fall of the Kuru (Kaurava) princes at the hands of their relatives the Pandavas (sons of Pandu), directed by the hero-god Krishna. The *Bhagavad Gita* was interpolated into the *Mahabharata* about the first century A.D. In every respect a remarkable poem, it has been more admired and more used for devotional and intellectual needs than any other Hindu work—this in spite of its eclectic character, philosophically and otherwise.* Its verve and emotional power have won many converts to its doctrines.

The Gita's greatest historical significance lies in its endorsement of bhakti as a true way of salvation and release. This endorsement comes in the course of a story dramatically conceived and told. Arjuna, the

---

* Also called Bhakti Yoga.
† In India he may add: "In some future existence I'll be a Brahmin."

* It makes the eclectic attempt, for example, to interweave into one way of life *all three* ways of release— knowledge, works, and devotion. It grants that knowledge leads to unconditioned release, and that the doing of good works is not to be underrated. But it protests against the performance of the prescribed works merely out of desire for the rewards that accrue, and says that such working for rewards secures only certain transient blessings in the next existence. It goes on, however, to take a position far in advance of the common Brahmin opinion when it declares that the performance of works, if carried out without any desire for reward, but only for the god, or for righteousness' sake, can win release on the basis of such works alone.

great warrior of the family of Pandavas, hesitates suddenly when on the point of leading his brothers and their allies into battle against the Kuru princes, sons of his uncle, the blind Dhritirashtra, and thus his close relatives. The hero-god Krishna is his charioteer and stands at his side poised for instant action. But it is not Arjuna who acts; it is the Kuru leader, his uncle, who orders the conch-shell to be blown as the signal for battle.

> Then at the signal of the aged king,
> With blare to wake the blood, rolling around
> Like to a lion's roar, the trumpeter
> Blew the great Conch; and, at the noise of it,
> Trumpets and drums, cymbals and gongs and horns,
> Burst into sudden clamor; as the blasts
> Of loosened tempest, such the tumult seemed!
>   Then 'twas—
> Beholding Dhritirashtra's battle set,
> Weapons unsheathing, bows drawn forth, the war
> Instant to break—Arjuna spake this thing
> To Krishna the Divine, his charioteer:
> "Drive, Dauntless One! to yonder open ground
> Betwixt the armies; I would see more nigh
> Those who will fight with us, those we must slay
> Today!"[F1]

But when Krishna drives the chariot, with its milk-white steeds, between the lines, Arjuna marks on each hand

>   the kinsmen of his house
> Grandsires and sires, uncles and brothers and sons,
> Cousins and sons-in-law and nephews, mixed
> With friends and honored elders; some this side,
> Some that side ranged.[F2]

At this sight his heart melts with sudden compunction. He addresses his charioteer in tones of anguish:

> "Krishna! as I behold, come here to shed
> Their common blood, yon concourse of our kin,
> My members fail, my tongue dries in my mouth,
> A shudder thrills my body, and my hair
> Bristles with horror; hardly may I stand.
>
>   . . . What rich spoils
> Could profit; what rule recompense; what span

> Of life seem sweet, bought with such blood?
> Seeing that these stand here, ready to die,
> For whose sake life was fair, and pleasure pleased,
> And power grew precious:—grandsires, sires, and sons,
> Brothers, and fathers-in-law, and sons-in-law,
> Elders and friends!"
>
> So speaking, in the face of those two hosts,
> Arjuna sank upon his chariot-seat,
> And let fall bow and arrows, sick at heart.[F3]

When Krishna tries to stir the reluctant warrior with the charge: "Cast off the coward-fit! Wake! Be thyself! Arise, Scourge of thy foes!" Arjuna's only reply is to reiterate his doubts and ask Krishna's counsel. Krishna's answer is made in the course of a long dialogue whose design, in the first instance, is to exalt caste-duty above every other consideration, no matter what is entailed and without thought of reward. Arjuna is told that his duty as a Kshatriya is to fight, when just war is joined, whether in doing so he kills his relatives or not. If he shuns the honorable field—he, a Kshatriya—if, knowing his duty and his task, he lets duty and task go by, that would be sin! If he fights and is killed, he will enter the Swarga-heaven; if he is victorious, he will mount a king's throne. As to those he may slay, grief for them would be lacking in reflection. The soul cannot be slain.

> "Thou grievest where no grief should be! thou speak'st
> Words lacking wisdom! for the wise in heart
> Mourn not for those that live, nor those that die.
> Nor I, nor thou, nor any one of these,
> Ever was not, nor ever will not be.
> All, that doth live, lives always! . . .
>   . . . Indestructible,
> Learn thou! the Life is, spreading life through all . . .
> But for these fleeting frames which it informs
> With spirit deathless, endless, infinite,
> They perish. Let them perish, Prince! and fight!
> He who shall say, 'Lo! I have slain a man!'
> He who shall think, 'Lo! I am slain!' those both
> Know naught! Life cannot slay. Life is not slain!"[F4]

Having thus looked philosophically at the immediate difficulties, Krishna proceeds to tell the still emotionally disturbed warrior that there are two ways of reaching the goal of salvation. One is the way of meditation (Jnana Yoga), and the other is the way of action (Karma Yoga). Both lead to final peace. But these paths, as it were, cross, and even coalesce. For no one can ever rest in thought even for a moment without action, while properly disciplined action requires, and ends in, knowledge. As a hero-god counseling a warrior, Krishna seems at one point to say that retirement from action to engage in meditation is inferior to disciplined action undergirded by the truth found in Krishna himself, but he says even more emphatically that both meditation and action are ways to final self-identification with Ultimate Reality.

However, both action and thought must be rightly oriented. To begin with, action must be disinterested action—action performed from duty alone, without thought of fruits (rewards).

> "Let right deeds be
> Thy motive, not the fruit which comes from them.
> And live in action! Labor! Make thine acts
> Thy piety, casting all self aside,
> Contemning gain and merit. . . .
> "Therefore, thy task prescribed
> With spirit unattached gladly perform,
> Since in performance of plain duty man
> Mounts to his highest bliss. . . .
> "For My sake, then,
> With meditation centered inwardly,
> Seeking no profit, satisfied, serene,
> Heedless of issue—fight!"[F5]

As for meditation, it should be disciplined by the knowledge that all things—all actions—proceed from and are infused by the eternal World-Spirit, Brahman. Here the word *Brahman* is not to be understood as having a strictly impersonal connotation. *Brahman is Vishnu and Vishnu is Krishna.* He who attaches himself to Vishnu through Krishna, which Arjuna is invited to do, may therefore experience the reality of union with Brahman. The yogin whose greatest desire is to enjoy the ecstasy of perfect release by absorption into the Ultimate may find such release through meditative absorption in a Person—that of Vishnu, if

he considers the deity on high, or that of Krishna, if the incarnation in the gallant charioteer attracts his trust.

> Sequestered should he sit,
> Steadfastly meditating, solitary,
> His thoughts controlled, his passions laid away,
> Quit of belongings. In a fair, still spot
> Having his fixed abode,—not too much raised,
> Nor yet too low,—let him abide, his goods
> A cloth, a deerskin, and the Kusa-grass.
> There, setting hard his mind upon The One,
> Restraining heart and senses, silent, calm,
> Let him accomplish Yoga, and achieve
> Pureness of soul, holding immovable
> Body and neck and head, his gaze absorbed
> Upon his nose-end, rapt from all around,
> Tranquil in spirit, free of fear, intent
> Upon his Brahmacharya vow, devout,
> Musing on Me, lost in the thought of Me.
> That Yojin, so devoted, so controlled,
> Comes to the peace beyond,—My peace, the peace
> Of high Nirvana! . . .
> He who thus vows
> His soul to the Supreme Soul, quitting sin,
> Passes unhindered to the endless bliss
> Of unity with Brahma[n]. He so vowed,
> So blended, sees the Life-Soul resident
> In all things living, and all living things
> In that Life-Soul contained. And whoso thus
> Discerneth Me in all, and all in Me,
> I never let him go; nor looseneth he
> Hold upon Me; but dwell he where he may,
> Whate'er his life, in Me he dwells and lives.[F6]

In this remarkable passage the Gita seeks to assimilate the doctrines of the Upanishads to its partial theism. (The theism is only partial, because it has so pronounced a pantheistic side.) With the same purpose, in later passages Krishna declares, "I Brahma[n] am! the one eternal God!" Hence:

> "I am the Sacrifice! I am the Prayer!
> I am the Funeral-cake set for the dead!
> I am—of all this boundless Universe—
> The Father, Mother, Ancestor and Guard!
> The end of Learning! That which purifies
> In lustral water! I am OM! I am
> Rig-Veda, Sama-Veda, Yajur-Ved;
> The Way, the Fosterer, the Lord, the Judge,

The Witness; the Abode, the Refuge-House,
The Friend, the Fountain and the Sea of Life
Which sends and swallows up! Seed and Seed-sower,
Whence endless harvests spring! . . .
Death am I, and Immortal Life I am,
Arjuna! SAT and ASAT, Visible Life
And Life Invisible!"[F7]

And then, as Arjuna looks on with wonder, Krishna is transfigured before him into Vishnu, the eternal Brahman in god-form, displaying to the astounded warrior his true reality, endowed with numberless mouths, countless eyes, "all-regarding" faces turned in every direction, and clothed in ornaments, wreaths, and divine apparel scented with heavenly fragrance.

If there should rise
Suddenly within the skies
Sunburst of a thousand suns
Flooding earth with rays undeemed-of,
Then might be that Holy One's
Majesty and glory dreamed of![F8]

At this sight, which makes his every hair bristle with awe, Arjuna gives voice to his adoration, and then prays that the too sublime vision be removed and the god return to the kindly disguise of Krishna, the charioteer. The god accedes to this request and then proceeds to deliver the heart of the Gita's message; he demands the uttermost surrender of perfect faith in himself—unconditioned bhakti—as the way to full and final release.

"Cling thou to Me!
Clasp Me with heart and mind! so shalt thou dwell
Surely with Me on high. But if thy thought
Droops from such height; if thou be'st weak to set
Body and soul upon Me constantly,
Despair not! give Me lower service! seek
To read Me, worshipping with steadfast will;
And, if thou canst not worship steadfastly,
Work for Me, toil in works pleasing to Me!
For he that laboreth right for love of Me
Shall finally attain! But, if in this
Thy faint heart fails, bring Me thy failure! find
Refuge in Me! let fruits of labor go,
Renouncing all for Me, with lowliest heart,

So shalt thou come; for, though to know is more
Than diligence, yet worship better is
Than knowing, and renouncing better still.
Near to renunciation—very near—
Dwelleth eternal Peace! . . .

"Take my last word, my utmost meaning have!
Give Me thy heart! adore Me! serve Me! cling
In faith and love and reverence to Me!
So shalt thou come to Me! I promise true.
Make Me thy single refuge! I will free
Thy soul from all its sins! Be of good cheer!"[F9]

These passages have had historic importance, not only because of their beauty, but also because of their influence on the intimate life of thousands of Hindu leaders and holy men, down to Mahatma Gandhi in recent years. Though philosophically the *Bhagavad Gita's* whole conception of reality and of the meaning of life is shot through with unresolved inconsistencies, its practical effect has been to stimulate and deepen Hinduism on its religious side and to make the Bhakti Marga of popular Hinduism intellectually respectable. It must be quite evident at this point that neither the Way of Knowledge, which is so highly intellectual and self-disciplinary, nor the Way of Works, which is so largely moral and practical, can satisfy fully the religious need of the average man as can the Way of Devotion. The *Bhagavad Gita*, therefore, has won for itself a unique place in the esteem of all Hindus, and though the followers of Vishnu lay first claim to it as their most blessed scripture, educated Hindus of all sects honor it as a worthy expression of the emotional factor in religion.

There is yet another reason why the *Bhagavad Gita* is so appreciated in India. In it Krishna throws wide open the gate of the Way of Devotion and invites all wayfarers, whatever their sex or caste, to enter.

"Be certain none can perish, trusting Me!
O Pritha's Son! whoso will turn to Me,
Though they be born from the very womb of Sin,
Woman or man; sprung of the Vaisya caste
Or lowly disregarded Sudra,—all
Plant foot upon the highest path."[F10]

Nothing could be more suited to meet the profound and unspoken need of millions in India for a ray of hope in their troubled bondage to social and religious restrictions.

IV   The Six Acceptable Systems of Hindu Philosophy

The Hindu word for "view of the nature of things" is *darshana,* and perhaps it should not be translated as "system of philosophy," for it does not aim, as Western systems do, to arrive, as nearly as possible, at a detached or uninvolved view of things, but rather seeks to dispel the ignorance that prevents liberation from Maya through "seeing the Real." "In India," says Mircea Eliade, "metaphysical knowledge always has a soteriological purpose,"[G1] that is, it seeks salvation, by liberation of soul or spirit. But if we remember that in the present context the word *philosophy* is to mean what it originally did, "love of wisdom" (rather than "scientific objectivity"), we can safely use it.

During the millennium from 500 B.C. to 500 A.D. the acceptable systems of Hindu philosophy took shape. In another thousand years they were refined into final fixed form. Their number is far greater than six, but Hindus themselves have singled out that many as the most significant, because among them they cover the whole ground gone over by all the acceptable philosophical views. These six make the one assumption that is considered necessary by Hindus to meet the conditions of orthodoxy, namely, that the Vedas are the inspired and final rule of faith. It is usually understood that in this case the Vedas include the early commentaries and interpretations (the Brahmanas and Upanishads) that are appended to the original four books.

We shall not follow the Hindu savants in considering each of the six philosophies in order; we are chiefly interested in those that have had the greatest effect on religion. (The rest will be treated briefly in footnotes.*)

The Sankhya System

This important darshana, the Sankhya philosophy, stands in sharp contrast with the monism expressed in the Upanishads. Indian tradition considers it the oldest darshana of all. In a preliminary form—an early, unsystematized dualism perhaps older than the earliest Upanishads—it may have been the common source of much that is in Jainism, the Upanishads, early Buddhism, and the *Bhagavad Gita.* Its mythical (or semi-mythical) founder is said to have been one Kapila, born at Kapilavastu a century before Gautama Buddha. He is said to have made his views known to Asuri, who transmitted them to Panchashikha, who in turn passed them on to Ishvarakrishna, but this gives us a time-scale that is certainly foreshortened, for the last named is the author of the oldest systematic statement of the Sankhya philosophy, the *Sankhya-karika,* which propably was not written before 200 A.D.

The Sankhya philosophy is staunchly atheistic and dualistic, maintaining that there are two eternal (and only two) categories of being: (1) matter (*prakriti*), which when structured becomes the natural world, and (2) souls or spirits (*purusha,* selves). Neither are

---

* Hindu scholars have arranged the six philosophies in their logical rather than their chronological order, beginning first with the philosophy that is most concerned with logic and epistemological method. This is the Nyaya system, based upon a text ascribed to a philosopher bearing the same name as the founder of Buddhism, i.e., Gautama. A complete analysis of correct reasoning is attempted. True knowledge is said to follow upon four processes of knowing: sense-perception, inference, comparison of fact or analogy, and trustworthy testimony. Emphasis is placed on testing knowledge by the findings of the five senses, whose report of the reality of the external world, for example, is accepted as correct. A major conclusion is that all misery follows from false notions, for such notions give rise to activities having bad consequences in successive rebirths. Hence, emancipation depends on sound knowledge.

maya, illusory; both equally real. The former, the natural world, is given its structure by three modes of activity, called *gunas* (strands, bonding agencies): a luminous, wise, and happy one known as *sattva* (purity and goodness matched with insight), an active, driving, energetic one named *rajas* (energy, passion), and a brooding, inert, moody one called *tamas* (darkness, inertia, obscurity). The mere presence of souls or spirits activates these modes, as dancers are activated by the presence of a king, and the characteristics of everything in the natural world are determined by the way in which they combine. Physical objects (bodies, inanimate or animate) result from the clusterings of dense elements under the impulsion of tamas; psychological phenomena in multi-sensed creatures (sense-experience, emotions) rise from the stimulus of rajas; mental and psychic activities spring from a predominance of sattva. The world of nature is composed of twenty-three elements (*tattvas,* that-nesses), including the five gross elements (*sthula-bhutani:* ether, air, fire, water, earth), higher intellect (*buddhi*), mind (*manas*), and ego-consciousness (*ahankara*), each with a different combination of the gunas. The special characteristics of a human individual at any one moment are due to the degree to which any one of the gunas predominates. If he is intelligent, pure, happy, sattva predominates; if emotional or energetic, rajas; if dull or crude, tamas. What is asserted, therefore, is that prakriti evolves into a wide range of phenomena from the grossest matter to the highest manifestations of intelligence, but they are all aspects of Nature and are not to be identified with or derived from souls or spirits.

As for the realm of souls (purusha), it is not constituted of a single All-Soul, like Brahman-Atman, but of an infinite number of individual souls, each independent and eternal. These souls or spirits have awareness, are "free," and are "without qualities," i.e., without such qualities as human experience discerns in objects. Each spirit, says Ishvarakrishna, "is that which sees [witnesses]; [but] it is isolated, indifferent, a mere inactive spectator."[62] Why it

should be associated as it is with a body and mind in life after life is an insoluble mystery, in some way tied in with karma. The soul or spirit needs to be liberated from its association with its polar opposite (lively matter, prakriti), but it cannot free itself; the freeing comes from the natural, not the spiritual side. What ought to happen in the realm of nature is that the higher intelligence (buddhi), which knows in its moments of insight the true character of the soul or spirit with which it is associated, should free itself from the suffering brought on by its lack of insight (avidya, ignorance). It can do this by ridding itself of the mistaken identification of the soul with bodily and mental processes, an identification that is not only entirely in error and a source of suffering but that prevents the soul's final freedom. If it destroys this illusion (the true maya), and in the process destroys (unstructures) itself as well, it will enable the soul to realize its freedom by final passage into a state of eternal but unearthly existence in the purity of the spirit. Here, too, salvation is sought by the Way of Knowledge.

In summary, the Sankhya philosophy emphasizes the conviction that the soul is forever an alien in the natural world and that its liberation consists in remaining uninvolved with it. In its true being it is free and detached, but its presence attracts prakriti elements (tattvas) to it, and these must be led by insight (buddhi) to relinquish their attachment to it and allow it a final freedom.

The Yoga System

The Yoga system of mental discipline has been greatly developed since it was first mentioned in the Upanishads, and it has won an important place in the practice of the Way of Knowledge. It became a highly refined technique in the hands of Patanjali (second century A.D.), a yogin who derived most of his ideas from the Sankhya system, though he differed from it in accepting as a part of his world-view a modified theism (reliance on Ishvara, an eternally

203

pure spirit who helps yogins). The philosophical basis of Yoga is, however, not as important historically as the practical measures, the technique of meditation and concentration developed in connection with it. These practical measures are a psychologically sophisticated modification of the purely metaphysical way to "release and liberation." It was as apparent then as now, that the Way of Knowledge, as at first formulated, required an intellectual effort most difficult to attain, because concentration of pure thought to the proper degree is beyond the capacity of all but the clearest minds and strongest wills. Hence, when a modification of its intellectual rigors, leading in the end to the same experience, was found, it was eagerly taken up. Yoga's greatest appeal lies in its physiological and psychological measures to assist the mind in the effort to concentrate. It consists largely of special postures, methods of breathing, and rhythmical repetition of the proper thought-formulas. The typical procedure, that of the classic Raja Yoga of Patanjali, has eight steps:

1. Performing the five desire-killing vows, or Yama, a step by which the yoga-aspirant abstains from harming living things (that is, he practices ahimsa), from deceit, stealing, unchastity (he takes the brahmacharya vow), and from acquisitiveness.

2. Observance, or Niyama, of self-disciplinary rules—cleanliness, calm, mortification, study, and prayer.

3. Sitting in the proper posture, or Asana; for example, with the right foot upon the left thigh, the left foot upon the right thigh, the hands crossed, and the eyes focused on the tip of the nose.

4. Regulation of the breath, or Pranayama, where the aim is to reduce the whole of being alive to one or two simple and rhythmic processes, all the muscles, voluntary and involuntary, and the nerve-currents being brought under control. The aspirant is advised to sit upright, with head, neck, and back in a straight line, and to breathe in and out rhythmically, while, perhaps, inwardly repeating the sacred word *AUM*. (Later refinements of this step suggested breathing up the left nostril, then out of the right, holding the breath between times, in order to allow nerve-currents to descend the spinal column and strike forcefully the reserves of nervous energy at the base of the spine and release them.)

5. Withdrawal of the senses from all sense-objects, or Pratyahara, much as a tortoise retreats under his shell by drawing in its head and limbs. This step shuts out the outside world.

6. Concentration, or Dharana, during which the mind is held steadily to the contemplation of a single idea or object until it is emptied of all else.

7. Meditation, or Dhyana, a half-unconscious condition affording a transition to the last step.

8. Samadhi, a trance in which the mind, now emptied of all content and no longer aware of either object or subject, is absorbed into the Ultimate and is one with the One.

The central feature of Yoga practice, whether in this or its other forms, is the use of the mind to suppress its own conscious movements, the whole body being so disciplined as to aid in the gradual suspension of consciousness and the bringing on of a state of pure ecstasy that is without thought and without sensation. The result is felt to be a complete freeing of the true self from the external world and natural causation. Extraordinary claims of psychic power are made by those who accept the intuitions that precede or follow this state: for example, that the yogin actually achieves levitation, can transcend the limits of space and time and be in several places or times at once, or can acquire the powers and qualities of anything upon which he chooses to concentrate. But, of course, the chief aim of Yoga is none of these things; it is, rather, the experience of utter and complete freedom of the self from earthly bonds.

The Vedanta System

The name of the Vedanta system is derived from the source of its leading doctrines, the Upanishads, which were commonly called the Vedanta—that is, "the concluding portions of the Vedas." An exciting basis for future speculation was contained in the Upanishads, especially in the treatises that tended toward philosophical monism or pantheism. The conservatives, following the lead of literalists like Jaimini,* might refuse to budge from their funda-

* Founder of the Purva-Mimansa system, listed by scholars as the fifth of the orthodox systems. This is the

mentalist positions; the mediationalists, like Kanada* and Kapila, might continue in their commonsense way to affirm the reality both of the world and of individual souls. But the liberals and the radicals, who were sure that intuition superseded and transcended common sense, rushed on with speculative enthusiasm to propound the monistic doctrine that the external world and human consciousness are alike maya or aspects of the world-illusion arising from

---

least philosophical of the six systems. It clings with unique consistency and simplicity to its doctrine of the literal inspiration of the four Vedas. Jaimini scorned to philosophize in the manner of the Upanishads; his thought ran, rather, in the molds provided by the Brahmanas. So highly did he regard the truth of the Vedas that he asserted they never had an author, but were themselves uncreated and eternal. In fact, they were in the language (sound, *shabda*) of Being Itself; hence, they had a magical power which prevailed even over the gods. So, he felt under no necessity to postulate a Supreme Being as the source of the revelation contained in them. He did not know whether there was such a being. It was enough to know that the Vedas and Brahmanas contained the whole Dharma or duty of man, and that by determining their literal meaning and carrying out the rites and ceremonies described in them liberation could be attained. When so much eternal and absolute truth was at hand, it seemed a monstrous impiety for men to want to spin their vainglorious speculation about the universe out of their own desire-filled heads. ("Mere rationalizations!" he would perhaps have said had he been a modern.) Jaimini's position in this matter was not essentially altered by his later followers, even though they became theists who declared that the Dharma, still considered literally true in every part, should be studied and practiced as an offering to a supreme god, who waited to redeem them as a reward for their faithfulness.

* Founder of the Vaisheshika system, the second of the orthodox systems. His school of thought applied logical methods (specifically, seven "categories") to the study of the external world. In accordance with the postulates of an atomic theory resembling in its initial (but not final) positions the philosophy of the Western philosopher Democritus, the external world is declared to be a self-existent reality, formed of eternal and indivisible atoms combining and recombining eternally. Later thinkers of the school say that this process is not purely mechanistic, for it takes place by the power of Advishta ("the unseen force" of deity). Thus, alongside the eternal atoms and individual souls is an eternal Soul, the source of all transmigrating souls. The cosmos thus conceived will, it is argued, never be destroyed, for both atoms and souls will abide indestructible forever.

primal creative energy, and claimed the authority of the Upanishads for it. Advanced Indian thought has usually sided with them.

The first attempt to set forth the monistic teachings of the Upanishads in a consistent philosophic system is contained in the difficult aphorisms of the *Vedanta Sutra*. These are said to have been prepared by Badarayana, a noted teacher who lived, it seems probable, during the first century before the Christian era. His aphorisms were meant to be committed to memory and were so pithy as to be ambiguous and confusing in effect. Even during his lifetime his own oral commentary was necessary to render them intelligible. During the centuries that followed, such oral interpretation, often rather dubiously supported by the original text, was continued and resulted finally in the rise of three different systems of Vedanta philosophy—those founded by Sankara, Ramanuja, and Madhva.

Sankara's system of thought is called "non-dualism" (*advaita*), because it holds that the world (prakriti), the individual ego (*jiva*), and Brahman, while not absolutely one, do not really exist separately but are in reality "not different," "not-two" (nor three or more). The impersonal and indescribable Brahman is wholly beyond the reach of human experience (absolutely non-empirical). Besides It, the eternal, the undecaying, the full of being, all else is "transient, impure, unsubstantial, like a flowing river or a burning lamp, lacking in fibre like a banana, comparable to foam appearance, a mirage, a dream"; in short, a product of maya. The empirical world is thus phenomenal, neither existent nor non-existent, and truly unexplainable; it "rests on" Brahman as its basis, but Brahman is in no way directly involved in it causally, for the universe has actually been developed, through maya, by Ishvara, the creative and personal manifestation of the unmanifest Brahman.

The source of this view is traced back to the later Upanishads, in which, as for example in the *Shvetasvatara Upanishad*, it is declared:

Sacred poetry, the sacrifices, the ceremonies, the ordinances,

205

The past, the future, and what the Vedas declare—
This whole world the illusion-maker [*mayin*] projects out
of this Brahman,
And in it by illusion the individual soul [*jiva*] is confined.
Now, one should know that Nature [*Prakriti*] is illusion,
And that Mighty Lord [*Ishvara*] is the illusion-maker.[E5]

But the illusion is not said to be absolute. Sankara was true to the spirit of Indian philosophy in treating this point with great subtlety. He started with an initial advantage. By denying the ultimacy of the phenomenal world and regarding it as maya, he avoided both the difficulty encountered by the Sankhya philosophy of maintaining that the universe and the soul, both equally real, are in association but not in junction, and the problem in Buddhism arising from its doing away with the soul while at the same time affirming the fact of ever-recurring rebirth. A human being, according to Sankara, is dealing with something real when he looks about him, but he relies on his senses for knowledge. The everyday world in which his experience takes place is the subjective spatio-temporal frame of reference through which his ignorance (avidya, non-knowledge) self-deceivingly perceives the Real. The notion that the objects of sense-experience are "realities" is the work of this ignorance. Ignorance is, indeed, the active force that constructs the everyday world by a process just the same as that by which the piece of rope lying by the roadside is seen in the twilight as a snake, or the distant post as a man. To believe that one has seen a snake or a man in such circumstances is to submit uncritically to Avidya, the illusion-making power in man that produces the phenomenal world.

Furthermore, to believe in the independent reality of the individual soul, as is the common experience, is to move in the world of maya and to have only the lower kind of knowledge, but to know that our selves and Brahman-Atman are not-two is to apprehend reality and have the higher knowledge. Similarly, to credit the world of sense-experienced objects in space and time, if one accepts their reality, to the work of the Creator, Ishvara, the living god-principle, worshiped and sacrificed to by the people under such names as Vishnu, Shiva, and Rama, is to apprehend the absolute truth through the appearances created by ignorance. In reality, there is only Brahman-Atman, solely existent, spaceless, timeless, and eternal. The Upanishads have rightly said: *Tat tvam asi!* ("That art thou!"). Emancipation from the long-drawn-out nightmare of the cycle of rebirth comes only with the lifting of the veil of ignorance that prevents one from knowing that the soul is and always has been identical with Brahman.

This, it may be seen, is the logical culmination of the monistic speculations of the Upanishads.

Sankara wrote out his commentary on the *Vedanta Sutra* about 800 A.D. Three hundred years later Ramanuja, the most renowned of Vishnuite scholars, undertook to interpret the Upanishads differently. His revision of Sankara's darshana—for so it might be called—was of the greatest importance, for it had a profound influence in supporting the trend toward belief in God as the ultimate power.

Ramanuja was a monist insofar as he based himself on such passages in the Upanishads as *Brihadaranyaka* III.vii.3, where Brahman is declared to be him who is the Inner Controller of the whole universe in its every part. (See supra, p. 104.) But he qualified his monism (whence one of its names, "qualified monism") by finding in the Upanishads, and certainly in the *Bhagavad Gita,* a stress not only on the unity of all things and beings in Brahman, but also a differentiation. He asserted that the physical world, individual souls, and the ultimate Reality or Supreme Being are each real, although non-divisible, for the first two make up the "body" of the last; they are the forms through which God manifests himself. The ultimate Reality is a personal and not an impersonal being. His name is Vishnu. In short, Vishnu is Brahman. The ultimate Reality is, therefore, not as Sankara said, abstract, without qualities, and unknowable, but a concrete person endowed with every desirable quality, possessing omniscience, all-pervading, all-powerful, all-loving, and merciful. He reveals himself as God in five ways. First, he shows himself to the liberated souls in a heavenly city, where under a jeweled canopy he sits on Shesha, the world serpent, and is attended by Lakshmi and other consorts (infra, p. 213). Second, he manifests himself in accumulation of knowledge, creation, preservation, persistence, ruling might, and ability to overcome opposition (the six *vyuhas*). Again, he appears in the ten *avataras* (to be described later, on pp. 214 f.). Fourth, he dwells within the human heart, accompanies his devotees wherever they go, and sometimes appears in visions. Lastly, he presents himself in the images men make of him. The best goal of man—and the happy lot of those who render Vishnu proper devotion (bhakti) —is not absorption in an impersonal Absolute (although this can be achieved) but a going to heaven to enjoy Vishnu's presence in full consciousness.

The third version of the Vedanta, that of Madhva (fourteenth century A.D.), has been called the "duality school." Madhva maintained that the individual soul is not one with nor to be identified, here or hereafter, with an Absolute or Supreme Soul. His view is monotheistic, for he believed that the souls that are saved will enjoy bliss in the presence of the Supreme Soul (Vishnu); others are doomed to spend eternity either in the hells or in endless transmigration. How does salvation come? It comes, Madhva said, through Vayu, the wind-god, the son of Vishnu. He is the vehicle of the grace of God, and a sort of holy spirit who breathes his life-giving power into those whom he saves. This version of the Vedanta contains more than an echo of Islam and Christianity, which were by Madhva's time known in India. It has had, like Ramanuja's version, an immense influence not only on the followers of Vishnu but on all India. Many modern liberal thought movements credit their general attitude, if not the substance of their beliefs, to Ramanuja or Madhva or both.

V Popular Hinduism

The Hindu masses may not be said ever to have had a clear conception of any of these matters that we have just discussed. They go about being religious in the manner that has been traditional in their localities. In the complex of their rituals and beliefs Western observers have found demonolatry, animal-veneration, and devotion to village spirits and godlings —all these with or without the worship of the great deities of the Hindu pantheon. In the past, British officials often expressed in their state papers and reports judgments like this:

The ordinary villager, who in his everyday life takes no thought for the morrow of a subsequent existence, is content to worship the village godlings to whom he looks for rain, bountiful harvests, and escape from plague, cholera, and small-pox. . . . There are, as it were, two religions: a work-a-day religion to meet the requirements of everyday existence and a higher religion, known only to the Brahmin, . . . which the ordinary man does not attempt to understand.[H]

In some regions Hinduism may hardly be said to exist; a primitive animism takes its place. This sub-Hinduism is common among the fifty million "untouchables." But it is not so usual outside of the outcaste group. Most people in India practice orthodox Hinduism conjointly with the primitive forms of religion common in their locality. In the same village, shrines for the worship of the great gods of Hinduism, with Brahmins in attendance to perform the ritual properly, exist side by side with wayside stones, trees, or small shrines sacred to village godlings and spirits. To these last the villagers resort for worship "without benefit of clergy." The need that impels them is that of the common man all over the world, and few in India would attempt to check them. The Brahmins tolerate the practice but keep more or less aloof.

The Great Triad of Gods

In the more universal forms of Hinduism a triad of great gods appears. These beings—Brahmā* the Cre-

* Masculine. The terminal *ā* here receives an accent to distinguish it from the neuter *Brahman* (unaccented), the name for the Absolute (Brahman-Atman).

ator, Shiva the Destroyer, and Vishnu the Preserver —are recognized by the Brahmins as undoubtedly standing for realities within the frame of the universe. In any event, they command the believing trust and devotion of millions of the common people of India. In the course of years these three great deities have among them gradually absorbed the functions of scores and hundreds of local aboriginal gods. Their existence is rationalized by the Brahmins in the following way: they say that Brahman-Atman, the impersonal ultimate reality, achieves a religiously significant threefold manifestation or *trimurti* through the three personal deities who represent the divine functions of creation, destruction, and preservation respectively.

Literature

This idea was first developed in the *Mahabharata*. During a period of five hundred years or more it was carried further and taken up by the sects, especially the Vishnuites (Vaishnavas) and Shivaites (Shaivas), to which we shall come later (pp. 218 f.). As special loyalties were developed, a considerable literature sprang up to extend speculation and mythology in one direction or another. These writings are the numerous Puranas ("Ancient Stories") and Tantras ("Threads," "Basic Teachings"). Although originally the three members of the great triad were thought to be of equal importance and complementary to each other, later on the rivalries and antagonisms that sprang up between the followers of one or the other were expressed in the Puranas, eighteen of which are generally held to be authoritative. Neatly divided into three groups of six each, they exalt, as the case may be, Brahmā, Vishnu, or Shiva above the rest. Taken together, the Puranas are an inexhaustible treasury of folklore and myth, some of its extraordinarily rich in symbols. When the female counterparts or shaktis of Shiva occupy the center of attention, we have the numerous Tantras, the manuals or textbooks

that are the basis of the Tantrism already discussed in the last chapter (p. 181).

Brahmā

Of the three great gods, Brahmā, the Creator, is the least widely worshiped. Scarcely half a dozen temples are now dedicated to him. He may be compared with the "high god" of primitive peoples, no longer active on earth after having finished the work of creation. Yet he is deeply respected. In art he is depicted as a kingly personage with four heads, severely reading the Vedas, and is shown riding a white wild goose, symbolic of his aloofness.

Shiva

Shiva is one of the great gods of Asia. His followers have given him the title "Mahadeva," "the great god," and he measures up to the name. His character is most complex and has some fascinating aspects. As the later form of the dread god Rudra of Vedic days, he still is (in an important aspect) the Destroyer. In the words of the *Yajur-Veda*, he is "the threatener, the slayer, the vexer, and the afflicter." His presence is felt "in the fall of the leaf," and he is the bringer of disease and death, and, hence, a "man-slayer." His presence is felt at the funeral pyre, and he should be honored there. But he is not purely evil. His name shows that he is, or can be made, "auspicious" (*shiva*). It is of some interest to speculate about the origin of this name. At the end of the Vedic Age Rudra seems to have been so feared that his name was never mentioned. This was all in the spirit of the European proverb, "Speak of the devil, and he is sure to appear." Like the peasants of Europe in similar circumstances, the Indo-Aryans spoke of him preferably through descriptive titles. At length the word *shiva*, at first applied to other deities also, came to stand for him alone. Not only *could* he be auspicious, if he would, but perhaps a flattering reference to him as such would *make* him so?

Moreover, there were reasons for believing he had a constructive and helpful aspect. Originally, he was a mountain-god given to destructive and punitive raids on the plains, but those who penetrated to his mountain fastnesses discovered that under his kindly care grew medicinal herbs for the healing of men. Could it be that his sole interest was destruction? Was not his coming often "a blessing in disguise"? Gradually it came to be felt that Shiva destroyed in order to make room for new creation. No doubt he was "in the fall of the leaf"; yet he was primarily concerned with fulfilling the hope so well expressed by Shelley:

> If winter comes, can spring be far behind?

After all, pure destructiveness achieves no lasting results in tropical countries; the death and decay of vegetation is but the prelude to the rise of new forms of life, all the more vigorous for having humus to feed on. Besides, in a land where reincarnation is an accepted belief, death means almost instantaneous release into new life. By suggestions flowing from realizations such as this, the functions of Shiva received a meaningful enlargement.

He became identified with the processes of reproduction in every realm of life—vegetable, animal, and human. He seemed to have taken over the phallic emblems and characteristics of the fertility-gods of pre-Aryan India. The sex-energy that was identified with him was represented to the eyes of his worshipers by the *lingam* and *yoni*, conventional emblems of the male and female organs of generation. With a wholly reverent sense of the mystery of divine and human creative force, Shiva's worshipers, in their homes as well as in their temples, approach these symbols in devout worship. In the same reverent spirit the Shiva-worshiping sect founded in the twelfth century A.D., called the Lingayats, numbering some three millions today, carry with them, usually in a capsule hung around the neck, a soapstone

Shiva as Nataraja. This bronze from the Madras Museum (one of many like it) shows Shiva dancing within a ring of fire. His upper right hand holds a small drum for beating out his rhythm, his upper left a devouring flame. His lower right hand is raised in the "fear not" gesture, although the arm carries a cobra, while his left points to a foot lifted to symbolize "release." The other foot is planted on the squirming body of the demon of ignorance and heedlessness. The whole figure dramatizes the vital processes of the universe, bringing both death and new life. (The Metropolitan Museum of Art, Harris Brisbane Dick Fund, 1964.)

lingam without which they would never think of appearing in public.

By a further development of this association of ideas, Shiva stands for Life itself, as pure energy or force. He is often shown dancing on the squirming body of the demon of delusion, with his four arms gracefully waving in the air, one hand holding a small drum, another a flame or fire-pot. Poised on one leg, his whole figure shows a tremendous vitality, and it is felt that the dance is speeding the cycles of birth and death. Further evidences of vitality are suggested by endowing Shiva with a third eye placed vertically in the middle of the forehead and picturing him as having a blue body and a dark throat encircled by a necklace of serpents. Some of his images display him with five or six faces varying in expression, all of which, taken together, suggest his multiple attributes and energies.

At first view it may come as a surprise that Shiva is also the patron of ascetics and holy men. He is often represented as being himself deep in meditation, his naked body smeared with ashes and his hair braided after the fashion of an ascetic. The rationale of the ascription to him of ascetic interests seems to be something like this: the ascetic "destroys" his lower self to allow his higher or spiritual self to come to expression; the body must be curbed to free the soul; all worldly affections and lusts must be rooted out. The result will be a great access of power. But such regeneration is just what Shiva most desires to further. He is therefore on the side of the ascetics.

Sir Charles Eliot justly observes:

As an idea, as a philosophy, Shivaism possesses truth and force. It gives the best picture . . . of the force which rules the Universe as it is, which reproduces and destroys, and in performing one of these acts necessarily performs the other, seeing that both are but aspects of change. . . . The Creator is also the Destroyer, not in anger but by the very nature of his activity. . . . The egg is destroyed when the chicken is hatched: the embryo ceases to exist when the child is born; when the man comes into being, the child is no more.[1]

Shiva's Consorts and Associates

That Shiva has come to represent life-energy in all its aspects is amply attested by the character of his

Shiva and Parvati. Among the extant murals is this study of Shiva supporting in his arms the most lovely and feminine of his shaktis, Parvati, the daughter of a Himalayan god and mother of Ganesha. Together they symbolize the total nature of the cosmos, with its union of male and female energies. (Courtesy of the Government of India Tourist Office.)

various consorts and associates. His divine spouse is many persons in one and bears different names in the various regions of India. As Parvati, "the mountainer," or Uma, "light," she is gracious and kind. As Durga, "the unapproachable," Chandi, "the wild," or Kali, "the black," she is helpful and baleful and terrible at once; a spreader of disease, thereby awaking men's terror, yet an implacable enemy of the demons, thereby filling them with gratitude; kindly to her favored ones, yet accustomed to devour men and animals. Durga, the unapproachable, has been the patroness of the robber caste bearing the name of Thugs. Kali, the black, wears round her dark neck a necklace of skulls and uses her four strong arms as flails to demolish her victims before she fills her mouth with their flesh, but she is infinitely generous and kind to those whom she loves and who love her in return. In Bengal she is adored as the great Mother; mystics and seers like Ramakrishna and Vivekananda have devoted themselves to her with the most intense kind of passionate attachment (bhakti).

Associated with Shiva also are Ganesha, the elephant-headed god, and Nandi, the white bull. Ganesha is Shiva's son by Parvati, his mountaineer consort. The elephant head, found everywhere in Shiva's temples, symbolizes Ganesha's cunning and his elephantlike ability to remove obstacles by great strength. Nandi, whose milk-white or black bull-image reclines in Shiva's temples, and whose representative, the live white bull, wanders in the temple courts and down the streets in freedom is Shiva's temple chamberlain and the guardian of quadrupeds (see his image overleaf).

Shaktism

As a general rule, the worship of Shiva's consorts, conceived as forms of his shakti or active power displayed in female energy, constitutes a minor theme in the adoration addressed primarily to himself. But a distinct subdivision of Hinduism concerns itself with the worship of Shiva's spouse or spouses, and in northeastern India particularly, it almost attains the status of a separate religion. As such, it is a form of Tantrism, but because, as we have seen in the previous chapter, there is a Buddhist Tantrism, this worship is more precisely called shaktism. As practiced, it has what have been called its "right-hand"

Ganesha, the elephant-headed son of Shiva. The good-natured Ganesha's pot-belly attests to his huge appetite for food. He has the elephant's ability to remove obstacles and is besought by his devotees before any undertaking to overcome possible difficulties. He is learned in the scriptures and wise. Among the symbols he carries, the most prominent is a goad such as elephant-drivers use. (*Nelson Gallery, Atkins Museum, Kansas City, Missouri.*)

and "left-hand" forms. Right-hand shaktism has a refined and philosophic aspect; it centers attention

211

*Nandi the bull, Chamundi Hills, Mysore.
The worshipers have placed garlands on
the head of the carrier of Shiva, draped the
bell of his necklace with flowers, and then
made their offerings. Nandi, when not
actually bearing Shiva on his back, serves
as a chamberlain protectively stationed
before every temple of the great god. He is
the representative and guardian of all four-
footed creatures. (Courtesy of the
Government of India Tourist Office.)*

on the white or benignant side of shakti, that is, the benevolent phases of the energy of nature, considered under the symbol of a mother-goddess, "combining in one shape life and death." Recent Bengali poets and swamis, like Tagore and Ramakrishna, have made much of this aspect of the mystery and reality of the universe. They identify shakti with maya, the illusion-creating power that has produced the beautiful and terrible phenomenal world. Thus Ramakrishna, in adoring the black goddess Kali as the fitting symbol of Reality truly and justly understood, could exclaim:

"When I think of the Supreme Being as inactive, neither creating, nor preserving, nor destroying, I call him *Brahman* or *Purusha*, the impersonal God. When I think of him as active, creating, preserving, destroying, I call him *Shakti* or *Maya* . . . the personal god. But the distinction between them does not mean a difference. The personal and the impersonal are the same Being, in the same way as are milk and its whiteness, or the diamond and its lustre, or the serpent and its undulations. It is impossible to conceive of the one without the other. The Divine Mother (Kali) and *Brahman* are one."[J1]

"Kali is none other than He whom you call *Brahman*. Kali is Primitive Energy (Shakti). . . . To accept Kali is to accept *Brahman*. . . . *Brahman* and his Power are identical."[J2]

Left-hand shaktism is both primitive and highly sophisticated. Its rites are essentially magical and esoteric. Our earlier discussion of Vajrayana Buddhism (p. 181) has indicated its general outlook. Here, in the Hindu setting, Durga and Kali, as representatives of the black and violent side of shakti, are the favorite manifestations of divine energy. Being identified with them means being swept into conventionally forbidden expressions of natural impulse. In secret rites, the details of which are not fully known, the carefully screened adherents meet in "circle worship" marked by dances of naked women, drinking of wine and blood, and ritualistic sex acts. The five *M*'s, ordinarily forbidden, are indulged in, namely, wine (*madya*), meat (*mansa*), fish (*matsya*), parched grain (*mudra*), and sexual union (*maithuna*). It is understood to be highly dangerous to the participant's welfare (karmic position) if pleasure is sought. Rightly, the aim is to have such tight control of the senses as to rise entirely above pleasure to a complete self-identification ("non-dualistic union") with holy natural force, ultimately with the purpose of riding the back of this "tiger" into Nirvana.

Vishnu

The third member of the great Hindu triad is called the Preserver. He is always benevolent, primarily the conservator of values and an active agent in their realization. Unlike the complex Shiva, he is the perfect and patient exemplar of winsome divine Love. He watches from the skies, and whenever he sees values threatened or the good in peril, he exerts all his preservative influence in their behalf. He therefore rivals Shiva in popularity among the masses. The stories of his divine activity attract a growing following. He is usually represented with four arms, in two hands holding the symbols of his royal power, the mace and the discus, and in two others the emblems of his magic power and stainless purity, the conch and the lotus respectively. His head is surmounted by a high crown and diadem, his feet are blue, his vesture yellow, and he has the lotus eyes so much admired by Hindus. When reclining, he is shown resting on the world-serpent, Shesha or Ananta; his vehicle is the bird Garuda, and a fish is his symbol. His shakti or spouse is the lovely goddess of fortune and beauty Lakshmi.

Vishnu's rise to high popular favor is in part due to Vedic mythology. In the Vedas, as we have seen, he is a solar deity. Taking their cue from the fact that the sun redeems the earth from darkness in his passage between earth and sky, the Vedic people

Vishnu and Lakshmi. As Shiva has his Parvati (or Devi), so Vishnu has his faithful and loving Lakshmi, who takes form as his consort in every one of his avatars (as Radha, Sita, etc.). This stone panel from the temple at Khajuraho (ca. 1000 A.D.) shows the mutual devotion of the pair. She shares in Vishnu's activities as Preserver. (Courtesy of the Government of India Tourist Office.)

developed the myth relating how, when the demon-king Bali seized control of the earth, Vishnu appeared in the form of a dwarf and meekly asked and obtained from the amused giant the promise of as much ground as he could traverse in three steps. The bargain concluded, Vishnu at once returned to his own shape and restored heaven and earth to gods and men by encompassing them in two swift strides. By not taking a third stride across hell, he left it in the demon's possession. This myth provided the intimation concerning the character of Vishnu's interests and activity that has led to his rise in popular esteem. It was seen that he "comes to earth" in *avataras* or "descents" when needed. He has not come down once only, his devotees have urged. Besides descending as a dwarf, he was incarnate in Rama, the Galahad-like hero of the *Ramayana*, and in Krishna, the warrior-hero and pastoral Don Juan of the *Mahabharata* and folklore. Indeed, a fast-developing my-

thology went on to relate that he has had animal as well as human avatars.

The Avatars of Vishnu

The avatars of Vishnu have been traditionally set at ten, though popular belief has much enlarged the number. Of the traditional list, nine avatars are said to have already occurred, while the tenth is yet to

The main temple at Angkor Vat, Cambodia. Although now in Buddhist territory and a place of Buddhist pilgrimage, Angkor Vat was originally dedicated to Vishnu. An outstanding example of twelfth-century Kmer architecture, its sculptures and reliefs show Vishnu in his various avatars and depict scenes and characters from the Ramayana *and other stories involving him. (Courtesy of the United Nations.)*

come. We have already mentioned three of them. In the other avatars Vishnu became in turn a fish, which rescued the first man, Manu, being swept away in a world-flood; a tortoise, which swam under Mt. Mandara and assisted the gods in using it to churn the nectar of immortality and other valuable products from the ocean of milk; a boar, which, with its tusks, lifted the sunken earth above the depths of the sea into which it had been plunged; a man-lion, who tore to pieces a demon-father attempting the life of his son because he prayed to Vishnu; a Brahmin warrior-hero, who twenty-one times utterly defeated the Kshatriya caste and finally established Brahmin supremacy; and Gautama, the founder of Buddhism. The tenth avatar is to be that of Kalki, a messiah with a sword of flame, riding on a white horse,* who shall come to save the righteous and destroy the wicked at the end of the fourth and depraved world period.

It is significant that the Buddha is in the list. One suspects the name of the great founder of Buddhism was added to Vishnu's avatars as a tactical maneuver, designed, and successfully too, to reconcile Buddhism and Hinduism. How well it served to facilitate Indian Buddhism's return to the mother-fold of Hinduism has already been seen on pp. 161 f., in the chapter on the religious development of Buddhism.

Incomparably the most popular of the avatars are those of Rama and Krishna. Rama is the ideal man of the Hindu epics, and his wife is the ideal woman. As the *Ramayana* relates, Rama's happy marriage to Sita, a beauteous princess of the royal house of Mithila, was followed by great trouble. The demon-king of Ceylon, Ravana, treacherously seized Sita and carried her off to his island home. In great distress, Rama enlisted the aid of Hanuman, the monkey-king (the earliest detective in world literature, by the way, and now a Hindu god in his own right). The monkey-king was able to conduct an extensive search from the vantage point of the treetops, and Sita was finally found. Rama fought and slew Ravana,

* To some the horse is so prominent that they name this avatar the *Ashvatara* (the "Horse Avatar").

and Sita, after successfully passing through an ordeal of fire to prove her chastity, rejoined her mate. Because of the currency in all parts of India of the various versions of the Ramayana, Rama is widely revered. Millions make him the object of their devotion, and his image is often worshiped in a manner to suggest that he is no mere savior-hero but the all-God. There are, in fact, two phases of Rama-worship: (1) reverential respect for Rama as a hero who was an avatar of Vishnu, and (2) theistic worship of Rama, which gives him exclusive devotion as the supreme deity.

It would be interesting to explore, as we cannot here, the theological doctrines evolved as a result of the theistic attitude to Rama. Yet one doctrinal issue calls for mention. It has to do with the famous controversy as to whether Rama saves by the "monkey-hold" or by the "cat-hold"—that is, with man's cooperation or without it. One group of Rama devotees contends that Rama saves only through the free cooperation of the believer with him; the believer must cling to the god as a baby monkey clings to its mother when the latter is swinging off to safety through the trees. The other group believes that salvation is of God only, and that Rama saves his chosen ones by carrying them off as a cat carries a kitten by the scruff of the neck.

Highly regarded though Rama is, Krishna is even more popular, both as an avatar and as a god. His character is more complex than Rama's, presenting two distinct aspects not a little difficult to reconcile. The *Mahabharata* shows him in one phase, pastoral poetry and folklore in another. In the Mahabharata he is serious and severe, a resourceful war-hero. Throughout the strenuous episodes of the epic he seems primarily anxious to direct man's attention to Vishnu, the god-form of the Absolute, of whom he is the incarnation. In this connection (as we have already noted in our summary of the episode called the *Bhagavad Gita*) he asks for the unconditioned devotion of true bhakti toward himself as the earthly form of Vishnu, the supreme Lord of the World. The other Krishna is a gay youth, the pivotal

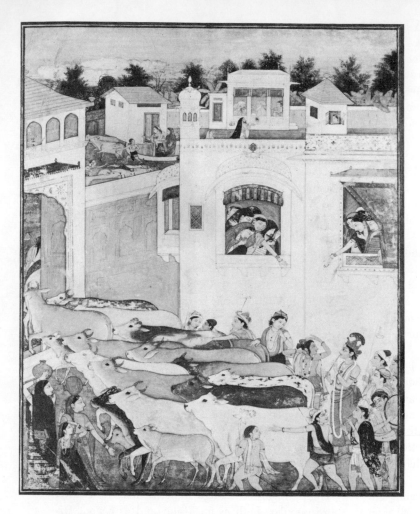

Krishna at the hour of cowdust. In this late-eighteenth-century Rajput painting Krishna, blowing on his flute and accompanied by cowgirls (gopis), brings the cows home from the pasture as evening comes. Love-smitten women lean from the windows, waving. Maidens with water pots on their heads pause to gaze rapturously at him. (Courtesy, Museum of Fine Arts, Boston.)

figure in a vast folklore. Hindu imagination has dwelt lovingly on his childhood as a pantry-haunting "butter-thief" and fat little play-fellow. Thousands of Hindu women daily worship him in this phase, gazing upon his chubby infant-images with as much devotion as Italian women regard their beloved Bambino, the child Jesus. But this Krishna is more representatively portrayed as an enchanting pastoral figure. In most of the folk-tales he is a sprightly and amorous cow-herd, a melodious flute at his lips, piping as he moves among the cattle the ravishing airs that win him the love of the *gopis* or milk-maids, with whom he dallies in dark-eyed passion. He unites himself with hundreds of these adoring ones, but

values above all the beautiful Radha, his favorite mistress.* The erotic literature that has sprung up to describe this phase of the god's activity bears some resemblance in general tone to the literature of Shaktism, though it prefers expression in story to the latter's philosophy and Tantrism.

The sects that give Krishna a more or less exclusive devotion rank him as high as the Rama-worshipers do their paragon. In Bengal one sect sets Radha beside Krishna as his eternal consort and directs worshipers to seek the favor of both diligently, in the hope of being transported at death to the

* One Purana says sixteen thousand adoring ones!

216

pleasure groves of the Brindaban heaven, where Krishna and Radha make love forever, in ever-young delight. It is not unexpected that the excesses of left-hand Shaktism occur in some Krishna cults, yet virtually all the devotees of Krishna stress love of the god as a spiritual rather than a carnal passion. The infatuation of the gopis for the divinely adorable cow-herd is given a symbolic meaning; even their transports of love, the thrilling sensation at the roots of the hair, the choking emotion, and the swooning, are said to give a true picture in sensuous imagery of the exaltation produced in the worshiper who is looking upon the image of Krishna and thinking of his love.

The Common Man's Worship at Home and Abroad

The common man of India is uncritically and perhaps limitlessly polytheistic. Even though experience or family habit leads him to adopt one god or goddess as a patron or tutelary deity whose image or symbol he enshrines in his house and whose name he repeats with special devotion at dawn and dusk, he honors nevertheless all supernatural beings whatever. The number of these is uncountable. Hindus are accustomed to saying their deities number some thirty-three crores, that is, some 330 millions. With so polytheistic an outlook, the average villager goes from shrine to shrine as need arises. If he wishes to have obstacles to some undertaking removed, he worships Ganesha, the elephant-headed son of Shiva; if he wishes to have greater bodily strength for some heavy work, he prays to Hanuman, the monkey-god; if his father is dying, he offers his anguished supplications to Rama; his hopes for immunity from smallpox or cholera, or for safety on a journey, or for the enjoyment of good fortune, or plenty of children, or the health of his cattle, take him to still other deities. His reverence is expressed not only at the shrines or before images; he may worship anywhere, recognizing in round stones lifted from the river bed to the roadside symbols of Shiva, in trees decorated with vermillion paint the divine fertility-force in nature, and in dark caves suggestions of Yama, the god of the dead, and so on.

In his life of devotion, the common man feels not only his personal need to express his religious consciousness but also the necessity of worship going on in his behalf all the time. Worship in his own locality takes three different forms simultaneously. First, he himself worships as need arises either at home or in a temple or elsewhere through his own devotional acts. Second, a priest or someone in the family (one of the women, or it may be his father or brother, or himself) conducts the simple domestic rites in behalf of the family before an image or symbol of the household god. Third, in his and the whole community's behalf, the local priests conduct several times daily a ceremony of homage—a *puja*—at the local temple or shrine.

But the common man's need is not fully met even by all this. He craves to go to some holy place of pilgrimage where he may receive a special blessing. It would not be wide of the mark to say that millions of Hindus derive their chief religious satisfaction from the pilgrimages they make and the temple festivals they attend. By these activities not only do they give testimony and expression to their faith through puja (the ritual of worship), but they enjoy themselves hugely in an earthly as well as spiritual sense.

Given a religion as polytheistic as Hinduism, it is to be expected that sacred places should multiply during the years. Indeed, from the Hindu point of view India may be said to be growing in sanctity all the time, owing to the slowly increasing number of sacred places to be found in it. Sacred places are of two general types: (1) sacred places as such, whose holiness made inevitable the rise of temples and shrines there, and (2) places that have become sacred *after* temples or shrines were erected on them. It is sometimes difficult, however, to know in which group to put the oldest sacred places.

Sacred places of the first type may come into being at almost any spot on mountain or plain where a cavern, strangely formed rock, fissure in the ground, hot spring, or natural wonder has given rise to a tale of spirit-visitation or of miracle, but in most cases they are along the great rivers. Hindus have long regarded their mightiest streams as holy from source to mouth. The Puranas have glorified almost every bend and every tributary with stories of some theophany—a visit of Shiva or one of his shaktis, an exploit of Rama, Krishna, or some other divine being who came to the spot to consecrate it by a significant conversation or wondrous deed. Consequently, it is a work of great merit to follow the course of a holy river from its source to its mouth and back along the other bank to the source again, stopping always at every sacred spot to read or hear again the sacred legends, visit the holy shrines, and engage in pious devotions there. But pilgrims do not often take this long and arduous journey. It is enough for them if they can go to one or more of the many temples that line the holy stream's banks, throw flowers on the river's sacred surface, bathe in the purifying flood, and carry its water home in small containers for last offices to the dying and other ministrations.

The holiest river of all—the Ganges—is known throughout India as "Mother Ganga." Its sacredness is explained by the myth that it issues from the feet of Vishnu in heaven and falls far below upon Shiva's head and flows out of his hair. One of the most sacred spots along its entire course is the place where it issues, strong and clear, from the Himalayas. That is the site of the famous pilgrim center Hardwar, with its long lines of steps going down into the river and its crowds of bathers seeking purification in the icy water. Equally sacred is the juncture of the Jumna River with the Ganges, at which spot a third river, the holy Saraswati, is supposed to rise to the surface. Here lies Allahabad, the city that attracts millions of pilgrims to its *melas* or religious fairs. The mouths of the Ganges, emptying through a great delta into the Bay of Bengal, are also holy, and particularly is this true of Saugor Island, which lies within the delta and is the site of a sacred bathing festival at the beginning of the year.

But it is to Benares that most pilgrims go to wash away their sins. The pilgrims who enter on its hallowed territory are often so overcome with joy at the sight of its temple towers in the distance that they prostrate themselves and pour the dust of the ground on their heads as a sign of their spiritual submission. They proceed joyfully to the bathing *ghats* (steps) along the river and are purified by immersion in the cleansing waters of sacred Mother Ganga. And when they finally turn homeward, it is with the joyous conviction that all past sins have been atoned for and the future made secure. Had any pilgrim been seized by a mortal illness while within the sacred territory, all would still have been well, for whoever dies upon that sacred soil, especially if his feet be immersed in the sacred river and his body cremated with due ritual on a burning ghat, goes to Shiva's heaven of unending delight.

The Sects

During the Gupta period (200–700 A.D.), when Indian culture entered a golden age, and particularly under the Gupta emperors themselves (320–570), teachers of the masses appeared, seeking to meet the popular need for rituals, symbols, and images that would provide the people with a clearer conception of some personal god or Ishvara who, besides having cosmic powers, was nearby enough to be approachable through bhakti and puja (worship). Sects thus arose that have widely dominated the religious scene until the present time. *Sectarian* is undoubtedly too strong and partisan a word to characterize most Hindus, because they preserve their freedom to worship different deities as need arises, but many Hindus nevertheless find greater satisfaction by becoming part of a distinctive religious group with its own literature, leaders, and rituals. The largest sects have been the Shaiva (Shivaite) and the Vaishnava (Vishnuite). The former, in their several varieties, seem to have been dominant over other groups during the thousand years after 100 A.D. Then the Vaishnavas

Bathing ghats at Benares. For many miles along the Ganges, steps or ghats lead down into the holy waters in which the pilgrims bathe. Umbrellas provide pilgrims and holy men with shade, and the spires and pavilions of temples rise above them. Special platforms offer places for rest and meditation. At nearby ghats cremation of the dead takes place, and the ashes are strewn on the waters. (Courtesy of the Government of India Tourist Office.)

took their turn in winning the greater part of popular adherence from about 1100 A.D. to the present.

Astrology

Since Gupta times there has been much horoscope-casting and use of astrology in India. Although Vedic India had already begun the study of the stars (with enough exactitude to warrant our calling the study astronomy), the preferred methods of foretelling the future were interpretation of omens and dreams and also readings taken from the size and shape of face and limbs and from such special features as birth-marks and lines appearing on the palms of the hands and soles of the feet. (The Buddha, for example, 219

The Brihadisvara temple at Tanjore in south India.
The spire or pyramid here shown rises on a square base, the shrine proper, in eleven stories. It was completed in the eleventh century by Rajaraja Deva Chola in honor of Shiva. It is in the Dravidian style, marked by horizontal lines, and is surmounted by a dome on a hexagonal base. (Courtesy of the Government of India Tourist Office.)

was examined, legend says, by soothsayers shortly after his birth, and the marks on his body and the soles of his feet—"the thirty-two marks of the superman"—told them he was destined for greatness.) But in Gupta and medieval times astrology, partly because it could be resorted to without delay as needed, came into daily use and is relied upon constantly throughout India today. It is considered especially necessary in the fixing of dates for weddings and journeys. Also it is thought that there is more luck in the name given to a child if its first letter is taken from the stars under which the child was born. When a go-between finds a suitable girl for a boy to marry, the betrothal does not take place until the horoscopes

The Jagannatha temple at Puri. Built in the twelfth century to house the image of Jagannatha (Vishnu), this temple has a main tower 192 feet in height, crowned by the mystic wheel and flags of Vishnu. In June or July the god is drawn by ropes attached to his huge car (the fabled "juggernaut") to his "country house," less than a mile away. Stories of people throwing themselves under the wheels are misinterpretations of deaths due to the crush of the crowds. (Courtesy of the Government of India Tourist Office.)

of the couple are found favorable. Even educated Hindus who no longer believe in the practice themselves nevertheless consult astrologers before important family events to make certain that all the participants are comfortable in their minds about what is to occur.

Cow Protection

Scholars who readily appreciate the importance of the idea of reincarnation have sometimes failed to give like recognition to an equally widespread feature of Hindu religious life—the veneration of the cow. Perhaps there is less disposition to overlook this unique feature of Hindu religious practice since Katherine Mayo's *Mother India* made it a factor in an acrimonious controversy spreading over three continents. Hindus, said Miss Mayo, hold the cow in *such* honor that they let her wander in inviolate loneliness, suffering and starving along the parched roads of India! There was an immediate reaction from India, all of it indignant. No less an advocate than

Mahatma Gandhi led in the defense of "cow-protection," as he liked to call it. He even named it "the central fact of Hinduism, the one concrete belief common to all Hindus," and justified it in the memorable words:

Cow-protection is to me one of the most wonderful phenomena in human evolution. It takes the human being beyond his species. The cow to me means the entire subhuman world. Man through the cow is enjoined to realize his identity with all that lives. . . . She is the mother to millions of Indian mankind. The cow is a poem of pity. Protection of the cow means protection of the whole dumb creation of God.[K]

The sincerity of the feeling here is beyond question. Certainly there is much to be said for the symbolism. Hindus are not without a case in saying that the exaltation of the cow is morally far above that of the eagle or the lion. But the Hindu attitude is rather more unreserved than the words of Gandhi just quoted would indicate. Ancient India came to *worship* the cow. In the words of Monier-Williams, who has written what is often quoted as the classic summary of Hindu cow-worship:

Reverence for cows. Sacred cows are being fed at the Sadpur fair grounds near Calcutta, where they are kept for ceremonial worship. The cows have had garlands placed around their necks and heads during a previous ritual. The cow, Gandhi said, "is the mother to millions of Indian mankind," and represents "the entire subhuman world." (United Press International Photo.)

The cow is of all animals the most sacred. Every part of its body is inhabited by some deity or other. Every hair on its body is inviolable. All its excreta are hallowed. Not a particle ought to be thrown away as impure. On the contrary, the water it ejects ought to be preserved as the best of all holy waters—a sin-destroying liquid which sanctifies everything it touches, while nothing purifies like cow-dung. Any spot which a cow has condescended to honor with the sacred deposit of her excrement is forever afterwards consecrated ground, and the filthiest place plastered with it is at once cleansed and freed from pollution, while the ashes produced by burning this hallowed substance are of such a holy nature, that they not only make clean all material things, however previously unclean, but have only to be sprinkled over a sinner to convert him into a saint.[L]

The merit of the cow has in some degree been passed on to the ox and the bull. To free oxen dedicated to Shiva so that they may wander through the streets is a work of high merit, and when done in the name of one recently deceased is of great benefit to him in his next life.

The killing of cows has in times past been visited with capital punishment; men are still out-casted for it. It has been a major source of conflict between Muslims and Hindus that, on the day annually commemorating Abraham's offering up of Isaac, the former sacrifice the gentle creature that spends its life in the selfless giving of its nourishment to others.[*] Since the partition of India into Hindu and Muslim states, the Hindu areas have attempted to suppress this practice.

In many parts of India cows receive at certain seasons of the year the honor given to deities. Garlands are placed around their necks, oil is poured on their foreheads and water at their feet, while tears of affection and gratitude start into the eyes of bystanders.

Cow dung is today used in most of the villages of Hindu India in many ways: as a fuel, as a disinfect-

ant element dissolved in the water used to wash floors, thresholds, and walls, as an ingredient in clay-mortar and mud-plaster, and as a medicine. In some rural regions, when a man is dying and wishes to assure himself a safe passage from this life into the next, he grasps the tail of a cow backed up to his bedside, or should the room be inaccessible to the animal, he holds a rope fastened to a cow's tail outside the room.

One observer, after a year's residence in a remote northern village, says with evident justice:

The charge that India is consciously cruel or indifferent to cattle is certainly not substantiated by anything I saw in my village. As a rule, out of self-interest, if for no higher reason, the villagers give the cattle the best care they can provide. If they go half-starved, so do their owners.[M]

The Holiness of Brahmins

Holiness as a potent element in human personality has fascinated India in the past, and still does. Although men of other castes may be recognized as holy (witness Gandhi and the title given him), Brahmins have had sanctity above all others. The *Code of Manu* long since made this clear. It placed the Brahmin in the position of "the lord of this whole creation," whose birth is "an eternal incarnation of the sacred law."[C10] As priest, or as *guru* (teacher), or in any occupation, the Brahmin is "the highest on earth," and "whatever exists in the world is his property"; on account of the excellence of his origin he is entitled to all.

A Brahmin, be he ignorant or learned, is a great divinity, just as the fire is a great divinity. The brilliant fire is not contaminated even in burial places, and, when presented with oblations of butter at sacrifices, it again increases mightily. Thus, though Brahmins employ themselves in all sorts of mean occupations, they must be honored in every way; for each of them is a very great deity.[C11]

---

[*] The British ran into trouble during the Indian Mutiny in 1857, when both Hindu and Muslim recruits refused any longer to bite percussion caps onto cartridges greased with fat from cows and pigs.

Today the mysterious quality of his person can only with difficulty be preserved, but it is being preserved. No matter what his manner of life may be, to kill or to maltreat him is always a heinous sin. Yet it would be erroneous to conclude that each individual Brahmin is necessarily revered. He is indeed theoretically a great lord among men, whatever his occupation, but then one may regard the person of a king as sacred and still despise his spirit or mock at his acts. Today, when Brahmins engage in all sorts of occupations, it is perhaps natural that in some cases they should be ridiculed, as were the monks of medieval Europe, for their petty vices, especially if they belie even while they adopt an air of ultrarespectability. But even those who laugh at a Brahmin may wish themselves in his place and hope after death to become a Brahmin in the next life.

Among the most highly honored Brahmins in India are the gurus. As a group, they exhibit Hinduism's conscious effort in the direction of religious education. Their function is to teach Hindus those tenets of their religion most directly bearing upon home-life and household ceremony. The wealthy often permanently retain a guru in their homes as a family tutor and religious mentor, but in most cases he serves a number of families and goes the rounds among them. He is usually a high-minded, conscientious person who is an effective force for good. His special function is to train boys in religious knowledge and the duties of caste and to initiate them into manhood (in the case of the three upper castes) by ceremonially investing them with the sacred cord. Not all gurus are Brahmins, but those who are not are religious authorities in their own right.

We must not overlook the "holy men," the *sadhus,* *sannyasis,* and *yogis,* who are so distinctive of India. Some slight differences distinguish them. The yogis are, as their name implies, those who hope that their practice of Yoga will someday give them the insight and status of sannyasis and sadhus. Sannyasis are today usually ash-smeared followers of Shiva imitating the great god's ascetic ardors, but in the classical Hindu conception they win their status by reaching the fourth stage of the ideal life-career. The sadhu is so called because he is acknowledged to be a person of great sanctity, one who has "attained" or "arrived" at his goal of spiritual unity with whatever he considers to be ultimate reality. He has probably enjoyed more than one experience of samadhi or trance, and is now truly holy. Most live fully clothed among their fellowmen and exercise a great influence over them; a few, in the zeal of concentrated effort, go half-clothed or naked, smeared with ashes, or frozen in unbroken silence; some are half-mad or even quite insane. The sacred places of India are like a lode-stone to the more fanatic among them. During festivals these eccentric sadhus—a special sect—march along naked, hundreds strong, and after they have passed, the people run to scoop up the dust made sacred by their footprints, that they may rub it on themselves or carry it away.

The West is familiar with pictures of Hindu holy men displaying their self-mastery by reclining on beds of spikes, sitting between fires or hanging with head down in the smoke, wearing feathered barbs set in their flesh, holding one or both arms (or legs) in the same position until atrophy renders them useless, looking at the sun with undeviating gaze until the eyes go blind, wearing heavy clanking chains wrapped around the legs and body, and so on. In these positions, or cumbered with these hampering weights, they remain for hours, days, weeks, or years together. The Western observer is filled with amazement at the mere thought of so much self-imposed suffering and such indomitable patience and endurance. But it would be too much to expect equal sincerity and devotion in every instance. The more philosophic holy man bears his self-inflicted torment in the silence and solitude of his forest or mountain retreat, perfecting himself in the quietude of his own thought. Others crave the presence of the multitudes and live by the offerings of the pious. All this is not without its logic. It may seem a strange sort of reasoning that leads to such maltreatment of the body, but the earnest basic purpose is there—to control the flesh for the sake of freedom of the spirit.

VI Issues and Problems of the Present

The story of Hinduism as we have so far told it suggests something that ought to be stated clearly. The originality and diversity of thought in this complex culture defy a simple setting forth. It would be quite impossible even in a long book—not to mention a single chapter like this—to give due consideration to the astonishing variety of opinion and range of disagreement that have accompanied the unfolding of Hinduism. Few Hindu doctrines have ever stood for long without being challenged. This is true even of what might be called the essentials of Hinduism—the beliefs, namely, that the doctrines in the Vedas and Upanishads, properly interpreted, are true, and that the caste system represents what is right and just, according to the Law of Karma. The heretical views in Jainism, Buddhism, and Sikhism only partially suggest the conflict of view shown by men of original minds and reforming zeal. In the space remaining to us it seems best to look into this interesting matter by raising and discussing some of the issues and problems of recent Hinduism, especially those that have made for change.

A. THE REACTION TO WESTERN RELIGION AND SCIENCE. Hinduism is paradoxically both one of the most liberal and one of the most conservative of religions. Its liberalism flows from the intellectual freedom granted to its adherents, a freedom whereby they may even deny the inspiration of the Vedas, the holiness of Brahmins, or the orthodox conceptions of the caste system, and yet remain Hindu—*provided* that they do not break completely with the accepted moral practices of their localities or the code of social regulations to which they have been bred, especially the dietary restrictions, marriage laws, and cow-veneration; in short, provided that they seek to reform Hinduism from within and are not complete rebels.

In the course of the centuries a large number of Hindu sects were allowed to adopt with little change the leading doctrines of heretical or foreign religions. The Brahmins complained and objected at times, but there was no marked disturbance of the religious peace, unless some sect broke utterly with caste law, or, as occasionally happened under Muslim influence, ate the flesh of the cow.

During the nineteenth century a new type of liberalism made its appearance. It was the direct result of the favorable impressions created by the teaching of Christian missionaries and by education in Western history and science in schools established under European auspices. When this liberal movement got under way, other movements followed, some reactionary, some radical, some latitudinarian. They may be briefly described under the following four heads.

1. *The Brahmo Samaj,* or the liberal movement of rapprochement with the West. The Brahmo Samaj is an important movement within modern Hinduism, not so much because of the number of its members as because of its influence. It was founded in Calcutta in 1828 by Ram Mohan Rai, a Brahmin of brilliant mind, whose religious heritage contained strong Vishnuite and Shivaite influences, from which he was partially weaned away by an education which brought him in touch with Buddhism, Zoroastrianism, Islam, and Christianity. He found in all the religions he learned to know a similar spiritual core and was therefore led to organize a religious society devoted to the essence that seemed to him to be central in every religious faith. His own creed grew out of the conviction that the truth underlying all religions is the unity, personality, and spirituality of God, "the Eternal, Unsearchable and Immutable Being who is the Author and Preserver of the Universe." Accordingly, he denounced all forms of polytheism and idolatry and advocated purging Hindu ceremonies of these elements. He welcomed any witness to the unity and personality of God. The precepts of Jesus were from his point of view, he said, "the Guide to Peace and Happiness." In seeking to formulate a universal religion he gave up many of the general beliefs of Hinduism, such as the doctrine of the transmigra-

tion of souls and the theory that the soul is destined to be eventually absorbed into the World-Soul.

From the beginning no pictures or images and no animal sacrifices were permitted in the religious services of the Brahmo Samaj. The worship was conducted (for the first time by Hindus) congregationally, as in European Protestantism, with hymns, sermons, and scripture readings. Social reforms, such as abolition of suttee (to whose official outlawing Ram Mohan Rai contributed not a little) and prohibition of child-marriage and polygamy, were urged but not actively sought. Agitation rather than action was the objective. The reason for this moderation lay in part in the fact that Ram Mohan Rai remained true to the social restrictions of his own caste and never ceased to wear the sacred cord of the Brahmin. He did not wish to break off communion with his fellow Hindus. He was thus able to win gifted aristocrats to his movement. The grandfather, and later the father, of the famous Bengali poet, Rabindranath Tagore, became leaders in the Brahmo Samaj.

The Brahmo Samaj split in two in the 1860's, when the socially-minded Keshab Chandra Sen, who was brought up in an English school and had learned to love the figure of Christ as a divine social reformer, began to attack the caste system root and branch and pled for a radical sweeping away of caste restrictions, including those placed upon intercaste marriages. A rupture between the radicals and conservatives followed. Keshab's adherents followed him in organizing a new society, called the Brahmo Samaj of India, to distinguish it from the Adi (or Original) Brahmo Samaj, which was the name given to the old society. Later, most of his followers left him to form the Sadharan (or General) Brahmo Samaj. Keshab renamed his diminished society the Nava Bidhana Samaj or Church of the New Dispensation. During the few years of life that remained to him he came to feel more and more that he was continuing the work of Christ on earth. After his death, this startling phase of his thought was played down as much as possible by his followers.

Today the Adi Brahmo Samaj and the Nava Bid-hana Samaj are less influential than the Sadharan Brahmo Samaj, but all three groups continue to stand for a universal religion based on the Fatherhood of God and the Brotherhood of Man.

2. *The Arya Samaj,* or the movement "back to the Vedas." Here is an effort to establish a universal religion which has had some success in India. It was founded in 1875 by Swami Dayanand, a Brahmin who had had the interesting religious experience of revolting in boyhood from the worship of Shiva and then of passing as an ascetic through a period of belief in the monism of the Upanishads into a period of belief in the dualism of the Sankhya philosophy. He finally arrived at the conviction that the religion of the Vedas is the oldest and purest of all religions. He found it to be untainted by superstition, idolatry, or erroneous conceptions like the doctrine of avatars, and free from the objectionable features of the caste system. The Vedas, he taught, were a direct revelation from the one God and, properly understood, do not teach either polytheism or pantheism. Not only do they furnish the one true key to the past, but they anticipate all future developments of thought. They have forecast all the recent discoveries of science, including the steam engines, railways, buses, ocean liners, and electric lights of today! In them are set forth the basic principles of such sciences as physics and chemistry. The Vedas are therefore the ideal charts or blueprints of nature; there is an exact correspondence between them and the structure of the world.

Two branches of the Arya Samaj now exist. One is liberal, the other conservative. Both engage in educational and philanthropic work throughout north India. In their schools modern science, "based on the Vedas," is taught. Their adherents number perhaps a half-million.*

---

* A related but unclassifiable modern religious movement is *Theosophy.* Though this movement was founded in New York City, its headquarters since 1878 have been in India, where its real inspiration lies. The realization of its aim—the establishment of a real brotherhood amongst all peoples—is held to be dependent on an esoteric, ancient wisdom, expressed in the Vedanta, and transmitted

3. *The Ramakrishna movement,* or the response of tolerance and inclusion. The broad-minded acceptance of the essence of the Western religious tradition and its inclusion in the teachings of Hinduism may be seen very clearly in the life and opinions of perhaps the outstanding Hindu saint and seer of the nineteenth century, called Ramakrishna.* Born a Brahmin in Bengal, he followed the family tradition in becoming one of the priests of a Kali temple near Calcutta. With a spiritual hunger that was not appeased by the performance of his priestly functions, he longed for an immediate experience of the divine. He concentrated on the image of Kali, the Divine Mother. In gazing at her image he experienced trance (samadhi) not once but many times and with increasing intensity, often seeing her move and come to him. He understood from the first that this was but one way of knowing God. He set out to try all the other ways. In a twelve-year period he meditated like a yogi, worshiped like a bhakta, practiced Jainism, Buddhism, and shaktism, and experienced the reality both of Brahman without attributes (the impersonal Brahman) and Brahman with attributes (i.e., the personal God). Dressed like a Muslim, he prayed until he knew God as Allah. He turned to Christianity and found God in Christ. God also became real to

---

through "masters" or "Mahatmas" who appear from age to age. These "great souls" have occult powers which give them unique control over their own bodies and over natural forces. Under their guidance humanity, bound to the ever-turning wheel of reincarnation by the Law of Karma, will someday gain happiness—in a world which will drink as one from the one wonderful Fountain of Wisdom from which all religions have drawn their hitherto partial truths. Two women have been outstanding in the leadership of the Theosophical Society, Madam Blavatsky, its co-founder (along with Colonel Olcott), and its English president, Mrs. Annie Besant. Dreamy, fanciful, and tolerant, the Theosophists have defended prophecy, second sight, Hindu idol worship, and caste. The Society has done some useful educational work in India, Mrs. Besant being the founder of Benares Hindu University. Today it lends its support to Indian nationalism. This is natural enough, for Theosophy is, in spite of its professed hospitality to all religions, Hindu at heart.

* This was his title; his original name was Gadadhar Chatterji.

him as Rama, as Krishna, as Sita, as Muhammad. All religions were to him different ways to God, and all creatures were God in so many different forms. He made friends with the members of the Brahmo Samaj; Keshab Chandra Sen particularly befriended him. He once told the latter, in a typical expression of conviction:

"Everything is in the mind. Bondage and freedom are in the mind. You can dye the mind with any color you wish. It is like a piece of clean white linen: dip it in red and it will be red, in blue it will be blue, in green it will be green, or any other color. Do you not see that if you study English, English words will come readily to you? Again, if a pandit studies Sanskrit, he will readily quote verse from Sacred Books. If you keep your mind in evil company, your thoughts, ideas, and words will be colored with evil; but keep in the company of Bhaktas, then your thoughts, ideas and words will be of God. The mind is everything."[N1]

A revealing bit of reminiscence is the following:

One day I went to the Zoological Garden in Calcutta. I desired to see the lion, but when I beheld him, I lost all sense-consciousness and went into samadhi. Those who were with me wished to show me the other animals, but I replied: "I saw everything when I saw the king of beasts. Take me home." The strength of the lion had aroused in me the consciousness of the omnipotence of God and had lifted me above the world of phenomena.

Another day I went to the parade ground to see the ascension of a balloon. Suddenly my eyes fell upon a young English boy leaning against a tree. The very posture of his body brought before me the vision of the form of Krishna and I went into samadhi.

Again I saw a woman wearing a blue garment under a tree. She was a harlot. As I looked at her, instantly the ideal of Sita appeared before me! . . . For a long time I remained motionless. I worshiped all women as representatives of the Divine Mother.[N2]

Typical of the inclusiveness of his teaching is this parable concerning the various aspects of God:

There was a man who worshiped Shiva but hated all other deities. One day Shiva appeared to him and said, "I shall not be pleased with thee so long as thou hatest the other gods." The man was inexorable. After a few days Shiva again appeared to him and said, "I shall never be pleased with thee so long as thou hatest." The man kept silent. After a few days Shiva again appeared to him. This time he appeared as Hari-har, namely, one side of his body was that of Shiva, and the other side that of Vishnu. The man was half pleased and half displeased. He laid his offerings on the side representing Shiva, and did not offer anything to the side representing Vishnu. Then Shiva said, "Thy bigotry is unconquerable. I, by assuming this dual aspect, tried to convince thee that all gods and goddesses are but various aspects of the one Absolute Brahman."P

An organized group of disciples gathered round him during the last six years of his life, led by a young student of the law who became his successor, under the name of Swami Vivekananda. A brilliant speaker and ardent apologist for the Vedanta, Vive-kananda, after Ramakrishna's death, founded the Ramakrishna movement and spread it all over the world. He was the spokesman for Hinduism at the Parliament of Religions in Chicago in 1893, where he made a great impression that electrified India. He was instrumental in founding Vedanta societies in New York and other American cities. He also founded Ramakrishna centers in Europe, on the Ganges, and in the Himalayas. A marked result of his success in interpreting Hinduism to the world was a revival of interest in the Vedanta in India itself, an interest that has continued to the present time.

4. *Secularism,* or the acceptance of science and technology and the rejection of all religion. Though most Hindus exult in the "spirituality" of India, there has been in the last century a pronounced drift toward materialism and secularism. This has caused great concern among the traditionalists of India. Under the influence of modern trends of thought, some intellectuals are showing less and less interest in organized religion. They view it coldly as a mass of superstition built around an antiquated view of life and the world. They condemn its pessimistic tone, its world-denying attitude. Observing religion and religious men with more detachment and critical judgment than has ever before been possible in India, thousands have ceased to believe in the old Hindu Dharma and its ceremonies. And yet in many cases, even though religious convictions have been given up, the attitude of belief has been maintained for family and social reasons.

Of late, Western humanism and new departures in ideology like Marxism have increased the process of religious dissolution. In some circles, especially where Communism has penetrated, a new attitude of de-fiant atheism has been voiced. However prepared one may be to hear it, one is nevertheless startled by the knowledge that young Hindus have written for publi-cation: "Of all the people in the world it is we In-dians that require more and more materialism. We have had too much religion."Q

B. SOCIAL REFORMS. Not only have there been changes in intellectual outlook; the past century has also seen, as our sketch of the Brahmo Samaj must have indicated, vigorous advocacy of far-reaching social changes. This has been especially true of pro-posed changes in caste and marriage laws, regulations which from their beginnings have constituted major sources of social and religious difficulty.

1. *Caste problems.* In ancient India the rigidity of the caste system was predicated upon the presumed finality of the economic structure, then relatively simple. But the social order could not be kept simple; it became more and more complex. Accordingly, the castes of ancient times virtually broke up, and the many so-called functional castes in reality superseded them. As one authority tells us:

There is a separate caste, or group of castes, for every one of the occupations that were followed in earlier times before the introduction of machinery. . . . They include numerous groups of ordinary cultivators; . . . of artisans such as . . . potters, goldsmiths, blacksmiths, workers in brass and bell-metal, tailors, cloth-printers and dyers, etc.; of village servants, such as cowherds, barbers, washer-men, watchmen, and scavengers; and various other occu-pations, such as . . . boatmen, fishermen, cattle-breeders, musicians, actors, salt- and earth-workers, rice-huskers, hunters, fowlers, etc.R

As can well be imagined, industrialization, to the degree that it has been introduced, has produced still further variations in caste structure.

Besides these functional castes there are race castes

(tribal and national groups taken into the Hindu fold), sectarian castes (originating from sects which, ironically enough, rejected the caste system and withdrew from it, only to become yet another caste), and castes formed by invasion, by migration, or by crossing.

The lowest castes have been separated into the "clean" and the "unclean." The clean may be generally grouped under the ancient name of Shudra. They do not follow degrading occupations, are in some sense orthodox in their social and religious practices, and are able, at least on occasion, to engage reputable Brahmins as their priests. The unclean are in general those engaged in a degrading occupation, one involving, say, defiling contacts with dead bodies, human or animal, or entailing sweeping up the dirt and refuse of the streets. The unclean castes include the leather-cutters and shoemakers, the sweepers or scavengers, the cane-chair makers, and the Kulis (coolies) or unskilled day-laborers.

The members of these unclean and degraded castes have long been regarded by the higher castes as "out-castes" and "untouchables." * Technically, there are more than fifty million of them in India today. In the past their plight was pitiable. Like the despised Chandala of the *Code of Manu,* who was ranked with the village pig and homeless dog, the untouchable was an object of contempt, despised by all. Not his touch only but even his shadow polluted a person of high caste. In some parts of India therefore he was required to announce his presence loudly as he came down the street, in order that those who might be defiled by him might draw their skirts away or move out of reach. Passage through certain public roads and bazaars was forbidden to him. He was not permitted to come within so many feet of certain temples. He was not allowed to draw water from the public wells, but had to go to those used only by his own group. If a Brahmin neared, he had to get off the road into a field. Should he approach the Brahmin too closely, the latter bathed, renewed his sacred cord, and underwent other purification. In some places an out-caste could not take purchases out of the hand of the merchant, but waited until the latter deposited them on the ground and walked away, or tossed them to him. It would seem to have been the object of the higher castes to reduce the untouchable to such a beaten, abject creature that he would never so much as attempt to better his lot.*

It is easy to see why Hinduism has witnessed one attempt after another, by persons who have gained fresh insight, to get around untouchability and other restrictions imposed by the caste system, or to get rid of the caste system altogether. These attempts have been mainly of two sorts.

The earliest attempts to deal with caste restrictions were made by heretical thinkers with a large following. Converts were invited to give up their caste positions, retire from the world, and join a new religious fellowship, a brotherhood of monks in which caste distinctions were erased. Jainism and Buddhism furnish the best instances of this attempt to deal with caste by saying "Come ye out from among them." And yet, lay members who did not enter the circle of monks continued to live under the old caste regulations. Not only did no real reform of the caste system result, but the lay members married and gave in marriage according to the old caste laws, and this led to the entrenchment of caste rather than to its opposite, except only among those who actually retired from the world to monasteries. More pronounced social effects occurred when a religious leader, inspired by a revelation, formed a new sect in which all converts, as equals in the sight of God no matter what their previous caste affiliations had been, were free to eat, visit, and intermarry with other members of the new sect. But because they could not marry outside the sect, either because they did not desire to

---

* Technically speaking, the out-castes are of no caste. They are "pariahs," unorganized, casteless people "outside the pale." This was quite true of them in ancient times. But the out-castes in course of time organized themselves along caste lines. A score of such "castes" now exists, as our quotation on functional castes indicates.

* It will be remembered that the higher castes invoked the Law of Karma to justify this morally; the untouchable was suffering retribution for past sins.

do so or could not arrange it, the new sect in time became to all intents and purposes just another caste. The Shiva-worshiping Lingayats of Bombay and southern India, numbering nearly three million members, and the Baishtams of Bengal furnish excellent examples of this type of protest against the Brahmin-dominated caste system.*

A second type of assault on the caste system sought its reform from within. This is a comparatively recent type of reform, and is usually motivated by a high social idealism, directly or indirectly influenced by Christianity and studies of Western social organization. One liberal proposal, with which Mahatma Gandhi was identified, may be summed up thus: let occupations be hereditary (on a kind of guild principle) but let the other restrictions be done away. Especially should untouchability be abolished.

Since his death, Mahatma Gandhi has finally prevailed. Hindu India's Constituent Assembly late in 1948 abolished untouchability and forbade its practice "in any form." What is on the statute books, however, will probably be a long time in being realized, for as the United States can bear witness, integration is a slow social process.

What has come to pass is that the political leaders of India are reacting constructively to the common-sense realization that the old order is disintegrating under modern industrialized and mechanized conditions of society. The old-time exclusiveness of the castes is crumbling away. The unavoidable mixing of high and low caste people in the trains and at railroad stations has made it a modern convention that a man of high caste may relax his observance of the old rules while on a journey, provided he is unbendingly strict when he is in his own village. While traveling he may sit beside persons whose nearness would defile him at home. In a big hotel he is not required to be as particular as he once had to be about the food and drink served to him, for he cannot demand

that every dish be prepared only by ritualistically clean hands.

In the rural parts of India a practical solution for problems of this kind is to refer them to the local governing council—the *panchayat*—and submit to its decision. The central government encourages this as a form of village democracy. See picture overleaf.

The masses of the people in the congested cities are meanwhile being shaken out of the grooves in which their lives have run for so many generations. Changes even in village life, although less pronounced, are following upon the growth of modern trade and the increasing industrialization of the country. Century-old village crafts are no longer being pursued because mills, mines, and factories are driving them out of business. People are deserting their traditional occupations for new and more profitable vocations. A man's caste now less certainly suggests his occupation. Thus change has entered the very heart of the caste system.

2. *Child-marriage and widowhood.* Child-marriage has existed in India for many centuries. It is usually traced to a family law, going back to the fifth century B.C., which required the marriage of all girls before puberty. This law (only imperfectly observed until eight or nine hundred years ago) may have originated out of a desire to forestall romantic attachments between young people of different castes, but there were other factors in the situation. For one thing, the old caste law prohibiting marriages outside of one's caste made it urgent that fathers search out eligible girls for their sons as soon as possible, lest there be none left; so parents took to betrothing their children when they were but a few months old, and marriage was frequently celebrated when bride and groom were only seven or eight years old. Another factor—ultimately important—was the great practical usefulness of child-marriage to the family system, insofar as it helped to keep the family group united. Daughters-in-law coming into the family in the late teens were comparatively hard to assimilate to a family's fixed habits; but a bride of eight could easily be molded and fitted into the family routine

---

* The above description applies to the *beginnings* of a religious movement, not to its whole history. The Lingayats began as a casteless community, but now have their own castelike subdivisions.

Session of an Indian panchayat. In the compound of an old temple in the Kulu Hills, the elders of a village meet to discuss its problems, judge its disputes, and assess penalties when necessary—an ancient form of democracy at the local level. (Courtesy of the Information Service of India.)

to become an integral part of it. From this point of view child-marriage became a demand of the patri-archal family system. To this day, as a result, many Hindu wives hardly remember having lived anywhere else than with the family of their husbands.

A tragic consequence of the very early marriages has been the widowhood, through the death of boy-husbands, of many virgin child-wives, who, according to the *Code of Manu,* may never remarry, and there-fore must spend long years of unhappy subjection to the members of the husband's family, with no hope of being regarded as anything but a burden on the family and no prospect of being given a higher status than that of a servant obliged to work if she wishes to eat.*

* There are more than five hundred thousand child widows under fifteen years of age in India. It should be said, however, that the unorthodox lower classes have not always followed the higher castes in forbidding the remar-riage of widows, and so the situation described in this and the following paragraphs does not universally exist.

Widowers are not so unfortunate. They may re-marry, if they can find a suitable bride. But this has often led to unequal marriages between middle-aged men and child-wives, it being impossible for the men to contract themselves to widows or to find unmarried women of their own age.

Until recently, this situation was shrugged off as inevitable and unavoidable, but, largely through the criticisms of Christian missionaries, the protests of Hindu reformers, and the adverse reports of medical authorities, an acute consciousness of the problem has been aroused among Hindus. The government, after an experimental trial with laws progressively lifting the age of consent, passed in 1930 the Child Mar-riage Restraint Bill, which made marriage of girls under fourteen and of boys under eighteen illegal, but the law was confined to what was then called British India. Today the whole of India is feeling the effect of a Marriage Act passed by the Indian Parlia-ment that restores the ancient practice of postponing the full consummation of any marriage until after puberty.

C. RECENT CHANGE. 1. *Religious liberalism and reaction.* In recent decades two Hindus have earnestly sought an integration of *Eastern Religions and Western Thought* (the title of a book by one of them).* One, the late Aurobindo Ghose, a Bengali Brahmin, abandoned nationalistic politics for philosophy, in order to urge the possibility that "integral yoga," as he called it, may enable man to become a superman. In the eternal shakti he saw the downward movement of Reality (i.e., of the infinite, all-inclusive Brahman) in "descents, eruptions, messages or revelations." After this has had its spiritual effect on the human mind, there can be an "ascent" from the ordinary human to the superman level of being.

Dr. Sarvepalli Radhakrishnan, former president of India, was an internationally known scholar and lecturer, whose cordiality to Western religion and philosophy was accompanied by consistent stress on mysticism as the very heart of religion. Consequently, Hinduism emerges in his numerous writings as the greatest of the religions. He defended Hinduism against the criticism that it is "non-ethical" (a criticism made by Albert Schweitzer) by emphasizing the moral growth that is the necessary preparation for mystic union with the ultimately real and by pointing to the duty of applying the spiritual lessons of religion in social and political activity.

Opposing this cordiality to the West are such groups supporting orthodox Hinduism as the Mahasabha and the Rashtriya Swayamasevak Sangh (the "National Service Organization"), which advocate making India officially a Hindu state. It was a member of the second group that assassinated Mahatma Gandhi.

Traditionally, Hindus have been tolerant of other faiths, but although this is still the case, paradoxically the prevailing view throughout India now is that conversion from one religion to another should

* It is by the late S. Radhakrishnan (see bibliography).

be discouraged.* One's native religion is always the best. But efforts to embody this principle in the law have not succeeded at this date (1969).

2. *Political change.* To pursue this topic in detail would take us far beyond the scope of this volume; yet not to pursue it at all would, on the other hand, narrow our study unduly; for it is not possible to divorce Indian politics from religion.

In the generation-long, organized struggle of the peoples of India for self-determination, three factors have been of supreme importance. The first is the well-founded feeling of the leading minds of India that in the intellectual sphere they have established their competence to engage in the life of reason on at least an equality with the world's greatest. Why then should they be kept in the role of a subject people?

The second factor is the personality and leadership of Mahatama Gandhi. With great patience, and a moral imagination not matched by any other individual in our time, he planned and led the political struggle for national self-determination. He fought with Hindu weapons—non-violent resistance, soulforce, a baffling use of tolerance and inclusive good will when confronted with strong opposition, but firm insistence on *swadeshi* (loyalty to one's own inherited

* Conversion is viewed either as an effect of proselytization or as a "migration" which as its social consequence leaves the convert culturally alien and displaced, breaks up homes, separates kinsfolk, and unsettles the social and national order. Memories of Muslim pressures toward conversion and of British favor toward missionaries, who, as an extreme view puts it, "invaded" India and other Asiatic countries as "an integral part of the domination of the white races over Asia," have reinforced the nationalist desire to preserve Indian unity and prevent "religious nationalism" from developing among minority religious groups, e.g., the Sikhs and some aboriginal peoples under the influence of Lutheran and Roman Catholic missions. When Hindus turn from these objective considerations to the subjective factors in conversion, they tend to make a distinction between yielding to the improper outside pressures of proselytization and the experience of genuine conversion, which they are inclined to view sympathetically. Conversion, they think, if it is from inward conviction, is not so likely to alienate the convert from his Hindu heritage, since, subjectively considered, all religions are essentially the same.[5]

religion and way of life). With astonishing practicality as to means but unyielding idealism in matters of principle, he morally guided the often divergent elements in the Congress Party up to and beyond the agreement with the British Raj which established national self-determination for Hindu India.

The third factor has been the mounting sense of deep difference between Hindu and Muslim. At first the Hindus refused to believe that such a difference existed, but the highly organized Pakistan movement proved at last convincing, and the Hindus consented to the formation of the separate Muslim state. It is hardly necessary to add that there was tragedy in this not only for Gandhi and Nehru, the leaders of the nationalist cause in India, but for millions of Muslims, Sikhs, and Hindus who suffered death and displacement when partition came in 1947. Gandhi himself was assassinated in the aftermath.

But one may be permitted to reflect, in conclusion, that so far as Hinduism is concerned, incalculable consequences were bound to flow from so startling a circumstance as this: a great religion of escape has produced leaders in this modern day who have not sought Nirvana in the solitude of the forests, but have rather come forth into the world to engage realistically and practically in the task of human betterment by social action. The leaders of the other great religions of the world cannot fail to see how great is the portent of this *volte-face* of the most influential recent leaders of the Hindu world.

SUGGESTIONS FOR FURTHER READING

ARNOLD, SIR EDWIN. *The Song Celestial* (The Bhagavad Gita). A good current edition: Routledge & Kegan Paul, Ltd., London, 1961

AUROBINDO, SRI. *The Synthesis of Yoga.* New York, Aurobindo Library, 1950

BANERJEA, J. N. *The Development of Hindu Iconography.* University of Calcutta, 1956

BROWN, D. MACKENZIE. *The White Umbrella: Indian Political Thought from Manu to Gandhi.* University of California Press pb, 1958

BÜHLER, GEORG, TR. *The Code of Manu.* Vol. XXV, *Sacred Books of the East* series, 1886

CHANDAVARKAR, G. A. *A Manual of Hindu Ethics.* 3rd rev. ed., Poona, Oriental Book Agency, 1925

CHATTERJEE, S. *The Fundamentals of Hinduism.* Calcutta, Das Gupta & Co., 1950

DASGUPTA, SURENDRANATH. *A History of Indian Philosophy.* 5 vols., Cambridge University Press, 1922–1955

DUTT, M. N. *A Prose English Translation of the Mahabharata.* 3 vols., Calcutta, M. N. Dutt, 1895–1905

EDGERTON, FRANKLIN, TR. *The Bhagavad Gita.* Harvard Oriental Series, 1944; Harper Torchbook pb, 1964

ELIADE, MIRCEA. *Yoga: Immortality and Freedom.* Pantheon Books, 1958

ELIOT, SIR CHARLES. *Hinduism and Buddhism.* 3 vols., Routledge and Kegan Paul, 1954. Earlier ed., Edward Arnold, 1921

FARQUHAR, J. N. *An Outline of the Religious Literature of India.* Oxford, 1920

GANDHI, MAHATMA. *An Autobiography; or The Story of My Experiments with Truth.* Tr. by Mahadev Desai. Ahmadabad, Navajivan Press, 1927; Beacon Press, 1959

GHURYE, G. S. *Caste and Class in India.* 2nd ed., Bombay, Popular Book Depot, 1957

———. *Indian Sadhus.* Bombay, Popular Book Depot, 1953

GROWSE, F. S., TR. *The Ramayana of Tulsi Das.* 7th ed., Allahabad, Ram Narain Lal, 1937

HIRIYANNA, M. *Outlines of Indian Philosophy*. Allen and Unwin, 1932

KANE, PANDURANG VAMAN. *History of Dharmasastra*. 5 vols., Poona, Bhandarkar Oriental Research Institute, 1930–1962

KEITH, A. B. *The Samkhya System*. Calcutta, Association Press, 1918

LEWIS, OSCAR. *Village Life in North India*. University of Illinois Press, 1958

MACNICOL, N. *Indian Theism from the Vedic to the Muhammaden Period*. Oxford University Press, 1915

MASCARO, JUAN, TR. *The Bhagavad Gita*. Penguin Books pb, 1962

MONIER-WILLIAMS, M. *Brahmanism and Hinduism*. Macmillan, 1891

MORGAN, K. W., ED. *Religion of the Hindus*. Ronald Press, 1953

NEHRU, JAWAHARLAL. *Toward Freedom: An Autobiography*. John Day, 1941; Beacon Press, 1958

NIKHILANANDA, SWAMI, TR. *Prophet of New India*. Abridged from the *Gospel of Ramakrishna*. Harper, 1948

O'MALLEY, L. S. S. *Popular Hinduism*. Macmillan, 1935

RADHAKRISHNAN, S. *Eastern Religions and Western Thought*. Oxford University Press, 1940; Galaxy Book pb, 1959

RADHAKRISHNAN, S. AND MOORE, CHARLES, EDS. *Source Book in Indian Philosophy*. Princeton University Press, 1957

RAI, LALA LAJPAT. *The Arya Samaj, an Account of its Origin, Doctrines, and Activities, with a Biographical Sketch of the Founder*. Longmans, Green & Co., 1915

RENOU, LOUIS. *Hinduism*. George Braziller, Inc., 1961; Washington Square Press Book, 1963

ROLLAND, ROMAIN. *Prophets of the New India*. Albert and Charles Boni, 1930

SARMA, D. S. *The Renaissance of Hinduism*. Benares Hindu University Press, 1944

SHASTRI, S. *History of the Brahmo Samaj*. 2 vols., Calcutta, R. Chatterji, 1911–1912

STEVENSON, MRS. S. *The Hindu View of Life*. Macmillan, 1927

———. *Rites of the Twice-Born*. Oxford, 1920

WOOD, JAMES H., TR. *The Yoga Sutras of Patanjali*. Harvard University Press, 1913

WOODRUFFE, SIR JOHN. *Shakti and Shakta*. Luzac, 1929

ZIMMER, H. *Myth and Symbol in Indian Art and Civilization*. Pantheon, 1946; Harper Torchbook pb, 1962

———. *Philosophies of India*. Pantheon, 1951; Meridian Books pb, 1956

8 Sikhism: A Study in Syncretism

SIKHISM IS a little known religion in Europe and America. It was for a long time known to few save British colonial administrators and army officers, who thought it a way of life useful to them because its adherents, being neither Hindu nor Muslim, although at certain points they were a little of both, thus stood apart from the two major religious groups. Colonial administrators were gratified at the combination of qualities that made Sikhs ideal police recruits: they were a stalwart, meat-eating people of exceptionally fine physique, trained to meet the hazards of war and violence with fierce courage, and at the same time not religiously abhorrent to Hindus or Muslims.

Another reason for Sikhism's obscure fame is that it is one of the world's youngest faiths. Its founding dates only from the fifteenth century.

It is not in any absolute sense new. Its basic tenet —monotheism—coincides with Muslim conviction; many of the other doctrines it professes are in more or less agreement with Hinduism. Indeed, Sikhism is an outstanding example of a working syncretism, one of the few that have ever proved viable.

On the other hand, Sikhism is not simply two old religions made one. It is, rather, a genuinely fresh start. Its followers believe it to have been authenticated by a new divine revelation to the founder, Nanak. It is therefore felt by its adherents to be the opposite of an intellectual reconstruction of faith arrived at after an academic examination of the articles of older religions. God—"The True Name"— appeared to Nanak and charged him with a redemptive mission to a lost world. It is thus evident that the religion of the Sikhs is not to be confused with the rationalistic syncretisms whose adherents have been engaged in a reworking of philosophy rather than in a revival of religion, properly conceived.

I The Life and Work of Nanak

The Historical Antecedents of Nanak

Before Nanak appeared on the historical scene, the ground was prepared for him by men who had no thought of founding a new religion but who saw a need of cleansing and purifying what seemed to them a decadent Hinduism. Their recurrent efforts at reform were the indirect effects of the severe and militant monotheism of the Muslims, who had reached India in the eighth century A.D. and wielded an enormous power. By the eleventh century the Muslims (known in India as Musalmans) firmly dominated the whole of northwest India, and then, with remorseless pressure, extended their suzerainty over most of India. As early as in the twelfth century a Hindu reformer-poet called Jaidev used the phrase that was to be the key word of Sikhism at a later date. He taught that the practice of religious ceremonials and austerities was of no value compared with "the pious repetition of God's name." This is an Islamic teaching adapted to Hindu use. Two centuries later another reformer, by the name of Ramananda, established a Vishnuite sect that sought to purge itself of certain Hindu beliefs and practices. He excited great discussion by "liberating" himself and his disciplies both from accepted Hindu restrictions of social contacts between castes and from prohibitions against meat-eating. But his chief claim to fame today rests upon the fact that he had a follower greater than himself, who in turn won the admiration of the founder of Sikhism. This disciple—Kabir (1440–1518)—has given his name to sects still flourishing in India, the Kabir-panthis (those who follow the path of Kabir). Kabir, reared by Muslims, had a hatred of idols, and, like the Hindu poet Namdev a generation before him, he scorned to believe that God can dwell in an image of stone. He took no satisfaction in the external forms of religion—rituals, scriptures, pilgrimages, asceticism, bathing in the Ganges, and such like—if these are unaccompanied by inward sincerity or morality of life. As a monotheist, he declared that the love of God was sufficient to free anyone of any class or race from the Law of Karma. In other words, the all-sufficient means of bringing an end to reincarnation is the simple, complete love of God that absorbs the soul into the Absolute. He denied the special authority of the Hindu Vedas, wrote in the vernacular rather than in Sanskrit, attacked both Brahmins and

Muslims for their barren ritualism, and set up in place of their standards of belief the person of the inspired spiritual leader and teacher (the guru), apart from whom, he held, the right life-attitudes cannot be gained. Clearly, a combination of Hindu and Muslim elements appears in Kabir's teaching.

Upon a similar foundation of ethical monotheism Nanak was to rear his own doctrinal position.

Nanak's Life and Work

As nearly as the facts can be ascertained, Nanak was born in 1469 A.D. at the village of Talwandi, about thirty miles from Lahore, the capital of the Punjab. His parents were Hindus belonging to a mercantile caste locally called Khatri (probably an offshoot of the ancient Kshatriya caste), but they were comparatively low in the economic scale, his father being a village accountant and farmer. His mother, a pious woman, was very devoted to her husband and son. The town of Talwandi, at the time of the birth of Nanak, was governed by a petty noble named Rai Bular, who was of Hindu stock but had been converted to the Muslim faith. He maintained, however, a tolerant attitude toward the adherents of the old faith and encouraged attempts to reconcile the two creeds. Nanak was in due time to excite his friendly interest.

The stories of Nanak's youth are typical examples of historical fact transmuted into wonder-tales. It is said that he was a precocious youth, a poet by nature, and so much given to meditation and religious speculation as to be worthless in the capacity of herdsman or store-keeper, two occupations chosen for him by his solicitous parents. His father agreed with some relief to his acceptance of a brother-in-law's offer of a government job in Sultanpur. Nanak set out for the district capital. During business hours he worked, it is claimed, hard and capably. Meanwhile he married and had two children, but he spent the evenings singing hymns to his Creator. His friend, the minstrel Mardana, a Muslim who was to have an important part to play in his career, came on from Talwandi to join him. Gradually they became the center of a small group of seekers.

The inward religious excitement of Nanak was approaching a crisis. Suddenly there came a decisive experience, which was described over a hundred years later in terms of a theophany.*

One day after bathing in the river Nanak disappeared in the forest, and was taken in a vision to God's presence. He was offered a cup of nectar, which he gratefully accepted. God said to him, "I am with thee. I have made thee happy, and also those who shall take thy name. Go and repeat Mine, and cause others to do likewise. Abide uncontaminated by the world. Practice the repetition of My name, charity, ablutions, worship, and meditation. I have given thee this cup of nectar, a pledge of My regard."[A1]

Modern Sikh scholars are convinced that this story is a reconstruction of the original experience by use of symbols of spiritual events, that the cup of nectar was in fact the thrilling revelation of God as True Name, and that the words attributed to God perceptively interpret a profound experience of being called to prophecy. They find in Nanak's own hymns a better account:

> I was a minstrel out of work;
> The Lord gave me employment.
> The Mighty One instructed me:
> "Night and day, sing my praise!"
> The Lord did summon this minstrel
> To his High Court;
> On me He bestowed the robe of honor
> Of those who exalt Him.
>
> On me He bestowed the Nectar in a Cup,
> The Nectar of His True and Holy Name.[B1]

Under the stress of his feelings Nanak is said to have then uttered the preamble of the Japji, a composition that is silently repeated as a morning devotional rite by every devout Sikh to this day.

* Kartar Singh, in his *Life of Guru Nanak Dev* (Lahore Book Shop, 1958, p. 62), traces the story to "the Old Chronicle (*Puratan Janamsakhi*), written about the year 1635 A.D., i.e., in the time of Guru Hargobind. In this chronicle the writer tried to describe the events of the spiritual world in the language of this world."

"There is but one God whose name is True, the Creator, devoid of fear and enmity, immortal, unborn, self-existent, great and bountiful.

"The True One was in the beginning, the True One was in the primal age.

"The True One is, was, O Nanak,* and the True One also shall be."[A2]

After three days Nanak emerged from the forest.

He remained silent for one day, and the next he uttered the pregnant announcement, "There is no Hindu and no Musalman."[A3]

This was the opening statement of what was to become a wide-ranging campaign of evangelism that had as its object the purification and reconciliation of religious faiths.

Setting out on an extended tour of north and west India, which lengthened into years of wandering, he took as his sole companion his friend, the minstrel Mardana, who, while Nanak was singing his evangelistic hymns, played an accompaniment upon a small stringed instrument called a rebeck. The far-traveling pair visited the chief places of Hindu pilgrimage, including Hardwar, Delhi, Benares, the Temple of Jaganatha, and holy places in the Himalaya Mountains. Undaunted by the rebuffs and hostility of religious authorities, Nanak sang and preached in marketplaces, open squares, and on street corners, pausing only to make a few converts before proceeding on his way, apparently in faith that God, the True Name, would cause the seed he broadcast to spring up and bear fruit of itself. He devised for his own wear a motley garb that at sight proclaimed his attempt to combine the two great faiths. In addition to the Hindu lower garment (*dhoti*) and sandals:

He put on a mango-colored jacket, over which he threw a white safa or sheet. On his head he carried the hat of a Musalman Qalander,† while he wore a necklace [rosary] of bones, and imprinted a saffron mark on his forehead in the style of the Hindus.[A4]

* It was the custom of Persian and Indian poets to address themselves by name at the end of their compositions—a kind of oral signature.
† A Muslim anchorite corresponding to the Hindu sannyasi, usually called a dervish.

But it was not until they reached the Punjab that they had any marked success. There groups of Sikhs (literally, disciples) began to form.

Late in life he took Mardana with him, it is said, into the heart of the Arab world. In the blue dress of Muslim pilgrims, staff in hand, and carrying cups for their ablutions and carpets for prayer, they eventually reached Mecca after many months. According to tradition:

When the Guru arrived, weary and footsore, he went and sat in the great mosque where pilgrims were engaged in their devotions. His disregard of Moslem customs soon involved him in difficulties. When he lay down to sleep at night he turned his feet toward the Kaaba. An Arab priest kicked him and said, "Who is this sleeping infidel? Why hast thou, O sinner, turned thy feet towards God?" The Guru replied, "Turn my feet in the direction in which God is not." Upon this the priest seized the Guru's feet and dragged them in the opposite direction.[A5]

He turned home to India. At Kartarpur, Mardana fell ill and died. He had grown old and was wearied out with wandering. Nanak, now sixty-nine years old, did not long survive him. Knowing his end was drawing near, and with his eye upon the future growth of his following of Sikhs, he made a decision that was to have far-reaching consequences. He determined to appoint a successor. His own sons were not worthy; they had not shown spiritual qualities. So he appointed a disciple, Angad, to be his successor.

In October 1538 he laid him down to die. The tradition says that Sikhs, Hindus, and Muslims gathered round him, mourning together. The Muslim converts, so runs the tale (which is also told of Kabir), said they would bury him after his death; the Sikhs of Hindu extraction said they would cremate him. When they referred the matter to the Guru, he said: "Let the Hindus place flowers on my right, and the Musalmans on my left. They whose flowers are found fresh in the morning may have the disposal of my body." So saying, he drew the sheet over his head and became still. When the sheet was removed the next morning, "there was nothing found beneath it. The flowers on both sides were in bloom."[A6]

Thus, even in death, Nanak reconciled Hindu and Muslim.

II Nanak's Teaching

The doctrinal position of Nanak has a surprisingly simple form, in spite of its blending of the insights of two widely differing faiths. The consistency is due to adherence to a single central concept—the sovereignty of the one God, the Creator.

Nanak called his god the True Name because he meant to avoid any delimiting term for Him, like Allah, Rama, Shiva, or Ganesha. He taught that the True Name is manifest in manifold ways and in manifold places and is known by manifold names, but He is eternally one, the sovereign and omnipotent God. If any name is to be used, let it be Hari (the Kindly), for that is a good description of His character. At the same time, God inscrutably predestinates all creatures and ordains that the highest of the creatures, man, be served by the lower creation. (This removed the Hindu taboo against meat-eating.) In these articles of Nanak's creed the Muslim element is evident.

On the other hand, Nanak subscribed to the Hindu doctrine of maya, but he did not give maya the connotation of pure illusion. By it he intended to say that material objects, even though they have reality as expressions of the Creator's eternal Truth, may build around those who live wholly in the mundane world a "wall of falsehood" that prevents them from seeing the truly Real. God, he held, created matter as a veil about himself that only spiritual minds can penetrate. By its mystic power, maya "maketh Truth dark and increaseth worldly attachment."[B2]

Maya, the mythical Goddess,
Sprang from the One, and her womb brought forth
Three acceptable disciples of the One:
Brahmā, Vishnu and Shiva.
Brahmā, it is said, bodies forth the world,
Vishnu it is who sustains it;
Shiva the destroyer who absorbs,

He controls death and judgment.
God makes them to work as He wills,
He sees them ever, they see Him not:
That of all is the greatest wonder.[B3]

God, ultimately, is the true creator, not maya.

God Himself created the world and Himself gave names
to things.
He made Maya by His power.[A7]

The world is, then, immediately real but ultimately
unreal. "The world is very transient, like a flash of
lightning,"[A8] Nanak sang, and did not shrink from
the parallel thought that man is in like case. Retaining the Hindu doctrine of the transmigration of souls,
together with its usual corollary the Law of Karma,
Nanak warned his hearers not to prolong the round
of their births by living apart from God and accumulating karma. Let them think only of God, endlessly
repeat his name,* and be absorbed into Him; in such
absorption alone lies the bliss known to Hindus as
Nirvana. For salvation is not going to Paradise after
a last judgment, but absorption—individuality-extin-
guishing absorption—in God, the True Name.

Nanak swung away from the firm Muslim emphasis
on divine transcendence to a Hindu insistence that
God pervades the world and is in man's heart.

Search not for the True One afar off; He is in every
heart, and is known by the Guru's instruction.[A9]

With almost a Quaker's distrust of ritual and ceremonial, he denounced Hindus and Muslims for going
through the forms of worship without really thinking
about God. In fact, he felt that ritual was a positive
distraction; it turned the current of men's thoughts
away from God to mere forms and motions of worship. On every hand he found illustrations of his
thesis. In the first Muslim religious service that he

---

* Sikhs call this Nam- (Name-) Marg to distinguish it
from the Hindu Karma Marga. To act always in the
name and for the sake of God is better, they say, than
Karma Marga, which Hindus tend to follow for self-
seeking motives instead of in the spirit of the *Bhagavad
Gita,* i.e., without thinking of rewards.

attended after his call to be the Guru of God, he is
said to have laughed aloud. The Muslims could
scarcely wait till the service was over before pounc-
ing on him for an explanation.

The Guru replied that immediately before prayer the
Qazi had unloosed a new-born filly. While he ostensibly
performed divine service, he remembered there was a
well in the enclosure, and his mind was filled with apprehension lest the filly should fall into it.[A10]

Therefore the Qazi's prayer was not accepted of God,
Nanak said.

He felt a similar distrust of Hindu rites, going on
pilgrimages, asceticism of the extreme type, and idolatry of any sort. In the last case he not only thought
that idols distracted men's thoughts from God's
reality, but, as he declared with all but Muslim fervor, God could not be contained in an image of wood
or stone. As for pilgrimages, merely repeating the
True Name is equal to bathing at the sixty-eight
places of pilgrimage. In regard to the ascetic retreat
from the world, "Why go searching for God in the
forest? I have found Him at home," Nanak cried.[C1]

Religion consisteth not in a patched coat, or in a Yogi's
staff, or in ashes smeared over the body;
Religion consisteth not in earrings worn, or a shaven
head, or in the blowing of horns. . . .
Religion consisteth not in wanderings to tombs or places
of cremation, or sitting in attitudes of contemplation.
Religion consisteth not in wandering in foreign countries, or in bathing at places of pilgrimage.[A11]

What he meant by religion is expressed in this
injunction to Muslims:

Let compassion be thy mosque,
Let faith be thy prayer mat,
Let honest living be thy Koran,
Let modesty be the rules of observance,
Let piety be the fasts thou keepest;
In such wise strive to be a Muslim:
Right conduct the Ka'ba; Truth the Prophet,
Good deeds thy prayer;
Submission to the Lord's Will thy rosary;
Nanak, if this thou do, the Lord will be thy Protector.[B4]

The good man and the good Sikh is pure in motive and in act, prefers the virtuous, seeks brotherhood with high and low without regard to caste, craves the Guru's word and all divine knowledge as a man craves food, loves his wife and renounces all other women, avoids quarrelsome topics, is not arrogant, does not trample on others, and forsakes evil company, associating instead only with the holy.

Nanak's creed and practice were distinctly conciliatory and irenic, and yet it was the singular fate of the religion he established to be obliged by persecution to change with the years into a vigorously self-defensive faith, its adherents resorting to the arbitrament of the sword. This is a fascinating story, to which we now turn.

III   The Political History of Sikhism

Nine gurus, as official heads of the Sikh religion, succeeded Nanak, and the body of believers grew.

Of the first four, Guru Amar Das (1552–1574) is typical. He was noted for his humility and freedom from pride of class, saying: "Let no one be proud of his caste. . . . The world is all made out of one clay."[A12] The quietism of early Sikh religion was evident in all he did. The Sikhs of his time lived by the truly pacifist rule: "If anyone ill-treat you, bear it three times, and God Himself will fight for you the fourth time."[D]

But the fifth guru, Guru Arjan (1581–1606), marks a period of transition to something more militant. This was due partly to a changed attitude on the part of the Muslim authorities, and partly within Sikhism itself to the vigor and leadership of the handsome Arjan. In addition to completing the ambitious project of his predecessors—the artificial lake of Amritsar and the Har Mandir (Temple of God) on its island—Arjan did two things of lasting significance. First, he compiled the *Granth*, the Sikh Bible. Realizing that the devotional hymns used by the Sikhs

in their worship were in danger of being lost, he brought them together into one collection. He was himself a talented poet, and half of the collection consisted of hymns of his own composition. The rest were mostly by Nanak, with a number by the second, third, and fourth gurus, and by Jaidev, Namdev, Kabir, and others. This compilation was at once recognized as notable by persons both within and outside the ranks of the Sikh following. The Muslim Emperor Akbar of the Mughal dynasty was told of it by his advisers, who considered it a dangerous infidel work, but Akbar was a tolerant monarch, and after hearing some readings from the Granth declared he discovered no dangerous ideas in it. He even paid Arjan a respectful visit and thus indicated his general approval. But the liberal-minded Akbar was succeeded by his cruel and fanatical son Jahangir, who, on the charge of political conspiracy, had Guru Arjan seized and tortured to death. Before he died, however, Arjan did the second thing whose significance was to be lasting: he left the injunction to his son, Har Govind, to "sit fully armed on his throne, and maintain an army to the best of his ability."[C2]

Guru Har Govind (1606–1645) obeyed the last injunction of his father. At his installation he refused to wear, as too suggestive of quietism, the ordinary turban and necklace that had come down from his predecessors. His intention was clearly expressed: "My *seli* [necklace] shall be a swordbelt, and my turban shall be adorned with a royal aigrette."[A13] He lost no time in suiting his actions to his words. He surrounded himself with an armed bodyguard, built the first Sikh stronghold, and in due time drew to his standard thousands of Sikhs eager for military service. He was able to provide rations and clothing, as well as weapons, out of the moneys in the treasury of the Temple. The Muslim world around him had been getting more and more hostile as the Sikhs, provided now with a capital city and a rich and beautiful temple, began to develop a national feeling. The Sikhs were no longer, from the Muslim point of view, an inconveniently close-knit yet otherwise harmless sect; they were a political and social reality

The golden temple at Amritsar.
On the tiny island in the lake at
Amritsar the temple housing the
Holy Granth, or Sikh scriptures,
receives pilgrims who come to
behold the sacred book under its
jeweled canopy and join in the
worship of God, the True One.
(Courtesy of the United Nations.)

**Sikh pilgrims preparing
for worship.** Before
entering the golden tem-
ple at Amritsar, three
Sikh pilgrims wash their
feet and cleanse their
lips. It is forbidden to
approach the divine
source of truth while
unclean. (Courtesy of
the United Nations.)

that menaced the balance of power in northwest India. So the Muslims began to bestir themselves. And the Sikhs on their part found in themselves the qualities of fighting men. Things did not go too well at first, however. Guru Har Govind fought and was imprisoned by the same Jahangir who had put his father to death, but when, soon after that, Jahangir died, the payment of a fine released him—to fight again.

Peaceful but wary consolidation of Sikh strength marked the rule of the next three gurus, the last of whom was imprisoned and executed by the Emperor Aurangzeb. Then the unequal struggle broke out in renewed military conflict in the time of the tenth guru, Govind Singh (1675–1708). On his accession this guru was called Govind Rai, but he is better known as Govind Singh, Govind the Lion. He found the Sikhs aroused for a major struggle. They were, he declared, not animated by enmity to any man but only fearlessly resolved to declare and defend the Truth. Only if they must would they seek a separate Sikh state. He hoped the Muslims would not force the issue. Meanwhile he exhorted the Sikhs to stand firm in the faith. While he awaited a possible clash of arms, he fortified the spirits of his followers by writing hymns, after the manner of the first gurus, but at times in a very martial style. For example:

I bow to Him who holdeth the arrow in His hand; I bow to the Fearless One;
I bow to the God of gods who is in the present and the future.
I bow to the Scimitar, the two-edged Sword, the Falchion, and the Dagger. . . .
I bow to the Holder of the Mace. . . .
I bow to the Arrow and the Cannon. . . .[C3]

These words are prefaced with the startling invocation:

Hail, hail to the Creator of the world, the Savior of creation, my Cherisher, hail to Thee, O Sword!

These and his other less militant hymns were later compiled into *The Granth of the Tenth Guru* and

made an authoritative supplement to the First (or Adi) Granth. Among them is this moving proclamation of human brotherhood:

One man by shaving his head
Hopes to become a holy monk,
Another sets up as a Yogi
Or some other kind of ascetic.
Some call themselves Hindus;
Others call themselves Musulmans. . .
And yet man is of one race in all the world. . . .
Worship the One God,
For all men the One Divine Teacher.
All men have the same form,
All men have the same soul.[B5]

Of himself and his mission he sang:

For this mission God sent me into the world,
And on the earth I was born as a mortal.
As He spoke to me, I must speak unto men:
Fearlessly I will declare His Truth,
But without enmity to any man.
Those who call me God
Shall fall into the depths of Hell.
Greet me as God's servant only.[B6]

There can be no question of the fact that Govind Singh was thoroughly convinced of his divine authority. When, after months of brooding, the inspiration came to him to institute his greatest innovation, the Khanda di-Pahul or Baptism of the Sword, he felt it was of God. One day after testing the sincerity of five followers, three of whom were from the so-called lower castes, by giving them an opportunity to prove they were willing to die for the faith, he poured water into an iron basin and stirred it with a double-edged sword, mixing in an Indian sweetmeat the while. He then bade each to drink five palmsful of the sweetened water and then sprinkled the water five times on each man's hair and into his eyes. Thus baptized into a new order of life they were made to repeat what became the war-cry of the Sikhs, *Waheguru ji ka Khalsa, Sri Waheguru ji ki Fateh*—"The Pure are of God, and the victory is to God." These men formed the group of the Khalsa or Pure; and they bore the name of Singhs or Lions. They were

241

charged to wear even after the five *K's*: (1) the *Kesh*, or long uncut hair on head and chin, (2) the *Kangha* of comb, (3) the *Kachh* or short drawers, (4) the *Kara* or steel bracelet, and (5) the *Kirpan* or sword. Beyond this, they pledged themselves to worship the one invisible God, to reverence the one visible holy object, the *Granth*, to honor the gurus, to rise before dawn to bathe in cold water and then meditate and pray. They gave up all stimulants, especially alcoholic liquors, and eschewed tobacco. They were encouraged to begin the eating of meat, provided it was from an animal slain in the prescribed manner, that is, by a single stroke of the sword.

Guru Govind himself became a Singh, by obliging the first five neophytes, after he had initiated them, to baptize him in turn. Then he threw the new cult open to men of every class, regardless of caste. To the open distress of the higher castes, many individuals from the lower classes, and even pariahs, flocked to join the guru's organization and, thrilled by the baptism of the sword, were transformed from shrinking untouchables and timid low-caste men into free and fearless soldiers, equal to the best. Clean living and the all-round diet gave them strong physiques; the enthusiasm of a confident faith gave them courage in battle; confident and independent leaders gave them direction.

Not all Sikhs became Singhs. Some remained Nanak-panthis ("Followers of Nanak"), displaying various shades of quietism and remaining dubious of war-making.

Although Govind Singh was successful in fighting off nearby hostile hill chieftains, his struggles with the resourceful Muslim ruler Aurangzeb were without advantage to the Sikhs. The guru lost his four sons on whom his hopes of succession depended, two in battle and two by execution, and the Sikh army was routed. After the doughty Mughal emperor died, Govind Singh was on friendly terms with his successor, Bahadur Shah, only to be himself the next to fall—by the knife of a Muslim assassin in 1708. He had provided, however, for such an event, and told his Sikhs, disappointed as he was in his hopes of succession, that after his death they were to regard the Granth as their guru; there was no need of other leadership than the teaching of the holy book.

The Sikhs were obedient. They have had no human guru since then; instead, they have reverenced the Granth as their one divine authority. At the Golden Temple in Amritsar it daily receives the honors of royalty. "Every morning it is dressed out in costly brocade, and reverently placed on a low throne under a jewelled canopy. Every evening it is made to repose for the night in a golden bed within a sacred chamber, railed off and protected from all profane intrusion by bolts and bars."[E] But though its words, as read from a duplicate copy, resound daily in the temple, it is written in so many languages and archaic dialects that, except for their scholars, the people must learn the meaning from popular expositions and translations into the vernacular.

The political history of Sikhism since Govind Singh's day has been one of great military renown. The Sikhs won many battles, and in due time dominated the whole Punjab. When the British came to subdue them in 1845 and 1848, they put up an exciting struggle. In 1849 the last Sikh ruler, Maharajah Dhulip Singh, surrendered to the victorious British arms, and as a pledge of loyalty gave over to Queen Victoria the world-renowned Koh-i-nur diamond. After that the Sikhs responded to the respect their conquerors felt for them, and never went back on their word to them. When the Indian Mutiny broke out, the Singhs of the Khalsa, remembering the oppressions of the Muslims, rushed to the British colors and helped save India for the British crown. The crown rewarded them with trust. All over the East they were the favorite soldiery and constabulary of the British colonial power. They could be seen in Hong Kong and Shanghai as well as in the nearer areas of Singapore and Burma.

But the Sikhs were not happy. Their frustration became manifest in the tensions between the sects that developed among them. Above all, they mourned the fact that their "slavery" under the British Raj had brought to an end all hope of developing in independence the form of democracy instituted by their gurus, in which the people, as represented in the Panth or General Assembly, were the real sovereign in temporal matters, each Sikh being the equal of any other, while the Granth (and not any one man, however high in authority) was the ultimate and absolute spiritual ruler.*

The partition of India in 1947 was initially a tragedy to the Sikhs. Some of their holy places, including the birthplace of Nanak, were given to Pakistan, and many thousands of Sikhs fled as refugees

* Women also were granted considerable freedom. Sikh religious convocations were thrown open to them, and they were allowed to engage freely in most religious and social observances.

to the towns, Amritsar among them, that were given to India. Some reverted briefly to the role of Lions of the Punjab and turned to violence to relieve their grief and fury. All Sikhs are now within the boundaries of India. Their status within India is not satisfactory to them. Some demand complete political independence; others oppose the formation of a separate Sikh state, believing that Sikhism has a role to play in the development of Indian democracy. The Indian government has recognized the legitimacy of the plea of still others for more autonomy within the Indian Commonwealth and has granted to some six million Sikhs, within what remains of the old Punjab in India, a measure of statehood or home rule.

SUGGESTIONS FOR FURTHER READING

ARCHER, J. C. *The Sikhs.* Princeton University Press, 1946

FIELD, DOROTHY. *The Religion of the Sikhs.* In the *Wisdom of the East* series, John Murray, 1911

GUPTA, H. R. *History of the Sikhs.* Dawson, 1950

KHARTAR SINGH. *The Life of Guru Nanak Dev.* Lahore, 1958

———. *The Life of Guru Gobind Singh.* Rev. and enl., Lahore, 1951

KHUSHWANT SINGH. *The Sikhs.* Allen & Unwin, London, 1953

———. *A History of the Sikhs.* Vol. I, 1469–1839, Allen & Unwin, London, 1963

MACAULIFFE, M. A. *The Sikh Religion: Its Gurus, Sacred Writings, and Anthems.* Oxford, 1909

The Sacred Writings of the Sikhs. Tr. by Trilochan Singh, Jodh Singh, Kapur Singh, Bawa Harkishen Singh, Khushwant Singh. Allen & Unwin, London, 1960. UNESCO Collection

243

Three

The Religions of the Far East

THE CHARACTERISTIC of preserving the old with the new that we noted in the religions of India is clearly present in the religions of the Far East. So far no religion has been able to transcend its past; even in the cases of those religions that at their inception consciously rejected the older faiths they sought to replace, much of the old re-entered the new at a later date. But rejection of the past is a rather unusual procedure. In India and the Far East, indeed, the old is seldom cast away, even when it is left behind in an advance, because it is felt that there is truth still there.

However, despite this and other likenesses, the general religious attitude in the Far East differs from that of India in important respects. India tends to give the value of an illusion to nature, or at least yearns to triumph over it in thought as a thing of secondary or tertiary value. The Chinese and Japanese do not do this easily. In general they have cultivated an aesthetic appreciation of nature, which, apart from Buddhist and Taoist influences, has reached such heights of satisfaction as to make the Far Easterner want to prolong life in this world as long as possible. Nature is not the ultimate reality, but it has a valuable role to play in the life of man. It is a real and not deceptive structure of forms and forces, and it displays sublime order and beauty in both action and being. The only dissenting opinion here might be that of the Taoists, who, especially in the case of the witty Chuang-tzu, have considered nature to be of value chiefly in signifying the operational presence of the only wholly real entity in the universe—the mysterious and wonderful Tao. But even here Chuang-tzu has been an inspiration to Chinese artists and poets, for he has helped them to treat the forms and forces of nature either as passively beautiful exteriorizations or as aesthetically effective dynamic expressions of the Tao. The Japanese, moved by a lively wonder and delight, have come to love the trees, flowers, and scenic glories of their land as surpassingly beautiful in form and structure, and not only lovely when committed in their essential lines by brush to paper, but also worthy of being graphically suggested in the objectively descriptive phrases of the world's briefest poems, the Japanese *haiku*. Consider this characteristically Oriental episode in the life of Prince Taira no Tadanori, fleeing for his life into the mountains of the western provinces. In the gravest peril though he was, he waited as twilight fell around him to write down in the required seventeen syllables the serene reflection:

> Twilight upon my path tonight,
> And for mine inn tonight
> The shadow of a tree,
> And for mine host a flower.*

---

* *An Anthology of Japanese Poems,* tr. by Miyamori Asataro, Tokyo, 1938, p. 174. (This *haiku* translated by James A. B. Scherer.) Quoted by permission.

Nature and the life of the spirit are but the obverse and converse of the same reality. In the opinion of F. S. C. Northrop:

The Orientals are an exceedingly concrete, practical, and realistic people; and their religion is best thought of by Westerners as something nearer to what the West regards as aesthetics than it is to what the West has regarded as religion. . . . But in saying this care must be taken. For . . . the aesthetic must be conceived in its Oriental sense as the aesthetically immediate for its own sake and not in its Western sense as the handmaid of commonsense beliefs in external, three-dimensional objects, or of more sophisticated . . . scientific, philosophical, or theological objects. In short, the Oriental uses the purely aesthetic to constitute the nature of the divine. . . . As Chiang Yee has written of Chinese painting—

"Perhaps the most important mental process in it is that movement of the sympathies where the onlooker loses his own identity and becomes one with the 'observed' and eventually with the Great Spirit of the Universe, which informs everything that has life." *

There is a further aspect of the Far Eastern religious consciousness that needs to be noted. Not to see it is to fail seriously in understanding. Man and nature are organically, not externally or accidentally, related. The basic concepts of Chinese religion may be cited in illustration. It is the central belief of the ancient Chinese that heaven, earth, and men are so sensitively related to each other that any untoward development affects them all. The misbehavior of men, or even of the emperor alone, throws the whole of nature off stride, and Heaven is disturbed; the pleasure of heaven and earth in the obedience of men to the law of nature's being (the Tao) causes a universal harmony to obtain: the crops will thrive and men will be at peace and prosperous. The various parts of the universe therefore are not externally related to each other as are the parts of a mechanism; they are mutually sensitive to each other as are the elements within an organism. Something of this same feeling has long been present among the Japanese. It is common among those who still live under the influence of the old traditions to consider that the emperor, his people, the mountains of Japan, and the heavens above form an interrelated community in which all the vital forces are acutely sensitive to each other.

There is a hidden pantheism here, or shall we call it the spiritual conception of things?

* F. S. C. Northrop, *The Meeting of East and West*, pp. 403–404. Copyright 1946 by the Macmillan Co. Reprinted by permission of the publishers.

9 Chinese Religion and the Taoists

THE ANCIENT CHINESE SCHOLARS living in the times of Lao-tzu and Confucius believed they were enjoying the ripe results of a nearly two-thousand-year-old culture. Their backward look, if they were right, traversed a stretch of time so long that to experience anything comparable we should have to think of the landing of the Pilgrims as having taken place not in 1620, but at the time of Augustus Caesar. They were perhaps looking back too far—recent historical and archeological investigations do throw considerable doubt on the traditional dates—but they were not wrong in the main, in assuming that their culture was both old and thoroughly Chinese.

The Chinese have embodied their recognition of this fact in their popular traditions. In many myths concerning the beginnings of their history, they have told of the clever Yu Ch'ao,* who taught the ancient Chinese to build "nests" (the first houses); of the ingenious Sui Jen, who made fire by twirling one dry stick upon another; of the great hunter Fu Hsi, emperor and originator extraordinary, who taught the early men of China how to domesticate animals, use iron in making hunting and fishing implements, fish with nets, write with pictograms, forecast with the Eight Trigrams, and play upon the musical instruments that he invented; of Shen Nung, the Divine Farmer, who while emperor invented ox-drawn carts and instructed men in the arts of agriculture and medicine; and of the Yellow Emperor, Huang Ti, most famous of all in after-times, who invented bricks, vessels of wood and clay, the calendar, and money, and whose principal wife introduced the people to silkworm culture. These great personages, the myths relate, were by no means the first to appear in China. Long ages lay behind them. In the distant

* Pronunciation of the Chinese names transliterated in this and the following chapter conforms to the rules of the Wade-Giles system: any consonant or group of consonants followed by an apostrophe should be pronounced about as in English. In this instance (*Yu Ch'ao*), pronounce the *ch* as in *church*. When not followed by an apostrophe *ch* = *j*, *t* = *d*, *ts* = *dz*, and *j* and *ih* are approximately *r*. Thus in this paragraph *Sui Jen* = *swee run; Huang Ti* = *hwang dee*. Elsewhere *Tao* = *dao*, *Chuang-tzu* = *jwang-dz*, *Shih Ching* = *shir jing*, etc.

past, but badly jumbled together by the confusing accounts, there reigned through ten great epochs, totaling two million years (!), groups of human, half-human, and animal-like sovereigns, who often occupied the throne for periods lasting up to eighteen thousand years. Yet even these sovereigns did not go back to the absolute beginnings, for there lived and labored, more than two million years ago,* P'an Ku, the first man, four times the size of ordinary men to begin with, and destined to grow larger with his toil. He came when the world was still in chaos, and with hammer and chisel, during a period of epic labor lasting eighteen thousand years, he separated heaven and earth, hewed out places in the heavens for the sun, moon, and stars, dug out the valleys on the surface of the earth, piled high the mountains, and finally enriched the scene of his labors by his own self-distribution. "When he died his remains fell apart and formed the Five Sacred Mountains of China. His head became T'ai Mountain in the East; his body Sung Mountain in the center; his right arm Heng Mountain in the North and his left Heng Mountain in the South; his two feet Hua Mountain in the West."A His breath became "winds and clouds, his voice thunder, his flesh the fields; his beard was turned into stars, his bones into metals; his dropping sweat increased to rain, and lastly the insects which stuck to his body were transformed into people."B

These fanciful stories accent the Chinese belief in the great age of their native culture. But, of course, no great culture anywhere is entirely indigenous. The Chinese undoubtedly learned much from others. Certain production techniques, like the baking of pottery and the making and casting of bronze, seem to have come in from central Asia. It is uncertain now whether these borrowings were the results of contacts made through trade or whether they followed upon the immigration or invasion of moving peoples. The latter seems likely in view of the appearance within China, about 1300 B.C., of bronze arms and armor, together with horses, chariots, and the compound bow (one strengthened with bone and sinew, probably a central Asian invention). It is not to our purpose to speculate further on this point. So impossible is it now to untangle the complex pattern of the indigenous and borrowed elements of Chinese culture that we may well leave the matter to the archeologists to solve, if they can.

Turning then from this problem, let us consider the religious conceptions that the common people of China have held. They are old, too.

I   The Basic Elements of Chinese Religion

The religions of China are a blend of many elements, native and foreign, sophisticated and naive, rational and superstitious. Because we have already glanced at Buddhism in China and are about to consider separately Taoism and Confucianism, our present topic is limited to those elements of popular religion that serve as background and foil to the more highly developed systems of thought and faith just mentioned. But even this limited topic is hard to discuss within a brief compass; so many of the old and superseded beliefs and practices of China must be considered along with the beliefs and practices that have supplanted them. Moreover, since the triumph of the Communists in 1949 and the lowering of the Bamboo Curtain, present changes cannot be observed. No doubt they are incalculable and are probably accelerating. However, not even the most radical revolution can be total. Some of the old beliefs and habits undoubtedly still remain.

First, let us ask what the cosmology of Old China was.

The Cosmology of Ancient China

About the time that the monistic idealism of the Upanishads was being formulated in India, there

---

* Ninety-six million years ago, says another account!

249

arose in China an attempt to order the spirits, that is, to see in all the processes of heaven and earth a display of fundamental regularity and harmony of operation.

As have many other peoples, the ancient Chinese believed that the earth is a flat, motionless disc with bowed heavens above. To their mind, China occupied the central place on the earth's surface. It was "The Middle Kingdom." The farther one went from the heart of China, which was where the emperor's palace and the imperial altars to heaven and earth stood, the less cultured and respectable one found the people.

When they looked up into the heavens, with the "natural piety" with which agricultural peoples view the dome of heaven by day and by night, they were impressed by the order and harmony of the celestial movements. Each heavenly body followed its appointed order and course, from year to year the same. If heaven in anger summoned meteors and thunderbolts to crash to earth in pursuance of the ends of justice and order, that would be because it had been disturbed out of its wonted equilibrium by some occurrence on earth, perhaps some human crime.

Earth also showed a like, if less apparent, obedience to law. There was order in the unvarying succession of the seasons, the growth of plants, the upward leap of flame, the down-flowing of water, and in thousands of instances of natural process. Here, too, demonic powers, or heaven's punishing will, caused disturbance, delay, or miscarriage. Floods, tornadoes, earthquakes, drought, and unseasonable cold were not uncommon. And yet, where earth was left to work out her processes without molestation, there was order and harmonious functioning everywhere.

The Yang and the Yin

As they pondered this matter, some early, now unknown Chinese philosophers, several centuries before Confucius, perhaps even as early as 1000 B.C., distinguished within every natural object two inter-

acting energy-modes, the *yang* and the *yin*. Everything that is in existence, they and their successors amplifying upon them[*] said, is constituted by the interplay of these two modes of energy, and therefore has the characteristics of each. The yang is described as masculine in character—active, warm, dry, bright, procreative, positive. It is seen in the sun, in anything with heat in it, the south side of a hill, the north side of a river, male properties of all kinds, fire. The yin is an energy mode in a lower and slower key; it is fertile and breeding, dark, cold, wet, mysterious, secret, the female or negative principle in nature. It is seen in shadows, quiescent things, the north side of a hill, the shadowed south bank of a river. A single object may at one moment show yin characteristics and at another become a yang object aflame with energy. Thus, a dried-out log is to all appearance wholly yin in character, but if put in the fire it will prove to have yang qualities in abundance. This is not because its substance has altered, but because its inner activity has changed from one mode to another. The like is true of anything else, although there may be things in which either the yin or the yang remains a deeply dormant mode of being. Examples of objects in which one or the other mode is dominant are the ever-fiery sun, earth as a whole (predominantly yin in character), and heaven (which is full of yang energy-modes). That this way of regarding the compound objects of nature is not unlike the theories of modern physical science is an inference one might draw from the following description:

The Chinese physical world is a world of action. . . . Things are differentiated, not by the stuff of which they are composed, but by the way they act. Stuffs pass from a state of having one sort of properties to a state of having another; in the latter state they have a different name, but the only difference is one of activity. . . . To say the

[*] A whole school of Chinese philosophers devoted themselves to Yin-Yang interactionism in the second century B.C. Outstanding among them were Huai-nan-tzu and the Confucians Tung Chung-shu and Wang Ch'ung. (See Fung, *A History of Chinese Philosophy*, Chapters III and VII. See also infra pp. 304 and 308 ff.)

same thing otherwise, the Chinese seem to have lacked a conception of substance, matter, as such, since this can only exist over against that which is not material. To the ancient Chinese thinker, the differences between things consist in degree of density (itself a kind of activity) and nature of activity.[c]

Men and women are, not less than inanimate things, the product of the interaction in varying degrees of the yang and the yin. They show differing proportions of the qualities of each activity-mode, men being celestial (that is, predominantly yang) and of great worth, whereas women are earthy (predominantly yin) and of little account on the whole!

Looking in another direction, one sees that the *shen* (or good spirits) are yang in character, the *kwei* (or evil spirits) are yin.

In still another direction, the "five elements"—metal, wood, water, fire, and earth—are the result of the interaction in the cosmic sphere of yang and yin, earth being a kind of sedimentary deposit, whereas the others are more volatile.

Finally, events reveal yin and yang influences in the alternation of success and failure, rise and fall, fluorescence and decay in all things.

The Conception of the Tao

But the ancient Chinese thinkers were not content with framing a theory to account for the becoming, being, and passing away of single objects. They wished also to account for the evident harmony and order in nature as a whole. To what was *this* due?

The concept at which they arrived by way of answer was the Tao. The harmony and orderliness displayed in heaven and earth were, they said, the result of the cosmic energy of the Tao. Literally, the word *Tao* means "a way" or "a road." Sometimes it denotes the "channel" of a river. In general, it means "the way to go." It refers to the standard procedure of things, the correct method of their operation or behavior.

This Tao of the universe is conceived to be eternal.

It would seem that the ancient Chinese distinguished between the mechanism of the universe and the powerful way in which, as if by inner necessity, it ran. To their minds it seemed that the way in which the universe runs must have existed before the universe itself did. First, the preordained Plan, the proper Way-to-Go; then the physical universe going that way.

The next step was to see that this way of nature's functioning has been a way of perfection. It is a pre-established pattern into which all things ought to fall if they are to be in their proper place and do their proper work. The Tao is emphatically a way of harmony, integration, and cooperation. Its natural tendency is toward peace, prosperity, and health. If it were not for the perverse men and demonic beings that refuse to adjust themselves to it, this would quickly become evident. In fact, if the Tao were ever to be followed everywhere, heaven, mankind, and earth would form a single, harmonious unit, in every part cooperating toward universal well-being.

This state of perfection, the Chinese dreamed, did obtain in the Golden Age, when the good Emperors Yao and Shun ruled their subjects by knowing and following the Tao. That was a time of universal felicity; men then lived in an earthly paradise. Such a state of perfection could return to earth if the conditions for its restoration were met. The possibility appeared to lie largely with the emperor. If he lived according to the Tao, he became, as we learn under the next topic, the earthly instrument of a cosmic power making for peace and harmony among men, animals, and natural forces, and so prosperity existed throughout his realm.

The Ancient Chinese Theory of History

The casual reader of Chinese history and folklore might too easily conclude that imperial authority in times past was absolute and uncontrolled, and that the emperor had no wishes to consult save his own. But this impression, however well supported by tales of imperial extravagance and arbitrary rule, would be wide of the mark. Chinese emperors schooled in the old imperial tradition carried a heavy load of responsibility, such as few monarchs in other parts of the world have had to bear. In ancient times it was believed that both crops in the fields and law and order among men were dependent on the sacrifices he performed. In his exalted position he excelled all others in *te,* or inherent power and virtue, and hence was the only one who could give the sacrifice its greatest efficacy. When an emperor regularly worshiped the spirits and lived in conscientious regard for the welfare of his people, he was highly revered for fulfilling the duty of a son of Heaven, who had been set upon the throne by its holy decree. But he was never entirely comfortable; he lived in the uneasy knowledge that his people held him strictly accountable for any failure to live by the celestial mandate, for if he did less he endangered the prosperity of the realm. If he failed to carry out the divine mandate and became licentious, lazy, and careless, calamity befell the nation as a sign of celestial displeasure, and the people had the right to revolt and depose their ruler. In such case Heaven guided some rebel to the throne who was more amenable to its will.°

Among the most pathetic scenes in history are those in which we see Chinese emperors going before Heaven to plead for mercy for their people—and some light on what they themselves had wrought amiss! What had they done? They wished they knew! Let Heaven inform them, they prayed. One of the emperors of the Chou dynasty is pictured by the *Book of Poetry* as having been in this predicament.

> Grand shone the Milky Way on high,
> With brilliant sun athwart the sky,
>   Nor promise gave of rain.
> King Seuen long gazed; then from him broke,
>
> In anguished tones the words he spoke . . .
> "The drought consumes us. Nor do I

° For many centuries war-lords justified themselves by this theory. The Communists have discarded the theory, but have at the same time appealed to the tradition that poor rule should be overthrown by revolution.

> To fix the blame on others try . . .
> Why upon me has come this drought?
> Vainly I try to search it out,
>   Vainly, with quest severe.
> God in great heaven, be just, be kind!
> My cry, ye wisest spirits, hear!
>   Why do I this endure?"[D]

By the second century B.C. this idea had reached so formidable an elaboration as this:

If the king and his ministers do not practice the ritual courtesies; if there be no majesty (on the one hand) and no reverence (on the other), then the trees will not grow (as they should), and in summer there will be an excess of high winds. . . .

If the king's mind fail to be penetrating, then the sowing and reaping will not be completed, so that in autumn there will be an excess of rumbling thunder.[E1]

Earth-Worship

The religion of ancient China faithfully mirrored the agricultural character of early Chinese civilization. It made much of a mound of earth symbolizing the fertility of the soil, called the *she,* which was raised in every village, surmounted sometimes by a tree or placed in a sacred grove. This mound was the center of an agricultural cult, whose rites in honor of the local gods of the soil sought to insure increase of the fertility of the ground and the growth of crops. In the spring a festival celebrated before the she included dancing and ceremonial songs, in general character resembling the European Maypole festival. The she also provided in the early autumn the scene of a Chinese harvest-home. When China became a feudal empire, the land was dotted with larger mounds, one in each provincial or state capital, symbolizing the territory of the feudal lord, while one at the imperial capital, composed of earth of five different colors, represented the earth-principle (or soil-spirit) of the whole realm. At the last mound the emperor himself, at the time of the summer solstice, ploughed a furrow and conducted a ceremony of earth-worship in behalf of the empire as a whole, a practice that was continued down to modern times.

Worship of Heaven

With the passage of time the worship of Earth lessened, while the worship of Heaven steadily increased. In the time of the Shangs, a deity by the name of Ti or Shang Ti was worshiped. Shang means "upper," and Ti is usually translated as "ruler" or "emperor." This deity was, then, the god of the upper regions or the heavens. The Shangs asked him for rain and believed he had oversight over the whole earth. Before they went into battle they bade their diviners find out whether Shang Ti approved. When the Chous began their rule, another name appeared and alternated with Shang Ti. It was the word *T'ien* —heaven. This was in general use a rather impersonal designation. Originally it meant "the abode of the Great Spirits," that is the heavens, or the sky, where the higher spirits dwelt.

The Chou and subsequent emperors, because of their reputed close relation to heaven, bore the title "T'ien Tzu" or "Son of Heaven." They worshiped Heaven in the people's behalf at regular annual ceremonies. In later centuries at Peking, the Chinese emperors used to perform during the winter solstice a solemn sacrifice to Imperial Heaven on the beautiful marble terraces of the Altar of Heaven south of the city (across the city from the Altar of Earth). After the Spirit of Heaven had been invited to come down and take up its abode in a large tablet inscribed "Imperial Heaven, Supreme Ruler," the emperor offered during the various stages of the ceremony incense, jade, silk, broth, and rice wine, and pressed his forehead nine times to the pavement while statutory prayers were recited by an official in a loud voice. Without this ceremony and its attendant appeals to the imperial ancestors it was felt that the harmony between earth and heaven would be disrupted.

The Worship of Localized Spirits

The Chinese believed that all nature is alive with spirits of many different kinds. Heaven throngs with spirits, and so does earth. On the second terrace of the Altar of Heaven stood tablets for the spirits of the sun, moon, the five planets, the seven stars of the Great Bear, the twenty-eight principal constellations, the stars considered collectively, the winds, the clouds, rain, and thunder. The spirits were, of course, not all in the sky. They were in hills and streams and even in roads and cultivated fields. The Yellow River and the principal mountains of China were from time immemorial the objects of special official worship.

Not all spirits were considered beneficent. From the earliest times it was a prevailing belief that devils and demons of many sorts and kinds thronged about every human dwelling, haunted lonely spots, and infested all roads, especially when at night-fall travelers thinned out along the way and were few and far between. They lurked, too, in the shadows of forests and mountains. The different species of demons make a long list, for there were demons in water, soil, and air, all varieties of animal-demons (were-tigers, -wolves, -foxes, -dogs, and domestic animals that were demons in disguise), bird-demons, fish-demons, and snake-demons. So extensive is the list that it includes plant-demons and demons in inanimate things. Very terrible were the man-eating specters, the vampires, ghouls, and gigantic devils with horned foreheads, long fangs, and a complete covering of fuzzy red hair.

Some nature-spirits had a high potency for destructiveness but were inclined toward benevolence if encouraged by human respect and veneration. Among these was the fearsome-looking dragon (see overleaf).

After a long period of hesitation of thought, all these spirits were finally° regarded as falling into two classes: the *shen,* good, and the *kwei,* bad or unpredictable. Both kinds of spirits were considered to be almost infinite in number, crowding the universe in

° Perhaps in the time of the first Han dynasty (206 B.C.–8 A.D.).

A Chinese dragon. From a Ming temple ceiling a lacquered and gilded dragon, coiled like a serpent, peers down with bulging eyes. Although his appearance is frightening, he is not the dreadful monster that European dragons are, for he is associated with water, the friend alike of men, animals, and plants, although in storm and flood it can get out of hand and be dangerous. (Philadelphia Museum of Art.)

all its parts. The shen were believed to animate heaven, the arable earth, sun, moon, stars, winds, clouds, rain, thunder, fire, mountains, rivers, seas, trees, springs, stones, and plants. Ancestors, too, were shen.

The kwei or untrustworthy powers of the universe were ubiquitous, affecting human fate in manifold ways and making night and darkness everywhere terrorsome—unless one had a lantern.

Perhaps no people have gone to such lengths to keep the good spirits on their side as the Chinese, because no people have been more afraid of demons. The sun was supposed to be the chief dispeller of devils, and because the cock by his crowing announces the sunrise, he was held to have power over the kwei. Earthenware cocks were thought to have special power to ward off demons and were placed on housetops and over gateways. The triumphant march of the season of spring (so full of shen potencies) was seen in peach blossoms. Therefore from the oldest times branches of peach trees, peach boards with mottoes drawn from the sayings of the sages inscribed on them, sheets of red paper in imitation of peach blossoms, and similar objects were nailed to doors and gates on New Year's Day. Bonfires, torches, candles, lanterns, and firecrackers scared off the kwei effectually and were used during popular festivals, especially on New Year's Day, when a general house-cleaning of evil spirits was effected by their means.

Ancestor-Worship

We have already seen in our study of the attitudes to the dead of contemporary primitives how natural it is for the living to be vividly aware of the continued being of persons who have recently died, especially if such persons have filled a large place in the lives of the survivors. Just the thought of them is enough to evoke their presence. One feels it not unnatural to want to talk to them, but if one should do so, they would not speak; they would merely be vaguely approving or disapproving. It is clear that faith may build upon such experiences and subsequently convince itself of the reasonableness and truth of its assumptions.

The Chinese always have tied their belief in survival after death to their tremendous sense of family solidarity. When they spoke of "the family," they did not mean merely father, mother, and children. They meant all that would be comprehended in an American family reunion, *and more.* For included in the family group were the ancestors, conceived as living and powerful spirits, all vitally concerned about the welfare of their living descendants, but capable of punitive anger if displeased. The relationship of the living and the dead was markedly one of interdependence. On the one hand, the dead were dependent upon the living for the maintenance of the strong bond tying them to the living, which bond was renewed every time prayers or sacrifices were offered to them. Prayers kept their memory alive, and sacrifices provided them with the food they needed. Not that they actually ate the meat and drink proffered them, for when the sacrifice was placed before them it did not disappear. What they availed themselves of, obviously, was its essence, which they inhaled, not its substance, the latter remaining for the priests and sacrificers to eat after a proper interval. On the other hand, the living were just as dependent upon the dead. Ancestors, if themselves properly provided for, actively promoted the prosperity of the family. Any favor done to the family was one done to them, any injury their injury, a fact of which the friends or the enemies of a powerful family were very well aware.

In the past, burials were momentous and expensive occasions. In ancient China ancestors of wealthy families were buried with bronze vessels and hunting weapons, and sometimes also with dogs, horses, and human attendants. Some Shang kings, according to surviving bone inscriptions, were buried with anywhere from a hundred to three hundred human victims, who were to be his attendants in the next world. (This practice links ancient China with Egypt, Africa, Japan, and other places, where similar sacrifices were made.)

In 621 B.C. Duke Mu of the state of Ch'in died with the request that three of his ablest subjects be sent after him. An ode in the *Book of Poetry* (Bk. XI, Ode 6) recounts the events of the sacrifice that took place by the grave of the noble lord. Consider the touching and natural reaction of one of the doomed men:

> Who followed Duke Mu to the grave?
> Tzu-ch'e Chen-hu.
> And this Chen-hu
> Could withstand a hundred men.
> But when he came to the grave,
> He looked terrified and trembled.[F]

This poem, full as it is of considerate human feeling, anticipates coming changes. Though human sacrifice continued late into Chou times, it was gradually discontinued as barbarous, and first pottery and then later on paper substitutes, not only for the human but also the animal victims, were evolved.[*]

If any single place in the home could be selected as the center of family life, it was the ancestral shrine. Even in the homes of the poor this shrine occupied an alcove built specially for it and contained wooden tablets inscribed with the names of the ancestors. Local clan organizations maintained family temples, often elaborately furnished. In front of the domestic shrine or inside the ancestral temple food sacrifices were offered and other ceremonies took place. Here in the presence of the ancestors proposals of marriage were received by a girl's father. Here the bridegroom's father asked approval of his marriage plans. Here the bride, by joining in the family ceremonies, became a full member of the new family. Here announcements were made to the ancestors when a journey or an important business venture was undertaken. Here all sorts of decisions were referred to the ancestors for endorsement.

In G. E. Simon's *La Cité Chinoise* there is an interesting and vivid description of the ancestor-worship of a few generations ago as he observed it being performed by Chinese families of high standing. A part of it is here quoted:

At the back of the room, standing against the wall and taking up almost the whole length of it, a long table of varnished wood forms the altar. On this altar are stands holding small lacquered tablets, chronologically arranged, on which the names of the ancestors are inscribed. Hanging at the very top of the wall is the sign of deity [T'ien]; and in front of the tablets are lights and incense burners. Lastly, at some distance from the altar, there is a common square table with chairs round it, and in the middle of the table a register with books on each side of it.

Everybody has put on his best clothes and is waiting. The father and mother, who in preparation for the cere-

---

[*] The manufacture of these paper substitutes and of paper money to be burned at the grave for the use of the dead has been a major industry in China.

mony have been abstinent from the evening before last, enter, followed by two acolytes, and take their places in front of the altar. They address a short invocation to Heaven, and those present chaunt the ancestral hymn. . . . A variety of things are offered . . . : a pigeon or a chicken, fruits, wine and grain, either rice or wheat, whichever is grown in the district. Or wine alone, with rice or wheat, may be offered. The two acolytes go to fetch these offerings, the wife takes them from their hands and gives them to her husband, who lifts them above his head, his wife standing beside him, and places them on the altar in sign of thanksgiving. The father then reads the names of the ancestors inscribed on the tablets, and recalling them more particularly to the memory of the family, he speaks in their name and makes them as it were arise from the grave. The corn and wine that he has just consecrated to them, which are a symbol of the efforts made and the progress realized, he now returns, on behalf of the ancestors to those present, in token of their indissoluble union. Lastly, the officiator exhorts the family to meditate on the meaning of this true communion, on the engagements that it implies, which all present swear to carry out: and then, after a last prayer, a meal is served, in which the consecrated offerings are included.[G]

Here we have ancestor-worship at its best. But this was only the first part of the ceremony that Simon saw. In the next or second part (the third part was a solemn family council) the father read from the family register the record of recent events, that the whole family, and the ancestors, too, might be fully informed, and then he read the biography of one of the ancestors.

He makes comments on it, emphasizing the claims of the said ancestor to be remembered by his descendants, and exhorts everyone to follow the example he gave.—A new biography is read in this way at every meeting * till the whole series is finished, after which they go back to the first, the second, and so on until everyone knows them all by heart, and none at least of the worthier ancestors remains unknown.[G]

An important part of ancestor-worship was and probably still is the family pilgrimage in spring and autumn to the graves of ancestors, in order to make sacrifices and leave offerings there. The spring visit usually includes the sweeping and rebuilding of the

grave mounds. In the autumn sheets of paper with pictures of warm blankets and clothing are burned at the grave in order to provide the dead with protection against the coming cold.

It cannot be surprising that in the past anyone who was believed to have abandoned or betrayed his family was regarded as an outcast, despised by men and pursued by the vengeance of his ancestral spirits. When such a person died, he became luckless ever, a hungry ghost, unhonored and unsung, without any family to sustain his lonely spirit with their sacrifices and their affection. Though Confucius made it his life-mission to restore the rightful authority of the state over its citizens, he is thought not to have approved of the implications in the statement of the Duke of She: "Among us there are those who may be styled upright in their conduct; if their father has stolen a sheep, they will bear witness to the fact"; for he countered with the reply: "Amongst us, in our part of the country, those who are upright are different from this. The father conceals the misconduct of the son, and the son conceals the misconduct of the father. Uprightness is to be found in this."[H] Significantly, China accepted the principle formulated by Confucius, although since 1912 the sense of duty to the nation has grown stronger. The Communists, of course, demand the highest priority for such a sense, and they consider the Confucian principle criminal.

The Grading of Social and Religious Functions in the Ancient Feudal Era

It is an interesting fact that the feudal system of ancient China, which Confucius was so anxious to conserve, was a graded hierarchy of an exceedingly thorough-going sort. In the heyday of the Chou dynasty China was divided into several hundred vassal states,* whose ruling princes were lieges of

* Each was small, and their total area did not much exceed the region lying north and south of the Yellow River.

* Twice a month.

the emperor and directly responsible to him. These states were again divided into prefectures or districts, ruled by governors and other officers. In well-regulated states each district was as nearly as possible divided into approximately square areas, which were, in the standard cases, subdivided again into eight outer and one central field (the well-field system), the outer ones cultivated by single families for their own use and the central one cultivated in common by all eight families for the overlord. The villages of China were therefore surrounded by neatly divided areas, so parceled out that groups of families cultivated a public field whose produce and cattle were destined for the overlord. Almost as neat was the grading of the population. The emperor, as liege lord, had under him the vassal lords holding their offices in hereditary perpetuity, in four descending ranks (dukes, marquises, earls, viscounts and barons). The vassal lords had under them the governors of the prefectures. The governors of the prefectures had under them officers, the officers subalterns, the subalterns petty officers, the petty officers assistants, the assistants employees, the employees menials, the menials helpers!* Emperors, noble, officials, and common people were subject to detailed rules of conduct governing all their interrelations and duties.

Nor was this by any means the whole story. Long before the time of Confucius there was a general recognition of the impropriety of ordinary men or even lesser officials sacrificing to the major cosmic or earth spirits. No prince was allowed to perform any of the sacrifices that were the emperor's function, and no ordinary man could take over a prince's religious duties. The mountains and rivers were not to be addressed by unauthorized individuals, lest their spirit-forces be offended or else induced to act in a way not consonant with the general welfare. In later China, therefore, from about the second century B.C. on, it became the settled practice for the common man to worship only his ancestors and such

* Or, under another nomenclature, the officials were classified thus: chief ministers, great officers, upper scholars, middle scholars, and low scholars.

household and personal spirits as the guardians of the door and of the stove and the gods of health and luck. He let the feudal lords or their officers worship the hills and streams of the province for him, as well as certain roads and cultivated fields, for they could do this acceptably, and he could not. The emperor, on his part, made a tour of the empire every seven years to perform sacrifices near or on the chief rivers and mountains of the land. And, of course, the emperor alone addressed Shang Ti, or sublime T'ien, in the ceremonies at the Altar of Heaven outside the capital of the empire.

The Peoples of the South

Although it was part of the theory of history of the Chou dynasty that an emperor who ruled by the mandate of Heaven was a universal king and that all people should defer to him as the "Son of Heaven," in actual fact the Chou empire during its first two centuries did not reach to the Yangtze River. When during the later Chou period the war-lords who took power into their own hands pushed Chinese authority to the south somewhat beyond the Yangtze, the two states involved, Ch'u and Wu, found themselves dealing with, and to some extent accommodating themselves to, the Lao people (lao meaning "old"). The latter were known to the Chinese as "aborigines" even through Han and later times.* Among these less highly organized peoples social stratification was in its beginnings and their religion was concerned with old gods, spirits of rivers, hills, and stars, and spirits of the dead. It was still a religion of rural people, and its human leaders were the wu (shamans), who, like their counterparts in central Asia, attracted or exorcised the spirits or visited them in trance states induced by dancing, drugs, and incantations. (See again p. 14 n.) Taoism, next to be encountered among the religions, may have drawn some of its perspective and motivation from this native, rural faith. Lao-tzu, its reputed founder, is said to have come from Ch'u.

* Note that Hui-neng was called an aborigine, p. 173.   **257**

At any rate, some authorities say that "there is a close parallel between the images of the flight of the soul in trance used by the shamans of the south and the descriptions of the trance state in the Taoists' philosophical classic *Chuang Tzu*."[1]

The Decay of the Feudal System and the Rise of the Schools

The period from 722 to 221 B.C.—a period of five hundred years—saw the gradual decay of the feudal system that we have just outlined and its replacement by a less rigid organization of society, which allowed men of lowly rank—farmers and merchants —to climb to positions of political importance and thus break up the aristocracy of hereditary vassal lords. On the one hand, many of the old noble families were impoverished by conflicts with upstart usurpers within their realms. On the other hand, the inability of the Chou emperors to protect their domain from invasion by Tartar hordes, pushing in from the northwest, led to the rise of powerful nobles, each fortified for his own protection with private armies and virtually supreme in his own territory. In due time these great lords thrust the emperor to one side and sprang at each other. At the same time, the agricultural serfs began to shake themselves free from the land system that denied them possession of property and confined them to small areas. They became the owners of their own fields, and some of them by joining field to field rose to power as landed proprietors. With the rise of a money economy, merchants appeared in the villages and attained wealth. Some aristocratic families now found themselves so stripped of power and brought down to the level of common people that they were obliged to take positions and earn their livelihood by their own labor. (Confucius came, it would seem, of a noble family, and found himself so obliged.) The decay of the feudal system finally culminated in a two-hundred-year period of violent civil disorders, called the Warring States Period. The smaller states disap-

peared, and the seven larger states that remained fought savagely for supremacy. The emperor by this time was an impotent figurehead, the puppet of the strongest feudal prince. Finally, in 221 B.C. Duke Cheng of the state of Ch'in conquered all his rivals and, as the great Emperor Shih Huang-ti, completely unified China under his arbitrary rule. The royal families of all the states were brought tumbling down into the ranks of the common people, and the feudal system was dealt a blow from which it never recovered.

In the period of the dissolution of the old order, and while the new was struggling to establish itself, a number of differing schools of thought arose to lay claim to the assent of thinking men—as always happens during a period of transition and change. Some of these schools attacked the feudal system and wished it done away; these were the Legalists. Others wanted the feudal system to be restored in a rationalized and idealized form, and among these were the Confucians. Still others would have nothing to do with any political system requiring a high degree of centralization; the Taoists took this point of view. A few, like the Mohists, advocated, from the standpoint of utility and common sense, a return to the old-time religion and the cultivation of a universal benevolence that would seek the welfare of all men together.*

* Lin Mousheng, in his interesting *Men and Ideas* (John Day, New York, 1942, p. 9), puts the situation thus: "The Confucian school apparently was the school of gentlemen—princes and dukes. The Taoist school was made up of disillusioned intellectuals. The Mocian [Motsean] school represented the lower middle class—free artisans and free farmers. The Legalist school stood for the interests of the upper middle class—plutocrats and landlords." Chinese scholars are, however, not in agreement on this. Many contend that the various schools sprang not from classes of the population, but from localities. For example, Confucianism issued from the Yellow River region, dominated by the Chou culture; Taoism from the Yangtze, where lived the less feudalistic suppressed people of Yin, who were in opposition to Chou culture; and so on. See in this connection Francis C. M. Wei, *The Spirit of Chinese Culture* (Scribner's, 1947).

A more recent view is that of the Communists. According to them (cf. Hou Wai-lu, *A Short History of Chinese*

It shall now be our task to examine some of these proposals for social change or restoration, and to see what religious consequences they had during the long history of Chinese religion to the present day.

II   Taoism

Taoism is an ambiguous term signifying either the thought system that in ancient times gave the Tao centrality in all thinking and living, or a mixture of magic and religion dating from the two Han dynasties (206 B.C.–221 A.D.). Under either aspect it has been the vehicle of beliefs and practices which, during a long emergence from the soil of popular faith and superstition, have expressed the philosophical and mystical aspects of Chinese thought and life.

The Legendary Lao-tzu

It all began, we have been told, with Lao-tzu or Lao Tan, a legendary scholar or seer of whom so little can be learned, even on the hypothesis that he lived, that it has been common for some authorities in the matter to be sceptical about his having lived at all. He was born, the old tradition relates, in the state of Ch'u in 604 B.C.,* and obtained the important

post of curator of the imperial archives at Loyang, the capital city. But he began to question the wisdom of having any sort of government; he thought the search for knowledge itself was vain, for it led only to a perversion of the simplicity in which men are meant to live. So, having found his position as an official a false one, he resigned from it and returned to "his own house." The rest of the story is even more questionable. Driven, it is said, by an unceasing desire for escape into the unknown, fed by his aversion to curious visitors, Confucius among them, the aged philosopher decided upon flight into the west. In a two-wheeled carriage drawn by black oxen, he set out, prepared to leave the world of deluded, society-corrupted men behind him. But the keeper of the gate at the western pass, his friend Yin-hsi, persuaded him to write down his philosophy. Lao-tzu thereupon lingered in the gatehouse long enough to compose the treatise that has come to be called the *Tao Te Ching*, or *Treatise of the Tao and Its Power*. In short crisp sentences, some of them obscure and cryptic, he expounded his views, and then he departed over the pass, to be heard of no more.

That even in the Warring States Period this romantic story was not firmly established in tradition is all too apparent from the fact that the fourth-century scholar Chuang-tzu makes the old master die in his bed!

The legendary Lao-tzu may have lived—that possibility exists *—but authoritative scholarship is con-

Philosophy, Peking, 1959), the revolutionary rising class of freemen were represented in various respects by the Taoists, Motseans, and Legalists (see infra, pp. 293–298), insofar as these schools rested on natural laws and aided freemen in coming to terms with the material world ("materialism"). But the Confucians sought to preserve the interests of the declining clan aristocracy both by stressing the moral code and social arrangements of the aristocracy and by strengthening religious and spiritual ties with Heaven and the ancestors as an opiate for the people.

  * Even on the assumption that the Lao-tzu of the traditions is historical, this date is in dispute. Some scholars think the records do not bear it out, and find on fresh computations that the date 570 B.C. is preferable. This would bring Lao-tzu much closer to Confucius in time. But many Chinese and Western scholars distinguish between Lao Tan, a legendary person, and Li Erh, presum-

ably nicknamed Lao-tzu, who lived in the 4th century B.C., long after Confucius. Others even say the traditional Lao-tzu is a fictitious character invented by Taoists in order to establish their historical priority to Confucianism. See Arthur Waley, *The Way and Its Power;* Y. L. Fung, *The History of Chinese Philosophy*, Vol. I, Chapter VIII; Homer H. Dubs, "The Date and Circumstances of the Philosopher Lao-dz," in *Journal of the American Oriental Society*, Vol. LXI, No. 4, Dec. 1941, pp. 215 f. But Hu Shih continues to think the evidence for the tradition is sufficient. See his "A Criticism of Some Recent Methods Used in Dating Lao Tsu," in *The Harvard Journal of Asiatic Studies*, Vol. II, Nos. 3 and 4, Dec. 1937.

  * So this writer feels. There is a strong Confucian tradition for his existence. But the writer agrees that we know nothing certainly about him, if he did exist.

vinced that even if such a person actually fathered the Taoist philosophy in the period prior to Confucius, he did not write the Tao Te Ching. That great classic of religious thought had a later origin. Of its dating, this must be said: the Tao Te Ching expresses an attitude toward life and nature that presupposes a rather advanced disintegration of the feudal order; moreover, its conceptions had the freshness of a new idea for a number of brilliant minds in the Warring States Period. It may be supposed it was they who gave to Taoism the permanently significant form of the Tao Te Ching. And this was a great achievement. Their thinking was in part an aroused and determined effort, in sorry times, to come to grips with unchanging reality, and in part an expression of temperamental revulsion from the ritual-minded Confucian school that came into being about the same time.

Because it was the destiny of Taoism to pass through three periods or phases, it will be convenient to consider in turn: (A) the philosophical or formative phase, characterized by strong mystical interests, (B) the magical phase, and (C) the phase of intermittent recognition by the Chinese government as the official religion of the empire.

A. The Formative Philosophical Phase of Taoism

The philosophical formulation of Taoism took place during the fifth and fourth centuries B.C.

Some contributory developments came first. There were forerunners (let us assume that a Lao Tan, an obscure originative figure, moved among them) who prepared the way. Already in the sixth century, Confucius seems to have met some nameless representatives of a pre-Taoist school. They were recluses who rejected "civilization." After his time other forerunners, more clearly seen by us now, appeared. Some of them were critics of human ways and institutions resembling the Sophists and Cynics even then stirring

up the Greeks.* Few more interesting and engagingly impudent persons have ever pressed their opinions on their fellows. They spoke with wit and pungency, and a certain unconventionality in their point of view made their sayings all the more intriguing.

This unconventionality is well illustrated by Yang Chu, who lived at the end of the fifth and the beginning of the fourth century. His problem seems to have been how to preserve his life whole and undamaged—the general personal problem of the early Taoists. Seeing that China was in a chaotic state beyond all help that he could devise, he concluded that turning his back on society and cultivating his own personal life was the only true good. Unabashed by the consequences of this reasoning, he said quite smartly, "Each one for himself!" and shocked the Confucians by asserting that even if all he had to do to be given the whole world would be to pluck a single hair from his shank, he would not do so. This was because he valued his own life above even the sum of all external things. "Not allowing outside things to entangle one's person"[J1] was his cardinal principle. (Some contemporary "hippies" talk thus.)

Even more unconventional were P'eng Meng and his followers, T'ien P'ien and Shen Tao. They resolved to discard knowledge, be impartial and nonpartisan, adopt an easy-going and unobtrusive manner, have no anxiety for the morrow, and let events just take their course without interfering. Perhaps the later Taoist Chuang-tzu was thinking of them when he made Tzuyü, a Confucian (!), say in carefree acceptance of fate: "If my left arm should be transformed into a cock, I would mark with it the time of night. If my right arm should be transformed into a crossbow, I would look for a bird to bring down and roast. If my rump-bone should be transformed into a wheel, and my spirit into a horse, I would mount and would have no need of any other steed."[J2] It was their opinion that the wise man who has acquired the secret of the good life "follows the

---

* From them, and the exponents of divers other viewpoints, sprang the "Hundred Schools" so often referred to in later times.

inevitable" and "simply moves with things." Of one of them we read:

Shen Tao discarded knowledge, abandoned self, followed the inevitable, and was indifferent to things. . . . He said: "Knowledge is not to know." He was one who despised knowledge and would destroy it. Stupid and irresponsible, he ridiculed the world's way of preferring the virtuous; careless and impractical, he condemned the world's great Sages; shifting and slippery, he changed about with circumstances; disregarding right and wrong, he was only concerned with avoiding trouble; learning nothing with knowledge and thinking, paying no attention to past or future, he stood loftily indifferent to everything.

He went where he was pushed and followed where he was led, like a whirling gale, like a feather tossed in the wind, like a turning mill-stone. He was complete without defects; in action or at rest he was free from mistakes and never offended others. How could this be? Because creatures without knowledge are freed from the trouble of self-assertion and the entanglements of knowledge; in motion or at rest they do not depart from the principles of nature. . . . Therefore, he said: "Let us be like creatures without knowledge. That will be sufficient. . . . For a clod of earth does not miss the Way [Tao]."[J3]

While Yang Chu and Shen Tao were thus venturing their own persons, so to speak, in an attempt to find the course (Tao) that nature prescribes for those who wish to be right, superior, and happy, other and more profound, more discriminating minds were assembling the Tao Te Ching and the essays of Chuang-tzu.

THE PHILOSOPHY AND ETHICS OF THE TAO TE CHING. As it stands, the Tao Te Ching is hardly the product of one mind. Interpolations and repeated editing have altered its original form. But doubtless most of the present version comes from the fourth century B.C.

The Tao Te Ching accepts unquestioningly the theory that when things are allowed to take their natural course, they move with a wonderful perfection and harmony. This is because, in such case, the Tao (the eternal Way of the universe) is not hindered in its smooth operation.

What is the Tao? Its definition is acknowledged to be difficult. The opening sentences of the Tao Te Ching say it is impossible. The Tao that can be expressed in words is not the eternal Tao; the name that can be named is not the real, the absolute name. The Tao is wrapped in cosmic mystery, and reaching for it is grasping through mystery into deeper mystery. Yet the whole world, all that has being, has emerged from its unactualized essence, its unrealized potentiality (non-being), and it is the sole source of the active power (Te) in all existent things.

The mightiest manifestations of active force flow solely from the Tao.

The Tao in itself is vague, impalpable,—how impalpable, how vague! Yet within it there is Form. How vague, how impalpable! Yet within it there is Substance. How profound, how obscure! Yet within it there is a Vital Principle.[K1]

Inquiry concerning the Tao takes us into the realm of pre-existence and non-being (potentiality), yet who can prevent the question from arising: how does the Tao operate in the realm of actuality or being? This is for the Tao Te Ching the central question, really, for it considers that the chief aim of human existence must be to attain fullness of life by present harmony with the Tao.

How important a matter this is for the Taoist may readily be seen. For just as heaven and earth attain complete harmony and order only by letting the Tao take its course, and even as the emperors of the Golden Age brought health and prosperity to themselves and their people by attuning themselves to the Tao, so any man can attain the highest well-being only by arriving at thorough conformity with it. Man has the power, and he has used his power, to choose his own way and build up his social habits after his own plan rather than after the eternal plan of the great Tao. But thence have sprung all the ills and pains of man, in the midst of the strange, queer "civilization" he has formed. He has chosen to move contrariwise to the eternal Tao, and it has been like swimming against the current: Nature is fighting him by flowing the other way. Perhaps he thinks he is big enough to overcome nature. But he is not. Men have the power to think and feel and act as they like, and the Tao allows, or rather does not disallow, them. But not to the extent of ceasing to be itself!

Nature is not benevolent; with ruthless indifference she makes all things serve their purposes, like the straw dogs we use at sacrifices.[K2]

What is contrary to the Tao soon perishes.[K3]

He who is self-approving does not shine. He who exalts himself does not rise high. Judged according to the Tao, he is like remnants of food or a tumour on the body—an object of universal disgust.[K4]

The Tao is quiet, so quiet that its presence goes easily undetected, save by intuition.

The Way of Heaven is not to contend and yet to be able to conquer,
Not to declare its will and yet to get a response,
Not to summon but have things come spontaneously.[E2]

Tao produces all things; . . .
It produces them without holding possession of them.
It acts without depending upon them, and raises without lording it over them.[L1]

Therefore heaven and earth—and men, too, if only they would—may safely resign themselves to it, and experience complete fulfillment of being.

The Tao is ever inactive,
And yet there is nothing that it does not do.[L2]

This brings us to a very important point in the Tao Te Ching. People who do not follow the Tao-way may meet with temporary success, but let them beware! For there is an invariable law in things, that if any movement goes to its extreme of development, it necessarily has to execute a "return" or "reversion."

All things come into existence,
And thence we see them return.
Look at the things that have been flourishing;
Each goes back to its origin.[L3]

Returning is the motion of the Tao.[L4]

Stretch a bow to the full,
And you will wish you had stopped in time;
Temper a sword-edge to its very sharpest,
And you will find it soon grows dull.
When bronze and jade fill your hall
It can no longer be guarded.
Wealth and place breed insolence
That brings ruin in its train.
When your work is done, then withdraw![M1]

The man "who moves on the even Tao (Path) seems to go up and down"![N1]

So universal and constant in all things is the process of reversion and return that all natural process is marked by the sameness of coming into being, reaching maturity, and reverting to non-being (death). All things go back to their common origin; ultimately they all blend into one. The Tao at work in each of the "ten thousand things under heaven" is the same Tao, obscure but originative, hidden but all-encompassing.

Because the eye gazes but can catch no glimpse of it,
It is called elusive.
Because the ear listens but cannot hear it,
It is called rarefied.
Because the hand feels for it but cannot find it,
It is called the infinitesimal.
These three, because they cannot be further scrutinized,
Blend into one.[M2]

Tao begets One; one begets two; two begets three; three begets all things.[L5]

Therefore the Sage embraces the One.[N2]

The sage knows that he is himself one with all things in the One. He himself, and all the distinguishable phenomena of nature, the events in space and time that make their appearance to the senses, are at heart indistinguishable. They are the same in their rise and fall, their growth and decay, but above all in the derivation of their being from original non-being and their return to non-being. All this is the way of nature and is the destiny of all things.

The sage therefore yields himself to nature (the Tao) and does not struggle to assert himself aggressively nor strive for a sharply distinguishable being of his own. He humbly seeks union with the All-Encompassing as the first condition of his own well-being.

> The ancient saying "Be humble and you shall remain entire"—
> Can this be regarded as mere empty words?[L6]

Above all, he wants to behave "naturally," "spontaneously." He won't insist that things should go on and on as he wants them to.

> Nature does not have to insist,
> Can blow for only half a morning,
> Rain for only half a day,
> And what are these winds and these rains but natural?
> If nature does not have to insist,
> Why should man?[P]

Leave all things to take their natural course, and do not interfere.[K5]

It may be objected that there is little of religion here. For one thing, it may be urged, the Tao is impersonal, and although persons are its expressions in some areas, it is itself without form and void. Therefore one meditates on the Tao but does not engage in formal worship of it. The Tao is not aware of nor does it make a compassionate response to persons; it is but the cosmic mode of action by which non-being becomes being. Yet religion may breathe in this rare air—a one-sidedly philosophical and intuitional type of religion no doubt, but something more than bare philosophy. For the Tao determines des-

Landscape with waterfall and two figures. This ink drawing on silk by Chou Ch'en, a Chinese artist of the fifteenth to sixteenth centuries (Ming dynasty), shows a scholar and his friend contemplating a waterfall among the mountains. The cliffs, the waterfall, the drifting mist, and they themselves are in accord with the Tao and "going where they are pushed, following where they are led." (Courtesy, Museum of Fine Arts, Boston.)

263

tiny, may even be said to be a ruling force (Te), and conformity to it is a species of religious mysticism. The study of the Tao begins in philosophy: what is the ultimate reality? and concludes as religion: how may I be in complete accord with this reality?

We turn now to the Tao Te Ching's ethics. What we have said has already suggested it.

The central consideration may be expressed in two sentences—one positive, the other negative. Positively stated, the principle is that one must exhibit within himself the procedure of the Tao and be characterized by its quietude of power, its production without possession, action without self-assertion, development without domination. Negatively, the principle runs: do not meddle with the smooth course of nature going on her blessed way. As the Tao Te Ching puts it, it is wise to practice *wu-wei* (quietism, non-aggression, non-meddlesome action). It is possible to achieve without doing.

Therefore, the sage carries on his business without action, and gives his teaching without words.[L7]

The sage exhibits a retiring, not to say a stay-at-home disposition. He says to himself:

Without going out of the door
One can know the whole world;
Without peeping out of the window
One can see the Tao of heaven.
The further one travels
The less one knows.
Therefore the sage knows everything without traveling;
He names everything without seeing it;
He accomplishes everything without doing it.[L8]

He has no ambitions, no desire for fame. He is egoless and knows that the admiration of other men, which most men seek, tends to bind him to a false image of himself that would prevent his acting freely and spontaneously. He must quietly be himself.

Such a one will appear "stupid" or "out of this world." Other people are wide-awake, knowing; he alone appears dull, confused, even uncomprehending, like a baby who is as yet unable to smile. But this is

his only way to guard from prying eyes and interfering wills the precious Te or natural ability that is the Tao's power at work in him.

This seems negative at first glance, but not so, says the Tao Te Ching. There is affirmative power in the quietism of wu-wei; its attendant virtues in human life are kindness, sincerity, and humility. If one does not meddle with others, human relations will fall as the Tao brings them to pass, naturally and simply. There will be a spontaneous birth of true love, real kindness, simplicity, and contentment in the lives and relationships of men. Just the restraint of self from anger, ambition, and meddlesome action is never merely negative in its consequences; power is in it, power for good.

To those who are good to me I am good; and to those who are not good to me, I am also good;—and thus all get to be good. To those who are sincere with me, I am sincere; and to those who are not sincere with me, I am also sincere;—and thus all get to be sincere.[°Q]

Oft-repeated is the conviction that in the presence of natural kindness the strong become harmless, and by its means the weak become irresistible.

There is nothing in the world more soft and weak than water, yet for attacking things that are hard and strong there is nothing that surpasses it. . . . The soft overcomes the hard; the weak overcomes the strong.[K6]
The highest goodness is like water. . . . It stays in places which others despise. Therefore it is near to Tao.[L9]

In developing the implications of this doctrine the Tao Te Ching went so far as to suggest that the Taoist sage possessed, through being in accord with the Tao, a magical power, more passive than active, which made him invulnerable to the attack of fierce beasts or violent men and immune to the assaults of death itself. It seems to be implied that when a man is possessed of the Tao he lives long, and during life

° The obverse of this is given in another section of the Tao Te Ching:

"It is by not believing in people that you turn them into liars."[M3]

he is exempt from decay. In one passage this idea is put forward with a modest "I have heard," but it came later to have great significance:

I have heard that he who possesses the secret of life, when traveling abroad, will not flee from rhinoceros or tiger; when entering a hostile camp, he will not equip himself with sword or buckler. The rhinoceros finds in him no place to insert its horn; the tiger has nowhere to fasten its claw; the soldier has nowhere to thrust his blade. And why? Because he has no spot where death can enter.[K7]

Elsewhere it is said:

He who is endowed with ample virtue may be compared
    to an infant.
No venomous insects sting him;
Nor fierce beasts seize;
Nor birds of prey strike him.[L10]

He who attains Tao is everlasting.
Though his body may decay he never perishes.[L11]

We shall see presently where pursuit of this conviction led the later Taoists.

Meanwhile, a word on the Tao Te Ching's distinctive theory of government.

It will readily be seen that the only political principle consistent with the Tao Te Ching's philosophy of life is laissez-faire. Non-interference by government in the lives of citizens is the one way to peace and freedom.

Tao is eternally inactive, and yet it leaves nothing undone. If kings and princes could but hold fast to this principle, all things would work out their own reformation.[K8]

Now this is how I know what I lay down:—
As restrictions and prohibitions are multiplied in the Empire, the people grow poorer and poorer. When the people are subjected to overmuch government, the land is thrown into confusion. . . . The greater the number of laws and enactments, the more thieves and robbers there will be. Therefore the Sage says: "So long as I do nothing, the people will work out their own reformation. So long as I love calm, the people will right themselves. If only I keep from meddling, the people will grow rich. If only I

am free from desire, the people will come naturally back to simplicity."[K9]

An interesting passage gives us the Tao Te Ching's picture of the ideal community—a small village-state, quiet, self-contained, and always keeping at home within its tiny boundaries.

Take a small country with a small population. It might well be that there were machines which saved labor ten times or a hundred times, and yet the people would not use them. . . . They would not emigrate to distant countries. Although there might be carriages and boats, no one would ride in them. Although there might be weapons of war, no one would issue them. It might well be that people would go back to using knotted cords.*
Make the people's food sweet, their clothes beautiful, their houses comfortable, their daily life a source of pleasure. Then the people will look at the country over the border, will hear the cocks crowing and the dogs barking there, but right down to old age and the day of their death, they will not trouble to go there [and see what it is like].[E3]

Of course, there was no room in this scheme of things for war, and we find the Tao Te Ching very firm on the point that "weapons, however beautiful, are instruments of ill omen, hateful to all creatures. Therefore he who has Tao will have nothing to do with them."[K10] But we are hardly prepared for the breath-taking insight:

Therefore, if a great kingdom humbles itself before a small kingdom, it shall make that small kingdom its prize. And if a small kingdom humbles itself before a great kingdom, it shall win over that great kingdom. Thus the one humbles itself in order to attain, the other attains because it is humble. If the great kingdom has no further desire than to bring men together and to nourish them, the small kingdom will have no further desire than to enter the service of the other. But in order that both may have their desire, the great one must learn humility.[K11]

We may not, perhaps, be in sympathy with the Tao Te Ching's political and social primitivism, but this is an amazing vision of international altruism that is still too high for us. Ironically enough, China

---

* In keeping records.

Scholar walking by a river. In this leaf from an Album of Paintings After Ancient Masters, *the scholar is faceless because his feelings are to be inferred from his surroundings, which present opposing themes. The trees, stripped by autumn, convey a sense of frailty and the brevity of life, but the crane symbolizes longevity, and the land masses in the background have solidity and strength that defy the mist creeping over them. He broods on both themes, much as Chuang-tzu did. (Wango H. C. Weng Collection.)*

in the past has not been unmindful of the possibilities suggested in it.

THE ESSAYS OF CHUANG-TZU. Chuang-tzu (or Chuang Chou) is, except for the legendary Lao-tzu himself, the most famous of the philosophical Taoists. He lived during the fourth century B.C. and skillfully popularized the teachings of his presumed master, performing for him in this respect the same service that Mencius, Chuang-tzu's contemporary, performed for Confucius. Thirty-three essays, which may contain considerable amounts of material from his own hand, have come down to us. In their present form they were probably compiled some centuries later from fragments of his own and his followers' writings. They are brilliantly written, with many a witty anecdote, entertaining allegory, and imaginary conversation to enhance their literary charm. He espe-

cially enjoyed tilting at the ideas expressed by contemporary Confucianism.[*]

Chuang-tzu was true to Taoist teaching in giving the Tao centrality. But he went beyond the Tao Te Ching in elaborating a doctrine of "transformations of the Tao" that resembles at some points the fluxionist speculations of Western philosophers. Objects originate in a whirl of being and becoming, out of preceding states of existence. Times succeed each other circularly; the seasons mutually produce and destroy each other without end. The yin and yang, springing from the Tao, produce each other, influence each other, and destroy each other in a never-ceasing

[*] He seems to have used the ironic propaganda device of making Confucius repudiate his love of learning and duty to society, talk like a Taoist, but not quite be one! This will appear in some of our quotations later on.

process. In the moral realm, he said, we have attractions and repulsions, loves and hates, distinctions of the sexes and their union for reproduction, but no lasting state either of peace or its opposite. Adversity and prosperity, security and danger succeed each other according to a law of reciprocal causality.

For there is (the process of) reverse evolution (uniting opposites). . . . The succession of growth and decay, of increase and diminution, goes in a cycle, each end becoming a new beginning. In this sense only may we discuss the ways of truth and the principles of the universe. The life of things passes by like a rushing, galloping horse, changing at every turn, at every hour. What should one do, or what should one not do? Let the (cycle of) changes go on by themselves![N2]

What seemed to Chuang-tzu to justify the Taoist restraint from action was the fact that in such a world of perfectly natural change absolute truth and absolute good are unknowable. All things are equal in their right to be and act. Whatever nature (Tao) brings to pass is at least as good and necessary as anything else it brings to pass. This is another way of saying that every creature has its own tao and its own te, and these are right for it. There is no standard or uniform way of doing things, no truth or right to which all creatures must conform. Each creature should be true to its own tao and te, not to another's. As to man, he may well ask: When is anything just right, or not just right? There is no means of knowing.

If a man sleeps in a damp place, he gets lumbago and dies. But how about an eel? And living up in a tree is precarious and trying to the nerves;—but how about monkeys? Of the man, the eel, and the monkey, whose habitat is the right one, absolutely? Human beings feed on flesh, deer on grass, centipedes on snakes, owls and crows on mice. Of these four, whose is the right taste, absolutely?[R1]

In regard to man's desires or interests, if we say that anything is either good or bad according to our individual (subjective) standards, then there is nothing which is not good, nothing which is not bad.[N4]

This point of view led Chuang-tzu to make the unconventional statement about the Three Dynasties:

Those who came at the wrong time and went against the tide are called usurpers. Those who came at the right time and fitted in with their age are called defenders of Right. . . . How can you know the distinctions of high and low and of the houses of the great and small?[N5]

Chuang-tzu likened the confusions of men to the puzzlement that would surely reign in the non-human world if the creatures could make comparisons of excellencies and defects.

The walrus envies the centipede; the centipede envies the snake; the snake envies the wind; the wind envies the eye; the eye envies the mind.

The walrus said to the centipede, "I hop about on one leg, but not very successfully. How do you manage all the legs you have?"

"I don't manage them," replied the centipede. "Have you never seen saliva? When it is ejected, the big drops are the size of pearls, the small ones like mist. They fall promiscuously on the ground and cannot be counted. And so it is that my mechanism works naturally, without my being conscious of the fact."

The centipede said to the snake, "With all my legs I do not move as fast as you with none. How is that?"

"One's natural mechanism," replied the snake, "is not a thing to be changed. What need have I for legs?"

The snake said to the wind, "I can manage to wriggle along, but I have a form. Now you come blustering down from the north sea to bluster away to the south sea, and you seem to be without form. How is that?"

"'Tis true," replied the wind, "that I bluster as you say; but any one who can kick at me, excels me. On the other hand, I can break huge trees and destroy large buildings. That is my strong point."[R2]

The wind was wise. It did not weaken itself by false value judgments issuing in envy. It realized that though, on an intellectual analysis of its differences from other things, it was relatively weak ("any one who can kick at me, excels me"), whenever it let itself go as nature intended it should, it was mighty and strong. Using similar logic, Chuang-tzu contends that a man should not argue about large and small, high and low, right and wrong, but let happen what will according to the transformations of the Tao. In so doing he will join the wind, the snake, and the centipede in the economy of nature.

267

Take no heed of time, nor of right or wrong. But passing into the realm of the Infinite, take your final rest therein.[R3]

This is the way of the sage, the truly natural man, who can seat himself by the sun and moon and hold the universe in his grasp, because:

He blends everything into one harmonious whole, rejecting the confusion of this and that. Rank and precedence, which the vulgar prize, the sage stolidly ignores. The revolutions of ten thousand years leave his unity unscathed.[R4]

The wise man does not wear out his senses trying to know individually and in detail the changing objects and beings of the material world. He dwells in the generality of a comprehensive view of all things. He makes his spiritual home in the Tao, in which all things lose their distinctions and merge into one.

The experience here referred to is not attainable by the searchings of reason, for the reason is too actively concerned with the discrimination of particulars. Real knowing is passive, receptive.

Hear not with your ears, but with your mind; not with your mind, but with your spirit. Let your hearing stop with the ears, and let your mind stop with its images. Let your spirit, however, be like a blank, passively responsive to externals. In such open receptivity only can Tao abide.[N6]

The final goal is the ecstasy of absorption into the quietude and ultimate truth of the Tao. One cannot push his way into this ecstasy; it must come of itself, in utter spontaneity. But when it comes, it changes the one who has experienced it. The "artificial and illusory self" has now been eliminated, and the "heavenly" has taken "full possession."[8]

Thereafter the sage cultivates an air of stupidity to keep people from rousing him out of his aloofness from the "ten thousand things" of which the world is composed. His mind is cool and tranquil under the realization that thoughts and dreams have little importance, for they are subjective phenomena. In a world of rapidly shifting and changing appearances, he knows it is best to be calm and not active, to accept life and not take it seriously. He is like Mr. Mengsun.

Mr. Mengsun knows not whence we come in life nor whither we go in death. He knows not which to put first and which to put last. He is ready to be transformed into other things without caring into what he may be transformed.[N7]

True to this conviction, Chuang-tzu, if we are to trust the anecdotes supplied by his followers, lived without worry or fret. He would not let his emotions upset his tranquility. It is said that when his wife died, his friend Hui-tzu, the logician, went to condole with him, according to custom, and found him seated on the ground singing and beating time on a metal bowl, which he held between his legs. Shocked at this sight, Hui-tzu said to him: "To live with your wife, and see your eldest son grow up to be a man, and then not to shed a tear over her corpse—this would be bad enough. But to drum on a bowl, and sing; surely this is going too far." "Not at all," replied Chuang-tzu. "When she first died, how could I help being affected? But then on examining the matter, I saw that in the Beginning she had originally been lifeless. And not only lifeless, but she had originally been formless. And not only formless, but she had originally lacked all substance. During this first state of confused chaos, there came a change which resulted in substance. This substance changed to assume form. The form changed and became alive. And now it has changed again to reach death. In this it has been like the passing of the four seasons, spring, autumn, winter, and summer. And while she is thus lying asleep in the Great House (i.e., the Universe), for me to go about weeping and wailing, would be to show myself ignorant of Fate. Therefore I refrain."[J4]

Another tale illustrates Chuang-tzu's philosophic pride. While he was walking along the road in a coarse, patched robe, and with shoes fastened to his feet with strings, he met the Marquis of Wei. "Master," said the marquis, "what distress is this that I see you in?" "Pardon," replied Chuang-tzu, "poverty, not distress. The scholar who possesses knowledge of the Principle [Tao] and its action is never in distress!"[T1]

But the most famous story about Chuang-tzu is the one concerning the offer of office made to him while he was fishing with line and float on the bank of the river P'u. The marquis of Ch'u sent two of his officials to offer Chuang-tzu the post of minister. Chuang-tzu went on fishing without turning his head and said, "I have heard that in Ch'u there is a sacred tortoise which has been dead now some three thousand years. And that the prince keeps this tortoise carefully enclosed in a chest on the altar of his ancestral temple. Now would this tortoise rather be dead and have its remains venerated, or be alive and wagging its tail in the mud?" "It would rather be alive," replied the two officials together. "Then," cried Chuang-tzu, "begone! I too will wag my tail in the mud."[R5]

The indictment that Chuang-tzu brought against his age was powerful. He idealized the past, as both his Taoist predecessors and the Confucians did, but he saw it from a point of view quite different from the Confucians', whose moralism he criticized as a forced matter that badly confused the true issues of life; under it men could not be simple and natural.* As he viewed it:

In the days when natural instincts prevailed, men moved quietly and gazed steadily. At that time, there were no roads over mountains, nor boats, nor bridges over water. All things were produced, each for its own proper sphere. Birds and beasts multiplied; trees and shrubs grew up. The former might be led by the hand; you could climb up and peep into the raven's nest. For then men dwelt with birds and beasts, and all creation was one. There were no distinctions of good and bad men. Being all equally without knowledge, their virtue could not go astray. Being all equally without evil desires, they were in a state of natural integrity, the perfection of human existence.

But when sages appeared, tripping people over charity and fettering with duty to one's neighbor, doubt found its way into the world. And then with their gushing over

* For more of this criticism see Section III of the next chapter, pp. 293 f.

music and fussing over ceremony, the empire became divided against itself.[R6]

In this primitivism of his, Chuang-tzu went much further than the Tao Te Ching. His thesis plainly is that none of the forms and institutions of social life under the Chou culture did anything but confuse men about their natural equality and thus corrupt their native integrity. With social institutions, he said violently, "gangsters appeared. Overthrow the Sages and set the gangsters free, and then the empire will be in order."[N8]

His animus against all social institutions died away when he turned his admiring eye toward nature. He taught Chinese artists in which direction to look for truth in their art. Since his time nature has been their first love, and, we are told, "he still is today the main fountain of [their] inspiration and imagination."[U]

And yet Chuang-tzu must not be supposed to have led artists to look merely at the outward forms of nature, for how much reality is there in forms taken by themselves? His inspiration for them has been in enabling them to look at the eternal Way *within* nature; that is, at the reality of which every form the poet or painter beholds is an expression, just as the poet or painter himself is. In one piquant illustration he posed for artists—and for philosophers—one of the knottiest problems of human knowledge: how to assess the reality of forms within the mind.

Once upon a time, I, Chuang-tzu, dreamt I was a butterfly, fluttering hither and thither, to all intents and purposes a butterfly . . . suddenly, I awaked. . . . Now I do not know whether I was then a man dreaming I was a butterfly, or whether I am now a butterfly dreaming I am a man.[R7]

But Taoism was not going to continue for long in this intriguing vein, philosophically defining the nature of things and the meaning of life. It was going to be turned into a species of magical theory and practice, and Chuang-tzu, as we shall see, was to share the responsibility for giving it an impetus in this direction.

269

B. The Magical Phase of Taoism

The problem of how to prolong life by mastering one's body and preventing the processes of natural decay from setting in has always interested the Chinese. No people have looked forward more than they have to old age—the period of patriarchal ease and leisure.

But there has been also a strong interest in "eternal life." And Taoism seemed to promise help. The Tao Te Ching, we have seen, suggested that anyone who possesses the secret of the Tao becomes immune to the attack of armed men and wild animals. He who is endowed with the ample virtue that the Tao engenders may be compared to an infant whom no venomous reptiles sting, no birds of prey strike.* Furthermore, "He who attains Tao is everlasting." Chuang-tzu (along with others, probably) added his speculations by way of further development. The mythical Emperor Fu Hsi, he said, obtained Tao, "and was able to steal the secrets of eternal principles." "The Yellow Emperor obtained it, and soared upon the clouds of heaven. . . . The Western (Fairy) Queen Mother obtained it, and settled at Shao Kuang, since when and until when, no one knows."[N9]

It is, of course, possible that Chuang-tzu was not entirely in earnest about all this, yet he brought this discussion, which had been confined to very ancient worthies, down to his own period in this lively dialogue:

Nanpo Tzek'uei said to Nü Yü (or Female Yü), "You are of a high age, and yet you have a child's complexion. How is this?"

Nü Yü replied, "I have learnt Tao."

*It may be remarked that this doctrine had some justification psychologically. Infants, aged people, and innocents are notoriously safe among violent men. As a rule animals, reptiles, and the larger insects are known to do no harm to people unafraid and gentle in movement. It may well have been that the complete Taoist sage enjoyed a comparatively high degree of personal safety in town and field. But such immunity from death and harm could be easily misconstrued as evidence of superhuman or magical potencies.

"Could I get Tao by studying it?" asked the other.

"No! How can you?" said Nü Yü. "You are not the type of person. There was Puliang I. He had all the mental talents of a sage, but not Tao of the sage. Now I had Tao, though not those talents. . . . I had to wait patiently to reveal it to him. In three days, he could transcend this mundane world. Again I waited for seven days more, then he could transcend all material existence. After he could transcend all material existence, I waited for another nine days, after which he could transcend all life. After he could transcend all life, then he had the clear vision of the morning, and after that, was able to see the Solitary (One). After seeing the Solitary, he could abolish the distinctions of past and present. After abolishing the past and present, he was able to enter there where life and death are no more."[N10]

Down this road of mysticism and magic Taoist speculation and experimentation turned. In the second century B.C. the Emperor Wu Ti of the Han dynasty was, in spite of his patronage of Confucianism, attracted to Taoism by the empress dowager and her associates. Ssu-ma Ch'ien, the famous Chinese historian of the first century B.C., records the tradition, whether true or not, that the geomancer Li Shao-Chin urged the emperor to apply himself to the alchemy furnace, for thus he would gain the good graces of the spirits and learn from them the formula for converting cinnabar into gold, after which he could have eating and drinking vessels made of the gold produced from the cinnabar and acquire longevity from the food and drink served in them. (Somehow the Chinese had come to connect "eatable gold" with immortality—if such gold could be had.) The geomancer further advised the emperor that if he performed on the sacred mountain T'ai Shan the ceremony known as feng-shan (in honor of Heaven or the Sovereign on High), he would not die anymore. It was thus, said the geomancer, that the Emperor Huang-ti had obtained immortality. From that time on, we are told, Wu Ti surrounded himself with Taoists and at their suggestion introduced many innovations into the practice of Chinese religion, against the wishes of the Confucians.*

*But in due time he was thoroughly disillusioned.

By the first century A.D. the magical emphasis in Taoism had become supreme. At that time a certain Chang-ling, better known as Chang Tao-ling, migrated from eastern to western China and founded a secret society devoted primarily to alchemy and the cultivation of the Taoist meditative trance, but availing itself also of ideas probably borrowed from Zoroastrian circles in western China. Because all who joined his society had to pay him with five pecks of rice, his sect was tauntingly called the Wu Tou Mi Tao, "The Five Pecks of Rice Way." On the foundation thus laid his son and grandson built an organization that attracted the superstitious adherence of many followers and through vigorous military activity acquired great political power. In course of time Chang Tao-ling was apotheosized as a "Celestial Teacher," for he was said to have been personally ordained by Lao-tzu, who appeared to him out of the spirit world. In addition, he was said to have discovered the formula for the potion of immortality, a powerful elixir of life, and to have ascended alive to heaven from the top of Mount Lung-hu (Dragon-Tiger Mountain) in Kiangsi on the back of a tiger, after having prolonged his life by the use of his elixir to the ripe age of 122 years.

His influence proved to be lasting, for in the course of centuries his successors became a line of high priests or "popes," living on Dragon-Tiger Mountain. Each pope was thought to be a reincarnation of Chang Tao-ling, and for some centuries flourished on the endowment provided for his see's expenses by the Sung Emperor Chen Tsung (998–1023 A.D.). But at length serious decay of power and inner vitality set in. In the turmoil of recent years the popes have been driven from their mountain, probably never to return.

Another of the Taoist sects, the Yellow Turbans, headed by a Chang-Chüeh and his two brothers, numbered hundreds of thousands of adepts, and in an attempted rising in the second century A.D. held for a time the whole of the Yellow River. In spite of the subsequent decline and failure of this and similar movements, the Taoists always hoped someday to make a serious bid for power.

Meanwhile Taoist magic continued to develop. The scholar Ko Hung of the fourth century A.D., who wrote a famous book on magical matters and himself spent the last years of his life on Lo-fu Mountain experimenting with the pill of immortality,* has described in detail the breathing exercises (a technique clearly taken over from Indian mysticism), dietetics, alchemy, and magic of the time, so that a dip into his storehouse of facts is illuminating. The object of the breathing exercises was to increase the spiritual powers of the body and mind, and of the dietetics to prolong life and particularly to enable one to live exclusively on air and dew, in a state immune to illness, though death from old age could not be prevented by this method alone. The alchemy had as its object the discovery of liquid or eatable gold, a commodity that should confer immortality on those who would swallow it.† This amalgam had to be other than one based on mercury, which is a yin substance and produces death. Cinnabar was thought to be the proper substance, but the alchemists never quite succeeded in attaining the results they desired, in spite of instances cited by Ko Hung of individuals who passed on into the immortal state, but who, alas! took the secret of their formulas with them! As to the magic, it could do all sorts of things in establishing control over natural processes. Ko Hung describes certain charms, which, if swallowed or worn on the person, rendered one invulnerable to warlike weapons, though immunity could be gained only from

* While most of his influence is due to his book, *Pao P'u-tzu*, much of his popular fame comes from the story that when he was eighty-one years old a friend whom he had invited to visit him found only his empty clothes—proof enough that he had disappeared among the Immortals! But he was not the only one thus to achieve immortality. He himself told the story that the author of another book on occult matters succeeded in preparing pills of immortality, and gave one to a dog, only to see it drop dead, but he had so much faith in his pill that he took one himself, and fell to the ground. His elder brother, faith unshaken, took the pill with the same result. A younger brother was about to bury them, when they came back to life. They were Immortals!

† Salt, says Ko Hung, preserves dead meat; it must be possible to find some preservative for live flesh!

the weapons specifically named in the charms. Care should therefore be taken to name every weapon by which one might ever conceivably be injured, for otherwise one might be caught like the magician "who being proof against every pointed or edged weapon, was killed by a blow from a cudgel, a common weapon he had not foreseen." Other charms are mentioned for making oneself invisible, for changing one's shape at will, for freeing oneself from all bonds, and for raising and transporting oneself through space. And then there was the little pill making one able to walk on water. It was only necessary to take "seven, three times a day, for three years, without forgetting a single time." In another place Ko Hung describes a magical seal, which, "impressed on the dust or mud, prevents ferocious beasts or malignant goblins from passing. The same, placed on the doors of storages and stables, protects the provisions and the animals."T2

In these last sentences, of which many parallels could be cited, there is to be seen the reason for the power of the Taoist priests among the common people of China down to this day. They were notable geomancers and doctors of thaumaturgy. But to attain this power over the common people these wonder-workers had to have all the sanctions of religion. And Taoism became a religion.

C. Taoism as a Religion

The third phase of Taoism was prefigured in 165 A.D. by the act of the Emperor Huan of the second Han dynasty in ordering for the first time official offerings to Lao-tzu and the building of a temple in his honor. But what was thus anticipated did not get under way until the seventh century when Li Shih-min, who established the great T'ang dynasty, gave Taoism imperial recognition as an organized religion.

By this time Buddhism had made its appearance as a great and significant factor in Chinese religious life. Neither Confucianism, the rather stiff and formal mode of thought and behavior known chiefly to the literati and officials, nor Taoism, still the preoccupation either of intellectuals on the one hand or of students of the esoteric and the occult on the other, was wholly satisfactory to the unlearned and lowly masses. Hinayana Buddhism was no better in the eyes of these unlettered but spiritually hungry souls, but the Mahayana was another matter. The beneficent Bodhisattvas who gave aid in daily life, and the Dhyani Buddhas who admitted one to paradise, were soon being plied with gifts and prayers by millions.

As Buddhism swept across China and into Korea, the Taoists, struck with amazement and yet sure that China had her own resources, so to speak, in the way of gods and spirits, began to look into their own heritage, and finding much to value, they began to ape the powerful faith brought in from India. One cannot be too positive that the effort was a sustained and self-conscious process, but what actually happened was that Chinese history was searched for personages that might compare in popular appeal with the Buddhas. Lao-tzu was formally apotheosized, with the title "Emperor of Mysterious Origin," and he was provided with heavenly associates in imitation of Buddha and the Lohans. The Taoist writings were united into a canon, temples were erected, and groups of ascetics were called together in close copying of the Buddhist models. But this as yet was not sufficient to give Taoism the status among the populace of a satisfactory religion. It was still not clearly theistic. So the Taoist gods and spirits were brought together into a systematized pantheon. The motivation may well have been as sincere as it was nationalistic: why resort to foreign gods, when the Chinese had long had on their own soil beings who were near at hand and able to help them with a proven sympathetic response to their immediate needs? *

But the Taoists' reconstruction of Chinese religion was not utterly sincere. There was some outright

---

* This would not necessarily, and did not, mean that Buddhist beings were to be denied value as efficacious helpers *in their own sphere*—i.e., release from suffering and admission to heaven of persons who would rather go to a Buddhist than a Taoist paradise.

fabrication. One of the most amazing incidents in all religion-making took place when the Emperor Chen Tsung, of the Sung dynasty, effected by fraud the final step in the transformation of Taoism into a complete theism. His ulterior purpose was the recovery of his own prestige, which needed bolstering badly. At the turn of the year 1005 A.D. the emperor "lost face" because, being unable to drive back the nomad invaders from the northwest, the dreaded Kitan Tartars who were pouring into China across the Great Wall, he had been forced to make a disgraceful peace by which he ceded away large portions of north China. He consulted the Taoist soothsayers and geomancers for advice. How could he reinstate himself in the favor of his people? The tradition has it that his minister, the wiley Wang Ch'in-jo, surprised the emperor by advising a fabricated revelation from heaven, and when the emperor protested, said brazenly: "Bah! the Ancients had no such scruples. Each time the need was felt the Sages caused Heaven and the spirits to intervene in order to bring their policy into popular favor. It is precisely in this that their wisdom consisted."T3 The emperor, much impressed, visited the imperial library and consulted the scholars there. In 1008 A.D. he called his ministers together and told them he had been informed in a dream that Heaven was about to send him a letter, and that the governor of the capital had just reported seeing a yellow scarf hanging from one of the cornices of the Gate of Heaven. The emperor then went on foot to watch the scarf being lowered. It proved to contain a letter, ostensibly from a celestial being writing in the style of Lao-tzu. Officers were dispatched throughout the empire to make known the news. Another revelation followed in six months. And then in 1012 A.D. it was disclosed that the celestial being thus communicating with the emperor was Yü Huang. This being had not been heard of in China before the ninth century, but he was now raised to supremacy, and by succeeding emperors declared to be the Pure and Great One, Author of the visible heaven and of physical laws, the Controller of Time and of the processes making divination valid, and the Em-

bodiment of Good and the Way (Tao). It was said finally that the celestial sovereign whom the ancients had called Imperial Ruler on High (Shang-ti) was and always had been none other than Yü Huang, the Jade Emperor!

There was a widespread popular response. The people were apparently well pleased to have so many of their favorite folklore gods given imperial recognition, and they soon became accustomed to thinking of Shang-ti and the Jade Emperor as one and the same being. The stories that began to circulate, giving the latter's history, entered the body of popular tradition without difficulty.

The popular satisfaction was increased by another sort of invention. Heaven and hell were added to the scheme. Paradise was found in various places, but most delightfully in the Three Isles of the Blessed (San Hsien Shan), long held in Chinese folklore to be located somewhere in the Eastern Sea (between the Chinese and Japanese mainlands, but nobody who had gone there had come back). Hell was given every appurtenance of torture and punishment, becoming a place full of ogres and goblins of every malevolent and horrifying kind. It became a major concern of the living to procure release of relatives from this terrifying place.

Whether the final product of Taoist religion-making should be called Taoist in any proper sense of that word is a question, but the Taoist priests had no hesitations, assured that because the common people shared in the decision as to which of the deities and spirits, old and new, should be the most important to them, there was no need to hold back. Although as a matter of course the Jade Emperor was granted the highest place and was commonly associated with Lao-tzu and a third being, Ling Pao, marshal of the supernatural beings, the three together forming the official Taoist trinity (the Three Purities), more interest and affection were shown toward adoptions from popular, originally non-Taoist, religion: the Eight Immortals, the God of the Hearth, the Guardians of the Door, and the City God. To these therefore we turn for a brief description.

273

The Eight Immortals have long been beloved figures of folklore. They are wholly and delightfully Chinese. Their abode is usually thought to be either somewhere in the mountains or on the Three Isles of the Blessed. They are supposed to have been (and most of them probably originally were) human beings, but they are also thought to have been ascetics to such good purpose that they achieved immortality and now live on in their old bodies with minds and spirits ever young. Four of them are often represented together as seated under a pine tree, two of them sipping the wine heated for them by a third, while a fourth pipes upon a flute in entertainment. The others are usually portrayed singly. The "Maiden Immortal," Ho Hsien Ku, was long ago a mortal, of course, but while at home with her shop-keeping parents, she lived on a diet of powdered mother-of-pearl and moonbeams and thus became immortal. She has often appeared to men floating on the clouds, carrying in her hand a lotus blossom or, at times, the peach of immortality. Because they are fairies, the Eight Immortals belong to a larger group whose presiding spirits are, for the females, the very popular Fairy Queen Mother, who is the subject of countless tales, and for the males, Tung Wang Kung, a less well-known being.

The God of the Hearth, Tsao Shen (not exclusively Taoist, once the spirit of the alchemy furnace honored by the Han Emperor Wu Ti in the second century B.C.), has been honored throughout China as the kitchen-spirit who sits in the chimney-corner viewlessly watching all that the family does. His presence used to be constantly recalled to the remembrance of naughty children. On the twenty-fourth day of the twelfth moon, food and wine offerings were presented to his paper image, and when this image and the paper money, horses, and chariots accompanying it were burned together below the chimney, he ascended up the flue to heaven to make his annual report on the behavior of the family.

At New Year, invocations used to be offered to two Guardians of the Door, the Men Shen, both spirits of great antiquity, and their paper images, in military garb and carrying swords or spears, were attached to the two halves of the front door to ward off evil spirits during the coming year.

The City God, Cheng Huang, was worshiped in almost every Chinese city, for five centuries officially. He was first adopted by the religion-makers of the T'ang dynasty, but it was not until the fourteenth century that his worship was made an official requirement. Today he belongs to the past.

Of all the other spirits honored by the Taoists there is no space here to tell. They were many. One could linger, not only with the river-, soil-, mountain-, and star-spirits and with the patron deities of all the trades and occupations, but also with the apotheosized national heroes, the gods of health and luck, and the many animal and vegetable spirits, the dragons and phoenixes and unicorns. But these must be found described in some other place.

Taoism has for many years been in decline. According to the latest reports, as a religion it is now dead. The government frowns upon it and is determined to suppress it. But many still cling to it as magic, no matter how secret they must be about it nor how carefully they must try to elude the vigilant eye of the Communist district leaders.

Suggestions for Further Reading

Blakney, R. B. *The Way of Life: Lao Tzu.* Mentor pb, 1955

Bodde, Derk. "Myths of Ancient China," in *Mythologies of the Ancient World.* Ed. by Samuel N. Kramer. Anchor Books pb, 1961

Carus, Paul. *The Canon of Reason and Virtue.* Open Court, 1913. Available in pb

Chan, Wing-tsit. *Religious Trends in Modern China.* Columbia University Press, 1953

CREEL, H. G. *The Birth of China.* John Day, 1937

————. *Sinism.* Open Court, 1928

DUYVENDAK, J. J. L., TR. *Tao Te Ching, Lao Tzu.* John Murray, London, 1954

EBERHARD, W. *Chinese Festivals.* Henry Schuman, New York, 1952

FERGUSON, J. C. "Chinese Mythology," in *The Mythology of All Races.* Ed. by J. A. MacCulloch. Marshall Jones Co., Boston, 1930

FUNG, Y. L. *A History of Chinese Philosophy.* Tr. by Derk Bodde. 2 vols., Princeton University Press, 1952

————. *Chuang Tzu, A New Selected Translation With An Exposition of The Philosophy of Kuo Hsiang.* Commercial Press, Shanghai, 1931

GILES, H. A. *Chuang Tzu—Mystic, Moralist and Social Reformer.* Kelly and Walsh, Shanghai, 1926

GILES, LIONEL. *The Sayings of Lao Tzu.* In the *Wisdom of the East* series, John Murray, 1905

GOODRICH, L. C. *A Short History of the Chinese People.* Harper, 1943

GRAHAM, A. C. *Lieh Tzu.* John Murray, London, 1960

GROUSSET, RENÉ. *The Rise and Splendour of the Chinese Empire.* 1st Amer. ed., University of California Press, 1953

HODOUS, L. *Folkways in China,* Probsthain, London, 1929

HUGHES, E. R. *Chinese Philosophy in Classical Times.* Everyman's Library, J. M. Dent, 1941

LANG, OLGA. *The Chinese Family and Society.* Yale University Press, 1950

LATOURETTE, K. S. *The Chinese, Their History and Culture.* Macmillan, 1934

LEGGE, JAMES, TR. *The Texts of Taoism.* In the *Sacred Books of the East* series, Oxford, 1891

LIN YUTANG. *The Wisdom of China and India.* Random House, 1942. An anthology. Includes new translation of *Tao Te Ching* and a revision of Giles' *Chuang Tsu*

————, TR. AND ED. *The Wisdom of Laotse.* Modern Library, 1948

TSUI CHI. *A Short History of Chinese Civilization.* Putnam, 1943

WALEY, ARTHUR, TR. *The Book of Songs.* Allen and Unwin, 1937

————. *The Way and Its Power, a Study of the Tao Te Ching.* Allen and Unwin, 1934

————. *Three Ways of Thought in Ancient China.* Allen and Unwin, 1939. Available as Anchor pb

WANG GUNG-HSING. *The Chinese Mind.* John Day, 1946

WEI, FRANCIS C. M. *The Spirit of Chinese Culture.* Scribner, 1947

WELCH, HOLMES. *The Parting of the Way: Lao Tzu and the Taoist Movement.* Beacon, 1957

YANG, C. K. *Religion in Chinese Society.* University of California Press, 1961

YANG, Y. C. *China's Religious Heritage.* Abingdon-Cokesbury, Nashville, 1943

10 Confucius and Confucianism: A Study in Optimistic Humanism

We are fortunate in the case of Confucius in having fairly reliable information about his attitudes and his opinions. His disciples made attempts to preserve his teachings from the first, and the descriptions they left of his personal habits are detailed and probably accurate. We cannot say as much for the accuracy of the later, traditional biographies, for they present us with much questionable history, containing many obviously legendary incidents. But even these doubtful accounts have value: they incorporate authentic material left by Confucius' disciples, and thus manage to present us with what seems on the whole a dependable portrait of the man.

That after all is the important thing. The kind of man Confucius was is of major importance. That the Chinese have eagerly studied and followed his teachings in the past, and have founded not only their educational procedure but much of their governmental practice, until very recently, on the principles he was understood to have laid down is due in large part to the fact that they have had such confidence in his character, shining nobly through the traditions of his life and permeating his teachings. He was not only a wise man or a clever one, they have said; he was an incorruptible man, a human-hearted man. He was a model gentleman.

But there is something more. The character of Confucius has seemed to exemplify the principles of order and harmony for which he stood in his teachings. During most of their history the Chinese have felt that their land would be well off indeed if the application of his principles could produce more men with his character. Not only would there then be better order in men's personal lives, but a superior order as well in the family and in the state and harmony between earth and heaven. The moral influence of truly Confucian men would make this a certainty.

It is not strange that Confucius rather than the Taoists should have laid the foundation for traditional Chinese education. The Taoists turned for the secret of life to nature and her laws, but Confucius was a humanist; he found the secret of life in men and their better relationships.

Let us see first of all what kind of man Confucius was and what his beliefs were, and then we shall be prepared to trace out the effects of his character and teaching on the rich development of Chinese thought.

I The Man Confucius

The best source of information on Confucius is the *Analects,* the famous collection of his sayings by his disciples, but the biographical matter in it is scant. Later Confucian tradition therefore busied itself with supplying an abundance of biographical detail, from birth to old age. As we have already observed, much of this later material is of doubtful historical value. Is then one to credit none of it, and to stand firm on the *Analects* alone? Or is it better to go part of the way with Ssu-ma Ch'ien (China's famous ancient historian, who died about 80 B.C.) and consider the body of tradition sound where it is not actually incredible? ° Neither course is satisfactory. The former does not sufficiently account for the clear-cut political aims of the Confucian school; the latter is apt to go too far in its acceptance of tradition.

If we pursue the moderate course of accepting just so much of the tradition as is needed to account for the eagerness of Confucius' disciples to take office and to set up a school of thought devoted to the training of officials and teachers, something like this brief biography results:

Confucius came of a poor but respected family in the ancient province of Lu, at the base of the Shantung peninsula. His ancestors were reputed to have been aristocratic refugees who fled from the state of Sung to Lu when a revolution overthrew the ducal house. Shortly after his birth (probably in 551 B.C.) his father died, and he and his young mother were left in straitened circumstances. According to the

Analects (IX. 6), Confucius said later that he was a poor man's son and could therefore do many menial things that are done by the common man—things that the princely (or superior) man does not have to do. Perhaps reflection on these early struggles led him to observe in after days, "It is hard not to chafe at poverty."[A1]

In spite of their straitened circumstances, Confucius was provided by his self-sacrificing mother with the proper intellectual training to be a gentleman. He apparently studied under a village tutor and became a life-long student of the poetry and historical tradition of ancient China. He also developed a consuming interest in the several varieties of Chinese classical music (now lost to us), which he performed on the lute, often singing the old songs to this accompaniment. According to the famous autobiographical summary in the *Analects,* at fifteen he began to be seriously interested in these studies, that is, he determined to be a scholar.

But the same source of information indicates that he did not spend all his time at his books. He did a good deal of hunting and fishing, but always with an aristocratic sense of sportsmanship, for his disciples noted: "The Master angled, but did not fish with a net; he shot, but not at birds sitting."[A2] He enjoyed chariot- and carriage-driving, and was well aware of the high sportsmanship demanded in archery: "A gentleman has no rivalries—except perhaps in archery; and then, as, bowing, he joins the winners or steps down to see the loser drink, throughout the struggle he is still a gentleman."[A3]

In his late teens he accepted a minor government post as a collector of grain and livestock due as taxes to the Duke of Lu, and also contracted a not too successful marriage, which, however, realized one major objective, the bringing of a son into the world to carry on the family line. In his middle twenties, his mother died. To Confucius this was a great personal tragedy. He at once retired from public life for twenty-seven months—a period reckoned in Chinese funerary tradition to be equivalent to three full years. Tradition insists that he more than fulfilled the con-

---

° The radical procedure of going on the *Analects* alone is sketched out for us in Arthur Waley's *Analects of Confucius,* p. 14. On the other hand, Carl Crow in *Master K'ung* accepts nearly all of the tradition.

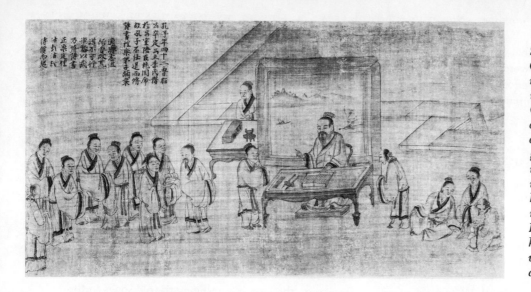

Scene from the life of Confucius. In this drawing from the Ming dynasty (1368–1644), Confucius lectures out of doors to a large band of disciples who have gathered round him. He is forty-two years old and is the headmaster of his own private school in the state of Lu. Like his disciples, he keeps his hair in place with a comb. (Philadelphia Museum of Art.)

ventions; at the end of the mourning period he took up his lute, but he played haltingly and was unable to sing to the notes for another five days, thus furnishing China with a classic instance of filial piety.

He now set himself up as a teacher, offering instruction in history, poetry, government, propriety, music, and divination (the traditional "Six Disciplines"). Disciples joined him, some remaining with him for years. But though his reputation was great, and the scions of the best families in Lu were sent to him, he kept saying that his principles could be made effective in improving the now decadent social system only if he and his disciples took office in the higher echelons of government.

Tradition, not verifiable on the evidence of the *Analects,* insists that he took office in the cabinet of the Duke of Lu when fifty years of age, and that he ascended through the offices of minister of public works and minister of justice to the position of prime minister, but that, through intrigue occasioned by his highly successful and upright administration, he was placed in a position where he "lost face" and resigned.

Whether this is true or not, at the age of fifty-five he left Lu, accompanied by some of his disciples, and wandered for thirteen years from state to state, seeking a post under some government, and all in vain. The great feudal lords entertained him courteously, tongue in cheek. Some thought him a very wise and great man, yet even in this event his idea of governing by the sheer force of moral example aroused no response. But if the feudal lords listened to him with respect, the officials intrigued to get rid of him. In some districts he was met with open suspicion, at the town of K'uang mobbed and imprisoned, at P'u surrounded and forced to accept armed protection, and in Sung, the state whence (perhaps) his ancestors had come, obliged to escape on foot into Cheng. In this last instance his disciples, knowing that a certain military officer called Huan T'uei was close on their heels, kept urging him to hurry, but he replied, "Heaven begat the power (Te) that is in me. What have I to fear from such a one as Huan T'uei?"[B] Although he was fundamentally a serious man, he was not above regarding his plight humorously.* In passing through Tahsiang, a man

* According to Ssu-ma Ch'ien, his lightheartedness offended the members of his party on one occasion, when between Ch'en and Ts'ai they were surrounded by a guard of hostile soldiers, who were instructed not to let them escape into the state of Ch'u. Food supplies ran short, some of the party fell sick and were confined to bed, but Confucius kept on reading and singing, accompanying himself with his lute. Only Yen Huei, his favorite disciple, understood his mood. He said to Confucius: "What do you care if [your ideas] are not accepted? The

taunted him, "Great indeed is Confucius! He knows about everything and has made no name in anything!" Confucius turned to his disciples in mock dismay. "Now what shall I take up? Shall I take up charioteering? Shall I take up archery?"[A4]

Through the good offices of one of his disciples who held a high official appointment in Lu, a cordial invitation to return was extended to Confucius by Duke Ai in 484 B.C., and Confucius, now sixty-seven years old, came home. Sometimes called into consultation by the duke, he otherwise passed his last years in retirement. Late Confucian tradition gave rise to the belief that he spent his time compiling the materials he used in his teaching into the famous Confucian Classics, the *Shu Ching* or Book of History, the *Shih Ching* or Book of Poetry, the *Li Chi* or Book of Rites, the *I Ching* or Book of Changes, and the *Ch'un Ch'iu* or Annals of Spring and Autumn, the first four being anthologies of older source material, the last his own composition.* But all this is, as we shall see in a moment, highly doubtful. Just before his death in 479 B.C. he expressed discouragement about his own career, yet left his disciples more determined than ever to carry out his political and social aims.

II   The Teachings of Confucius

Present Estimate of the Sources

A discussion of our sources of the teaching of Confucius is important, first of all, because it is generally agreed upon today that the Five Classics are

---

at least not wholly from Confucius' hands—if they have come from his hands at all. For one thing, his disciples edited, altered, and amplified the materials they inherited. Thus, Ssu-ma Ch'ien says that Mencius, over a hundred years after Confucius, "put the *Shih* and *Shu* in order."[D1] It is especially true of the *Li Chi* that it cannot possibly be called, as it now stands, the product of Confucius' editorial work, but seems rather to date from the early years of the Han dynasty (second century B.C.). Apparently, Confucius' materials were often re-issued in revised editions.

But there is a more fundamental point to make: a careful scholarship must recognize it as a possibility that Confucius used, rather than first assembled, the materials of the earlier editions of the Classics, and that these collections were already in existence and may have been in use by teachers before his time.*

If we assume that Confucius adopted the Classics as already-known and valued anthologies, then his chief purpose was to point out the lessons contained in them. As a matter of fact, the *Analects* is full of evidence of this. It was in this that we may see his originality. It is possible that he may have done some editing while he was about it, editing that had decisive effects. But even when we assume such

---

very fact that they are not accepted shows that you are a true gentleman [with ideas too great to be accepted by the people]." And Confucius was pleased with this flattery. "Is that so? Oh, son of Yen, if you were a rich man, I would be your butler!"[C1]

* He is also said to have compiled a sixth book, the *Yüeh* or Book of Music, of which only a portion has survived (in Chapter X of the *Li Chi*).

* This is the contention of Dr. Y. L. Fung in *A History of Chinese Philosophy* (Henri Vetch, Peiping, 1937, pp. 46–47). He says: "The *Kuo Yü* informs us concerning a crown prince of Ch'u, son of King Chuan of Ch'u (613–591 B.C.), that the prince was given instruction in such works as the 'Odes,' 'Rites,' 'Music,' 'Spring and Autumn,' and 'Old Records.' Both the *Kuo Yü* and *Tso Chuan* record numerous conversations between important personages, in which the 'Odes' and 'History' are frequently mentioned; while the 'Rites' (*Li*) were used in diplomatic relations, and the 'Changes' (*I*) in divination. This indicates that an education of this sort was acquired by a portion, at least, of the nobility of that time. Confucius was the first man, however, to use the Six Disciplines for teaching the common people." It must be granted, this Chinese authority says also, that Confucius had a special connection with the Six Disciplines, for both the New Text school in its claim that Confucius organized the Six Disciplines himself, and the Old Text school in its contention that he was merely their transmitter, agree that he was very closely connected with them.

279

editing, we cannot know where or on what materials he did it.＊

Another fact should be made clear. The possibility that Confucius made changes in the Five Classics cannot be ruled out, but if he did so, he behaved as an editor should. He did not intrude his private convictions into these collections; he conceived his function to be merely that of a "transmitter," and that is

＊ Present critical opinion concerning the Five Classics comes to something like this:

The *Shih Ching* or Book of Poetry is authentically old, a valuable treasure-trove of information about Chou times. Its archaic language and simple grammar mark it as a genuine survival from the Chou dynasty's heyday (1000–600 B.C.).

The *Shu Ching* or Book of History contains some later forgeries and has lost a good deal of its once great historical authority, but the greater bulk of it may be judged from its archaic style to have been composed in some part during early Chou times (but not earlier), and in other parts during late Chou and early Han times (600–50 B.C.).

The *Ch'un Ch'iu* or Annals of Spring and Autumn is in two parts: the original extremely concise year-by-year annals of the state of Lu, and a commentary, the Tso Chuan, traditionally ascribed to Tso Chiu-Ming, a personal disciple of Confucius. The first part probably antedates Confucius; the second part seems to have been composed not earlier than the fourth century B.C., if not later.

The *I Ching* or Book of Changes is also in two main parts. The original sixty-four hexagrams, with a list of very brief oracles to accompany each line in them, probably dates from somewhere around 1000–800 B.C. The number of explanatory appendices, called the Shih I or Ten Wings, assigned by tradition to Confucius, seem rather to have been written by Confucians some time after him, perhaps during the early years of the Han dynasty, when the original I Ching (mysterious even to Confucius) needed to have the proper interpretations supplied from the oral tradition preserved by the Confucian school.

As it stands, the *Li Chi* or Book of Rites, as has been noted, is very late. Its sixty-four chapters may contain earlier material but are in their present form a compilation not earlier than early Han times.

For the student, the most easily accessible brief discussions of these matters may be found in *A History of Chinese Philosophy* by Fung Yu-Lan, Vol. I, translated by Derk Bodde (see the bibliography and index at the end of the volume), and in the brief introductions written for each part of *Chinese Philosophy in Classical Times*, edited and translated by E. R. Hughes (No. 973 in the Everyman's Library).

actually what he said he was. The *Analects* records two sayings of his that testify to his great respect for the learning of the "ancients": "I am a transmitter and not a creator. I believe in and have a passion for the Ancients,"E1 "I'm not born a wise man. I'm merely one in love with ancient studies and work very hard to learn them."F1 The Classics, then, are not a source of Confucius' original ideas. His private views and interpretations can be judged uncertainly, or at best to a limited degree only, from his textbook materials.

This might seem at first glance a serious difficulty, but we have other sources of his teaching that are far more revealing. When he was using or studying the Classics, he offered his comments and interpretations to by-standers freely and in ample detail. He went further, and developed his own conception of what men must do to preserve, and live by, the best insights contained in the literature he so highly valued. These comments and discussions seemed so important to those who heard them that they wrote them down on slips of bamboo, at first fragmentarily, then more fully by way of interpretation and paraphrase. The details of Confucius' own teaching have thus come to us through his disciples and owe much to their phrasing. Their recollections and interpretations are found in the Four Books, which are:

1. The *Analects* (the *Lun Yü*). This is a collection of the sayings of Confucius and of some of his disciples and might be called the salient points of his and their conversations removed from the context and condensed. Although it is of very composite origin, and though "not much more than half [of it] can be really trusted even as good second-hand evidence," as one estimate puts it,G1 nevertheless, in spite of its inaccuracies, Confucius vividly and in his own person speaks to us through it. It is our most important source of material on him.

2. The *Great Learning* (*Ta Hsüeh*). This was originally Chapter 39 of the *Li Chi*, but since Chu Hsi's time ＊ it has been removed for separate use. We

＊ The twelfth century A.D. For Chu Hsi, see pp. 307 ff.

cannot consider it to be from Confucius. Rather, it seems to be dependent for its point of view upon Hsün-tzu (298–238 B.C.). Obviously a treatise in itself, it was initially designed to serve as the basis of the education of gentlemen in general, princes in particular. In classical Chinese education it was the first text studied by school boys.

3. The *Doctrine of the Mean* (*Chung Yung*). This also was a part of the *Li Chi* (as Chapter 28). It is an excellent exposition of the philosophical presuppositions of Confucian thought, dealing particularly with the relation of human nature to the underlying moral order of the universe. Its contents have been traditionally attributed to Confucius' grandson, Tzu Ssu, but this is now regarded as subject to serious qualification. For one thing, it is apparently composed of two parts, one later than the other. The earlier, central part *may* have come from Tzu Ssu, but the later portion appears to have been written after the time of Mencius, perhaps in the second century B.C.

4. The *Book of Mencius,* dating from the third century B.C. This is a collection of the writings and sayings of the most original of the earlier Confucian thinkers and constitutes the first attempt to reach a rounded and systematic exposition of Confucian philosophy.

It would be foolish to say the Four Books have removed all our difficulties. Though perhaps hardly anyone ever lived who succeeded as well as Confucius in reshaping the minds of his disciples into accurate reflections of his own, it has to be recognized that the Four Books changed with the passage of time through the editing of later hands, as must be evident from the descriptions of them just given, and therefore any competent exposition of Confucius' teachings must take these changes into account wherever they can be detected.

One final difficulty remains. It can be said to have arisen historically and been settled for us historically. The long history of the Five Classics and the Four Books is punctuated at one point with a great threat to their survival. The first real emperor of all

China, and perhaps its greatest, was Duke Cheng of Ch'in, the founder of the short-lived Ch'in dynasty, who conquered and in 221 B.C. forcibly unified the provinces of China as that had never been done before, and who accordingly took the proud title "Shih Huang-ti" or the First Emperor. We have referred to him before (p. 258). An administrative and military genius, he established a new imperial capital, abolished the old feudal system, concentrated authority in himself, redivided the empire into thirty-six new administrative districts, built the Great Wall, introduced a new currency, instituted reforms among the officials (many of whom lost their jobs), substituted silk painted with a soft hair brush for the old bamboo records incised with a metal stylus, and encouraged the simplification of the writing of Chinese characters which followed, and which resulted in a new script. He found amidst all these changes that his attempts to establish a new order were obstructed by traditionalists and conservatives, chief among whom were the Confucian-trained school-masters and officials, who clung on to the feudal traditions of the first three dynasties (the Hsia, the Shang, and the Chou) and openly resisted his innovations as destructive of public order and morality. On the advice of his prime minister, Li Ssu, who was an advocate of the doctrines of the Legalists,* the emperor in 213 B.C. ordered the famous "Burning of the Books" for which Chinese scholarship has since so execrated him. His purpose was to standardize the thinking of the common people, and therefore he wished to destroy every privately owned copy of the writings that preserved the knowledge of past ways of conducting public affairs, except such books as the *I Ching* (useful in divination) and manuals on agriculture and medicine. Special wrath was vented on the *Book of Poetry* and the *Book of History*. He decreed that any persons who failed to deliver up to the prefects their copies of the proscribed books should be branded with hot iron and compelled to work for four years at hard labor on the Great Wall.

* Opponents or rivals of the Confucians discussed in Section III of this chapter, pp. 296 ff.

Some 460 scholars, many of them Confucian, were buried alive for treason, it is said, in the years that followed.

But three years after he issued his decree, Shih Huang-ti died, and all his animus against the past came at last to nothing. To do him justice, he had "merely burned the books which existed among the people, but did not burn those in the official archives."D2 During the Han dynasty that succeeded his within five years after his death, the Confucian Classics were restored to public use, with, if anything, a heightened renown.

Were they the worse for their misadventure? Curiously enough, not as the result of their suppression, but as the result of their recopying, for they were recopied in the new script! The scholars now wrote rapidly on long pieces of silk instead of slowly on short pieces of bamboo, and they began to fill out the bare bones of the Old Texts with the interpretative glosses they had learned in the schools. Without any conscious wish to make grave alterations, they practically rewrote the *Li Chi* and added to the *Shu Ching*, to the *I Ching*, and to the *Chung Yung*. Included in these additions were certain ascriptions of divinity to Confucius, the tradition that he was the first to compile the Five Classics, and stories of his miraculous birth. Then gradually there was a recovery of some writings, composed in the old script, that contradicted the new script writings in matters of fact, and at once the Old Text school was born. The battle between the Old Text and the New Text schools was to continue intermittently for nearly two thousand years, but it had this good result: as a consequence of the enormous amount of textual criticism that was done down the centuries, and especially by the Ch'ing scholars of the seventeenth to nineteenth centuries, forgeries (largely Old Text) have been located, variant readings reduced, and conflicting passages clearly defined.

And now, after this long excursus, let us proceed to the most careful statement of Confucius' own teaching that we can achieve in the light of present knowledge.

The Ethical Principles of Confucius

The ethical thought of Confucius sprang from a double realization: first, that the China of his day was disturbingly corrupt, but second, that the moral condition of the country was not beyond redemption. The situation was bad, but not hopeless. Man's practices had grown corrupt, but man himself had not yet become corrupt; he was still as apt to good as to evil. But why had man's practices grown corrupt? Confucius answered this question quite simply: men had failed from moral causes to live by *jen* (approximately "run"), or the will to seek the good of others, as those of their ancestors who were devoted to the common good had lived by it.

The common good was to be secured by the attainment of five cardinal virtues: *jen* (the root), *yi*, or righteousness by justice (the trunk), *li*, or the religious and moral ways of acting (the branches), *chih*, or wisdom (the flower), and *hsin*, or faithfulness (the fruit). "These five," Confucius might have said, "but the greatest of these is *jen*."H We shall consider two of these at some length: (a) li and its underlying principles and (b) jen or the motivating force in the moral life.

(a) The word *li* is one of the most important words used by Confucius to formulate his program for the recovery of China. It is a difficult word to translate, for it means different things in different contexts. In one connection or another it means "propriety" (the usual translation, but not always adequate), "courtesy," "reverence," "rites and ceremonies," "the correct forms of social ceremony," "ritual," "ritual and music," "the due order of public ceremony," "the ideal standard of social and religious conduct," "the religious and moral way of life." Put into its historical perspective, it means in the words of Lin Yutang, "an ideal social order with everything in its place, and particularly a rationalized feudal order, [like that] which was breaking down in Confucius' days."C2

In the *Li Chi* (the Confucian Classic on the subject) comprehensive and illuminating discussions of the meaning of li are attempted. The following passages are particularly worthy of study: *

> Duke Ai asked Confucius, "What is this great *li?* Why is it that you talk about *li* as though it were such an important thing?"
>
> Confucius replied, "Your humble servant is really not worthy to understand *li.*"
>
> "But you do constantly speak about it," said Duke Ai.
>
> Confucius: "What I have learned is this, that of all the things that people live by, *li* is the greatest. Without *li,* we do not know how to conduct a proper worship of the spirits of the universe; or how to establish the proper status of the king and the ministers, the ruler and the ruled, and the elders and the juniors; or how to establish the moral relationships between the sexes; between parents and children, and between brothers; or how to distinguish the different degrees of relationships in the family. That is why a gentleman holds *li* in such high regard."[C3]
>
> Confucius said [in conversation with Tsuyu]: "The principles of *li* and righteousness serve as the principles of social discipline. By means of these principles, people try to maintain the official status of rulers and subjects, to teach the parents and children and elder brothers and younger brothers and husbands and wives to live in harmony, to establish social institutions, and to live in groups of hamlets. . . ."
>
> "Is *li* so very important as all that?" asked Tsuyu again.
>
> "This *li,*" replied Confucius, "is the principle by which the ancient kings embodied the laws of heaven and regulated the expressions of human nature. Therefore he who has attained *li* lives, and he who has lost it, dies. . . . *Li* is based on heaven, patterned on earth, deals with the worship of the spirits and is extended to the rites and ceremonies of funerals, sacrifices to ancestors, archery, carriage driving, 'capping,' † marriage, and court audience, or exchange of diplomatic visits. Therefore the Sage shows the people this principle of a rationalized social order (*li*) and through it everything becomes right in the family, the state, and the world."[C4]

These passages reveal, upon examination, certain basic Confucian principles.

---

* These passages show the influence of later Confucian thought, particularly that of Hsün-tzu, but with due caution in their use we may get from them authentic glimpses into Confucius' mind. For Hsün-tzu see pp. 301 ff.

† The ceremony of putting a cap on a boy when he reaches maturity.

1. Li is of vital importance in ordering and regulating the principal human relationships. These relationships are five in number. They are the relationships between ruler and subject, father and son, husband and wife, the oldest son and his younger brothers, and elders and juniors (or friends). Besides these five relationships others are incidentally mentioned, such as the relationships between men and the spirits of the universe, between rulers and their ministers, and between diplomats, but the five relationships given above are the "great" ones, because they are judged fundamental to the social order.

2. By the practice of li the principal relationships in society can be so regulated and set straight that complete harmony may reign in every home, in every village, and throughout the empire. Ultimately—and here Confucius and his school proved themselves to be true to the deepest feelings of the Chinese people about the ultimate nature of the universe—the goal is to obtain a cosmic harmony between men, earth and heaven, and thus put into actual operation among men the Tao or the will of Heaven.

3. The forms of social ceremony that best exemplify the practice of li are observable in the manners of those ancients who sought the common welfare and exhibited a humane spirit of mutual respect and courtesy.

The last of these principles deserves more than passing notice. The ancients lived harmoniously and courteously together in a social order that was profoundly just, Confucius believed. Superiors and inferiors knew their places and behaved politely according to their several stations. So he reverently studied and tried to embody in his own conduct the ceremonial procedures of the olden time. He wished to be instrumental in getting all China to do the same. This won him the mocking criticism of the Taoists, who raged at his formalism as being unnatural and futile. But Confucius believed he stood for "the crystallization of what is right" *[C5] in terms of formal behavior. For the sake of giving his conduct

---

* One of the definitions of li in the *Li Chi*.

the force of a moral example, he acted out his principles with obvious symbolism. This accounts for his supposed meticulous behavior in the ducal court of Lu, described in Book X of the *Analects*. Consider this description of his conduct.*

When the duke bade him receive guests, his face seemed to change, his knees to bend. He bowed left and right to those beside him, straightened his robes in front and behind, and sped forward, his elbows spread like wings. When the guest had left, he always reported: "The guest has ceased to look back."

Entering the palace gate he stooped, as though it were too low for him. He did not stand in the middle of the gate, nor step on the threshold.

Passing the throne, his face seemed to change, his knees to bend, he spake with bated breath.

Mounting the dais, he lifted his robes, bowed his back and masked his breathing, till it seemed to stop.

Coming down, his face relaxed below the first step, and bore a pleased look. From the foot of the steps he sped forward, his elbows spread like wings; and when again in his seat he looked intent and solemn as before.

When bearing the sceptre, his back bent, as under too heavy a burden. He held his hands not higher than in bowing, nor lower than in giving a present. He wore an awed look and dragged his feet, as though they were fettered.

On the duke coming to see him in sickness, he turned his face to the east and had his court dress spread across him, with the girdle over it.

When summoned by the duke, he walked, without waiting for his carriage.

In mounting his chariot he stood straight and grasped the cord. When in his chariot he did not look round, speak fast, or point.[A5]

This description, whether it describes Confucius himself or merely an imagined ideal Confucian official, raises the question, was Confucius just a narrow formalist, or was he a social philosopher to be taken seriously? The answer would seem to depend

on whether he lived by purely formal rules or by a deeper principle.

That Confucius found in the practices of the ancients a profound principle that provided him with a key to ideal relationships among men is more than once indicated in the *Analects* and elsewhere.

Tzu-kung asked, saying, "Is there one word which may serve as a rule of practice for all one's life?" The Master said, "Is not Reciprocity (*shu*) such a word? What you do not want done to yourself, do not do to others."[11]

In these words Confucius formulated a law of human relationships identical with the Golden Rule of the New Testament. He happened to define reciprocity (shu) negatively (and hence won from some Western scholars the grudging judgment that he had given China the "Silver Rule"), but the word means "fellow-feeling" or "mutual consideration," and its definition need not have been put negatively. In the *Doctrine of the Mean* Confucius is in fact quoted as having explained this central ethical principle in positive terms making it quite comparable with Jesus' Golden Rule. He is there found saying:

"There are four things in the moral life of man, not one of which I have been able to carry out in my life. To serve my father as I would expect my son to serve me: that I have not been able to do. To serve my sovereign as I would expect a minister under me to serve me: that I have not been able to do. To act towards my elder brother as I would expect my younger brother to act towards me: that I have not been able to do.* To be the first to behave towards friends as I would expect them to behave towards me: that I have not been able to do."[J1]

However, it is true that Confucius did not go as far as Jesus (or, for that matter, the Taoists of his own land) in defining the scope of the application of this ideal of ethical conduct. He made a significant reservation when confronted with the Taoist rule of

---

* There is serious doubt as to whether this is an authentic description. Arthur Waley, for example, considers it simply a collection of traditional ritual maxims altered to apply to Confucius. This may be the fact. But even so, Confucius would have approved in another the behavior here attributed to him.

* Here, of course, he is being made to speak by one who lived after his time—by his grandson perhaps—and we note that he is using the word *brother* in the most general sense.

returning good for evil. Someone asked him: "What do you think of repaying evil with kindness?" He replied, "Then what are you going to repay kindness with? . . . Repay kindness with kindness, but repay evil with justice."[F2] It would seem that Confucius limited the operation of the law of reciprocity, in its complete sense, to the circle of the good, because evil persons were judged unworthy of the mutual consideration prompted by fellow-feeling.

(b) It cannot be emphasized too strongly, however, that Confucius' primary purpose was to persuade all men to cooperate in securing the general good. True virtue, he taught, lay in the expression of jen or the will to seek the good of others. (The Chinese character for jen is a composite of two characters, one for man and the other for two. It therefore stands for a man's inclusion of a second person in his plans.) It consisted in the recognition of the worth of any human being of any rank or station, and kindly behavior toward one's fellows as a consequence of this recognition. Many instances could be cited of Confucius' insistence that government should be directed toward the welfare of the whole people, that families must safeguard the good of each of their members and bring harmony into the interrelationships of old and young, and that in society at large men, knowing that all who live within the four seas are brothers, should display to each other in action their real humane and kindly character (their jen).

Confucius wanted government to be by jen. He was not aware (he did not live in a culture that permitted him to know) that government may be based on the democratic process of election to office by ballot, but he did demand that government be for if not by the people and that feudal lords be responsive to the needs of the people at large.*

* For a strong treatment of the "democratic" aspect of Confucius' teaching see H. G. Creel, *Confucius, Man and Myth* (John Day, 1949) and *Chinese Thought from Confucius to Mao Tse-tung* (University of Chicago Press, 1953). If Professor Creel's thesis is to be accepted, the word *democratic* must be used in a rather broad sense.

The Five Great Relationships

The *Li Chi* presents the following scheme as growing out of Confucius' study of shu as applied to the Five Relationships: *

Kindness in the father, filial piety in the son

Gentility in the eldest brother, humility and respect in the younger

Righteous behavior in the husband, obedience in the wife

Humane consideration in elders, deference in juniors

Benevolence in rulers, loyalty in ministers and subjects

If these ten attitudes (known as the ten *I* or appropriate attitudes) are generally present in society, then the highest propriety (li) will be actualized, and perfect harmony will reign between all individuals. Then people will show their real human character (jen). No quarrels, no disturbance, no injustices will exist. There will be happiness among friends, harmony in the home, peace in the state. The *Doctrine of the Mean* quotes approvingly from the *Book of Poetry:*

> "When wives and children and their sires are one,
> 'Tis like the harp and lute in unison.
> When brothers live in concord and at peace
> The strain of harmony shall never cease.
> The lamp of happy union lights the home,
> And bright days follow when the children come."[J2]

And the *Great Learning* (Chapter VII) quotes from the same source lines which may be translated:

> A prince by courteous carriage may create
> Concord at court and order in the state.

To see that Confucius was a practical sort of philosopher and did not lose himself in vague contemplation of an ideal that was conceived only in general terms, let us turn now to the subjects concerning

* It is very doubtful whether Confucius developed so schematic a treatment of this matter, but it follows logically from his teaching.

which he most often spoke when amplifying upon what he meant by practicing li: the relationship of fathers and sons, the relationship of rulers and subjects, and the nature of the superior man.

Filial Piety (*Hsiao*)

Confucius did not, of course, bring into being the fact that the whole of Chinese culture has rested upon the basis of the family. Yet what he said helped to make the interests of the family the first consideration of Chinese. In the past, nothing has stood higher. In China, loyalty to the family has been one's first loyalty. No lad in China ever comes of age, in the Western sense. It is still true that his whole service is expected to be devoted to the family until death, and he is expected to obey his father, and when his father dies, his eldest brother, with a perfect compliance.* This has meant in the past that every father has a great and grave responsibility to fulfill toward his family. He must seek to produce virtue in his sons by being himself the best example of it.

Confucius considered this so self-evident a proposition that he laid far heavier stress on the filial piety without which the father's goodness would remain ineffective. Here he touched a chord that has had the most resounding response in the Chinese consciousness since his time. It struck home. Consider a few of the many important utterances of Confucius on the subject (and thereby glimpse an essential aspect of the folk-mind of China):

The Master said, "Whilst thy father lives look for his purpose; when he is gone, look how he walked. To change

* This statement presumes that the old order in China has not been entirely swept away by the Communist regime. However, it is being said by escapees from behind the Bamboo Curtain that the present Chinese state is determined to make itself "the father and elder brother" by breaking up the old family system and instituting "communes" in its place, and, above all, by claiming the first loyalty (or filial piety) of every citizen. The last paragraph on this topic shows how they are able to explain this.

nothing in thy father's way for three years may be called pious."K1

Meng Wu asked the duty of a son.

The Master said, "He shall not grieve his father and mother by anything but illness."K2

Tsu-yu asked the duty of a son.

The Master said, "He that can feed his parents is now called a good son. But both dogs and horses are fed, and unless we honor our parents, what is the difference?"K3

The Master said, "Whilst thy father and mother are living, do not wander afar. If thou must travel, hold a set course."K4

The *Doctrine of the Mean* lays down these very influential precepts:

Confucius remarked: "The Emperor Wu and his brother, Duke Chou, were indeed eminently pious men. . . .

"In spring and autumn they repaired and put in order the ancestral temple, arranged the sacrificial vessels, exhibited the regalia and heirlooms of the family, and presented the appropriate offerings of the season. . . .

"To gather in the same places where our fathers before us have gathered; to perform the same ceremonies which they before us have performed; to play the same music which they before us have played; to pay respect to those whom they have honored; to love those who were dear to them—in fact, to serve those now dead as if they were living, and now departed as if they were still with us: this is the highest achievement of true filial piety."J3

Confucius may not have been as firm about it, but the majority of his followers concluded that the duty of a son is to obey his father in all things while he lives and to honor and still obey him in all things after he is dead. Indeed, the filial relationship has been made since Confucius' time the type and symbol of all life-enriching and wisdom-conserving subordination to the leadership of the old and wise. "By the principle of filial piety the whole world can be made happy and all calamities and dangers can be averted"L is one of the claims made for treating not only one's father as a father should be treated, but also such superior spirits as one's ancestors, one's elders, noted scholars, and one's emperor or prince as they should be treated. The attitude of filial piety can thus be almost indefinitely extended.

Political Philosophy

But Confucius was equally emphatic about the importance of the relationship between rulers and their subjects. Here he merged ethics and politics. He told everyone who would listen to him that if rulers adopt and act upon the highest moral principles, then the spiritual climate of a whole state may be changed, and all the people from the higher officials on down to the poorest and least of citizens may be led to live more virtuously in their several stations. The reform of society begins at the top, among the rulers, and thence reaches down to the lower orders of society.*

On one occasion the head of the Chi clan in Lu, Baron Chi K'ang Tsu, a person of importance, asked Confucius how to rule. The sage replied: "To govern is to keep straight. If you, Sir, lead the people straight, which of your subjects will venture to fall out of line?"M1 The same baron in another conversation asked, "Ought not I to cut off the lawless in order to establish law and order? What do you think?" To this crucial question Confucius made the sort of reply that won him profound respect as the enunciator of ultimate ethical principles, but that made the legalistic smile in derision: "Sir, what need is there of the death-penalty in your system of government? If you showed a sincere desire to be good, your people would likewise be good. The virtue of the prince is like unto wind; that of the people like unto grass. For it is the nature of grass to bend when the wind blows upon it."M2

For an understanding of his point of view, too much stress can hardly be laid upon this fundamental conviction of Confucius. People, he held, being at heart good, are responsive to good in those above them to whom they look for leadership. "If a country," he insisted, "had none but good rulers for a hundred years, crime might be stamped out and the death-penalty abolished." He added for good measure. "How true this saying is!"M3

* The Communists can make good use of this principle, too.

One of the main conclusions that Confucius' followers, thinking in his spirit, drew from his study of history is contained in this curious piece of close-linked logic that is to be found in the *Great Learning:*

> The ancients [i.e., the ancient kings] who wished to cause their virtue to shine forth first ordered well their own states. Wishing to order well their states, they first regulated their families. Wishing to regulate their families, they first cultivated their persons. Wishing to cultivate their persons, they first rectified their hearts. Wishing to rectify their hearts, they first sought to be sincere in their thoughts. Wishing to be sincere in their thoughts, they first extended to the utmost their knowledge. Such extension of knowledge lay in the investigation of things. Things being investigated, their knowledge became complete. Their knowledge being complete, their thoughts were sincere. Their thoughts being sincere, their hearts were then rectified. Their hearts being rectified, their persons were cultivated. Their persons being cultivated, their families were regulated. Their families being regulated, their states were rightly governed. Their states being rightly governed, the whole kingdom was made tranquil and happy.[12]

In this, perhaps the most famous of all Confucian paragraphs, and in the previous quotations, it is apparent that according to Confucian teaching the good life is a spiritual rather than a legal attainment. A good example may prevent crime, but statutory law breeds it. A well-ordered state cannot be legislated into existence; it grows out of a contagious spirit of good will and earnestness in well-doing. Love or cooperative good will makes law unnecessary.

The *Doctrine of the Mean* quotes Confucius as saying to the Duke of Lu: "When the men are there, good government will flourish, when the men are gone, good government decays and becomes extinct. . . . The conduct of government, therefore, depends upon the men. The right men are obtained by the ruler's personal character. To cultivate his personal character, the ruler must use the moral law (Tao). To cultivate the moral law, the ruler must use the moral sense [jen, or the principles of true manhood]."J4 In the words of the *Book of Poetry* concerning the good Emperor Shun:

That great and noble Prince displayed
The sense of right in all he wrought;
The spirit of his wisdom swayed
Peasant and peer; the crowd, the court.[J5]

Because Confucius believed in government by moral example, he took no interest in written laws. In fact, he is quoted as saying: "Guide the people by law, keep them in line by punishment, and they may shun crime, but they will be shameless. Guide them by mind, keep them in line by courtesy, and they will learn shame and grow good."[K5] A high hope!

He used to admit the truth of the old saying, "To be a good king is difficult." But he went on to say: "He who realizes the difficulty of being a good king —has he not almost succeeded in making his country prosper?"[M4] What he meant was, obviously, that when a king pauses to think long enough about being a good king, he will feel within him the strong native tendencies toward virtue, and the result will be a virtuous and prosperous people. No one has defined more clearly the best hopes for a paternalistic state.

The Rectification of Names

A place was made for logic. (It was a sort of semantics.) Moral and political reorganization had a side that was to be called "the rectification of names." We must consider this concept, if Confucius discussed it,* his chief contribution to straight thinking in politics and morals. The crucial passage is in the *Analects*.

Tsu-lu said: "The prince of Wei is awaiting you, Sir, to take control of his administration. What will you undertake first, Sir?" The Master replied: "The one thing needed is the rectification of names."[D3]

The disciple then says in bewilderment, "That is far-fetched, Sir! Why rectify them?" Confucius re-

* He may not have done so, although, as we shall see, eminent authorities believe he did. For the view that the whole "language crisis" must be dated not earlier than the fourth century B.C., see Arthur Waley, *The Analects of Confucius*, pp. 22 f.

bukes him for showing lack of logical acuteness and proceeds to explain that if names are incorrect, words will be misused, and when words are misused, nothing can be on a sound footing. Li and music will languish, law and punishments will not be just, and people will not know where to place hand or foot. This is why one cannot be too careful about words and names.

In another conversation Confucius declared that only when the ruler is ruler, the minister is minister, the father is father, and the son is son can there be good government. He meant to say that only when men know what names stand for and then act as the definitions indicate can there be true social order. Morality cannot exist apart from precision of thought and speech. To quote one eminent modern Chinese scholar: "Confucius considered [there was] an inseparable connection between intellectual disorder and moral perversity." Hu Shih, whose statement this is, explains Confucius' point of view further, thus:

The rectification of names consists in making real relationships and duties and institutions conform as far as possible to their *ideal* meanings. . . . When this intellectual reorganization is at last effected, the ideal social order will come as night follows day,—a social order where, just as a circle is a circle and a square a square, so every prince is princely, every official is faithful, every father is fatherly, and every child is filially pious.[N]

The principle, then, is that everyone must act in life in accordance with the highest, that is, the socially-agreed-upon ideal of his true place and function in society.

The Superior Man

The kind of man Confucius most firmly believed in and was always talking about was the man whose mind was perfectly clear about names and duties, and who moreover acted with an altruistic uprightness (jen) and good taste (li). He called him the Higher Type of Man, or the Superior Man, one who is truly a *chün-tzu* (literally, a superior person, a prince).

One must take seriously Confucius' description of this true gentleman, who as a son is always filial, as a father just and kind, as an official loyal and faithful, as a husband righteous and judicious, as a friend sincere and tactful. It is this ideal that constitutes Confucius' greatest claim to distinction as a moral philosopher.

The Superior Man, he said, displays the Five Constant Virtues, for "moral virtue simply consists," he asserted, "in being able, anywhere and everywhere, to exercise five particular qualities: self-respect, magnanimity, sincerity, earnestness, and benevolence,"M5 the qualities of the Superior Man.

This list of virtues suggests that though Confucius loved the order that punctilious observance of rules and ceremonies brings, he saw the fallacy of a merely legalistic formalism. The harmony he sought could issue only from inward uprightness, a sincere and basic feeling of mutuality with others. He had no use for the insincere politeness that comes from mere etiquette. He emphatically rejected "the glib talker," "the smoothie," "the goody-goody." Mencius quotes him as saying: "I hate things that resemble the real things but are not the real things. . . . I hate the ingratiating fellows, because they get mixed up with the good men. I hate the glib talkers because they confuse us about honest people. . . . I hate goody-goodys because they confuse us about virtuous people."F3 In the *Analects* we hear him saying: "Your goody-goody people are the thieves of virtue."M6 In another connection he remarked, "If a man is not a true man, what is the use of rituals? If a man is not a true man, what is the use of music?"F4 This touches on the very heart of Confucius' philosophy of life, which demands integrity in one's good will.

The Superior Man *feels* like practicing li, because he is realizing his own magnanimity (jen) through it. This is an important moral point, and Dr. Y. L. Fung suggests it in these words:

The *li* are imposed on man from outside. But besides this outer mould, we each still have within us something which we may take as a model for our conduct. If we "can find in ourselves a rule for the similar treatment of others"; if we do to others what we wish for ourselves, and "do not do to others what we do not like ourselves," then the outpourings of our nature will of themselves be in accord with what is proper. Hence while there are still occasions on which one's own natural uprightness (*chih*) cannot be followed, there is none upon which *jen* (which is one's own uprightness conforming to what is proper) may not be acted upon. This is why *jen* is the "all pervading" principle of Confucius' teaching, and the center of his philosophy.D4

Because of the perfect adjustment he has achieved between his manners and his motives, the Superior Man embodies in his conduct a golden mean, something that Confucius said was rare among men. To the Superior Man decorum is as natural as breathing. He has a compelling sense of duty, but no difficulty in carrying it out. "In his progress through the world he has neither narrow predilections nor obstinate antipathies."M7 His uprightness never takes the form of rudeness, because he controls its expression by the rules of good taste. He is modest. He is catholic-minded. He is simple, honest, and a lover of justice. "He weighs men's words and observes the expression on their faces."M8 Then his response is tactful but conscientious and truthful. In trying to establish his own character, he also tries to establish the character of others. "The higher type of man makes a sense of duty the groundwork of his character, blends with it in action a sense of harmonious proportion, manifests it in a spirit of unselfishness, and perfects it by the addition of sincerity and truth."M9 Surely a noble ideal of manhood—whether attainable or not on the basis of Confucius' ethics! And this noble man never forgets himself. He obeys the inner law of self-control. He keeps his head, and with it his equilibrium and his virtue. "Not even whilst he eats his meal will the superior man forget what he owes to his fellowmen. Even in his hurried leave-takings, even in moments of frantic confusion, he keeps true to his virtue."E3 He is a real gentleman because he lives by a superior law—a law of proportion and equilibrium in acting on his inner motives, and of mutuality and fellow-feeling as regards others.

It was left to the Confucian school to develop the

Portrait of Confucius. Confucius, speaking animatedly, looks at all of his six feet. His hands are joined under his voluminous sleeves. The girdle lying high on his stomach shows he is no ascetic. In this rubbing from stone from the Ch'ng dynasty (1644–1912), Confucius wears the ceremonial hat of a high official, replete with hat-pin. He looks very much the Superior Man. (Philadelphia Museum of Art.)

doctrine of the Golden Mean. Confucius spoke of it, apparently, only suggestively and in passing:

"Since I cannot find people who follow the Golden Mean to teach, I suppose I will have to work with those who are brilliant or erratic (*k'uang*) and those who are a little dull but careful (*chuan*). The brilliant but erratic persons are always ready to go forward (or are too active), and the dull but careful persons always hold themselves back (or are not active enough)."F5

One of his sayings had the ambiguous but profoundly suggestive character that always excites speculation and leads to further development of thought. It has been both narrowly and broadly translated, as the following two English versions show. The succinct, less explanatory rendering is:

"That virtue is perfect which adheres to a constant mean."M10

In the more philosophically phrased translation this becomes:

"The use of the moral sentiment, well balanced and kept in perfect equilibrium,—that is the true state of human perfection."D

Perhaps Confucius (if he used the word at all) meant by *chungyung* (the word in dispute) something like the Middle Way of early Buddhism, even then being worked out in India. And, if we sense his meaning aright, he was as well touching upon a theme that the Greeks, in the person of Aristotle, far away

290

"across the roof of the world," were soon to place at the center of their ethics.

There is no doubt, whatever suggestions he may have made along this line, that Confucius himself was a good example of "the higher type of man" who walks the middle way and does nothing in excess. He had true decorum. He himself was modest about his achievements. "In three ways I fall short of a gentleman. Love is never vexed; wisdom has no doubts; courage is without fear."[A6] But he knew he possessed one qualification of the superior type of man; he had a compelling sense of duty. "To divine wisdom and perfect virtue," he said, "I can lay no claim. All that can be said of me is that I never falter in the course which I pursue and am unwearying in my instruction of others—this and nothing more."[M11] "There are men, I daresay, who act rightly without knowing the reason why, but I am not one of them. Having heard much, I sift out the good and practice it; having seen much I retain it in my memory. This is the second order of wisdom."[M12] "I am a transmitter and not an originator, and as one who believes in and loves the ancients, venture to compare myself with our old P'eng"[E3]—an ancient sage of the eleventh (?) century B.C. who was said to have disappeared, as Lao-tzu was said to have done years later, into the west. There is little boasting here, and yet in his old age he is quoted as saying calmly, as from a great height: "At fifteen I had my mind bent on learning. At thirty I stood firm. At forty I had no doubts. At fifty I knew the decrees of Heaven. At sixty my ear was an obedient organ for the reception of truth. At seventy I could do what my heart desired without transgressing what was right."[I3]

Religious Teaching

It may be granted that Confucius was primarily a teacher of ethics. Some would say that little more need be added; he was no more than that. But this is a contention that cannot be maintained. In private belief and in public practice he exhibited faith in religious reality. So carefully, moreover, did he adhere to the established religious ceremonies of his time that he set an example that was, until this century, officially considered to be the Chinese ideal.

However, his attitude in religion was critical and discriminating, even marked by an evident restraint, for he was rationalistic and decidedly humanistic in his outlook. Only in the milder sense of the word can he be called mystical or supernaturalistic. His position in matters of faith was this: whatever seemed contrary to common sense in popular tradition, and whatever did not serve any discoverable social purpose, he regarded coldly. In his teaching he avoided discussing such subjects as prodigies, feats of strength, crime, and the supernatural, apparently because he did not wish to spend time discussing perturbing exceptions to human and natural law. "Absorption in the study of the supernatural is most harmful," he said,[M13] not that he disbelieved in the supernatural, but that it would not do to let the pressing concerns of human welfare suffer neglect. It is from this point of view that we should weigh two sayings of his that have perhaps received overmuch attention. His disciple Tsu-yu asked him about one's duty to the spirits of the dead. He replied: "Before we are able to do our duty by the living, how can we do it by the spirits of the dead?"[M14] He defined what he believed was the proper attitude with great exactness thus: "To devote oneself earnestly to one's duty to humanity, and, while respecting the spirits, to keep aloof from them, may be called wisdom."[D5]

Yet the effect of his desire to support whatever made for unity in the state and harmony in the home was that he went as far as he could in observing the rites and ceremonies of his time. One might even hazard the opinion, with Dr. Lin Yutang, that "Confucius would undoubtedly have been a High Churchman," could he have been a Christian.[C6] Perhaps his interest in the stabilizing moral effect of the old inherited rituals was strengthened by his own aesthetic satisfaction in them. At any rate, at the village exorcisms he put on court dress and stood on the east steps. He took seriously the ceremonial bath before religious worship. When one of his disciples (Tzu Kung) suggested doing away with the sheep offering at the new moon, he disagreed, saying: "Tzu, you love the sheep; I love the ceremony!"[14] On going into the Great Temple he asked about everything. This once brought from a by-stander the criticism that he knew shockingly little about the rites, but when he heard this, he said that asking about everything was part of the rite. In offering sacrifices to ancestors, he behaved as if they were physically present, and this was also his attitude toward the other spirits to whom sacrifices were made. He felt it his duty to participate in the sacrifice actively, saying, "For me, to take no part in the sacrifice is the same as not sacrificing."[K6] Asked the meaning of the Grand Sacrifice to the Imperial Ancestors, he said, "I do not know. He who knew its meaning would find it as easy to govern the Empire as to look upon this"—pointing to his palm.[M15]

His endorsement of ancestor-worship seems to have been unreserved. In a quotation from the *Doctrine of the Mean,* given on an earlier page, we were assured that he judged the Emperor Wu and his brother, the Duke of Chou, to be eminently pious men, because they repaired and put in order the ancestral temple each spring and autumn, carefully arranging the sacrificial vessels, the regalia, and the heirlooms of the family and presenting appropriate sacrifices at the same time. He is said to have thought that the great emperors of the past were fortunate indeed; after their deaths their descendants continued to sacrifice to them for many generations.

What, in view of all this, was Confucius' own philosophy of religion? Was he teasing his disciples when, while he was seriously ill and Tsu-Yu asked to be allowed to say prayers for him, he parried with "Are such available?" "Yes," said Tsu-Yu; "and the *Manual of Prayers* says, 'Pray to the spirits above and to those here below!' " Thereupon Confucius said: "My praying has been going on a long while."[E4] The exact meaning of this remark is difficult to determine, of course, and so we must turn elsewhere for further evidence.

The clue to his own belief is contained in the conviction that when a man practices the moral law he does the will of Heaven. The writer of the *Doctrine of the Mean* (reputed, but probably apocryphally, to be Confucius' grandson) says that Confucius made it evident that the truths handed down from the ancient Emperors Yao and Shun "harmonize with the divine order which governs the revolutions of the seasons in the Heaven above and . . . fit in with the moral design which is to be seen in physical nature upon the Earth below."[J6] This seems to be a pretty accurate statement of Confucius' real, though perhaps never expressed, intent. One can hardly call such an attitude supernaturalistic or monotheistic. It is vaguely mystical, and at the same time aloof from the concerns of popular religion. An inquirer once asked, "Why do people say it is better to be on good terms with the kitchen god than with the god of the southwestern corner of the house?" (two deities popularly believed to dwell in every house and to intercede for those under their protection). Whereupon Confucius replied sharply: "Nonsense; if you have committed sins against Heaven, you haven't got a god to pray to."[F6]

The basic fact is that, for himself, he felt that he had the backing of Heaven. He must indeed be ranged with the other religious leaders whom we have studied. He had a prophetic consciousness all his own. Once, in the city of K'uang, he was surrounded by a threatening crowd, and his disciples feared for his life; but he said: "Since King Wen [the founder of the Chou feudal order] died, is not the tradition of King Wen in my keeping or possession? If it be the will of Heaven that this moral tradition should be lost, posterity shall never again share in the knowledge of this tradition. But if it be the will of Heaven that this tradition shall not be lost, what can the people of K'uang do to me?"[*][F7] We have heard him on another occasion exclaiming "Heaven begat the power (Te) that is in me. What

---

* There is a play on words here which may be suggested by a similar pun in English: "The Great Wan is dead, but is not *this one* preserving his Way?"

have I to fear from such a one as Huan T'uei?" *
There were thus moments when he felt clearly that
his message to his times was one that carried eternal
significances, because it had its origin in the moral
order of the world. His teaching seemed to him to be
firmly grounded in the ultimate nature of things. It
was a conviction to which we cannot justly deny the
adjective religious.

III   The Confucian School—Its Rivals and Champions

The Formation of the Confucian School

In a famous passage Mencius gives the tradition
concerning the mourning of Confucius' disciples:

> When Confucius died, after three years had elapsed,
> his disciples collected their baggage, and prepared to
> return to their several homes. But on entering to take
> their leave of Tzu Kung, as they looked toward one an-
> other, they wailed, till they all lost their voices. After this
> they returned to their homes, but Tzu Kung went back,
> and built a house for himself on the altar-ground, where
> he lived alone three years, before he returned home.Q

This was, presumably, the beginning of the Confucian school. Most of its members—said to have
numbered seventy in all—scattered and offered their
services to the feudal lords. "The important ones,"
says Ssu-ma Ch'ien, "became teachers and ministers
(of the feudal lords). The lesser ones became friends
and teachers of the officials or went into retirement
and were no longer seen."D6 Some started schools
devoted to spreading the teachings of the master.
All helped during the next generation to gather the
material that was ultimately fashioned into the *Analects*. Gradually, during a period of three or four
centuries the Confucian school produced the *Great
Learning*, the *Doctrine of the Mean*, the *Book of
Filial Piety* (the *Hsiao Ching*, destined to become a

* See supra, p. 278.

great favorite but not to be listed in the canon of the
Four Books), the present *Book of Rites*, and the
commentaries on the *Book of Changes* and on the
Annals of Spring and Autumn. Some other writings,
which have not survived, came from their hands.
Among the leaders of the school in the second generation was Tzu Ssu, the scholarly grandson of
Confucius, who, like his grandfather, devoted himself to teaching.

The spread of Confucian thought was impeded,
however, by two factors, the rapid decay of the Chou
feudal system during the Warring States Period
(403–221 B.C.), and the rise in this period of the
many different schools of thought that proposed
moral and political solutions for the perplexities of
the times. Only the princes descended from the old
feudal families and the usurpers who wished to keep
their positions by a prolongation of the feudal order
listened readily to the Confucian scholars. But though
many of the feudal princes would have liked to see
Confucianism make headway, they thought it had no
chance. The world was changing. And furthermore,
in the community at large there was widespread scorn
of the highbrow *ju chiao* (the "scholar—or literatus
—school") and its advocates.

We can understand this better if we look briefly
now at some of the rival schools of thought.

Rival Views: (1) The Taoists

The compilers of the *Tao Te Ching* were not gentle
toward the Confucians. The scorn they felt toward
all advocates of social discipline or managed economy
was directed especially at the Confucians (although
Mohists and Legalists were just as abhorrent to
them). Consider the implications of these verses:

The man of superior virtue never acts,
  Nor ever (does so) with an ulterior motive.
The man of inferior virtue acts,
  And (does so) with an ulterior motive . . .
(When) the man of superior *li* acts and finds no response,
He rolls up his sleeves to force it on others.

293

Therefore:
After Tao is lost, then (arises the doctrine of) kindness,
After kindness is lost, then (arises the doctrine of) justice.
After justice is lost, then (arises the doctrine of) *li*.
Now *li* is the thinning out of loyalty and honesty of heart.
And the beginning of chaos.[F8]

Or of these, which seem directly aimed at Confucians:

On the decline of the great Tao,
   The doctrines of "love" and "justice" arose.
When knowledge and cleverness appeared,
   Great hypocrisy followed in its wake.

When the six relationships no longer lived at peace,
   There was (praise of) "kind parents" and "filial sons."
When the country fell into chaos and misrule,
   There was (praise of) "loyal ministers."[F9]

Though Chuang-tzu writes at greater length, and with equal scorn, he does not achieve a more rapier-like thrust than this, even when he says:

Of old the Yellow Emperor first interfered with the natural goodness of the heart of man, by means of charity and duty. In consequence, Yao and Shun . . . tortured the people's internal economy in order to conform to charity and duty. They exhausted the people's energies to live in accordance with the laws and statutes. Even then they did not succeed. . . . By and by, the Confucianists and the Motseanists° arose; and then came confusion between joy and anger, fraud between the simple and the cunning, recrimination between the virtuous and the evil-minded, slander between the honest and the liars, and the world order collapsed. . . .

Then, when dead men lay about pillowed on each other's corpses, when . . . criminals were seen everywhere, then the Confucianists and the Motseanists bustled about and rolled up their sleeves in the midst of gyves and fetters! Alas, they know not shame, nor what it is to blush![F10]

But sometimes Chuang-tzu preferred to laugh at Confucius by making him say Taoist things, as in this delicious bit of mockery:

Yen Huei spoke to Chungni (Confucius), "I am getting on."
"How so?" asked the latter.

"I have got rid of charity and duty," replied the former.
"Very good," replied Chungni, "but not quite perfect."
Another day, Yen Huei met Chungni and said, "I am getting on."
"How so?"
"I can forget myself while sitting," replied Yen Huei.
"What do you mean by that?" said Chungni, changing his countenance.
"I have freed myself from my body," answered Yen Huei. "I have discarded my reasoning powers. And by thus getting rid of my body and mind, I have become One with the Infinite. This is what I mean by forgetting myself while sitting."
"If you have become One," said Chungni, "there can be no room for bias. If you have lost yourself, there can be no more hindrance. Perhaps you are really a wise one. I trust to be allowed to follow in your steps."[F11]

Rival Views: (2) The Mohists

Another sort of rivalry was expressed by the philosopher Mo-tzu or Mo Ti (ca. 468–390 B.C.). He was an earnest, humane sort of man who thought that the government should operate strictly under religious sanctions, always insist on simplicity and thrift everywhere, and do away with all Chou institutions, in order to build up a community of workers generally alike in station and filled with homely good will and brotherly kindness toward each other and all men. In some ways he was a proto-Communist.

Even though his school of thought died out and his name was for two thousand years known only to Chinese scholars, Mo-tzu was an important figure in his time and remains so in any history of Chinese philosophy and religion. He lived at the height of the dislocations of the Warring States Period, for he was born not long after the death of Confucius, probably in Lu. He seems to have spent his early life under Confucian influence and for a short time became an official in Sung and then an envoy from Sung to Wei. He broke away from Confucianism and adopted a less formal, more broadly democratic attitude, perhaps as a result of living in Sung, where the Chou culture was apparently regarded by the inhabitants as an oppressive system.

294   ° Or Mohists. See next topic.

Mo-tzu was motivated by two major aims. The first was to unite all his fellow-men in a working brotherhood altruistically devoted to the common good, and the second was to have all men do the will of Heaven and the spirits, Heaven being conceived as the Sovereign on High (Shang-ti), from whom a universal love or benevolence is flowing out to all creatures.

In pursuing the first aim, Mo-tzu combined love of mankind with a hard-headed utilitarian logic:

Mutual attacks among states, mutual usurpation among houses, mutual injuries among individuals; the lack of grace and loyalty between ruler and ruled, the lack of affection and filial piety between father and son, the lack of harmony between elder and younger brothers—these are the major calamities in the world.

But whence did these calamities arise? . . .

They arise out of want of mutual love. At present feudal lords have learned only to love their own states and not those of others. Therefore they do not scruple about attacking other states. The heads of houses have learned only to love their own houses and not those of others. Therefore they do not scruple about usurping other houses. And individuals have learned only to love themselves and not others. Therefore they do not scruple about injuring others. . . . Therefore all the calamities, strifes, complaints, and hatred in the world have arisen out of want of mutual love. . . .

How can we have the condition altered?

It is to be altered by the way of universal love and mutual aid.

But what is the way of universal love and mutual aid?

It is to regard the states of others as one's own, the houses of others as one's own, the persons of others as one's self. When feudal lords love one another there will be no more war; when heads of houses love one another there will be no more mutual usurpation; when individuals love one another there will be no more mutual injury. When ruler and ruled love each other they will be gracious and loyal; when father and son love each other they will be affectionate and filial; when elder and younger brothers love each other they will be harmonious. When all the people in the world love one another, then the strong will not overpower the weak, the many will not oppress the few, the wealthy will not mock the poor, the honored will not disdain the humble, and the cunning will not deceive the simple. And it is all due to mutual love that calamities, strifes, complaints, and hatred are prevented from arising. Therefore the benevolent exalt it.[R1]

Lest anyone should think that this is all impractical idealism, Mo-tzu asserts: "If it were not useful then even I would disapprove of it. But how can there be anything that is good but not useful?"[R2]

The essence of his thesis is that the principle of universal love and mutual aid "pays off," as we say today. "Whoever loves others is loved by others; whoever benefits others is benefited by others; whoever hates others is hated by others; whoever injures others is injured by others."[R3] Love pays all around, but hate never works. Unfortunately, "the gentlemen of the world" fail to see that this is so.

Within the state there should be no waste of wealth nor of the time of the laboring man that means wealth. Time-consuming and expensive rituals, ceremonies with long passages of music, and the like were to be pared down to a minimum. It was not that they were evil in themselves, but they took too much time and were useless in promoting increase of wealth and of population. He condemned for like reasons the economic waste of the funerals so beloved of the Confucians. Funerals and mourning periods should be simplified and shortened, he insisted. All pious and cultural embroideries on life should be minimized until the common welfare was better served. Even recreation was out of the question.

This reasoning brought down on Mo-tzu the wrath of Confucians and Taoists alike. They said he sacrificed culture and the amenities that make life pleasant for bare economic benefit. In words of condemnation that were to carry great weight in the future and help to keep the tide running against Mo-tzu, the Confucian scholar, Mencius, whom we shall soon be meeting, said:

The words of Yang Chu° and Mo Ti fill the empire. If you listen to people's discourses throughout it, you will find that they have adopted the views of the one or the other. Now, Yang's principle is—"Each for himself"—

° See the preceding chapter, p. 260.

which does not acknowledge the claims of the sovereign. Mo's principle is—"To love all equally"—which does not acknowledge the peculiar affection due to a father. To acknowledge neither king nor father is to be in the state of a beast.[R4]

But Mo-tzu, who never lived to hear but actually anticipated these criticisms, found justification for his way of life in the sanctions of Heaven. He was sure of two things: first, that Heaven *wanted* men to love each other equally, and second, that this belief had a high utility. It is a great incentive to universal love if men just believe that Heaven is the source and sanction of it. He severely condemned his contemporaries for scepticism with regard to the spirit-worship that the ancient sage-kings of the Hsia dynasty practiced, and he taught with religious fervor that heaven above and earth below are spheres in which a universal love is operating.

I know Heaven loves men dearly. . . . Heaven ordered the sun, the moon, and the stars . . . the four seasons . . . sent down snow, frost, rain, and dew . . . established the hills and rivers, ravines and valleys . . . appointed dukes and lords to reward the virtuous and punish the wicked. . . . This has been taking place from antiquity to the present. . . . Heaven loves the whole world universally. Everything is prepared for the good of man.[R5]

Now, what does Heaven desire and what does it abominate? Heaven desires righteousness and abominates unrighteousness. . . . For, with righteousness the world lives and without it the world dies; with it the world becomes rich and without it the world becomes poor; with it the world becomes orderly and without it the world becomes chaotic. And Heaven likes to have the world live and dislikes to have it die, likes to have it rich and dislikes to have it poor, and likes to have it orderly and dislikes to have it disorderly. Therefore we know Heaven desires righteousness and abominates unrighteousness.[R6]

Mo-tzu was very well aware, it seems, that "the gentlemen of the world" would reject his proposals as impractical and revolutionary. Hence it is touching to hear him say:

The gentlemen of the world would say: "So far so good. It is of course very excellent when love becomes universal. But it is only a difficult and distant ideal." . . . This is simply because the gentlemen of the world do not recognize what is to the benefit of the world, or understand what is its calamity.[R7]

Rival Views: (3) The Legalists

But of greater force at the time than Mo-tzu's attack upon the Confucians was the opposition of the so-called School of Law. This loosely associated group was composed of thinkers of a wide variety of views who agreed on one thing—that the disjointed and easy-going feudal system must give place to a social order held together by a tough, all-embracing law in all the states. The Confucian ideal of government by moral example and polite ideal behavior seemed impracticable to these hard-headed realists. Many of them laid down rules that startlingly anticipate present-day fascist totalitarianism. Others took a position closely resembling Machiavelli's; the prince should, they said, make and unmake laws and alliances according to expediency and immediate advantage, *or* according to the changing drift of the Tao! Above all, because man is a creature to be ruled for his own good by playing upon his desire for material rewards and his fear of suffering and punishment, the laws must be made clear and strong, so that he will know what will bring rewards and what punishment. From the standpoint of the prince, men taken in the mass are like a flock of geese or a herd of deer—they need the discipline of strong laws to make them into one homogeneous whole, obedient to the prince in peace and war.

The Legalists were powerful in the councils of the various states during the two centuries of the Warring States Period (from 403 to 221 B.C.) and left a permanent impress on Chinese political and ethical theory. One of their earliest representatives was the ultrarealistic Shang Yang (Lord Shang), who served for some time as minister in the far western state of Ch'in, but finally became involved in a bloody intrigue that led to his falling in battle and having his body crushed by chariots (338 B.C.). He advised his prince to confine his people to two activities, farming and fighting.

That through which the country is important and that through which the ruler is honored is force. . . . Bring about a condition where people find it bitter not to till the soil, and where they find it dangerous not to fight.[G2]

Among the Legalists he was held to be the leader of those who emphasized strict administration of the law (*fa*). Another group, headed by Shen Tao, a contemporary of Mencius, emphasized princely power or authority (*shih*), alleging: "The reason why . . . subjects do not dare to deceive their ruler, is not because they love him, but because they fear his awe-inspiring power (*shih*)."[D7] A third group emphasized *shu* or statecraft in the handling of men and affairs. Their leader was Han Fei.

Han Fei (d. 233 B.C.) was, like Shang Yang, an official in the state of Ch'in. He was, however, a more brilliant man and served under a more brilliant prince—the same who conquered and unified China not long after Han Fei's tragic death, the totalitarian Emperor Shih Huang-ti. Along the way Han Fei acquired a deep admiration for the *Tao Te Ching*. He studied, too, under the Confucian scholar Hsün-tzu. These influences appear in his writings (the *Han-fei-tzu*) and give them a richness and depth not found in other Legalist treatises. Unfortunately, Han Fei fell a victim to intrigue, and while in prison was either poisoned or, as one story has it, committed suicide on the secret advice of his jealous erstwhile friend Li Ssu.

Han Fei believed that every man is naturally selfish and materialistic. His religion, his obedience to the ruler, his relations to parents, wife, and children, and his dealings with his fellow-men are all permeated by his desire for advantage.

That people love each other Han Fei did not deny, but such love, he maintained, was secondary to the desire for advantage.

There is nothing like the warm feelings between sons and fathers; and anyone who wants to act on the basis of

public morality and issue prohibitions to those under his jurisdiction must needs take into account the intimacy of the flesh-and-blood relation. But there is something more [than love] in the relationship of fathers and mothers with their sons. If a son is born, then they congratulate each other. If a daughter is born, they (may) kill it. Both these have come out of the mother's womb, and when it is a boy, congratulations, when it is a girl, death! The parents are thinking of convenience later on. They calculate on longterm profit. Thus it is that even fathers and mothers in their relation to their children have calculating minds and treat them accordingly.[G3]

He makes a better case of his thesis when he turns to the farm:

When a man sells his services as a farm hand, the master will give him good food at the expense of his own family, and pay him money and cloth. This is not because he loves the farm hand, but he says: "In this way, his ploughing of the ground will go deeper and his sowing of seeds be more active." The farm hand, on the other hand. exerts his strength and works busily at tilling and weeding. He exerts all his skill cultivating the fields. This is not because he loves his master, but he says: "In this way I shall have good soup, and money and cloth will come easily." Thus he expends his strength as if between them there were a bond of love such as that of father and son. Yet their hearts are centered on utility, and they both harbor the idea of serving themselves.[D8]

Han Fei was impressed by certain lessons he had learned from a study of the *Tao Te Ching*. Men are as they are because of the Tao. The prince should emulate the Tao and be not too active nor too deeply involved in arranging every matter himself.

Be too great to be measured, too profound to be surveyed. . . . Hence the saying, "The ruler must not reveal his wants, for if he reveals his wants, the ministers will polish their manners accordingly. . . . If the likes and dislikes of the ruler be concealed, the true hearts of the ministers will be revealed." . . . Accordingly the ruler, wise though he may be, should not bother but let everything find its proper place.[G4]

Han Fei warns his prince that statecraft and wu-wei have a close connection. He draws a clear and deadly picture of the perils that surround a prince if he fails to be properly aloof and Taolike.

Ministers, in relation to the ruler, have no tie of kinship, but serve him solely because constrained by the force of circumstances. Therefore those who minister to a ruler always watch the mental condition of their master without stopping even for a moment; whereas the lord of men remains idle and arrogant over them. . . .

If the lord of men has much confidence in his son, then wicked ministers will utilize his son to accomplish their selfish purposes. . . . If the lord of men has much confidence in his wife, then wicked ministers will utilize her. . . .

The physician sucks patients' cuts and holds their blood in his mouth, not because he is intimate with them like a blood relation, but because he expects profit from them. Likewise, when the cartwright finishes making carriages, he wants people to be rich and noble; when the carpenter finishes making coffins, he wants people to die early. Not that the cartwright is benevolent and the carpenter is cruel, but that unless people are noble, the carriages will not sell, and unless people die, the coffins will not be bought. Thus the carpenter's motive is not hatred for anybody, but his profits which are due to people's death. For the same reason, when the clique of the queen, the princess, the concubine, or the crown prince is formed, they want the ruler to die early; for, unless the ruler die, their positions will not be powerful. Their motive is not hatred for the ruler, but their profits are dependent on the ruler's death.

The hard, realist conclusion is then drawn:

Therefore the lord of men must specially mind those who will profit by his death.[65]

It was these thinkers of the School of Law who, as we have previously noted, prepared the ground for the ruthless and autocratic Shih Huang-ti, the "First Emperor." But we have run a little ahead of our story. Han Fei and his associates (but not Lord Shang) came after Mencius and Hsün-tzu, the great Confucian champions, for they came at the end of the two-century movement that culminated in the political triumph of their conceptions. Meanwhile, the Confucians had been struggling without much success for influence and power. Fortunately for their long-term prospects, a series of brilliant variations on the Confucian theme appeared from the pens of Mencius and Hsün-tzu, and Confucianism took on added significance.

Mencius: The "Orthodox" Champion

We turn first to the celebrated scholar whom Confucians many centuries later regarded as having come closest to Confucius' true meaning.* Born a little over a hundred years after the death of Confucius, Mencius, the greatest writer of the Confucian school, magnified and gave studied emphasis to the master's belief in the innate goodness of man and the adequacy of the feudal system to develop and maintain that goodness. Mencius (or Meng K'o) was a native of T'sou, a small state near Lu, and early came under Confucian influence. The way in which his love of learning was aroused is told in a delightful tradition that caused later Chinese to regard his mother as an ideal parent. According to this apocryphal tale, his father died young, and his mother lived alone with her small son near a cemetery. After a while she began to worry, because she noticed that he was playing constantly at the etiquette of attending funerals, so she moved with him to a house near a market-place, whereupon the boy, influenced again by his environment, began to play at buying and selling. She liked this so little that she made haste to take a house near a school, in the expectation— which was fulfilled—that he would pattern his behavior after the pupils and teachers whom he observed.† In time he became a scholar in his own right, in a school that was, it is likely, conducted by disciples of Tsu Ssu, Confucius' grandson. Later he sought office under the Duke of Ch'i, but the duke proving beyond "reform" (in the Confucian sense,

---

* The orthodoxy of Mencius was not finally determined until the time of Chu Hsi (see p. 307).

† This story, incidentally, neatly illustrates Mencius' teaching that surroundings so greatly influence human beings that all they need is the right kind.

of course), he departed, and like his master, wandered from state to state, exhorting rulers to follow the Confucian way, but always in vain. So he found it expedient to retire to T'sou, his native place, to spend the rest of his days—until his death in 289 B.C. at the age of eighty-one—teaching and writing in the graceful, if somewhat academic style that won favor for the doctrines of Confucius among the intelligentsia of the time.

The mellow flavor and genial atmosphere of Mencius' writings are evident in almost any quotation from him.

He believed wholeheartedly in the innate goodness of human nature. Here are two famous passages in exposition of this theme:

> The tendency of man's nature to good is like the tendency of water to flow downwards. There are none but have this tendency to good, just as all water flows downwards.[15]
>
> If men become evil, that is not the fault of their original endowment. The sense of mercy is found in all men; the sense of shame is found in all men; the sense of respect is found in all men; the sense of right and wrong is found in all men. The sense of mercy is what we call benevolence or charity. The sense of shame is what we call righteousness. The sense of respect is what we call propriety. The sense of right and wrong is what we call wisdom, or moral consciousness. Charity, righteousness, propriety and moral consciousness are not something that is drilled into us; we have got them originally with us.[G7]

All men possess these fundamental qualities as "tender shoots"[G6] within them, ready to grow. Sometimes they ripen into the fullness of the virtue that is seen in the moral nature of a sage. No man is born without them. Oft-quoted by the Chinese themselves is this argument:

> All men have the sense of compassion for others. . . . What I mean by all men having a sense of compassion is that if, for instance, a child is suddenly seen to be on the point of falling into a well, everybody without exception will have a sense of distress. It is not by reason of any close intimacy with the parents of the child, nor by reason of a desire for the praise of neighbors and friends, nor by reason of disliking to be known as the kind of

man (who is not moved by compassion). From this point of view we observe that it is inhuman to have no sense of compassion, inhuman to have no sense of shame over wickedness, inhuman to have no sense of modesty and the need for yielding place to a better man, inhuman not to distinguish right and wrong.[G7]

And yet, all men, though morally equal in the sense that they are all alike essentially good, or good at heart, are not equal in moral achievement. Some use their minds; others do not. This creates distinctions among them that alter their status in a properly constituted society.

> There is a saying, "Some labor with their minds, and some labor with their strength. Those who labor with their minds govern others; those who labor with their strength are governed by others. Those who are governed by others support them; those who govern others are supported by others." This is a principle universally recognized.[16]

This fact is so puzzling to one of Mencius' disciples that he asks: "All are equally men, but some are great men, and some are little men;—how is this?" Mencius replies: "Those who follow that part of themselves which is great are great men; those who follow that part which is little are little men."[17]

But why are not more great men in evidence? Mencius would seem to suggest that environment and circumstances have a great deal to do with the extent to which different men fulfill their natural powers.

> In good years the children of the people are most of them good, while in bad years the most of them abandon themselves to evil. It is not owing to their natural powers conferred by heaven that they are thus different. The abandonment is owing to the circumstances through which they allow their minds to be ensnarled and drowned in evil.[18]

The best environment and the most encouraging circumstances for the flowering out of men's essential goodness are found under a paternalistic feudal system, provided the latter is administered for the benefit not of the aristocrats, but of the people. It is recorded that when Mencius went to see King Hsüan of Ch'i, the king, who had ambitions to become the emperor of China, asked what virtues a man must display to gain imperial sway. Mencius answered, "The love and protection of the people."

The king asked again, "Is such a one as I competent to love and protect the people?" Mencius said, "Yes. . . .

"Treat with the reverence due to age the elders in your own family, so that the elders in the families of others shall be similarly treated; treat with the kindness due to youth the young in your family, so that the young in the families of others shall be similarly treated:—do this, and the empire may be made to go round in your palm. . . .

"Now, if your Majesty will institute a government whose action shall be all benevolent, this will cause all the officers in the empire to wish to stand in your Majesty's court, and the farmers all to wish to plough in your Majesty's fields, and the merchants, both travelling and stationary, all to wish to store their goods in your Majesty's market-places."[19]

It may thus be seen that though Mencius is conservative so far as the form of his ideal society is concerned—it is the old feudal system—yet he makes a strong point of it that:

The people are the most important element in the state. . . . Therefore to gain the peasantry is the way to become Emperor.[D9]

He hit hard at the Machiavellian councilors who made common cause with Shang Yang and later Legalists.

Those who nowadays serve their sovereigns say, "We can for our sovereign enlarge the limits of the cultivated ground, and fill his treasuries and arsenals." Such persons are nowadays called "Good ministers," but anciently they were called "Robbers of the people."[110]

Mencius realized full well from studying his times that war destroyed the possibility of attaining his ideals of government, and so he constantly inveighed against it. War-makers are also "robbers of the people." Furthermore, war not only harms the state but it signifies Heaven's punishment for offenses against its dispensations. When a kingdom is badly

governed, Heaven lets the strong triumph over the weak, until corruption is unbounded. Then the righteous, thoroughly aroused, unite in rebellion and, with Heaven's sanction, drive the hopelessly corrupt ruler from his throne.

This brings us to Mencius' religious views, a type of mysticism. He believed like Confucius in a guiding will or appointment of Heaven. Heaven sees and hears, and "there is an appointment for everything."[111] One who exercises his mind to the utmost and studies his own nature knows Heaven and Heaven's will. It is Heaven that creates the inner disposition.

What belongs by his nature to the superior man cannot be increased by the largeness of his sphere of action, nor diminished by his dwelling in poverty and retirement;—for this reason, that it is determinately apportioned to him by Heaven.[112]

To look with sincerity into this inner disposition is to know Heaven through it. In contradistinction to the Taoists, Mencius believed that the predispositions toward moral order are complete within us. So, as Dr. Chan Wing-tsit puts it, "instead of looking to nature in order to know ourselves, we look within ourselves in order to know nature."[S1] It is thus that we may fulfill our destiny as Heaven prepares it for us.

At this point Mencius made a suggestion that was to have great influence, over a thousand years later, on the Neo-Confucians. He believed that within each person there is a "vast-flowing vital energy";[G8] he called it ch'i, a sort of élan vital. Anyone who lives rightly removes within himself the obstructions to the free flow of this spiritual force. It will not do to try to help its growth, he said. It is already there as a great potential of force, and all it needs is to have the channels cleared for it by uprightness, and then it will flow. The spiritual man thus gains a power that projects his influence far and wide.

Such is the nature of this energy that it is immensely great and immensely strong, and if it be nourished by uprightness and so sustain no injury, then it pervades the whole space between the heavens and the earth.[G9]

Later generations were to play down Mencius' confidence in the goodness of man, but his optimism, gentleness, love of wisdom, and pacifism were eventually to increase his influence among the literati, so that he ultimately took rank next to Confucius in Confucian eyes.

Hsün-tzu: The "Heterodox" Champion

Born a little before the death of Mencius, Hsün-tzu had greater immediate influence. This was in part due to his many-sidedness. He came to some extent under the influence of the Taoists on the one hand and of the Legalists on the other. Like the latter, he exalted the functions and prerogatives of the state and was brutally realistic about the weaknesses of human nature.

Hsün-tzu, or Hsün Ch'ing (*ca.* 298–238 B.C.), was a native of Chao, but much of his life was spent in Ch'i, where he was one of the "great officers" of the court and an active member of a group of scholars and teachers at the capital. He taught Han Fei and Li Ssu, who became leaders in Legalist circles. On being the victim of slander, he went to Ch'u, where he spent his declining years as a magistrate at Lanling.

In developing his philosophy Hsün-tzu rejected the two cardinal principles of Mencius: that man's nature is innately good, and that Heaven watches over earth with something of a personal concern. He held that "man is by nature bad; his goodness is only acquired training."[T1] Though he is capable, under proper conditions, of indefinite improvement, left to himself he grows crooked, like some sapling that must be tied into position before it will grow straight. The restraints that force improvement on his unruly nature are the rules of propriety and the laws compelling respect for property and the personal rights of others. Education of the right kind helps to subdue the bad in human nature and develop the good.

These views led Hsün-tzu to emphasize, even more than Confucius did, the importance of li, the ceremonies and rules of proper conduct that are the legacy left by the great sage-kings to after-times. The state should undertake to enforce education in li upon disorderly humanity.

The nature of man is evil. . . . Therefore to give rein to man's original nature, to follow man's feelings, inevitably results in strife and rapacity. . . . Crooked wood needs to undergo steaming and bending to conform to the carpenter's rule; then only is it straight. Blunt metal needs to undergo grinding and whetting; then only is it sharp. The original nature of man is evil, so he needs to undergo the instruction of teachers and laws, then only will he be upright.[T2]

Against the Mencian view that the rules of proper conduct arise from or out of man's nature, Hsün-tzu argued:

The relation of the Sage to the rules of proper conduct (Li) and justice (Yi) and accumulated acquired training is the same as that of the potter and the clay: he brings the pottery into being [by pounding and molding the clay].[T3]

The sage-kings knew that man's nature is evil, corrupt, rebellious, and disorderly. Hence they set forth clearly the rules of proper conduct to reform him. They were aware that:

If a man is without a teacher or precepts, then if he is intelligent, he will certainly become a robber; if he is brave, he will certainly become a murderer; if he has ability, he will certainly cause disorder; if he is a dialectician, he will certainly go far from the truth. [But] if he has a teacher and precepts, then if he is intelligent, he will quickly become learned; if he is brave, he will quickly become awe-inspiring; if he has ability, he will quickly become perfect; if he is a dialectician, he will quickly be able to determine the truth or falsity of things.[T4]

In his attitude toward Heaven (T'ien), Hsün-tzu leaned far over in the direction of the Taoists' impersonal, naturalistic Way (Tao). Heaven is not to be anthropomorphically viewed, for it is just our name for the law of compensation operating within cosmic events, and one cannot ever expect it to respond to prayer.

One ought not to grumble at Heaven that things happen according to its Way (Tao). . . . When stars fall or the sacred tree groans, the people of the whole state are afraid. They ask, "Why is it?" I answer: There is no reason. This is due to a modification of Heaven and Earth, to the mutation of *Yin* and *Yang*. . . . If people pray for rain and get rain, why is that? I answer: There is no reason for it. If people do not pray for rain, it will nevertheless rain.[T5]

Heaven will not abolish winter just because mankind does not like cold weather. Nor will Earth shrink because we object to long distance. . . .

As long as we practice thriftiness and enrich the sources of our wealth, Heaven is powerless to make us poor. Likewise, Heaven can hardly make us sick if we nourish ourselves well, take proper care, and exercise regularly. . . .

The way to do things is neither the way of Heaven nor that of Earth but that of Man.[U1]

All natural events, then, come to pass according to natural law. There are no supernatural agencies anywhere. So sure was Hsün-tzu of this that he took the radical step of denying the existence of spirits: neither the popular gods nor the demons nor even the ancestral spirits exist. Divination may have some uncertain bearing on the future, but when the knowing decide an important affair after divination, this is not because they think in this way they will get what they seek, but only to "gloss over the matter"!

The people think it is supernatural. He who thinks it is glossing over the matter is fortunate; he who thinks it is supernatural is unfortunate.[T6]

Hsün-tzu was obliged in the light of these naturalistic views to re-evaluate the funeral and sacrificial ceremonies inherited from the great sage-kings. He took a down-to-earth view of the matter. Rites and ceremonies are good for people. Nothing supernatural occurs during them, but they have a valuable subjective effect in allowing the expression and catharsis of human feeling, while also introducing beauty into human life and cultivating the sense of propriety.

Hence I say: Sacrifice is because of the emotions produced by memories, ideas, thoughts, and longings; it is the extreme of loyalty, faithfulness, love and reverence.

Among superior men it is considered to be a human practice; among the common people it is considered to be serving the spirits.[T7]

The aesthetic value of ceremony appealed especially to Hsün-tzu.

All rites, if for the service of the living, are to beautify joy; or if to send off the dead, they are to beautify sorrow; or if for sacrifice, they are to beautify reverence; or if they are military, they are to beautify majesty.[T8]

On the whole, Hsün-tzu was unwilling to go beyond what was required to guide the living. In funerals, for example, the living properly desire to "send off" the dead as if they were still living and to beautify their departure. Therefore the living perform the traditional rituals with thoroughness and care. The carriages and all the other articles traditionally sent along with the dead are duly burned or buried, but:

The horses are sent away and informed that they are not to be buried. . . . The metal rein-ends, the reins, the horse-collars do not go into the grave. . . . Things for the dead are showy, but not useful.[T9]

This may be called a strictly rational propriety, expressing and yet reining in the emotions, lest they lead to extravagance, an unreasoning waste. The emotions have their place, but they are not to be allowed too much scope. There should be balance here as elsewhere. Each age should judge for itself what is useful in its traditions.

The rules of proper conduct (Li) cut off that which is too long and stretch out that which is too short; they diminish that which is too much and increase that which is insufficient; they attain to the beauty of love and reverence, and they strengthen the excellence of character and right moral feeling. . . . They provide for weeping and sorrow, but do not go so far as an undue degree of distress and self-injury. This is the middle path of the rites (Li). . . . Anything beyond this is evil.[T10]

Hsün-tzu was no narrow Confucian. He found such values in the Taoist point of view that he was led to equate li with the Tao, the latter being in his conception the cosmological principle "whereby

Heaven and Earth unite, whereby the sun and moon are bright, whereby the four seasons are ordered, whereby the stars move in their courses," and "whereby joy and anger keep their proper place."[T11] He also showed the extent of Taoist influence upon him in holding that meditative reflection confirms the faith that the universe at large tends steadily toward perfection and in its impersonal way is on the side of the righteous.

The Triumph of the Confucians Under the Early Han

The Legalists scored their greatest victory in the reign of Shih Huang-ti, but with the fall of his dynasty their school gradually disintegrated. Only those Legalist doctrines that were taken up by the Confucians ultimately entered the accepted body of Chinese political thought, for China had not taken kindly to the arbitrariness of the regime of Shih Huang-ti and his attempted complete reordering of their lives and thinking. During the first years of the early Han dynasty the nation breathed a sigh of relief and relaxed into a Taoistlike quietude, as though worn out by the late disturbances. The first Han emperors encouraged this psychological reaction. Taoism met with their approval. The people turned from fighting to dreaming. The Taoist geomancers were able to attract widespread attention to their alchemy and experimentation with the pill of immortality. But the Confucians were also busy. Gradually they were repossessing themselves of copies—in the new script—of the books that Shih Huang-ti had taken from them and burned. They had not liked the regimentation of life under Shih Huang-ti, but they liked anarchistic drifting and disorganization less, so they appealed to the Han emperors to reinstitute order and proper procedure in official life.

Not, however, until the reign of the great Han Emperor Wu Ti, to whom we have already referred, were their pleas heeded. It was probably in 136 B.C., in the fourth year of that reign, that the Confucian scholar Tung Chung-shu (179?–104 B.C.) presented his famous memorial to the emperor. Knowing the emperor to be desirous of greater national unity, he reminded that monarch that general unification would not come so long as the teachers and philosophic schools of the day had such diverse standards. The people did not know what to cling to, and the government statutes were in a state of confusion. The only way out, said Tung Chung-shu, was a return to the Six Disciplines of Confucius. All other standards should be "cut short" and not allowed to progress further. Only thus could the government statutes be made consistent and the people know what to follow. He accompanied this firm and unequivocal proposal with the suggestion that the emperor found an imperial academy or college for the training of officials in the uniform procedures that the Confucians had worked out on the basis of the best experience of the past. The emperor was impressed. He adopted Tung Chung-shu's suggestions. The Confucians were put in charge of a government-sponsored system of education designed to train officials.

Thereupon Confucianism began a two-thousand-year reign as the predominant intellectual discipline used in the training of the governing class. It was not the Confucianism of earlier times that triumphed, however; it was Confucianism (1) modified by a tendency to magnify Confucius into a more than human being, (2) infused with Legalist ideas as to the nature of the enlarged bureaucracy that was needed to cope with the problems of an empire grown so vast as to lie on the borders of India, stretch into central Asia, and penetrate Korea, and (3) tempered with Mo-tzu's conviction that a government that was to win and hold the common people must have back of it the sanctions of religion—the approval of Heaven above and the spirits below.

Confucian Scholasticism and Rationalism

From the intellectual standpoint, Confucianism reached the end of its formative period when the later

303

Han dynasty (23–220 A.D.) began. In fact, it would be correct to say, with Dr. Y. L. Fung, that this was true even earlier, for "with the putting into practice of Tung Chung-shu's suggestion, the Period of the Philosophers came to an end, and that of the Study of the Classics commenced."D10 The shift was from formative thinking to textual criticism, systematization, and syncretism.

This appears in the writings of Tung Chung-shu himself. Self-consciously more a scholar than an imperial counselor, he followed Hsün-tzu rather than Mencius and sought to absorb into Confucianism the truth elements, as he saw them, in Taoist yin-yang interactionism and in the Five Forces theories. His pure scholasticism may be seen in a sentence or two from his treatises.

Heaven has Five Forces, first Wood, second Fire, third Soil, fourth Metal, fifth Water. . . .
These Five Forces correspond to the actions of filial sons and loyal ministers. . . . Thus, as a son welcomes the completion of his years (of nurture), so Fire delights in Wood; and, as (the time comes when) the son buries his father, so (the time comes when) Water conquers Metal. Also the service of one's sovereign is like the reverent service Soil renders to Heaven. Thus we may well say that there are Force men, and that there are both Five Forces, each keeping its right turn, and Five-Force officials, each doing his utmost.G10

And so forth. This sort of scholasticism was to absorb the Confucians for centuries.

But the systematizers were not to have it all their own way. Realizing, perhaps, that scholasticism already had or would become "a matter of intellectual sport, a game of puzzles, and finally a superstition,"S2 Wang Ch'ung (ca. 27–100 A.D.), a left-wing rationalist of the Confucian school, strove for a less theoretical and a more empirical viewpoint. He attacked the superstition and supernaturalism he found in religion. He was a thorough-going naturalist and humanist, armed with all the vigor and clarity of style characteristic of so many of the Chinese writers whom

we have quoted.* It would be too bad not to quote him. The following passages speak for themselves:

The Scholars at the present day have a passion for believing that what their teachers say is (genuinely) old, and they regard the words of worthies and sages as all of the very essence of truth. In expounding and learning these words off by heart, they do not realize that there are any difficulties requiring explanation.G11
The common idea is that the dead become ghosts, have knowledge, and can injure people. . . . (I maintain that) the dead do not become ghosts, have no consciousness, and cannot injure people. How do I prove my position? By means of other beings. Man is a being and other creatures also are beings. When they die, they do not become ghosts: why then should man alone when he dies be able to become a ghost?G12
At the height of summer, thunder and lightning come with tremendous force, splitting trees, demolishing houses, and from time to time killing people. The common idea is that this splitting of trees and demolishing of houses is Heaven setting a dragon to work. And when the thunder and lightning rush on people and kill them, this is described as due to hidden faults, for example, people eating unclean things, and so Heaven in its anger striking them and killing them. The roar of the thunder is the voice of Heaven's anger, like men gasping with rage. . . . This is all nonsense.G13

Wang Ch'ung tried also to reverse the tendency to convert the fallible man Confucius into some kind of infallible authority touched with the qualities of divinity. In his treatment of the sayings in the *Analects*, he examined the teachings of Confucius as casually and critically as though he were looking into the opinions of a person who had to establish his authority like anyone else—by winning the assent of the reason.

* If this were a history of philosophy rather than a history of religions, it would be necessary to go into the well-developed tradition of atheism and naturalism ("materialism" in Communist terms) which forms a persistent theme in Chinese thought, beginning with Hsün-tzu and Wang Ch'ung and continuing with Fan Ch'en (*ca.* 450–515 A.D.), Lu T'sai (600–665), Lin Tsung-yuan and Liu Yu-hsi (*ca.* 800), Wang An-shih (1021–1086), Yah Hsi and Ch'en Liang (*ca.* 1175), and others down through the nineteenth century to the present.

Confucianism and Buddhism

The coming of Buddhism to China put Confucianism to a severe test. Taoism felt far less antipathy to the new religion when it first appeared and was aroused to resistance only by jealousy. But all orthodox Confucians remained stiff in opposition. Buddhism seemed to them too other-worldly and nihilistic. They did not like the concentration of attention on transmigration, birth, and death. Above all, they condemned the Buddhists, as they already had the Taoists, for diverting men from the service of society to self-salvation. Yet two factors operated to make their protests without much effect: the novelty and freshness of Buddhism, and the formal and lifeless character of their own scholasticism and of the official ritualism and ceremony practiced in the court and at the Confucian temples which by this time had appeared.* Moreover, the later Han dynasty had collapsed in the turmoil in which the Three Kingdoms (220–280 A.D.) rose up to divide China. For 350 years China was to suffer inroads by "barbarians" from the north and to know disunion and misery. Many brilliant minds, distracted by the chaos, were unable to embrace Buddhism, yet were equally repelled by Confucian traditionalism, formalism and "ineptitude."

Caught between the scoffing Taoists on the one hand and the Buddhists on the other, who were riding high on the success of the spectacular and glamorous Mahayana, the Confucians weakened. Except for a few stern Old Text die-hards who would not yield, they began to add semi-Buddhist touches to their Confucian temples and warmed up their beliefs about Confucius with stories of miracles and signs in heaven and on earth. Original Confucianism had been singularly free from legend and miracle, but now that even the Taoists attributed miracles to Confucius, the Confucians insensibly veered from their orthodox course toward meeting the Buddhist

and Taoist challenges. They adopted stories of the appearance of a unicorn before Confucius' birth, saying his mother even tied a ribbon on its horn. On the night of his birth two dragons appeared, and the five planets drew near in the shapes of interested old men. Heavenly harmonies sounded, and a voice said: "Divine harmony strikes the ear, because Heaven has caused a saint to be born. His doctrine will be the law of the world."ᵛ Other stories, circulated perhaps by the Taoists before the Confucianists themselves believed them, told how when Confucius was dying, a meteor descended and turned into an inscribed jade tablet, and how when Shih Huang-ti ordered his soldiers to open Confucius' tomb, they found within it a written prophecy of this very event and a prediction of the death of the First Emperor, which was later exactly verified.

One should not, probably, lay all this entirely to the influence of Taoism and Buddhism; it might have happened anyway.

What could not have occurred, however, without the presence of rival faiths was the rise of scholars who attempted a syncretism of the San Chiao ("The Three Religions").* On the Taoist side there was T'an Ch'iao (probably sixth century), who held that the Tao is the central or underlying principle of all three religions. The Buddhists on their part proved not averse to this type of thinking, for they quoted favorably Li Shih-ch'ien (*ca.* 590 A.D.), who said Buddhism was the sun, Taoism the moon, and Confucianism the five planets. Later on a Buddhist monk founded a cult that had official sanction for a long time and that placed the images of Confucius, Lao-tzu, and Buddha side by side on the altar. Among the Confucians there was Wang T'ung (583–616 A.D.), who held that the Doctrine of the Mean or Middle Way is the common ground between the three religions.

---

* See Section IV of this chapter for an explanation of how these temples appeared.

* We have already seen in Chapter 6, "The Religious Development of Buddhism," how Buddhism combined with Chinese thought to produce such varieties of Buddhism as the Ch'an (or Zen) sects.

But Confucianism was able nevertheless to maintain its distinctive character. It had a steadying factor to keep it on a straight course—the curriculum of its school. So long as the imperial academy and the lesser schools drilled their students in the *Analects* and the Five Classics—particularly the *Li Chi* and the *Ch'un Ch'iu*—Confucianism was safe from the temptation to stray too far from its historic basis. Indeed, its hard, resistant core finally gave rise to a Confucian revival.

Neo-Confucianism

The first sign that such a revival would eventually come about was the famous protest made by the scholar Han Yü to the thirteenth emperor of the T'ang dynasty, Hsien Tsung, concerning the bone of the Buddha. Han Yü (or Han T'ui-chih, 767–824 A.D.) was a valiant champion of the Mencian point of view in Confucianism. His protest was made in 820 A.D., when the emperor made a great pageant of receiving from the Buddhist priests, marching to him in public procession, a bone that was reputed to be a relic of the Buddha. Han Yü addressed a vigorous memorial to the emperor, reminding him that the founder of the T'ang dynasty had contemplated exterminating Buddhism because its founder was a foreigner who could not speak Chinese, wore outlandish clothes such as a barbarian would wear, and had no conception of the sacred ties that bind ruler and subject or father and son. At that time, he went on, Kao Tsu had unfortunately been prevented from carrying out his intention by his foolish ministers. But now, Han Yü begged, let the present emperor give the noxious, putrid bone to the public executioner so that he might throw it in the water or burn it in a fire—and, if the Buddha became angered at such action, let the blame be upon him, Han Yü, as alone responsible!

For these spirited words the audacious scholar was banished to an official post in the far south, where he languished in virtual exile.

The Confucian revival foreshadowed by Han Yü came two centuries later during a period of distressing social change. The Sung dynasty (960–1279 A.D.), which, after an interval of civil wars, succeeded the brilliant T'ang dynasty, was perhaps equally great in cultural matters but was dogged by disastrous military and political failures. Whereas the T'angs had come to grips with and mastered the "barbarian" tribes that surrounded China and had extended the domain of their empire from Korea in the northeast to Afghanistan on the west, the Sungs, made inept and weak by internal corruption, failed to prevent the resurgence of the border tribes. First the Kitans, then the Chins, and finally the Mongols, fiercer yet, poured across the Yellow River and down to the Yangtze. The Mongols eventually were able, under Kublai Khan, to wipe out the dynasty altogether by conquering the regions south of the Yangtze and even rolling on into Indo-China and Burma.

It was natural that the Chinese should from the very beginning of these events react to conquest by withdrawing into themselves until their conquerors should once more be absorbed and made over by Chinese culture. In particular there was a return to the older Confucianism. Han Yü had been a very early voice presaging this, but the true Neo-Confucian revival did not begin until it was evident that the Sung dynasty was to fall on evil days. The two figures within the movement whom we shall consider are only the most celebrated of a large group of scholars expressing the related views that these two ably brought together and systematized. Some of the names are worth rehearsing: Hu Yüan (993–1059), who started the movement, Chou Tun-yi (1017–1073), Shao Yung (1011–1067), Chang Tsai (1020–1076), and the inimitable Cheng brothers (Hao, 1032–1086, and Yi, 1033–1107), who between them gave rise to two divergent schools among the Neo-Confucians, although this was not realized at the time. The younger brother, Yi, initiated the school of laws and principles that Chu Hsi systematized, while Hao, the elder brother, started a trend that led to the rise of the school of mind championed by Wang

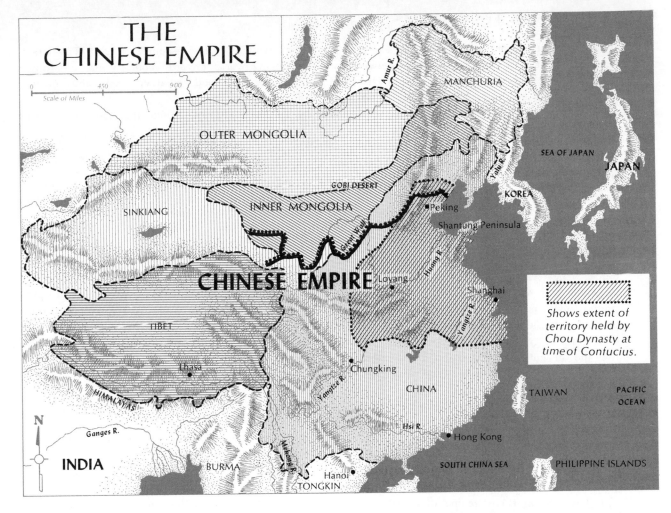

THE CHINESE EMPIRE

Scale of Miles
0   450   900

OUTER MONGOLIA

MANCHURIA

SEA OF JAPAN

JAPAN

SINKIANG

GOBI DESERT

INNER MONGOLIA

KOREA

Peking

Shantung Peninsula

CHINESE EMPIRE

Loyang

Shanghai

TIBET

Lhasa

HIMALAYAS

Chungking

CHINA

TAIWAN

PACIFIC OCEAN

Yangtze R.

Hsi R.

Hong Kong

Ganges R.

N

INDIA

BURMA

Hanoi
TONGKIN

SOUTH CHINA SEA

PHILIPPINE ISLANDS

Shows extent of territory held by Chou Dynasty at time of Confucius.

Yang-ming. What the Neo-Confucians professed to do was to get back to pure Confucianism, before there had been any manifest borrowing from Taoist and Buddhist sources.

Chu Hsi (1130–1200) was a scholar of the first rank, whose commentaries on the Confucian Classics were immediately recognized as the final words on the subject. In his distress at the invasions of the Chin tribes, he said such bitter things about the official appeasement policy that he incurred imperial displeasure. But his lectures at the White Deer Grotto drew distinguished audiences of scholars. Of his austere personal habits we learn from a Chinese biographer:

Rising at dawn, he clothed himself decently and paid homage to his ancestors and to Confucius. Then he went to his study and attended to his daily work. Sitting or sleeping he held himself erect; working or resting he behaved according to the model of behavior prescribed by Confucius in his Classics. Everything in his home was permanently in good order, and in this way he lived from youth to old age.[w]

To Chu Hsi fell the lot of determining finally the question of Hsün-tzu's orthodoxy. He pronounced the earlier thinker a heretic for departing from Confucius' belief in the original goodness of human nature. This proved enough to set up Mencius, Hsün-tzu's rival, as the orthodox interpreter of Confucius' thought. But it was only one of Chu Hsi's services to Confucianism that he thus distinguished between the "sound" and "unsound" interpretations. His chief contribution to the Confucian school lay in his clarification of the orthodox attitude toward the themes appearing in Taoism and Buddhism. In other words, he led the Neo-Confucians in their attempt to discuss the philosophical concepts of the rival religions and to adapt what was sound in them.

The way in which Chu Hsi went about his task was to take key passages from the Confucian texts and use them as touchstones of truth and error. To cite one (the chief) instance, he selected the passage from the *Great Learning* in which appears the sentence, "To extend their knowledge to the utmost they [the ancients] investigated things." Chu Hsi interpreted this to mean that the ancients examined the world about them objectively, in order to increase their grasp of general truth. He concluded, in short, that the ancients thought nature, quite apart from human nature, embodied laws or principles independent of the human mind.

In his objective examination of the cosmos, Chu Hsi, speaking for his fellow-Confucians as well as himself, was, he said, led to the view that all things are brought into being by the following two elements mentioned by Confucius and Mencius: vital (or physical) force (ch'i), and law or rational principle (li). The latter in its cosmic operations, where it may be called the *T'ai Chi* or Great Ultimate, impels the vital force to generate movement and change within matter, and thereby are produced the two energy-modes (yang and yin) and the five elements (fire, water, wood, metal, and earth). Every object in nature exhibits some aspect of the rational law (li) or Great Ultimate that works within it. In the words of his summary:

With reference to the entire universe, there is in it one Great Ultimate. With reference to the myriad things, there is a Great Ultimate in each of them.[53]

This is true of man also. What we call his soul or nature is the supreme regulative principle of the universe working in him as mind or spirit. This law of his being works toward good, so man's nature is fundamentally good, whatever evil habits he may display.

The rational principle and the vital force interact in mutual dependence.

There is no Reason independent of the vital force, and there is no vital force independent of Reason. . . .
The Great Ultimate is Reason, whereas activity and tranquility are the vital force. The two are mutually dependent and never separated. The Great Ultimate may be compared to a man, the activity and tranquility may be compared to a horse. The horse carries the man and the man rides on the horse. As the horse comes and goes, so does the man.[54]

Though the description so far might suggest it, this was not conceived to be a purely non-physical process, for it results in the creation of matter. The Great Ultimate or reason, constituting the metaphysical principle, "rides on" the activating or physical principle, ch'i, and when the pace is swift, the yang energy-mode is generated; when the pace slows down, the yin mode is produced. Once brought into being, the yang and yin, by their eternal interaction and alternation of dominance over each other, give rise to the energy-structures that are the Five Elements or the physical constituents of the "myriad things" of the material world.

Chu Hsi found in the concept of the Great Ultimate what he felt to be the truth element in Taoism, for the law or reason of any entity was its "right way to go" or tao. But he did not regard his T'ai Chi, as the Taoists did their Tao, as something "still and silent," nor did he think it operated to reduce all things ultimately to equality and indistinguishability. By its cooperation with vital energy it exhibits itself as a differentiating principle that may at any moment produce something new. At this point also, Chu Hsi disagreed with Buddhism. He could not conceive of reality as a void (a something devoid of any assignable attributes), nor did he expect the universe to return again to the void. There is a central harmony, but it is not a static nor a qualityless harmony; it is a dynamic harmony. The Great Ultimate never ceases to act, and therefore it is not to be identified with the Buddhist Ultimate within which the universe forms, flowers, deteriorates, and is finally swallowed up again. To use an American phrase, "there is always something doing."

Though he had gone pretty far toward rendering the older terminology no longer usable, Chu Hsi tried to make some concessions to the ancient conception of Heaven. He refused to be anthropomorphic and, indeed, spoke of Heaven in such abstract language that he encouraged the agnostic tendency in Confucianism, but because his Great Ultimate is reason, he sensed behind the cosmos something like an ordering will. In a passage in which he summed up the opinion of the Classics, he wrote:

"These passages indicate that there is a man, *as it were,* in the heavens ruling all."[X]

In other respects he gave religion in its traditional forms little place. Worship of spirits and offerings to images even excited his contempt, and although he granted to ancestor-worship the slight basis that is found in biological and social immortality, he denied that the souls of ancestors exist; ancestor-worship has the appropriateness and value that are derived from gratitude to forebears piously felt and expressed.

In his personal practice Chu Hsi found his spiritual and moral development best served by devoting a certain portion of each day to solitary meditation, something he called "silent sitting." It resembled the Buddhist dhyana or meditation. He wrote:

Introspection is most effective when employed quietly. One should with eternal vigilance constantly examine himself. If he finds himself too talkative, he should quiet down. If he is careless, he should learn to be prudent. If he is too fresh and shallow, he should balance this with dignity and dependability.[U2]

But he denied that this "self-correction through introspection"[U3] was actually the Buddhist dhyana (or *Ch'an-ting*).

Silent-sitting is not the Buddhist type of *Ch'an-ting* which requires the cessation of all processes of thinking. Mine is to help aim our mind so that it will not be distracted by conflicting streams of thought. When our mind is calm and undisturbed, concentration is a matter of course.[U4]

As a matter of fact, for Chu Hsi meditation, as was natural in a Confucian, had more a moral than a metaphysical or mystical bearing. Feeling that "centrality is the order of the universe and harmony is its unalterable law,"[Y1] he wished to get himself into the equable state that enabled him to apprehend this order and harmony and to feel at one with the reason in it. When he succeeded in doing so, he found that "all people are brothers and sisters, and all things are my companions."[Y2]

Because of his combination of many-sidedness with practicality, Chu Hsi became, as we have little difficulty in understanding, the almost infallible interpreter of Confucianism from his time on. He has been called the Thomas Aquinas of Confucianism.

Yet he did not dominate the scene so completely that no other interpretations were countenanced. He perhaps carried the majority with him, but there were many Neo-Confucians, more under the spell of Buddhism and Taoism, who thought that the clue to the reason in things is to be found not so much in the investigation of the reason in nature as within the mind or consciousness of man. They therefore gave chief emphasis to an examination of the mental content disclosed in introspection. The greatest name of this group is that of Wang Yang-ming (1473–1529 A.D.), a scholar appearing two and a half centuries after Chu Hsi, when both the Sung and the Yüan (or Mongol) dynasties had passed into history and the Ming dynasty (1368–1644 A.D.) had for more than a hundred years demonstrated, in spite of licentiousness and corruption, its staying power. For offending a corrupt eunuch who had acquired great power in the imperial court, Wang Yang-ming was exiled for a time to a distant province, but he was able to summon up sufficient interior resources to spend the time in developing his philosophy. His reflections led him to say that objects are not independent of the mind, for the mind shapes them within itself. This emphasis on the part mind plays in constituting objects as they are known in experience may have been due to an experiment Wang Yang-ming performed when he was twenty-one. It seems he took seriously Chu Hsi's suggestion that to know the reason in things one must investigate to the utmost all sorts of external objects. He chose his father's bamboo grove for a test of this method. For three days and nights, it is said, he sat among the bamboos to see what they would teach him, and caught a bad cold without arriving at any satisfactory results. He concluded that because objects do not put reason into the mind, the mind must put reason into them. In a modern interpreter's words:

> In the case of bamboo, for instance, . . . if one views it as a plant which is humble enough to be hollow inside, hardy enough to stay green the year round, plain enough to adorn itself with slender leaves instead of luxurious blossoms, and dignified enough to stand straight and erect, then one perceives a number of reasons in its worth as a garden companion.[U5]

Our own minds, then, are the source of reasonableness in things.

All this had for Wang Yang-ming important moral bearings. The reason in us is a moral reason and is not only intelligent but good. It is an inner light, an innnate goodness. Knowledge of the good is not imparted to us from without, but is inborn, and if the inborn knowledge is clouded over, then all that is necessary is to have the reflective surface of the mind polished by teaching and experience.

> The mind may be compared to a mirror. . . . When, after effort has been made to polish the mirror, it is bright, the power of reflecting has not been lost.[85]

The mind has the native ability to know. If one follows his (pure) mind, he naturally is able to know (what is morally good). When he sees his parents, he naturally knows what filial piety is; . . . when he sees a child fall into a well, he naturally knows what commiseration is. This is inborn knowledge of the good, without any necessity of going beyond the mind itself.[86]

In a further point that Wang Yang-ming makes we perceive resemblances to a central belief of Socrates. Knowledge of the good leads immediately to practice of the good. ("Knowledge," said Socrates, as we know, "*is* virtue.") Wang Yang-ming put it thus:

> There has been no one who really has knowledge and yet fails to practice it. . . . As soon as one perceives a bad odor, one already hates it.[87]

It is important, then, to keep the mirror of one's mind clear by eliminating the selfish desires that cloud it. This may be done only by practicing a "tranquil repose" resembling the meditative self-discipline of Ch'an (Zen) Buddhism, by which one may be purged of such desires.

This is not all of the story of the Confucian school. We might, were space available, go on to tell of the Neo-Confucians of the Ch'ing period. But what has been told must surely exhibit Confucianism in its true light as a highly evolved philosophy of religion with a complexity and competence comparable to those we have already examined elsewhere in the world.

IV   The State Cult of Confucius

All this time a state cult honoring the spirit of Confucius had been in existence. It had developed slowly. The reason for this tardiness of growth is not far to seek. Confucius was in his own time unsuccessful as a public figure. Mencius, like his master, was also unable to make a great mark in public affairs. For several hundred years after the master's death no Confucian came anywhere to power long enough to make permanent changes in the official outlook on problems of government. But then, suddenly, when the ways and works of Shih Huang-ti, the First Emperor, had been swept away, and the Confucian Classics had been recovered, the Emperor Wu Ti of the Han dynasty (who reigned 141–87 B.C.) took up Confucianism and made its teaching the policy of the state. For officialdom this was a momentous decision, for from this time on, even when Taoist or Buddhist emperors sat on the throne, Confucius was honored by the state as a great sage and was periodically advanced in official status.

The progressive elevation of Confucius to higher and higher official rank makes an interesting story. At first only the K'ung family and perhaps Confucius' immediate disciples rendered to his spirit a regular worship. Later on, sacrifices were made at the grave of Confucius by politically-minded sovereigns, anxious to conciliate local feelings. The first of these to do so was the Han Emperor Kao Tsu. Though himself inclined toward Taoism, he sacrificed three victims— an ox, a sheep, and a pig—when in 195 B.C. he passed through Lu on a tour of the empire and stopped at the grave of Confucius. Thereafter other emperors with an eye to political effect stopped off at the sage's grave to render tribute. In the year 1 A.D. the Emperor P'ing of the Han dynasty ordered the repair of the nearby temple of Confucius and elevated the sage to the rank of duke. By this time readings, prayers, and gifts of money and silk were added to the sacrifices made at the grave. The habit of bestowing posthumous titles grew. At intervals during succeeding centuries various emperors bestowed upon Confucius honorific titles, such as "The Venerable, the Accomplished Sage," "The Sage of Former Times," and the like. He acquired a long string of such titles. His descendants also were elevated to nobility and made the recipients of state honors.

Another step in the development of the state cult came in 630 A.D., when the T'ang Emperor T'ai Tsung issued a decree obliging every prefecture of China to erect a state temple to Confucius in which regular sacrifices to him were ordered. The same emperor converted these temples into national halls of fame by placing tablets to distinguished scholars and literary men alongside that of Confucius, thus honoring both him and them. In the eighth century, and under the influence of Buddhism, a T'ang emperor adopted and carried out the suggestion that images of Confucius be placed in the great hall of the state temples and pictures of his chief followers be painted on the walls. For the next eight centuries Confucian temples had little to distinguish them from Buddhist counterparts. (See picture overleaf.)

The sacrifices offered to the spirit of Confucius became progressively more elaborate. The T'ang emperors came with great pomp, in spring and autumn, to the state temple at the capital to add the dignity of their presence to the celebrations. It was customary that a bull, a pig, and a sheep be offered to Confucius' image, while dances and pantomimes were performed to stately music and prayers were solemnly presented. By the time of the Mongol rulers the ritual of the sacrifices became still more impressive. Incense was freely used, and much formal kow-towing took place before the image of Confucius and the various altars. Hundreds of bronze, wood, and porcelain vessels were required for the ceremonies, two kinds of wine were offered, and an ox, five sheep, and five pigs, as well as much food, were presented. It was the opinion of the time that the music and rites used in this worship of Confucius were those of an emperor, though the actual title of "Emperor" (*Ti*) was withheld because it was not deemed consistent with the practices of antiquity, and particularly not in accord with Confucius' teaching condemning bestowal of this title on men of less than imperial rank. However, there were those who said it would not have been too much if Confucius had been regarded as equal to Heaven.

In 1530 a remarkable reform in the cult of Confucius was effected, and proved permanent. The Ming Emperor Chia Ching, on the advice of a learned Confucian scholar, revoked the lengthy and cumbrous titles borne by Confucius and called him simply "Master K'ung, the Perfectly Holy Teacher of Antiquity." The temples to Confucius were ordered restored to their historic simplicity, the ceremonies were revised in accordance with the practices of antiquity, and the images of Confucius were replaced by tablets in the antique style or by plain wood panels with written characters inscribed on them.

At the beginning of the present century, when the Manchus were vainly seeking to recover the good

311

Chinese temple hall. *The architecture of this hall from the Chih-hua temple at Peking, dated 1444 A.D., is relatively severe, although the ceiling is decorated with ornate wood carvings. It lends itself to Buddhist use, as the image of Kwan Yin and other Bodhisattvas indicate, but the hanging tablets might just as well have been Confucian, and the image of Confucius been placed where Kwan Yin sits. (Philadelphia Museum of Art. Photograph by A. J. Wyatt, staff photographer.)*

opinion of the Chinese, an edict was issued abolishing the old classical examination system in favor of more modern educational training. To make good whatever disrespect to the memory of Confucius was involved in this significant change, another edict was issued in 1906 making the sacrifices to Confucius equal with those offered to Heaven and Earth, but this signal honor to the great sage came too late to save the Manchus from the revolution that brought into being the Republic.

After 1911 the cult of reverence for Confucius languished. With no emperor to participate in the worship of Heaven at the altar in Peking, the famous marble terraces fell into such neglect that sometimes grass grew in their crevasses. Only the Temple of Heaven nearby was kept in order. Elsewhere, except for the temple at Confucius' birthplace, the state temples either fell into disuse, many of them even becoming dilapidated in their utter abandonment, or were put to secular uses.

V Recent Changes

In intermittent attempts after the Revolution of 1911 to recover itself, Confucianism had some bad moments. After the Republic had written into its constitution a grant of religious liberty to all, the attempt of the scholars who formed the Confucian Society to have Confucianism made the state religion failed. But the situation was not without some hopeful signs from the Confucian point of view. Although the Kuomintang, or Nationalist Party, in forming for political action, committed itself to no particular religious views, its motto was nevertheless a reassertion of the eight Confucian virtues: loyalty, filial piety, benevolence, human-heartedness, fidelity, just attitudes, harmony, and peace. And when in 1934 Chiang Kai-shek inaugurated the New Life movement, it proved to have a distinctly Confucian coloring. (Even after he was baptized a Christian, he still saw China's problems through Confucian eyes.) The movement was announced as having "four binding principles": *Li* or courtesy and good manners, *I* or justice and uprightness, *Lien* or integrity, and *Ch'ih* or modesty and self-respect.

At the same time it should be said that the New Life movement was never officially affiliated with Confucianism. It was meant to be principally a movement of moral regeneration, and it found the traditional ethical concepts expressive. More indicative of national goals was the temple that the government erected in 1937 at Nanking. This imposing structure was intended as a national shrine. In the highest

place was the tablet of Confucius and just below it a marble bust of Dr. Sun Yat-sen, "the father of modern China." On surrounding pillars were portraits of great Western "sages": Newton, Pasteur, Lavoisier, Galileo, James Watt, Lord Kelvin, Dalton, and Benjamin Franklin! The meaning seemed to be that the China of the future would make a synthesis of the old and the new, combining the best of its philosophy and ethics with the best of the science and culture of the West.

But now all this is in doubt. Chinese Communism has gained the strength to remake China. Not only is it the present government's intention to alter permanently the economic and social structures of China; the mental outlook is to be thoroughly reoriented to a "materialistic" point of view. The entire history of Chinese philosophy and religion is being rewritten. A government-sponsored text, issued for international distribution and published in Peking in 1959 under the title *A Short History of Chinese Philosophy*, says the chief issue in the development of Chinese thought is one between "the feudal, bourgeois, reactionary culture and the democratic, socialist revolutionary culture"; ideologically, this is the issue between "the idealist, metaphysical theory and the dialectical, materialist theory." Confucius in this perspective becomes a metaphysical idealist who tried to preserve the interests of the declining clan aristocracy, his one "progressive" achievement being his innovations in private education. Mo Ti represented, on the other hand, the interests of the rising class of freemen and pitted his materialistic theory against the idealism of the Confucians. Lao-tzu was on the whole an idealist and mystic who considered the Tao a transcendental absolute, but he was progressive in two respects: in discussing natural laws (*teh*) he accepted some elements of materialism, and in seeing an opposition of yin and yang he developed the rudiments of dialectics. In his quietist political theory he reflected the feeling of the peasants and their naive attitude of non-resistance. Chuang-tzu was so much of an idealist and mystic that he settled for relativism, pessimism, and "philistinism" (i.e., opposition to the true

313

trend of historical forces). Yang Chu as a rebellious egoist was in some sense progressive in reflecting the desire of the freemen of the time to seek personal interest. As for Mencius, in turning for knowledge of right and wrong from objective reality to an innate power to distinguish them, he used an idealist logic that savors of sophistry. Hsün-tzu, on the other hand, was against idealism. He was materialistic and atheistic and said that man should conquer and exploit nature by using his mind to give him power over the objective world. He was a true progressive, and so was Han Fei of the Legalist school. Han Fei represented the interests of the freemen in stressing that human nature is selfish and society is a battleground of calculating minds. All this time materialism was taking a firm hold on the Chinese mind, and so was a gradually emerging vision of a Great Togetherness, a cosmopolitan society in which all men are brothers and there exists a world community. This vision was as yet idealist (Confucian in name) and seemed but a dream so transcendent that it could not be realized, but it laid the groundwork for future, more realistic and materialistic planning and action. In combating Confucian scholasticism Wang Ch'ung, who came of a poor family and was a true democrat, is a "glorious example" of rationalism, materialism,

and rebellious struggle against idealist authoritarianism. There were others like him, before and after, who spoke for the true nature of historical forces. Meanwhile, Buddhism, "a foreign religion" with a mistaken theory of transmigration and retributive justice, lured men into fancying that they could, by conscious effort, free themselves from the world of reality and attain a mysterious, spiritual world of eternal bliss. Buddhism emasculated the will of the people to free themselves from the existing feudal order. It influenced the socially conservative Neo-Confucians to support methods of thinking that led to unrealistic objective and subjective idealisms. Yet all the same, strains of materialism and atheism appeared also in Chinese thought then and later. At long last, from the sixteenth century onward there came the beginnings of enlightenment and a brilliant development of materialism and atheism that prepared the way for a culmination of the wisdom of the Chinese people in the philosophy of Mao Tse-tung. So reads the government-sponsored text.

It remains only to ask, is the Confucian element in Chinese culture ineradicable enough to modify the Communists' will-to-change and to add one more culture-saving compromise to those of China's long past? Or will the Communist opposition prevail?

SUGGESTIONS FOR FURTHER READING

BRUCE, J. P. *Chu Hsi and His Masters.* Probsthain, 1923

CHAN WING-TSIT. *Religious Trends in Modern China.* Columbia University Press, 1953

CHANG, CARSUN. *The Development of Neo-Confucian Thought.* Twayne Publishers, New York, 1957

CREEL, H. G. *Confucius, The Man and The Myth.* John Day, 1949

———. *Chinese Thought from Confucius to Mao Tse-tung.* University of Chicago Press, 1953. Available as Mentor pb, 1960

DEBARY, THEODORE, ED. *Sources of the Chinese Tradition.* Columbia University Press, 1960

DUBS, H. H. *Hsüntze, the Moulder of Ancient Confucianism.* Probsthain, 1927

———. *The Works of Hsüntze.* Probsthain, 1928

FUNG, Y. L. *A History of Chinese Philosophy.* Tr. by Derk Bodde. 2 vols., Princeton University Press, 1952

———. *A Short History of Chinese Philosophy*. Ed. by Derk Bodde. Macmillan, 1948. Macmillan pb ed., 1960

GILES LIONEL, TR. *The Sayings of Confucius*. In the *Wisdom of the East* series, John Murray, 1917

HENKE, F. G. *The Philosophy of Wang Yang-ming*. Open Court, 1916

HUGHES, E. R. *Chinese Philosophy in Classical Times*. Everyman's Library, J. M. Dent, 1941. An anthology

———. *The Religion of China*. Hutchinson, 1950

KU HUNG MING. *The Conduct of Life*. A translation of The Doctrine of the Mean. *Wisdom of the East* series, John Murray, 1906

LEGGE, JAMES. *The Works of Mencius*. Clarendon Press, Oxford, 1895

LIN MOUSHENG. *Men and Ideas*. John Day, 1943

LIN YUTANG. *The Wisdom of Confucius*. The Modern Library, Random House, 1938

LIU, WU-CHI. *A Short History of Confucian Philosophy*. Penguin Books, 1955.

LYALL, L. A., TR. *Mencius*. Longmans, Green, 1932

MEI YI PAO. *The Ethical and Political Works of Motse*. Probsthain, 1930

———. *Motse, the Neglected Rival of Confucius*. Probsthain, 1934

MOORE, CHARLES A., ED. *Philosophy—East and West*. Princeton University Press, 1944

SHRYOCK, JOHN. *The Origin and Development of the State Cult of Confucius*. Century, 1932

WALEY, ARTHUR. *The Analects of Confucius*. Allen and Unwin, 1938

———. *Three Ways of Thought in Ancient China*. Allen and Unwin, 1939. Available as Anchor pb, 1956

WARE, J. R. *The Sayings of Confucius*. Mentor pb, 1955

WEI, FRANCIS C. M. *The Spirit of Chinese Culture*. Scribner's, 1947

WILHELM, RICHARD. *Confucius and Confucianism*. Harcourt, Brace, 1931

YANG, K. C. *Religion in Chinese Society*. University of California Press, 1961

YANG, Y. C. *China's Religious Heritage*. Abingdon, 1943

11 Shinto: A Religion from Ancient Japan

Shinto, the native religion of Japan, is not fundamentally a system of doctrines, although before World War II it took on doctrines. It is basically a reverent loyalty to familiar ways of life and familiar places. The rank and file of any country do not, unless they are submitted to a process of indoctrination, readily express themselves through a dialectic or an ideology built on premises and logical inferences. At least it is true to say that for the masses in Japan love of country, as in other lands, is a matter of the heart first, and of doctrinal substance second.

The Japanese love their land with great constancy. It is a love of the country as a whole, and of each part of it, existing less in abstract idea than in an aesthetic love of things and places. Every hill and lake, all their mountains and rivers, are dear to them, so dear that they can only with difficulty think of parting from them. Their cherry trees, their shrines, their scenic resorts seem indispensable to a full enjoyment of life. Among these scenes their fathers lived and died. Here, with the ancestral spirits looking on, their families abide and have their complex being. Moreover, their country has always been their own. Until 1945 no armed invaders ever crossed their shores. It is unthinkable to them that any but Japanese should live where they live, and to most Japanese it is unthinkable that they should live anywhere but where they do. It goes without saying that when their country is in peril, they will die for it. All of this aligns them with those who love other lands.

There is nothing doctrinaire about this. This is emotional disposition or feeling, so bred in the bone that psychologists of an earlier generation would have called it innate. It is the sort of feeling that readily expresses itself in myth. And so it did express itself in Japan—in myth first, in nationalistic ideology afterwards. The Japanese came early to the belief that their land was divine, but late to the nationalistic dogma that no other land is divine, that the divinity of Japan is so special and unique, so absent elsewhere, as to make Japan "the center of this phenomenal world."

I The Background of Shinto

The word *Shinto* is derived from the Chinese *shen-tao*, meaning "the way of the higher spirits or gods." Its equivalent in Japanese is *kami-no-michi* or "the *kamis*' way," kami meaning in general gods or deities, but also, in a more inclusive sense, beings possessing sacred power or superior potency but of less than divine status, even though endowed or charged with a numinous or charismatic force. It has been part of the myth of Shinto that Japan was once peopled exclusively with kami. The early Japanese regarded the whole of nature as imbued with kami-powers, from the gods in the upper regions to spirits in mountains, lakes, and trees on earth, not to speak of powers in the sea and under the ground. Shinto thus expresses a religious faith about Japan and its past. The customs of old Japan were the way followed by kami, the awe-inspiring spirits from whom the Japanese people have descended. But this faith, as faiths often do, has ignored or has been unaware of certain historical facts about the true origins of the Japanese people.

The Japanese are in reality a mixed people, partly Korean, partly Mongolian, and partly Malayan. Their ancestors came at different times from the Asiatic mainland and South Pacific islands, and succeeded in uniting with or displacing and driving northward the aboriginal tribes. Apparently, the civil condition of ancient Japan was that of a loose conjunction of tribes and clans, each more or less independent and with its own traditions of nature- and chieftain-worship. Magic, taboo, and religion were commingled in the fashion that is characteristic of a primitive society. The fox was worshiped as a messenger of the gods. Bows and arrows were fetishes of so high an order that they were offered the reverence accorded to the gods. The constant warfare with the slowly yielding but still fierce aboriginal tribesmen gave a military color to the whole of life. Great warriors were treated with exaggerated respect, whether living or dead.

Clothed though they were in rough garments, and primitively housed, the Japanese already showed the passion for personal cleanliness that is so characteristic of them today. Their attitude toward the dead was marked by a dread of pollution, so that when a death occurred, the funeral was immediately held, and after the ten-day mourning period was at an end, the whole family went into the water to wash. In many cases the survivors abandoned the primitive structure that had been the home of the dead person and built a new one. This practice imposed a peculiar difficulty upon the early emperors. Each new emperor perforce abandoned the old capital and built a new palace in another part of the country, and this meant that with each accession to the throne the government was temporarily disorganized, and the people were obliged to orientate themselves afresh to yet another capital.

There were, it seems likely, three main centers of culture about the time of the first century B.C.: one in the southwest on the island of Kyushu, another at Izumo, on the western verge of the main island, and a third at Yamato, at the northern end of the Inland Sea. Far to the north were the Ainu, originally immigrants from the subarctic areas of Siberia, who doggedly preserved their own cultural life down through the years. (They are now in Hokkaido.) It may be an oversimplification, but there are indications that on the island of Kyushu the tribal cults were mainly concerned with gods of the sea, and upon the central island the Izumo clans worshiped the storm-god Susa-no-wo, while the Yamato clans adored the sun-goddess, regarded as the ruler of the heavens and the ancestress of their chieftains. The Yamato clans, probably in the fourth century A.D., sealed their ascendancy over the other groups by placing their chieftain on a somewhat shaky imperial throne as a descendant of the sun. But perhaps they had to overcome the opposition of other groups who preferred as rulers women reigning in the matriarchal tradition and credited with special powers as diviners and shamanistic mediums.[A1]

317

The Effect of Chinese Religion and Culture on Old Shinto

But, however arrived at, Old Shinto was formless and without any particular sense of direction. It became a clearly worked out pattern of national culture only when Chinese civilizing influences began to operate in Japan in the fifth century A.D. These influences were initially Sino-Korean, for the immediate teachers of the Japanese were Koreans. But because the Koreans had learned from the Chinese, the Japanese were not long in going directly to the Chinese for their further advances in knowledge and skills. The transformation effected then in the national life and outlook * is one of the most remarkable instances of its kind in history. The Japanese eagerly made their lives over by adapting Chinese ideas and procedures to their needs. They went about it very thoroughly.

Always adept in improving their methods and skills in the practical arts, once the way is shown, they quickly learned all that the Koreans and beyond them the Chinese could teach them about pottery-making, metal working, wood carving, farming, horticulture, gardening, silkworm culture, road and bridge building, and canal dredging. Almost at a bound the people passed from a primitive to a relatively advanced type of material culture. In the realm of social relations, Confucian ideas brought about permanent changes of emphasis in morals. There followed in particular a powerful re-enforcement of the ideal of filial piety. Old Shinto had been mainly a haphazard cult of nature-worship, loosely tied in with ancestor-worship. It now took on the aspect of history's most comprehensive ancestor-cult. Not only did the emperor's descent from the sun-goddess receive stress, but the higher officials began to trace their own descent from the deities most closely related to the sun-goddess, and the common people were supposed

* Sometimes called "the first great transformation of Japan," to distinguish it from "the second great transformation" in the nineteenth century. (See p. 325.)

to be descendants of the more distantly related deities. In this way the mythological basis was laid for the claim (so greatly emphasized during the last decades of the nineteenth century and the beginning of this) that the whole people were organically related to the emperor by a divine family relationship.

But an even greater impact was made upon the Japanese by Buddhism, coming first by way of Korea and then from China. When this religion came to Japan in the sixth century, it brought with it an exciting literature, a new, rich art, an emotionally satisfying ritual, and fresh insights in every field of human thought and action, including logic, medicine, and social service. Buddhism broke down Japanese provincialism by bringing the overseas world into the religious picture, for in the eyes of the Buddhist priests, the seats of religious reality and authority lay not in Japan, but in India and China. Some conservative, provincial-minded clan leaders were affronted by this, but Buddhism had so much to contribute to Japan that its best, most progressive minds were irresistibly attracted to it. Certain clan leaders and their clans adopted the new faith. After a short period of resistance, the members of the imperial family also accepted Buddhism. The aristocracy of the court followed suit. As temples multiplied in the centuries that followed, the common people were widely won over (pp. 159 ff.).

One important result of the new ferment of ideas was the attempt, under imperial sanction, to put into writing the native myths and traditions still current among the local clans. In 620 A.D. appeared the *Kujiki*, or Chronicle of Old Events, which gave the history of the emperors from the legendary Jimmu Tenno onward. In 712 A.D. the more comprehensive *Kojiki*, or Chronicle of Ancient Events, was completed, it being intended as a history of Japan from the creation of the world to the middle of the seventh century. Paralleling it, with variations and additions that give it greater historical accuracy, was the *Nihongi*, or Chronicles of Japan, issued in 720 A.D. Almost a century later, about 806 A.D., during the first decade of the Heian era,* appeared the *Kogoshui*, or Gleanings from Ancient Stories, a defense of the practices of one of the ancient priestly families connected with Shinto. Still later, in the first quarter of the tenth century, came the *Engi-shiki*, an impor-

* Japanese history is divided into periods and eras. There is no general agreement about the names for two of them, i.e., the prehistoric period and the period of the Yamato kingdom established in the fourth century, which saw the first introduction of Sino-Korean influences. But it is usual to name the periods of Japanese history from the eighth century on, as follows: (1) The Nara period (710–794 A.D.) when Nara was the capital city and Sino-Korean influences were at their peak. The *Kojiki* and *Nihongi* were compiled, and Nara was the center around which Buddhist schools and monasteries gathered, namely, the Ritsu ("Vinaya"), Kusha ("Abhidarma"), Jojitsu ("Satyasiddhi"), Sanron ("Madhyamika"), Hossō ("Yogacara"), and Kago ("Avatamsaka"). (2) The Heian period (794–1193) when Kyoto was the capital, a period during which the imperial court lived the elegant and graceful life reflected in the *Tale of Genji*, the Nara Buddhist schools began to decline, and the Tendai and Shingon schools rose and flourished (see pp. 177 ff.). (3) The Kamakura period (1192–1336), which was dominated by the military rule of the Minamoto and Hōjō families, and saw not only the rise of Zen Buddhism (pp. 173–177) but as well the spread of Amidism (pp. 170 f.) and the establishment of the Nichiren sect (pp. 179 f.). (4) The Ashikaga or "Warring States" period (1336–1573), during and at the end of which (a) the Ashikaga military regime failed to prevent civil disorder and virtual chaos, (b) the arts—drama, literature, painting —flourished, (c) Christianity was introduced to Japan by the Jesuits (1549) and was even favored by the "strong man" Oda Nobunaga, who (d) in the hope of unifying the quarreling feudal lords got rid of the last of the Ashikaga shoguns (1573) in a pacification program which was carried on and completed by two other strong men, Toyotomi Hideyoshi and Tokugawa Iyeyasu. (5) The Tokugawa period (1603–1867), inaugurated by the last-named strong man, the period of the famous, long-lasting dictatorship which at its start turned upon Christianity, tried to stamp it out, and closed Japan to the outside world (p. 324). (6) The Meiji (Enlightenment) era (1868–1912), so named for the Emperor Meiji (Mutsuhito), once again raised to supremacy, a period during which Japan underwent its "second great transformation" (p. 325). (7) The Taisho era (1912–1926), the era of the political parties of the "Taisho democracy." (8) The Showa era (1926 to date), with Hirohito the emperor. This last era might well be called that of "the third great transformation of Japan."

tant compendium of Shinto traditions, in fifty parts, the first ten of which contain lists of ritual prayers or litanies for various ceremonial occasions, called *norito*. The norito served then and for centuries afterward as the models, if not the actual words, of prayers in all Shinto shrines, whether in the country at large or in the court. All these treatises showed the influence of Chinese and Buddhist ideas. Foreign modes of thought were evident, for example, in the opening paragraphs of the *Kojiki* and *Nihongi*, much as the influence of Greek philosophy shows in the first chapter of the Fourth Gospel. The *Kojiki* and *Nihongi* were deeply indebted to overseas thought for their political orientation, which led them to endow the imperial line with a sovereignty reaching back to remote time and grounded in a divine order of things.

More undilutedly Japanese were two extraordinary works of the Heian period reflecting Japanese life, love, and religion. They came into being when Japanese minds were stirred to creativity by the exciting opportunity presented by the Chinese characters to put old and new thoughts into writing. One was the *Manyōshū*, a collection of old and new poems, four thousand in number, compiled toward the end of the eighth century. The other was a work of genius, Lady Murasaki's long novel *The Tale of Genji*, dealing with the sensuous, beauty-oriented court at Kyoto in its early years.

II The Shinto Myth

There can be no doubt of the interest the imperial court took in the formulation of an official version of the Shinto folk-traditions. On the one hand, the court had displayed a desire to follow Chinese models in its official procedure and hierarchical structure, for it wished to be judged civilized or cultivated. But on the other hand, it had no wish to become un-Japanese, for inevitably and naturally it reflected in thousands of ways well-established Japanese folk-ways. The court therefore became the scene of elaborate rites and ceremonies, some in imitation of the procedures of the Chinese and Korean courts, but others based on quite ancient Shinto beliefs and practices. Among these were rituals for purification from pollution, which were of great importance, sacred dances performed for their beauty as well as their magico-religious effects, taboos against moving in certain directions when the position of the moon and other objects was not favorable, and devout obeisance (kneeling with head lowered to the hands along the floor) toward spirits (kami) present in the surrounding world.

In another direction, it seemed required both by national pride and by Chinese standards of rationality and order that the native myths concerning the early history of Japan and its people be woven into a more or less unified sequence. The result was what we may call the Shinto myth. (For definition of *myth*, see p. 11 n.) Of the slightly variant forms of the officially approved versions of this myth we have chosen that of the *Kojiki*, mentioned above. The story runs as follows: [B1]

The Japanese islands are a special creation of the gods. After the primal chaos had in the course of events separated into heaven and ocean, various gods appeared in the heavenly drift-mist, only to disappear without event, until finally there came upon the scene the two deities who produced the Japanese islands and their inhabitants. These were the primal male and female, Izanagi, the Male-Who-Invites, and Izanami, the Female-Who-Invites. Their heavenly associates commanded them to "make, consolidate, and give birth to" the Japanese islands. These two beings descended the Floating Bridge of Heaven (a rainbow?), and when they reached its lower end, Izanagi pushed down his jeweled spear into the muddy brine and stirred it until the fluid below them became "thick and glutinous." Then he drew the spear up, whereupon "the brine that dripped down from the end of the spear was piled up and became an island." Stepping down on the island, they came together,

and Izanami bore from her womb the eight great islands of Japan. After that they brought into being a populace of thirty-five deities, the last of whom, the fiery heat-god, Kagu-Tsuchi, at his birth fatally burned his mother. So enraged was Izanagi at Kagu-Tsuchi for causing Izanami's death that he hacked him up with rapid strokes of his sword, only to produce other deities out of the flying fragments.

The historically important part of this story is its sequel. When Izanami died and went to the underworld (the Land of Yomi), in due time the inconsolable Izanagi followed after her, hoping to get her to return to the upper world with him. But he had not come in time. She had begun to decompose and was unsightly. When he neared her in the darkness, she asked him not to look at her. But he lit the end tooth of the comb by which he kept his hair in place and saw her lying before him horribly swarming with maggots. "Thou hast put me to shame," she screamed, and as he fled back, sent the Ugly Females of Yomi to pursue him. When by various stratagems he delayed this pursuit, she sent after him eight thunder deities, generated in the decay of her own body, and fifteen hundred warriors of Yomi. When he fought these off, she herself took up the chase. As he fled into the upper world, he picked up a rock that would have taken a thousand men to lift and blocked up the pass of the underworld with it. The two erstwhile loving deities, standing on opposite sides of the rock, exchanged angry farewells. Finally, Izanagi, who was now covered with pollution, went down to the ocean to bathe his august person. As he threw away his staff, his girdle, and the rest of his apparel, each item turned into a deity. But the major event was still to come. According to the *Kojiki*, when he stepped into the water and, in a typically Japanese act of purification, washed away the filth out of his left eye, he produced the most highly revered of the Japanese deities, Amaterasu, the goddess of the sun. This was an important creation. After that, he produced the moon-god, Tsuki-yomi, from the washing of his right eye, and the storm-god, Susa-no-wo, from his nostrils.

Years later, we find the sun-goddess, Amaterasu, looking down from her seat in heaven and becoming concerned about the disorder in the islands below. The storm-god's son was ruling there, but she was not satisfied. She finally commissioned her grandson Ni-ni-gi to descend to the islands and rule them for her. Her charge to him was in words that many a child in Japan once knew by heart: "This Luxuriant-Reed-Plain-Land-of-Fresh-Rice-Ears shall be the land which thou shalt rule." Ni-ni-gi obeyed. He first ruled from the island of Kyushu. In a later time, his great-grandson Jimmu Tenno, the first human emperor, embarked from Kyushu on a conquest of the province of Yamato, on the central Japanese island, Honshu, and set up his capital there, in the year set by tradition at 660 B.C.

Meanwhile, the leading families of Japan and the whole Japanese people descended from the minor deities, or lesser kami, residing on the islands.

Thus, we are to understand that the emperor of Japan is a descendant in an unbroken line from the sun-goddess, Amaterasu, and that the islands of Japan have a divine origin, and so also the Japanese people.

It will be observed that this Old Shinto account of things is concerned with Japan alone; no other countries are considered. Moreover, Japan is regarded as full of gods and goddesses. The polytheism is almost unlimited. It was characteristic of the earlier Japanese to deify everywhere, to see a god or godling in every kind of force or natural object. Hence it was that they called their country "the Land of the Gods," and in later times estimated that their deities must number some "eighty myriads" or even some "eight hundred myriads." We may observe further that the chief place in the pantheon was given to the sun-goddess, Amaterasu, whose temple at Isé is the holiest shrine in Japan, but she has never been regarded as more than the first among her peers. Associated with her were not only those born with her—Tsuki-yomi, the moon-god, and Susa-no-wo, the unmoral and capricious storm-god—but also a vast company of deities, such as the wind deities, "Prince of the Long

Wind" and "Lady of the Long Wind"; the god of lightning, "Terrible Swift Fire Deity"; the thunder-god, "Fierce Thunder Male Deity"; the rain-god, "Fierce Rain Chief"; the general mountain-god, "Dark-Mountain Possessing Deity," under whose aegis many local mountain deities, like the goddess of Mount Fuji, performed their functions; the fertility-deities, such as "High August Producing God" and "Divine Producing Goddess"; the food-deities—Inari, who is the grain-goddess, and the still very popular Toyo-Uke-Hime, the food-goddess, today widely worshiped by peasants and especially honored at the outer shrine of Isé; phallic deities; the gods of healing and purification; star-gods and goddesses; the deities of the sea (of whom there are those of the middle, the bottom, and the surface of the sea); not to mention river-gods, harbor-gods, mist-gods, and deities of trees, leaves, rocks, earthquakes, volcanoes, and so on.

We need draw out the list no further. It is obvious that the Shinto myth pictured a pristine Japan thronging with deities.

The Composite Nature of the Myth

That the myth reflects a primitive response to nature, not far advanced above animism, is clear. It is the opinion of D. C. Holtom, a leading authority, that Izanagi and Izanami are Japanese forms of those familiar figures in the world's cosmogonic myths, "the Sky-Father and the Earth-Mother," and that the details of the myth fit into the general pattern of worldwide descriptions of seasonal change in vegetation, typified by the Cybele-Attis myth of the Western World. He urges that the death of Izanami is caused by the earth-burning god of summer heat (which is his interpretation of the meaning of Kagu-Tsuchi), so that when Izanagi hews up the fiery god with his sword, thus producing lightning-, thunder-, and rain-deities, what is signified is the vengeful onslaught of the quenching rainstorm upon the drought-child that has burned its earth-mother. The

321

search of Izanagi for Izanami in the underworld is, Dr. Holtom says further, clearly in line with the chthonian myths of the West: the disappearance of the earth-mother has brought about the death of vegetation, and the sky-father endeavors to find her and return her to the world. His is a seeking that "re-echoes the search of the Egyptian Isis for the body of Osiris."[C1]

Much may be said for this interpretation of the Japanese myth, but it explains the myth only in part, for interwoven with this portion of the story, and cutting it short, are other parts dealing with the sun-goddess and her struggles with her unruly brother, the storm-god. The story of these quarrels is susceptible of two different interpretations. The first interpretation sees in them a mythological treatment of the unending contest between sun and storm-cloud; the other reading finds in their geographical references an indication that Amaterasu represents the people of the southern island of Kyushu, and Susa-no-wo the settlers in Izumo, two groups that in the early years of immigration from the continent of Asia struggled with each other for ascendancy. The total myth represents, therefore, the combination of several strands of tradition originating from different clans among the ancient population of Japan.

III Shinto in Medieval and More Recent Times

By the eighth century, when Buddhism had obtained a dominant influence in governing circles, an accommodation between Shinto and Buddhism became desirable. Shinto was still a vital and independent force in the rural areas and in villages and provincial towns. Members of families and local clans still felt bound to the kami who had been much in evidence in their histories. Many Shinto shrines still received subsidies from aristocratic families and were more closely regulated than ever by their priests, if only because the Buddhist temples were. But even

such shrines began both to give a place to Taoist and Buddhist rituals and to encourage accommodation and cooperation. "At first the kami," says Professor Kitagawa, "were considered to be the 'protectors of Buddha's Law.' . . . Soon, however, this belief was reversed so that the kami were considered to be in need of salvation through the help of Buddha. . . . Some of the honored kami also received the Buddhist title of *bosatsu* (bodhisattva)."[A2] By the ninth century these conceptions of the relationship between the still-separate kami and Buddhas were replaced by the idea that the former were to be equated with the latter. An assertion that this could be the case seems to have been made by Kōbō Daishi, founder of the Shingon school, who taught that the Buddhas and Bodhisattvas appeared as various gods in different countries and had so appeared in Japan (see p. 179). Dengyo Daishi, founder of the Tendai school (p. 178), made a similar suggestion. Subsequently, priests of various Buddhist sects reported having visions and intuitions that were later accepted as proof that the gods of Japan were in reality Buddhas and Bodhisattvas who "appeared" as gods of the Japanese islands. Amaterasu, the sun-goddess, was identified as a manifestation of the Buddha Maha-Vairocana; Hachiman, the war-god, was found to be the guise assumed on Japanese soil by the Bodhisattva Kshitigarbha; and so on.

Ryobu or Mixed Shinto

As a result of all this there emerged throughout the land by the twelfth century the so-called Ryobu or Mixed Shinto (literally, "the Twofold Way of the Gods"*). In this syncretism the deities of the Buddhist pantheon were given the honored position of "the Originals," whereas the deities of the Shinto pantheon were thought to be their Japanese appearances or manifestations (*gongen*).

It is not surprising that Shinto almost succumbed

*Another translation is "two-seated," i.e., seated abroad and in Japan at the same time.

in this crisis. Certainly, Ryobu, or Two-sided Shinto, had immense influence on the people of Japan. It won the majority to its interpretation. In ensuing years most of the Shinto shrines made room for Buddhist worship in the "inner sanctuary" and were quite generally served by Buddhist priests. The latter introduced into the old Shinto rites images, incense, sermons, and elaborate ceremonies. The simple primitive appearance of the Shinto shrines was greatly altered by the exterior application of the intricate ornament of Buddhist temples and by the addition to the shrine property of pagodas, drum-towers, large bells, assembly-halls for preaching services, and the like. Even the unadorned Shinto gateway, or *torii*, was supplied with curves and ornate decoration. So

pervasive did the Buddhist influence become that it is quite true to say with W. M. Horton that "down to the Meiji era, Japan might fairly be described as a Buddhist nation," though one adds, as Dr. Horton aptly does, the qualification that this only holds good "in the same sense in which certain western nations have been described as 'Christian.' "[D] A deadly parallel!

Japanese appropriation and adaptation of Buddhism continued to the fourteenth century, when public order dissolved in three hundred years of feudal strife, during which the emperor, his headship of the nation thoroughly obscured, was condemned to impotence, while dictators (*shoguns*) vainly strove to control the powerful nobles and the *samurai*, or

Kasuga shrine at Nara. Founded in 768 A.D., *this is one of the oldest Shinto shrines in Japan. Under the influence of Buddhist temple art, it has been painted a bright vermillion and boasts some three thousand colorful lanterns, many of them centuries old, about half of which are hung within the shrine, the rest from the eaves outside, as here. The shrine's sacred maidens are emerging from the temple's inner precincts. (Courtesy of Japan National Tourist Organization.)*

military class. At the end of the sixteenth century a shogun arose, as we have seen (p. 319 n.), who brought an end to the centuries of feudal warfare. This marked the beginning of the period of the Tokugawa regime (1603–1867 A.D.). It was a period of some importance to Shinto, for during it occurred its own revival or renaissance.

The Revival of Shinto

The revival of Shinto was a slow and gradual process. During the disorders that attended the end of the Kamakura period in the first half of the fourteenth century, those who supported the Emperor Go-Daigo in his unsuccessful effort to gain control of the nation could not have failed to raise the question whether the descendant of the sun-goddess should have been rejected. That Shinto and its central themes should be so nearly submerged in Buddhism also worried many. As the fourteenth century wore on, several of the hereditary priests of the Watarai family who took care of the outer shrine at Isé sought without great success to free Shinto (their "Isé Shinto") from Buddhist and Chinese infusions, and a century later one of the Urabé priests at the Kasuga shrine at Nara wrote a treatise that tried to distinguish the ancient Shinto elements from the current Buddhized (Ryobu) Shinto. Then suggestions were made by the Watarai priests and others that the thesis of Ryobu Shinto should be reversed, that is, that the Japanese kami be declared the "originals" and the Buddhist deities their "appearances." But their voices were at first scarcely more than faint cries against the prevailing wind. Other Shintoists were not yet ready to give them a hearing. Moreover, they could not free even themselves from Buddhist and Confucian thinking when they set forth their own arguments.

But a purer Shinto had friends in other quarters. Support for its independence of Buddhism was unwittingly evoked by the Tokugawa shogunate. By the seventeenth century, Christianity was being sup-

pressed, and the ports of Japan had been closed to all but a few Dutch and Chinese traders. (As the saying goes, Japan had become "a hermit nation.") After a desperate uprising of Christians in 1637–38, the government attempted to smoke out all remaining Christians by ordering every Japanese to secure a certificate (*tera-uke*) from a Buddhist temple to prove that he or she was not an adherent of the proscribed religion. This greatly upset some Shinto priests, who, obliged to have recourse to Buddhist temples, asked recognition as representatives of an independent religion. They received immediate support from a number of Japanese Confucian scholars, who also desired the disengagement of Shinto from its Buddhist entanglements. There was even a proposal of a Confucian-Shinto amalgamation, to be called Suiga Shinto, to displace Ryobu Shinto.[A3]

It was clear, too, that the Japanese masses still loved the "purer" Shinto rites, especially those performed at the grand shrine of the Sun-goddess, Amaterasu, at Isé, to which in times of plentiful harvests (and falling consumer prices) they flocked in great numbers to express their thanks for the sunshine that had favored the crops. Encouraged, the Isé priests toured the countrysides promoting the practice of visiting Isé at least once in a lifetime.

All this heartened scholars of the Shinto classics in a nationalistic concentration on "native ancient learning." During the eighteenth and early nineteenth centuries three outstanding scholars, Kamo Mabuchi, Motoōri Norinaga, and Hirata Astutane, took advantage of the anti-foreign atmosphere to revive what came to be called "Pure Shinto," or the "True Ancient Way." The second of this group was perhaps the greatest scholar in Japanese history. His commentary on the *Kojiki* is still authoritative. But his conclusions were as subjective as his scholarship in other respects was factual. Scorning to take the position of his contemporaries, who saw and unhesitatingly acknowledged the dependence of Japanese learning on Chinese sources, he firmly upheld the superiority of the ancient way of Japan, declaring:

"From the central truth that the Mikado is the direct descendant of the gods, the tenet that Japan ranks far above all other countries is a natural consequence. No other nation is entitled to equality with her, and all are bound to do homage to the Japanese sovereign and pay tribute to him."[c2]

He repudiated the suggestion that because the Japanese had no native system of ethics, they must borrow one from Confucianism. Only a depraved people need an ethics, he said; the Japanese, by reason of their divine motivation, were so naturally upright in their lives that they were in no need of a moral code, and consequently had never had one. They should therefore give up forever all foreign modes of thought and action and walk in simplicity the ancient way of Shinto.

But these were scholarly opinions. Not until the nineteenth century did a political triumph of Shinto come to pass.

The Restoration of 1868

The efforts made in the eighteenth century revival to disentangle Shinto from its Buddhist infusions did not change the habits of the people. It aroused discussion and little more. Nevertheless, the fruitage of the movement and the vindication of the Shinto myth came in the second half of the nineteenth century, when the "second great transformation of Japan" took place.

The necessity for this transformation was borne in upon the Japanese rather suddenly. Though they strove to remain a "hermit nation," they could not prevent American whaling ships from appearing off their coasts and from time to time suffering shipwreck. The sailors who reached shore were sometimes killed as "foreign devils," and it took many months for those who did not meet this fate to be repatriated through the Dutch traders who were the only foreigners allowed in Japanese waters. But this was not the sole problem of the whalers. Their vessels often ran out of water and provisions by the time they reached Japan, and they naturally desired to be able to put into port to stock up. President Fillmore, aware of this need, and also anxious to open Japan to foreign trade, appealed by letter to the ruler of Japan to open up a few ports to American ships. Carrying this letter, Admiral Perry entered Tokyo Bay in 1853 with four gunboats and managed to deliver the president's message to the shogun. He sailed away to China, promising to return in the spring for an answer. The shogun circulated the president's letter among the Japanese feudal lords, who thereupon formed into three parties: the liberals, the compromisers, and the anti-foreign party, the last being much the largest and rejoicing in the adherence of the anti-foreign emperor, Komei. Admiral Perry returned in 1854 with ten ships and a force of two thousand men. The shogun yielded to this persuasion and concluded a treaty providing for kind treatment of shipwrecked sailors, permission for foreign vessels to obtain stores and water ashore, and the opening to trade of three unimportant ports. In concluding this treaty, the shogun did not obtain the sanction of the throne—an old habit of the shoguns. Although the emperor restrained the anti-shogunate forces of his court while he lived, after his death they entered into a determined struggle aimed at unseating the shogun. In the course of this struggle the shogun was at last led to abolish his own office, retire to the background, and leave the way open for restoration of the emperor to sovereignty over the nation, an event that occurred in 1868.

But the shogun had allowed a process of Westernization to begin that could not be stopped. The reactionary clan leaders tried to stop it, but after the startling experience of having some of their coastal defenses shattered by the guns of American, British, French, and Dutch ships, the anti-foreign leaders began to realize the military impotence of Japan and abruptly about-faced. They decided then and there to bring the military might of Japan up to a par with that of the Western powers, and therefore entered, along with the liberals, upon the process of modernizing and industrializing Japan. It was a mighty task of transformation, and it was accomplished with amazing speed and thoroughness.

The conservatives soon found that the adoption of Western economic and industrial methods, even when these were adapted to Japanese requirements, involved momentous changes in culture and outlook. But this made them all the more resolved to preserve somehow the ancient military ideals and values in the modern setting. They saw to it that in the Constitution of 1889—an important step in the national reorganization—the army and navy were not placed under civilian control but were made responsible to the emperor alone. And, what is of chief interest to us here, they raised the old Shinto myth of the emperor's descent from the sun-goddess to high place in the national life by incorporating it, by indirection, in the Constitution itself,* and then went about developing a state cult that could be expected to give it a continuing force in the nation's life. To this end they felt that the myth should be isolated from its Buddhist involvements and made to stand clear.

Accordingly, one of the first acts of the Emperor Meiji, after the restoration, was to disestablish Buddhism, make Shinto the state religion, and order the elimination of all Buddhist elements, including priests, from the Shinto shrines. A good deal of purging was done, some of it violent; even Buddhism as such was brought under attack. But so closely were Shinto and Buddhism intermingled that the national return to a "pure" Shinto proved impracticable. The common people continued to favor both religions. In 1877 Buddhism was given leave to exist by being granted autonomy. In the Constitution of 1889 the complete religious liberty of all citizens was guaranteed, though the government showed where its official heart lay by retaining a department, called the Department of Shrines, to express its attitude of special regard and care for the refurbished and redefined national faith. This department was subsequently

divided into a bureau of Shinto shrines, under the Department of Home Affairs, and a bureau of religions, under the Department of Education. The division was made advisable by the official distinction drawn by the government between "State" Shinto and "Sectarian" Shinto, a matter that requires our further attention.

IV   State Shinto to 1945

State Shinto may be defined as the government-fostered program of patriotic rites that was conducted until 1945 * in shrines removed from sectarian control and made national property. Its purpose was the systematic cultivation of patriotic feeling within the nation. Age-old traditions were stressed by it, because it rose initially out of the need of keeping the Japanese people true to "the spirit of ancient Japan" through all the revolutionary changes wrought in the economic, educational, and political life of the nation by the adoption of the civilization of the West.

Western Ideas and Agnosticism in Japan

The upheaval of Japanese life and culture that accompanied the wholesale importation of Western ideas in the post-restoration era at first adversely affected the fortunes of Shinto. Thousands, in estrangement, turned away for a time from the officially sanctioned state shrines. The simultaneous resurgence of Buddhism, fighting for its life, and the re-entrance of Christianity, raised as it were from the dead, helped to produce a religious attitude among the people that portended the end of the old native faith. But all religions suffered. Disbelief and agnosticism became widespread. The impact of Western

---

* "Article I: The Empire of Japan shall be reigned over and governed by a line of Emperors unbroken for ages eternal.
"Article III: The Emperor is sacred and inviolable."

* The American occupation authority caused its compulsory features to be abolished in that year. Worship at the former state shrines is now on a purely voluntary basis. See further infra.

science upon the students in the newly founded universities hastened this tendency. Students began to laugh all religions out of court, and so far did this scepticism ultimately extend that a census of student opinion in the University of Tokyo two decades after the opening of the present century showed that "out of a total of 4,608, 2,989 listed themselves as agnostic, 1,511 as atheists, and only 118 as adhering to Christianity, Buddhism or Shinto"E—a truly extraordinary expression of religious disbelief and indifference.

The Government Attitude Before 1945

The Japanese government from the first took measures to save Shinto from extinction. Its strategy was both defensive and offensive. On the side of defense, it encouraged a reinterpretation of the Shinto myth that would make it acceptable to the critical intelligence of the nation. The view that received semi-official sanction was to the effect that the deities of the national myth were originally human beings with superior gifts. The sun-goddess was a noble woman ruler of a clan that had flourished in the dawn-age of Japanese history, and she laid the foundations of Japanese culture and national organization. This view took advantage of the ambiguity of the Japanese term *kami*, which, we have said, means any being that has unusual power or is exceedingly awe-inspiring or superior in potency.* In the words of the famous scholar Motoōri, uttered over two hundred years ago:

"Speaking in general, it may be said that *kami* signifies in the first place, the deities of heaven and earth that appear in the ancient records and also the spirits of the shrines where they are worshipped. It is hardly necessary to say that it includes human beings; also such objects as birds, beasts, trees, plants, seas, mountains, and so forth. In ancient usage, anything whatsoever which was outside of the ordinary, which possessed superior virtues, or which was awe-inspiring was called *kami*."

* A close analogy exists between this potency and the South Sea conception of *mana*.

Motoōri added:

"The *kami* of the Divine Age were for the most part human beings of that time, and because the people of that age were all *kami*, it is called 'the Age of the Gods.' "C3

Availing themselves of this interpretation of the meaning of the word for deity, Japanese scholars humanized and rationalized the whole of Japanese mythology, and thus tried to make their peace with historical science as that is understood in the Western World. To cite a typical instance, a Japanese professor declared:

"Shinto, as the Chinese characters read, is the way of the Gods. What are gods? There are many things which go by the name 'gods.' In Greece, there is a god of stars; in India, Buddha is a god; in Occidental countries, they have one god, the ruler of Heaven. Thus, we find there are various gods in the world. Gods, in our country, are our forefathers. It is hardly necessary to mention that the Goddess Amaterasu is enshrined in Isé shrine; so are the Emperor Jimmu in Kashiwabara shrine, Emperor Ojin in Hachiman shrine, Emperor Kammu in Heian shrine and Emperor Godaigo in Yoshino shrine. To enshrine forefathers as gods is peculiar to our people. It is not seen in any other civilized countries of the world. It is true that in our country there also existed and exists even now to a certain extent the worship of animals, rocks, trees and mountains, but gods as taught by Shinto are our ancestors worshipped as gods. . . . In mystical groves, with sacred torii, the spirits of our forefathers are enshrined."F

This argument, besides being inaccurate in its references to other religions, has no sound historical basis so far as the major Shinto gods are concerned, because it flies in the face of the fact that in the Shinto myth Amaterasu, Susa-no-wo, Izanagi, and Izanami stand for aspects of nature—the radiant sun, the storm, ancient sky-father, teeming earth-mother—and by no means for apotheosized human beings of the past. The argument nevertheless has had an attraction for intelligent Japanese, anxious to be in harmony both with science and the national tradition.

In another direction, the Japanese government endeavored to save Shinto by making it over into a

327

positive force, a national institution of an ethical and historical character. The official government view was that Shinto was not a religion, properly speaking, but a formulation of national ethics and a cult of loyalty to national institutions. In order to make this clear, the restoration (or Meiji) government in 1882 officially separated what is known as *Jinja-Shinto* or State Shinto, from *Kyoha-Shinto* or Sectarian Shinto. The latter was declared ineligible for government financial support and was given the status of an independent religion on the same footing with Buddhism and Christianity. State Shinto was declared to be no more than a system of state ceremonials whose patriotic object it was to unify the popular mind in accordance with "the national morality." The official position was based on declarations made by the Emperor Meiji from 1870 to 1890, when Japan was being reorganized to take its place in the modern world. Especial stress was laid on the famous Imperial Rescript on Education, issued in 1890 and regarded as the basis of the school system of Japan. The rescript reads:

Know Ye, Our Subjects:
Our Imperial Ancestors have founded our Empire on a basis broad and everlasting, and have deeply and firmly implanted virtue; Our subjects ever united in loyalty and filial piety have from generation to generation illustrated the beauty thereof. This is the glory of the fundamental character of Our Empire, and herein lies the source of Our education. Ye, Our subjects, be filial to your parents, affectionate to your brothers and sisters; as husbands and wives be harmonious, as friends true; bear yourselves in modesty and moderation; extend your benevolence to all; pursue learning and cultivate arts and thereby develop intellectual faculties and perfect moral powers; furthermore, advance public good and promote common interests; always respect the Constitution and obey the laws; should emergency arise, offer yourselves courageously to the State; and thus guard and maintain the prosperity of Our Imperial Throne coeval with heaven and earth. So shall ye be not only Our good and faithful subjects but render illustrious the best traditions of your forefathers.
The Way here set forth is indeed the teaching bequeathed by Our Imperial Ancestors, to be observed alike by their descendants and the subjects, infallible for all ages and true for all places. It is Our wish to lay it to

heart in all reverence, in common with you, Our subjects, that we may all attain the same virtue.[G]

It was generally accepted in Japan that this declaration not only laid down the best possible ethical principles—we may note these were Confucian in substance—but also called for the kind of complete loyalty to emperor and country upheld by State Shinto. For this reason successive ministers of education issued orders like the following to school officials:

Especially on the days of school ceremonies or on some date determined according to convenience, the pupils must be assembled and the Imperial Rescript on Education must be read before them. Furthermore, the meaning must be carefully explained to the pupils and they must be instructed to obey it at all times.[H1]

Another order, dated 1911, goes further:

The sentiment of reverence is correlative with the feeling of respect for ancestors and is most important in establishing the foundations of national morality. Accordingly, on the occasion of the festivals of the local shrines of the districts where the schools are located, the teachers must conduct the children to the shrines and give expression to the true spirit of reverence.[C4]

These and subsequent orders, involving a daily bowing in school assemblies before the picture of the emperor, gave no end of trouble to Christian groups. But leading Japanese nationalists, refusing to see the ambiguity in the government's position, contended that Shinto shrines had no more than the significance of the memorial statues to be seen in London, Paris, or Berlin. "Foreigners," one spokesman said, "erect statues, we celebrate at shrines."[H2] So they saw no reason why all citizens might not, without inconsistency, present themselves on patriotic occasions at the shrines and participate in the ceremonies conducted there.

State Shrines Before 1945

Before World War II the shrines that the government put under the control of the home ministry numbered about 110,000. Of these about a hundred were maintained by the government. Others received partial government support. The rest were locally supported. Not included in the government count were many thousands of wayside shrines too small to mention in the records of the Home Ministry or too remote to be readily accessible. Many of these were memorial in character, being dedicated to legendary heroes or ancient clan figures. Others were small temples erected in honor of the fox, the messenger and symbol of the grain-goddess, Inari. Still others were placed in factory compounds, on the roofs of department stores, or in the small space between stores in a business district. The chief state shrines were served by some sixteen thousand priests, who were appointed by the government and were officially instructed not to conduct unmistakably religious ceremonies, such as funerals, but only those officially prescribed rituals that were intended to establish the "national morality." (These ceremonies were said to be religious in form but not in intent.) In rural and out-of-the-way districts one priest often served

a large number of scattered shrines, but at the great shrines a staff of ten or more were in attendance.

The state shrines were, as tradition demanded, in appearance just what their name, *jinja,* implies—"god-houses." In most cases they were unpainted Japanese houses of an ancient design, and because the exposed wood surfaces showed the effects of weathering in course of time, it was common for some of the major shrines to follow the example set at the Grand Imperial Shrine at Isé and tear down the shrine at regular intervals and rebuild it. (At Isé this was done every twenty years, at other places at longer intervals.)

The Grand Imperial Shrine at Isé

The most honored of all state shrines was the Grand Imperial Shrine at Isé, sacred to the sun-goddess, Amaterasu. This shrine was of such importance to the government's nationalistic aims that citizens were for years bred up in the notion that

The grand shrine at Isé. Dedicated to the worship of the sun-goddess Amaterasu, its sacred precincts secluded behind one outer and two inner sacred fences, the shrine at Isé, and its accompanying buildings, conforms to the ancient architecture of Japan. It is rebuilt of unpainted wood every twenty years, and we see it here after it has been renewed. (Courtesy of Japan National Tourist Organization.)

from ancient times the people of Japan made pilgrimages to this shrine once in a lifetime "without fail." Isé is situated some two hundred miles southwest of Tokyo near the mouth of the beautiful bay that bears its name. There the shrine of the sun-goddess still stands, linked with that of the food-goddess, Toyo-Uke-Hime, and between is a shrine-lined avenue four miles long, running through a forest of magnificent cryptomeria trees. Both shrines are made of unpainted cedar wood and are in the style of Old Shinto. In each case the superstructure rests on piles driven into the ground. The roofs are thatched and are secured at the top by three long planks, two fitted to form a ridge, and the third laid flat along the ridge to keep the rain from entering there. This third plank is weighted down by the very ancient device of laying short sections of round logs at right angles to it along the whole interval between the end-rafters. A narrow, railed veranda, also on piles, runs around the building.

From time immemorial Amaterasu has had "the inner shrine." * The shrine itself stands within two sacred fences, through which only authorized priests and officials of the government were in times past allowed to enter. The most treasured possessions of the shrine have been the "divine Imperial regalia," the three precious symbols of the sun-goddess—a mirror, a sword, and a string of ancient "curved" stone jewels. The most highly valued of these, both in itself and for its symbolic meaning, has been the mirror, long declared to be the one with which the sun-goddess was lured from the cave to which she once retreated in high dudgeon at the misdeeds of her brother, Susa-no-wo.† How the "divine Imperial

regalia" reached earth is explained by the story that the sun-goddess gave them to Ni-ni-gi, her grandson, when she sent him down from heaven to rule the Japanese empire.* The school books of Japan used to teach that from that time on the successive emperors, in a single dynasty unbroken through the ages, handed on the three sacred treasures as "symbols of the Imperial Throne."C5

Such was the sacredness of these treasures that so great a person as the emperor directly concerned himself with the conduct of the state ceremonies of the Grand Imperial Shrine of Isé, though he was seldom present in person. An old school text explains the matter thus:

The reverence accorded the Grand Imperial Shrine by the Imperial Family is of an extraordinary nature. . . . At the time of the Festival of Prayer for the Year's Crops

---

* Being less holy, the shrine of the food-goddess stands in a smaller area than that of the sun-goddess and is called "the outer shrine of Isé."

† The old story is that the sun-goddess locked herself in the rock-cave of heaven and left the world in darkness, save for the light of the moon and the stars. So the deities of the world (eighty myriads of them!) gathered outside the rock door and put on a serio-comic show to draw the offended deity out again into the open. They placed in front of the door a freshly dug-up sakaki tree, the most sacred of all trees, and hung on its branches a newly

forged and very brightly polished metal mirror, a string of "curved" stone jewels, and blue and white offerings of cloth made from the inner bark of the sacred tree. Then Ame-no-uzume, the phallic goddess, danced so outrageously, to the rhythmic chanting of the other deities, that the sound of the laughter shook heaven and earth. Overcome with curiosity, the sun-goddess peeked out, saw her own face reflected in the mirror hanging from the branches of the sakaki tree, and took a half-step to meet the beautiful rival she thus beheld. Immediately, Te-chikara-wo (strength-of-hand deity) took her by the arm and drew her forth, while all the other deities shouted for joy. From this ancient myth of the reappearing of light in the world (after an eclipse?) Shintoists have derived the symbols of the mirror and the string of jewels and also their practice of using in their ceremonies and on altar-tables purification wands, called *nusa* and *gohei*, made to simulate branches of the sacred sakaki tree. The myth also provides the rationale for the two tall poles set up for formal ceremonies in front of the "worship sanctuary," on either side of the approach from the torii, the pole on the right bearing suspended, amid a flutter of silk streamers in five colors, a metal mirror and a string of stone jewels, and the pole on the left a small sword. In this latter case, the sword-symbol refers back to the exploit of the storm-god Susa-no-wo, in slaying a dragon, whose tail terminated in an imbedded sword blade, of a miraculous potency, which the storm-god extracted and presented to the sun-goddess.B2

* There are good grounds for believing, however, that they are really ancient gifts from the Chinese court.

(Kinen Sai), at the Festival of Presentation of First Fruits (Niiname Sai), he dispatches messengers and presents offerings. At the time of dispatching the Imperial messenger the Emperor personally views the offerings and delivers a ritualistic report to the messenger. Also, the Emperor does not withdraw prior to the departure of the Imperial messenger. Again, on the day of the Festival of the Presentation of First Fruits a solemn ceremony of distant worship (toward the Grand Imperial Shrine) is carried out. Each year at the Ceremony of Beginning State Affairs the first thing done is to receive a report relating to the Grand Imperial Shrine, and whenever there is an affair of great importance either to the Imperial Family or to the nation it is reported to the Grand Imperial Shrine. Furthermore, at the time when the Emperor carries out the Ceremony of Accession to the Throne, he worships in person at the Grand Imperial Shrine.[C6]

On at least one other occasion of national importance the emperor customarily went to the Grand Imperial Shrine at Isé. It was when war was declared upon some foreign power. He reported this solemn fact in person, as a matter of life and death import for the nation.

In the past, the emperor also played a part in the greatest of all Shinto ceremonies, the *O-Harai*, or Great Purification. This was performed not only at Isé but at many other shrines throughout the country, twice each year, in June and December. It was in essence a national purgation by a purification ritual. Before the ceremony the priests sought for a month to attain inward as well as outward cleanliness by abstention (*imi*) from strong drink, sex, and food

Procession at Toshogu shrine, Nikko. Large crowds gather as the white-clad Shinto priest and his attendants lead the festival procession along the grand avenue between the huge cypresses and through the torii, decorated with a taboo rope, tassels, and paper symbols in zigzag shapes. (Courtesy of Pan American Airways.)

not purified by ritual fires. During the ceremony itself they waved slowly above the people a *nusa* or purification wand, read the ritual, and accepted penalty offerings (*harai*). In olden times the people rubbed their bodies with small straw or paper effigies representing themselves, thus transferring their guilt to their person-substitutes. The priests collected and threw the effigies into some body of water—lake, river, or ocean as the case might be—and the guilt of the people was thus borne away. At the proper moment during the festival, the emperor, as a descendant of the forgiving sun-goddess, pronounced from the imperial capital the absolution of the defiling impurities of the nation.

The waving of the purification wand during this and other ceremonies has been an important feature of Shinto ceremonies. The origin of the wand itself, though traced back to the ritual use of the branches of the sacred sakaki tree by the deities of heaven, is clearly magical. Its many analogues in the aversive magic of primitives throughout the world would make a long list. Other practices before and during Shinto ceremonies have a similar magical derivation. Instances are the hanging of a taboo rope between the uprights of the torii and beneath the eaves of shrine buildings, the flying of streamers, banners, and flags from poles, the use of straw and paper objects twisted or cut into zigzag shapes and set in the interior of the shrines or hung from the torii, and the wearing of grotesque masks by performers in festival processions.

Although in the past the emperor customarily took part in the great ceremonies of the year, the priests at Isé and elsewhere conducted by themselves the day-to-day ritual of the shrines. The services were of the utmost simplicity, consisting merely of a ceremonial approach to the inner shrine with offerings, the ritualistic presentation of the offerings, the reading of ritualistic prayers (*norito*), the removal of the offerings, and finally the quiet withdrawal of the worshipers and priests. The offerings have usually been of two kinds, food-offerings and cloth-offerings. The former have consisted typically of raw or cooked

rice, rice-brandy (*saké*), fish, fruit, vegetables, cakes, salt, and similar food-stuffs. The cloth-offerings have sometimes included money, paper, jewels, or art-objects, but normally consist of lengths of silk, cotton, and linen. These offerings are not only made to the gods but are also often proffered in the spirit of thanksgiving to the ever-glorious ancestress of the imperial family and the local clan leaders and heroes, whose spirits from remote time have guided the nation.

V   Shinto and the Warrior

The way of the gods has from the beginning been easily reconcilable with the way of the warrior. In fact, the affinity of Shinto with the warrior's way was long ago made clear in the code practiced by the samurai, the military class of the feudal period of Japan. This code was called Bushido, literally "the warrior-knight-way." It was the Japanese equivalent of the code of chivalry of medieval Europe and had a comparable influence. Indeed, when its general provisions became known, the entire nation came under its spell, to the extent at least of applauding those who adhered to it.

The Bushido Code

Bushido did not consist of finally fixed rules. It was a convention; more accurately, it was a system of propriety, preserved in unwritten law and expressing a spirit, an ideal of behavior. As such, it owed something to all the cultural and spiritual forces of the feudal era. Shinto supplied it the spirit of devotion to country and overlord, Confucianism provided its ethical substance, Zen Buddhism its method of private self-discipline, and the feudal habit of life contributed to it the spirit of unquestioning obedience to superiors and a sense of honor that was never to be compromised.

A missionary who knew the Japanese well has set forth the Bushido ethical code in the following eight attitudes:

1. Loyalty.

This was due first of all to the Emperor and under him to the lord whom one more immediately serves. One of the most familiar proverbs says, "A loyal retainer does not serve two lords."

2. Gratitude.

It may surprise some to hear that this is a Japanese characteristic, but the Christian doctrine that the spring of a right life is not duty, but gratitude, is one that is readily appreciated by the Japanese.

3. Courage.

Life itself is to be surrendered gladly in the service of the lord. An American cannot fail to be touched by the noble words of a young warrior of ancient times to the effect that he wanted to die in battle for his lord and feared nothing so much as dying in bed before he had a chance to sacrifice his life for the object of his devotion.

4. Justice.

This means not allowing any selfishness to stand in the way of one's duty.

5. Truthfulness.

A knight scorns to tell a lie in order to avoid harm or hurt to himself.

6. Politeness.

It is the mark of a strong man to be polite in all circumstances, even to an enemy.

7. Reserve.

No matter how deeply one is moved, feeling should not be shown.

8. Honor.

Death is preferable to disgrace. The knight always carried two swords, a long one to fight his foes, a short one to turn upon his own body in the case of blunder or defeat.[1]

The readiness to commit suicide last mentioned is perhaps the most startling feature of the Bushido code. Yet suicide was the accepted form of atonement for failure or misjudgment. The warrior-knight was always preparing himself in thought and in mood for it. The kind of suicide he mentally rehearsed was *harakiri,** a ceremonial method of disembowelment, carried out coolly and deliberately according to rule,

* Or *seppuku,* the more classical term.

without any expression of emotion. (Women in a similar action cut their jugular veins by a method called *jigai.*)

No story better illustrates the Bushido spirit than the famous tale of old Japan, known as "The Forty-Seven Ronins." A certain lord, we read, was repeatedly insulted by a superior, till, goaded beyond endurance, he aimed a dagger at his tormentor, and missed. A hastily summoned council of court officials condemned him to commit harakiri and ordered his castle and all his goods to be confiscated to the state. After the noble lord had ceremonially killed himself, his samurai-retainers became *ronins,* that is, men cast adrift by the death of their lord but in duty bound to avenge him. The court official who had brought on the tragedy and was the object of their vengeance thereafter kept to his castle, surrounded by a heavy guard. His spies reported that the leader of the ronins had embarked on a career of drunkenness and debauchery, evidently too craven to do his duty by his dead lord. They did not suspect that this was a ruse adopted by the ronin leader to throw the enemy off guard. The ruse succeeded. A less strict watch began to be kept in the enemy castle, and finally half of the guard was sent away. Then the forty-seven ronins secretly came together, and on a snowy night stormed the castle and captured the enemy of their dead lord. The leader of the ronins respectfully addressed the captive noble, saying: "My lord, we are the retainers of Asano Takumi no Kami. Last year your lordship and our master quarreled in the palace, and our master was sentenced to harakiri, and his family was ruined. We have come tonight to avenge him, as is the duty of faithful and loyal men. I pray your lordship to acknowledge the justice of our purpose. And now, my lord, we beseech you to perform harakiri. I myself shall have the honor to act as your second, and when, with all humility, I shall have received your lordship's head, it is my intention to lay it as an offering upon the grave of Asano Takumi no Kami."[J] But the enemy lord sat speechless and trembling, unable to perform the act required of him, so the leader of the ronins leaped upon him and cut off

333

his head with the same dagger with which his own lord had killed himself. All the ronins then went in a body to the grave of their dead lord and offered to his spirit the washed head of his enemy. After that they waited quietly until the government sent word that they should atone for their crime by committing harakiri themselves, and this they all did, without exception. The whole of Japan rang with their praises, and ever since they have lived in Japanese imagination as peerless exemplars of the Bushido spirit.

Bushido and the Modern Warrior

That Bushido has greatly influenced the ideals cherished by modern Japanese is beyond doubt. When General Nogi, who became the military hero of the Russo-Japanese War, heard in 1894 that war with China had been declared, he left home for the front instantly, without stopping to say goodby to his wife, and when the Emperor Meiji died in 1912, the old general and his wife committed suicide (harakiri and jigai respectively), believing that by this devoted act they had made possible their personal attendance on their sovereign in the next world. Many other instances of the Bushido or samurai spirit could be cited. One such instance has been supplied by a certain Lieutenant Sakurai, who was crippled in the siege of Port Arthur during the Russo-Japanese War and afterwards wrote a book entitled *Human Bullets,* which was for many months a best-seller throughout Japan. The title of this book is an apt description of the soldiers who flung themselves at Port Arthur with an unparalleled disregard of self-preservation, a swarm of men whom the machine guns of the Russians, which poured death into them at point-blank range, could not stop. Many of them exhibited an incredibly eager desire to make the supreme sacrifice in battle, for such a death was always thought of as patriotism's perfect gift. Lieutenant Sakurai himself, burning with devotion to emperor and country, gathered his men around him before one assault and passed among them a cup of

water, saying: "This water you drink, please drink as if at your death-moment."* They resolved to be a "sure-death" band and went into battle with a firm determination to give their lives in the attack, or at any rate to fight with complete disregard of personal safety, until they should either conquer or die.

Experts on the subject of Bushido would probably say that the suicide-complex is a distortion of the original spirit of the warrior-way. Warriors were to be loyal to lord and country and filial to parents, they were to be brave and fearless in battle, incapable of flinching from danger or death, but they were not to throw their lives away in unthinking bravado. On the contrary, they were to make them count to the utmost in preserving the security of home and country, that is, they were to make their lives last as long as possible. However, this rule was subject to one

* His intense patriotism always had this touch of formality in it. Thus, when at three o'clock in the morning the cannon which roared from the hilltop of the old castle in his hometown told him he was to depart for the front, he jumped out of bed, cleansed his body with pure water, donned his best uniform, bowed to the east where the emperor resided, solemnly read over His Majesty's declaration of war, and told His Majesty that his humble subject was just starting for the front. While he offered what he thought were his last prayers before the god-shelf, he felt a thrill going through him, as if his ancestors were solemnly saying: "Thou art not thine own. For His Majesty's sake, thou shalt go . . . to bear the crushing of thy bones and the tearing of thy flesh. Disgrace not thine ancestors by any act of cowardice."[K2]

About the same time, an acquaintance of his, who "had promised his parents, brothers and friends that he would be among the first to help win battles," was lodged in a Buddhist temple to wait for a later summons. "This was too great a humiliation for him to bear," says our lieutenant. "He thought it better to kill himself so that his spirit, freed from the shackles of the body, might be at the front to work with his living comrades. . . . Late one night when his friends were fast asleep, he scribbled a line of farewell to this effect: 'I am more sorry than I can possibly bear not to be at the front with the others. No one would take me in spite of my entreaties; I will prove my loyalty with death.' Thus prepared, he drew a dagger from a white-wood sheath and cut across the abdomen. . . . But good Heaven seemed to take compassion on such a faithful soldier. His friends awoke and came to the rescue. He was sent to the hospital." "Cold reason may call this man a fool, or a fanatic, but his heart was pure and true," adds our lieutenant.[K3]

exception: unbearable humiliation or disgrace justified honorable men in committing harakiri. Thus, a warrior, especially one charged with responsibility, was expected to commit harakiri when captured in battle or unsuccessful in carrying out an important mission.

Shinto and Official Militarism Before World War II

The high regard in which warriors have been held in Japan led, before and during World War II, to special commemorative services dedicated to the soldiers who had laid down their lives for their country. Throughout Japan, on the designated memorial day, Shinto priests said liturgies before special shrines called "soul-inviting-altars," in which the spirits of the heroic dead were invited to reside during the ceremony to receive homage. The Japanese government maintained in Tokyo a Shinto shrine where an annual ritual of national importance was performed in honor of the army and navy dead. This shrine, the Yasukuni-jinja, was regularly used by military and naval leaders for ceremonies designed to instill in the armed forces the highest patriotism. The names of all the war dead were preserved in it—and still are.

In those years the military ardor of the warrior was fed from yet another source, the publications of professors in various departments of the imperial universities. The extremes to which a religious nationalism sometimes goes is well illustrated in the following interesting argument by a well-known professor. He declared that Shinto is the faith at the basis of all religion; it is the religion of religions. The proof he offered for this broad assertion was that in the opening sentences of the *Kojiki* the first deity mentioned, Ame-no-mi-naka-nushi-no-kami ("The Deity Who Is the August Lord of the Center of Heaven"), is none other than the god who has been recognized in all other religions and philosophies as the unchanging foundation of all things, "the great Life of the Universe." Shinto thus has had from the beginning, he

declared, a conception of a great all-inclusive spirit, manifested in the life of each individual human being, and this makes it so comprehensive a faith that it may be regarded as including all other religions! Buddha, Confucius, Lao-tzu, and Jesus Christ were all missionaries of Shinto, unconscious of it though they may have been.* But Shinto has been unique in one respect, argued the professor, and in this fact has demonstrated its superiority. The uniqueness consists in this: politics and religion have not been divorced by it. The Japanese emperor, supreme politically, has also been supreme religiously, for his line goes back unbroken to the sun-goddess, Amaterasu, and behind her to the all-inclusive spirit that is "the great Life of the Universe." The emperor therefore has represented in living person the wall of the great Spirit-behind-the-Universe, who is being worshiped under many names in other lands, but who has expressed his original intent best through the emperor of Japan. The professor therefore declared: "The Emperor is god revealed in men. He is manifest Deity." "The Emperors of our country are persons equipped with qualities without parallel in the world; they are both the centers of (religious) faith and of temporal power." Hence:

The center of this phenomenal world is the Mikado's land. From this center we must expand this Great Spirit throughout the world. . . . The expansion of Great Japan throughout the world and the elevation of the entire world into the Land of the Gods is the urgent business of the present and, again, it is our eternal and unchanging object.[H3]

The Japanese military were not slow in availing themselves of this point of view. They made it part of their war talk that conquest was the holy mission of Japan. Certainly in such words we may see the logical outcome of a nationalism infused with all the values of religion. From the military point of view,

* In seeking to show that Jesus was Shinto at heart, several books have in fact attempted to give plausibility to a story that he did not die on the cross; a younger brother was crucified in his stead, and Jesus then traversed Asia and died in northern Japan, his spiritual homeland!

it seemed a useful faith. Inspired by its hopes, the Japanese people were empowered to fight for what seemed to them their manifest destiny in Asia, and ultimately in the entire world.

But the military point of view brought disaster. Perhaps that disaster may yet be retrieved, if the Shinto myth is relegated to the realm of poetry and folklore and the Japanese people move on to a synthesis of the best of their cultural and aesthetic values with the science, religion, and philosophy of the West—a synthesis wrought out while living under a new democratic order of life.

VI   Shrine Shinto Today

When in 1945 the 110,000 shrines formerly under the control of the home ministry were cut off from state supervision and subsidies, the first effect of this disestablishment and of the return of the shrines to local control was a measure of confusion and paralysis. Attendance at the shrines fell off sharply, and the priests, accustomed to the by-then obsolete rituals and prayers that had been supplied by the Home Ministry, were thrown on their own resources, although they were sometimes untrained and unprepared. But after a period of readjustment a more genuine religious atmosphere than before was established, and the shrines began to regain their popularity. Although a number of shrines have fallen into disuse, others are kept in repair by local shrine associations, and some eighty-six thousand are maintained by a nationwide Shrine Association supported by private funds and voluntary gifts. Most of the shrines are therefore back in business and enjoy genuine popular support.

The typical village shrine occupies a low knoll, where it reposes among cryptomerias and pines that give it a delightful woodland setting. Its rectangular space is hedged about by a sacred fence, pierced on one side by an exactly centered opening. Here stands the torii, the world-famous Shinto gateway, which

has been to its shrine what a pagoda is to the Chinese temple or a minaret to a Muslim mosque.* Behind the torii a shaded path leads through other torii to the outer shrine or *haiden,* which is the sanctuary for worship. This is a small building with a bell hung under its eaves.

As the worshiper draws near the haiden, he steps aside to wash his hands and cleanse out his mouth at the "water-purification place." He removes his hat, coat, and scarf. Then he approaches the outer shrine, bows before it, claps his hands decorously (the distinctive Japanese way of obtaining the gods' attention), bows, rings the bell, bows again—or, if he has ascended the steps of the outer shrine, kneels on the top step and bows, head low to the floor—leaves an offering on a cloth or drops it in the treasury-box provided for the purpose, prays, bows again in meditation and reverence, and then retires quietly, pausing to turn round and bow low as he goes.

A little beyond the outer shrine, and often connected with it by a covered passageway, stands the inner sanctuary or *hondon.* This the worshiper does not enter, but he knows that the chief treasure of the shrine is housed within it, an object called the *shintai* or "god-body," a precious object that is never allowed to be seen, except in those rare instances where it is a large rock, a hill, or a tree. Usually it is small enough to go into a treasure chest. It is often an object of little value in itself, perhaps an old sword, a mirror, a crystal ball, or a bit of ancient parchment with writing on it. In all likelihood it is an object that the ruling local clan in olden times prized as an intimate possession, or manufacture, of the powerful clan ancestors. In any case, it has become symbolic of the superhuman and is therefore often called the "spirit-substitute," that is, the outward representation of an invisible spiritual presence. Being precious, it is usually wrapped in finely woven cloths and enclosed

---

* In its simplest and oldest form a torii is constructed of three smooth tree trunks, two forming the uprights and one lying horizontally across their tops so as to project on either side, a cross-brace two or three feet from the top holding all in place. On the next page is a more elaborate one.

The torii of Itsukushima. This most famous gateway in Japan is partly submerged by the sea at high tide. It is off the shore of Miyajima Island and is dedicated to Itsukushima-Hima, daughter of the storm-god Susanowo. On sacred Miyajima no one is allowed either to be born or to die, unless this is unpreventable. But the tame deer are under no such rule. (Courtesy of Japan National Tourist Organization.)

in several sacred caskets, one inside the other, the whole covered over with another fine cloth. Seldom moved, it is carried once a year during the annual village festival in a shrine-on-wheels (the *mikoshi*), or in a palanquin, through the streets, while before and behind it, amidst banners and streamers, musicians in colorful masks play traditional music, actors on floats portray historical scenes drawn from local story, and singing girls posture to the sounds of drum and flute.

The meaning of the shintai has varied, of course, with the faith and education of the worshiper. The more devout among the common people have clearly associated the sacred object with one of the old gods of the land or with a deified ancestor and have even offered prayers to it as though it had ears to hear. Perhaps, however, the majority no longer find in it a distinctly religious value; it signifies instead the locus of a magical power of some sort or the seat of a good-luck agency to be coaxed into friendliness. The edu-

cated person is more discriminating and comes to regard it as an object symbolic solely of the ongoing virtue and spirit of deified ancestors and great men of the past.

Shrine Shinto has always enjoyed the indirect support of the Japanese love of festivals, to which old and young rally at every season of the year with much gaiety. When the festival procession comes down the street, great crowds gather to look on. Five festivals are traditionally grouped as the *go-sekku*. At the beginning of the year comes the New Year Festival (or First Moon's Festival), accompanied by national holidays. On the third day of the third month (March) the Girls' Festival (also called the Peach Festival) is celebrated, and on the fifth day of the fifth month (May) occurs the famous Boys' Festival (coinciding with the Sweet Flag or Iris Festival). These two festivals will be described further under the next topic. The seventh day of the seventh month is devoted to the Festival of the Star Vega, a summer

337

festival, and on the ninth day of the ninth month comes the Indian Summer or Chrysanthemum Festival. Not to be forgotten is the Cherry Blossom Festival in the spring. It is customary also to celebrate the emperor's birthday early in November and important dates in the long years of imperial history in other months. In October and November occur the festivals of the offering of the first-fruits of harvest and the tasting of the first-fruits by the emperor. At the end of the year at a sort of New Year's Eve feast each person present eats mixed in with his rice one more bean than the number of the years of his age. Even this is not a complete list of all the feasts and festivals of the year. Not yet mentioned are the rites of the agricultural year, when the seed is sown, the rice plants are springing up, and the first tasting of the new rice is celebrated (the Niiname Feast). Even though in the great cities these events of the ritual year are being infiltrated by such new festivals as Christmas, which is very popular in Tokyo (especially among merchants and advertisers), there is strong sentiment for continuing the old ceremonies as links with a meaningful and honorable past.

VII   Domestic and Sectarian Shinto

The ambiguity that once enshrouded the government position has been absent in domestic and sectarian Shinto. Although among the sects there have been ethical culture groups committed to a disavowal of religious interests, the motives of the majority of those supporting the sects have been frankly and unreservedly religious.

Shinto in the Home

The heart and center of domestic Shinto (the Shinto of the home) has been the *kami-dana* or godshelf. Most private homes possess one. On it are placed memorial tablets made of wood or paper,

A dragon in procession. During an autumn festival a dragon is carried on poles by young men through smoke curling under the eaves of a temple. The dragon, an importation from China, is associated with water, good fortune, and harmony with the animal world. (Courtesy of Pan American Airways.)

each inscribed with the name of an ancestor or of a patron deity of the household or locality. Sometimes Amaterasu, sometimes Inari, the goddess of rice, or both, are honored by the presence of their symbols. In most cases a miniature shrine containing a sacred mirror, or strips of paper with sacred texts written on them, or talismans obtained at Isé or elsewhere, occupies the center of the god-shelf. The god-shelf itself in this case becomes a temple area in miniature. It may be the repository of any object surcharged with family history and significance. (The writer knows of a Japanese farmer, so grateful for kindness rendered during illness in his family by a Christian missionary, that he rescued a pair of the latter's cast-off shoes from an ash-pile and put them on his god-shelf. One can scarcely conceive of a higher compliment.)

Unless in abeyance through neglect or discontinuance, the domestic rites are still performed daily. They may involve no more than the bringing of a small offering of food and the murmuring of a prayer. However, special occasions or crises in the family life call forth more elaborate rites, such as the lighting of tapers, and the offering of rice-brandy, sprigs of the sakaki tree, and cloth as supplements to the usual food-offerings, while the whole family, after prostration, head to floor, sits before the god-shelf with bowed heads, while a prayer is said.

Usually, domestic religious life is not exclusively Shinto in character. Buddhist priests are often called in to perform rites connected with important aspects of family life. This is especially true after a death, the Buddhist priest being a "funeral specialist" whose services are nearly as indispensable in Japan as those of a funeral director in the West. The family may also maintain in addition to the kami-dana, but usually in another room, a Buddhist altar (or *butsu-dana*, the Buddha-shelf), on which are placed wooden tablets bearing the "heavenly names" of the departed, which the Buddhist priest makes known. The priest may say masses here at stated intervals—another instance of how Buddhism vies with the native religion for the adherence of the family.

Family life is greatly enlivened by the two annual festivals, heretofore mentioned, for the boys and girls in the family. The Girls' Festival, also called the Dolls' Festival, takes place in March and features within the home a display of beautiful dolls on ascending ceremonial shelves, with the highest shelf occupied by a brilliantly costumed emperor and empress. At a lower level are the dolls' furniture and utensils. The Boys' Festival enables the family to report to the community the number of boys belonging to it. On a special pole erected outside the house, brightly colored paper carps, one for each boy, are suspended one below the other in order of age, through the yawning mouths of which the breezes of early May enter to inflate and float them like banners. Inside the home, it has been traditional to set out an array of samurai dolls and their weapons, not simply to simulate war and martial exercises, but also to symbolize courage and patriotism. But it is common nowadays to omit such a display as no longer appropriate in an age of peace and industry.

The Shinto Sects

During the years that the government sponsored the supposedly non-religious ceremonies of State Shinto, a sphere for sectarian, that is to say religious, Shinto was allowed. Under the provisions of the Constitution of 1889, which granted religious liberty to all citizens, Shinto sects were free to formulate their own beliefs and ceremonies, but obliged also to find their own means of support, just as were the various branches of Buddhism and Christianity. Of the thirteen sects recognized by the Bureau of Religions before the Second World War, about one half came into existence after the restoration of 1868. Any attempt to classify these self-propagating religious orders reveals their generally eclectic character. In D. C. Holtom's classification only three of them can be called pure Shinto sects. Of the others, two have sought amalgamation with Confucianism. Three have been called mountain sects, because they have specialized in the ascent of steep mountain slopes, the object being to experience on the summits ecstatic communion with the great spirits of Japan. Of these last-named sects two have centered their faith upon Mount Fuji as the best symbol of the national life and the most sacred object in the world. The purification sects, so-called, of which there are two, have emphasized the regard for ceremonial purity that ran through Old Shinto, but they have also adopted Hindu methods of cleansing the soul and mind, especially deep breathing and even fire-walking. The most interesting and the most influential of the sectarian orders have been the faith-healing sects, three in number. One of them, the Tenri Kyo, has been aptly called the Christian Science of Japan. It was founded by a woman, and has had strong popular appeal.

Since World War II, with the withdrawal of the government from the sphere of religion, hundreds of sects, Shinto and other, have formed, and some sixty or so have registered with the government as Sectarian Shinto denominations. Many other recently formed groups make no claim to be Shintoist, except in the most tenuous sense, and should be called new religions, for they include every variety of religious belief. These more syncretistic sects adapt to their needs not only the doctrines of many foreign religions but also certain theories drawn from psychology and other sciences, in the hope of attaining ultimate truth and personal spiritual security.

SUGGESTIONS FOR FURTHER READING

ANESAKI, M. *The History of Japanese Religion.* K. Paul, Trench & Trubner, Ltd., 1931

ASTON, W. G., TR. *Nihongi.* George Allen & Unwin, Ltd., 1956

BUNCE, W. K. *Religions in Japan.* Tuttle pb, Vermont, 1955

CHAMBERLAIN, BASIL H., TR. *The Kojiki.* 2nd ed., J. L. Thompson and Co., Kobe, 1932

DE BARY, WILLIAM THEODORE, RYUSAKU TSUNODA, DONALD KEENE, EDS. *Sources of the Japanese Tradition.* Columbia University Press, 1958

GROOT, G. J. *The Prehistory of Japan.* Ed. by B. S. Kraus. Columbia University Press, 1951

HOLTOM, D. C. *The National Faith of Japan.* E. P. Dutton, 1938

———. "The Political Philosophy of Modern Shinto," in *Transactions of the Asiatic Society of Japan,* XLIX (1922), Part 2, pp. 1–325

KIDDER, JONATHAN E. *Japan Before Buddhism.* F. A. Praeger, New York, 1959

KISHIMOTO, H., ED. *Japanese Religion in the Meiji Era.* Tr. and adapted by J. F. Howes. Tokyo, Obunsha, 1956

KITAGAWA, JOSEPH M. *Religion in Japanese History.* Columbia University Press, 1966

NIELSON, NIELS C., JR. *Religion and Philosophy in Contemporary Japan.* Rice Institute Pamphlet, Houston, 1957

REISCHAUER, EDWIN O. *Japan—Past and Present.* Rev. ed., Alfred A. Knopf, 1953

REISCHAUER, ROBERT K. *Early Japanese History.* 2 vols., Princeton University Press, 1937

SANSOM, G. B. *Japan: A Short Cultural History.* Century, 1931

SAUNDERS, DALE. "Japanese Mythology," in *Mythologies of the Ancient World,* ed. by Samuel N. Kramer. Anchor Books, 1961

THOMSEN, HARRY. *The New Religions of Japan.* Tuttle, Rutland, Vt., 1963

Four

The Religions of the Near East

THE AVERAGE WESTERN READER will find himself in a more familiar
atmosphere when he turns from the religions of the Orient to those of
the Near East. The prevailing ideas are more easily comprehended.
It is not that the religions of India and the Far East are so difficult, as that they
have created in him a sense of strangeness. He is not fully at home with the
pantheists, for example, or with the believers in reincarnation; he has not
experienced enough aesthetic self-identification with nature and its underlying
structural forces to share in full the Orient's distinctive mysticism. Nor does he
readily impersonalize God, as Heaven, the Tao, Brahman-Atman, or the
Dharmakaya are impersonalized in the East. Accustomed as he is to having
religion lay down a moral code for daily observance, he misses in the Oriental
religions the preoccupation with ethics that he expects to find in them.

In the religions of the Near East he finds a more familiar perspective.
God is a person, more or less anthropomorphically conceived, with a very
pronounced interest in good moral behavior. Pantheism gives place to a spiritual
pluralism, in which God, the creator and sustainer of the universe, joins with
the spiritual host of good men and angels in forming a community of beings
devoted through good and evil to the realization of the Good. Religion is a way
of mastering life and the world, not of negating nor of identifying oneself with
them. Asceticism is a minor and not quite natural kind of behavior. Nature is
a subordinate reality, a created thing, merely the stage on which the drama
of divine-human relationship is enacted. When its usefulness is at an end,
it will be destroyed.

Let us say, then, that in their most representative forms the Near East religions,
with some minor exceptions here and there, give a high value to human
individuality and conceive of the relationship between God and man as a
person-to-person encounter, in which the moral element is prominent.

Above all, man stands apart from nature in a spiritual relationship with God,
and is not caught up along with nature, as the Orient tends to believe, in the
multiple self-manifestation of a reality more ultimate than all gods, men, and
other natural forms and forces taken together. The divine, the human, and the
natural are not merged together into the ineffable One, but stand out distinctly
in a situation that is fundamentally interactive.

A consequence of this is that in the Near East religions the characteristic
question of the religious man is, What does God want me to do? What is his will?
And a further development naturally follows: God is seen to have revealed
himself and his will in history. Two marked characteristics of the Near East
religions are therefore great interest in the historical religious fact and intense
moral activity as the issue of personal encounter with the one God.

In our study of the structure of religious experience around the world we have come to an interesting point. More clearly than is usual in the history of human thought, we see in the evolution of Zoroastrianism and its neighboring faith Hinduism the effect of environment on the beliefs and attitudes of kindred peoples. The religion of Zoroaster had the same source as the religion of the Vedic Aryans. When the Indo-European wanderers who sometime at the beginning of the second millennium before Christ, or earlier, came to a parting of the ways somewhere near the Caspian Sea, one portion, perhaps the larger, went on to India, the other penetrated into present-day Armenia, Azarbaijan, and the mountain valleys forming the northwest fringes of the Iranian plateau. This physical separation was destined to be paralleled by a cultural one.

In the land of Iran, as the historians prefer to call ancient Persia, the soil was hard and arid, the climate dry and rather bracing. The inhabitants therefore tended to be aggressive and realistic, because it was necessary for them to be attentive farmers and herdsmen. In the somewhat enervating climate of India, on the other hand, human life tended to become recessive physically, yet rich in romantic and philosophical interests. There is more time for thought in India, perhaps because more time is taken for it. On the Iranian plateau the situation was quite otherwise. Thought and life were concerned largely with this world and the exciting, if difficult, struggle for existence. Morality while pursuing the business of life became one of the chief concerns of religion, and the mood of asceticism was far removed from most men's minds.

Suppose that the Aryans of India and the Aryans of Iran had remained together, living side by side on the plains somewhere in southeastern Europe, as they once did. Would they have developed so great a difference as that between Zoroastrianism and Hinduism? It is fruitless to ask. They separated, and time and circumstance swung them poles apart.

The story of Zoroastrianism is not easy to tell. Our sources are not clear and authentic, as they were in

12 Zoroastrianism: The Religion of Ethical Dualism

our study of the religion of the Vedas. The sacred book of the Zoroastrian faith, the *Avesta,* was for centuries preserved orally; it was not written down before the third or fourth centuries A.D. during Sassanian times. It is more or less a miscellany, without cohesion; indeed, it is but the remnant of a far larger body of literature, a great part of which has perished. The portion of the *Avesta* most important for us is the *Yasna,* because it contains the Gathas or Hymns of Zoroaster, written in an ancient dialect (Gathic, a dialect predating the Avestan language and closely related to the Vedic). These hymns give us our only really trustworthy information on his life and thought. The other portions of the *Avesta*—the *Yashts* or "songs of praise," the *Visperat,* containing invocations and rituals, the *Videvdat* (or *Vendidad* of the older scholarship), full of spells against demons and prescriptions for purification, and the *Khordah Avesta* or "Little Avesta"—are less reliable because of their later date and change in emphasis and world-view. In addition to the *Avesta* there are the so-called Pahlevi Texts, written down in Pahlevi, the language of the Parthians, two-hundred years or more after the humbling Muslim conquest (p. 359). Chief among them are the *Bundahishn,* an account of the creation and structure of the world, and the *Denkhart,* a compendium of Zoroastrian lore. They give us an insight into late Zoroastrianism.

Our best course, in view of the difficulties, is to begin with Iranian religion before Zoroaster, then take up the life and teaching of Zoroaster himself, and finally mark the changes that were introduced into his religious system in later times.

I   Iranian Religion Before Zoroaster

There is difficulty in determining the facts here because virtually all we know of the popular religion of Zoroaster's day is derived from the hostile references to it in the *Avesta.* Some further light is obtained from recently discovered inscriptions that confirm and supplement what we gather from the *Avesta,* but that is all.

We know, however, that the popular religion of the Iranians was practically the same as that reflected in the Vedas.

The common people worshiped powers known as *daevas,* a name identical with the *devas* or "shining ones" of the *Rig-Veda.* They were associated with the powers of nature—sun, moon, stars, earth, fire, water, and winds. The priests recognized also *ahuras* ("lords") among the gods, who were considered to be high in the heavens and concerned with cosmic order. There was, therefore, a hierarchic organization of the gods that is not too clear to us now.

Among the gods was Intar or Indara (the Vedic Indra), the dragon-slayer and rain-god, but he was not of as paramount importance as he was among the Aryans of India. He was overshadowed by Mithra (Vedic Mitra), a very popular god, who seems to have been widely known among Aryan folk everywhere. In a Hittite document of 1400–1300 B.C., found in Asia Minor, he is mentioned under the name of Miidraashshiil, and he was, it appears, the chief god of the Mitanni, an Aryan group then controlling the mountain areas fringing the Mesopotamian plain on the north. The Iranians on their part gave him highest honors. He was to them the god of war and the god of light (whence the Greeks and Romans drew the inference that he was a sun-god, and this may have been true). Particularly, he stood for the quality of loyalty and faith-keeping. In a later yasht (song) of the *Khordah Avesta* he is portrayed as the god "to whom the princes pray when they go forth to battle," and in his function of supporter of the sanctity of treaties (Mithra seems to mean "treaty" or "pact") he sees to it that wherever bad faith exists—

The steeds of the deceivers refuse to bear their riders; though they run they do not advance, though they ride they make no progress, though they ride in their chariots they gain no advantage; backwards flies the lance hurled by the enemy of Mithra. Even if the enemy throw skillfully, even if his lance reach his enemy's body, the stroke does not hurt. The lance from the hand of Mithra's enemy is borne away by the wind.[A]

Along with Mithra there appears a god called in the Hittite document Uruwanaashshiel, who was known to the Greeks as Ouranos and is to be identified with the Vedic Varuna, the god of the domed sky and lord (ahura) of the moral order. He had a high ethical character. We shall have need to mention him again.

We learn also of a conception of an underlying order of the world, whether natural or moral, called Asha or Arta, whose attributes are right, justice, and divine order (this is certainly the Vedic Rita); of the heavenly twins, the Nasatya or Asvins (in the Hittite document called the Nashaadtianna), who were reduced by the later Persians to one being; of Vayu, the Wind, under the double aspect of good and bad winds, blowing from the beginning of time; of the ruler of the dead, the first man to die, Yima (the Vedic Yama); and of the Fravashi or Fathers, the beloved and protective ancestral spirits.

These divine powers (and others whose names are lost to us, but were in every case probably akin to the names of gods in the *Rig-Veda*) were worshiped and sacrificed to under the open sky, beside altars, with the aid of priests, fire-worship, and the sacramental use of the intoxicating beverage prepared from the sacred *haoma* plant (the Vedic soma).

The fire-worship of the ancient Iranians is of particular interest, not only because of its likeness to the fire ceremonies of ancient India, but also because of its historical importance in Zoroastrianism down to the present day. The Vedic name Agni is not mentioned in the literature, but undoubtedly it was he who was invoked and worshiped. Along with the ceremony by which the sacrificial fire was lit and reverenced, the grass around the altar was consecrated, sprinkled with haoma-juice, and made the table upon which were laid portions of the sacrifice for the invisible divine guests, the gods. The sacrifice might be a cereal one, but was usually that of an animal of some kind. In the latter case the victim about to be sacrificed was touched with the *barsom,* a bundle of boughs that was worshiped as supernatural and held before the face during the adoration of the sacred fire. The ceremony of the pressing of the haoma-juice and the sacramental use of the sacred liquid were, one is led to conclude, so similar to the ceremonies of the kind in Vedic India that the reader is referred to the chapter on Hinduism for details (p. 92).

In general, the ancient Iranians, for the most part settlers who cultivated gardens and put their livestock out to graze, followed a religion ill suited to their mode of life and developing economy. Its animal sacrifices were becoming increasingly burdensome. What to nomads seemed natural and reasonable enough and involved no great economic sacrifice, to settlers was far too costly. Change at last became overdue. So doubtless it seemed to many a good husbandman, whose inarticulate religious experience ran counter to much of the teaching of the priests. The priests were complacent with the traditional state of affairs and desired no reform, but the need they ignored they ignored at their peril, for Zoroaster was not an easy-going person.

II   The Life and Teachings of Zoroaster

Life

Zoroaster was the son of a landed proprietor, probably of Aryan stock. This seems to be the inference from his teachings and career best supported by the facts. His name itself suggests a rural setting. Zoroaster, the designation by which he is known in Europe, is taken from the Greek corruption of the old Iranian word *Zarathustra,* and the last part of the old name, *ustra,* means "camel."[*]

[*] Suggestive proposals for the translation of all of Zoroaster's name are "one who plows with camels" and "one whose camels are old."

The date of Zoroaster's birth is very uncertain. Persian tradition places the time at 660 B.C., which may be thirty or more years too early. This date, with misgivings, is accepted by most modern scholars, but others, with some plausibility, contend that Zoroaster must have lived at an earlier period, perhaps as early as 1000 B.C. or as late as the first half of the sixth century B.C.

Another elusive matter is the determination of his birthplace. Was he born in western or eastern Iran? It seems likely he was born somewhere in central Iran, but did his work farther to the east. One modern authority ventures to be quite specific: "The region in which he proclaimed his message was probably ancient Chorasmia—an area comprising what is now Persian Khorasan, Western Afghanistan and the Turkmen Republic of the U.S.S.R."[B]

According to tradition, he received instruction in youth from a tutor, assumed the *kusti* or sacred thread (note once more the parallelism with Indian custom) at the age of fifteen, was known for his compassionate nature, expressed especially in solicitude toward the aged and toward cattle in time of famine, and at twenty left his father and mother and the wife they chose for him to wander forth, seeking an answer to his deepest religious questionings. He sought enlightenment from all he met who would submit to inquiry.

On one occasion, upon inquiring in open assembly, what may be accounted as the most favorable for the soul, he is told, "to nourish the poor, to give fodder to cattle, to bring firewood to the fire, to pour Hom-juice into water, and to worship many demons." Zoroaster gives proof of his eclectic tendency by performing the first four of these injunctions as worthy of a righteous man to do; but demon-worship he absolutely denounces.[C1]

According to Greek sources, he kept silent for seven years and lived in a mountain cave, and this tradition reached Rome in the form of the wonder-rousing story that he lived for twenty years in desert places subsisting on cheese!

At the critical age of thirty (so often a time of crisis in the lives of religious geniuses) he received a revelation. Legend magnifies the original event into a series of miraculous visions. The traditional scene of the first and most startling vision is laid on the banks of the Daitya River near his home. A figure "nine times as large as a man" appeared before Zoroaster. It was the archangel Vohu Manah (Good Thought). Vohu Manah questioned Zoroaster and then bade him lay aside the "vesture" of his material body and, as a disembodied soul, mount to the presence of Ahura Mazda, "the Wise Lord" and Supreme Being, holding court among his attendant angels.[C2] A curiously vivid detail of the account records the fact that as soon as Zoroaster appeared in the celestial assembly, he no longer beheld his own shadow upon the floor, "on account of the great brilliance of the archangels" who encircled him.[C3] Ahura Mazda then instructed Zoroaster, called now to be a prophet, in the doctrines and duties of the true religion.

During the next eight years Zoroaster is said to have met in vision each of the six principal archangels, and each conference made more complete the original revelation. So runs the tradition.

But in the Gathas, where presumably we have Zoroaster's own words, the references to these revelations furnish us with more authentic, if fragmentary, details. Thus:

"As the holy one I recognized thee, Mazda Ahura, when Good Thought (Vohu Manah) came to me and asked me, 'Who art thou? to whom dost thou belong? By what sign wilt thou appoint the days for questioning about thy possessions and thyself?'

"Then said I to him: 'To the first (question), Zarathustra am I, a true foe to the Liar, to the utmost of my power, but a powerful support would I be to the Righteous, that I may attain the future things of the infinite Dominion, according as I praise and sing thee, Mazda.'

"As the holy one I recognized thee, Mazda Ahura, when Good Thought came to me. To his question, 'For which wilt thou decide?' (I made reply), 'At every offering of reverence to thy Fire, I will bethink me of Right [Asha] so long as I have power. Then show me Right, upon whom I call.' . . .

"And when thou saidst to me, 'To Right shalt thou go for teaching,' then thou didst not command what I did not obey: 'Speed thee, ere my Obedience* come, followed by treasure-laden Destiny, who shall render to men severally the destinies of the two-fold award.' "ᴰ¹

The ten years that followed his divine call were to Zoroaster years of private exaltation but of public discouragement. He began immediately to preach, but without success. Discouraged, he was visited by a severe temptation, in which the Evil Spirit, Angra Mainyu, bade him renounce the religion of the worshiper of Mazda. "But Zarathustra answered him: 'No! I shall not renounce the good religion of the worshipers of Mazda, not though life, limb, and soul should part asunder.' "ᶜ⁴

At last he was rewarded. After ten years he won his first convert—his own cousin Maidhynimaonha.

Then somewhere in eastern Iran he found himself, it is said, in the court of an Aryan prince by the name of Vishtaspa.† With renewed hope he began a two years' effort to win this ruler to his faith. Vishtaspa, all but hidden from view in the mass of laudatory tradition gathered round him, gives the impression of being an honest-hearted man, simple and sincere in his habit of life. But he was dominated by the Karpans so detested in the *Avesta*, a greedy throng of priests. With their numerous animal sacrifices, and their magical procedures designed to make the crops grow, protect the cattle, keep the marauding nomads of the north (the Turanians) at a distance, and frustrate demonic influences of all sorts, they roused Zoroaster's intensest opposition. During the struggle with him they managed to have him cast into prison, but in the end, after two hard years, aided, tradition tells, by his wondrous cure of Vishtaspa's favorite black horse and helped by the sympathetic support of Vishtaspa's consort, Hutaosa, he won the monarch over to his faith.

The conversion was complete and unreserved. Vishtaspa put all his power behind the propagation

* Sraosha, Obedience, the angel of judgment, under whose care the dead are.

† Or Hystaspes. Some authorities think he may have been the father of Darius, who bore this name and was satrap of Parthia. But this supposition seems in conflict with the linguistic age of the Gathas.

of the faith. The whole court followed the monarch into the new religion. The king's brother, Zain, and his gallant son, Isfendir, were of special importance as converts. Two brothers, both nobles who stood high in the councils of Vishtaspa, Frashaoshtra and Jamnaspa by name, became Zoroaster's kin by marriage; the former gave Zoroaster his daughter, Huovi, to wife, and the latter married Pourucista, Zoroaster's daughter by his first wife.

The next twenty years, as the late and not too trustworthy tradition records, were spent in vigorously promulgating the faith among the Iranians and in fighting two holy wars in its defense. The first of these saw the rise of Isfendir to great heights of heroism in routing the invading Turanians. But, if tradition can be credited, the second invasion of the Turanians, which took place when Zoroaster was seventy-seven years of age, was at first successful and led to Zoroaster's death. The later writers of the *Avesta* state, over a thousand years after the event, that when the Turanians stormed Balkh, one of their number surprised and slew him before the fire-altar at which he was officiating.

Whether or not this was the manner of it, Zoroaster's death did not mean the extinction of the faith. He had planted the roots of his new faith deeply in the rich soil of Iranian folk-consciousness, where it was destined to flourish.

Teachings

The religion that Zoroaster taught was a unique ethical monotheism. Like the Hebrew monotheist Moses, he was a great original, even though he based himself solidly on inherited beliefs.

In calling the supreme god of his unquestioning faith Ahura Mazda ("Wise Lord"), he did not resort to invention. The name was already current. Nor was the god denoted by it hitherto unknown. Ahura Mazda was, there is little doubt, no other than the god of the moral and natural order whom the Aryans of India worshiped under the name of Varuna. It seems that Zoroaster's clan had long given their special allegiance to this highly ethical deity. Though the god was no longer called Varuna, many scholars, seeing in what aspects he was viewed (he is described in the Gathas as "clad with the massy heavens as with a garment"[D2]), have concluded that the honorific title had come to take the place of his ancient name, just as in India the title "Auspicious" (Shiva) dispossessed the ancient name Rudra. That Ahura Mazda was an honorific designation is quite apparent. Mazda means "the wise" or "the full of light." Ahura is the same word as the Vedic Asura, meaning "lord," and was an Indo-European name for outstanding figures among the devas or gods.

Incidentally, it is interesting to follow out the curious twist given by Zoroaster on the one hand and the Vedic Aryans on the other to the words for lord and god. The Indo-Aryans, like the Romans and Celts on the other side of the world, called their good spirits devas (Roman *deus*, Celtic *divin*, and English *deity* or *divinity*), but their experience of the capricious natural forces of India somehow caused the name asura (lord) to be applied exclusively to evil spirits, the sublime and awful lords of mischief. (This shift in meaning may be seen taking place between the earlier and later hymns of the *Rig-Veda*.) In Iran, on the other hand, Zoroaster attached to these words quite the opposite meanings. In Mazda he saw the one true Ahura to whom his entire devotion should be paid, the sublime and awful "Lord" who was perfect wisdom and goodness. But he feared that Mazda would not be recognized in the same way by the masses of his people. Under the leadership of the priests of the old religion, they worshiped a host of daevas, gods called by many ancient Aryan names. They even ignorantly adored as daevas the fire on the altar and the intoxicating juice of the haoma plant. The corrupt priests made magic with the aid of these deities. The wild nomads to the north, who were the scourge of all good settlers, sacrificed to these deities before they made their raids on Iran to carry off the grain and cattle and gut the barns and homes with fire. There could be only one conclusion

for Zoroaster. One and all, he declared roundly, these daevas were malicious devils masquerading as good spirits, fathers of lies deceiving the very elect. They wrought evil and turned men from following Ahura Mazda. Their worship must be stamped out!

Opposing himself squarely and uncompromisingly, therefore, to the popular religion, Zoroaster set forth his religious system in a few clear-cut conceptions.

1. He took a firm stand, to begin with, on the revelation he had received. The Gathas again and again set forth his claim that he had been called to his prophetic mission by Ahura Mazda himself and that the religion he taught was the final and true religion.

2. He gave all his devotion to one god. Ahura Mazda was, to him, the supreme deity—that is to say, supreme in creation, supreme in value, and supreme by anticipation of the final apocalyptic event by which he would forever crush all evil and establish right and truth. In contradistinction to some of his later followers, Zoroaster believed that by the will of the one supreme Lord Mazda all things had come into being. As the following sentences from the Gathas declare, Mazda caused darkness as well as light.

Who is by generation the Father of Right (Asha) at the first? Who determined the path of sun and stars? Who is it by whom the moon waxes and wanes again? . . . Who upheld the earth beneath and the firmament from falling? Who made the water and the plants? Who yoked swiftness to winds and clouds? . . . What artist made light and darkness, sleep and waking? Who made morning, noon, and night, that call the understanding man to his duty? . . . I strive to recognize by these things thee, O Mazda, creator of all things through the holy spirit.[D3]

3. He had a rich conception of Ahura Mazda's way of accomplishing results. Mazda expresses his will through a Holy Spirit (Spenta Mainyu) and various modes of divine action, called the "Immortal Holy Ones" or Amesha Spentas (the Ameshaspands of later Persia). These modes of ethical activity bear such names as Vohu Manah (Good Thought or Sense), Asha (Right), Kshathra (Power or Domin-

ion), Haurvatat (Prosperity), Armaiti (Piety), and Ameretat (Immortality). Asha (or Arta) is the Vedic Rita. Vohu Manah is the divine mode that conducted Zoroaster to Ahura Mazda for his first revelation (here the allegorical meaning that Zoroaster was led by inspiration to the true God seems to suggest itself). Armaiti, Kshathra, Haurvatat, and Ameretat are gifts of Ahura Mazda to man and also forces and facts in their own right. All of them are abstract qualities or states, and it is a little perplexing to know just what Zoroaster's conception of them was, whether he felt that they were good genii of Ahura Mazda, with their own being and individuality, or whether he meant to give them no more than the force of conveniently personalized abstractions.*

* If the latter was his meaning, he was using language in much the same way as poets do, as in the lines of W. W. Story:
  "Brothers, unite—rouse in your might,
  For Justice and Freedom, for God and the Right!"
James Hope Moulton was one leading authority who inclined toward this interpretation of Zoroaster's use of his abstractions. He wrote: "The inference seems inevitable that Asha and Vohu Manah are not archangels at all, but divine attributes within the hypostasis of Deity. Piety (Armaiti) and the Ox-Creator would seem to be likewise definable. And if so, there is no reason why we should not include Dominion (Kshathra), Welfare or Salvation (Haurvatat), and Immortality (Ameretat), which are clearly concepts of the same order, although we cannot make a dogmatic statement. In any case we see that this profound thinker's instinct not only grasped the supreme truth of the Oneness of God, but realized the vital corollary that there must be diversity within the Godhead if the unity is to be a fruitful doctrine."[E1] But that this high abstractness was modified by Zoroaster or his immediate followers was admitted by Moulton in an earlier book, in noting the fact "that Armaiti is clearly the genius of the Earth in the Gathas," that there is a connection between Kshathra and metals, and "that Haurvatat and Ameretat are Water and Plants." One might almost suggest, he added, that Zarathustra "drew from the popular religion what suited him."[D4] The German scholar B. Geiger and the American authority A. V. W. Jackson are more inclined to think the Amesha Spenta were real archangels who were endowed with abstract names to accent the changed character they now displayed in Zoroaster's purified faith. More recently, Jacques Duchesne-Guillemin in *Zoroastre* (Paris, 1948) draws the following parallels: the two Vayus with the two Mainyus, Varuna with Rita or Arta, Mitra with Manah (Thought), the two Nasatya

Other modes of divine expression are named besides the Amesha Spentas—for example, Obedience (Sraosha), the Ox-Creator or Spirit that protects cows (Geus Urva), and still others. But none of these are very clearly visualized as divine beings with independent personalities. At all events, they are kept subordinate to Ahura Mazda as agents of his divine self-expression. In short, Zoroaster gives us a rich conception of deity without abandoning monotheism.

4. But, though Ahura Mazda is supreme, he is not unopposed. This is an important belief of Zoroaster. Over against Asha (Right or Truth) is Druj (the Lie). Truth is confronted with Falsehood, Life with Death. The Good Spirit (Spenta Mainyu) is opposed by Angra Mainyu, literally, "the Bad Spirit." It is characteristic of the Gathas to lay continual emphasis on the fundamental cleavage in the world of nature and in the life of man between right and wrong, the true religion and the false. This cleavage began at the time Ahura Mazda created the world and established freedom of choice for his creatures.

Now the two primal Spirits, who revealed themselves in vision as Twins, are the Better and the Bad in thought and word and action. And between these two the wise once choose aright, the foolish not so. And when these twain Spirits came together in the beginning, they estab-

with Haurvatat and Ameretat, and the river- or water-goddess with Armaiti. In the over-all Zoroastrian scheme, "at the height of the hierarchy" Ahura Mazda is "the father" of Spenta Mainyu (*Yasna* 47.3), Arta or Asha, and Vohu Manah, the first of these three being especially close, almost to the point of complete identity. At any rate, the Holy Spirit proceeds from the father as a son. If the father and this son are regarded as one, then a trinity emerges, composed of the Wise Lord, Justice (or Right), and Good Thought. R. C. Zaehner recasts the data into this picture: in the beginning Ahura Mazda had twin "sons," identical in potentialities; they and Ahura Mazda himself were faced by free choice, the constant condition of being a person; one by choice of Truth and Right became Spenta Mainyu, the Good or Holy Spirit; the other by misguided choice of the Lie became Angra Mainyu, the Evil Spirit. (See *The Dawn and Twilight of Zoroastrianism*, G. P. Putnam's Sons, 1961.) The variety of opinions here depends on the linguistic analysis of the words used presumably by Zoroaster in the Gathas.

lished Life and Not-Life, and that at the last the Worst Existence (Hell) shall be to the followers of the Lie, but the Best Thought (Paradise) to him that follows Right. Of these twain Spirits he that followed the Lie *chose* doing the worst things; the holiest Spirit *chose* Right.[D5]

Again:

I will speak of the Spirits twain at the first beginning of the world, of whom the holier thus spake to the enemy: "Neither thought nor teachings nor wills nor beliefs nor words nor deeds nor selves nor souls of us twain agree."[D6]

Thus, at the beginning of the world, the good spirit going forth from Ahura Mazda was met and opposed by an evil spirit—the spirit called in later times Shaitin or Satan.

5. Although only a few words are needed to state it, it was perhaps Zoroaster's cardinal moral principle that each man's soul is the seat of a war between good and evil. This war in the breast is of critical importance. In creating man, Ahura Mazda gave him freedom to determine his own actions and hence the power to choose between right and wrong. Though Ahura Mazda seeks always by the power of his Good Spirit (Spenta Mainyu) and through Vohu Manah to commend the right, he has not made man inaccessible to Angra Mainyu's evil suggestions. So it is required of each man to decide the issue of the war in his own bosom, and to choose either the good or the evil. The good man chooses aright.

6. Good and evil are not clearly defined, but we cannot rightly expect the Gathas, which are devotional hymns and not theological treatises, to be precise. The Gathas, however, give us an indication of the *practical difference* between right and wrong. The good people, for example, were to Zoroaster those who accepted the true religion, and the evil were those who rejected it, especially those who continued to practice the old popular religion with its worship of the daevas. The daevas, it seemed clear, had allied themselves with Angra Mainyu, the Evil Spirit, and so those who followed them were living in a condition fraught with evil. Such people were not merely to be shunned: "Resist them with the weapon!"[D7] If it is good always to speak the truth and to aid all those who follow Asha and Vohu Manah, it is evil to help the bad, to do them favors, or give them gifts. The good—and here is an insight into Zoroaster's practical common sense—till the soil, raise grain, grow fruits, root out weeds, reclaim wasteland, irrigate the barren ground, and treat kindly the animals, especially the cow, that are of service to the farmers. In their personal relations they are truth-speakers; they never lie. The evil have no such interests. They do not concern themselves about agriculture. That is their condemnation.

He that is no husbandman, O Mazda, however eager he be, has no part in the good message.[D8]

Angra Mainyu is always busy against husbandry:

The Liar stays the supporters of Right from prospering the cattle in district and province, infamous that he is.[D9]

The Turanian nomads represented evil at its worst. They prepared for their raids by worshiping the daevas, after wickedly slaying cattle as sacrifices for the altar. Then they fell upon the fields and destroyed their produce. Such is the evil one may expect from daeva-worshipers!

The good man would say, in the words of an old Zoroastrian pledge:

"I repudiate the Daevas. I confess myself a worshipper of Mazda, a Zarathustrian, as an enemy of the Daevas, a prophet of the Lord, praising and worshipping the Immortal Holy Ones (the Amesha Spentas). To the Wise Lord I promise all good; to him, the good, beneficent, righteous, glorious, venerable, I vow all the best; to him from whom is the cow, the law, the (celestial) luminaries, with whose luminaries (heavenly) blessedness is conjoined. I choose the holy, good Armaiti, she shall be mine. I abjure theft and cattle-stealing, plundering and devastating the villages of Mazda-worshippers."[F]

7. Of religious ceremonial little is left. The old Aryan ritual is purged (almost to the vanishing point) of magic and idolatry. Animal sacrifices are eliminated, and the ritual intoxication attendant upon drinking haoma-juice is condemned.

But there was one feature of the old ritual that Zoroaster retained. According to tradition, as we have seen, he was done to death while serving before the sacred fire. In a previous quotation from the Gathas we have heard him say, "At every offering to thy Fire, I will bethink me of Right so long as I have power." Elsewhere he declares the sacred fire to be a gift of Ahura Mazda to mankind. But Zoroastra did not worship *the fire*, as his ancestors had done, or as some of his followers later did; it was to him a precious symbol of Ahura Mazda, and no more, through which he could realize the nature and essence of the Wise Lord. So, at least, his language and the logic of his whole position seems to have led him to believe.

8. What, finally, is to be the issue of the long struggle between good and evil? Will Ahura Mazda forever be opposed? Will Angra Mainyu, the Liar, always afflict man and lead him astray?

Whatever misgivings his later followers may have had on the subject, Zoroaster had no doubt that Ahura Mazda would, in the fullness of time, triumphantly overthrow all evil. He did not believe that the influence of evil is as eternal as good. He was thoroughly optimistic. Good would yet outlast and outwit evil.

How?

Here, as among the Celts and Teutons, eschatology, the conception of "last things" or the end of the world, comes into prominence. According to Zoroaster's teachings, a general resurrection will take place at the end of the present world order. The good and evil will then be subjected to an ordeal of fire and molten metal. By this fiery test, as a later amplification of the original teaching declares, the evil will be made known by their terrible burning, but the rightous will find the fire kindly and the molten metal harmless, as soft and healing as milk. In the Gathas the picture is much less clearly defined, so that it remains in doubt whether the forces of evil, including Angra Mainyu, will be entirely consumed by the fiery ordeal or will survive to be hurled into the abyss of the "Abode of Lies" (hell).

If the latter conception is the correct one, some consistency can be read into the rather confused imagery of individual judgment. Individual judgment follows shortly after death, and the state of the soul remains fixed thereafter until the general resurrection at the end of the world. The references to it —marked by excessive brevity—may, with a little interpretation, be made to yield a picture replete with picturesque detail. Each soul, good or bad, must face judgment at the Bridge of the Separator (the Chinvat Bridge), which spans the abyss of hell and at its farther end opens on paradise. At this bridge the record of the soul is read. The balance of merits and demerits is cast. If good deeds predominate over evil, the "pointing of the hand" (of Ahura Mazda?) will be toward paradise, but if evil overbalances good, the hand will point to the abyss below the bridge. The crossing of the bridge is most dramatically conceived. The righteous, guided by Zoroaster, will have no difficulty, but the evil, already condemned by the judges, will find themselves in no case able to go beyond its center. Why? Zoroaster held the profound doctrine that a man's self fixes his destiny. He said of the evil:

"Their own Soul and their own Self* shall torment them when they come to the Bridge of the Separator. To all time will they be guests for the House of the Lie."[E2]

Staggered by their own guilty consciences, they will of themselves fall to their doom.

They will dwell in "The House of the Lie," the Gathas' hell, a place called "the worst existence," the abode of "the worst thought," an ill-smelling region, most dreadful to the Iranian imagination because it is so foul. In its lightless depths sad voices cry out, but each sufferer is forever "alone." On the other hand, the righteous will dwell beyond the great bridge in "The House of Song," the Gathas' paradise, described as "the best existence," the abode of "the best thought," where the sun shines forever, and the

---

* Or "their own *daena*." *Daena* is variously translated. It stands for the moral center of the personality, the higher nature—specifically, the conscience.

righteous enjoy spiritual bliss, happy in their ever-joyous companionship.

Zoroaster believed so earnestly that the good religion of Ahura Mazda would win enough adherents to bring about the eventual defeat of evil that he had the stout hope that some of these adherents would be, like him, "deliverers."* He therefore had no doubt of Ahura Mazda's ultimate triumph—but he also felt strongly, let no man who sees the nature of the struggle between truth and falsehood fail meanwhile to ally himself with truth!

Such was the militant note with which Zoroaster brought his moral challenge to the folk of his time. How far he was in advance of his age, those who read further may judge.

III   The Religion of the Later Avesta

It is typical of the fragmentary records of early Zoroastrianism that we cannot trace in them the growth and spread of that faith through the plateau of Iran and in the Zagreus Mountains. When again Zoroastrianism emerges clearly into the light of history, it is the religion of the kings of the Achaemenian dynasty, the rulers of the Persian empire founded by Cyrus the Great, who in 538 B.C. overthrew Babylon and put an end to the Chaldaean empire. What had happened meanwhile is largely a matter of conjecture. There was probably a rapid spread of Zoroastrianism among the Aryan princes, wars in its behalf were doubtless freely and fiercely fought, and at least in Media Zoroastrianism rose to ascendancy and won the influential support of a Median group known as the Magi.

It is somewhat of a mystery who the Magi were. They probably were not of Aryan stock. But they were known as far west as Jerusalem for their skill

in the practice of magical arts. (The word *magic* is, of course, derived from them.) Babylon knew of them, even before that great city fell under the successful onslaught of Cyrus. It appears that when Zoroastrianism first came on the scene they opposed it, but becoming convinced that their special talents as priests could be used in its propagation, they adopted it and became its leading exponents in the Mesopotamian world.

Cyrus the Great was a Zoroastrian, but not a very strict one, because for political reasons, when he first extended his sway over the Chaldaeans, he sought their support by appearing to be a worshiper of the Babylonian god Marduk. But Darius I and Xerxes after him did less compromising; they honored Ahura Mazda, in their many inscriptions, as supreme Lord of heaven and earth. Their religion was not precisely that of Zoroaster as presented in the Gathas, but they believed firmly that Ahura Mazda and the agencies of his divine working and favor were with them.

It was in these days that world history hung in the balance. Cambyses first, then Darius, and Xerxes later, turned to world-conquest. Summoning the resources of the great Persian empire to their aid, they marched into Egypt and then toward Europe. Xerxes invaded Greece, and perhaps only the disaster of Salamis prevented Zoroaster's faith from becoming a major religion of the Western World.

In so brief a time Zoroastrianism rose to the apex of its claims to worldwide validity.

However, it made its way to this height of influence at a cost—the cost of modification of the ideas of the founder, the sacrifice of the integrity of his philosophy of life to the brightening of its color and popular appeal.

The account of these developments, which follows, strives to present within the briefest compass consistent with truth a picture of the changes that entered Zoroastrianism—changes that must be called typical of any religion founded by a prophetic personality but propagated at a later time by priests and kings.

* The word here used is *saoshyant*, and after Zoroaster's day it was destined to have a significant history, as we shall see.

1. A highly worshipful attitude came to be taken toward Zoroaster himself. To the adoring eyes of his later followers, that very human man, "the shepherd of the poor" who appears in the Gathas, became a godlike personage whose whole existence was attended by supernatural manifestations. Heaven and hell were thrown into commotion by him. His coming was known and foretold three thousand years before by the mythical primeval bull, and King Yima, in the Golden Age, gave the demons warning that their defeat was impending. The demons, thus forewarned, strove to prevent the occurrence of what they so much feared. They noted with consternation the manner of Zoroaster's conception. The Glory of Ahura Mazda united itself with Zoroaster's future mother at her birth and rendered her fit thereby to bear the prophet. At the same time a divinely protected stem of a haoma plant was infused with the *fravashi** of the coming prophet, and at the proper time the parents of Zoroaster drank its juices mixed with a potent milk, which the demons vainly sought to destroy and which contained the material essence (body protoplasm) of the child about to be conceived. After his birth, at which all nature rejoiced, and at the moment of which he himself laughed aloud, demons and hostile wizards surrounded him with every sort of hazard. His own father was rendered by magic arts indifferent to his fate. The baby was almost killed in his cradle, burnt in a huge fire, and trampled to death by a herd of cattle (whose leading ox, however, stood above him and saved him, exactly as did a leading horse, in a similar event where demons stampeded a herd of horses). He was placed in a cave with wolves whose young had been killed, and sad would have been his plight if these savage creatures had not allowed a ewe to enter and suckle him!

According to the highly elaborated tradition, the same sort of miracle attended his adult life. The *Zartusht Namah* (composed about 1200 A.D. from earlier material) thus tells the famous story of the healing of Vishtaspa's horse. Zoroaster had been imprisoned as the result of a plot of the hostile nobles (Kavis) and priests of the daevas (Karpans). Thereupon King Vishtaspa's horse fell to the ground, unable to move, its four legs drawn up toward its belly. Zoroaster sent word from his cell that he could cure the animal. But he promised to act only on one condition—that the king would grant a boon for each leg he restored. Zoroaster was summoned to the king's presence. The first boon asked was that Vishtaspa accept the faith. When the king agreed, the right front leg was straightened. As readily the king granted the other three boons—that the king's son, Isfendir, should fight for the faith, that the queen should also become a convert, and that the names of those in the plot against Zoroaster should be revealed and the plotters punished—in consideration of which, one by one the quivering charger's other legs were restored to use and it leapt to its feet, full of strength and fire. At one stroke Zoroaster had routed his enemies and multiplied his converts.

His miraculous powers should have afforded no one surprise, one observes, if his first appearance at Vishtaspa's court was, as some writers record, an entrance through the palace roof, which opened of itself to admit the prophet, holding in his hand "a cube of fire with which he played without its hurting him."C5

Zoroaster was highly venerated in antiquity. The Greeks and Romans were much impressed by what they heard of him and his religion. How greatly they were impressed is evidenced by the astonishingly numerous references to him in the extant literature and by the fact that Plato was reportedly prevented, shortly after the death of Socrates, from going to Persia to study Zoroastrianism at first hand only by the outbreak of the War of Sparta with Persia in 396 B.C.

2. A change came over the monotheism of Zoroaster. In theory—that is to say, according to the official creed of the later *Avesta*—Ahura Mazda (or Ormazd as he came to be called) was always adored as a supreme deity, transcendent and without equal.

* See below, p. 354.

353

He was held to be too great and spiritual to have images made of him, as though he could be contained in wood or stone. But he was no longer godhead undivided. The old Aryan nature gods whom Zoroaster condemned and fought, crept back into the faith and provided powerful figures around him to share his powers. Thus Vohu Manah (Good Thought), upon hearing in the lowing of the cattle a prayer to him to plead their cause, assumed certain agricultural functions and became the guardian divinity of the cattle. Asha (Right) became the guardian divinity of fire, and Kshathra (Dominion) the lord of metals. Because the other Amesha Spentas had feminine names they became female archangels. Armaiti (Piety) became the goddess of the soil, Haurvatat (Prosperity) the goddess of waters, and Ameretat (Immortality) the goddess of vegetation.

But these Holy Immortal Ones, perhaps because of a certain artificial quality about them (they were at least not suited to popular mythology), seemed much less important than the *Yazatas*, or angels, of whom about forty are named. That they came back into Zoroastrianism trailing clouds of glory from a far past is evident in the Yasht that speaks of the Yazatas as rising by "hundreds and thousands." They bore a distinct Aryan character, with many reminders of the *Rig-Veda*, for included among them were Ushas, the dawn-goddess, and Vayu, god of the wind. But greatest of them all was Mithra. Though Zoroaster apparently would have nothing to do with this radiant divinity, the people clung to him. In the later *Avesta* he returns to his earlier prominence. His name is regularly mentioned along with Ahura Mazda's in the inscriptions of the later Achaemenian kings, those of Artaxerxes, for instance. Theologically he was, of course, subordinate to Ahura Mazda, but in the religion of the masses he attained a supreme stature as the god of light, the rewarder of those who spoke truth and kept faith, and the chief support of those who relied on him to aid them in the struggle with the powers of darkness in this life and the next. One of the unique features of this later Zoroastrianism is the extraordinary claim that Ahura Mazda himself offers sacrifices to Mithra!* No wonder that one leading scholar says, "It must be allowed that monotheism is submitted to a severe strain when Ahura Mazda himself offers worship to angels like these."E3

Also brought back (albeit refined of the character of excess) was Haoma, the sacred intoxicant, "the enlivening, the healing, the beautiful, the lordly, with golden eyes." Animal sacrifices—this would have horrified Zoroaster—were made to him. He became again "the averter of Death," associated, as in the *Rig-Veda*, with long life and the immortality of the soul.

There were also the *Fravashis*. These beings are hard to describe because of their rather mixed character. Originally, they seem to have been the ancestral spirits, guarding, and in return expecting worship from, the living. But later their significance broadened, until they stood for ideal selves, who were also guardian genii, both of men and gods. Each living man was finally thought to have a fravashi, or eternal element, and so also certain beings not yet born, namely, "the Saoshyants who are to restore the world." Much more, the Amesha Spentas, the Yazatas, and Ahura Mazda himself were assumed each to have a fravashi! Carefully narrowing down this meaning, we arrive at the conclusion that such fravashis are the spiritual or immortal parts of living personalities, which, like the human souls in Plato's philosophy, exist before birth and survive after death. Here they have the added function of subsisting as ideal or better selves separately from men and pulling them heavenward and away from danger. Prayer and sacrifices were owing to ancestral fravashis in return for their indispensable service in the work of salvation.

So far did the process of fitting out Ahura Mazda's realm with assistant deities go that the Persians availed themselves of opportunities provided outside the Aryan scheme of things. In one of his inscriptions, Artaxerxes II (404–358 B.C.) for the first time mentions a female deity named Anahita, "the Spotless One." His high regard for her is evidenced by the fact that he erected images to her in Babylon, Susa,

* And both Ahura Mazda and Mithra worship Vayu, the wind! (Yasht 10:123, 15:2–4.)

Ecbatana, Damascus, and Sardis. Her origin was not of the best. She was, it appears, one of the many forms taken by the Babylonian goddess Ishtar, whom we have met in other connections. In the Yasht in which Anahita's praises are sung, she is called the goddess of the waters let down from heaven to fructify the earth in all its seven regions. She brings fertility to vegetation and to flocks and herds, and she awakens in human beings, Ishtar-like, the powers of reproduction, her blessing resting especially on women, that they may have easy births and abundant milk.

In all this we see monotheism relapsing into polytheism, a not uncommon fact in the history of religions. In all faiths there is a joyful acceptance of prophetic utterances and ideals in difficult and degenerate days, but reform is generally succeeded by relapse, a falling away from "thoughts that are high and deeds that are noble" to a more comfortable accommodation of doctrine and practice to the easygoing ways of the masses of men "who like not thinking better than to follow habit."

3. The doctrine of evil was developed further and approached an almost complete ethical dualism. Like the good angels, the spirits of evil were more sharply individualized than they were by Zoroaster. Angra Mainyu, of whom Zoroaster had spoken bitterly, although not in very concrete terms, as being from the beginning of creation in opposition to Ahura Mazda's Spirit of Good, now became the arch-fiend, and was set over against Ahura Mazda in dualistic fashion. Portions of the later *Avesta* almost made Angra Mainyu co-equal with as well as the contradiction of Ahura Mazda. For example, the world was regarded as their joint creation. In the first chapter of the *Videvdat*, Ahura Mazda is portrayed as telling Zoroaster the story of his struggle with Angra Mainyu at the creation of the world. He pictures himself creating the various Iranian districts and endowing them with every excellence; unfortunately, as he admits, Angra Mainyu was on hand, too, busily creating an evil for every good—killing frost of winter, excessive heat of summer, snakes, locusts, ants, the wicked

rich, evil sorcerers, non-Aryan lords of the land, human vices, lusts, witchcraft, doubt, disbelief, and so on, not to speak of such unpardonable offenses as burying of the dead or cooking of carrion, practices peculiarly abhorrent to the orthodox Zoroastrians of later days. Angra Mainyu's capacity for mischief was in fact boundless. The twenty-second chapter places the number of diseases created by him at 99,999, a stupendous number to the people of that time. But there was a final touch. He was the author of death.

The evil power that Angra Mainyu possessed was many times multiplied by the demons he created to assist him, such as Aka Manah (Bad Thought), Andar (the Vedic Indra), Naonhaithya (the Vedic Nasatyas, "the heavenly twins," here reduced to one being), Sauru, Fauru, Zairi, and others. Besides these there were also "numberless myriads" of evil spirits, daevas (devils) all of them. In this connection we must not overlook Druj (the Lie), now appearing in the likeness of a female demon so destructive of righteousness among men that even Ahura Mazda, in one Yasht, exclaims: "Had not the awful Fravashis of the faithful given help unto me . . . dominion would belong to the Druj, the material world would belong to the Druj!"[G]

This is one way to solve the problem of evil, to say that all good comes from God, all evil from the Devil. But consistency demands that the Devil, if he is the true author of evil, be co-eternal with God from the beginning of time; otherwise, God created evil in the beginning. Only a few Zoroastrians embraced this logical corollary of their position.

4. Another solution to this problem was offered in what is called Zervanism. A powerful group among the Magi, attempting to avoid the unsatisfactory conclusion outlined above, proposed as early as the fourth century B.C. a doctrine that was rejected by the main body of Zoroastrians but that seems an interesting foreshadowing of a modern physical theory. They suggested that both Ahura Mazda and Angra Mainyu sprang as twins from a unitary world-principle called Zervan (Time or Space, or was it Space-Time?). God and Devil were thus made co-

355

equal in length of years. But even in the working out of this doctrine, the ultimate victory of Ahura Mazda was declared to be certain, and opposition to evil was still made the first duty of every right-thinking man.*

5. Though man's conflict with the demons on the great battlefield of life is described as fundamentally moral, in the later *Avesta*, especially in the *Videvdat*, it becomes more and more a struggle against the demonic attempt to fasten ceremonial impurity on man. In consequence of this shift of interest, ancient procedures designed to preserve life by aversive magic made their way back into the religion of Zoroaster. To counteract the power of demons over a man involved in ceremonial impurity, the *Videvdat* provided not ethical and moral instruction but directions for the use of powerful *manthras* (cf. the Vedic and Hindu *mantras*), passages taken from the Gathas of Zoroaster for use as spells and incantations. In fact, all the Gathas become useful primarily as "spells of ineffable power, to be repeated without flaw, by men who may or may not understand them."[E4]

Besides the manthras, an effective means of daunting evil and avoiding its touch, defiling as pitch, was the offering of libations of haoma-juice. To this day the Parsis of India take the twigs of a sacred plant, pound them in a mortar, and mix the juice pressed from them with milk and holy water, the resulting fluid being in part offered as a libation and in part drunk by the officiating priests. This procedure is almost identical with that performed thousands of years ago by the Indo-Aryans on the banks of the Indus River.

* Some scholars consider the idea of Zervan a later one than is here suggested, arguing that it arose in the minds of upper-class intellectuals in Sassanian times in order to offer a solution to Zoroastrian dualism satisfactory to Babylonian and Greek critics, but that it did not give rise to distinctive cult practices nor survive the fall of the Sassanian dynasty. On the other hand, a number of scholars consider the idea an old one, a belief, in fact, of the Magi before the time of Zoroaster, which the Magi managed to synthesize with Zoroastrian beliefs and keep more or less to themselves, until the idea emerged finally in Pahlevi literature.

But more directly effective were the methods of cleansing one's person of defilement and thus getting rid of contaminating influence. According to the *Videvdat,* contact with the human dead is the source of greatest defilement. Anyone touching a corpse must immediately be purified by ablutions with water, or, in certain contingencies, with the urine of cattle. To modern as to ancient Parsis, corpses have always been so defiling that they are not allowed to enter the earth, lest they corrupt the ground, nor fall into the water, lest they render it unfit for any use, nor be burned on a funeral pyre, lest they defile the flame. In the early days of Zoroastrianism the dead were laid on a bed of stones or a layer of lime or encased in stone to keep them isolated from earth and water. Today they are placed in stone "towers of silence," open to the sky, so that birds of prey may feast on them. Any portion of a dead body, or, for that matter, any part severed from a living body— as for example nail-parings or hair cut from the head or beard—is unclean. Spitting, especially in the presence of another person, is forbidden. Even the exhaled breath is defiling, so that, down to the present day, priests wear cloths over their mouths while tending the sacred fire. Creatures that are known to feed on dead flesh—maggots, flies, and ants—are loathed. They are creations of Angra Mainyu, as are also snakes and frogs. In times past the Magi have killed hundreds of thousands of them as an act of piety. Direct contact with any of them requires that the person involved must be cleansed and purified without delay.

This shift from moral regeneration to considerations of ceremonial purity marks much of the history of Zoroastrianism.

6. In one more direction the religion of Zoroaster grew ever more elaborate: the doctrine of the future life was worked out in graphic detail, highly stimulating to the imagination.

Much attention was paid to the drama of individual judgment. This was not supposed to take place until the fourth day after death. For three nights, it was thought, the soul of the dead man sits at the

Tower of silence. On a remote and barren hilltop the vultures gather to accomplish the desire of the Parsi mourners—the stripping of the corruptible flesh from the bones of the dead without contamination of the soil. The shallow pits in which the corpses are laid appear in the central enclosure. A minority of Zoroastrians now advocate cremation, with scattering of the ashes at sea. (Drawing based on photographs.)

head of its former body and meditates on its past good or evil thoughts, words, and deeds. During this time it is comforted, if it has been a righteous soul, by good angels, and tormented, if it has been wicked, by demons hovering about ready to drag it off to punishment. On the fourth day the soul makes its way to the Chinvat Bridge, to stand before its judges, Mithra and his associates Sraosha and Rashnu, the last of whom holds the dread scales for the final weighing of merits and demerits. Judgment rendered and sentence passed, the soul then walks onto the Chinvat Bridge. Here, according to the Pahlevi text called the *Bundahishn,* in the middle part of the bridge,

there is a sharp edge which stands like a sword; . . . and Hell is below the Bridge. Then the soul is carried to where stands the sharp edge. Then, if it be righteous, the sharp edge presents its broad side. . . . If the soul be wicked, that sharp edge continues to stand edgewise, and does not give a passage. . . . With three steps which it (the soul) takes forward—which are the evil thoughts, evil words, and evil deeds that it has performed—it is cut down from the head of the Bridge, and falls headlong to Hell.[11]

In a further account of the crossing, this text adds an attractive picture of how the righteous soul is guided over the bridge by its own *daena,* or conscience, in the form of a beautiful maiden, and how the wicked man is confronted by an ugly hag (the personification of his own bad conscience). A late text gives us this amplified description:

When (the righteous soul) takes a step over the Chinvat Bridge, there comes to it a fragrant wind from Paradise, which smells of musk and ambergris, and that fragrance is more pleasant to it than any other pleasure.

When it reaches the middle of the Bridge, it beholds an apparition of such beauty that it hath never seen a figure of greater beauty. . . . And when the apparition appears to the soul, (the soul) speaks thus: "Who art thou with such beauty that a figure of greater beauty I have never seen?"

The apparition speaks (thus): "I am thine own good actions. I myself was good, but thine actions have made me better."

And she embraces him, and they both depart with complete joy and ease to Paradise.

But if the soul be that of a wicked man,

when it takes a step over the Chinvat Bridge, there blows to him an exceedingly foul wind from Hell, so foul as is unheard of among all the stench in the world. There is no stench fouler than that; and that stench is the worst of all the punishments that are visited upon it.

357

When it reaches the middle of the Chinvat Bridge, it sees an apparition of such extreme ugliness and frightfulness that it hath never seen one uglier and more unseemly. . . . And it is as much terrified on account of her as a sheep is of a wolf, and wants to flee away from her.

And that apparition speaks thus: "Whither dost thou want to flee?"

It (the soul) speaks thus: "Who art thou with such ugliness and terror that a figure worse than thou art, uglier and more frightful, I have never seen in the world?"

She speaks (thus): "I am thine own bad actions. I myself was ugly, and thou madest me worse day after day, and now thou hast thrown me and thine own self into misery and damnation, and we shall suffer punishment till the day of the Resurrection."

And she embraces it, and both fall headlong from the middle of the Chinvat Bridge and descend to Hell.[H2]

Thus did the later Zoroastrians elaborate the doctrine of their founder that a man's own self—his own moral consciousness—determines his future destiny.

In these later accounts it was held that those whose merits and demerits exactly balanced were sent to Hamestakan, a sort of limbo, located between earth and the stars. Hell, they believed, had several levels, the lowest being down in the bowels of the earth, where the darkness could be grasped by the hand and where the stench was unbearable. Heaven, on the other hand, presented ascending levels, corresponding to good thoughts, good words, and good deeds, and located respectively in the regions of the stars, the moon, and the sun. Through these ascending stations the good soul passed, until it reached highest heaven, Garotman or Garo-demana, "The House of Song," the realm where the Best Thought dwells, and where it would enjoy felicity beyond earth's highest joy until the day of resurrection and the final judgment of all souls.

In estimating when the final judgment would come, the later Zoroastrians developed a theory of world-ages, each lasting three thousand years. They said Zoroaster had appeared at the beginning of the last of these aeons. He would be succeeded by three savior-beings, each appearing at intervals of a thousand years: one, Aushetar, born a thousand years after Zoroaster; the second, Aushetarmah, two thousand years later; and the last, Soshyans (Saoshyant) at the end of the world; and Zoroaster would be their father! For it was said that Zoroaster's seed was being miraculously preserved in a lake in Persia, and at intervals of a thousand years three pure virgins would bathe there and conceive the great deliverers.

With the appearance of Soshyans, the last Messiah, the "final days" would begin. All the dead would be raised; heaven and hell would be emptied of their residents, in order to make up the great assembly where the final judgment would be passed upon all souls. The righteous and the wicked would be separated, and a flood of molten metal would pour out upon the earth and roar through hell, purifying all regions with its scorching fires. Every living soul would have to walk through the flaming river, but to the righteous it would seem like warm milk, because there would be no evil in them to be burned away. To the wicked it would bring terrible agony, a purifying burning proportioned to their wickedness, which would sear all the evil out of them and allow the survival only of their goodness. In a final conflict, Ahura Mazda and his angels would hurl Ahriman and his devils into the flames and they would be utterly consumed.[*] Then all the survivors of the fiery trial would live together in the new heavens and the new earth, in utmost joy and felicity. Adults would remain forever at forty years of age and children at fifteen; friends and relatives would be reunited forever. Even hell, at last made pure, would be brought back "for the enlargement of the world," and the world in its totality would then be "immortal for ever and ever-lasting."[I]

---

[*] This conception of Ahriman's end is not the only one. Some of the later conceptions assert that at the resurrection men will drive him into outer darkness, there to hide himself forever, or, as others say, to be destroyed at last.

IV The Zoroastrians of the Present Day

The changes in Zoroastrian doctrine that we have just reviewed began during the reigns of the Achaemenian kings and were resumed, after a prolonged period of disturbance occasioned by the invasion of Alexander the Great, during the time of the Sassanian dynasty (226–651 A.D.). The influence that Zoroastrianism during this time wielded on orthodox Judaism and the pre-Islamic Arabs, among them a young camel-driver from Mecca, was very considerable, so far as ideas were concerned. Indeed, the young camel-driver was so obsessed by visions of the approaching last judgment foretold alike by Zoroastrians, Jews, and Christians that he became a warning prophet among his own amused and scornful townsmen, and then, in flight from his native place, began a career as soldier-prophet that in its effects not only transformed Arabia but shook the Jewish and Christian worlds to their foundations and almost extinguished Zoroastrianism.

The Effects of the Muslim Conquest

The successors of Muhammad conducted their conquests with almost incredible swiftness and thoroughness. In 636 they took Syria from the Christians, and in 639 Egypt. During the decade following 637 the empire of the Sassanids was overrun, and in 651 (or 652) the last of the Sassanid rulers was surprised and slain, and Zoroastrianism suffered a severe blow. But for a century or more, the Arab conquerors attempted no wholesale methods of force in bringing about conversion, because the Qur'an provided that peoples "to whom a Book (i.e., a scripture) has been given" were to be treated generously, and the Zoroastrians, like the Jews and Christians, had "a Book," in fact a whole library of sacred texts. It was some time after the Muslim conquest that pressure was exerted, and then the Arabs were not directly responsible.

Nevertheless, within a hundred years of the Arab conquest, a great number of Zoroastrians determined to leave Persia. They first moved to a city far down the coast, near the mouth of the Persian Gulf, then removed to an island off the coast of India, and finally to India itself. Other emigrant bands of Zoroastrians joined them, and among the tolerant Hindus, by whom they were called Parsis (i.e., Persians), all were allowed to pursue their religious rites and duties in freedom. We shall see shortly how well they fared.

Their co-religionists who remained behind in Persia were not so fortunate.

The Gabars

The Zoroastrians of Persia did not name themselves Gabars (a name that was fastened upon them by the Muslims and means, loosely, "infidels"). They called themselves Zardushtians ("Zoroastrians") or Bahdinan ("those of the good religion"), but long persecution made them keep this name to themselves and hide away their light. To this day their clothes are rough and of a dull yellow, and their manners are subdued. But they have clung tenaciously to their faith. The priests are initiated according to the ancient rituals, keep the sacred fires fed in their unpretentious fire-temples, and follow strict rules in performing all their offices. The lay-folk are faithful to the old rites. They want no abbreviations of ceremony at the investiture of their boys with the sacred shirt (the *sudra*) and the sacred thread (the *kusti*, a three-ply cord symbolizing good thought, good words, and good deeds, and worn as a girdle), and they want the full rites at marriages and at funerals, which end with placing the corpse for the vultures to eat in "towers of silence" (*dakhmas*, for further description of which see below). They are careful, too, to observe the ancient purification rites on the many occasions when they are polluted by contact with unclean things and persons. Like the Jews, they suffered for centuries from the old vicious circle into which religious persecution drew them: their sufferings made them secretive, and their secretiveness made them suspect. But recently, the more tolerant government of modern Iran has removed their civil disabilities, and their lot has greatly eased. They number about eleven thousand now.

The Parsis in India

More fortunate, the Parsis of India have increased to over one hundred thousand souls, most of them still in Gujurat, the province in the Bombay Presidency to which they first came. An outsider in Bombay soon recognizes them, not only by their relatively light complexion and Aryan features, but also by their dignified mixture of ancient and modern dress. The men commonly wear European clothes, except for the snugly fitting white trousers that give their legs a spidery appearance, and they never appear with uncovered heads in or out of doors, the common head-gear being a shiny hat of stiffened cloth, darkly colored, rimless, and sloping back from the forehead. The women drape their brightly colored Indian saris over dresses of European style and go about freely with unveiled faces. The priests with their white turbans, full beards, and immaculate white garments appear in purely ancient garb.

The Bombay Parsis are often seen by travelers gathering at evening on the sands of the city's Back Bay, in order to face the setting sun and "adore" for a few moments, according to ancient custom, the shining waters rolling in from the west.

As a class the Parsis are wealthy and may deserve their reputation of being the most progressive community in India. They are frequently described as India's best businessmen and most competent industrialists; they are said to control the best hotels, the biggest stores, and the new Indian air service. Not only can they make money, but they are famous for their many and large benefactions. Yet in their dealings with non-Zoroastrians they still preserve a certain self-protective dignity, a kind of ceremonial coldness, and, like the Gabars of Iran, they let no outsiders,

however trusted, share their more sacred rites or look upon the holy fires burning in their fire-temples.

The ceremonial life of the Parsis is regulated by the priesthood, which is hereditary and traces its descent to the ancient tribe of Magi. Their high priests are called *dasturs,* and many of them are highly educated. Yet the ceremonies in the fire-temples are performed not by them, but by a specially trained class of priests called *mobeds,* whose ritual of initiation is very exacting and who keep themselves constantly purified by cleansing rites. These priests memorize fully half of the *Avesta,* without as a rule understanding a word of it because it is composed in what is now a dead language. In this they do not greatly differ from the ordinary worshipers, who also memorize the more sacred passages of the *Avesta* and repeat them during ceremonial procedures.

The Fire-Temples and Their Worship

In both Iran and India the fire-temple is not distinguishable from other buildings when viewed from the street. But the worshipers know the fire is kept there, and that it is better if the outsider is not made too curious by a distinctive exterior. In Iran the fire-temple may be merely a room in a quiet part of a dwelling; in India the whole building usually is devoted to the fire-keeping and the ceremonies. Not all the Indian temples are equally holy, however. Some, where the fire is more ancient or is purified to a greater degree, are holier. This matter of purifying the fire is distinctive of Zoroastrians and is of more than ordinary interest. The more holy fire has to be compounded of sixteen different fires, all purified after a long and complicated ritual. One such fire is obtained from the cremation of a corpse.

A number of sandalwood logs are kindled from the cremation. Then above the flame, a little too high to touch it, a metal spoon is held, with small holes in it, containing chips of sandalwood. When these ignite, the flame is made to kindle a fresh fire. This process is repeated ninety-one times, to the accompaniment of recited prayers.[E5]

Other fires, purified to a greater or lesser degree by a similar use of spoons, are obtained from flames kindled by a bolt of lightning, from fire produced by flints, and from fires in idol-temples, distilleries, and homes. Finally, the sixteen purified fires are brought together by priests (who hardly dare to breathe through the covering over their mouths) into one urn, and placed in the fire-chamber of the temple.

The fire occupies the center of an inner room, resting in its ash-filled urn on a four-legged stone pedestal. It is fed day in and day out by the attendant priests with pieces of sandalwood. During the performance of their duties in the fire-chamber the priests always wear a cloth over their mouths, so as to prevent a single breath from coming directly upon and contaminating the pure flame, and they may not cough or sneeze, at any rate not near the fire.

The worshipers come individually, at any time they wish to. Inside the entrance each washes the uncovered parts of his body, recites the Kusti prayer in Avestan, and then, putting off his shoes, proceeds bare-footed through the inner hall to the threshold—no further—of the fire-chamber, where he gives the priest his offering of sandalwood and money and receives in return a ladleful of ashes from the sacred urn, which he rubs on his forehead and eyelids. Bowing toward the fire, he offers prayers (but not *to* the fire, for it is only a symbol), and then he retreats slowly backward to his shoes and goes home.

Perhaps the most important visit to the fire-temple is on the Parsi New Year's Day. On that day the worshipers rise early, bathe, put on new clothes, go to the fire-temple, worship, and, after giving alms to the poor, spend the rest of the day in exchanging greetings and in feasting.

That Parsi practices in general are based on the religion of the later *Avesta* and not simply on the religion of Zoroaster himself is evident from the briefest study of the annual ceremonies. One festival honors Mithra, whose seat is the sun, and who enjoins upon his devotees truth and friendship—faith-keeping. A very solemn festival is that in honor of Farvadin, the deity who presides over the Fravashis or the spirits of the departed ancestors. During this festival, which lasts for ten days, the Fravashis revisit the homes of their descendants. To give them welcome the worshipers attend special ceremonies for the dead on the hills before the towers of silence. Still another festival honors Vohu Manah, regarded as the guardian of cattle; during this period the Parsis practice special kindness to animals. Other feasts commemorate the six phases of creation—heaven, water, earth, trees, animals and man.

The Towers of Silence

The *dakhmas*, or towers of silence, provide the Parsis with an approved way of disposing of their dead without contaminating soil and water with spoiling flesh. A dakhma is traditionally a stone floor with a circular brick or stone wall around it. The floor is built with a pit in the center and is in three sections—the highest section for men, the next for women, and the lowest for children. The corpse is brought to the dakhma by six bearers, followed by the mourners, all in white. After a final viewing of the remains by the funeral procession, the body is taken inside the tower, laid in a shallow pit on its proper level, and partially uncovered by a thorough slitting of its clothes with scissors. As to what follows:

As soon as the corpse-bearers have left the Tower, the vultures swoop down from their post of observation round the wall, and in half an hour there is nothing left but the skeleton. Quickly the bones dry, and the corpse-bearers enter again after some days, and cast the bones into the central well, where they crumble away.[E6]

For obvious reasons, the towers of silence are situated on hill tops in vacant land. There are seven in the vicinity of Bombay, where deaths occur frequently enough to attract a constant attendance of vultures. In other parts of India where the Parsis are not numerous, as in Calcutta, there is occasional difficulty in attracting vultures at the right time. In communities too small to have a dakhma, interment in lead coffins or in underground stone chambers is common.

At this point we conclude our study of the Zoroastrian faith. A great deal more might have been discussed—for example, the fact that the Parsis are divided into two sects over the question of the yearly calendar, and much else. But enough has been told to give a clear picture, it is hoped, of the course run by any religion that has had only one great prophet in its history.

Suggestions for Further Reading

DARMESTETER, J., TR. *The Zend Avesta*. Vols. IV, XXXI, XXXIII in the *Sacred Books of the East* series, Oxford, 1883

DHALLA, M. N. *History of Zoroastrianism*. Oxford, 1938

———. *Zoroastrian Civilization*. Oxford, 1922

DUCHESNE-GUILLEMIN, JACQUES. *Zoroastre*, Paris, 1948

———. *The Hymns of Zoroaster*. London, 1952

GHIRSHMAN, R. *Iran from the Earliest Times to the Islamic Conquest*. Penguin Books pb, 1954

GRAY, L. H. *The Foundations of the Iranian Religions*. Bombay, 1925

HENNING, W. B. *Zoroaster, Politician or Witch Doctor?* Oxford, 1950

HERZFELD, ERNEST. *Zoroaster and His World*. 2 vols., Princeton University Press, 1947

JACKSON, A. V. W. *Zoroaster, the Prophet of Ancient Iran*. Columbia University Press, 1898

———. *Zoroastrian Studies*. Columbia University Press, 1928

MODI, J. J. *Religious Ceremonies and Customs of the Parsis*. 2nd ed., Luzac, 1954

MOULTON, JAMES HOPE. *Early Zoroastrianism*. Constable, 1913

———. *The Treasure of the Magi*. Oxford, 1917

PAVRY, JAL DASTUR CURSETJI. *The Zoroastrian Doctrine of the Future Life*. Columbia University Press, 1926

ZAEHNER, R. C. *The Teachings of the Magi*. George Allen & Unwin, 1956

———. *The Dawn and Twilight of Zoroastrianism*. G. P. Putnam & Sons, 1961

———. *Zurvan: A Zoroastrian Dilemma*. Oxford, 1955

It may be said that one great theme dominates the course of Jewish religion. This is the theme that a single, righteous God is at work in the social and natural order. This theme was not immediately arrived at, but somehow it seems implicit from the beginning. Only morally and socially sensitive minds could conceive of history in such terms or develop a group-consciousness of such a god.

Being socially sensitive, the Hebrews were historical-minded, and not in any casual or intermittent way, but steadily. This fact needs stressing. The Old Testament is as complete a record of the nation's history as the Hebrew historians could make it. That their work, from the eighth century B.C. onward, was fundamentally sound is more and more evident as modern archeological research proceeds with the task of unearthing the vestiges of the early Palestinian cultures. At the same time, it should not be overlooked that the Hebrews wrote religious, not secular, history, and the facts they cited and the traditions they used no longer have quite the values for us that they had for them. In fact, their narratives contain hidden meanings and significances to which they paid no heed because they took them for granted. But we must bring these matters out into the light. It is highly rewarding to do so. When the necessary interpretations and reconstructions have been made, the Old Testament record gains in meaning.

13 Judaism: Encounter with One God in Nature and the Social Process

I The Religion of the Pre-Mosaic Hebrews

The Hebrews were Semites, originally bred in the Arabian Desert near its northern borders, where they wandered for centuries. As have other Semitic groups before and since, they camped on Arabia's northern steppes, beside oases or in areas of sparse vegetation, crossing and recrossing the desert's undulating wastes of flat stone, thinly covered with pebbles or shifting sand. At each encampment they erected straggling camel- or goat-skin tents, pitched close to the ground. Under such shelter their communal life ran its self-contained course. Each tribe lived to itself, and the day's routine was ordered by a single authoritative voice, that of the ruling elder or patriarch, to whom the word *sheikh* is now applied. In those far-off times the implements and weapons they possessed were of stone, and their beliefs were in their early formative stages. Suspicious of all strangers, and yet open-handed to a fault to any they received into their tents, they huddled together in the vast expanse of the desert, as if back to back against a hard and grudging world.

That their lives had the character of comradely cohesion at home but fear and caution as they faced outward toward the world is attested by their religious beliefs and practices.

Animism and Tribal Gods

The desert heritage with which the Hebrews began suggests a transition from animism to polytheism and monotheism. The earlier types of belief persisted alongside of, or as vestiges contained within, the later.

The veneration of stones and pillars was universal. Certain heaps of stones were particularly viewed with respect. A desert people will honor its landmarks. The Semitic name for a pillarlike rock that was sacred (*mazzebah*) was often on the lips of the earliest Hebrews, and the word *gilgal,* used later by the Hebrews as the name of a town in Palestine, meant a circular series of pillars. Stones and pillars provided convenient objects around which religious ceremonies and sacrifices might be conducted, but originally they had their own awesome significance, perhaps because of their odd shape, or suggestively human appearance, or striking position on a mountain top or athwart a much traveled way. At first the stones were themselves felt to have life (dynamism or animatism); then they were regarded as the abiding-places of indwelling-spirits (animism); finally, de-

mons, or godlings and goddesses were thought to make their local habitation there (polydemonism or polytheism).

It was natural among a desert people, unused to seeing enough of them, that wells, springs, and streams had a specially sacred character and usually were credited to the creative power of spirits or gods that had brought them into being and could readily, if angered, dry them up again.

Trees in general, but evergreen trees in particular, were, it was felt, full of spirit-energy. Groves became holy places. But trees were sometimes as much dreaded as beheld with rejoicing, for a desert people must fear being entangled in a thicket—the lair of wild beasts and the ambush of demons—and, moreover, trees may draw down the lightning or even be animated demonic beings themselves. On the other hand, some trees whispered wisdom in the rustling of their leaves. They were protective spirits, giving relief and shelter, and under certain conditions they were capable of delivering oracles, should the rare individual who could understand their language be there to hear.

Of the "beasts of the field," serpents were universally feared (and as universally revered) for being demoniacally sly and cunning, if not indeed possessed by fiery spirits (known to the later Hebrews as *seraphim,* "burning ones"). Goats were regarded as incarnations of "hairy ones" (Hebrew *se'irim*). As for the untameable wild things of the desert—the panthers, leopards, hyenas, wolves, and foxes—they were the savage flock of demon-gods of the wasteland. The untameable, swift-footed ostrich and the birds of prey were demonic, too.

But the first Hebrews believed in many more spirits besides these. They believed in spirits having a human shape, though possessed of an inhuman character, like the *jinn* of later Arabia, and they let their imaginations play with the thought of seductive female night-demons (like glamorous Lilith in the Hebrew tradition, who led Adam astray). The raging desert wind that brought the sandstorm was a malevolent demon; he was connected with pestilence and ruin. There were many others of a like evil disposition, but, of course, there were as well multitudes of beneficent spirits.

And here we come upon a fact of some importance in the present study. Many spirits that possessed a high degree of power or dynamism were given a name universally current among Semitic peoples—it was *el* (sing.) or *elim* or *elohim* (pl.), a word with the general meaning of "superhuman being" or 'divinity." This term was broad and inclusive; it was applicable to major and minor divinities alike, and although it usually designated the more beneficent powers, it was also applied to demons. As a rule it referred to no specific supernatural individual, unless hyphenated with a descriptive adjective or with the name of a locality. This held good until among the Aramaeans and the Hebrews it came to mean, whether in its singular or plural form, but one God. (Just so in Europe *god* became *God*.)*

Other words used as appellations of the gods in the Semitic world were Adonis or Adoni (Hebrew, Adonai) meaning "Lord"; Malak or Moloch (Hebrew, Melech) meaning "King"; Bel or Baal meaning "Land-Lord" or "Possessor of the Land"; and Rabb (Hebrew, Rabbi) meaning "Master."

An examination of these names for the gods reveals a significant fact. The Semites thought of their relationship to their high-gods as being direct and personal. Perhaps the desert simplified the relationship of god and man by reducing nature to an empty waste. At any rate, the Semites adopted toward their gods an attitude that was not like that of frightened or wondering humans approaching the more or less impersonal and mysterious powers of nature, but rather like that of subjects in the presence of a king or, more intimately, like that of sons before a father.

By the time this point was reached, we note further, a distinctive choice had been made, either by

* How the plural of *el* (*elohim*) could stand for one being may perhaps be explained thus: the many gods were eventually considered to be names of but one true God (as we have already seen happen elsewhere in the world), and then the plural term signified "The One who is All," or "the All-god."

the gods or by men. Not all the gods could be "father" or "personal lord" to the same men; intimacy cannot be general. What happened was this: one, or at most several, gods chose, or were chosen by, a larger or smaller group of men (a clan) for closer, more intimate connection than that of all the gods to all men. The bond was "peculiar" and familiar and tended to be binding on both sides.

From the beginning, the Hebrews seem to have had this sense of being "chosen" and of making a choice. The case of Abraham is instructive.

Abraham and the Migration to Palestine

Abraham stands in a somewhat new light today. Recent discoveries of long-buried documentary material in Iraq, Syria, and Palestine have placed him in rather exciting setting, highly fluid and shifting. As the biblical tradition tells us, his forefathers pressed out of the desert in the same way that other Semitic groups had done—the groups that earlier became Babylonians, Aramaeans, Phoenicians, Amorites, and Canaanites. His tribe dwelt for a time in Babylonia, near a place called Ur of the Chaldees, and there Abraham is said to have been born. Under the leadership of their patriarchs his people migrated along the border of the Mesopotamian plain westward to Haran, a semi-barren place on the extreme northern verge of the Arabian Desert. This migration was made possible for them because the social situation there had for some time been so disturbed that population shifts were constantly taking place; at any rate, newcomers were not immediately driven away. But the tribe of Abraham did not stay long. It had reasons to move again.

Briefly, in the nineteenth century B.C., after the death of its great Amorite king, the law-giver Hammurabi, the Sumero-Akkadian empire in the Mesopotamian valley suddenly crumbled under the onslaughts of barbarians from the northwest and northeast. These barbaric invaders were themselves pushed into action. Behind them was the enormous

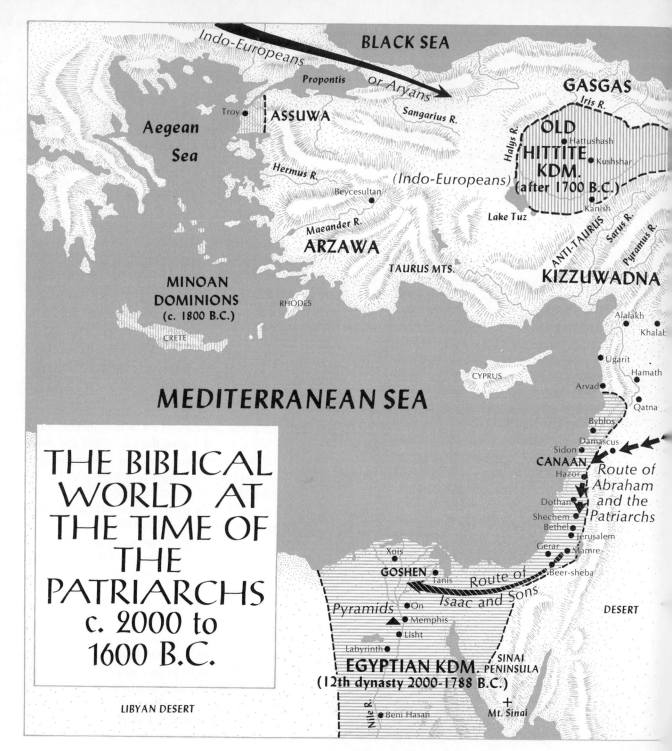

THE BIBLICAL WORLD AT THE TIME OF THE PATRIARCHS c. 2000 to 1600 B.C.

BLACK SEA

Indo-Europeans

Or Aryans

Propontis

Sangarius R.

GASGAS

Iris R.

Troy

ASSUWA

Aegean

Sea

Hermus R.

Beycesultan

(Indo-Europeans)

OLD HITTITE KDM. (after 1700 B.C.)

Halys R.

Hattushash

Kushshar

Kanish

Lake Tuz

Maeander R.

ARZAWA

TAURUS MTS.

ANTI-TAURUS

Sarus R.

Pyramus R.

KIZZUWADNA

MINOAN DOMINIONS (c. 1800 B.C.)

RHODES

CRETE

Alalakh

Khalab

Ugarit

Hamath

Arvad

Qatna

Byblos

Damascus

Sidon

CANAAN

Hazor

Route of Abraham and the Patriarchs

CYPRUS

MEDITERRANEAN SEA

Dothan

Shechem

Bethel

Jerusalem

Gerar

Mamre

Beer-sheba

Xois

GOSHEN

Tanis

Route of Isaac and Sons

DESERT

Pyramids

On

Memphis

Lisht

Labyrinth

EGYPTIAN KDM. (12th dynasty 2000-1788 B.C.)

SINAI PENINSULA

Nile R.

Beni Hasan

Mt. Sinai

LIBYAN DESERT

366

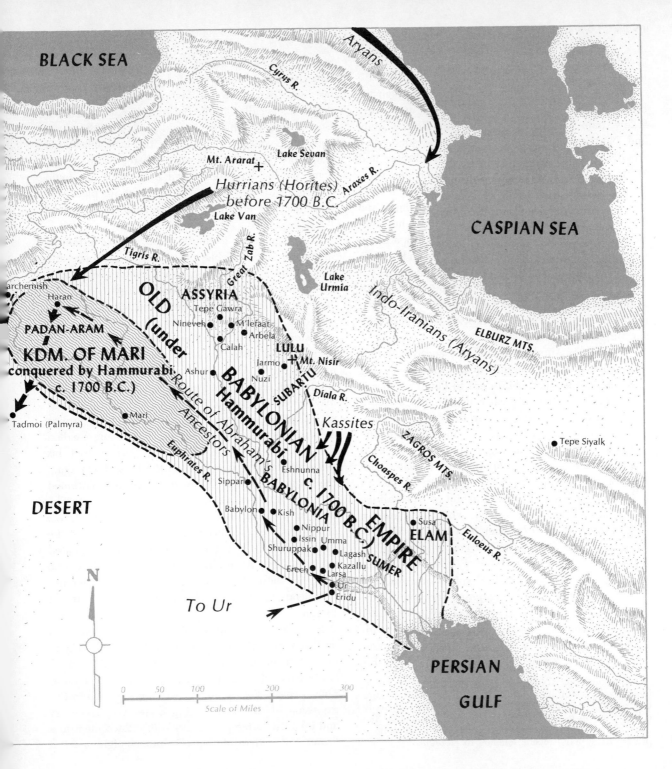

BLACK SEA

Aryans

Cyrus R.

Lake Sevan

Mt. Ararat ✛

Araxes R.

Hurrians (Horites)
before 1700 B.C.

Lake Van

CASPIAN SEA

Tigris R.

archemish

Haran

OLD

Great Zab R.

ASSYRIA

Tepe Gawra

Nineveh M'lefaat

Arbela

Calah

LULU

✛ Mt. Nisir

Lake Urmia

Indo-Iranians (Aryans)

ELBURZ MTS.

PADAN-ARAM

(under

KDM. OF MARI

conquered by Hammurabi
c. 1700 B.C.)

Ashur

Jarmo

Nuzi

BABYLONIAN

SUBARTU

Diala R.

Route of Abraham's

Hammurabi

Kassites

ZAGROS MTS.

Tepe Siyalk

Tadmoi (Palmyra)

Mari

Ancestors

Euphrates R.

Eshnunna

BABYLONIA

c. 1700 B.C.)

EMPIRE

Choaspes R.

DESERT

Sippar

Babylon Kish

Nippur

Issin Umma

Shuruppak

Erech Kazallu

Larsa

Ur

Eridu

Lagash

SUMER

Susa

ELAM

Euloeus R.

N

To Ur

0   50   100   200   300

Scale of Miles

PERSIAN

GULF

367

pressure of a chariot-borne Indo-European (Aryan) irruption into the southlands. (Once more we are confronted by these extraordinary people, whom we have already followed into India and Iran, and whose fellow Indo-Europeans we found in Greece, Italy and Northern Europe.) Syria and Palestine were equally, if not more, disturbed. The Hittites and Hurrians of Asia Minor were driven, some westward, some southward. The population of Palestine was swollen with refugees of many kinds: Hurrians (the biblical Horites), Amorites, Aramaeans, and non-Semitic peoples from further north. And, apparently, the early nomadic tribe with which tradition has associated Abraham followed or was swept along in the general movement southward. A moving group of associated peoples, most of them Semitic, whom the Egyptians were to call the Hyksos, was gathering and surging toward the Nile.

The story of Abraham as told in Genesis is the interweaving of several strands of tradition of varying age. This has led some historians to doubt all that is told about him. But so great a degree of scepticism seems, on present evidence, unwarranted. It is fairly certain that he was not the only tribal leader of the Hebrew (Habiru?)* migration, but he may have been so typical of his group that legend later centered on him. The gist of the story is this: Abraham's personal religious experience led him to place all his faith in a single protective deity, whom he chose, or who chose him, an *El* whom he called El-Shaddai ("the El of the Mountains"), a god who was probably from the vicinity of Haran. For him, this being far overshadowed the ancestral spirits or household gods represented by the *teraphim*—the wooden or stone images kept by his family for use in domestic magic and worship. When he longed to migrate with the group of which he was the leader to the safer and more favored grazing lands in the southwest, El-

* See infra pp. 374 ff. for discussion of this suggested identification. Abraham is the first Old Testament figure to be called a Hebrew. His descendants were commonly called after his grandson Jacob or Israel and thus bore the name *the children of Israel* or *Israelites*. This last name is preferred by many recent scholars to *Hebrews*.

Shaddai encouraged him to go there. So Abraham took the long journey, in full faith in the promises of his divine patron (whose favor he enjoyed to such a degree he is called in the old tradition "the friend of God"), and with his flocks and herds and the members of his small tribe came to the land where the Canaanites dwelt. Once safely there, he made his home on the limestone ridge that forms the main contour of the land, and after his death his place was taken successively by his son Isaac and his grandson Jacob.

Then, according to the tradition, a terrible famine smote the land. Unable to eke out an existence any longer, the descendants of Abraham migrated once more, this time to the borders of Egypt—here the story of Joseph explains the sequence of events—where lay the fertile Land of Goshen.

Historians are now inclined to supplement this account considerably. They suppose Abraham to have migrated from Haran at the time when an Indo-Iranian invasion seemed near (about 1800 B.C.). He may have been in the forefront of the push of displaced peoples toward the south. Scattered groups of these peoples, coalescing into the invaders called the Hyksos ("Foreign Rulers"?), pushed past his descendants, who were still on the hills, down along the sea to Egypt, which they mastered and continued to dominate from about 1750 to about 1580. The tribe of Abraham, and no doubt others, were drawn along, or simply followed behind, to the more fertile lands of the Nile delta, where the Hyksos treated them as allies. At any rate, the Hyksos used Semitic terms for the names of towns and appointed Semites as officials under them (as in the famous case of Joseph).

For generations all went well. The Israelites in particular prospered and multiplied. Then the Egyptians arose and expelled the Hyksos (1580–1560 B.C.) and recovered control of the whole eastern Mediterranean coast. The Israelites were not included in this expulsion of the hated ruling caste. For a century and a half no attempt was made to reduce them to a lowier status than of their Egyptian neighbors. But there came to the throne of Egypt a mad pharaoh (Ramses II?) whose passion was the building of great public works, including whole cities and monumental temples. Needing large forces of free labor, he turned his eyes toward the northeastern border upon the Israelites, pounced on and made slaves of them. They were compelled, under the lash, to give their forced labor to the pharaoh's public works. Nothing appeared able to save them except either a catastrophe overwhelming Egypt or a leader arising in their own midst to rescue them from their plight. One at least, if not both, of these conditions for their escape was met.

II Moses and the Covenant with Yahweh

The high place that Moses has held in Hebrew-Jewish devotion is richly deserved. Recent scholarship, though denying to him the authorship of the Pentateuch and the extremely complicated legal provisions of the Law (the Torah),* has vindicated his place of highest honor in the early history of Israel. He was a creative personality of the first order. Unfortunately, the exact details of his work are shrouded from us in tradition.

The story of Moses has come down to us in the narratives (known to scholars as "J" and "E") intertwined in Exodus and Numbers. The written form of these traditions dates from three or four hundred years after his time. They have preserved for us the famous tale of Moses' infancy.

Then a new king arose over Egypt, who . . . said to his people, "See, the Israelite people have become too numerous and too strong for us; come, let us take pre-

* Here and in the rest of this chapter the Law or Torah is identified with the first five books of the Bible (the Pentateuch). It should be said that many Jews use the word *Torah* more broadly to mean God's teaching or guidance, and thus would use it to refer to the whole of the Old Testament or even to the Jewish faith as a whole.

cautions against them lest they become so numerous that in the case of a war they should join forces with our enemies and fight against us." . . .

So Pharaoh commanded all his people, "Every boy that is born to the Hebrews, you must throw into the Nile, but you are to let all the girls live." Now a man belonging to the House of Levi went and married a daughter of Levi. The woman conceived and bore a son, and seeing he was robust, she hid him for three months. When she could no longer hide him, she procured an ark of papyrus reeds for him, and daubing it with bitumen and pitch, she put the child in it, and placed it among the reeds beside the bank of the Nile. His sister posted herself some distance away to see what would happen to him. Presently Pharaoh's daughter came down to bathe at the Nile, while her maids walked on the bank of the Nile. Then she saw the ark among the reeds and sent her maid to get it. On opening it, she saw the child, and it was a boy crying! She took pity on him, and said, "This is one of the Hebrews' children." Thereupon his sister said to Pharaoh's daughter, "Shall I go and summon a nurse for you from the Hebrew women, to nurse the child for you?" "Go," said Pharaoh's daughter to her. So the girl went and called the child's mother, to whom Pharaoh's daughter said, "Take this child away and nurse it for me, and I will pay the wages due you." So the woman took the child and nursed him; and when the child grew up, she brought him to Pharaoh's daughter, and he became her son. She called his name Moses (drawn out); "For," said she, "I drew him out of the water."A1

The tradition continues that Moses, when grown to manhood, saw one day an Egyptian beating an Israelite, "one of his people." Moved by ungovernable rage, to which he allowed full scope because they were in a lonely place, he smote the Egyptian and killed him. The next day, finding that the deed was becoming known, he fled eastward beyond the Red Sea to the land of Midian, where, while in hiding, he joined the household of a Midianite priest by the name of Jethro (or Reuel). He married Jethro's daughter Zipporah and had two sons by her.

"In the course of this long time," continues the story, "the king of Egypt died," and far away in Midian the greatest single event in Hebrew history took place.

While Moses was tending the flock of his father-in-law, Jethro, the priest of Midian, he led the flock to the western side of the desert, and came to the mountain of God, Horeb. Then the angel of the Lord appeared to him in a flame of fire, rising out of a bush. He looked, and there was the bush burning with fire without being consumed! . . . When the Lord saw that he turned aside to look at it, God called to him out of the bush "Moses, Moses!" he said. "Here I am!" said he. "Do not come near here," he said; "take your sandals off your feet; for the place on which you are standing is holy ground.". . . Then Moses hid his face; for he was afraid to look at God. "I have indeed seen the plight of my people who are in Egypt," the Lord said, "and I have heard their cry under their oppressors; for I know their sorrows, and I have come down to rescue them from the Egyptians and bring them up out of that land to a land, fine and large, to a land abounding in milk and honey, to the country of the Canaanites, Hittites, Amorites, Perizzites, Hivvites, and Jebusites. . . . So come now, let me send you to Pharaoh, that you may bring my people, the Israelites, out of Egypt.". . . "But," said Moses to God, "in case I go to the Israelites and say to them, 'The God of your fathers has sent me to you,' and they say to me, 'What is his name?' what am I to say to them?"

The reply of God to Moses' question is a very important one, no less to the modern historian than to the Moses of this tradition, who did not know the answer.

"I am who I am," God said to Moses. . . . God said further to Moses, "Thus you shall say to the Israelites: 'Yahweh* . . . has sent me to you.' "A2

Behind the elaboration of later tradition embroidering the original historical incident, we may perceive the element of fact. Moses had had a direct,

personal experience with a god of strong and determined character. It became evident that this vital being, Yahweh, was not just a nature-god, although he dwelt on the wild slopes of a wilderness mountain and descended upon it in fire and smoke.* These elements of nature were his instrumentalities; he himself was distinct from them, a god behind the scenes, who could take into his keeping the destinies of a whole nation and swear a solemn compact with them, promising to give them in return for their loyalty and obedience peace, prosperity and plenty, rain and sun in their season, cattle on a thousand hills, victory in war, children, and long life. He was a just god, but a god of strong feelings, happy in the loyalty of those who obeyed him, but jealous if they were unfaithful.

The full character of Yahweh was, of course, not known to Moses at once. Moses' experience simply made him aware of a task, this task being the leading of the Israelites out of Egypt to Sinai, where the God who wanted a people could make a covenant with the people who needed a God.

It is not necessary here to go into the well-known story of how Moses hurried to Egypt to win the Israelites over to his plan, how during their farewell Passover Yahweh, according to Exodus 12, "passed over" them but slew Egypt's firstborn, and how Moses finally led the exodus by crossing the Red (or Reed) Sea with all his people, just before the pursuing Egyptians drove up in their chariots in the attempt

---

* That this was a new name for the Israelites to give to the God of Abraham, Isaac, and Jacob seems evident. Little doubt now exists that Moses introduced them for the first time to the worship of Yahweh (or Jehovah, as another vowel pointing reads). It is significant that in Exodus 6:3 Yahweh is seen admitting that though he appeared to Abraham, Isaac, and Jacob as El-Shaddai, he was not known to them as Yahweh. The word *Yahweh* can be variously translated as meaning "I will be what I will be" or "I am that (or who) I am," or yet again "I am he that causes to be," i.e., the Creator. Jews have long considered the word too holy to pronounce, and when they come to it in their reading, they say instead "Adonai," "Lord."

* The ascriptions of nature-power are vivid enough. According to Exodus 19:18, "Mount Sinai was completely enveloped in smoke, because the Lord had descended upon it in fire." In Deut. 4:9–12, passim, we read: "Take care . . . that you do not forget the things that you saw with your own eyes . . . ; but that you impart them to your children and your children's children—the day that you stood before the Lord your God at Horeb . . . at the foot of the mountain, while the mountain flamed with fire up to the very heart of the heavens, shrouded in darkness, cloud, and gloom." Similarly, we read in Exodus 24:17: "The glory of the Lord looked to the Israelites like a consuming fire on the top of the mountain." Translations from *The Bible: An American Translation* (University of Chicago Press, 1935). Quoted by permission of the publishers.

to turn them back. Apparently, the Egyptians could not spare enough fighting men to prevent the Israelites' escape. There seems to be some historical warrant for saying that the exodus came at a time when catastrophe threatend Egypt from the north and west, as a result of invasions of barbaric enemies from Libya and of pirates sailing up the mouths of the Nile to lay waste the wealthy cities along its banks. The distraction of Egypt by these dangers could have, and perhaps actually, furnished the Israelites with their opportunity.

However, the leadership of Moses made its greatest contribution not in Egypt, but at the foot of the sacred mountain, called in one strand of tradition Sinai and in another Horeb. The exact location of this mountain is still debatable. It has traditionally been located on what is known as the Sinaitic Peninsula, but many recent scholars place it nearer the head of the Gulf of Aqaba or in the region of Kadesh-Barnea, a little to the southwest of the Dead Sea. The location matters little. What took place, in any event, is that Moses served as the intermediary between his followers and Yahweh, the God who had sent Moses to deliver them out of Egypt, had thus far saved them from all their perils, and now desired to make a covenant relationship with them. According to the tradition, the terms of the covenant were made known in the following manner. Leaving the people at the foot of the mountain, Moses went up the slope to commune with Yahweh, and after some days he returned with the knowledge of Yahweh's will for the people. This will, summarized in "commandments" inscribed on two tablets of stone, was subsequently amplified into the many provisions of the Torah or Law.

Two lists of commandments are given in the records. One, the formulation of a high ethical code, is familiar to us as the Ten Commandments. It is doubtful, however, that we have it in its original form. Evidently what we have is the full and elaborated form of later days. For one thing, it was not until much later than the time of Moses that Yahweh was identified as the maker of sky and earth and sea and all that they contain. The reader will also remember that the commandments assume that the Israelites live in homes, own livestock, and must deal with aliens in the community.

The other list of commandments is not nearly as fine nor as influential as the first. It is indeed largely ritualistic in character. Some scholars, seeing in this fact evidence of priority in time, prefer it as the earlier list. It is very interestingly introduced in the records thus:

The Lord said to Moses,
"Cut two stone tablets* . . . and in the morning ascend Mount Sinai, and present yourself there to me on the top of the mountain. No one is to ascend with you, nor is anyone to be seen anywhere on the mountain, nor must the flocks and herds graze in front of that mountain."
So Moses cut two stone tablets . . . and rising early next morning, he ascended Mount Sinai, as the Lord had commanded him, taking the two stone tablets in his hand. Then the Lord descended in a cloud, and took up a position with him there, while he called upon the name of the Lord. The Lord passed in front of him, proclaiming,
"The Lord, the Lord, a God compassionate and gracious, slow to anger, abounding in kindness and fidelity, showing kindness to the thousandth generation, forgiving iniquity, transgression, and sin, without leaving it unpunished however, but avenging the iniquity of fathers upon their children and grandchildren down to the third or even the fourth generation."
Then Moses quickly bowed his head to the ground, and made obeisance.[A3]

This passage is followed by Yahweh's announcement that he wishes to make a compact or covenant with the Israelites in the following specific terms:

You must not make any molten gods for yourselves.
You must keep the festival of unleavened cakes, eating unleavened cakes for seven days, as I commanded you . . . .

* The account adds, "like the former ones." This is considered by scholars an editor's addition necessitated by the earlier use of the story (from the "E" narrative) telling of the inscribing by Yahweh's finger of the Ten Commandments on two tablets of stone, tablets which Moses later broke (see infra). The account here quoted is from the "J" narrative, the older of the two traditions.

Whatever first opens the womb belongs to me, in the case of all your livestock that are male, the firstlings of oxen and sheep; a firstling ass, however, you may redeem with a sheep, but if you do not redeem it, you must break its neck; any first-born son of yours you may redeem.

None may visit me empty-handed.

Six days you are to labor, but on the seventh day you must rest, resting at ploughing-time and at harvest.

You must observe the festival of weeks, that of the first-fruits of the wheat harvest, and also the festival of ingathering at the turn of the year; three times a year must all your males come to see the Lord God, the God of Israel . . . .

You must not offer the blood of a sacrifice to me with leavened bread.

The sacrifice of the passover feast must not be left over night until morning.

The very first of the first-fruits of your land you must bring to the house of the Lord your God.

You must not boil a kid in its mother's milk.[A4]

Very clearly, however, this could not have been the original compact with Yahweh, because, like the Ten Commandments, it presupposes an agricultural, not a nomadic, community, and one, moreover, long established in its own land.

The precise terms of the covenant are therefore irrecoverable. Later tradition has too thoroughly obscured the original situation. Nevertheless, the nature of the ceremony by which the pact was sealed between Yahweh and those who were thenceforth to be his people may be preserved in this important passage:

Then Moses . . . recounted to the people all the regulations of the Lord and all the ordinances; and the people all answered with one voice,

"All the regulations that the Lord has given we will observe."

So Moses . . . built an altar at the foot of the mountain, along with twelve sacred pillars, one for each of the twelve tribes of Israel. Then he sent the young men of the Israelites to offer burnt-offerings and to sacrifice oxen as thank-offerings to the Lord, while Moses himself took half of the blood, and put it in basins, dashing the other half on the altar. He then took the book of the covenant, and read it in the hearing of the people, who said,

"All that the Lord has directed we will obediently do."

Then Moses took the blood and dashed it on the people, saying,

"Behold the blood of the covenant which the Lord has made with you on the basis of all these regulations."[A5]

Later times were well aware of the significance of such a ritual. One and the same blood was splashed on Yahweh's altar and on the people, and this made them "of one blood," that is, indissolubly joined in a single whole and made one body. It was a very solemn act of union and community. Other Semitic groups sometimes practiced rituals similar to it. This covenant had a markedly legal and contractual character. The people bound themselves to Yahweh by a solemn legal agreement, such as men might contract with each other and ratify in blood, as if pledging their very lives.

When the Israelites prepared to journey on, they had the problem, not so much of leaving Yahweh behind on his mountain (for they believed he could go with them in spirit and power), but the problem of providing a medium of communication with him. At Sinai Moses went up the mountain, and God talked to him. If they left the mountain behind, what then? The solution of the problem was the ancient one of providing a meeting-place for God and his people, that is, a shrine or sanctuary. So they devised a portable "tent of meeting" (the "tabernacle of the Lord") and reserved it for purely sacred use. At each encampment it was set up by ritualistically proper persons (tradition says these were members of the tribe of Levi, from whom sprang the priests of later days), and in the silence of its interior Moses was able to listen as Yahweh spoke to him.

It is quite unlikely that the tabernacle had an unfurnished interior. The persistent and early tradition may be accepted that within it stood a box or chest in which were contained two stone tablets marked with the terms of the covenant. This was the famous Ark of the Covenant, which played such a vital part in later Hebrew history. In Moses' day, tradition insists, whenever the Israelites were on the march, they reverently bore the ark in the van. Carried into battle, it gave strength to the warriors' arms. So holy a thing did it become that none but priests dared to touch it, for fear of being felled by the power it possessed.

In a very natural way a ritual of worship was developed that became more and more elaborate with the passing of years. The oldest elements of this ritual were the annual celebration of the Passover and the weekly observance of the Sabbath. The Passover was an ancient Semitic festival appropriated to Israelite uses. Through it they celebrated the memory of their escape from Egyptian bondage. It was a spring festival, taking place during the night of the full moon nearest the spring equinox, and centering in each family's hurried eating between twilight and dawn of a sacrificial sheep (or goat) taken from the flock, after its blood has been smeared on the doorposts of the tent or on the lintel and doorposts at the entrance to a dwelling. The whole sheep was to be consumed, either by the eaters or in the fire, nothing was to be left over. The Sabbath day also appears to have an ancient date, originating long before the time of the exodus, from the custom of taking one day of every "moon" for worship and recreation. Gradually, it became customary to set aside the seventh day of the week as a pious period of rest, sacred to the Lord.

Of an early origin also were the new-moon festivals (more or less frowned upon and modified by the strict of later days), the feast of sheep-shearing, circumcision (common to most Semites and to adjacent peoples), the taboo upon food before battle, and blood revenge.

Mosaic religion may thus be seen to be in transition from the primitive to the more developed ethical type of religion. That the people were not quite prepared for the practice of Yahwism in its purity is implied by the story of the apostasy of Aaron at the foot of Mt. Sinai. The story* runs that when Moses

went up the mountain for forty days and forty nights, the people became restive.

When the people saw that Moses was long in coming down from the mountain, the people gathered about Aaron, and said to him,

"Come, make us a god to go ahead of us; for this is the way it is with Moses, the man who brought us up out of the land of Egypt,—we do not know what has become of him."

So Aaron said to them, "Tear off the gold rings which are in the ears of your wives, your sons, and your daughters, and bring them to me."

So all the people tore off the gold rings which were in their ears, and brought them to Aaron, who took the material from them, and pouring it into a mold, made it into a molten bull, whereupon they said,

"Here is your god, O Israel, who brought you up out of the land of Egypt!"

On seeing this, Aaron built an altar in front of it, and Aaron made proclamation, "Tomorrow a feast shall be held to the Lord."

So next day the people rose early, and offered burnt-offerings, and presented thank-offerings; the people sat down to eat and drink, after which they rose to make merry.

Then the Lord said to Moses, "Go down at once; for your people whom you brought up out of the land of Egypt have acted perniciously. . . ."

Moses then turned and descended from the mountain . . . .

As soon as he came near the camp, he saw the bull and the dancing, whereupon Moses' anger blazed, and he flung the tablets [of the Commandments which he was carrying] from his hands, and broke them at the foot of the mountain; then he took the bull which they had made, and burned it up, and grinding it to powder, he scattered it on the surface of the water, and made the Israelites drink it. Then Moses said to Aaron,

"What did this people do to you, that you have let them incur such great guilt?"

Aaron said, "Let not my Lord's anger blaze; you know yourself how bad the people are. They said to me, 'Make us a god to go ahead of us!' . . . So I said to them, 'Whoever has any gold, let them tear it off'; and when they gave it to me, I threw it into the fire, and out came this bull!"A6

This sort of apostasy was to be not infrequent in the years to come.

* So much edited by later hands as to contain obviously self-contradictory elements.

III   Yahweh and the Baals

After wandering in the wilderness for a number of years (forty, according to tradition), the Exodus-Hebrews or Israelites felt themselves strong enough to invade Canaan.

It is not easy to reconstruct the story of the "conquest" from the accounts of Joshua and the Book of Judges. According to them, the main assault of the invaders was led by the "Joseph tribes," Ephraim and Manasseh, which fought their way across the Jordan under the generalship of Joshua,* took Jericho, and from this base spread their bloody conquest through central Palestine, in time capturing Shechem, Shiloh, and Samaria, to make good their control of the central territory. Judah and Simeon, invading from the south, possessed themselves of the highlands in the vicinity of the walled city of the Jebusites. In this they were assisted by the non-Hebraic Kenites on the south. Two tribes, Reuben and Gad, remained behind east of the Jordan. Others made their way among the northern Canaanites (with less of fighting than immigrating), slowly penetrating and permeating the valley of Esdraelon and the north country. Dan, after an abortive settlement in the south, eventually occupied the extreme north, and Zebulun went northwestward toward the Phoenician coast and came to amicable terms with the Hittities. Still other tribes, like Issachar, Asher, and Naphtali, were content with agricultural serfdom to Canaanite overlords who lived in the walled towns near the Lake of Galilee. In the process of occupying the land some of the tribes were either dissipated or absorbed, like Simeon and Benjamin.

The tradition does not hide the fact that this was a long process. The Canaanites had strong walls around their principal cities and villages and possessed chariots and arms far superior to the crude weapons of the Israelite fighting men. On the heights where Jerusalem stood, a powerful tribe of Jebusites lived secure within the city's thick stone walls and repelled every attack made on them for two hundred years. Elsewhere as well, the Israelites had to content themselves with possession of the open country, because the Canaanites beat off their attacks on the towns from the top of their battlements. But the invaders in the end, by whatever means, made the land theirs.

Their dominance of the land was not secure, however, until their external enemies were beaten off. This was a long-drawn-out struggle. Their Semitic enemies from the east, the Edomites, Moabites, and Ammonites, constantly harassed them by seeking to enter the land. But the most formidable enemies were the Philistines, a non-Semitic people who had descended upon the southwestern coastal plain from the islands of the Mediterranean. Their original home, we learn from other sources, was Crete, and when driven out of it, they turned pirates. They may actually have assisted the Israelites in their escape from Egypt by harrying the cities of the lower Nile. Unable to make a landing in Egypt, they sought a territory to colonize further north and found it on the south Palestinian shore. Gradually they spread inland and, with five fortified towns at their back, began to ascend the hills. The Israelites fought with them for generations and barely held them off.

This story is now being amended and supplemented by historians, who do not question its substance so much as its narrowing of attention too exclusively to but one group—the Israelites or Exodus-Hebrews. New evidence has come to light of turmoil within Canaan caused by "outsiders" or "wanderers" known as Habiru, some of whom may be unhesitatingly identified as non-Exodus-Hebrews, who had not gone down to Egypt but who joined forces with the Exodus-Hebrews (the Israelites) when they entered Canaan. Others of the same or similar grouping had for years been appearing in Mesopotamia, Syria, and northern Egypt. They were probably Semites from the desert and had no fixed location or occupation, for they wandered about sometimes as shepherds, sometimes as musicians, smiths and craftsmen, and sometimes as mercenaries for hire or free-roving

374   * Moses' successor. Moses died just before these events.

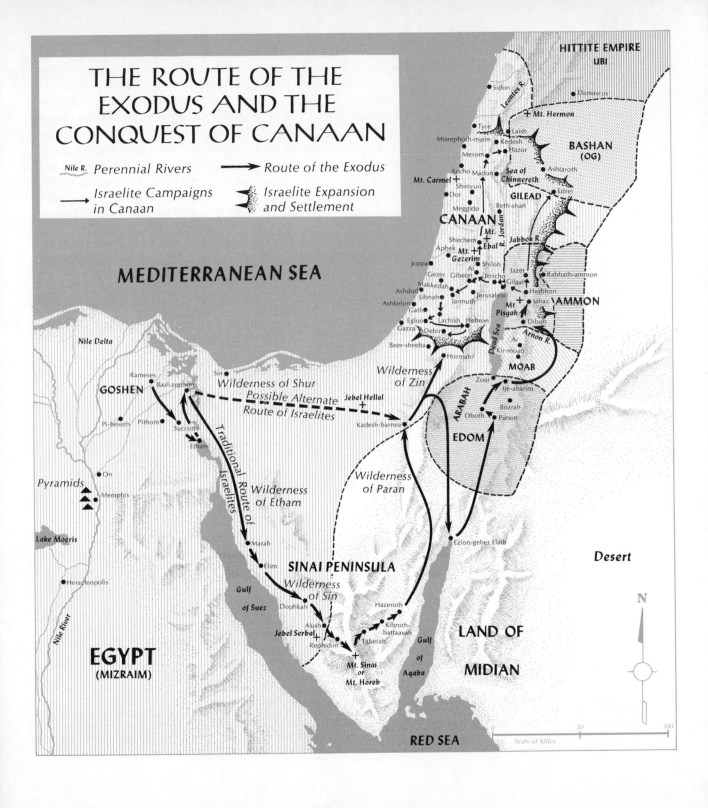

THE ROUTE OF THE EXODUS AND THE CONQUEST OF CANAAN

Nile R. Perennial Rivers   → Route of the Exodus

→ Israelite Campaigns in Canaan   Israelite Expansion and Settlement

HITTITE EMPIRE
UBI

MEDITERRANEAN SEA

Sidon
Leontes R.
Damascus
Mt. Hermon
Tyre
Misrephoth-maim
Merom
Kedesh
Laish
Hazor
BASHAN (OG)
Accho
Madon
Ashtaroth
Sea of Chinnereth
Mt. Carmel
Shimron
Dor
GILEAD
Edrei
Meggido
Beth-shan
CANAAN
Mt. Jordan
Shechem
Ebal
R. Jordan
Aphek
Mt. Gezerim
Jabbok R.
Joppa
Shiloh
Jazer
Gezer
Gibeon
Jericho
Rabbath-ammon
Ashdod
Ai
Gilgal
Libnah
Jerusalem
Heshbon
AMMON
Ashkelon
Jarmuth
Mt. Pisgah
Jahaz
Gath
Lachish
Hebron
Eglon
Gazza
Debir
Dibon
Beer-sheeba
Dead Sea
Ar
Kir-moab
Arnon R.
Hormah?
MOAB

Wilderness of Zin

Zoar
Ije-abarim
ARABAH
Oboth
Bozrah
Punon
EDOM

Nile Delta

Sin
Wilderness of Shur
Possible Alternate Route of Israelites
Jebel Hellal
Rameses
GOSHEN
Baal-zephon
Kadesh-barnea
Pi-beseth
Pithom
Succoth
Etham
Traditional Route of Israelites
On
Pyramids
Memphis
Wilderness of Etham
Wilderness of Paran
Lake Moeris
Ezion-geber Elath
Desert
Heracleopolis
Gulf of Suez
Marah
Elim
SINAI PENINSULA
Wilderness of Sin
Hazeroth
LAND OF
N
Dophkah
Alush
Kibroth-battaavah
Jebel Serbal
Rephidim
Taberah
Gulf of Aqaba
MIDIAN
EGYPT (MIZRAIM)
Mt. Sinai or Mt. Horeb
Nile River

RED SEA

0   50   100
Scale of Miles

guerrillas. (The Akkadians called them Khapiru and the Egyptians Apiru.) They were often very troublesome to local authorities and needed only organization into a group with common beliefs and purposes to be a menace. The famous Tell-el-Amarna Letters, found in Egypt by a peasant woman in 1887 and identified as dispatches sent by the Egyptian governors and minor officials in Canaan to the pharaohs from about 1400 to 1350 B.C., contain frantic appeals for help against groups of Habiru who were coming from the east and northeast and threatening to overrun the country.

"There are no lands left to the king, my lord. The Habiru plunder all the countries of the king!"
"The country of the king is fallen away to the Habiru. And now also a city of the country of Jerusalem (its name is Beth-Shemesh), a city of the king, has gone over to the men of Keilah. May the king send mercenaries that the land may remain unto the king. If there are no mercenaries, lost is the land of the king to the Habiru!"[B]

The alarm of the officials gradually subsided. The Habiru did not make a conquest. Their inrush was an infiltration process in the main, for the Canaanites were able to retain a string of fortresses and walled towns across the land, while the seminomadic "outsiders" settled in the unoccupied hill country and made themselves at home.

Some time later, if our reconstruction—a precarious matter at best—is correct, the Exodus-Hebrews, inspired by the Mosaic faith in Yahweh, entered the land, made common cause with the Habiru (whence their own later name of Hebrews?), and by vigorous assaults on important Canaanite towns put themselves in the position to become masters of the whole land eventually, and what is equally important for our story, so impressed their Habiru allies with their superior *élan* that Yahweh was adopted by the latter as their own Lord of Hosts.*

* All this must be regarded as conjectural. There are other interpretations of the historical evidence. Some authorities would make the Exodus-Hebrews enter the south a century or so *after* the Habiru, led by Joshua, invaded the central areas of Canaan. More recent views

But this, assuming it occurred, was not the only triumph of the Exodus-Hebrews. As the years passed, they succeeded in imbuing their Canaanite neighbors as well as themselves and their allies with a sense of nationhood. The increasing menace of the Philistines caused the feeling of difference to be forgotten, especially when, under the seer Samuel and the first king, Saul, strong efforts were made to throw the Philistines back upon their coastal plain. These efforts began to bear fruit at last, for though in the generation before Saul the Philistines had captured the Ark of the Covenant in battle (and then, in fear induced by bad luck, had returned it in a cart drawn by cows turned loose across the frontier), they now began to taste repeated defeat. Saul took his own life when defeated at Mt. Gilboa, but his successor, David, finally routed the Philistines and broke their fighting spirit.

David also captured at long last the city of the Jebusites (Jerusalem), made it his capital, and planned a temple in it to house the Ark of the Covenant properly, a project that was left for his son Solomon to carry out, as indeed he did.

All this while, the religion of Yahweh had undergone many changes, resisted many more, and risen to new heights of insight.

Great changes were necessarily involved in the passage from nomadic to agricultural and urban life. When the Israelites came in from the desert, they

support the order of events suggested in the text above. See W. F. Albright, *The Archaeology of Palestine* (fully revised, Pelican Books, 1960); Kathleen Kenyon, *Archaeology in the Holy Land* (1960); G. Ernest Wright, *Biblical Archaeology* (1957); and *Adam to Daniel,* an illustrated guide to the Old Testament and its background, printed in Israel (published by The Macmillan Co., N. Y.), the editor being Gaalyahu Cornfield, assisted by biblical scholars, historians and archeologists in Israel. These books achieve a noteworthy reconciliation of the biblical narratives with the latest archeological findings.

It may be added that W. F. Albright and the Israeli scholars, B. Mazar and S. Yeivin, consider that the conquest of Canaan occurred in two or more waves and was carried out by different groups of tribes over several generations, first by the Joseph (or Rachel) tribes, then by the Leah tribes.

moved among a people with a well-developed culture and religion. They had much to learn from their new neighbors.

The Canaanites had developed a thorough-going nature-religion, growing out of their agricultural life. Their gods were, in general character, farm-gods. The class name by which they were known was *baal*, which, as we have seen, means "owner" or "possessor" (of the soil). Every stretch of fertile ground owed its fertility to the presence of some baal, who held sway, like a feudal lord, within his own boundaries, though, like a feudal lord, he himself was in turn subject to the two supreme lords of all lesser baals, the elevated but inactive god El, who, if we can judge from recently recovered documents, resided in the "Source of the Two Deeps" in highest heaven, and the subordinate but active storm-god and chief of the lower gods, the great Baal of Heaven. El's consort was Ashirat, known to the Hebrews as Asherah, and the great Baal was associated with his sister Anath and the equally virgin but fertility-giving and fruitful Astarte. One may conclude that these heavenly powers were represented on earth by baals acting in the soil, and that each earthly baal in his sphere of operation at will imparted or withheld fertility power in the soil. The plant-cycle was so closely associated with him that its various stages were considered his birth, life, and death and were ritually celebrated. At his death (the decay of vegetation*) those who owed most to him ceremonially wept at the remembrance of his past goodness. In a number of districts it was even the custom to tear the hair in grief at his passing. At his birth (revival), it was common to hold festivals of rejoicing during which, in their gayest attire, the celebrants streamed together to the nearest shrine, to dance and sing and give themselves up to orgiastic ceremonies, designed in part to assist him and in part to make recognition of his fertility-power renewed in them.

The numerous baals whose presence was recognized on the hill tops, in the valleys, and at springs

---

*In Palestine vegetation dried up at the beginning of summer and revived with the autumn rains.

and wells all over the land had each their places of worship. On elevated ground, either within the walls or upon a nearby dominating height, each city built a sanctuary in honor of its patron baal, whose name was hyphenated with that of the city. The priests in charge of these "bamoth" or "high-places" conducted the worship in an open-air court facing the shrine of the god. An image of the god might occupy the shrine and be dimly seen by the worshipers, and near the altar outside stood a stone pillar, the mazzebah, a phallic symbol of the god. Perhaps also there would be a wooden column or pole, called the asherah, representing the goddess who was the god's consort (the baalah). Many sanctuaries boasted also bull-images and bronze snakes, these being very popular representations of the fertility-power of the god.

Sacrifices were of two kinds: (1) gift sacrifices, either of the first fruits of field or tree (a debt necessarily owing) or of animal flesh burnt upon the altar, and (2) communion sacrifices, through which the god and his people partook together of the sacrifice and thus strengthened the bond between them.

There were three main festivals, in spring, early summer, and fall, and during them the role played by the fertility-goddesses was given prominence. By far the most important was Astarte (Hebrew, Ashtoreth; Babylonian, Ishtar). She embodied all the qualities of the Egyptian Isis, the Grecian Demeter, and the Roman Venus. The cypress, the myrtle, and the palm were sacred to her, as being evergreen, and her special symbol was a two-horned cow. In her own person, she was usually represented naked, like Anath and other baalahs, who played similar roles. Nor was she always thought of as gentle and kindly. There was something of the uncontrollable about her; she was, when roused, a very primitive force and, like Kali in India, had a black or terrible side: she sometimes took sword in hand, sprang naked upon a horse, and rode forth to bloody slaughter—perhaps because sex has its deadly as well as life-giving side. It was in connection chiefly with her worship that the Canaanites practiced temple-prostitution. The men and women attendants who ministered in her sanctuaries for this purpose were called Kedeshoth, meaning "consecrated persons," a euphemistic term of respect. In the divine marriage between Astarte and Baal, which the Canaanites celebrated in the autumn, she was literally the soil become a wife, and he was the husband of the land who fertilized her.

The Hebrews found it natural to adopt the greater part of these concepts. Those among them who continued to be herdsmen, or who still lived in a semi-nomadic condition, felt no need of other help than that given by Yahweh, the god of mountain and storm, who had been their guide in the wilderness and was mighty still in war and in peace. But those who took up agriculture found themselves in a different case. They had practically everything to learn; the art of husbandry had to be acquired by them almost in its entirety. The educational feat here required was as great as that which would confront an Eskimo taking up farming in Connecticut. The analogy is far from perfect, however, because, though the modern farmer must know his tools and seeds and have at least a rudimentary knowledge of the chemistry of the soil, the ancient farmer had to have in addition to an understanding of his materials a thorough grasp of the spirit-lore of his locality, and this involved so much of magic and religion as to make it difficult for him to resist taking over the whole of the local religion. This is why, in the more fertile north, Israel* was less true to the religion of Yahweh than were the people of rock-bound Judah, with its large class of shepherds, not dominated by Canaanite influences. Without resigning their faith in Yahweh as the God who presided over the destiny of the whole people and guided them in war, the Hebrew farmers went with the Canaanites to the village high-places, gave of their first-fruits to the local baals and ashtoreths, brought gift offerings and peace offerings, and learned how to make whole burnt offerings. They also observed the festivals of their Canaanite neighbors at the beginning and end of the wheat harvest and in the autumn.

Only gradually did the conviction arise that Yahweh controlled the processes of agriculture too. This insight may have come first to those who on the highlands and in the border regions remained true through thick and thin to the Mosaic tradition, but it probably also dawned as well on others who participated freely in baal-worship, but who saw for themselves: "Under these forms of baal-worship we worship Yahweh, for he is the Baal of Heaven and all the power behind the ashtoreths." Though in the period of the Book of Judges the Yahweh shrine at Shiloh held only the Ark of the Covenant, in later times the sanctuaries at Bethel and at Dan contained bull-images (golden calves), which were regarded as symbols of Yahweh. This could have only one meaning, namely, that Yahweh had taken over in addition to his older functions those that the bull represented: the God who had led the Israelites through the desert was now proving his capacity to bring fertility to field and flock.

The sense that Yahweh was over all and in all was thus being engendered. And yet the transition to this insight was precariously made. It looked for a time as if Yahweh was not assimilating baalism to himself but was instead being absorbed by it, even submerged beneath it. Hence the prophet Hosea was moved vehemently to exclaim:

> "My people ask a piece of wood to guide them,
> a pole gives them their oracles!
> For a harlot-spirit has led them astray,
> they have left their God for a faithless way;
> they sacrifice on mountain heights,
> and offer incense on the hills,
> below the oak, the terebinth, the poplar—
> so pleasant is their shade.
> So your daughters play the harlot,
> matrons commit adultery.
> But I will not punish your daughters for harlotry,
> nor your matrons for adultery,
> when the men themselves go off with harlots,
> and sacrifice with temple-prostitutes.
> This brings a senseless people to their ruin—
> liquor and lust deprive them of their wits."[C1]

At long last, inspired by a conception of Yahweh that made him greater than he ever was before, the prophets had risen to protest.

* The ten northern tribes.

IV Prophetic Protest and Reform

The danger that lay in the baalization of Yahweh has been well expressed by several modern scholars. It might be called the danger of naturization, that is, of absorption into the agricultural milieu. As Max Loehr puts it: "Baalism saw the activity of the god in natural phenomena. In the annual cycle of the sprouting and decay of vegetation, in the fertilizing rain and the destructive heat of the sun, in the swelling and ripening of the fruits of garden and field, or in their destruction by the forces of nature, the benignant or wrathful god made himself known, the god whom the Old Testament usually names Baal. It was a nature religion whose worship issued in the materializing of the godhead. Genuine Yahwehism, on the other hand, regarded history as the sphere of divine action. It separated nature and God."[D] Rudolph Kittel says even more emphatically: "Those who take a short-sighted view of the period succeeding the death of Moses always take it amiss when it is described as a retrograde period. This was the fact. . . . The nature-elements in Yahweh, instead of being overcome by the higher aspect of his being, were associated in Canaan with the nature-elements in Baal and threatened to submerge the moral and spiritual elements. . . . This was the situation in Israel against which the later prophets waged so fierce a war; for they saw that the exalted God of Moses was in danger of being degraded into a mere local nature-power. This then was the root cause of the appearance of the great prophets and of their frequent opposition to their nation."[E1]

The Origin of Hebrew Prophecy

The great prophets did not appear suddenly without a background of preparation. Predecessors "made straight the way" for them. These early "prophets" came during the time of the Book of Judges, before 1000 B.C., and were known as *nebiim*. Like the dancing dervishes of the Orient today, they were ecstatics, who felt that when they were excited with religious frenzy they were full of the spirit of Yahweh and had access to his truth. In I Samuel 10:5 f., Saul, who had just been anointed as the future king, is sent off by the aging Samuel with this prediction: "As you approach the town [of Gibeah], you will meet a band of dervishes [nebiim] coming down from the height with lutes, drums, flutes, and lyres playing in front of them, while they prophesy; the spirit of the Eternal [Yahweh] will then inspire you till you prophesy along with them and become a different man." But when this befalls Saul, he learns that he has not won favor with the people. They say scornfully, "Is Saul now numbered among the prophets?"

The first nebiim, leaping in convulsive frenzy, were prone to irrational utterance, unintelligible even to themselves, but alongside of and perhaps associated with them arose men of a cooler spirit, who were the real predecessors of the later prophets: such were Nathan in the time of David, and Ahijah in the time of Solomon, prophets who appeared before kings and people to speak the unvarnished, sensible truth from Yahweh. Their intelligent and inspired behavior may be explained as due perhaps to a new kind of training for prophecy instituted about that time. Some of the nebiim were being gathered into organized schools or guilds and trained to serve their function with greater intelligibility. This certainly was done in Elijah's time, for he belonged to such a group.

Elijah and Elisha

With Elijah, the prophetic protest against degrading the ethical religion of Yahweh to a mere nature-religion was begun in earnest. Appearing in the northern kingdom in the time of King Ahab, when that monarch was yielding to the strong pressure of his "wicked" wife, Jezebel, to make the Tyrian variety of baalism dominant in Israel,[*] Elijah made a truly noteworthy stand in behalf of Yahwism. The Hebrew his-

---

[*] Baal-Melkart, god of Tyre, was the deity put forward.

torians say that when he began his reforming work there were only seven thousand men in Israel who had not bowed the knee to the Tyrian Baal, nor kissed him, but that before he was done he had reduced the worshipers of this Baal to so much less than that number that they could be crowded into one building. He was not a merciful man. Yahweh was to him a god of stern, unyielding righteousness and justice. When Jezebel contrived to have Naboth stoned, so that Ahab could take his vineyard, Elijah stormed into the presence of the king standing in the vineyard and uttered such terrible imprecations in the name of Yahweh that the king rent his garments, hastened away to put on sackcloth, and fasted in terror. In the story of the trial of the respective powers of Yahweh and the Tyrian Baal on Mt. Carmel, which, as it stands, is one of the most dramatic in religious literature, Elijah keeps to the stark issue—who is real, Yahweh or Baal-Melkart?—and makes good his claim that Yahweh is real and Baal-Melkart is not.

But during Elijah's lifetime no substantial progress could be effected in permanently discrediting baalism. The opposition of the royal house was too strong, and the people as a whole were hard to change. When Elijah suddenly and, it was felt, supernaturally disappeared, his reforming work was continued by his disciple Elisha, who encouraged a certain Jehu to carry out a sweeping political and religious revolution. This was one of the most bloody in Hebrew history. Jehu, a violent man, whose headlong charioteering gave rise to the saying, "He drives like Jehu," annihilated the royal house and then destroyed every vestige of the cult of the Tyrian Baal. So great was the slaughter that a century later Hosea denounced it.

The sum of the matter is this: baalism in general received a very telling blow from the activities of Elijah and Elisha, yet not a death blow; it recovered. One permanent and important result, however, was accomplished—the right of Yahweh to supremacy in Palestine was never afterward denied or even doubted. Baalism could be practiced only as a local cult, either because Yahweh's function was not conceived to be locally agricultural or because Yahweh was held to have made over the local baals into his ministrants. This was a great gain for the stricter followers of Yahweh, for it put them in a tactically good position. On the other hand, it was a gain that was not immediately apparent. Too large a loophole had been left for the continued practice of Canaanitish rites, and during the next century the common people, reluctant to part with the baals, availed themselves to the limit of their opportunity in this direction.

Or so Amos and his successors charged.

Amos

Amos, the first and perhaps greatest of the eighth-century prophets, came from the borderland of the south, where the debasement of Yahwism to the level of a nature-cult had not progressed as far as elsewhere. He thus resembled in place of origin his great predecessor Elijah, who also sprang from the borders of Canaan, from the town of Tishbe, beyond Jordan. This fact has significance, because it suggests that prophetic reform was motivated by the more spiritual insights of the outlying districts that had remained true to the Mosiac tradition. Amos came from Tekoa, a small town about twelve miles south of Jerusalem, and was by occupation a herdsman and pruner of sycamore trees. In marketing sheep he drove them to the populous commercial centers of the north* and thus became acquainted with social and religious conditions there. This was about the year 760 B.C., during the reign of Uzziah in Judah and Jereboam II in Israel. What he saw set him to brooding. As a herdsman who enjoyed social equality among his fellows in Tekoa, he could not fail to note that under the more complex economic conditions of the north the independence of the farmers had been destroyed in the rise of great landlords, who had bought up farm after farm and who manipulated the grain

* The Northern Kingdom (Israel), formed by the rebellion of the ten northern tribes against Rehoboam, the son of Solomon.

markets to their own enrichment. The whole social structure had become abnormal. The wars of the past had nearly wiped out the middle class. Rich and poor alike were morally adrift. There was increasing laxity in religion and morals everywhere. Integrity was gone, and justice, mercy, and spiritual religion with it. While he reflected upon all this, suddenly he had visions foretelling the doom imminent over the north. Though he came from Judah, he did not hesitate. He hastened into the Northern Kingdom. Yehweh had called him to prophesy.

What he said in Bethel and elsewhere he (or some associate) set down in writing, casting his messages into poetic diction and rhythm to give them a high literary quality and a measure of permanency. His thundering words were a prophecy of doom grounded in deeply significant convictions.

That he was appalled at the social injustice and moral laxity on every hand is evident from the strength of his condemnation:

The Eternal* declares:

"After crime upon crime of Israel
I will not relent,
for they sell honest folk for money,
the needy for a pair of shoes,
they trample down the poor like dust,
and humble souls they harry;
father and son go in to the same girl
(a profanation of my sacred shrine!),
they loll on garments seized in pledge,
by every altar,
they drink the money taken in fines
in the temple of their God. . . .

"Woe to the careless citizens,
so confident in high Samaria,
leaders of this most ancient race,
who are like gods in Israel!—
lolling on their ivory diwans,
sprawling on their couches,
dining off fresh lamb and fatted veal,
crooning to the music of the lute,
composing airs like David himself,
lapping wine by the bowlful,

* This is one possible translation of *Yahweh*.

and using for ointment the best of the oil—
with never a single thought
for the bleeding wounds of the nation!"[C2]

To punish these social sins and injustices, Amos predicted, the dreaded Foe from the north would overrun the land, laying its forts level, plundering the palaces, and carrying the citizens away into exile.

But his indictment did not rest on charges of social iniquity alone. Amos declared that Yahweh was sick of the national apostasy in religion and despised the heathenish temple rites, even though they might be offered in his name.

Your sacred festivals? I hate them, scorn them;
your sacrifices? I will not smell their smoke;
you offer me your gifts? I will not take them;
you offer fatted cattle? I will not look at them.
No more of your hymns for me!
I will not listen to your lutes.
No. Let justice well up like fresh water,
let honesty roll in full tide."[C3]

No wonder that Amaziah, the high priest at Bethel, feared the fiery prophet from Judah and charged him in the king's name: "Be off to Judah and earn your living there; play the prophet there, but never again at Bethel, for it is the royal shrine, the national temple." But Amos answered: "I am no prophet, no member of any prophets' guild; I am only a shepherd, and I tend sycamores. But the Eternal took me from the flock; the Eternal said to me, 'Go and prophesy to my people Israel.' Now then, listen to what the Eternal says. . . ."[C4] He had his say. He would not rest with less.

Amos opens a new epoch in creative religion. In the course of uttering his fearsome indictment, he revealed a conception of the nature and jurisdiction of Yahweh far in advance of the people of his time. Yahweh was going to *send* the foe from the north, and was about to punish, along with Israel, the Philistines, the Ammonites, the Moabites, and the people of Damascus. Phoenicia and Edom were not beyond his chastisement. Unlimited power over the forces of nature was his; he had brought on a drought three months before the harvest, smitten the fields with blight and mildew, settled a cloud of locusts on the land, slain the soldiers of the army of Israel with an Egyptian plague, and sent a shattering earthquake, resembling the shaking of Sodom and Gomorrah. His might had been exhibited on a world-wide arena.

Hosea

If Amos was the prophet of the righteousness of God, then a younger contemporary of his, Hosea, must be called the prophet of God's love. Unlike Amos, Hosea was a native of the north and enough accustomed to the social conditions there to be less appalled by them; his deepest concern was therefore not moral but religious. The state of the text of his prophecies leaves us in some doubt as to the exact circumstances of his personal life. It seems probable, however, that he married a woman who was unfaithful to him and left him. He could not acknowledge her children as his own; yet, after years of infidelity on her part, he was able to take her back into his home, reclaimed and regenerated. As Hosea contemplated his domestic trials, he began to see a similarity between his inner history and the experience of Yahweh with Israel. Yahweh, too, suffered on account of the unfaithfulness of his people. Unfaithful they were in more than one way. Too blind to see that the political and social doom overhanging them was the inevitable result of abandoning the true God, they were seeking to forestall disaster by the political device of running after "foreign lovers," one party courting Damascus, another Egypt, a third climbing to the throne through alliance with Assyria. Religiously, they were wooing alien gods and futile native baals, their unholy religious paramours. Hosea put into Yahweh's mouth these woeful words, ending on the note of inalienable love, anxious still to forgive:

"Bid her* clear her face of harlotry,
and her breasts of adulterous charms;

or I will strip her naked,
bare as the day she was born;
I will make her like a land forlorn. . . .
On her children I will have no mercy,
for they are born out of wedlock;
their mother has played the harlot,
she who conceived them has been shameless;
she said, 'I will follow my lovers,*
who give me my bread and water,
my wool, flax, oil, and wine.' . . .
Little she knew it was I who had given her
the grain and oil and wine. . . .

"I will bring all her gaiety to an end,
her festivals, new-moons, and sabbaths,
to punish her for all the days
when to the Baals she offered incense,
decking herself with rings and jewels,
running after her lovers,
and forgetting me," says the Eternal.

"Now then I will block up her path
with a thorn-hedge,
and bar the road against her,
till she cannot find her way;
she will pursue her lovers and miss them,
seek them and never find them.
Then at last she will say,
'Let me go back to my first husband,
I fared better with him than today.'

"So I will allure her, . . .
and speak to her heart; . . .
then shall she answer me
as in her youthful days,
when she came up from Egypt's land. . . .

"On that day, the Eternal declares, she shall call me,
        "My husband,' no more 'My Baal';
I will betroth her to me for ever,
betroth her in a bond
of goodness and of justice,
in kindness and in love."C5

It is doubtful whether Hosea received in his time the hearing that Amos did. He quotes his contemporaries as shouting angrily: "A prophet is a crazy fool, a man inspired is a man insane!"C6 He discovered that within the very temple of God men are hostile to the prophet, God's watchman. Surely, if he lived to see

* I.e., Israel.

* I.e., the Baals.

the holocaust of the Assyrian conquest of the Northern Kingdom, he must have felt that the God of love had wooed Israel in vain, and that all he had predicted in that event had been fulfilled.

Isaiah

The Southern Kingdom, meanwhile, came in for its share of prophetic admonition. About 740 B.C., at the close of the reign of King Uzziah, a young man of good family appeared on the streets of Jerusalem in a prophetic role. His name was Isaiah. He had just had an experience of the reality of Yahweh that had moved him deeply. He told of it in these awe-struck words:

"In the year that king Uzziah died, I saw the Lord seated on a high and lofty throne; his trailing robes spread over the temple-floor, and seraphs hovered round him, each with six wings—two covering the face, two covering the body, and two to fly with. They kept calling to one another.
    'Holy, holy, holy, is the Lord of hosts,
    his majestic splendour fills the whole earth!'
At the sound of the chant, the foundations of the threshold shook, and the temple began to fill with smoke. Then I said, 'Alas! I am undone! man of unclean lips that I am, living among a people of unclean lips! I am undone, for mine eyes have seen the King, the Lord of hosts!' But one of the seraphs flew towards me with a live coal in his hand, which he had lifted with tongs from the altar; he touched my mouth with it, saying,
    'Now that this has touched your lips,
    your guilt is gone, your sin forgiven.'
Then I heard the voice of the Lord saying,
    'Whom shall I send?
    Who will go for us?'
I answered, 'Here am I; send me.' "[C7]

Conscious of his divine commission, Isaiah remained active for nearly forty years as prophet to the people at large and special adviser to the Judean kings. In a time of uncertainty he stood unswervingly for trusting in the providence of God. He was the prophet of faith, of confidence in Yahweh beyond doubt or shaking, and he was forever warning the rulers of Jerusalem that the city's safety lay in ceasing to make leagues with the nations round about and relying upon the only trustworthy ally, Yahweh. "Your strength," he warned, "is quiet faith."[C8] In giving advice to Judah's kings this was his constant declaration. Thus, when the Northern Kingdom had been destroyed by the Assyrians (722 B.C.), and the Assyrians were camped before Jerusalem under their mighty general, Sennacherib, he sent panic-stricken King Hezekiah, who besought him to call upon Yahweh, assurances that the city would not be taken.[C9] His prophecy was wondrously fulfilled. The Assyrians suddenly raised the siege.*

But Isaiah was certain that the faithless and wicked would not survive to enjoy future security. They would perish by the sword or languish in miserable exile, far from the comfortable hills of home. As he looked about him, he saw many who were doomed to death or exile. In the manner of Amos, he saw nothing but woe in store for the socially sinning "soldier and warrior, governor and prophet, seer, sheikh, and official," for "the men who add house to house, who join one field to another, till there is room for none but them," for "those who get up early for a drinking bout, who sit far into the night, heated by their wine," or for "those who think themselves so wise, . . . who let off guilty men for a bribe, and deprive the innocent of his rights," "the unruly men," the rulers of the city, "hand in hand with thieves, every one fond of his bribe, keen upon fees, but careless of the orphan's rights, and of the widow's cause."[C10]

Like Amos, too, he records Yahweh's impatience with the elaborate ritual of the temple. Slaughtered rams, the fat from fatted beasts, the blood of bullocks and goats, offerings, the smoke of sacrifice, gatherings at the new moon and on the Sabbath, fasts and festivals are "a weariness" to Yahweh. Though the worshipers stretch out their hands, he will never look at them, and though they offer many a prayer, he

* According to tradition, a plague struck them. But there is evidence that Sennacherib accepted a heavy ransom to withdraw his forces.

383

will not listen. Their hands are stained with blood! They are not really true to Yahweh!

It is not just blind fate that determines events. Yahweh is the moving force and contriver behind human history. He will punish and destroy the wicked everywhere, in Moab, in Edom, in Damascus, in Egypt, but no less in Judah. The wicked will destroy each other by Yahweh's contrivance. Assyria is doomed like all the rest, but meanwhile Yahweh has use for this exterminator of the nations, a use like that of a club swung in anger or a rod wielded in wrath. It will do its work well. Justice will be done even in the plundering and spoiling of the nations.

If Isaiah was as inflexible as Amos in the pronouncement of doom, he saw, however, like Hosea, that pity and love are at the heart of Yahweh's divine plan. The purging of the nations is in the interest of spiritual betterment, a kindlier world.

> "Come, let me put it thus,"
>   the Eternal argues:
> "Scarlet your sins may be,
>   but they can become white as snow,
> they may be red as crimson,
>   and yet turn white as wool.
> If only you are willing to obey . . ."[C11]

After the day of doom, there will be a return of blessedness to the "remnant" who have lived through all the trouble and relied upon Yahweh for all good. Peace, prosperity, and health will be theirs. Upon them Yahweh will have mercy; them he will abundantly pardon.

And here we come to the passages in Isaiah that have had great historic importance—the golden dreams of the new age that shall dawn after the terrible day of wrath and doom is past. After-generations lingered over them and relied upon Isaiah's authority in indulging the eager hope of their fulfillment. Some scholars, it is true, and with good warrant, dispute the authenticity of these passages. In them Isaiah is seen, perhaps before the time was ripe for such prevision, painting a rosy picture of a warless world and of the benign rule of a great prince

of peace, the Messiah, who should spring from the seed and lineage of David and bring in the new day. But these poems of hope and vision came out of the afflictions of his period in history, and so, for our interests in this study, it matters little whether they are from Isaiah's own hand or not. Isaiah was a grieving witness of the spoliation and dismemberment of the Northern Kingdom, and he would quite naturally have dreamed these dreams and seen these visions, which forecast the gathering together from the four corners of the earth of the scattered both of Judah and of Israel too.

Of the prophecies attributed to Isaiah, consider the two notable passages that follow, both probably reworked or even written by later hands, the first dealing with the New Jerusalem, the second with the peaceful prince who is to sit on David's throne in the new age.

> In after days it shall be
> that the Eternal's hill shall rise,
> towering over every hill,
> and higher than the heights.
> To it shall all the nations stream,
> and many a folk exclaim,
> "Come, let us go to the Eternal's hill,
> to the house of Jacob's God,
> that he may instruct us in his ways,
> to walk upon his paths."
> For instruction comes from Sion,
> and from Jerusalem the Eternal's word.
> He will decide the disputes of the nations,
> and settle many a people's case,
> till swords are beaten into ploughshares,
> spears into pruning hooks;
> no nation draws the sword against another,
> no longer shall men learn to fight.
> O household of Jacob, come,
> let us live by the light of the Eternal![C12]

> From the stump of Jesse a shoot shall rise,
>   and a scion from his roots shall flourish;
> on him shall rest the spirit of the Eternal,
>   and the spirit of wisdom and insight,
> the spirit of counsel and strength,
>   the spirit that knows and reverences the Eternal. . . .
> Justice shall gird him up for action,
>   he shall be belted with trustworthiness.

The wolf shall couch then with the lamb,
    the leopard's lair shall be the kid's;
the lion shall eat straw like any ox,
    wolf and lion shall graze side by side,
    herded by a little child;
the cow and the bear shall be friends,
    and their young lie down together;
the infant shall play at the hole of an asp,
    and the baby's feet at the nest of a viper.
None shall injure, none shall kill,
    anywhere on my sacred hill;
for the land shall be as full of the knowledge of the
Eternal as the ocean-bed is full of water.
And the scion of Jesse who is to rally the peoples,
him shall the nations then consult,
    and his seat shall be famous.[C13]

Micah

Inspired by Isaiah, a young man who came up from the country to Jerusalem, Micah by name, began to prophesy on the eve of the fall of the Northern Kingdom in 722 B.C. The prophecies attributed to him are remarkable for two utterances, here quoted, one against the prophets who truckled to popular self-complacence about the supposed inviolability of Jerusalem, the other a notable definition of the essence of spiritual religion.

"And as for the prophets," the Eternal says,
"who lead my folk astray,
who cry 'All's well!' if they get food to eat,
and open war on any who refuse them,
it shall be night for you, devoid of vision,
so dark you cannot divine;
the sun shall set upon the prophets,
daylight shall darken over them,
till seers are shamed,
and the diviners blush,
in mourning, all of them,
because no answer comes from God."
. . . . Listen to this, you. . . .
priests pattering oracles for pay,
prophets divining for money,
. . . saying, "Surely the Eternal is among us;
no evil can befall us!"
Therefore on your account
shall Sion be ploughed up like a field,

Jerusalem shall become a heap of ruins,
    the temple-hill a mere wooded height.[C14]

How shall I enter the Eternal's presence,
    and bow before the God of Heaven?
Shall I come to him with sacrifices,
    with yearling calves to offer?
Would the Eternal care for rams in thousands,
    or for oil flowing in myriad streams?
Shall I offer my first-born son for my sin,
    fruit of my body for guilt of my soul?
O man, he has told you what is good;
    what does the Eternal ask from you
but to be just and kind
and live in quiet fellowship with your God?[C15]

The Deuteronomic Reform

After Micah, the prophets were silent for seventy years. Were they suppressed? That seems likely. For, when the danger of an Assyrian siege of Jerusalem had passed, and King Manasseh sat upon the throne, a serious relapse from ethical Yahwism again set in. Two factors seem to have been in operation. One was a popular ebb-movement back to the Canaanitish form of Yahweh worship. The people were loath to give up the festive gaiety of the high-places and altars. They feared the possible ill effects of relinquishing the magic arts, amulets, household spirits, and images on which they had depended for so long. Besides, the sternly ethical religion of the prophets appeared to them bare and cold compared with the half-heathenish syncretistic religion that so pleased their senses and their imagination. Apostasy became well-nigh universal.

The other factor in the relapse was an official sponsoring of Assyrian cults for reasons of state. Judah was, it must be remembered, a tribute-paying vassal of Assyria. In the very temple itself, therefore, shrines were erected and offerings made to the gods and goddesses of Assyria. Something like this had happened before, but not to the same extent. In an earlier time Solomon had sought to please his many wives by filling Jerusalem with shrines to foreign deities, but he had not erected them in the temple

THE RELIGIONS OF THE NEAR EAST

area, and at best they had only a sub-rosa status. When King Ahaz, in Isaiah's day and against the protests of that prophet, tried to save Judah by accepting vassalage to Assyria and paying tribute for the "protection" of the great king, the obsequious monarch set up an altar before the temple that was a faithful copy of those used in the imperial Assyrian worship. The old Yahweh altar was put to one side; images of Assyrian sun-steeds were given a place in the temple area, and an arbor for the worship of Tammuz (Adonis) was erected on the roof of a temple building. These profanations of Yahweh's holy shrine were suppressed in the puritanical reforms instituted under Isaiah's guidance by the next monarch, Hezekiah, but Assyrian pressure and popular religious laxity sufficed to restore them in the reign of King Manasseh, which followed. But Manasseh went far beyond the point reached by his grandfather, Ahaz. He built altars for the sun- and stargods of Babylon and Nineveh in both the inner and the outer courts of the temple. He set up an asherah within the temple area in honor of Ishtar, queen of heaven, to whom the people flocking there burnt incense, poured out libations, and offered cakes baked with her image on them. Not neglecting the nearer Semitic deities, Manasseh erected altars to various Baals and sacrificed a son by giving him to the fires of the child-devouring Molech.

Between the state policy of fostering Assyrian forms of worship and the popular drift away from strict ethical conduct, the religion of Yahweh seemed about to suffer entire eclipse.

But not so. Two things happened. Suddenly the prophets began to find again their voices—Zephaniah, Habakkuk, Nahum, and the greatest of all, Jeremiah. And as the Assyrian world-empire began crumbling and falling, the grandson of Manasseh, the good King Josiah, directed a great religious reform.

King Josiah's reform came in this way. In 621 B.C. the king authorized the high priest to make a number of overdue repairs on the temple, and the high priest subsequently reported a momentous "find." A previously unknown "book of the Law" had, he said, been discovered, laid away in a hiding place. This book, he declared, dated from the Mosaic era.* When the king saw it and heard its provisions, he rent his garments and charged his councilors to find out from Yahweh if it was genuine, a true statement of divine law. The councilors consulted a prophetess called Huldah, who vouched for its authenticity. The king then summoned the people to a great assemby and led them in swearing a solemn covenant to keep with all earnestness and zeal the statutes written in the newly discovered code.

The reform thus determined upon began with a clean sweep of all the religious practices condemned by the code. The Second Book of Kings gives a vivid account of this phase of the reform:

Then the king commanded Hilkiah, the high priest, and the second priest and the keepers of the threshold to bring out of the temple of the Lord all the vessels that were made for the Baal and the Asherah and for all the host of the heavens; and he burned them outside Jerusalem in the limekilns by the Kidron, and carried their ashes to Bethel. He also removed the idolatrous priests . . . and those who offered sacrifices to the Baal, to the sun, the moon, and the constellations, and all the host of the heavens. . . . He tore down the houses of the devotees of the fertility cult which were in the house of the Lord, where the women wove tunics for the Asherah. . . . He tore down the high places of the Satyrs, which stood at the entrance of the gate of Joshua. . . . He also defiled Topheth, which is in the valley of the son of Hinnom, that no man might make his son or his daughter pass through the fire to Molech. He took away the horses which the kings of Judah had given to the sun, . . . and he burned the chariots of the sun with fire. Also the altars which were on the roof, and the altars which Manasseh had made in the two courts of the house of the Lord the king demolished and beat them down there, and cast the dust into the Brook Kidron. Moreover the high places that were east of Jerusalem, which Solomon had built for Ashtart, the abomination of the Sidonians, and for Chemosh, the abomination of Moab, and for Milcom, the

* Now embodied in the Book of Deuteronomy, this document is known to scholars as "D" or the Deuteronomic code. It was undoubtedly a contemporary attempt to codify Hebrew ethical law; its "finding" was *possibly* a pious fraud, honestly intended to promote the public good.

abomination of the Ammonites, the king defiled. He shattered the sacred pillars, and cut down the sacred poles, and filled their places with the bones of men.[A7]

The king did not stop with Jerusalem and its immediate environs. He ranged through the whole of Judah and as far as Bethel, demolishing and beating to dust the altars, pillars, and asherahs of the high-places and sanctuaries.

One very important feature of the reform followed upon this. The king fetched away all the priests from the sanctuaries of Yahweh outside of Jerusalem and centralized Yahweh worship at Jerusalem. It was held that proper sacrifices could be offered only there.

Further phases of the reform were concerned with the ethical injunctions of the Deuteronomic code. A new social idealism spread through the land. The code called for greater humanitarianism toward slaves, more consideration for the needs of the poor. The old law of blood-vengeance stood condemned in the light of the new law running: "Everyone is to be put to death for his own sin."[A8] Though savage and cruel elements still remained to mark the new code with reflections of a more primitive era, there was genuine ethical advance toward justice and righteousness.

But the reform begun with such thoroughness failed of complete success. This was in large part due to its too great severity in one respect—the centralizing of religion in Jerusalem. This had the effect of subtraction from the local community for the sake of addition to Jerusalem. The Jerusalem priesthood now had an absolute control over Yahwism and, moreover, a vested interest in it. The rural and village priesthoods were abolished, and the rural common people, expected now to go to Jerusalem "to find their chief joy," suffered a greatly diminished sense of the immediacy of the divine presence in their localities. Yahweh, truly enough, had become ineffably holy and transcendent, and his stern will was clearly known from the pages of a sacred book, but he was a less intimate presence, not so near as before. The common people, finding it hard to attain to so high and intellectual a faith, relapsed disastrously into the

emotionally more satisfying rites outlawed now by the Law as well as by the prophets.

Jeremiah

This great prophet, a man of intensely human quality but condemned by circumstances to the distasteful public role of a Cassandra, began to prophesy when in his early twenties. He came of a priestly family, which before the Josianic reforms ministered in the sanctuary at Anatoth, a small town four miles northeast of Jerusalem. Stirred by the disaster threatening his wayward nation, he felt called by Yahweh to prophecy.

The word of the Lord came to me, saying,
"Before I formed you in the womb I knew you,
And before you were born I set you apart,
I appointed you a prophet to the nations."
  Then said I,
"Ah, Lord God! I cannot speak;
For I am only a youth."
  But the Lord said to me,
"Do not say, 'I am only a youth';
For to all to whom I send you shall you go,
And all that I command you shall you speak . . ."
  Then the Lord stretched forth his hand, and touched
my mouth. And the Lord said to me,
  "See! I put my words in your mouth."[A9]

The prophetic ministry that Jeremiah performed was mostly that of warning the nation—always in vain—of disasters that might be forestalled or averted with Yahweh's help. So difficult was his task that at times, in later days, his heart failed him, and he gave vent to very human outbursts at the thanklessness of it all.

I have become a laughing-stock all day long,
Everyone mocks me.
As often as I speak, I must cry out,
I must call, "Violence and spoil!"
. . . . If I say, "I will not think of it,
Nor speak any more in his name,"
It is in my heart like a burning fire,
  Shut up in my bones;

387

I am worn out with holding it in . . .
Cursed be the day on which I was born,
The day on which my mother bore me—
      Let it not be blessed!
Cursed be the man who brought the good news to my
    father,
"A son is born to you"—
      Wishing him much joy!
. . . Why came I out of the womb,
To see trouble and sorrow,
That my days might be spent in shame?[A10]

But although he became highly unpopular, Jeremiah never shrank from saying exactly what he felt the Lord meant him to say. When kings consulted him, he never broke the bad news gently. No threatening mob could make him speak softly. He was not an ingratiating person. Only one loyal friend stood by him through all the bitter days when he was reviled by kings, princes, common people, and fellow prophets. This was Baruch, his private secretary, the man who wrote down Jeremiah's prophecies at the prophet's dictation and afterward added valuable biographical notes to explain how the prophecies came to be uttered and what consequences then ensued.

Jeremiah came at one of the most difficult and perplexing periods in Judah's entire history. He began his career when the Assyrian empire was in decline and a terrifying invasion of Scythian plunderers swept down through Syria and along the Palestinian coast toward Egypt. Judah was in a panic of fear. Not long after the Scythian hordes withdrew into the north, a momentous change occurred in the east: Nineveh fell, and the Assyrian empire gave place to the Babylonian. Immediately there began a titanic contest between Egypt and Babylon for supremacy in the east. Judah became the seat of international intrigue, Egypt hoping to win to its side the little hill country, with its almost impregnable fortress-capital, and in good part succeeding. Yet during the tortuous contest the good King Josiah fell in battle opposing the very Egyptians who proposed to be his allies. Shortly afterward, Egypt met with a stunning defeat at the hands of the Babylonians at Carche-

mish. Judah, now bereft of its good king and of its boastful ally from the Nile, came again under the control of an Oriental power. Heavy annual tribute was exacted of her by the Babylonians. Then Egypt resumed her intrigues, making fresh promises. In Jerusalem king and people, hoping for relief from the paying of tribute, lent a ready ear.

But Jeremiah had the clear eye and good sense to see the folly of rebelling against the mighty Chaldaean power. He aroused the fierce displeasure of his compatriots by denying that Yahweh would keep the city inviolable, should Judah rebel and the Babylonians attack. Rather the contrary, he declared. He appeared one day in the temple to deliver a scathing arraignment of the apostate people, and shouted: "Thus says the Lord: 'I will make this house like [ruined] Shiloh, and will make this city a curse to all the nations of the earth.'" His life was immediately in danger, for we read:

When Jeremiah had finished speaking all that the Lord had commanded him to speak to all the people, the priests and the prophets laid hold on him, saying,

"You shall die! How dare you prophesy in the name of the Lord, saying, 'This house shall become like Shiloh, and this city shall become an uninhabited waste'?"

Thereupon all the people crowded around Jeremiah in the house of the Lord.

When the princes of Judah heard the news, they came up from the palace and took their seats at the entrance to the new gate of the house of the Lord. Then the priests and the prophets addressed the princes and all the people saying,

"This man deserves to die; for he has prophesied against this city in the terms which you have heard."

Then Jeremiah addressed the princes and all the people, saying,

"The Lord sent me to prophesy against this house and this city all the words which you have heard. But now, if you amend your ways and your doings, and listen to the voice of the Lord your God, the Lord will repent of the evil which he has pronounced against you. As for myself, see! I am in your hands. Do to me as you think right and proper. Only be well assured of this, that, if you put me to death, you will be bringing innocent blood upon yourselves, upon this city, and upon its people; for the Lord has truly sent me to you, to speak these words in your hearing."

This firm speech completely changed the situation. Jeremiah was saved.

Then the princes and all the people said to the priests and the prophets,
"This man does not deserve to die; for he has spoken to us in the name of the Lord our God."[A11]

It required only that the elders of the land should remind the assembly how Micah had prophesied in an earlier day that Jerusalem should become a ruin,* and Jeremiah was released.

It will be noted that Jeremiah's fellow-prophets united with the priests against him. Their constant opposition was a sore point. On one occasion he appeared in the streets with a wooden yoke upon his neck. This, he said, symbolized the yoke of the king of Babylon that would be laid upon the necks of the people. While he was walking through the temple, a rival prophet named Hananiah stepped forward, bringing an opposite word from the Lord. He took the yoke from Jeremiah's neck and broke it, saying: "Thus says the Lord: 'So will I break the yoke of Nebuchadnezzar, king of Babylon, from the neck of all the nations within two years.'" Jeremiah retired to ponder this, and then came back to cry out that Hananiah, the false prophet, had made the people trust in a lie, and that the Lord would bind them with iron. He would put an unbreakable "yoke of iron on the neck of all the nations," that they might "serve Nebuchadnezzar, the king of Babylon."[A12]

The other prophets in Jerusalem seemed to Jeremiah no better than Hananiah. He pronounced severe judgment on them:

> Thus says the Lord of hosts:
> "Listen not to the words of the prophets
>   who prophesy to you!
> They fill you with vain hopes;
> They speak a vision from their own minds,
> Not from the mouth of the Lord. . . .

"Behold, I am against the prophets who deal in lying dreams," is the oracle of the Lord, "and tell them, and

* Micah 3:9–12. See p. 385, supra.

mislead my people by their lies and their bombast—when I neither sent them nor commissioned them."[A13]

When Judah recklessly revolted against Babylon and the city was invested by the army of Nebuchadnezzar, Jeremiah exhausted the patience of the princes by openly telling the people that the city was doomed, and that those who stayed in it would die by the sword, famine, and pestilence, but those who would go and surrender to the Babylonians would escape and have their lives given them as a prize of war. The rulers of Jerusalem naturally complained to the king that Jeremiah was disheartening the soldiers defending the city, and they urged that he be put out of the way. So Jeremiah was thrown into a dry cistern in the court of the royal guard, where he sank in the mud and was left to die. Had not an Ethiopian guard pricked the king's conscience with a description of Jeremiah's plight, he would surely have perished; as it happened, the king had the prophet secretly drawn up to terra firma. He was not set at liberty again until the city fell to the Babylonians.

This was not the first nor the last time Jeremiah was in danger. Once he had been arrested and put in the stocks for twenty-four hours; at one time his fellow-townsmen at Anatoth had plotted to put him to death. He and Baruch had had to go into hiding during the reign of King Jehoiakim after that monarch became coldly enraged during a private palace-reading of a scroll of Jeremiah's sermons; the king cut up the scroll with his penknife piece by piece as it was being read to him and flung the pieces into the fire in the brazier before him, and then ordered Jeremiah's arrest. The danger passed, but the prophet was never to know peace thereafter. When Jerusalem was destroyed in 586 B.C., Nebuchadnezzar freed him as a friend and allowed him to remain in Judah along with the handful of citizens—the rabble really—who were not taken into exile. Jeremiah tried to reconcile those left behind with him to their lot, but Gedaliah, the able governor appointed by Nebuchadnezzar, was assassinated, and the conspirators kidnapped Jeremiah and carried him to Egypt, where he prophesied briefly before he came to his unknown, perhaps violent, end.

A reading of Jeremiah's sermons brings clearly before us his forthright, gloomy, suffering personality. The passages in which he predicts dire doom are still harrowing to read and must have been almost unendurable to hear. Certainly they burn with the prophet's own anguish. Yet Jeremiah was not an ultimate pessimist; he had grounds for hope. He predicted that after Yahweh had finished using Babylon as the means of accomplishing his just punishment of the nations, Babylon itself would be punished. Then the people of Judah, and those also of Israel, would "serve aliens no more" but would return to Judah to "serve the Lord their God, and David their king," whom Yahweh would raise up for them.

> "For I am with you to save you,"
>   is the oracle of the Lord;
> "And I will make a full end of all the nations
>   among whom I scattered you;
> But of you will I not make a full end."[A14]

Having corrected them "in just measure," Yahweh would make a "new covenant" with his people, Jeremiah said.

At this point Jeremiah made an original and distinctive contribution to the prophetic tradition. The new covenant that was to be made was to be between Yahweh and redeemed *individuals*. Former prophets had concentrated on the public, socially experienced relationship between Yahweh and the Hebrews—the basis of the old covenant. Jeremiah advanced the idea of a valid, subjective experience of relationship between Yahweh and the individual.

"Behold, days are coming," is the oracle of the Lord, "when I will make a new covenant with the household of Israel and with the household of Judah, not like the covenant which I made with their fathers on the day that I took them by the hand to lead them out of the land of Egypt—that covenant of mine which they broke, so that I had to reject them—but this is the covenant which I will make with the household of Israel. . . . I will put

my law within them, and will write it on their hearts . . . And they shall teach no more every one his neighbor, and every one his brother, saying, 'Know the Lord'; for all of them shall know me, from the least of them to the greatest of them."

Jeremiah accompanied this prediction with a succinct statement of individual responsibility:

"In those days shall they say no more,
    'The fathers have eaten sour grapes,
    And the children's teeth are set on edge';
but everyone shall die for his own guilt—everyone who eats the sour grapes shall have his own teeth set on edge."[A15]

In other words, Jeremiah brought men face to face with God as individuals who were responsible directly to him for their conduct. They could no longer say that he dealt with men only through their group relationships.

This was a proposition of great importance, for its logical corollary was: if the human relationship to God is a direct and personal relationship, then the approach to God through temple sacrifice may not be all-important, may even be no longer requisite to the highest spiritual living of the individual.

V   The Babylonian Exile

As so often happens with fanatical nationalist groups, the pro-Egyptian party in Jerusalem brought about the very disaster they most hoped to avert— the collapse of Hebrew national sovereignty. They persuaded the aging King Jehoiakim to withhold tribute from Nebuchadnezzar, king of Babylon, and to make a stand for national independence, relying upon Egypt's military backing. When Nebuchadnezzar learned of this, he moved quickly, displaying in every decision an unyielding determination to crush Judean rebelliousness for good and all. In 597 B.C., he invested Jerusalem with his full forces. After a three months' siege the new king, Jehoiakin, who had just succeeded to the throne,* surrendered the city in order to avoid its total destruction. Nebuchadnezzar looted the temple and carried away captive to Babylon the king and ten thousand of the citizens, or, as the Second Book of Kings describes them, "all the nobles, and all the renowned warriors, and all the craftsmen, and all the smiths," as well as "all the strong men fit for war."[A16] At Babylon the king was thrown into prison and the people were settled as colonists on the river Chebar, a large canal running to the southeast out of Babylon. Those who were left behind in Judah were placed under the rule of the deported king's uncle, Zedekiah, the third son of Josiah. In 588, after nine years of wavering loyalty to Nebuchadnezzar, Zedekiah too rebelled.

This time Jerusalem was not spared. In 586 B.C. after a siege lasting a year and a half, during which the Egyptians coming up to relieve the beleaguered city were decisively driven back by the besiegers, Jerusalem was taken. The Babylonians and their allies † systematically looted, burned, and destroyed all the buildings in the city, including the temple, whose holy ark was never again heard of, and they laboriously tore down the city walls. The city was so thoroughly laid in ruins that it was not completely rebuilt for over a century and a half. Before being carried away in chains to Babylon, King Zedekiah was forced to witness the execution of his sons and then had his own eyes put out. All of the inhabitants of Jerusalem, except Jeremiah and a handful of the poorest and lowliest citizens, were taken away. The towns around Jerusalem were drained of their upper classes. Meanwhile, many of those who could do so fled southward toward Egypt. The nation was disrupted. One part was in Babylonia. Another portion reached Egypt and settled in scattered communities along the Nile and its delta. A third portion stayed on in the ruined homeland. So profound was the change in national status that historians referring to the people who survived the fall of Jerusalem in 586

drop the name Hebrew and speak of them henceforward as Jews.

Yet the Babylonian exile was not as disastrous to the Judean captives as the Assyrian deportation had been to the lost ten tribes. Nebuchadnezzar's hostility was of a political kind; it had only been directed against the continuance of Hebrew national sovereignty and not against the people as individuals. Once the Jews had been transported to the environs of Babylon, he allowed them comparative freedom. They could live together and follow their old ways of life and culture without disturbance. The region in which they were settled was part of a rich alluvial plain, intersected by irrigating canals, and therefore from an agricultural standpoint far superior to Palestine. Moreover, it lay between two of the greatest cities of the world—Babylon and Nippur—and hence provided economic advantages of an unusual kind, so that those who made themselves at home and developed their opportunities throve wonderfully.

At first, of course, it was hard to feel at home. Of this we have the clearest sort of evidence. The Old Testament contains no passage so full of mingled pathos and unhappy rage as the Psalm that runs:

> By the rivers of Babylon,
> There we sat down, and wept,
> When we remembered Zion.
> Upon the poplars, in the midst of her,
> We hung up our harps.
> For there our captors
> Demanded of us songs,
> And our tormentors, mirth:
> "Sing us some of the songs of Zion."
>
> How could we sing the songs of the Lord
> In a foreign land?
> If I forget you, O Jerusalem,
> May my right hand fail me!
> May my tongue cleave to my palate,
> If I do not remember you;
> If I set not Jerusalem
> Above my highest joy!
>
> Remember, O Lord, against the Edomites,
> The day of Jerusalem!
> They who said, "Raze it, raze it,

---

* Jehoiakim died during the siege.
† The Edomites, Samaritans, Ammonites, and others who came in for the kill.

To its very foundations!"
O daughter of Babylon, destructive one,
Blessed be he who requites to you
The treatment that you dealt out to us!
Blessed be he who seizes your little ones,
And dashes them to pieces upon a rock!"[A17]

But the mood of irreconcilability with their lot passed. Economically the situation became better than tolerable. Those who farmed the rich soil found themselves harvesting big crops. Stony Judah had never yielded such. Many Jews, freed from farming, entered government service as soldiers and officials. Others, turning their economic opportunities to advantage, became merchants and traders, following a direction that many of their ethnic brethren were even now pursuing in Egypt and Syria and were to pursue increasingly down the centuries. It would not be long now before their great success would lead a Jewish writer (the author of Esther) to recognize the existence of anti-Semitism in Babylonia. He would make Haman say to King Xerxes in Susa: "There is a certain people scattered abroad and dispersed among the peoples throughout all the provinces of your kingdom, and their laws are different from every other people. . . . If it please the king, let it be prescribed that they be destroyed."[A18] The Jews had entered upon the long and troublous course of anti-Semitic persecution across the face of the earth.

The Origin of the Synagogue

Yahwism had now to pass a crucial test. Would the exiled people consider that their Palestinian God had failed them and that the deities of foreign peoples were greater? Or would the viewpoint of the major prophets, that Yahweh was with his people everywhere and directed the destinies of other peoples besides the chosen race, prevail? Apparently, some gave up Yahweh to follow the gods that had prospered Babylon. An older apostasy recurred in Egypt. Among the refugees who kidnapped Jeremiah and dragged him off to Egypt were men and women who thus defied the old prophet: "We will not listen to you, but will assuredly . . . [offer] sacrifices to the queen of the heavens,* and . . . [pour] libations to her, as we did, both we and our fathers, our kings and our princes, in the cities of Judah and in the streets of Jerusalem. For then we had plenty to eat, and were well, and met with no trouble; but since we gave up offering sacrifices to the queen of the heavens . . . we have been destitute of all things, and have been consumed by sword and famine."[A19] These folk were lost to Yahwism. But those with whom the future of Judaism lay were not shaken in their faith: it widened and deepened. Yahweh was in Egypt and in Babylonia with them; of this they were assured.

To the faithful in Babylonia there was only one place in the world where sacrifices could be offered to Yahweh, and that was on the altar in the temple at Jerusalem. This means of approach to the High God was now denied to them. But they could draw near to him in other ways. They could, for example, gather together on the Sabbath day in their homes, read to each other the scrolls of the Law and the writings of the prophets. Besides these they could read aloud the early histories of their people, in various recensions, not yet finally combined into a canonical text. After reading from these texts, someone might lead in prayer. It became a practice to hold such gatherings every Sabbath day.† Out of them came the synagogue of later days. The sermon so familiar to Christian church-goers originated here too, for one of the chief features of the Sabbath meetings of the Jews in Babylon came to be an exposition and interpretation of some portion of the sacred texts directed to the correction or comfort of the hearers.

Along with the establishment of this form of worship there came a marked increase in literary activity. Copies of the older writings were prepared for use on

---

* Ashtart (= Ishtar).
† Some authorities think this custom had already been begun in the villages of Judah after the Deuteronomic reform, as an attempt to worship God without animal sacrifice.

the Sabbath day and during the festivals of the Jewish year, and those who feared that the new generation growing up in Babylon might forget the traditions that were still unrecorded made haste to write these traditions down and to revise and enlarge the older histories and codes by addition and expansion. Writings also appeared reflecting contemporary religious insights. Many psalms, such as the one quoted on a previous page, were composed. And two great prophets appeared to pour out their inspired thoughts in speech and writing.

Ezekiel

Very little is known about the life of Ezekiel. It is possible that much of the book credited to him was written in his name at a later time. He was apparently a leader of what has been called the Deuteronomic circle among the exiles—those who leaned heavily upon the Deuteronomic code and interpreted the whole of Hebrew history in its light, going so far as to rewrite much of Judges, and the books of Samuel and Kings in accordance with Deuteronomic value judgments. Ezekiel came of a priestly family of Jerusalem, was carried captive to Babylonia in 597 B.C., and lived in the Jewish community by the river Chebar. For twenty-two years or more he was active as prophet and self-styled "watchman to the household of Israel,"[A20] exercising pastoral oversight and care over his fellow-exiles and dreaming always of the restoration and regeneration of his people.

In his visions and allegories, written down in fervid and florid phrase, a major concern emerged: when the exile should end, as it soon would, and the people returned to the homeland, what was to be the constitution under which they were to live, and especially, how were the services in the restored temple to be conducted? Here Ezekiel showed himself to be what he has been called, "a priest in the prophet's mantle."[E2] Whereas Jeremiah realized in his day that the temple and its divine services would soon come to an end, but that he could do without them, Ezekiel knew that "it was only a question of time before the temple and its divine services would be restored, and he could not do without them."[E3] So he concentrated on envisioning their restoration and did it in detail and with great enthusiasm. His minute descriptions of the temple-to-be and its ceremonies and his statement of the philosophy of worship that inspired him had a very great influence on later Judaism.

Ezekiel's philosophy of worship combined the new emphasis on individual responsibility—new since Jeremiah and the issuance of the Deuteronomic code—with an exalted conception of Yahweh as a being sublimely transcendant and holy. The sinner needing pardon would not find Yahweh melting with love and forgiveness at the first sign of remorse. The holiness of Yahweh required the sacrificial approach of chastened individuals gathering in the temple in a state of physical and ritual purity, under the guidance of expert priests. In his infinite sanctity, Yahweh had now withdrawn so far from the world of men that it was only through intermediaries, human and divine,* that he could be reached.

Perhaps this emphasis on the remoteness and absoluteness of the Lord God was an effect of the expanding view of his movements in history that the exiles had. Did not the Lord God rule the nations with a rod of iron? Was he not using individual men and single nations as means to inscrutable but holy and righteous ends? Was he not bent upon making his name known to all mankind? Questions such as these oppressed the minds of Ezekiel and his contemporaries and made them aware that God had other objects in view than just the showing of loving kindness and tender mercy to a chosen few. Ezekiel expressed their awareness in one saying of his:

"Thus says the Lord God: It is not for your sake that I am about to act, O household of Israel, but for my holy name which you have caused to be profaned among the nations to which you came. . . . and when I restore my holiness in their sight, through my dealings with you, the nations shall know that I am the Lord."[A21]

* Priests and angels.

Nevertheless, the temple alone could offer the conditions of a proper approach to such a God—an approach of purified persons, in the beauty of holiness, seeking to add to the glory of God by fulfilling his Law.

Deutero-Isaiah

To Deutero-Isaiah, the great unknown prophet of the exile, scholars have given a cumbrous name meaning Second Isaiah. His prophecies are preserved in the latter part of the book of Isaiah, approximately from the fortieth chapter on. Nothing about his life or identity is known, but fortunately his mind and spirit do not thus elude us. In ethical and religious insight his prophecies bring us to the culminating point of the Old Testament.

The central problem with which Deutero-Isaiah was concerned loomed large in the minds of the exiled Jews. It was the problem of the evil that had befallen them. Why had Yahweh brought so much suffering upon them? The old answer that it was because of their sins, although acknowledged to explain much, was not wholly satisfactory, for it was evident that the people of Babylonia, who now prospered, were as bad as, even worse than, the Jews had ever been. Deutero-Isaiah did not reject the conventional explanation; he saw truth in it. But he did not think the sufferings of the Jews could be entirely explained on that basis. He set his people's trials against a world background. They were, he declared, a part of Yahweh's plan of eventual world redemption.

The conception here is magnificent in scope. Yahweh becomes without any qualification the only God: "there is no other." His sphere of action is the whole world. Whatever he does must be seen against a cosmic background.

> Have you not known? have you not heard?
> The Lord is a God everlasting,
> The Creator of the ends of the earth.[A22]

He is the first, and the last: "before me was no God formed, and after me there shall be none."[A23] He alone created the heavens and the earth, and he gives breath to the peoples. He controls all history, forms the light and creates darkness, makes peace and creates evil. This holy Lord of Hosts, who says from his seat of world power, "As the heavens are higher than the earth, so are my ways higher than your ways, and my thoughts than your thoughts,"[A24] nevertheless dwells as an immanent savior and redeemer in the hearts of the contrite and humble in spirit.

> For thus says the high and exalted One,
> Who dwells enthroned for ever, and whose name is Holy:
> "I dwell enthroned on high, as the Holy One,
> But with him also that is contrite and humble in spirit."[A25]

Furthermore, God's redemptive purpose is not limited to one area or one people. It is universal; he means to save all mankind, Gentiles as well as Jews.

At this point Deutero-Isaiah brought forward his most original conception, the finest fruit of his experience of living among the Gentiles. To bring the saving knowledge of himself and his holy will to all mankind God needs a messenger, a servant. Israel is that servant and may say:

> Listen, you coast lands, to me;
> Hearken, you peoples afar!
> The Lord called me from birth,
> From my mother's womb he gave me my name. . . .
> He said to me, "You are my servant,
> Israel, through whom I will show forth my glory."[A26]

> "I the Eternal have called you of set purpose,
> And have taken you by the hand;
> I have formed you for the rescuing of my people,
> For a light to the nations."[C16]

The Jews were thus a chosen people, chosen not to be the recipients of unearned favors, but to serve as bearers of light. It was not that they were to be active missionaries, it would seem, but that in their characters and lives the nations would see the presence of the Lord.

But, alas, they had been blind and deaf to their

world mission and had had to be refined and purified "in the furnace of suffering." The Lord had to give up the chosen people to spoilers and plunderers because they had sinned and would not walk in his ways, nor listen to his instructions. "So he poured upon them the heat of his anger, and the fierceness of war."[A27] This punishment had to be. It was forced upon God by the chosen people's sins. But the prophet brought comforting word that the Lord God now declared that Jerusalem's guilt was paid in full, and her people would therefore not have to suffer any more afflictions.

The suffering had not been in vain. Not only had it purified the nation, but it had gone straight to the hearts of onlooking Gentiles and vicariously redeemed them. This conception is wrought out in one of the greatest religious odes ever written. The nations of the earth are heard saying of the Suffering Servant:

He was despised, and rejected of men;
A man of sorrows, and acquainted with grief:
    And as one from whom men hide their face he was
      despised,
    And we esteemed him not.

Surely he hath borne our griefs,
And carried our sorrows:
    Yet we did esteem him stricken,
    Smitten of God, and afflicted.

But he was wounded for our transgressions,
He was bruised for our iniquities:
    The chastisement of our peace was upon him;
    And with his stripes we are healed.

All we like sheep have gone astray;
We have turned every one to his own way:
    And the Lord hath laid on him
    The iniquity of us all.[F]

Deeply moved, the Gentile kings and their people understand at last that through the sufferings of God's servant, Israel, righteousness is recommended to them and they are led to practice it. The ethical character of the true God has been revealed to them in the moral nature of his stricken servant.

Thus Deutero-Isaiah justified the ways of God to the Jews. But he not only looked into the past, he saw into the future. The next phase of God's redemptive plan, he declared, was a glorious restoration of the Jews to Jerusalem, where the work of redemption could proceed into all the world as from a center, amid the joy of all believers. This was to be effected through Cyrus, the Persian war-lord, who by God's direction would tread down rulers as a potter tramples clay, overthrow Babylon, and release the Jews. (We shall see that Cyrus fulfilled these expectations.) Then, after their return to the homeland, the Jews would minister to the nations in the Lord's name. All the world would flock to Jerusalem to worship God, saying,

"With you alone is God, and there is no other,
      no God besides;
  Truly with you God hides himself,
      the God of Israel is a savior."[A28]

But not only would the world come to Jerusalem; Israel would go out into the world.

Thus says the Lord God:
"Behold! I will lift up my hands to the nations, . . .
And they shall bring your sons in their bosom,
And your daughters shall be carried on their shoulders.
And kings shall be your foster fathers,
And their queens your nursing-mothers."[A29]

Salvation would reach to the ends of the earth. Evil would be destroyed. Eternal light would arise.

Through the appeal of his high moral idealism, Deutero-Isaiah was to have a great influence on the best minds of later Judaism, and even more was he to influence early Christianity. Some understood him; others did not. His prophecies were searched again and again by those who waited expectantly for the coming of a Messiah. His descriptions of the suffering servant were so concrete and individualized that later generations readily concluded that he was speaking in them not of a nation but of a Messiah, and so they looked for a person who should some day redeem the world through his suffering. The early Christians found in Jesus of Nazareth one who fitted these descriptions perfectly.

VI The Rise of Judaism in the Restoration Period

In 538 B.C. Cyrus the Great took Babylon and made it the capital of a new empire, which was ultimately to stretch from the Persian Gulf to the Black Sea and from the Indus River to the Greek cities on the Ionian coast. When he looked about him, he found grouped together in the heart of Babylonia an unassimilated captive people, with ways different from the ways of other peoples, and on inquiring about them, he heard their plaints. In order to win their friendship and at the same time to have them go off to the border near Egypt and set up a buffer state, he gave them permission to return to Jerusalem. The return so longed for by the first generation of exiles was now possible.

The Return to Judah and Jerusalem

An expedition of returning Jews was organized at once. According to later Jewish historians, Cyrus issued a decree giving them a privileged status; he not only restored to them the temple vessels carried away by Nebuchadnezzar in 586 B.C., but even made funds available for the expedition! Apparently, the leaders of the return were two: Zerubbabel, a grandson of King Jehoiakin and hence as a lineal descendant of King David a person with Messianic possibilities, and Joshua, a priest of the highly revered Zadokite branch of the Levite tribe. Though it was evident from the first that many Jews were not going to return, for Babylonia was their home now, thousands did. The latter were idealistically described by Ezra a century later as those "whose spirit God had aroused to go up to build the house of the Lord which is in Jerusalem."[A30]

Upon arrival at Jerusalem, the first act of the returning exiles was to erect an altar on the site of the ruined temple and begin regular morning and evening sacrifices. The rebuilt altar was made the center of a communal life organized on lines like those suggested by the prophet Ezekiel. The temple area was gradually cleared of debris, and amid shouts of joy and the weeping of the older folks the foundation stone was laid for the reconstruction of the temple.

But the community soon proved unable to proceed with the task. Most of the people chose to live in the surrounding fields and villages, not in Jerusalem itself, where the heaps of burnt-over ruins discouraged home-making. But conditions outside of Jerusalem were scarcely better. Virtually no economic opportunities awaited the newcomers. Moreover, the "peoples of the land," that is, the non-exiles, had taken possession of the properties of the exiled upper classes and were undoubtedly annoyed to see so many returning claimants to old homesteads, for they could themselves claim sixty or seventy years of squatter's rights. But there were further factors of contention. The returning exiles had for seventy years idealized Jerusalem and the Law, and they looked with disdain upon the non-exiles, because they had lapsed from the Deuteronomic standard and had, moreover, intermarried with Edomites, Ammonites, and Samaritans. So, on their part, the non-exiles, disgruntled at being treated as religious and social inferiors, withheld cooperation from the rebuilding of the temple and other reconstruction projects. No wonder, then, that a stubborn depression, both spiritual and economic, overwhelmed the community, and for fifteen years the temple lay untouched.

Then, at the urging of the prophets Haggai and Zechariah, the rebuilding was resumed. Haggai had indignantly scolded: how could the people expect prosperity as long as they left the Lord's house in ruins? Both prophets encouraged the community to resume the work quickly because of the great hope they held out: there would be a shaking up of the world powers and Judah would again become an independent kingdom, with Zerubbabel, the descendant of David, becoming their crowned head as Yahweh's Messianic "Chosen One." This hope animating them, the Jews made haste to complete the temple. It was not like Solomon's, but it was strongly built and in the correct dimensions. Then they settled back to wait for signs of the Lord's favor. And no change in the situation came.

A century passed. The prophetic hopes concerning the restoration were plainly unrealized. Were they unrealizable? Some apparently thought so, for on every hand there were multiplying signs of ebbing faith. The writer of the book of Malachi, who prophesied at this time, accused the people of slackening zeal, of cynicism, of lack of respect for Yahweh. He said they did not pay their tithes properly, brought defective animals to the sacrifices, were not reverent during the temple ceremonies. How could they hope for the Lord's blessing?

When knowledge of this state of affairs reached Babylonia, the faithful Jews there were disturbed. One of their number, a young man who was a favorite cup-bearer to King Artaxerxes (I or II?), on receiving fresh reports of the woeful condition of Jerusalem and its inhabitants, came before the king at Susa with a sad countenance. The king inquired the reason for his melancholy and, learning the cause, generously sent the young man, whose name was Nehemiah, upon a special mission, with the powers of a governor, to Jerusalem to oversee the rebuilding of the city's walls and to reorganize the community. Nehemiah set out for Jerusalem, accompanied by army officers and horsemen and provided with enabling letters to the authorities. Before or about the same time Ezra the Scribe and some seventeen hundred Babylonian Jews, many of them hand-picked for the work of reform, left for Jerusalem to push the spiritual renewal that was to parallel Nehemiah's rebuilding of the walls.* The story of Nehemiah's successful leader-

* It is here assumed that Ezra and Nehemiah were in Jerusalem about the same time. The facts are open to another interpretation. It is possible that Ezra arrived first and that Nehemiah came later and completed the work which Ezra had begun. Scholars are divided on the sequence of events.

ship is dramatically told in the autobiography bearing his name. It was due entirely to his executive genius and energy that the breaches in the walls and the burnt gates of the city were repaired at last, after over 150 years of lying in ruin.

The Establishment of a Priestly State

Seeking the spiritual renewal of the community, Ezra the Scribe summoned the Jews before the Water Gate. Here the assembly heard read to them a book of the Law (presumably the holiness code from Leviticus*) and bound themselves by a solemn covenant and oath to observe its provisions. A new theocratic state was inaugurated, with power vested in the priests. It re-established the Mosaic covenant, but it might be called a new one at the same time. What occupied the center of attention—then and for the next four hundred years—becomes clear in the following quotation from the pledge the assembly adopted under oath:

"We make and sign a binding covenant . . . and take oath, under penalty of a curse, to walk in the law of God which was given by Moses the servant of God, and to be careful to observe all the commands of the LORD our Lord, and his ordinances and his statutes; and that we will not give our daughters to the peoples of the land or take their daughters as wives for our sons; and that, if the peoples of the land bring wares or any grain on the Sabbath day to sell, we will not buy from them on the Sabbath or on a holy day; and that in the seventh year we will leave the land fallow and refrain from the exaction of any debt.

"We also lay upon ourselves the charge to give the third part of a shekel yearly for the service of the house of our God, for the bread that is arranged in layers, and for the regular burnt-offering, for the sabbaths, the new moons, the fixed festivals, and the holy things, and for the sin-offerings to make atonement for Israel, and for all the work of the house of our God. Moreover, we will cast lots, the priests, the Levites, and the people, concerning the wood-offering, to bring it into the house of our God, . . . to burn upon the altar of the LORD our God . . . ;

* Leviticus xvii–xxvi.

and to bring the first produce of our ground and the first of all fruit of every kind of tree year by year to the house of the LORD; also the first-born of our sons and of our cattle, as it is written in the law, and the firstlings of our herds and our flocks, . . . and our first batch of baking, our contributions, the fruit of every kind of tree, the wine, and the oil, to the priests in the chambers of the house of our God; and the tithes of our ground to the Levites, since they, the Levites, take the tithes in all the cities dependent on our agriculture. Now the priest, the son of Aaron, shall be with the Levites, when the Levites tithe, and the Levites shall bring up the tithe of the tithes to the house of our God, to the chambers into the treasure house."[A31]

In thus laying primary stress on first-fruits, and tithing, and sacrifices, and fixed festivals, the Jews of Ezra's time established upon the foundation of the old pre-exilic faith—called, conveniently, the Religion of Israel—the clear-cut, legalistic religion named Judaism. The chief figures of the reorganized faith were priests; its infallible guide was a book of the Law (the Torah); its concern was directed toward matters of ritual: what was clean and unclean, purifications and expiations, permissions and prohibitions, and general obedience to the scriptural Law. And when, after a struggle in which Ezra and Nehemiah had to exert all their authority, foreign wives were put away, together with their children, and intermarriage with non-Jews prohibited on pain of ostracism, the Jews entered upon the process of becoming a racially as well as religiously exclusive group.

Much future history, however, is anticipated in a revealing passage from Nehemiah, written of his second governorship, when presumably Ezra was dead and he himself had been away in Susa:

In these days I saw in Judah men treading wine presses on the Sabbath and bringing heaps of grain loaded on asses, also wine, grapes, figs, and all kinds of burdens which they brought into Jerusalem on the Sabbath day; and I protested on the day when they sold provisions. Tyrians also dwelt therein, who brought in fish and all kinds of wares, and sold them on the Sabbath to the Judeans and in Jerusalem. Then I contended with the nobles of Judah and said to them,

"What evil thing is this that you are doing, and thereby profaning the Sabbath day? Did not your fathers do this and did not our God bring all this misfortune upon us and upon this city? Yet you are bringing more wrath upon Israel by profaning the Sabbath."

Accordingly when the gates of Jerusalem began to be in darkness, before the Sabbath, I commanded that the gates be shut; and I gave orders that they should not be opened until after the Sabbath. Also I put some of my servants in charge of the gates, that none should bring in a burden on the Sabbath day. Then the traders and sellers of all kinds of wares lodged outside Jerusalem once or twice. So I warned them and said to them,

"Why do you lodge in front of the wall? If you repeat it, I shall arrest you."

From that time on they came no more on the Sabbath.[*][A32]

These details have been given to show the situation. The common people continued to err, and yet the way of life established for them in law and in authority—a theocratic, ceremonial legalism—was laid inescapably upon their consciences and dominated all thought. As time went on it would claim them more and more. In considering the postexilic period down to the end of the fourth century B.C., we cannot fail to see that however great their laxity at times, the people gave their increasing loyalty to the regular round of religious duties prescribed for them. The weekly Sabbath day observances drew them to the temple at Jerusalem or to the gathering places in the outlying towns and villages that later acquired the Greek name for such places, synagogues. The annual festivals and fasts became a matter of ingrained custom. These were the Passover and the week-long

* Nehemiah found to his horror that the portion of the Levites had not been given them, so that the Levites and the singers at the services in the Temple were obliged to cultivate their own fields for a living. So he had to bring pressure upon the Judeans to pay their tithes. Also he found that some Jews had married foreign women, and that their children spoke foreign languages and "none of them could speak in the Jews' language." Here he felt he had to take direct action, reporting: "I contended with them and cursed them and beat some of them and pulled out their hair and made them swear by God";[A33] after which they sent their foreign wives off. He even found a prominent priest married to a foreign woman and exiled him.

Feast of Unleavened Bread that accompanied it in the first month of the year (March or April); the Feast of Weeks (or First Ripe Fruits) ending in Pentecost in the spring; and the Feast of Trumpets (later called "Rosh Hashanah" or New Year, followed ten days later by the fast of the Day of Atonement or Yom Kippur, and in fifteen days by the Feast of Booths or Tabernacles, all in the seventh month (September or October). The purely ethical religion of the prophets could not by itself firmly hold the common people, but these observances did.*

Further, as the years passed, the racial exclusiveness of the Jews threw them more and more upon their own religious authorities, both human and literary. Their supreme ecclesiastical personage was the high priest, who lived in the temple at Jerusalem. He was a descendant of Zadok, a royally appointed priest of King David's time, said to be descended from Aaron, the brother of Moses. He was both the religious and the civic ruler of Jerusalem. Under him were the ordained priests, who ministered in the temple during religious ceremonies, and the Levites, who had the status of temple servitors and were in charge of the musical services and the temple property. Authority was also vested in the learned profession of scribes, from which the rabbis sprang. The scribes had once been a more or less secular order, but they were now a religious class devoted to copying and interpreting the Torah and other sacred writings. Those of their number who developed a special talent for preaching in the synagogues came to be known as rabbis or "teachers." The rabbis performed a double service for the common people, which gave them increasing importance as time went on. In the first place, they met the growing need for a professional exposition of the sacred books, all the more necessary because Hebrew was being superseded as a spoken language by Aramaic, the mixed language that prevailed throughout Syria and Palestine, so that the common people could no longer

understand their own Hebrew writings without the aid of an interpreter.* In the second place, the rabbis helped to decentralize religious worship and make genuine group religious experience possible again in the villages—something that King Josiah's reformation in 621 B.C. had made difficult.

The priests and the scribes were not idle in providing authoritative religious literature for the people. Though the days of oral prophecy had virtually ended, testifying through the written word to the power of the holy and transcendent God of Israel in nature and history had become more and more common. In Babylonia and in Jerusalem the priests and scribes were diligently engaged in literary labors. They circulated copies of the writings of the more recent prophets—Malachi, Obadiah, Ezekiel, Haggai, Zechariah, and Second Isaiah—and they re-edited the writings of the older prophets. The five books of the Torah were being finally completed: "J," "E," and "D" were dovetailed into one complete work, then recombined with "P" or the priestly code. This last document, newly written, furnished the strictly monotheistic first chapter of Genesis and many legal provisions interspersed through the five books, including "H," the holiness code used by Ezra and Nehemiah in their reforms. Joshua, Judges, Samuel, and Kings were further revised and expanded by the addition of new material. A group of priests, with a Deuteronomic slant, worked on Chronicles, Ezra, and Nehemiah. The singers in the temple were using and composing the chants that were later to furnish much of the Book of Psalms. Quite another type of poetry, the erotic, had already found embodiment in the Song of Songs. Fully two thirds of the Old Testament as we know it today was in existence.

The significance of the new shift in interest has been well stated by a Jewish historian, thus:

All through the 5th century there was a steady reaction against religious laxness, a reaction sponsored by

---

* For a fuller description of these observances as practiced at a later time, see the last topic in Section XI of this chapter, beginning on p. 417.

* A translation of important texts into Aramaic was finally made and called the Targum. An earlier translation into Greek, begun in the third century B.C. in Alexandria, is known as the Septuagint. See p. 403 for further details.

the scribes, who were becoming ever more influential. The scribes, forerunners of the Pharisees, were the interpreters of the law, the leaders in the synagogues. . . . "Turn it and turn it again," the scribes admonished their people, "for everything is in it." And the Jews responded with unparalleled devotion. All existence was centered in the law. The Jews became a people of the book. The early Hebrews had created the Bible out of their lives; their descendants created their lives out of the Bible.[G1]

Or, as a group of Jewish scholars has pointed out in commenting on the effects of Ezra's reform:

Henceforth, the distinguishing mark of a Jew would not be political identity but adherence to the Torah, even if he lived outside Palestine and did not participate in the Temple cult. After the Exile, Jewish nationality became identified with ethnic solidarity—common descent, destiny, religion, and culture—rather than territorial status.[H]

"Schools of expounders" arose to deduce new laws from the old, in order that the ancient Torah might be made applicable to and practical in the life of later generations. These schools of the scribes were ultimately to become the solidly learned Pharisaic schools of the second and first centuries B.C. From the first they provided valuable insight on the problem of devising workable laws for conditions not dreamt of in the day of Moses. Improvements were made in civil law and Sabbath practices. But that there were drawbacks is also indicated by the historian we have just quoted:

It was inevitable that the endless spinning of meanings from the old texts should go to extremes and become burdensome. The Biblical law which prohibited the eating of meat torn in the field was based upon the sensible hygienic principle that carrion was dangerous as food. In the hands of the dialecticians the law was elaborated into a complex dietary machinery. If meat torn in the field was prohibited, why not also meat torn in the city? But what was torn meat? If it were not properly slaughtered, it was surely torn. What was proper slaughter? A whole code, the basis for the practice of *Shehita* (ritual slaughter), grew up to meet these problems—rules governing the knife to be used and the manner of using it, rules governing the competency of the ritual slaughterer and

his training, the prayers to be recited when the throat was cut and when the blood was covered with ashes.* A simple Biblical precept grew into a labyrinth of observances.[G2]

VII New Trends of Thought in the Greek and Maccabean Periods

In 332 B.C. the Palestinian theocracy came under a new control—that of far-away Greece. Alexander the Great drove the Persian armies out of Asia Minor and Syria and then seized Palestine on his way to the conquest of Egypt. After founding on the Egyptian coast, and naming after himself, the new city of Alexandria, which he hoped would become a culture center that would revolutionize the civilization of the regions bordering on the southeastern Mediterranean, he turned his attention to what was left of the Persian empire and brought it tumbling down at his feet.

General Characteristics of the Hellenistic Influence

In Alexander's motivation his personal ambition played the more considerable part without a doubt, but he also started out with an uncritical and altruistic passion for the spread of Greek civilization through the Near East. Yet he had no notion of imparting Greek civilization by force. He believed in the self-evidencing power of truth and planned to convert the world to the Greek view of life by education and example. So, in Alexandria and at other strategic points he ordered the establishment of new cities, which were to be laid out by Greek architects and provided with colonnaded municipal buildings, gymnasiums, open-air theaters, and libraries like those at Athens. He encouraged Greek, Egyptian,

* Without such slaughter the flesh would not be *kosher* or "fit."

Persian, and Jewish colonists to live in these model cities, under municipal governments that allowed each national group to live in its own quarter of the city and yet have a democratic share in certain processes of city government.* Of course, no little pressure was brought to bear on each citizen to induce him—entirely of his own free will!—to put on Greek dress, speak in Greek, build and furnish his home in the Hellenistic modes, and read and discuss Greek philosophical and political works, so far as his education allowed.

Alexander seemed to respect and favor the Jews. He wanted them in Alexandria, and in later days they filled two of the city's five sections. (They may have numbered one million souls there!) He hoped to make places for them elsewhere. The Jews, for their part, were more influenced by his cultural proposals than by those of any foreigner in their whole history. For one thing, the Hellenism for which he stood combined a new breadth of culture with unprecedented religious and racial tolerance. For another, it seemed to hold a great promise of vital world relationships overflowing into the economic and political back-eddy that was Judah. The Jews wanted to be on good terms with the rest of the world. They may have been suspicious at first of the Hellenic colonists set up in model communities throughout Palestine, but these colonists proved after all to be persuasive exponents of Hellenism, because they were amusing, fraternal, and peaceful. In three generations the higher-class Jews were freely admitting Greek words into their everyday speech and calling their children by Greek names. The cultured classes, and especially the Jerusalem priests, were, as might be expected, more profoundly influenced than the common people. Without giving up their religion, they welcomed the external features of Hellenistic civilization, so much so that in the heyday of the Greek influence the sacrifices were sometimes left half-burnt on the altar at Jerusalem while the priests rushed off to some stadium to see the Greek

* For example, each city was to be ruled by a council annually elected by the people.

athletes performing in the games! Yet there was a strong counter-current. The plain people were slow as always to adopt foreign ways. And the scribes and rabbis held back. With a stubborn loyalty to the Torah and the Jewish way of life, they kept resistance to Hellenism and all its ways and works alive among the "quiet in the land," the conservatively Jewish "pious ones" or *hasidim,* as they were called then and later.

The process of Hellenization was retarded but not interrupted by the contention for the possession of Palestine that followed Alexander's early death in Babylon. During a hundred years unhappy Palestine was overrun again and again by the armies of the Seleucids (of Syria) and the Ptolemies (of Egypt). Though the latter, the kindlier and therefore the preferred overlords of the Jews, were in the ascendancy most of the time, at the beginning of the second century B.C. the Seleucids finally triumphed. There was peace after that for a while, and Palestinian Judaism might have gone over even more completely to Hellenism than had yet been the case had not a headstrong Seleucid king caused his Jewish subjects to revolt against him and return to the ways of their fathers.

The Period of Independence Under the Maccabees

It had now become a fact that as long as their religious life was not interfered with, the orthodox Jews endured a good deal of oppression, but when their religion was endangered, they incontinently rebelled. This was something that Antiochus Epiphanes, king of Syria, did not understand. Anxious to hasten the lagging process of welding all the peoples of his kingdom into a Hellenistically-minded whole, he determined to use force to make the Jews worship Zeus, of whom he claimed to be the earthly manifestation (hence his title of Epiphanes, "God-made-manifest"). He therefore forbade the Jews, on pain of death, to keep the Sabbath, own any copies of their sacred writings, or practice circumcision. He erected on the altar of burnt offering in the temple at Jerusalem an altar to Zeus of Olympus, and here sacrificed pigs (always an abomination to the Jews). Further, he commanded all Jews to join in similar sacrifices, not only at Jerusalem but in the villages. The horror and indignation of the faithful passed all bounds. When, then, an aged priest called Mattathias was ordered by a Syrian commissioner to participate in a sacrifice to Zeus at the village of Modein, he murdered the commissioner and raised the standard of revolt. With his five sons at his side, and backed by many followers from among the hasidic Jews who rushed to him from every quarter, he took his stand in the wilderness. His able son Judas Macca-beus astounded the Syrian commanders by defeating four of their armies and forcing a fifth to retreat. In 165 B.C. Judas accomplished the surprising feat of recapturing all of Jerusalem except its garrisoned castle. The temple was then purged of its "abomina-tions," and the Jewish worship restored. Palestinian Judaism had been saved. In the subsequent phases of the campaign, the Syrians were obliged to quit Judea. Judas was killed in 161 B.C., and the leader-ship passed to his brother Jonathan, and after him to the last of the brothers, Simon, who was made high priest. Simon's son, John Hyrcanus, jeopardized the future by imperialistically adding Idumea (Edom), Samaria, and Perea (the region beyond Jordan) to Judea, so that his kingdom approached King David's in size. He forced the Idumeans to accept Judaism at the point of the sword—a bad precedent. Though the Jews seemed here to be over-reaching themselves, the period of Jewish inde-pendence lasted to 63 B.C., and might have lasted longer had it not been for the strife that broke out between divergent parties among the Jews them-selves.

Before we tell that story and add the tragic after-math, we need to examine the foreign ideas and modes of thought that now made an influx into Judaism and laid the basis for the rise of the post-exilic Jewish parties.

Gentile Influences on Thought During the Greek and Maccabean Periods

In the theology and literature of these periods may be seen the influence of Greek and Persian ideas about nature and history. Written or being written were the books of Proverbs, Job, and Ecclesiastes, now in the Bible, and Ecclesiasticus and the Wisdom of Solomon, contained in the Apocrypha. Considered together, they are usually referred to as the Wisdom Books. Ruth, Esther, Jonah, and the Book of Psalms made their appearance at this time, too. The last of the Old Testament books to be completed was Daniel, and along with it a host of extra-canonical books in like vein, giving expression to fervid Messianic hopes.

The Wisdom literature shows the influence of Greek ideas, although one cannot say that these ideas were either dominant or the basic motivating factors. One may only say that Hellenism confirmed many thoughtful Jews, discouraged by the trend of their history, in their disillusionment and quiet scepticism, and that, beyond this, it developed in them the ra-tionalistic attitude of submitting every belief to the test of reason, and thus encouraged a taste for the more intellectual types of speculation. To take an example, the latest portions of Proverbs assimilate certain speculative concepts of Greek philosophy. Most of Proverbs is very old. It was begun in the days before Solomon as a translation and paraphrase of Egyptian collections of wise sayings about the na-ture and conduct of life. Solomon is said to have been attracted to these sayings and to have added some generalizations of his own. The collection grew slowly with the years by the accession to it of other inde-pendent collections, until by about 250 B.C. it as-sumed its present form. On the whole, it is pitched in a key of quite unecclesiastical lay-wisdom, in the spirit of *Poor Richard's Almanack,* Benjamin Frank-lin's contribution to the practical wisdom of early America. Morality is for the most part regarded not so much as the law of God (though that is not denied, certainly) but as the demand of reason and common sense. In its latest sections, however, Wisdom is personified as God's consultant at creation—a Greek notion, the word for *Wisdom* being *Sophia* or *Logos,* and signifying in either case a combination of reason and sound judgment.

Another book that requires for its explanation the presence of Hellenism is Ecclesiastes. The writer seems to have had a knowledge of both Judaism and Hellenism, but to have been thrown into such mental confusion by the attempt to reconcile them that he could see no worth in human thought or effort. All that seemed to him good he summed up in such words as these: "I know there is nothing good for man but to be glad and enjoy himself while he lives." Everything else involved futility, a vain striving to hold the wind. Perhaps the writer had read the older book, Job, and had been unable to solve its fundamental problem: Why does not God make it the rule that the righteous prosper and the wicked suffer? But no, the righteous suffer and the wicked prosper. Ecclesiastes only vaguely catches Job's suggestion that the wise and pure in heart may transcend their suffering by rejoicing in the wisdom and majesty of God revealed in the awesome design of the world.

The Hellenistic influence on Judaism reached its height at Alexandria in Egypt rather than in Palestine. There near the time of Christ it made itself felt in the book called the Wisdom of Solomon and in the writings of the Jewish philosopher Philo, who consciously tried to synthesize Greek and Jewish thought by identifying the Wisdom of Jewish theology with the Logos of Greek philosophy. His teaching that contact with the Supreme Being, in the fullest spiritual sense, was the work of the divine Logos as the mediator of the power or activity of God was to have great influence on the thought-forms to be found in the prologue of the Fourth Gospel and in the writings of the early Christian Fathers.

Another effect of the pervasive Greek influence was the translation of the books of the Old Testament into Greek by a group of scholarly translators, traditionally said to have numbered seventy (whence the name of the translation, the Septuagint). This translation was begun in the third century B.C. but was not completed until near the time of Christ.*

But the influence of Hellenism on the religious conceptions of the main body of Jews was less enduring than that of Zoroastrianism, chiefly because the former was philosophical and secular in spirit, whereas the latter was religious and could offer supplementation to already existing beliefs.

It is easy but hazardous to seek exact conclusions concerning so elusive a thing as "influence," but the Jews came to know Zoroastrianism from observations near at hand in Babylonia, and certain Persian beliefs about Satan, the angels, the after-life, and the Messianic deliverer supplied what must have seemed missing elements in the old Jewish beliefs. Before they met the Satan of the Zoroastrians, the Jews had pondered the old stories about the serpent in the Garden of Eden and the fallen angels who had taken wives from among the daughters of men before the days of Noah. Then, too, there was the Adversary among the heavenly beings surrounding Yahweh who obtained permission to afflict Job and make him curse God. These stories antedated the exile, and in none of them is there the suggestion that the Spirit of Evil is a cosmic being, manifested from the beginning of time, and of a strength and creative power almost equal to that of the Spirit of Good. But after the exile the Adversary among the heavenly beings became, for at least some of the Jews, an evil and

---

* A word should be said about the importance of this translation. It is now apparent that the translators used only the most authentic manuscripts. Scholars have long believed this to be the case. The Septuagint proved to be the most reliable check they had upon the accuracy of the Hebrew manuscripts that had survived up to 1947, none of which could be dated before the tenth century A.D. The discovery from 1947 on of the Dead Sea Scrolls has confirmed this earlier belief, for these oldest of Hebrew manuscripts (dated from the two centuries before Christ) are in accord at nearly every point with the Septuagint.

It may be added that the Dead Sea Scrolls have also confirmed the belief that the Latin translation (the Vulgate) made by St. Jerome in the fourth century A.D. was the result of his careful choices among variant readings in the Hebrew manuscripts he was able to gather. **403**

infinitely malicious power, wholly in opposition to God—in fact almost a rival sovereign, with attendant devils to match the angels who stood before God. In another direction, She'ol, the shadowy land of the dead, was replaced by a heaven and a hell, and some Jews began also to speak of a resurrection from the dead at the last day and of a last judgment, a final reward of the good and condemnation of the evil. Long before the exile the prophets had foretold, of course, a day of doom and a purging of the nations, but now many Jews believed this with Persian alterations. Let us see what some of these changes specifically were.

1. The ancient Hebrew belief in demons, which scarcely rose above the animistic level and never implied strong resistance to Yahweh, much less a systematic or sustained opposition, now became the belief that the demons were *organized;* they had a leader, a head. This head was variously named, but the most common name for him was Satan (Shaitin). One of his first appearances under this name is in a passage in the prophecies of Zechariah, where he is described as contending with an angel-messenger of the Lord. As the Tempter, he was also read back by editors and revisers into the historical books, and the writers of "P" put him into the Garden of Eden.

2. The angels who, according to old belief, were Yahweh's divine messengers now were thought of as arranged in a hierarchy. In the Hellenistic and Maccabean periods this hierarchy consisted of seven archangels: Raphael, Uriel, Michael, Raguel, Saraqiel, Gabriel, and Jeremiel. The most prominent of these was Michael, with Gabriel coming next in importance.

3. The older Jewish belief that the dead descend to a colorless existence in the pit of She'ol, a land of forgetfulness not unlike the Greek Hades and the Babylonian Aralu, was in large part superseded by a belief in the resurrection of the body to an after-life of full mental vigor and awareness.

4. The prediction of the older prophets that there would be a Day of Yahweh in which the enemies of Israel would be carried down to doom, after which

a new kingdom would be set up with a Messianic king of Davidic lineage on the throne, underwent a radical change. This may have been a natural development and not a Zoroastrian suggestion; probably it was both. At any rate, the older hopes being unfulfilled and seemingly unfulfillable, the expectation now was that the coming of God's agent of deliverance would be from the clouds of heaven at the end of the world.

5. It looks as if the idea of a last judgment, a comparatively new concept, was taken over into Jewish apocalypticism with little basic change from Persian sources, although the locale was shifted.

This must suffice as a brief and somewhat speculative account of the influx of alien thought into Judaism. It raises a question for us. Was there, then, little opposition among the Jews to Gentile thought-pressures? Not so, at all. Considerable opposition did arise, as we shall see in the next section. Yet, as one might suspect, attitudes were sharply divided. Some did not accept anything alien; some did. The books of Esther, Ruth, and Jonah reflect these differences. Esther was written by a Jewish nationalist, fired by a fierce hatred of the peoples who had anti-Semites among them. But the more tolerant and forgiving view toward aliens was given immortal expression in two stories, one concerning Ruth, the beautiful Moabitess, who found acceptance among Jews, married one of them, and became an ancestress of King David, and the other concerning Jonah, the rebellious and anti-Gentile prophet, whom the Lord firmly bent to his more inclusive purposes.

The Rise of the Postexilic Jewish Parties

Had Judea remained isolated from the rest of the world, there might perhaps have been among its people no divisions into parties. There might have been only the old clash between the popular majority and prophetic minority that characterized the pre-exilic era.

Choices between cultures are seldom clear and

simple. In any one instance of choice it is not often possible to leave out the bearing of what is desired by parties in power and what coincides best with local opinion, personal popularity, and means of livelihood. In Judea it was the priests, or at least the higher orders of the priesthood, who were the internationalists. This certainly seems a paradox, for priests are notoriously conservative and careful in their tolerances. But in this case the priests were the party in power. The high priest had become the civic as well as religious head of the country and raised taxes, collected tribute money, and grew wealthy along with the other members of the high priestly families. His actions were subject to some slight check by the Gerousia, the council of Jewish elders later known as the Sanhedrin, but in most respects he was archbishop, prime minister, and foreign secretary all in one. This meant that the higher orders of priests were constantly engaged in regulating the international relations of Judea. The psychological effect of this was to make them discriminate for purposes of official policy between the essential or unchangeable in Judaism, as they saw it, and the matters that seemed open to change and compromise. The rule that they evolved, without much thought, was this: new and foreign ideas in religion, that is, ideas not found in the Torah, were to be frowned upon, but cultural innovations tending to improve foreign relations abroad and living conditions and standards at home were to be welcomed.

Out of this rose the important party of the Sadducees (a name very likely derived from "Zadokites," a name for the group of great families that formed the ruling clan of priests). The members of this wealthy, aristocratic, and worldly group dissociated themselves from the emotional ardors of the masses, believed in the "reasonable" views of the ancient fathers, as embodied in the written Law, and thought well of the teachings of the Greek intelligentsia. In the realm of religion they rejected the spreading popular belief in angels, the new apocalyptic ideas, and particularly the conceptions of the resurrection of the body to full consciousness in after-life. In matters of culture they were so liberal to foreign points of view that they were called "Hellenizers," the implication being that they were active propagandists for the Greek view of life.

This kind of thing was held quite unacceptable by the Hasidim, the "pious ones" or "puritans" already mentioned, who were described as "the quiet in the land." These were the ones who rallied so quickly to fight beside Judas Maccabeus in the war for independence. They had no interest in politics as such, much less in internationalism or Greek culture. Their one major intellectual passion was the Jewish religion. From their ranks sprang the powerful party of the Pharisees, to which most of the scribes and rabbis and many of the lower orders of the priesthood belonged. The Pharisees believed that the Sadducees were lost souls. The world with which the Sadducees compromised was under a sentence of doom; God meant to destroy it and bring in a new age. The Pharisees eagerly embraced the new Messianic concepts involving the resurrection of the dead and the last judgment. Yet their dreams were harnessed to some very practical considerations. In the interim before the end of the world, which would come only when God judged the time was ripe, they believed their prime duty was to be loyal to the Law "written" and "unwritten." That meant study of the scriptures and "traditions," together with moral obedience, ceremonial purity (they had to keep themselves unspotted from unclean persons and things), and, above all, spiritual growth and development, the result of "living unto the Lord."

When John Hyrcanus and his Maccabean successors became too enamored of their despotic power and over-sympathetic with Sadducean ideas, the Pharisees swung from support of the ruling family to fierce opposition. Sporadic open revolt was met with violent suppression and bloody massacre. When, in their turn, the Pharisees won an advantage, they took revenge in retaliatory bloodshed. The final result was civil war. But a stalemate resulted, and the Roman general Pompey, then resident in Syria, was called upon to arbitrate the issue. In 63 B.C., Pompey came down from Syria and promptly took the country over. It became a Roman province.

VIII   The Roman Period to 70 A.D.

The Romans had been called in to umpire a dispute. That they seized the opportunity to make themselves masters of Palestine hardly pleased the Jews. The swift and bewildering succession of political changes that followed increased the sense of frustration and outrage. One source of deep resentment was the fact that a certain Antipater, an Idumean, and therefore, even though he professed Judaism, racially unacceptable to the Jews, had been active behind the scenes in winning Roman favor and gaining personal power. The grudging approval he won from the Jews when he got the Romans to make Hyrcanus II, of the Maccabean family, the high priest was withdrawn after the overthrow of Pompey, when Julius Caesar rewarded him for his services by making him a Roman citizen and the procurator of Judea, for thus an Idumean became the civil ruler of Judea and the political superior of the high priest. In 40 B.C. Antipater's son Herod, whose favorite wife was a Maccabean princess, was chosen by Augustus Caesar to be king of Judea. It took three years of fighting, but Herod established himself as the absolute ruler of Palestine. In spite of the peace and prosperity that he brought and his remodeling of the temple into a thing of marble beauty, the Jews hated him. When he died horribly of a cancer in 4 B.C., they rejoiced loudly.

Meanwhile, significant factors in the religious situation were operating.

The Messianic Expectation at Its Height

From the coming of the Romans to the time of the destruction of Jerusalem in 70 A.D., the Messianic expectation increased its hold on thousands of suffering Jews. Deep in their hearts was the feeling that if God cared at all for his chosen people, he would act soon. The ardent hope of a supernatural deliverance from their unmerited suffering grew by what it fed on—an increasing flood of apocalyptic literature. Most of it followed the pattern of Daniel,* which had set the fashion of rehearsing the history of the Jews, from the exile to the time of writing, in the cryptic terms of beasts with wings and images breaking under blows, to signify in symbols the end of the wicked world-order and the resurrection of the righteous dead to join the righteous living in the enjoyment of a better world. There is not space here, nor necessity, to mention by name and assign to their decades the books that followed Daniel's pattern.† It will be enough to give a general picture of the Messianic expectation when it reached its height.

The central belief was that divine intervention would bring about a radical change in the world order. Through his Messiah, God was going to gather together "his own," both living and dead, and live with them in blessedness forever. That necessitated first the "end of the age," as some held, or the end of the world, as others believed. The "end" would be foreshadowed by certain last evils—wars and rumors of wars, distress, fear, famine, plagues, the rise to power of even more wicked rulers on the earth, and the like. The discerning would recognize in them the "signs of the end." At the last moment, with the sounding of "the last trump," the Messiah would appear in the clouds, with all the heavenly angels round him. He would be a supernatural personage, someone "like a man," and to be called the Son of Man, but bearing as well other titles, such as the Christ, the Elect One, the Son of David, the Lord's Anointed, the Righteous Judge, the Prince of Peace, and the like. At his appearing the righteous on earth would be caught up to him in the air (many said),

---

* Written during the early years of the Maccabean revolt.

† Many of the books were lost, and the dates of those existing are hard to determine in any case.

and the dead would rise from their graves. The older views held that only the justified Jews would join the Messiah, but later expectations offered hope to the righteous Gentiles that they also would be among the redeemed. Finally, the Zoroastrian view was accepted that all human souls, good and bad, would be summoned to a last judgment. Before the Messiah's seat they would be separated into the redeemed and the lost. The bad would be sent away into ever-lasting hell-fire, and the good would enter a state of blessedness with their Lord and King. This state of blessedness was variously conceived. Some writers thought it would be enjoyed on earth in a restored Garden of Eden, an earthly paradise; others placed it in one of the lower heavens. (There were thought to be seven heavens in all, God occupying the highest level along with his attendant angels.) Some combined the divergent conceptions, picturing an earthly paradise centered in a New Jerusalem to be inhabited by the Messiah and his chosen ones for a millennial period before the last judgment, and a heavenly paradise to be occupied by the redeemed after judgment was given. The heavenly paradise was most enthusiastically described as a place of green meadows, flowing streams, and fruit trees, where the righteous would banquet together with great joy and sing to the glory of God forever.

So great was the distress of devout Jews in the period we are describing, and yet so high their faith, that the near fulfillment of these dreams seemed completely reasonable. In fact, the world would not have seemed rational otherwise.

But not all the Jews believed alike about these matters.

New Jewish Parties in the Roman Period

Throughout this period the old parties continued to function. The Sadducees were more concerned than ever in politics, and the Pharisees, with a majority representation in the Sanhedrin, the deliberative body of organized Judean Judaism, regarded themselves as the true carriers of the Jewish religion. The schools that the latter maintained were the best in Jewry and boasted such great teachers as Shammai and Hillel.

But two new parties with a distinct political orientation now sprang up. One went by the name of Herodians, because they supported the house of Herod. They came into existence as a party in 6 A.D. when Augustus Caesar, at the request of a Jewish deputation, deposed Herod's son Archelaus as ethnarch of Judea and appointed a Roman procurator in his stead. The Herodians were not inhospitable to Greco-Roman culture, but they wanted home rule at all costs.

A far different group were the Zealots. They were passionate upholders of a policy of rebellion against Rome. The northern district of Galilee was their home base and stronghold. As an organized group they made their first appearance in 6 A.D. under the leadership of a certain Judas the Gaulonite or Galilean, who led a revolt against the taking of a census by the Romans. The revolt was bloodily suppressed by the Roman general Varus, but this did not bring to an end the Zealot agitation. The Zealots all believed that meek submission to "Roman slavery" meant forsaking God, their only Lord and Master, and they were convinced that by taking the sword they could hasten the Messiah's coming or even be rewarded by finding the Messiah in their midst. (On occasion they thought one of their own number was the Messiah.) The Romans called these super-patriots, who hid out in the hills and fought in guerrilla fashion, "bandits" and "robbers"—a not unfamiliar proceeding among conquerors.

A third new group, which entirely dissociated itself from politics, bore the name of Essenes. They lived in various places throughout Palestine, some in the villages, others in the open country. In preparation for the Messiah's coming, they withdrew from the "corruption" of civilized society into monastic seclusion, where they fasted and prayed, ate together, washed themselves frequently in prescribed ceremonial ablutions, observed the Sabbath strictly, and

407

engaged in daily chores of farming and handicraft. They practiced non-violence, meekly awaiting the world's end. As we learn from the famous Dead Sea Scrolls, the main group withdrew to a level hill top south of Jericho under the cliffs rimming the western shore of the Dead Sea. As early as in the second century B.C. they sought this especially barren and isolated site in order to remain unmolested in their utter absorption in religious study and devotion. The founder of the community, as an expounder of the Law or Torah, bore the name "The Teacher of Righteousness." From his time on they held property in common, ate common meals, and worshiped and studied together, devoting themselves especially to copying scrolls for their library on a long table of solid plaster. Under the regimen described in the scroll known as the Manual of Discipline, they formed a decidedly other-worldly covenant community. They practiced baptism as a rite of cleansing following on confession and repentance of sins, and it was repeated in individual cases whenever this seemed spiritually necessary. They called themselves, in a manner suggestive of the early Christians, followers of "the way" and "sons of light," for they conceived themselves to be under the rule of "the Prince of Light" and opposed themselves therefore to the "sons of darkness" under the "Angel of Darkness"— a set of concepts with a Zoroastrian rather than Hebrew coloring. Leadership of the community, until its complete destruction in 68 A.D., during the Jewish War, by a Roman legion, was exercised by a group of chosen priests and laymen, perhaps twelve in number.*

And then, as always, there were the unorganized common people, many of them indifferent to religion, though keeping up some of its forms like circumcision and hanging up the mezuzah on the doorpost. (See p. 430 n.) Others were pious in a quiet way. These, when confronted by the challenging point of view of a young carpenter from Nazareth, listened to him

gladly, just as with some astonishment they had earlier given ear to the prophetic personality John the Baptist, who counseled repentance because, he insisted, the end was near. Both won large followings, but Herod Antipas beheaded the one, and the other was crucified. The mainstream of Judaism was tending elsewhere, irresistibly, toward tragedy.

IX   The Great Dispersion

The discontent of the Jews had been leading steadily to a gruesome climax. Bloodshed and turmoil, with only brief intervals of quiet, kept all Palestine seething for sixty years after the desperate revolt of Judas the Galilean in 6 A.D. The Romans were aware that the one indispensable condition of keeping the peace was to let the Jewish religion alone, and they made it their policy to do so. In other directions they used a grim force. At the beginning of the first century Palestine was divided into four districts—three ruled by sons of Herod, the fourth (Judea, Idumea, and Samaria) governed by a Roman procurator residing at Caesarea on the coast below Jerusalem. In deference to Jewish feeling the procurators never brought the Roman imperial standards with their image of Caesar into Jerusalem, nor required that the statue of the emperor be erected in the temple and made the object of worship. They were satisfied officially with the Jewish agreement to offer a daily sacrifice *for* the emperor on the temple altar. But the Jews were touchy, or, from another point of view, forever on their guard. When Pilate thought that he might meet with no objection if he brought the imperial standards into Jerusalem in the darkness of the night, he found he had failed to reckon with Jewish alertness. When, again, he assumed that the Jews would take no offense at his seizing and applying temple funds to the extension of an aqueduct into Jerusalem, he discovered they were offended to the point of revolt. A slight improvement of the condition of ill-will came during the

---

* If we are to go by a rather obscure reference in the Manual of Discipline, twelve may have been the number, but this is conjectural.

reigns of Caligula and Claudius when Herod Agrippa I, a grandson of Herod the Great, ruled the whole of Palestine and the procurators were recalled. But when the well-liked Herod Agrippa died, the sending of procurators was resumed. As one succeeded another, disorder mounted; there were "bandits" everywhere, and rioting broke out in Jerusalem; a lax high priest was assassinated; there was conflict between Jew and Gentile, Jew and Samaritan, Jew and Roman. A frightened people was struggling desperately for self-determination.

The stage was now set for open rebellion. It came in 66 A.D., toward the close of Nero's reign. The war was begun with terrible determination on both sides. The Jews had been divided among themselves about having a war at all, but once the issue was joined, they entered the struggle together, still quarreling. The Romans on their part had lost all patience and would stand for no more "folly." Their forces were led by Vespasian, until Nero's death took him to Rome to be crowned emperor; he then appointed his son Titus to subdue the Jews. Titus did so. The struggle was unbelievably savage and bitter. After Titus finally invested Jerusalem, he more than once pled with the Jews to surrender, but they would not. The superhuman resistance of the city's defenders nearly baffled their besiegers, even though the Roman catapults threw huge stones a quarter of a mile into the defenses, and the battering-rams, devastating in their weight and force, broke down wall after wall. Yet, as soon as one wall was breached, another was found behind it. The defenders, starving and half-maddened with horror, were driven back until they were at bay within the temple area. The heroic resistance continued even after a brand hurled through the air set the temple on fire and the assaulting forces broke into the enclosure. Then the defenders retired to make a last stand in the upper city. At the end of another month they could resist no more. Amid indescribable slaughter, the city was razed, and Titus went away to Rome, laden with plunder, to be borne in triumph under the beautiful arch that bears his name and stands proudly still in the ruins of the

Roman Forum, a mute testimony to Jewish valor.

More than the city was destroyed. The priests and their sacrifices, and with them the Sadducean party, passed from the scene of history, never to have importance, or even reality, again. The Zealots, Essenes, and Herodians were the next to follow them off the stage. Only the party of the rabbis—that is, the Pharisees—and a rising heretic sect called the Christians were destined to wield influence through the coming years. The Romans had succeeded, for the moment, in decentralizing the Jewish religion. The bonds joining each outlying synagogue with the temple were sundered. Set adrift, the Jews had no reason to turn their faces in worship to Jerusalem, except in sorrow and mourning.

After 70 A.D. the Jewish dispersion reached the proportions of a national migration. Some of the inhabitants of Jerusalem fled east to Babylonia and southeast into the Arabian Desert, where they were beyond the power of Rome. Others went to join friends and relatives all over the Mediterranean world. Many who had no such ties emigrated to Jewish communities in Syria, Asia Minor, Rome, Egypt, North Africa, and far-off Spain.

But not all went away. Some retired to the rural parts of Palestine, hoping to be able to go back to Jerusalem some day and restore it. The Zealots, unwilling to believe their cause hopeless, continued active in the hills, eluding the Romans who lay in wait for them.

Then, sixty years after the fall of Jerusalem, a last, bloody revolt broke out in Palestine. On a visit to Judea the Emperor Hadrian had seen for himself that Jerusalem still lay in ruins after over half a century and had reissued his previous order, drawn up in Rome, that the city be rebuilt and that a temple to Jupiter Capitolinus be erected on the site of the razed Jewish sanctuary. As soon as Hadrian left Syria, Judea rose to arms. The most learned Jew of the day, Rabbi Akiba, had urged a Messianic aspirant called Bar Kokba to be the military leader of a new war for liberation. In high anger Hadrian ordered the Jews to be butchered into submission, at the

The Wailing Wall of Jerusalem. One of the most sacred of all Jewish sites is this west wall, all that remains of the temple begun by King David, completed by his son Solomon, razed by the Baby-lonians in 586 B.C., and finally destroyed by the Romans in 70 A.D. Jews come to it to pray and recite from the Torah. In 1967 the wall for the first time since the first century came into Jewish hands. (Courtesy of the Israel Government Tourist Office.)

same time intensifying their opposition by forbidding the observance of the Sabbath, the practice of circumcision, and the study of the Torah. The struggle lasted three and a half years. Judea was virtually depopulated. The Romans then proceeded to the rebuilding of Jerusalem as planned, but it was constituted a Roman colony in which only non-Jews were allowed to live, and its name was changed to Aelia Capitolina. With despairing eyes the patriots who drew near the city beheld the new temple to Jupiter standing where the old sanctuary had been, but they were forbidden by imperial edict to set foot in the city or linger near it, on pain of death. Only on the anniversary of the destruction of the temple—the ninth day of the month Ab—were they permitted to pay the sentries for the forlorn privilege of leaning against a remnant of the foundation wall of the old temple and bewail the loss of their national home and the complete dispersion of their nation. That "Wailing at the Wall," begun then, continued, except when interrupted, until a very recent date. But now at the time of writing (1969), the wall is, as a result of the Jewish victory in the war of June, 1967, in Jewish control for the first time since 70 A.D.

X   The Making of the Talmud

But the Jews would not give up. Though cured apparently—then—of the Zealot delusion, and persuaded also of the truth in the saying of the rejected Jesus, "Those that take the sword shall perish by the sword," they defended themselves until this century by a religious and cultural cohesion, a form of non-violent resistance, under the direction of their intellectual and moral leaders, the rabbis, which was destined to survive every persecution of the future.

In the year 69 A.D., while Titus was before Jerusalem, a leading rabbi, with the name of Johanan ben Zakkai, escaped through the Roman army to the seaside town of Jabneh (Jamnia), where he began teaching in a "house of learning" * in a far-sighted endeavor to save Judaism from extinction by systematizing its laws and doctrines and adapting it to the changes now upon it. He was a follower of the great Rabbi Hillel of the previous century, and he took his task seriously. Not only did he gather about him students and scholars who were to devote themselves earnestly to study and interpretation of the scriptures and the traditions, but now that the Sanhedrin was defunct, he organized the leaders among them into a new council to fix the dates of the Jewish calendar—a task that had to be done each year—and to make such necessary regulations for Judaism as a whole as needed to be made. Gradually, this body became the one recognized authority throughout the Jewish world that could pronounce on the true meaning and right practice of Judaism. Its president, with

the title of patriarch, was officially recognized by the Romans (until 425 A.D.) as the supreme head of all the Jews in the Roman empire.

During the sixty years of the school's existence at Jabneh much work was accomplished. In addition to making a detailed study of the written Law (the Torah), the school exactly recorded and defined the unwritten Law (the Halakah) conveyed through the traditions of the past and in the interpretations and opinions (the Midrash) of learned rabbis. This produced a vast accumulation of rules and judgments, which had at last to be sorted out. It was Rabbi Akiba (the same who backed up Bar Kokba in the disastrous rebellion during the reign of Hadrian) who discovered how to group the material of the unwritten law under six major heads, and thus simplified the task of classifying and codifying the whole body of tradition.

The repressive measures following in the train of the war under Hadrian brought a sudden end to the school at Jabneh. Akiba perished during the conflict, and other rabbis and scholars lost their lives. But those who survived smuggled the scrolls of Jabneh into Galilee, where work on them was presently resumed at Usha, near the seaport of Haifa, and then at various other places, such as Sepphoris and Tiberias, further inland. Such repeated removals only increased the rabbis' sense of urgency.

The Mishnah

The schools in Galilee developed outstanding "masters," chief among them being Rabbi Meir and Rabbi Judah.* Their names are associated with the compilation of the great Mishnah (Repetition), a voluminous collection, under Akiba's six headings, of some four thousand precepts of rabbinic law, intended to "interpret" and adapt the original Torah to the conditions of the second century. The Mishnah was a large and rambling work that quoted the legal

* Or "school," such as existed in connection with most synagogues throughout the Jewish world.

* Who was also patriarch.

decisions of the outstanding rabbis of past generations, pausing sometimes to give the varying points
of view of noted rabbis on disputed points. After it
left Rabbi Judah's hands, it acquired an authority
almost as great as that of the Torah itself. Certainly
it met a real need. The "Law of Moses" was all but
inapplicable in the second century, and the Mishnah
provided detailed guidance for the Jews who needed
new ways to hold fast to their ancient faith. Completed by about 220 A.D., the Mishnah contained
the decisions and judgments of almost 150 of the
sainted teachers (Tannaim) of Israel and gathered
its material from a period of six centuries. The range
of its subjects was great, as may be seen by a glance
at its contents. One section was concerned with the
seasonal festivals and fasts; another with prayers,
agricultural laws, and the rights of the poor; a third
with "women," that is, the laws relating to marriage
and divorce; a fourth with civil and criminal law;
a fifth with "consecrated things," particularly the
ritual of offerings and sacrifices; a sixth with laws
respecting what was clean and unclean in persons
and things and prescriptions as to how a Jew was to
purify himself when polluted.

One reads the Mishnah's pages with a sense of
wonderment at its microscopic examination of every
phase of Jewish life and cannot withhold his sympathy, in spite of the overstrained interpretations and
tortuous reasonings. It may seem hard to believe, as
Lewis Browne suggests, that the rabbis who compiled the laws in the Mishnah were sane. "But they
were very sane, those rabbis. They saw how near
their people were to death. Panic-stricken, they
clutched at every imaginable regulation that might
keep Israel alive."[11]

The schools in Galilee flourished for a century and
then declined in importance. The Mishnah proved to
be their one *magnum opus*. The economic and spiritual inanition of the Palestinian area somehow operated to rob them of their creative power. Their
schools continued to exist for two centuries more
and made a contribution to Jewish learning through
the Palestinian Talmud, but this was an incomplete

and inferior work. Intellectual leadership had long
since passed to the scholars of Babylonia.

The schools in Babylonia were of long standing.
They were the expression, in fact, of an uninter-
rupted community life going back as far as 586 B.C.,
when Nebuchadnezzar carried away into exile the
greater part of the people of Jerusalem. It is estimated that after the destruction of Jerusalem in 70
A.D. the refugees who fled to Babylonia swelled its
Jewish population to nearly a million persons. The
importance of this group was increased during the
Parthian dominance of Babylonia by the fact that
the government recognized a Jew of reputedly
Davidic lineage, called the Resh Galuta or Chief of
the Exile, as their civil head. But far greater importance for Judaism at large can be claimed for the
deep learning and great ability of the rabbis in the
Babylonian schools. Out of their labors came the
ponderous work known as the Gemara (or Supplementary Learning).

The Gemara and the Talmud

The completion of the Mishnah did not bring an
end to the process of exploring and defining the details of orthodox Jewish religion and life. Indeed, the
Mishnah itself became the basis of further commentary, for in many parts it was so concise as to be
very nearly cryptic, and therefore itself in need of
elucidation. Moreover, it was devoted chiefly to the
study of the unwritten Law (the Halakah) and
contained a relatively small portion of the oral traditions that the Jews called the Haggadah, a name by
which they meant the non-juristic traditions, the
historical, moral, and religious instruction included
in rabbinic lore. The Haggadah was the remembered
substance of countless school and synagogue homilies.
In itself it was more interesting by far than the
Halakah or legal traditions, for its purpose was the
instruction and edification, if not entertainment, of
the layman through graphic discourse illustrating the
meaning of moral and religious truths. It abounded in

stories from Jewish history, anecdotes of great and wise men, vivid anticipations of reward and punishment here and hereafter, and pithy comments on Bible truths by the great rabbis and teachers of Israel. Therefore, when the basic and indispensable Mishnah was completed, the Palestinian and Babylonian scholars busied themselves with recording and coming to agreement on the unrecorded portions of the Haggadah and indeed of every scrap of Jewish learning that was not in the Mishnah, so that nothing might be lost.

Then, in the second quarter of the third century, just after Jewish intellectual leadership had passed to the scholars of Babylonia, the tolerant Parthian rule was replaced by the severe reign of the Sassanian dynasty, dominated by the Magi—that is, the Zoroastrian priesthood. After centuries of security and prosperity the Babylonian Jews began to experience persecution. They were forbidden to bury their dead in the ground, because in the Zoroastrian view that would pollute the soil, and were ordered to send in a portion of all their table meat to be sacrificed on the Zoroastrian altars. Because the Magi of that period had a fanatically high regard for fire as a symbol of deity, they prohibited its religious use by all non-Zoroastrians. Immediate difficulties with the Jews arose as a result, for the Mishnah instructed them to light a Sabbath lamp before dark on Friday and keep it burning until the holy day ended, an observance that is orthodox practice to this day. Attempts to enforce the prohibition led to rioting and massacre. In the ensuing troubles some of the schools and academies were raided and closed.

The upshot of the new difficulties—which, however, never reached the proportions of an annihilating persecution—was a still greater zeal to preserve Jewish learning. The vast accumulations of rabbinic commentary were at last put in order. All unrecorded Halakah and Haggadah were brought together in the Gemara, the *magnum opus* of the Babylonian schools. When this was combined with the Mishnah, the Talmud was the result.

The Talmud was completed by the end of the fifth century. It marked an epoch in Jewish history. In all the years since its completion it has never been superseded as an authoritative compendium or even encyclopedia of descriptions and definitions in detail of every aspect of orthodox Jewish belief and practice. Its six major parts and sixty-three volumes have been as meat and drink to the tragic Jews who fled from east to west and back again during the long ordeal of the Middle Ages. Its physical bulk has had —and this constitutes a rather exceptional circumstance—no little relation to its spiritual inexhaustibility. It has served as a rampart of moral resistance that rose higher and stood firmer than the brick and stone of the ghetto walls that Europe raised to hem the Jew in. Though condemned as magic and as devil's lore, burned in the market-places by angry civil authorities or torn apart page by page and thrown on the waters, the Talmud always survived to feed the souls of a persecuted people determined to live by its regulations or have no further part in life. Others might laugh at what was contained in it, but to the Jew it was the wisdom that is of God.

XI   The Jew in the Middle Ages

At the beginning of the Middle Ages the situation of the Jewish people was profoundly affected by the impact upon them of two religions, Christianity and Islam. The first was inclined to be hostile; the second tolerant, if not friendly.

The relationship between the Jews and the Christians had never been good, even from the beginning. Because, from the first century on, the official attitude of Judaism was always defined by the rabbis, the Christian claim that Jesus was the Christ (that is, the Messiah) was flatly denied by the Jews from the moment it was made. The Christians, however, never quite gave up hope that the Jews might be persuaded to accept Jesus as the Christ. For two centuries and more, their missionaries and apologists tried with earnest persistence to win the Jews over to their faith, but their success was small in proportion to the efforts they expended. The Jews were for the most part adamant against the Christian teaching, especially after St. Paul carried the Christian gospel into Europe and the Greeks who entered the Church, in giving expression to their fine flair for philosophical interpretation, placed the life of Jesus in the cosmological setting of Greek philosophy and developed a theology around the figure of Jesus that was breathtaking in its speculative sweep and daring. It should be remembered that the rabbis, primarily concerned as they were with saving Judaism from dissolution seldom strayed from the study of conduct of life. Meticulous in details, they kept their eyes on what was written in the Law, not disdaining to be common-place and even humdrum in their interpretations. Above all, they took off on no high flights of philosophizing; the Talmud is proof of that. Consequently, they viewed "the Hellenizing of the Christian religion" with scorn, refusing to see any virtue in it. Why should they accept the vague and cloudy propositions of theological speculation in exchange for the concrete ethical realities of a holy way of life sanctioned by long tradition and deriving from God? The antagonisms implicit in this situation became a political actuality after the conversion of the Emperor Constantine in 312 A.D. and the subsequent elevation of Christianity to the status of the state religion. The Christian bishops, who now became great powers in the world, were in no amiable mood when they found that the Jews only stiffened their resistance to Christian pressure with the state behind it. As the Middle Ages advanced, hostility between Christians and Jews intensified and occasionally broke out into violence.

The Muslims at first treated the Jews better. In Palestine, Syria, and Babylonia they displayed toward the Jews not only tolerance but kindness, partly because the Jews looked upon them as deliverers from the Christians and Zoroastrians and therefore lent them their service as spies and scouts, and partly for the reason that culturally, racially, and religiously there was a marked resemblance between them. The

rabbinical schools in Babylonia therefore throve once more. The "Prince of the Exile" (the exilarch) became a powerful figure in the Muslim court at Baghdad, and the Jewish traders, following in the wake of Muslim conquerors, turned almost overnight into wealthy merchants who trafficked from one end of the Mediterranean world to the other. But it was too good to last. Economic conditions took a turn for the worse. The Turks came; the Jews again began to be oppressed. So, in the tenth and eleventh centuries many Babylonian scholars took their precious scrolls and set forth with their folk for Spain, at the other end of the world, where, since the eighth century, Jewish learning had been enjoying a heyday under the tolerant rule of the Moors. Here they joined forces with their Spanish brethren in creating the "golden age" of Jewish science, religious philosophy, and mysticism in the West.

New Thought in Babylonia and Spain

It took the combined resources of Eastern and Western Judaism to produce this notable Spanish interlude. Jewish scholarship in the West had at least these advantages: it was the beneficiary, first of Arabic science, which excelled in mathematics and astronomy and had rediscovered Aristotle, and next of a renaissance of Jewish poetry and *belles-lettres,* then in progress (eleventh century). But the scholars from Babylonia were also ripe for creative advance. They were not narrow Talmudists; something had happened to them before they left Babylonia that freed them from too confined an adherence to the Talmud's text. This was the Karaite heresy and the corrective reaction, led by the great scholar Saadiah, which followed in its wake.

Acceptance of the Talmud as an infallible guide of life never was universal throughout the Jewish world. Occasionally, Messianic aspirants would release their followers from obedience to its regulations and lead them "back to the Torah." But this was perhaps the least important reaction against the Talmud. There was greater disturbance when it was argued that the Talmud was a departure from the truths divinely revealed to ancient Israel. A significant protest of this kind was led by the scholar Anan ben David of Baghdad, a candidate for the title of exilarch, rejected (767 A.D.) for his heretical views, who declared that the supreme authority in Jewish life was what we call today the Old Testament and not the Talmud. The new sect he founded was nicknamed "the Children of the Text" and more commonly bore the name of Karaites (Readers). As a movement, it resembled in some respects the Protestant Anabaptist reaction against Catholic scholasticism and ritual, though it was even more extremely literalistic. Generally, among the Karaites the eating of almost any meat was forbidden, the Sabbath lights enjoined by the Mishnah were not kindled, recourse to physicians was regarded as lack of faith in the scriptural promise "I am the Lord that healeth thee," and many ancient practices that had fallen into disuse were revived in spite of the anachronisms involved. Although, because it stressed the full validity of individual interpretations of the ancient scriptures, it broke up into many divergent sects (like Protestantism again) and subsequently declined, the Karaite sect spread thinly through the Jewish world and up into Russia, where a remnant of the sect still survives. Its chief historical importance lies in the fact that it awoke orthodox Jews from their complacency with strictly logical juristic deductions from divine Law and stimulated a re-examination retrospectively of the Talmud's indebtedness to the Old Testament and, in terms of contemporary interests, of its general suitability to the times. Just this was attempted by Saadiah ben Joseph (882–942 A.D.), head of the Sura Academy in Babylonia.

Saadiah, realizing that the Karaites were obeying a sound impulse in returning to the original Hebrew scriptures (now no longer read by the rabbis themselves, because Hebrew was by this time a dead language), began the translation of the Old Testament into Arabic, in order that his fellow-Talmudists might see to what extent their position was based in scripture. He also tried to demonstrate the reasonableness of that position by reference to the Arabic translations of Greek philosophical and scientific works. Revelation and reason (scripture and philosophy) were, he said, complementary; both were needed. So he attempted a new systematization of Jewish thought, harmonizing it with the best in world thought, and thus became the father of medieval Jewish philosophy.

When the Babylonian scholars migrated to Spain, they took Saadiah's liberal conceptions with them, and these ideas of his helped to shape the course taken by enlightened Jewish opinion there.

In Spain, the fruitful meeting of Eastern and Western influences produced a mental quickening so marked that Spain quickly became the chief center of Jewish learning and culture. In the Jewish Academy of Cordoba, founded in the tenth century, a succession of distinguished scholars encouraged the fresh expression of Jewish learning and insight in literature. In the eleventh and twelfth centuries Ibn Gabirol, Judah Halevi, and Ibn Ezra wrote books of verse and learned treatises with great clarity and power. So deeply devotional were many of their hymns and religious essays that portions of them have since found their way into the liturgy of the synagogues.

Moses Maimonides

Even more famous was the great twelfth century scholar Moses ben Maimon (1135–1204), who is usually called Moses Maimonides. Born in Cordoba, he and his family fled during his youth from persecution (this time Muslim), which drove them through Spain and across the world to Cairo, where he wrote two great commentaries, the one systematizing the Mishnah and reducing it to thirteen cardinal principles,* the other simplifying and condensing the

---

* These were in brief: "I believe with perfect faith that God is the creator of all things and he alone; that he is one with a unique unity; that he is without body or any form whatsoever; that he is eternal; that to him alone is

whole of rabbinical law by what amounted to a re-writing of the Talmud. His greatest work was his *Guide to the Perplexed,* a rational examination of the Jewish faith, conceived in a spirit more than cordial to Aristotle, even while it stood firm on the doctrine of the divine revelation of the Hebrew Law. Reason, he said, could take one far, even though revelation was needed to supplement it. Such revelation, when it came, could not be contrary to reason but was rational in all its parts. Hence, the miracles are to be explained rationally, and the anthropomorphisms of the scriptures so interpreted that they become mere figures of speech, charged with ethical meanings. The account of creation in Genesis must be interpreted allegorically. By such use of our understanding we get to know the highest truth about God and his will for mankind.

But many Jewish scholars were not taken with Maimonides' rationalism. They would have none of him, in spite of the mental stimulus his works provided. Religion, they said, was mystical and dealt with hidden meanings not accessible to reason but known only to the truly devout. The most able spokesman for these views was Nahmanides (1195–1270), born in Gerona, Spain, who felt that man cannot compass God's truth with his finite and fallible reason; one must have faith and deep feeling that God is all in all. In similar vein, Hasdai Crescas in the fourteenth century contended that man can reach God only through love and submission, not through a purely rational search.

---

it proper to pray; that all the words of the prophets are true; that Moses is the chief of the prophets; that the law given to Moses has been passed down without alteration; that this law will never be changed and no other will be given; that God knows all the thoughts and actions of men; that he rewards the obedient and punishes transgressors; that the Messiah will come; that there will be a resurrection of the dead." See *Judaism,* edited by Arthur Hertzberg (Washington Square Press, 1963, pp. 222 f.). It is interesting that these articles appear in the Jewish Daily Prayer Book (in a more amplified form and in rhyme) to serve as an introduction to the morning service, although they have never been completely accepted and are in no way binding.

The Kabbala

But the conviction that religion has hidden meanings was to receive another kind of statement—that of the Kabbala, the books of speculative theology and mystical number symbolism that gave new currency to old accumulations of secret wisdom and esoteric lore and fascinated their hopeful readers by mysterious arrangements of words and numbers, purporting to reveal the "deeper meaning" in the scriptures. The fact that the ten Hebrew numbers (the Sephiroth) are letters of the alphabet had the effect of turning any word or sentence into a number series, and this seemed to the Kabbalists to yield significant results in the case of the various names and attributes of God. Even rabbis and scholars of note gave themselves up to acrostic anagrams and other forms of esoteric word-play.

But the Kabbala also addressed itself to serious metaphysical problems, the problem, for example, of how a perfect God could produce an imperfect or incomplete world, or, to put it in other terms, how the Infinite could bring forth the finite without damaging subtraction from himself. In finding a solution of this problem in the theory of emanations, the Kabbala went back ultimately to such ancient sources as Philo and the Gnostics. A typical line of speculation started with the concept of God as the Boundless (Ensoph). From him as light springs from a sun proceeded various emanations, like the Divine Will, which generated Wisdom (male) and Knowledge (female), these in turn generating Grace (male) and Power (female), which latter by their union produced Beauty; from the last three sprang the natural world. Not to carry the matter further, the upshot of these speculations was the conviction that man, who has all these qualities, is the universe in miniature, a microcosm filled with magical cosmic forces, the direction of which can be controlled by efficacious formulas, names, and symbols. The Messiah himself will be identified at his coming by his mysterious name and symbol.

The exciting implications which flowed from these

considerations produced in central Europe an abundant crop of false Messiahs who only disappointed the faithful. Since the middle of the sixteenth century Kabbalism has had its chief center in Safed in northern Galilee.

The Crusades and the Ghettos

The Jews had by this time long since spread out into France, England, and the Rhineland, where they settled in little clusters, followed similar occupations, and remained true to their faith. Because their religious ceremonies were carried out in virtual seclusion and never came under the direct observation of the general public, they excited curiosity and suspicion. Many on the outside took the attitude that the Jews were a secret order of conspirators against the public welfare. They were charged with every form of malevolent purpose. The launching of the Crusades at the end of the eleventh century produced such excitement against "infidels" that an open butchery of the Jews began, starting in Germany, where wholesale massacres took place, and spreading to the rest of Europe. After the butchery ran its course, orders of expulsion followed. In Germany one town after another drove the Jews out completely. They were expelled, at least in law, from England in 1290, and after two centuries of periodic expulsion and restoration, in 1394 they were denied residence in France. In Spain persecution of the Jews accompanied the expulsion of the Moors, and in 1492 all unconverted Jews were ordered driven out.

Fleeing in the only direction open to them, eastward, the Jews of Spain and southern European areas found refuge in Turkey, Palestine, and Syria (where they spoke Ladino, basically a Spanish dialect interspersed with Hebrew). These Jews of the Near East have acquired the name Shphardim. Their tendency has been to develop on the base of the Torah and Talmud an intense mysticism and speculation, Kabbalic in form. The Jews of northern areas went in large numbers to Poland and western Russia, where

they brought the welcome arts of trade and money-lending to that then sparsely settled land. But they were not assimilated by the Poles. They spoke a dialect compounded of German and Hebrew, now called Yiddish. They have come to be called Ashkenazim. Their orientation, on the whole, has been provided by the Talmud and its legalism, although they have had mystics among them (see p. 420).

As for those who remained in Italy and the towns of Austria and Germany that had not totally excluded them, they were forced to live in segregated quarters called ghettos, usually located in the worst part of town. To add to their distress, in most places where the Catholic Church was supreme there was enforcement of the thirteenth-century law forbidding Jews on pain of death to appear on the streets without the Jew badge—a colored patch of cloth sewn on to their clothing. This badge became a mark of shame. In many towns high walls were built around the ghettos, and the Jews were locked in at night. To be seen abroad after dark often meant death, and always a fine.

The Medieval Festivals and Fasts

Meanwhile, the calendar of Jewish festivals and fasts had undergone development and reinterpretation. The ancient Palestinian and Babylonian liturgies, somewhat divergent to begin with, were further but not radically modified to meet the particular needs or preferences of the Jews of Spain, Italy, North Africa, Turkey, Persia, and central and western Europe, or to admit Spanish, Kabbalistic and other devotional materials.* Of great importance was the fact that the agricultural interests expressed in the

* At times, also, for longer or shorter periods and more or less radically, the ritual was affected by leading Jewish personalities, such as Anan ben David, the Karaite leader, Maimonides, Isaac Lurya, a Shephardic Jew, and others. Such rites are today mostly extinct. Rites now differ according to each congregation's leanings, whether Orthodox, Reform, Conservative, etc., and reflect Ashkenazic, Shephardic, or other orientations.

ancient Hebrew rites and ceremonies were no longer in the forefront, and therefore the inherited forms had to be charged with historical and ethical meanings that would call out the continued loyalty and devotion of the Jews in every sort of occupation and environment.

The chief festivals and fasts of the year, with considerable local variation, were assigned the procedures, meanings, and dates (determined according to the lunar calendar) that have been standard for orthodox Jews to the present day. They had by now taken approximately the following forms (which are in use today):

In late March or during April, Passover (Pesakh), "the anniversary of Israel's natal day," basically a spring festival of thanksgiving for the birth of lambs and the sprouting of grain, was ritually associated with the idea of individual and group liberation and renewal in all periods, beginning with the Exodus and continuing through history. As in the ancient period, nothing leavened was eaten for a full week (whence the name "the Feast of Unleavened Bread"). The biblically prescribed eating of the paschal lamb had from the time of the great dispersion been gradually set aside, and the chief event of Passover had become the Seder Feast, observed on the eve of the first (or else the second) day, by the whole family assembled together, some from a distance, in the home. A ritual called the Haggadah—or Narrative—was read throughout the ceremony. After the Kiddush cup had been passed, the male head of the family washed his hands and assumed the function of the family priest. Parsley dipped in salt water was eaten in remembrance of the trials of captivity. At other intervals further cups of wine, bitter herbs and roots, and unleavened bread were passed. Accompanying each act was the running account of the Haggadah, generally in the form of question and answer, designed to retell the story of the Exodus and explain the purpose of the Passover rite itself—that is, its challenge ever to seek freedom from any bondage. Psalms were sung, and finally the evening meal was served. Afterwards a door was opened, amid a recitation of psalms and

lamentations, and Elijah, the hoped-for precursor of the Messiah, was invited to come in and drink of the Elijah Cup, which had stood untouched on the table during the preceding rite. The service ended with a psalm of praise, a prayer, or the recitation of a grace. The solemnity then melted into general rejoicing in which the children present were encouraged to take a leading part.

For forty-nine days after the Seder Feast, except at the new moon or on the thirty-third day, no joyous occasions, including marriages, were allowed. Then on the fiftieth day came Shebhuoth—the Feast of Weeks or Pentecost, a day of rejoicing once set aside to commemorate the first-fruits of the spring wheat harvest, now modified to include thanksgiving for the giving of the Law at Sinai, which was held to have occurred at the same time of year.

The next great holiday came in September (or early October). It was Rosh Hashanah, or New Year's Day. This name took the place of the ancient biblical names, Day of Memorial and Day of Blowing the Alarm (signalized by the sounding of the *shofar* or ram's horn, a custom still solemnly observed as a means of summoning the Jew "to ponder over his deeds, remember his Creator, and go back to Him in penitence"). In recognition of the significance of the day, the Talmud called it the Day of Judgment. After it followed the Days of Repentance, and on the tenth day the solemn Day of Atonement (Yom Kippur), during which "repentance, prayer, and righteousness" were enjoined upon all the participants in the fast, who, as free agents, were urged to exert their wills to turn from wrong-doing and in true atonement for sin do God's will henceforth.

Five days later came Succoth, the eight-day Feast of Booths or Tabernacles, basically a thanksgiving festival devoted to expression of gratitude for the autumnal fruits of vine and tree, and now associated with the thought of God's provident goodness in the days of Israel's wandering in the wilderness and during later times. In addition to the decoration of the synagogue with all sorts of fruits and flowers, a feature of the services was the ritualistic carrying in procession of four products of Palestine tied together, namely, a citron and a palm-branch bound with branches of the myrtle and the willow. Those who could do so erected a booth or tabernacle in or beside their homes and ate their meals under it during the period of the festival. (Some even slept there.)

Close on the termination of the festival a special day, Simkhath Torah (the Rejoicing over the Law), had as its feature the carrying of the scrolls from the ark in procession around the synagogue.

Two festivals not based upon the Mosaic tradition were the Hanukkah in December and Purim in February or March. The former—the Feast of Lights —was celebrated for eight days, one light being lit in the synagogues and in every home on the first night, two on the second, three on the third, and so on, this being interpreted to commemorate the rededication of the temple by Judas Maccabeus in 165 B.C.

Purim or the Feast of Lots was associated with the biblical Book of Esther and thus was made to celebrate the deliverance of the Jews from persecution through Esther's patriotic intervention. Gifts were exchanged within the family and sent to friends and to the poor, in the spirit of carnival. There was dancing and singing in the homes.

XII Judaism in the Modern World

The Protestant Reformation was the product of many causes. Not least among the contributing factors was the return by the Reformers to the study of the Bible in the original Hebrew and Greek. So impressed was Luther in his earlier years by his discovery of the close genetic relation of the Jewish and Christian faiths that he published in 1523 a pamphlet *Jesus Was Born a Jew,* in which he pleaded: "They (the Jews) are blood-relations of our Lord; and if it were proper to boast of flesh and blood, the Jews belong to Christ more than we. . . . Therefore it is

The shophar or ram's horn. The old man is reverently preparing the shofar for use in the synagogue. The holy ram's horn is blown during the services of New Year's Day (Rosh Hashanah), at the conclusion of the Day of Atonement, on the seventh day of the Feast of Tabernacles, and during the entire month of Elul after the supplications. It has a loud, piercing tone and symbolizes God's call or summons. (Courtesy of the Israel Government Tourist Office.)

my advice that we treat them kindly. . . . We must exercise not the law of the Pope, but that of Christian love, and show them a friendly spirit. . . ."[12] But Luther retraced in his own life the first three centuries of the Christian era. When he found the Jews solidly resistant to conversion, his anger slowly mounted, until in his later years he began to abuse them savagely. In a pamphlet *Concerning the Jews and Their Lies* (1542) he repeated in a passion of credulous rage all the old rumors concerning the Jews —that they poisoned the wells of the Christians or that they murdered Christian children (presumably, as the current rumor had it, to get blood for the Passover). In his last sermons he hinted that Jewish doctors knew and therefore practiced the art of poisoning their Christian patients. "If the Jews," he growled, "refuse to be converted, we ought not to suffer them or bear with them any longer!"[G3]

Luther was typical of his age in this. The Reformation brought no permanent improvement in the condition of the Jews of Europe. In fact, in the sixteenth and seventeenth centuries their fortunes reached a very low point, as low as any in their history. Not only did they live in physical ghettos devised by their oppressors, but they themselves retired into mental ghettos of their own creation, which shut the world out—its science, art, and culture as well as its hostility and evil. Improvement in their lot came, but came slowly.

Eastern Europe

In eastern Europe the Jews were (and have largely remained up to the present time) true to their heritage of ancient patterns of thought and life. In the seventeenth century a terrible pogrom was wreaked upon them, especially in Poland, by the Cossacks, when these furious Russians rose in rebellion against their feudal lords and went on to slaughter five hundred thousand Jews. This and other pogroms have only confirmed the eastern Jew in his unrelaxing grip upon every article of his inherited faith. But there are characteristic differences in the different areas. In Lithuania and White Russia the emphasis has been on intellectual study of the Talmud and the original Hebrew texts. In these regions the Jews have been consistently anti-mystical; a dry, matter-of-fact scholarship has been rated above emotional fervor. Their characteristic personality was the eighteenth-century scholar, Elijah of Vilna, who be-

came their ruling rabbi. He was an intellectual giant, at once Hebrew grammarian, astronomer, author, bitter foe of the mystical Hasidim (about to be described), and founder of a famous academy to which students came from all over Europe during the nineteenth century to study the Talmud in the traditional manner of the Babylonian schools of over a thousand years earlier.

South of the Pripet Marshes, in southern Poland and the Ukraine, eastern Talmudism took a warmly emotional and mystical turn, which led finally to the virtual abandonment of the Talmudic point of view and a joyous espousal of the pantheistic vagaries of the Kabbala. Messianism ran riot for awhile, and more than one unstable soul encouraged by the hopeful ran a career among them as Messiah, only to dash their hopes at last by some false step that brought ruin or disgrace. However, one notable religious personality emerged among them, Israel of Moldavia, affectionately renamed Baal Shem Tob ("The Good Master of God's Name"), a kindly, itinerant faith-healer of the eighteenth century, who scorned the Talmudists for studying the Law so narrowly that they had no time to think about God. Thinking about God meant to him realizing that God is everywhere—in nature, in human life, and in every human thought. Religion was feeling God in everything and praying joyously in the wholesome consciousness of God's indwelling. "All that I have achieved," he used to say, "I have achieved, not through study, but through prayer."[G4] Reviving a name used in postexilic times two thousand years earlier, he called his followers, who were mostly common people, Hasidim or "Pious Ones." Hence, the movement initiated by him is called Hasidism.

Central and Western Europe

In central and western Europe the matter of chief import during the last two centuries has been the experience of slow but exhilarating liberation from civil disabilities, followed by what might be called "a return to the world." The justice of such a liberation was admitted by the leaders of the European Enlightenment during the eighteenth century and was made an actuality by the revolutionary movements in France and Germany in the eighteenth and nineteenth centuries.

The rationalism and scepticism of the eighteenth-century intellectuals in Europe, which tended to hold all religions up to mockery, led to a lowering of religious and class barriers in the centers of culture. It was thus that Moses Mendelssohn, perhaps the greatest modern Jew, broke through the restrictions barring Jews in Berlin and reached the center of its intellectual life. While pursuing his studies there, he became the friend of Lessing, the literary lion of Berlin, and was accorded the signal honor of having the liberal drama, *Nathan the Wise,* Lessing's masterpiece, created around his personality. That the great Lessing should choose a hump-backed Jew as his intimate and enshrine him in a serious work of art was at first astounding, then thought-provoking. Mendelssohn wrote German, not as the Jews spoke it, but as the Germans themselves desired to write it. A dialogue on immortality, which he composed on the Platonic model, was read throughout Europe. In the hope of doing a service to his fellow Jews, he translated the Pentateuch and other parts of the Old Testament into accomplished German prose (written out in Hebrew characters) and added a commentary of an advanced liberal character. But the chief work of his life was his earnest pleading in behalf of his people, that they might be freed from the ghettos to enter the stream of modern life on a basis approaching equality with other people. He did not live to see this happen, but in his own person he showed Europe how worthy the Jews were to be freed.

Liberalism and Reform

The revolutionary changes wrought by the rise of democracy in America and Europe eventually gave the Jews their full civil freedom. The American Revolution established the political principle that all men are created free and equal. During the French Revolution the Jews of France received the rights of full citizenship. Wherever Napoleon went, he abolished the ghettos and released the Jews into the world at large. After him reaction set in. All through Europe the Jews were faced with the choice: back to the ghettos or become a Christian. Many chose the latter alternative; others submitted to the reimposition of restrictions but entered avidly into all underground revolutionary movements looking toward the overthrow of reactionary governments, thereby providing conservatives and future reactionaries with the argument that Jews are by nature subversive. (Those Jews who had never tried to enter European life but clung to their ancient ways had, of course, no part in this.) Finally came the social upheavals of 1848 and after, which had as their consequence, for the Jews of all Europe, the granting of complete equality with other men before the law. The universities opened their doors. From them Jewish doctors, politicians, dramatists, professors, and scientists poured forth into the communal life of Europe. In the vast processes of change accompanying the victory of political democracy, the Jews stood to benefit most.

Not least among the far-reaching consequences of the freeing of the Jews was the effect upon Judaism itself. The Jews found themselves in a world fast throwing aside the vestiges of the past that stood in the path of the liberal movement, and it was natural that they should consider doing the like among themselves. The educated Jew, engaged in the activities of the modern world, began to feel that Judaism should no longer stand aloof behind self-protective barriers but should resume its ancient progressive character. One result of this realization was the movement called Reform Judaism. It made a beginning in such synagogues as the Reform rabbis could control, its usual first innovation being the simplifying and modernizing of the synagogue worship. The Sabbath service was condensed, and most of it was translated into the vernacular. References to the coming of the

Messiah, the resurrection of the dead on the last day, or to the re-establishment of Jewish nationality and of the sacrificial rites of ancient Palestine were stricken out. Organ and choir were installed, and hymns in the vernacular were sung. The fundamental conviction of the movement was stated by Abraham Geiger, its leading exponent, in the words: "Judaism is not a finished tale; there is much in its present form that must be changed or abolished; it can assume a better and higher position in the world only if it will rejuvenate itself."[J1] There were both moderates and radicals in the Reform movement. The latter shocked the Jewish world by declaring in 1843 that their principles were: "*First,* We recognize the possibility of unlimited development in the Mosaic religion. *Second,* The collection of controversies, dissertations, and prescriptions commonly designated by the name Talmud possesses for us no authority from either the doctrinal or practical standpoint. *Third,* A Messiah who is to lead back the Israelites to the land of Palestine is neither expected nor desired by us; we know no fatherland but that to which we belong by birth and citizenship."[J2] But after 1848 the conservatives fought the Reform movement to a halt, and even drove it into retreat. The movement then transferred itself largely to America, where it is now very powerful.

The Orthodox Jews earnestly fought Reform from its beginning because it denied the orthodox view that the divine revelation in the Law is final and complete and awaits only its fulfillment. But the proposed changes in belief seemed less dangerous than the threatened changes in way of life. It is perhaps fair to say that the Orthodox Jew of today lays a heavier emphasis on practice than on belief. One need not believe exactly as the rabbis do, but one must adhere with absolute fidelity to the practical admonitions of the Law of Moses, as they are interpreted and applied to daily life by the Talmud: the Sabbath lights must be lit and the Sabbath kept as of old; none of the ancient Jewish festivals may be skimped or abbreviated; the dietary laws, with their prohibitions of certain foods and their regulations as to kosher meat, must be observed exactly, and one's life must never be regarded as "holy" or "acceptable to the Lord" unless defilement is avoided precisely as the ancient laws prescribe. So far as conditions permit, the ancient Palestinian mode of life—minus only the daily sacrifices on the altar of the temple at Jerusalem—must be carefully followed by the Jewish community.

Zionism and the Establishment of a New Nation

Neither Reform nor Orthodox Jews have had plain sailing, however. The astonishing economic and professional successes of the Jews in the second half of the nineteenth century stirred up a new wave of anti-Semitism in Europe, where pogroms in Russia, vindictive Jew-baiting in Germany, and the famous Dreyfus case in France convinced many Jews that their only hope of permanent security lay in the re-establishment of a national home in Palestine. A landmark in the crystallization of this viewpoint was the book by Theodor Herzl, on *The Jewish State,* issued in 1896. Based on its premises, a Jewish movement called Zionism rose rapidly to international notice. From the start it gained wide support among Orthodox Jews and has by now won over many Reform Jews, who at first opposed it as reactionary and impracticable. The Balfour Declaration during the First World War, to the effect that the British government viewed with favor "the establishment in Palestine of a national home for the Jewish people" and would seek to "facilitate the achievement of this object," changed the political status of the movement overnight. Thousands of Jews went to Palestine during the next two decades, and under the protection of the British Mandate laid the foundations of Jewish national life there. The monstrously brutal and murderous persecution of the Jews by the Nazis and the displacements of the Second World War accentuated the pressures brought to bear by world Jewry toward the formation of an independent Jewish state. While the world watched, the United Nations Assembly finally, in 1947, voted to partition Palestine and make a Jewish state an actuality. The new state calls itself Israel. It has maintained itself as a nation with vigor and success. Yet the intensity of Arab opposition has not abated. The wars that have occurred and the guerrilla raids that continue across the frontiers augur stormy times ahead for the eastern Mediterranean littoral.

Other Developments

Meanwhile, the need to find a median position between Orthodoxy and Reform resulted in the establishment of neo-Orthodoxy and Conservatism in Europe. These movements were founded in the mid-nineteenth century and made some headway. In America the Conservative movement experienced a rapid growth. With its own seminary in New York City, and its congregations organized into the United Synagogue of America, it has striven to find common ground between extreme Zionism on the one hand and the position taken, say, by the Conference of Reform Jews meeting in Chicago in 1918 some six months after the Balfour Declaration was issued, at which time that body announced:

We hold that Jewish people are and of right ought to be at home in all lands. Israel, like every other religious communion, has the right to live and assert its message in any part of the world. We are opposed to the idea that Palestine should be considered *the home-land* of the Jews. Jews in America are part of the American nation. The ideal of the Jew is not the establishment of a Jewish state—not the reassertion of Jewish nationality which has long been outgrown. We believe that our survival as a people is dependent upon the assertion and the maintenance of our historic religious role and not upon the acceptance of Palestine as a home-land of the Jewish people. The mission of the Jew is to witness to God all over the world.[J3]

The Conservatives see no inherent contradiction in witnessing to God all over the world and having a Jewish state in Palestine as a center from which Jewish culture may be disseminated among the nations. In effect, the Conservatives endorse the *religious* aspects of both right and left. In an essay surveying "Current Philosophies of Jewish Life," Milton Steinberg says:

Conservative Judaism had its origin simultaneously in America and Western Europe among those Jews who either in theory or practice could no longer be orthodox, and who yet refused to accept what they regarded as the extreme nontraditionalism of Reform. . . . Two motifs dominate conservative Judaism. The first is the assertion of the centrality of religion in Jewish life. . . . The second theme, heavily underscored, is the sense of tradition, of history, of the continuity of Jewish life both through time and in space. It is this feeling of the organic unity of one Jewry with other Jewries which Professor Solomon Schechter, the leading figure in American Conservatism, caught in the phrase "Catholic Israel." This phrase is more than a description. It is intended to serve as a norm for the guidance of behavior. That shall be done by Jews, it implies, which is normal to Catholic Israel: . . . to hold on to the traditional, to sanction modifications slowly, reluctantly, and, if at all possible, within the framework of Jewish law.[K]

Recently, a group a little left of center has arisen among the Conservatives calling themselves the Reconstructionists. They advocate wide liberty in doctrine and "creative adjustment" to the conditions of modern life.

The future of Judaism would seem to lie between these divergent groups, each as yet feeling its way more or less anxiously to solid foundations in a tragically unstable modern world. These groups are not sharply divided from each other, for each yearns to have its unity with the others made possible in word, deed, and faith.

SUGGESTIONS FOR FURTHER READING

ALBRIGHT, W. F. *From the Stone Age to Christianity.* 2nd ed., with new introduction, Johns Hopkins Press, 1957. Also available in Anchor pb

————. *The Archaeology of Palestine.* Penguin Books; 3rd ed., fully revised, 1960. A Pelican pb

————. *Archaeology and the Religion of Israel.* 3rd ed., Johns Hopkins Press, 1959

ANDERSON, BERNARD W. *Understanding the Old Testament,* Prentice-Hall, 1957

BARON, S. W. *A Social and Religious History of the Jews.* 3 vols., Columbia University Press, 1952

———— AND BLAU, JOSEPH L., EDS. *Judaism. Postbiblical and Talmudic Period.* Liberal Arts Press, 1954. An anthology in pb

BEVAN AND SINGER, EDS. *The Legacy of Israel.* Oxford, 1927.

BRIGHT, JOHN. *History of Israel.* Westminister, 1959

BUBER, MARTIN. *Tales of the Hasidim.* Thames & Hudson, London, 1956

BURROWS, MILLAR. *The Dead Sea Scrolls.* Viking Press, 1955

————. *More Light on the Dead Sea Scrolls.* Viking Press, 1958

CHARLES, R. H. *Religious Development Between the Old and New Testament.* Holt, Rinehart & Winston, 1914

COHEN, A. *Everyman's Talmud.* J. M. Dent, 1937

CORNFIELD, GAALYAHU, ED. *Adam to Daniel: An Illustrated Guide to the Old Testament and Its Background.* Printed in Israel, distributed by Macmillan, New York, 1961

FINKELSTEIN, L., ED. *The Jews: Their History, Culture and Religion.* Harper & Brothers, 1960

GINSBERG, L. *Legends of the Jews.* 7 vols., Jewish Publication Society of America, Philadelphia, 1909–1938

————. *Legends of the Bible.* One-vol. condensation of above. Jewish Publication Society of America, 1956

GRAETZ, H. *History of the Jews.* Jewish Publication Society of America, Philadelphia, 1891; frequently reprinted

GRAYZEL, S. *A History of the Jews.* Jewish Publication Society of America, 1947

KAUFMANN, Y. *The Religion of Israel.* Abr. and tr. by M. Greenberg. University of Chicago Press, 1960

KITTEL, RUDOLPH. *The Religion of the People of Israel.* Macmillan, 1925

KOHLER, K. *Jewish Theology, Systematically and Historically Considered.* Macmillan, 1918

MARGOLIS, M. L. AND MARX, A. *A History of the Jewish People.* Jewish Publication Society of America, 1927; frequently reprinted

MOORE, GEORGE FOOT. *Judaism in the First Centuries of the Christian Era.* 3 vols., Harvard University Press, 1927–1930

NOTH, MARTIN. *The History of Israel.* Harper, 1958

OESTERLEY AND ROBINSON. *A History of Israel.* 2 vols., Oxford, 1932

————. *Hebrew Religion, Its Origin and Development.* Macmillan, 1937

PEDERSEN, J. *Israel, Its Life and Culture.* 4 vols., Oxford University Press, 1926–1946

PFEIFFER, ROBERT H. *Introduction to the Old Testament.* Harper, 1941

PRITCHARD, JAMES B., ED. *The Ancient Near East.* An anthology of texts and pictures compiled from two earlier works: *Ancient Near Eastern Texts* and *The Ancient Near East in Pictures*. Princeton University Press, 1958

ROBINSON, H. WHEELER. *Inspiration and Revelation in the Old Testament*. Oxford, 1946

SCHÜRER, EMIL. *A History of the Jewish People in the Time of Jesus*. Abr. and tr. by N. N. Glatzer. Schocken Books pb, 1961

SCHOLEM, G. G. *Major Trends in Jewish Mysticism*. Schocken Books, 1946

TCHERIKOVER, V. *Hellenistic Civilization and the Jews*. Tr. by S. Appelbaum. Jewish Publication Society of America, 1959

WRIGHT, G. E. *Biblical Archaeology*. Westminster, 1957. With illustrations

14 Christianity in Its Opening Phase: The Religion of Jesus

THE STORY of Christianity is the story of a religion that has sprung from the faith that in its founder God was made manifest in the flesh and dwelt among men. Other religions have developed a conception of incarnation, but none has given it such centrality. In the belief that Jesus is the clearest portrayal of the character of God all the rest of Christian doctrine is implied.

It is not easy to tell the story briefly and clearly. The first Christian century has had more books written about it than any other comparable period of history. The chief sources bearing on its history are the Gospels and Epistles of the New Testament, and these—again we must make a comparative statement —have been more thoroughly searched by inquiring minds than any other books ever written. Historical criticism has been particularly busy with them during the last seventy-five years and has reached the verdict that in the New Testament the early Christian religion *about* Jesus has overlaid and modified the record of the religion *of* Jesus himself, but there is no unanimity about the degree of modification. It is known that Jesus himself did not write down his teachings but relied upon his disciples to go about preaching what he taught, from memory. It is generally assumed by historians that after his death some of them did write down his sayings, with occasional notes of the historical setting, before they should be forgotten, and that thus a document, or group of documents, came into being that scholars call "Q" (from the German word *Quelle* or "source"). It is generally considered that "Q" was somewhat colored by the prepossessions of the early Christians and may have had sayings added to it that were mistakenly ascribed to Jesus, but on the whole it was authentic and quite naturally became primary source material for the compilers of Matthew and Luke. These compilers used a great deal of other material also, both oral and written; for example they drew much of their material from Mark, already existent (65–70 A.D.). The Gospel of John was not written until the end of the century and then largely from private historical sources that were primarily concerned with the theological implications of Jesus' life and death.

Through all of these records runs the often unseen division between what is from Jesus himself and what is from the Apostolic Age. But when scholars are asked to separate the material that authentically reveals the historical Jesus from the material that reflects the growing Christology of the early Christians, they vary widely in their interpretations. At certain points each student is thrown back, after careful study, upon his own judgment, even his intuitive feeling of what is from the historical Jesus and what is from the early Church. In many cases these decisions on the quality of the evidence are crucial. There is some warrant therefore for saying that every life of Jesus is in some sense a *confessio fidei*. And yet, on many other points there has been wide agreement, and the future may see the development of a greater consensus among authorities as to the finally valid interpretation of the life of Jesus. The present chapter contains an essay in that direction.

I   The World into Which Jesus Came

That Jesus was born into a part of the world that had only recently been brought under Roman dominion is of some significance, to begin with. One of the last acquisitions of Roman arms was Palestine. The Jews, as we have seen in the chapter dealing with them, had been subjected over and over to a foreign yoke, yet the Roman rule came to seem more intolerable than any. This was due in large part to the fact that the Romans were an aloof, administrative group. They had in particular a purely regulatory feeling concerning local populations; there was no fellow-feeling at all. It had been different with the Greeks, who were an imaginative and responsive people, able to enter into the spirit of a locality and weigh its ideas as though they deserved respect. But the Jews and the Romans were poles apart. There was so little of seeing eye to eye that they were enig-

mas to each other and gave up trying to arrive at an understanding.

This hardening of the heart toward each other's natures and cultures precluded any possibility of adjustment and therefore made it inevitable that their living together in the same land would produce social tumult. This was so much the case throughout Palestine that in his childhood Jesus must have gained little better than a confusing impression of swift political and social changes taking place all around him. He grew up in an atmosphere of argument, conflict, and bitterness. There was endless talk. Older minds were bewildered by events and torn by mounting tensions. Even now the historians' picture of the period remains confusing. What then must contemporaries have felt!

The Political Divisions of Palestine in Jesus' Time

About the time of Jesus' birth Herod the Great died. Three of Herod's sons had escaped the fatal consequences of exciting his suspicion, and so survived. In his will he divided Palestine among them. While that unhappy country trembled on the brink of insurrection, the three sons hurried to Rome to have their bequests confirmed. Augustus Caesar assigned Judea, Samaria, and Idumea to Archelaus, Galilee and Perea to Herod Antipas, and the region northeast of the Lake of Galilee to Philip. Archelaus was, however, not given outright control of his district, as the other two sons were. The caution of Augustus proved well founded, for after nine years of incompetence and brutality Archelaus was accused before the emperor on a number of serious charges and banished to Gaul. His place was taken by a Roman official called a procurator, who was made responsible to the governor of Syria.

Procurator followed procurator in regular succession. They ruled Judea from Caesarea, on the coast below Jerusalem. Few of them had any sense of the historic forces at work beneath the surface of the **427**

PALESTINE IN THE TIME OF CHRIST

- ▨ Tetrarchy of Lysanias
- ▥ Tetrarchy of Philip
- ▥ Tetrarchy of Herod Antipas
- ⬚ Territory under Roman Procurator
- ▥ Areas Tributary to Salome
- ▤ Decapolis*
- ▨ Independent*
- ▧ Roman Province of Syria

*The Decapolis and Ascalon retained their independence under the Roman governor of the Province of Syria.

MEDITERRANEAN SEA

Damascus
ABILENE
ITURAEA
Sidon
Sarepta
Leontes R.
Mt. Hermon
PANIAS
PHOENICIA
Mount Lebanon
Tyre
Dan
Caesarea Philippi
SYRIA
ULATHA
TRACHONITIS
Lake Semechonitis
BASHAN
Gischala
Ptolemais
GALILEE
Chorazin
GAULANITIS
Seleucia
BATANAEA
Capernaum
Bethsaida
Raphana
Sea of Galilee
Gergesa
Cana
Gamala
+ Mt. Carmel
Sepphoris
Tiberias
Hippos
Dion
Nazareth
Yarmuk R.
Abila
Mt. Tabor +
Nain
Gadara
Edrei
Dora
Capitolis
Caesarea
Scythopolis
Bethabara
DECAPOLIS
En-gannim
Pella
SAMARIA
Plains of Sharon
Samaria
Mt. Ebal
Gerasa
Apollonia
Shechem + Sychar
Amathus
+ Mt. Gezerim
Jabbok R.
Antipatris
PERAEA
Joppa
Arimathaea
Phasaelis
Lydda
Gophna
Archelais
Philadelphia
Bethel
Ephraim
Bethnimrah
Gezer
Ramah
Jericho
AMMON
Jamnia
Emmaus
Mt. of Olives
Julias
Heshbon
Ekron
Nicopolis
Jerusalem
Bethany
Azotus
Bethlehem
X Qumran
[Dead Sea Scrolls]
Herodium
Dead
Callirhoe
ARABIA
Ascalon
Mareshah
Machaerus
Hebron
Wilderness
Dibon
JUDAEA
Juttah
Ziph
of
En-gedi
Gaza
Gerar
Carmel
Judah
Sea
Arnon R.
Masada
Raphia
Rabbath Moab
Beersheba
Kir-moab

NABATAEANS
NABATAEANS

Zered R.
Scale of Miles

N

Jewish scene. Some of them were rapacious and un-scrupulous men, anxious only to make enough money to retire in comfort to Rome. Though they allowed the Jews as much civil and religious liberty as politi-cal considerations (that is, Roman imperialism) per-mitted, they insisted on a kind of remote control over the Jewish religion. For example, they kept the robes of the high priest stored in the Tower of Antonia and released them only for the ceremonies in which they were worn. This meant that they could control the appointment of the high priest by signifying to whom they would be pleased to release the robes. They also from time to time tried to introduce into Jerusalem battle-standards and shields displaying the image of Caesar as emperor-god, but the Jews angrily pro-tested each time, and the procurators for the sake of preserving the peace did not insist.

Under these conditions Judea was scarcely happy. Indeed, perplexed almost to despair by the difficulties besetting them, the Jews "strove among themselves" —Pharisees with Sadducees, and Zealots and Herod-ians with the rest. (See again pp. 407–409.)

The Situation in Galilee

In Galilee, on the other hand, the irritation was less pervasive. There Herod Antipas ruled over a very mixed population. The Jews were barely in the major-ity. There were many Greek-speaking citizens, as well as Phoenicians from the coast and Syrians from inte-rior regions to the north. In some districts the Jews were outnumbered by these Gentiles. Furthermore, across the Jordan and not under Herod's authority directly, though within the borders of Perea, there were ten self-governing towns,* leagued together on the pattern of Hellenic city-states. These were the Palestinian expression of Alexander the Great's dream of a new international order. Their presence helps to explain why Herod Antipas pursued a policy of internationalism. He hoped that a patient infusion of

* Hence called, from the Greek, the Decapolis, the "tenfold city."

world-culture into his area would unify his people under his rule. But the Galilean Jews, though pre-disposed to "suffer fools gladly" so long as their religion was not threatened, were more than a little disturbed when he began to make their key towns over into Greco-Roman cities. One of these cultural ventures was the rebuilding of the largest city in Galilee, Sepphoris, not more than four miles north of Nazareth. This city was, however, outshone in mag-nificence, if not in size, by the new town of Tiberias on the western shore of the Lake of Galilee, a city provided with a colonnaded forum and named by Herod after the reigning Roman emperor. Here the Hellenistic influence reached its apogee in Herod's domain.

Many of the Jews in Galilee might have reconciled themselves to all this, and even welcomed it, if they had not been obliged to foot the bill. It had formerly seemed onerous enough to have to pay the direct, personal tax for administrative expenses, for only part of it went to Herod Antipas, the rest to far-away Rome. Now they were obliged to pay additional taxes in the form of burdensome customs duties, not only on goods imported into or exported from the region, but on those shipped from city to city and from farm to market. Tolls were collected, too, at bridges and harbors. And there was a salt tax—always irritating anywhere. The Jews thus found themselves contrib-uting to the expenses of their own subjection. So, when in 6 A.D. Quirinius, the governor of Syria, or-dered a census taken of the inhabitants of Palestine, in order that an even more thorough form of tax-assessment might be worked out, there were imme-diate hostile repercussions among the people. Jesus may have been ten or twelve years old at that time and must have been keenly aware of the general excitement of the Galilean Jews, which boiled up swiftly into insurrection.

A certain Judas the Galilean, assisted by a Pharisee called Zaddok, organized the Zealot party by calling around him the Galilean hotheads and forming a rebel army that stood ready to fight on the principle: "No God but Yahweh, no tax but to the Temple, no friend

429

but the Zealot."* Judas and his followers surprised the city of Sepphoris, seized the armory, provided themselves with its store of weapons, and made the city their headquarters. So serious did the revolt become that the Roman General Varus had to bring up two Roman legions to suppress it. He burned and destroyed Sepphoris and crucified several thousand Zealots in a bloody attempt to stamp the movement out, but its secret spread continued. Jesus was faced with the realities created by it all his life, for one at least, if not two, of the Twelve † had been affiliated with the Zealot party, and he himself was crucified finally, when the crowd in Pilate's courtyard shouted to have Barabbas, known to them as a Zealot, released to them instead of himself.

Not all the Jews of Galilee supported the Zealot cause. The Essenes were opposed to violence on principle. They were even opposed to animal sacrifices—a radical departure for that day. Fairly numerous in Galilee, they paid little attention to the strife of the times but waited patiently for the Lord's Anointed One, the Messiah. Meanwhile, they lived by strict rules in celibate communities, holding their possessions in common, keeping the Sabbath day, laboring in their fields during the other days of the week, and devoting themselves to fasting, prayer, and frequent ceremonial ablutions, much as the Dead Sea community did. (See again p. 407 f.)

The Pharisees, on their part, held themselves from violence largely out of considerations of prudence.

They were by far the largest party in Galilee and were led by scribes and rabbis whose consciousness of mission was heightened by systematic training. The Jewish parties had all caught the concept of organization from the Greeks and Romans and knew their hopes of survival depended upon unified leadership. Many attended schools that the Pharisees maintained —academies, we might call them, for in attitude and method they resembled the academies of Greece. The largest of these schools was in Jerusalem and boasted great teachers like Shammai and Hillel. Caught, all of them, in a world of rapid and unpredictable change, the Pharisees made it their principle to live as nearly as conditions permitted according to their traditions. They felt that the only way to hasten the coming of the Messiah, and in the meantime save Judaism in their perverse and wicked generation from extinction, was to be scrupulous in religious practices that linked tradition with every detail of daily living. This meant that they endeavored to keep every one of the Sabbath laws, to fulfill to the letter the regulations for keeping the Jewish festivals, to tithe, to repeat the Shema constantly, to have a mezuzah inside the door and a phylactery on the brow,* to be very particular about ceremonial purity, correct treatment of "holy things," and dietary rules, to have no legal dealings with anyone in the civil courts (because Jews should have recourse only to the judicial proceedings set up by their own tribunal, the Sanhedrin), and so on. Though the time was not long distant when they would be obliged to alter many of their old rites and introduce others that would be new, they were at this time critical of all those who did not keep the Law as they interpreted it.

The Sadducees, by comparison, were less influen-

---

* According to their contemporary, Josephus, "These men agree in all other things with the Pharisaic notions; but they have an inviolable attachment to liberty, and say that *God* is to be their only Lord and Master. They also do not mind dying any death, nor indeed do they heed the deaths of their relations and friends, nor could the fear of death make them call any man their master. And . . . I fear that what I have said does not adequately express the determination that they show when they undergo pain." Antiquities, XVIII, 1, 6. The fanaticism of the Zealots was due in some measure to the fact that many of them had a family history of death by violence for rebellion. Judas the Galilean's father was killed fifty-two years earlier while engaged in insurrection.

† Simon the Zealot and possibly Judas Iscariot.

* A mezuzah is a tube or case attached inside the doorpost and containing a piece of cowhide parchment inscribed with Deuteronomy 6:4–9 and 11:13–21. A phylactery is a black calf-skin case with thongs for binding it on the forehead or left arm, containing a strip (or strips) of parchment inscribed with Exodus 13:1–10 and 11–16 and Deuteronomy 6:4–9 and 11:13–22. Today the orthodox do not wear the phylactery constantly but only during weekday morning prayers.

tial in Galilee, but even more conservative. They were certain that the old cultus and Torah were unalterable, whereas the Pharisees, after much heart-searching, were willing with changed circumstances to alter old customs, if that meant preserving Jewish communities against religious dissolution. But Sadducees and Pharisees alike opposed looseness, opportunism, and radicalism.

Some of the common people, perhaps most of them, were tolerant and easy-going in these things, readily influenced by "the world," and only loosely and vaguely religious. Many, on the other hand, considered themselves strict Jews, attended the services of the synagogues, revered the Law and the Prophets, kept the Jewish festivals and fasts, and went up annually to the temple in Jerusalem at the Passover. This was not enough, the sterner Pharisees held. If they did not keep themselves free from ceremonial defilement, observe the strict dietary rules, tithe, wash their hands before meals, ceremonially cleanse their persons, their clothes, cups, jugs, basins, and all the food bought in the markets, and do no work on the Sabbath day, they were impure and could not be considered pious. Many of the devout among the common people, however, were sure that one could be deeply devotional, truly religious, without being narrowly legalistic in obeying "the tradition of the elders." It was to this group that the parents of Jesus seem to have belonged.

II   The Life and Teachings of Jesus

Youth

It seems paradoxical to say it, but Jesus was born in 4 B.C. or a year or two earlier. Herod the Great was still alive, and this fact, together with other evidence, such as the testimony of Luke that Jesus was crucified in "the fifteenth year of Tiberius Caesar," compels us to put his birth further back than the year

hallowed by long use.* Matthew and Luke are authorities for the fact that he was born in Bethlehem, south of Jerusalem, while Joseph and Mary were on a visit there. Luke says they were there to register for a census, but he alone suggests such a reason. All the evangelists agree that the home of the family was in Nazareth of Galilee. It was there that Joseph pursued his trade as a carpenter, and up to about his thirtieth year all but a few weeks of Jesus' life were spent there.

Of Jesus' childhood and youth we know little directly. The internal evidence of the Gospels leads us to assume that his parents belonged to the common people, the 'Am ha'aretz, but were deeply religious. Jesus not only went to the synagogue services with them but came to know by heart long passages from the Law and the Prophets. It may be that he attended the local synagogue school. Somehow he came to know enough of the prophetic tradition to develop a distrust of whatever arid scholarship and legalism the scribes and Pharisees were given to. As to his trade, he was trained to be a carpenter. As a result, his feeling for the common people was strong. We know from the Gospels that he grew up in a large family. There were at least six other children: four boys—James, Joses, Simon, and Jude—and "sisters," how many is not said.† Luke gives us one revealing glimpse into his religious experience as a child. The story of the boy Jesus in the temple is a witness to many things, but above all to the fact that he was capable of sustained interest in religious matters, an absorption so deep that he did not think of the effect his absence must be having upon his relatives and friends.

The next eighteen years of Jesus' life are often called the silent years, for we have no direct evidence

---

* It was not until the middle of the sixth century A.D. that the Church began to reckon time as before and after the birth of Christ. The monks whose calculations were followed made a mistake in computing the year.

† Mk. 6:3. Roman Catholic tradition, however, says the other children were not Mary's but children of Joseph by an earlier marriage or of Mary's presumed sister, Mary Cleophas.

Church of the Nativity, Bethlehem. From the bell tower of this church in Bethlehem we get a far-ranging view of the fields where "the shepherds watched their flocks by night." The silhouetted bells ring out each Christmas Eve to celebrate the birth of Jesus in the little town now the subject of bitterly disputed claims by Jordan and Israel. (Courtesy of the Arab Information Center.)

on what took place during them. We may assume, from the fact that Joseph drops out of the story completely, that he died in this interval, and that Jesus, as the oldest son, took over the management of the carpenter business, his brothers helping him. It has been an interesting surmise of recent scholarship that in the early part of this period Jesus worked as a carpenter in Sepphoris, four miles to the north, when that city was rebuilt by Herod Antipas after its burning during the Zealot rebellion of 6 A.D. If that was so, he had first-hand experience of working in a city being rebuilt after the Greek manner. But we have

greater warrant for assuming that as a carpenter Jesus hewed and installed the woodwork that went into Galilean homes and constructed ploughshares, yokes, and carts for the farmers near Nazareth.

Baptism and Temptation

When he was about thirty years old Jesus passed through one of the most profound experiences of his life. His baptism by John brought to him the same double experience of mystic vision and call that came to Amos, Isaiah, and Jeremiah. It terminated the quiet years at Nazareth and changed the direction of his life completely.

John the Baptist had appeared suddenly on the banks of the Jordan with an urgent message, "Repent! for the Kingdom of Heaven is coming!" He had emerged from the desert region beyond the Jordan, where he had been meditating on what appeared to him the crisis of the hour. We are told by the Gospels that he "wore clothing made of hair cloth, and had a leather belt around his waist, and he lived on dried locusts and wild honey,"[A1]—that is, he had assumed the life of a solitary ascetic. His periods of lonely brooding increased his feeling that the end of the present age was at hand; the Messiah who should judge the world was about to appear and bring in the day of wrath that the repentant alone would be able to face. So near did this day seem to him that he is reported to have used the vivid figure, "The axe is already lying at the roots of the trees." Another startling image of his was drawn from the threshing floor; he said the Messiah had already taken up the winnowing fork in his hand and would "clean up his threshing-floor, and store his wheat in his barn," but would "burn up the chaff with inextinguishable fire."[A2] He was not alone in so believing. The Essenes had a similar sense of the imminence of the end, but John did not join them. He had too much of the feeling of social responsibility to retire into mere watchful waiting. He therefore left the desert and began a career of fiery preaching, in order to warn the unwary. He succeeded in drawing people from all over Palestine to hear him. When these listeners became distressed about their spiritual condition, he took them down into the Jordan and immersed them in the water, to signify their repentance and the washing away of their sins. He became known as the Baptist. He was more, however, than a ceremonialist. His instructions to his converts were on an ethical plane of highest urgency. In the interim before the coming of the Messiah, they were to practice the strictest individual and social righteousness. The crowds would ask him, "What ought we to do?" He

answered, "The man who has two shirts must share with the man who has none, and the man who has food must do the same."[A3] He told tax-collectors not to collect more than they were authorized to, and soldiers not to extort money or make false charges against people, but to be satisfied with their pay. Though he roused the anger of Herod Antipas by condemning his illegal marriage with Herodias, his brother's wife, and was arrested and finally executed while in prison, he had raised up a loyal following that became self-propagating. St. Paul found a circle of his followers in Ephesus thirty years later.

It was natural that Jesus should be attracted. In the first chapter of Mark we have the story given barely and briefly:

It was in those days that Jesus came from Nazareth in Galilee, and was baptized by John in the Jordan. And just as he was coming up out of the water he saw the heavens torn open and the Spirit coming down like a dove to enter into him, and out of the heavens came a voice: "You are my Son, my Beloved! You are my Chosen!"[A4]

This experience was profoundly moving and convincing. Ever since his twelfth year Jesus had felt, and been known by his acquaintances to feel, a more than ordinary interest in religious matters. His sensitive intelligence and quick social conscience predisposed him toward a prophetic role in life. Now he was clearly called to assume such a role.

It is significant that he at once retired into the wilderness beyond Jordan to think through the course that he must in future take. In the Christian tradition, this time of meditation and decision is described as a period of forty days during which Satan tried to tempt him. As told by Matthew and Luke, the temptation had three phases. Back of the imagery used we may see the elements of very real issues. Should he continue to work for a livelihood— for bread? Not any longer. Should he use spectacular methods that might attract attention but put him in jeopardy? No, he must not force God's hand, must not put God's choice of him to trial. Should he seek political power as a precondition of redeeming Israel?

433

No, that would be indeed compromising with Satan.

In making his decisions Jesus was guided by what he well knew differentiated his position from those taken by the leading Jewish parties. He rejected the methods of the Zealot, because he saw they were futile and self-destructive. Those who take the sword, he later said, will perish by the sword. This conviction others shared with him. Many in Nazareth and Sepphoris knew by bitter experience that the Zealot rebellion of 6 A.D. had brought upon them only death and destruction.* As to the Pharisees, he differed from them chiefly in emphasis. In the diatribe in the 23rd chapter of Matthew he is quoted as saying: "Alas for you, you hypocritical scribes and Pharisees, for you pay tithes on mint, dill, and cummin, and you have let the weightier matters of the law go—justice, mercy, and integrity. But you should have observed these, without overlooking the others." With the Sadducees he had little contact, but he seems to have sided with the Pharisees against them. In another direction, he could not be an Essene. Like John the Baptist, he was too sensitive to his social duty to go into monastic seclusion. Moreover, he was no ascetic. Thoroughly at home with the plain people from among whom he had sprung, he enjoyed wedding feasts and banquets, insomuch that the scandalized Pharisees, afraid of all forms of ceremonial defilement, went about complaining that Jesus ate with tax-collectors and irreligious people, did not observe the dietary rules, and never fasted. They pointed out that even John the Baptist's disciples fasted. But Jesus insisted that fasting should be done in private; not by rule or rote, but in accordance with personal need. And this was not the only respect in which he differed from John the Baptist. He came too freshly from the carpenter's bench and from vital contacts with village folk absorbed in the concrete problems of the everyday world to be carried away by John's fanatic persuasion that the world was about to end

* The people of Sepphoris and the surrounding towns actually refused in 66 A.D. to support the Zealot-inspired Jewish War that led four years later to the destruction of Jerusalem and the dispersion of the nation.

434

suddenly. Moreover, John was too much the preacher: the people had to come to him. Jesus resolved to go to the people and change them where he found them.

The Beginning of the Galilean Ministry

About the time of John's arrest, Jesus crossed the Jordan and made his way to Galilee, "proclaiming," says Mark, "the good news from God, saying, "The time has come and the reign of God is near; repent, and believe this good news!' "A5 He produced such conviction of his divine calling that he was immediately followed by four disciples—Simon Peter, and his brother Andrew, James, and his brother John, the sons of Zebedee—all fishermen who dropped their nets and followed him. The Lake of Galilee was then surrounded by thriving towns—Tiberias, Taricheae, Capernaum, Chorazin, and Bethsaida. Jesus began his ministry among them, choosing Capernaum as his headquarters because Simon Peter's home was there. At first he spoke in the synagogues, and when the crowds grew too large for that, he preached in the market-places and open fields.

The first chapter of Mark contains a full description of what befell Jesus on the first Sabbath day in Capernaum. It will serve our purpose well to analyze it at some length as a typical day in the early ministry of Jesus. First of all, "he went to the synagogue and taught." Probably there was more than one synagogue in Capernaum, and he went to the one to which he was invited.* The interior of the synagogue was bare

* The synagogues were controlled, in matters of doctrine and polity, by the scribes and Pharisees, but the local administration was in the hands of a council of elders, one of whom was elected the "ruler of the synagogue" and had charge of the religious services. He would be in a position to invite Jesus to speak in the synagogue. Another officer, the *chazzan* or attendant, was the synagogue's librarian, having in his care the rolls of the scriptures which were in the "ark"; he was also the caretaker of the building, and if a person with scribal training, the teacher of the synagogue school. Every synagogue had in addition a group of men who collected and disbursed the alms. It was in imitation of them that the Christians appointed deacons.

and simple. The worshipers faced Jerusalem. Before them was a raised platform with a reading desk on it, and against the wall or within a recess was a cabinet containing the rolls of scripture. This was the ark. A curtain hung before it, and in front of the curtain stood a lamp, which was always alight. During services the "chief seats" were occupied by the elders and the leading Pharisees, who sat facing the other worshipers. Their voices led in the unison repetition of the Shema, an essential part of every service. At times the worshipers stood, as when the ruler of the synagogue recited prayers and the congregation repeated the appropriate responses. After the chazzan took from the ark the rolls of the Law and the Prophets, the scripture readings of the day were recited, first in Hebrew, then in Aramaic. After that the ruler himself, or a person chosen by him, addressed the congregation by way of "teaching."

Such was the setting of Jesus' first important utterance in Capernaum. When he began speaking, we are told, his audience was amazed at his teaching, for he spoke "like one who had authority," that is, with great freedom of interpretation and from the fullness of his heart, not drily "like the scribes." Whereupon a startling thing occurred. A man in the audience who believed he had a devil in him that had caused his abnormal physical and mental condition—the universally accepted explanation of certain ailments in that day—suddenly and hopefully interrupted the preacher.

"What do you want of us, Jesus, you Nazarene? Have you come to destroy us? I know who you are, you are God's Holy One!"

Jesus reproved him, and said,

"Silence! Get out of him!"

The foul spirit convulsed the man and gave a loud cry and went out of him.*

Jesus was probably as much surprised as anyone at this evidence of his healing power. (That seems to

* This and the next four quotations are from Mark 1:21–45. Translation is from *The Bible: An American Translation,* University of Chicago Press, 1935. Reprinted by permission of the publishers.

be indicated in what he did early the next morning.) It should be kept in mind in judging the situation that he had no reason to question the diagnosis of puzzling ailments that was universal in his time, that is, that they were caused by an indwelling demonic power entering the person from elsewhere. His audience certainly had no doubt. We read further:

And they were all so amazed that they discussed it with one another, and said,

"What does this mean? It is a new teaching! He gives orders with authority even to the foul spirits, and they obey him!"

And his fame immediately spread in all directions. . . .

After the synagogue service, the story continues, Jesus went with his disciples to the home of Simon Peter, where Simon's mother-in-law was in bed, sick with a fever. Jesus went up to her, and grasping her hand, made her rise. "And the fever left her, and she waited on them." Then followed one of the crucial episodes of Jesus' early ministry.

In the evening, after sunset, they brought to him all who were sick or possessed by demons, and the whole town was gathered at the door. And he cured many. . . .

The wording here deserves close study. It is interesting to note that the other evangelists in copying from Mark at this point change the word *many* to *all,* but Mark undoubtedly preserves the original tradition. Jesus could not heal people except by their "faith," and in his perfect honesty he always refused the credit, but said to every healed person such words as: "Go in peace, and sin no more. Your faith has healed you."*

* The healing miracles of Jesus, as preserved for us in tradition, present many difficulties, but if we could speak of a "minimum view," it would be something like this: in a world like that of Jesus' time, where spiritual and nervous tensions were so great, there must have been many instances of functional disorders, greatly aggravated by fears and repressions and exhibiting many of the symptoms of organic disease, among all classes of the people. The nobility of Jesus' own faith, mediated through a wholesome, sympathetic, and challenging per-

That Jesus was disturbed by his new-found power and the kind of renown it brought him is implied in the next words:

Early in the morning, long before daylight, he got up and left the house and went off to a lonely spot, and prayed there. And Simon and his companions sought him out and found him, and said to him,

"They are all looking for you!"

He said to them,

"Let us go somewhere else, to the neighboring country towns, so that I may preach in them, too, for that is why I came out here."

But his experience in the other towns was like that in Capernaum. For some days he could no longer go into a town openly but stayed in unfrequented places, and people came to him from every direction. His popularity was tremendous. People "ran" to him. There seemed to be great promise in him. They were hopeful of great things. When he came again into Capernaum, "such a crowd gathered that there was no room even around the door." On another occasion there were so many people in the house it was impossible to prepare a meal; on still another, so many people gathered along the lake shore that for fear of being crushed, Jesus had his disciples keep a boat ready to remove him. Subsequently, he found the crowd so great "he got into a boat and sat in it, a little way from the shore, while all the people were on the land close to the water,"[A6] and from this vantage point, he taught them.

The Content of Jesus' Teaching

What was it in Jesus' preaching that so attracted the crowds during the early part of his ministry? The answer is that, for one thing, he spoke in simple and untechnical language about the central issues in religion, always with the use of homely illustrations drawn from nature and human life. He was a plain man speaking to plain people. Many of his most profound lessons were given through parables—brief stories that set life in its true perspective. But it would not have been enough if the manner of his teaching had been its only attraction. What he really had achieved was a new synthesis of the religious insights of his people, perfectly exemplified and illustrated in his own personality and experience.

A. RELIGIOUS TEACHING. One thing is obvious in all the teaching his disciples remembered: the centrality of the religious point of view. From the time of his baptism by John the Baptist, and throughout the rest of his life, the reality of God and of his own intimate relationship with God occupied the central place in Jesus' thinking and determined the consistency of his point of view. He was never moved to set in order his reasons for believing in the reality of God. In that age of universal faith in the divine existence, no one ever asked him to. What men desired to know then was what kind of a god God was, and what, in view of his character, he might be expected to do. On this point Jesus spoke with profound assurance. God was the sovereign moral personality ruling the universe, the moving spirit behind the course of history, a transcendent being, sternly righteous, who never departed from perfect justice in determining the course of events or the destiny of an individual. But God was also forgiving and merciful, primarily occupied with human redemption, in character and action paternal. Jesus' favorite name for God was Father (or Father in Heaven). It is implied in his teaching that though God allows men to make their own decisions and, like the prodigal in the famous parable, take the means at their disposal and waste them in riotous living, he continues to love them throughout the redemptive process of punishment and suffering that inevitably follows and will forgive them when they return to him. God therefore is utterly good as well as holy. Men should trust him beyond all shadow of doubting, be unanxious, and regularly seek spiritual enlightenment through prayer,

sonality, remade many lost or sick souls, restored their faith, and caused their alarming symptoms to vanish in an instant. To this minimum view a great deal might be added.

especially private prayer in one's chamber or in the solitude of the fields and hill tops.

Jesus' attitude toward nature was conditioned by his conception of God. He was truly Jewish in thinking of nature as the stage-setting of the sublime drama of human redemption. Nature was not the ultimate reality. God worked behind and through nature. (One might generalize and say that Jesus was like the Jews in looking through nature at God, and did not follow the Greek tendency to look through the gods at nature.) At the same time it is apparent in Jesus' teaching that he looked at nature directly with delight and trust. The lilies of the field, more beautifully arrayed than Solomon in all his glory, were of God's making and were, like the birds of the heaven—the ravens and sparrows—fully sustained by God's care. Surely, if men would know how to live with each other in the righteousness of God's kingdom, they too would find in nature all they needed.*

Jesus' attitude toward his body and the impulses of the natural man within him (to follow the traditional phrasing for a reference to the native impulses of human beings) was similarly confident and trustful, and again typically Jewish. He apparently accepted the body as functionally integrated with the mind and spirit in a working unity. As we have observed earlier, he was no ascetic. He enjoyed wedding feasts and banquets. He never suggested that the body is inherently corrupting and defiling, or that the soul is foully imprisoned in the flesh. The body may indeed become the dangerous instrument of an evil will, or it may be divided between good and evil because the will is so divided. In the latter case, Jesus said, one might use drastic means to regain unity of the personality: "If your foot makes you fall, cut it off."[A7] But on the positive side, his follower, St. Paul, who had received a Jewish training, put the whole matter clearly enough in the suggestion that the body may become the temple of the Holy Spirit.* Jesus, in short, did not distract his followers from the pursuit of personal and social goodness by suggesting that the body is the chief enemy of good and ought first to be subdued.

His attention was directed elsewhere. His primary interest was in man's doing the will of God. What God most wanted was that men should become fit for the coming Kingdom of Heaven by living together as persons religiously oriented toward him as sons toward a father and ethically oriented toward each other as brethren. No person was to be excluded from attempting to reach such fitness. No person was natively unworthy either of God's grace or man's fellowship. All through Jesus' teaching appears the concept of the infinite worth of human personality—the principle that is often called today respect for personality. He invoked this principle particularly in the case of little children, but also in the case of the disinherited, the sinful, and alien folk, with whom he was constantly in association. There were to be no exceptions to the law of love; it was to be interracial and international.

These might be called the universal and fundamental elements in Jesus' religious teaching. They were, of course, clothed in and colored by the thought-forms of his day. That was inevitable. This places us in some difficulty, however. Although some of the thought-forms he used may properly be called fugitive and now largely unusable, they had great importance at the time, and hence it is necessary to give them serious consideration. We are here in a hard field of discussion, providing some of the thorniest problems of interpretation in historical research, but if the strictest objectivity in seeking to determine the facts be as nearly as possible realized, one may hope to approximate the truth of history.

It is apparent that Jesus shared with his people the expectation that the Messianic Kingdom long

---

* It is a simplification, but the sense of Jesus' teaching at this point is: the trouble lies in the fact that men seek food and clothing *first,* but if they would seek first the Kingdom, food and clothing would come in course; that was God's plan. If we shed the thought-forms of Jesus' time, this is at the heart of his faith.

* St. Paul, however, was sufficiently influenced by Greek modes of thought to say elsewhere that the flesh and spirit are "in opposition, so that you cannot do anything you please."[A8]

foretold was about to be ushered in. The religious feeling of the Jewish people then centered in this expectation. From his youth on Jesus was under the influence of the hopes raised by it. So that he was responding normally to his environment when he entertained along with his people their general and passionate hope of a new order of things.

Consider the following passages from "Q":

And he said to his disciples,
"The time will come when you will long to see one of the days of the Son of Man. . . . Men will say to you, 'Look! There he is!' or, 'Look! Here he is!' Do not go off in pursuit of him, for just as when lightning flashes, it shines from one end of the sky to the other, that will be the way with the Son of Man. . . . In the time of the Son of Man it will be just as in the time of Noah. People went on eating, drinking, marrying, and being married up to the very day that Noah got into the ark and the flood came and destroyed them all. . . . It will be like that on the day when the Son of Man appears."[A9]

In the Gospel of Mark there are passages (modified by the language of the Apostolic age) that have a similar meaning:

And he said to them, "I tell you, some of you who stand here will certainly live to see the reign of God come in its might."[A10]
"I tell you, these things will all happen before the present age passes away. . . . But about that day or hour no one knows, not even the angels in heaven, nor the Son; only the Father. You must look out and be on the alert, for you do not know when it will be time."[A11]

If we accept these sayings as going back to Jesus —and they would seem in essence to be his—what is to be said of their meaning? In the first place, the conviction clearly is that the "end of the age" is imminent, possibly very near. The thrill of expectancy produced by this conviction is hard for us to recreate even in imagination. That it is a strange belief to the twentieth century is, of course, no argument at all that only a strange or unhealthy mind could believe it then. The marvel of it is that Jesus did not make more of it. If the critical dissection of the records is on the right track, his disciples made much more of it than he did. For it was almost an obsession among the greater number of unhappy Jews of Palestine and was a large factor in the lives of the Jews who lived abroad. Not to believe it was unreasonable. In a world where the concept of social evolution and progress did not exist, and where faith in God's direct intervention in human affairs was unquestioned, no pious mind among the Jews doubted that God was soon to work his deliverance, just as he had in the past when his people were suffering beyond endurance.

But in his analysis and weighing of the situation Jesus showed distinct originality.

A careful examination of his use of the more or less fugitive thought-forms of the eschatology of his time conclusively shows that though Jesus shared the general apocalyptic hope, he transformed it. He took the narrowly conceived, exclusively Jewish Messianic kingdom of the less liberal Judaism and made it the universal kingdom of the Father of all men. The "elect" are from the four corners of the earth. A passage from "Q" puts it with the utmost directness:

"You must strain every nerve to get in through the narrow door, for I tell you many will try to get in, and will not succeed, when the master of the house gets up and shuts the door, and you begin to stand outside and to knock on the door, and say, 'Open it for us, sir!' Then he will answer you and say, 'I do not know where you come from. . . . Get away from me, all you wrong-doers!' There you will weep and gnash your teeth when you see Abraham and Isaac and Jacob and all the prophets in the Kingdom of God, while you are put outside. People will come from the east and west and the north and south, and take their places in the Kingdom of God. There are those now last who will then be first, and there are those now first who will be last."[A12]

Matthew renders part of this passage still more clearly, thus:

"I tell you, many will come from the east and from the west and take their places at the feast with Abraham, Isaac, and Jacob, in the Kingdom of Heaven, while the heirs to the kingdom will be driven into the darkness outside, there to weep and grind their teeth!"[A13]

The Kingdom is thus not a collection of righteous Jews only, but a brotherhood including Gentiles.

Entrance into the Kingdom is not conditioned by the keeping of the Law of Moses, but by broader ethical qualifications. Matthew's paraphrase of the Lukan beatitudes is not false to the fact. It is the pure in heart who shall see God; it is the meek who shall inherit the earth.

Further, it is to be noted that Jesus distinctly lessened the tension of expectation by teaching that the Kingdom is in a real sense already present. It is from "Q" that we derive this teaching: the Kingdom is like a bit of yeast in a large measure of flour; it is like a mustard seed, the smallest of the seeds, but sure in process of time to grow into a tree. Jesus was in no hurry for the consummation of the eschatological hope. We see everywhere that the essential thing to him was *present* unbroken union with God.

And this brings us to the very knotty problem of Jesus' conception of his own relationship with God. Did he consider himself the Son of Man and Son of God in a special sense? Did he think of himself as the Messiah from the time of his baptism, or did he grow gradually into the conviction that he was the Lord's Anointed? Or did his followers endow him with Messiahship toward the end of his career and after his death, without any intimation from him that this was due him?

These questions are crucial and can perhaps never be answered finally. Nevertheless, some very definite things can be said about Jesus' sense of unique relationship with God.

God was much more to Jesus than the great august presence to whom one owes a morning and an evening prayer. The intimacy and rapport of his communion with God in prayer exceeded anything he experienced among men. In teaching his disciples to pray, he communicated something of this experience to them, but there was as well something incommunicable about it, so that they were reduced to wonder. Whatever his use of the terms *Son of Man* and *the Christ* was, it is quite beyond doubt that he knew he was "sent." God had commissioned him to establish his Kingdom. As with Amos, so with Jesus: God "took" him and sent him to men.

Hence he could choose twelve men to follow him. He could preach and teach and heal with authority. He could propound a law superseding that of Moses. And he could read to the congregation in Nazareth the great passage from Isaiah:

"The spirit of the Lord is upon me,
For he has consecrated me to preach the good news to the poor,
He has sent me to announce to the prisoners their release and to the blind the recovery of their sight,
To set the down-trodden at liberty,
To proclaim the year of the Lord's favor!"

and say calmly, "This passage of Scripture has been fulfilled here in your hearing today!"[A14]

The sum of the matter is that Jesus had found a master principle for his life and that he was completely possessed by it. The central reality in his environment as he saw it, the ultimate fact giving religious value and character to all his world, was God, and in an act of surrender he gave himself up to the consciousness of the presence and will of God. Thenceforth, completely unified in person and attitude, he went among men, possessed of absolute certitude, never hesitant, never doubting, clothed with power and authority, his whole unified life crying aloud: Nothing is so important to you as that you should hear me, everyone of you: by me God speaks!

B. ETHICAL TEACHING. This religious consciousness of Jesus—analogous to that of the prophets—carried over into his ethical teaching. He spoke with the authority of moral assurance. And because he could himself move swiftly and easily from one moral decision to another, without prolonged hesitancy, his teaching contains a constant challenge to will whatever may hasten the coming of the Kingdom of God and to be firm in that will.

Taking for granted their knowledge of the scope and requirements of the Kingdom of God, Jesus expected his followers, as truly religious men, to be sincere, immediately and thoroughly sincere in acting on their insight. According to Luke this seemed so

439

urgent a matter to him that once, when he challenged a man to follow him, and the man said, "Let me first go and bury my father," Jesus said to him, "Leave the dead to bury their own dead; you must go and spread the news of the Kingdom of God!" Yet another man said to him, "Master, I am going to follow you, but let me first say goodbye to my people at home," to which Jesus replied, "No one who puts his hand to the plough, and then looks back, is fitted for the Kingdom of God."[A15]

Besides calling for sincerity and complete self-commitment, Jesus asked his followers to put their moral obligations above all social, legal, or ceremonial demands. It was at this point that he felt most critical of the Pharisees. They* were guilty of certain obvious faults: complacency, self-seeking, the desire for honor and applause, spiritual pride, hypocrisy. But, more profoundly, their gravest shortcoming lay in their neglect of the primary imperatives of the moral law. They had substituted legal and ceremonial practices for a creative and truly regenerating morality. They strained out the gnat, yet swallowed the camel; they cleaned the outside of the cup and the dish, but were themselves full inside of greed and self-indulgence; they were like white-washed tombs, looking well on the outside but full inside of the bones of the dead and all that is unclean. Though they paid tithes on mint, dill, and cummin, they let the weightier matters of the Law go—justice, mercy, and integrity. They took the relatively unimportant for the central and significant, and so their religious position had lost all vital significance.

It was indeed characteristic of Jesus, in all his ethical precepts, to transfer attention from the external features of moral behavior to its inward motivation, the spirit or attitude behind it. To concentrate upon outwardly correct behavior according to Jewish law was perversely short-sighted, if not downright immoral! Only if one's heart is right and one is in addition sincere in doing as the heart directs can one

* One should perhaps note here that Jesus was referring to the Pharisees who had not yielded to the liberals of their own party.

be called a truly moral person. Spirit and motive are all-important. Out of the heart are the issues of life.

Before we look at the application of this principle to morality, we should see clearly that Jesus linked it up with a twofold concern: concern for one's own inner integrity and concern for the inner health of others. Woe, said Jesus, to anyone who hurts another at the center of his moral being! All three Synoptic Gospels repeat the solemn warning that anyone who causes a humble believer to fall might better have a great millstone hung around his neck and then be thrown into the sea. Harming the moral nature of another is the gravest of crimes.

With the same stress on the inward condition of the personality Jesus reviewed and rephrased the old Hebrew laws. Matthew assembles a series of teachings in which Jesus looks behind a prohibited act to the motive that might cause it. Two examples may be cited. There was the law against murder that had been given to the men of old. "But I tell you that anyone who gets angry with his brother . . . and anyone who speaks contemptuously to his brother . . . and anyone who says to his brother 'You cursed fool!' will have to answer for it."[A16] There was the law against adultery. "But I tell you that anyone who looks at a woman with desire has already committed adultery with her in his heart."[A17]

But the stress on the spiritual and the inward in morality reached its most significant form in Jesus' teaching about love. This is a teaching that still requires the utmost effort of understanding, for although the command to use the method of love toward friend and foe alike is an absolute principle, its application to the details of conduct is always marked by such relativity that sincere Christians often differ in their judgments as to what that conduct should be.

The absolute principle is contained in the familiar words:

You have heard that [the men of old] were told, "You must love your neighbor and hate your enemy." But I tell you, love your enemies and pray for your persecutors, so that you may show yourselves true sons of your Father in heaven, for he makes his sun rise on bad and good alike, and makes his rain fall on the upright and the wrongdoers. . . . You are to be perfect, as your heavenly Father is.

You must always treat other people as you would like to have them treat you, for this sums up the Law and the Prophets.

"You must love the Lord your God with your whole heart, your whole soul, and your whole mind." That is the great, first command. There is a second like it: "You must love your neighbor as you do yourself." These two commands sum up the whole of the Law and the Prophets.[A18]

Recent studies of his disciples' understanding of Jesus' teaching about the love of God and the love of man clearly show that to them God's love for man is so boundless and unlimited that it is poured out on good and bad alike without regard to merit or need and does not diminish when it gets a bad reception. It hates evil, but it loves persons with the same unqualified good will with which a mother loves her child or the father in the parable loved the prodigal son. It was understood that every follower of Christ must love his fellow-men, regardless of merit or desert, in the same unqualified fashion. Evil must be opposed with vigor, but persons must be loved unendingly and with an unlimited capacity to forgive.

The application of this principle to the details of conduct must be left to the judgment of the moment, for the moment often contains unpredictable surprises, and one finds himself faced with the quandary, "Which side shall I take in this conflict between groups of my fellow-men? What is evil here, and what is good?* And what form of opposition to evil must I adopt that will be consistent with inclusive love for all?" It cannot be said that Jesus' teaching, as it has been preserved, deals specifically with such a dilemma. Just the central principle is stated, and the application of it at any juncture is left to the conscience of the individual who espouses it.

In one direction, however, clear guidance is given. The hard rule is laid down that one should not resist with violence evil done to one's own self.

* Or, "Which is the lesser evil?"

You have heard that [the men of old] were told, "An eye for an eye and a tooth for a tooth." But I tell you not to resist injury, but if anyone strikes you on your right cheek, turn the other to him too; and if anyone wants to sue you for your shirt, let him have your coat too.[A19]

The correct interpretation of these words would seem to be, do not engage in embittering and futile personal retaliation; it will only add to the moral confusion if one answers a personal injury with some similar one. Rather, then, one should endure a wrong without any display of vengefulness or hatred, and without doing the things that would prolong the bad situation indefinitely, with no improvement. Yet, on the other and more positive side, the wrong should be endured without moral surrender or compromise. The wrong-doer should be made to understand that his wrong-doing is being resisted, man to man, yet only with answering goodness, immediately expressed by a gesture—the turning of a cheek, the giving of a coat, the second mile—symbolizing with shattering clearness the complete willingness of the wronged individual to live in fellowship with the wrong-doer, should that be made possible.

A complementary teaching warns against rash or ill-considered criticism of another's conduct. For one thing, it is all too often true that the rash critic is himself in need of moral correction. For another, it is always best to be generous and thus call forth love from others.

Pass no more judgments upon other people, so that you may not have judgment passed upon you. . . . Why do you keep looking at the speck in your brother's eye, and pay no attention to the beam that is in your own? How can you say to your brother, "Just let me get that speck out of your eye," when all the time there is a beam in your own? You hypocrite! First get the beam out of your own eye, and then you can see to get the speck out of your brother's eye.[A20]

You must be merciful just as your Father is. Do not judge others. . . . Excuse others. . . . Give, and they will give to you; good measure, pressed down, shaken together, and running over, they will pour into your lap. For the measure you use with others they in turn will use with you.[A21]

441

In other words, goodness in any form has an all-conquering power to call forth a response of the same kind.

The Growth of Opposition and the Retirement to the North

The furor of excitement and interest that attended the journeys of Jesus through the towns and villages of Galilee attracted the attention of the Pharisees and Sadducees in Jerusalem. The former as guardians of the Law and the latter as guardians of the temple sent investigators to spy on Jesus and render a full report of him. The report when it came in was adverse. Thereupon selected Pharisees and Sadducees were sent to Galilee to heckle and oppose him. Verbal encounters between them and Jesus became frequent and always threw the radical tendency of Jesus' proposals into sharp focus. A typical encounter occurred when, in passing through the wheat fields on the Sabbath, Jesus' disciples began to pick the heads of the wheat as they made their way through. The Pharisees protested against this as a breaking of the Sabbath law forbidding the gathering of produce from the fields. Jesus retorted: "The Sabbath was made for man, not man for the Sabbath."[A22] The Pharisees would not have denied the truth of this assertion, but they disliked its radical tone. They were critical also of other elements in Jesus' teaching. Because physicians were prohibited from working on the Sabbath day, they attacked Jesus' healings on the Sabbath. On more than one occasion they obliged Jesus to defend himself on this score. They noticed, too, that some of his disciples ate their food without first giving their hands a ceremonial washing to purify them, and accused Jesus of allowing the laxity. Jesus replied: "Listen to me all of you, and understand this. Nothing that goes into a man from outside can pollute him. It is what comes out of a man that pollutes him."[A23] Asked by his disciples to explain, he said: "It is from inside, from men's hearts, that designs of evil come; immorality, stealing, murder, adultery, greed, malice, deceit, indecency, envy, abusiveness, arrogance, folly—all these evils come from inside, and they pollute a man."

What offended the Pharisees most, however, was the freedom with which Jesus interpreted the Law and the Prophets without respecting tradition. Too often the formula that Matthew uses in recording the Sermon on the Mount appeared in Jesus' discourse: "You have heard that the men of old were told . . . but I tell you. . . ." In short, Jesus had his authority from within. Some Pharisees pitched on this with eagerness. They began to go among the people, zealously spreading the rumor that Jesus' eloquence and ability to draw the people away from the Pharisaic line of reasoning to a broader and (to their mind) dangerously free point of view were proof that he was possessed by an evil spirit that had entered into him. His apparent sincerity was the result of delusion; in truth he was going against the revelation of God, contradicting Moses, and leading the people astray.

The rumor that Jesus was "possessed" was implanted at Nazareth. When he returned to his hometown and taught in the synagogue on the Sabbath day, he wondered at the lack of faith. "A prophet is treated with honor everywhere except in his native place and among his relatives and at his home," he is reported to have said.[A24] Mark records that on an earlier occasion his relatives had come to Capernaum to stop him because, being not yet won over, they were alarmed at his behavior. The story has a grim note:

His mother and his brothers came. And they stood outside the house and sent word in to him to come outside to them. There was a crowd sitting around him when they told him,
"Your mother and your brothers are outside asking for you."
He answered,
"Who are my mother and my brothers?"
And looking around at the people sitting about him, he said, "Here are my mother and my brothers! Whoever does the will of God is my brother and sister and mother."[A25]

The only answer that Jesus could make to the open accusations against him was, "How can Satan drive Satan out? . . . If Satan has rebelled against himself and become disunited, he cannot last."[A26] But the Pharisees brushed this aside.

The Zealot group in Galilee meanwhile turned against Jesus because he held the position that those who take the sword will perish by the sword. He could not be the Messiah, with such views, they felt, even though he healed the sick, cast out demons, and drew the multitudes to him with enthralling discourses on matters of religion and morals.

Many of the common people began therefore to fall away from Jesus, in doubt and disappointment. They had been so often deceived and misled; were they being imposed on once more? The enemies of Jesus redoubled their attacks, and threats against his life began to be breathed.

It was under these circumstances that Jesus made his way northwestward into the regions about Tyre and Sidon that were outside of Palestine, and then into southern Syria. This retirement to the north was apparently for the purpose of gaining time to consider further fateful decisions and to prepare his disciples for them. The Twelve were with him when he reached the inland town of Caesarea Philippi.° Here occurred the famous confession of Peter. Jesus said to them, "Who do people say that I am?" They said to him, "John the Baptist; others say Elijah, and others that you are one of the prophets." (It was thus clear that the people had not thought he was the Messiah.) "But," he said, "who do you say I am?" Peter answered: "You are the Christ."[A27] The record says that Jesus warned the Twelve not to say this about him to anyone, and he went on to tell them that he must go to Jerusalem and face suffering and death for the consummation of his mission. The frightened protest of the Twelve, voiced by Peter, met with his stern rebuke. This final step had now become necessary. He began to make his way steadily and quietly toward Jerusalem, timing himself to arrive during the Passover Festival.

° The capital of the Tetrarchy of Philip.

Passion Week and Crucifixion

Jews from all over the world had come to Jerusalem to attend the great annual festival of the Passover. The Roman procurator, Pilate, had moved up to the city from the coastal town of Caesarea to be on hand to see order kept and to quell any attempted uprising. Herod Antipas had come down from Galilee to enjoy the festivities and to go through the motions of being a faithful Jew. There was no room in the inns. The Galileans came prepared to live in tents in the valley between the city and the Mount of Olives. Many of them knew Jesus and would welcome him if he put in an appearance. On a borrowed colt, he rode down the Mount of Olives, accompanied by his disciples, and into the city. The Galileans greeted him with shouts of joy and spread palm branches in the way, but the people of the city said, "Who is this?" and the people in the procession responded, "This is Jesus, the prophet of Nazareth in Galilee!"

With his disciples, Jesus did a startling thing. He went to the temple and overturned the tables of the money-changers and drove out the pigeon-dealers and all who were buying or selling things in the precincts of the temple. He cried out: "Does not the Scripture say, 'My house shall be called a house of prayer for all the nations'? But you have made it a robbers' cave."[A28] This act must have had wide popular support, for the authorities did nothing in direct reprisal.

But the Jewish leaders did not intend to let Jesus go scot free. They began verbal hostilities, in the hope of discrediting him before the people. For several days, while he taught in the temple, they attempted to trap him into some treasonable or blasphemous utterance, but he eluded them. He urged the plain people to join his movement as the inauguration of the true Kingdom of God, and they listened to him eagerly.

His opponents damaged him in the people's eyes, however, when he refused to make a declaration against paying the poll-tax to the Roman emperor. Presented with the dilemma, "Is it right to pay taxes

443

to Caesar or not?" he made the disappointing reply, "Give Caesar what belongs to Caesar, give God what belongs to God!"[B] The sheer weight of the opposition to him must have impressed the people unfavorably; even the Herodians joined in the opposition. Seeing that this was so, Jesus began to tell the people, in pungent parables, that though the Jews had received the first invitation to sit at God's banquet table, now because they had refused the invitation, God was going to bring in to the feast of the Kingdom outcasts and aliens. Matthew represents Jesus as saying pointedly to the Sadducees and Pharisees, "I tell you, the tax-collectors and prostitutes are going into the Kingdom of God ahead of you. . . . The Kingdom of God will be taken away from you, and given to a people that will produce its proper fruit."[A29]

All the evangelists agree that Jesus knew the opposition would contrive his death and that he prepared himself for it. In their treatment of events they clearly reflect the consuming interest of the early Christians in these final hours and especially in the Last Supper in an upper room in Jerusalem. As the early Christians told and retold the story, Jesus not only foresaw his death but knew who should betray him, and he performed a simple ceremony, during that last meal, to bring home to the Twelve the significance of his death.

As they were eating, he took a loaf and blessed it, and he broke it in pieces and gave it to them saying,
"Take this. It is my body."
And he took the wine cup and gave thanks and gave it to them and they all drank from it. And he said to them, "This is my blood."[A30]

Later, in the Garden of Gethesemane, he was betrayed by Judas to a crowd of men with swords

The Via Dolorosa. The steep street in Jerusalem, said to have been the one along which Jesus attempted to carry his cross before he fell under its weight, is visited on Good Friday by a group of Franciscan monks, who are shown kneeling at one of the traditional Stations of the Cross. (Courtesy of the Arab Information Center.)

and clubs, who had been sent out by the high priest. He was haled before the Sanhedrin and condemned to death by Jewish law for blasphemy. Pilate, when asked to carry out the sentence, passed Jesus over to Herod Antipas, as the governor of Galilee, but Herod sent Jesus back to Pilate. The latter endeavored to procure Jesus' release, the early Christians asserted, by offering him to the crowd in his courtyard as the prisoner to be released to them for that year. But the crowd cried for the release of Barabbas, known to Pilate as a robber, but to them as a Zealot insurrectionist. At their demand, Pilate turned Jesus over for crucifixion. At three o'clock in the afternoon, forsaken by all but the women who would not leave him, amidst a howling mob for whom he breathed out the prayer, "Father, forgive them, for they know not what they do," he cried out with a loud voice, "My God, my God, why have you forsaken me?" and, resigning himself into God's care, expired.

No single death in the world's history has so affected the human imagination. To the Christians who have used the cross as a symbol of their faith, it has seemed that in his willingness to suffer death for the redemption of his fellow-men Jesus has given to them their clearest insight into the quality of the redemptive love of God himself.

To avoid having the body hanging on the cross over the Sabbath day, Joseph of Arimathaea, a member of the Sanhedrin, offered the use of his empty tomb, and the body of Jesus was taken there.

SUGGESTIONS FOR FURTHER READING

BORNKAMM, G. *Jesus of Nazareth.* Tr. by Irene and Fraser McLuskey with James M. Robinson. Harper, 1960

BRANSCOMB, H. *The Teachings of Jesus.* Abingdon-Cokesbury, 1931. Available as Apex pb

BULTMANN, R. *Jesus and the Word.* Tr. by L. P. Smith and E. Huntress. Scribner, 1934. Available as Scribner pb

DIBELIUS, M. *Jesus.* Tr. by Hedrick and Grant. Westminster Press, 1949

FULLER, R. H. *The Mission and Achievement of Jesus.* Student Christian Movement, London, 1954

GOGUEL, M. *The Life of Jesus.* Tr. by Olive Wyon. Macmillan, 1945. Available in 2 vols. as Harper Torchbooks pb

JEREMIAS, J. *The Parables of Jesus.* Tr. by S. H. Hooke. Scribner, 1955
———. *The Eucharistic Words of Jesus.* Blackwell, London, 1955

KLAUSNER, JOSEPH. *Jesus of Nazareth.* Macmillan, 1925. A Jewish interpretation

MAJOR, MANSON, AND WRIGHT. *The Mission and Message of Jesus.* Dutton, 1946. See especially the section by Manson

MANSON, T. W. *The Teaching of Jesus.* Cambridge, 1931

RICCIOTTI, G. *The Life of Christ.* Tr. A. L. Zizzamia. Bruce, 1945. A Catholic interpretation

RICHARDSON, A. *The Miracle Stories of the Gospels.* Student Christian Movement, London, 1941

SCHWEITZER, ALBERT. *The Quest of the Historical Jesus.* A. & C. Black, London, 1910; reissue, with new Introduction by James M. Robinson, Macmillan, 1968

SCOTT, E. F. *The Ethical Teaching of Jesus.* Macmillan, 1923

TAYLOR, VINCENT. *The Life and Ministry of Jesus.* London, 1954

15 The Religious Development of Christianity

To THE CHRISTIANS of the first century, the events that followed upon the death of Jesus were of greater importance than those that preceded it. It was true for them that the life and teachings of Jesus were of priceless value for their daily life and thought; but yet his resurrection from the dead was of higher value still, for it was their proof of his *living* reality as a person, that is, as the undying Lord of Life who was the assurance of their own immortality and the pledge of their unbreakable spiritual oneness with God the Father.

I The Apostolic Age

The Resurrection

At the time of Jesus' arrest in the Garden of Gethsemane, the disciples scattered and fled. None of them, except John, dared draw near to the place of crucifixion. Peter had waited nearby while Jesus was being tried, but on being identified by a maidservant in the courtyard of the high priest as a follower of Jesus, he denied it. Sick with despair and fear, the disciples remained in hiding during the Sabbath day. On the morning of the third day some of the women, before starting back to Galilee, sought out the tomb to which the body of Jesus had been taken. They found it empty. When they were about to turn away, perplexed, they saw, so they later told the at first unbelieving disciples, an angel who convinced them that Jesus had risen from the dead. Then Peter and others saw Jesus himself. These experiences were repeated in Galilee when they returned there. By this time despair had given way to an invincible confidence and hope, which was to spread a great new faith throughout the Mediterranean world.

The earliest extant account of the appearances of Jesus after the resurrection is that of St. Paul. About the year 52 A.D. he wrote to the church he had founded in Corinth:

Now I want to remind you, brothers . . . [that] I passed on to you, as of first importance, the account I had received, that Christ died for our sins, as the Scriptures foretold, that he was buried, that on the third day he was raised from the dead, as the Scriptures foretold, and that he was seen by Cephas [Peter], and then by the Twelve. After that he was seen by more than five hundred brothers at one time, most of whom are still alive, although some of them have fallen asleep.* Then he was seen by James, then by all the apostles, and finally he was seen by me also, as though I were born at the wrong time.†A1

Pentecost

The resurrection appearances convinced the disciples that Jesus had been raised from the dead so that he might soon return on the clouds of heaven as the promised Son of Man who should judge the nations at the great assize of the last day. His mission on earth, they now believed, had been to prepare the way for his second coming. So all the disciples who could do so, about 120 in number, left Galilee and went to live in Jerusalem, where they met in a large upper room for prayer and counsel. The Book of Acts says that among them were Mary, Jesus' mother, and his brothers. The Apostles were the official leaders of the group, but James, Jesus' brother, soon became a prominent figure.

The next great moment in their common experience is thus recorded:

On the day of the Harvest Festival [the Jewish festival called Pentecost], they were all meeting together, when suddenly there came from the sky a sound like a violent

* The early Christians spoke of death as "going to sleep" until the Judgment Day.
† The interesting thing about what Paul says next is that he goes on the assumption that Jesus rose in a spiritual body, not in a physical one. "It is so with the resurrection of the dead. The body is sown in decay, it is raised free from decay. . . . It is a physical body that is sown, it is a spiritual body that is raised. . . . I can tell you this, brothers: flesh and blood cannot share in the Kingdom of God, and decay will not share in what is imperishable." This is not what the Church later declared about the resurrection of Jesus, namely, that it was a resurrection of his physical body, nor is it the view of Luke and John, but it is worth noting that one who was converted two years after Jesus' death should hold it.

blast of wind, and it filled the whole house where they were sitting. And they saw tongues like flame separating and settling one on the head of each of them, and they were all filled with the holy Spirit and began to say in foreign languages whatever the Spirit prompted them to utter.A2

To the early Christians the resurrection was their proof of the truth of the Gospel, and the descent of the Holy Spirit at Pentecost was their guarantee that the power that was in Jesus Christ their Lord was in them too. The Apostles now took courage and began preaching boldly in the streets where but a few weeks before Jesus had encountered an opposition that had ended in his crucifixion.

They met with startling success. Hundreds of converts joined them. The Pharisees and Sadducees in alarm arrested Peter and John, brought them before the Sanhedrin, and ordered them to cease speaking as they did "in the name of Jesus." But on their release they continued their preaching undeterred. Once more they were arrested, with others of their number, and haled before the Sanhedrin. Reminded that they had been ordered to refrain from speaking in the name of Jesus, Peter and the Apostles, we read, answered: "We must obey God rather than men."A3 During the disturbance that followed, one of the leading Pharisees checked the rising anger of the other members of the Sanhedrin by suavely suggesting that fanatical Messianic movements always destroy themselves in time; one may therefore safely let them alone. This man was Gamaliel, a grandson of Hillel, and like his grandfather one of the great teachers of the rabbinical schools. He proceeded to draw upon history for his argument: "Men of Israel, take care what you propose to do with these men. For some time ago Theudas appeared, claiming to be a person of importance, and a group of men numbering some four hundred joined him. But he was killed and all his followers were dispersed and disappeared. After him, at the time of the census, Judas of Galilee appeared, and raised a great following, but he too perished, and all his followers were scattered. So in the present case, I tell you, keep

447

away from these men and let them alone, for if this idea or movement is of human origin, it will come to naught, but if it is from God, you will not be able to stop it."[A4] This counsel prevailed, the authorities contented themselves with flogging the Apostles, in order to disgrace them in the eyes of the people, and let them go.

The Jerusalem Church

Two factors seem to have saved the Jerusalem church from annihilating persecution: first, the Apostles were followers of a dead leader and might be expected to lose their fervor with the passage of time, and second, the Apostles obviously kept all the provisions of the Jewish Law. In fact, the Palestinian followers of Jesus went daily to the temple and honored the Law of Moses as much as any Jew, requiring circumcision of every convert not already circumcised, as if they were just a Jewish sect. But they had made some unorthodox additions to the accepted faith and practice. They believed that Jesus was the Messiah foretold in the Jewish scriptures and that he would shortly reappear on the clouds of heaven as the Son of Man. They met in private homes, such as the home of John Mark's mother in Jerusalem, for group gatherings, which were devoted to "the breaking of bread and prayers." The believers shared everything they had with one another, sold their property and belongings, and divided the proceeds according to their special needs, and they all had a vigorous proselyting spirit and baptized their converts.

But if it appeared true of the Palestinian followers of Jesus that they acted as if they were just a Jewish sect, this was not true of all the converts. Some began to take the liberties Jesus had taken with the Law of Moses. There were synagogues in Jerusalem for the Jews who had returned from foreign lands and spoke Greek, and these Greek-speaking Jews were notably less impressed by the temple sacrifices than the Palestinian Jews and more given than the latter to stressing the passages in the prophetic writings condemning externalism in the practice of the Law. So, when any of the Greek-speaking Jews became Christians, they eagerly applied the more radical passages from the Prophets to the life and sayings of Jesus and stressed Jesus' criticism of the practices of the Sadducees and Pharisees.

Tension appeared not only between these Christians and the Jewish authorities, but within the Christian group itself. On the one hand, the Apostles began to lose touch with the Greek-speaking radicals. On the other hand, the latter made complaints against the Palestinian Christians "that their [i.e., the Greek-speaking] widows were being neglected in the daily distribution of food."[A5] To allay this tension, the whole Christian group met and solved the problem by appointing from their number seven men who were not Apostles to take charge of the distribution of food and the keeping of accounts. One of these seven was a Greek-speaking man by the name of Stephen, who was a leader of the more libertarian wing of the Christian movement. All went well until the Jewish authorities brought him before the Sanhedrin, condemned him, and stoned him to death.

This violent action signalized the outbreak of a great persecution of the church in Jerusalem. The Jewish authorities apparently directed it against those who did not keep the Jewish Law, for the Book of Acts says, "They were all scattered over Judea and Samaria, except the apostles."[A6]

Thenceforth the Christian movement in Palestine was to have two parties within it, which never lost their sense of being bound together under the name of Christ, but which struggled with each other for the right to be the final interpreters of what Christianity meant. On the one side stood James, the brother of Jesus, now the chief "pillar" of the Jerusalem church, and with him most of the Apostles. They held that Christians must not only follow Christ, but please God by also obeying the Law of Moses. One of the requirements for which they stood was circumcision, and they sent out their emissaries to the out-lying churches to insist that this requirement be met before baptism. It was also considered necessary to observe the distinctions between clean and unclean and to refuse to sit down to a meal with the uncircumcised. Although some of the members of the Jerusalem church showed a willingness to compromise, the extremists carried their insistence to great lengths. They are often called the Judaizers. In time they formed an exclusive group of Jewish Christians called Ebionites or Nazarenes.

Among the Jerusalem Christians who were disposed to make compromises was Peter. He saw that the Holy Spirit had descended freely upon the more liberal Christians. What was more, on visits to the coast towns he found the new faith spreading among uncircumcised foreigners, and the Holy Spirit had come upon them too. He approved of their being baptized and sat down to eat with them without being overly careful concerning the Jewish dietary restrictions. But when he was back in Jerusalem, he was severely criticized by the Judaizers, and thereafter vacillated before his narrower brethren, without being able to take a bold stand.*

Yet the more liberal elements in the Christian movement were to win the day and remake the heretical Jewish sect into a powerful independent religion that was to spread rapidly through the Gentile world. The leader of the liberals was their one-time fiercest persecutor, a man from Tarsus called Saul (or Paul).

Paul and the Spread of Christianity to Europe

Paul has been frequently called "the second founder of Christianity." Certain it is that he fought and defeated the Judaizers, who thereafter steadily lost importance in the Christian movement, but more important, he developed certain basic theological concepts for stating the spiritual effects of Jesus upon the lives of his followers, concepts that enabled Christianity to win the Gentile world. To that world he

* Subsequently, he went to Rome, where presumably he was able to follow a freer course.

brought intact the religion *of* Jesus in the vehicle of a religion *about* Jesus.

All this Paul accomplished only after an early career of fierce opposition to Christianity. He was a non-Palestinian Jew, born, about the same time as Jesus, in the town of Tarsus in Cilicia, then an important city and the seat of a university where the Stoic and Cynic philosophies were taught. Probably Paul here learned something of the Greek mystery-cults and the desire of their adherents to achieve immortality by identification with dying and rising savior-gods. His family was apparently well-off, for his parents had purchased Roman citizenship, and he therefore had the legal status of a free-born Roman. But he reacted adversely to the religious ideas of his Hellenistic environment and remained a strict Pharisee. Filled with an earnest desire for "the righteouness which is from the Law," he went to Jerusalem and "sat at the feet" of Gamaliel, the leading Pharisaic teacher. Of this period of his life he later wrote: "I surpassed many of my own age among my people in my devotion to Judaism, I was so fanatically devoted to what my forefathers had handed down."[A7] He joined furiously in the persecution of the early Church. He was present as an approving spectator at the stoning of Stephen.

When the Christian believers fled northward to Damascus and beyond, he went to the high priest and asked for letters to the synagogues in Damascus, "so that if he found any men or women there who belonged to the Way, he might bring them in chains to Jerusalem." "But," says the Book of Acts, "as he was approaching Damascus, a sudden light flashed around him from heaven, and he fell to the ground. Then he heard a voice saying to him, 'Saul! Saul! Why do you persecute me?' "[A8] Blinded by the bright vision, Paul was led by the hand into Damascus, where for three days he could not see and neither ate nor drank. He believed that the resurrected Jesus, in whom the Christians now centered their faith, had appeared also to him.

So vast a change in Paul's life was now made necessary that he went off into upper Arabia to think things through. Then he returned to Damascus. He became a Christian leader not only there but also far to the north at Antioch, the third largest city in the Roman empire, where the new religion was making many converts among the Gentiles. Except for a two-week visit to Jerusalem after three years to become personally acquainted with Peter and James, he confined himself to the districts of Syria and Cilicia. Then he set out on his famous missionary journeys, accompanied by men like Barnabas and John Mark. On his first journey he sailed to the island of Cyprus, traveled through it from end to end, embarked for Asia Minor, and established self-propagating Christian groups at Perga, Antioch in Pisidia, Iconium, Lystra, and Derbe. On his second journey he revisited the churches he had already established and then proceeded to Troas (ancient Troy), whence he sailed to Macedonia on the continent of Europe. After establishing congregations in the principal cities along the coast, he went south to Athens and then to Corinth, where he founded an important church. On his return he sailed to Ephesus in Ionia before going home. His third journey took him around the same circuit.

Although he suffered from some physical malady, which he refers to as "a thorn in the flesh," in these journeys he displayed tremendous energy, zeal, and courage. His strength abounded, he said, because when he felt physically weak, he threw himself upon the strength of Christ, who dwelt within him.

Five times (he wrote) I have been given one less than forty lashes, by the Jews. I have been beaten three times by the Romans, I have been stoned once, I have been ship-wrecked three times, a night and a day I have been adrift at sea; with my frequent journeys, [I have been] in danger from rivers, danger from robbers, danger from my own people, danger from the heathen, danger in the city, danger in the desert, danger at sea, danger from false brothers, through toil and hardship, through many a sleepless night, through hunger and thirst, often without food, and exposed to cold.[49]

Two great spiritual facts animated Paul and gave him his dynamic faith: the "Lordship of Christ Jesus," and "the freedom of the Spirit."

He came to know the freedom of the spirit during the early days of his conversion. The Christians of Syria and Cilicia were for the most part uncircumcised and without the knowledge of the Jewish Law. In his great hunger to know the secret of true righteousness, Paul had long held the Law (the Torah) to be the one and only condition of a good life enjoying the Lord's favor. But now he was surprised and delighted to discover that those who followed Christ were, quite apart from the Law, more profoundly good than those who obeyed the Law. The righteousness that was in Christ was greater than the righteousness that was from the Law. The reason was that Christ changed a man's inward disposition and gave him the right relationship to his fellow-men and to God, so that he did what is right from the heart, without having to refer constantly to outward legal requirements. Love was the fulfillment of the Law. Therefore the weary bondage of the Law could be cast aside for the freedom of the spirit. There was no further need, Paul declared, for circumcision, dietary restrictions, and distinctions between clean and unclean.

It was at this point that the Judaizers came into conflict with Paul. He had it out with Peter, James, and John at Jerusalem, and they gave him their cooperation on the basis that he was to consider himself called to work among the uncircumcised, while they were called to work among the circumcised. At the same time, they were not willing to yield all, but insisted on the compromise that the Gentiles need not be circumcised if they pledged themselves to be chaste, to eat no meat that had been sacrificed to idols, and to refrain from the meat of strangled animals and the tasting of blood. This compromise was a great victory for Paul, for it meant that the Christians would no longer be asked to regard the Jewish Law as in all respects binding.

The Lordship of Christ was another article of faith at the heart of Paul's conviction. To him it meant more even than the Messiahship of Jesus. He had joyously accepted Jesus as the Messianic savior who had inaugurated the Kingdom of God and would soon return on the clouds of heaven to judge the

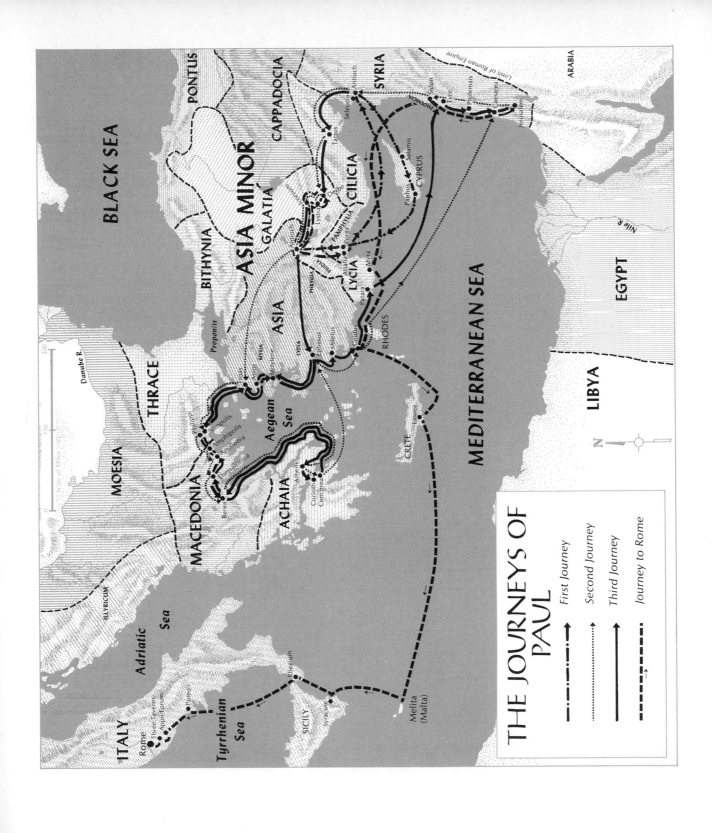

BLACK SEA

PONTUS

CAPPADOCIA

ASIA MINOR

GALATIA

BITHYNIA

ASIA

Propontis

LYDIA

Mysia

Assos
Mitylene
Ephesus
Miletus
Cnidus

RHODES

PHRYGIA

PISIDIA

Iconium
Lystra
Derbe

Antioch

PAMPHYLIA
Perga
Attalia

LYCIA
Patara
Myra

Tarsus
Seleucia

CILICIA

SYRIA

Antioch

PHOENICIA
Tyre
Sidon
Ptolemais

Caesarea

Jerusalem

ARABIA

Limit of Roman Empire

Salamis

Paphos

CYPRUS

MEDITERRANEAN SEA

Nile R.

EGYPT

LIBYA

N

THRACE

MOESIA

Danube R.

Scale of Miles

300

750

0

ILLYRICUM

Adriatic
Sea

MACEDONIA

Philippi
Neapolis
Amphipolis
Apollonia
Thessalonica
Berea

Aegean
Sea

Athens
Corinth
Cenchreae

ACHAIA

CRETE
Lasea

ITALY

Rome
Three Taverns
Appii Forum
Puteoli

Tyrrhenian
Sea

SICILY

Syracuse

Rhegium

Melita
(Malta)

THE JOURNEYS OF PAUL

First Journey

Second Journey

Third Journey

Journey to Rome

quick and the dead on the last day. But as a missionary to the Gentiles (to whom the Messiahship of Jesus, a purely Jewish concept, meant little), he was quick to see and to herald the power of Christ to redeem individuals from sin and death by uniting them to himself by faith. And here Paul made an original contribution to the interpretation of Christ's death and resurrection. Christ, he ardently declared, was a divine being who possessed the nature of God but who had humbled himself and come down from heaven and assumed human form, and, humbling himself still further, died on the cross, in order that he might rise again, after his victory over death, to the right hand of God as the Lord of life and death. In setting forth this new and glorious mystery, Paul ascribed unqualified divinity to the pre-existent Christ: "He is a likeness of the unseen God, born before any creature, for it was through him that everything was created in heaven and earth, the seen and the unseen, angelic thrones, dominions, principalities, authorities,—all things were created through and for him."A10

By this great conception—through which Paul expressed his intuition that Jesus was the expression in human history of God's redemptive spirit and love at work since the dawn of creation—Paul quite captivated the Gentiles. They had been brought up under the influence of the Greek mystery religions, which, as we have seen, satisfied the yearning for immortality by providing an experience of union with a resurrected savior-god, thereby deifying and immortalizing the corrupt and perishable self.* But Paul's conception was far more profound and regenerative than any they had known. He not only offered assurance of immortality through union with Christ but provided a means of salvation from guilt and sin in this

---

* To help them to understand properly the significance of the redemption which Christ wrought in their lives, Paul put it thus: by the mystical experience of baptism, those who believe may identify themselves with Christ in his death and resurrection, for "through baptism we have been buried with him in death, so that just as he was raised from the dead through the Father's glory, we too may live a new life." "You must think of yourselves as dead to sin but alive to God, through union with Christ Jesus" (Romans 6:4, 11).

life. For Christ the deified Lord of life and death had been the blameless Jesus of Nazareth of Galilee, who had proclaimed a high and noble ethics that led to individual and social remaking on the moral plane. Thus mysticism and ethics were in Paul's teaching one and inseparable. To follow Christ meant not only identifying oneself with him through baptism, the Lord's Supper, and the ecstasy of speaking with tongues, but even more, doing as Jesus did, living as he did.*

This was important in the development of Christianity, for here Paul saved it from an extreme—that of non-ethical mysticism—as dangerous to its balance and truth as the extreme of legalism from which he had earlier rescued it.

The letters that Paul sent to the churches he established furnish abundant proof of the importance he attached to ethics. With eagle eye he watched over his congregations and scolded them like a father for every infraction of the high Christian code of morality. He was far from believing that a capacity for religious ecstasy covers a multitude of sins.

His generosity toward his Christian brethren in Jerusalem brought to a sudden end his missionary career. He had taken upon himself the obligation to raise a collection for the poor in the Jerusalem church, and having done so, carried the funds to Jerusalem himself. Here he ran afoul of the Jews, who mobbed him and caused his arrest. As a Roman citizen, he appealed to Caesar, anxious as he was at any rate to get to Rome. He was taken under arrest to the Imperial City, but if he expected to be released after his trial, he was disappointed. The authorities continued to hold him in custody. He had time to write letters to churches and individuals, but after a period of confinement whose length is not known, he was executed as a troublesome character, a disturber of the Roman peace.

---

* "If I can speak the languages of men and even of angels, but have no love, I am only a noisy gong or a clashing cymbal. . . . I want you all to speak ecstatically. . . . But in public worship I would rather say five words with my understanding so as to instruct others also than ten thousand words in an ecstasy" (I Cor. 13:1; 14:5, 19).

But he had by this time fully demonstrated the power of the Christian religion to bring together Jew, Greek, and Roman, mystic, legalist, and rationalist, all under a common sense of their vital spiritual community in Christ. To such of the culturally divided and spiritually drifting people of the Roman Empire as heard them, words like these from the powerful letter to the Ephesians—a letter that some scholars now attribute to a follower of Paul rather than to him, but that in any case is warmed and vitalized by his spirit—contained "good news":

You also were dead because of the offenses and sins in the midst of which you once lived under the control of the present age of the world. . . . We all lived among them once, indulging our physical cravings and obeying the impulses of our lower nature and its thoughts, and by nature we were doomed to God's wrath like other men. But God is so rich in mercy that because of the great love he had for us, he made us, dead as we were through our offenses, live again with the Christ. It is by his mercy that you have been saved. . . . It is not by your own action, it is the gift of God. It has not been earned, so that no one can boast of it. . . .

So remember that you were once physically heathen. . . . At that time you had no connection with Christ, you were aliens to the commonwealth of Israel . . . ; with no hope and no God in all the world. But now through your union with Christ Jesus you who were once far away have through the blood of Christ been brought near. For he is our peace. He has united the two divisions, and broken down the barrier that kept us apart; . . . for it is through him that we both with one Spirit are now able to approach the Father. So you are no longer foreigners or strangers, but you are fellow-citizens of God's people and members of his family.[A11]

II   The Early Church (50–150 A.D.)

The World-Spread of the Early Christian Communities

But in calling Paul "the second founder of Christianity," we should not exaggerate his immediate in-

fluence. Before his time other leaders than he had successfully carried Christianity to Antioch, Alexandria, and Rome. Besides the Apostles we hear of Barnabas, Symeon Niger, Lucius the Cyrenian, Manaen, "who had been brought up with Herod the governor," Apollos, and others, all actively engaged in organizing new Christian churches. So rapidly, in fact, were Christian converts springing up along the coasts of the eastern Mediterranean that it was Paul's ambition to proceed from Rome to Spain in order to carry Christianity to the farthest bounds of the known world.

The chief successes of early Christianity were in the commercial centers of the Roman empire, largely because there were synagogues, or at least Jewish quarters, in them, and the Christian message could make its best appeal in places where the Jewish religion was already known. But when the orthodox Jewish communities rejected the new faith and refused to harbor it, independent Christian communities sprang up among the tradesmen and working people of the great cities and towns, first among the Greek-speaking citizens and then among those who spoke other languages. And not only did the new religion spread westward; it was also carried to the Tigris-Euphrates valley and into Ethiopia.

Opposition and Persecution

By the middle of the second century the Christian religion had become a major problem to the governors of the Roman provinces, especially in Syria and Asia Minor. For one thing, the Romans disliked mystery and secrecy. For another, the Christians considered themselves *in* the world but not *of* it. Though a few of them here and there joined the armed services of the Roman empire and took office in the administrative branches of the government, the greater number dissociated themselves from all worldly power. In purely secular matters they were obedient, but on the whole indifferent, to the civil authority. But they absolutely refused to take part in the official patriotic cult that required citizens to take an oath "by the genius" (the divine spirit) of the emperor and to offer incense and wine in honor of the emperor's godhead on the altar before his image. This refusal was a particularly sore point with the Roman administrative officials, less for religious reasons than because it signified disloyalty and rebellion. Moreover, the Christians met secretly, almost always at daybreak or at night, because so many of them were employed during the day. Distorted conceptions of their worship "orgies" were current. The Christians were accused of sexual perversions ("love-feasts") and cannibalism, the eating of human flesh. ("Take, eat; this is my body . . . this is my blood.") In addition, their staying away from theaters, gladiatorial combats, and popular festivals was interpreted as narrow and intolerant and aroused rage. "The Christians to the lions!" became a common cry.

A classic expression of official perplexity is contained in the letters of Pliny the Younger, governor of Bithynia (in Asia Minor), to the Roman Emperor Trajan. Wrote he:

> It is my custom, my lord, to refer to you all questions about which I have doubts. . . . I have no little uncertainty whether pardon is granted on repentance, or whether when one has been a Christian there is no gain to him in that he has ceased to be such; whether the mere name, without crimes, or crimes connected with the name are punished. . . . Those who were accused before me as Christians . . . asserted that the amount of their fault or error was this: that they had been accustomed to assemble on a fixed day before daylight and sing by turns a hymn to Christ as a god; and that they bound themselves with an oath, not for any crime, but to commit neither theft, nor robbery, nor adultery, not to break their word and not to deny a deposit when demanded; after these things were done, it was their custom to depart and meet together again to take food, but ordinary and harmless food; and they said that even this had ceased after my edict was issued, by which, according to your commands, I had forbidden the existence of clubs. On this account I believed it the more necessary to find out from two maid-servants, who were called deaconesses, and that by torture, what was the truth. I found nothing else than a perverse and excessive superstition. I therefore adjourned the examination and hastened to consult you. The matter seemed to me to be worth deliberation.[B1]

Pliny reported, however, that when he found Christians who persisted three times over in saying they were Christians, he ordered them to be executed, "for," said he blandly, "I did not doubt that, whatever it was they admitted, obstinacy and unbending perversity certainly deserve to be punished!" The Romans, on principle, expected obedience.

Christians were publicly done to death in Rome as early as 64 A.D., in the time of Nero. During the century that followed, Roman officials frequently made examples of Christians who refused to worship Caesar's image by throwing them to the lions or burning them at the stake. The number of martyrs was not large, perhaps, but the public commotion was sometimes great and had far-reaching effects both on the Christians themselves and on the public at large, especially in sharpening the feeling that the Christian religion was to its adherents worth not only living by but dying for as well.

Developments in Worship and Ecclesiastical Organization

Meanwhile, the Christian communities were developing into self-contained units with an organized life of their own.

At the time of the Apostle Paul, when the Christians were beginning to look upon themselves as a Church called out of the world into a separate fellowship, their services were of two kinds: (1) meetings on the model of synagogue services, open to inquirers as well as believers, and consisting of readings from the Jewish scriptures,* prayer, preaching, and the singing of psalms; and (2) the *agapé* or "love-feast," for the believers only, an evening meal in which all present shared and during which a brief ceremony, recalling the Last Supper, commemorated the sacrifice of Jesus' body and blood. Because this ceremony was couched in terms of thanksgiving, the

---

* Not until the second century were the Jewish scriptures supplemented with readings from the Gospels and Epistles.

Greek name for it was *eucharist* ("the giving of thanks").

As the Christian communities grew larger, the common meal was gradually discontinued as impracticable, and the Lord's Supper was observed thereafter at the conclusion of the public portion of the Sunday services, when the unbaptized withdrew in order that the baptized might celebrate together this inner mystery of the Christian faith.

At the same time, entrance into the Christian community was formalized into definite steps. Candidates for church membership, of all ages, were first given a systematic course of instruction and testing (catechization), lasting for several months and ending in the rite of baptism, by immersion or sprinkling. (Commonly, the catechizing was during Lent and the baptizing at Easter.) The believers appeared in white robes for their baptism, and that rite was followed by confirmation, or the laying on of hands, that the Holy Spirit might descend upon each new member. After the laying on of hands came unction (anointing with oil), concluded with making the sign of the cross, while each new member vowed to give up the old gods and the old morality and to follow the law of Christ, in perfect assurance of faith.

At first the churches were loosely organized, but by the end of the first century the congregations were directed by a board of elders, including one or more superintendents or "bishops." These officers were assisted by deacons. Preaching and instruction were still, however, in the hands of prophets and teachers, who either belonged to the congregation or came from elsewhere, perhaps as traveling evangelists. Out of this type of government there very naturally developed a more rigid and centralized form of organization. By the first quarter of the second century we read of congregations being headed by a single bishop, assisted by elders and deacons, and, when this became general, this permanent head of the congregation included among his functions those of teaching and preaching, with the result that the prophets and traveling evangelists of the early Church gradually disappeared from church life.

Doctrinal Developments to the Year 150 A.D.

Growth in doctrine more than matched the growth in institutional forms.

By the year 100 A.D. a Christian literature distinct from that of the Old Testament and in some respects consciously designed to serve as a new scripture (it eventually became the New Testament) had come into being. Its appearance had become necessary with the gradual fading of the first generation's expectation of the imminent return of Jesus on the clouds of heaven—a faith that had once made the writing of a scripture seem superfluous. The eyewitnesses of Jesus' ministry were rapidly dying off by the time fifty years had passed, and the second-generation Christians, most of whom now lived far from Jerusalem, demanded a record of the master's life and teachings. The destruction of Jerusalem in 70 A.D. increased the urgency of this demand among those living outside of Palestine.

In the introduction to the preceding chapter we reviewed the beginning of this literature. Something further needs to be said here about the nature and content of the completed literature that sprang from these beginnings, for each portion of it is significant of the greater and greater estimates placed upon Jesus' teaching and person as time went on, and all combine to give us a sense of the factors, both Jewish and Greek, that operated in the first century of Christian history to make Christianity a great and rich religion.

Of the earliest portions of the New Testament—the Epistles of Paul—we need say nothing more, for their doctrinal significance has already been discussed. So it is to the Gospels that we first turn, for each had a distinct Christological purpose in view.

The Gospel of Mark, the earliest and briefest of the Gospels, was probably written in Antioch during the years 65–70. According to Papias, a Christian writer of the early second century, it was based upon the recollections of St. Peter as set down by John Mark, who had lived in Jerusalem before he came to Antioch. This Gospel shows no interest in Jesus' birth and youth, but begins with his baptism and gives a vivid account of his ministry, with pointed descriptions of his human feelings. But Jesus is much more than an average human being in Mark; he is the Son of God through the experience of divine election at his baptism, and the true Messiah, the "Holy One of God." No doctrine of divine incarnation nor any conception of pre-existence such as Paul exhibits is found, however.

Matthew and Luke, going further, provide a basis for the doctrine of the incarnation. Both relate the stories of the virgin birth and of supernatural incidents occurring during Jesus' infancy. They concentrate throughout on the divine character of the Messiahship of Jesus and the manner in which, as one who came from heaven, he fulfilled Hebrew prophecy of the coming of the Son of Man to redeem mankind.

But it is in the Fourth Gospel that we find the divine character of Jesus most clearly presented. The writer sought to write a Gospel that would find the living, subjectively experienced Lord of Paul in the historic, objectively known Jesus of the first three Gospels. The fundamental thesis of this Gospel is, "The Word (the Logos) became flesh and blood and lived for a while among us, . . . and we saw the honor God had given him, such honor as an only son receives from his father."[A13] Though we are not allowed to forget the man Jesus, who was an objective personage in a world of real persons and things, the divinity of Jesus is the characteristic note of this Gospel. Jesus Christ is above all else "the Son of God." He is more than the Son of God in the Hebrew sense of being the Messiah, for though this simpler Messianic significance is implicit, it is merged, even submerged, in the more comprehensive meanings found in the prologue of the Gospel. There Christ is represented as the visible bodying forth of the creative impulsion (the Logos) of the unseen and eternal Father and the mode or manifestation in a human person of the love of the Father for men. The Fourth Gospel therefore follows Paul in thinking of Christ as personally come from God—that is, from

a state of pre-existence—and connects him not only with the work of redemption on earth but with the creation of the world. In the body of the Gospel he is represented as remembering his preincarnate life, or at least that he had a preincarnate life. This pre-existence, and not his human experience, accounts for his knowledge of God, to whom, therefore, he bears "true" witness. For, having come from heaven, "it is to what he has seen and heard that he gives testimony." What is more, not only are his words "the words of God," but he is himself the Word (the Logos); he is himself that to which he bears witness. To know him is to know the Father.

The Epistle to the Hebrews, written in the decade before the Fourth Gospel, does not use the term *logos* (Word), but it is apparent that the writer had something like it in mind. In the first sentence he says that God, who spoke fragmentarily through the prophets, has now spoken to us fully "in a Son, whom he had destined to possess everything, and through whom he had made the world." The Son while on earth resembled his human brethren in every respect; he shared their flesh and blood and participated in their nature, even to suffering temptation and agonizing "with tears." But, because in his essential nature he was divine, his spiritual and psychological endowment was unique. The human Jesus and the divine Father were mutually accessible to each other at all times. In this Jesus differed from his brethren, who can have no such free access to the Father without his redemptive mediation as high priest.

A simpler and less doctrinal conception of the person and work of Christ appeared in the epistles of James and Peter and in the non-canonical writings of the so-called Apostolic Fathers: Clement of Rome (writing ca. 93–97), Hermas of Rome (ca. 115–140), and the authors of such works as *The Epistle of Barnabas* (ca. 130), *Second Clement* (ca. 160), and *The Teachings of the Twelve Apostles* (ca. 130–160). For the most part, these various writings gave expression to a straight-forward adoration of Christ as the heaven-descended revealer of the true nature of God and the giver of a new law of life on the loftiest ethical plane.

Addressed directly not to the religious needs of the growing Christian communities but rather to the world at large were the writings of the Apologists. These were men educated in the best Greek and Roman schools and well versed in ancient philosophy, who sent their defenses of Christianity to the Roman emperors or to other non-Christians of high rank and reputation. Among their number were Aristides of Athens, Melito, bishop of Sardis, Minucius Felix, a cultivated gentleman of Rome, and most famous of all Justin, called the Martyr because of the nature of his death, who, like his disciple, Tatian, had been successively a Stoic, Aristotelian, Pythagorean, and Platonist. When he turned Christian, he found in his new faith the perfect philosophy. He was far from believing that all other thought-systems were untrue. The divine Logos was at work in the world before the time of Christ, enlightening Socrates and Heraclitus and imparting truth to such "barbarians" (a truly Greek expression) as the patriarchs of the Old Testament, so that the Greek philosophers and the Hebrew prophets, insofar as the Logos enlightened them, were to this degree Christians before Christ. But Christianity was superior to all other thought-systems, because the Logos not only spoke through Christ, the Logos *was* Christ. Christ perfectly revealed the truth of divine reason and was the peerless teacher whom all humanity should accept.

The significance of Justin Martyr and his fellow apologists is that they successfully demonstrated how Christianity, when it chose to appear in Greek dress, could, at whatever sacrifice of its original Hebraic form, not only continue to make a powerful religious appeal but hold its own with any of the classic philosophies of the ancient world—Platonism and Stoicism especially. It became easier now for Christian writers to invade the field of general philosophy and to speak of the Christian religion as truly universal in its scope and application. *Catholic* was the word they used.

III   The Ancient Catholic Church (150–1054 A.D.)

The word *catholic* was first applied to the Christian Church in its meaning of "universal." Descriptively, this was an apt designation for a religious faith that now reached into all the provinces of the empire and into every class of society. But it was too good an adjective to escape a more technical use. It became, in fact, part of the name of *the single* organized institution that expressed the Christian religion after the middle of the second century. With this name the Catholic Church could stand united in the resolve to maintain itself against its external foes and also to combat heresy and schism within.

In striving to keep both its outer and inner integrity, the ancient Catholic Church developed two things: (1) a system of doctrine, clarified, purged of error, and declared to be orthodox, and (2) an ecclesiastical organization characterized in its own eyes by apostolicity, catholicity, unity, and holiness. We shall now describe the several steps by which these developments were effected.

The Gnostic and Marcionite Heresies

It was Jesus' fortune to appear not only at a time when the Jews were looking for a Messiah but when the rest of the world was seeking an incarnation of godhead and had, at the same time, evolved the concept of the Logos, without realizing with what richness of meaning it might be endowed were it to be applied to a savior-god appearing in the flesh of a human personality. When Christian thinkers brought the Logos-concept to bear upon Jesus, a whole theology sprang, almost without effort, into being, a theology that combined in the most satisfactory measure both religion and philosophy. Yet there were dangers in the process. A just balance of elements had to be preserved, or the religious value of the new synthesis would be destroyed. It became the task of

457

the Christian bishops and teachers of the second and third centuries to find that balance and to outlaw all deviations from the orthodox view.

Among the interpretations of the work and person of Christ during the second century that were later declared heretical were the Gnostic and Marcionite doctrines.

The view called Gnosticism (from *gnosis*, or esoteric knowledge) had a marked characteristic running through all its varieties: instead of assimilating philosophy to the Christian religion, it adopted the figure of Christ as the final ingredient of a Greco-Oriental syncretism. The Gnostics started with a dualism that radically divided spirit from matter and regarded the material world as so vile and degrading that God could have had nothing to do with making it. Surrounded by a society of male and female spiritual beings, called aeons, the pre-existent Jesus among them, God dwelt far above the evil world. At a lower level lived and labored the creator of the earth, the Jehovah of the Old Testament, a spiritual vulgarian, who produced the evil mass that is the world of matter. The Old Testament and its way of life is hopelessly infected with Jehovah's inferior conception of things. To the Gnostics the serpent in the Garden of Eden, in bringing Adam and Eve to the Tree of Knowledge (that is, of Gnosis!), was a benefactor, not a vile tempter, and did his best to save the parents of the human race from Jehovah's misleading guidance! When Jesus, the compassionate divine aeon, saw how badly things were going on earth, he came down in the masquerade of a body (but his flesh could not have been real, it was appearance merely*) and showed the human souls struggling in their defiling envelopes of flesh how, by an ascetic discipline of the body and the acquisition of saving wisdom for the mind, they could free themselves from their bondage in the material world and gain immortality by an escape from the flesh into pure spirituality of being.

Here were doctrines that the Church as a whole

felt indeed it could not countenance without violence to its own historic foundations: that God does not control the entire universe, that the Jehovah of the Old Testament is an inferior being, that the Old Testament must be rejected as valueless, that Jesus was not really born and did not truly suffer and die, and that there can be no resurrection of the flesh.

The suggestion that the Old Testament is valueless found, however, a tempestuous advocate in a citizen of Rome called Marcion. Without joining any of the Gnostic schools (which flourished chiefly in Egypt and Asia Minor), he nevertheless followed their lead in excoriating the God of the Old Testament as a cruelly legalistic and merciless deity, who, though he created the material world, was of an inferior moral quality. The really good God, who created the invisible, spiritual world, was not known to the prophets of the Old Testament; Christ was the first to reveal him. Men are in bondage to the bodies they have received from the God of the Old Testament, but their souls may find redemption through faith in the God of Jesus. Let them then follow Christ and St. Paul in ascetism, celibacy, and scorn of the physical world and strive to enter the Kingdom of the good God, here and hereafter. Marcion increased the alarm his views created by attempting to provide a scripture for his followers, in doing which he edited and brought together the writings of Paul and the Gospel of Luke, but first expurgated all passages linking Jesus with the God of the Old Testament, Furthermore, he broke away from the church at Rome and organized a new congregation.

This kind of thing aroused the Christian world to inquire into its basic positions.

The Answer of the Church: The Apostles' Creed and the Canon of the New Testament

The first clear voice within the Church to propose a program for dealing with heretical opinions was Irenaeus, a native of Asia Minor and the bishop of Lyons (in the province of Gaul). About 185 A.D. he

---

* This view, called Docetism, was an early heresy, not confined to the Gnostics.

issued a famous book, *Against the Heresies*. It was of determinative importance. In it he argued that the sign of a sound Christian doctrine is its apostolicity. The Apostles had perfect knowledge of the Gospel, and what is not in agreement with their teachings as transmitted in the Gospels and Epistles cannot be accepted. By this touchstone Gnosticism and Marcionism stood condemned. To the retort that Jesus must have imparted a private and esoteric teaching to an elect few—a claim made by the Gnostics—Irenaeus replied that such private wisdom, if it ever existed, would have had to be handed down through the churches founded by Apostles. Yet, he pointed out, the churches of apostolic foundation had no such traditions. On the whole, then, Irenaeus urged, one must go for sound doctrine to the apostolic writings, the apostolic churches, and their bishops.

This was the answer that appealed to the churches of the West. It was especially pleasing to the church at Rome, where between 150 and 175 A.D. a creed for use at baptism had been framed both to express the faith and to avoid the Gnostic and Marcionite doctrines. It came to be called, in accordance with Irenaeus' criterion of orthodoxy, the Apostles' Creed, and in its early form it ran (the crucial words being here italicized) as follows:

I believe in God the Father *Almighty**;
And in Jesus Christ, his *only begotten* Son, our Lord, who was *born* of the Holy Spirit and the Virgin Mary, *crucified* under Pontius Pilate and *buried;* the third day he rose from the dead, ascended into heaven, being seated at the right hand of the Father, whence he shall come to judge the living and the dead;
And in the Holy Spirit, holy Church, forgiveness of sins, and *the resurrection of the flesh*.[c]

The later emendations and refinements of this creed sharpened its signficance as a summary of orthodox and apostolic doctrine.

Another result of the Church's attempt to define apostolic tradition was an endeavor to fix a canon of

authentic scripture. By the end of the second century the present New Testament canon was virtually agreed upon.* The books now in the New Testament apocrypha were excluded from the canon when a careful weighing of their value had thrown doubt on their apostolicity.

The Church was by these measures placed in a position to preserve itself from dissolution into countless sects, "borne about by every wind of doctrine" and doomed to quick disappearance.

The Triumph of Christianity as the Imperial State Church

Meanwhile, the central Roman government remained officially opposed to Christianity. It had come to realize during the second century that the growing Christian Church was the institutional expression of a powerful new religion in the empire, and that it presented an increasingly serious challenge to the old pagan faiths. Because the latter had given to the Roman and Greek civilizations their distinctive moral and spiritual tone, it began to trouble the government, and the schools, that the old religious values were now threatened with total overthrow. Would the empire survive? The barbarian hordes that were poised along the Danube and the Rhine, ready to come plunging into the empire whenever the restraints were relaxed, would not be resisted by the pacifist Christians—nor by the Roman themselves, should they be even partially infected by Christian pietism and otherworldliness. Something had to be done. Therefore Marcus Aurelius (161–180 A.D.), himself an admirable person imbued with the highest ideals of Stoicism, initiated during the last years of his reign severe persecutions of Christians in the provinces. Septimus Severus, Caracalla, and Maximimus followed with like attempts to curb the Christian movement.

---

* In order to make the point against the Gnostics clear there was added later the phrase *Maker of heaven and earth*.

* This is roughly true, though the canon was not finally fixed until 400 in the West and still later in the East. Several books were removed from the original list, others added.

459

But not until the middle of the third century did the central government become thoroughly alarmed. The Emperor Decius, returning from the endangered frontier and sensing in the apathy of the people to their peril weaknesses due to Christianity, issued an order in 250 that every citizen of the empire must be required to get a certificate from a government official affirming that he had sacrificed to the emperor's image. Failure to possess such a certificate was to be visited with death. In the persecutions that followed there were conspicuous martyrs, the bishops of Rome and Antioch among them. Multitudes were painfully tortured, and yet refused to yield. A great many others surrendered to the government's pressure, whether through fear or weakness, and joined the number of "the lapsed," as the more faithful Christians called them. Still others bribed officials to issue them certificates without their actually having sacrificed in the prescribed manner. In the eyes of the loyal "confessors" they, too, were apostate. The persecution soon ended, and most of the apostates tried to get back into the Church, with the result that some of the stricter Christians created schisms in the churches in protest against the readmission of the returning penitents.* Under the Emperor Valerian the persecutions were fiercely renewed; much church property was confiscated, and many among the higher clergy met martyrdom. But when the emperor fell a prisoner to the Persians, his orders were rescinded. A final terrible persecution began under Diocletian in 303. Successive decrees ordered all churches destroyed, Christian scriptures confiscated, bishops and lesser clergy put to the torture until they sacrificed to Caesar's image, and ordinary Christians forced to sacrifice likewise. But before the persecutions had gone very far, Diocletian retired from the burdens of office and left four coordinate "Caesars" in control. Thereafter the persecutions became more sporadic. Clashes among the Caesars soon upset the balance

* One such schism at Rome was widely discussed. During the persecutions under Diocletian a similar and more widespread schism developed in North Africa and persisted until the Muslim invasion.

among them, and the son of one of them, a man favorable to Christianity, named Constantine, finally overcame all opposition and became in 323 the sole ruler of the empire.

Constantine changed the entire situation. Already in 313 he had issued jointly with another contender for power an edict granting freedom of conscience to Christians and equality with other religions to Christianity. Constantine was said to have affirmed meanwhile—whether truthfully or not—that early in his upward struggle he had seen in the heavens the cross of Christ with the inscription *In hoc signo vinces* ("In this sign you shall conquer"), and although he was not baptized, he had vowed to rest his hopes of conquest in the Christian God.* When, therefore, Constantine became undisputed emperor, he set himself to the task of strengthening the Catholic Church. Not only did he restore to the Church its lost properties; he allowed it to increase its holdings. He frowned upon heretical sects and sought to heal all schisms, for he wanted unity in the empire and hoped to obtain it through a united Christendom. He made the Christian Sunday a legal holiday. He built new churches and ordered others built at pagan expense. Indeed, his interest was almost too great; it amounted to a form of active control. His successors followed in his steps. Christianity was declared in 383 the imperial state religion.

The Arian Controversy and the Nicene Creed

While all these events were in progress, the theological formulation of the Catholic faith had gone steadily forward. Tertullian and Cyprian in North Africa, and Clement and Origen in Alexandria began to clarify and define the still-inchoate doctrines concerning the relation of Father, Son, and Holy Spirit and to set forth the claims of the Church to power and authority. But lack of complete agreement among them gave scope to acrimonious disputes.

* This may be a legend with only general truth to sustain it.

Turin cathedral. The Cathedral of St. John the Baptist in Turin is a Renaissance version of an early Christian basilica, the Renaissance architects having made it cruciform and added a dome mounted on a hexagonal base and a campanile or bell tower standing apart. Behind it looms the Chapel of Sudario, which preserves a shroud said to be that in which Joseph of Arimathea wrapped the body of Jesus. (Religious News Service Photo.)

Constantine felt that the issues had to be settled by a world council of the churches. The circumstances were these. A learned presbyter of Alexandria, called Arius, differed with his bishop on the question of whether Christ was a finite or an eternal being. Arius held that Christ, even as the Logos, was a created being. He was made like other creatures out of nothing, and so he could not be eternal; neither could he be of the same substance as God. The Son, he argued, had a beginning, whereas God was without beginning. Arius' bishop took issue with him hotly, asserting that the Son was eternal, uncreated, and of like essence with God. Summoning a synod, the bishop had Arius deposed, but this only caused the controversy to spread all over the East. This was in 321, and Constantine, after failing in conciliatory efforts, called a council of the whole Church to settle the issue once and for all. In the summer of 325 some three hundred delegate bishops, mostly from the East, met at Nicaea, across the Bosphorus from Constantinople, and produced the famous formula of the Creed of Nicaea. With its crucial phrases italicized, its text was:

We believe in one God, Father Almighty, maker of all things, visible and invisible. And in one Lord Jesus Christ, the Son of God, begotten of [literally, "out of"] the Father, as His only Son, that is, from the substance of the Father, God from God, light from light, true God from true God, *begotten, not made, of the same substance [homo-ousios] with the Father,* through whom all things in heaven and earth were made; who for us men and our salvation came down and was made flesh, became man, suffered, and rose on the third day, ascended to heaven, and is coming to judge the living and the dead. And (we believe) in the Holy Spirit.

Attached to this creed was a rider declaring anathema those who say, "There was a time when he was not"   **461** or assert, "The Son of God is of a different subsistence or substance, or is created."

This creed, adopted under pressure from the emperor, who wanted peace, did not immediately solve the doctrinal difficulties or save the peace. The phrases we have italicized were bitterly denounced by many and were actually revoked by later councils.* Indeed it was perhaps only the ardent, indefatigable, and patient defense of it by Athanasius, bishop of Alexandria, in tract after tract that finally overbore opposition and led to its ultimate acceptance. And even then it was several generations before it became infallible in the eyes of the Church.†

What Athanasius successfully urged upon his at first unbelieving contemporaries in the East was that the issue at stake was no mere verbal matter, no question of words; it was the issue of whether Christ is truly a savior. For the East in general held to the Greek conception of salvation, that it consists in making divine and immortal the sinful mortality of the human being. Athanasius was eventually able to convince the East that only God can bring immortal life down into the realm of mortality, and so Jesus must have been true God, truly so in substance or essence, not just a created being of lower quality, as Arius had urged.

---

* One such council substituted for the *homo-ousios* of the Creed of Nicaea *homoiousios*, that is, "of *like* substance." "We call the Son *like* the Father, as the holy scriptures call him and teach."[B2] But the decision of this council did not stand. The Church later went back to the Nicene formula.

† The familiar Nicene Creed which is recited in certain Christian churches today, it should be said, is not the original creed adopted at Nicaea in 325, but an expanded form of it (often called the "Constantinopolitan Creed") which came into use after the time of the General Council of 381. For completeness, we may add that the later formulation says firmly that the Godhead of Father, Son, and Holy Spirit is *one in essence* (or substance), though *in three hypostases* (subsistences or individualized manifestations). When this formulation was translated into Latin, the rather abstract Greek for *individualized manifestation* became the rather concrete word *persona*, and connotations of distinct and self-contained personality were suggested in a way not intended by the original Greek wording.

The Christological Controversies and the Creed of Chalcedon

The story of theological difficulties is not ended. Other issues now arose to divide the mind of Christendom. When the Creed of Nicaea laid down the dogma that the Logos or Christ was not of a lower grade of deity but equal in divinity with God the Father, it said nothing about the mode of union of the divine Logos with the human Jesus. So the incarnation itself now became the center of heated theological argument.

Once the distinction was drawn between the divine and the human natures of Christ, it was possible to regard them as being so distinct as to make it difficult to account for Jesus' unified personality. On the other hand, it was equally easy to see such a dominance of the one nature over the other as to suggest the absorption of the one nature in the other.

The West had no great difficulty here, for among the definitive statements of Tertullian, made over a century earlier, was the generally accepted formula: "We see (in Christ) a twofold state, not confounded but conjoined in one person, Jesus, God and man."[D1] The practical-minded West puzzled over the matter no further.

Not so the East. It was soon fiercely, and deeply, divided. The great sees of Alexandria and Antioch became especially irreconcilable—until the Muslim conquests hammered them down in common disaster.

The controversy first became heated when Apollinaris, a bishop in Syria, perhaps reacting adversely to the views of his nearest colleagues, asserted that Christ could not have been perfect man united with complete God, for then there would not have been one Son of God, but two sons, one by nature and one by adoption, the first with a divine, the second with a human will. Such a thing seemed inconceivable, religiously abhorrent. Therefore, in Christ a human body with its animating principle ("animal soul" was the actual phrase) was indwelt by the Logos, as the reasoning principle, the union, on the analogy of the unity of a human personality, being so complete that the body of Christ was the body of God, and in cruci-fying this body the Jews crucified God. Immediately, his opponents of the school of Antioch pointed out that under this conception Christ was not truly human, for his manhood was incomplete, without a reasoning intelligence or the power of choice. The Antiochians declared that in Christ a *whole* human being must have been divine; the Jesus of history had a complete human nature, endowed with reason and free will like all other men, and the Logos dwelt in him as in a temple, in perfect moral unity, such that the Logos and Jesus willed the same things. Nesto-ius, their chief spokesman, excited riots among the monks of Constantinople, where he became bishop, when he preached a sermon against calling the Virgin Mary "the mother of God," declaring she did not bear a deity, she bore "a man, the organ of deity."[B3] Cyril, bishop of Alexandria, now entered the fray on the other side. He admitted that Christ's humanity pos-sessed body, rational soul, and spirit, but it was with-out personality; the Logos was its personality.

Charges and counter-charges flew thick and fast. A general council was called in 431 and found itself unwholesomely involved in political machinations and imperial pressures. Nestorius was deposed and banished. But the issues remained unsettled. Finally, a general council met in 451 at Chalcedon in Asia Minor and formulated a definition of the relation of Christ's natures that became standard Catholic doc-trine. It reads:

Following, therefore, the holy Fathers, we confess and all teach with one accord one and the same Son, our Lord Jesus Christ, at once complete in Godhead and complete in manhood, truly God and truly man, and, further, of a rational soul and body; of one essence with the Father as regards his Godhead, and at the same time of one essence with us as regards his manhood, in all respects like us, apart from sin; as regards his Godhead begotten of the Father before the ages, yet as regards his manhood—on account of us and our salvation—begotten in these last days of Mary the Virgin, bearer of God; one and the same Christ, Son, Lord, Only-begotten, proclaimed in two natures, without confusion, without change, with-out division, without separation; the difference of the natures being in no way destroyed on account of the union, but rather the peculiar property of each nature being preserved and concurring in one person and one hypostasis—not as though parted or divided into two persons, but one and the same son and Only-begotten God the Logos, Lord, Jesus Christ, even as the prophets from of old and the Lord Jesus Christ taught us concern-ing him, and the Creed of the Fathers has handed down to us.

This creed, like the Nicene, was a triumph for the West, and of course the West accepted it without demur. But the East did not find it so satisfactory. Those who followed the Alexandrian lead dissented as "partisans of the *one* nature" and were called ac-cordingly Monophysites. From them sprang the Cop-tic Church of Egypt and Abyssinia and the "Jacobite" churches of Syria and Armenia, which dissent to this day.

The Nestorians were already declared unsound when the general council convened at Chalcedon. They persisted as a sect in Syria, however, and they found the peoples to the east of them receptive. So they took their doctrines into Persia, and from thence to India and China, which they reached in the seventh century. In Syria Nestorianism survived the Muslim conquest. Nestorian churches also still exist in southern India and northwestern Iran.

The Growth of the Papacy

It was the good fortune of the church of Rome to be on the victorious side in the great doctrinal con-troversies of the second and fourth centuries. During the Gnostic crisis it was the church of Rome that framed the Apostles' Creed, and it was the same church that led in the formation of the New Testa-ment canon. The superior dignity of the church of Rome was acknowledged by eminent authorities of the West. Irenaeus, from his place in Gaul, urged the Western churches to agree with Rome in all mat-ters involving the apostolic tradition. Cyprian, from his place in North Africa, thought of Rome as "the chief church whence priestly unity takes its source."[D2]

Aware of all these things, and sure that if civil authority rested at Constantinople in the person of the emperor, spiritual authority rested at Rome in his own person, Pope Leo I (440–461) declared that because St. Peter was the first among the Apostles, St. Peter's church should be accorded primacy among the churches. He based his claim on the doctrine that Peter's powers, as defined in Matt. 16:18, 19,* had been passed on to each of his successors. This was a special application, we note, of the doctrine of "apostolic succession," a doctrine that had early been formulated, e.g., by Clement of Rome at the close of the first century, and that was generally understood to apply to *all* bishops as the successors, through the laying on of hands at ordination, of *all* the Apostles. But Leo held that St. Peter was the first in rank among the Apostles, and hence the successors of Peter were the first among bishops.

He and his successors took steps to make good this claim, but their success was in suspense while the Roman empire fell. Well was it for the pope, indeed, that most of the empire's invaders—Visigoths, Ostrogoths, Vandals, Burgundians, and Lombards—had already been converted to Christianity by missionaries of the heretical Arian sects.† They were heretics, but they were Christians, so that when Alaric the Visigoth captured Rome, he treated the pope with favor and spared the churches, while ravin and ruin overwhelmed all else around.

As the inroads of the barbarians swelled to a disastrous flood-tide and civilization faltered, the popes drew some consolation from the fact that the Arian invaders were after awhile persuaded to become Catholics.‡

---

* "I tell you, your name is Peter, a rock, and on this rock I will build my church, and the powers of death will not subdue it. I will give you the keys of the Kingdom of Heaven, and whatever you forbid on earth will be held in heaven to be forbidden, and whatever you permit on earth will be held in heaven to be permitted."

† By the great missionary Ulfilas and others.

‡ As a result of the conversion of Clovis, king of the Franks, and the efforts of the British missionary Boniface.

The Rise of Monasticism

Monasticism grew rapidly in the Catholic Church after Christianity was made the imperial state religion. Early tendencies in its direction appeared in the individuals who followed St. Paul's suggestion that men and women believers might well practice sexual abstinence and live as "virgins." But as a movement involving a definite break with society, it did not begin until toward the end of the third century. Its first great representative was St. Anthony of Korma in Egypt. After trying to practice asceticism in his own village, an attempt that failed, he went away into the solitude of the desert. There he was beset by his famous temptations, at peace only when asleep, when awake fasting and praying ceaselessly, but haunted by demons, in male and female form, enticing him to every sin. Egypt was full of lonely exiles and friendless men; its climate was favorable for, and its people respectful toward, austerity. The belief was prevalent (in accord with the Gnostic and Alexandrian theologies) that the world and the body were defiling, so Anthony attracted many followers. It was soon apparent, however, that those who strove to live entirely alone often went mad and just as often failed through lack of guidance, so a communal type of hermit life (cenobitism) was developed by Pachomius, a convert to Coptic Christianity in southern Egypt, who organized monasteries (and one nunnery) under a rule of balanced work and meditation, directed by an abbot.

Both the solitary and communal types of monasticism quickly spread to Syria and Asia Minor. The solitary hermits drew great attention to themselves. Some retired to caves and desert places; some, like Simeon the Stylite, lived on the tops of pillars in ruined cities and had their food lifted up to them on poles; others (the Dendrites) resided in trees; still others, in the same manner as Buddhist monks in China and Tibet, walled themselves up in narrow enclosures and had food tossed in to them or pushed through slits in the wall. But this form of asceticism was never more than the rage of the moment. By far the greater number of hermits gathered together in monasteries (that is, became monks) and maintained themselves by their own husbandry. They early won the favor of Basil, bishop of Caesarea, one of the three great Cappadocians still honored by the Eastern Orthodox churches, and he laid down for them a rule that is universal in the East to this day. By it the monasteries submit themselves to the bishops of their localities and, in addition to the monastic practices shared with the West, prohibit strong drink and outside or non-canonical reading. Social service among the poor and orphaned is prescribed.

In the West the monastic movement was slow in getting started, but when the Germanic invasions turned society upside-down, it became popular and developed many independent orders. For some time each monastery had its own rule, and some were shockingly lax. In the sixth century, therefore, appeared the order of St. Benedict, whose founder prescribed for those who joined his order a full life of manual labor in the monastery's fields or shops, serious directed reading, and above all, worship throughout the day and part of the night. That the Benedictine monasteries, which eventually spread through western Europe, had libraries was in itself a fact of great consequence for the future.

Just how consistent monasticism was, at least in the case of some individuals, with an active purpose of serving society at large was apparent in the life, first, of St. Jerome, who while in monastic seclusion in Palestine completed the Vulgate, the translation of the Old and New Testaments into Latin; and in the career also of St. Chrysostom, the "golden-mouthed," who emerged from hermit life to attract great congregations in Antioch by his sermons and was therefore called to the bishopric of Constantinople (and the jealousies that plunged him into the obscurity of ill-deserved exile).

Another influential representative of the hermit life was Gregory the Great, the first monk to be chosen to the papal office (590–604). An administrator with great personal gifts, he so managed the financial resources of the papacy* that he virtually ruled Italy like a monarch. He laid the foundations of later papal authority in England, in whose conversion to Christianity he took great interest,† and increased his ecclesiastical power in France and Spain. His emphasis on penance and his stress on belief in purgatory brought these aspects of belief and practice for the first time to the forefront in Catholicism. He anticipated later practice by recommending penitents to seek the aid of the saints. He took it to be a fact that as the apostolic successor to St. Peter, who was "the prince of all the Apostles" to whom "by the Lord's voice the care of the whole church was committed," he should be acknowledged to be the head of the whole Church. He thus was the forerunner and model of the powerful medieval popes.

St. Augustine

But the greatest personality of the ancient Catholic Church was Augustine (354–430), bishop of Hippo in north Africa. He was a person in whose temperament almost every human quality was present in great intensity, yet such was the clarity and strength of his mind that he was able to master his unruly passions and harness them to a Christian purpose. Born of a pagan father and Christian mother, he attended the schools of his native north Africa, and at seventeen, while pursuing the study of rhetoric, he followed the promptings of his ardently sensuous nature and took a concubine. He rejected the New Testament at first as "unworthy to be compared with the dignity of Cicero,"[E1] whose works he was study-

---

* The church at Rome now had great land-holdings in Italy.

† England was converted by a kind of Christian pincers movement—from the north by way of Ireland and Scotland, from the south by missionaries sent out from Rome directly. Ireland had been converted earlier by St. Patrick. His converts crossed to Scotland; after they won it, missionaries entered England from Scotland.

465

ing. But Cicero was not enough, so he became an adherent of Manichaeism.* He derived only small comfort from this doctrine, however, for he never became one of the "perfect"; he could only be a "hearer," because he was unable to give up the lusts of the flesh, as Manichaeism demanded. His prayer at that time, he says in his famous *Confessions,* was, "Grant me chastity and continence, but not yet."E2

At twenty-nine he went to Italy. There, in Milan, he heard the powerful sermons of Ambrose, another of the great personalities of the ancient Catholic Church. His conscience was touched. When his mother, on joining him, urged him to enter upon betrothal to someone of his own class, he sorrowfully sent away his faithful concubine, who had borne him a son, and agreed to do as his mother asked, though on account of the tender years of the girl to whom he contracted himself, he put his marriage off. Then, finding himself still a prey to desire, he took another concubine. He almost despaired of himself now, for it seemed indeed true to him, as the Manichaens taught, that the flesh is incurably evil.

Radical changes in his point of view followed from an awakened interest in Neo-Platonism.† He began

---

* This was a philosophical system evolved by a Persian called Mani (215–276). Combined of elements drawn from Zoroastrianism, Buddhism, Judaism, Gnosticism, and Christianity, its characteristic tenet was the dualism of light and darkness, spirit and matter, good and evil. The soul of man is in bondage to vile matter and must follow the way of asceticism to freedom from the lusts of the flesh. Organized like a religion, it became for a time one of the chief rivals of Christianity. Though its influence waned after Augustine's time, it is interesting that some of the Crusaders returned to western Europe with a revived form of its doctrines and founded the sect of Cathari in southern France.

† An Alexandrian school of philosophy, of which Plotinus (205–270) was the chief representative. All reality consists, according to this school, of a series of emanations, at various removes, issuing from the One, the perfect Form, which is the source of all being everywhere. Like water from an overflowing spring, the realities closest to the source of being are the purest and best. Mind or intelligence is the emanation nearest to the One, soul or psyche is further removed, and matter is at the outer edge of being, at such a remove from its source as to suffer from an absence of indwelling divine reason or worth. Man

to consider it true that the temptations of the flesh follow from a falling away from God rather than from the presence of any positive and inherent element of badness in the flesh. In fact, he came to believe that God is the source of all things, and that matter and evil are to be defined in terms of an absence of the creative energy of God, due to spiritual remoteness from the one eternal good Being.

His conversion to Christianity occurred with apparent suddenness. Learning of a Neo-Platonist who had turned Christian, and then of some Egyptian monks who overcame their temptations by simple faithfulness to their monastic discipline, he ran distractedly from his friend Alypius into the farther reaches of a garden and heard a child's voice from across the wall saying, "Take up and read." Returning to his friend, he seized a copy of the Epistles of the New Testament lying on the bench, and opening it, read: "Not in rioting and drunkenness, not in chambering and wantonness . . . ; but put ye on the Lord Jesus Christ, and make not provision for the flesh to fulfil the lusts thereof." These words brought him to a decision.E3 Thenceforth he lived in strict continence. Baptized by Ambrose, he left for north Africa, resolved to found a monastery. There he became the bishop of Hippo, wrote voluminously for the next thirty years, and died while the Vandals were besieging his city.

Augustine was so many-sided that his theology is a synthesis of various trends. One sees in it a Neo-Platonist strain that modifies his basic reliance on Hebraic insights. But he yielded to no one tendency exclusively. So germinal was his thinking that we should not take leave of him without briefly summarizing his doctrines of God, man, and the Church and his philosophy of history.

Augustine's mystical personal experience of God kept him from thinking of God as a pure abstraction.

---

is a union of matter, soul, and mind. His salvation depends on his moving away from immersion in the realm of matter and achieving knowledge of true reality by an intuitive and mystical union with the One. As his soul becomes more intelligent and rational, it becomes more spiritual and divine.

God is near and very real, and both in the person of Jesus and through the activity of the Holy Spirit has broken into history and is continuously at work in human hearts. And yet, Augustine's conception had a Neo-Platonist tinge. God is the one eternal Being, alone absolutely real and absolutely good. He is the source of all other things, and they depend upon him at every moment for their continued existence. The physical universe especially has only a derived reality and is scarcely worthy of study in itself.

Augustine adapted this conception of God to his Christian conviction that God is "one in three." In the Trinity he saw no subordination of one member to another, as earlier theologians did. "There is so great an equality in that Trinity," he wrote, "that not only the Father is not greater than the Son, as regards divinity, but neither are the Father and the Son together greater than the Holy Spirit."[E4] Going further, he suggested that the Holy Spirit, though equal with the Father and the Son as regards divinity, "proceeds not only from the Father but also from the Son (*filioque*)."[E5] Yet again, the Trinity is as united as lover, loved, and love, or as memory, understanding, and will, of which he said: "Since, then, these three, memory, understanding, will, are not three lives, but one life; nor three minds, but one mind; it follows certainly that neither are they three substances, but one substance."[E6]

In forming his doctrine of man—which had enormous influence not only on Catholic theologians but also on the Protestant Reformers—Augustine drew upon his bitter experiences of his own moral weakness in youth. Man in and of himself is depraved, "the entire mass of (his) nature ruined,"[E7] "bound by original sin."[E8] This is the inheritance we all have from Adam. Adam was created good and with a fine intelligence. But he was endowed with free will, and though he could have chosen not to sin, he, along with Eve, ate of the forbidden fruit in willfulness and pride. After that he and all his descendants have been in a state of original sin, from which no one can now escape by his own efforts. It is as though the whole human race were morally diseased.

But God is merciful. Those whom he chooses, he saves by divine grace. Not that they deserve such mercy; it is entirely a free gift. This is the love of God, on which no human claims can be made. And when the divine grace comes, no one can resist it. Uplifted to effort and perseverance—"the perseverance of the saints"[E9]—the sinner is changed, justified, sanctified. To others the grace never comes, for they are doomed to damnation.

This hard doctrine involved Augustine in fierce controversy with a British monk called Pelagius, and with others. These men contended that there is no such thing as original sin, all men having an aptitude for goodness. Adam may have left to his descendants a bad example, but no inherited and inescapable moral weakness. Anyone who has faith is justified. But Augustine fought stoutly for his view. He knew from experience how inescapable are pride and lust in a life spent apart from God and how irresistible is God's sudden grace.

The Church, according to Augustine, is the divinely appointed institution to perform the sacraments that are the means of grace. There is only one Church, and none who are outside of it, whether heathen or heretic, can be saved. In opposition to a purist group in north Africa called the Donatists, who maintained that the sacraments performed by unworthy priests were ineffectual, Augustine held that the sacraments are instituted of God, not of men, and therefore they communicate grace regardless of the unworthy character of any man who performs them.

Augustine expressed his philosophy of history in his treatise *The City of God*. When he wrote it, Rome, "the mistress of the world," had been sacked by barbaric conquerors, and the pagan writers of the time were loudly lamenting what they conceived to be the fact that the city had declined and fallen because the grand old gods that had brought greatness to her had been abandoned for the enfeebling god of the Christians. In defending Christianity against this charge, Augustine boldly contrasted the Earthly City, which in history reached its clearest forms in Babylon

467

and Rome, with the City of God, to which God's elect in every generation have belonged. In his own day, he said, not all those who formed the visible Church were members of the invisible City of God. They, the non-elect, together with all those outside the Church, belonged to the Earthly City, which must decline and pass away. But the City of God will survive even the death of "civilization" and ultimately inherit the earth. So wrote Augustine even while the barbarians hammered at the gates of the cities of his Africa.

It cannot be said that the Roman Catholic Church adopted all of the Augustinian theology. Other influences, as we shall see, intervened. But the Protestant Reformation was a return to Augustine just as much as it was a return to Paul and Jesus.

The Division of the Church into East and West

Not only was the Roman empire brought low by invasions from the north; in the seventh century other invaders appeared in the southeast and rapidly overran Palestine, Syria, Asia Minor, north Africa, and Spain. The staunch defense of Constantinople checked them for a time in the East, and a Frankish chieftain by the name of Charles Martel turned them back in France in 732. Otherwise, perhaps, the Muslims would have taken Europe.

The effect of the Muslim conquests on what was left of the Roman empire was to divide it more seriously than ever. The Emperor Leo III at Constantinople incurred the displeasure of Pope Gregory II by his efforts to obtain reform in the face of the onrushing Muslim peril. Recoiling sharply from the criticisms coming from Arab (and Christian) quarters concerning the "idolatrous" veneration of images and pictures in the Christian churches, the emperor forbade, in 726, their further use—thus fathering the first iconoclastic movement in Christian history. There was immediate remonstrance both in the East and in the West. In the East Leo used his army to enforce his decree. But Rome was far enough away to make

good its disobedience. What was more, the pope called a Roman synod and obtained an action excommunicating those who opposed the use of pictures, namely, the emperor and those who sided with him. The emperor then retaliated by removing Sicily and southern Italy from the pope's spiritual jurisdiction. This left the pope in a precarious situation, for northern Italy was occupied by Lombards, and they had their hearts set on the conquest of Rome. So the pope called for help from Charles Martel, whose prowess against the Muslims made his aid worth seeking. Both Gregory and Charles were to die before that help was forthcoming, but Charles's son Pippin the Short, invaded Italy, brought the Lombard king to terms, and made a present of the province of Ravenna to the pope. He thus caused the pope to fix the orientation of the papacy toward the trans-Alpine lands rather than toward the East and, without knowing it, laid the foundations of a huge, unstable, Western empire.

The pope gained much. He was now not only the largest land-holder in Italy, with an annual income of over a million dollars, but a temporal sovereign, the ruler of "the states of the Church," as they came to be called, and very important these were to him.* Pippin's son, Charlemagne, gained much too. He built up an empire that included almost all of western Europe—in modern terms, France, northeastern Spain, Belgium, Holland, most of Germany, Austria, Hungary, and northern Italy. Cordial to the Church, Charlemagne came to Rome and on Christmas Day, 800, was formally crowned Holy Roman Emperor by Leo III. This act signalized the fact that West and East were at the parting of the ways, a fact accepted some years later by Emperor Leo V in Constantinople when he officially recognized the title of Charlemagne, and thus acknowledged that the empire had fallen in two.

---

* From 740 to 1870 the popes held firmly to their States of the Church, and, when bereft of them by King Victor Emmanuel, were outraged. In 1929 Mussolini restored the pope's temporal sovereignty over the Vatican and the grounds immediately around it.

Meanwhile, a serious doctrinal split between East and West had been preparing. We have already seen that Augustine thought the Holy Spirit proceeds from the Father *and* the Son. In 589 a Western council, meeting in Spain, added to the Nicene Creed (the creed of 381 A.D.) the word *filioque* ("and from the Son") immediately after the words saying that the Holy Spirit proceeds from the Father. The theologians of the East protested the change strongly, believing that to make it meant denying that God is the source of all things. The West held out generally for the *filioque*. The rift of opinion hung fire for several centuries. Finally, in 876 a synod at Constantinople condemned the pope both for his political activities and because he did not correct the heresy of the *filioque* clause. This action was part of the East's entire rejection of the pope's claim of universal jurisdiction over the Church. A bitter break came in 1054, when the long-smoldering schism led a papal legate, without authorization, to excommunicate the patriarch of Constantinople and the patriarch to hurl back anathemas in return. Since then the two branches of the Catholic Church have gone their separate ways.

However, as individuals brought the final break, its decisiveness was in doubt for a time, but after Good Friday in 1204, when Crusaders from northwestern Europe, on their way to delivering Jerusalem from the Muslims, inexcusably sacked and pillaged Constantinople, the break became final and complete.

IV The Eastern Orthodox Churches

Although until recently the patriarch of Constantinople claimed spiritual supremacy over them, the various bodies of the Eastern Orthodox Church have been virtually independent of each other, divided as they are into units corresponding more or less to the national states in which they have existed. Yet none of them has departed to any great degree from the Orthodox tradition accepted in the East. Inasmuch as the ancient sees of Alexandria, Jerusalem, and Antioch early fell into Muslim hands, theological development in those areas virtually ceased after the eighth century. It ceased elsewhere as well. The only real changes have been in liturgy and religious practice. Here leadership was for a long time held by the patriarch of Constantinople, and when Constantinople fell to the Turks in 1453, it passed to the Slavic Orthodox churches, and particularly to the largest of them all, the Russian Orthodox Church, whose patriarch once said that even as Constantinople had been the second Rome, so Moscow should be the third.

The unity of the Orthodox churches has never been really broken. Although, as a consequence of international changes and conflicts, the various nationalized churches have sometimes had such violent disputes concerning jurisdiction that more than once one branch of the Church has excommunicated another, they have all learned to fall back finally on a doctrine of expediency, called "economy," whereby acts of excommunicated Church leaders have been first tolerated, and then validated, on the grounds of keeping the churches operating without loss of power and authority. Basically, this reaction to occasional divergence rests on a sense of "wholeness" or essential indivisibility (the Orthodox interpretation of catholicity) of the Church, which preserves its unity even in the diversifications that arise from the exercise of freedom.

The General Doctrinal Position

In spite of differences of administration, the various branches of the Eastern Orthodox Church have remained more or less united in matters of doctrine. The ancient creeds are accepted as infallible definitions of orthodox apostolic teaching. There have been local divergences in faith and practice, but in general the churches have not departed from the doctrinal position reached by the last of their acknowledged

469

ancient fathers, John of Damascus, who one century after the Muslims seized Syria made a last effort on the basis of the completed creeds and the writings of preceding fathers to systematize the Eastern faith.

The position taken by John of Damascus fairly well characterizes the general attitude of the Orthodox churches—a mystical emphasis on the life-giving incarnation of God in Christ conveyed down to the present time through the seven sacraments and the other rites and devotional practices of the churches. The Western interest in the practical, juridical (analytical and individualistic) aspects of the relation between God and man had no great place in the concern of John of Damascus, or, for that matter, of the Eastern Church before or after him.

There are some interesting aspects in this position. John of Damascus appeared at a time when the Byzantine type of church architecture had been highly developed. The chief external mark of the Eastern churches had become a dome resting on a rectangular or octagonal substructure, supported by half-domes and buttresses. In the interior, the nave led to a chancel within which was the altar and to the rear of it a semi-circle of seats for the bishops and presbyters. The pulpit stood outside of the chancel, nearer to the congregation. The floor, walls, ceilings, and screens were richly decorated with pictures and mosaics, representing in the formal manner of symbolical and devotional art the Holy Trinity, the Virgin Mary, Christ, the Apostles, and many saints and martyrs. Icons, with images shown in low relief against a plaque (such as Christ on the cross and Mary as the Mother of God) were colored in red, gold, and blue, and these, together with multicolored mosaics of the same subjects, were venerated by the worshipers, prayers being addressed in their direction and even kisses and strokings bestowed on them. In due time some of these images and pictures were credited with miraculous powers and became objects of special pilgrimage. When the Emperor Leo III was moved to order the suppression of such veneration, and there ensued the uproar in the East and West that we have described, John of Damascus

came to the defense of images. He declared that the question of icons "is a question for Synods and not for Emperors." He went on to argue that the synods would see in images an incarnation of the Holy Spirit analogous to the incarnation of God in Christ. Again, icons were analogous to the sacraments, in that they conveyed divine grace to the believer. Yet again, they were analogous to books, for "what a book is to the literate, that an image is to the illiterate." Indeed, the reverend father went so far as to put all the rites, creeds, and institutions of the Church in the same position: all alike are chiefly means of conveying divine life and grace to the believer.

It was in accordance with this reasoning that in 787 the Seventh General Council—the last in which the Greek and Roman churches concurred—declared that pictures and images, the cross, and the Gospels "should be given due salutation and honorable reverence, (though) not indeed that true worship which pertains to the divine nature. . . . For the honor which is paid to the image passes on to that which the image represents, and he who shows reverence to the image shows reverence to the subject represented in it."[B4] (So far the East and West could agree.)

Differences Between the Eastern and Roman Churches

But even in the attitude toward images the Eastern and Roman churches have differed. In the East icons are not humanized, and the figures remain symbols, simplified representations of "essential" meanings. As such they are rendered in formalized bas-relief rather than in the round as in the Roman Church. In other words, the East regards icons as signifying divine nature and spirit, whereas the Roman Church on the whole uses images to bring the Virgin and the saints within human range. Hence the attitude to Jesus' mother differs fundamentally in the two churches: the Roman Catholics venerate the Blessed Virgin as one who loves her child and is compassionate and humane to her suppliants; the Eastern churches worship her as the holy Mother of God, the exalted being in whom the human and the divine met in the Incarnation.

These differences in attitude are considered by representatives of the Eastern churches as not contradictory but complementary. As one puts it: "The Western mind, being more analytical, approaches spirit and matter as distinct and even opposite entities, whereas Orthodoxy conceives matter and spirit as two interdependent manifestations of the same ultimate reality. These attitudes are not contradictory but complementary to each other; yet in their own way they color every aspect of Church life, and, as a result, the same terms are differently understood by the Christian East and West. . . . An example of this is the word 'Catholic,' which in the West has acquired the meaning of universal in the sense of the geographical extension of the Church throughout the world. . . . In the East 'Catholic' means 'integral' or 'whole'; the word signifies the inner quality of the true Church as opposed to heresies or sects. . . . The same difference in interpretation applies to the word 'Orthodoxy.' In the West this word stands for 'correct doctrine'; in the East it is also interpreted as 'right praise,' for the Eastern mind links teaching with worship, and considers that only those Christians who pray to God in the spirit of love and humility have proper access to Orthodox belief and profess it in the right way."[F]

Other points of difference persisting down to the present may be briefly mentioned. The East has sacraments differing from those of the Roman Catholic Church in certain respects: baptism in infancy by triple immersion, chrismation (anointing after baptism with oil consecrated by a bishop), the eucharist or sacrament of communion in both kinds (bread and wine), confession only after reconciliation with those wronged or estranged, the taking of holy orders only after the congregation has given its unanimous approval, marriage with the bride and groom wearing crowns of glory, and extreme unction, which is given not, as in the West, only before death,

but in serious illness to encourage recovery. It is held that in the eucharist the bread and wine become the body and blood of Christ, not as in Roman belief by transubstantiation,[*] but rather by a transformation due to the operation of the Holy Spirit. The liturgy of the eucharist has been developed into an elaborate work of devotional art enriched by antiphonal choral chants, sung in different voices, without instrumental accompaniment, by priests in gorgeous vestments. Long recitatives at a high level of devotional poetry and beauty precede and follow the central act of elevating the sanctified bread and wine before the altar. The sign of the cross is made by the priest with candles, of which two in the left hand, with lighted tips meeting, symbolize the union of the divine and human natures in Christ, and three in the right hand, similarly joined, symbolize the Trinity of Father, Son, and Holy Spirit.

The list of differences could be extended. It must suffice to mention but one or two more. In addition to refusing to add filioque to the Nicene Creed, the East repudiates the belief in purgatory taught in the Roman West. The Orthodox churches do not demand celibacy of all the clergy, allowing those to marry who are content to remain among the "lower" clergy. Of course, the Eastern churches firmly "renounce" as "erroneous" the belief "that a man, to wit, the Bishop of Rome, can be the head of Christ's Body, that is to say, of the whole church." With equal firmness they reject "the erroneous belief that the Holy Apostles did not receive from our Lord equal spiritual power, but that the holy Apostle Peter was their Prince: and that the Bishop of Rome alone is his successor: and that the Bishops of Jerusalem, Alexandria, Antioch, and others are not, equally with the bishops of Rome, successors of the Apostles."[G] They contend that the pope of Rome cannot be infallible in matters of faith and morals, because several of the popes have been condemned as heretics by the Church councils; and certainly, they say, the

---

[*] The doctrine that during the celebration of the mass the substance of the bread and of the wine is converted into the actual or real body and blood of Christ.

471

pope cannot claim to be superior to the Church councils.

The Present Situation

The Orthodox churches outside the Iron Curtain have to a large extent recovered from the setbacks received during World War II. Since their admission to the World Council of Churches, they have participated in its activities with considerable evidence of vitality.

As for the Orthodox churches in Russia and the satellite countries, it has been difficult to gauge accurately the developments taking place within them. The old national Church of Russia was so clearly identified with the Czarist regime that the 1917 revolution was a major catastrophe to it. But the situation of its disestablished successor, the Orthodox Church of Russia, seems rather to improve with time. Its work in society continues to be restricted, for the Church may engage only in religious activity. It may maintain a certain number of buildings, train and employ priests, and conduct religious services, but formal religious education of the young is prohibited. However, although for some time the Russian government kept the Russian Church from joining the World Council of Churches, it reversed itself in 1961. In November of that year not only the Russian but also the Bulgarian, Roumanian, and Polish churches sent delegates to the meeting of the World Council at New Delhi, India, and entered its membership. In his letter requesting such membership, the patriarch of Moscow reported that the Russian Church had at that time thirty thousand priests, twenty thousand parishes, seventy-three bishoprics, eight theological schools, and forty monasteries. Apparently, as long as there is no "subversion" or "counter-revolutionary activity" within the Church, it is allowed to minister religiously to its estimated forty million adherents. However, there is constant surveillance and an obvious wish on the part of the government that the Church would die out.

As members of the World Council of Churches, the Eastern Orthodox churches, whose senior prelate is Patriarch Athenogoras I of Constantinople, are seeking closer ecumenical ties with both the Protestant and Roman Catholic churches. The Third Pan-Orthodox Church Conference held at Rhodes in 1964 considered proposed discussions with the Roman Catholic Church on reunion but postponed, until "adequate provisions" had been effected, conferences of committees empowered to arrange for such union. Meanwhile, Athenogoras met with Pope Paul in Jerusalem (1964) as a first step in achieving closer relations. In 1965 the mutual excommunications that were pronounced in 1054 were annulled simultaneously in Rome and Constantinople.

V The Roman Catholic Church in the Middle Ages

The Great Period of the Papacy

The Roman Catholic Church entered the Middle Ages with a head who was a temporal sovereign quite equal in political and financial position to some of the secular sovereigns of the West. Not only that. The Donation of Constantine, so-called, suggested that he was destined to be the theocratic ruler of the entire West.* Whether the popes of the time actually desired such a position or not, there seemed to be no insurmountable obstacle to their attaining it if they wanted it.

The kings and chieftains of the West, on their part, were willing to concede the spiritual supremacy of

* The pope's territorial ambitions were bolstered by an extraordinary forgery that was circulated at this time and won widespread acceptance as genuine. Known as the Donation of Constantine, this forgery represented Constantine as granting to the popes not only spiritual supremacy over the whole Church but also temporal dominion over Rome, Italy, and the "provinces, places, and cities of the western regions." Not until the middle of the fifteenth century was the forgery successfully discredited.

472

the Roman pontiff, but they were equally sure that the pope ought not to intrude himself into their purely temporal affairs.

Hence arose vexing conflicts between the popes and secular powers. Such churchmen as were elevated to high office at the behest or by the appointment of kings and princes were often easy-going and worldly-minded. Some of them had even bought and paid for their appointment—a practice called simony. They were prone to take their churchly honors as a personal prerogative, to do with as they liked, and the farther they were from Rome the more this was the case. In northern areas, especially in Germany, bishops even married and passed their bishoprics on to their sons, in complete disregard of the rule laid down long before by Pope Leo I that all the clergy, even to the sub-deacons, should be celibate. Again, northern bishops were frequently complaisant toward, and sanctioned, easy divorce among kings and princes when political marriages proved unsatisfactory. In another direction, conflicts arose between canon law (the law of the Church drawn from the decrees of councils, synods, and popes) and the civil law of the various states, and where the state was strong, the canon law was often violated in the administration of parishes and monasteries.

A head-on contest between pope and emperor could not long be avoided. Its outbreak simply awaited the appearance of personalities sufficiently strong to enter upon it. This occurred when Hildebrand became pope in 1073, under the name of Gregory VII. He wasted no time. A new emperor, Henry IV, had ascended the throne in Germany. The pope ordered Henry to conform to the decree that bishops receive their staff of office from the pope and not from the emperor, and he charged the married bishops of Germany to give up their wives. But Henry IV was to prove a formidable opponent. He defiantly appointed a cleric of his own choice to the bishopric of Milan, then under his control. Hildebrand called him to task. Henry held a council with his nobles and bishops and led them in rejecting Hildebrand's authority as pope. Hildebrand replied

Chartres cathedral. The facade of this most praised of Gothic cathedrals is interestingly asymmetrical, its two spires being in different styles. Its doorways are decorated with spirited sculpture of great refinement. In the interior the stained glass windows, seen from between columns and arches faultlessly executed, are the finest in the world. It is seven hundred years old. (Religious News Service Photo.)

with a decree falling like a thunderbolt upon Henry, excommunicating him and releasing his subjects in Germany and Italy from their oaths of allegiance to him. Though Henry sent the pope a fierce letter calling him "now no pope, but a false monk," and telling him to "come down, to be damned through all eternity," he was merely blustering. In reality he was hard hit. His nobles told him that if he were not released from his excommunication within a year and a day, they would depose him.

In great trouble Henry crossed the Alps. It was mid-winter. He followed the pope to a castle at Canossa, and for three days stood in the snow of the courtyard, a white-clad, bare-footed penitent, while Gregory considered what to do about him. Finally, the pope, utterly avenged, admitted Henry to an audience and released him from his excommunication.

The pope's great triumph—one of the most dramatic in history—was short-lived. Three years later he made the mistake of excommunicating Henry again. Henry's answer was a march on Rome that enabled him to drive the pope out of it and set up a rival pontiff. But the contest had reached an inconclusive stage. Soon Gregory and Henry were both dead, and their successors, Henry V and Pope Calixtus II, came to a compromise. Bishops everywhere and in all cases were to be chosen by the Church in accordance with canon law, yet before their consecration the German bishops were to appear before the emperor to be invested by the touch of the royal scepter with the temporal possession of their sees. In other words, all new German bishops were to be acceptable to the emperor. Furthermore, it was agreed that bishops should be celibate. Hildebrand's reforms had in great part been achieved.

More powerful even than Hildebrand was Pope Innocent III (1193–1216) a hundred years later. Innocent entered on his office when papal prestige had reached a new height, largely due to his predecessor's effective discipline of Henry II of England.*

Although Innocent III was conceded, on his accession, to be without qualification the spiritual superior of every terrestrial sovereign, he acted on the principle that he was the first among his peers in the temporal sphere also. When Germany was torn between rival claimants to the throne, he crowned one of them, Otto III, Holy Roman Emperor—after wringing large promises from him. When the new emperor forgot his promises, the pope put a rival in the field and with the help of the king of France established him on the imperial throne. He thus proved that he could make and unmake kings. The king of France, too, felt the pope's whip-hand. Resolved to rid himself of his unloved queen, the Swedish princess Ingeborg, the French monarch divorced her. The pope then put all France under an interdict (i.e., a ban on all religious services), and the king, yielding to popular clamor, took back his queen. In Spain the pope first assumed control of Aragon and then granted it back as a fief to its king, Peter. He imposed a similar status upon the rebellious English. Richard the Lion-Hearted's unpopular brother, King John, tried to force his candidate for archbishop on the see of Canterbury, and the pope placed England under an interdict, to last until Stephen Langton, his choice, should be made archbishop. When King John resisted, the pope excommunicated him, declared his throne vacant, and proclaimed a crusade against him. John capitulated but was not restored to grace until he acknowledged his kingdom to be a fief of the papacy from which a thousand marks were due annually to the pope as a feudal tax!

Within the Church itself Innocent III became the undisputed head of the whole ecclesiastical domain. All disagreements of the higher clergy were ordered

---

* From the security of his island kingdom Henry II had challenged the Roman pontiff by passing laws limiting the application of canon law in ecclesiastical cases and putting the election of bishops into the hands of the king, to whom these prelates were required to do homage. The archbishop of Canterbury, Thomas à Becket, an old friend of Henry's, had sternly opposed him at this juncture, and Henry's expressions of anger caused four knights to ride to Canterbury and murder the archbishop before the cathedral's very altar. The pope, capitalizing on Becket's popularity, canonized him; streams of pilgrims (precisely like those pictured in *The Canterbury Tales*) poured through the cathedral's doors and wore down the stone floor by kneeling before the new saint's tomb. The king, full of dismay and remorse, withdrew the offending laws, and as a penitent submitted himself to being scourged before Becket's tomb!

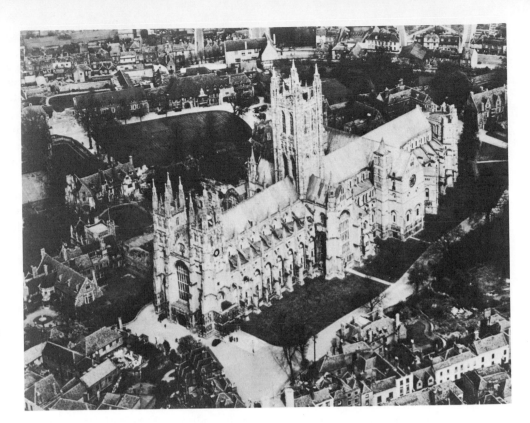

Canterbury cathedral. The seat of the archbishop of Canterbury and the scene, in the twelfth century, of the murder of Thomas à Becket, this cruciform cathedral is in the Perpendicular Gothic style. It was begun as a basilica as early as 950 and completed, after much restyling, five hundred years later. This picture was chosen to show how the old town, which made it a community project, surrounds it. (Religious News Service Photo.)

to be referred to him, and his decisions were final. He reserved the right to move bishops about among their sees. He forced through the Fourth Lateran Council (in 1215) the acceptance of the dogma of transubstantiation and the rule that the good standing of a Catholic was conditioned upon periodic confession, absolution, and communion.

The papacy had reached its all-time height of spiritual and earthly power.

Medieval Monasticism

Monastic reform was in the air before the Crusades. (In fact, the Crusades were first projected by popes schooled in the reforms initiated by the Cluny movement of the tenth century.) Significantly, the whole monastic scene in Europe during the Crusades was dominated by the reforming Cistercian order—French and Benedictine, like the Cluny group—its greatest exponent, as organizer and preacher, being the saintly Bernard of Clairvaux. But the most notable expressions of medieval monastic piety were achieved a little later by the Dominican and Franciscan orders.

The Dominican order was in origin a missionary movement, whose first objective was the conversion of the heretical Cathari of southern France. But Dominic (1170–1221), its Spanish founder, had the inspiration to send his "preachers," as imitators of the Apostle Paul, to many other parts of Europe, especially to the university towns, and their success caused his order to grow swiftly. The friars, as his monks were called, were devoted to learning because they were primarily preachers and teachers sent to the uninstructed and the unconvinced. They dressed plainly in black (whence their name of Black Friars) and were vowed to a mendicant poverty, begging

475

their daily food in the spirit of Matt. 10:7–14. The order was headed by a "master-general" who supervised the work of the "provincial priors" in the Dominican "provinces." At the head of each monastery or nunnery was a "prior" or "prioress," chosen for a term of four years by the monks or nuns themselves, something of a democratic innovation. It was the misfortune of the Dominicans that the popes chose them as inquisitors; they had no original leaning in that direction. When they followed their own natural path, they had wide success among the higher classes and produced great writers and teachers, like the theologians Albertus Magnus and Thomas Aquinas; the reformer of Florence, Savonarola; and the mystics, Eckhart and Tauler.

The Franciscans had their great success among the common people. The founder of their order, St. Francis of Assisi (1182–1226), is one of the world's great personalities—as an individual the most winsome of saints, as a world-figure Christ in a medieval incarnation. After a gay and frivolous youth, during which his father, a businessman, disinherited him for showing no interest in accumulating riches, he underwent after illness a religious experience that led him back to the "rule of Christ" as described in the New Testament. Thereafter he said he was "married to Lady Poverty," ate the plainest food, wore unadorned grey garments, possessed no other property than his immediate personal belongings, worked when he could, not for money, which he would not take, but just for the needs of the hour, or begged for his food when work failed. He preached to the poor or, when afield, to birds and beasts, in a love of nature that was a revelation to his hard-headed and practical age. He ministered to the unfortunate, the lepers, the outcast with a compassion drawn both from his own nature and from his imitation of Christ. His way of life immediately attracted others, and he prescribed for them no more than the New Testament "rule of Christ." When twelve men had joined him, he went with them to Pope Innocent III for recognition of their order, and it was at once granted. Francis attempted no organization beyond sending his

grey-clad friars out two by two on preaching missions. Even so, his movement spread like wildfire. It became necessary for others to step in and organize it, putting at its head a "minister-general" who directed the "provincial ministers" of the "provinces," which were composed in turn of local groups under a "custos." A second order, for nuns, was formed under Clara Sciffi of Assisi, and later a third order was created for lay people who wished, while pursuing a livelihood, to fast, pray, and practice benevolence in association with the order. St. Francis did not oppose the organizers who came to help him, but he regretted the necessity of putting a spiritual movement in leading strings.[*]

Both the Dominican and Franciscan orders had enormous influence in suggesting that the Christian religion transcends all organization and reaches into every department of life with an elemental appeal addressed directly to every man's reason and conscience.

Scholasticism

While all this occurred, the schools were busy, for a new world had risen at last out of the ruins of the old, and men now began to study their intellectual heritage.

Since the time of Charlemagne the cathedrals and monasteries had devoted more and more attention to the schools they had founded for boys and young men. Some of the teachers, pursuing truth for its own sake, began to develop an interest in every kind of subject matter. They not only taught what was in the old books—the Vulgate, the creeds, collections of canon law, fragments of Aristotle, Plato, the Stoics, the writings of the Neo-Platonists, the works of St. Augustine, and so on—but they began to compose

[*] Today the order consists of three branches of varying degrees of strictness: the Friars Minor (dressed in dark brown tunics), the more rigorous Capuchins (grey-clad), and the less rigorous, property-accumulating Conventuals (in black tunics).

new treatises, which were circulated among the various monasteries and aroused debate, controversy, and dialectical discussion. As the fame of individual teachers increased, students came from far and near, and the conditions were created for the founding of universities, the first of which were established late in the twelfth century. Soon Bologna became famous for canon and civil law, Salerno for medicine, and Paris and Oxford for theology.

Scholasticism was the brain-child of these medieval schools. It quite naturally concerned itself with the logic of the faith. After its first tentative emergence in the time of Charlemagne, it became with time more responsible, philosophically more weighty.[*] Its dialectical method was applied at last to the really great problem of theology: how to reconcile reason and revelation—a problem that becomes in one direction the problem of the reconciliation of science and religion and, in another, that of the reconciliation of philosophy and theology.

Augustine had laid one of the bases of Scholasticism by saying, "Faith seeks the support of the intelligence" (*fides quaerit intellectum*), meaning that the intelligence explores and corroborates or finds added reasons for believing in the divinely revealed dogmas of the Church. The other basis of Scholasticism was suggested by Anselm (1033–1109) in one of his works: *credo ut intelligam*, "I believe in order that I may understand." On the one hand, then, the

Education of the Virgin. Conceived according to the Hildesheim school (ca. 1500), the young Virgin, already crowned, is responding to the affectionate, slightly admonitory instruction of her teacher. The canopy over their heads is clearly Gothic, resembling a miniature Gothic cathedral. (Philadelphia Museum of Art.)

[*] It is generally agreed that some of the early efforts of scholastic logic were scarcely profound. In the words of Guignebert, *Christianity, Past and Present* (Macmillan, 1927, p. 257): "To tell the truth, the dialecticians of the ninth century, and even those of the first half of the tenth, do not always deal in their arguments with really lofty subjects; little by little they perfect their methods through discussions which appear to us extremely puerile. They inquire, for instance, whether God can choose as a Redeemer a woman or a demon or an ass, or even a plant or a stone; they discuss the question whether a prostitute can become a virgin again through Divine grace, or whether a mouse that nibbles a consecrated wafer really eats the Lord's body!" But our possible amusement at this turn of discussion should be tempered with the thought that it was not characteristic of scholasticism generally or of any one place for long.

scholastics proceeded on faith: the revelation was to be accepted as true, and then understanding of God, man, and world would follow. On the other hand, revelation was supported and defended by reason, as Augustine had suggested. It was in this spirit that Anselm developed his famous ontological argument for God's existence.

When Scholasticism was in full swing one hundred years later, its exponents were committed roughly to the following procedure: they took their starting point from the incompletely systematized doctrines set forth in the scriptures and the creeds, erected these into a general structure of truth, and then proceeded to fill in this framework with the proper details—that is to say, with the deductions, inferences, and related data necessary to a fully developed systematic theology—all the while using as a test of validity each detail's coherence with the revealed dogma.

The early schoolmen started out with high hopes, drawing heavily upon the opinions of the Church fathers and the great pagan philosophers. But they soon hit upon serious snags, which no amount of discussion seemed entirely to remove. Among them, as Anselm had pointed out, was the problem of the status to be assigned to unchanging ideas or universals. Were universals real (the position of medieval realism) or names only (the position of nominalism)?* Much depended—much that did not at once meet the eye—upon the answer. Take the Church, for example. "Church" is a universal. Did the Church exist as an ideal form prior to all individual churches, which must then have come into existence to exemplify its nature, or is "Church" a name given to individual institutions with certain marked resemblances and thus bestowed after they came into existence? If the answer was in terms of the first alternative, then the Church was indeed a divine institution; if the answer was in terms of the second alternative, then it was a much more human institution than it claimed to be.

The Church was actively behind the realists, yet

nominalism had sown such doubts, left such problems, and won so many followers that the effort of the scholastic theologians to bring philosophy wholly into the service of theology (which they called "the queen of the sciences") proved at last a failure. By the fourteenth century Catholic theology had to let philosophy go upon its own way of free intellectual inquiry, untrammeled by tradition and authority.

The recovery late in the twelfth century of the Aristotelian writings helped to win for philosophy this freedom from theology. Up to the twelfth century only fragments of Aristotle's writings had survived the wreck of Roman civilization, but then from Spain there came translations of his works from the Arabic texts studied in the University of Cordoba. These translations were later checked against recovered Greek texts. For the first time in seven hundred years the West had before it a systematic treatment of natural science. The final result of its study was a "new theology," ably presented by Thomas Aquinas, the greatest of the scholastics. His synthesis of faith and philosophy, which reconciled without discrediting either, proved to be the most influential scholastic achievement.

Thomas Aquinas

Born in 1227, Thomas Aquinas was a native of Italy, a member of a noble family of part Roman and part German blood. He became a Dominican friar, of such promise that he was sent to Paris and Cologne to study under Albertus Magnus, another Dominican friar and one of the encyclopedic minds of his time. Afterwards he taught, first at Cologne, then at Paris, and finally in Italy, where he wrote his great books—now the standard theological guides of the Roman Catholic Church—the *Summa Contra Gentiles* and the *Summa Theologica*.

In the endeavor to reconcile reason and revelation, philosophy and theology, Aristotle and Christ, he tried to show that natural reason and faith are lower and higher forms of apprehension that are comple-

* To put the issue more technically, do universals (class terms) like *man* or *house* exist, as Plato claimed, prior to and as patterns determining the nature of the individual objects bearing their names (realism), or are such universals merely designations (names) for resemblances between objects, and do they have no existence except in thought (nominalism)?

478

mentary to each other. By itself human or natural reason, that is, such reason as Aristotle used, can go very far, not only in exploring the natural world but also in proving the existence of God. It is possible for human reason by its own efforts to establish God's existence, using at least five cogent arguments: an argument from motion to an unmoved mover, an argument based on the necessity of a first efficient cause, an argument from possibility to necessity, an argument accounting for the gradation to be found in things, and a teleological argument drawn from consideration of design in the structure of the world. Nor is this all that reason can do. It can discover without divine help the nature of God; that is, it can by itself establish that God is pure actuality, one and unchanging, perfect and therefore good, infinite and therefore possessed of infinite intelligence, knowledge, goodness, freedom, and power. But reason is unable to establish more than general propositions. It cannot know what God hath wrought historically unless it receives divine supplementation of its knowledge. Therefore, it needs to have added to its conclusions what revelation alone can supply, namely, knowledge of the tragic nature of the fall of Adam, by which mankind has been infected with original sin, the facts of the Incarnation and the Atonement, the doctrine of the Trinity, the fact of saving grace through the sacraments, assurance of the resurrection of the body, and knowledge of hell, purgatory, and paradise. Thus a faith based on revelation knows things that are *above* reason, that is, that are beyond reason's unaided power to establish.

Yet faith needs reason none the less. Nothing should be accepted by faith that is contrary to reason. There is no risk in this. Candid examination of the Christian revelation shows it to be in no part contrary to reason, but in all its parts according to reason.

Similar reasoning enabled Thomas Aquinas to reconcile philosophy and theology. Philosophy begins with the world of sense-experience and by the exercise of scientific reflection (reason) ascends to God. Theology begins with the revealed truths that are

from God and descends to man and the world. Both supplement and need each other.

In his doctrine of man Aquinas combined Aristotle with the Christian revelation. With Aristotle, he considered that body and soul (matter and form) are functionally necessary to each other. The body without the soul cannot live, and the soul, though immortal, can neither develop nor maintain the characteristics of an individual self without the body. Hence, it is a great comfort to be assured by Christian revelation of the resurrection of the body.

Aquinas clarified the Catholic conception of the sacraments by a similar Aristotelian distinction of lower and higher elements. Every sacrament has two elements in it, a material element (water, bread, wine, oil) and a formal element (the liturgical formulas). Together they make an organic union and supply a means of grace. Present during the performance of each sacrament are the human or affected and the divine or causal elements. When the conditions are duly present, supernatural grace is conveyed through the sacraments to the human recipients as regenerating power. In each case a miracle takes place. Especially is this so in the celebration of the mass. There, at the words of consecration by the priest, the unleavened bread and the wine are transubstantiated, so that without changing in shape or taste they are the very body and blood of Christ. The miracle of the Incarnation is thus repeated at each celebration of the mass.

Penance, though a sacrament, is not highly sacramental. It is more prolonged and requires greater human participation. It involves contrition, confession (to a priest), satisfaction, and absolution (by a priest). Here, as in all human regeneration, there is a lower and a higher side. In his life on earth the individual finds himself able to attain a certain degree of natural virtue. Without God's aid he may exemplify wisdom, justice, courage, and temperance. But these will not redeem him; these are but the virtues of the natural man. To attain to eternal life, he must attain the theological virtues, which have God for their source and their object and are nourished by God's

479

grace alone. These virtues, which he cannot achieve by himself but must have from God, are faith, hope, and love.

To go no further with the summary of Aquinas' synthesis, we may see how orthodox and yet how flexible it is. The whole system is dogmatic from beginning to end, yet science is granted competence in the discovery of truth. Theology is in highest place, but humanism and naturalism are also given roles to play.

Medieval Mysticism

While, under the leadership of men like Thomas Aquinas, the schoolmen were pursuing what the Hindus would call "the way of knowledge," and while at the same time the common man was following "the way of works," there were others who cultivated a mystic "way of devotion" that was deeply rooted in the Church's past. Monasticism had always had its mystic aspect. When the monk retired to solitary meditation, he sought to purge himself of evil and lift his soul to ecstatic union with God and the saints. The mystics were those who refused to believe that the direct vision of God himself, or of Christ, or of the saints had to await the passage from this world to the next; the mystic vision was possible here on earth.

Medieval mysticism had both an individual and a cultic form. In the twelfth century the Cistercian leader, Bernard of Clairvaux, tried to bring new vigor into the religious life of his time by preaching and writing of the blessing that came from the mystic's love of the Virgin and of Christ. In his *Homilies on the Song of Songs* he provided later mystics with valuable concepts for the description of their feelings. He saw in Christ the bridegroom of the soul and so vividly defined this relationship of the Redeemer and his adorers that he made it possible for mystics to interpret their raptures as ideal and heavenly love. It seemed to Bernard that such a relationship would transcend earthly feeling. Love for Jesus can be so

warm and personal that the entire being of the enraptured mystic becomes flooded with a sense of tenderness, fervor, and sweetness.*

Hugo St. Victor and Bonaventura in the twelfth and thirteen centuries carried mysticism into the schools. The Dominican preachers Meister Eckhart and John Tauler, in the late thirteenth and early fourteenth centuries in Germany, succeeded in developing an influential mystic cult in central Europe. Both were impatient with the externalism of the then current Catholicism. To Eckhart even "individuality" was something to be laid aside; it was "nothing." Only the divine spark in the soul is real; it alone matters. Following the same path, the Dominican ascetic Henry Suso illustrated in his own life the privations that extremer mystics determinedly underwent. As long as he felt within himself any element of self-love and fleshly desire, he submitted his body to the extremes of self-torture, carrying on his back a heavy cross studded with nails and needles and sometimes lying down upon it in stern self-chastisement, until at last God did "gladden the heart of the sufferer in return for all his suffering with inward peace of heart, so that he praised God with all his heart for his past suffering."[H]

Around these German mystics a cult calling itself The Friends of God arose and spread through south-

---

* How profoundly stirring this idea was, may be seen in the hymn which comes down from his day, perhaps from his own hand:

> Jesus, the very thought of thee
>   With sweetness fills my breast;
> But sweeter far thy face to see,
>   And in thy presence rest. . . .
>
> O Hope of every contrite heart,
>   O Joy of all the meek,
> To those who fall, how kind thou art!
>   How good to those who seek!
>
> But what to those who find? Ah, this
>   Nor tongue nor pen can show;
> The love of Jesus, what it is
>   None but his loved ones know.

western Germany, Switzerland, and Holland. In Holland the movement led to the founding of a group called the Brethren of the Common Life, whose members, renouncing sex, lived in separate houses of brethren and sisters, practicing the mystic discipline in semi-monastic seclusion. The finest literary product of this group was a book of simple and earnest piety called the *Imitation of Christ*, by one Thomas a Kempis. No book produced during the Middle Ages has reached so many readers as this, for it commended itself long after as much to Protestants as to Catholics.

In other parts of the Catholic world the disorders of the Church beginning in the fourteenth century caused many individuals to turn to mysticism for truth and grace. Two great women found in their mystic raptures the power to work for reforms in the Church and in the world. Catherine of Siena (1347–1380), energized by a mystic experience of "marriage" with Christ, the heavenly bridegroom, worked among the victims of the Black Plague and, being distressed by the "Babylonish Captivity" of the popes at Avignon, personally persuaded Gregory XI to move the seat of the papacy back to Rome. Almost two centuries later, Teresa of Avila in Spain (1515–1582), after similar experiences, reformed the Carmelite order. She found guidance and help from a fellow mystic, the ascetic John of the Cross.

It is needless here to extend the list. One and all displayed the irrepressible longing of all high religions to transcend the formal and external limits of human experience and meet God face-to-face.

The Decline of the Papacy

The papacy was unable to maintain itself on the height of authority and power reached during the thirteenth century. The factors that led to its decline were many. The unremitting papal pressure at the top only accentuated the divisive effect of a new sense of nationalism rising among the different European peoples from below. France and England, par-

ticularly, were able to move toward independence. Indeed, the Holy Roman Empire (now "neither holy, nor Roman, nor an empire") broke up into a collection of loosely united petty kingdoms. When this happened, France began to wield a more powerful influence than Italy. There was an immediate clash of interests. The French clergy, forced to take sides, began to distinguish between the spiritual and the temporal authority of the pope and often sided with the king of France in disputes involving temporal matters. When Pope Boniface VIII (1294–1303) and Philip the Fair fell out, the latter did an epochal thing, a demonstration both of the force of rising nationalism and of the stirring of democracy in western Europe. He called together a parliament such as the English already had; it was the first French States-General and had representation from clergy, nobility, and commoners. This body gave him full support. The pope thereupon issued the famous bull, *Unam Sanctam,* containing the unqualified words: "We declare, we say, we define and pronounce that to every creature it is absolutely necessary to salvation to be subject to the Roman pontiff." This attempt to bring him to heel only led Philip to call another session of the States-General, during which the pope was defiantly arraigned as a criminal, a heretic, and immoral, and an appeal was issued for a general council of the churches to put the pope on trial. Because neither side would yield, the pope, a spiritual authority without military power, at length suffered the indignity of imprisonment by some of Philip's armed supporters. He was soon released, but the harm was done: in the name of nationalism, rough men had seized the pope's person and put him under duress.

A succession of French popes followed (1305–1377). Fearing violence in Italy, they retired to "Babylonish Captivity" at Avignon, where the power of the king of France over them was so unlimited that rival popes were elsewhere put in the field (1378–1417), thus to the great damage of papal prestige producing what is known as the Great Schism. Thenceforth France and England became

481

increasingly independent. The papal power waned. In the great chorus of liberated voices that was rising, the popes were no longer able to command a hushed silence when they spoke.

The Movement Toward Individualism, Freedom, and Reform

Meanwhile, during the Crusades and especially after the fall of Constantinople in the fifteenth century—an event that brought many scholars fleeing to Italy with the literary masterpieces of the ancient Greeks in the original tongue—there began that revival of classical learning known as the Renaissance. Poets and tale-tellers like Petrarch and Boccaccio were the literary masters who joined the great Renaissance painters and sculptors in popularizing the "humanist" outlook, with its ever-fresh delight in man and nature. Even the popes became zealous patrons of art and learning and all but forgot the duties they owed to the Christian world as Holy Fathers.

This was not lost on the common man. With the world rapidly expanding and enlarging his view—as stories first of the Crusades, then of the discoveries of Marco Polo, of Columbus, and later of Magellan and others were conveyed to him—and with his own life vastly altered by the rise of commercial towns independent of lords and princes, the common man began, in guild-hall and market-place, to question the manners and morals of the clergy, from the pope down, and to criticize the practices of the Church that had recently been established—the sale of indulgences,* obligatory confession, and papal taxation in the form of money fees for baptisms, weddings, funerals, and all appointments to office in the Church, and for hundreds of other transactions. Moreover, the common man began to want learning for himself. He

knew he could not master the classics of antiquity known to the learned, but he became curious about the Bible. He reveled in the mystery plays that dramatized for him episodes from the Biblical story and moral dilemmas from everyday life. These whetted his appetite for direct acquaintance with the literary sources of these productions.

The common man's criticism of the Church and his hunger for scripture reached more intense forms in northern Europe than elsewhere, and there aroused the English priest John Wyclif to condemn papal taxation as greed and the doctrine of transubstantiation as unscriptural and to send his Lollard priests among the people of England to teach them the leveling doctrines of the Bible directly from translations out of the Vulgate into the English tongue. Wyclif influenced John Huss in Bohemia to lead a popular religious revolt of such proportions that the Council of Constance in 1415 condemned Huss to be burned at the stake. A quite unrelated reform later in the fifteenth century was led by the Dominican monk Savonarola in the city of Florence, which, after a brief triumph over the lives and spirits of the entire citizenry, procured for Savonarola finally only his own death by hanging.

In vain the Church at large attempted, through the cooperation of bishops, kings, emperors, and by the councils called at Constance and at Basel in the first half of the fifteenth century, to introduce needed reforms in Church life and administration. The only reform they seemed able to effect was the healing of the scandalous papal schism, an accomplishment brought about by forcing the rival popes from office and then restoring a single pontiff to the see of Rome. Otherwise, the situation remained fundamentally unaltered and provocative of greater upheavals to come.

VI   The Protestant Reformation

The Protestant Reformation split Western Christianity into two irreconcilable groups. It was long in

---

* It was held that the pope possessed a treasury of the superfluous merits accumulated by the saints and that he had unlimited dispensation of these credits. Indulgences were sold in the form of documents transferring credits to the purchaser's spiritual account.

preparation, as any study of medieval thought, even one so brief as ours, shows. It remained only for certain new developments, chief among which was the rise of the middle class to economic and cultural self-sufficiency, to bring it to pass. When the people of Europe gathered into towns along the rivers and coasts, as a consequence of the increase of commerce and trade, wealth was no longer immobilized in land or in produce offered for near-at-hand barter. It became fluid in the form of money, and modern capitalism was born. Gradually, the lords and princes were forced to relax their hold upon the growing middle class, and thousands of townspeople began to be true individuals. With no immediate overlords save only burgomaster and town councilors, they gained rapidly in self-confidence and ability to meet life's problems on their own initiative. Politically, they began to evolve a point of view that was later to issue in democracy. One John Ball, the so-called "mad priest of Kent," cried out in England as early as in the fourteenth century:

"My good friends, matters cannot go on well in England until all things shall be in common; when there shall be neither vassals nor lords; when the lords shall be no more masters than ourselves. . . . Are we not all descended from the same parents, Adam and Eve? So what reason can they give why they should be more masters than ourselves? They are clothed in velvet and rich stuffs, ornamented with ermine and other furs, while we are forced to wear coarse linen. They have wine, spices, and good bread, while we have only rye-bread and the refuse of the straw; and when we drink it must be water. They have handsome seats and manors, while we have the trouble and the work, and must brave the rain and the wind in the fields. And it is by our labor they have wherewith to support their pomp."[1]

In such words lay the seeds of the peasant revolts of the fourteenth and fifteenth centuries in England and central Europe.

It is not surprising that the common man of Europe began to want his religious competence recognized too, whether in the use of reason or in the exercise of conscience. Martin Luther very well expressed the feeling of laymen when he passionately asserted:

"I say, then, neither pope, nor bishop, nor any man whatever has the right of making one syllable binding on a Christian man, unless it be done with his own consent. Whatever is done otherwise is done in the spirit of tyranny. . . . I cry aloud on behalf of liberty and conscience, and I proclaim with confidence that no kind of law can with any justice be imposed on Christians, except so far as they themselves will; for we are free from all."[11]

The spiritual fact was that at the very time when the layman began to feel his own competence most, the Church seemed to him most corrupt. The Church had become identified in his mind with a vast system of financial exactions, rapaciously draining gold from every corner of Europe to Rome, where luxury, materialism, irreverence, and even harlotry seemed to reign unchecked among the clergy. Not only was the Church in his eyes corrupt, it seemed also to be left behind in the onward sweep of progress. In a changing world it represented cramping institutionalism, conservatism, conformity from age to age to one inflexible law, one worship, one order of life for every individual. Worse still, a yawning gulf had opened between religion and life, and the disparity between the Church and man's need increased more and more, until the pious layman, just a little appalled anyway by the secularizing effects of capitalism and nationalism, began to wish for changes in the Church that would make it serve the needs of men better.

All that was lacking was a leader who should precipitate the needed reforms.

The Lutheran Reformation

In Germany such a man appeared. He was Martin Luther (1483–1546), an honest, impetuous, heavy-set German, who linked conviction immediately and as a matter of course with appropriate action. Born in Saxony of peasant stock, he absorbed from his environment no particular respect for priests, but a great fear of the wrath of God. His father wanted him to become a lawyer, but mid-way in his study of the law he responded to his intense religious need and entered a monastery of the Augustinian order, bent on winning God's favor by a pure and arduous conformity to monastic discipline. He punctiliously obeyed all the rules of his order; he swept the floor, fasted, bent over his books, almost froze. But though he wept and prayed and became mere skin and bone, he failed to make God gracious. Indeed, he was not sure of his salvation. In 1507 he was ordained to the priesthood and later was appointed a professor in the new university established at Wittenberg by Frederick the Wise, elector of Saxony. There he came to despise Aristotle as an "accursed, proud, knavish heathen" who had led many of the best Christians astray by his emptiness and "false words."[J2] The reason for this animus seems to have been the lack in Aristotle of any profound religious conviction. Luther obtained what he most needed directly from the Bible, and on its books, especially the Book of Psalms and the epistles of Paul, he lectured with growing enthusiasm and comfort to himself.

A journey to Rome in the meantime, even while it deepened his love of the Holy City, confirmed him in the conviction that the papacy had fallen into unworthy hands. He saw in the lives of the priests at Rome not the poverty and humility of Christ but pomp, worldliness, and pride. He was later to say:

"It is of a piece with this revolting pride that the Pope is not satisfied with riding on horseback or in a carriage, but though he be hale and strong, is carried by men like an idol in unheard-of pomp. My friend, how does this Lucifer-like pride agree with the example of Christ, who went on foot, as did also all the Apostles?"[J3]

His own inner life was illuminated suddenly by a sentence from St. Paul; its words were determinative in clearing up his own uncertainty: "The just shall live by faith" (Romans 1:17). Faith! It alone was sufficient! God cannot be *made* gracious by good works; God, like a father, *is* gracious toward his own. All who live in this love and trust know that they are justified by their faith alone and will gratefully live a life of good works, without any urging, like a child who knows his father loves him. Gratitude, not fear, is the spring of the Christian life.

While Luther was forming these convictions, he was disturbed by the arrival of Tetzel, a papal agent, to sell indulgences in a nearby town. When members of his Wittenberg congregation (he preached in the castle church besides teaching in the university) went to buy these indulgences, he spoke out against their doing so. Urged by friends who felt as he did, on October 31, 1517, he posted on the door of the castle church the famous Ninety-Five Theses, a detailed attack on the selling of indulgences, drawn up in the form of propositions for public discussion. In accordance with the prevailing academic etiquette, he politely invited debate on each point he made, but he hardly anticipated the effect of his action. So great was the demand both for copies of the Latin original of his Theses and for its German translation that the university press could not issue copies fast enough to meet the demand from every part of Germany.

The fat was in the fire now. All north Germany began to buzz with talk. There was no thought then on anyone's part of leaving the Church; there was only a demand for reform. Yet there was present a deeper desire—scarcely conscious—for greater freedom from Rome. It was natural that Luther should be immediately attacked by Tetzel and others. His own bishop sent a copy of the Theses to the pope, who promptly ordered Luther to appear at Rome for trial and discipline. The elector of Saxony, who was proud of Luther, intervened, however, and the pope modified his demand to the order that Luther appear before the papal legate at Augsburg, which he did.

All this pressure had the effect, in itself a basic reaction of the entire Reformation, of making Luther search the scriptures to verify his position and justify his actions. His examination of the Bible convinced him that the Catholic Church had so far departed from its scriptural basis that many of its practices were actually anti-Christian. He was driven to question not only the sale through indulgences of the infinite merits of Christ and the superfluous merits of the saints, but the whole medieval attitude toward penance and good works conceived as transactions made with God for his favor through the necessary mediation of priest, bishop, and pope. True repentance is an inward matter and puts a man into direct touch with the forgiving Father. Therefore, in the words of the 36th Thesis: "Every Christian who feels true compunction has of right plenary remission of pain and guilt, even without letters of pardon."[J4] Forgiveness of sins comes through the change wrought in a man's soul by his direct personal relationship with Christ and through Christ with God. Gradually, Luther reached the position that the true Church is not any particular ecclesiastical organization but simply the community of the faithful whose head is Christ. The only final religious authority is the Bible made understandable to believers by the Holy Spirit through their faith. So competent is every man of faith that he is potentially a priest. The Church should therefore proclaim "the universal priesthood of all believers." Said he:

To put the matter plainly, if a little company of pious Christian laymen were taken prisoners and carried away to a desert, and had not among them a priest consecrated by a bishop, and were there to agree to elect one of them, born in wedlock or not, and were to order him to baptise, to celebrate the mass, to absolve, and to preach, this man would as truly be a priest, as if all the bishops and all the popes had consecrated him. That is why in cases of necessity every man can baptise and absolve, which would not be possible if we were not all priests.[J5]

Further, because believers should be enabled to participate in religious exercises to the full, services should be in German rather than Latin, and they should be simplified and given a clearer intent.

Luther's appearance before the papal legate proved inconclusive. Ordered to recant, he refused and made good his escape back to Wittenberg. A lull in the papal agitation against him followed, produced by political developments in the empire, but it ended abruptly when Luther was led into a debate with the Catholic theologian John of Eck and forced to admit that he thought the Council of Constance had erred in condemning John Huss. Was Luther now repudiating the authority of the Catholic Church wherever it ran counter to his own judgment of what the Bible meant? It appeared so, and the pope issued a bull of condemnation against him. The Emperor Charles V being called upon to act, Luther was summoned in 1521 to appear before the imperial Diet, meeting at Worms. The elector of Saxony consented to this only if Luther were promised safe-conduct, which being assured, Luther appeared. He readily acknowledged that the writings issued under his name were his, but would not retract, he said, unless he should be convinced from scripture that he was in error. While some of his admirers among the German princes looked on, he boldly told the emperor and assembled delegates of the Church: "Unless I am convinced by the testimony of Scripture or by evident reason—for I confide neither in the Pope nor in a Council alone, since it is certain they have often erred and contradicted themselves—I am held fast by the Scriptures adduced by me, and my conscience is taken captive by God's Word, and I neither can nor will revoke anything, seeing that it is not safe or right to act against conscience. God help me. Amen."[K] Because he was under safe-conduct, Luther left Worms unharmed, but it was understood that as soon as he returned home, he could be apprehended for punishment. The Diet therefore put him under a ban, ordered him to surrender, and forbade anyone to shelter him or read his books. But Luther could not be found. His prince, the elector Frederick, had had him seized on the way home, and he was hidden away in Wartburg Castle.

Luther used his enforced leisure to good purpose. He set to work on a translation of the New Testament into German. (Some years later, in 1534, he issued a complete translation of the Bible, an epochal achievement in more than one sense. Not only did it carry out the Reformation principle that the Bible must be put into the hands of the common man, but it also gave the Germans for the first time a uniform language, through which they could achieve national cultural unity.)

The Edict of Worms was never enforced. When

Luther emerged from hiding, the emperor was busy with wars and quarrels elsewhere, and moreover, it was apparent that the German people were largely on Luther's side. Whole provinces became Protestant at one stroke when their princes renounced allegiance to the pope and turned Lutheran. By the time of Luther's death in 1546 his reforms had spread from central Germany into much of southern Germany, all of northern Germany, and beyond into Denmark, Norway, Sweden, and the Baltic states.

Luther did not leave to his followers a fixed system of theology and polity. He himself showed many inconsistencies, due in no small degree to his caution and growing conservatism. He was not a radical. He had repudiated Thomas Aquinas and Aristotle, yet, as though he were appealing from medieval Catholicism back to the ancient Catholic Church, he found in St. Augustine a man after his own heart, and back of Augustine he rested, of course, on St. Paul. So vehemently did he cling to what he conceived to be Augustine's doctrine of determinism and predestination that he alienated the humanist Erasmus. Others found him too conservative in matters of worship, inasmuch as he retained the use of candles, the crucifix, the organ, and certain elements of the Roman mass.* When an attempt was made to bring Luther and the Swiss Reformer Zwingli together, the conference between them broke down because Luther insisted that although there is no transubstantiation in the Lord's Supper, the body of Christ is spiritually present in, with, and under the elements of bread and wine (consubstantiation). His conservatism appeared, too, in his social and political views. He showed traces of anti-Semitism in later life, and in the peasant revolt of 1524 he disappointed many by siding with the princes. In fact, he laid the basis of German statism by commanding submissive obedience to state authorities on the part of all Lutherans.

Wherever the Lutheran Reformation spread, the Catholic monks and nuns either left the district or abandoned their former way of life and dress and joined the Lutheran community as parish priests, teachers, and lay-folk, free to marry and raise families. Luther himself married a former nun and enjoyed a happy family life with the five children he had by her. In organizing the new Lutheran communities, he concerned himself most with three functions: the pastorate, charity, and the training and educating of the children. The monasteries that were appropriated by the town councilors or by princes were often turned, on his advice, into schools and universities.

Luther did not live to see the religious war that brought Germany during the mid-century years to the brink of chaos and resulted in the compromise Peace of Augsburg (September 1555), by which equal rights were guaranteed to Catholics and Lutherans, but which left the religion of each province to the determination of its prince, on the principle *cujus regio, ejus religio* ("whose the rule, his the religion"). The Lutheran Reformation had really put the ruling prince where the bishop had formerly been, that is, in a position to exercise general jurisdiction over the churches.

The Swiss Reformation

A more radical Reformation came in Switzerland, when Ulrich Zwingli (1484–1531), a highly educated parish priest whose sympathies lay from youth with the Humanists, especially in their war on superstition and irrationalism, advocated a return to the New Testament as the basic source of Christian truth. In Zurich, therefore, he began a systematic public exposition of the books of the Bible, beginning with the Gospels. By 1522 he reached the conviction that Christians are bound by and should practice only what is commanded in the Bible—a far more radical position than that of Luther, who held that Christians need not give up the elements in Catholic practice that are helpful and not forbidden in the Bible. In accordance with his convictions, Zwingli persuaded

---

* But he removed the priestly sacrificial aspects of the Roman mass and may be said to have moved back toward the Lord's Supper as described in the New Testament.

the people of Zurich to remove all images and crosses from the churches and to sing without organ accompaniment. In putting a stop to the celebration of the mass, he took the view that when Jesus said "This is my body," he meant "This *signifies* my body." It was irrational to suppose, he contended, that Christ's body and blood could be at once in heaven and with equal reality on ten thousand altars on earth all at the same time, as Luther argued. The bread and wine must be regarded as symbolic in character; they were blessed memorials of Jesus' sacrifice of himself upon the cross. The proper way to celebrate the Lord's Supper was to reproduce as nearly as possible the atmosphere and situation of the early Christian eucharist. Ritual should be at a minimum. And as to the regular church services, the sermon should be the central element in worship. It was the chief means by which the will of God could be made known. Local church government was to be reposed in the hands of the elders of each congregation, called collectively the spiritual council, for this seemed a close approximation to early Christian church organization.

The Zwinglian Reformation spread in his lifetime to Basel, Berne, Glarus, Mulhausen, and Strassburg. Ultimately it produced civil war between Catholic and Reformed forces, and Zwingli fell in one of the battles (1531).

In the southwestern part of Switzerland an intense young preacher called Farel won Geneva over to the Reformation. The task of producing a thorough-going religious reform proved so difficult that he prevailed upon a young French scholar by the name of John Calvin (1509–1564) to stay and help him. Calvin was at the time (1536) in flight from France, where he had just published, at twenty-six years of age, the first edition of the Reformation classic *The Institutes of the Christian Religion,* a crystal-clear definition of the Protestant position, which was destined to lay the foundations of Presbyterianism.

Because the public policies of Calvin flowed logically from his religious convictions, it would be well to list at once the chief affirmations of the *Institutes.*

1. The central fact of religion is the sovereignty of God. God wills whatever happens in the physical world and in human history and thereby assures his own glory. His will is inscrutable, and from the human point of view he may seem to follow merely his good pleasure, but his character is holy and righteous, and all his decisions are just.

2. Man is possessed of a certain natural knowledge of God as the moving spirit in nature and history, but his understanding is dimmed by his innate depravity, inherited from Adam, and so his knowledge must be supplemented by the revelation of holy writ.

3. Man's depravity vitiates not only his understanding but his whole nature. With a conviction going straight back to St. Augustine, Calvin wrote:

Original sin may be defined as an hereditary corruption and depravity of our nature, extending to all parts of the soul, which makes us obnoxious to the wrath of God, and then produces in us those works which the Scripture calls "works of the flesh." . . . We are, on account of this corruption, justly condemned in the sight of God. And this liableness to punishment arises not from the delinquency of another; for when it is said that the sin of Adam has made us obnoxious to the justice of God, the meaning is not that we, in ourselves innocent and blameless, are bearing his guilt. The Apostle himself expressly declares, that "death has passed upon all men, for that all have sinned" (Rom. 5:12), that is, have been involved in original sin, and defiled.[L1]

4. But not all men are lost. There is a justification by faith that saves some, and these go on to sanctification. Justification comes through the work of Christ in the believer's behalf and is "the acceptance with which God receives us into His favor, as if we were righteous."[L2] But God justifies only those believers in Christ whom he *elects* to receive into favor.

5. This idea of election leads into the Calvinistic doctrine of predestination. "By predestination we mean," wrote Calvin, "the eternal decree of God, by which he determined with himself whatever he wished to happen with regard to every man. All are not created on equal terms, but some are preordained to eternal life, others to eternal damnation."[L3]

6. Like Augustine, Calvin considered the Church under two aspects. The Church invisible is consti-

487

tuted of all the elect of God in heaven and on earth; the Church visible is the company of professing believers on earth, organized in accordance with God's word in the scripture. In the Church visible the believer is not saved by his works, for it is God's election alone that saves him. Yet he is saved unto a righteousness abounding in good works; in fact, his righteousness is the only assurance he has of his election. "We are justified not without, and yet not by works," said Calvin.

This reasoning led Calvin to regard life with more than usual gravity and seriousness. Duty and self-discipline were to him uppermost. One must live as under God's eye. Frivolous people who spent their hours in worldly pleasures, light-heartedly preferring card-playing, dancing, and masquerades to sober reflection, reading the Bible, and doing God's will, might fear the worst. They were to be regarded as already the Devil's own, doomed to the fires of hell. On the other hand, those who were moved by the Holy Spirit to go about the Lord's solemn business on earth were earnest, industrious, and thrifty and valued these attributes in themselves as signs of their election to salvation. By this chastening logic, from which there seemed no escape, Calvin changed the mood of the citizens of Geneva to a puritanical righteousness. There was no room in Geneva for Luther's playfulness and laughter, his roaring, lusty voice raised in song around the organ, nor for his glad sense of the passing of God's wrath and the outpouring of his gracious love. Calvin's joy was a more secret thing, an inward peace and satisfaction, not expressed in the joviality of convivial fellowship. It was intellectual rather than emotional in quality and expression.

In Geneva arose a new kind of community. Working with the Small and General Town Councils, over which he gained increasing if sometimes stormy ascendancy, Calvin instituted both a church life and an educational system that gave Geneva a trained ministry and a people sufficiently informed regarding their faith to be able to give a clear account of it. Refugee scholars and exiles from all over Europe

flocked to Geneva as to an asylum, so that the city increased its original thirteen thousand population by six thousand. Among the brilliant men who came there were Beza, one of Europe's leading humanists, Cordier, perhaps the ablest of European educators, Caraccioli, an Italian noble, Michael Servetus, who scarcely reached Geneva before he was condemned to death in a public trial and burned at the stake for heretical unitarian views, and the Scottish refugee John Knox.

The Reformation in France and the Low Countries

Beza and Cordier came to Geneva when the fires of affliction were being kindled for the Protestants of France. The Reformation had begun rather quietly in that land, yet with every prospect of soon sweeping the country. Then all at once it was very nearly drowned in blood. The forces on either side were brought into such violent conflict that civil war engulfed the country. Much more completely than in Geneva, the French Protestants, or Huguenots, adopted John Calvin's conception of church organization. The local congregation "called" its own ministers through the elders and deacons who formed the "consistory."* The Catholic clergy and the French court took alarm and resorted to suppression

---

* T. M. Lindsay, in *A History of the Reformation* (Scribner's Sons, 1919, II, p. 165), gives the following clear summary: Calvin "proposed to revive the simple three-fold ministry of the Church of the early centuries— a congregation ruled by a bishop or pastor, a session of elders, and a body of deacons. This was adopted by the French Protestants. A group of believers, a minister, a 'consistory' of elders and deacons, regular preaching, and the sacraments duly administered, made a church properly constituted. The minister was the chief; he preached; he administered the sacraments; he presided at the 'consistory.' The 'consistory' was composed of elders charged with the spiritual oversight of the community, and of deacons who looked after the poor and the sick. The elders and deacons were chosen by the members of the congregation; and the minister by the elders and deacons." This was Christian democracy. Kings and bishops naturally opposed it.

by fire and sword. When Catherine de Medici became regent, she first courted, then turned upon the Huguenots. It was she who persuaded the weakling King Charles IX to order the Massacre of St. Bartholomew (August 1572), which is said to have brought death to twenty thousand Protestants. But the Huguenots were served by great military leaders, notably Admiral Coligny, and after each renewal of the bitter civil war they were able, howsoever reduced in numbers, to secure at least a measure of toleration, and at last by the Edict of Nantes (1598) won complete liberty of conscience, full civil rights, and the control of two hundred towns. Protestantism in France had not grown strong, but it had won the protection of the state. However, Louis XIV revoked the Edict of Nantes in 1685, and made Protestantism illegal again. It was Napoleon who finally restored Protestant rights.

Bitter, too, was the struggle in the Low Countries. The Spaniards were in control there, and both the Emperor Charles V and his son, Philip II of Spain, were determined to stamp out the Reformed faith wherever it showed itself. The people of the Low Countries were in some sense prepared for the Reformation by the Brethren of the Common Life, already described, who had expressed what was really a people's movement toward personal piety, accompanied by a strong love of biblical learning. Luther's writings were eagerly circulated when they appeared; later Zwingli won devoted adherents; and still later Calvin's conception of church organization was to prevail. Some Netherlanders were attracted to the radical Anabaptists (see below). Open rebellion against Spain came when Philip II sent the cruel Duke of Alva to suppress every form of heresy at any necessary cost of blood. The struggle was long-drawn-out, but at last William the Silent was able to form a group of northern states that won independence as the nation of Holland. Holland became a Calvinistic land, sturdy and self-reliant, with its churches (the Dutch Reformed) organized on the democratic principles already established among the French Protestants.

The Reformation in Scotland

If the antagonism of Philip II and William the Silent may be called dramatic, that of Mary Queen of Scots and John Knox was highly so, for the first two never met face-to-face, but Mary and John Knox confronted each other more than once, with decisive results.

In a sense, the case of Scotland was critical for the whole Reformation. To many at the time it seemed very possible that Mary, either by her marriage with Francis II of France (through which she became an adherent of the French Catholic party in European politics) or by making good her claim to the English throne as a Stuart (which she never was able to do), might bring both Scotland and England back to the Catholic fold.

But Mary's marriage to the French king actually gave the Protestants of Scotland a chance they were not slow to seize. She was long absent in France, and during that time John Knox led his Protestant colleagues in the rapid development of a Calvinistic church. Knox did not introduce the Reformation to Scotland; he was himself a product of it. Captured in youth by a French force sent to Scotland to apprehend a group of Protestant rebels there, he was carried to France and compelled to row in the galleys for nineteen bitter months. On release he went to England, then under the Protestant government of Edward VI, and served in various towns as a royal chaplain. On the accession of Mary Tudor he escaped to the continent and made his way to Geneva, where he became an enthusiastic disciple of Calvin. Ultimately he returned to Scotland and in 1560, not long after his return, had the great triumph of having the Scottish Parliament ratify the "Confession of Faith Professed and Believed by the Protestants within the Realm of Scotland," which he and five others prepared and which remained the creedal formula of the Church of Scotland until it was replaced by the Westminster Confession in 1647. A week later the Parliament decreed that "the bishops of Rome have no jurisdiction nor authority in this realm," and

489

forbade the saying, hearing, or being present at mass. Eventually, the Roman Catholic bishops and priests were expelled from the Church lands, which then came largely into the possession of the Scottish nobles.

In subsequent developments the so-called Presbyterian system of church government was worked out on a national scale. In its complete form it established a representative democracy. The congregation elected and called the minister, who thereafter was alone responsible for the conduct of public worship. But this was his only unlimited prerogative. All local matters affecting the discipline and administration of the parish were entrusted to the kirk-session, composed of the minister, who presided, and the elders, chosen by election. Above the kirk-session was the presbytery, which consisted of the ministers of the parishes of a designated area and an equal number of elders representing each parish. Above the presbyteries was the Synod, with jurisdiction over certain groups of presbyteries, and over all was the General Assembly, the supreme judicatory of the national Church, consisting of delegate ministers and an equal number of elders. The center of gravity of this system was the presbytery, which was small enough to be vitally representative of its locality and large enough to have plenty of fight in it when its survival was threatened.

It was a bad moment for the Scottish Reformers when the fascinating and calculating Mary Queen of Scots came back from France a widow. They knew she was a devout Catholic and meant to overthrow the Reformation in Scotland if she could. When she first arrived, she pursued a moderate course, insisting only on having mass for her own household but promising to maintain elsewhere the laws that made it illegal in Scotland. She summoned Knox to five interviews in which she used all her skill to win him over, but he remained firm in opposition to any concession to the papacy. In other quarters Mary had more success and might have won all had she not fallen into disgrace through her intrigue with Bothwell and been deposed in favor of her year-old son,

who later became James I of England. With her fall the Protestant forces recovered their strength, and Scotland was made secure for the Reformation.

In the meantime, the Reformation in England had won a similar firm footing.

The English Reformation

The English Reformation was one of those more or less inevitable outcomes that thrive upon accidents. A king's private whim opened the way for the religious revolution that the nation basically wanted. With the moderation so characteristic of them, the English leaders nourished a desire to enjoy at least the degree of religious self-determination that the Reformation had brought to the continental Protestants, and yet they bowed to the forms of legality in their national life and patiently waited. Eventually, they made their will felt, which was as soon as the opportunity presented itself.

The uninhibited Henry VIII, in the grip of a personal desire for a change in his marital status, vowed that if the Roman Curia would not annul his marriage to Catherine of Aragon in order that he might marry Ann Boleyn, he would break with the pope! The Roman Curia turned him down, and Henry did not hesitate to act. Though much that he did and said shocked all shades of opinion in the nation, he had powerful elements among his people with him when he got Parliament to declare that "the bishop of Rome" had no more jurisdiction in England than any other foreign ecclesiastic, that the only true head of the Church of England was the king of England, that bishops in England were thenceforth to be nominated by the king and were to give their oath of obedience to him instead of to the pope, and that denial of the king's supremacy in the Church was an act of high treason. Henry quickly won the support of his nobles by first suppressing the monasteries in his realm and then distributing generous grants of land to them from among the great possessions thereby confiscated. Besides winning these powerful supporters, he cut off the flow of papal taxes to Rome and satisfied the growing desire of the English people for national self-determination in all things.

But Henry VIII was theologically conservative. He did not intend that there should be a doctrinal break with the past to match his jurisdictional break with the pope. In 1539 he had Parliament pass what is known as the "Bloody Statute." It declared the doctrine of transubstantiation to be the faith of the Church of England and denial of it to be punishable by burning at the stake and confiscation of goods. It forbade the marriage of priests, and disallowed communion in both bread and wine. The only considerable concession he made to liberal views, aside from his break with Rome, was in having a copy of the Bible in English placed in all the churches.° Many English followers of Luther and the Swiss Reformers were put to death under the Bloody Statute. More fled to the continent, where they found their chief asylum in Switzerland.

These exiles returned when Henry was succeeded by his nine-year-old son, Edward VI, for then it became apparent that under the protectorate established for the immature king the national policy would shift religiously to the left. The young king's advisers, especially Somerset and Northumberland, strongly favored doctrinal as well as political changes. The Bloody Statute was repealed, communion in both kinds was allowed, private masses were brought to an end by the confiscation of the chapels where they were said, priests were permitted to marry, and images were removed from the churches as instances of papish idolatry. But Edward died when only fifteen and was succeeded by his sister Mary, an ardent Catholic, who loved and married the Spanish heir-apparent.† She led the return to Rome by restoring the pope's jurisdiction over the English churches, and herself earned the name of "Bloody Mary" by the ruthlessness with which leading Protestants were at her behest apprehended and burned at the stake. When she died after a reign as brief as Edward's, her sister, Elizabeth, the daughter of Ann Boleyn, brought the nation finally to the Protestant fold. "Good Queen Bess," as her subjects affectionately called her, completed the unfinished work of her young brother's reign. The Prayer Book of Edward VI was revised so as to be made palatable to Catholics and Protestants alike, and under the name of *The Book of Common Prayer* was, by the Act of Uniformity of 1559, prescribed for use in all churches without alteration or deviation. The beliefs of the Church were stated clearly in the famous creedal statement "The Thirty-Nine Articles of the Church of England," which is to this day the formally authoritative summary of its doctrines. England remained Protestant henceforth, even when Catholic monarchs were on the throne.

The Protestant Radicals

While the national Reformation movements just described were coming to terms in one way or another with the civil powers, quiet searchers of the scriptures all over Europe were finding their own way to a much more radical break with constituted authority. Some were moved by the Word of God alive within them; some followed reason solely.

Among the former were the Anabaptists (literally "rebaptizers"), groups largely recruited from the common people—peasants and artisans—and led in the first instance by immediate associates of Luther and Zwingli. Most took the New Testament literally and with great seriousness, determined to depart in no way from the manner of life they saw depicted in it. Others felt themselves not bound thus by the "letter" of scripture, because the "Word" is a "living spirit" expressed in but not confined to scripture nor present equally in all parts of it. The living Word of God is heard in prophetic personalities and in the

° The so-called Great Bible, drawn largely from the translation of Tyndale, but with some parts taken from Coverdale's version.

† Charles V's son, soon to become the intolerant Philip II.

inner consciousness of all who are justified by faith.

It seemed to all the Anabaptists that the first requisite of being a Christian is that one should grasp clearly in his own mind the meaning of each aspect of the Christian life and practice and then act upon that understanding no matter what the cost. Ceremonies and rituals must, they thought, have a clear meaning to the participants or cease being real and vital. Accordingly, they rejected infant baptism; plainly, the baby could not know what was being done, and so the rite could mean nothing. Those who had been baptized in infancy therefore baptized each other all over again (hence the name they bore). In the wider realm of conduct, a clear understanding and sincerity, they held, are just as imperatively needed. The New Testament teaches the principle of overcoming evil with good instead of resisting one injury with another. Most Anabaptists concluded that they should not join the armed forces of the state, contribute to warfare in any way at all, or even take part in the civil administration during peacetime, because of the policy of force all states adopt. They found New Testament warrant for never taking oaths; so, when taken to court, they insisted that their simple word be taken for truth: their yea was yea and their nay nay. Because they felt that priests and ministers were prone to please worldly powers and make compromises in vital areas, the Anabaptists were anti-clerical and met outside the regular church circles in their own houses; churches were to them idolatrous "steeple-houses." They did not agree on all matters, but they made it a principle to exercise tolerance where differences as to the literal meaning of scripture appeared. Some, for instance, took with greater literalness than others the apocalyptic or millenarian passages of the New Testament expressing the expectation that Christ would return on the clouds of heaven to be the judge on the last day. Others practiced the communism of the early Christian fellowship in Jerusalem. Occasionally, an Anabaptist would proclaim himself a prophet, as did the noted Hans Hut, who won many of the working people of Austria and adjacent parts of Germany

to the view that a Turkish invasion would be followed by the appearance of Christ to inaugurate the millennium.

The finality with which the Anabaptists separated themselves from the established churches and the state (whence the name Separatists that they also bore) and the radical views that many of them espoused led to intense persecution. Luther parted company with them, or, rather, they with him. Zwingli engaged them in bitter public debates, which were usually followed by the decision of the Swiss cantonal authorities that his views alone were to be recognized as lawful. A few Anabaptist leaders were executed as criminals. In 1527 Felix Manz was put to death by drowning in Zurich, Michael Sattler was burned and his wife drowned at Rottenburg; the following year Balthasar Hubmaier and his wife met the same fates in Vienna; a year later Georg Blaurock was burned in the Tyrol. One desperate group of millenarian Anabaptists seized control of the German town of Münster and so radically revolutionized both the religious and social life there that the Catholics and Lutherans joined forces in storming the city and putting the leaders to death by torture. The erratic behavior of these Anabaptist leaders, marked as it was by communism, polygamy, and violence, gave Anabaptism an undeserved bad name in Europe.

Later on, this bad name was partially redeemed by the gentle and reasonable Anabaptist leader Menno Simons (1492–1547), whose followers in the Netherlands and the United States were called, after him, Mennonites. They were pacifists, espoused an Arminian theology that softened the harshness of Calvinism,* and practiced a person-to-person toler-

* In the Reformed churches, especially in Holland, the harsh predestinarianism of the strict Calvinists—and no less of the "Formula of Concord" (1580), which was meant to unify the Lutherans—could not be stomached by many who felt that damnation was not due solely to God's determination but also to man's erring choices. In their heartfelt conviction (for "God is love"), God has elected not just some but *all* men to salvation through the atonement of Christ, which has saving efficacy for every member of the human race, but not all men reach the pitch

ance that enabled individual Mennonites to house, with simple Christian charity, such exiles as the ostracized Jew Spinoza and certain refugee English Separatists.

But the Anabaptist revolt was not the only expression of radical Christianity. The basis of Unitarianism was now laid. At a time so early in the period of the Reformation that the doctrines of the Reformers had not yet been fixed in set forms, such as the Augsburg Confession or the Heidelberg Catechism, and the extent of the doctrinal departure from Catholic dogma was not yet clear, excited minds, stirred by the possibilities opening up to a thorough-going rational test of Christian doctrines, proposed unrestricted reason as the sovereign guide to sound reconstruction in theology. Such a one was the Michael Servetus whom we saw burned at the stake in Calvin's Geneva. A Spaniard by birth, he was struck on a close reading of the New Testament, while traveling in the retinue of a Catholic prelate, by the fact that the Nicene doctrine of the Trinity, in whose name so many of his own countrymen were being burned at the stake or exiled, was not to be found in it, and that, moreover, his reason found fault with the doctrine itself. So he wrote down his ideas secretly and audaciously and in 1531 published his famous heretical treatise, *Concerning the Errors of the Trinity*. Hopeful of winning the Reformers to his views, he went to Switzerland, but found the leaders whom he met cool, though still not committed to any clear position. Servetus could not imagine how his reasoning failed to carry conviction. The doctrine of the Trinity he felt to be a Catholic perversion and himself to be a good New Testament Christian in combating it. He himself was far from denying the

divinity of Christ. According to his conception, a Trinity composed of three distinct persons in one God is a rational impossibility; he proposed instead "a manifestation of the true substance of God *in* the Word (or Christ) and its *communication* in the Holy Spirit,"[*] a view that seemed to him to preserve the full deity of Christ without destroying the unity of God. There seemed to be no good reason, he felt, to deny the virgin birth or miracles.

Finding himself in danger, Servetus now changed his name, went to France, studied and practiced medicine with success, and became the first scientist to advance the theory of the pulmonary circulation of the blood. Meanwhile, he was being sought by the Inquisition, and from motives of prudence, when he opened up an acrimonious and to himself fatal correspondence with Calvin, he wrote under his assumed name. But Calvin's friends looked him up, made his identity known, and thus obliged him to flee. At the moment, Calvin's position in Geneva was not altogether secure, and for this or some other reason Servetus went there, only to fall afoul of Calvin's supporters, have condemnation passed upon him with Calvin's assent, and perish at the stake (1553).

Servetus was associated with no organized group. He was something of an individualist and worked alone. But his writings stirred groups of already existent anti-Trinitarians, who, when made the object of persecution both by the Inquisition and Protestants, took refuge in the only areas that would at that time harbor them, Poland and Transylvania, now part of Roumania. Some asserted the Arian position which maintained that long before the Incarnation Christ proceeded from the Father and was subordinate to him. Others denied Christ's pre-existence but believed he should be adored as virgin-born and risen from the dead to God's right hand (whence they were called "Adorantes"). Still others (the "Non-adorantes"), led by the great Transylvanian preacher Francis David, would worship God only, for to them Christ was not God but a man born of Joseph and

---

of faith which makes forgiveness and justification available to them; hence they perish through their own lack. Those who held these views were called Arminians, after the Dutch theologian Arminius who gave expression to their convictions. The Reformed churches condemned their position at the Synod of Dort (1619), but it has spread through the Methodist churches and has gained more than a foothold in Presbyterian and other Reformed circles.

[*] *"Verae substantiae Dei manifestatio in Verbo et communicatio in Spiritu."*

Mary, who grew into fullness of divine powers—a view shared with certain Anabaptists and common to Unitarians today. The reconciliation of these divergent views was to a large degree effected by Faustus Socinus (1539–1604), an Italian, who, after living in Switzerland and in Transylvania, finally established himself in Poland. He denied the pre-existence of Christ, holding that he was only a man, but he asserted, more positively, that Christ's life was so exemplary and his consciousness so flooded with divine wisdom that he was resurrected in triumph from the dead and elevated to God's right hand, and so one may adore and address prayers to him. In the Racovian Catechism (1605), published by his followers after his death, this median position was explained and proved widely acceptable, becoming known as Socinianism.

Poland was then a hospitable refuge for the oppressed, and in the atmosphere of freedom of thought that there existed these views met with a warm reception. But after 1632 the Catholics returned to power, and the Unitarians were suppressed, together with all other Protestants in Poland. Driven into exile, they fled to eastern Germany, Holland, and England. When the English passed a law in 1648 making the denial of the divinity of Christ a crime punishable by death, some of the more liberal Unitarians were obliged to flee again to Holland. During the eighteenth century many of them quietly appeared in New England, and in the early nineteenth century, under the preaching of Ellery Channing and Theodore Parker, they grew in strength, formed the American Unitarian Association (1825), and received many Congregational ministers and churches into their organized fellowship.

The Nonconformists

The Anabaptists and Unitarians were generally considered to be too immoderate in their radicalism to be tolerated. The Nonconformists, a much larger group, were not so fiercely set upon by the duly constituted authorities of church and state. Not that there was no persecution of the more moderate radicals—we shall see there was plenty of it—but the authorities were unable to maintain the sterner attitude with unbending harshness.

The Noncomformists were in general neither as non-cooperative with the state as the Anabaptists nor as heterodox as the Unitarians. They were willing to render civil obedience as long as they were granted freedom of conscience in their religion. So far as their theological position was concerned, they generally subscribed to the ancient creeds as standard interpretations of holy writ; hence their Trinitarianism was never in question. But in matters of polity or denominational organization they differed quite widely from the so-called established churches. In church administration they demanded self-determination as their Protestant right. We now turn to them.

The Puritans

The Puritans got their name in the time of Queen Elizabeth. Her accession in 1558 brought back to England, as we have seen, many exiles who had fled from "Bloody Mary." Their residence abroad in Calvinistic areas had inclined them toward presbyterial forms of church government and simplicity of worship and life, but they had no wish to be Separatists. Rather, they desired only to purify the worship of the Church of England of what they called its "Romish" elements* and to give emphasis to preaching the Word rather than to ritual and sacraments. Most of them resigned themselves, at least for the time being, to episcopacy—bishops, archbishops, archdeacons, and the like—provided locally they could be served by sympathetic parish ministers, but a few openly advocated a presbyterial system such as existed in Scotland. When these presbyterial

---

* Such as kneeling to receive the bread and wine at communion services, the sign of the cross at baptism and confirmation, the use of the ring at weddings, and special clerical garb for ministers.

Puritans increased in numbers, the Puritans became divided. Those who wished to reform the Church of England from within retained their membership in it in patience and hope; those who could not wait broke away from time to time as Separatists and found the government so determined to crush them that they emigrated to Holland. They were the first Congregationalists and Baptists, and we shall return to them shortly.

The Puritans still within the Church of England found the government hardening against them when James I became king. Charles I after him was more resolved even than his father not only to make the English Puritans conform in full to the practices of the Established Church but to carry further his father's attempt to force episcopacy on the Scots. It was a literally fatal attempt on his part. To his astonishment, he provoked the Scots (thousands of them as "Covenanters" sworn to a life-and-death struggle against him) to rebellion, and their success in arms brought him to such a pass that he had to summon Parliament, only to find that the Puritans were now in the majority in that body! The Puritans had not for some time been faring so well. They had fared so ill while Archbishop Laud was in power, that twenty thousand of them in the period from 1628 to 1640 followed the Pilgrims over the sea and in Massachusetts and Connecticut became New England Congregationalists. But now in 1640 they were in such majority in Parliament that they could cast Laud into prison. When the angered king opposed them, they as angrily rose to arms as representatives of the people driven by their sovereign's stubbornness to make war upon him. So came about Charles I's beheading and the Puritan Revolution under Oliver Cromwell. For twelve years England was a Puritan land, and all the people were bound by a stern religion's purifying restraints.

Not only the Puritan way of life but also Presbyterianism seemed about to triumph in England, for in 1646 the Westminster Assembly, called to advise Parliament and composed of English ministers and laymen, with Scottish commissioners sitting in an advisory capacity, presented to Parliament the "Westminster Confession," the last of the great confessional standards of the Reformation and still the doctrinal norm of the Presbyterians throughout the world. The Parliament rather hesitantly adopted it, as well as the Larger and Shorter Catechisms prepared to accompany it. But, as it happened, little came of the Parliament's action, for the return of Charles II to England in 1660 brought with it the Restoration, and reaction was thereafter so triumphant that by the Act of Uniformity of 1662 the Puritans were forced out of the Church of England into the ranks of the Dissenters, ultimately to become Congregationalists, Baptists, Quakers, Presbyterians, and Unitarians.

The Congregationalists and Baptists

Meanwhile, the Separatists who had left England prior to the Puritan Revolution had had an interesting and important history abroad. One group that settled at Amsterdam about 1607 was led by a John Smyth, formerly a Church of England minister, who, upon learning from Mennonite neighbors their views on adult baptism and being convinced by study of the New Testament that it was not the early Christian practice to baptize infants, rebaptized himself and his whole flock. Members of his congregation returned to London and established there about 1612 the first Baptist Church in England that endured. This was the beginning of the Baptist denomination, soon to spread throughout the British Isles. Though some Baptists are Arminian and others Calvinist in theology, they finally found unity in one distinctive position: baptism of believers only, and that by total immersion. In 1639 a group of Baptists, to whose number Roger Williams belonged, founded a church in Rhode Island. Baptists subsequently appeared in all the American colonies, especially in the south.

Other emigrants in Holland passed their first years of exile there quietly enough. At Middelburg in 1582 Robert Browne, a Cambridge man, published the clearest definition of Congregationalism ever to be penned. His logic was firm. Said he, the Church of Christ, in the view of true Christians, is not an ecclesiastical organization but a local group of believers who have experienced union with Christ, the only real and permanent head of the Church, and by a voluntary covenant with each other have consented to be ruled by officers—pastor, elders, deacons, teachers—chosen by themselves as moved by the spirit of Christ. Each church is absolutely self-governing, none has authority over any other, but all are under the Christian obligation to extend each other brotherly help and good will.

But if all this was quietly done and said, a notable course in history was run by one group among them. In 1609 a Congregationalist group that had come over from Scrooby, England, under the leadership of John Robinson and William Brewster, with William Bradford of their number, settled in Leyden. Not content there, they made a momentous decision: to return to England in order to send their more adventurous and able-bodied members to America. On the *Mayflower*, then, in 1620 the Pilgrims crossed the Atlantic, and, in the spirit of their solemn covenant made at sea founded the colony of Plymouth. Other immigrants, mostly Puritans from England, followed them over the waters, until the whole of New England, except Rhode Island, was won for Congregationalism. There it enjoyed the status virtually of a state religion for two centuries.

The Quakers

One more English Noncomformist group of this period, the Quakers, requires our attention. They were in many respects the most radical of all. Founded during the civil war that resulted in the Puritan Revolution, the Quaker movement was in essence a

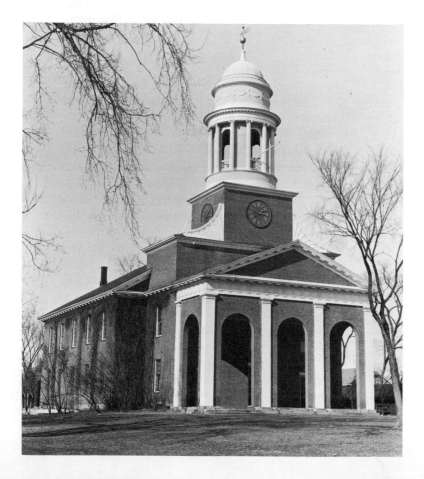

First Church of Christ, Lancaster, Massachusetts. Built in 1816 to 1817, this church is considered the masterpiece of Charles Bulfinch in his Adamesque or late Georgian style. A fine example of colonial architecture, it suggests both the dignity and the simplicity of New England Protestantism. Whereas the conventional New England steeple rises into a high spire, this church is surmounted by a graceful dome on engaged columns.

revolt against formalism and sham. The Quakers were nicknamed so, but preferred to call themselves the Society of Friends. Their founder was George Fox (1624–1691), a religious genius who may be reckoned one of the world's great mystics. In a profound experience of conversion, which occurred in 1646, he came to a belief much like that of some of the early Anabaptists. True Christianity was to him not a matter of conforming to a set of doctrines or of believing in scripture without having "a concern" as the result of so doing, nor was it going to a "steeple-house" to listen to a sermon or prayers read by a professional priest. It was being illuminated by an inner light. The Word of God is a living thing not confined to the scriptures, though it is there. It comes directly into the consciousness of the believer whom God chooses for the purpose of speaking through him.

Fox would not hear of training a professional clergy. God speaks through whom he will when he will. Every man—or woman, for that matter—is potentially God's spokesman. Fellow-men are to be treated as friends, with infinite reverence for the divine possibilities in any personality. War and any violence are therefore thoroughly wicked. Slavery is abhorrent. The requirement to take an oath should not be imposed upon a Christian, for he always speaks soberly and truthfully.

At a religious meeting of Friends there were no sacraments (sacraments by their material symbolism are the occasion of leading the mind out of its subjective state of contemplation into the idolatry of fixation on an object) and no prepared discourses (God will stir up thought in someone present, at need). It was admitted that prayer is appropriate to begin with, but let it be followed by silent meditation, until the inner light illumines someone's understanding.

Fox and his followers promptly obeyed every prophetic impulse to action. Fox, for instance, would march boldly into a "steeple-house," if inspired to do so, interrupt the "priest" in the middle of his sermon, and denounce the proceedings, to the accompani-

ment of outcries and tumult. Consequently, the authorities vigorously opposed Quakers as disturbers of the peace. Thousands were imprisoned or heavily fined. Fox himself was often jailed. But no persecution could quench his ardor.

During the intensely repressive persecutions of the Restoration period, William Penn (1644–1718) became a Quaker, and after obtaining in 1681 the grant of Pennsylvania from Charles II, he threw it open to colonization by all who might desire freedom of religion, the Quakers being especially invited to Philadelphia. In England it was not until the "Glorious Revolution" that accompanied the accession of William and Mary (1689) that full religious toleration for the Quakers and all other dissenting groups was made into law.

Pietism

Common to most of the Nonconformists was a shift of emphasis from doctrinal orthodoxy (which was taken for granted) to conversion or new birth. Conversion seemed the one infallible test of the possession of true Christianity. Abandonment of the conception of human sin and depravity was not contemplated, nor were the standard Reformation theologies called in question. All that was sought was a heightened sense of reality in the emotional life. The accent lay on having *new life* in Christ. Everyone was dead in sin, lost, guilty before God, certain to be damned, until "reborn," made a "new man in Christ Jesus," by the quick inflow of divine grace, bringing joy and peace to the distracted sinner and a sense of divine forgiveness crowned by reconciliation with God and personal communion with Christ. It cannot be overemphasized that to most of these men and women of deep personal piety Christ had the reality of a living presence, who, though he was a visitant from another world, was as real and near as any earthly person.

We see all this with particular clarity in Pietism, which was in origin a reaction from seventeenth-century German doctrinalism, the latter being regarded by the Pietists as infected with moral unconcern and a cold indifference toward right *feeling* in religion. The cultivation of right feeling was held to lead not to a coming to terms with the world, as worldings might expect, but to its opposite, an ascetic emphasis on purity and holiness of life. This is the reason that Pietism was initially separatist in tendency.

Two figures were important in the development of Pietism. One, Philipp Spener (1635–1705), was an earnest Lutheran minister who felt keenly the lack of "heart" and "life" in the current Lutheran absorption in "pure doctrine." He invited a group of similarly-minded people to meet in his home as a "church within the church" (as he put it, as an *ecclesiola in ecclesia*) for Bible study, prayer, and the further discussion of Sunday sermons. The result was their common conviction that the world was too much for them: the state was too interfering, the clergy quarreled too much over theological matters to live a holy life, the clergy were even morally lax, and the laity were immoderate in eating, drinking, and dress and spent too much time on worldly amusements, dances, the theater, and cards. In his writings Spener advocated the formation everywhere of similar study groups and found immediate response in all German-speaking areas, but the movement, spreading rapidly, soon ran into stiff opposition on the part of the clergy, who did not relish a church within the Church nor criticisms of their piety or morality. Their hostility increased when some of Spener's followers, against his wish, exhibited their separatist tendency by refraining from church attendance and the sacraments.

The other leader of Pietism was Hermann Francke (1663–1727), an instructor in the University of Leipzig, who introduced Pietism into German academic circles by establishing a *collegium philobiblicum* (a "gathering of Bible lovers"). Driven from the university by the opposition of his colleagues, he ultimately joined Spener and others at Halle, where the elector of Brandenburg, who was to become King Frederick I of Prussia, founded a university and

encouraged, without becoming identified with, their activities. In this new environment Francke proceeded to demonstrate the implicit social consciousness of Pietism by successively founding a school for poor children, a Latin school, an orphans' home, and a Bible institute, all of which had great contemporary support. The Halle group also displayed a zeal for missions, a development of interest that prompted the earliest Protestant attempts to evangelize India.

After the time of Spener and Francke, Pietism gradually declined, perhaps because it had largely attained its initial objectives, but it survived as a special form of impetus in the revival of the Moravian Brethren. This occurred under the guidance of Count Zinzendorf, a land-owner in eastern Saxony to whose estates came a group of refugee Moravian Hussites displaced by the turmoil of the Thirty Years' War. Zinzendorf had had a Pietist education at Halle, modified by law studies at Wittenberg, a center of orthodox Lutheran influence, and by travels in Holland and France. He had the compassion to allow the Hussites to establish a Moravian village on his estates, which they called Hernhut, and it was also in his nature to enter into their communal life, with the result that a communion service into which he entered with them led in 1727 to a revived and revitalized form of the Moravian Church. Though Zinzendorf strove to keep it within the Lutheran fellowship, the new church gradually became a separatist sect with a special life of its own and a sense of mission to the world. Missions, in fact, became the hallmark of the movement. Zinzendorf himself inspired the first Moravian missionaries to go to the Danish West Indies, Greenland, and Georgia. When Lutheran opposition caused him to be expelled from Saxony, he traveled widely, first in the European areas to which the Moravians spread, including London, then in the West Indies and the American colonies. He also instituted missions among the American Indians. But he did not live to see the full extent of the far-flung missionary efforts of the Moravian Church, the successful establishment of missions in Egypt, South Africa, Surinam, Guiana, and Labrador.

VII Catholicism Since the 16th Century

The Protestant Reformation resulted in intensifying latent Catholic self-criticism and stirred up a Church-wide call for reform. The popes, however, were not among the motivating forces; they were too much on the defensive. It was the Emperor Charles V, anxious like Constantine in the fourth century to reduce sources of disunity, who earnestly sought for reforms in the Church and a redefinition of Catholic doctrine in order to offset the effectiveness of Protestant critical propaganda. He came to this position only after his prolonged efforts to bring about a reconciliation of Catholics and Protestants on the basis of projected reforms had failed. It was he who brought pressure on Pope Paul III to call the Council of Trent.

This pressure was decisive, because it had behind it all the accumulated power generated by the cries for reform, both clerical and lay, which had been heard in Europe for centuries. John Wyclif, John Huss, Savonarola, and Erasmus, not to mention Luther and Zwingli before they left the mother church, were simply the more powerful figures among those who advocated reform. But the Catholic Reformation (by Protestants labeled the Counter-Reformation) did not get under way until momentum was imparted to it by the determined and militant forces for reform and enlightenment in Spain, where the expulsion of the Moors in the fifteenth century had been followed by the reform of the clergy under Ximenes, the great archbishop of Toledo and confessor to Queen Isabella. The Spanish Church had been purified of unworthy monks and priests, universities for the training of the clergy had been founded, the union of church and state under Ferdinand and Isabella had been made very close, and the means of keeping church and state purified had been found in the reorganization of the Inquisition on a national basis, with inquisitors appointed by the Spanish monarchs. The result had been a revitalization of the Spanish Church to match the rapid rise of Spain itself to the position of the first power in Europe. When, therefore, the Spanish king became the Holy Roman Emperor, in the person of Charles V, the drive for reform, all the more urgent because of the Protestant menace, had secured powerful support.

St. Peter's cathedral, Rome. A notable example of the Renaissance style, St. Peter's is a basilica rebuilt in the form of a Roman cross. Its dome and cupola were designed by Michelangelo, its splendid plaza and colonnade by Bernini. The Vatican Palace, the residence of the pope, adjoins it. The whole is known as Vatican City, the ecclesiastical center of the Roman Catholic Church. (Courtesy of the Italian Government Travel Office.)

The Catholic Reformation

The wave of Catholic reform had three chief expressions.

A. THE COUNCIL OF TRENT. When Charles V got Pope Paul III to call the Council of Trent in 1545, he hoped first to get needed reforms and afterwards a redefinition of the Catholic position. It was thus that he planned to conciliate the Protestant leadership and follow up his military victories over the German Protestant princes with a psychological master-stroke that would bring the recalcitrants back into the Catholic fold. But the Catholic leaders insisted that doctrine be discussed alternately with reform and soon made reconciliation with the Protestants impossible by firmly redefining the medieval Catholic doctrines. The council met over a period of eighteen years (1545–1563) and during its course declared:

1. Catholic tradition is co-equal with scripture as a source of truth and in authority over Christian life.
2. The Latin Vulgate is the sacred canon.
3. The Catholic Church has sole right of scriptural interpretation.
4. The sacraments are the seven recognized by the medieval Church, not just the two of the Protestants. They are, as Thomas Aquinas declared, the visible forms of invisible grace bestowed through the Church on the worthy.
5. Justification rests on faith, but not on faith alone as the Protestants assert. Good works also procure God's grace.

In the sphere of discipline and church management, the council turned to the broad task of preserving morals and furthering education. It ordered stricter regulation of the issuance of indulgences and the veneration of saints, it limited the number of holy days observed during the year (in deference in part to demands of economic interests), and it ordered bishops and priests in the larger towns to make public expositions and interpretations of scripture and in general to preach and teach what is necessary for salvation. Of far-reaching effect was the council's instruction to the pope to prepare an index of prohibited books, a step that helped to limit the reading of Protestant literature by Catholics.

B. THE REORGANIZATION OF THE INQUISITION FOR CHURCH-WIDE OPERATION. In 1542 Pope Paul III was persuaded by his advisers to reorganize the Inquisition on a scale that made its immediate use possible in any part of Europe where the civil authorities asked for it or were willing to support it. The Catholic Reformation thus acquired the instrumentality by which Catholic areas could quickly be purged of Protestants. The first country to be thus cleared was Italy.

C. THE JESUITS AND OTHER RELIGIOUS ORDERS. Of the greatest importance for the revival of Catholic spirit and zeal was the rise of new religious orders, the most famous of which has been the Jesuit order founded by Ignatius Loyola.

The Jesuits

Loyola (1491–1556) was a Spanish nobleman, who, after being a page at the court of Ferdinand and Isabella, became a soldier and was seriously wounded in a battle with the French. During convalescence he read the lives of Christ, St. Dominic, and St. Francis and resolved to become a "knight of the Virgin." He accordingly hung his weapons on the Virgin's altar at Monserrat and at a Dominican monastery began the self-directed visualizations of the life and work of Christ and of Christian warfare against evil that he later systematized as the Jesuit spiritual "exercises." While on a pilgrimage to Jerusalem he came to feel the need of more education, so he hurried home to study in Spain and at the University of Paris. He gathered around him student associates with whom he practiced his spiritual exercises. It was thus that he attracted to himself Francis Xavier, who became the famous missionary to India and

Japan, and men like Diego Lainez and Simon Rodriguez. In Paris in 1534 he organized these friends into a military "company of Jesus" vowed to go to Jerusalem, if possible, as missionaries to the infidel Muslims, or, failing that, to offer their services to the pope. When war with the Turks barred the way to Jerusalem, they went to Rome and in 1540 obtained the authorization of the pope, Paul III, to establish The Society of Jesus, with Loyola as the first general.

Known as the Jesuits, they dedicated themselves to study and to translate into their own everyday activities the life and spirit of Christ himself. To this end, as "good soldiers of the cross," they bound themselves to a life of strict militialike discipline, spiritual exercises, and absolute obedience to their superiors short of sin, never ceasing to train their wills to serve Christ absolutely, unreservedly, and unselfishly. Yet "sin" was so defined that it was seldom confronted in the course of carrying out the instructions of their superiors, for they held that there could be no sin in a doubtful course of action if "probable" grounds for it existed or it had been accepted by men of greater experience or had authority for it. Moreover, so sure were they that a good end justifies secrecy about means that they sanctioned "mental reservation" on being required to tell the whole truth: one was not bound to give the whole truth even under oath. The main thing was absolute self-commitment to the aims of the Jesuit order and unreserved and complete surrender of self in doing what one's superiors considered to be in the interests of Christ. This sacrificial devotion was intensively cultivated in each Jesuit during his novitiate, a regimen that included a unique and very effective four weeks of spiritual exercises under the point-to-point direction of a spiritual drill-master. On the basis of the capacities revealed during this period, each Jesuit was assigned by his superiors to the tasks he was judged best suited to, and when sent to some post, no matter how far away, he was under obligation to send back a continuous stream of reports to his superiors who had sent him.

The Jesuit order had spectacular success in the field of missions. Not only did Francis Xavier and his associates carry Catholicism to India, Japan, and China, but others during the sixteenth and seventeenth centuries won their way into South America, the St. Lawrence and Mississippi valleys, Mexico, and California.

Here it is important to observe that the natives sensed that the priests had come not to exploit and rob them, as the conquistadors often did, but to save them. In Europe itself Jesuits diligently and intelligently sought and occupied important commercial and governmental posts, which took them into far-flung places abroad as well as into the council chambers of kings and princes at home. Their political influence in France, Portugal, Spain, and Austria during the sixteenth and seventeenth centuries was very great. They led in checking the spread of Lutheranism into south Germany and were powerful factors behind the scenes when the Huguenots in France were fought and massacred. But they aroused the enmity eventually not only of all Protestant but also of many Catholic groups. In the eighteenth century they found Portugal, France, and Spain successively closed to them. At last they lost their temporal power, but they have continued to this day to promote the supremacy of the pope implied in the decrees of the Council of Trent.

Other Orders

The Jesuit was not the only new organization to witness to the forces of Catholic renewal. The sixteenth and seventeenth centuries saw the rise of the Oratorians, Theatines, Ursulines, Visitandines, and Lazaristes. The first two sought respectively the reform of the breviary and the improvement of preaching; the last three were orders for women that laid emphasis on education for women and remedial social work.

These movements were both effects and causes. They sprang from the heightened Catholic sense of the seriousness of the Church's mission in the world, and they caused the older organizations in the Church to look into their ways and to replace their former laxity with greater earnestness. The Franciscan and Dominican orders were thus revitalized. Even the papal office was affected. The popes from this time forward were uniformly men of more austere character and earnestly Catholic aims.

Doctrinal and Ecclesiastical Developments From 1700 to 1900

The eighteenth century saw much of the force of the Catholic Reformation wane. In France Louis XIV had already stemmed the power of the papacy by appropriating the income of vacant bishoprics and by encouraging the French clergy to assert openly their right to certain "Gallic liberties," which included the view that the pope was not infallible because general councils are superior to him. The rise of the rationalistic spirit among great numbers of Frenchmen during the eighteenth century reached a climax in the French Revolution, when anti-clericalism developed to the point of violence and Christianity itself was for a time "abolished." Although religious freedom for all men was later proclaimed, Napoleon, in coming to terms with the Catholic Church, was determined to keep it within government control. In Germany the Catholics painfully recovered from the effects of the Thirty Years' War, which had reduced the population of the German states by 65 per cent without effecting any real changes in the lines separating Catholics and Protestants. Not until after the Napoleonic wars, when romanticism led the reaction against the rationalistic spirit of the eighteenth century, did the Catholic Church revive some of its old power.

In Europe generally, during the nineteenth century, the assertion of papal supremacy in the name of worldwide Catholic unity reappeared in Ultramontanism, or the movement among Catholics north of the Alps in favor of the view that final authority

lay "beyond the mountains," that is, in the Vatican and the regularized channels of the papal government (the Roman Congregation). The popes for obvious reasons encouraged this opinion to the limit of their influence.

Two major doctrinal developments mark the nineteenth century. In 1854 Pius IX, after consulting with cardinals concerning a doctrine that had been discussed since the Middle Ages, proclaimed the Immaculate Conception of the Virgin to be a dogma of the Catholic Church. The meaning of this was that all Catholics must believe that Mary, in order to be fitted to conceive Christ while still a virgin, was freed from original sin by the immaculate purity in which her parents conceived her. More important was the declaration in 1870, under the same pope, of the doctrine of papal infallibility. It was not said that *all* utterances of the pope are without error, but only those that he pronounces *ex cathedra* in exposition of "the revelation or deposit of faith delivered through the Apostles," and the Catholic tradition. The declaration affirms:

The Roman pontiff, when he speaks *ex cathedra,* that is, when in discharge of the office of pastor and doctor of all Christians, by virtue of his supreme apostolic authority, he defines a doctrine regarding faith or morals to be held by the universal church, by the divine assistance promised to him in blessed Peter, is possessed of that infallibility with which the divine Redeemer willed that His church should be endowed.

This doctrine elevated the pope to a supreme height in the field of faith and morals. But it did not save him from the consequences of the rise of Italian nationalism in the wake of agitations of Mazzini and Garibaldi. For no sooner had the Vatican Council made its declaration than King Victor Emmanuel came along to capture Rome, and after a plebiscite of the inhabitants overwhelmingly directed him to do so, took from the pope the States of the Church, leaving only the Vatican, the Lateran, and Castel Gondolfo as the area where papal secular sovereignty could be exercised.

Some Recent Developments

Toward the end of the nineteenth century many thoughtful Catholics, both clerical and lay, began to see the need of taking into account the discoveries of modern historical and biblical criticism and of modern science, especially in the realms of biology and geology, where the theory of evolution was applied. There thus came into being the short-lived movement called Catholic Modernism. It sought a reconciliation of Catholicism and modern scientific and critical knowledge. Modernist voices were heard suddenly in all parts of Europe. Notable were those of George Tyrrell in England, Alfred Loisy in France, and Hermann Schell in Germany. But Pope Pius X found their thought dangerous and firmly condemned it in an encyclical in 1907, which effectively brought the movement to an end.

More successful as an attempt to put Catholic doctrine into current thought-forms is recent Neo-Thomism—so-called because its representatives, Jacques Maritain and others, seek to state the entire philosophy of Thomas Aquinas in modern terms and to apply it to modern issues. But the pope is still the final arbiter of what is sound in theology and morals and what is not.

In fulfilling his theological responsibilities, the pope (Pius XII) in 1950 proclaimed as a dogma of the Church the assumption of the uncorrupted body of the Virgin Mary to heaven after her death.

The pontiffs have also been conscious of worldwide responsibility in overseeing morals. Recent years have found them more and more disposed to make moral pronouncements, international in scope, in the name of God and the Church. Recent popes have taken a strong anti-Communist stand.

In like manner, the Catholic Church as a whole has become intensely aware of the value of action on an international scale. One of the significant new features of its effort is the institution of Church-wide Eucharistic Congresses, held every few years, when world conditions permit, in different parts of the Catholic world.

The concern throughout the Christian world with Church unity has affected the Catholic Church. Pope John XXIII issued in 1959 a summons to an ecumenical council (Vatican II) embracing the entire Catholic world. The council met for its first session in 1962 in Rome and was attended by 2,500 bishops of the Catholic Church. It met in three further sessions in 1963, 1964, and 1965, at the call of Pope Paul VI, the successor of Pope John, who died in 1963. Official observers from Protestant and Orthodox Churches (including the Russian but not the Greek) and selected laymen and women "auditors" were present. The council during its four sessions sought adjustment to the twentieth-century world and the promotion of Christian unity. Its decisions included the following: authorization of a more extensive use of vernaculars in the celebration of the sacraments and in public worship (with worldwide effects upon liturgical change and increased congregational participation in ritual responses and singing); endorsement of "collegiality" or the principle that all bishops as successors of the Apostles share with the pope in the government of the Church; provision for greater lay participation in church administration by creation of a permanent separate order of deacons, to include mature married men and not merely celibate youths preparing for the priesthood as heretofore; approval of a declaration that no man should be forced to act against his conscience and that nations should neither impose religion nor prohibit freedom of religious belief and association; authorization of worship by Catholics with non-Catholics in special circumstances; recognition of the possibility of salvation outside the Catholic Church; and a declaration that Jews are not to be held collectively responsible for the death of Christ.

In opening the second session of the council Pope Paul said that the long-range goal of the council was the complete and universal union of all Christians. Having visited Palestine and India in 1964, the pope addressed the United Nations assembly in 1965. The archbishop of Canterbury visited the Vatican in 1966 for the first time since the Reformation and signed

with the pope a declaration calling for "serious dialogue" on unity between the Churches.

VIII Protestantism in the Modern World

With perhaps one exception, the basic diversifications within the Protestant world all occurred before
the eighteenth century. The exception might be
Methodism. Methodism, however, was not really a
Reformation movement. It was essentially an awakening in response to new conditions created by the
development of science and the rapid rise of industrial capitalism, and it is therefore to be considered
a phenomenon not immediately related to the Reformation. Methodism stands in fact at the beginning
of the shifts and changes characteristic of modern
times.

To these changes we now turn, in a final general
survey.

Deism in the Eighteenth Century

It was not until the eighteenth century that Western science in its modern sense became generally
diffused among thinking men. When it did, the
eighteenth century Enlightenment came. Religion
was for the first time in the Western world compelled
to justify its case inductively. The empirically-minded
men of the eighteenth century were so little content
with the dogmas of the Church that they asked
themselves curiously what made primitives religious,
or what "natural religion" was. The whole structure
of revealed religion was abandoned, and in the estimation of many wide-eyed men of reason it came
tumbling down. In their awe before the iron laws of
the beautifully running mechanical universe, viewed
as through the eyes of a Galileo or a Newton in
mathematical terms, they ruled out all miracles and

special divine providences. God was no longer invoked to explain immediate causes; he was not any
longer necessarily *inside* the physical frame of nature.
He seemed distant both in space and time. The
Deists, who adopted these views, "ushered God to
the frontiers of the universe." To them he was the
Ancient of Days, who was to be revered as the creator
who made all, but they virtually "bowed Him out
over the threshold of the world," courteously but
firmly.

The Deists were representative of their age in
avoiding a clash between religion and science by
thus separating God from his creation and conceiving
that the latter ran by itself and could therefore be a
separate object of study.

A great many of the clergymen of the English
churches, and many also on the continent, highly
educated as a class, held views similar to those of
the Deists. Indeed, they were at heart Unitarians, or
even privately agnostic, and so lukewarm were their
devotions, so utterly non-mystical their public utterances, that it was inevitable that something like
Methodism should appear to bring heart and soul
back into English Christianity. When this renewal
of religious warmth among the clergy came to pass
the people responded eagerly.

Methodism

The industrial revolution was in the making.
Drawn from the land to the towns, the people had
lost anchorage. Drunkenness was so widespread
among them as to menace the national well-being.
The spiritual hunger of the common people was not
satisfied by the sceptical intellectualism of the
sermons they heard in the Established Church—mere
discourses, virtually essays, prepared as an accompaniment to the formal reading of the Book of
Common Prayer. John Wesley and his associates, en-
hungered too, brought them the emotional fire and
hearty conviction which they most needed.

The name *Methodist* was applied at first in sarcasm

by Wesley's fellow-students at Oxford to the little group—also derisively called the "Holy Club"—of which he was a leader, and which met regularly for *methodical* study and prayer in their rooms, endeavoring to bring God down to them out of the skies to which he had been relegated by their Deist teachers. They strove to cultivate something of the sense of the immediacy of God's presence in human lives that the Quakers felt. In an unmistakably decisive experience, since known as conversion, they underwent a complete change of life and faith and came to know that religion was real and vital for every act of existence. Afterwards, in seeking to "revive" their fellow-Christians of the churches, they had no intention of leaving the Church of England; they hoped only to reform that Church from within. But when the Wesley brothers and George Whitefield began to preach up and down the British Isles, and the people flocking to them in all the towns were converted in astonishing numbers, it was natural to form a new denomination, and to call it the Methodist Church.

John Wesley had been born in an Anglican manse in 1703, the fifteenth child of Samuel and Susannah Wesley. His brother Charles was the eighteenth. After their years at Oxford, during which the most important accession to their Methodist Club was George Whitefield, the talented son of an innkeeper, John and Charles Wesley went as missionaries to Georgia, where neither met with much success, though John Wesley made fruitful friendships with Moravians. On return to England both brothers resorted to a Moravian, Peter Böhler, in London, who convinced them that they would not be true Christians until they had experienced genuine conversion. That experience subsequently came to both. Together with Whitefield, also changed, they were soon preaching in the open fields to tens of thousands of deeply stirred miners and workmen in England, Scotland, and Ireland. It was common for their hearers to exhibit their emotion in ecstasies, bodily excitement, cries and groans, and lapses of consciousness. Methodist "chapels" were soon erected for more orderly worship, and as circumstances showed the need for them, characteristically Methodist innovations appeared: "classes," "bands," "circuits," "stewards," "superintendents," and the like. On the devotional side, Charles Wesley contributed to the cause the highly emotional hymns that were to have the usefulness to envangelistic Christianity that the hymns of Isaac Watts and of the Lutherans and Moravians had to the older Churches.

The new Church spread to the American colonies. Whitefield had prepared the way by seven immensely successful visits that greatly extended the area swept by an earlier wave of revivals, also marked by the experience of conversion, that had begun under Jonathan Edwards' powerful preaching in Northampton, Mass., and was called "The Great Awakening." Systematic organizational work in behalf of Methodism was begun in New York by 1766, and the epic labors of Francis Asbury (1745–1816), the great "circuit-rider," secured the spread of Methodism across the Alleghanies into the vast spaces of the Middle West. Since then, the Methodist Church has become one of the great denominations of the United States.

The Missionary Movement

The nineteenth may be reckoned a great Protestant century. It opened with a second "great awakening" in the United States, a series of revivals that much increased the number of Baptists and Methodists in the midwestern states. In Great Britain the Church of England was powerfully moved by a pietistic Evangelical movement, which in later decades issued in the Oxford or Tractarian movement, the formation of the Young Men's Christian Association (in London in 1844), and the organization of the Salvation Army (by William Booth in 1865). In Germany the theologians Schleiermacher (1768–1834) and Ritschl (1822–1889) gave a new and liberal turn to Protestant religious thought. But perhaps the two most significant developments of the century were the organization of worldwide Protestant missions and the rapid expansion of the Sunday School movement, two developments to which we now turn.

In missionary activity the Catholics had long shown the way. The Protestants gathered momentum more slowly. When the Dutch established trading stations in the East Indies in the seventeenth century, they encouraged missionaries to follow behind them. In the same century the Church of England felt a responsibility for the American Indians and organized the Society for the Propagation of the Gospel in New England, a group that at the beginning of the eighteenth century was largely superseded by the Society for the Propagation of the Gospel in Foreign Parts. The Quakers from the start sent missionaries to the West Indies, Palestine, and various parts of Europe. We have already seen how vigorously the Moravians fostered missions during the eighteenth century.

A new phase of missionary effort began with the publication of the globe-circling Captain Cook, whose vivid descriptions of the condition of the primitives of the many South Pacific islands that he visited from 1768–1779 stirred up William Carey to go to India as the first missionary of the Baptist Society for Propagating the Gospel among the Heathen, which he helped to organize in 1792. In 1795 an interdenominational group formed the London Missionary Society, which sent its first appointees to Tahiti. (This society has since been Congregationalist.) There followed the formation of the Edinburgh Missionary Society, the Glasgow Missionary Society, the Church Missionary Society (of the Church of England), and the Wesleyan Methodist Missionary Society.

To match these British efforts with like devotion to the expansion of the Christian world, a group of students at Williams College in Massachusetts joined in mutual commitments that led in 1810 to the birth of the famous missionary organ of American Congregationalism, the American Board of Commissioners for Foreign Missions. Subsequently, like organizations were formed in the other American churches.

Continental Europe was not idle. Similar societies appeared in Denmark, Germany, France, and Switzerland.

In the years that followed, the reports brought back by the missionaries from every part of the world had a pronounced quickening effect on the life of the churches at home. The whole tone of Christian life was raised. With the dawn of the twentieth century incalculable benefits to Christendom as a whole were seen to have sprung from the development of worldwide fellowship among Christians of every culture and color. Recent changes in missionary objectives have led to the concept of total service in every area of life. Indigenous church leadership is encouraged, and one missionary aim is now the eventual development of "two-way evangelization"—the mission fields producing interpretations and interpreters of Christianity to minister to the churches at home.

The Sunday School Movement and Religious Education

The older Protestant churches were conscious from the very beginning of the need to instruct their young people in the doctrines and duties of the Christian religion before confirming them as members of the church. This, of course, was the origin of catechetical instruction. But the religious education thus attempted was brief and of limited effect, and it did not embrace all the children of the community. There was therefore great need for more freqeunt instruction, and particularly for instruction open to the children of the religiously illiterate and the unchurched. Realization of this need came in Gloucester, England, to Robert Raikes, whose interest in prison reform led to his study of the social conditions producing delinquency in city slums. In order to provide schooling for the neglected waifs of Gloucester, he organized in 1780 the first Sunday School, in part designed to teach them how to read the Bible.

Thus began the Sunday School movement that became so significant a feature of the religious life of the nineteenth century. It spread rapidly through the British Isles, in the Protestant areas of the European continent, and on the other side of the Atlantic. The Sunday School Society of London, its analogues on the continent, and the state Sunday School associations of the United States held, during a century of effort, numerous conventions to advance the cause. These societies actively fostered teacher-training programs, prepared and published lesson-materials, and worked with each other on an international basis. In 1907 they organized the World's Sunday School Association.

So valuable were the Sunday Schools and their teachers to the churches during this period that no Protestant congregation could afford to be without them. Indeed, they were the chief source of the new members brought into the churches by confirmation. Their altruistic purpose shone clear and strong. The teachers and superintendents, with very rare exceptions, served without salary on a purely voluntary basis. The instruction was too often inadequate and ill-prepared, but it was always meant to supply the highest kind of moral and religious guidance.

The shortcomings of the Sunday Schools of the nineteenth century have been clearly seen in the twentieth. A better-informed leadership has been seeking to turn them into an effective means of Christian education by applying the principles and techniques discovered in secular public instruction. The Sunday School has now acquired the more comprehensive and dignified name of the Church School.

No more serious and sustained educational effort to bring Christianity home to men's hearts and lives as a discipline for the whole of human life has ever been attempted in any period of the history of the Christian Church.

Protestantism and Science

The nineteenth century dawned with little inkling of the hazards that science was to place in the way of faith, but long before the century was out, a momentous struggle between orthodox religion and a naturalism bred by science was joined, and many a devout Christian felt his heart turn faint within him as he watched and listened.

One of the earliest controversies was precipitated by the development of historical criticism and the rewriting of history. Hume and Gibbon in the eighteenth century had cast doubt on many a feature of Christian belief, but they did not subject the life of Jesus, nor the Bible as a whole, to detailed examination. The nineteenth century was to supply such "biblical criticism." David Strauss and Ernest Renan, in epoch-making German and French works, radically rewrote the life of Jesus. Lower (or textual) and higher (or historico-literary) criticism of the Bible demonstrated that its books were the work of many different authors at many different times. The Pentateuch was shown to have had a composite authorship stretching over at least five centuries. The New Testament was dissected into "Q," "M," "L," and other strata of tradition. Violent controversy over these findings, as they were made, divided Protestantism into two camps, later to be called Fundamentalists (who rejected biblical criticism as gross unbelief) and Modernists (who accepted it as sound).

But though bitter and long-drawn-out, this controversy was all but overshadowed during the last half of the nineteenth century by the chorus of angry protest that followed the publication of Darwin's *Origin of Species*. For Darwin, and his predecessor in formulating the evolutionary theory, Lamarck, were interpreted not only to deny the story of creation in the first chapters of Genesis but to rule out any theory of creation whatever. At the same time, some of the philosophic successors of Hegel had transformed his spiritual monism into materialism, and they loudly welcomed the support of the theory of evolution. Ludwig Büchner and Ernst Haeckel, particularly, sprang forward as champions of a mechanistic materialism that left no room for God. (Feuerbach had concluded thirty years earlier, in 1841: "Anthropology is the secret of theology. God

507

is man worshiping himself. The Trinity is the human family deified."ᴹ) And in England, Thomas Huxley and Herbert Spencer increased the sense of outrage among the conservatives by rejecting the doctrine of an impassable gulf between man and the beasts and arguing instead for the theory that man has emerged by slow evolution from the anthropoid apes, and is not a separate, special creation of God.

To all these views orthodox Christians entered a heated denial in the name of the immutability of the species God had separately created. When geologists had worked out Lyell's theory of gradual evolutionary change in the history of the earth and presented fossils taken from the rocks as evidence of the biological evolution of the various species, the only reply the orthodox could make was that God had planted the fossils in the rocks on the day of creation to confound the judgment of unbelievers, whose rejection of God's truth was thus made manifest and their damnation justified. Confronted, by the end of the century, with bio-chemical theories that sought to explain away as non-existent the vital principle in living things, and psychological theories that denied the existence of the soul (and later of the mind and consciousness as such), many devout believers felt they were faced by an inflexible choice between irreconcilable positions: one that science is true and religion is false, and the other that science is preposterous guess-work and the biblical revelation God's own infallible word, true from beginning to end exactly as it is contained in the Bible.

But amidst the clamor, liberal Christians remained sure no such irreconcilability between science and religion existed. Men like Henry Drummond in Scotland (in his *Natural Law in the Spiritual World*) and John Fiske in New England (in *Outlines of Cosmic Philosophy* and *The Idea of God as Affected by Modern Knowledge*) endeavored to show that on the theory that evolution is God's method of creation, religion and science can indeed be reconciled. The biblical story of creation has to be taken as devout, prescientific theorizing, poetically if not literally true, its essence not disproved, though its form re-

quires reinterpretation. With this beginning, the liberals proceeded confidently to a task of reconstruction, assured that the essentials of the Christian faith are never shaken by the findings of a careful, non-metaphysical (or "pure") science. Science itself, they pointed out, moves on assumptions that are beyond proof, and these are *its* faith. More recently, the liberals have been saying that the dogmatic materialism of the nineteenth century is no longer tenable. Scientists, for lack of any definite indication of what electrons and protons are made of, must be more open-minded toward organic as against mechanistic conceptions of the universe. Even psychology, with its emphasis on integrations, configurations, or *gestalts,* can no longer be dogmatically sure about the detailed analyses that once seemed to destroy any evidence of the existence of the soul. The Christian faith is thus, say the liberals, unshaken in its major assumptions, and its adherents may give credence to the assured findings of science. For truth is one and indivisible, and to see life steadily and to see it whole is still to gain the pure heart of those who see God.

This liberal view, so confident and optimistic in its faith in God and man, was itself severely shaken by the catastrophe of the First World War. There emerged thereafter a Neo-Orthodoxy, which accepted the findings of science and of historical criticism but insisted that God is not immanent in nature and history in the way in which the liberals say he is, but is transcendent, existing quite apart from nature and man, indeed is the Wholly Other, the Absolute, who must break through the wall of human error and self-contradiction that separates him from men in order to appear in human history. Without such breaking through, man is lost. The dour champions —Karl Barth and his followers—of a going "beyond fundamentalism and modernism" to a theology resting on a dualism of God and the world have not yet won the field. It remains to be seen whether the liberals will yield to their attack and abandon their faith in the divine in man, that is, in the eternal immanence of God in the nature of man.

508

The Social Gospel

With the advent of the era of "big business" and the onset of labor-capital tension, socialism took on new life. In Europe, as the nineteenth century approached and passed its half-way mark, it had great and increasing political significance. The social upheavals of 1848 brought sharply home to thoughtful churchmen the need of finding a Christian solution to poverty and social injustice. In England, Frederick Maurice and Charles Kingsley made a beginning of discussing the application of the Christian gospel to these social problems. Liberals in the Church of England were moved to form the Christian Social Union and the Church Socialist League (subsequently renamed the League of the Kingdom of God). Bishops and archbishops associated themselves with these and later efforts to bring Protestantism to bear on social issues. In the United States men like Francis G. Peabody, Washington Gladden, Shailer Mathews, and Walter Rauschenbusch searched the scriptures and discovered a neglected theme in the teaching of Jesus—the Kingdom of God. They brought together all the sayings of Jesus referring to it and found in the carpenter of Nazareth a prophet of social justice whose principles seemed still the key to happier human relationships in every variety of social context. Here was a social gospel whose practice would solve modern man's economic, industrial, political, racial, and international problems; it could bring peace to the nations, justice among the peoples, and good will among the races.

A new note had been sounded in Protestant Christianity. In general, the liberals rallied to the ardent exposition of the social gospel; the conservatives as generally drew back, decrying the dabbling in politics and the involvement in merely worldly matters that they declared was the pit into which the preachers of the social gospel fell. The critics complained that the New Testament contained no social message to speak of, the appeal of Jesus being almost exclusively to individuals that they might be saved one by one. But advocates of the social gospel replied that although the redemption of the individual is a necessary aim of all religion, it is almost impossible to bring about the moral redemption of individuals in an immoral society, and that the Church will lose all relevance to modern life, as it seemed to have already lost relevance for a large part of the laboring classes, unless the Christian religion is brought to bear on the moral redemption of society. If the Christian religion, they cried, has nothing to say and no program to offer on the chief problems of the hour, it is no longer of any use to men! Its day is over!

The critical question of how much social gospel there is in the New Testament is not yet settled and may never be settled, but the great Protestant denominations, at least of the English-speaking world, have all formulated detailed social policies and programs and in all their major conferences devote a large part of their attention to questions of Christian social action. The determination of the social bearing of Christianity is indeed one of the principal factors now drawing Protestantism together. This has been quite evident in the participation by both the clergy and laity of all denominations in civil rights movements, anti-poverty programs, and anti-war demonstrations.

Movements Toward Union of the Churches

The fissions and separations within Protestantism have slowed down markedly in the last fifty years and have now virtually ceased. Rapprochement and union are now sought. In part this is due to the attitude of the liberals in all denominations who have stressed the fact of agreement on essentials as a basis for unity. But there are many other factors: the social changes that an economy marked by rapid communications and general interdependence have brought about; the fact that scientific scepticism and widespread secularism have tended to drive adherents of religion together; the very expansion of the Christian effort into all the world; the growing interchange

509

between denominations of helpful literature, such as hymns, lesson-materials, and devotional aids; the meeting and intermingling of ministers and laymen from many different denominations on interdenominational boards and committees and at conferences and camps; and, not least, the realization that a divided Protestantism is a weakened Protestantism, particularly in a day when the problems of society are no longer those of the frontier, nor yet those of the village or town, but those arising from the closely interwoven destinies of the peoples of the entire world. All these factors suggest that only a united Church can effectively seek social and individual redemption.

Union of the churches has been urged for over a century, both in Europe and America. Heads of states have frequently expressed a desire for it. A prime example of government-initiated union was the Prussian national church formed in 1817 by the organic union of Lutheran and Reformed Churches (the Evangelical Church of Prussia). But the steps toward union rising from within the churches have greater significance. The most natural expression of the urge to union has been the creation of interdenominational agencies and boards, like the American Tract Society, the American Bible Society, the Home Missions Council, and the Foreign Missions Conference of North America. Federation on a yet wider scale has long been urged and has been in good part responsible for the forming of societies on both sides of the Atlantic looking toward united Christian action.

From such beginnings the ecumenical movement (or the movement for worldwide unity of the churches) has grown into one of the most significant features of modern Protestantism. Just the bare rehearsal of the chief results of the trend to union is impressive. In the area of interdenominational cooperation, lesser and greater federations of churches (city, county, state, and nationwide) have been organized. The outstanding example of a nationwide federation was the Federal Council of Churches of Christ in America organized in 1908, the predecessor of the present National Council of Churches. Although the latter body meets only biennially, it functions constantly through standing committees dealing with home missions, race relations, international justice and good will, mercy and relief, and relations with churches abroad. In Europe the first great achievements in unity were in the area of foreign missions. The problems of interdenominational comity on the mission fields led to the calling of the great Edinburgh Missionary Conference of 1910, which resulted in the formation of the International Missionary Council (1921) and the calling of the world conferences held at Jerusalem in 1928 and at Madras in 1938. Episcopal or Church of England hopes of serving as the mediator between the Protestant and Catholic worlds shone forth strongly in the Lambeth Conference of 1920 and the World Conference on Faith and Order at Lausanne in 1927. But a papal encyclical in 1928 temporarily dashed all hopes of reunion with Rome except by "return" and submission to the Roman Church. The Eastern Orthodox Church, however, proved more open-minded, and its representatives participated in the World Conference on Faith and Order held in Edinburgh in 1937 and the two World Conferences on Life and Work meeting in Stockholm in 1925 and in Oxford in 1937. Held in close succession, for the sake of the delegates who came from all parts of the world, the 1937 Oxford and Edinburgh conferences gave rise to the World Council of Churches, designed to parallel on a worldwide scale the Federal Council of Churches of Christ in America. The first assembly of the World Council of Churches was held in Amsterdam, Holland, in 1948, the second in Evanston, Illinois, in 1954, and the third in New Delhi, India, in 1961. The last of these meetings was significant for three things especially: (1) the integration of the International Missionary Council with the World Council of Churches, (2) the admission of the Orthodox Churches of Russia, Roumania, Bulgaria, and Poland to membership, an event signalizing the first organizational penetration of the World Council behind the Iron Curtain, and (3) the presence throughout the sessions of official observers from the Roman Catholic Church.

Two separate methods of union have emerged: federal union of the churches without abolishing the member denominations, as in the World Council of Churches and in certain proposed smaller federal unions, and (2) complete organic union through merger. Of the latter kind was the organic union in Canada of Presbyterians, Methodists, and Congregationalists in the United Church of Canada (1925). Along denominational lines separate branches of the Lutheran and also of the Presbyterian Churches in the United States have more recently united. Ecumenically more significant was the organic union in 1961 of the Congregational-Christian Church (itself the result of the union of the Congregational and Christian Churches) and the Evangelical and Reformed Church (formed from the Reformed Church in the United States and the Evangelical Synod of North America), under the name of the United Church of Christ. Great interest is now being shown in a proposed union of this new denomination with other major Protestant bodies in the United States. The discussions at first began as an official consultation on church union involving four denominations—the United Presbyterian, the Episcopal, the Methodist, and the United Church of Christ—and has since involved the Evangelical United Brethren, the Disciples of Christ, the Presbyterian Church in the U.S., the African Methodist Episcopal Church, and its offshoot the African Methodist Episcopal Zion Church. Others are considering participating. The participants

in the consultation do not anticipate an early union but express the hope that a concrete plan for eventual merger can be arrived at and that, once it is ratified, some years of federal union will see the emergence of a constitution resulting in a merger. While these discussions are proceeding, smaller unions have been or are in course of being effected—e.g., the Methodist Church with the Evangelical United Brethren, the Presbyterian Church in the U.S. with the (Dutch) Reformed Church in the U.S., and the Unitarian with the Universalist Church.

On an international level some thirty Reformed and Presbyterian Churches in more than twenty countries on five continents are engaged in consultations on union. Other major union projects are those of the Anglican Churches with the Methodists, the Anglicans with the Presbyterians in South Africa, the Anglicans with the United Church of Canada, the Presbyterians with the Congregationalists in England, and others. The reunion of Christians throughout the world is a major phenomenon of the twentieth century.

Our space is at an end. Perhaps the story here unfolded suggests that basic Christianity is not a way of looking back into the past but a way of going forward into the future; not an escape from the world into solitariness, but a way of spending one's life for others in order to find it; not a retreat into ultimate truth, but a redemptive mission, a way of salvation leading into the world and through the world, in the love of God and man.

Suggestions for Further Reading

Augustine, St. *City of God.* 8th ed., T. & T. Clark, Edinburgh, 1934

———. *Confessions.* Any ed.

Bainton, R. *Here I Stand, a Life of Martin Luther.* Abingdon-Cokesbury, 1950. Available as Mentor pb

Battenhouse, R. W., ed. *A Companion to the Study of Saint Augustine.* Oxford University Press, 1955

Beach, W. and Niebuhr, H. R., eds. *Christian Ethics: Sources of the Living Tradition.* Ronald Press, 1955

BRAUER, J. C. *Protestantism in America: a Narrative History*. Westminster, 1954

BULTMANN, R. *Theology of the New Testament*. 2 vols., Scribner, 1951 and 1955

———. *Primitive Christianity in Its Contemporary Setting*. Meridian Books pb, 1956

CADOUX, C. J. *The Early Christian Church and the World*. T. & T. Clark, Edinburgh, 1925

CAIRD, G. B. *The Apostolic Age*. Duckworth & Co., London, 1955

CROSS, F. L., ED. *The Early Christian Fathers*. Duckworth & Co., 1956

CRUMP, C. G. AND JACOB, F. *The Legacy of the Middle Ages*. Oxford, 1926

DEISSMAN, A. *Paul*. 2nd ed., Hodder and Stoughten, 1926. Available in Harper Torchbooks pb

DENZINGER, H. J. D. *The Sources of Catholic Dogma*. Herder, 1957

DIBELIUS, M. *Studies in the Acts of the Apostles*. Tr. by Mary Ling. Charles Scribner's Sons, 1956

——— AND KUMMEL, W. G. *Paul*. Westminster, 1953

DODD, C. H. *According to the Scriptures: The Substructure of New Testament Theology*. Charles Scribner's Sons, 1953

DUCHESNE, L. *The Early History of the Christian Church*. Tr. from the 4th French rev. ed. by Claude Jenkins. 3 vols., John Murray, London, 1909–24

ENSLIN, M. S. *Christian Beginnings*. Harper, 1938. Available in Harper Torchbooks pb, 2 vols.

FLEW, R. N., ED. *The Nature of the Church*. Student Christian Movement Press, 1952

FRENCH, R. M. *The Eastern Orthodox Church*. Hutchinson, 1951

GILSON, E. *History of Christian Philosophy in the Middle Ages*. Random House, 1954

HOPKINS, C. H. *The Rise of the Social Gospel in American Protestantism, 1865–1915*. Yale University Press, 1940

HULME, E. M. *The Renaissance, the Protestant Reformation, and the Catholic Reformation*. 2 vols., Century House, 1914

KELLY, J. N. D. *Early Christian Doctrines*. Harper, 1958

KIDD, B. J. *A History of the Church to 461*. 3 vols., Oxford, Clarendon Press, 1922

———. *Documents Illustrative of the History of the Church*. 2 vols., Macmillan Co., 1920

KLAUSNER, JOSEPH. *From Jesus to Paul*. Macmillan, 1943. Available as Beacon pb. A Jewish view

LATOURETTE, K. S. *History of the Expansion of Christianity*. 7 vols., Harper, 1937–1945

———. *A History of Christianity*. Harper & Brothers, 1953

LEFF, G. *Medieval Thought: St. Augustine to Ockham*. Penguin Books, 1958

LIETZMANN, H. *The Beginnings of the Christian Church*. Nicholson & Watson, London, 1937

———. *The Founding of the Church Universal*. Nicholson & Watson, 1938

———. *From Constantine to Julian*. Lutterworth Press, London, 1950

———. *The Era of the Church Fathers*. Charles Scribner's Sons, 1952

LOSSKY, V. *The Mystical Theology of the Eastern Church*. James Clarke, 1957

MACKINTOSH, H. R. *Types of Modern Theology*. Charles Scribner's Sons, 1937

McARTHUR, A. A. *The Evolution of the Christian Year*. Student Christian Movement Press, London, 1953

MILBURN, R. L. P. *Early Christian Interpretations of History*. Adam & Charles Black, London, 1954

PEGIS, A. C., ED. *Basic Writings of St. Thomas Aquinas.* Modern Library, 1948

ROUSE, R. AND NEILL, S. C., EDS. *A History of the Ecumenical Movement.* Westminster, 1954

WALKER, WILLISTON. *A History of the Christian Church.* Rev. by Richardson, Pauck, and Handy. Charles Scribner's Sons, 1959

16 Islam: The Religion of Submission to God in Interaction with Various Cultures

ON ROUTE 22 in eastern Pennsylvania not long ago a big Greyhound bus drew over toward the shoulder of the highway. It was late in the afternoon, and when the considerate bus-driver opened the door, a Muslim emerged with his prayer-rug, performed his ablutions with the dust he could gather from the ground (remembering how the Qur'an says, "If you can find no water, then have recourse to wholesome dust, and wipe your faces and your hands"), and spreading out his prayer-rug, prostrated himself toward the east and prayed to the all-seeing, all-compassionate One to whom he had since childhood daily offered his surrender. The other passengers in the bus, whether or not it was an example to them, were witnesses to an act of faith and a rite of surrender and commitment.

A "Muslim" is "one who submits" or "one who commits himself to Islam." The word *Islam* is a noun formed from the infinitive of a verb meaning "to accept," "to submit," "to commit oneself," and means "submission" or "surrender." Of this word Charles J. Adams says: "By its very form [as a verbal noun] it conveys a feeling of action and ongoingness, not of something that is static and finished, once and for all, but of an inward state which is always repeated and renewed. . . . One who thoughtfully declares 'I am a Muslim' has done much more than affirm his membership in a community. . . . [He is saying] 'I am one who commits himself to God.' "A

Although the challenge of Islam appalled those who resisted it, its force and clarity appealed to those who accepted it. Four hundred and fifty million people, by a conservative estimate, are now numbered among its willing adherents, and their number is increasing. They accept it as the absolute and final faith, and they are proud to be able to follow it. In general, it has kept to one basic scripture, preserved from the first in a state of textual purity such that comparatively few variant readings have arisen to confuse the commentators. What is in the Qur'an* all

* Or Koran, the traditional spelling, and therefore to be found in some of the quotations of this chapter, but Qur'an more accurately suggests the real pronunciation.

true Muslims accept for absolute truth, for it is the word, of God himself.

The Muslim's pride in his faith is not decreased by the convincing evidence that can be gathered to show that Muhammad's teaching was not completely new, for it is Islam's proud claim that the Qur'an as the last and final revelation from heaven, completes and goes beyond the revelations that other religions before it haltingly declared.

But in the study of Islam we are met by an initial difficulty. Though its doctrinal and ethical character is finally determined by an absolute standard or rule of faith, the Qur'an, it is not from the Qur'an that we get most of the information we possess concerning the life of Muhammad and the early spread of his religion. This information comes to us first through the Hadith, the body of tradition originating from the first generation of Muslims and handed down orally to those who finally committed it to writing, and secondly, through Muslim biographies of the Prophet that appeared during the first centuries of Muslim history.* These sources contain unreliable material, but as early reports of what Muhammad, said and did, or was believed to have said and done, they are extremely valuable.

I Arabian Beliefs and Practices Before Muhammad

Racial and Economic Factors

The Arabians, like any other people that might be mentioned, were not racially homogeneous. The pure

* One of the earliest of these, Musa ibn 'Uqbah's account, survives only in fragmentary form, but others appearing later are better preserved; for example, the connected narrative of Ibn Ishaq (b. 707), whose text was edited and abridged a generation later by Ibn Hisham and has come down to us in this version, and the biography of Al-Waqidi (ca. 797–874), whose follower Ibn Sa'd also set down the life of the Prophet. These biographies were used by Al-Tabari (d. 923) when he wrote his notable history of the early days of Islam.

Semites among them outnumbered very greatly all the representatives of other ethnic groups, but a considerable proportion of the population had in their blood a mixture of both Semitic and non-Semitic strains. In the south Ethiopians crossed the Red Sea to establish settlements along the coastal plain; in the northeast conquests dating as far back as the second millennium B.C. somewhat altered the racial composition there by infusion of Sumerian, Babylonian, and Persian elements. From Egypt a Hamitic strain entered the population.

Divisive modes of thought produced further variations. Cultural differences that often proved irreconcilable were introduced when Semites who left the desert returned again after the passage of centuries. During periods of international convulsion many refugees from lands to the north and west retreated into the desert wastes that their fathers had put behind them. In the time of Muhammad the western portions of Arabia contained considerable numbers of Jews who had fled from their enemies—Assyrian, Babylonian, Greek, and Roman. It was they who introduced the intensive cultivation of the oases in western Arabia. They were numerous in Medina (the ancient Yathrib) and its neighborhood and had even at times held this region under armed control.

There were some rather marked differences between northern and southern Arabs. The huge Arabian peninsula (natively and aptly called Jazirat al-'Arab, "the Island of the Arabs," because it is virtually isolated by its surrounding waters and its own sands) is geographically divided by a clam-shell-shaped tract of red sand, a third of a million square miles in extent, which even the bedouins avoid (it being known to them as Al-Rub 'al-Khali, "the Vacant Quarter"). To the north of this bad land are stretches of more habitable desert steppe, containing oases and arable valley-bottoms. This more hospitable territory is bounded by a band of desert resembling a crescent moon and reaching from Al-Rub 'al-Khali for five hundred miles to another desert, the Great Nefud, lying in the northwest. The Nefud's shifting dunes of red and white sand stretch mid-way between Medina

THE SPREAD OF CHRISTIANITY AND THE EXTENT OF MUSLIM CONQUESTS

NORTH SEA

BALTIC SEA

Clonard

IRELAND

York

Lincoln

BRITAIN

Caerleon

London

Canterbury

Bremen

Pomeranians
(1122-1130)

Marienbur

Utrecht

Saxons (785-805)

Magdeburg

Gnesen

Cologne

Poles
(962-1025)

Fulda

Rouen

Reims

Trier

Mainz

Thuringians
(8th Cent.)

ATLANTIC OCEAN

Paris

Luxeuil

Regensburg

Czechs
(C. 1000)

Nantes

Tours

Allamanni
(7th Cent.)

Bourges

Augsburg

GAUL

Esztergom

Lyons

Vienne

Milan

Aquileia

Siscia

Bordeaux

Verona

Sirmium

Astorga

Leon

Toulouse

Arles

Genoa

Ravenna

Salona

Duero R.

Marseille

Florence

SPAIN

Narbonne

Pisa

Ancona

Saragossa

ITALY

Tagus R.

Tarragona

Evora

Merida

Toledo

Rome

Beneventum

Faro

Cordova

Valencia

SARDINIA

Puteoli

Naples

Seville

Cadiz

Malaca

Cartegena

Messina

Tingis

SICILY

Caesarea

Hippo Regius

Syracuse

Cirta

Carthage

Madaura

Lambaesis

Hadrumetum

MEDITERRANEAN

Leptis Magna

Berenic

▨	200-325 (by the time of Constantine)
▨	Areas known to contain Christians at the time of Irenaeus, c. 185
▨	200-325 (by the time of Constantine)
▨	325-600 (by the time of Gregory I)
▨	600-800 (by the time of Charlemagne)
- - -	800-1300 Northern limit of area permanently lost to Islam

516

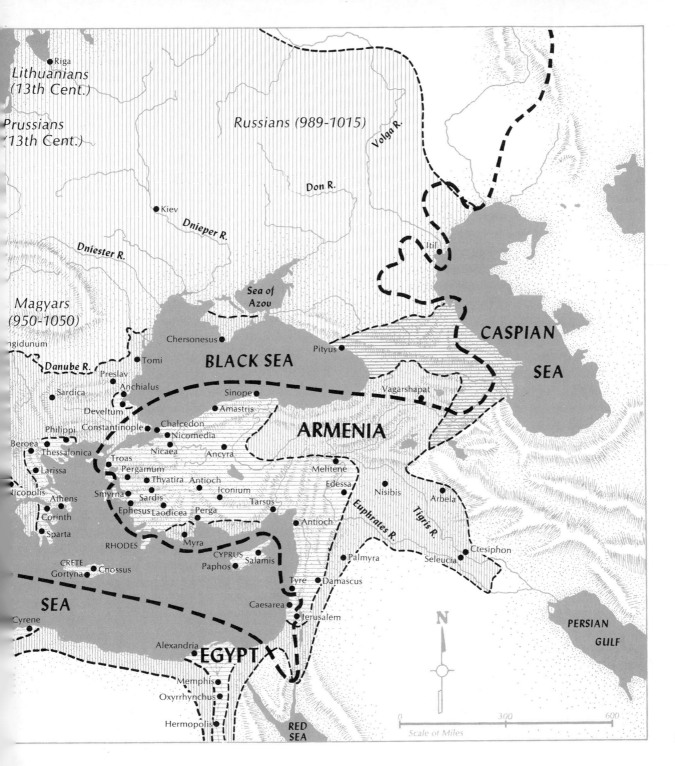

Lithuanians
(13th Cent.)

Prussians
(13th Cent.)

Russians (989-1015)

•Riga

Volga R.

Don R.

Dnieper R.

•Kiev

Dniester R.

Itil

Magyars
(950-1050)

Sea of
Azov

CASPIAN

Chersonesus

Pityus

SEA

ngidunum

Danube R.

BLACK SEA

•Tomi

Preslav

Sinope

Vagarshapat

Sardica•

Anchialus

Amastris

Develtum

Chalcedon

ARMENIA

Philippi•

Constantinople

Nicomedia

Beroea•

Nicaea

Ancyra

Thessalonica•

Troas

Melitene

Larissa•

Pergamum

Thyatira

Antioch

Edessa

Nisibis

Arbela

Nicopolis•

Smyrna

Sardis

Iconium

Athens•

Ephesus

Laodicea

Perga

Tarsus

Euphrates R.

Tigris R.

Corinth•

Myra

Antioch

Sparta•

RHODES

Ctesiphon

CYPRUS

Salamis

Palmyra

Seleucia

CRETE

Gortyna•

Cnossus

Paphos

Tyre•

Damascus

SEA

Caesarea

PERSIAN

Cyrene•

Jerusalem

GULF

N

Alexandria

EGYPT

Memphis•

Oxyrrhynchus•

Scale of Miles

0   300   600

Hermopolis•

RED
SEA

517

and Damascus. On the steppeland the coarse soil supports a sparse, hardy verdure that springs up when the infrequent winter rains fall and provides grazing for the camels, sheep, goats, and horses of the bedouin tribes. Southwest of the "Vacant Quarter" is the rain-bathed area of Yemen or South Arabia— the classical Arabia Felix—bounded on the southeast by the Gulf of Aden and on the southwest by the lower end of the Red Sea. This was the region so famed among the Greeks and Romans for its frankincense and spices. The geographical separation of north and south Arabia was paralled by ethnic differences among the people. The north Arabians of Muhammad's day were long-headed, wiry nomads, who spoke a pure Arabic and were by nature liberty-loving and imaginative. Thousands of years of hungry struggle had schooled them in predatory habits. They were quite different in speech and customs from their comfortable brethren below the "Vacant Quarter," the round-headed, hook-nosed southerners, who were farmers and horticulturists and spoke a Semitic dialect, with Ethiopic loan-words, that sounded strange in northern ears. Before the time of Muhammad the north Arabians, although they had many outside contacts, never knew a conqueror, but the south Arabians, blessed with fertilizing rain and sun, grew prosperous through trade, built cities, and towns surrounded by green fields and gardens, and brought down upon themselves in consequence raids from the desert, wars from abroad, the expense of fortifications, heavy taxes, economic rivalries, commercial anxieties, and recurrent depressions coming close on the heels of boom times. And when the Ptolemies (and the Romans after them) learned how to sail past them to India, they went into permanent decline.

A third section of Arabia happens to be more important to us. It consists of the mountain range running parallel with the Red Sea from the Gulf of Aqaba to Yemen. Rising at some points over ten thousand feet above sea level, this range falls swiftly to the Red Sea, but its eastern slope declines gradually through bare, volcanic lava-tracts, scoured with deep wadis or water-courses, toward the red sands of the central desert and the flat coastal plains bordering the far-away Persian Gulf. Although at places like Ta'if or Medina subterranean waters rising to the surface moisten an arable soil, this mountain range is for the most part dry and barren. Violent rainstorms sometimes visit it, but then the water rushes off in floods that wash out more deeply the gullies or wadis. Yet, it figures historically as the most vital part of the peninsula, for it once furnished a connecting link between the southern spice-lands and the markets of the Mediterranean world. On the cool, hard surface of its uplands, caravans long before the time of Christ plodded their way through the trading-posts of Ta'if, Mecca, and Yathrib (Medina), and at Petra forked off west or north to Egypt or Syria. The pre-Islamic prosperity of the communities of Al-Hejaz, this mountain home of Islam, was primarily due to the passage through them of the spice-laden caravans of the south.

Religious Conceptions

The religion of pre-Islamic Arabia was a development out of the primitive Semitic desert-faith already sketched in the chapter on Judaism. In some parts of Arabia that development had gone pretty far in one or another direction. In south Arabia, for example, a rather advanced astral cult prevailed, centered in the moon-god and reflecting Babylonian and Zoroastrian influences. In other regions where Jews and Christians had secured a foothold (which was in most of the commercial centers of Arabia), the native converts to these faiths abandoned their primitive beliefs and espoused monotheism. But the great majority of Arabs, both in the towns and on the steppes, worshiped local gods and goddesses. Some of these deities were strictly tribal; others presided over certain geographical areas and obliged all who entered their domains to worship them, like Hubal at Mecca and Dushara at Petra. There was also widespread veneration of certain astral deities. Some of these had names that were obviously foreign, Babylonian for the most part, and were readily identified by Greek and Roman visitors as local forms of Jupiter, Mercury, Canopus, and other deities. In Mecca three almost indistinguishable goddesses were adored: Al-Lat, a mother-goddess (perhaps the sun), Al-Manat, the goddess of fate, and Al-'Uzza, the morning star, a pale sort of Venus, their idols being the center of a phallic-worship much like that accorded across the frontiers in olden times to Ishtar and Isis. They were reckoned to be "the daughters of Allah"—Allah[*] being vaguely conceived as the creator, a far-off high-god, venerated by Muhammad's tribe, the Quraysh.

In addition to these beings of the rank of high divinity, there were lesser spirits, scarcely less honored—namely, angels and various sorts of jinn, some friendly (fairylike), some hostile and demonic. It is interesting to mark the differences in character that seem to have existed between these lesser spirits. The angels were, of course, morally irreproachable and of a uniformly beneficent nature.[†] The jinn were, according to fable, created from fire two thousand years before Adam and could at will appear to human eyes or remain invisible. They could assume animal or human forms and have sexual relations and progeny. The friendly jinn were beautiful in form and kind in disposition. By way of contrast, the desert-ranging jinn, a predominantly demonic group, struck terror to Arab hearts as active agents of evil. Yet some of them could be bent to good use, for anyone who could control their movements might convert them into helpful agents to the attainment of beneficial ends, like finding treasure, building palaces, or whirling young men away on the wings of the wind to far places and new fortunes. Among the demonic beings who were always evil were the ghouls, who lay in wait where

men were destined to perish, that they might satisfy their depraved appetite for corrupt human flesh, or who robbed graves of their bodies to furnish the main dish for their midnight orgies. The ever-active imagination of the Arabs and their Persian co-religionists, which came to such colorful expression in after-times in the tales of *The Thousand and One Nights*, whiled away the hours weaving innumerable stories out of these concepts.

Particularly among the bedouin, but in every part of Arabia, animism existed. Pillarlike stones and noteworthy rocks, caves, springs, and wells were held in great respect. In some districts there were sacred palm trees on which offerings of weapons and cloth were hung. Totemism may or may not have been involved in the reverence paid to the gazelle, the eagle, the vulture, and the camel.

Mecca

Mecca offered the most conspicuous instance of veneration given to a stone—that given to the meteorite built into the corner of the Ka'ba,[*] one of the holiest shrines in Arabia. The Roman historian Diodorus Siculus (*ca.* 60 B.C.) already refers to it. In some far past the people of that part of Arabia had been startled by the rush of a meteor, which quenched its heaven-fire in Mecca's sandy glen. Afterwards the awed inhabitants worshiped it, calling it "the black stone which fell from heaven in the days of Adam." From far and near across the desert the tribes of Arabia, year after year, came on a *hajj* (pilgrimage) to offer near it sacrifices of sheep and camels and to run the circuit of the stone seven times and kiss it, in the hope of heaven's blessing on them. In the course of years the cube-shaped Ka'ba was erected in honor of the stone and to give lodgment to the gods associated with it by the pilgrims. The holy stone was placed in the southeast corner at a height that per-

---

[*] Meaning God or "the deity," like the Hebrew *El* and the Babylonian *Bel*. Arabic accent falls on second syllable.
[†] It is likely that this concept was derived from Jewish and Zoroastrian sources, through the currency in Arabia of the stories of the Old Testament and the Avesta.

[*] Literally, "the cube," for it was a cubelike structure with no exterior ornament. To enhance its appearance, it was later covered with a tissue of black cloth.

519

mitted it to be kissed by those who made the seven-fold circuit. Images of local and distant deities were placed in the dark interior. Borrowing from the stories of the Hebrews, the Meccans declared that the great patriarch Abraham, while on a visit to his outcast son Ishmael, had built the Ka'ba and imbedded the Black Stone in it.*

Only a few steps away from the Ka'ba was the holy well Zamzam, whose water was sacred to the pilgrims who ran the circuit of the shrine. Meccan tradition endowed it with a curious history. In the third century A.D., when the men of the Bani-Jurhum tribe were driven from Mecca by the Bani-Khuza'a, their sheikh, so it was said, before giving up the town, threw down into the well some suits of armor, several swords, and two gazelles of gold, and then covered all up with tamped-down earth and sand, so that when the captors of the city entered it, the location of the well was not known to them. After the Quraysh came into control of Mecca, Muhammad's grandfather, 'Abd-al-Muttalib, the leading chief, relocated the well and restored it. The Meccans could not thank him enough, for they had an old tradition that after Hagar was expelled from Abraham's tent,† she came with her little son Ishmael to the future site of their city, at that time a barren valley, and because her child was dying of thirst, she left him lying on the hot earth while she searched despairingly for water; behind her the child, in a tantrum, kicked his heels into the ground, and the waters of Zamzam welled up into the depression. In recognition of this fabled event, it was considered meritorious for pilgrims to add to the circling of the Ka'ba an exercise called the Lesser Pilgrimage, which involved a rapid pacing back and forth seven times between two hills and the Ka'ba in imitation of Hagar's anguished search. And because Ishmael was declared to be the founder of the city, it was thought well to extend this exercise into

something more arduous, called the Greater Pilgrimage. This was performed during the holy month Dhu-al-Hijja and required besides the exercises of the Lesser Pilgrimage, a tour of the hills east of Mecca taking several days and including in its scope visits to places celebrated for great events in Arabian history.

Within the Ka'ba itself a number of idols were ranged around Hubal, the chief male deity. Next in importance to him were the three goddesses, Al-Lat, al-Manat, and Al-'Uzza. Together with their associates, including the far-off Allah, who was imageless, these deities constituted a sort of pantheon for Arabia, designed to draw to Mecca the people of every region. So holy did Mecca become, in fact, that the city and its immediate environs were declared sacred territory, and pilgrims were obliged to disarm when entering it.

By agreement throughout Arabia, four months were reserved out of each year for pilgrimage and trade. During them no violence or warfare was permitted, and Mecca, along with many other places, profited by the fairs and markets that then sprang up.

In spite, however, of her pre-eminent station as the chief pilgrim-center and one of the chief crossroads towns of Arabia, Mecca had a hard struggle to keep going. There were three reasons for this, all rooted in long-standing conditions, the first geographical, the second economic, the third civic. The trouble with Mecca physically was that it lay in a barren mountain pass. Not only the city but the sacred territory around it could not sustain gardens and date palms. Hence, the city's chief reliance was upon its commerce. This was extensive enough to keep the inhabitants fairly prosperous, for Mecca was the focus for caravan routes reaching all over Arabia. Its fortunes, however, declined considerably after the Arab monopoly in the spice trade was broken by the re-opening of the old Egyptian maritime route through the Red Sea. This was a serious blow not only to the Al-Hejaz transport towns but to south Arabia as well, for it forced down prices by bringing India and Somaliland into play as trade rivals. In the

---

* Tradition was not content with this legend, however; it asserted that the first Ka'ba was built by Adam from a celestial prototype, and was rebuilt by Abraham and Ishmael.

† The Arabs learned this story from the Hebrews.

subsequent decline of Arab commerce, some hill towns had to fall back on agriculture for survival, but barren Mecca could have recourse to no such expedient. Fortunately, its position athwart the trade routes of Arabia remained secure, and her power to attract pilgrims to her Black Stone was undiminished. This saved her from the fate of Petra to the west, the marvelous rock-hewn city that by Muhammad's time had lain uninhabited for five centuries. The margin of security was none too large. Should the city be overrun, a crisis of real magnitude would threaten. Tradition had it that such a crisis actually developed in the very year in which Muhammad was born. This was the year known in Arabia as "the year of the elephant," because the Abyssinian (and Christian) governor of south Arabia marched upon Mecca in force, with a battle elephant, professing a vengeful desire to destroy the heathen shrine, but he had to retreat, just when Mecca lay defenseless before him, because of an outbreak of smallpox among his troops.

What endangered Mecca more was the civic tension between her rival factions. Civic peace was of that hair-trigger variety dependent on the precarious balance maintained by the law of vendetta. Exactly like the free-roaming bedouin tribes, the rival clans that camped together within the city's limits subscribed to the ancient principle that the murder of any member of one's own clan called for the answering death of a member of the murderer's clan. If the murder was done within a clan, the murderer would be without defense; if he was caught he was put to death, and if he escaped he became an outlaw, a member of no clan, with every man's hand against him. But when a member of a clan was murdered by an outsider, his whole clan rose up to avenge him. The principal deterrent to violent crime in Arabia and also the guarantee of civic order was, it is clear, the fear of blood vengeance.

Before the time of Muhammad the two chief tribes that contended for mastery in Mecca were the Quraysh and Khuza'a, the former having risen to dominance about the middle of the fifth century and driven the latter out. But the Quraysh tribe was itself inwardly at tension among its twelve clans, the Hashimite clan to which Muhammad belonged being one of those less inclined to civic struggle.

II The Prophet Muhammad

Muhammad belongs to the charismatic company of the prophets who by a display of complex personal traits and qualities—particularly vitality, intelligence, articulateness, and dedication—effected momentous changes in the lives of other persons. These traits and qualities did not lie dormant or merely latent but were stirred to vigorous expression. Even with the supposition of divine inspiration, it is always something of a mystery how this comes about in the development of any great man. In Muhammad's case, his genius is not any more susceptible of easy explanation than in other instances of prophetic power.

The date of Muhammad's birth is uncertain; it was perhaps in 571 A.D. According to tradition, his father, a Quraysh of the Hashimite clan, died before his birth and his mother when he was six years old. He then became a ward first of his grandfather, 'Abd-al-Muttalib, and then of his uncle, Abu Talib. It would seem that the Hashimite clan, although sharing with the rest of the Quraysh the office of trustee of the Ka'ba, its idols, its Black Stone, and the nearby sacred well, was at that time in needy circumstances. The Qur'an attests that Muhammad grew up in poverty (Sura 93, v, 6 f.). He began by sharing the religious beliefs of his community—their worship of Hubal and al-'Uzza, their belief in jinn, Satan, good and evil omens, and the like—but as he came to maturity he more and more looked upon the Meccan religion with a critical appraisal born of questioning and distaste. He was disturbed by incessant quarreling in the avowed interests of religion and honor among the Quraysh chiefs. Stronger still was his dissatisfaction with the primitive survivals in Arabian religion, the idolatrous polytheism and animism, the immorality at religious convocations and fairs, the drinking, gambling, and dancing that were fashionable, and the burial alive of unwanted infant daughters practiced not only in Mecca but throughout Arabia. He must have been puzzled by the senseless bloodshed and intertribal anarchy that accompanied the so-called "sacrilegious wars" that occurred during his youth. There was little to commend these conflicts, called sacrilegious because they broke out during the sacred month Dhu-al-Qaʻda, at the time of the fair annually held at Ukaz, three days east of Mecca. The Quraysh were involved, and Muhammad is said to have attended his uncles during one of the skirmishes, but without enthusiasm.

Why were his views changing? And particularly, how did he become receptive to ideas of God, the last judgment, and the religious life paralleling those of the Jewish and Christian religions? Our information is so scanty that we are driven largely to conjecture. There is no evidence that he had direct knowledge of the Old and New Testaments, although the Qur'an is full of references to ideas and stories that are to be found in these writings. Certainly he always expressed a high regard for written scriptures and the people who used them ("the peoples of the Book"). The venerable tradition that he learned about Judaism and Christianity during caravan trips to Syria, the first when he was twelve in the company of Abu Talib and the second when he was twenty-five and in the employ of Khadija, whom he subsequently married, must be set aside as untrustworthy. Greater importance should be given to the possible influence of Christians and Jews in caravans passing through Mecca, foreign merchants trading in Mecca, and Jews and Christians at the commercial fairs, where representatives of these faiths used to address the crowds. As a matter of fact, the Qur'an contains references that indicate that his curiosity was aroused by the exposition of these faiths which he so heard. Traditions that may be given some weight say that some of his acquaintances in Mecca were versed in the traditions of the Jews and Christians, in particular a cousin of Khadija, Waraqa by name, and the poet Umaiya (born Abi'l-Salt). What he learned he

acquired gradually and from a variety of sources. So far as Christianity is concerned, he was most influenced by Nestorian conceptions and popular traditions that reflected apocryphal as well as canonical Christian literature.°

His need to resolve his religious perplexities became more urgent during the leisure that his marriage to Khadija, a rich Qurayshite widow, brought him. Muslim traditions describe how Khadija, fifteen years his senior, mothered as well as loved him and encouraged his religious interests. The two sons, possibly three, she bore him died in infancy, to Muhammad's lasting grief; of their four daughters only Fatima survived him.†

Religious Awakening

Muhammad now seems to have entered a period of spiritual stress. He had apparently been struck by the belief common to both Jews and Christians that there would be a last judgment and a punishment of idolaters by everlasting fire. The one true God, they said, could not be represented by any image but only by

° Two things need to be said here in deference to Muslim conviction. The first is that when listing the "influences" that possibly helped the future Prophet to form his opinions we should at the same time stress the interior force that led him ultimately to transcend both his environment and what he learned from persons in it. Muslims have good grounds for contending that he was not molded and set in motion by his environment but reacted to and upon it. The second observation is that Muslims reject any implication that Muhammad took the information he received from other persons and incorporated it later in the Qur'an. The Qur'an, they believe, was not composed by Muhammad; it was revealed to him in its entirety either directly or by an angelic messenger sent down from God, and therefore could not have been his work. The most that they can acknowledge is that in the days before the revelations, he received from others a "foreknowledge," i.e., truths and moral laws made known through prophets such as Abraham, Moses, and Jesus, and by its means was enabled to understand and interpret what was later revealed to him.

† Their four daughters lived long enough to marry associates of Muhammad. Zainab married Abu-al-ʻAs; Ruqayya, Uthman, who became the third caliph; Fatima, ʻAli, the fourth caliph; Umm-Qulthum, Utayba.

522

prophetic spokesmen. Such spokesmen had in times past appeared in Palestine and Persia. Would no one come to Arabia to give warning? Surely God would send a prophet there.

His private thought during this period was quickened by persons brought close to him by marriage. Khadija's cousin, the blind Waraqa, a venerable old man who had some influence in her household, may have been a Christian, and though his information was apparently at many points misleading, Muhammad found him a useful source of knowledge concerning matters of faith and conduct. Less information was perhaps provided by a Christian slave-boy called Zaid, whom Muhammad liberated and adopted as a son, just as he had already adopted his cousin 'Ali, the child of his uncle Abu Talib. The thought that the last day and the last judgment might be near at hand began to agitate him. He wandered off to the hills about Mecca to brood privately. He was now about forty years old.

Prophetic Call

According to Muslim tradition, he visited a cave near the base of Mount Hira, a few miles north of Mecca, for days at a time. Suddenly one night ("The Night Of Power and Excellence," Muslims call it) there rose in vision before him an angel, the messenger of God, at about "two bows'-length," crying "Recite!"

> Recite: In the Name of thy Lord who created,
>   created Man of a blood-clot.
> Recite: And thy Lord is the Most Generous,
>   who taught by the Pen,
>   taught Man that he knew not. . . .[B1]

When the vision ended, Muhammad was able to reproduce the whole revelation (Sura 96 of the Qur'an, of which only the first lines are here given). He rushed home in great excitement, half doubting, half believing. Later, he was to defend the authenticity of his experience in these words (Sura 53):

> By the Star when it plunges,
> your comrade is not astray, neither errs,
>   nor speaks he out of caprice.
> This is naught but a revelation revealed,
>   taught him by one terrible in power,
>   very strong; he stood poised,
>   being on the higher horizon,
>   then drew near and suspended hung,
>   two bows'-length away, or nearer,
> then revealed to his servant that he revealed.
>   His heart lies not of what he saw;
> what, will you dispute with him what he sees?[B2]*

Yet at first Muhammad's heart did nearly belie that which he saw. He had fears for his sanity. According to an early tradition (recorded by al-Tabiri as having come first from 'A'isha, daughter of Abu Bakr and one of Muhammad's favorite wives), after meeting with Gabriel he hurried home to his wife Khadija.

> I said: 'I am worried about myself.' Then I told her the whole story. She said: 'Rejoice, for by Allah, Allah will never put thee to shame. By Allah, thou art mindful of thy kinsfolk, speakest truthfully, renderest what is given thee in trust, bearest burdens, art ever hospitable to the guest, and dost always uphold the right against any wrong.' Then she took me to Waraqa (to whom) she said: 'Give ear to [him].' So he questioned me, and I told him (the whole) story. He said: 'This is the *namus* [the Greek word *nomos*, Law] which was sent down upon Moses.'[C1]

But Muhammad was not at once comforted. Another early tradition has him say:

> Now it so happened that no creature of Allah was more loathsome to me than a poet or a man possessed by jinn,† the sight of neither of whom I could bear. So I

---

* It will be noticed that this passage from the Qur'an does not identify the angel nor the sura. The traditional account, that of Ibn Hisham, which says the angel was Gabriel, is therefore questioned even by some Muslim authorities. In other words, it is no longer unquestioned that Sura 96 was the first revelation and Gabriel the angel who brought it.
† In popular belief poets and soothsayers were inspired by a familiar spirit among the jinn. Muhammad seems to have been in doubt as to whether the voice he heard really came from a heavenly messenger or from a mere jinn. In the latter case he would be "possessed," or even "mad."

said: 'That one (referring to himself) has become either a poet or a man jinn-possessed. The Quraish will never say this about me. I shall go to some high mountain cliff and cast myself down therefrom so that I may kill myself and be at rest.' I went off with this in mind, but when I was in the midst of the mountains I heard a voice from heaven saying: 'O Muhammad, thou art (indeed) Allah's Apostle, and I am Gabriel.' At that I raised my head to the skies, and there was Gabriel in clear human form, with his feet on the edges of the skies. . . . I began to turn my face to the whole expanse of the skies, but no matter in what direction I looked there I saw him.[C2]

Other traditions somewhat vary this account, but without attempting to straighten out the tangle of fact and tradition, we may conclude that Muhammad, after a period of self-questioning lasting perhaps many months, finally came to look upon himself as being, miraculously enough, a true prophet (*nabi*) and apostle (*rasul*) of Allah, that is to say, a messenger of the one and only God already known to the Jews and Christians. When it began to appear that the strange experiences, in which rhapsodies in Arabic flowed across his lips, would continue to occur spontaneously, without his willing them, he came to believe that Allah was using him as a mouthpiece; the verses he uttered, half in trance, were real revelations. His first doubts about them disappeared. He now saw what his wife and friends asserted was true, that they made sense. At last Arabia was being provided with a scripture—of later date and greater authority than the scriptures of the Jews and Christians.

The Meccan Ministry

After a short period of consultation with relatives and friends, he appeared in the streets and in the courtyard of the Ka'ba to recite "in the name of the Lord" the verses of the revelations. The listening Meccans gaped and then, hearing strange doctrine, broke into ridicule. The man must be mad! The incredible substance of his preaching seemed to be a warning of a divine judgment day, together with predictions of the resurrection of the body and of a consuming fire. They gave him a poor reception, but in spite of that he kept coming back day after day to recite the rhythmically composed verses that had come to him.

> When the sun shall be darkened,
> when the stars shall be thrown down,
> when the mountains shall be set moving,
> when the pregnant camels shall be neglected,
> when the savage beasts shall be mustered,
> when the seas shall be set boiling,
> when the souls shall be coupled [reunited?]
> when the buried infant shall be asked for what sin she was slain,
> when the scrolls shall be unrolled,
> when heaven shall be stripped off,
> when Hell shall be set blazing,
> when Paradise shall be brought nigh,
> then shall a soul know what it has produced.[B3]

Could much credence be accorded to such an utterance? his critics cried, or to what follows?

> And when the Blast shall sound,
> upon the day when a man shall flee from his brother,
> his mother, his father,
> his consort, his sons,
> every man that day shall have business to suffice him.
> Some faces on that day shall shine
> laughing, joyous;
> Some faces on that day shall be dusty,
> O'erspread with darkness—
> those—they are the unbelievers, the libertines.[B4]

But he defied his critics as "criers of lies";

> Woe that day unto those who cry it lies,
> who cry lies to the Day of Doom;
> and none cries lies to it but every guilty aggressor.
> When our signs are recited to him, he says,
> 'Fairy-tales of the ancients!'
> No indeed; but that they were earning has rusted
> upon their hearts.
> No indeed; but upon that day they shall be veiled
> from their Lord,
> then they shall roast in Hell.
> Then it shall be said to them, 'This is that you cried lies to.'[B5]

There was in the early revelations not so much on the unity of God (which was taken for granted) but a great deal on the power and final judgment of God. The verses quoted God as speaking in the first person plural:

Behold, We shall cast upon thee a weighty word. . . .
Surely We have sent unto you a Messenger
as a witness over you, even as We sent to
Pharaoh a Messenger.[B6]

Unimpressed though they were at first, his hearers, especially those of the Quraysh tribe, at last became seriously disturbed. They did not object so much to Muhammad's insistence that there is but one God, but they stiffened with opposition at his claim to be a prophet, for this seemed to them to be a claim to leadership, as if he intended to assert his dominance over the whole community. He could talk all he liked about his belief in the resurrection of the dead and a last judgment, but he was not entitled to authority over the city.

It would not serve our purpose to go into the chronology of the ensuing trials and tribulations of Muhammad during a whole decade of disheartening community opposition. His following seemed doomed to be small. Khadija was perhaps the first to accept his mission, believing in it even before he himself did. Her faith was quickly echoed by his adopted sons, Zaid, the liberated slave-boy, and 'Ali, the son of Abu Talib. A very important convert, one of the first and destined to be Muhammad's first successor, was Abu Bakr, a kinsman from the Quraysh tribe, a merchant and therefore a person of some prestige. Abu Bakr's proselyting for the new faith secured five other early converts, among whom Uthman, son of Affan and later the third caliph, was outstanding. But conversions came slowly. In the first four years they numbered only about forty, including wives of male believers and liberated slaves.

Muhammad's revelations were meanwhile continuing. When he appeared to recite them, the hostile members of the Quraysh did all they could to break up his gatherings. They scattered thorns about, threw filth and dirt on him and his hearers, and stirred up the rowdies to hurl insults and threats. They longed to be able to use violence, but from this they were deterred by the stout protection of his uncle, Abu Talib. In an attempt to prevent his public appearances, the Ummayads, and other hostile elements of the Quraysh issued a solemn ban against the Hashimites, the branch of the tribe to which Muhammad belonged, and forced them to retire to the quarter of the town where Abu Talib lived—a narrow defile among the hills—for over two years. But the rest of the community brought pressure to have the ban removed. Then greater blows were to fall on Muhammad. Khadija, his greatest support, died, and five weeks later his protector, faithful Abu Talib, still unconverted but nonetheless always loyal. This severe double bereavement weakened the position of Muhammad in the eyes of his enemies, and though the vendetta law still shielded him, it was apparent that some of the Hashimites were becoming disaffected and might be persuaded to consent to his imprisonment or execution.

He therefore began to look afield. An attempt to establish himself in Ta'if, some sixty miles to the southeast, proved abortive. His cause seemed almost hopeless. Then suddenly, hope revived. During the truce period of 620 A.D. he held a lengthy conference at the Ukaz fair with six men from Yathrib (Medina), who thought he might be their man. Their native city, three hundred miles to the north, had not recovered from the effects of open dissension caused by blood feuds between two Arab tribes, the Aws and the Khazraj, and stood to benefit if someone could be brought in to impose a firm rule over them. They agreed to prepare their town for the Prophet's coming. By the next pilgrimage season they reported progress, and in the following year the preparations for Muhammad's assumption of prophetic leadership were complete.

The Hijra (622 A.D.)

Secrecy had been well maintained, but at the last moment the Meccans got wind of the matter, and the hostile Quraysh (chiefly Ummayads under the leadership of Abu Sufyan) determined to strike and strike quickly. But Muhammad and Abu Bakr escaped to a cave on Mt. Thaur, and when the pursuit died down, mounted camels and successfully made the Hijra (the Migration) to Yathrib, ordinarily eleven days off, in the short time of eight days.

Establishment of the Theocracy at Medina

After several years of establishing himself as an unquestioned prophet, Muhammad was given astonishingly unrestricted power over the town, whose name was changed in his honor to Medina (*Madinat an nabi,* the City of the Prophet). He set about the erection of a house of worship, the first mosque. Rapidly and simply, he evolved a new cultus. Weekly services on Friday, prostration during prayer (at first toward Jerusalem, but when the Jews in Medina withstood conversion, toward Mecca), a call to prayer from the mosque's roof (at first only for the Friday services, and then every day at the times for private prayer), the taking up of alms for the poor and for the support of the cause—these and other practices were soon established.

Perhaps to supply his followers with arms, and treasure, or perhaps to strike at Mecca's source of power, he led out a small force to waylay a Meccan caravan. War with Mecca was the result. In the first engagement Muhammad had the better of it, in the next the Meccans, and then the Meccans prepared for a grand assault. With ten thousand men they invested Medina, but Muhammad, probably on the advice of a Persian follower, had a trench dug around the town. The "Battle of the Ditch" that followed persuaded the Meccans that Muhammad was beyond their taking. In January 630 Muhammad in his turn marched forth with ten thousand men. Mecca, whose trade routes had been severed by Muhammad, surrendered. The Prophet of Allah, at a bound, reached the stature of the greatest chief in Arabia. As such he acted with great magnanimity toward his former fellow-townsmen, excluding only a handful of them from the general amnesty he proclaimed.

One of his first acts was to go reverently to the Ka'ba; yet he showed no signs of yielding to the ancient Meccan polytheism. After honoring the Black Stone and riding seven times around the shrine, he ordered the destruction of the idols within it and the scraping of the paintings of Abraham and the angels from the walls. He sanctioned the use of the well Zamzam and restored the boundary pillars defining the sacred territory around Mecca. Thenceforth no Muslim would have cause to hesitate about going on a pilgrimage to the ancient holy city.

Muhammad now made sure of his political and religious ascendancy in Arabia. Active opponents near at hand were conquered by the sword, and tribes far away were invited sternly to send delegations offering their allegiance. Before his sudden death in 632 he knew he was well on the way to unifying the Arab tribes under a theocracy governed by the will of the one and only God, Allah. Because he was no longer so conscious of imminent divine judgment on the world, an immediate task absorbed him—the moral elevation and unification of the Arab tribes. On his last visit to Mecca, just before his death, tradition pictures him as preaching a memorable sermon in which he proclaimed a central fact of the Muslim movement in these words: "O ye men! harken unto my words and take ye them to heart! Know ye that every Muslim is a brother unto every other Muslim, and that ye are now one brotherhood."[D1]

Muhammad's death was unexpected, and the problem of choosing a new leader almost split up his followers, but in a desperate move to forestall such a disaster Abu Bakr, whom Muhammad had often designated to lead the prayers when he had to be absent, was chosen to be his successor (or caliph). Muhammad's death therefore only momentarily checked the rapid spread of his movement.

III The Faith and Practice of Islam

The teachings of Muhammad became after his death the basis of the faith (*iman*) and obligation or duty (*din*) of Islam. Many elements, not so much of the faith as of the practice, were, so far as their final formulation is concerned, the product of later times, for the process by which Muhammad's utterances were put into permanent form and distilled into a creed and way of life did not take place overnight. But this matter was never allowed to have secondary importance. Divergent groups appealed to Muhammad's remembered talk and conduct; faithfulness to his instruction and example was from the first required. The differences in interpretation and action that gave rise to the sects, still to be described, were in no case marked by consciousness of departure from the example set by Muhammad.

Because the faith and practice of Muslims after Muhammad's time were so very closely related to his teaching and personal example, it seems well to consider them now, even before we follow the story of the spread of Islam, for in essence what the Qur'an said and what Muhammad did, although still not finally condensed into fixed articles of faith and prescribed practices, inspired, motivated, and guided that spread.

Ultimately, Muslim authorities subsumed most of Islam under three heads: *iman,* or articles of faith, *ihsan,* or right conduct, and *'ibadat,* or religious duty. Because faith (iman) and conduct (ihsan) were set forth in the Qur'an, and religious duty ('ibadat) was defined later, we shall consider the former two first.

A. ARTICLES OF FAITH. In the famous Muslim creedal formula the first part reads: *la ilāha illa Allāh* "(There is) no god but God." This is the most important article in Muslim theology. No statement about God seemed to Muhammad more fundamental than the declaration that God is one, and no sin seemed to him so unpardonable as associating another being with God on terms of equality.* God stands alone and supreme. He existed before any other being or thing, is self-subsistent, omniscient, omnipotent ("all-seeing, all-hearing, all-willing"). He is the creator, and in the awful day of judgment he is the sole arbiter who shall save the believer out of the dissolution of the world and place him in paradise.

In one respect, however, in its numerous references to God's "guidance," the Qur'an is varied and loose enough in statement (as is not unusual in the world's scriptures) to be open to differing interpretations. Does God "guide" men by challenging them to choose aright in freedom, or by determining their choices in advance (predestination)? Some passages imply free will, but more suggest predestination. (This variance should occasion no surprise. Muhammad was a prophet who over a period of twenty years or more spoke out of ecstatic states. His motives were not to write a systematic theology but rather to speak to the people and tell them what they needed at a particular time to hear.) Although Sunni Muslims have, as we shall see later (p. 544), generally come to the conclusion that the Qur'an comes down on the side of predestination, it is possible to reconcile the variant passages, if one keeps in mind the conditions of desert life, as Muhammad must have.† To follow I.

---

* The Arabian idolaters who worshiped many gods and goddesses represented by stocks and stones were obviously guilty of this sin of sins, but so also were the Christians who said, "God is the third of three."

† Typical of the variant passages are the following. Freedom of choice is implied in: "Say: 'The truth is from your Lord; so let whosoever will believe, and let whosoever will disbelieve.' "B7 A Meccan passage says: "If you do good, it is your own souls you do good to."B8 This is matched by a Medinan passage: "Whatever evil visits thee is of thyself."B9 Freedom of action is implied also in passages dealing with the forgiveness of God, as for instance in this: "Whoever does evil, or wrongs himself, and then prays God's forgiveness, he shall find God All-forgiving, All-compassionate;"B10 or this: "God shall turn [in forgiveness] only towards those who do evil in ignorance, then shortly repent."B11 But many other passages say God not only has perfect foreknowledge of men's actions but controls their choices as well. As to foreknowledge: "Very well he knows you, when He produced you

527

Goldziher's illuminating comments: "If, in many passages of the Koran it is said: 'Allah guides whom he will, and lets whom he will go astray,' such passages do not imply that God directly brings the latter class into the evil path. The decisive word *adalla* is not to be taken in such a connection as meaning to 'lead astray,' but to allow to go astray, not to trouble about a person, not to show him the way out. . . . Let us conjure up the picture of a lonely wanderer in the desert,—it is from this idea that the language of the Koran concerning leading and wandering has sprung. The wanderer errs in the boundless expanse, gazing about for the right direction to his goal. So is man in his wanderings through life. He who, through faith and good works, has deserved the good will of God, him he rewards with his guidance. He lets the evildoer go astray. He leaves him to his fate, and takes his protection from him. He does not offer him the guiding hand, but he does not bring him directly to the evil path. . . . Guidance is the reward of the good. 'Allah does not guide the wicked.' (Sura 9, v. 110)."[E1]

Allah reveals his will and guides men in three distinct ways: through Muhammad, his messenger; through the Qur'an, his revelation; and through the angels. (Considered in another way, the three are part of one process: revelation came to Muhammad by the agency of an angel. Revelation is the thing.)

The second half of the Muslim creedal formula declares: *Muhammad rasūl Allāh,* "Muhammad is the messenger (or prophet) of Allah." It seems self-evident to Muslims that God must reveal himself through prophets, else men could not know him. God would not leave himself without witness, and so there has been a long line of such prophets, including Abraham, Moses, and Jesus. But Muhammad is the last and greatest of them all, the "seal" of those who appeared before him. None is his equal, either in knowledge or in authority; none has received or handed down so perfect a revelation. But though his authority is supreme, he was not a divine being appearing in the flesh. He was human like the rest of men. Nor did he pretend to supernatural powers; he performed no miracles, instituted no mystical, deifying sacraments, ordained no holy priesthood, set apart none to a sacred office by ordination or a mystical laying on of hands. He was simply man at his best, and God was still the wholly Other, with whom he was united in will but not in substance. The most celebrated suggestion in Muslim tradition that Muhammad had a special relationship with heaven is to be found in the traditions (hadiths) concerning the Mir'aj or Night Journey of the Prophet to paradise. These traditions are based on a passage in Sura XVII, 1, which says: "Glory be to Him Who carried His servant by night from the Holy Mosque [at Mecca] to the Further Mosque [at Jerusalem], the precincts of which We have blessed, that We might show him some of Our signs."[B19] The traditions vary with those who tell or attest to them, but they add up to something like this story: On a certain night while the Prophet still lived in Mecca (a night whose anniversary is celebrated each year throughout the Muslim world) Gabriel came, cleansed him within, and took him through the air (on the back of the winged steed Buraq) first to Jerusalem and then up through the seven heavens, where as he passed through he spoke successively with Adam, John the Baptist and Jesus, Joseph, Enoch, Aaron, Moses, and (in the seventh heaven) Abraham. Finally, without Gabriel, who could go no further perhaps, he was lifted on a flying carpet (*a rafraf*) into the great space beyond to the very pres-

---

from the earth, and when you were yet unborn in your mothers' wombs."[B12] More to the point: "Whomsoever God will, He leads astray, and whomsoever He will, He sets him on a straight path."[B13] God declares indeed: "We elected them, and We guided them to a straight path."[B14] Furthermore, God rules men's inner lives. "Whomsoever God desires to guide, He expands his breast to Islam; whomsoever He desires to lead astray, He makes his breast narrow, tight."[B15] An early sura is even more explicit: "But will you shall not, unless God wills."[B16] And yet there are still other passages that seem to fall between the two extremes. In Sura 6:78 we hear Abraham saying: "If my Lord does not guide me I shall surely be of the people gone astray."[B17] Freedom and divine determinism seemingly appear side by side in a Medinan passage: "Whomsoever God leads astray, no guide he has; He leaves them in their insolence blindly wandering."[B18]

The Dome of the Rock, Jerusalem. At the foot of Mt. Moriah, within the southeastern end of the city wall, stands this fine example of early Muslim architecture. Known to many as the Mosque of Omar, it marks the site of the temple of Solomon and the rock where, reputedly, Abraham prepared to sacrifice Isaac. Muslim tradition says that from the rock Muhammad ascended to heaven on the steed Buraq. (Courtesy of the Arab Information Center.)

ence of Allah, who spoke with him about many un-utterable matters and told him: "O Muhammad, I take you as a friend just as I took Abraham as a friend. I am speaking to you just as I spoke face to face with Moses." C3 Thus Muhammad is demonstrated to have a status in God's sight at least equal to that of any of his prophetic predecessors. But even

with such a story to give it encouragement, no claim is made by Muslims that Muhammad was other than human, even though Allah viewed him with special favor.

The second way by which Allah guides men is through the Qur'an. The Qur'an, revealed to Muhammad, is the undistorted and final word of Allah to mankind. The traditional Muslim position is that the Qur'an is identical with words transmitted, without change, from "the well-preserved tablet," "the mother of the Book," an eternal and uncreated archetype that are the very words of God himself. Previous authoritative revelations, such as the Jewish and Christian scriptures, are also genuine transmissions from the Umm-ul-Kitab, the uncreated heavenly archetype, but they have been changed and corrupted by men and are therefore not absolutely true like the Qur'an.*

The third means by which Allah makes known his will is through the angels. Of these the chief is Gabriel, the agent of revelation, who is described in terms reminiscent of Zoroastrian angelology as "the faithful spirit" and "the spirit of holiness." Allah sits in the seventh heaven on a high throne, surrounded by angels who serve him exactly as kings are served by their ministers and attendants.

The Devil (called either *Iblis,* a contraction of Diabolos, or *Shaitin,* the Zoroastrian Satan) is an

angel who fell through pride and is now an accursed tempter. He and his assistants busy themselves on earth to obstruct the plans of Allah and tempt men to go astray. This sounds worse than things really are, for—at least in the light of the later Medina suras—because Allah wills all, the scope of the Devil's operations is in fact restricted to Allah's permissive decrees and calculated noninterferences.

As to the last judgment, Muhammad's revelations contain phrases resembling those of Zoroastrian, Jewish, and Christian apocalypticism. There will be "signs" of its imminence: portents, ominous rumblings, strange occurrences in nature; then, the last trumpet, at whose sound the dead will rise and all souls will assemble before Allah's judgment throne. During the judgment itself the books in which each man's deeds have been recorded will be read, and eternal judgment will be passed accordingly.

Heaven and hell are concretely described.

> God has cursed the unbelievers, and prepared
> for them a Blaze,
> therein to dwell for ever; they shall find
> neither protector nor helper.

Upon the day when their faces are turned about in the Fire they shall say, 'Ah, would we had obeyed God and the Messenger!'[B20]

> The Companions of the Left (O Companions of the Left!)
> mid burning winds and boiling waters
> and the shadow of a smoking blaze
> neither cool, neither goodly; . . .
> Then you erring ones, you that cried lies,
> you shall eat of a tree called Zakkoum. . . .[B21]

> It is a tree that comes forth in
> the root of Hell;
> its spathes are as the heads of Satans,
> and they eat of it, and of it fill
> their bellies,
> then on top of it they have a brew
> of boiling water. . . .[B22]

> Lo, the Tree of Ez-Zakkoum
> is the food of the guilty,
> like molten copper, bubbling in the belly
> as boiling water bubbles.
> 'Take him, and thrust him into the midst of Hell,

---

* This conviction concerning the infallibility of the Qur'an assumes that the text was transmitted without error. Part of the Qur'an, it seems certain, was written down in Muhammad's lifetime under his supervision and arranged into suras. It was not completely left to oral transmission. It is further assumed that the "Memorizers" (*huffaz*) who preserved part of the Qur'anic materials before they were reduced to writing, made no errors of recollection. There can be little doubt that even though Muhammad might have arranged the materials differently and made some revisions in the text had he seen it, the Qur'an as now preserved conveys the original content he gave it. According to tradition, in the year which followed Muhammad's death Abu Bakr, on the advice of Umar, who feared the companions might all die off or perish in battle, ordered Muhammad's secretary, Zaid ibn Thabit, to make a collection of the revelations. The collection was composed from "ribs of palm-leaves and tablets of white stone and from the breasts of men," we read. There is strong evidence that other collections were made that varied in containing more or less materials and to a certain extent in wording. A second and variant tradition says that the final canonical text resulted from the work of a committee appointed by the Caliph Uthman and headed again by Muhammad's secretary. Four identical copies were made, and all previous texts were pronounced defective. The Uthmanic text met some resistance, but finally prevailed.

then pour over his head the chastisement of
　　boiling water!'
'Taste! Surely thou art the mighty, the noble.
This is that concerning which you were doubting.'[B23]

On the other hand, the Companions of the Right, especially those who "outstrip" their fellows in faithfulness, enter gardens of delight.

Surely the godfearing shall be in a station secure
　　among gardens and fountains,
robed in silk and brocade, set face to face.[B24]

　　Upon close-wrought couches
　reclining upon them, set face to face,
immortal youths going round about them
with goblets, and ewers, and a cup from a spring
　　(no brows throbbing, no intoxication)
and such fruits as they shall choose,
and such flesh of fowl as they desire,
　　and wide-eyed houris
　　as the likeness for that they laboured. . . .
a recompense for that they laboured. . . .
and We made them spotless virgins,
　　chastely amorous, like of age
　for the Companions of the Right.＊[B25]

B. RIGHT CONDUCT. Muhammad gave much thought to the behavior of his followers and must be said to have legislated for them so comprehensively and with such a uniform purpose of elevating their morals to a higher level than before—the high level of an inclusive brotherhood instead of the lower level of divisive tribal organization—that a wide range of the acts of the Muslims of his time, of either sex, from

---

＊ It is an interesting fact that these promises of houris in paradise date from Muhammad's early Meccan days. But later on, perhaps to correct false conclusions, he more than once suggested that the faithful take their *wives* with them to paradise. E.g., Sura 13:23: "Gardens of Eden which they shall enter, and also those who were righteous of their fathers, and their wives, and their descendants."[B26] These predictions can be reconciled, as follows: "Although the Koran hardly provides a basis for such a view, the earliest tradition of Islam supports the definite conception that the virgins of Paradise were once earthly wives. The Prophet himself is supposed to have said: 'They are devout wives, and those who with grey hair and watery eyes died in old age. After death Allah re-makes them into virgins' (Tabari, Tasfir xxvii)."[F]

birth to death, was provided for. The following selection of some of the principal moral regulations of Muhammad will show how reformatory they initially were. The laws prohibiting wine and gambling, as well as the regulations covering the relations of the sexes and granting a higher status to women, must have meant to his early followers a considerable change in their way of life.

It is not piety, that you turn your faces
　　to the East and to the West.
　　True piety is this:
to believe in God, and the Last Day,
the angels, the Book, and the Prophets,
to give of one's substance, however cherished,
　　to kinsmen, and orphans,
　　the needy, the traveller, beggars,
　　　and to ransom the slave,
to perform the prayer, to pay the alms.
And they who fulfil their covenant
when they have engaged in a covenant,
　　and endure with fortitude
　　misfortune, hardship and peril,
these are they who are true in their faith,
　　these are the truly godfearing.[B27]

. . . and to be good to parents,
　　whether one or both of them
　　attains old age with thee;
　　　say not to them 'Fie'
　　　neither chide them, but
　　speak unto them words
　　　respectful,
　　and lower to them the
　　wing of humbleness
　　out of mercy and say,
　　　'My Lord,
　　have mercy upon them,
　　as they raised me up
　　when I was little.'[B28]

And slay not your children for fear of poverty;
　We will provide for you and them;
surely the slaying of them is a grievous sin.
　And approach not fornication;
surely it is an indecency, and evil as a way.[B29]

Give the orphans their property, and do not exchange the corrupt for the good; and devour not their property with your property; surely
　　that is a great crime.

If you fear that you will not act justly
towards the orphans, marry such women
as seem good to you, two, three, four;
but if you fear you will not be equitable,
then only one, or what your right hands own;
so it is likelier you will not be partial.
And give the women their dowries as a gift
spontaneous; but if they are pleased
to offer you any of it, consume it
    with wholesome appetite. . . .
Test well the orphans, until they reach
the age of marrying; then, if you perceive
in them right judgment, deliver to them
their property; consume it not wastefully
    and hastily
ere they are grown. . . .
Those who devour the property of orphans
unjustly, devour Fire in their bellies,
and shall assuredly roast in a Blaze.[B30]

Marry the spouseless among you, and your
slaves and handmaidens that are righteous;
if they are poor, God will enrich them
of His bounty; God is All-embracing,
    All-knowing.
And let those who find not the means to
marry be abstinent till God enriches them
of His bounty.[B31]

When you divorce women, and they have reached
their term [three months], then retain them honourably
or set them free honourably; do not retain them
by force, to transgress.[B32]

And fight in the way of God with those
who fight with you, but aggress not: God loves
  . not the aggressors. . . .
Fight them, till there is no persecution
and the religion is God's; then if they
give over, there shall be no enmity
    save for the evildoers.[B33]

Permitted to you is the beast of the flocks,
except that which is now recited to you. . . .
    Forbidden to you are
carrion, blood, the flesh of swine,
what has been hallowed to other than God,
the beast strangled, the beast beaten down,
the beast fallen to death, the beast gored,
and that devoured by beasts of prey—
excepting that you have sacrificed duly—
as also things sacrificed to idols.[B34]

O believers, wine and arrow-shuffling [gambling],
idols and divining-arrows are an abomination,
some of Satan's work; so avoid it; haply
    so you will prosper.
Satan only desires to precipitate enmity
and hatred between you in regard to wine
and arrow-shuffling, and to bar you from
the remembrance of God, and from prayer.
Will you then desist? And obey God
and obey the Messenger, and beware.[B35]

C. RELIGIOUS DUTY. We come now to that part of Muslim religious practice that, except for the fast of the month of Ramadan, which is prescribed in the Qur'an, took some time to fix in tradition. It is summed up as the "Five Pillars" (al-Arkan). For many centuries now, all Muslims have felt obligated to engage in the following:

1. *Repetition of the creed* (*Shahada*). *La ilāha illa Allāh; Muhammad rasūl Allāh:* "There is no god but Allah, and Muhammad is the prophet of Allah." Acceptance of this confession of faith and its faithful repetition constitute the first step in being a Muslim. These simple words are heard everywhere in the Muslim world and come down as if out of the sky from the minaret in the muezzin's calls to prayer.

2. *Prayer* (*Salat*). The good Muslim reserves time each day for five acts of devotion and prayer. The first comes at dawn, the second at midday, the others at mid-afternoon, sunset, and at the fall of darkness. In town or country or on the desert, the devotee goes through a ritual of ablution, rolls out his prayer-rug, and bows down toward Mecca, to offer to Allah less a petition than ascriptions of praise and declarations of submission to his holy will. It is common simply to repeat the Fatiha, the Arabian Lord's Prayer (Sura 1):

Praise belongs to God, the Lord of all Being,
the All-merciful, the All-compassionate,
    the Master of the Day of Doom.

Thee only we serve; to Thee alone we pray for succour.
    Guide us in the straight path,
the path of those whom Thou hast blessed,
not of those against whom Thou art wrathful,
    nor of those who are astray.[B36]

Friday is the special day of public prayer for all adult males, when the faithful assemble in the mosque, under the leadership of the *imam,* usually at noon, or perhaps at sunset. The service is in the mosque's paved courtyard, or where the worship area has been covered over, under the dome or vault.* The men have assembled at the call from the minaret, have left their shoes at the entrance, have gone to the pool or fountain to perform their ablutions (of hands, mouth, nostrils, face, forearms, neck, and feet), have sat for a few minutes to hear a "reader" (*qari*) recite from the Qur'an, and then on the appearance of the imam have taken their places in long rows, facing Mecca and spaced so as to allow their throwing themselves forward in "prostration" on their prayer-mats. During the ritual prayer (or *salat*) the imam recites all the necessary words and all the worshipers silently and as one follow him in his motions, standing erect when he does so, or inclining the head and body, or dropping on their knees to place their hands upon the ground a little in front of them and press their foreheads to the pavement, in "prostration," at the exact moment they see him do so. After the prayers, the imam usually preaches a sermon having for its purpose the exposition of Muslim doctrine.

3. *Almsgiving.* This is called *Zakāt.* Its general meaning is that of a free-will offering, consisting of gifts to the poor, the needy, debtors, slaves, wayfarers, beggars, and charities of various kinds. In the early days of Islam it was a "loan to Allah", exacted from Muslims in money or in kind. It was gathered by religious officials into a common treasury and distributed in part as charity to the poor and in part to mosques and imams for repairs and administrative expenses. It was a fund quite apart from the tribute (the *jizyat*) exacted of non-Muslims for political and military expenses. The Zakāt was once universally obligatory, although not, strictly speaking, a tax. It is now in most regions voluntary, yet even there no one is expected to neglect it, on pain of exciting contempt.

---

* If women attend, they ordinarily stay behind screens and are not seen.

4. *The fast during the sacred month of Ramadan.* Except for the sick and ailing, this fast is laid upon all as an obligation and is carried out in this manner: as soon as it becomes possible to distinguish between a white thread and a black at dawn, no food and drink are to be taken until at sundown the difference between the threads is no longer perceptible to the eye.

5. *Pilgrimage (Hajj).* Once in a lifetime every Muslim, man or woman, is expected, unless it is impossible, to make a pilgrimage (a hajj) to Mecca. The pilgrim should be there during the sacred month Dhu-al-Hijja so as to enter with thousands of others into the annual mass observance of the circumambulation of the Ka'ba, the Lesser and Greater pilgrimages, and the Great Feast.

When war or other untoward conditions do not interfere, a great part of the pilgrims nowadays go by rail and ship or by air to the coast below Mecca or to Cairo or Jerusalem. In ancient times they joined far-traveling over-land caravans, which in the last stages of the journey crossed the desert from Basra in Iraq, or followed the trade routes from Yemen, Cairo, or Damascus. Each such caravan had as an indispensable part of its insignia (at least since the thirteenth century) a camel bearing on its back an unoccupied *mahmil,* or richly ornamented litter, the resplendent symbol of the piety and sacrificial spirit of the pilgrims.

Since Muhammad's day all pilgrims have been required, whether rich or poor, to enter the sacred precincts of Mecca wearing the same kind of seamless white garments and practicing the proper abstinences: no food or drink by day, continence, and no harm to living things, animal or vegetable. This is the first of a long series of leveling practices by which people of all countries and languages are made to mingle in one unifying mass observance without distinction of race or class.

The principal ceremonies in Mecca begin with circumambulation of the Ka'ba. The pilgrims start at the Black Stone and run three times fast and four times slowly around the building, stopping each time at the southeast corner to kiss the Black Stone, or, if

The Ka'ba at Mecca. *Pilgrims in white robes (including women with covered heads, some in black) gather around the holy shrine on marked lines establishing the distances for prayer. The Ka'ba is covered with a black silk cloth embroidered with inscriptions in ornamental Arabic characters. The pilgrims have come to circle the Ka'ba seven times and kiss or touch the Black Stone. (Courtesy of Saudi Arabian Public Relations Bureau.)*

the crowd is too great, to touch it with hand or stick, or perhaps just look keenly at it. The next observance is the Lesser Pilgrimage, which consists of trotting, with shoulders shaking, seven times between Safa and Marwa, two low hills across the valley from each other—this in imitation of frantic Hagar seeking in despair for water for wailing little Ishmael.

On the eighth day of Dhu-al-Hijja the Greater Pilgrimage begins. The pilgrims in a dense mass move off toward Arafat, a day's foot-journey to the east. Some pass the night at Mina, the half-way point, the rest go on. The next day the pilgrims, all arrived, stand or move slowly about, from noon to sunset, over the Arafat plain, absorbed in pious meditation. After sunset they begin running en masse, and with the greatest possible noise and commotion, to Muzdalifa, a fourth of the way back to Mecca, where they pass the night in the open. At sunrise they continue to Mina, where each pilgrim casts seven pebbles down the slope below the mountain road, crying out at each throw: "In the name of God! Allah is almighty!" Those who are able to do so then make the Great

Feast possible by offering as a sacrifice a camel, sheep, or horned animal, keeping in mind the injunction in the pilgrimage sura of the Qur'an (Sura XX:37):

> Mention God's Name over them, standing in ranks;
> then, when their flanks collapse, eat of them
> and feed the beggar and the suppliant.[B37]

That is to say, the sacrificer eats part of the meat and gives the rest of it to the poorer pilgrims who stand by, whoever they may be.

The three days following are spent in eating, talking, and merry-making, and then as a final act of the pilgrimage all return to Mecca and make the circuit of the Ka'ba once more.

IV   The Spread of Islam

It may be doubted whether the spread of Islam, at least in its early stages, was the result of calculation. Neither the devout Muslim view that it was a purely religious movement engaged in a far-sighted effort to save the world, by force if necessary, nor the medieval Christian view that it was the outgrowth first of pure imposture and then of greed, will bear scrutiny. Both religion and greed may be granted to have played their part as motivating impulses, but it would be closer to the mark to say that Muhammad unified the bedouins for the first time in their history and thus made it possible for them, as a potentially powerful military group, to yoke together their economic need and their religious faith in an overwhelming drive out of the desert into lands where plenty beckoned. They began with scarcely more than the hope of carrying out a gigantic raid for booty that might be brought back into the desert, but the weakness of the Byzantine and Persian empires, exhausted by years of strife with each other, made a permanent conquest of the Near East easy. Only then did calculated efforts to extend the spread of Islam make their appearance. On the whole, then, the Muslim con-

quests represent one more of the long succession of Semitic migrations from the Arabian desert—the last and the greatest.

Abu Bakr and the Unification of Arabia for Conquest

When Muhammad died so suddenly, he had designated no successor (caliph). His followers had to decide who should exercise that function. Should the principle of succession be that of heredity, or should the caliphs be elected by (and from) some properly qualified group? The answer to these questions was supplied differently at different times by the three major political parties of early Muslim history. The Companions (so-called because they were composed of Muhammad's closest associates, the Muhajirin, or Emigrants, and the Ansar, or Supporters) assumed that the caliph should be elected from their number. A later group, the Legitimists, following the hereditary principle of succession, thought the caliphs should be Muhammad's descendants through Fatima and her husband, 'Ali, Muhammad's son-in-law and cousin. Later still, the Ummayads, as the leaders of Muhammad's tribe, sought to be the sole determinants of the question who should occupy the caliphate.

The Companions were the first to act and gained the initial decision. Abu Bakr was their choice for caliph, the first of four thus chosen. His caliphate lasted only a year, for he soon followed the Prophet in death, but his administration was notable for two things: great firmness in bringing to heel not only those tribes which took the opportunity provided by Muhammad's death to break away from control but also those who had not yet "submitted" (which was accomplished by the so-called Riddah wars), and secondly, the fusing of these forces in the first organized assault on the outside world. Three armies, totaling ten thousand men, whose ranks were soon swollen to twice that number, took separate routes into Syria, in accordance, it was said, with Muhammad's own well-laid plans. Abu Bakr did not live to see their startling triumphs.

Umar and the Conquests

The second caliph, Umar (in office A.D. 634–644) dispatched and from a distance directed the great General Khalid ibn al-Walid in the stroke that altered beyond all calculation the destiny of the Near East, the capture of the ancient city of Damascus after a six months' siege (635). Christian forces were at once summoned to restore the situation, but Khalid sagaciously retreated to a more favorable location when the force of fifty thousand men sent by the Byzantine Emperor Heraclius came to drive him away, and on a day of smothering heat and dust, such as perhaps only bedouins could endure, he turned and won a decisive victory in which Theodorus, brother of Heraclius and general of the Christian forces, fell. The whole of Syria, up to the Taurus Mountains, fell too, and the deeply agitated emperor, departing for good, is said to have exclaimed: "Farewell, O Syria, and what an excellent country this is for the enemy!"

But the Jewish and Christian inhabitants, even of Damascus, felt differently. They were not altogether displeased! They had felt oppressed by Heraclius in the aftermath of the wars of their liberation from the Persians. The Arabs were, moreover, comparatively magnanimous. They acted in the spirit of the Qur'anic injunction, "If they desist (from fighting), let there be no enmity," as the terms for the surrender of Damascus suggest:

In the name of Allah, the compassionate, the merciful. This is what Khalid would grant to the inhabitants of Damascus if he enters therein: he promises to give them security for their lives, property, and churches. Their city wall shall not be demolished, neither shall any Moslem be quartered in their houses. Thereunto we give to them the pact of Allah and the protection of His Prophet, the caliphs and the believers. So long as they pay the poll tax, nothing but good shall befall them.[D2]

It is historically sound to say, with Philip Hitti, that the "easy conquest" of Syria had its own special causes: "The Hellenistic culture imposed on the land since its conquest by Alexander the Great (332 B.C.) was only skin-deep and was limited to the urban population. The rural people remained ever conscious of cultural and racial differences between themselves and their masters,"[D3] that is, between themselves as the Semitic population of Syria and their Hellenistic rulers. The Muslim historian Baladhuri attributed to the people of the Syrian town of Hims this confession to their Arab conquerors: "'We like your rule and justice far better than the state of oppression and tyranny under which we have been living."[D4]

The Muslim victories in Syria were decisive elsewhere. Jerusalem fell in 638, and Caesarea, relieved by sea and invincible until a Jew within the walls gave the necessary secret information, in 640. The whole of Palestine then surrendered to the Arabs. Cut off from needed aid, Egypt was the next conquest (639–641), and the Arabs pushed on rapidly through North Africa, to be in Spain within a century. Back in the Near East, the attack shifted to the Sassanids (Persians). First Iraq, with its fabulously rich cities (in 637), and then Persia (from 640 to 649) were subdued. Persia offered the stiffest opposition the Arabs had yet encountered. Its conquest took longer because the population was non-Semitic, well unified, and firmly Zoroastrian. To the northwest a twelve-year campaign (640–652) reduced the greater part of Asia Minor to subjection.

It may be asked in astonishment how the comparatively ill-equipped and outnumbered Muslim warriors, armed initially with bows and arrows and bamboo-shafted spears and riding on camels and horses, could overthrow one after another the disciplined hosts and even the navies of the Byzantine world. The answer is to be found partly in the war-weariness and disaffection of the resident populations, partly in the expert use of cavalry and the high mobility of Arab camel transport, but equally, perhaps, in the intense eagerness of the Muslim warriors, which was fed on the one hand by their acceptance of the Prophet's word that if they survived the battle they could keep four fifths of the booty and if they died they would go to paradise, and on the other hand by their sense of wonder and discovery: they were invading countries that seemed to their scarcity-bred minds literally earthly paradises. No untraveled country lad ever felt more wonder-struck by a metropolis than these warriors of the desert felt when they beheld the richly appointed cities lying ready for their taking in the ancient lands that were the "cradle of civilization." And what also greatly animated the better minds among them was the exciting prospect of learning the Greek and Persian arts, philosophies, and sciences—ripe and beckoning fields of learning as yet unharvested by their hungry minds and spirits.

Subsequent campaigns took the Muslim armies, now no longer predominantly Arab, northeastward and to the back of the Himalayas into Chinese Turkestan and Mongolia and southeastward into India. Far to the west the Spanish Muslims, but for Charles Martel, might well have overrun France; only the slender margin of the victory of the Franks in the Battle of Tours (732) turned them back into Spain. The resistance of the Byzantines in Asia Minor kept them also from crossing the Bosphorus for a long time.

But we must return to the caliphs and the internal history of the rapidly expanding Muslim empire.

Umar, who himself lived very simply, was soon in receipt of a swelling stream of tribute money, pouring into the treasury at Medina from all sides. Muhammad could never have dreamed of so much wealth. Umar determined to distribute it in the form of yearly stipends, first to Muhammad's widows and dependents,* next to others of the faithful, such as the Companions (the Emigrants and the Supporters), and finally, in lesser amounts, to all Arab warriors and tribesmen ($10–$30). In consideration of this income and in order to keep the Arabian Muslims together as a military unit, with home addresses, so

* 'A'isha, Muhammad's favorite wife, was assigned 12,000 dirhems, or about $2,400.

to speak, always in Arabia, he forbade any Arab to acquire lands outside that peninsula. Simultaneously, he dispossessed and drove from Arabia resistant members of other religions, especially Jews, Christians, and Zoroastrians.

Appearance of the First Power Struggles

In addition to the moneys distributed to them and their families as an annuity, the Arab warriors were, as has been noted, entitled to four fifths of all the booty they gathered in the form of movable goods and captives. (All moneys seized during campaigns were kept in the common treasury.) The economic advantages of being an Arabian Muslim were obvious. It became a matter of first importance to the various Arab groups close to the seat of power to control the caliphate. Umar himself was incorruptible, but a Christian captive stabbed him one day with a poisoned dagger, and the road to political maneuvering at once lay open.

It was significant of the internal political situation beginning to develop that Uthman, another of Muhammad's close associates, a son-in-law in fact, was next chosen (in office 644–656). An Ummayad, he yielded weakly to the pressures of his family and appointed so many Ummayads to high office that the ensuing scandals led to his assassination in Medina by dissatisfied Muslims gathered to force his abdication.

'Ali, another of Muhammad's sons-in-law, an early believer, and father of the two boys who were Muhammad's only male descendants, became caliph in 656 A.D. over much opposition, including that of 'A'isha, who, tradition says, never forgave him for thinking her unfaithful with a camel-driver on the day she failed to keep up with Muhammad while returning from a desert raid. He had had to triumph over two other aspirants, and after his assumption of office a third appeared in the person of the governor of Syria, Mu'awiya, an Ummayad, the son of Abu Sufyan. So formidable did the movement to depose him become that 'Ali, who had moved the administrative capital from Medina to the Muslim camp at Kufa in Iraq, raised an army, marched west, and was about to defeat his chief rival, Mu'awiya, when he consented to arbitrate the issue and was immediately immobilized. While Mu'awiya was busily establishing himself as the chief contender in Egypt, Arabia, and Yemen, 'Ali remained disappointingly passive. Disgusted followers, concluding that Allah had not chosen 'Ali after all and that both he and Mu'awiya should be eliminated, murdered him—a never-to-be-forgotten fact, as we shall see.

Summary of Political Events, 661–1900

The Ummayads now seized the caliphate, Mu'awiya declaring himself 'Ali's successor (661). Thus began the Ummayad caliphate, ruling from Damascus and encompassing an enormous territory, stretching from India to Spain. But in 750 the Abbassids overthrew them everywhere except in Spain and moved the capital to Baghdad, which they built up into a great city, on the "crossroads of the world," famous both in the Orient and in the Occident for its wealth, culture, and gaiety, qualities all exemplified in the person of their most distinguished representative, the Caliph Harun al-Rashid (736–809). Then came slow political decadence; the Muslim empire fell apart into separate states. In two regions anti-caliphates declared themselves. In Spain survivors of the Ummayad caliphate established an independent rule, and in Egypt and neighboring areas, including Palestine, a Shi'ite anti-caliphate, the Fatimid, claiming for their imams (or caliphs) descent from Muhammad's daughter Fatima, ruled from 909 to 1171, with such success for a while that the Alid or Shi'ite cause (pp. 549 ff.) seemed about to attain ascendancy in the Muslim world. But the Seljuk Turks, moving down from the steppes of central Asia, seized power in Persia, Iraq, and Syria in the eleventh century and reached the borders of Egypt and Byzantium.

It was at this point that the Crusaders came, their first expedition resulting in the capture of Jerusalem. Then followed the Muslim counter-attacks and the emergence of the great leader Saladin. Saladin prepared the way carefully for his successes against the Crusaders by first putting an end to the Fatimid caliphate in Egypt and taking over its holdings in Palestine and Syria. Then he began slowly to contract the areas held by the Crusaders and finally recaptured Jerusalem (1187). He and his successors came to terms with the Crusaders who clung to the coast for a time before being ousted. Suddenly, seventy years later, came the Mongols, burning and pillaging as they went, with incredible massacres, advancing and receding in two separate waves of conquest. Repelled by the Mamelukes of Egypt, who managed to hold on to Syria and Arabia, the Mongols fell back into Iraq and Persia, where they held on for a century longer and were converted en masse to Islam.

With the receding of the Mongol tide, four new Islamic empires arose: the Uzbek in the Oxus-Jaxartes basin, the Safawi in Persia (or Western Iran), the Mughal in India, and the Ottoman in Asia Minor. The Ottoman Turks rose to power in Asia Minor in the thirteenth century, crossed the Bosphorus, took Byzantium (Constantinople) in 1453, and fought their way into the Balkans and along the Danube as far as Vienna before they were forced back into areas that they could hold (sixteenth century). The Ottoman empire also stretched southward through Palestine into Egypt. It endured to World War I.

But now we must return to earlier centuries.

V The First Five Centuries of Muslim Thought

That the simplicity and like-mindedness of the period of the first four caliphs did not long persist should afford no surprise. The Caliph Umar's laws, designed to keep the Arabs permanently in Arabia as a land-owning and military unit, were soon and inevitably modified. Multitudes of Arabs thereafter migrated out of their barren homeland to enjoy the possession of richer holdings elsewhere—and were changed in the process. In many cases they were culturally merged into the subject peoples (the Mawali or "client peoples"*) among whom they settled and as often won over the Mawali.

The Formation of the Hadith Canons

Lines of divergence appeared early in the Muslim "Traditions." We have already referred, in the opening paragraphs of this chapter, to the Hadith or Tradition. It consisted to a large extent of recollections of Muhammad's sayings and doings traced back through "attestors" or "authorities" to Muhammad himself or to a Companion in Medina. There were many of these, but they were not the only authenticated traditions. Many others dealt with the way things had been done in Medina during Muhammad's lifetime, either by himself or with his "silent approval" (taqrir)—in short, they described the customs, usages, or precedents established in Muhammad's days. They soon swelled to formidable bulk, and many of them were contradictory. Some lines of tradition were suspiciously favorable either to the partisans of 'Ali (the Shi'ites), or to the Ummayads, or, later on, to the Abbassids, and so on.† But not

until over two centuries had passed after Muhammad's death were critical attempts made to select the more trustworthy traditions and bring them into a collection, and then the criterion used was an "external" one: the trustworthiness of the contributors of each hadith was the measure of its authenticity. The traditions had to have, as it were, a good pedigree. The authenticity and value of a tradition were judged by its isnad or chain of attestors, each of whom had to stand up under examination for veracity. The traditions were then declared either "genuine" or "fair" or "weak." At last six separate (and overlapping) collections made their appearance and won general acceptance. Of these the most highly regarded is the book of al-Bukhari, a Persian Muslim who diligently visited all through Arabia, Syria, Egypt, and Iraq gathering a vast number of hadiths (reportedly numbering six hundred thousand!) and then sifted them down to the 7,275 that he found "genuine." In influence this collection ranks next to the Qur'an itself.

But the six canonical books were not the only collections of hadiths in common use among Muslims. Such collections as the *Muwatta* of Malik or the *Musnad* of Ibn Hanbal, founders of two schools of the law, have been used more often and given more authority than some of the six canonical books. Their authority derives from that of their compilers. (For Malik and Ibn Hanbal, see pp. 543 f.)

The interpretation and reconciliation of the "genuine" traditions, being as they are the basis of the *Sunna*, or Custom, of traditionalist Islam, became a preoccupation of Muslim minds, and they allowed plenty of room for divergence of thought.

---

* For some centuries the Arabs normally functioned within the conquered territories according to the tribal relations to which they were accustomed. They granted the status of "clients" to some of the conquered peoples; that is, they treated them as adopted members of the Arab tribes. In this case clientship was a way of assimilating some of the conquered peoples no less than a way of becoming assimilated. Culturally, the process worked both ways.

† As traditional Islamic scholarship itself points out, there was outright invention or fabrication. One Ibn-abi-al-'Awja confessed before his execution 150 years after the Hijra that he had profited financially by fabricating four thousand hadiths. There was evidence also (though

Muslims were inclined to shut their eyes to it) of fertility of imagination and bias even among those who bore all the marks of trustworthiness. 'A'isha's prejudice against 'Ali appeared in her 2,210 traditions, and there seemed to be a very ready remembrance indeed on the part of Abu-Hureira, one of the Companions, with his 5,300 traditions. There were others only slightly less voluble. And always there were those who had it from someone, who had it from someone else, that still another person had heard a Companion say, "Muhammad used to do so and so." It became a major concern of the Muslim scholars and theologians to sift and weigh this evidence.

539

The First Controversies

Should expediency or political considerations have any weight in the choices of a Muslim? Was a Muslim to hew straight to the line of what he felt to be the true Islamic principles, without compromise or delay, or was he to let events sometimes take their course and leave the ultimate decision or action to Allah? These were the issues underlying the first Muslim controversies. For there was no fixed standard of orthodoxy, and never would be.

When 'Ali was chosen caliph, he was supported by fiercely anti-Ummayad elements who watched him narrowly to see if he would be as firm and decisive as Muhammad had been. But midway in the struggle with Mu'awiya, he had, as we have seen, agreed to arbitrate the issues, whereupon twelve thousand disgusted warriors marched out of his camp, so disillusioned with him that some of them later assassinated him. They became the Kharijites, "separatists" or "secessionists." Viewing with hostile eyes the political developments occurring behind the scenes among the Muslim leaders, this group of Muslims concluded bitterly that the only sure way of getting the right caliph was to select the best qualified person, not necessarily a person from just the Prophet's family nor just his tribe. The caliph need not come from either group, they said. Not enough of them were true Muslims! The Ummayads, for instance, had joined the Muslim movement at the last minute, just before it would be too late, obviously less from conviction than from expediency. No, the true caliph could be the choice only of true Muslims, men of proven good works acting solely on the religious principle of doing the will of Allah in complete self-surrender. All those who had become Muslims for political or economic reasons, or who were "trimmers," or who went through the practices of Islam as a mere outward form, were not true Muslims at all and must be destroyed in a great purge. This was imperative to save the cause of Allah and Muhammad from their hands. It was natural that these fierce puritans should find the full force of the Ummayads arrayed against them. The more radical and uncompromising were wiped out in bloody slaughter as heretics. Yet, their beliefs spread in time to the utmost fringes of the Muslim empire and still persist in Zanzibar and Algeria.

Opposed to them were the Murjites, the advocates of "delayed judgment." Their position was that only God can judge who is a true Muslim and who is not. When one sees a believer sinning, he cannot call him forthwith an infidel or without faith. Therefore, believers should treat all practicing Muslims, tentatively at least, as real Muslims, leaving to the last judgment, that is, to Allah, the fixing of their final status. Hence, even the Ummayads were to be tolerated—not to mention the converted Christians and Jews who appeared to be merely half-hearted in their "submission."

When it appeared that the weight of Muslim opinion agreed more with the Murjites than the Kharijites, the outlines of a coming traditionalist position began to emerge, but with some definition only after the Mu'tazilites had stirred up further controversy.

The Mu'tazilites

These vigorous defenders of the faith appeared first in Syria and Iraq during the Ummayad caliphate among the converts to Islam who were familiar with Greek, Jewish, Christian, and Zoroastrian thought. Initially, they may have been politically motivated, but in large part they were moved by a desire to convince the unpersuaded non-Muslims of the soundness of the Muslim position. They thus provide a Muslim analogue to the Christian apologists (p. 457). In any case, they were among the first Muslims to engage in what came to be called *kalam* or reasoned argument in defense of the faith.

In an attempt to find firm ground between the Kharijites and the Murjites, they laid emphasis upon the free response of men to the moral demands of Allah in the Qur'an, particularly when confronted by the "promise and threat" of Allah contained there.

But they were also sure, and believed that they were acting in the spirit of Muhammad in affirming, that not only does Allah challenge the consciences of men, he also seeks their rational assent. Hence, the Mu'tazilites took it for granted that the theological doctrines that might be erected on the foundation supplied by the Qur'an, whose truth they never questioned, were subject to rational testing. Their reading of translations of works of Greek philosophy, which may not have been extensive, made it seem to them a foregone conclusion that no doctrine could be true that did not survive such a test. How could a true doctrine be contrary to reason?

Reason, for example, the Mu'tazilites argued, insists on both the justice and unity of God. Doctrines that throw doubt on either cannot be accepted. In defense of the justice of God, the Mu'tazilites made an all-out attack on the doctrine that *all* men's doings are decreed by the inscrutable will of Allah, and that therefore man is not the author of any of his acts. Because the inconclusiveness of the Qur'an on this point allowed some room for further clarification, the Mu'tazilites insisted that no final position ought to be taken that would put to the question the justice of Allah: Allah *must* be just; it would be monstrous to think him moved by arbitrariness alone or by mere good pleasure. How could it be just for God to predestine a man to commit mortal sin or to maintain an attitude of heresy or unbelief, and then punish him for being guilty of either? It would not be fair or right. Hence, Allah must allow men enough freedom to choose between right and wrong, truth and falsehood. Only then could men be held responsible for their acts.

That Allah *had* to do anything whatever, as of necessity, was a doctrine that many Muslims viewed with distaste and horror. But the Mu'tazilites nevertheless insisted further that because Allah most certainly was the Merciful, the Compassionate, and desired the good of all creatures, he *had* to send down revelations to the Prophet to indicate the way of salvation—an act that showed both graciousness and an inner necessity to be just and merciful. Hence, a "necessary grace" is to be seen in the delivery to men of the Qur'an.

And this brought the Mu'tazilites to the declaration that stirred up the greatest dissension. They denied that the revelation—that is, the Qur'an—is eternal and uncreated. Allah created it when the need arose and sent it down. To suppose that it was uncreated and eternal would destroy the unity of God by setting up beside him something else co-eternal with him, and this would be polytheism, which the Qur'an itself condemned.

So persuasive did this point seem, perhaps more on political than intellectual grounds, to one of the Abbassid caliphs (al-Ma'mun), that in 827 A.D. he proclaimed it a heresy to assert the eternity of the Qur'an and went so far as to set up an inquisition to purge all government departments of those who held such a view. But twenty years later another caliph thought the reverse view the true one, called the Mu'tazilites heretical, and began a purge of them in turn.

Before their final overthrow in the tenth century, the Mu'tazilites turned their rationalistic method upon the anthropomorphism inherent in the literal interpretation of the Qur'an. They refused to take literally the descriptions of Allah as sitting on a throne in heaven among the angels and as having hands and feet, eyes and ears.[*] Allah is infinite and eternal and nowhere particularly in space. It endangered the unity of God, they said, to be too literal about his agents or about his attributes or qualities, as though these last could be his "members," as some of the orthodox maintained. It would be consistent with the unity of God only to speak of his attributes as being of his essence or as being his modes or states, not as being additions or accretions of an external kind. God is one as to his essence, without division or quality. This sort of reasoning was applied also to the language of the Qur'an about heaven and hell. The imagery was to be taken figuratively, or at any rate modified by the consideration that those who

---

[*] Some of the literalists said God is a being made of flesh and blood.

541

are intellectual or spiritual will not, in paradise for example, go in for sensual delights, because they are above that.

But though the Mu'tazilites did manage to teach the Muslim thinkers who came after them the value of using a rational method of exposition, the weight of opinion turned against them, and the tenth century saw their school as such come to an end. But their ideas survived among the Shi'ites (see p. 550), and many modernists have revived them.*

The Sunnis or Traditionalists

The downfall of the Mu'tazilites came about when the more conservative defenders of the Sunna adopted the methods of rationalism (the construction of logical systems) in order to confute them. It was

---

* The Mu'tazilites used the rationalistic methods and tools of philosophy to argue from within Islam about its meaning and message; there were others who, without giving up their Muslim faith, moved amid the concepts and issues of Greek philosophy. They were known as the *falasifah*, which is how the Arabs pronounced *philosopher*. It appeared to these thinkers that the Muslim faith, as the final truth in religion, should be stated in philosophical terms to gain the full assent of reason. In doing this they were ready to reject whatever reason rejected. But their tradition-nurtured fellow-Muslims were distrustful, and after seeing where their reasoning led them, agreed with al-Ghazali, whom we shall meet on a later page, when he condemned the falasifah for self-contradiction in espousing such Greek doctrines as the eternity of the world, the impossibility of resurrection from the dead, and God's having no knowledge of particulars. Nevertheless, during the first five centuries of Muslim thought, powerful intellects, displaying an encyclopedic learning, appeared among the philosophers. Perhaps the greatest was ibn-Sina (Avicenna), who lived in Persia, 980–1037. His predecessors, the Arab al-Kindi of Basra and Baghdad (died 873) and the Turk al-Farabi (870–950), were scarcely less able. In Spain ibn-Rushd (Averroës, 1126–98) was to follow in Avicenna's steps, seeking like him to forge a syncretism of Islam, Plato, Aristotle, and Plotinus. These men all gained the respect of Christian thinkers of their times, because their grounding in Greek philosophy was sounder than was then possible in the West, with its large loss of classical learning. But Muslims came to think they had stepped outside Islam onto alien ground.

a man trained in a Mu'tazilite school, named al-Ash'ari, who thus turned the tables on them.

But before we see how he did so, we should look at another development even more important to the Sunnis and antedating both the Mu'tazilites and al-Ash'ari. The earliest systematic activity of Islamic thought was concerned with the law (*fiqh, shari'a*), not with reasoned argument concerning the faith (*kalam*).

1. *The Four Schools of the Law.* Islam has seldom made a distinction between law and religion. The word finally chosen and now used for the law of Islam—Shari'a—means the Way, that is, the true path of religion. The word in earlier use, fiqh, or "understanding," was at first applied equally to law and theology, although in common usage it has usually referred to the former. It is well said that "Muslims conceive of their religion as a community that says 'Yes' to God and His world, and the joyful performance of the Law, in most areas of the Islamic world, is looked on as a positive religious value."G Accordingly, the recognized scholars of religion (the *'ulama,'* "the learned") have ceaselessly watched over the observance of the law in human life, and the *muftis*, the jurists appointed to be consultants to the religious courts, have framed with care each legal opinion (*fatwa*) followed on the bench by the *qadis* (judges).* Sometimes, however, the situations confronted by Muslims outside of Arabia have been such that the injunctions of the Qur'an have proved either insufficient or inapplicable. Reason and common sense have been needed then to work out legal

---

* A distinction must be drawn between the religious courts and those established by local governments. Sometimes the latter have completely ignored the Shari'a, which in such a case serves as the ideal law according to Islam as opposed to the actual working law of the civil courts. A more practical difference exists in jurisdiction. The religious courts have usually passed judgment in private and family affairs of Muslims, such as marriage, divorce, inheritance, and individual moral and religious conduct, whereas the civil courts have administered the statute laws laid down for a particular country by sovereigns and officials to regulate the actions of the citizenry of whatever faith.

solutions that appear compatible with the Qur'an.

To attain such a result, a certain amount of "speculation" was needed. As a rule, Muslims recoiled from speculation lest it carry reason into conflict with revelation. It was safest simply to examine the revelation reverently and arrange it into order or system. However, some use of speculation to fill in gaps or to meet new contingencies had to be allowed, provided it was speculation that built upon what had already been revealed.

Of the four schools the first in time, the Hanifite, was the most liberal in its use of speculation, by which, of course, is meant juridical, not theological, speculation. It was founded in Iraq by Abu Hanifa (died 767 A.D.), a Persian whose followers put down his teachings in Arabic. The essence of his position was that he began with the Qur'an (taking little notice of the Hadith) and asked himself how its precepts could be applied by analogy to the somewhat different situation in Iraq. If a particular situation for which Muhammad legislated was closely analogous to a situation existing in Iraq, he applied the Qur'an as it stood. If, however, the two situations differed widely, he developed by deduction an analogy applicable to Iraq, and if he ran into difficulties, he consulted *ra'y*, "opinion" or "preference" derived from the local situation and then made a ruling. The ruling might in this last case even supersede the Qur'an. (For example, the Qur'an prescribes cutting off the hand for theft, but that was meant for a situation not analogous to the one obtaining in more diversified Iraq; so it was not meant for Iraq. By analogical deduction from other parts of the Qur'an we derive for Iraq other, more effective punishment, namely, imprisonment.) It was natural for the easygoing Abbassids and the Ottoman Turks after them to follow the Hanifite rulings on laws and religious rites. They are still followed in Iraq, Iran, northern India, and central Asia.

The second school, the Malikite, founded in Medina by Malik-ibn-Anas (*ca.* 715–795 A.D.), interpreted laws and rites in the light of the Qur'an and the Hadith together, and when in difficulty leaned heavily on the "consensus of opinion" (*ijma'*) that prevailed in Medina. For especially perplexing situations he used analogy, and when analogy conflicted with opinion, he fell back on "public advantage." This school is still generally followed in north Africa, parts of Egypt, and eastern Arabia.

The *Shafi'ite*, the third school in time, is important because it can be said to have scrutinized the other two schools and arrived at a science of the law based on what had been previously determined. It was founded by al-Shafi'i, an Arab born in Persia but descended from the Quraysh tribe. He clearly distinguished four sources of the law: the words of God (the Qur'an), the words and deeds of the Prophet (the sunna discerned within the Hadith), the consensus of the community (ijma'), and analogy (*qiyas*). This formulation has been accepted by all schools of the law as the classical theory of the sources of the law, but each school reserves the right to stress these sources differently. The Shafi'ite school gives equal weight to the Qur'an and the hadiths that authentically reflect the words and deeds of the Prophet, but sometimes, where one of the prophetic hadiths may be more specific and clear, prefers it even to the Qur'an. At times the traditions, it is held, represent the Muslim world in expansion and therefore the more developed situation, but although liberal in this respect, the Shafi'ites reject "opinion" in any form as using speculation in an unwarranted manner. The Shafi'ite school still prevails in lower Egypt (Cairo), eastern Africa, southern Arabia, Palestine, southern India, and the East Indies.

The most conservative of the four schools is the Hanbalite. It was founded at Baghdad in the loose and merry days of Harun-al-Rashid by the shocked Ibn-Hanbal, a student of al-Shafi'i, who was even more uncompromising than his master toward "opinion." He seems to have been in special opposition to the Mu'tazilites and adhered strictly to the letter of the Qur'an, with less reliance on the Hadith. For refusal to deny the eternity of the Qur'an he was put in chains by the Abbassid Caliph al-Ma'mun, and by a succeeding caliph scourged and imprisoned. The

543

Hanbalite laws and ritual are followed today in the Hejaz and in Saudi Arabia as a whole.

2. *The thought of al-Ash'ari.* Born in Iraq about 873, al-Ash'ari made his home in Baghdad, where he early became a Shafi'ite; he died there in 935 (or 936). He became one of the two great thinkers most honored by conservative Muslims, the other being al-Ghazali. After studying and publicly advocating the Mu'tazilites' teachings, he found himself at the age of forty suddenly and violently disagreeing and went on to develop a rational exposition of the Islamic revelation.* He accomplished this by making God

* He now swung all the way over to connection with the ultraconservative Hanbalite school of law.

Page from the Qur'an. The Arabic text appears here in the Kufic script. It comes from the thirteenth century but aims to be a worthy resemblance to the eternal Umm-ul-Kalib, the uncreated heavenly archetype that is the source of the whole Qur'an, transmitted without error or change to Muhammad. (Courtesy, Museum of Fine Arts, Boston.)

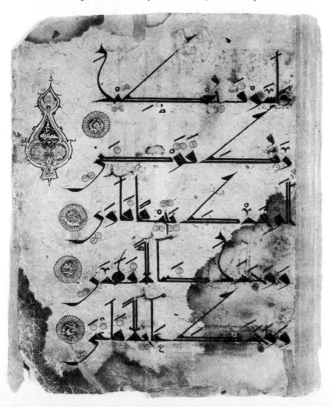

not only one but all in all. All life, all knowledge, power, will, hearing, sight, and speech—the seven divine attributes—no matter where or when experienced, are Allah in action, for Allah has created men and all their acts. Men cannot see, hear, know, or will anything of themselves; it is Allah who causes what happens in and through them. This position enabled al-Ash'ari to supply logical grounds for traditionalist doctrines, whether drawn from the Qur'an or the Hadith. For example, because it is Allah who immediately causes all events, internal and external, it is he who determines men to think of him as he is described in the Qur'an. Allah, then, really sits on a throne and has hands and feet, eyes and ears; the Qur'an says so. But because the Qur'an also declares that he is "not like anything" in the universe, men must believe what they are told "without thinking how" it may be so. Similarly, the concrete imagery of heaven and hell supplied by the Qur'an is to be taken as descriptive of reality. The believers in paradise will really have a vision of Allah sitting on his throne, though it must not be supposed that the seeing or the sitting are to be compared with this world's seeing or sitting. As for the Qur'an, al-Ash'ari said its words are, as ideas in the mind of Allah, eternal, but the letters on sheets of paper forming the words read and recited on earth are produced by men and are of temporal origin—a solution of the old puzzle as to the uncreated nature of the Qur'an that was immediately satisfactory to most Muslims. Finally, that the conception of Allah as being the immediate cause of every act made him responsible for evil as well as good did not daunt al-Ash'ari: it was just a fact that Allah created the unbelief of the infidel and damned him for it. Allah has his own reasons, which are not like human reasons and which men cannot know and should not have the temerity to seek to know. But al-Ash'ari modified this hard teaching by saying that even though man's actions are predestined, he "acquires" guilt or righteousness by acting as if he were free, thus personally involving himself in his actions, bad or good.

The Mystics

But what concerned the majority of Muslims more than the kalam of al-Ash'ari and the Shari'a of the schools of the law were such immediate and present things as (1) the practice of the Five Pillars and the ceremonies of the ritual year, (2) the vaguely mystical experience of the presence of God in worship and daily life, with both its "promise and threat," and (3) assurance of the vitality and reality of Islam in the lives and persons of true men of God. For certainly millions of Muslims had within themselves the natural human need to feel their religion as a personal and emotional experience. Islam had no priests, then or now, ordained and set apart for a life dedicated to the worship of God and the pursuit of holiness,* and yet everyone knew that Muhammad had been a true man of God, wholly dedicated to his mission, who in the period before the revelations came had retired at times from the world to meditate in a cave. It was thus that he had become an instrument of God's truth.

It was the popular yearning for the presence among them of unworldly men dedicated to God, asceticism, and holiness that encouraged the eventual emergence of Islamic mysticism.

The forerunners of the mystics appeared almost as soon as Islam reached Syria. Early in the Ummayad caliphate, Syrian Muslims, yearning to know Allah in this strange context and influenced by, among other things, passages from the New Testament, wandered about, neither begging nor yet working for a living, but endlessly reciting a litany of the "beautiful names" and titles of Allah and resigning themselves to his care, in trustful dependence on such a promise as that contained in the saying of Jesus: "Take therefore no thought for the morrow: for the morrow shall take thought for the things of itself." Ascetics rather than mystics, they practiced an utter indifference toward hunger and illness or the abuse they received

from men, saying that they must be under the hand of Allah "as passive as a corpse under the hand of him who washes it."[H1] In Iraq there was al-Hasan of Basra (died 728), an ascetic who was at the same time a religious scholar. His holy life caused him to be revered as a saint in his own lifetime. He rejected this world (*dunya*) as a "lower" place full of wretchedness and grief and called upon his hearers to seek heavenly "mansions which long ages will not decay nor alter."

The first Sufis to bear the name (meaning "wool-wearers," i.e., wearers of the ascetics' coarse, undyed woolen robe) appeared in the eighth century, but they soon went beyond their forerunners in the development of intellectual and mystical interests that took them into directed contemplation. Eventually, although they based themselves on the Qur'an, they sought philosophical aid from Neo-Platonism and Gnosticism, while Christian monasticism supplied them with hints toward organization. They adopted a monkish rule of life, practiced long vigils and stated periods of meditation, and finally gathered into fraternities (this by the twelfth century) with communal religious services, marked by Muslim rituals and music much like that of the Christian churches.* Their consuming interest was union with God now rather than after death. Because there were no distinctively Muslim lines of thought to guide them, they strained at the leash of Muslim orthodoxy toward mysticism and pantheism.

When the Sufis were establishing themselves, they were influenced by what they heard of the mystical speculations of an Egyptian Muslim, Dhu'l-Nun al-Misri, who perhaps received the name "the Man of the Fish from Egypt," i.e., the Jonah of Egypt, because he said that individuality is a deadly sin and

---

* The imams who lead the prayers in the mosques have always been laymen who serve full or part-time to the glory of God.

* The Sufis claimed Muhammad as their example (witness his use of caves on Mount Hira), but they had to overlook the hadith quoting Muhammad as being critical of "monkery" (e.g., in the saying attributed to him: "Either you propose to be a Christian monk; in that case, join them openly! Or you belong to our people; then you must follow our custom [sunna]. Our custom is married life.")[H2] The hadith may be spurious.

the soul must be "swallowed up" in God by complete mystic union. But neither he nor the Sufis in general thought that the swallowing up of the soul could be achieved at once without the soul being prepared for it. There were stages to pass through. To follow the figure of Harith al-Muhasibi of Basra (died 857 A.D.), the Sufi was a pilgrim on the road that leads to "the truth," and there were way-stations he must pass, under the guidance of a director, such as repentance, abstinence, renunciation, poverty, patience, trust in God, and satisfaction (the "seven stages" most commonly prescribed). Final entrance into the transcendental realm of knowledge and truth would crown the various "states" of longing, fear, hope, love, intimacy, and trust that Allah had bestowed. The climactic state would be experienced as an intoxicating and ineffable flash of divine illumination, bringing with it the certainty of divine love—the goal of the mystical theist in all lands.

But a few mystics were not theists. They defined Allah as the realm of true being, and when certain Buddhist influences penetrated Iraq, the Sufis there moved perilously close to atheism (as did some *zindiq* or free-thinking Muslims) and emphasized self-annihilation, conceived as complete absorption into True Being, as the entire goal.

These and others among the more extreme Sufis (the "ecstatics") were recognized by conservative Muslims as heretics. There was more than one martyrdom. A Persian Sufi called al-Hallaj was in 922 scourged, mutilated, nailed to a gibbet, and then beheaded for crying out publicly, "I am the True (*al-Haqq*)," by which his hearers, accustomed to hearing Allah named "The True," judged he was committing the ultimate in blasphemy. They were right in understanding that he felt he and his creator were one, but he meant no blasphemy. He felt much as did the Persian mystic Bayazid, to whom the saying was attributed: "Thirty years the transcendent God was my mirror, now I am my own mirror—i.e., that which I was I am no more, for 'I' and 'God' is a denial of the Unity of God. Since I am no more, the transcendent God is His own mirror. I say that I am

my own mirror, for 'tis God that speaks with my tongue, and I have vanished."[J1]

To al-Hallaj the hope of mystic union with God is that of the lover who suffers with separation from his beloved, and in his famous verses he bewails any absence of perfect harmony with the Great Beloved. When he can, he celebrates its presence with intimacy and tenderness:

Betwixt me and Thee there lingers an "it is I" that
  torments me.
Ah, of Thy grace, take away this "I" from between us![J2]

I am He whom I love, and He whom I love is I,
We are two spirits dwelling in one body.
If thou seest me, thou seest Him,
And if thou seest Him, thou seest us both.[J3]

Condemned for heresy though he was, Hallaj was to be echoed by more than one of the Persian poets. Consider the words of the mystical poet Jalal al-Din Rumi, born in Balkh in 1207 A.D. (three hundred years later), the famous author of the *Mathnavi* ("the Qur'an of the Persian language"), whose disciples formed on the foundations he laid the Maulawi (Mevlevi) order of whirling dervishes:

When God appears to His ardent lover the lover is absorbed in Him, and not so much as a hair of the lover remains. True lovers are as shadows, and when the sun shines in glory the shadows vanish away. He is a true lover of God to whom God says, "I am thine, and thou art mine!"[K1]

Let me then become non-existent, for non-existence
Sings to me in organ tones, "To him shall we return."
Behold water in a pitcher; pour it out;
Will that water run away from the stream?
When that water joins the water of the stream
It is lost therein, and becomes itself the stream.
Its individuality is lost, but its essence remains,
And thereby it becomes not less nor inferior.[K2]

In the world of Divine Unity is no room for Number,
But Number necessarily exists in the world of Five and
  Four.
You may count a hundred thousand sweet apples in your
  hand:
If you wish to make One, crush them all together.[K3]

In the house of water and clay this heart is desolate
  without thee;
O Beloved, enter the house, or I will leave it.[K4]

For his disciples Rumi wrote the famous "Song of the Reed Flute," celebrating the love of God that the flute symbolized. It begins:

Hearken to the reed-flute, how it discourses
When complaining of the pains of separation—
"Ever since they tore me from my osier bed,
My plaintive notes have moved men and women to tears.
I burst my breast, striving to give vent to sighs,
And to express the pangs of my yearning for my
  home. . . ."

A central passage cries out in celebration of the ecstasy of the love of God:

Hail to thee, then, O LOVE, sweet madness!
Thou who healest all our infirmities!
Who art the physician of our pride and self-conceit!
Who art our Plato and our Galen!
Love exalts our earthly bodies to heaven,
And makes the very hills to dance with joy!
O lover, 'twas love that gave life to Mount Sinai,
When "it quaked, and Moses fell down in a swoon."

Did my Beloved only touch me with his lips,
I too, like the flute, would burst out in melody.[K5]

The references here to the Greeks point to the fact that the Sufis, especially in their manifestation as dervishes, were hospitable to any point of view that lent aid to their quest. They felt the essential oneness of all seekers of union with God, no matter what their name or sign. Said Rumi:

If the picture of our Beloved is found in a heathen temple, it is an error to encircle the Ka'bah: if the Ka'bah is deprived of its sweet smell, it is a synagogue: and if in the synagogue we feel the sweet smell of union with him, it is our Ka'bah.[E2]

And an earlier philosopher-poet, Ibn 'Arabi (born 1165 A.D.), who was an outright pantheist, declared:

There was a time, when I blamed my companion if his religion did not resemble mine;

Now, however, my heart accepts every form: it is a pasture ground for gazelles, a cloister for monks,
  A temple for idols and a Ka'bah for the pilgrim, the tables of the Torah and the sacred books of the Koran.
  Love alone is my religion.[E3]

But the accent by the mystics on the immanence and omnipresence of God was so at odds with the Sunni emphasis on the transcendence and omnipotence of God that there was great need of a reconciliation of these themes, and this need was met by al-Ghazali, the great synthesizer of Muslim thought.

The Synthesis of al-Ghazali

After the tension between the traditionalists and the Kharijites and Mu'talizites, and the straining in different directions of the jurists and the mystics, the kalam of al-Ghazali, when it was understood, "came like a deliverance."[L] In recognition of the fact that he rescued the schools from the barren scholasticism into which they had fallen after al-Ash'ari, Muslims have called him Muhyi al-Din, "The Restorer (or Reviver) of Religion."

And yet his value was not immediately recognized. It was only after his synthesis had been before them awhile that the Muslim schoolmen began to appreciate its balance and wisdom.

Born in a Persian village in 1058 A.D., he attained his fame elsewhere but returned home before he died in 1111. After an education in jurisprudence in a Shafi'ite school and in theology under a famous Ash'arite imam, he was invited to Baghdad as a lecturer in the Nizamiyah, a newly founded university where the Ash'arite doctrine predominated. During his four years of teaching he reached a spiritual crisis. Not satisfied with scholasticism, he veered to scepticism, then to Sufism. His intellectual curiosity was great, but his desire to find himself left him physically and morally exhausted. Later in life, when he was past fifty (and near his end), he wrote:

Ever since I was under twenty (now I am over fifty) . . . I have not ceased to investigate every dogma and

547

belief. No Batinite did I come across without desiring to investigate his esotericism; no Zaharite, without wishing to acquire the gist of his literalism; no philosopher (Neo-Platonist), without wanting to learn the essence of his philosophy; no dialectical theologian, without striving to ascertain the object of his dialectics and theology; no Sufi, without coveting to probe the secret of his Sufism; no ascetic, without trying to delve into the origin of his asceticism; no atheistic *zindiq*, without groping for the causes of his bold atheism and *zindiqism*. Such was the unquenchable thirst of my soul for research and investigation from the early days of my youth, an instinct and a temperament implanted in me by God through no choice of mine.[D5]

The swing to Sufism proved decisive. He left the university, went to Syria to find out for himself, under the Sufis there, whether their way was the right path to religious certainty, and after two years of meditation and prayer made a holy pilgrimage to Mecca before returning to his home and children. He practiced mysticism thenceforth and began writing. Though at the command of the sultan he returned to teaching for a short time, he soon resumed his meditation and writing in his native village until his death at fifty-three.

His greatest book was *The Revivification of the Religious Sciences*. As a fundamentally religious person, he was not satisfied with the legalism and intellectualism of the Sunnis. He had the same need that the German Pietists were to have after Lutheran scholasticism had reduced the German Reformation to a tough shell of theology and ritual. His quietism, like theirs, was motivated by his sense of the unreality of religion without religious experience. In fact, all human thinking and life itself were flat and unprofitable without God. He took the time to analyze in detail the philosophies of certain Muslim followers of Aristotle, only to condemn them as self-contradictory and essentially irreligious rational systems. To him the universe was not eternal but was created out of nothing by the creative will of Allah. The relation between men and the great being who has produced them and the world about them should be fundamentally moral and experiential. It is not enough to observe the laws and rites of Islam or to have a kalam that one is ready to defend against all comers. A humble soul may be profoundly religious even though he be ignorant of the details of Qur'anic interpretation or theology. The core of religion—which may be practiced even by a non-Muslim—is to repent of one's sins, purge the heart of all but God, and by the exercises of religion attain a virtuous character. And here, he said, the Sufi methods of self-discipline and meditation, if practiced with common sense and wisdom, are of great value. Of priceless value, too, are the Five Pillars of the faith, accepted as obligatory for all Muslims; yet they do not yield their full profit unless they are performed from the heart and with the right attitude of mind. Only thus could the Muslim hope to escape punishment on the last day.

The vigor with which al-Ghazali censured the teachers of law, theology, and philosophy for their lack of religious fire and for encouraging sectarian tendencies caused his works to be bitterly assailed when they were first published. But on second thought, all but the more extreme sects in areas dominated by formalistic jurisprudence, like far-off Spain, acknowledged the sanity and general truth of his position. Ultimately, he was given the rank of the greatest of Muslim thinkers and was at last revered as a saint. And just as Catholic schoolmen have not gone far from the positions of Aquinas, so Muslim thinkers have remained in the main content with al-Ghazali's formulations, his word being taken as all but final.

VI The Great Dissent

It must be obvious by now that Islam is not and never has been a monolithic faith. Divergences in doctrine, divisions of a political nature, and variations in law and the development of the spiritual life have frequently occurred. Even the conservative position was long in emerging and then proved unable to achieve a fixed and final form. But we have not seen so far any major deviation. There was one, however, and it falls to us now to examine it. It occurred before there existed any Islamic standard or norm to block it effectively, and it could not have been blocked anyway perhaps, for it was motivated by a very powerful desire: to have Islam directed by Muhammad's own descendants through his daughter Fatima, the wife of 'Ali.

The Shi'ites

The tragedy that befell the House of 'Ali, beginning with the murder of 'Ali himself and including the deaths of his two sons, grandsons of Muhammad, has haunted the lives of "the party (*Shi'a*) of 'Ali." They have brooded upon these dark happenings down the years as Christians do upon the death of Jesus. A major heretical group, they have drawn the censure and yet also have had the sympathy of the Sunnis and Sufis. They were among the sects whose radical elements al-Ghazali attacked as guilty of resting their claims on false grounds and sinfully dividing Islam. And yet, although agreeing with this indictment, the Muslim world at large has suppressed its annoyance at them out of a kind of pity, because their movement goes back to the very beginnings of Islam and has a kind of perverse justification, even in orthodox eyes. Their critics agree that there is little sense in it, yet it has an appeal all its own.

The partisans of 'Ali only gradually worked out their final claims made by the various Shi'ite sects. In the beginning there was simply the assertion—which as events unfolded became more and more heated—that only Muhammad's direct descendants, no others, should have been given first place in the leadership of Islam. This could be called their political and dynastic claim, and at first this seems to have been all that they were interested in claiming. But this was not enough for adherents of their cause in Iraq, who over the years developed the religious theory, perhaps as an effect of Christian theories about God being in Christ, that every legitimate leader of the Alids, beginning with 'Ali, was an *imam*

mahdi, a divinely appointed and supernaturally guided spiritual leader, endowed by Allah with special knowledge and insight—an assertion that the main body of Muslims, significantly enough, called *ghuluw,* "exaggeration," rather than heresy. The political claim of the earlier days was, then, gradually supplemented by such sincere convictions as these: that Allah was determinedly behind 'Ali and his descendants, that he would not be frustrated by death, and that he would surely conduct the Shi'ite cause to a final triumph, even if this might mean bringing a descendant of 'Ali back from death or "withdrawal" to be a Messianic figure capable of accomplishing the aims that Muhammad and 'Ali had espoused when they were leaders of the Muslim world. Such expectations were at first scarcely more than hopes born of frustration and faith, but gradually the hope and faith became a firm conviction.

In the eyes of the Shi'ites, Muhammad was the divinely chosen Prophet of Islam, and 'Ali, his cousin and son-in-law, the Imam, the divinely designated "leader" and commander-in-chief of the faithful, and also their "pattern," for they came to believe that before his death Muhammad, the revealer of the truth in Arabia, under the guidance of Allah, chose 'Ali as the successor (caliph) who should establish this truth throughout the earth. Muhammad's designation of 'Ali as his successor therefore conferred on 'Ali the same kind of supernatural status as Catholics claim Jesus bestowed on Peter at Caesarea Philippi. Hence, the appointment of Abu Bakr, Umar, and Uthman as caliphs was a usurpation—a usurpation with disastrous consequences, for when 'Ali at last was elected caliph, the opposition had developed so much power that it was able to bring his caliphate to a tragic conclusion. So bitter are all but one of the Shi'ite sects about this great "betrayal" that to this day they curse Abu Bakr, Umar, and Uthman as usurpers in their Friday prayers.

The Shi'ites found the same kind of tragedy overwhelming 'Ali's sons, who by heritage were endowed with his unique spiritual quality. Al-Hasan, the older of the two sons 'Ali had by Fatima, was led by the

549

opposition to resign his imamship for a mere pension and shortly thereafter died. The younger son, al-Husain, the third imam according to this reading of history, fell a martyr (680 A.D.), together with his little son, in a night battle at Karbala during a futile attempt to establish himself as the rightful caliph over the Ummayad incumbent, Yazid.

While this interpretation of history was still in its formative stage, the Shi'ites struggled against the Ummayads and gave their support to the rebellions that led to the triumph of the Abbassids. (The Abbassids, who derived their name from Muhammad's uncle, al-'Abbas, were thus blood relations of the descendants of 'Ali.) But the Shi'ites were no better treated by the Abbassids than by the Ummayads, and in seeking attainment of their aims broke up into different sects (which we shall examine shortly). Nevertheless, they continued to regard the descendants of al-Hasan and al-Husain as "nobles" and "lords" and among their number distinguished, according to their various sectarian principles, certain individuals as divinely ordained imams, who had inherited from 'Ali and the intermediate imams two extraordinary qualities: infallibility in interpreting the law and sinlessness. Historically, it was not until about the time of the sixth imam after 'Ali (Ja'far al-Sadiq) that these claims assumed a clear-cut form. Back of them were two principles: that of the *nass* (designation of the next imam by the preceding one), a principle that was read back into history all the way to Muhammad, as we have seen; and that of the *'ilm* (special knowledge, such as would give an imam the warrant to exercise authority, impose discipline, and make decisions of a binding character in cases at issue).

Eventually another belief was to be added. It came later and concerned the expected return of some one of the imams as a "divinely guided" Messianic personage, the *Mahdi*. Where their line of imams ended, various sects were to believe that the last of these divine leaders had just "withdrawn" from sight and would return again as the Mahdi before the last day, to gather his own about him once more.

Shi'ite loyalty to these imams has been stubborn. When persecution or compulsion proved too strong, they allowed themselves the leeway provided in their principle of dissimulation (*taqiyah*), which permitted them to conform outwardly to the requirements laid upon them by the persecuting authorities while making a secret mental reservation. By this means they were able to survive as an underground movement in the areas where their views were proscribed. But though their fanaticism was sharpened by persecution in respect to their distinctive views, in other respects the very fact of their being in opposition to the Sunni Muslims made them sympathetic with the more liberal theological positions. Like the Mu'tazilites, they did not believe the Qur'an to be eternal, nor men to be without any freedom of the will. They believed, too, that Allah *must* be just and holds men responsible only for their own acts.

The Shi'ite Sects

The repressions suffered by the Shi'ites have had a result that might well have been expected. Underground sects and terrorist groups, often outlawed by the main body of the Shi'ites themselves, have kept forming. Some of them have preyed upon whole communities or built states within states; some have seized large areas and ruled them as outlaw kingdoms; others have conspired secretly to annihilate their enemies by poison and dagger. These have, of course, been the violent minority.

Let us begin with the less extreme sects. In order to do so without too much confusion, the reader is invited to consider the chart or tree* on the next page showing the family relationship of the successors of 'Ali who figure so largely in the thoughts of the Shi'ite world.

Following down the extreme left side of this chart, we find the three general groups that form the Shi'ite sects. A discussion of each follows below.

* Adapted from Hitti, *History of the Arabs.*

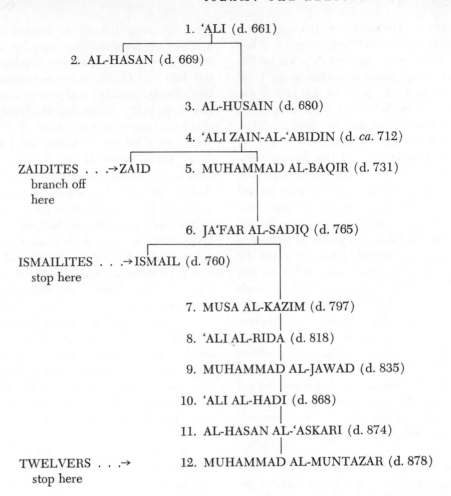

1. 'ALI (d. 661)

2. AL-HASAN (d. 669)

3. AL-HUSAIN (d. 680)

4. 'ALI ZAIN-AL-'ABIDIN (d. *ca.* 712)

ZAIDITES . . .→ZAID   5. MUHAMMAD AL-BAQIR (d. 731)
branch off
here

6. JA'FAR AL-SADIQ (d. 765)

ISMAILITES . . .→ISMAIL (d. 760)
stop here

7. MUSA AL-KAZIM (d. 797)

8. 'ALI AL-RIDA (d. 818)

9. MUHAMMAD AL-JAWAD (d. 835)

10. 'ALI AL-HADI (d. 868)

11. AL-HASAN AL-'ASKARI (d. 874)

TWELVERS . . .→   12. MUHAMMAD AL-MUNTAZAR (d. 878)
stop here

A. THE ZAIDITES. The Zaidites are the Shi'ites who approximate most closely the traditionalist (Sunnite) position. They differ with the other sects in considering Zaid (see chart) as the fifth imam instead of Muhammad al-Baqir, the fifth imam of the other sects. The Zaidites did not realize that they were a separate sect until the time of Ja'far al-Sadiq and have quite generally shied away from the principle of the nass, especially if it is interpreted as having a supernatural significance. It is typical for them to assert that 'Ali, not having been designated as the first caliph by Muhammad, freely gave Abu Bakr and Umar his allegiance when they were chosen, and therefore these two caliphs are not cursed in the Friday prayers. Some of them execrate Uthman for being an Ummayad who displaced 'Ali as the third caliph, but not all the Zaidites feel the same resentment, though all agree that the Ummayads who succeeded 'Ali were usurpers of the lowest kind: they were and are accursed. As a force in history the Zaidites have maintained a dynasty (now on the point of extinction) since the ninth century in Yemen (south Arabia) and in the past have had dynasties for periods varying from sixty to two hundred years in Tabaristan, Dailan, Gilan, and Morocco.

B. THE TWELVERS. The sect of the Twelvers claims the great majority of the Shi'ites as members. They get their name from reckoning through to the twelfth imam, Muhammad al-Muntazar. This imam is of great importance to them. They say that in 878 A.D. he "disappeared" or "withdrew" into the cave of the great mosque at Samarra, up the river from Baghdad. He had left no issue, but the Twelvers refused to believe that Allah could have let the divinely instituted line of imams come to an end. The twelfth imam therefore had simply gone into concealment; he had withdrawn from human sight until the fullness of the time when he will return as the Mahdi, "the divinely guided one" who will usher in a period of righteousness and peace before the end of the world and the last judgment.° The "concealed imam," while remaining in his hidden state where death cannot touch him, has not left his waiting followers without guidance, many have said; he has selected representatives on earth to lead them. In Persia (now Iran), where almost the whole population of about twenty million is Shi'ite (and Twelver) and where Islam has been since the beginning of the sixteenth century the religion of the state, the shah was once regarded as such a representative. During the last two centuries this claim has not been made officially.

C. THE ISMAILITES OR SEVENERS AND THEIR OFFSHOOTS. Although moderate as a group, the Ismailites have produced offshoots that have sometimes shocked and stirred the whole Muslim world. The Ismailites are so called because they have remained loyal to Ismail, the first son of the sixth imam. After being designated by his father as the next imam (by the nass) Ismail was set aside for his younger brother when his father was told of his drunkenness. But the

Ismailites have refused to believe the accusation against their favorite. They have considered that the father must have yielded to a slanderous attack that was false, for Ismail, as imam-designate, and therefore already infallible and sinless, simply could not have been guilty of the charge against him. The fact that Ismail was reported to have died (760 A.D.) five years before his father excited the Ismailites all the more. They concluded that he was not dead but hidden: he would come again as the Mahdi.° In their fervid belief, Ismail was the very incarnation of God himself and would soon return. In order to find support for these views in the Qur'an, they began to interpret it allegorically (as many Christian eschatologists today interpret the Bible) and arrived at an esoteric, hidden doctrine, which was so heretical that they spread it to others only through secret missionary activity.

This aspect of Ismailite thought attracted men disposed to rebellion against authority. An early and startling manifestation of the political effects that might flow from secret Ismailite activities occurred near the head of the Persian Gulf. There the ambitious Persian 'Abdullah ibn-Maimum (d. *ca.* 874), claiming to be the earthly representative of the concealed Imam Muhammad ibn-Ismail, built up a secret society devoted to the cause of destroying the Abbassid caliphate and putting 'Abdullah or his descendants on the throne. Though this scheme was not carried out, because 'Abdullah had to flee for his life to northern Syria, his organization succeeded after his death in founding (909 A.D.) the Fatimid caliphate that for centuries ruled Egypt, Tunis, and Syria (p. 538). This proved to be one of the major Shi'ite assumptions of temporal power.

Another group that developed from 'Abdullah's secret organization was the Qarmatians. They were led by one of 'Abdullah's disciples, a certain Hamdan Qarmat, from whom they took their name. His secret society, formed toward the close of the ninth century,

---

° A widely accepted hadith declares that Muhammad prophesied there would come in the last days a man of his own family who would do this. He would be known as the Mahdi. The Shi'ites seized upon the phrase "of his own family" and made the prophecy apply to the Alids, which meant the Imams. But another hadith contradicts all this with the saying: "There is no Mahdi but Jesus the Son of Mary!"H3

° Some admitted that he did die, but left a son, Muhammad ibn-Ismail, who "disappeared" in India and would return as the Mahdi.

was along communistic lines and succeeded in setting up an independent kingdom on the western shore of the Persian Gulf, with complete control from Yemen to the borders of Iraq. This rebel state was able to defend itself successfully against the caliphs at Baghdad, and in one remarkable and hair-raising sortie dared to capture and loot Mecca during the pilgrimage season! In this astonishing assault on the holy city they carried off the Black Stone and returned it after twenty years only because the Fatimid (fellow-Ismailite) caliph, the powerful al-Mansur, requested it. The Qarmatians cut the roads from Iraq to Mecca, and pilgrims over these routes either paid heavily for the privilege or were turned back. Before they finally fell, the Qarmatians set a record of a century

of revolutionary violence and bloodshed—all at bottom a kind of vengeance of the Persians upon the Arabs who had conquered them, a vengeance disguised, indeed, perhaps even to themselves, as religious obedience to the will of a divine imam descended from Muhammad.

Actually less dangerous but even more dreaded were the mysterious Assassins, who as exponents of what they called "the new propaganda" developed to a high point the terrorist art of worming one's way in disguise into the presence of Muslim rulers and officials and striking them down with a poisoned dagger. It did not matter how public the occasion was—the Friday prayers at the mosque, the holding of court by a prince or king—the more people present

The royal Badshadi mosque in Lahore, Pakistan. This handsome mosque was built for the Mughal ruler Aurangzeb in the seventeenth century. To save the pavement from soiling, pilgrims proceed to the mosque on marked walk-ways. (Courtesy of the United Nations.)

the better. The assassin aimed and struck and was himself struck down, or else seized and put to death after torture, but he endured all in the confident expectation of going directly to paradise, the promised reward he was seeking.

The founder and first grand-master of this order was Hasan Sabbah (d. 1124 A.D.), probably a Persian, though he claimed descent from a line of kings in south Arabia. It was he who had the inspiration to seize the mountain stronghold of Alamut, in Persia, perched on a high narrow ledge of rock three-quarters of a mile long and several hundred feet wide, which he and his men fortified so expertly that it remained impregnable for two centuries. Here they supported themselves by their own farming and gardening of the land beneath the heights of their fortress. By sorties in force from their mountain fortress the Assassins captured other strongholds in northern Persia, and by sending missionaries into northern Syria, they were also able to start a vigorous movement there, which eventually led to the establishment of a powerful mountain kingdom with ten or more fortresses in the order's hands. It was here that the Crusaders came to know and to fear them and to be in awe of their leader, Rashid-al-Sinan, whose title "sheikh al-jabal" was translated for them into "The Old Man of the Mountain." It is said that twenty thousand of them still survive as a now peaceful sect in the Lebanon Mountains.

Another aberrant Ismaili movement, that of the Druses of the Lebanon Mountains, was the result of the missionary efforts of al-Darazi (from whom the Druses take their name) in the eleventh century. He persuaded these mountain-dwellers that the Fatimid Caliph al-Hakim, who mysteriously disappeared, was the last and most perfect of ten successive incarnations of God and would return as Mahdi. It is said that the Druses, who have formed a closed society for centuries, number today some one hundred thousand in several separate locations.

Still another Ismaili group, an offshoot of the Assassins, the Nizarites of Pakistan, India, Persia and Syria, numbering some 250,000, have as their present head Agha Khan IV. He is a descendant of the chief of the Assassins and a Harvard graduate.

VII Two Deviations from the Established Norms

The Dervishes

As we have seen, the Sufi movement early gave rise, after observation in Syria of the value of certain types of Christian organization, to the nearest approach in Islam to church worship and ecclesiastical organization. Under masters or guides the devotees of Sufi mystical experiences drew apart into retreats or monastic houses, to live fraternally in something like communistic societies and to enjoy social fellowship along with their mystical raptures. Those of them who began a wandering life, dependent on charity, came to be called dervishes (from the Persian *darwish*, meaning "one who comes to the door," i.e., to beg). Because of their distinctive dress, their begging baskets,* and their known addiction to ecstatic experiences, they excited great interest.

The poets celebrated them, some in fun, others in order to pay them grave respect. The "nightingale of Shiraz," the poet Sa'di, believed in the dervishes and himself practiced meditation with them, but he warned them that a dervish is not made such by his clothes.

The dervish's course of life is spent in commemorating, and thanking, and serving, and obeying God; and in beneficence and contentment; and in the acknowledgement of one God and reliance on Him; and in resignation and patience. Everyone who is endued with these qualities is, in fact, a dervish, though dressed in a tunic. But a babbler, who neglects prayer, and is given to sensuality, and the gratification of his appetite; who spends his days till nightfall in the pursuit of licentiousness, and passes his night till day returns in careless slumber; eats whatever is set before him, and says whatever comes upper-

---

* Not all the dervishes beg, however. Many dervish orders raise their own food.

most; is a profligate, though he wear the habit of a der-vish.[M]

Since the twelfth century a number of widespread dervish orders or brotherhoods have been founded, each with its own monastic retreats, special rites, and methods of inducing ecstasy. The Qadariya were the first of these orders. Founded in Baghdad by Abd-al-Qadar al-Jilani (1077–1166), it has spread, thinly to be sure, to Java in the East and Algeria in the West. The so-called Howling Dervishes (the Rifa'iya) came next, being founded in the second half of the twelfth century by Ahmad al-Rifa'i. The widely known Whirling Dervishes (the Maulawiya) are members of an order founded by disciples of the Persian poet Jalal al-Din Rumi, whom we have quoted on a previous page (pp. 546 f.), and who be-queathed to his followers not his verses only but also, to accompany them, a method of using music as an important and stimulating element in their rites, whereby they were made to whirl about in ecstasy.

The more extreme of the dervishes have turned out to be little more than shamans. They astonish the pious, in the manner of their Hindu prototypes, by swallowing live coals and snakes and by passing needles, hooks, and knives through their flesh. Many wear special badges, use rosaries, and venerate the founders of their orders as saints.

The dervish orders parallel the Franciscans of Europe in admitting lay members, who live and work in the world but have stated times, usually in the evening, when they come to the monasteries to take part in religious exercises directed by a leader.

It should be added, perhaps, that though the sort of dervishes who have whirled, or howled, or lashed themselves into frenzy by using whips or knives have given dervishes as a group much notoriety, the ma-jority are content to practice their quiet devotional life in the fellowship of their houses and do not show themselves often in public. Their popular following has been often quite large, for in medieval times, for most people, the sufi orders *were* religion in its most sincere form.

Veneration of Saints

The mention above of the practice by dervish orders of the veneration of their founders as saints, brings before us another variation on the standard Muslim themes, the veneration of saints. In early Muslim literature the name *wali* (pl. *waliya*) is given to persons who are "near or close in feeling" or who play a protective role as benefactors. In a religious context the term comes to mean "friend of God" or "one who is near to God," as in Qur'an X.64. But the Sufis made *wali* mean saint, that is, a person possessed by God. R. A. Nicholson in *The Mystics of Islam* shows how human and natural this was, for the wali privately conversing with a small circle of friends became, first a teacher and spiritual guide gathering disciples around him during his lifetime, and finally the sainted head of a religious order bear-ing his name. But saints are not exclusively Sufi. The Muslim world has produced them everywhere, as the long list of saints in Baghdad ("the city of saints"), Turkey (where each province had a saint), Arabia, Egypt, north Africa and India attests. These saints have usually been placed in a hierarchical order differing slightly with the area. Those who are on earth are not always apparent or known even to themselves (hundreds live "hidden" in the world), whereas those who know one another and act to-gether are arranged in an ascending order of merit, with decreasing numbers on the higher levels, until at the top or pole of the hierarchy stands the figure of the greatest saint of his age or time. Saints are sometimes distinguished from prophets, the holy pro-claimers of the word of God; their special merit is to experience the ecstasy of union with God and after-wards to exhibit God in their own persons. In doing so, particularly those associated with the Sufis and the dervish orders perform miracles (*karamat*, "favors" that God bestows), such as flying through the air, walking on water, being in several places at once, resurrecting the dead, turning earth into gold or jewels, and the like.

Although the practice is not Qur'anic, the Sufis

555

The Taj Mahal, Agra, India. Erected by Shah Jahan in memory of his wife, this marble mausoleum is considered by many the most perfect building in the world. Only the Greek Parthenon is compared with it. Although the other buildings around it quite obviously belong to a particular century, it has a timeless character, as though in its perfection it is dateless and eternal. (*Courtesy of the Government of India Tourist Office.*)

and the common people, fairly generally throughout the Muslim world, visit the tombs of Muslim saints to leave votive offerings, pray for the intercession of the saints, and ask their blessing (*barakah*) upon them personally. Many of these tombs are found in the vicinity of mosques and may quite often be surrounded by the graves of those whose last wish it was to be buried nearby. Of course, to worship the sainted dead is in direct conflict with the spirit, if not the letter, of the Qur'an, but most of the 'ulama' have tolerated and even joined in it, because the consensus of the community (ijma') has almost everywhere overridden the objections of the critics.

VIII The Feasts and Festivals of the Muslim Year

Although the Sunnis, Sufis, and Shi'ites have tended at certain points to differ to the extent of irreconcilability, it must be said that powerful unitive forces have always been at work. Chief is the Qur'an itself, and running a close second are the Five Pillars, especially the observance of the five daily times of prayer and the pilgrimage to Mecca. Not far behind in bringing a sense of over-all unity to the Muslim world are the recurring feasts and festivals of the Muslim year. They were gradually developed through the centuries to the number of five. (Five plays a role in Islam comparable to three in Christianity.) These feasts and festivals are observed differently in the various Muslim lands, but they have a common intention.

The feasts are two:

1. The so-called "little feast" at the end of the fast of Ramadan, called '*Id al-Fitr*. It is the occasion of great merriment and occurs on the first day of the month Shawwal.

2. The Feast of Sacrifice ('*Id al-Adha*) or the "great feast." It falls on the day (the tenth day of the month Dhu-al-Hijja) when the pilgrims outside Mecca have returned half-way from the Great Pilgrimage and are making a feast of sacrifice by ritually offering up the

allowed animals and joining in a joyous sharing of their flesh (pp. 534 f.).

The festivals are three:

1. The New Year Festival (*Muharram*), observed during the first days of the first month. The Shi'ites take this occasion to commemorate the death of al-Husain and his little son in the night battle of Karbala; they do so by dedicating the first ten days to lamentation, at the end of which a passion play is performed with much attention to the suffering and death of the son and grandson of 'Ali.*

2. The Festival of the Prophet's Birthday (*Mawlid an-Nabi*), held traditionally on the twelfth day of the month Rabi 'al-awwal. (In point of time this is the last of the festivals to be evolved.)

3. The Festival of the Prophet's Night Journey (*Lailat al-Mir'aj*), observed as a rule on the night preceding the twenty-seventh day of the month Rajab. Mosques and minarets are lighted in honor of the famous "night journey," and the hadiths concerning the event are reverentially read.

IX Recent Developments

That Islam has continued in the more recent past to give rise to powerful new movements within itself

---

* It could be said that whereas the celebration of the New Year throughout the Muslim world is unitive, this particular observance is divisive, for the "passion play" of the Shi'ites magnifies the tragedy of Karbala and perpetuates its memory. The story of the assault which caused the death of Husain's son by a flying arrow, the slaying of a nephew by mutilation by the sword, and Husain's own death and mutilation under the hooves of horses is dramatically re-enacted, its effects heightened by amplifications bringing in angels, prophets, and kings. Also stressed are such peculiarly Shi'ite assertions as the pre-existence of Muhammad (who is said to have designated 'Ali as his rightful successor some days before he "went back to heaven"), the divine powers and attributes of 'Ali, and the savior roles of Hasan and Husain, the latter portrayed, like Christ, as vicariously atoning by his death for the sins of mankind. Little wonder that Shi'ites have at times been so aroused that they have rioted in vengeful fury, not without the sympathy of non-Shi'ite witnesses of the dramatic episodes.

—movements even of a disruptive kind—is plain in the history of the last two centuries. These movements may generally be said, on analysis, to emphasize in various degrees purification, secularism, conservatism, reformulation and, in at least one heretical development, syncretism.

Before we survey these more recent movements, a general observation needs to be made. It might be thought that the reformulations that have occurred within modern Islam must be the inevitable effect of the influx of new ideas and practices from western Europe and America. There can be no doubt that this effect is mounting in significance, but it constitutes only part of the total situation. Muslims themselves find that the recent diversifications within their faith are principally due to two forms of Islamic self-searching: (1) revival and reform due strictly to internal causes reaching back to the fourteenth century, and (2) a defensive restatement of the essential and central elements in Muslim belief and practice, attempted in the face of the encroachment of the modern West and in order to render Muslim minds immune to foreign subversion. Western science and technology have begun to penetrate the Muslim defenses, but Western thought has not done so to the same extent. Alien modes of looking at life and the world, whether in the form of the universalism of missionaries seeking to convert the Muslims to a world Christianity or of Western philosophy from Thomas Aquinas to Marxian dialectical materialism, have had an extraordinarily widespread negative effect in alerting the whole Muslim community to the threat of disintegrative change.

The prime instance of the first form of Islamic self-searching is the *purification* begun in inner Arabia in the eighteenth century—the Wahhabi movement, a stern puritan reform that grew to great strength through the support of the emirs of the house of Sa'ud. It represented a return to earlier Hanbalite theories of conduct and was greatly influenced by the anti-Sufism of the fourteenth-century writer Ibn Taimiya. The movement took its name from its originator Muhammad ibn 'Abd al-Wahhab, whose aim was to lead Muslims in a return to Muhammad and

557

the Qur'an. To this end he rejected all modifications of Muslim belief and practice traced to "the consensus of community opinion" (ijma'), except for those that went back authentically to the Medina community immediately after the death of Muhammad. "Sufi innovations" were especially frowned upon. Accordingly, the Wahhabis (or *Ikwan*, "brothers") condemned all blood feuds and tribal distinctions and urged the utmost purity and simplicity of life, without wine or tobacco. Through the years they have firmly emphasized Muslim unitarianism, and so fierce has been their rejection of Sufi-inspired intercessory prayers at the tombs and shrines of holy men and women (which they denounce as saint-worship, and therefore polytheism) that when they captured Mecca in 1806, they destroyed the tombs before which pilgrims did reverence. Again, in 1924–1925, when the deposed sultan ceded Mecca and Medina to Saudi Arabia, they turned the birthplace of Muhammad himself into a camel's resting-place and demolished the markers on the graves of Muhammad's family and of his Companions. To accept as true any belief not confirmed by the Qur'an, the authentic hadiths, or strict reasoning is an act of infidelity. Houses and clothes must be plain; joking, music, and gold ornaments are forbidden. Such games as chess should be given up because they may make the players forget the hours of prayer.

The extremism of the Wahhabis has been generally rejected by the Muslim world, but their devotion to historic Islam pure and undefiled has had pronounced reformative effects in north Africa, India, and the East Indies.

Ironically enough, the faithful in Saudi Arabia now find the outside world intruding mightily into their way of life. Their civil leaders have concluded agreements and treaties with the great powers with respect to the oil reserves under their sands, and Saudi Arabia has experienced not only a quick inflow of vast wealth but also the introduction in increasing measure of Western inventions and conveniences, such as automobiles, trailer-trucks, airplanes, air-conditioned housing, radios, movies, hospitals, sanitary devices, artesian wells, and much else of a like kind. It is a question whether the orthodox in Saudi Arabia can preserve their puritan simplicity and conservatism much longer.

The Sufis, meanwhile, have had too great a measure of support among the common people to worry overmuch because the Wahhabis assailed them. In the name of long-corroborated religious experience they have continued to uphold the validity of personal religious response, intuition, the practices of their religious orders, and reverence for sainted leaders. This is true especially in the non-Arab areas and particularly among the Berbers, Iranians, and Turks. But even the Sufis have been chastened by Wahhabi puritanism and orthodoxy; in fact, they have abandoned many a practice to which they were once devoted.

When most of Africa and much of Asia came under the rule of the European powers, it was inevitable that Western books and periodicals, Western-sponsored schools and academies, and still more the colonial administrations themselves, with all the political and economic changes that accompanied them, should introduce into the occupied areas new concepts of law and political organization, new forms of commercial and industrial enterprise, new modes of transport by land, sea, and air, improvements in agriculture, scientific medicine, and never-before-dreamed-of wealth through the exploitation of newly discovered natural resources, particularly oil. Conservatives who cling to the old Muslim way of life naturally view these developments with more than a little alarm.

Muslims, liberal or conservative, have learned how to use the printed page. From about the middle of the nineteenth century there began to appear Muslim books and periodicals that have enjoyed wide circulation from West to East, their general aim being to save Islam by uniting the Muslim world to meet the challenge of the contemporary scene, although the final effect has been to increase the diversity of opinion as to how this may be done. Perhaps the most important fact here is this: Muslims began to reason again as they had not actively done so in centuries.

Indeed, the 'ulama' or conservative scholars have had some difficulty controlling the effects of this recovery of the use of reason, especially in the bold expression of private judgment. On the other hand, the *conservatism* of the 'ulama' has had wide support in every part of the Islamic world where the fear prevails that revelation may be corrupted by reason, if restraints are not imposed.

In attempting here to cope with the vast amount of detail that has been accumulated concerning recent developments in Islam, perhaps the simplest and most clarifying thing to do is to review events in some of the major areas of the Muslim world.

The most startling political and cultural changes have occurred in Turkey. There *secularism* has reached an open form. The Young Turks, led by Mustapha Kemal, overthrew the Ottoman caliphate in 1924 and went on to revolutionary changes that were openly designed to Westernize and secularize Turkey. The separation of church and state and new laws affecting marriage, divorce, the family, the status and dress of women, education, and public conduct in general have brought about drastic changes. The effect has been to remove Turkey from vital interrelationships with the rest of the Muslim world.

During the last hundred years Egypt has been the scene of religious and political developments that have had great importance in Muslim eyes. The revival of Egyptian influence began with the untiring efforts of Jamal al-Din al-Afghani (1839–1897), the founder of the pan-Islamic movement to unite the Muslim peoples against European domination and to incite them to rid themselves of certain religious and social departures from a pure Islam based on Qur'anic orthodoxy, and thus enable them to meet the challenge of the European world. Concentrating upon the latter objective, his disciple, Muhammad Abduh (1849–1905), a teacher and later a member of the administrative committee of the old University of Cairo (al-Azhar), urged not only the necessity of renewed study of the classical Arabic theological works but also the introduction into the university curriculum of courses in modern science, geography, and European history and religion. He was resolved to take seriously the orthodox position that reason cannot contradict revelation but can only confirm it. Reason is, moreover, of decisive importance not only in moral conduct and the quest of happiness, to which all men are entitled, but also in the understanding of the principles of the Qur'an.

One of the consequences of his teaching has been the strengthening of tendencies toward a "modernism" that advocates a *reformulation* of Muslim doctrines and laws using modern as opposed to traditional language. But, on the other hand, his return, in the spirit of Wahhabism, to Muhammad and the traditions of the early Medina community resulted in formation of a back-to-the-Qur'an religious group called the Salafiya, led by his Syrian disciple Rashid Rida, the editor of a periodical that was read from one end of the Muslim world to the other. The Salafi movement spread to North Africa, India, and the East Indies.

The Egyptian influence may be seen in another form: the rise of religious societies, such as The Young Men's Muslim Association (inspired by the Y.M.C.A.) and the stern Wahhabi-motivated Muslim Brotherhood, a powerful factor in Egyptian politics before and since the independence of Egypt.

Potentially more decisive for Egypt abroad, as well as at home, is the military regime established by Jamal Abd al-Nasir ("Nasser"). In seizing the Suez Canal and in establishing the United Arab Republic, Nasser has attempted to achieve two aims: to rid Egypt of the last vestiges of colonialism and to seek pan-Islamic unity. He has succeeded in his first aim but not so far in his second, for Syria withdrew in 1961 from the U.A.R. and spiked his initial plans.

Turning now to India before its partition, we find a type of reformulation by a number of the Muslim liberal leaders that recalls that of the Hindu founders of the Brahmo Samaj. The readiness of intellectuals in India through the centuries to consider openmindedly every variety of thought is reflected in the broad-mindedness of Sir Sayyid Ahmad Khan (1817–

1898). He was aided rather than hindered, curiously enough, by the spread of the Wahhabi movement among Indian Muslims, for, as we have seen, its rejection of Sufi emotionalism and its insistence on a return to Muhammad and the early Medina community gave new importance to reason as a guide in religion. He took his stand upon the supreme authority of Muhammad, the Qur'an, and the early traditions, asserting that both nature and reason confirm any open-minded man in such a stand. Because Allah supports nature as well as revelation, reason can find no real contradiction between them. Hence, science or the study of nature, when properly pursued, cannot conflict with the Qur'an but only confirm it. Accordingly, Sir Sayyid founded a Muslim university at Aligarh in 1875 with a curriculum that accompanied the study of the Muslim religion with courses in Western social and natural sciences (an advanced position from which the university, now in Pakistan, has since retreated).

Among the Indian intellectual leaders who were encouraged to take liberal positions influenced by Western thought was Sayyid Amir Ali, a Shi'ite, whose book *The Spirit of Islam* (first published in 1891 with the title *The Life and Teachings of Mohammad*) defends Islam as a liberal religion based on the perfect moral personality of Muhammad and the reasonableness of the Qur'an. This book is a classic among Muslim liberals and is widely used also by conservatives who wish to know what a modernist might believe. Even more liberal are the lectures delivered in English in 1928 by Sir Muhammad Iqbal and published under the title *The Reconstruction of Religious Thought in Islam*. A poet inspired by Sufi mysticism, Iqbal proposed a reconstruction of Muslim thought in quite non-Wahhabist terms; he stressed the validity of personal religious experience, the immanence of God, creative evolution à la Bergson, and the emergence of the superman à la Nietzsche. So radical is this position that it is doubtful whether Iqbal has had many followers outside of India.

We should not exaggerate the influence of such

intellectuals as these, for we need to be reminded, in the words of H. A. R. Gibbs, that "the illiterate Muslim, the villager, is in no danger yet of losing his faith, and, even if he were, the educated town-bred modernist would have no word to meet his needs. His spiritual life is cared for by the Sufi brotherhoods, regular or irregular, by the imam of the local mosque, or by the itinerant revivalist preacher."[N]

On August 14, 1947, the status of Muslims in India changed; the "Partition" took place. In two areas, West Pakistan and East Pakistan, a Muslim state was born. In India fifty million Muslims became a religious minority, with the political right to be represented in the Indian Parliament. As to Pakistan, Wilfred Cantwell Smith has said: "Before August 14, 1947, the Muslims of India had their art, their theology, their mysticism; but they had no state. When Jinnah proposed to them that they should work to get themselves one, they responded with a surging enthusiasm. Their attainment, on that date, of a state of their own was greeted with an elation that was religious as well as personal. It was considered a triumph not only for Muslims but for Islam."[P] But what is an Islamic state? The framers of the constitution decided against making Pakistan a theocracy, for they did not wish the final decisions to be the prerogative of the 'ulama'; the decision was to lie with the people as the final political authority. But the people have yet to become used to the practice of democracy, and so the intention to create a truly Islamic state is still just that, for Pakistan, after twenty years of experience and trial, is still in the formative stage.

As to revivalist preachers, one such developed an organized religious movement that has distinctly heretical aspects in the eyes of the orthodox. Its leader, Mirza Ghulam Ahmad of Qadrian (d. 1908) accepted homage as a Mahdi in the closing decades of the nineteenth century. A reading of the Bible convinced him he was also the Messiah (Jesus in a second coming), and in 1904 he proclaimed himself an avatar of Krishna. But he remained a Muslim in the sense that he said he was not a prophet in himself but only in and through Muhammad. In his teaching he made it clear that holy war is not to be carried on by the use of force but only through preaching. His followers, the Ahmadiya, are therefore at once pacifists and ardent missionaries. The Ahmadiya have split into several branches. The original or Qadiani branch is *consciously syncretist* and all but outside the Muslim community. The Lahore branch is devotedly Muslim in character and has rejected the extreme claims that Ahmad made for himself, although they consider him to be a genuine "renewer of religion." Ahmadiya missionaries of both these branches are active in England, America, Africa, and the East Indies, where they make considerable use of the printed page and regard Christian leaders as their chief adversaries. They often maintain, as for example on the outskirts of London, their own mosques, to which they cordially welcome all comers, including conservative Muslims.

Persia (or Iran) has unwillingly given rise to another syncretistic movement, one that has, like Sikhism, become a separate and distinct faith. This is Bahai. Its background is Shi'ite. Influenced by the teachings of a heretical Shi'ite to the effect that the imams of the Twelver sect were "gates" by which the believers gained access to the true faith, and that the hidden imam seeks further "gates" to conduct men to himself, a certain Mirza Ali Muhammad in 1844 added his name to the list and called himself Bab-ud-Din ("Gate of the Faith"). His followers were called after him Babis. He proclaimed that his mission was to prepare the way for a greater than himself who should come after him and complete the work of reform and righteousness that he had begun. When he said his writings were scripture equaling, if not superseding, the Qur'an, and on their basis advocated sweeping religious and social reforms, he was executed in 1850 as a heretic and disturber of the peace. Among his followers was a well-born youth who, following Babi custom, took the name of Baha'u'Lah ("Glory of God"). He was accused of complicity in an attempt by a fanatical Babi to assassinate the shah in 1852 and was exiled to Baghdad. After some ten years there, when he and his followers were on the point of departure, he announced that he was the one-who-should-come of whom the Bab had spoken. Moving with his followers, who now called themselves after him Bahais, he sought asylum in the Muslim areas to the west and was finally imprisoned by the Turks in Acre, Palestine, for the balance of his life. His writings reached the outside world. They advocated a broad religious view upholding the unity of God and the essential harmony of all prophecy when rightly understood. He called upon all religions to unite, for every religion contains some truth, because all prophets are witnesses to the one Truth that Bahaism supremely represents. The human race is one under God and will be united through his spirit when the Bahai cause is known and joined. Outlawed in Iran, Bahai, with its headquarters in Haifa in Palestine, is active in many countries, and especially in the United States.

Although many observers have felt during the past quarter of a century that Islam has been yielding on all sides to the disintegrative influences of Western culture, it remains still to be seen whether or not the establishment of the state of Israel in Palestine will have the effect, for a period at least, of drawing the Muslim world together into a tighter unity and a heightening of resistance to change.

Finally, what is Islam? We have come far enough to see that it cannot be treated simply as a set of more or less narrowly defined "religious" beliefs, for it is also a way of life, and more—an entire cultural complex, including philosophical and literary works. It also includes many vital activities, each interacting with the others and with non-Islamic religions and cultures. In this study we have become aware of these various aspects of Islam as we have pondered what constitutes the Islamic tradition, a tradition no more immune to inner movements of change, growth, and diversification than the other religions of the world.

561

Suggestions for Further Reading

ADAMS, C. C. *Islam and Modernism in Egypt.* Oxford, 1933

'ALI, MUHAMMAD. *The Religion of Islam.* Lahore, 1950

'ALI, SAYYID AMIR. *The Spirit of Islam.* Christopher's, London, 1922

ANDRAE, TOR. *Mohammed: the Man and His Faith.* Tr. by Theophil Menzel. Allen and Unwin, 1936. Available as Harper Torchbooks pb

ARBERRY, A. J. *The Koran Interpreted.* George Allen & Unwin, 1955. A translation of the *Qur'an* in 2 vols. Combined in a one-vol. pb by Macmillan

————. *Sufism.* George Allen and Unwin, 1950

————. *Reason and Revelation in Islam.* George Allen & Unwin, 1957

ARNOLD, T. W. *The Caliphate.* Oxford, 1924

ARNOLD AND GUILLAUME, EDS. *The Legacy of Islam.* 2nd ed., Oxford, 1948

ASAD, MUHAMMAD. *Sahih al-Bukhari.* Lahore, Arafat Publications, 1938. A portion of the Traditions gathered by al-Bukhari

AL-ASH'ARI. *al-Ibanah 'an Usul ad-Diyanah.* Ash'ari's principal work tr. by Walter Klein. American Oriental Society, New Haven, 1940

BELL, R. *Introduction to the Qur'an.* Edinburgh University Press, 1953

————. *The Qur'an.* 2 vols., Edinburgh, 1937–1939

————. *The Origin of Islam in its Christian Environment.* London, 1926

CRAGG, KENNETH. *The Call of the Minaret.* Oxford University Press, 1956

DONALDSON, D. M. *The Shi'ite Religion.* Luzac, 1933

————. *Studies in Muslim Ethics.* London, 1950

FARIS, NABIH AMIN, ED. *The Arab Heritage.* Princeton University Press, 1944

GAUDEFOY-DEMOMBYNES, M. *Muslim Institutions.* Macmillan, 1951

GIBB, H. A. R. *Modern Trends in Islam.* University of Chicago Press, 1947

————. *Mohammedanism, an Historical Survey.* Oxford, 1949. Mentor pb, 1955

————. "The Structure of Religious Thought in Islam," in a vol. of Gibb's writings ed. by S. J. Shaw and W. R. Polk, *Studies on the Civilization of Islam.* Beacon Press, 1962

———— AND KRAMER, ET AL, EDS. *Shorter Encyclopaedia of Islam.* E. J. Brill, Leiden, 1953

GOLDSACK, WILLIAM, TR. *Selections from Muhammadan Traditions.* Christian Literature Society, Madras, 1923

GOLDZIHER, I. *Mohammed and Islam.* Tr. by K. C. Seelye. Yale University Press, 1917

GRUNEBAUM, G. E. VON. *Medieval Islam.* University of Chicago Press, 1953

————. *Islam: Essays in the Nature and Growth of a Cultural Tradition.* Menasha, 1955

————. *Muhammadan Festivals.* New York, 1951

GUILLAUME, ALFRED. *Islam.* Penguin Books pb, 1954

————. *The Traditions of Islam.* Oxford, 1924

————. *Life of Muhammed.* Oxford, 1955

HITTI, P. K. *History of the Arabs.* 5th ed., Macmillan, 1951

HOLLISTER, JOHN N. *The Shi'a of India.* Luzac & Co., London, 1953

IQBAL, MOHAMMED. *Reconstruction of Religious Thought in Islam.* 2nd ed., Oxford, 1934

IVANOW, W. *Brief Survey of the Evolution of Ismailism.* Ismaili Society, Bombay

IZUTSU, TOSHIHIKO. *The Structure of the Ethical Terms in the Koran.* Keio Institute of Philological Studies, Tokyo, 1959

JEFFERY, ARTHUR, ED. *Islam.* Liberal Arts Press pb, 1958. Readings on Muhammad and his religion

————. *A Reader on Islam.* 's Gravenhage, Mouton and Co., 1962

————. *The Qur'an as Scripture.* Moore Publishing Co., N.Y., 1952

LANE, EDWARD. *Manners and Customs of the Modern Egyptians.* Any ed.

LEVY, R. *The Social Structure of Islam.* Cambridge, 1957

LEWIS, B. *The Arabs in History.* London, 1950

MACDONALD, DUNCAN B. *Development of Muslim Theology, Jurisprudence, and Constitutional Theory.* Scribner's Sons, 1903

————. *The Religious Attitude and Life in Islam.* University of Chicago Press, 1909

NICHOLSON, R. A. *The Mystics of Islam.* London, 1914

————. *A Literary History of the Arabs.* 2nd ed., Cambridge, 1930

————. *Studies in Islamic Mysticism.* Cambridge University Press, 1921

————, ED. AND TR. *The Mathnawi.* Luzac & Co., London, 1925–40

O'LEARY, DELACY. *Arabic Thought and Its Place in History.* Routledge & Kegan Paul, 1922

PADWICK, CONSTANCE. *Muslim Devotions.* London, Society for Promoting Christian Knowledge, 1961

SCHACHT, JOSEPH. *Origins of Muhammadan Jurisprudence.* Clarendon Press, Oxford, 1950

SMITH, MARGARET. *The Sufi Path of Love.* Luzac & Co., London, 1954

SMITH, W. C. *Modern Islam in India.* Lahore, 1943

————. *Islam in Modern History.* Princeton, 1957. Available as Mentor pb, 1959

SMITH, W. ROBERTSON. *Religion of the Semites.* Cambridge University Press, 1885; republished as Meridian Books pb, 1956

TRITTON, A. S. *Muslim Theology.* Luzac & Co., London, 1947

WATT, W. M. *Free Will and Predestination in Early Islam.* Luzac, London, 1948

————. *Muhammed: Prophet and Statesman.* Oxford University Press, 1961

————. *Islam and the Integration of Society.* Routledge & Kegan Paul, London, 1961

WENSINCK, A. J. *The Muslim Creed: Its Genesis and Historical Development.* Cambridge, 1932

WILLIAMS, JOHN A., ED. *Islam.* George Braziller, N.Y., 1961. Washington Square pb, 1963. Readings

References for Quotations

REFERENCES ARE ARRANGED in the order in which they are first quoted in the body of the text. They are preceded in the left-hand margin by the capital letters, that are their identifying symbols. The page numbers of the books from which quotations are taken are immediately preceded, in small type, by the number that is affixed to the end of the quotation in the body of the text. Where a book has been more than once quoted, as often happens when original sources are drawn upon, page numbers are arranged in the order of quotation in the text.

Chapter 1. Religion in Prehistoric and Primitive Cultures

A. Brontislaw Malinowski, article "Culture," *Encyclopaedia of the Social Sciences*. Macmillan Company, New York, 1931, p. 630.

B. E. B. Tylor, *Primitive Culture*. 2 vols. G. P. Putnam's sons, New York, 1871, Vol. II, p. 185.

C. E. W. Hopkins, *The Origin and Evolution of Religion*. Yale University Press, 1923, p. 13.

D. Mabel Cooke Cole, *Savage Gentlemen*. D. Van Nostrand Company, New York, 1929, p. 15.

E. Vergilias Ferm, ed., *Forgotten Religions*. Philosophical Library, New York, 1950, p. 275.

F. A. W. Howitt, *The Native Tribes of South-East Australia*. Macmillan and Company, London, 1904. [1] p. 395; [2] p. 798; [3] p. 650; [4] p. 661.

G. Rai Bahadur Sarat Chandra Roy, *The Birhors; A Little Known Jungle Tribe of Chota Nagpur*. Ranchi, India, 1925. [1] pp. 70–76; [2] p. 352; [3] p. 241; [4] pp. 284–285; [5] p. 237; [6] p. 369; [7] pp. 378–384

H. Hugh Stayt, *The BaVenda*. Oxford University Press, publishing for the International African Institute, London, 1928. [1] p. 262; [2] p. 276; [3] p. 276; [4] p. 162; [5] p. 230. Reprinted by permission of the publishers.

Chapter 2. Representative National Religions of the Past

A. Henri Frankfort, et al., *Before Philosophy*, Pelican Books, 1949, p. 74.

B. Rudolph Anthes, "Mythology in Ancient Egypt," in *Mythologies of the Ancient World*, edited by S. N. Kramer, Anchor Books, 1961, p. 22.

564

C. J. H. Breasted, *The Dawn of Conscience*. Charles Scribner's Sons, New York, 1934. [1] pp. 25, 27; [2] p. 281; [3] pp. 284–286. Reprinted by permission of the publishers.

D. *The History of Herodotus*. Translated by G. C. Macaulay. Macmillan and Company, London, 1914, Vol. I, p. 153. Reprinted by permission of the publishers.

E. J. H. Breasted, *Development of Religion and Thought in Ancient Egypt*. Charles Scribner's Sons, New York, 1912. [1] p. 295; [2] pp. 299–300. Reprinted by permission of the publishers.

F. Sir W. Flinders Petrie, *Religious Life in Ancient Egypt*. Constable and Company, Ltd., London, and Houghton Mifflin Company, Boston, 1924, p. 118. Reprinted by permission of the publishers.

G. W. F. Albright, *From the Stone Age to Christianity; Monotheism and the Historical Process*. Johns Hopkins Press, 1940, p. 166. Reprinted by permission of the publishers.

H. Samuel N. Kramer, *Sumerian Mythology*. Harper Torchbooks, 1961, p. 73 f.

I. James B. Pritchard, ed., *Ancient Near Eastern Texts Relating to the Old Testament*. Rev. ed. Princeton University Press, 1955. [1] p. 161; [2] p. 162 f.; [3] p. 107; [4] p. 108; [5] pp. 384–85. Reprinted by permission of Princeton University Press.

J. R. W. Rogers, *The Religion of Babylonia and Assyria*. Eaton and Mains, New York, 1908. [1] pp. 124–126; [2] p. 201; [3] pp. 202–204.

K. Morris Jastrow, *Aspects of Religious Belief and Practice in Babylonia and Assyria*. G. P. Putnam's Sons, New York, 1911. [1] p. 374; [2] p. 303. Reprinted by permission of the publishers.

L. Gilbert Murray, *Five Stages of Greek Religion*. Oxford, Clarendon Press. 1925. [1] p. 87; [2] p. 94. Reprinted by permission of the publishers.

M. Jane E. Harrison, *Mythology*. Marshall Jones, Boston, 1924, p. 94.

N. *The Iliad of Homer*. Translated by Edward Earl of Derby. Everyman's Library, J. M. Dent and Sons, London, 1910. [1] p. 2 (Bk. I); [2] p. 94 (Bk. V), substituting Hera for Juno in the translation; [3] p. 212 (Bk. XIII); [4] p. 239 (Bk. XIV); [5] p. 281 (Bk. XVI).

P. Jane E. Harrison, *Prolegomena to the Study of Greek Religion*. Cambridge University Press, London, 1903, p. 321.

Q. *Greek Religious Thought from Homer to the Age of Alexander*. Edited by F. M. Cornford. J. M. Dent and Sons, London, and E. P. Dutton and Company, New York, 1923. [1] p. 94; [2] p. 50, arranging lines in verse forms; [3] p. 51, arranged as verse; [4] p. 87; [5] p. 85. Reprinted by permission of the publishers.

R. *The House of Atreus, Being the Agamemnon, Libation-bearers, and Furies of Aeschylus*. Translated by E. D. A. Morshead. The Macmillan Company, London, 1901, pp. 18, 22 (Agamemnon, 380–385, 467–476).

S. *The Plays of Euripides*. Translated into rhyming verse by Gilbert Murray. George Allen & Unwin, London, 1914. [1] "Hippolytus," 1347 ff.; [2] Ibid., 1144 f.; [3] Ibid., 1102 f.; [4] "The Trojan Women," 884–888. Reprinted by permission of the publishers.

T. *The Dialogues of Plato*. Translated and edited by Benjamin Jowett. Oxford University Press, London, 1893. [1] Bk. II, 378; [2] Bk. II, 364–365.

U. Carl Clemen, ed. *Religions of the World; Their Nature and History*. George G. Harrap and Company, London, and Harcourt, Brace and Company, New York, 1931. [1] p. 204; [2] p. 220. Quoted by permission of the publishers.

V. Cyril Bailey, *The Religion of Ancient Rome*. Constable and Company, London, 1907, pp. 18–19. Reprinted by permission of the author.

W. George Foot Moore, *History of Religions*, 2 vols. Charles Scribner's Sons, New York, and T. & T. Clark, Edinburgh, 1913, 1919, Vol. I, p. 541. Reprinted by permission of the publishers.

Y. Cyril Bailey, *Phases of the Religion of Ancient Rome*. University of California Press, 1932, p. 74.

Chapter 3. Early Hinduism

A. *The Hymns of the Rig Veda*. Translated by Ralph T. Griffith. E. J. Lazarus and Company, Benares, 1896. [1] VI. 23.6, 7; [2] X. 90.10–13; [3] I. 50.2; [4] X. 139.1, I. 35.11; [5] X. 14.1, 2, 7, 8; [6] V. 85.7, 8; [7] VII. 98.7, 8; [8] I. 164.46. Reprinted by arrangement with the publishers.

B. *The Satapatha Brahmana* in the *Sacred Books of the East*. Oxford, Clarendon Press, 1879–1910. [1] X. 6.4.1 (Vol. XLIII, p. 40); [2] XIII. 3.1.1 (Vol. XLIV, p. 328); [3] II. 4.2.8–24 (Vol. XII, pp. 363–369).

C. *Vedic Hymns*. Translated by Edward J. Thomas. *Wisdom of the East* series. John Murray, London, 1923. [1] p. 45 (Bk. I. 32.2, 3); [2] pp. 48–51 (II. 12.7–9, 15); [3] p. 70 (I. 114.7–9); [4] pp. 65–66 (V. 57.4–5); [5] p. 31 (I. 113.7). Reprinted by permission of the publisher.

D. Franklin Edgerton, *The Beginnings of Indian Philosophy*. George Allen & Unwin, London, 1963, p. 18 f.

E. *Hymns from the Rig Veda*. Metrically translated by A. A. Macdonell. Association Press, Calcutta; printed by the Wesleyan Mission Press, Mysore, without date, p. 80 (Bk. VIII. 48.3).

F. *Sacred Books of the East*, Vol. XLII, *The Hymns of the Atharva Veda*. Translated by Maurice Bloomfield. Oxford, Clarendon Press, 1897. [1] p. 163 (Bk. VI. 26); [2] p. 31 (VI. 136). Reprinted by permission of the publishers.

G. Surendranath Dasgupta, *History of Indian Philosophy*. 3 vols. Cambridge University Press, 1932, Vol. II, pp. 300–301. Reprinted by permission of the Syndics of the Cambridge University Press.

H. *The Thirteen Principal Upanishads*. Translated by R. E. Hume. Oxford University Press, London, 1934. [1] Svet. 6.17, p. 410; [2] Mait. 6.17, p. 435; [3] Chand. 3.14.1, p. 209; [4] Mait. 6.3, 7, p. 425; [5] Brih. 2.1–20, pp. 92–95; [6] Kath. 5.2, p. 356; [7] Mund. 2.2.11, p. 373; [8] Brih. 3.7.1–23, pp. 115–117; [9] Chand. 6.8.6, p. 246 f.; [10] Brih. 1.4.7, p. 82; [11] Chand. 3.14.3, p. 210; [12] Chand. 6.12, p. 247; [13] Tait. 2.4, p. 285; [14] Chand. 5.10.7, p. 233; [15] Mait. 1.4, p. 413. Reprinted by permission of the author and publishers.

I. S. Radhakrishnan, *The Philosophy of the Upanishads*. George Allen and Unwin, London, 1924. [1] p. 36; [2] pp. 36–37; [3] p. 23. Reprinted by permission of the publishers.

J. Sir Charles Eliot, *Hinduism and Buddhism*. 3 vols. Edward Arnold and Company, London, 1921, Vol. I, lix. Reprinted by permission of the publishers.

K. George Foot Moore, *The Birth and Growth of Religion*. Charles Scribner's Sons, New York, and T. & T. Clark, Ltd., Edinburgh, 1923, p. 118. Quoted by permission of the publishers.

L. *Sacred Books of the East*, Vol. XXV, *The Laws of Manu*. Translated by G. Bühler. Oxford, Clarendon Press, 1886, pp. 484, 496–498 (XII. 9, 54–67). Reprinted by permission of the publishers.

Chapter 4. Jainism

A. *Sacred Books of the East*, Vol. XXII, *The Gaina Sutras*. Translated by Hermann Jacobi. Oxford, Clarendon Press, 1884. [1] pp. 192–193; [2] p. 250; [3] p. 194; [4] p. 194; [5] p. 200; [6] pp. 80, 79, 82, 79, 87; [7] pp. 82, 83, 86, 82, 86; [8] pp. 80, 84, 85; [9] p. 201; [10] p. 264; [11] p. 52; [12] p. 152; [13] p. 33; [14] pp. 202–210; [15] p. 21; [16] p. 81; [17] p. 264. Reprinted by permission of the publishers.

B. James Bissett Pratt, *India and Its Faiths*. Houghton Mifflin Company, Boston, 1915, p. 255.

C. Carl Clemen, ed., *Religions of the World: Their Nature and History*. George G. Harrap & Co., Ltd., London, and Harcourt, Brace and Company, New York, 1931, p. 106, quoting Otto Strauss. By permission of the publishers.

Chapter 5. Buddhism in its First Phase

A. Kenneth J. Saunders, *Gotama Buddha: A Biography Based on the Canonical Books of the Theravadin*. Association Press, New York, 1920. [1] p. 9 (quoting Anguttara Nikaya 1.45); [2] p. 8; [3] p. 21 (quoting Jataka 1.71); [4] p. 112 (Samyutta IV). Quoted by permission of the publishers.

B. *Asvaghosa's Life of Buddha* (Buddha Carita). Translated from the Chinese version by Samuel Beal. The World's Great Classics, Colonial Press, New York, 1900. [1] p. 306; [2] condensation of a lengthy passage from Bk. XII (following L. Adams Beck, *The Story of Oriental Philosophy*, p. 133).

C. Henry Clarke Warren, *Buddhism in Translation.* Harvard University Press, 1922. [1] p. 55 (Jataka 1.58.7); [2] p. 122 (Majjhima Nikaya 63); [3] p. 129 (Milindapanha 25.1); [4] p. 234 (Ibid. 71.16); [5] p. 239 (Vissudhi Magga 17); [6] p. 136 (Maha-Nidana-Sutta of the Digha-Nikaya, 256.21); [7] p. 436 (Vissudhi Magga 3). Reprinted by permission of the publishers.

D. Sir Charles Eliot, *Hinduism and Buddhism.* 3 vols. Edward Arnold and Company, London, 1921. [1] Vol. I, p. 135 (Anguttara Nikaya 3.35); [2] Vol. I, p. 139 (Majjhima Nikaya 1.22); [3] Vol. I, p. 160 (Maha-Parinibbana 5.25); [4] Vol. I, p. 227 n. (Puggala Pannati 1.39). Reprinted by permission of the publishers.

E. *Further Dialogues of the Buddha.* Translated from the *Majjhima Nikaya* by Lord Chalmers. For the Pali Text Society, Oxford University Press, London, 1926. [1] I. 115 (1.163); [2] I, pp. 115–117 (1.163–166); [3] I, p. 117 (1.166); [4] I, p. 173 (1.240–241); [5] I, p. 174 (1.242); [6] I, p. 56 (1.80); [7] I, p. 176 (1.246); [8] I, p. 15 (1.22); [9] I, p. 17 (1.24); [10] I, p. 118 (1.167). Reprinted by permission of the publishers.

F. For various accounts see **C** above, p. 71 f. (*Jataka* 1.68), which provides the more elaborated version condensed in the text; and Clarence H. Hamilton, ed., *Buddhism, A Religion of Infinite Compassion,* p. 18 f., the *Sutta-Nipata's* version, which makes Mara little more than the personification of Gautama's own doubts and inner states.

G. *Sacred Books of the East,* Vol. XIII, *Vinaya Texts.* Translated by T. W. Rhys Davids and Hermann Oldenberg. Oxford, Clarendon Press, 1883, p. 94. By permission of the publishers.

H. *Buddhist Scriptures.* Translated by Edward J. Thomas. *Wisdom of the East* series. John Murray, London, 1913, p. 52 (Khuddaka Patha 2). Quoted by permission of the publisher.

I. T. W. Rhys Davids, *Buddhism.* Society for Promoting Christian Knowledge, London, 1890, pp. 81–83.

J. George Foot Moore, *History of Religions.* 2 vols. Charles Scribner's Sons, New York, and T. & T. Clark, Ltd., Edinburgh, 1913–1919, Vol. I, p. 296. Quoted by permission of the publishers.

K. A. C. Bouquet, *The Christian Faith and the Non-Christian Religions.* Harper & Bros., 1958, p. 81 (quoting a translation of *Udana* VIII.3 "by a Buddhist").

L. *Sacred Books of the East,* Vol. XI, *Buddhist Suttas.* Translated by T. W. Rhys Davids. Oxford, Clarendon Press, 1881, pp. 148–150. Quoted by permission of the publishers.

M. *Sacred Books of the East,* Vol. X, *The Dhammapada.* Translated by F. Max Müller. Oxford, Clarendon Press, 1881. [1] XVI.211; [2] 1:2–5. Quoted by permission of the publishers.

N. James Bissett Pratt, *The Pilgrimage of Buddhism.* The Macmillan Company, New York, 1928. [1] p. 30 (Udana VIII.8, following the German of Seidenstucken); [2] p. 30 (Samyutta 21, following Mrs. Rhys Davids); [3] p. 54 (Majjhima Nikaya, XXXI.). Reprinted by permission of the publishers.

P. Mrs. T. W. Rhys Davids, *Psalms of the Brethren.* Published for the Pali Text Society by Henry Frowde, London, 1913, p. 362 (CCLXI).

Q. Bikshu Sangharakshita, *A Survey of Buddhism.* Indian Institute of World Culture, Bangalore, 1957, p. 175 (Samyutta-Nikaya, III.235).

R. Edward Conze, ed., *Buddhist Texts Through the Ages.* Harper Torchbooks, 1964, p. 94 (changing *perception* to *ideation*).

S. *Sacred Books of the East,* Vol. X, Part 2, *The Sutta Nipata.* Translated by V. Fausböll. Oxford, Clarendon Press, 1881. [1] p. 6 f. (Khaggavissana Sutta 1–13); [2] p. 25. Quoted by permission of the publishers.

Chapter 6. The Religious Development of Buddhism

A. Carl Clemen, ed., *Religions of the World: Their Nature and History.* George G. Harrap and Co., Ltd., London, and Harcourt, Brace and Company, New York, 1931, pp. 308–309. Quoted by permission of the publishers.

B. Vincent A. Smith, *Asoka, the Buddhist Emperor of India.* Oxford, Clarendon Press, 1920. [1] p. 186; [2] pp. 150, 178. Reprinted by permission of the publishers.

C. T. W. Rhys Davids, *Buddhism.* Society for Promoting Christian Knowledge, London, 1890, pp. 170–171.

D. Bikshu Sangharakshita, *A Survey of Buddhism.* Indian Institute of World Culture, Bangalore, 1957. [1] p. 371 f.; [2] pp. 64 and 66.

E. Sir Charles Eliot, *Hinduism and Buddhism.* 3 vols. Edward Arnold and Company, London, 1921. [1] Vol. II, p. 30 (quoting the Lesser Sukhavati-vyuha); [2] Vol. II, p. 43 (quoting Nagarjuna); [3] Vol. III, p. 404; [4] Vol. II, p. 284 n. 2. Reprinted by permission of the publishers.

F. *Sacred Books of the East,* Vol. XLIX, *Buddhist Mahayana Texts.* Translated by E. B. Cowell, Max Müller, and I. Takakusu. Oxford, Clarendon Press, 1893, pp. 153–154. Reprinted by permission of the publishers.

G. Heinrich Zimmer, *Philosophies of India.* Edited by Joseph Campbell. Bollingen Foundation, 1951; reference here is to Meridian edition, 1956. [1] pp. 447–448, quoting *Majjhima Nikaya,* 3.2.22.-135; [2] p. 485, quoting *Astsahasrika Prajnaparamita,* 1.

H. James Bissett Pratt, *The Pilgrimage of Buddhism.* The Macmillan Company, 1928, p. 480 (quoting Coates and Ishizuka, *Honen, the Buddhist Saint,* pp. 185–187). Quoted by permission of the publishers.

I. Dwight Goddard, ed., *A Buddhist Bible.* Dwight Goddard, Thetford, Vermont, 1938, pp. 497–498 (Sutra Spoken by the Sixth Patriarch). Quoted by permission of the Dwight Goddard estate.

J. Erik Haarh, "Contributions to the Study of Mandala and Mudra," in *Acta Orientalia,* Vol. XXIII, nos. 1–2 (1958), pp. 57–91.

Chapter 7. Later Hinduism

A. *Sacred Books of the East,* Vol. XII, *Satapatha-Brahmana.* Translated by Julius Eggeling. Oxford, Clarendon Press, 1882, pp. 190–191 (1.7.2.5). Reprinted by permission of the publishers.

B. W. Crooke, article "Ancestor-Worship (Indian)," in *Encyclopaedia of Religion and Ethics.* T. & T. Clark, Edinburgh, and Charles Scribner's Sons, New York. Vol. I, p. 453. Reprinted by permission of the publishers.

C. *Sacred Books of the East,* Vol. XXV, *The Laws of Manu.* Translated by G. Bühler. Oxford, Clarendon Press, 1896. [1] p. 195 (V. 148); [2] p. 196 (V. 154); [3] p. 196 (V. 157, 158); [4] p. 197 (V. 161, 164); [5] pp. 87–88 (III. 68–70); [6] p. 198 (VI. 2); [7] pp. 199–205 (VI. 3–6, 8, 16, 29, 33); [8] p. 213 (VI. 82); [9] pp. 206–213 (VI. 42, 43, 55, 56, 44, 45, 65, 81, 79); [10] p. 25 (I. 93, 98); [11] p. 398 (IX. 317–319). Reprinted by permission of the publishers.

D. This quotation is from a newspaper clipping, which is now untraceable and which does not identify the passage except to say it is from the *Padmapurana.* The author has been unable to track it down, although he believes it is from *Padmapurana* IV. 110.

E. R. E. Hume, *The Thirteen Principal Upanishads.* 2nd ed. Oxford University Press, London, 1934. [1] Svet. 1.6, p. 395; [2] Mun. 3.2.8, p. 376; [3] Mun. 2.2.8, p. 373; [4] Mait. 6.18, p. 435; [5] Svet. 4.9, p. 404. Reprinted by permission of the author and publishers.

F. Sir Edwin Arnold, *The Bhagavad Gita: The Song Celestial.* In any edition. [1] 1.13–23; [2] 1.24–26; [3] 1.28–47; [4] 2.11–20; [5] 2.47–51; 319, 30; [6] 6.10–15, 25–31; [7] 9.16–19; [8] 11.12; [9] 12.8–12; 18.64–66; [10] 9.28–30.

G. Mircea Eliade, *Yoga: Immortality and Freedom.* Pantheon Books, published for and copyrighted by Bollingen Foundation, New York, 1958. [1] p. 13; [2] p. 16 (quoting Sankhya-Karika, 19).

H. *Bombay Census Report for 1911,* Part I, pp. 66–67 (as quoted by L. S. S. O'Malley, *Popular Hinduism,* 1935).

I. Sir Charles Eliot, *Hinduism and Buddhism.* 3 vols. Edward Arnold and Company, London, 1921, Vol. II, p. 144. Reprinted by permission of the publishers.

J. Romain Rolland, *Prophets of the New India.* Translated by E. F. Malcolmn-Smith. Albert and Charles Boni, New York, 1930. [1] pp. 42–43; [2] p. 43 n.

K. Mohandas Gandhi, *Young India, 1919–1922.* Huebsch, New York, 1923, p. 804.

L. Sir Monier-Williams, *Brahmanism and Hinduism.* The Macmillan Company, London, 1891, p. 318.

By permission of J. Murray, author's publisher.

M. Gertrude Emerson, *Voiceless India.* Doubleday, Doran and Company, New York, 1931, p. 110. Reprinted by permission of the John Day Company, publisher.

N. *The Gospel of Ramakrishna,* Vedanta Society, New York, 1907. [1] pp. 158–160; [2] pp. 207–214.

P. *The Sayings of Ramakrishna,* compiled by Swami Abhedananda. Vedanta Society, New York, 1903, p. 54.

Q. Charles S. Braden, *Modern Tendencies in World Religions.* The Macmillan Company, 1933, p. 31.

R. E. A. Gait, article "Caste," in *Encyclopaedia of Religion and Ethics.* T. & T. Clark, Edinburgh, and Charles Scribner's Sons, New York, Vol. III, p. 231. Reprinted by permission of the publishers.

S. Paul D. Devanandan, "The Contemporary Attitude to Conversion," in *Religion in Life,* Vol. XXVII (1958), pp. 381–392.

Chapter 8. Sikhism

A. M. A. MacAuliffe, *The Sikh Religion; Its Gurus, Sacred Writings and Anthems.* 6 vols. Oxford, Clarendon Press, 1909. Vol. I: [1] pp. 33–34; [2] p. 35; [3] p. 37; [4] p. 58; [5] p. 175; [6] pp. 190–191; [7] p. 219; [8] p. 377; [9] p. 328; [10] p. 40; [11] p. 60. Vol. II: [12] p. 238. Vol. IV: [13] p. 2. Reprinted by permission of the publishers.

B. *The Sacred Writings of the Sikhs.* Translated by Trilochan Singh, Jodh Singh, Kapur Singh, Bawa Henkishen Singh, and Khushwant Singh, under the auspices of the National Academy of Letters, India. George Allen & Unwin, London, 1960. [1] p. 82; [2] p. 105; [3] p. 46; [4] p. 77; [5] p. 268; [6] p. 270. Reprinted by permission of the publishers.

C. Dorothy Field, *The Religion of the Sikhs. Wisdom of the East* series. John Murray, 1914. [1] p. 54; [2] p. 19; [3] p. 106. Quoted by permission of the publisher.

D. Duncan Greenlees, *The Gospel of the Guru Granth Sahib.* The Theosophical Publishing House, Adyar, Madras, 1960, p. lxiv.

E. Sir Monier-Williams, *Brahmanism and Hinduism.*

The Macmillan Company, London, 1891, p. 177. By permission of J. Murray, author's publisher.

Chapter 9. Chinese Religion and the Taoists

A. Tsui Chi, *A Short History of Chinese Civilization.* G. P. Putnam's Sons, New York, 1943, p. 3. Reprinted by permission of the publishers.

B. S. Wells Williams, *The Middle Kingdom.* Charles Scribner's Sons, New York, 1899, II, p. 139 (slightly condensed). Reprinted by permission of the publishers.

C. H. G. Creel, *Sinism: A Study of the Evolution of the Chinese World-View.* Open Court Publishing Company, Chicago, 1928, p. 21.

D. *The Shi-King.* Metrically translated by James Legge. The World's Great Classics, Colonial Press, New York, 1900, pp. 195–199.

E. E. R. Hughes, *Chinese Philosophy in Classical Times.* Everyman's Library, No. 973, J. M. Dent and Sons, London, and E. P. Dutton and Co., Inc., New York, 1941. [1] p. 308; [2] p. 163; [3] p. 154. Reprinted by permission of the publishers.

F. *Sacred Books of the East,* Vol. III, *The Texts of Confucianism.* Part I. Translated by James Legge. Oxford, Clarendon Press, 1879, p. 443 f., arranged in verse. Reprinted by permission of the publishers.

G. L. A. Lyall, *China.* Ernest Benn, London, and Charles Scribner's Sons, New York, 1934, pp. 28–33 (translating G. E. Simon, *La Cité Chinoise*). Reprinted by permission of publishers.

H. *The Analects of Confucius,* etc. A translation by Charles A. Wong, published in China without imprint of publisher or date. (A partial American reprint is to be found in Robert O. Ballou, *The Bible of the World,* Viking Press, New York, 1939, p. 398 f.) Analects, Bk. XIII. 18.

I. *A Reader's Guide to the Great Religions.* Edited by Charles J. Adams. The Free Press, Collier-Macmillan, Ltd., London, 1965, p. 39.

J. Y. L. Fung, *History of Chinese Philosophy (From the Beginnings to Circa 100 B.C.).* Translated by Derk Bodde. Henri Vetch, Peiping, 1937. [1] pp. 133–134 (quoting Mencius and Huai-nan-tzu); [2] p. 156 (quoting Chuang-tzu); [3] p. 153

(Chuang-tzu); [4] p. 237. Reprinted by permission of the publisher.

K. Lionel Giles, *The Sayings of Lao Tzu. Wisdom of the East* series. John Murray, London, 1905. [1] p. 20 (XXI); [2] p. 43 (V); [3] p. 23 (XXX); [4] p. 25 (XXIV); [5] p. 32 (LXIII); [6] p. 46 (LXXVIII); [7] p. 50 (L); [8] p. 30 (XXXVII); [9] p. 38 (LVII); [10] p. 41 (XXXI); [11] p. 34 (LXI). Reprinted by permission of the publisher.

L. Ch'u Ta-kao, *The Tao Te Ching*. A translation published by the Buddhist Society, London. [1] LI; [2] XXXVII; [3] XVI; [4] XL; [5] XLII; [6] XXII; [7] II; [8] XLVII; [9] VIII; [10] LV; [11] XVI. Reprinted by permission of the publishers.

M. Arthur Waley, *The Way and Its Power*. Houghton Mifflin Company, Boston, and George Allen and Unwin, London, 1934. [1] p. 152 (IX); [2] p. 159 (XIV); [3] p. 164 (XVII). Reprinted by permission of the publishers.

N. Lin Yutang, ed., *The Wisdom of China and India*. Random House, New York, 1942. From the *Tao Te Ching:* [1] p. 606 (XLI); [2] p. 594 (XXII). From *Chuang-tzu:* [3] p. 686; [4] p. 685; [5] p. 686; [6] p. 647; [7] p. 664; [8] p. 672; [9] p. 660; [10] p. 660–661. Reprinted by permission of the publishers.

P. Witter Bynner, *The Way of Life*. John Day Company, New York, 1944, p. 38 (XXIII). Reprinted by permission of the publishers.

Q. *Sacred Books of the East*, Vol. XXXIX, *The Texts of Taoism*. Translated by James Legge. Oxford, Clarendon Press, 1891, p. 91. Reprinted by permission of the publishers.

R. H. A. Giles, *Chuang Tzu: Mystic, Moralist and Social Reformer*. Kelly and Walsh, Shanghai, 1889. [1] II. 4; [2] XII. 2; [3] II. 5; [4] II. 5; [5] XII 3; [6] VIII. 2; [7] II. 6. Reprinted by permission of the publishers.

S. Edward J. Jurji, ed., *The Great Religions of the Modern World*. Princeton University Press, 1946, p. 27. Quoted by permission of the publishers.

T. Leon Wieger, *A History of the Religious Beliefs and Philosophical Opinions in China*. Translated by E. C. Werner. Hsien-hsien Press, China, 1927. [1] p. 187; [2] pp. 395–401 passim; [3] p. 603.

U. Chan Wing-tsit, "The Story of Chinese Philosophy," in *Philosophy—East and West,* edited by Charles A. Moore. Princeton University Press, 1944, p. 45. Quoted by permission of the publishers.

Chapter 10. Confucius and Confucianism

A. James Legge, *The Analects of Confucius*. Vol. I of *The Chinese Classics*. 2nd ed. Oxford, Clarendon Press, 1893–1895. [1] XIV. 11; [2] VII. 26; [3] III. 7; [4] IX. 2; [5] X. 1–17 (changing *king* to *duke* in the translation); [6] XIV. 13. Reprinted by permission of the publishers.

B. Arthur Waley, *The Analects of Confucius*. Houghton Mifflin Company, Boston, and George Allen and Unwin, London, 1938, p. 127 (VII. 22). Reprinted by permission of the publishers.

C. Lin Yutang, *The Wisdom of Confucius*. The Modern Library, Random House, 1938. [1] p. 83; [2] p. 13; [3] p. 216 (LiKi XXVII); [4] pp. 228–229 (LiKi IX); [5] p. 238; [6] p. 14; [7] p. 280 (Mencius VI. I). Reprinted by permission of the publishers.

D. Y. L. Fung, *A History of Chinese Philosophy (From the Beginnings to Circa 100 B.C.)*. Translated by Derk Bodde. Henri Vetch, Peiping, 1937. [1] p. 108 (quoting Sse-ma Ch'ien); [2] p. 15; [3] p. 59 (An. XIII. 3); [4] p. 72; [5] p. 58 (An. VI. 20); [6] p. 106; [7] p. 318; [8] p. 327; [9] p. 113; [10] p. 17. Reprinted by permission of the publisher.

E. Brian Brown, *The Story of Confucius*. David Mackay Company, Philadelphia, 1927. [1] p. 94 (An. VII. 1); [2] p. 137 (An. IV. 5); [3] p. 94 (An. VII. 1); [4] p. 100 (An. VII. 34). Reprinted by permission of the publishers.

F. Lin Yutang, *The Wisdom of China and India*. Random House, New York, 1942. [1] p. 816 (An. VII. 19); [2] p. 828 (An. XIV. 36); [3] p. 838 (Mencius); [4] p. 833 (An. III. 3); [5] p. 835 (An. XIII. 21); [6] p. 819 (An. III. 13); [7] p. 817 (An. IX. 5); [8] p. 604 (Tao-Te-Ching, XXXVIII); [9] p. 592 (Tao-Te-Ching, XVIII); [10] p. 677 (Chuang-tzu); [11] p. 665 (Chuang-tzu). Reprinted by permission of the publishers.

G. E. R. Hughes, *Chinese Philosophy in Classical Times*. Everyman's Library No. 973, J. M. Dent and Sons, London, and E. P. Dutton and Co., Inc., New York, 1941. [1] p. 12; [2] p. 87; [3] pp. 265–266; [4] p. 261; [5] pp. 259–260; [6] p. 101; [7] pp. 100–101; [8] p. 102; [9] p. 102; [10] pp. 294–295; [11] p. 317; [12] pp. 335–336; [13] pp. 324–325. Reprinted by permission of the publishers.

H. The Chinese characters are translatable into a variety of terms suggesting the many facets of each word. This is the translation (and assignment of analogies from a tree) of Y. C. Yang, in *China's Religious Heritage*. Abingdon-Cokesbury Press, New York and Nashville, 1943, p. 81.

I. Charles A. Wong, *The Analects of Confucius, The Great Learning, The Doctrine of the Mean, and the Works of Mencius.* Translation published in China without the imprint of a publisher or date. A partial American reprint is to be found in Robert O. Ballou, *The Bible of the World* (Viking Press, New York, 1939). Because of the great rarity of the original work, the following references are made, for reader convenience, to this American reprint. [1] p. 413 (An. XV. 23); [2] p. 420 (Gr. Learn.); [3] p. 399 (An. II. 4); [4] p. 400 (An. III. 17); [5] p. 451 (Men.); [6] p. 444 (Men.); [7] p. 455 (Men.); [8] p. 452 (Mem.); [9] pp. 431, 433, 434 (Men.); [10] p. 458 (Men.); [11] p. 459 (Men.); [12] p. 460 (Men.).

J. Ku Hung Ming, *The Conduct of Life: A Translation of the Doctrine of the Mean. Wisdom of the East* series. John Murray, London, 1906. [1] p. 26 (XIII); [2] p. 28 (XV); [3] p. 42 (XIX); [4] p. 29 (XVI); [5] p. 39 (XVII); [6] p. 53 (XXIX). Reprinted by permission of the publisher.

K. L. A. Lyall, *The Sayings of Confucius*. 3rd ed. Longmans, Green and Company, 1935. [1] p. 2 (I. 11); [2] p. 4 (II. 6); [3] p. 5 (II. 7); [4] p. 15 (IV. 19); [5] p. 4 (II. 3, slightly modified); [6] p. 10 (III. 12). Reprinted by permission of the publishers.

L. Ivan Chen, *The Book of Filial Duty. Wisdom of the East* series. John Murray, London, 1920, p. 22 (Chap. VIII). Quoted by permission of the publisher.

M. Lionel Giles, *The Sayings of Confucius. Wisdom of the East* series. John Murray, London, 1917. [1] p. 41 (XII. 17); [2] p. 42 (XII. 19); [3] p. 45 (XIII. 11); [4] p. 46 (XIII. 15); [5] p. 69 (XVII. 6); [6] p. 108 (XVII. 13); [7] p. 57 (IV. 10); [8] p. 64 (XII. 20); [9] p. 68 (XV. 17); [10] p. 60 (VI. 27); [11] p. 87 (VII. 33); [12] p. 86 (VII. 27); [13] p. 94 (II. 16); [14] p. 102 (XI. 11); [15] p. 95 (III. 11). Reprinted by permission of the publisher.

N. Hu Shih, *The Development of the Logical Method in Ancient China.* The New China Book Company, Shanghai, 1917, p. 26.

P. Ku Hung Ming, *The Discourses and Sayings of Confucius.* Kelly and Walsh, Shanghai, 1898, p. 46 (An. VI. 27).

Q. James Legge, *Mencius.* Vol. II of *The Chinese Classics.* 2nd ed. Oxford, Clarendon Press, 1893–1895, III. 1, 4, 13. Reprinted by permission of the publishers.

R. Yi-pao Mei, *Motse, the Neglected Rival of Confucius.* Probsthain, London, 1929. [1] p. 80 f.; [2] p. 89; [3] p. 83; [4] p. 87; [5] p. 145; [6] p. 142; [7] p. 83. Reprinted by permission of the publisher.

S. Chan Wing-tsit, "The Story of Chinese Philosophy," in *Philosophy — East and West.* Edited by Charles A. Moore. Princeton University Press, 1944. [1] p. 30; [2] p. 50; [3] p. 57; [4] p. 58; [5] p. 63; [6] p. 63–64; [7] p. 64. Reprinted by permission of the publishers.

T. H. H. Dubs, *The Works of Hsüntse Translated from the Chinese.* Probsthain, London, 1928. [1] p. 301; [2] pp. 301, 302; [3] p. 310; [4] pp. 113–114; [5] pp. 179, 181; [6] p. 182; [7] pp. 244–245; [8] p. 237; [9] pp. 236–237; [10] pp. 232–233; [11] p. 223. Reprinted by permission of the publisher.

U. Gung-hsing Wang, *The Chinese Mind.* John Day Company, New York, 1946. [1] p. 46; [2] p. 138; [3] p. 139; [4] p. 139; [5] p. 145. Reprinted by permission of the publishers.

V. John K. Shryock, *The Origin and Development of the State Cult of Confucius.* The Century Company, New York, 1932, p. 123. Reprinted by permission of Appleton-Century Company.

W. Tsui Chi, *A Short History of Chinese Civilization.* G. P. Putnam's Sons, New York, 1943, pp. 168–169. Reprinted by permission of the publishers.

X. P. J. MacClagan, *Chinese Religious Ideas*. Student Christian Movement Press, London, 1926, p. 112.

Y. Dagobert D. Runes, ed., *The Dictionary of Philosophy*. Philosophical Library, New York, 1942. [1] p. 52 (article, "Chinese Philosophy," by Chan Wing-tsit); p. 53 (Ibid.).

Chapter 11. Shinto

A. Joseph M. Kitagawa, *Religion in Japanese History*. Columbia University Press, 1966. [1] p. 68; [2] p. 167 f.

B. *The Ko-ji-ki*. Translated by Basil H. Chamberlain. 2nd ed. J. L. Thompson and Company, Kobe, 1932, pp. 17–51, 127–129.

C. D. C. Holtom, *The National Faith of Japan*. Kegan, Paul, Trench, Trubner and Company, London, 1938. [1] p. 113; [2] p. 49; [3] p. 23; [4] p. 73; [5] pp. 81–82; [6] pp. 133–134. Reprinted by permission of George Routledge & Sons, Ltd., London.

D. Wieman and Horton, *The Growth of Religion*. Willett, Clark and Company, Chicago, 1938, p. 88. Quoted by permission of the publishers.

E. Charles S. Braden, *Modern Tendencies in World Religions*. The Macmillan Company, New York, 1933, p. 169. Quoted by permission of the publishers.

F. Yoshito Tanaka, "The True Import of Shinto," in *The University Review*. Issued by the National League of Japanese University Professors, 1938, Vol. I, No. 2, p. 4.

G. N. Hozumi, *Ancestor-Worship and Japanese Law*. 6th ed. Hokuseido Press, Tokyo, 1940, pp. 107–108.

H. D. C. Holtom, *The Political Philosophy of Modern Shinto*. Vol. XLIX, Part II, of Transactions of the Asiatic Society of Japan, Tokyo, 1922. [1] p. 73; [2] p. 88; [3] pp. 107–108.

I. Christopher Noss, *Tohoku, The Scotland of Japan*. Board of Foreign Missions of the Reformed Church in the United States, Philadelphia, 1918, pp. 87–88.

J. A. B. Mitford (Lord Redesdale), *Tales of Old Japan*. Reprint of 1928, The Macmillan Company, London, p. 13.

K. Tadayoshi Sakurai, *Human Bullets: A Soldier's Story of Port Arthur*. Translated by Masujiro Honda and Alice M. Bacon. 9th ed. Teibo Publishing Company, Tokyo, 1911. [1] p. 221; [2] pp. 16–17; [3] pp. 10–11.

Chapter 12. Zoroastrianism

A. Carl Clemen, ed., *The Religions of the World: Their Nature and History*. George G. Harrap & Co., Ltd., London, and Harcourt, Brace and Company, New York, 1931, p. 142. Quoted by permission of the publishers.

B. R. C. Zaehner, "Zoroastrianism," in *Concise Encyclopedia of Living Faiths*. Edited by R. C. Zaehner. Hawthorn Books, New York, 1959, p. 209.

C. A. V. Williams Jackson, *Zoroaster, the Prophet of Ancient Iran*. Columbia University Press, New York, 1898. [1] p. 33; [2] p. 41; [3] p. 41; [4] p. 52; [5] p. 60. Reprinted by permission of the publisher.

D. James Hope Moulton, *Early Zoroastrianism*. Constable and Company (for Hibbert Trust), London, 1913. [1] pp. 365–366 (Yasna 43.7 f.); [2] p. 350 (Ys. 30.5); [3] p. 367 (Ys. 44.3–7); [4] p. 98; [5] p. 349 (Ys. 30.3–5); [6] p. 370 (Ys. 45.2); [7] p. 354 (Ys. 31.18); [8] p. 53 (Ys. 31.10); [9] p. 373 (Ys. 45.4). Reprinted by permission of the publishers.

E. James Hope Moulton, *The Treasure of the Magi*. Oxford University Press, London, 1917. [1] p. 24; [2] p. 37 (Yasna 46.11); [3] p. 87; [4] p. 89; [5] p. 142; [6] p. 149. Quoted by permission of Rev. H. K. Moulton.

F. George Foot Moore, *History of Religions*. 2 vols. Charles Scribner's Sons, and T. & T. Clark, Ltd., Edinburgh, 1913–1919, Vol. I, p. 366 (Ys. 12). Quoted by permission of the publishers.

G. *Sacred Books of the East*, Vol. XXIII, *The Zend Avesta*. Translated by J. Darmesteter. Oxford, Clarendon Press, 1883, p. 183 (Ys. 13.12). Reprinted by permission of the publishers.

H. Jal Dastur Cursetji Pavry, *The Zoroastrian Doctrine of a Future Life*. Columbia University Press, New York, 1926. [1] pp. 92–93; [2] pp.

44–45 (from Sar Dar Bundahish 99.5–20). Reprinted by permission of the publishers.

I. *Sacred Books of the East,* Vol. V, *The Pahlavi Tests,* Part I. Translated by E. W. West. Oxford, Clarendon Press, 1880, p. 248 (Bundahish 30). Reprinted by permission of the publishers.

Chapter 13. Judaism

A. Smith and Goodspeed, *The Bible: An American Translation.* University of Chicago Press, 1935. [1] Ex. 1:8–10, 22; 2:1–10; [2] Ex. 3:1–15; [3] Ex. 34:1–8; [4] Ex. 34:17–26; [5] Ex. 24:3–8; [6] Ex. 32:1–24; [7] II Kings 23:4–14; [8] Deut. 24:16; [9] Jer. 1:4–9; [10] Jer. 20:7–18; [11] Jer. 26:5–24; [12] Jer. 28:10–14; [13] Jer. 23:16, 31–32; [14] Jer. 30:11; [15] Jer. 31:27–34; [16] II Kings 24:14–16; [17] Ps. 137; [18] Esther 3:8–9; [19] Jer. 44:17–18; [20] Ezek. 3:17; [21] Ezek. 36:22–23; [22] Is. 40:28; [23] Is. 43:10; [24] Is. 55:9; [25] Is. 57:15; [26] Is. 49:1–3; [27] Is. 42:25; [28] Is. 45:14–15; [29] Is. 49:22–23; [30] Ezra 1:5; [31] Neh. 9:38–10:39; [32] Neh. 13:15–21; [33] Neh. 13:25. Reprinted by permission of the publishers.

B. George A. Barton, *Archaeology and the Bible.* 6th ed. rev. American Sunday School Union, 1933, p. 442, 444 (substituting *Habiru* for *Habiri*).

C. James Moffatt, *The Holy Bible: A New Translation.* Hodder and Stoughton, Ltd., London and George H. Doran Company, New York, 1922, 1924, 1926. [1] Hosea 4:11–14; [2] Amos 3:6–8; 5:7–11; 6:1–6; [3] Amos 5:4–6, 21–24; [4] Amos 7:1–17; [5] Hosea 2:2–19; [6] Hosea 10:7; [7] Is. 6:1–9; [8] Is. 30:15; [9] Is. 7:1–9; [10] Is. 3:2; 5:8, 11; 6:21–23; 1:23; [11] Is. 1:18–19; [12] Is. 2:1–5; [13] Is. 11:1–10; [14] Micah 3:5–12; [15] Micah 6:6–8; [16] Is. 42:6. Reprinted by permission of Hodder and Stoughton, Ltd., and Harper and Brothers, present publishers.

D. Max Loehr, *A History of Religion in the Old Testament.* Ivor Nicholson & Watson, Ltd., London, and Charles Scribner's Sons, New York, 1936, pp. 51–52. Quoted by permission of the publishers.

E. Rudolph Kittel, *The Religion of the People of Israel.* The Macmillan Company, New York, 1925. [1] p. 71; [2] p. 162; [3] p. 162. Reprinted by permission of the publishers.

F. R. G. Moulton, *The Modern Reader's Bible.* The Macmillan Company, New York, 1907, Is. 53.3–6. Reprinted by permission of the publishers.

G. Abram Leon Sachar, *A History of the Jews.* Alfred Knopf, New York, 1930. [1] p. 88; [2] p. 89; [3] p. 229; [4] p. 265.

H. Gaalyahu Cornfield, ed., *Adam to Daniel.* Macmillan, New York, 1961, p. 381.

I. Lewis Browne, *Stranger than Fiction: A Short History of the Jews.* The Macmillan Company, 1931. [1] p. 171; [2] p. 249. Reprinted by permission of the publishers.

J. David Philipson, *The Reform Movement in Judaism. Rev. ed.* The Macmillan Company, 1931. [1] p. 54; [2] p. 122; [3] p. 363. Reprinted by permission of the publishers.

K. Oscar I. Janowsky, *The American Jew: A Composite Portrait.* 2nd ed. Harper and Brothers, New York, 1932, pp. 214–215. Quoted by permission of the publishers.

Chapter 14. Christianity in Its Opening Phase

A. Smith and Goodspeed, *The Bible: An American Translation.* University of Chicago Press, 1935. [1] Matt. 3:4; [2] Matt. 3:12; [3] Lk. 3:11; [4] Mk. 1:9–11; [5] Mk. 1:15; [6] Mk. 4:1; [7] Mk. 9:45; [8] Gal. 5:17; [9] Lk. 17:22–24; 26–27, 30; [10] Mk. 9:1; [11] Mk. 13:30–33; [12] Lk. 13:24–30; [13] Matt. 8:11–12; [14] Lk. 4:18–21; [15] Lk. 9:59–62; [16] Matt. 5:22; [17] Matt. 5:28; [18] Matt. 5:43–48; 7:12; 22:37–40; [19] Matt. 5:38–40; [20] Matt. 7:1–5; [21] Lk. 6:36–38; [22] Mk. 2:27–28; [23] Mk. 7:14–15; [24] Mk. 6:4; [25] Mk. 3:31–35; [26] Mk. 3:24–26; [27] Mk. 8:27–29; [28] Mk. 11:17; [29] Matt. 21:31, 43; [30] Mk. 14:22–24. Reprinted by permission of the publishers.

B. James Moffatt, *The Holy Bible: A New Translation.* Hodder and Stoughton, Ltd., London and George H. Doran Company, New York, 1922, 1924, 1926, Mk. 12:14–17. Quoted by permission of Hodder and Stoughton, Ltd., and Harper and Brothers, present publishers.

Chapter 15. The Religious Development of Christianity

A. Smith and Goodspeed, *The Bible: An American Translation.* University of Chicago Press, 1935. [1] I Cor. 15:1–8, 42–44, 50; [2] Acts 2:1–4; [3] Acts 5:29; [4] Acts 5:35–39; [5] Acts 6:1; [6] Acts 8:1; [7] Gal. 1:14; [8] Acts 9:2–19; [9] II Cor. 11:24–27; [10] Col. 1:15–16; [11] Eph. 2:1–19; [12] John 1:14. Reprinted by permission of the publishers.

B. Joseph Cullen Ayer, Jr., *A Source Book for Ancient Church History.* Charles Scribner's Sons, New York, 1913. [1] pp. 20–21; [2] p. 319; [3] p. 501; [4] pp. 696–697. Reprinted by permission of the publishers.

C. Williston Walker, *A History of the Christian Church.* Charles Scribner's Sons, New York, 1918, p. 61. Reprinted by permission of the publishers.

D. *The Ante-Nicene Fathers.* Edited by Alexander Roberts and James Donaldson. 10 vols. American reprint of the Edinburgh edition, revised and rearranged. Buffalo, The Christian Literature Publishing Company, 1885–1887. [1] Praxeas 27 (Vol. III, p. 624); [2] Letter 54.14 (Vol. V, p. 344).

E. *A Select Library of Nicene and Post-Nicene Fathers.* 1st ser., 14 vols. New York, The Christian Literature Company, 1886–1890. [1] Confessions 2.5 (Vol. I, p. 62); [2] Ibid. 8.7 (Vol. I, p. 124); [3] Ibid. 8.12 (Vol. I, p. 127); [4] On Trinity, Bk. 8, pref. (Vol. III, p. 115); [5] Ibid. Bk. 4.20 (Vol. III, p. 84); [6] Ibid. Bk. 10.11 (Vol. III, p. 142); [7] On Original Sin, 2.34 (Vol. V, p. 249); [8] Marriage and Concup., 1.27 (Vol. V, p. 275); [9] Gift of Perseverance, 1 Vol. V, p. 526 f.).

F. Nicolas Zernov, "Christianity: The Eastern Schism and the Eastern Orthodox Church," in *The Concise Encyclopedia of Living Faiths.* Edited by R. C. Zaehner. Hawthorn Books, Inc., New York, 1959, p. 98.

G. Isabel Florence Hapgood, ed., *Service Book of the Holy Orthodox Catholic Apostolic (Greco-Russian) Church.* Cambridge, Mass., 1922, pp. 455–456.

H. D. C. Somervell, *A Short History of Our Religion.* G. Bell and Sons, London, 1922, p. 190. Reprinted by permission of the publishers.

I. Froissart, *Chronicles.* Translated from the French by Thomas Johnes. Vol. I of rev. ed. The World's Great Classics, Colonial Press, New York, 1901, pp. 212–213 (Chap. IX).

J. Henry Wace and C. A. Bucheim, *Luther's Primary Works.* Lutheran Publication Society, Philadelphia, 1885. [1] pp. 194–196; [2] p. 78; [3] p. 53; [4] p. 9; [5] p. 21.

K. J. MacKinnon, *Luther and the Reformation.* 4 vols. Longmans, Green and Company, London, 1925–1930, Vol. II, pp. 301–302. Reprinted by permission of the publishers.

L. John Calvin, *Institutes of the Christian Religion.* Translated by Henry Beveridge. 3 vols. Calvin Tract Society, Edinburgh, 1845. [1] Bk. II, chap. 1.8 (Vol. I, pp. 292–293; [2] Bk. III, chap. 11.2 (Vol. II, p. 303); [3] Bk. III, chap. 21–25 (Vol. II, p. 534).

M. Alfred Weber, *History of Philosophy.* Translated by Frank Thilly from 6th French ed. Charles Scribner's Sons, New York, 1896, p. 562, quoting Feuerbach, *Essence of Christianity*, 1841, in footnote 1.

Chapter 16. Islam

A. Charles J. Adams, ed., *A Reader's Guide to the Great Religions.* The Free Press, New York, 1965, p. 287 f.

B. A. J. Arberry, *The Koran Interpreted.* 2 vols. George Allen & Unwin Ltd., London, 1955. (A one-vol. paperback edition has been issued in New York by The Macmillan Company.) Reprinted with permission of The Macmillan Company from *The Koran Interpreted* by A. J. Arberry. Copyright © George Allen & Unwin Ltd. 1955. [1] XCVI.1–5 (Vol. II, p. 344); [2] LIII.1–13 (II, 244); [3] LXXXI.2–14 (II, 326); [4] LXXX.33f. (II, 325); [5] LXXXIII.6–18 (II, 329); [6] LXXIII.5–15 (II, 308); [7] XVIII.28 (I, 319); [8] XVII.7 (I, 302); [9] IV.82 (I, 112); [10] IV.110 f. (I, 117); [11] IV.21 (I, 103); [12] LIII.34 (II, 245); [13] VI.39 (I, 153); [14] VI.84 (I, 159); [15] VI.125

(I, 164); [16] LXXXI.27 (II, 327); [17] VI.77 (I, 158); [18] VII.185 (I, 194); [19] XVII.1 (I, 302); [20] XXXIII.64 f. (II, 129); [21] LVI.40, 50 (II, 255); [22] XXXVII.63 f. (II, 152); [23] XLIV.44–50 (I, 209); [24] XLIV.51 (II, 209); [25] LVI.15–23, 34 f. (II, 254 f.); [26] XIII.23 (I, 270); [27] II.173 f. (I, 50 f.); [28] XVII.24 f. (I, 304 f.); [29] XVII.34 (I, 305); [30] IV.2–5, 10 (I, 100 f.); [31] XXIV.33 (II, 50); [32] II.231 (I, 60); [33] II.187, 189 (I, 51 f.); [34] V.1–4 (I, 127); [35] V.93 (I, 142); [36] I (I, 29); [37] XXII.37 (II, 31).

C. Arthur Jeffery, ed., *Islam: Muhammad and His Religion*. Liberal Arts Press, New York, 1958, p. 45.

D. Philip K. Hitti, *History of the Arabs*. The Macmillan Company, New York, 1937. [1] p. 120; [2] p. 150; [3] p. 153; [4] p. 153; [5] p. 431. Reprinted by permission of the publishers.

E. I. Goldziher, *Mohammed and Islam*. Translated by K. C. Seelye. Yale University Press, 1917. [1] pp. 97–98; [2] p. 183; [3] p. 183. Reprinted by permission of the publishers.

F. Tor Andrae, *Mohammed: The Man and His Faith*. Translated by Theophil Menzel. Allen & Unwin, London, 1936, p. 77. Available as Harper Torchbook.

G. John A. Williams, ed., *Islam, A Book of Readings*. George Braziller, New York, 1961, p. 79.

H. George Foot Moore, *History of Religions*. 2 vols. Charles Scribner's Sons, New York, and T. & T. Clark, Ltd., Edinburgh, 1913–1919. [1] II, p. 442; [2] II, p. 441; [3] II, p. 435. Reprinted by permission of the publishers.

I. *The Legacy of Islam*. Edited by Sir Thomas Arnold and Alfred Guillaume. Oxford, Clarendon Press, 1931. [1] pp. 215–216; [2] p. 217; [3] p. 218; [4] p. 218. Reprinted by permission of the publishers.

J. *The Persian Poets*. Edited by N. H. Dole and Belle M. Walker. Thomas Y. Crowell, 1901. [1] p. 216; [2] p. 219; [3] p. 241; [4] p. 242; [5] p. 207–209; [6] p. 289.

K. Carl Clemen, ed., *The Religions of the World*. George C. Harrap & Co., Ltd., London, and Harcourt, Brace and Company, New York, 1931, p. 454.

L. John C. Archer, *Faiths Men Live By*. Thomas Nelson and Sons, New York, 1934, p. 447.

M. H. A. R. Gibb, *Modern Trends in Islam*. University of Chicago Press, 1947, p. 69.

N. Wilfred Cantwell Smith, *Islam in Modern History*. Princeton University Press, 1957, p. 213.

THE PRONUNCIATION of words that are not found in standard dictionaries (Oriental words in particular) is indicated by a system of diacritical marks that are to be sounded approximately like the italicized letters in the following words: ärtistic, ădd, ȧsk, bĕll, fāme, ēve, hĭt, pīne, gō, ŏdd, ôr, fŏŏt, fōōd, oіl, bŭt, menü, bûrn, ūnite, säuerkraut, chin, H like ch in German ach or Scotch loch. Where, however, pronunciation seems to present no difficulty, it is not suggested. This is especially true of Japanese words, which, besides being phonetically spelled, seldom have an accent. In the instances where the pronunciation of Chinese words is not indicated, the general rules for such pronunciation are given on page 248. It may be noted that Chinese, like Japanese, words are either only slightly accented or not at all. To avoid overburdening the index, names and topics only incidentally mentioned in the text are omitted, *except* when pronunciation might present a difficulty, in which case the word is included and the pronunciation indicated. In some cases where separate reference is made to some person(s), place(s), or subject(s) in both columns of the page being numbered, the page number will be followed by the symbol (1 & 2).

Many Hindu words ending in *a* or *ha* are pronounced today with only a slight exhalation of the breath. Jaganatha thus becomes almost jŭgänŭtt, ashrama becomes äshrŭmm, Jataka jŭtŭkk, ahankara ŭhŭnkŭrr, marga mŭrg, and so on. It should be added that a *v* is today usually pronounced like a *w*.

Note: The subentries are followed by semicolons and are as a general rule arranged in ascending order beginning with the lowest page number cited in each subentry.

Index

577

583

591